THE NINETEENTH MENTAL
MEASUREMENTS YEARBOOK

OTHER PUBLICATIONS
FROM THE BUROS CENTER FOR TESTING

THE NINETEENTH MENTAL MEASUREMENTS YEARBOOK

JANET F. CARLSON, KURT F. GEISINGER,

and JESSICA L. JONSON

Editors

NANCY ANDERSON
LINDA L. MURPHY
Managing Editors

The Buros Center for Testing
The University of Nebraska-Lincoln
Lincoln, Nebraska

2014
Distributed by The University of Nebraska Press

Note to Users

TABLE OF CONTENTS

DEDICATION

Dedicated to Linda L. Murphy

Linda L. Murphy worked at the University of Nebraska-Lincoln (UNL) for 30 years, 29 of them with the Buros Center for Testing. For the great majority of those years, she served as the Managing Editor for Buros publications. After three decades of extraordinary service, Linda retired from her position as Managing Editor in January 2013.

During her tenure with the Buros Center, Linda was instrumental in a large number and wide variety of publications, as she advanced from an entry-level position to a managerial one, while earning her Master's degree and completing graduate courses in the doctoral program in Cognition, Learning, and Development. In total, she worked on all eleven of the *Mental Measurements Yearbooks* and all five of the *Tests in Print* volumes that have been published since the Buros Center moved to UNL in 1978. She served as Managing Editor for ten of the eleven yearbooks and as an Editor for all five *Tests in Print* volumes. In addition, she is an Editor of the volume *Pruebas Publicadas en Español*, a Spanish edition of *Tests in Print*, published for the first time in 2013. She also assisted in the publication of several other volumes, including the *Buros Desk Reference* series, *Yearbook Supplements* to the ninth through thirteenth yearbooks, and the *Buros-Nebraska Series on Measurement and Testing*.

Linda's editorial skills are legion and matched—or possibly exceeded—only by her warm interpersonal skills. Linda has been the voice of reason, caring, and calm insistence in countless communications with test publishers, test reviewers, graduate assistants, student workers, and colleagues. In addition to her editorial responsibilities, she has represented the Center at professional conferences, served on numerous search committees, proofread many dissertations and myriad documents, and offered encouraging words to those who needed them. It is unclear just how many graduate students received assistance from Linda in the editing of their doctoral dissertations. We wish her the very best in her well-earned retirement, and extend to her our gratitude for her many years of outstanding service to the Buros Center for Testing, the College of Education and Human Sciences, and the University of Nebraska.

For her broad and valuable service over many years, for her unwavering commitment to the mission of the Buros Center for Testing, for her keen editorial skills, and to honor her proud heritage as a "Nebraska farm girl," we dedicate this volume to Linda L. Murphy.

Janet F. Carlson
Kurt F. Geisinger
Jessica L. Jonson
and
The staff of the Buros Center for Testing

INTRODUCTION

Consistent with all volumes of this long-running series, *The Nineteenth Mental Measurements Yearbook* (*19th MMY*) serves as a guide to the complex task of test evaluation, selection, and use. With its initial publication in 1938, Oscar K. Buros (1905-1978) provided a historic forum that would allow the emerging field of testing to improve in both science and practice.

Criteria for inclusion in this edition of the *MMY* series are that a test be (a) new or substantially revised since last reviewed in the *MMY* series, (b) commercially available, (c) published in the English language, and (d) documented with sufficient test development information and technical data to allow for a comprehensive review process.

THE NINETEENTH MENTAL MEASUREMENTS YEARBOOK

The *19th MMY* primarily contains reviews of tests that are new or significantly revised since the publication of the *18th MMY* in 2010. Reviews, descriptions, and references associated with many older tests can be located in other Buros publications: previous *MMY*s and *Tests in Print VIII*. Criteria for inclusion in this edition of the *MMY* remain that a test be (a) new or substantively revised since it was last reviewed in the *MMY* series, (b) commercially available from its publishers, (c) available in the English language, and (d) published with adequate developmental and technical documentation.

Content. The contents of the *19th MMY* include: (a) a bibliography of 183 commercially available tests, new or revised, published as separates for use with English-speaking individuals; (b) 350 critical test reviews from specialists selected by the editors on the basis of their expertise in measurement and, often, the content of the test being reviewed; (c) a test title index with appropriate cross references; (d) an index of acronyms for easy reference when only a test acronym is known; (e) a classified subject index; (f) a publishers directory and index, including publisher addresses and other contact information with test listings by publisher; (g) a name index including the names of authors of all tests, reviews, or references included in this *MMY*; and (h) a score index to identify for users test scores of potential interest.

Appendix. Three separate listings appear in the *19th MMY* for users requiring additional information when a specific test cannot be otherwise located in the *Mental Measurements Yearbook* series. Beginning with the *14th MMY* (2001), for a test to qualify for review, its publisher must provide an adequate developmental history and sufficient evidence describing the instrument's technical properties. Not all tests submitted for evaluation meet these two criteria for review in the *MMY* series. A listing of tests received (but not reviewed) is included in the Appendix to make users aware of the availability of these tests, albeit without supporting documentation or reviews. The Appendix also provides a list of tests that meet review criteria but were received too late for review in this volume. It is expected that these tests (plus additional tests received in the following months) will be reviewed in *The Twentieth Mental Measurements Yearbook*. Test reviews that are completed prior to publication of the *20th MMY* are available electronically for a small fee on our web-based service Test Reviews Online (buros.org). A third list in the Appendix includes titles of tests requested from publishers but not yet received as of this volume's publication. This listing includes tests from publishers who refuse to allow their tests to be reviewed as well as those from publishers who routinely make their instruments available for review but who have failed at this point to provide a new or revised test for evaluation. We at Buros believe that to meet professional standards, test publishers should be willing to have their tests independently evaluated so that consumers are informed of the strengths and potential drawbacks of all measures that they are considering for use.

Organization. The current *MMY* series is organized like an encyclopedia, with tests being ordered alphabetically by title. If the title of a test is known, the reader can locate the test information immediately without having to consult the Index of Titles.

The page headings reflect the encyclopedic organization. The page heading of the left-hand page cites the number and title of the first test listed on that page, and the page heading of the right-hand page cites the number and title of the last test listed on that page. All numbers presented in the various indexes are test numbers, not page numbers. Page numbers are important only for the Table of Contents and are located at the bottom of each page.

TESTS AND REVIEWS

The *19th MMY* contains descriptive information on 183 tests as well as test reviews by 264 different authors. Statistics on the number and percentage of tests in each of 18 major classifications are contained in Table 1.

The percentage of new and revised or supplemented tests according to major classifications is contained in Table 2. Overall, 108 of the tests included in the *19th MMY* are new and have not

TABLE 1
TESTS BY MAJOR CLASSIFICATIONS

Classification	Number	Percentage
Vocations	46	25.1
Personality	33	18.0
English and Language	18	9.8
Behavior Assessment	13	7.1
Neuropsychological	13	7.1
Miscellaneous	12	6.6
Intelligence and General Aptitude	11	6.0
Developmental	10	5.5
Reading	8	4.4
Education	5	2.7
Sensory Motor	4	2.2
Speech and Hearing	4	2.2
Achievement	2	1.1
Mathematics	2	1.1
Fine Arts	1	0.5
Foreign Languages	1	0.5
Science	0	0.0
Social Studies	0	0.0
Total	183	100.0

TABLE 2
NEW AND REVISED OR SUPPLEMENTED TESTS BY MAJOR CLASSIFICATION

Classification	Number of Tests	Percentage New	Percentage Revised
Achievement	2	50.0	50.0
Behavior Assessment	13	76.9	23.1
Developmental	10	60.0	40.0
Education	5	80.0	20.0
English and Language	18	50.0	50.0
Fine Arts	1	100.0	0.0
Foreign Languages	1	100.0	0.0
Intelligence and General Aptitude	11	63.6	36.4
Mathematics	2	50.0	50.0
Miscellaneous	12	66.7	33.3
Neuropsychological	13	69.2	30.8
Personality	33	54.5	45.5
Reading	8	62.5	37.5
Science	0	0.0	0.0
Sensory Motor	4	50.0	50.0
Social Studies	0	0.0	0.0
Speech and Hearing	4	50.0	50.0
Vocations	46	52.2	47.8
Total	183	59.0	41.0

been listed in a previous *MMY* although some descriptions may have been included in *Tests in Print VIII* (*TIP VIII*; 2011). The Index of Titles may be consulted to determine whether a test is new or revised.

Test Selection. A new policy for selecting tests for review became effective with the *14th MMY* (2001). This policy requires at least minimal information be available regarding test development. The requirement that tests have such minimal information does not assure the quality of the test; it simply provides reviewers with a minimum basis for critically evaluating the quality of the test. We select our reviewers carefully and let them and well-informed readers decide for themselves about the essential features needed to assure the appropriate use of a test. Some new or revised tests are not included because they were received too late to undergo the review process and still permit timely publication. A list of these tests is included in the Appendix, and every effort will be made to have them reviewed for *The Twentieth Mental Measurements Yearbook* and included before then through our web-based service, Test Reviews Online (buros.org). These reviews also may be available electronically through EBSCO Publishing or Ovid Technologies at many university, medical, law, and research libraries.

There are some new or revised tests for which there will be no reviews although these tests are described in *Tests in Print VIII*. The absence of reviews occurred for a variety of reasons including: we could not identify qualified reviewers, the test materials were incomplete so reviews were not possible, the tests were sufficiently obscure that reviews were deemed unnecessary, the publisher advised us the test was out of print before reviews were completed, or the test did not meet our criterion for documentation. Descriptions of all these tests still in print were published in *TIP VIII* or will be published in *Tests in Print IX* and are included in the Test Reviews Online database.

Reviewer Selection. The selection of reviewers was done with great care. The objective was to secure measurement and subject specialists who would be independent and represent a variety of different viewpoints. It was also important to find individuals who would write critical reviews competently, judiciously, fairly, and in a timely manner. Reviewers were identified by means of extensive searches of the professional literature, attendance at professional meetings, and recommendations from leaders in various professional fields. Perusal of reviews in this volume also will reveal that reviewers work in and represent a cross-section of the contexts in which testing is taught and tests are used: universities, public schools, businesses, and community agencies. These reviewers represent an outstanding array of professional talent, and their contributions are obviously of primary importance in making this *Yearbook* a valuable resource. A list of the individuals reviewing in this volume is included at the beginning of the Index section.

Active, evaluative reading is the key to the most effective use of the professional expertise offered in each of the reviews. Just as one would evaluate a test, readers should evaluate critically the reviewer's comments about the test. The reviewers selected are competent professionals in their respective fields, but it is inevitable that their reviews also reflect their individual perspectives. *The Mental Measurements Yearbook* series was developed to stimulate critical thinking and assist in the selection of the best available test for a given purpose, not to promote the passive acceptance of reviewer judgment.

INDEXES

As mentioned previously, the *19th MMY* includes six indexes invaluable as aids to effective use of this volume: (a) Index of Titles, (b) Index of Acronyms, (c) Classified Subject Index, (d) Publishers Directory and Index, (e) Index of Names, and (f) Score Index. Additional comment on these indexes is presented below.

Index of Titles. Because the organization of the *19th MMY* is encyclopedic in nature, with the tests ordered alphabetically by title throughout the volume, the test title index does not have to be consulted to find a test if the title is known. However, the title index has some features that make it useful beyond its function as a complete title listing. First, it includes cross-reference information useful for tests with superseded or alternative titles or tests commonly (and sometimes inaccurately) known by multiple titles. Second, it identifies tests that are new or revised. Third, it may cue the user to other tests with similar titles that may be useful. Titles for the 14 tests not reviewed because of insufficient technical documentation are included in the Index of Titles. It is important to keep in mind that the numbers in this index, like those for all *MMY* indexes, are test numbers and not page numbers.

Because no *MMY* includes reviews of all tests currently in print, a particular test of interest may not be reviewed in this volume. To learn whether a commercially published test has been reviewed in this or an earlier volume of the *MMY*, users may visit the Buros website (buros.org). A search of Test Reviews Online (TROL) will indicate whether a test has been reviewed and also will indicate the yearbook in which the review can be found. TROL also provides electronic access to reviews provided in recent *MMY*s (the most current reviews only) and test reviews that have been finalized since the publication of the most recent *MMY*. Therefore, TROL provides ready access, for a nominal fee, to the majority of tests that have been reviewed in *The Mental Measurements Yearbook* series. As an alternative, *Tests in Print VIII* provides a cross reference to reviews of still-in-print tests in the *MMY* series.

Index of Acronyms. Some tests seem to be better known by their acronyms than by their full titles. The Index of Acronyms can help in these instances; it refers the reader to the full title of the test and to the relevant descriptive information and reviews.

Classified Subject Index. The Classified Subject Index classifies all tests listed in the *19th MMY* into 16 of 18 major categories: Achievement, Behavior Assessment, Developmental, Education, English and Language, Fine Arts, Foreign Languages, Intelligence and General Aptitude, Mathematics, Miscellaneous, Neuropsychological, Personality, Reading, Science, Sensory-Motor, Social Studies, Speech and Hearing, and Vocations. (No tests in the Science or Social Studies categories are reviewed in the *19th MMY*.) Each test entry in this index includes test title, population for which the test is intended, and test number. The Classified Subject Index is of great help to readers who seek a listing of tests in given subject areas. This index represents a starting point for readers who know their area of interest but do not know how to further focus that interest in order to identify the best test(s) for their particular purposes.

Publishers Directory and Index. The Publishers Directory and Index includes the names and addresses of the publishers of all tests included in the *19th MMY* plus a listing of test numbers for each individual publisher. Also included are the telephone and FAX numbers, email, and Web addresses for those publishers who responded to our request for this information. This index can be particularly useful in obtaining addresses for specimen sets or catalogs after the test reviews have been read and evaluated. It also can be useful when a reader knows the publisher of a certain test but is uncertain about the test title, or when a reader is interested in the range of tests published by a given publisher.

Index of Names. The Index of Names provides a comprehensive list of names, indicating authorship of a test, test review, or reviewer's reference.

Score Index. The Score Index is a listing of the scored parts of all tests reviewed in the *19th MMY*. Test titles are sometimes misleading or ambiguous, and test content may be difficult to define with precision. In contrast, test scores often represent operational definitions of the variables the test author is trying to measure, and as such they can define test purpose and content more adequately than other descriptive information. A search for a particular test is most often a search for a test that measures some specific variable(s). Test scores and their associated labels can often be the best definitions of the variable(s) of interest. The Score Index is a detailed subject index based on the most critical operational features of any test—the scores and their associated labels.

HOW TO USE THIS YEARBOOK

A reference work like *The Nineteenth Mental Measurements Yearbook* can be of far greater benefit to a reader if some time is taken to become familiar with what it has to offer and how it might be used most effectively to obtain the information wanted.

Step 1: Read the Introduction to the *19th MMY* in its entirety.

Step 2: Become familiar with the six indexes and particularly with the instructions preceding each index listing.

Step 3: Use the book by looking up needed information. This step is simple if one keeps the following procedures in mind:

1. Go directly to the test entry using the alphabetical page headings if you know the title of the test.

2. Consult the Index of Titles for possible variants of the title or consult the appropriate subject area of the Classified Subject Index for other possible leads or for similar or related tests in the same area, if you do not know, cannot find, or are unsure of the title of a test. (Other uses for both of these indexes were described previously.)

3. Consult the Index of Names if you know the author of a test but not the title or publisher. Look up the author's titles until you find the test you want.

4. Consult the Publishers Directory and Index if you know the test publisher but not the title or author. Look through the publisher's titles until you find the test you want.

5. Consult the Score Index and locate the test or tests that include the score variable of interest if you are looking for a test that yields a particular kind of test score.

6. If after following the above steps you are not able to find a review of the test you want, consult the Appendix for a list of tests that are not reviewed. Reasons tests are not reviewed include (a) they did not meet our selection criteria, (b) the reviews were not completed in time for publication in this volume, or (c) the publisher failed to respond in a timely manner to our request for testing materials. You also can consult *TIP VIII* or visit the Buros web page (buros.org) and use the Test Reviews Online service (TROL) to identify the yearbook that contains the description and any available reviews for a test of interest.

7. Once you have found the test or tests you are looking for, read the descriptive entries for

these tests carefully so that you can take advantage of the information provided. A description of the information in these test entries is presented later in this section.

8. Read the test reviews carefully and analytically, as suggested above. The information and evaluations contained in these reviews are meant to assist test consumers in making well-informed decisions about the choice and applications of tests.

9. Once you have read the descriptive information and test reviews, you may want to contact the publisher to order a specimen set for a particular test so that you can examine it firsthand. The Publishers Directory and Index has the address information needed to obtain specimen sets or catalogs.

Making Effective Use of the Test Entries. Although brief, the test entries include extensive information. For each test, descriptive information is presented in the following order:

a) TITLES. Test titles are printed in boldface type. Secondary or series titles are set off from main titles by a colon.

b) PURPOSE. For each test there is a brief, clear statement describing the purpose of the test. Often these statements are quotations from the test manual.

c) POPULATION. This field describes the groups for whom the test is intended. The grade, chronological age, semester range, or employment category is usually given. For example, "Grades 1.5–2.5, 2–3, 4–12, 13–17" means that there are four test booklets: a booklet for the middle of first grade through the middle of second grade, a booklet for the beginning of second grade through the end of third grade, a booklet for Grades 4 through 12 inclusive, and a booklet for undergraduate and graduate students in colleges and universities.

d) PUBLICATION DATE. The inclusive range of publication dates for the various forms, accessories, and editions of a test is reported.

e) ACRONYM. When a test is often referred to by an acronym, the acronym is given.

f) SCORES. The number of part scores is presented along with their titles or descriptions of what they are intended to represent or measure.

g) ADMINISTRATION. Individual or group administration is indicated. A test is considered a group test unless it may be administered only individually.

h) FORMS, PARTS, AND LEVELS. All available forms, parts, and levels are listed.

i) MANUAL. Notation is made if no manual is available. All other manual information is included under Price Data.

j) RESTRICTED DISTRIBUTION. This is noted only for tests that are made available to a special market by the publisher. Educational and psychological restrictions are not noted (unless a special training course is required for use).

k) PRICE DATA. Price information is reported for test packages (usually 20 to 35 tests), answer sheets, all other accessories, and specimen sets. The statement "$17.50 per 35 tests" means that all accessories are included unless otherwise indicated by the reporting of separate prices for accessories. The statement also means 35 tests of one level, one edition, or one part unless stated otherwise. Because test prices can change very quickly, the year that the listed test prices were obtained is also given. Foreign currency is assigned the appropriate symbol. When prices are given in foreign dollars, a qualifying symbol is added (e.g., A$16.50 refers to 16 dollars and 50 cents in Australian currency). Along with cost, the publication date and number of pages on which print occurs is reported for manuals and technical reports (e.g., 2009, 102 pages). All types of machine-scorable answer sheets available for use with a specific test are reported in the descriptive entry. Scoring and reporting services provided by publishers are reported along with information on costs. In a few cases, special computerized scoring and interpretation services are noted at the end of the price information.

l) FOREIGN LANGUAGE AND OTHER SPECIAL EDITIONS. This section concerns foreign language editions published by the same publisher that sells the English-language edition. It also indicates special editions (e.g., Braille, large type) available from the same or a different publisher. Readers interested in a Spanish version of a particular test may wish to consult another Buros publication, *Pruebas Publicadas en Español,* which provides descriptive listings of commercially published tests that are available in part or wholly in Spanish. Many of these tests are translations or adaptations of English language tests.

m) TIME. The number of minutes of actual working time allowed examinees and the approximate length of time needed for administering a test are reported whenever obtainable. The latter figure is always enclosed in parentheses. Thus, "50(60) minutes" indicates that the examinees are allowed 50 minutes of working time and that a total of 60 minutes is needed to administer the test. A time of "40–50 minutes" indicates an untimed test that takes approximately 45 minutes to administer, or—in a few instances—a test so timed that working time and administration time are very difficult to disentangle. When the time necessary to administer a test is not reported or suggested in the test materials but has been obtained from a catalog or through correspondence with the test publisher or author, the time is enclosed in brackets.

n) COMMENTS. Some entries contain special notations, such as: "for research use only"; "revision of the ABC Test"; "tests administered monthly at centers throughout the United States"; "subtests available as separates"; and "verbal creativity." A statement such as "verbal creativity" is intended to further describe what the test claims to measure. Some of the test entries include factual statements that imply criticism of the test, such as "1999 test identical with test copyrighted 1980."

o) AUTHOR. For most tests, all authors are reported. In the case of tests that appear in a new form each year, only authors of the most recent forms are listed. Names are reported exactly as printed on test booklets. Names of editors generally are not reported.

p) PUBLISHER. The name of the publisher or distributor is reported for each test. Foreign publishers are identified by listing the country in brackets immediately following the name of the publisher. The Publishers Directory and Index must be consulted for a publisher's address and other contact information.

q) FOREIGN ADAPTATIONS. Revisions and adaptations of tests for foreign use are listed in a separate paragraph following the original edition.

r) SUBLISTINGS. Levels, editions, subtests, or parts of a test available in separate booklets are sometimes presented as sublistings with titles set in small capital letters. Sub-sublistings are indented, and titles are set in italic type.

s) CROSS REFERENCES. For tests that have been listed previously in a Buros Center for Testing (or a Buros Institute of Mental Measurements) publication, a test entry includes—if relevant—a final item containing cross references to the reviews, excerpts, and references for that test in those volumes. In the cross references, "T7:467" refers to test 467 in *Tests in Print VII*, "16:121" refers to test 121 in *The Sixteenth Mental Measurements Yearbook*, "8:1023" refers to test 1023 in *The Eighth Mental Measurements Yearbook*, "T3:144" refers to test 144 in *Tests in Print III*, "P:262" refers to test 262 in *Personality Tests and Reviews*, "2:1427" refers to test 1427 in *The 1940 Yearbook*, and "1:1110" refers to test 1110 in *The 1938 Yearbook*. In the case of batteries and programs, the paragraph also includes cross references—from the battery to the separately listed subtests and vice versa—to entries in this volume and to entries and reviews in earlier *Yearbooks*.

ACKNOWLEDGMENTS

The publication of *The Nineteenth Mental Measurements Yearbook* could not have been accomplished without the contributions of many individuals. The editors gratefully acknowledge the talent, expertise, and dedication of our staff at the Buros Center for Testing who have made this most recent version of the *MMY* series possible. Linda Murphy, Managing Editor, was long essential to the publication of new editions of the *MMY*. Her historical base of knowledge, attention to detail, good humor, and steadfast commitment have been critical to this series and made our job as editors much more agreeable than it otherwise would be. She sorted out many inaccuracies and omissions as a matter of course, provided fine points on APA style, and alerted us to numerous errors that might occur save for her wise counsel. She also was generally responsible for communications with test publishers to receive new and substantially revised tests. Linda retired part way through production of the *19th MMY*. Her role has been ably filled by Nancy Anderson, who not only has substantial knowledge of testing and psychometrics, but also had a career in newspaper editing. She has already played a vital role in the publication of *The Eighteenth Mental Measurements Yearbook, Tests in Print VIII*, and *Pruebas Publicadas en Español* (our newest publication that is, essentially, a Spanish edition of *Tests in Print*). As Managing Editor, Nancy has largely been responsible for completion of the book and has carried on in the tradition of excellence established by her immediate predecessor.

Publication of this volume also would not be possible without the perseverance of our Assistant Editor, Gary Anderson, who among many other duties continually updates the website, helps to manage voluminous testing materials and databases, provides good-natured communication with all of our reviewers, and carefully proofreads each test review. We also wish to thank Jennifer Schlueter, Assistant Editor, for her assistance with numerous tasks related primarily to communications with test publishers, layout, and proofreading. Her contributions and personable nature made many processes easier and more efficient. We appreciate the many contributions by Rob Spies, whose commitment to the quality of our test review products has been unerring. We would like to acknowledge the efforts of Rasma Strautkalns, Staff Secretary, for key contributions to an efficient office environment and her warm reception for our clients. In addition, we would like to cite other members of the Buros Center for Testing for their support and encouragement during the publication of this edition of the *MMY*. Tzu-Yun (Katherine) Chin, Anja Römhild, Theresa Glanz, Elaine Rodeck, and Patrick Irwin have all made generous contributions to discussions of our current and future directions. We appreciate the efforts of all permanent staff, each of whom contributes more than their share to the development and production of our publications. We also enjoy the respect and collegiality of others within the University of Nebraska-Lincoln system. In particular, we wish to thank Ralph De Ayala, Chair of the Department of Educational Psychology, and Marjorie Kostelnik, Dean of the College of Education and Human Sciences, for their encouragement and support. Brett Bieber, senior web programmer, provided a great deal of data management assistance, and his expert contributions were especially valuable when compiling the indexes for this publication.

This volume would not exist without the substantial efforts of our test reviewers. We are very grateful to the many reviewers (and especially to those Distinguished Reviewers recognized in this and previous editions of the *MMY* series) who have prepared test reviews for the Buros Center for Testing (previously known as the Buros Institute of Mental Measurements). Their willingness to take time from busy professional schedules and to share their expertise in the form of thoughtful test reviews is very much appreciated. *The Mental Measurements Yearbook* series would not exist without their concerted efforts.

The work of many graduate and undergraduate students helps make possible the quality of this volume. Their efforts include writing test descriptions, fact checking reviews, verifying test references, proofreading, and innumerable other tasks. We thank our graduate research assistants Nancy Anderson (now Managing Editor), Allison Champion-Wescott, Kevin Dahlmann, Sara Gonzalez, Kristin Jones, Chelsi Klentz-Davis, HyeSun Lee, and Betty-Jean Usher-Tate for their assistance. We also wish to thank Kaley Smith and Kirstie Smith (yes, they are sisters), who contributed primarily in the areas of word processing and proofreading.

Appreciation is also extended to the members of our National Advisory Committee for their willingness to assist in the operation of the Buros Center for Testing and for their thought-provoking suggestions for improving the *MMY* series and other publications of the Center. During the period in which this volume was prepared, the National Advisory Council has included Angee Baker, Gregory Cizek, John Fremer, Paula Kaufman, Michael Rodriguez, Jonathan Sandoval, and Neal Schmitt.

The Buros Center for Testing is part of the Department of Educational Psychology of the University of Nebraska-Lincoln. We have benefited from the many departmental colleagues who have contributed to this work. In addition, we are grateful for the contribution of the University of Nebraska Press, which provides expert consultation and serves as distributor of the *MMY* series.

SUMMARY

The Mental Measurements Yearbook series is an essential resource for both individuals and organizations seeking information critical to the evaluation, selection, and use of specific testing instruments. This edition contains 350 test reviews of 183 different tests.

Test reviews from recent *MMY* editions are available electronically through EBSCO Publishing or Ovid Technologies at many university, medical, law, and research libraries. Test reviews also are available from the Buros Center website (buros.org) through our Test Reviews Online page.

For over 75 years the *MMY* series has worked to support the interests of knowledgeable professionals and to advance the purpose of an informed public. By providing candid reviews of testing products, this publication also serves test publishers who wish to improve their instruments by submitting tests for independent review. Given the critical importance of testing, we hope test authors and publishers will carefully consider the comments made by reviewers and continue to refine and perfect their assessment products.

Janet F. Carlson
Kurt F. Geisinger
Jessica L. Jonson
January 2014

Tests and Reviews

[1]

Adult Self-Report Inventory-4.

Purpose: Designed to be "a guide for conducting clinical interviews" and be used "as a tool to assist the clinician in making a diagnosis" and to help identify possible psychiatric disorders.

Population: Ages 18-75.

Publication Dates: 2004-2008.

Acronyms: ASRI-4; AI-4.

Scores, 20: Symptom Severity Score (Normative Data Model): Anxiety Disorders, Mood Disorders, Eating Disorders, Somatoform Disorders, Psychotic Disorders, Sleep Disorders, Impulse Control Disorders, Personality Disorders, Child-Onset Disorders, Other Disorders; Symptom Count Cutoff Score (Diagnostic Model): Anxiety Disorders, Mood Disorders, Eating Disorders, Somatoform Disorders, Psychotic Disorders, Sleep Disorders, Impulse Control Disorders, Personality Disorders, Child-Onset Disorders, Other Disorders.

Administration: Individual.

Forms, 2: Adult Self Report Inventory-4, Adult Inventory-4.

Price Data, 2011: $112 per Deluxe Kit including manual (2004, 173 pages), 50 Adult Self-Report Inventories-4, 5 Adult Inventories-4, 50 Symptom Count score sheets, and 50 Symptom Severity Profile score sheets; $235 per Deluxe Kit plus Scoring Program CD; $57 per 50 copies of Adult Self-Report Inventory-4 Checklist in Spanish or 50 copies of Adult Inventory-4 Checklist in Spanish; $44 per manual.

Foreign Language Edition: Spanish edition available.

Time: (15-20) minutes.

Comments: The assessments are taken by the patient and by a person who knows the patient well "(e.g., parent, partner, roommate)."

Authors: Kenneth D. Gadow, Joyce Sprafkin, and Margaret D. Weiss.

Publisher: Checkmate Plus, Ltd.

Review of Adult Self-Report Inventory-4 by TONY CELLUCCI, Professor and Director of the ECU Psychological Assessment and Specialty Services (PASS) Clinic, East Carolina University, Greenville, NC:

DESCRIPTION. The Adult Self-Report Inventory-4 (ASRI-4) is the adult instrument in a series of symptom inventories developed by the test authors. There is a preliminary section (e.g., demographics, prior treatment), whereas the instrument itself consists of approximately 136 questions grouped into 20 diagnostic-related areas (A-T). Respondents indicate the frequency of occurrence of each behavior or symptom on a 4-point scale (i.e., *never, sometimes, often,* or *very often*). The ASRI-4 explicitly does not provide diagnoses but rather serves as an aid in initial diagnostic assessment. It provides comprehensive screening for adult problems and allows efficiency in guiding and focusing the clinical interview. Separate profile sheets for males and females provide T scores for 20 symptom clusters. Actually, in the test manual, there are 40 specific diagnostic categories for which both symptom severity and symptom count cutoff scores are reported (said to provide dimensional and categorical information, respectively). Severity scores are simply the sum of item response scores, which range from 0 to 3, whereas the cutoff scores are the number of symptoms enumerated in the *Diagnostic and Statistical Manual of Mental Disorders, Fourth Edition* (DSM-IV; American Psychiatric Association, 1994) that must be present to suggest that diagnosis. There is a parallel version of the Adult Inventory (AI-4) designed to be filled out by a significant other. A comprehensive manual provides the history of the inventory, extensive description of diagnostic criteria, reliability information and prevalence rates calculated from both community and outpatient clinic samples, selected validity studies, and suggested clinical application.

The clinical application chapter is innovative–it includes for easy reference, interpretive guidelines, review of reliability, base rate information, and scale correlations in a table for each symptom category. For some disorders, illustrative case examples are provided in the associated narrative.

DEVELOPMENT. This measure was largely developed from the DSM-IV formulations of the various disorders. Tables are provided to compare the DSM-IV criteria and the ASRI-4 items. Beyond that, there is limited information about the development process or item generation. The test manual states that inclusion of diagnostic categories was based on prevalence and application, although the developers clearly extended a large screening net including many low frequency problems (e.g., narcolepsy, gender identity disorder). DSM-IV symptom statements were reportedly rewritten to be more understandable and some were revised during field testing. The test manual does not provide an assessment of required reading level. Many disorders are screened for by a single item. Twenty symptom categories include a minimum of 3 items with varying numbers of items within these categories; for example, there are 3 items related to anorexia, 11 related to major depression, and 22 for borderline personality disorder. The number of symptoms necessary for meeting symptom cutoffs follows the DSM-IV with some symptom categories including multiple ASRI-4 items when DSM-IV provides alternative examples (e.g., Posttraumatic Stress Disorder (PTSD) criteria require 2 or more of 4 listed items related to increased arousal). For substance use, the developers departed from the DSM-IV and simply asked about use as opposed to symptoms of substance abuse disorder.

TECHNICAL.

Standardization. The normative sample was recruited from Suffolk County, NY and consisted of 450 females and 450 males with the percentages at various (unspecified) age levels (18–75, mean 45 years) said to be in keeping with 2000 U.S. Census data. The ethnic distribution of the sample was 86% European American, 5% Asian American, 4% African American, 3% Hispanic American, and 2% other. Analyses indicated modest differences between age groups but enough significant gender differences (i.e., 23 out of 39 symptom categories) to warrant separate norms and profile sheets. No information is provided as to whether the scores of minority respondents differed from European Americans. The sample was highly educated with

only 16% indicating a high school diploma or less. The test manual appropriately notes that the symptom severity scores are highly skewed such that the linear T scores provided should not be interpreted in terms of a normal distribution. Approximately 3–5% of adults in the normative sample obtained scores equal to or greater than 70T (i.e., two standard deviations above the mean).

Reliability. Alpha coefficients are provided from multiple samples for the 20 symptoms categories with a minimum of three items. As would be expected, these estimates of internal consistency were low to moderate for categories with fewer items (i.e., anorexia .61) and higher (i.e., above .70) for most categories. A 2-week test-retest study involving 219 university students indicated a median correlation coefficient of .68 for symptom severity scores with kappas for most symptom cutoffs above .40 with the exception of bipolar personality disorder (BPD) (.29), Mania (.16), oppositional defiant disorder (ODD) (.35), and Schizoid Personality Disorder (.33).

The intercorrelations between ASRI-4 severity scores are also provided and suggest a number of symptom categories are highly related (e.g., PTSD was correlated .73 with generalized anxiety disorder [GAD] and .83 with major depressive disorder [MDD]); the test authors interpret these correlations as reflecting both symptom overlap within DSM-IV and comorbidity patterns. In addition, the degree of agreement between patient (ASRI-4) and other (AI-4) symptom ratings is reported as modest, indicating these respondents provide distinct information.

Validity. Several types of validity evidence are provided. First, the mean symptom severity scores and the symptom prevalence rates in the normative sample were compared to those from a diverse outpatient clinic sample composed of 487 adult referrals in various psychology practices located in six states. With few exceptions (mostly single item categories), the clinic outpatients scored higher on the ASRI-4. Also, where data were available (> 10 diagnosed patients), the patients diagnosed with a particular disorder obtained a higher severity score on the associated category than those without the disorder.

Second, the test manual provides a wealth of statistical information correlating ASRI-4 scores with other psychological measures (i.e., Brief Symptom Inventory, Conners' Adult ADHD Rating Scales, Hamilton Rating Scales, etc.). Of course, the degree of correspondence observed varied with the scale comparison. Although many of the correlations conform to the expected pattern, the correlations were generally modest with limited discrimination between some symptom categories.

The developers also examined the ASRI-4 prevalence rates in the normative sample relative to available epidemiological studies. They concluded that the rates were comparable for most symptom categories but that the ASRI-4 might underidentify PTSD and Antisocial Personality Disorder and overidentify anorexia, mania, sleep disorders, and BPD. Significantly, they recommend adjusting diagnostic cutoff scores based on the user's clinical setting.

COMMENTARY. This is a comprehensive adult symptom checklist for which the major use is to screen for DSM-IV symptoms in behavioral health settings as an aid in clinical assessment. Although the coverage is broad, too many symptom categories rely on a single screening item. Internal consistency for multi-item symptom categories is generally adequate but there is a need to examine stability of the scores in a clinical population. Many of the symptom severity scores are highly intercorrelated and probably have low discriminant validity as constructs. Psychometric limitations reflect the underlying DSM-IV model. Although mapping to the DSM-IV symptom criteria is an asset at one level, reliance on this model and criteria could also be considered a limitation when compared to instruments developed through or subjected to factor analytic techniques. Although the outpatient clinical group referenced in the test manual is reasonably diverse, the normative community sample on which T scores are based is restricted geographically and underrepresents minority groups. To avoid overidentifying individuals as likely having certain problems, clinical use would seemingly warrant examining base rates and cutoffs for particular populations and settings as the test authors of the ASRI-4 recommend.

A literature review indicated limited published research on the ASRI-4 beyond what is included in the test manual. A particular strength of the instrument is the inclusion of adult symptoms of childhood developmental disorder, particularly, attention-deficit/hyperactivity disorder (ADHD). In fact, examining patterns of comorbidity among ADHD subtypes and the continued distinctiveness of ODD symptoms among adults with ADHD (Gadow, Sprafkin, Schneider, Nolan, Schwartz, & Weiss, 2007; Sprafkin, Gadow, Weiss, Schneider,

& Nolan, 2007) appears to have been the major focus of research with this instrument. Some of the suggested uses in the test manual (e.g., screening in general medical practice, monitoring outcomes of psychotherapy) appear to need more research support at this time.

SUMMARY. The test developers have created a comprehensive adult screening checklist for DSM-IV symptom categories that is best used in behavioral health settings. A particular asset is the inclusion of ADHD and use of the ASRI-4 to assess for co-occurring problems in this population. However, mirroring the DSM-IV seems to limit the instrument psychometrically, and more research is needed to recommend some applications. Some diagnostic-related categories may become dated with the release of DSM-5. Readers may wish to compare the ASRI-4 to the Psychiatric Diagnostic Screening Questionnaire (PDSQ; Zimmerman, 2002), which focuses on screening a smaller number of disorders, but has a somewhat more developed research base.

REVIEWER'S REFERENCES
American Psychiatric Association. (1994). *Diagnostic and statistical manual of mental disorders* (4th ed.). Washington, DC: Author.
Gadow, K. D., Sprafkin, J., Schneider, J., Nolan, E., Schwartz, J., & Weiss, M. D. (2007). ODD, ADHD, versus ODD+ADHD in clinic and community adults. *Journal of Attention Disorders, 11*, 374–383.
Sprafkin, J., Gadow, K. D., Weiss, M. D., Schneider, J. S., & Nolan, E. (2007). Psychiatric comorbidity in ADHD symptom subtypes in clinic and community adults. *Journal of Attention Disorders, 11*, 114–124.
Zimmerman, M. (2002). Psychiatric Diagnostic Screening Questionnaire (PDSQ). Los Angeles, CA: Western Psychological Services.

Review of the Adult Self-Report Inventory-4 by BETH DOLL, Associate Dean, College of Education and Human Sciences, and JONATHON SIKORSKI, Doctoral Student, Department of Educational Psychology, University of Nebraska-Lincoln, Lincoln, NE:

DESCRIPTION. The Adult Self-Report Inventory-4 (ASRI-4) is a client-completed checklist describing symptoms of disorders identified in the *Diagnostic and Statistical Manual of Mental Disorders–Fourth Edition* (DSM-IV; 1994). It was developed for mental health practitioners to use when conducting clinical interviews of adults (aged 18 to 75 years) with possible mental disorders. The ASRI-4 manual also briefly describes a parallel form completed by someone who knows the client well, the Adult Inventory-4 (AI-4). Neither the ASRI-4 nor the ASI-4 is intended to be a diagnostic rating scale and results do not yield specific diagnoses. Rather, they are intended to streamline the process of gathering information so that qualified mental health professionals can make diagnoses. Only the ASRI-4 is described in this review.

The ASRI-4 consists of 136 items organized into 21 subsections describing the principal symptoms of most major mental disorders. The paper-and-pencil inventory can be completed in 15 to 20 minutes and is available in both English and Spanish. Respondents rate the prevalence of each symptom using a Likert scale from 0 (*never*) to 4 (*very often*). Those symptoms rated as occurring *often* or *very often* are considered to be clinically significant. Results can be summarized by comparing the clinically significant symptoms to the criteria of the DSM-IV diagnoses, or by computing a severity score for each symptom domain and comparing it to the normative sample. A summary score can be computed by hand using paper protocols, or can be created using a computer scoring program.

DEVELOPMENT. The test authors developed the ASRI-4 by identifying key symptoms for the major psychiatric disorders described in the DSM-IV. The checklist was then administered to a community sample and several clinical samples of participants, and results were examined to ensure that symptom severity was higher in the clinical samples, scores correlated with associated scores from other major psychiatric checklists, and scores supported accurate diagnostic decisions within the clinical samples. The ASRI-4 is the latest in a series of checklists developed to assist mental health professionals in gathering information about children's, adolescents', and adults' emotional or behavioral symptoms. Related inventories include the Early Childhood Inventory-4 (ECI-4; Gadow & Sprafkin, 1997) for 3- to 5-year-old children; the Child Symptom Inventory-4 (Gadow & Sprafkin, 2002) for children aged 5 to 12 years who are enrolled in special education programs; the Adolescent Symptom Inventory-4 (ASI-4; Gadow & Sprafkin, 1997) for adolescents (12 to 18 years); and the Youth's Inventory-4 (YI-4; Gadow & Sprafkin, 1999) for youth aged 12 to 18 years. The test authors consider the YI-4 to be a companion inventory to the ASRI-4, and the inventory shares similar rating scales.

TECHNICAL. In the opinion of the reviewers, evidence for the technical adequacy of the ASRI-4 is weak. The normative sample of the ASRI-4 is small and nonrepresentative. It consists of 900 adults recruited through public media in Suffolk County, Long Island, New York. Although the sample matched the 2000 U.S. Census for age, it did not match the Census for race, occupation, education, and marital status. In addition, the test manual describes a second nonclinical sample of 261 undergraduate students (the York University Study) in which the ASRI-4 ratings were compared to those of the Conners' Adult ADHD Rating Scale (Conners, Erkhardt, & Sparrow, 1999), the Wender Utah Rating Scale (Ward, Wender, & Rimherr, 1993), and the ADHD Behavior Checklist for Adults (Murphy & Barkley, 1995).

Results are also described for four studies of outpatient samples using the ASRI-4; means from the outpatient and normative samples were compared to verify that more symptoms were reported by clients of psychiatric practices. The first study, the Clinical Outpatient study, examined the prevalence of DSM-IV disorders for 487 clients of psychiatric practices in six states: Alabama, California, Georgia, Hawaii, Oregon, and Utah. The ADHD Randomized Clinical trial compared clients' DSM-IV diagnosis to ratings on the ASRI-4 for 81 adult participants with ADHD. The Follow-up Study compared 37 mothers' ratings of their sons (diagnosed 4 years earlier with attention-deficit/hyperactivity disorder) on the ASRI-4, Beck Depression Inventory (Beck & Steer, 1993), and the Symptom Checklist-90-R (Derogatis, 1994). Finally, the Child ADHD Study compared ratings using the ASRI-4 and the Brief Symptom Inventory (Derogatis, 1993) for mothers whose sons were referred for ADHD. None of the studies were referenced to peer-reviewed journals or national conference proceedings, and the test manual's incomplete description of study methods and results makes it difficult to tell whether their experimental control was adequate. Results of these studies, displayed in comprehensive correlation tables in the test manual, made a very weak case for the ASRI-4's discriminative power. Although the tables generally showed significant but modest correlations between the ASRI-4 symptom domains and associated subscales of other published measures, results also showed similarly mild to moderate relations with unrelated subscales or other psychiatric disorders.

Results of the six studies and those of additional conference proceedings are summarized into two chapters describing the ASRI-4's reliability. The internal consistency of the ASRI-4 symptom categories ranged from unacceptably low to high (alpha coefficients ranging from .52 to .92) depending on the sample. Test-retest reliability was moderately strong (.60 or higher) for ASRI-4 symptom categories when the symptom severity method was used to summarize results, but was not strong when the symptom count method was used.

The test authors also examined the accuracy of diagnoses made using the ASRI-4 for the outpatient samples. Results showed that ASRI-4 correctly identified over 70% of clients subsequently identified with borderline personality disorder, social phobia, and bulimia. It was moderately accurate in identifying over 70% of clients who were diagnosed with attention-deficit/hyperactivity disorder or general anxiety disorder and over 60% of clients who were diagnosed with major depressive disorder, post traumatic stress disorder, and schizophrenia. Fewer than half of clients were accurately identified who had been diagnosed with dysthymic disorder, mania/bipolar, and substance use.

COMMENTARY. The ASRI-4 is a brief and easy-to-use checklist of symptoms for the most common DSM-IV disorders. It could be a useful organizational tool for beginning mental health professionals by providing helpful prompts of the symptoms needed for differential diagnoses of mental disorders. However, there is only limited information about the technical adequacy of the ASRI-4, and studies examining the checklist's reliability or validity have not been subjected to careful peer review. The preliminary information available in the test manual provides limited evidence that the ASRI-4 is a reliable and valid measure. The checklist's reliability is inconsistent; it does not adequately discriminate among the various symptoms of mental disorders; and it has limited utility for diagnostic decision making. Normative interpretations of the ASRI-4 scores are unfounded given the small and geographically limited standardization sample. It is not clear that the ASRI-4 would add appreciably to the quality of diagnosis or treatment planning in mental health practices.

SUMMARY. In its current state, the ASRI-4 is a supplementary tool that mental health professionals could use to gather information about the DSM-IV symptoms of clients. Given gaps in methodological design, item development and analysis, standardization, and validity studies, the ASRI-4 cannot be recommended for clinical use.

REVIEWERS' REFERENCES

American Psychiatric Association. (1994). *Diagnostic and statistical manual of mental disorders* (4th ed.). Washington, DC: Author.
Beck, A. T., & Steer, R. A. (1993). Beck Depression Inventory. San Antonio, TX: Psychological Corporation.
Conners, C. K., Erkhardt, D., & Sparrow, E. P. (1999). Conners' Adult ADHD Rating Scale. North Tonowanda, NY: Multi-Health Systems.
Derogatis, L. R. (1993). Brief Symptom Inventory. Minneapolis, MN: National Computer Systems.
Derogatis, L. R. (1994). Symptom Checklist-90-R. Minneapolis, MN: National Computer Systems.
Gadow, K. D., & Sprafkin, J. (1997). *Adolescent Symptom Inventory-4 screening manual.* Stony Brook, NY: Checkmate Plus.
Gadow, K. D., & Sprafkin, J. (1997). *Early Childhood Inventory-4 norms manual.* Stony Brook, NY: Checkmate Plus.
Gadow, K. D., & Sprafkin, J. (1999). *Youth's Inventory-4 manual.* Stony Brook, NY: Checkmate Plus.
Gadow, K. D., & Sprafkin, J. (2002). *Child Symptom Inventory-4 screening and norms manual.* Stony Brook, NY: Checkmate Plus.
Murphy, K. R., & Barkley, R. A. (1996). Prevalence of DSM-IV symptoms of ADHD in adult licensed drivers: Implications for clinical diagnosis. *Journal of Attention Disorders, 1,* 147–161.
Ward, M. F., Wender, P. H., & Rimherr, F. W. (1993). The Wender Utah Rating Scale: An aid in the retrospective diagnosis of childhood attention-deficit hyperactivity disorder. *American Journal of Psychiatry, 150,* 885–890.

[2]
Advanced Multi-Dimensional Personality Matrix Abridged—Big 5 Personality Test.

Purpose: Designed to "measure five main personality traits ... for personal and professional development."

Population: Under age 17 through adult.

Publication Date: 2011.

Acronym: AMPM-Ab.

Scores, 5: Emotional Stability, Extroversion, Openness, Agreeableness, Conscientiousness.

Administration: Individual.

Price Data: Available from publisher.

Time: (15) minutes.

Comments: Self-administered online assessment. The test publisher advises that the test manual is being updated to include more information about methodology and theoretical background used in the development of the test. The test publisher also advises that this information is available to clients, as are benchmarks for relevant industries and racial/ethnic group comparison data. However, this information was not provided to Buros or the reviewers.

Author: PsychTests AIM, Inc.

Publisher: PsychTests AIM, Inc. [Canada].

Review of the Advanced Multi-Dimensional Personality Matrix Abridged–Big 5 Personality Test by SANDRA M. HARRIS, Assessment Coordinator, College of Social and Behavioral Sciences, Walden University, Minneapolis, MN:

DESCRIPTION. The Advanced Multi-Dimensional Personality Matrix Abridged–Big 5 Personality Test (AMPM-Ab) is a brief personality test that is completed online in about 15 minutes. The purpose of the test is to evaluate certain personality characteristics or specific skill sets. The results are computer scored, and the respondent receives a computer-generated report that describes his or her personality. Results from the test are used to generate five subscale scores: Emotional Stability, Extroversion, Openness, Agreeableness, and Conscientiousness. The test manual indicates that results from the test can be used for professional or personal development.

DEVELOPMENT. The 25-item AMPM-Ab is a shortened version of the Advanced Multi-Dimensional Personality Matrix Abridged, which contains 190 items. The test manual indicates the test is based on the Five Factor Model credited to Goldberg (1981) and McCrae and Costa (1987). However, no information is provided regarding how the AMPM-Ab relates to the Five Factor Model. The test manual does not describe the rationale, model, or other theoretical base that was used to guide the selection and inclusion of items appearing on the AMPM-Ab.

TECHNICAL.

Normative sample. The test manual presents a table of information regarding basic demographic information for participants in the normative sample. The standardization sample consisted of 36,087 participants. The sample contained 64% female and 28% male respondents, with 8% of participants not reporting gender. The test manual presents a summary table that categorizes the participants into seven age groups. All participants self-selected to participate in the validation study.

Psychometric properties. The test manual presents basic statistics such as mean and standard deviation for each of the five scales. However, data were presented for the entire sample. No additional data were presented for any of the other demographic variables identified in the test manual. One table presents the internal consistency estimates (alpha coefficients) for each subscale. Values ranged from .45 for the Agreeableness subscale to .79 for the entire 25-item scale.

Validity. Given that the test authors state that the AMPM-Ab is based on the Five Factor Model credited to Goldberg (1981) and McCrae and Costa (1987), it would be reasonable to expect the test authors to conduct studies to assess validity of test scores by comparing them with scores obtained by other means. For example, such studies might correlate scores obtained from the AMPM-Ab with scores of other validated instruments that measure the five personality factors (Emotional Stability, Extroversion, Openness, Agreeableness, and Conscientiousness). No information is given regarding the degree to which scores obtained on the AMPM-Ab correlate with scores from other instruments that measure the five factors of personality.

COMMENTARY. The AMPM-Ab is presented as a personality assessment that can be used to measure the five main personality traits that affect a person's attitudes and behavior. The test manual presents an extensive array of tables and charts of comparative analyses across a number of demographic variables. However, the test manual does not present narrative text to explain and contextualize the various analyses. There are bulleted statements that describe the overall statistical results, but there is no supporting narrative that provides the background or rationale for the analyses.

The test manual further falls short of providing background information on the development of the instrument. No explanation is given as to the theoretical, empirical, or other rationale that guided the selection of items retained in the abridged version of the instrument. Another shortcoming is that the test manual presents scant information on the psychometric properties of the AMPM-Ab. Limited information is presented regarding internal consistency estimates, but no information is presented regarding other types of reliability. There is also no information regarding validity of test score use, test bias, or standard errors of measurement.

SUMMARY. The AMPM-Ab may be a useful instrument for self-exploration or comparative analysis of how well a profile generated from it compares to a profile generated from other tests that measure the five factors of personality. The test manual indicates that results could be used for professional development; however, there are no directions or instructions to guide its use in that capacity. There is a need for additional information regarding the development, reliability, and validity of the instrument.

REVIEWER'S REFERENCES

Goldberg, L. R. (1981). Language and individual differences: The search for universals in personality lexicons. *Review of Personality and Social Psychology, 2* (1), 141–165.

McCrae, R. R., & Costa P. T., Jr. (1987). Validation of the five-factor model of personality across instruments and observers. *Journal of Personality and Social Psychology, 52,* 81–90.

Review of the Advanced Multi-Dimensional Personality Matrix Abridged–Big 5 Personality Test by STEVEN V. ROUSE, Professor of Psychology, Pepperdine University, Malibu, CA:

DESCRIPTION. The Advanced Multi-Dimensional Personality Matrix Abridged–Big 5 Personality Test (AMPM-Ab) is a 25-item measure of the personality traits comprising the Five Factor Model (FFM) of personality: Emotional Stability, Extroversion, Openness, Agreeableness, and Conscientiousness. Readers who are unfamiliar with the FFM should consult John, Naumann, and Soto (2008) for a comprehensive overview of the model, including a review of its history and its many methods of measurement. The AMPM-Ab manual provides a brief statement that the test is intended to be used to "evaluate certain personality characteristics and or specific skill sets" for personal and professional development purposes, but the manual itself does not provide guidance regarding how this information can be applied for these purposes. The company's website lists this test as one of their "Candidate Selection; General pre-employment tests," but neither the website nor the test manual provides recommendations concerning how results could be appropriately used for this purpose.

The test is administered online and results in an automatically generated web-based interpretive report. This report is divided into six sections. First, a paragraph-long description of a specific personality type (such as "The Altruist," "The Diplomat," or "The Balance") provides an overarching characterization of the individual based on the highest scores obtained from the FFM trait scales. Second, an introduction provides a brief description of the FFM and a sentence-long description of the five traits. Third, scores for each of the five traits are presented graphically. Fourth, paragraph-long interpretations of the five scores expand on the brief descriptions given in the second section. Fifth, "Strengths" (i.e., high scores on Emotional Stability, Agreeableness, Openness, and Conscientiousness), "Potential Strengths" (i.e., moderate scores on the same four scales), and "Limitations" (i.e., low scores on the same four scales) are listed. Sixth, "Advice" is provided in the form of several paragraph-long pieces of guidance. It does not appear that the advice is individualized for the test taker, because all three demonstration administrations provided to the reviewer included the same advice, despite distinctly different scores on the five scales.

DEVELOPMENT. No information is provided in the test manual to inform potential users about any aspect of the development of the test, nor does the test manual address the development or validation of the interpretive statements. In the absence of the availability of this developmental information, which is considered essential according to the American Educational Research Association (AERA), American Psychological Association (APA), and the National Council on Measurement in Education (NCME) (1999), potential users of the AMPM-Ab are unable to evaluate for themselves the psychometric integrity of the test development methods used.

TECHNICAL.

Standardization. The standardization sample is composed of 36,087 individuals who completed the

study through a website that makes tests available for self-exploration purposes (i.e., www.queendom.com). The sample is a self-selected one, and does not appear to be representative of the U.S. population; for example, women are overrepresented (64%) as are individuals ages 24 and below (65%). No information is provided regarding the representation of different races and ethnicities. Although the validation studies described below involved selecting subgroups for comparisons across groups for several variables (e.g., educational attainment, self-reported academic grades, and socioeconomic status), these comparisons only represent subsets of the standardization sample, and descriptive statistics on these variables are not provided for the full sample.

Reliability. The test manual presents reliability data in the form of alpha coefficients; for the five scales, the values range from .45 (Agreeableness) to .72 (Extroversion) with a mean of .64. Because these five scale scores are based on responses to five items each, these relatively low levels of reliability are not surprising. Interestingly, the alpha coefficient for the entire set of 25 items was .79. It is surprising, however, that an internal consistency coefficient was calculated for items measuring five theoretically uncorrelated characteristics. Alpha coefficients measure the covariance among all of the items being analyzed. As such, one would not expect a high alpha value for a set of items measuring five distinctly different constructs. Because the alpha coefficient for the entire set of 25 items was higher than that obtained for any one specific trait, this raises the hypothesis that the five trait scores have a higher level of intercorrelation than would be appropriate if the measure truly represents an orthogonal trait model (John et al., 2008). Other common forms of reliability data (such as test-retest reliability) are not provided.

Validity. The Validation section of the AMPM-Ab manual does not include the types of analyses that one would normally expect for a measure of the FFM. For example, because these traits represent five uncorrelated factors, a measure of these traits would be expected to provide data regarding the intercorrelations of the scores or the results of a confirmatory factor analysis, but these data are not provided. In addition, because of the large number of extant tests developed to measure the FFM, one would expect data regarding the correlations between the five AMPM-Ab scales and counterpart scales from other measures such as those listed by John et al. (2008). Instead of these standard pieces of validation evidence, the test manual presents a series of comparisons across various subgroups from the standardization sample. These comparisons, though interesting, do not constitute "validation data" because they provide no information regarding the extent to which the test scores measure the intended traits. For example, scores are contrasted across gender (with men obtaining higher scores on Emotional Stability and Openness, and women obtaining higher scores on Extroversion, Agreeableness, and Conscientiousness), Age (with older adults generally obtaining higher scores than younger adults on Emotional Stability, Agreeableness, and Conscientiousness, and lower scores on Extroversion), Education level (with college-educated individuals generally obtaining higher scores than non-college-educated on Emotional Stability, Openness, Agreeableness, and Conscientiousness, and lower scores on Extroversion), socioeconomic status (with those from higher income levels generally obtaining higher scores than those from lower income levels on Emotional Stability, Openness, and Agreeableness), and other similar variables. Interestingly, all five scales were correlated with a measure of overall happiness, with self-reported happy people obtaining higher scores on all five measures. In the absence of the intercorrelation and factor analytic data described above, this finding raises a concern that all five scores might share common variance with an underlying factor of subjective well-being or social desirability.

COMMENTARY AND SUMMARY. A test user wishing to measure the traits of the FFM has a large number of options from which to select, including the well-established and well-validated NEO Personality Inventory—3 (Costa & McCrae, 2011) and the Five Factor Inventory (John et al., 2008). Developers of a new test of this model would be expected to provide evidence of the ways in which their measure improves on extant measures. Even if this model was not as effectively measured as it is by existing tests, test developers should provide a manual that documents the basic aspects of test development and validity that are considered essential by the AERA, APA, and NCME (1999). However, the AMPM-Ab manual lacks the information that would allow a test user to choose this test with confidence. Moreover, the data provided in the test manual, such as the relatively low internal consistency estimates for the individual scales and the higher internal consistency estimates for the

entire item set of five theoretically uncorrelated factors, diminishes one's confidence in its use. In short, in the presence of well-established alternate measures and in the absence of basic supporting data, use of the AMPM-Ab is ill-advised for any purpose other than basic research, and even that is most appropriately limited to gathering data on the strengths and weaknesses of the test itself.

REVIEWER'S REFERENCES

American Educational Research Association, American Psychological Association, & National Council on Measurement in Education. (1999). *Standards for educational and psychological testing.* Washington, DC: American Educational Research Association.

Costa, P. T., Jr., & McCrae, R. R. (2011). *NEO Inventories: Professional manual.* Lutz, FL: PAR, Inc.

John, O. P., Naumann, L. P., & Soto, C. J. (2008). Paradigm shift to the integrative Big Five trait taxonomy. In O. P. John, R. W. Robins, & L. A. Pervin (Eds.), *Handbook of personality: Theory and research* (3rd ed. pp. 114–158). New York, NY: Guilford Press.

[3]

Anger Regulation and Expression Scale.

Purpose: Designed as "a self-report assessment of the expression and regulation of anger in children and adolescents."

Population: Ages 10-17.

Publication Date: 2011.

Acronym: ARES; ARES(S).

Scores, 25: 3 clusters, 13 scales, 8 subscales, Total Score: Internalizing Anger [Arousal (Physiological Arousal, Cognitive Arousal), Rejection, Anger-In, Bitterness (Resentment, Suspiciousness)], Externalizing Anger [Overt Aggression/Expression (Physical Aggression, Verbal Expression), Covert Aggression, Revenge, Subversion (Relational Aggression, Passive Aggression), Bullying, Impulsivity], Extent of Anger [Scope of Triggers, Problem Duration, Episode Duration].

Administration: Individual or group.

Forms, 2: Full-length, Short.

Price Data, 2012: $199 per online kit, including technical manual (114 pages), 15 online response forms, and 15 short online response forms; $299 per complete scoring software kit, including technical manual, unlimited use scoring software (USB key), 25 response forms, and 25 short response forms; $55 per 25 response forms (full-length or short); $132 per complete scoring software program (USB key); $2.50 per online response form (full-length or short); $89 per technical manual.

Time: (15) minutes for ARES; (5) minutes for ARES(S).

Comments: May be administered via paper-and-pencil or online; online scoring or software (USB key) is required for scoring paper-and-pencil assessments.

Authors: Raymond DiGiuseppe and Raymond Chip Tafrate.

Publisher: Multi-Health Systems, Inc.

Review of the Anger Regulation and Expression Scale by CYNTHIA E. HAZEL, Associate Professor of Child, Family, and School Psychology, University of Denver, and SUSAN McDONALD, Doctoral Stu-

dent, Child, Family, and School Psychology, University of Denver, Denver, CO:

DESCRIPTION. The Anger Regulation and Expression Scale (ARES) is a self-report assessment for evaluating expression and regulation of anger, as well as planning interventions and monitoring progress for anger control in youth, ages 10 to 17 years. The 75-item instrument is composed of five domains of anger functioning, broken into 13 scales. The 13 scales provide for three cluster scores (Internalizing Anger, Externalizing Anger, and Extent of Anger) and a Total score. The 13 scale scores, 3 cluster scores, and Total Score are reported as *T*-scores and categorized as Very Elevated, Elevated, Slightly Elevated, Average, and Low. A response validity scale assesses Positive Impression and Negative Impression. The instrument can be purchased with scoring software or scored through the publisher's website; it cannot be scored by hand. There is also a 17-item short form of the instrument (ARES[S]) that is composed of the 3 cluster scores (Internalizing Anger, Externalizing Anger, and Extent of Anger) and Total score. The ARES(S) can be used as a screener for individuals and/or groups to evaluate the need for more comprehensive assessment, additional supports, or universal intervention.

The test authors intend that the instrument be administered by psychologists, social workers, physicians, professional counselors, marriage and family therapists, criminal justice professionals, psychiatric workers, or pediatric/psychiatric nurses. They also require that interpreters of the ARES and ARES(S) have graduate-level coursework in assessment and measurement, be familiar with the technical manual, be familiar with educational and psychological testing standards, and be professionally licensed or have membership in a professional association with ethical standards relating to educational and psychological testing.

Test items are written at a fifth-grade reading level. Administration takes approximately 5 minutes for the ARES(S) and 15 minutes for the ARES. The technical manual provides instructions for oral administration if necessary to ensure that the youth understands each item. The test authors recommend that the instrument not be given to youth with severe neurological or intellectual impairment, with reading impairments, or who may not be English proficient.

DEVELOPMENT. The ARES was developed to assess features of anger experiences and expressions relevant to and understandable by youth, and to be a tool in treatment planning. The ARES is based on the same conceptual framework as the test authors' adult anger inventory, the Anger Disorders Scale (ADS; DiGiuseppe & Tafrate, 2004). This model assumes that anger is a clinical problem and not a personality trait and that there are five domains of anger (Provocations, Arousal, Cognitions, Motives, and Behaviors). Utilizing theories of child and adolescent development, the test authors developed items across the five domains distinctive to how youth express and regulate anger. The ARES technical manual contains a discussion of current research on the construct of anger and measures of anger in youth. The test authors designed the ARES to assess a broader range of anger characteristics than other available measures, provide more differentiation of clinically significant anger than other youth anger instruments, and better account for anger differences in age and gender through separate norms. The test authors propose criteria for an anger disorder, Anger Regulation and Expression Disorder, which is manifested in extensive, extended anger episodes or excessive or disruptive expressions of anger that impact social, family, school, or work relationships.

The ARES was piloted with 700 youth from a culturally diverse sample in New York City. Based on the pilot data, items were discarded, reworded, and added to create a reliable and valid preliminary factor structure. A multidimensional factor model with scales and subscales was developed through exploratory and confirmatory factor analyses, including separating respondents by gender and ages. The 21 empirically derived scales and subscales were organized into three clusters (Internalizing Anger, Externalizing Anger, and Extent of Anger). This model was tested through confirmatory factor analysis and found to meet fit criteria under several indices. The Validity Scale was developed to address concerns of youth presenting themselves overly positively or negatively.

The ARES(S) was developed by including one item from each scale or subscale based on regression analyses, resulting in a 17-item form. A multiple correlation coefficient of .97 between the total score on ARES(S) and ARES was found and confirmatory factor analysis found excellent model fit for the cluster scores on the ARES(S).

TECHNICAL.

Standardization of ARES and ARES(S). The ARES and ARES(S) were normed on 800 youth between the ages of 10 and 17, equally distributed by gender for each age and representative of the most recent U.S. Census on race and ethnicity. Utilizing multivariate analyses of variance (MANOVA), significant main effects were found on cluster scores, scales, and subscales with respect to gender and age. Therefore, separate norms are provided by age groups (10–12 years, 13–15 years, and 16–17 years) and gender. Only small effect sizes were found based on race and ethnicity, and so norms are not divided by race or ethnicity.

Reliability of ARES and ARES(S). Internal consistency estimates for the ARES across the normative sample and a clinical sample ranged from .97 to .99 for the Total score, .87 to .97 for the cluster scores, and .65 to .96 for the scales and subscales. Internal consistency estimates for the ARES(S) of .89 to .92 on the Total score and .35 to .90 on the cluster scores were reported. When adjusting for the lack of range in some scales, the test-retest reliability of the ARES over a 2-week to 4-week interval (mean of 17.4 days) ranged from .58 to .91 for the scales and subscales, and from .76 to .92 for the clusters, based on a sample of 58 youth (mean age 14.5). Test-retest reliability coefficients for the ARES(S) on Total score and cluster scores ranged from .79 to .88.

Validity of ARES and ARES(S). The technical manual presents evidence of discriminant and convergent validity. Discriminant validity was determined using data collected from youth with previous diagnoses of Conduct Disorder, Oppositional Defiant Disorder, and other clinical disorders (such as anxiety disorders, depression, and learning disabilities). MANCOVA results found significant main effects of clinical group membership for ARES scale scores, cluster scores, and total score (Wilks' Lambda = .53 to .64) and for ARES(S) cluster scores and total score (Wilks' Lambda = .65). Further, discriminant function analyses found the ARES to correctly predict classification of Conduct Disorder (CD) and Oppositional Defiant Disorder (ODD) with rates ranging from 83% to 91% and the ARES(S) to correctly predict classification of CD and ODD with rates ranging from 82% to 88%. Convergent validity evidence was provided based on the Conners Comprehensive Behavior Rating Scales (CBRS) and the Jesness Inventory–Revised (JI-R). Correlation coefficients between the ARES total score and the Conners CBRS (r = .64 to .70) and the JI-R (r = .42 to .52) were moderate to strong. Correlation coefficients between the ARES cluster

scores and the Conners CBRS (r = .52 to .70) and the JI-R (r = .26 to .66) also provide evidence of moderate to strong convergent validity.

COMMENTARY. Because the ARES and ARES(S) were first published in 2011, there are no published research studies that use the ARES and ARES(S) to date. Particularly because there is a lack of consensus on what constitutes problematic childhood anger, it is a great strength that the ARES has a firm theoretical basis. Studies that have used the ADS, which is also based on a model of disturbed anger, have found it to have clinical and empirical utility with adults (see, for example, Fuller, DiGiuseppe, O'Leary, Fountain, & Lang, 2010). Although the ARES looks extremely promising, the clinical and independent empirical support remain to be shown.

A benefit of the ARES and ARES(S) is that the scales focus exclusively on anger, in comparison to other broader assessments. Because these scales are focused solely on anger, they provide nuanced information about children and youth with problematic anger. The ARES(S), with only 17 items and estimated to take 5 minutes to administer, offers great possibilities for initial screening and progress monitoring.

SUMMARY. In summary, the ARES and ARES(S) are self-report measures designed to measure problematic anger regulation and expression in youth, ages 10 to 17. The scales are based on a model of disturbed anger and describe the youth's anger along the dimensions of Internalizing Anger, Externalizing Anger, and Extent of Anger. The scales were normed with a sample of 800 youth, representative of the demographics of the U.S.; with the norming sample, both scales show strong evidence in support of test score use as far as reliability and validity are concerned. The ARES and ARES(S) offer great promise to clinicians and researchers for assessing anger to design responsive interventions and to monitor progress for individuals and groups of youth.

REVIEWERS' REFERENCES

DiGiuseppe, R., & Tafrate, R. C. (2004). *Anger Disorder Scale technical manual.* Toronto, Canada: Multi-Health Systems, Inc.

Fuller, J. R., DiGiuseppe, R., O'Leary, S., Fountain, T., & Lang, C. (2010). An open trial of a comprehensive anger treatment program on an outpatient sample. *Behavioural and Cognitive Psychotherapy, 38*, 485-490. doi: 10.1017/S1352465810000019

Review of the Anger Regulation and Expression Scale by CHRISTOPHER A. SINK, Professor and Chair, School Counseling and Psychology, and LAUREN D. MOORE, Doctoral Student, Counselor Education, Seattle Pacific University, Seattle, WA:

DESCRIPTION. According to the test manual, the Anger Regulation and Expression Scale (ARES) and its abbreviated form, Anger Regulation Expression Scale–Short (ARES[S]), are self-report quantitative measurements of anger expression and regulation in older children and adolescents (ages 10 to 17). Specifically, the scales are designed to be clinically relevant in identifying patterns of feelings, behavior, and cognition that can be addressed in intervention programs. Whereas the test authors indicate that the ARES(S) is only to be used as a screening and monitoring tool, the ARES is particularly useful to mental health and school-based counselors who desire a comprehensive profile assessing aspects of anger that contribute to poor functioning and maladjustment. This review considers only the ARES. For those readers who are interested in the ARES(S), the test manual provides pertinent technical information.

The ARES (75 items) can be administered to client groups as well as individually either in person or remotely. In addition to the paper-and-pencil form, the assessment is also available online. Potential respondents need only possess a 5.5 grade-level reading ability to complete the instrument. Given that examinees respond to a series of item statements arrayed in a 5-point Likert-type fashion, the administration time required is 15 minutes.

The ARES estimates respondents' levels of Internalizing Anger (cluster 1 score; addresses angry thoughts and feelings), Externalizing Anger (cluster 2 score; addresses behaviors associated with anger such as coercive bullying), and Extent of Anger (cluster 3 score; addresses the scope and duration of respondents' anger level). Each cluster comprises multiple scales, several of which have subscales. Internalizing Anger is represented by four scales (Arousal [subscales: Physiological and Cognitive], Rejection, Anger-In, and Bitterness [subscales: Resentment and Suspiciousness]). Externalizing Anger has six scales (Overt Aggression/Expression [subscales: Physical Aggression and Verbal Expression], Covert Aggression, Revenge, Subversion [subscales: Relational Aggression and Passive Aggression], Bullying, and Impulsivity). Extent of Anger is composed of three scales (Scope of Triggers, Problem Duration, and Episode Duration). The ARES also has two validity scales: Positive Impression and Negative Impression. In all, 27 scores are generated.

Administration instructions are clearly outlined in the test manual and readily comprehensible for informed practitioners. The computerized versions are convenient and efficient to distribute; however, clinicians should consider potential computer and software logistical issues and glitches (see test manual for hardware and software requirements). To effectively utilize the ARES online, a reliable and fast internet connection with a current browser are optimal. To score the paper-and-pencil ARES, the most efficient approach is to use the publisher's software included as part of the test kit. The scoring process is not as straightforward and intuitive as one would expect from a professional appraisal tool. For example, data entry instructions are underdescribed in the test manual. Once item responses are correctly entered into the scoring program, a comprehensive anger profile/report summarizing the characteristics of anger that contribute to poor functioning and maladjustment is quickly generated. The findings reported include total, scale, and subscale scores, as well as for interpretation purposes, associated T-scores ($M = 50$, $SD = 10$), confidence intervals, and percentile ranks. The ARES software also provides score interpretation, intervention suggestions, and response validity information. After multiple survey administrations to the same respondents are performed, a progress report also can be produced.

DEVELOPMENT. The test manual outlines four phases that roughly correspond with accepted scale development processes (Netemeyer, Bearden, & Sharma, 2003; Nunnally & Bernstein, 1994). Apparently the measures discussed in the test manual are in their third iteration. Drawing from a variety of pertinent sources including clinical, developmental, and social psychologies, the test authors describe the measures' solid conceptual framework. The anger-related clinical research literature was consulted during test development (e.g., initial item generation and inclusion). In short, the fundamental constructs of the ARES appear to reflect elements of the five emotion domains that are assessed, in part, on the respective scales and subscales.

The test manual also discusses the involved pilot research conducted on the early versions of ARES with large clinical and nonclinical groups of older children and adolescents ($N = 700+$) living in the New York City metropolitan area. Although not detailed in the narrative, initial test version data were submitted to a series of item and factor analyses providing some evidence for scale reliability and validity.

To determine the final ARES's scales and subscales, derivation and confirmatory respondent sample data were gathered using what looks to be a stratified (on gender and ethnicity) convenience sampling process. Aggregated sample sizes for the derivation sample were largely acceptable (e.g., nonclinical respondents, $N = 510$; clinical samples, $N = 166$). Demographic data were comparable across the derivation and confirmatory clinical and nonclinical samples (e.g., relatively equal proportions of males and females and different ethnicities [White, African American, Hispanic Latino, Multiracial/other]). Regrettably, age frequencies were not reported.

The underlying dimensionality of the ARES scales was determined through exploratory factor analyses (EFA) and confirmatory factor analyses (CFA). Although the EFA and CFA results are underreported in the test manual, a four-factor model (Arousal, Bitterness, Subversion, and Overt Aggression/Expression) appears to be largely substantiated. Further CFAs were conducted generating the three general anger clusters (Internalizing, Externalizing, and Extent of Anger). These clusters differ in part from the initial ARES theoretical framework and its five emotion domains. Congruence analyses revealed high consistency between boys and girls (rs all greater than .90). As discussed below, in the final phase of test development, the authors collected sufficient data for the norming process.

TECHNICAL. Data collection for the standardization phase of test development lasted three years (2006–2009). ARES results ($N = 800$, equally divided into eight age groups [ages 10 to 17], 50% female, 62% White, 17% African American, 15% Hispanic/Latino, 7% Multiracial/other) were disproportionally collected across four geographic regions of the U.S. (approximately 80% were drawn from the Northeast and Southern regions) using convenience sampling. The overall standardization sample was matched to the general population on race/ethnicity (i.e., within about 1% to the most recent U.S. Census race/ethnicity distribution). However, Asian Americans seemed to be underrepresented in the norming sample; as such, the applicability of the ARES to Asian American older children and adolescents is questionable. Significant respondent gender differences were found on some scales. For example, whereas nonsignificant gender differences for Internalizing or Scope/duration scales were found, boys reported significantly higher levels of Externalizing Anger than girls. These disparities, as evidenced by the small effect sizes, were considered by the test authors to be of little practical significance. Perhaps more troubling, age main effects were reported across multiple scales, including total score. In comparison to the youngest and oldest respondents, on various anger scales adolescents in the 13 to 15 age range generally had the highest scores. Significant age by gender interaction effects were found on certain subscales and are summarized in the test manual. Thus, an atypical curvilinear response pattern was found for the Age and Gender variables. Based on these results, the test authors normed the ARES to three age groups (10 to 12, 13 to 15, and 16 to 17 years).

Other important psychometric properties of the ARES were generally well-described in the manual. In terms of reliability, internal consistency and stability coefficients are presented. For each age group (n greater than or equal to 200 for each of three groups) and gender ($n = 400$ for each) in the normative sample ($N = 800$), all scales and subscales revealed at least adequate internal consistency (greater than .70) for attitudinal, self-report measures (Nunnally & Bernstein, 1994), with exceptions noted for the 13–15 age group (for males and females) where values were at least .65 for Episode Duration. In addition, an alpha coefficient of .68 occurred for the Bullying scale among 10–12-year-old females. The alpha coefficients computed by gender for the clinical sample were satisfactory as well. For the normative and clinical ($N = 270$) groups, the three cluster scores and total score generated strong overall alpha coefficients, ranging from .89 to .98.

A 2-to-4-week test-retest interval (mean interval = 17.4 days) was used to determine scale stability (Ns range from 52 to 58). Pearson correlations (obtained and adjusted for restriction in range) were calculated from data gathered from nonclinical and clinical samples, and from disaggregated gender and ethnicity test scores. For the entire sample, all clusters, scales, and subscales generated acceptable stability coefficients (adjusted rs ranged from .58 [Passive Aggression subscale] to .92 [Extent of Anger cluster], $ps < .001$). Total score ($r_{adjusted} = .90$) and the other two clusters showed robust test-retest reliability (Internalizing Anger, $r_{adjusted} = .76$; Externalizing Anger, $r_{adjusted} = .88$).

To examine the ARES's validity, several conventional methods were employed. First, the scale's scores were subjected to a series of multivariate and discriminant function analyses (DFAs) to estimate their discriminative validity. MANCOVA (covariates: age, gender, and race/ethnicity) results yielded significant main effects for group membership across all analyses, differentiating, for example, conduct disorder (CD) and oppositional defiant disorder (ODD) groups from the general (nonclinical) group and a nonspecified other clinical (OC) group (omnibus results for cluster scores: Wilks' Lambda = .64, $F[9, 912.80] = 20.59$, $p < .001$, eta-squared partial = .14; scales: Wilks' Lambda = .53, $F[39, 1081.59] = 6.54$, $p < .001$, eta-squared partial = .19; subscales: Wilks' Lambda = .64, $F[24, 1073.71] = 7.37$, $p < .001$, eta-squared partial = .14). In summary, total and cluster scale (T-scores), as well as Internalizing Anger, Externalizing Anger, and Extent of Anger scales appeared to significantly differentiate respondent clinical groups (CD, ODD, OC) from the nonclinical sample, producing modest to large effect sizes (eta-squared partial range = .07 [Rejection] to .31 [Total]).

As a further examination of discriminant validity, DFAs were conducted to ascertain whether ARES scores (total and cluster) could accurately predict group membership into the clinical samples (respondents diagnosed with CD or ODD) or nonclinical samples. The relevant classification statistics were strong for predicting CD and ODD on total and cluster scores. For example, correct classification percentages ranged from 83% (predicting ODD with total score) to 91% (predicting CD with cluster scores).

According to the research presented in the test manual, scores on the ARES demonstrate satisfactory convergent validity. For example, a sample of older children and youth ($N = 92$) from the general, nonclinical population completed the ARES along with the Conners Comprehensive Behavior Rating Scales (CBRS; $N = 92$) and the Jesness Inventory–Revised (JI-R; $N = 47$). To determine convergent validity, correlation coefficients between the ARES total score and selected (anger related) Conners CBRS scales ranged from .64 to .70. Similarly, ARES cluster scores moderately correlated with selected Conners scales (coefficients ranged from .52 to .70). Total ARES and JI-R scores were also significantly correlated (coefficients ranged from .42 to .52). ARES cluster scores correlated with JI-R scales, with coefficients ranging from .26 to .66.

Finally, the test manual summarizes numerous statistical analyses aimed at ascertaining whether similar mean ARES scale T-scores would be found across varying ethnicities (African American, $N = 135$; Hispanic/Latino, $N = 116$; White, $N = 494$) drawn from the normative sample. Contrary to what one might predict, the omnibus MANCOVA (co-variates included pertinent demographic variables) conducted on the dependent variables (cluster, scale, and subscale scores) consistently generated significant main effects for ethnicity. Effect size estimates (eta-squared partial) were relatively weak, ranging from .04 (cluster scores) to .09 (scale scores). Follow-up univariate tests again showed significant differences among various ethnic groups across almost every scale (i.e., White respondents scored significantly higher than Hispanic/Latino group). On the Internalizing Anger scales, African American examinees tended to score significantly lower than the European American/White sample. Effect sizes generated for each analysis were small, fluctuating approximately from .02 to .05. Even though the test authors note that the reported ethnicity group score differences are consistent and small, sufficient caution is warranted when using the ARES with nonmajority clients or students.

In summary, the ARES appears to be psychometrically sound, demonstrating adequate to strong reliability for the older children and adolescent normative sample and various clinical populations. With some exceptions, validity evidence was sufficient to support test score use in the manner proposed. Reliability and validity data were less convincing for minority groups such as Asian American respondents.

COMMENTARY. At this juncture, the ARES can be tentatively utilized as a comprehensive assessment for understanding anger-related experiences, self-perceptions, and actions of various older children and adolescent groups represented in the normative sample (e.g., White, African American, certain clinical populations). If used with appropriate ethical care and psychometric training, the ARES may also be suitable for developing baseline anger-related client data and loosely monitoring anger intervention effectiveness.

Practically speaking, the ARES should be deployed primarily as an anger-related screening measure. Well-trained and experienced clinicians (e.g., child psychologists and other mental health professionals) should find the ARES particularly serviceable for a variety of reasons. First, the measures appear to be solidly based on applicable theory and research. Second, the test manual is well-organized, and the information is coherently presented with readable instructions, explanations, as well as figures, and tables. Third, the ARES is easy to administer and relatively uncomplicated to score and carefully interpret. Fourth, clinicians will appreciate the multiple illustrative case studies discussed in the test manual to assist with test administration and score interpretation. It is important to note, however, the manual is short on the specifics needed for nuanced intervention planning and treatment efficacy evaluations. In this regard, other sources should be consulted.

To their credit, the test authors, DiGiuseppe and Tafrate, counsel against interpretation, diagnosis, and treatment planning from ARES data alone. Rather, they rightly suggest a wide-ranging appraisal process, administering related psychometrically sound measures to clients in addition to ARES. Observational, interview, and other available data should be collected and synthesized into a full report. This recommendation is particularly germane to the test administration and score interpretation of underrepresented minority and clinical populations excluded from the norming process.

SUMMARY. The ARES is a promising measure to assess research-based anger characteristics in certain groups of U.S. older children and adolescents. Because this user-friendly measure is relatively new, its long-term psychometric properties and validity are unconfirmed. Moreover, the norms are restricted, and the test's underlying conceptual framework is moderately complex, requiring ARES administration, interpretation, and intervention planning only by examiners who are knowledgeable of and experienced in clinical assessment procedures and psychological testing. Any definite conclusions about respondents' anger issues and the threats to their mental health should be avoided. With further longitudinal and cross-cultural research, this instrument may become a welcome addition to the diagnostic and intervention planning efforts directed to anger issues.

REVIEWERS' REFERENCES

Netemeyer, R. G., Bearden, W. O., & Sharma, S. (2003). *Scaling procedures: Issues and applications.* Thousand Oaks, CA: Sage.
Nunnally J. C., & Bernstein, I. H. (1994). *Psychometric theory.* New York, NY: McGraw Hill.
U.S. Census Bureau, Population Division. (2010). *Race data: The Asian population in the United States.* Retrieved from http://www.census.gov/population/www/socdemo/race/Asian-slide-presentation.html

[4]

Assess Expert System.

Purpose: A web-based assessment system that provides assessment for selection and development of managers and professionals.

Population: Current employees, potential employees, and candidates for promotion in professional, managerial, and sales positions.

Publication Dates: 1997-2010.

Acronym: ASSESS.

Scores: Updated and shortened versions of the Guilford Zimmerman Temperament Survey (GZTS) and Dynamic Factors Opinion Survey (DFOS) provide normative results on 24 characteristics grouped in the areas of Thinking, Working, and Relating; Intellectual Ability Tests: 7 possible scores: Watson-Glaser Critical Thinking, Raven's Standard Progressive Matrices (Abstract Reasoning), Thurstone Test of Mental Alertness, Employee Aptitude Survey 7 (EAS-7)—Verbal Reasoning, RBH Arithmetic Reasoning Test, Employee Aptitude Survey 2 (EAS-2)—Numerical Ability, Employee Aptitude Survey 1 (EAS-1)—Verbal Comprehension.

Administration: Group or individual.

Parts, 8: Assess v2 Personality Survey, Watson-Glaser Critical Thinking, Raven's Standard Progressive Matrices, Thurstone Test of Mental Alertness, Employee Aptitude Survey 7 (EAS-7)—Verbal Reasoning, RBH Arithmetic Reasoning Test, Employee Aptitude Survey 2 (EAS-2)—Numerical Ability, Employee Aptitude Survey 1 (EAS-1)—Verbal Comprehension.

Price Data, 2011: $295 per one-time fee for account set-up and user training; $170 to $220 per report (depending on quantity); annual licenses for larger volume usage are available.

Foreign Language Edition: German version available.

Time: Administration time varies for each assessment.

Comments: The personality survey is the main component of the assessment. Intellectual ability tests are optional and may be given in any combination.

Author: Bigby, Havis & Associates, Inc., d/b/a Assess Systems.

Publisher: Bigby, Havis & Associates, Inc., d/b/a Assess Systems.

Cross References: For reviews by Peter F. Merenda and Stephen Olejnik of an earlier version called Assess Expert Assessment System Internet Version 1.3, see 14:21.

Review of the Assess Expert System by LAURA L. B. BARNES, Associate Professor of Research and Evaluation, School of Educational Studies, Oklahoma State University, Tulsa, OK, and R. EVAN DAVIS, Adjunct Instructor of Management, Spears School of Business, Oklahoma State University, Stillwater, OK:

DESCRIPTION. The Assess Expert System is described as an "expert system designed to model the judgments of psychologists in the interpretation of an assessment test battery and in the writing of reports based on these judgments" (manual, p. 1). The computer-based system of tests is designed for use in "hiring, promotion, placement, and developmental decisions" (manual, p. 1).

The system's main component is the Assess Personality Survey, which contains 24 scales organized under three constructs: Thinking, Working, and Relating. The other components include an abridged version of Raven's Standard Progressive Matrices (1958), Watson-Glaser Critical Thinking Appraisal Form S (1994), the Thurstone Test of Mental Alertness (1952), the Employee Aptitude Survey to measure verbal and numerical ability (1956), and the RBH Arithmetic Reasoning Test (1983).

The Internet interface appears to support online testing for the Personality Survey, the Watson-Glaser Critical Thinking test, and the abridged Raven's Standard Progressive Matrices. The 350-item personality test takes approximately 30 minutes to complete, but testing can be completed in more than one session if desired by the test administrator. The interface generates both competency-based reports and standard reports for hiring as well as developmental reports. Test scoring and interpretation are conducted within the expert system.

DEVELOPMENT. The Assess Personality Survey has undergone a number of revisions since its initial development in the 1970s when it was a combination of the Guilford-Zimmerman Temperament Survey (GZTS) and the Dynamic Factors Opinion Survey. Items have been deleted, others revised, new items developed, new scales added, scale names changed, and scales reorganized under different category labels for reporting. Additional changes from 1996–2001 were in response to item reviews by staff psychologists who identified items that were not compliant with the Americans with Disabilities Act, items that were not job related or that appeared to be associated with the wrong scale, or items that appeared to suggest negative personality traits or behavior. The current 350-item instrument, Assess v2, was released in 2003.

TECHNICAL. This review focuses on the Personality Survey; however, a few comments regarding the technical aspects of the aptitude measures are appropriate. Normative data are not provided in the manual for the aptitude tests. Although the technical manual states that Assess Systems developed norms for the Watson-Glaser test and that they appear in the manual (p. 38), there are no normative data in the manual for the Watson-Glaser. Standardization regarding the other ability tests is not addressed. Reliability information is absent, and validity evidence is, in some cases, entirely out of date. The most recent validity evidence shown in the test manual for the Thur-

stone Test of Mental Alertness was a 1968 study by Thurstone himself. Regarding the Arithmetic Reasoning Test, the Assess technical manual says, "The AR was originally developed in 1948 and was revised in 1961 to conform to current laws and procedures. Validity of the test is supported by numerous studies cited by the publisher (RBH, 1963)" (manual, p. 42).

For the Personality Survey, psychometric properties are reported for different versions, making it difficult to determine how up-to-date various components of the information are. For example, alpha coefficients are reported for original and shortened scales, but the scale names do not all match those for which test-retest coefficients are reported, nor is the number of scales the same. There are 21 scales with alpha coefficients but 24 scales with test-retest coefficients. Several scales share a common code, adding some confusion.

Test norms were developed using Assess candidate data. The total sample upon which these norms were based is said to be more than 55,000. The technical manual lists sample sizes used to develop "normative templates" for nearly 100 different job descriptions ranging from 46 (e.g., aviation manager) to 1,785 (executive, general). The sample sizes for the five most general job groups (executive, mid-manager, supervisor, professional, and sales) are 1,785; 8,165; 752; 14,979; and 2,822, respectively. Dates of data collection are not given, and because the test itself has changed considerably over the years, there is no way to evaluate the relevance of some of the normative data. A normative data table converting subscale scores on the Personality Survey and the positive response factors to percentiles is provided, although the reason for its inclusion in the manual is not clear given that scoring, percentile conversion, and interpretation are governed by expert system rules. Following the general norms table is a display of graphic profiles for the five general job groups. These profiles contain information about typical scores of people in specific job groups with comparisons to other professionals. The test manual says comparing job groups can help assess a respondent's fit with specific jobs.

Reliability. Internal consistency coefficients based on 5,050 professional and managerial respondents are provided for 21 scales. When the test was shortened from 480 to 350 items in 1996, both subjective and statistical analyses were used for item selection/revision. The statistical analyses for selecting 15 items per scale are described simply as multiple regression and item-scale correlations. The 16 original length scales had a range of alpha coefficients from .65 to .85 (*Mdn* = .795); the 16 shorter scales had alpha coefficients ranging from .57 to .85 (*Mdn* = .70). The authors suggest the lower reliability is to be expected because the scales were shortened and maintain that the coefficients still are at an "acceptable" (manual, p. 18) level. However, half of the coefficients are at or below the bare minimum threshold of acceptability for early stage research in the opinions of these reviewers.

Internal consistency coefficients presented for the five new scales are not much better, ranging from .64 to .78 (two scales below .70; *Mdn* = .76). The lack of stability reliability data noted in a previous review (Merenda, 2001) has been addressed by including one test-retest study. Test-retest coefficients are reported for 24 scales using a sample of 99 U.S. university students who took the test twice within 5 to 51 days (*M* = 16.8, *SD* = 9.5). Test-retest coefficients ranged from .67 to .89 (*Mdn* = .81). A German translation was given to a sample of 238 students and faculty at a university in Germany. In two administrations 24 to 65 days apart (*M* = 51.1, *SD* = 7.1), test-retest coefficients ranged from .72 to .91 (*Mdn* = .775).

Validity. Validity evidence is non-systematic and consists largely of tables of correlations that are not adequately explained or interpreted. Construct validation is discussed in the manual primarily with respect to the original Guilford-Zimmerman Temperament Survey and the Dynamic Factors Opinion Survey from which the Personality Survey was adapted. With one exception, the studies cited in the Assess technical manual were published in the 1950s, 1960s, and 1970s. A dissertation published in 1999 showed some relationship between the Assess shortened scales and the NEO-PI-R (a five-factor model) with a sample of 88 professionals. Correlations show some overlap between the Assess scales and the NEO-PI-R scales, but the included table shows no logical connection between the factors of the GZTS and the Big Five model. Another table shows scale intercorrelations for Assess v2, which could form the basis for an examination of the factor structure, but no attempt is made to interpret the correlation matrix. It is presented "for informational purposes" (manual, p. 26). Construct evidence of validity is lacking regarding the relationships among the scales and their clustering into the dimensions Thinking, Working, and Relating.

The section on criterion-related evidence of validity research presents a series of concurrent

validity studies of 15 different jobs in which a Success Profile Index was computed for each employee participant and correlated with supervisor ratings of key performance measures. All but five were based on the Personality Survey alone. Correlations with supervisors' ratings range from .19 to .57. The computation of the Success Profile Index depends on which dimensions were identified as important for the job and on the ranges identified as desirable for that dimension. The technical manual suggests that the correlations between supervisor ratings and Assess scale scores were the basis for identifying which scales would be included. This is inappropriate because if only the tests that correlated with the criterion were included in the index, then the validity index is inflated. A cross-validation strategy should be used so that a different set of respondents and supervisors would be used in the validation sample than in the calibration sample. It appears that all the criterion validity studies suffer from this same limitation. Another limitation is the lack of information regarding how the "desirable ranges" on the attributes were determined.

COMMENTARY. In recent years, the most commonly used personality measurement in both industrial and organizational psychology and organizational behavior research has been based on the Big Five model. The research connecting the GZTS to this widely used taxonomy is weak and underdeveloped, consisting of a single dissertation with a sample size of 88. This sample size is inadequate to evaluate the measurement model required by a 350-item instrument. Additionally, only certain aspects of the Big Five have shown consistency in predicting workplace outcomes across industries and careers.

The fatigue effects that could be experienced by individuals taking the Assess Personality Scale could be mitigated by eliminating many of the extraneous elements that do not measure significant variance in the outcome variables. With nine subscales as part of the larger GZTS instrument, one would expect significant shrinkage when trying to predict performance outcomes. More parsimonious models of the personality construct exist, and it is curious that these more recent revelations are eschewed for adherence to an older model that has not been subjected to rigorous academic evaluation for many years.

The meta-analytic results of Barrick and Mount (1991) on the Big Five personality dimensions showed that only conscientiousness is a consistent predictor of performance across industries and careers, but for certain types of jobs extraversion and openness to experience are also good predictors of certain outcomes. This conclusion brings into question the need for all nine factors to be included in each test administration. In a 20-year longitudinal study Harrell and Alpert (1989) employed the GZTS but found that only three facets (Energy, Ascendance, and Sociability) were of any significant use. The final instrument used in their data collection contained only eight GZTS items out of 480. These same factors (E, A, and S) were similarly related to "general executive competence" in a study by Bentz (1985).

The internal consistency of the measure raises another concern. The test authors cite Nunnally and Bernstein (1994) to justify having reliability coefficients of barely .70. However, what Nunnally (1978) actually said differs from this view and focuses on this type of test application. For early stages of research, Nunnally believed .70 was a lower limit of the acceptable range of reliabilities. For high stakes decision-making situations Nunnally called for reliability coefficients of at least .90. Nunnally noted that even when the reliability is .90, the standard error of measurement is almost one-third of the group standard deviation.

A final concern involves the lack of information regarding the language translation. The Assess Personality Survey is available for online or paper-and-pencil administration in many different languages, but no evidence regarding the quality of translated forms has been provided. The only piece of evidence reported for a language translation is test-retest reliability for a German form. There is no information regarding the norms or validity of the German form for international clients. No evidence is presented regarding the relevance of the Assess system to any market outside the U.S. Do the measures have the same predictive validity cross-culturally?

SUMMARY. The Assess system is a technologically sophisticated testing, scoring, and reporting system. Such a sophisticated system needs to be supported by equally sophisticated psychometric evidence. Unfortunately, the evidence is sparse. It seems that a great deal of effort has gone into revising the instrument and enhancing the interface and the expert reporting system, but the empirical evaluation of the psychometric underpinnings of the testing system has not reached the same level of success. Most reported changes to the test have been on the basis of subjective review by staff psychologists. However, the Personality Survey has not been subjected to rigorous empirical review nor have psychometric standards of reliability and validity been given serious consideration. Evidence regarding the reliability and validity of the ability tests needs to be addressed as well. There is a need also to revise the manual—not simply to add new information to the old, but to rewrite it—bringing the information up-to-date and reorganizing it so the consumer can evaluate the system in its most current state. Until adequate evidence is presented to support the quality of this system, it cannot be recommended.

REVIEWERS' REFERENCES

Barrick, M. R., & Mount, M. K. (1991). The Big Five personality dimensions and job performance: A meta-analysis. *Personnel Psychology, 44*, 1-26.

Bentz, V. J. (1985, August). A view from the top: A thirty year perspective of research devoted to the discovery, description, and prediction of executive behavior. In 93rd Annual Convention of the American Psychological Association, Los Angeles.

Harrell, T. W., & Alpert, B. (1989). Attributes of successful MBAs: A 20-year longitudinal study. *Human Performance, 2*(4), 301-322.

Merenda, P. F. (2001). [Review of ASSESS Expert Assessment System Version 5.X]. In B. S. Plake & J. C. Impara (Eds.), *The fourteenth mental measurements yearbook* (pp. 1033-1038). Lincoln, NE: Buros Institute of Mental Measurements.

Nunnally, J. C. (1978). *Psychometric theory* (2nd ed.). New York, NY: McGraw-Hill.

Nunnally, J. C., & Bernstein, I. H. (1994). *Psychometric theory* (3rd ed.). New York, NY: McGraw-Hill.

Review of the Assess Expert System by KATE HATTRUP, Professor, Department of Psychology, San Diego State University, San Diego, CA:

DESCRIPTION. The Assess Expert System is a computer-based system for the administration and scoring of several personality scales and cognitive ability measures used in personnel selection and development. The Assess Expert System uses a large normative database of respondents to compare examinees' scores and generate written narrative and graphical reports that describe a job applicant's scores on several personality dimensions and job-related competencies. As the manual states, the normative database consists of "professional level job candidates" who were seeking jobs that require education and training beyond a high school level, which are usually salaried rather than hourly, and which usually require some personal responsibility for work results. Therefore, the Assess Expert System may be less useful for entry-level unskilled jobs.

The personality measure included in the Assess Expert System consists of 350 items that are administered either via a web-based interface or by paper-and-pencil. The items are anchored with a simple binary choice: *agree* or *disagree*. Most of the items were taken from the Guilford-Zimmerman Temperament Survey (GZTS) and the Dynamic Factors Opinion Survey (DFOS). Thus, nine of the scales of the GZTS are retained in the Assess Expert System (Masculinity-Femininity was dropped because it was not considered job-relevant), along with seven of the scales of the DFOS (Aesthetic Appreciation, Adventure vs. Security, and Need for Diversion were dropped). The personality measure also includes items written to measure five additional dimensions and two experimental scales. There are also two positive response scales (Subtle Fake and Gross Fake), and scores on these scales may be used to flag unusual scores or to adjust scale scores; the magnitude of adjustment to test scores is not clarified in the manual.

The Assess Expert System also can accommodate the administration of up to seven cognitive ability tests, including the Watson-Glaser Critical Thinking Appraisal Form S; Raven's Standard Progressive Matrices; the Thurstone Test of Mental Alertness; the RBH Arithmetic Reasoning Test; and the Verbal Comprehension, Verbal Reasoning, and Numerical Ability tests of the Employee Aptitude Surveys. Scores are compared with the same database of professional and managerial applicants, and interpretations are provided in a separate section of the Assess report.

Detailed information is provided to examinees about the purpose of the test and about anonymity, privacy, and data sharing. There are no time limits indicated for the measure. The web interface is easy to use and understand. Examinees must respond to all of the items because the interface will not allow an examinee to change pages without first completing all of the items that are shown. It would be preferable to anchor the items with an odd number of response options, allowing a "neutral" or "no opinion" response, and to permit examinees to skip items or leave them blank.

DEVELOPMENT. The Assess Expert System originated in the 1970s as a computer-based system for interpreting scores on the GZTS and DFOS and writing professional reports. Over time, new items were added, and others were deleted to update the measure and to improve its face validity as an apparent predictor of job performance. Using multiple regression and item-scale correlations, each of the original scales was reduced in length by deleting items. Items were also deleted to ensure compliance with guidelines related to the Equal Employment Opportunity Commission (EEOC), Americans with Disabilities Act (ADA), invasion of privacy, and other legal and ethical standards. Correlations between the original and revised scales range from .85 to 1.0. In the most recent version

of the Assess Expert System, scores are also available for 38 job-specific competencies that fall into three broad areas: Thinking, Working, and Relating. Linkages between the personality scales and competencies were determined by expert judgment and prior research.

TECHNICAL. At various places in the manual, it is stated that the normative database consists of "over 55,000 professionals and managers" (p. 3) and "over 100,000" respondents (pp. 1, 2). As noted, the normative database consists of candidates for professional level jobs, and not for entry-level jobs, military occupations, or skilled trades. Overall percentile ranks are provided in the manual for each of the personality scales; these are not separated by age, experience, ethnicity, gender, or occupation. Templates are available for 96 occupations, allowing comparisons of an examinee's scores with successful employees in each of a wide variety of occupations. These templates are based on normative data collected from employees in specific occupations, with sample sizes ranging from 46 employees to 14,979 (mean sample size = 707.72). Normative information is not provided for any of the cognitive ability measures, and scores on these measures do not appear to be included in the job-specific templates.

The test manual reports internal consistency (alpha) reliability coefficients for each of the personality scales, ranging from .57 to .85 (N = 5,050 to 5,851), the lower end of which might be considered very low but the upper end perhaps acceptable for a test used in high stakes decision making (normally reliabilities should exceed .90 in this reviewer's opinion). Retest reliabilities were calculated in separate samples of U.S. (N = 99) and German (N = 238) university students and faculty. An average of 16.83 (SD = 9.54) or 51.13 (SD = 7.12) days passed between administration of the measure on the first and second occasions in the U.S. and German samples, respectively. Retest reliabilities ranged from .67 to .89 in the U.S. sample and from .72 to .91 in the German sample.

The manual also reports intercorrelations among all of the personality scales; a factor analysis of these correlations might provide useful insights about the factor structure of the overall measure. Evidence of the construct validity of specific scales is provided in the manual. Previous research reported expected patterns of correlations between the GZTS scales and scales from the 16PF Questionnaire, the California Psychological Inventory

(CPI), and Edwards Personal Preference Survey (EPPS). Other research reported in the test manual observed expected correlations between Assess scales and scales of the NEO-PI-R, which measures the five-factor model of personality. The manual also reports expected patterns of correlations between the cognitive ability measures and other measures of ability, academic performance (i.e., GPA), and job performance. Some of the correlations between the personality scales and the positive response factors (Subtle Fake, Gross Fake) are quite substantial. For example, correlations with Work Pace, Need for Task Closure, Optimism, Criticism Tolerance, and Sociability each exceed .45.

Results of 15 criterion-related validation studies are reported in the manual, and the reported validity coefficients range from .22 to .62, based on relatively small samples ranging from 49 to 221 participants. Each of these coefficients is based on a flawed design. In every case, a concurrent validation was undertaken, and then the Assess scales that correlated with criterion performance were used to create a tailored "Success Profile" for each new sample. Then, the Success Profile was correlated with the criteria, and these correlations are reported as criterion-related evidence of validity in the manual. Because there was no cross-validation of the Success Profiles in any of the samples, there is considerable potential for validity shrinkage in new samples, and this possibility is especially problematic given the small samples used in the validation studies. Although adverse impact ratios are provided for most of the studies, differential prediction analyses by ethnicity or gender are not reported.

COMMENTARY. The Assess Expert System is a sophisticated and flexible computer-based application for the administration, scoring, and interpretation of a set of standardized personality and cognitive ability measures. The Assess Expert System relies on several well-known and successful measures, including the GZTS, DFOS, and several published measures of cognitive ability. As such, a certain degree of psychometric quality is built into the Assess Expert System, and perhaps more is known about the constructs measured by the Assess Expert System than many competing computer-based test batteries. It is unfortunate that normative data are currently not available for a wider range of jobs, but that is easily corrected through additional data collection. Perhaps the most significant weakness of the measure is what this reviewer considers the limited evidence of criterion-related validity. The concurrent validity coefficients that are reported in the manual are no doubt inflated relative to their population values and are unlikely to replicate.

Moreover, users must consider carefully whether the tests used in the Assess Expert System, and the dimensions that it measures, meet their needs as well as competing Internet and computer-based assessments. Several vendors provide similar products; some, like the Assess Expert System, report scores on their own proprietary scales, whereas others report scores for more widely used dimensions, such as those in the five-factor model.

SUMMARY. The Assess Expert System is an adaptable computer-based system for administering, scoring, and interpreting several personality and ability scales. It relies on tests that are well-known and well-validated as measures of specific constructs, but although preliminary evidence is certainly available, its usefulness as a predictor of job performance has yet to be demonstrated convincingly. Although the Assess Expert System is engaging and easy to use, flexible, and provides detailed and colorful computer-generated reports, users are urged to make test adoption decisions on the basis of sound psychometric evidence, especially evidence of validation.

[5]

Assessment of Multiple Intelligences.

Purpose: Designed to "assess which of Gardner's Eight Intelligence Types a person possesses."
Population: Below age 17 to over age 40.
Publication Date: 2011.
Acronym: AMI.
Scores, 8: Bodily-Kinesthetic, Logical-Mathematical, Linguistic, Visual-Spatial, Musical, Intrapersonal, Interpersonal, Naturalistic.
Administration: Group.
Price Data: Available from publisher.
Time: (20) minutes.
Comments: Self-administered online assessment. The test publisher advises that the test manual is being updated to include more information about methodology and theoretical background used in the development of the test. The test publisher also advises that this information is available to clients, as are benchmarks for relevant industries and racial/ethnic group comparison data. However, this information was not provided to Buros or the reviewers.
Author: PsychTests AIM, Inc.
Publisher: PsychTests AIM, Inc. [Canada].

Review of the Assessment of Multiple Intelligences by GARY L. CANIVEZ, Professor of Psychology,

Department of Psychology, Eastern Illinois University, Charleston, IL:

DESCRIPTION. The Assessment of Multiple Intelligences (AMI) purports to measure "which of Gardner's eight intelligence types a person possesses" for use in pre-employment testing (manual, p. 1). The AMI is also "designed to facilitate improvement and increase the test-taker's suitability for this career" (p. 1). Unfortunately there is no description as to *how* the AMI is to be used in pre-employment testing or otherwise. It is computer administered and scored based on a self-report questionnaire or survey with 55 questions and presents results and scores for each of Gardner's eight hypothesized intelligences: Bodily-Kinesthetic, Logical-Mathematical, Visual-Spatial, Linguistic, Musical, Intrapersonal, Interpersonal, and Naturalistic. The AMI contains nine questions asking the examinee to indicate which response (out of four to nine options) best answers a question about what they would or might do, think, or remember, or about how others might perceive them; six questions that ask the examinee to check all activities, jobs, hobbies, previous best school subjects, venting feelings, and rating strengths that apply; one question with a list of careers they think they could be best at with adequate resources and training from which they select three; and 39 statements or characteristics rated on a 5-point scale ranging from *exactly like me* to *not at all like me*. Self-report responses related to each of the eight intelligences produce scores, but there is no indication of the type of score reported (raw score, standard score, percentile rank, etc.). It appears that the results are simply raw scores totaling item responses related to the particular intelligence dimensions.

A computer-generated report is produced that first summarizes the individual's "main" intelligence type, specified by the intelligence scale that results in the highest score. There is no explication in the manual as to how this "main" type is determined when there is not a significant difference between the highest and the next highest score; presumably the "main" intelligence type is simply the one with the highest score. The report includes a description of Gardner's theory and beliefs, followed by a graph, reflecting a profile, of the individual's scores on the eight intelligence scales. No standard error of measurement-based confidence intervals are presented on the graph or elsewhere. A presentation of each of Gardner's eight intelligences with a description, motto, list of common abilities/strengths/interests, and list of famous people who presumably represent that intelligence is included with the individual's score. Areas of concern are reported on a listing of so-called "Dominant Intelligence Types" (those with "high" scores), "Influencing Intelligence Types" (those with "medium" scores), and "Least Developed Intelligence Types" (those with "low" scores). However, like the determination of the "main" intelligence type, the manual provides no information or criteria for what constitutes a high, medium, or low score. Finally, the report ends with "Advice" regarding each of the eight intelligences presented with "Tips" on how to maximize that type (presumably by practicing or doing more of it). The vast majority of the report appears to be canned statements that do not differ regardless of responses. There are no peer-reviewed research publications or books referenced in the report or the manual.

DEVELOPMENT. The manual provided for this review provides little or no information about how the AMI was developed or about the procedures and iterations of item construction or evaluation. No rationale is provided for why a self-report survey was used in place of directly assessing intellectual skills and abilities through actual performance. There is no report of expert evaluation of essential content to guide construct representation, and there is no report of pilot testing, item analyses, item refinement, or criteria for decisions to add, delete, or modify items or item types. Statistical analyses and tables are included in the manual, but there is no description of a priori hypotheses stated for statistical comparisons across gender, age, education, grades, or occupational position that would guide interpretation of statistical results. The test manual presents statistically significant findings, but no discussion of the meaning or implications of these differences is provided.

TECHNICAL. Statistical information is presented in the manual, but there is no normative sample or transformation of raw scores to standardized scores. A total of 10,135 individuals (5,463 [54%] female, 3,595 [35%] male, 1,077 [11%] unknown gender) reportedly completed the AMI on Queendom.com, Psychtests.com, or PsychologyToday.com. The sample was uncontrolled, as respondents self-selected to participate in the validation data collection. Reported frequencies within age categories indicated 29% were below 17, 29% were 18-24, 11% were 25-29, 12% were 30-39, 11% were 40 and above, and 8% did not report their age. Disappointingly, descriptive statistics for age are not provided, so it is unknown how young the youngest or how old the oldest participants were. Also there is no indication why the specified unequal age ranges were selected or whether individuals reported exact ages that were later converted to age ranges.

Descriptive statistics for the eight intelligences include minimums, maximums, means, and standard deviations, but skewness and kurtosis indexes are not reported. Histograms presented for each of the eight intelligence dimensions illustrate that all eight were negatively skewed and indicate that participants tended to rate themselves more favorably on all dimensions. This is in contrast to performance-based intelligence tests in which subtests and composite scores are normally distributed. The manual contains tables of descriptive statistics of scores by gender, age, education, grades, and occupational position. Missing is any description of participant race, ethnicity, geographic region, community size, or country of origin.

The only method of reliability reported for the eight intelligence scale scores is internal consistency. Alpha coefficients for the scale scores ranged from .64 (Naturalistic) to .79 (Logical-Mathematical). The alpha coefficient for the overall scale was .82, even though there is no total or overall score provided by the AMI. The sample size and sample characteristics for these calculations were not disclosed. These internal consistency estimates are substantially lower than the criterion ($\geq$ .90) many measurement experts indicate is necessary for individual test use or clinical decision-making (Nunnally & Bernstein, 1994; Ponterotto & Ruckdeschel, 2007; Salvia & Ysseldyke, 2001). Although alpha coefficients are presented, no standard errors of measurement or confidence intervals (obtained score or estimated true score) are provided in either the manual or the report. Standard errors of measurement are necessary for proper test score reporting and interpretation (AERA, APA, & NCME, 1999). Because intelligence is a construct that is assumed to be stable across time, it is further disappointing that short-term test-retest (stability) estimates are not provided as is customary.

Prior to reporting what were described as validity analyses, t-test and ANOVA procedures were noted, and sample size was acknowledged to be an issue in interpreting statistically significant differences that might not have practical importance. Presentation of effect size estimates (i.e., Cohen's

d; Cohen, 1988) would have easily illustrated such differences, but the manual is devoid of these important estimates. It was further noted that when the number of subjects in validation samples were not equally balanced, a smaller random sample from the larger group was made to "conduct the analyses effectively" (p. 3). Reductions in sample sizes were apparently made for females, individuals under age 25, and in an unknown manner across education, grades, and occupation. Resulting sample sizes across subgroups were not identical but were closer than those in the total sample. There are no multivariate analyses (MANOVA) or factorial analyses examining interactions between the five validity variables on the eight intelligence dimensions.

It was noted in the manual that all data provided were self-reported; there was no report of an attempt or ability to verify the accuracy of data obtained. Participants were asked to reply to questions regarding their gender, age, educational level (10 categories from grade school through Ph.D./Doctoral Degree), grades (top, good, average, or below average), and position (entrepreneur, managerial, non-managerial, or not employed). The manual notes that age, education, grades, and position variables were "recoded" but this adjustment is not explained. Presumably these variables were used to test the validity of AMI scores, but there is no discussion about expected differences or hypotheses for differences between various groups. Only t-tests (gender) or univariate ANOVAs (age, education, grades, position) and descriptive statistics are presented; given that the AMI includes eight scales (eight dependent variables), multivariate analyses should have been reported first. Significant ($p < .05$) or "marginally" significant ($p < .10$) post hoc comparisons are reported, but effect sizes are not presented. Following presentation of statistically significant differences across subgroups, bar graphs of group means are presented to illustrate the subgroup differences. To judge these results, this reviewer calculated effect sizes based on the largest mean differences reported in the tables in the manual across the five comparision variables. The majority of comparisons reported to be statistically significant were of trivial or small effect sizes (Cohen, 1988) and thus not of practical or clinical importance. Several medium effect sizes were found, but no mean comparisons achieved a large effect size. Particularly troubling is the fact that mean differences between those reporting Ph.D./Doctoral Degrees and those reporting Some

High School produced Cohen's *d* effect sizes of only .59 (Logical-Mathematical), .68 (Linguistic), and .032 (Visual-Spatial); other effect sizes were much smaller, including for those reporting only a Grade School education. It is also clear that the graphs in the manual illustrating group differences are presented in a manner that grossly exaggerates group differences visually because of stretching out the vertical axis and starting it well above zero.

COMMENTARY. Tests and assessment instruments are constructed in a manner that reflects both theoretical constructs and practical applications. Instruments have specific applications, and psychometric research is conducted to provide evidence for the various uses and interpretations proposed by authors and publishers. In addition to a test demonstrating strong evidence for reliability, validity, and utility of scores, there must be a detailed manual that provides ample evidence for the theoretical background and research supporting the construct being measured; explicit description of the methods and procedures of test construction including item development, analysis, and modification; detailed description of a normative sample from which norm referenced scores would be derived based on a representative sample from the population; detailed description of various methods of psychometric evaluation of reliability, validity, and utility; and, finally, detailed description of interpretation procedures for application of scores for groups and individuals. The AMI and its manual fall far short of approximating any of these important qualities.

With respect to the underlying theory of the AMI, there are many critics of Gardner's theory, and many have pointed out major shortcomings (e.g., Barnett, Ceci, & Williams, 2006; Brody, 2006; Jensen, 1998; White, 2006). Generations of psychologists have studied intelligence for more than a century and have measured and quantified aspects such as quantitative reasoning (Logical-Mathematical), verbal reasoning (Linguistic), and spatial visualization (Visual-Spatial). These aspects seem to be the only intelligences in Gardner's theory with strong evidence and that others would consider intelligence. Although other abilities or characteristics Gardner calls intelligence do constitute differences across individuals, very few agree with Gardner that they are intelligence or should be considered so.

Messick (1989, 1995) argued for validity of tests to be examined along a number of important dimensions and to be based on evidence from (a)

test content, (b) response processes, (c) internal structure, (d) relations with other variables, and (e) consequences of testing. These areas are specifically noted in the *Standards for Educational and Psychological Testing* (AERA, APA, & NCME, 1999). The only reported approach to assessing validity of AMI scores was with relations with other variables related to general comparisons across demographic subgroups without specified hypotheses or expectations from theory or past research. There were no correlations between the eight AMI scales presented, no internal structural analyses (exploratory or confirmatory factor analyses), no predictive validity analyses, and no diagnostic efficiency or utility analyses. There were no comparisons of the AMI self-ratings with objective measures of the actual skills of the individuals. Without such data it is impossible to meaningfully interpret AMI scores. There are no inferences one can make based on AMI scores without such validity data. The available evidence in the AMI manual showing inadequate reliability and the general dearth of information in the manual is not consistent with *Standards for Educational and Psychological Testing* (AERA, APA, & NCME, 1999), and the AMI should not be used in individual clinical decision-making. In the words of Weiner (1989), the ethical psychologist will "(a) know what their tests can do and (b) act accordingly" (p. 829). In the case of the AMI, this test (a) has not demonstrated acceptable levels of reliability, validity, or diagnostic utility of scores and (b) ought not be used in individual assessment situations, pre-employment or otherwise.

SUMMARY. The AMI was reportedly designed to assess which of Gardner's eight intelligence types individuals possess, to be used in pre-employment testing, to suggest improvement, and to increase the individual's career suitability. Based on the extreme lack of information provided in the AMI manual and the apparent lack of published peer-reviewed research, it appears that the AMI can do none of these. It is strongly recommended that the guidance of Clark and Watson (1995) and *Standards for Educational and Psychological Testing* (1999) be followed and that the AMI not be used in any clinical, pre-employment, or other individual evaluation situations until it is revised and refined and strong reliability, validity, and utility evidence is provided. Individuals who complete the AMI and the professionals attempting to make sense of and use scores from the AMI are sadly provided scores that are not normatively based, are insufficiently reliable, disregard error in measurement, lack validity data to make interpretations, and lack utility data regarding whether scores assist in correctly identifying or classifying individuals. At best, the AMI is a novelty test like those commonly found on Internet sites. Should one be interested in assessing intelligence then one of the many well normed, standardized, and research abundant skill-based measures of intellectual or cognitive abilities should be used.

REVIEWER'S REFERENCES

American Educational Research Association, American Psychological Association, & National Council on Measurement in Education. (1999). *Standards for educational and psychological testing.* Washington, DC: American Educational Research Association.

Barnett, S. M., Ceci, S. J., & Williams, W. M. (2006). Is the ability to make a bacon sandwich a mark of intelligence?, and other issues: Some reflections on Gardner's theory of multiple intelligences. In J. A. Schaler (Ed.), *Howard Gardner under fire: The rebel psychologist faces his critics* (pp. 95–114). Chicago, IL: Open Court.

Brody, N. (2006). Geocentric theory: A valid alternative to Gardner's theory of intelligence. In J. A. Schaler (Ed.), *Howard Gardner under fire: The rebel psychologist faces his critics* (pp. 73–94). Chicago, IL: Open Court.

Clark, L. A., & Watson, D. (1995). Constructing validity: Basic issues in objective scale development. *Psychological Assessment, 7,* 309–319.

Cohen, J. (1988). *Statistical power analysis for the behavioral sciences* (2nd ed.). Hillsdale, NJ: Lawrence Erlbaum Associates.

Jensen, A. R. (1998). *The g factor: The science of mental ability.* Westport, CT: Praeger.

Messick, S. (1989). Validity. In R. L. Linn (Ed.), *Educational measurement* (3rd ed., pp. 13–103). New York, NY: American Council on Education and Macmillan.

Messick, S. (1995). Validity of psychological assessment: Validation of inferences from persons' responses and performances as scientific inquiry into score meaning. *American Psychologist, 50,* 741–749.

Nunnally, J. C., & Bernstein, I. H. (1994). *Psychometric theory* (3rd ed.). New York, NY: McGraw–Hill.

Ponterotto, J. G., & Ruckdeschel, D. E. (2007). An overview of coefficient alpha and a reliability matrix for estimating adequacy of internal consistency coefficients with psychological research measures. *Perceptual and Motor Skills, 105,* 997–1014.

Salvia, J., & Ysseldyke, J. E. (2001). *Assessment* (8th ed.). Boston, MA: Houghton Mifflin.

Weiner, I. B. (1989). On competence and ethicality in psychodiagnostic assessment. *Journal of Personality Assessment, 53,* 827–831.

White, J. (2006). Multiple invalidities. In J. A. Schaler (Ed.), *Howard Gardner under fire: The rebel psychologist faces his critics* (pp. 45–71). Chicago, IL: Open Court.

Review of the Assessment of Multiple Intelligences by ELEANOR E. SANFORD-MOORE, Senior Vice-president of Research and Development, MetaMetrics, Inc., Durham, NC:

DESCRIPTION. The Assessment of Multiple Intelligences (AMI) was developed and published by PsychTests AIM, Inc. in 2011. The test is based on the work of Howard Gardner and is designed to assess "the manner in which a person learns best. It will identify which specific type of intelligence an individual possesses and how it can be used to his or her advantage" (ArchProfile catalog, 2012). The test reports scores related to eight intelligence types: Bodily-Kinesthetic, Logical-Mathematical, Visual-Spatial, Linguistic, Musical, Intrapersonal, Interpersonal, and Naturalistic. Scoring reports also provide advice "to facilitate improvement and increase the test-taker's suitability for this career" (manual, p. 1). In addition to the eight scores reported, the scores are categorized as Dominant Intelligence Types, Influencing Intelligence Types, and Least Developed Intelligence Types.

The AMI consists of 55 items and is administered online. The items include selected-response (Likert-type) items in which the examinee is asked to indicate the extent to which the statement describes him or her (self-assessment) and items in which the examinee is asked to select all of the statements that describe what he or she would do in a specific situation (situational). The test takes about 20 minutes to complete. The AMI is scored by computer and a printable report is provided to the test-taker with detailed information related to the descriptions of each of the eight scores and associated common capacities and strengths. No information concerning the scoring procedures is provided in the test manual.

DEVELOPMENT. The Assessment of Multiple Intelligences is based on the work of Howard Gardner and his Multiple Intelligence Theory. This theory was described in 1983 as a classical model that could be used to understand and teach many aspects of human intelligence, learning styles, personality, and behavior. The model has been used in both education and industry to provide an indication of people's preferred learning styles, as well as their behavioral and work styles, and their natural strengths.

No information is provided in the technical manual about the development of the items or the assessment. One table provides the number of items per scale, but no information is provided showing how the 55 items are incorporated into each of the eight scores (intelligence types). It is obvious from the table that most, if not all, of the items contribute to numerous scores (the number of items per scale ranges from 22 to 23). No information is provided as to the factor structure of the eight scores. Also, no information is provided related to the scaling of the eight scores and the criteria for the three categories of the scores.

TECHNICAL. No information is provided related to standardization of the results or norming populations.

Reliability was calculated using coefficient alpha. The reliability estimate of the overall scale was .82, and the reliability estimates of the eight scores (intelligence types) ranged from .64 to .79 across one study (N = 10, 135; examinees self-selected to take the assessment and opted in to participate in the study). No information related to test-retest reliability is presented.

The validity information presented in the manual consists of one study of 10,135 self-selected examinees. The distributions of each of the eight scores are negatively skewed with means between 70 and 80 (range of scores is from 0 to 100). The scores for the eight intelligence types are compared across various subgroups: gender, age, education, grades, and [employment] position (subgroup information provided by participants). No information was provided as to where differences should be expected. For the variable of gender, all differences between men and women were significant. For the characteristic age, a variety of comparisons for all eight scores were significant. Across levels of education, a variety of significant comparisons were observed for four of the eight scores (Logical-Mathematical, Linguistic, Intrapersonal, and Interpersonal). Comparing grades, a variety of significant comparisons were observed for seven of the eight scores (the exception being Musical). A variety of significant comparisons were observed for seven of the eight scores (the exception was Visual-Spatial) when vocational positions were compared.

COMMENTARY. The results from only one study were presented in the technical manual, and no interpretive information about the results was provided. In order for the test results to be useful, information should be provided within the developmental model for the assessment to explain when significant comparisons should be expected. An Internet search finds little empirical evidence to support the eight intelligence types in the Gardner model. Given the high degree (inferred) of overlap of items across the eight scores on the AMI (55 items total and each of the eight scores is based on 22 to 23 items), there does not seem to be support for all eight scores. In addition, although numerous subgroup comparisons were statistically significant, the actual observed score differences between the highest and lowest subgroups were often small (less than one-fourth of a standard deviation).

SUMMARY. The Assessment of Multiple Intelligences is administered and scored online. The technical manual provides limited psychometric information for the AMI and provides no information related to the development of the items and the assessment, scoring, or construct validation. Although the results do have "face validity" when comparing the scores and reading through the descriptions of the scores, construct validity information should be provided to support eight scores and the use of the results to "provide insight about what is important to the examinee and/or which settings the examinee would most likely thrive" (from online directions for AMI).

Assessment of Spirituality and Religious Sentiments.

Purpose: Designed to measure spirituality constructs "with individuals across a wide range of faith traditions."
Population: Ages 15 and over.
Publication Dates: 1999-2010.
Acronym: ASPIRES.
Scores, 7: Religiosity, Religious Crisis, Prayer Fulfillment, Universality, Connectedness, Total Religious Sentiments, Total Spiritual Transcendence.
Administration: Group.
Forms, 4: Self-Report, Observer Rating, Self-Report Short Form, Observer Rating Short Form.
Price Data, 2010: $.50 per Self-Report Long Form; $.50 per Self-Report Short Form; $.50 per Observer Rating Long Form; $.50 per Observer Rating Short Form; $25 per Scoring and Interpretive Manual; $50 per Scoring Software 2007 Excel; $50 per Scoring Software 2003 Excel.
Foreign Language Editions: Also available in Spanish, Tagalog, Czech, Polish, Chinese, Malay, and Korean.
Time: Administration time not reported.
Author: Ralph L. Piedmont.
Publisher: Ralph L. Piedmont [the author].

Review of the Assessment of Spirituality and Religious Sentiments by FRANK M. BERNT, Professor, Education Department, Saint Joseph's University, Philadelphia, PA:

DESCRIPTION. The Assessment of Spirituality and Religious Sentiments (ASPIRES) was developed to assess spirituality and religiosity dimensions for a range of faith traditions, as well as for nonreligious or agnostic persons. The instrument in its present form consists of two domains: the Spiritual Transcendence (ST) scale consists of 23 items and comprises three subscales: Prayer Fulfillment (a feeling of joy resulting from encounters with a transcendent reality), Universality (a belief in the unitive nature of life), and Connectedness (a belief that one is part of a larger intergenerational and transcultural human reality). The Religious Sentiments (RS) scale consists of 12 items and comprises Religiosity (one's involvement in religious rituals and activities) and Religious Crisis (the experience of difficulties or conflicts with one's God or faith community) subscales. The recently developed short forms of the two scales contain 9 and 4 items, respectively. There are both self-report and observer-report formats for all subscales.

The ASPIRES has been translated into Spanish, Tagalog, Czech, Polish, Chinese, Malay, and Korean. The test author reports that additional translations are currently being developed, and the technical manual provides suggested guidelines for those interested in generating new translations of the instrument. The revised version of the scale is written at a seventh grade reading level, making it accessible to a wide range of respondents. In addition, both short-form and observer-report formats make it versatile for use with populations who might have difficulty completing the standard self-report form.

The most recent version of the ASPIRES includes a computer-based scoring and interpretive program (Microsoft Excel-based) that generates a detailed four-page printout and includes age- and gender-normed T-scores for all scales as well as interpretive text.

DEVELOPMENT. The origin of the AS-PIRES lies in the development of the ST scale, which aimed to measure spirituality as "a motivational drive directed towards creating personal meaning for one's life" (Piedmont, 1999). A group of theological experts drawn from a range of faith traditions was used to identify common qualities of spirituality found in all faiths and to construct items reflecting those common qualities. Items developed by the test author were added to this pool and subjected to a series of correlational analyses, which yielded the three subscales that currently comprise the ST scale.

The current (second) revision of the ST scale aims at several improvements over its predecessor: elimination of esoteric vocabulary to enhance readability for younger and less educated respondents; modification of the Connectedness scale to increase internal consistency; and creation of a short form. The revised ST scale's 23 items are mostly new (13 of the 23 are changed from the original); however, correlations between original and revised versions of subscales and of the total ST scale range from .83 to .87 (with the exception of the Connectedness subscale, r = .55), evidencing continuity between the two versions. Six of the items in the RS scale had been included as an adjunct set used for convergent validity analysis of the original scale; they were integrated into the ASPIRES on the strength of their incremental and predictive validity (see below). To these 6, 2 more items were added to assess one's level of religious commitment; 4 more were included to address issues of religious crisis.

TECHNICAL. The technical manual is comprehensive and complete in its reporting of normative data for age and gender subgroups, reliability and validity information, and instructions for handscoring. Both overall (n = 2,999) and validation samples upon which psychometric data are based are sufficient in size as well as in representativeness, drawing from both student and community groups in four geographically distinct areas of the United States. The sample is somewhat overrepresented by Caucasians, Catholics, and undergraduate women; however, there are sufficient numbers to suggest generalizability across diverse groups, and cross-cultural studies have increased credibility for claims regarding spirituality as a universal construct.

Reliability. Internal consistency estimates for the total ST, Prayer Fulfillment, and Universality scales are satisfactory (r = .86–.95 for self-report; r = .79–.93 for observer-report). Estimates for the Connectedness scale continue to be less than adequate (.60 and .54, respectively), despite revision efforts. Internal consistency estimates for the two Religious Sentiment scales are also satisfactory (alpha coefficients range from .78 to .89 for self-report and observer-report formats). No test-retest or temporal stability estimates are reported. Alpha reliabilities for subscales of the short form of ASPIRES were comparable to those for the long form (median alpha = .73, range = .53–.90), with correlations to comparable subscales on the long form ranging from .85–.94. It should be noted that a single Religiosity score (4 items) is presented for the short form. Cross-observer convergence (correlations between observer ratings and self-report) tends to be moderate for scales and subscales (rs range from .42 to .75), with the exceptions of Connectedness (r = .25), Religious Crisis (r = .34), and Universality (r = .42).

Discriminant and incremental validity. A factor analysis of self-report and observer-report scores from the ASPIRES and the Five Factor Model (FFM) dimensions yielded two factors. When these components were obliquely rotated, the resulting factor loadings provided compelling evidence that the ST scale measures a construct distinct from traditional nonreligious measures of personality (the exception being the Religious Crisis self-report subscale, which loaded comparably on both components).

Multiple regression analyses using ASPIRES subscales as predictors and psychosocial outcomes as criterion variables yielded significant R^2 values (percentage of explained variance) in nearly every case (median R^2 = .15, range = .03–.30). Furthermore, in a series of stepwise regression analyses using the same outcomes as criterion variables and entering ASPIRES subscales in a third step after both demographic and FFM scales had been entered, the ASPIRES subscales still contributed statistically significant additional explained variance–an average of 5% (technical manual, p. 32).

Construct evidence. The technical manual reviews studies aimed at exploring the factor structure of ASPIRES. Structural equation modeling (SEM) by Piedmont, Ciarrochi, Dy-Liacco, and Williams (2009) led to a finding that "spirituality and religiosity represent two highly correlated, yet separate, dimensions" (technical manual, p. 36); the disattenuated correlation between the two dimensions was .71. The scale's author nonetheless maintains that the scales should not be collapsed, largely based upon each scale's incremental validity.

COMMENTARY. The ASPIRES's author presents it as a valuable measurement tool not only for conducting basic research in the area of psychology of religion and spirituality, but also for use in applied clinical and pastoral settings. It has been used to study the impact of religion and spirituality upon such psychological outcomes as burnout, recovery from substance abuse, sexuality, quality of life among arthritis sufferers, and psychological growth more generally. It is important to underscore evidence (presented in the technical manual and elsewhere) that the relationships between ASPIRES subscales and psychological outcomes are not simply mediated through nonreligious or nonspiritual personality variables, but that "measures of spirituality and religious sentiments have strong, unique relationships with psychological phenomena" (technical manual, p. 33).

The consistent inability of the Connectedness scale to meet minimal standards for internal consistency may say less about its psychometric inadequacy than about the complexity of what is being measured. The test author clearly acknowledges the Connectedness subscale's "peculiar behavior" and describes additional psychometric studies suggesting that the factor structure of the spirituality construct is slippery, defying any "neat internal structure" (technical manual, p. 24). There is clearly room for further research and refinement of the ASPIRES's underlying structure; however, in its present form, it combines careful psychometric support with an appeal to those interested in positive psychology; it goes far in achieving its aim to create a "relevant instrument for understanding . . . the creation of a

life-directing sense of personal meaning" (technical manual, p. 10).

SUMMARY. The ASPIRES offers several advantages over other available measures of spirituality and religiosity. It is easy to administer, and its short form and observer rating format make it versatile enough to use in a wide range of settings (especially health and mental health settings) where self-administration of the scale might be burdensome. It is also appropriate for use with a wide range of faith traditions and in even broader contexts of spiritual life. Among the myriad scales available for measuring facets of religiosity and spirituality, the ASPIRES holds promise for wide use among researchers and clinicians alike.

REVIEWER'S REFERENCES

Piedmont, R. L. (1999). Does spirituality represent the sixth factor of personality? Spiritual transcendence and the five-factor model. *Journal of Personality, 67*, 985-1013.
Piedmont, R. L., Ciarrochi, J. W., Dy-Liacco, G. S., & Williams, J. E. G. (2009). The empirical and conceptual value of the Spiritual Transcendence and Religious Involvement Scales for personality research. *Psychology of Religion and Spirituality, 1*(3), 162-179.

Review of the Assessment of Spirituality and Religious Sentiments by PATRICIA SCHOENRADE, Professor of Psychology, William Jewell College, Liberty, MO:

DESCRIPTION. The Assessment of Spirituality and Religious Sentiments (ASPIRES) is a self-report assessment of aspects of the respondent's spiritual motivation and religious sentiment. It includes 35 questions (preceded by 4 demographic items). Completion requires about 10 minutes; a short form, involving only 13 items, is also available. Both the long and short forms are also offered in an observer rating format, for use in situations where another perspective on the individual's religious and spiritual inclinations might be helpful.

The ASPIRES inventory includes two sections. The Spiritual Transcendence portion, 23 items, focuses on the individual's sense of meaning in life. This portion contains subscales named Prayer Fulfillment, Universality, and Connectedness. Prayer Fulfillment items (10) inquire about both the activity of prayer and the sense of connection with a divine being. Universality items (7) reflect a sense of common meaning that unites all of life. Connectedness items (6) center on connection to others, both those living and those who have died. Responses are given on a 1–5 scale (*strongly disagree–strongly agree*). The scale includes 10 items that are reverse-scored.

The Religious Sentiments scale, comprising 12 items, was a somewhat later addition to the instrument, but had undergone considerable development prior to its addition. The Religious Sentiments scale includes two subscales. The Religiosity subscale focuses on both devotion to religious beliefs and frequency of overtly religious behavior (e.g., praying, attending services). The Religious Crisis subscale attempts to discern whether the respondent is in a period of particular difficulty or struggle with regard to religion or relationship with the divine.

The test author explains an additional important distinction between the Spiritual Transcendence scale and the Religious Sentiments scale. Spiritual Transcendence, as assessed by the ASPIRES, is a motivation, and is a quality of the individual, or perhaps a personality characteristic. Religious Sentiment, as the term implies, reflects a more emotional quality.

The accompanying test manual includes extensive description and background, as well as normative tables, summaries of validity and reliability information, and scoring guides. A CD with which the user may obtain both scores and interpretive summaries is also available.

DEVELOPMENT. In at least 11 years of development, the ASPIRES has undergone extensive review and refinement, and more than a dozen scholarly publications by the test author and colleagues are cited in the description of its history. The Spiritual Transcendence Scale has a particularly intriguing beginning. At its inception, experts in the theology of at least six different religious traditions were gathered and asked for descriptions of spirituality; these experts then helped to identify the common elements that gave rise to the items in the initial version of the Spiritual Transcendence Scale. Applications of the scale with varied age groups subsequently pointed to the need for simplification of language (the current version reflecting appropriateness for readers of Grade 7 and above) and reworking of the items. Both tasks were accomplished to yield the current version.

The Religious Sentiments scale was in the process of development along with the Spiritual Transcendence scale. Recent research on religion and spirituality suggested to the test author that it was appropriate to combine the items into one instrument, while acknowledging that the two reflect different, though overlapping, components of human experience.

The ASPIRES arose in part from a concern that many of the inventories available for assessment of religiosity either originate in specific theological traditions or are not easily applied in certain

therapeutic contexts. It has been utilized in samples including conservative, reformed, and orthodox Jews, Indian Hindus and Muslims, and aboriginal Canadians in treatment for alcoholism. It has been translated into several languages including Spanish, Korean, and Tagalog, and the test manual includes guidelines for translators.

TECHNICAL. The normative data for the ASPIRES are drawn from a sample of 2,999 respondents from four states, two Eastern and two in the Midwest. The mean age of respondents in the validation sample was 21.23. The majority of respondents were of Christian traditions, though more than 20% were from non-Christian groups, and some 16% did not indicate their tradition. The sample included both students and community members, though we are not told how many of each. There is no information as to how these individuals were recruited; for example, if they were completing the inventory in the context of a religious fellowship, this might be important, given the nature of the inventory. Nonetheless, the normative data are extensive and clearly presented, offering means and standard deviations for each of the subscales within age ranges. Additionally, normative data for each of the specific items on the Religious Sentiments scale are included.

The reliability data reported in the ASPIRES manual are also quite extensive. Alpha coefficients for all of the subscales in the self-report version are above .70, with the exception of the Connectedness subscale (.60), which the test author acknowledges is a somewhat complex concept, and most are above .80. The reliabilities for the observer report version are slightly lower, but still generally strong.

The test manual offers several types of evidence to support the validity of test scores. The correlations between self and observer reports are presented with values ranging from moderately low to moderately high. The test author supplies reasonable explanations for these findings. With regard to discriminant validity, the test author notes that, although the subscales do correlate with components of the "Big Five" personality characteristics, these correlations are low and the ASPIRE subscales seem to reflect constructs beyond those oft-assessed personality characteristics. In relation to construct evidence, predictive relationships with numerous other related assessments–for example, Snyder's Hope Scale (Snyder et al., 1996) and Rosenberg's (1979) Self-Esteem Scale–are presented. Additionally, the test author notes the successful use of the instrument among a number of clinical and mental health populations. To further develop the constructs, the subscales were related to responses on a descriptive adjective checklist. This process allowed the test author to obtain a clearer picture of what a high scorer on a particular scale might be like.

COMMENTARY. The content of items generally have face validity with respect to each construct. One item on the Universality scale, a reverse-scored item that refers to humans as inherently bad, seems to reflect more a humanist philosophy than a yearning for connection and meaning, but it does load as expected in factor analyses. The ASPIRE subscales do indeed predict some of the variation of responses that occur in a number of other scales. Somewhat surprisingly, certain oft-used assessments within the psychology of religion, specifically Allport's Intrinsic Scale (see Allport & Ross, 1967) and Batson's Quest Scale (see, for example, Batson & Raynor-Prince, 1983), both frequently used in the psychology of religion, were not included. These might be considered for future work, as the two would seem to have close ties to the concepts underlying the Religious Sentiments and the Spiritual Transcendence Scales, respectively. There is little mention of the ability of the instrument to predict behavior beyond responses to self-report scales, but it seems likely that such work will be forthcoming. The original form is itself fairly brief and user-friendly, so the short form would probably be most useful for inclusion within a battery of scales.

SUMMARY. The ASPIRES inventory enters the complex arena of the relationship between religion and spirituality, allowing the individual to consider these issues with regard to his or her own journey. Its author is clearly interested in continued development and refinement. The ASPIRES seems to have especially strong potential for use among groups gathered around a religious or spiritual purpose (e.g., worship groups, support groups). Although it is likely to raise as many questions as it answers, scores can provide a useful starting point for those interested in how the two concepts are reflected in human development.

REVIEWER'S REFERENCES

Allport, G. W., & Ross, M. J. (1967). Personal religious orientation and prejudice. *Journal for the Scientific Study of Religion, 5,* 432-443.

Batson, C. D., & Raynor-Prince, L. (1983). Religious orientation and complexity of thought about existential concerns. *Journal for the Scientific Study of Religion, 22,* 38-50.

Rosenberg, M. (1979). *Conceiving the self.* New York, NY: Basic Books.

Snyder, C. R., Simpson, S. C., Ybasco, F. C., Borders, T. F., Babyak, M. A., & Higgins, R. L. (1996). Development and validation of a Hope Scale. *Journal of Personality and Social Psychology, 70,* 321-335.

Auditory Skills Assessment.

Purpose: Designed for the "early identification of young children who might be at risk for auditory skill deficits and/or early literacy skill difficulties."

Publication Date: 2010.

Acronym: ASA.

Administration: Individual.

Price Data, 2010: $174 per complete test kit including examiner's manual (53 pages), 25 record forms, stimulus book, and stimulus CD-ROM; $72 per 25 record forms; $70 per examiner's manual; $57 per stimulus book; $30 per stimulus CD-ROM.

Authors: Donna Geffner and Ronald Goldman.

Publisher: Pearson.

a) ASA FOR AGES 3-6 TO 4-11.

Population: Ages 3-6 to 4-11.

Time: 5 minutes.

Scores, 4: Speech Discrimination (Speech Discrimination in Noise, Mimicry, Total), Total ASA.

b) ASA FOR AGES 5-0 TO 6-11.

Population: Ages 5-0 to 6-11.

Time: 15 minutes.

Scores, 10: Speech Discrimination (Speech Discrimination in Noise, Mimicry, Total), Phonological Awareness (Blending, Rhyming, Total), Nonspeech Processing (Tonal Discrimination, Tonal Patterning, Total), Total ASA.

Review of the Auditory Skills Assessment by KATHLEEN D. ALLEN, Associate Professor of Education and Professional Psychology, and MAUREEN SIERA, Associate Professor of Education and Professional Psychology, Saint Martin's University, Lacey, WA:

DESCRIPTION. The Auditory Skills Assessment (ASA) is a screening tool to identify auditory skill deficits in young children, ages 3 years 6 months through 6 years 11 months that could impede their language, learning, and academic development. The assessment is individually administered and takes 5–15 minutes. A low overall cut score may indicate the need for further testing or intervention.

The ASA is a criterion-referenced test that samples a young child's auditory skills across three domains: Speech Discrimination, Phonological Awareness, and Nonspeech Processing. The Speech Discrimination domain has two sections. In Section 1: Speech Discrimination in Noise, the child hears "school noise" background and then a female voice says a word. The child then points to the correct picture. In Section 2: Mimicry, the child hears a nonsense word and repeats it. In the Phonological

Awareness domain, the Blending section has two parts. Part 1 requires the child to point to one of six pictures that illustrate the word heard in phonemes or morpheme parts. In Part 2, the child must blend the parts heard into the word. In Section 4: Rhyming, the child responds yes or no when asked if two words rhyme. The Nonspeech Processing domain uses nonlinguistic auditory stimuli. In the Tonal Discrimination section, tones from two instruments, a piano and an oboe, are played. The child is asked to determine whether the two sounds are the same and give a yes or no response. For the Tonal Patterning section, the child is asked which sound is heard last and to say or point to the picture of the instrument.

The instructions for administering and scoring the ASA are on the record form. The examiner follows the directions, which are scripted. Each assessment begins with practice items. If a child gives an incorrect response, it is corrected by the examiner. If the child is not successful on the practice items, that section of the test is skipped. The first domain is given to children ages 3 years 6 months to 4 years 11 months; the whole test is given to children ages 5 years to 6 years 11 months. The words or sounds for each test are on the CD. Scoring is either "1" if correct or "0" if incorrect. A total raw score is obtained and recorded on the answer sheet. The score is compared to a cut score by age, percentile by age, and performance descriptor on each domain indicated by low, average, or high by child's age. Appendix B, in the test manual, contains the score tables with cut scores and percentiles. The test authors caution that interpreting the scores is a complex task and only a qualified professional should explain the results.

DEVELOPMENT.

Theoretical framework. The ASA instrument was designed to quickly assess a young child's auditory skills in preparation for school. Geffner, one of the test authors, developed the tool from her four-component model of auditory skills. These components are Speech Discrimination, Auditory Verbal Memory, Phonological Awareness, and Nonspeech Processing. The test authors cite research evidence to establish the need to assess each of these domains, which play a significant role in the development of language and literacy skills.

Task development. Considerations for task development were utility of words, clarity of word-picture association, structure of words, and distinction of sounds.

Content development took into consideration words with which young children were familiar, ease of word-picture association, structure of words, and distinction of sounds.

Two national tryouts were conducted to study the ASA. An item level analysis was performed with the results to examine difficulty, validity, and bias as well as to evaluate reliability, validity, and score distribution. Other considerations were accuracy and appropriateness of materials (artwork, administration, and scoring directions).

A test-retest reliability study and a clinical study were then performed with the tryout version of the ASA. Based on these investigations, items were either revised or eliminated for standardization. Results indicated that the total ASA score was the best predictor for all age groups.

TECHNICAL.

Standardization. Standardization tests were conducted using over 600 children at 123 locations throughout the United States. The norm sample represented population distributions across age, sex, race, ethnicity, region, and mother's level of education. Cut scores and percentile ranks were determined for each 6-month age group.

Reliability. The test authors used a split-half method to determine internal consistency reliability. When the reliability of the scores were grouped by age, coefficients ranged from .52–.90. The lowest reliability coefficient range was .52–.72 for the age range of 3 years and 6 months to 4 years and 11 months. The test authors state that this is likely due to the lower attainable score in the test for this age group and the developmental capabilities of younger subjects. Internal consistency reliability coefficients for the scores of 5- and 6-year-old subjects ranged from .88–.92. These values offer strong evidence of internal consistency of scores.

The accuracy of the cut scores was analyzed to provide further evidence of internal consistency reliability. This analysis of standard error of measurement and standard deviation near the cut scores resulted in a .64–.77 (moderate) range of reliability coefficients for the 3- and 4-year-old subjects, and a .86–.92 (high) range for the older subjects.

To assess test-retest reliability, the ASA was administered a second time by the same examiner to 125 individuals using a 2–7-week interval. The demographic characteristics of these individuals are detailed in the test manual. The test-retest reliability coefficient adjusted by standard deviation for sample variability was .64 (ages 3–4) and .83 (ages 5–6).

For interscorer reliability, two different test administrators observed and scored the same child for the Mimicry and Blending sections of the test during the standardization trials. The 78 children tested were a representative cross section of the standardization population. The interscorer reliability coefficients were very good, ranging from .90–.99.

Validity. To substantiate content validity, the test authors provide a detailed description of the theoretical construct and clearly delineate the tasks that correlate with each component. The test authors' case for construct validity is based on expected increases in scores across age levels. For criterion evidence, sections of the ASA were correlated with three other assessments. During the standardization phase, portions of The Comprehensive Test of Phonological Processing (CTOPP), the SCAN-3:C Tests for Auditory Processing Disorders in Children (SCAN-3:C), and The Test of Auditory Skills, Third Edition (TAPS-3) were administered less than 14 days after the ASA. Demographic characteristics for this validity study are well described. For the ASA Phonological Awareness domain, phonological processing measures of the CTOPP and TAPS-3 demonstrate moderate to high coefficients of correlation (.65 and .76, respectively). The correlation coefficient of the ASA Speech Discrimination domain to the SCAN-3:C was low (.21). To demonstrate clinical validity, the scores of a subset of children classified as "at risk for auditory processing deficits" were compared to the scores of normal children with matching demographic characteristics. An analysis of the mean scores using t-test statistics indicates statistical significance ($p < .01$) across all three ASA domains for subjects from 4.0–6.11 years of age.

COMMENTARY. The Auditory Skills Assessment is useful for early identification of children with suspected auditory skill deficits, or as a universal screening instrument. A strength of this tool is that auditory skills are measured across three domains that assess the child's ability to identify and produce language. The ASA can also be re-administered to monitor children's progress.

The test manual provides substantial evidence that research supports these domains as critical to a child's academic and language development. The task development for the test items was systematic and methodical. The reliability and validity procedures and evidence are thoroughly described in the test manual. In general, the reliability was very good for school-age subjects, but less reliable for preschoolers. It is recommended that the test authors continue looking for a test correlated to the Speech Discrimination domain that would provide evidence of criterion validity for this age level.

The ASA is both quick and easy to administer. The test directions are explicit and detailed. The test authors even provide a suggested seating arrangement and layout for materials. The inclusion of practice items ensures that the child understands the task. The examiner acts as "teacher" explaining incorrect responses before proceeding with the test. The test session is discontinued if the child cannot perform the practice items. It should be noted that only those with professional qualifications should interpret the results. However, suggestions for additional testing and assistance for children having difficulties within the different domains are provided.

SUMMARY. The ASA is an appropriate resource for the early identification of auditory skill deficits that may interfere with language, learning, and academic development. Recommendations for interventions or accommodations are also addressed. The test is based on sound research and the test manual provides detailed descriptions of validity and reliability evidence. Therefore, the ASA is an instrument that should be highly considered when looking for an auditory skill screening assessment of young children.

Review of the Auditory Skills Assessment by CONNIE T. ENGLAND, Professor, Graduate Counseling & Guidance, Lincoln Memorial University, Knoxville, TN:

DESCRIPTION. The Auditory Skills Assessment (ASA) is "an individually administered criterion-referenced screening tool" (manual, p. 1) designed to provide early identification of young children at risk for auditory skill deficits and early literacy deficits. The ASA may be used in companion to routine acuity screening and for progress monitoring of auditory skills interventions.

DEVELOPMENT. The ASA is based on Geffner's four-component model of auditory skills development: Speech Discrimination, Auditory Verbal Memory, Phonological Awareness, and Nonspeech Processing. The model also identifies underlying process(es) related to auditory skills: (a) Speech Discrimination requires attention and listening skills; (b) Auditory Verbal Memory requires working memory for auditory stimuli; (c) Phonological Awareness requires phonetic representation skills;

and (d) Nonspeech Processing requires temporal processing skills. Field testing of the model consisted of the creation of a large pool of speech and nonspeech items specifically selected to limit the number of distinctive auditory features (i.e., nasal, non-nasal, continuous, explosive, vocal/nonvocal, and articulator[s] placement). For individual subtests, items were selected to reflect early childhood vocabulary and easy word-picture associations.

The ASA manual provides extensive coverage of the processes used during test development. National tryouts, conducted during 2007, scrutinized items for their difficulty, validity, and possible bias; evaluated reliability and validity of score distribution across ages; determined appropriateness of administration and scoring guidelines; and examined stimulus artwork. Demographic sampling characteristics included age, sex, race/ethnicity, mother or female guardian's education level, and geographic region. Based on these collected data, final items were chosen for standardization and formed the basis for various decisions regarding subtest selection, starting age, section order, and item sequencing.

TECHNICAL. The ASA's final standardization sample consisted of 475 children of normal hearing, ages 3 years 6 months to 6 years 11 months. The sample was divided into seven age groups of 6-month intervals. Classical item analyses such as item difficulty, item-total correlations by age group, score measures, and examiner feedback were used in final item selection. Cut scores were age-corrected to provide standard scores with a mean of 100 and a standard deviation of 15. Overall sensitivity and specificity of the ASA resulted in 77% of the clinical sample scoring at or below cutscores and 68% of the matched nonclinical sample scoring above cutscores. Two sets of percentile ranks corresponding to total raw scores were created for age groups 3 years 6 months to 4 years 11 months and for age groups 5 years 0 months to 6 years 11 months because children in these two age ranges were given different sections of the ASA.

Reliability estimates for overall and conditional internal consistency are reported as high for ages 5 and 6 and low to moderate for those at the younger ages. Standard errors of measurement based on split-half total raw score reliabilities range from 1.3 to 2.6 points. Test-retest reliability coefficients are higher for older students with only small differences (effect sizes) between first and second administrations of the test. Interscorer reliability is high, ranging from .90 to .99 for all age groups.

Evidence supporting content validity of test scores is described as being consistent with the American Speech-Language-Hearing Association Working Group on Auditory Processing Disorders' (2005) recommendations (i.e., auditory discrimination, differentiation of frequency, intensity and temporal parameters of auditory stimuli, auditory temporal processing, and, analysis of acoustic stimuli over time).

Construct evidence is based on age differentiation; that is, as children's auditory systems mature, so, too will their raw scores on the ASA. Criterion-related evidence derives from the following comparisons: three subtests (Elision, Blending Words, and Sound Matching) from the Comprehensive Test of Phonological Processing (CTOPP; Wagner, Torgesen, & Rashotte, 1999); one subtest (auditory figure ground +8 db/SN) from the SCAN-3 for Children: Tests for Auditory Processing Disorders (SCAN-3:C, Keith, 2009); and three subtests (Word Discrimination, Phonological Segmentation, and Phonological Blending) from the Test of Auditory Processing Skills–Third Edition (TAPS-3; Martin & Brownell, 2005). Correlation coefficients for ASA's Phonological Awareness subtest and the CTOPP's Phonological Awareness Composite and the TAPS-3 Phonological Index are reported as moderate (.65) for the CTOPP and high (.76) for the TAPS-3. Correlation of the SCAN-3:C's Auditory Figure Ground +8 db/SN and ASA's Speech Discrimination Domain is reportedly weak (coefficient reported as .21).

COMMENTARY. The ASA is a brief (5 to 15 minutes) screening tool designed to measure a young child's auditory skills across three domains: Speech Discrimination, Phonological Awareness, and Nonspeech Processing. According to the test authors, it may be used for early identification and intervention, for universal screening, and for progress monitoring of children at risk for auditory skills deficits. Its key strengths include provision of complex data in an easy-to-use record form, its extensive psychometric analyses of pilot study results for inclusion in final normative data, and its commitment to providing an evaluation tool suited to measuring a broad spectrum of auditory skills deemed necessary for children's early learning experiences. As previously mentioned, overall and conditional reliabilities for internal consistency based on split-half reliability are low to moderate for the younger age groups suggesting, perhaps, more rigorous efforts are needed to distinguish between clinical and nonclinical samples at the earlier ages. Also of concern is the low coefficient of correlation (.21) between the SCAN-3:C's Auditory Figure-Ground +8 db/SN subtest and the ASA Speech Discrimination domain, signifying the ASA may be less suitable for those children particularly sensitive to background noise interference. The test authors specifically recommend the use of other commercially available instruments that measure issues related to selective attention or discrimination, or both, as preferable for in-depth analysis of auditory processing disorders.

SUMMARY. The ASA is designed as a screening tool for early identification of children at risk for auditory skill deficits and/or early literacy difficulties, not a diagnostic instrument for identification of auditory processing disorders. As an auditory skill deficit measure, it meets its goal. However, as a predictor of early literacy difficulties, the ASA may fail to distinguish between clinical and nonclinical students' signal to noise ratio skills and the effects those differences may have on early literacy development.

REVIEWER'S REFERENCES
American Speech-Language-Hearing Association. (2005). (Central) Auditory Processing Disorder [Technical Report.] Available from www.asha.org/policy.

Keith, R. W. (2009). SCAN-3 for Children: Tests for Auditory Processing Disorders. San Antonio, TX: Pearson.

Martin, N. A., & Brownell, R. (2005). Test of Auditory Processing Skills–Third Edition. Novato, CA: Academic Therapy Publications.

Wagner, R., Torgesen, J. K., & Rashotte, C. A. (1999). The Comprehensive Test of Phonological Processing. Austin, TX: PRO-ED.

[8]
Autism Spectrum Rating Scales.

Purpose: Measures behaviors associated with Autism Spectrum Disorders.
Population: Ages 2-18.
Publication Date: 2010.
Acronym: ASRS.
Scores, 13: 5 ASRS scale scores (Total Score, Social/Communication, Unusual Behaviors, Self-Regulation, Short Form Score) and 8 Treatment scale scores (Peer Socialization, Adult Socialization, Social/Emotional Reciprocity, Atypical Language, Stereotypy, Behavioral Rigidity, Sensory Sensitivity, Attention/Self-Regulation).
Administration: Individual or group.
Levels, 2: 2–5 years, 6–18 years.
Price Data, 2013: $399 per complete hand-scored kit including 25 each of the ASRS 2-5 Parent, Teacher, and Short QuikScore forms, 25 each of the ASRS 6-18 Parent, Teacher, and Short QuikScore forms, and technical manual (167 pages); $529 per complete software scoring kit including technical manual, scoring software, 25 each of the ASRS 6-18 Parent, Teacher, and Short

response forms; $239 per particular age range hand-scored kit (2-5 years or 6-18 years) including 25 each of the Parent, Teacher, and Short QuikScore Forms for the appropriate age range; $379 per age range scoring software kit including the technical manual, age range response forms and scoring software; $150 pers scoring software; $86 per technical manual; $429 per complete online kit including technical manual, 25 each of the ASRS 2-5 Parent, Teacher, and Short online forms, 25 each of the ASRS 6-18 Parent, Teacher, and short online forms; $259 per age range online kit including the technical manual and age range online forms.
Time: (5-15) minutes.
Comments: All scales include a parent and teacher score form.
Authors: Sam Goldstein and Jack A. Naglieri.
Publisher: Multi-Health Systems, Inc.

Review of the Autism Spectrum Rating Scales by ANNETTE S. KLUCK, *Associate Professor, Auburn University, Auburn, AL:*

DESCRIPTION. The Autism Spectrum Rating Scales (ASRS) are a set of scales developed to assist mental health professionals in assessing symptoms associated with Autism Spectrum Disorder (ASD) diagnoses (i.e., Autism, Aspergers, and Pervasive Developmental Disorder) among children ages 2 to 18 using informant ratings. The ASRS was designed to allow for rapid assessment of parent and teacher report, can be administered individually or in a group format, and is available in English and Spanish. Separate forms and norms exist for parents and teachers/childcare providers to reflect environmental differences. The ASRS also contains a short form for rapid screening of problems associated with ASDs. There are separate versions of the full and short forms for preschool (ages 2–5) and school-aged (ages 6–18) children.

The ASRS administration is simple and the directions are clear. The evaluator gives the appropriate form (based upon the rater, child age, and preferred scoring method) to the individual rating the child's behavior, directing the rater to complete the demographic information section and indicate how often the child displayed each behavior over the past month. Administration takes 5 to 15 minutes and directions for oral administration are available. According to the manual, the evaluator need not be present for the ASRS to be completed and an online form (containing the same items) is available. Manual directions emphasize the need to speak with the rater prior to initiating the test to obtain informed consent and clarify how the responses will be used. Scoring can be done by hand, online, or through the ASRS scoring software. Hand scoring requires the use of the QuikScore forms (which contain information needed to compute the standardized scores). No information is provided regarding how long it takes to score the ASRS, but hand scoring will require more time than the computer scoring options. The ASRS yields a total score, two (Social/Communication and Unusual Behaviors for ages 2–5), or three (Social/Communication, Unusual Behaviors, and Self-Regulation for ages 6–18) ASRS subscales, a DSM-IV-TR scale (designed to align with diagnostic criteria within the diagnostic requirements for the disorders), and eight treatment subscales (Peer Socialization, Adult Socialization, Social/Emotional Reciprocity, Stereotypy, Behavioral Rigidity, Sensory Sensitivity, and Attention/Self-Regulation for ages 2–5 or Attention for ages 6–18) intended to aid in treatment planning/evaluation. Information is also available to allow for comparisons of scores over time or across raters.

DEVELOPMENT. The test authors sought to create an assessment tool that (a) would assess symptoms of ASDs, (b) be appropriate for use among children and adolescents, and (c) could be used with multiple informants. The literature and theory on assessment and diagnosis of ASDs was reviewed to generate test items and the test authors sought to include key content areas of "socialization (child and adult); stereotypies, behavioral rigidity, and sensory sensitivity; language; and attention" (technical manual, p. 43). However, minimal specific information on item generation is provided. After generating items, the psychometric properties of the initial items were examined in a pilot study using an ethnically diverse clinical sample. The test authors report that item discrimination analyses, item variance, and expert review were used to examine the pilot items but details and specific items for the pilot are not provided. The pilot study supported the use of 74 items to comprise separate forms for the preschool (70 items) and school-aged children (71 items) with nonshared items reflecting developmental differences. The short forms for the 2–5-years and 6–18-years forms were drawn from items that demonstrated the greatest predictive power for each form during standardization.

Factor analysis was used to generate the ASRS subscales, yielding two (Social/Communication; Unusual Behaviors) subscales for the 2-5 years and three (Social/Communication; Unusual Behaviors;

Self-Regulation) for the 6-18 years forms. The ASRS subscales show intercorrelations ranging from .45 to .66. The treatment subscales were formed by examining items (including expert judgment, item content, and intercorrelations) to fit with identified key concepts during the planning stages.

TECHNICAL. A total of 2,560 ratings (including 40 males and 40 females at each age) comprised the normative sample for the full-length ASRS forms. The standardization also included 700 ratings for children having an ASDs diagnosis and 500 ratings of children diagnosed with other clinical disorders. Ratings were collected from sites across North America. Most (83%) of the 1,280 parent ratings were from mothers. In both the parent and teacher rating norming samples, the individuals who were rated were selected to reflect population demographics for ethnic background based on U.S. Census data. Parental education data were available only for the parent normative sample and parents with at least some college (including those with a college degree and graduate education) were initially overrepresented, but all normative samples were weighted to match the U.S. Census. Clinical cases were included in the norming sample at a rate reflective of the population prevalence. Small age and gender effects were found. The test authors note that the gender differences (which consistently revealed higher scores for males) were reflective of higher prevalence rates in males. In addition to having separate forms for young and school-aged children, the older age group was subdivided into two age groups (6–11 years and 12–18 years) to address age effects. The short forms were developed from the full-length forms using a sample of 695 individuals for item selection and another 695 individuals to examine statistical properties.

Internal consistency estimates ranged from unacceptable to excellent (alpha coefficients for the 2–5-years form were between .67 and .95 for parent ratings and .59 to .95 for teachers; alpha coefficients for older children ranged from .77 to .97 for parents and .69 to .97 for teacher ratings) with better internal consistency for the ASRS subscales, DSM-IV-TR scale, and total scale (above .90 in nearly all cases). Test-retest reliability coefficients (on a subset of the norming sample) for a 2–4-week interval were adequate, falling between .73 and .94 across raters and age groups with higher values found for parent raters. Interrater reliability estimates were reported for two raters (either two parents or two teachers) and were adequate to excellent (.69 to .92) for parents, but lower for teachers (.50–.73), as would be expected if observations came from different classroom environments. The internal consistency of the short forms was good, ranging from .86 to .90 for the normative sample, and test-retest reliability coefficients and interrater reliability estimates were similar to those of the full-length ASRS.

Construct and criterion-related evidence supporting validity of test scores is provided in the manual and supports the use of ASRS test scores to examine severity of symptoms associated with ASDs. Children with ASDs diagnoses were compared to a nonclinical group and children with diagnoses other than ASDs to examine the extent to which the ASRS can differentiate between those with ASDs and other individuals. Mean scores were significantly higher across rater types and child ages for individuals with ASDs than those for the general clinical and nonclinical groups, and overall correct classification rates for individuals with ASDs and the general population ranged from 88.3% to 94.9% across all forms. The short forms were strongly correlated with their full-length counterparts (r values ranged from .84 to .92), supporting their use as screening instruments. Correlations between ASRS total scale scores with scores on pre-existing parent and teacher rating scales (the Gilliam Autism Rating Scale–Second Edition [GARS-2; Gilliam, 2006] and the Gilliam Asperger's Disorder Scale [GADS; Gilliam, 2001]) were moderate to high (rs = .63 to .83) and provide criterion-related evidence for the use of ASRS scores. Correlations between the ASRS and the Childhood Autism Rating Scale (CARS; Schopler, Reichler, & Renner, 1986), a clinician-based measure, were lower and in one case (teacher ratings of 2–5 years) was approximately 0 (r = .06), suggesting that the ASRS cannot be used to replace the clinician's evaluation of a child. Exploratory factor analysis was used to create the final ASRS subscales, and studies suggest that factor loadings were generally consistent across gender, age, race, and clinical status (coefficients of congruence ranged from .87 to .99 with most above .95).

COMMENTARY. The ASRS is easy to administer and can aid in the evaluation of severity of behaviors associated with ASDs. The use of a general population norming sample is a strength that allows for meaningful interpretation of elevations on ASRS subscales. In addition, key strengths include the use of a relatively representative norming sample, availability of software-based scoring,

and psychometric studies to support the intended uses of the measure. It is surprising that the test authors advocate for the use of individual items in guiding treatment planning and examining treatment outcome. Although the test authors provide normative information to allow for evaluation of statistically significant differences, the limitations involved in reliance upon a single item (and lack of any reliability or validity data by item) limit the confidence one can have in item scores, and item interpretation is not advised. Evidence for use of the short forms is sufficient to support their use as screening tools. The manual would benefit from better articulation of the theory guiding the development of the test and test items. Additional studies regarding the use of the treatment scales to effectively identify treatment domains and evaluate treatment progress are needed prior to use of these subscales in this way. Specifically, the same procedures employed to examine the factor structure of the ASRS subscales should be followed to select treatment subscale items rather than relying upon predetermined domains.

SUMMARY. The ASRS is a set of rating scales designed to assess severity of behaviors associated with ASDs using parent and teacher/childcare provider ratings to assist mental health professionals in diagnosis, evaluation, and treatment planning. The test meets its goals of serving as a screening instrument and tool to incorporate multiple raters' observations into an evaluation. The test contains sufficient evidence of reliability and validity and can be recommended for clinical use as a part of a battery that combines measures of cognitive functioning, interview, and other sources of data when evaluating a child for potential ASD diagnoses.

REVIEWER'S REFERENCES
Gilliam, J. E. (2001). *Gilliam Asperger's Disorder Scale examiner's manual.* Austin, TX: PRO-ED, Inc.
Gilliam, J. E. (2006). *Gilliam Autism Rating Scale–Second Edition examiner's manual.* Austin, TX: PRO-ED, Inc.
Schopler, E., Reichler, R. J., & Renner, B. R. (1986). Childhood Autism Rating Scale. Los Angeles, CA: Western Psychological Services.

Review of the Autism Spectrum Rating Scales by STEVEN R. SHAW, Associate Professor of Educational and Counselling Psychology, McGill University, Montreal, Quebec, Canada:

DESCRIPTION. The Autism Spectrum Rating Scales (ASRS) are designed to measure behaviors of children and youth aged 2 through 18 years that are associated with autism spectrum disorders (ASD) as reported by parents or teachers. The ASRS helps guide diagnostic decisions and can be used during treatment planning, ongoing monitoring of response to intervention, and program evaluation. The ASRS includes items related to Autistic Disorder, Asperger's Disorder, and Pervasive Developmental Disorder—Not Otherwise Specified (PDD-NOS).

The ASRS has both full-length and short forms. The short forms consist of 15 items, require 5 minutes to complete, and are designed for screening of large populations. The full-length forms consist of 70 items for ages 2 to 5 years and 71 items for ages 6 to 18 years. The estimated administration time is 15 minutes. There are separate forms for young children ages 2 to 5 years and school-aged children ages 6 to 18 years. The two age groups have separate forms for parent and teacher ratings. The ASRS is intended for use by a range of psychologists, medical professionals, and social workers. The test manual recommends that all test interpreters must meet the publisher's B-level qualifications.

The ASRS has multiple administration and scoring options. Administration can be completed via paper and pencil using carbonless forms or can be administered online. Scoring can be done by hand using the Multi-Health Systems, Inc. (MHS) QuikScore format available within the carbonless forms, online, or using scoring software. When using the online or scoring software three types of reports can be generated. These report types include an interpretive report, which provides detailed results from one administration; a comparative report, which provides multirater perspective by combining results from up to five different raters; and a progress monitoring report, which provides an overview of change over time when used as an intervention evaluation.

The ASRS consists of scores reported as *T*-scores, percentile ranks, and qualitative classifications. Multiple scales comprise the ASRS. These scales are Total score, Social/Communication, Unusual Behaviors, and Self-Regulation (6 to 18 years only). Items are further divided into DSM-IV-TR scale, which represent symptoms directly related to the DSM-IV TR (*Diagnostic and Statistical Manual of Mental Disorders: Fourth Edition-Text Revision*; American Psychiatric Association, 2000) diagnostic criteria for autism spectrum disorders. In addition, there are multiple treatment scales. The treatment scales are Peer Socialization, Adult Socialization, Social/Emotional Reciprocity, Atypical Language, Stereotypy, Behavioral Rigidity, Sensory Sensitivity, Attention/Self-Regulation (2 to 5 years only), and Attention (6 to 18 years).

DEVELOPMENT. The test manual devotes significant space to the complex development of the scales. Items were initially created for parent and teacher respondent rating scales based on current theory and literature on the assessment of ASD, the DSM-IV-TR criteria, and ICD-10 (*International Classification of Diseases;* World Health Organization, 2007) diagnostic criteria, as well as the test authors' clinical and research experiences. From this process 74 items were created. A pilot study consisted of using ratings from a sample of 128 parents (69 typical; 59 clinical) and 110 teachers (60 typical; 50 clinical) to reflect children who are typically developing and who have a clinically diagnosed developmental disorder (40% of the clinical sample was diagnosed with ASD, 50% diagnosed with attention-deficit/hyperactivity disorder [ADHD], and 10% received other diagnoses). In addition, multiple expert opinions were solicited to further identify and refine items. Exploratory factor analysis was used to help develop an item set where a two-factor model was most suitable for the parent and teacher forms for children aged 2 to 5 years and a three-factor model was most suitable for the parent and teacher forms for children aged 6 to 18 years. After all forms were finalized, Spanish forms were created using translations from bilingual school psychologists, back translations, and a review from Spanish-speaking experts in the field to determine appropriate content and cultural sensitivity.

TECHNICAL.

Standardization. The normative samples include 1,280 parent ratings and 1,280 teacher ratings. Of those, 640 ratings were for the 2- to 5-year-old form (320 males, 320 females) and 1,920 ratings for the 6- to 18-year-old form (960 males, 960 females). Over 80% of the ASRS parent forms in the normative sample were completed by the mother or female guardian of the child being rated, 13% of the sample was rated by the father or male guardian, and less than 4% of the sample was rated by other primary caregivers. All of the teachers or childcare providers knew the students they rated for at least 1 month, thereby meeting the minimum time requirement to complete the ASRS.

The normative samples were evenly proportioned in terms of age and gender with 40 males and 40 females at each age. The sample characteristics match the U.S. Census in terms of race and ethnicity. There was an uneven distribution by parent education level and geographic region relative to the U.S. Census. These characteristics were controlled by weighting the normative cases such that the normative sample demographics represented a statistical match to the U.S. Census. In the entire standardization sample there were 14 participants who had been diagnosed with ASD.

Reliability. The ASRS demonstrates strong internal consistency, test-retest reliability, and inter-rater reliability. For the 2- to 5-year form the total score mean alpha coefficient for the parent ratings and teacher ratings is .97. For the 6- to 18-year form the total weighted average alpha coefficient for the parent ratings is .97 and for teacher ratings is also .97. Across the normative and clinical samples the specific scales' internal consistency for parent ratings ranges from .67 (Adult Socialization) to .98 (Social/Communication). Internal consistency estimates for teacher ratings vary from .59 (Atypical Language, Sensory Sensitivity) to .98 (Social/Communication, DSM-IV-TR) across normative and clinical samples. Test-retest reliability was evaluated in a sample of 165 parents and 280 teachers across both age forms using mean intervals of about 2.5 to 3 weeks. Across the forms, the corrected coefficients ranged from .78 to .92 for the total score and from .72 to .93 for the ASRS scales, and from .70 to .92 for the treatment scales. Stability metrics indicate little change from Time 1 to Time 2. Interrater reliability is quite strong for the parent ratings. For the 2- to 5-year form the total score corrected r is .87. Coefficients range from .73 (Peer Socialization) to .87 (Social/Communication). For the 6- to 18-year form the total score corrected r is .89. Coefficients range from .83 (Atypical Language) to .92 (Sensory Sensitivity and Social/Communication). Interrater reliability for teachers is markedly lower. For the 6- to 18-year form the total score interrater reliability coefficient is .60. Coefficients range from .59 (Social/Communication) to .73 (Self-Regulation). These relatively low coefficients are not a serious problem as different teachers often observe children in different contexts and a common outcome in behavioral checklists is low interrater reliability among teachers.

Validity. Three types of validity were examined for the ASRS: criterion-related validity, construct validity, and content validity. Most compelling is a study of teacher ratings across groups. The study provided criterion-related evidence of validity using 227 children who were typically developing, 228 children who had been formally diagnosed with ASD, 147 children diagnosed with ADHD, and 69 children diagnosed with another clinical condition. The ASD group scored over 2 standard deviations above the mean, whereas atypical developing and other clinical populations scored at or below the mean. The ADHD population scored approximately 1 standard deviation above the mean. There was clearly a strong ability to discriminate children with ASD from other populations using both parent and teacher ratings at the 2- to 5-year and 6- to 18-year age levels. Also presented were a variety of diagnostic efficiency statistics. The results demonstrated strong sensitivity and specificity classification. Evidence was also provided for internal construct validity via factor analysis and criterion validity though correlations with other measures designed to assess ASD. In sum, the ASRS manual provides strong and compelling evidence for the validity of the utility of scores produced by this instrument.

COMMENTARY. Frequently, autism rating scales use standardization samples consisting entirely of persons currently diagnosed with ASD. Therefore, any individual scoring at the 50th percentile would have a score commensurate with the median score of others diagnosed with ASD. The ASRS uses a typically developing standardization sample. Scores consistent with ASD would need to be nearly 3 standard deviations above the mean to be consistent with estimated prevalence rates of ASD at 1.1% of the population (Centers for Disease Control, 2012). Extreme scores on norm-referenced measures tend to be less reliable and subject to artifacts such as regression to the mean. The ASRS is a high quality and professionally developed instrument of the continuum of behaviors comprising ASD; however, it is not entirely clear how the ASRS represents a significant improvement in diagnostic information when compared to the Autism Diagnostic Interview–Revised (Le Couteur, Lord, & Rutter, 2003), Autism Diagnostic Observation Schedule (Lord, Rutter, DiLavore, & Risi, 1989), and Childhood Autism Rating Scale (Schopler, Reichler, & Renner, 1980). As a measure of progress for intervention evaluation, norm-referenced measures are notoriously insensitive to change over time. This is because changes in scores reflect only relative standing to the standardization sample and not changes in a specific and observable behavior. The ASRS is most likely to be an excellent contribution to research and the short form is a truly outstanding screener for ASD. Yet, despite the outstanding and much-needed psychometric sophistication in the development and execution of the ASRS, most professionals who routinely assess and diagnose ASD are unlikely to incorporate this measure into their clinical repertoire.

SUMMARY. The ASRS is a norm-referenced grading scale to assist in the identification and diagnosis of behaviors consistent with ASD. The test is well-developed with strong standardization, reliability, and validity information reported. The test manual is also a detailed and well-written document that provides important technical information and helpful interpretation guidelines. However, using a norm-referenced instrument using typically developing children to assist in the diagnosis of a relatively low incidence disorder that is marked by qualitative, rather than quantitative, differences in language, socialization, and stereotyped or repetitive movements is not an entirely comfortable fit.

REVIEWER'S REFERENCES

American Psychiatric Association. (2000). *Diagnostic and statistical manual of mental disorders–Fourth edition-Text revision* (DSM-IV-TR). Washington, DC: American Psychiatric Association.

Centers for Disease Control. (2012, March). *Autism Spectrum Disorders: Facts about ASD.* Retrieved from: http://www.cdc.gov/NCBDDD/autism/facts.html

Le Couteur, A., Lord, C., & Rutter, M. (2003). Autism Diagnostic Interview–Revised. Torrance, CA: Western Psychological Services.

Lord, C., Rutter, M., DiLavore, P. C., & Risi, S. (1989). Autism Diagnostic Observation Schedule. Torrance, CA: Western Psychological Services.

Schopler, E., Reichler, R. J., & Renner, B. R. (1980). Childhood Autism Rating Scale. Torrance, CA: Western Psychological Services.

World Health Organization. (2007). *International classification of diseases: 10th edition.* Geneva, Switzerland: World Health Organization.

[9]

Barkley Adult ADHD Rating Scale-IV.

Purpose: Designed "for clinical purposes to evaluate the range of ADHD symptoms in clinic-referred or high-risk adults ... includes a section of items for assessing ... a subtype of ADHD known as sluggish cognitive tempo."

Population: Ages 18 to 89.

Publication Date: 2011.

Acronym: BAARS-IV.

Administration: Individual.

Price Data, 2011: $149 for manual (160 pages) containing forms and score sheets (includes permission to photocopy).

Author: Russell A. Barkley.

Publisher: Guilford Publications, Inc.

a) SELF-REPORT: CURRENT SYMPTOMS.

Scores, 9: Inattention, Hyperactivity, Impulsivity, Sluggish Cognitive Tempo, Total ADHD Score, Symptom Counts (Inattention, Hyperactivity-Impulsivity, Total ADHD, Sluggish Cognitive Tempo).

Time: (5-7) minutes.

b) SELF-REPORT: CHILDHOOD SYMPTOMS.

Scores, 6: Inattention, Hyperactivity-Impulsivity, Total, Symptom Count (Inattention, Hyperactivity-Impulsivity, Total).

Time: (5-7) minutes.

c) OTHER-REPORT: CURRENT SYMPTOMS.

Scores, 10: Inattention, Hyperactivity, Impulsivity, Total, Sluggish Cognitive Tempo, Symptom Counts (Inattention, Hyperactivity, Impulsivity, Total, Sluggish Cognitive Tempo).

Time: (5-7) minutes.

d) OTHER-REPORT: CHILDHOOD SYMPTOMS.

Scores, 6: Inattention, Hyperactivity-Impulsivity, Total, Symptom Counts (Inattention, Hyperactivity-Impulsivity, Total).

Time: (5-7) minutes.

e) SELF-REPORT: QUICK SCREEN.

Scores, 3: Current Symptoms, Childhood Symptoms, Total.

Time: (3-5) minutes.

f) OTHER-REPORT: QUICK SCREEN.

Scores, 2: Current Symptoms, Childhood Symptoms.

Time: (3-5) minutes.

g) SELF-REPORT: CURRENT SYMPTOMS INTERVIEW.

Scores, 5: Symptom Count (Inattention, Hyperactivity, Impulsivity, Total, Sluggish Cognitive Tempo).

Time: (5-7) minutes.

h) SELF-REPORT: CHILDHOOD SYMPTOMS INTERVIEW.

Scores, 3: Symptom Count (Inattention, Hyperactivity-Impulsivity, Total).

Time: (5-7) minutes.

Review of the Barkley Adult ADHD Rating Scale-IV by NANCY L. CRUMPTON, Adjunct Professor, Walden University, School of Counseling and Social Service, Mental Health Counseling Program; Troy University, College of Education, Counseling Department, Montgomery, AL:

DESCRIPTION. The Barkley Adult ADHD Rating Scale-IV (BAARS-IV) is an individually administered behavioral assessment used to evaluate the range of attention-deficit/hyperactivity disorder (ADHD) in clinic-referred or high-risk adults (ages 18–89). It is designed to quickly and inexpensively evaluate ADHD symptoms in daily life using a combination of rating forms. The BAARS-IV is composed of the Current Symptoms scale, the Childhood Symptoms scale, and the Quick Screen (all available in self-report and other-report versions), and an interview form (to be used when the clinician needs to interview a patient who cannot complete a rating form). The BAARS-IV is updated to the *DSM-IV-TR* symptom list (Items 1–18 on each rating form) and has added 9 items to evaluate symptoms of sluggish cognitive tempo (SCT; Barkley, 2010). The test author notes that individuals with this subset of symptoms are often diagnosed with the inattentive type of ADHD, but do not exhibit hyperactivity; impulsive actions, speech, or emotions; or difficulties with being distractible, which are more typical behaviors of ADHD. These 9 items are included only in the Current Symptoms scale, not in the Childhood recall version or in the short-form (Quick Screen) version.

The BAARS-IV scale items focus on problematic symptoms (deficit behaviors). In the present scale, individuals are asked to indicate impairment in home life, education, occupation, and social functioning, which represent the specific domains of the *DSM-IV-TR* diagnostic criteria. The reading level required for the rating scales is approximately eighth grade. BAARS-IV forms and score sheets for each scale are included in the test manual's appendix. The test author has authorized permission for reproduction of these forms for personal use.

On the Self-Report: Current Symptoms form, individuals are instructed to circle ratings 1 to 4 for each of 27 items representing areas of Inattention, Hyperactivity, Impulsivity, and Sluggish Cognitive Tempo. Ratings are defined as follows: 1 indicates a behavior occurs *never or rarely*, 2 = *sometimes*, 3 = *often* and 4 = *very often*. In the last section of the form, the individual answers "No" or "Yes" to experiencing any of the 27 symptoms *often* or *very often*, notes the age at which these symptoms began, and notes the settings in which functioning was impaired (school, home, work, or social relationships). On the Self-Report: Childhood Symptoms form, 18 items are rated using the same rubric (1–4) for behavior of the individual as a child between the ages of 5 and 12 years. Sections represent behaviors of Inattention (Items 1–9) and Hyperactivity-Impulsivity (Items 10–18). In the last section of the form, the individual answers "No" or "Yes" to experiencing any of these symptoms *often* or *very often* and reports the settings in which functioning was impaired (school, home, or social relationships). The Other-Report: Current Symptoms and Other Report: Childhood Symptoms forms have identical items rated by a family member, spouse, or friend. The interview forms for current and childhood reports include the same sections; however, instead of a 1–4 rating for questions, they are answered "No, this does not occur often" or "Yes, this occurs often or very often." The Quick Screen forms have an abbreviated list of symptoms rated 1–4 (8 items for Current Symptoms and 6 items for Childhood Symptoms).

Completing the BAARS-IV long version takes an average of 5–7 minutes, and the Quick Screen takes 3–5 minutes. Instructions for administration are easily understood, and scoring is convenient as the tables for scoring follow each report form. The self-report forms include norms for three age groups (18–39 years, 40–59 years, and 60–89 years). Raw scores are interpreted as percentile ranks, and values above the 76th percentile are considered marginally symptomatic. Scores in the 84th to 92nd percentile are considered borderline or somewhat symptomatic, scores in the 96th to 98th percentile are moderately symptomatic, and scores at or above the 99th percentile are markedly or severely symptomatic.

DEVELOPMENT. The BAARS-IV is the latest version of a rating scale for ADHD symptoms developed over a 16-year period of research. The initial scale was based on *DSM-III-R* symptoms for the diagnosis of ADHD and updated with the *DSM-IV* symptom list. The BAARS-IV expanded the size of the normative sample to extend local norms to adults in the general population, representative of the population of the U.S. based on 2000 Census data. Adding nine items to evaluate symptoms of sluggish cognitive tempo (SCT) in the current version evaluates adults with inattentive ADHD for whom hyperactivity is not problematic, extending the usefulness of the rating scale in diagnosis. In the BAARS-IV, noting impairment or no impairment in areas of home life, education, occupation, and social functioning–areas that were derived from the specific domains of the *DSM-IV-TR* diagnostic criteria–is used to evaluate the range of ADHD symptoms, rather than Likert scale responses in 10 domains of life activities that were used in previous versions.

TECHNICAL.

Standardization. To obtain a representative sample, adults ranging in age from 18–70+, defined in six age groups, with equal representation of males and females from all four regions of the U.S. were included in the norming population. A total of 1,249 adults completed the survey. Representation of the normative sample to the U.S. population was generally comparable in categories of sex, race/ethnic group, marital status, employment status, total household income, and education. Norming information is not available for the interview forms.

Reliability. The relationships among the scales (ADHD Inattention, ADHD Hyperactivity, ADHD Impulsivity, and SCT) for self-ratings, evaluated using Pearson product-moment correlations for all of the norming population (n = 1,249) were statistically significant at p < .001. Coefficients ranged from .77 (ADHD Inattention and SCT) to .42 (SCT and ADHD Impulsivity), indicating support for use in assessing adult ADHD symptoms. Results of prior studies of the correlation of self-ratings and other-ratings were noted in the BAARS-IV manual, as other-reports were not collected from the normative sample for this version. Earlier studies indicated correlations between self- and other-reports ranged from .67 to .70. Discussion of the nature of the relationship of those completing other-ratings indicated a marginally significant influence for ADHD symptoms but not for ratings of impairment and that spouse/partners provided somewhat higher ratings of ADHD symptoms than parents, friends, or siblings. Correlations for test-retest reliability (n = 62) ranged from .66 to .88, indicating a reasonable level of reliability over a 2- to 3-week period.

Validity. Validation studies have been completed by the test's developer for prior versions of the BAARS over an approximately 16-year period. Construct validity studies were conducted to evaluate the relationship between previous versions of the test and other frequently used scales that support the definitions of the BAARS in assessing ADHD. Individuals included in the BAARS-IV normative sample also completed a rating scale of executive functioning (typically lower in adults with ADHD), the Barkley Deficits in Executive Functioning Scale (19:10; Barkley, 2011). All correlation coefficients between the executive functioning subscales and the BAARS-IV scales were significant at p < .001 (Total ADHD coefficients ranged from .67 to .81). Other evidence supporting validity of test score use included the relationship of BAARS-IV scales to difficulties in life activities including education, occupational functioning, income, marital relationships, driving, health, parenting, and other psychopathology (Barkley & Murphy, 2010).

COMMENTARY. The years of research and development of the BAARS-IV have resulted in a measure that is easily administered and scored. The BAARS-IV assists in the understanding of ADHD behavior in a cross-section of individuals as well as being useful in assessing risk analysis in various life activities and in pre-post neurological injury or psychiatric change. The test author has included all forms and score sheets, which may be copied for use, in the appendix to the test manual providing an economical method of assessment. As the test author purports, further research and statistical analysis on the psychometric properties of the BAARS-IV will strengthen test users'

confidence in using it to assess ADHD behaviors. Research on SCT, the effects of this symptom, and the evaluation of items representing this subset of ADHD are specifically needed. The test author's website (www.russellbarkley.org) is a useful resource for individuals interested in additional information about adult ADHD.

SUMMARY. The BAARS-IV is an individually administered behavioral assessment of symptoms of ADHD in adults (ages 18–89). Development of the assessment has taken place over a 16–year period and has been correlated with numerous other studies and ADHD measures. Rating forms for ADHD symptoms in daily life evaluate behaviors. Self-report and other-report ratings provide comparisons and understanding of an individual's behavior based on the symptoms of ADHD defined in the *DSM-IV-TR*. Scores obtained on rating scales alone are not recommended for making an ADHD diagnosis, but may be used to support a more thorough clinical evaluation.

REVIEWER'S REFERENCES

Barkley, R. A. (2010). Against the status quo: Revising the diagnostic criteria for ADHD. *Journal of the American Academy of Child and Adolescent Psychiatry, 49,* 205–207.
Barkley, R. A. (2011). Barkley Deficits in Executive Functioning Scale (BDEFS). New York, NY: Guilford Press.
Barkley, R. A., & Murphy, K. R. (2010). Deficient emotional self-regulation in adults with attention-deficit/hyperactivity disorder (ADHD): The relative contributions of emotional impulsiveness and ADHD symptoms to adaptive impairments in major life activities. *Journal of ADHD and Related Disorders, 1,* 5–28.

Review of the Barkley Adult ADHD Rating Scale-IV by CAROLYN H. SUPPA, Licensed Psychologist, Coordinator of Human Services Education, Office of Career and Technical Instruction, West Virginia Department of Education, Charleston, WV:

DESCRIPTION. The Barkley Adult ADHD Rating Scale-IV (BAARS-IV) is a behavior rating scale of adult attention-deficit/hyperactivity disorder (ADHD) symptoms. It is intended for adults ages 18–89 living in the U.S. Several versions of the BAARS-IV are available to evaluate symptoms of ADHD in daily life and can be used in clinical, research, industrial, and organizational settings. Suggested clinical uses include: to screen for ADHD symptoms and to establish the age inappropriateness of these symptoms; to evaluate changes in symptoms that may result from interventions such as medication; to evaluate ADHD related mental status changes; and to evaluate changes pre-post neurological injury.

Scale items are derived from the 18 ADHD symptoms found in the *Diagnostic and Statistical Manual of Mental Disorders* (*DSM-IV-TR*; American Psychiatric Association, 2000) and the large body of related research. The test author claims that a unique feature of the BAARS-IV is the inclusion of items assessing a subtype of ADHD symptoms referred to as sluggish cognitive tempo (SCT). Although not included in the *DSM-IV-TR*, SCT is thought to represent a distinct form of inattention. BAARS-IV versions include self- and other-reports of current and childhood symptoms in long form, self- and other-report quick screens, and self-report current and childhood symptoms interviews. The self-report long forms assess the 18 symptoms of ADHD and 9 symptoms of SCT, age of onset, and impairment domains (Current Symptoms) and ADHD symptoms, age of onset, and impairment recollected between the ages of 5–12 (Childhood Symptoms). SCT symptoms are not included in the childhood forms. Other-report forms are completed by a collateral informant. The Quick Screen for both self- and other-report scales rates five current and four childhood symptoms identified from a community control group as most discriminating. The clinical interview form, based on the long form, is intended for use when the evaluated adult is unable to complete the rating scale. The test manual encourages use of the BAARS-IV rating scales whenever possible because the clinical interview form has no directly applicable norms. The reading level for an earlier version was reported to be approximately eighth grade.

Administration, scoring, and interpretation instructions are clearly detailed in the test manual. Long forms and interviews take 5–7 minutes for administration, and the Quick Screen takes 3–5 minutes. Score sheets with norm tables are provided for the Current and Childhood Symptoms and Quick Screen self-report scales. Scoring on these rating scales involves simple summing of section and total scores and translating scores to percentile ranks by age. Placement of scores on the score sheet results in graphic profiles. Normative data were not collected for other-report versions and the clinical interviews due to such difficulties as determining types of relationships. However, the test author does suggest examining the degree of disparity between the self-other reports. Also, the test author asserts that responses from the clinical interview may be compared to long form results for "a very rough approximation of the status of the respondent relative to others in the population" (manual, p. 96). All report forms and scoring sheets are provided in the appendices of the test manual, and limited copying is permitted for personal use

by individual manual purchasers. Research-based information for clinical uses and interpretations are provided throughout the test manual.

DEVELOPMENT. The BAARS-IV is an updated version of other ADHD behavior rating scales originally developed to screen for ADHD risk according to earlier *DSM* diagnostic criteria. With the publication of the *DSM-IV* (American Psychiatric Association, 1994), the scales were updated to reflect new criteria, and local norms were collected from a general population of adults in Massachusetts. The BAARS-IV update increased the size of the normative sample, expanded its national representativeness, and used an item pool reflecting the 18 ADHD symptoms in the then-current *DSM* (*DSM-IV-TR*) and nine items intended to evaluate the symptoms of SCT demonstrated in research with children. No research apparently exists regarding adult SCT, according to the author.

Factor analysis, scale construction, and item frequencies are reported in a comprehensive chapter of the test manual. The normative sample's initial self-reports were submitted to a principal-components factor analysis and a varimax rotation. Both approaches yielded a four-factor structure (table of factor loadings provided). Three factors–ADHD Inattention, ADHD Hyperactivity, and ADHD Impulsivity–were similar to those identified in other studies, including the study using the Massachusetts sample. The fourth factor was SCT, which accounted for 17.4% of the variance, thus giving support for its inclusion in the BAARS-IV as a dimension of attention. These factors were used for scale construction.

The test author elected to develop a scale for clinical diagnosis that was derived directly from diagnostic criteria. Therefore, the focus is on problematic symptoms as opposed to other ADHD assessments that have rephrased symptoms into positive equivalents. The BAARS-IV is intended to evaluate the range of ADHD symptoms in clinic-referred or high-risk adults as well as the likelihood that these adults are experiencing complaints severe or numerous enough to place them significantly outside the distribution of typical complaints for the general population. The earlier version of the BAARS assessed impairment in domains in addition to those in the *DSM*; the current version limits impairment domains to those found in the *DSM-IV-TR*. The test author has developed scales separate from the BAARS-IV for more in-depth assessment of impairment in both major life activities and executive functioning to augment clinical evaluation.

TECHNICAL. New to the BAARS-IV is a norming project examining ADHD symptoms in a sample of 1,249 U.S. adults (623 males, 626 females). The sample was obtained by a national survey company, Knowledge Networks, hired to conduct a survey using a panel designed to be representative of the U.S. population based on the 2000 Census. Detailed demographic characteristics of the 1,249 adults who completed the survey–including tables for regional distribution, sex, race/ethnic group, marital status, employment status, total household income, and education–are presented in the test manual.

Although the test author acknowledges that more research on the psychometric characteristics of the scale would be welcome (particularly with regard to SCT), technical information is provided in-depth and critiqued impartially. Data provided for subscale relationships, interobserver agreement and disparity, internal consistency, and test-retest reliability indicate satisfactory reliability of the scale. Pearson product-moment correlations for the relationships among the four subscales for the self-rating of Current Symptoms were all significant ($p <$ .001). Other measures of reliability were satisfactory.

Consistent with all other aspects of the test manual, detailed information was provided regarding validity. The test author states that "much of the research validating the BAARS-IV was done with the earlier prototype" of the rating scale, which did not contain the SCT symptoms (manual, p. 9). Because there is a high degree of consensus regarding the characteristics of ADHD and a large body of research, ample evidence of construct validity for ADHD exists. Although no current evidence is available concerning predictive validity of the scales, the test manual provides satisfactory evidence for concurrent and retrospective validity from numerous studies. Validity evidence provided is more than sufficient to recommend the use of BAARS-IV scores for their intended purposes.

COMMENTARY. The BAARS-IV is brief, user-friendly, and well researched and constructed. The test manual is comprehensive and practice-oriented with detailed and substantial technical evidence supporting reasonable reliability and validity of test score use. The test author openly comments on further research needs and other challenges. Because the evaluation of SCT is new to this version, further research on the SCT di-

mension is warranted. The BAARS-IV is a useful evaluation of four dimensions of adult ADHD symptoms in daily life activities providing varied efficient and cost-effective methods of collecting information. The addition of items relating to SCT and inclusion of items related to impairment in various domains of major life activities provide valuable clinical information for assessing deficits and risks that is not available from use of other ADHD assessments. Because norming is limited to a U.S. sample, generalizability to other populations is cautioned.

SUMMARY. The BAARS-IV succeeds in its goal of providing a clinically informative means of evaluating ADHD symptoms of U.S. adults ages 18 to 89 as reported by self and others. Technical information provided supports assessment of four interrelated dimensions of ADHD deficits, three of which reflect diagnostic criteria found in the *DSM-IV-TR*. Support for the fourth dimension, SCT, provides an additional basis for evaluating symptoms of inattention that may be impairing current activities of daily life but are not included among *DSM-IV-TR* diagnostic criteria. (Note: A fifth edition of the DSM was published in May 2013.) Due to extensive research and other information included in the test manual and the allowed use of copied forms by those who purchase this manual, the BAARS-IV is recommended for use as an adult behavior rating scale component of an overall clinical assessment of those who are clinic-referred or at high risk for ADHD according to *DSM-IV-TR* criteria.

REVIEWER'S REFERENCES
American Psychiatric Association. (2000). *Diagnostic and statistical manual of mental disorders* (4th ed., text rev.). Washington, DC: Author.
American Psychiatric Association. (1994). *Diagnostic and statistical manual of mental disorders* (4th ed.). Washington, DC: Author.

[10]

Barkley Deficits in Executive Functioning Scale.

Purpose: Designed "for evaluating dimensions of adult executive functioning in daily life."

Population: Ages 18-81.

Publication Date: 2011.

Acronym: BDEFS.

Scores, 8: Self-Management to Time, Self-Organization/Problem Solving, Self-Restraint, Self-Motivation, Self-Regulation of Emotions, Total EF Summary, ADHD-EF Index, EF Symptom Count.

Administration: Individual.

Forms, 4: Self-Report, Other-Report, Short Form, Long Form.

Price Data, 2011: $149 per manual (184 pages) including all forms and score sheets (includes permission to photocopy).
Time: (15-20) minutes long form; (4-5) minutes short form.
Author: Russell A. Barkley.
Publisher: Guilford Publications, Inc.

Review of the Barkley Deficits in Executive Functioning Scale by MARTIN W. ANDERSON, Deputy Commissioner, Connecticut Department of Administrative Services, Hartford, CT:

DESCRIPTION. The Barkley Deficits in Executive Functioning Scale (BDEFS) consists of a set of rating scales that can be completed (a) in long or short form by an individual, (b) by someone closely familiar with an individual, and (c) during a clinical interview by a clinician. The forms for the rating scales are printed in the test manual and persons who have purchased the manual are granted limited permission to copy the forms for their own use in their clinical or research practice.

The test author describes the BDEFS as the culmination of more than a decade of research and development to identify the most useful items for the assessment of deficits in executive functioning (EF) in daily life activities in adults. Interpretation of the scores on the BDEFS scales and subscales is said to require graduate-level training in a psychological, psychiatric, or medical specialty that requires training and coursework in the administration and interpretation of psychological measures.

The BDEFS-LF (long form, 89 items) has both a self-report and an other-report version. Norms are not available for the other-report, which is typically completed by a close relative to the person being rated such as a parent, sibling, or spouse/partner. Norms for the self-report form are available for adults in four age groups spanning 18 to 81 years, and percentile ranks are available for each scale score in four age groups for males, females, and both genders combined. The BDEFS-SF (short form, 20 items) has norms for the same four age groups as the BDEFS-LF, but there are no separate norms by gender.

The BDEFS-LF self-report form yields scores in Self-Management to Time, Self-Organization/Problem Solving, Self-Restraint, Self-Motivation, and Self-Regulation of Emotions from separate item sections that are answered on 4-point scales of *never or rarely, sometimes, often*, or *very often*. An EF Symptom Count is gleaned from the number of items answered *often* or *very often*, and an ADHD-EF Index score (the likelihood that the respondent may have adult ADHD) is tallied from 11 items found throughout the form. There is also a Total EF Summary Score. The higher the percentile rank represented by a person's score, the greater the likelihood that the individual may experience some impairment in major daily life activities as a consequence of his or her level of EF deficits.

DEVELOPMENT. The test author observes that the term *EF* is nothing new. After much discussion of the historical definitions and attribution of EF and associated functioning, Barkley operationally defines EF as "self-regulation across time for the attainment of one's goals (self-interests), often in the context of others" (manual, p. 13).

The original BDEFS item pool consisted of 91 items. A review of more than 200 charts of adults diagnosed with ADHD at a regional medical clinic led to additional item development. The prototype EF scale was developed for two large federally funded research projects on adults with ADHD. The first examined clinic-referred adults diagnosed with ADHD in comparison to both clinical and community control groups; the second was a follow-up study of hyperactive children into young adulthood (Barkley & Murphy, 2010). The items are described in the test manual as focusing on problematic symptoms ("deficit measurement"). According to the test manual, the measure "is intended to be used for clinical purposes, to evaluate the range of EF deficits in clinic-referred or high-risk adults; and to assess symptoms of executive dysfunctioning" (p. 25).

A 100-item BDEFS was normed in April 2010 on a sample of adults, ages 18 and older, in the United States. To accomplish this process, a company named Knowledge Networks of Menlo Park, California, was hired to obtain a norm group for administration of the scale and also to obtain test-retest statistics from the original norm group along with collecting demographic and other data. Subsequent analyses of the factor structure of the scale used with the norm group led to some item eliminations that yielded the final BDEFS-LF consisting of 89 items and the 20-item BDEFS-SF. The short form consists of the 4 items with the highest factor loadings on each of the five subscales found on the long form.

TECHNICAL.
Normative sample. Knowledge Networks was contracted to administer the scale to a sample of adults in the United States according to specific

parameters. The participants were first chosen by a random selection of telephone numbers and addresses. Persons with Internet access completed the 100-item scale online, and persons without access were provided a laptop and Internet access at no cost. Participants were paid for completing the survey. Knowledge Networks was to obtain completed scales on no fewer than 1,200 adults divided into six age groups with at least 100 males and 100 females in each. A subset of 62 participants (31 male and 31 female) selected across all of the age groups was retested after 2 to 3 weeks to obtain test-retest reliability statistics.

The norm group had nearly identical numbers of participants per age and gender group (that is, they were not proportional to actual U.S. Census numbers per age group) and were fairly representative across the four major regions of the United States, income levels, race/ethnic groups, marital status, and household income. For the final BDEFS-LF 89-item survey that resulted from item analysis and factor structure investigations, norms were developed for Self-Management to Time (21 items), Self-Organization/Problem Solving (24 items), Self-Restraint (19 items), Self-Motivation (12 items), Self-Regulation of Emotions (13 items), Total EF Summary (based on all 89 items), and the ADHD-EF Index (scores from 11 items selected from the subscales). Norms are presented in the form of percentile ranks for age groups 18–34, 35–49, 50–64, and 65–81 for males, females, and males and females combined. Norms for EF Symptom Counts (a tally of items answered *often* or *very often*) are provided for the separate age groups for both sexes combined. The BDEFS-SF 20-item survey supplies percentile ranks for the same age groups with both sexes combined. There are no norms for the clinical interview or for the other-report forms. The total normative sample consisted of 1,249 participants.

An inspection of mean BDEFS-LF raw scores plotted for gender by each age group showed that the Total EF Summary score, Self-Management to Time score, and Self-Restraint score were the scores on which there was clear group variability. The others were very consistent in the interaction and similarity of gender group and age group raw scores.

Reliability and scale relationships. Pearson product-moment correlations among the five subscales and the ADHD-EF index reveal coefficients ranging from .55 to .88 (all $p < .001$). In an earlier version of the BDEFS, correlations between the sub-

scales for the self-rated and the other-rated versions ranged from .66 for the Self-Organization/Problem Solving scale to .79 for the Self-Management to Time scale, showing a useful relationship between self-reported ratings and other-reported ratings of the same person.

Internal consistency estimates for the BDEFS-LF in the form of alpha coefficients were .95 for Self-Management to Time, .96 for Self-Organization/Problem Solving, .93 for Self-Restraint, .91 for Self-Motivation, and .95 for Self-Regulation of Emotion. The alpha coefficient for the ADHD-EF Index was .84 and the coefficient for the Total EF Summary score for the BDEFS-SF was .92. All coefficients were significant at $p < .001$.

Test-retest reliability estimates using a 2- to 3-week testing interval were .83 for Self-Management to Time, .90 for Self-Organization/Problem Solving, .78 for Self-Restraints, .62 for Self-Motivation, .78 for Self-Regulation of Emotions, and .84 for the Total EF Summary score (all $p < .001$). Test-retest correlation coefficients were .76 for the ADHD-EF Index and .80 for the BDEFS-SF Total EF Summary, again using a 2- to 3-week interval. Mean subscale scores were not significantly different between administrations. The BDEFS-LF has good temporal stability and internal consistency, and the short form is nearly as reliable over time as the long form.

Validity. Most of the validation work was conducted using a predecessor scale of the BDEFS, which the test author refers to as the P-BDEFS throughout the test manual. Although the P-BDEFS and the BDEFS are very similar instruments, they are not identical.

Across two major studies directed by the test author, it was notable that the scores on the P-BDEFS were far more effective than other tests and measures in identifying people with ADHD. One study compared children whose ADHD had persisted into adulthood with those whose ADHD did not persist and with a control group. The other study compared clinic-referred adults with ADHD to clinic and community control groups. Using what the test author employed as impaired designations on scale scores (that is, scores greater than the 93rd percentile rank), the P-BDEFS subscales were far better than an array of neuropsychological tests at classifying ADHD and clinical control adults as compared with community control adults. Similarly, the P-BDEFS subscales were better at classifying children whose ADHD persisted into adulthood compared with those whose ADHD did not persist and with the control group. Significant correlations were found within combined groupings of ADHD, clinical, and community groups with three ADHD symptom scores (inattentive, hyperactive-impulsive, and total ADHD) and for both the P-BDEFS scales and the norm group of the BDEFS-LF. Further, mean score differences on the BDEFS-LF scales were significant for persons with ADHD symptom scores greater than the 95th percentile and persons with symptom scores below the 84th percentile rank (the upper band of "normal" for that measure).

P-BDEFS scales also were found to be useful for showing differences in 10 occupational areas after controlling for IQ, such as percent of jobs from which a person was fired. One or more P-BDEFS subscales were significantly related to various occupational impairments such as scores on an employer-rated ADHD survey. Subscale scores on the BDEFS-LF showed significant relationships with education attainment on all but one subscale. P-BDEFS subscales showed significant relationships with adverse motor vehicle driving outcomes, credit ratings, arrests, health status, psychopathology, parenting stress, problems in offspring, and overall major life activities. Overall, greater EF problems reflected in answers on the BDEFS are associated with a greater likelihood of impairment or adversity in numerous life activities.

COMMENTARY. There seems to be sufficient research and statistical support indicating BDEFS scales have efficacy for clinical use in measuring important facets of EF that have a relationship with real world behavior.

There was inconsistency in the presentation of statistical studies and results in the test manual. For example, actual factor analysis results were presented for BDEFS items in some studies but not in others. Relationships between variables were reported as r (correlation coefficient) in some studies and r^2 (shared variance) in others. Finally, the number of subjects or degrees of freedom did not always accompany statistical results.

Further investigation of the relationship between obtained BDEFS scores and other neuropsychological or information processing assessments of EF, PFC functioning, and ADHD might prove useful. Although the P-BDEFS can successfully identify ADHD adults scoring in the clinically impaired range versus a control group, as compared to other measures of EF, it also identified other "clinical control adults" with it. So although

these EF symptoms have been shown to be further related in a meaningful way to ecological variables (income, job history, etc.) it is not entirely certain that the relationship exists because the BDEFS is measuring EF. Therefore, it is believed more work should be directed to this link, even though it is clear that adults scoring in the clinically impaired range on the BDEFS will show more differences on ecological variables than their non-impaired peers.

Additionally, a purpose might be served by investigating the relationships of the various BDEFS subscales to tests of personality. Such an investigation could help clarify the factor structure of the BDEFS items and build a knowledge base pointing to a fuller understanding of the subscale constructs. The BDEFS statements are very symptom-based and very personal. For example, respondents are not asked to compare whether they waste time more or less than other people but to indicate whether they believe they waste time *often* or *very often*. It is a curiosity if the scores operate independently of personality constructs because high or low BDEFS scores may be as much a reflection of the presence or absence of symptoms as how troubled by or aware of the symptoms the respondent might be or how much the symptoms impact daily living. High scores being a reflection of endorsing a large number of potentially troublesome symptoms could be one reason why the P-BDEFS so easily distinguished both ADHD and clinical control adults separate from community control adults in one study.

SUMMARY. The Barkley Deficits in Executive Functioning Scale (BDEFS) consists of a set of rating scales that can be completed (a) in long or short form by an individual, (b) by someone closely familiar with the individual, and (c) during a clinical interview by a clinician. The test manual, including forms, norms, and references is 184 pages. The long form takes 15 to 20 minutes to complete and the short form takes 4 to 5 minutes to complete.

The BDEFS long form and short form were normed with a group of 1,249 adults aged 18 to 81 representing the four major geographical regions of the United States. The BDEFS-LF yields percentile ranks for five main subscales meant to measure EF, an ADHD-EF Index, and an EF Symptom Count.

Evidence of internal consistency and test-retest reliability was presented. Strong validity evidence for the BDEFS or predecessor scales from factor analysis, effectiveness categorizing subject groups, and relationships with real-world ecological variables was also presented.

Overall, it is believed that there is more than sufficient evidence that the BDEFS can be used for its intended purpose. Further research to explore how performance on the BDEFS relates to other purported measures of EF as well as how the BDEFS relates to personality variables would be useful.

REVIEWER'S REFERENCES
Barkley, R. A. (1997). Behavioral inhibition, sustained attention, and executive functions: Constructing a unifying theory of ADHD. *Psychological Bulletin, 121,* 65-94.
Barkley, R. A., & Murphy, K. R. (2010). *The nature of executive function (EF) deficits in daily life activities in adults with ADHD and their relationship to EF tests.* Manuscript submitted for publication.

Review of the Barkley Deficits in Executive Functioning Scale by GREGORY SCHRAW, Professor, Department of Educational Psychology, University of Nevada-Las Vegas, Las Vegas, NV:

DESCRIPTION. The Barkley Deficits in Executive Functioning Scale (BDEFS) provides a self-report assessment of executive functioning deficits in everyday life in adults 18 to 81, but especially those with attention-deficit/hyperactivity disorder (ADHD). The BDEFS long form includes 89 items that measure five dimensions of executive functioning on a 4-point Likert scale that ranges from *never or rarely* to *very often.* The test takes 15–20 minutes to complete and is scored by the examiner using criteria described in the 184-page test manual. The test booklet includes a self-completed score profile and summary and interpretation guide for each of the five dimensions. There is a BDEFS short form as well with 20 items that takes 4 to 5 minutes to complete. Henceforth, this review focuses on the 89-item long form.

Barkley (1997, 2005) defines executive functioning as "self-regulation across time for the attainment of one's goals." The BDEFS includes five theoretically motivated components composed of self-organization, self-management of time, self-restraint, self-regulation of emotion, and self-regulation of motivation. High scores on each dimension and the aggregated total score indicate higher degrees of impairment in executive functioning and autonomous self-regulation, both of which facilitate academic and social regulation and achievement.

The test can be administered either as a self-reported or other-reported assessment. Several earlier versions were used to pilot and evaluate individual test items and underlying factors. These versions led to the 89-item instrument reported in the current manual.

DEVELOPMENT. The BDEFS manual includes an introductory chapter that provides an historical background about executive functioning and a brief review of contemporary theories. The second chapter describes the development of the current instrument within the context of executive functioning theory with an emphasis on common attributes of executive functioning such as working memory, planning, problem solving, and self-monitoring. This chapter also provides a detailed list of problems with previous assessments of executive functioning, as well as proposed conceptual and measurement improvements within the BDEFS.

TECHNICAL. The test manual is well written and provides detailed information regarding the theoretical or conceptual framework for the BDEFS, as well as norming, reliability, validity, and scoring information.

The five scales on the final version of the BDEFS are based on the work of Barkley and colleagues on ADHD and executive self-regulation to overcome ADHD-related symptoms. A preliminary set of 100 items was developed and revised based on the identification of five robust interpretative factors. A subset of these items was dropped due to poor factor loadings and replaced with new items. A new study reduced this set to the 89 items reported in the test manual.

The norming sample included 1,249 American adults between the ages of 18 and 96, including 623 males and 626 females. The sample included four educational strata (i.e., less than high school through bachelor's degree or higher), as well as a wide range of earned income strata. Overall, the norming sample was large and comprehensive of age, income, race, and geographical region of the country.

Detailed factor-analytic results used to provide evidence of construct validity are reported in the test manual. In summary, the principal components analyses with varimax rotation yielded a five-factor solution that explained 53% of sample variance. Each factor contained at least 10 items with loadings of .50 or higher. These scales each received a separate interpretation based on the factor interpretations described above, as well as an overall interpretation of executive functioning based on their aggregate. In addition, 11 items were identified as a separate scale (i.e., ADHD-EF Index) that could be used to identify executive functioning difficulties in individuals with ADHD.

The five main factors were correlated with demographic variables in the norming sample. Age demonstrated small but statistically significant correlations with most factors. Gender, ethnicity, and geographical region did not demonstrate statistically significant relationships with most factors. When significant differences were noted, they were small. For this reason, score interpretations are based on age bands of approximately 15 to 20 years. The test author opted to provide separate norms by gender, as well.

Several types of reliability data were provided. The intercorrelations between the five main factors ranged from .60 to .76 using Pearson correlation coefficients. Each of the five factors was correlated with the ADHD-EF Index in the .67 to .87 range. Each of the five main factors had an internal consistency reliability using coefficient alpha of .91 or higher, whereas the ADHD-EF Index was .84. Sixty-two individuals completed a retest 2 to 3 weeks after the first test. Test-retest correlation coefficients ranged from .78 to .90 except for on the self-motivation scale, which had a correlation coefficient of .62. A t-test of differences between test and retest scores revealed that none of the scores differed significantly between testing occasions.

The test manual includes detailed content, convergent, and discriminate validity information based on two versions of the BDEFS. The first version was the prototype of the BDEFS, referred to as the P-BDEFS. Two large validation studies using the P-BDEFS reported significant correlations between the five factors described above and a variety of executive functioning measures in individuals with ADHD. The second study utilized a large sample of students with ADHD who were followed to adulthood. Again, the five BDEFS factors showed significant correlations with self-reports and behaviors of those individuals, including inattentiveness and hyperactivity-impulsivity scores. The P-BDEFS factors also were correlated with a wide variety of occupational functioning measures, educational attainment, household income, marital satisfaction, driving, credit ratings, health status, arrests, parenting stress, and impairment of major life-activity domains. Many of these correlations were replicated using the 89-item BDEFS form of the assessment. Scores for the five factors on both versions were unrelated to IQ and academic achievement, suggesting that the BDEFS was not redundant with measures of intellectual ability. Collectively, these studies provided very strong convergent and discriminant validity evidence, which indicated that the five factors were significantly related to more than 20 different outcome measures among individuals with ADHD.

The test manual also includes a section on scoring and score interpretation of both the long and short forms. Two versions of the long form are provided (i.e., self-report and other-report), although norms are available only for the self-report version. Appropriate populations, scoring, and interpretation are discussed.

COMMENTARY AND SUMMARY. The BDEFS has many strengths and no major weaknesses. Strengths include the following: easy to administer, provides a clear definition and theoretical framework for executive functioning, provides a five-factor conceptual framework, defines and interprets five separate factors that are reliable and have credible validity evidence, has strong concurrent and predictive correlations with a wide variety of executive functioning indicators, and is not overly redundant with other measures of executive functioning.

Another advantage is that the assessment was developed within a strong research-based theoretical context by one of the leading scholars in ADHD and executive functioning disorders.

Overall, the instrument appears very sound, well researched, reliable, and valid based on several large validation samples. Examiners may use the instrument to identify executive functioning deficits, as well as to examine the relationship between executive functioning and five core self-regulatory dimensions of cognitive functioning in everyday life.

REVIEWER'S REFERENCES

Barkley, R. A. (1997). Behavioral inhibition, sustained attention, and executive functions: Constructing a unifying theory of ADHD. *Psychological Bulletin, 121*, 65-94.
Barkley, R. A. (2005). *Attention-deficit hyperactivity disorder: A handbook for diagnosis and treatment.* New York, NY: Guilford Press.

[11]

Barkley Deficits in Executive Functioning Scale–Children and Adolescents.

Purpose: Designed to "evaluate the major components of executive functioning in daily life activities of children … for whom there is concern about deficits in EF, such as children with neurological, developmental, or psychiatric disorders or those having psychological difficulties with which deficits in EF may be thought to be associated."

Population: Ages 6–17.

Publication Date: 2012.

Acronym: BDEFS-CA.

Scores, 9: Self-Management to Time, Self-Organization/Problem Solving, Self-Restraint, Self-Motivation, Self-Regulation of Emotion, EF Summary Score, EF Symptom Count, EF Summary Score–Short Form, ADHD-EF Index (optional).

Administration: Individual.

Forms: Long Form, Short Form, Interview.

Price Data, 2013: $126.65 per manual (192 pages), includes permission to reproduce forms and score sheets (found in manual) for repeated use.

Time: (10-15) minutes (Long Form); (3-5) minutes (Short Form).

Comments: "If an individual is unable to complete the BDEFS-CA Long Form or BDEFS-CA Short Form … the examiner may opt to use the BDEFS-CA Interview, which is based on the BDEFS-CA Short Form (20 items)."

Author: Russell A. Barkley.

Publisher: Guilford Publications, Inc.

Review of the Barkley Deficits in Executive Functioning Scale–Children and Adolescents by JOE W. DIXON, Licensed Psychologist, Private Practice, Tuscaloosa, AL:

DESCRIPTION. The Barkley Deficits in Executive Functioning Scale–Children and Adolescents (BDEFS-CA) by Russell A. Barkley is a downward age extension of his previously published Barkley Deficits in Executive Functioning Scale (BDEFS, Barkley, 2011; 19:10) for adults ages 18 to 81. The BDEFS-CA instrument is designed to screen for deficits in executive functioning (EF) in children and adolescents ages 6–17 based upon parent ratings of 70 observed behaviors. For those familiar with Barkley's earlier BDEFS, the transition to using the BDEFS-CA will be easy because both have similar theoretical underpinnings and both utilize rating scales of similar design.

The BDEFS-CA user's manual provides normative data, psychometric properties, and scoring and interpretation information. The actual rating scales are provided in the user's manual, which offers an unlimited right for purchasers to photocopy forms for personal use, making this instrument inexpensive to use. There is a 70-item long form and a 20-item short form. Also provided is a 20-item brief interview form based upon the short form for times when a parent is unable to complete the rating scale. Embedded within the long form are 10 items that are used to indicate risk of attention-deficit/hyperactivity disorder (ADHD). The rating subscales all employ a 4-point Likert rating system: 1 = *never or rarely*, 2 = *sometimes*, 3 = *often*, and 4 = *very often*. Point values are summed to obtain scores. There are no forms for teachers or self-report forms for completion by the children and adolescents themselves.

The test author recommends that the instrument be interpreted by professionals trained at the graduate level in clinical assessment of children and adolescents. It can be used in clinical settings to screen for EF deficits, to assess intervention effects, and for research.

Subscales assess five domains: Self-Management to Time, Self-Organization/Problem Solving, Self-Restraint, Self-Motivation, and Self-Regulation of Emotion.

DEVELOPMENT. The test author reports that the BDEFS-CA is based upon more than 17 years of research in identifying the most useful behaviors to include on the subscales to clinically assess EF in children and adolescents. This instrument is principally based upon the test author's well known theory of EF. In brief, Barkley's theory describes EF as self-regulation of goal-directed behavior, allowing for changes in the manner of achieving the goal, with at least five executive activities at work. These executive activities include self-inhibition, self-directed sensory-motor action, self-directed private speech, self-directed emotion and motivation, and self-directed play. In the test manual, the author reviews various theories of EF and describes how many neuropsychological tests are used in the field to measure EF although they were not designed for that purpose. Barkley proposes that if the purpose of evaluating EF is to render judgment about actual real-world impairment, then a better approach is to assess these impairments through the use of ratings by those who know the patient best. To this end, the test author originally developed the BDEFS, and, after experimental and commercial success with that instrument, developed the BDEFS-CA. The test manual includes many persuasive reasons for the use of rating scales, including: Raters who know the child or adolescent best can quickly and reliably provide useful clinical information; low frequency behaviors can be identified; normative data easily can be compiled and used clinically; and rating scales can be used for many different purposes.

Based upon descriptions of EF in the literature and the test author's own experiences, 91 original items were selected for study in the prototype adult instrument, the P-BDEFS. Using those data and findings in clinical use, the 89 final items on the BDEFS were used to select items for the child and adolescent version, the BDEFS-CA.

The BDEFS-CA was normed on a large, nationally representative sample of 1,922 parents in the U.S. who had children ages 6–17. The sample was stratified by socioeconomic status, nine geographic regions, and ethnicity. Details are provided in the test manual. Data about clinical diagnoses (23% of the sample reported diagnoses, which is roughly the same proportion as in the general population) and treatment were obtained as well. The BDEFS-CA sampling procedure compares quite favorably to the parent form of the Behavior Rating Inventory of Executive Function (BRIEF, 2000; 15:32), another widely used measure of EF in children and adolescents that employed a smaller and narrower normative sample.

TECHNICAL. The 14 items with the highest loadings on each of the five factors identified through factor analysis conducted on the BDEFS were selected for the BDEFS-CA. The five factors identified were: Self-Management to Time, Self-Organization/Problem Solving, Self-Restraint (Inhibition), Self-Motivation, and Self-Regulation of Emotion. The 70 items selected for the BDEFS-CA were then submitted to a principal components factor analysis. Five factors were identified with eigenvalues greater than 1.0, which accounted for 68.5% of the variance. These factors delineate the five subscales of the BDEFS-CA. All factor loadings on the first factor were positive, indicating a unitary executive dysfunction factor for the scale as a whole. The finding that EF is a unitary construct is consistent with the published literature. Varimax and promax rotation yielded the same five factors for the BDEFS-CA and the adult instrument. The test manual provides factor loadings for each item on the instrument grouped by factor. Additional analysis identified 10 items that classified children and adolescents with ADHD at 97% accuracy.

As a measure of internal reliability, the five scales plus the 10-item ADHD-EF Index were subjected to correlational analyses. Results indicated that all five scales were significantly (p < .001) intercorrelated (Pearson's r ranging from .63 to .83). The ADHD-EF Index score was highly correlated with all five subscales on the long form. The BDEFS-CA short form was found to correlate highly with the BDEFS-CA long form, (r = .98; p < .001). Thus, the subscales and the long and short versions of the BDEFS-CA are highly correlated indicating good internal reliability.

Coefficient alpha was computed as a measure of internal consistency. Alpha coefficients for the subscales were all higher than .95. For all 70 items on the long form, the alpha coefficient was .99; for the ADHD-EF Index, the alpha coefficient was .90. To determine whether the BDEFS-CA was stable over time, a test-retest analysis was conducted. Results revealed temporal consistency with 86 parents completing the scale for a second time 3–5 weeks after the first administration. The correlation coefficients for the EF Summary Score and the ADHD-EF Index were .82 and .79, respectively (p < .001).

Evidence of conceptual or face validity was demonstrated by basing item selection on the test author's definition of EF that emphasizes self-regulation as a means to modify one's own behavior. Further, items were selected based upon review of the relevant literature describing deficits believed to be associated with dysexecutive syndrome or deficits in EF. Inspection of the actual items on the scale leads one to believe that the BDEFS-CA does demonstrate face validity.

The test author argues that neuropsychological tests that purport to measure EF often fail to do just that given that such tests are poor predictors of functioning and impairment in major life activities in which EF is considered important. He goes on to say that most EF rating scales do not correlate well with neuropsychological tests per se and concludes that one cannot use neuropsychological tests as a criterion measure or standard for the validity of test scores from EF rating scales. No published research is available comparing the BDEFS-CA to neuropsychological tests inasmuch as the BDEFS-CA is a newly published instrument. A search of PsycINFO and PsycARTICLES found no published research on the BDEFS-CA in preparation for this review. The test manual does contain data comparing BDEFS-CA scores with those from the parent form of the BRIEF (n = 22). Results showed the BRIEF Total EF Score compared quite favorably to the EF Summary Score from the BDEFS-CA (r = .92, p < .001), providing significant support to the validity of the BDEFS-CA.

Another form of validity evidence stems from divergent or discriminant test scores from measures that should be unrelated to the subject construct. This approach assesses the degree to which one instrument fails to measure a construct that it was not designed to measure. To this end, the test author cites prior studies with the BDEFS and IQ measures that revealed low and insignificant correlation coefficients. This finding would seem to indicate that the BDEFS is indeed measuring something other than what intelligence tests measure, and arguably the same could be said of the BDEFS-CA. No such comparative studies with intelligence tests have yet been conducted using the BDEFS-CA. In the test manual, the author mounts a similar and parallel argument concerning achievement tests.

As an indicator of criterion validity, the BDEFS-CA was used to distinguish among disordered and normal groups where the disordered group was believed to have deficits in EF. Recall that clinical data were collected on the children in the normative sample for the BDEFS-CA. The results of that comparison showed significant differences in the subscale ratings and the total BDEFS-CA long and short form results for children who had received a diagnosis of ADHD (or attention-deficit disorder) compared to children in the normative sample who had not received such a diagnosis (EF Summary Score: $F = 396.32$, $p < .001$; ADHD-EF Index: $F = 390.32$, $p < .001$; EF Summary Score-Short Form: $F = 386.53$, $p < .001$).

Overall, the user's manual provides ample discussion, data, and analysis for the statistical properties of the BDEFS-CA.

COMMENTARY. The BDEFS-CA derives a great deal of its theoretical underpinnings and strength as a rating scale from its parent instrument, the BDEFS. Several of the arguments in the user's manual justifying item selection and inclusion, reliability, and validity draw heavily upon the parent instrument. Nonetheless, there is ample statistical analysis and excellent normative data provided for the BDEFS-CA for it to stand alone as a useful scale. The rationale for the selection of items, development of scales, and the validation arguments are strong. Executive functioning, as defined by the test author, is certainly directly assessed through the use of this parent rating form for children and adolescents in the age group 6 to 17. The theoretical model upon which the instrument is based has received wide support in the professional community.

SUMMARY. The BDEFS-CA is a well thought out, well designed, well crafted, and useful instrument for the assessment of deficits in executive functioning in children and adolescents. It arguably is the single best rating scale currently available for EF deficit measurement in this age group.

REVIEWER'S REFERENCES

Barkley, R. A. (2011). Barkley Deficits in Executive Functioning Scale (BDEFS). New York, NY: Guilford Press.
Gioia, G. A., Isquith, P. K., Guy, S. C., & Kenworthy, L. (2000). BRIEF: Behavior Rating Inventory of Executive Function–Professional manual. Odessa, FL: Psychological Assessment Resources.

Review of the Barkley Deficits in Executive Functioning Scale—Children and Adolescents by

KATHLEEN TORSNEY, Associate Professor, Department of Psychology, William Paterson University, Wayne, NJ:

DESCRIPTION. The Barkley Deficits in Executive Functioning Scale—Children and Adolescents (BDEFS-CA) is a parent-report scale for the assessment of executive functioning in children and adolescents who are 6–17 years of age and thought to have some deficits in executive functioning. The test author indicates that this scale is especially useful for evaluating how executive functioning (EF) deficits appear in the daily living activities of children and adolescents. The scale assesses five related aspects of EF deficits: Self-Management to Time, Self-Organization/Problem Solving, Self-Restraint, Self-Motivation, and Self-Regulation of Emotion. The BDEFS-CA consists of a 70-item long form, a 20-item short form, and an interview form of the short version. The items on the short form were chosen from a factor analysis of the long form; the 20 items are the four highest loading items on each of the subscales. The test author advises that the interview form be used only in rare instances when one of the other forms cannot be completed due to reading, language, or visual deficits. The scale is theoretically based on Barkley's theory of executive functioning and empirically supported by extensive research with the adult version of the instrument, the Barkley Deficits in Executive Functioning Scale (BDEFS; Barkley, 2011; 19:10). Barkley conceptualized executive functioning as both self-regulation to attain a goal and self-directed activities toward the goal. The BDEFS-CA asks respondents to rate the frequency of executive functioning deficits in daily living activities on a scale of *never or rarely* (1), *sometimes* (2), *often* (3), and *very often* (4), during the past 6 months and without medication, if the child is currently taking medication for a psychiatric or psychological disorder. The test author provides combined age and sex norms as well as norms for ages 6–11 and 12–17, for males, and for females. A deficit in executive functioning in one of the areas of daily living (e.g., Self-Management to Time, Self-Organization/Problem Solving, Self-Restraint, Self-Motivation, and Self-Regulation of Emotion) is indicated when the score is at or above the 93rd percentile. The scale also contains an EF Summary Score, an ADHD-EF Index (a sum of 10 selected items) and an EF Symptom Count (number of answers of *often* or *very often*). The scale may be employed in research, clinical practice, and educational settings. It not only indicates the presence of an executive functioning deficit, but also the important factor of how it manifests in the child's or adolescent's functional behavior (Biederman et al., 2007). The scale also can be used to demonstrate change in the level of executive functioning deficits from a variety of sources such as treatment, a neurological or psychiatric disorder, or a temporary episode of psychological dysfunction that may affect the child's or adolescent's EF in daily life.

DEVELOPMENT. The BDEFS-CA is based on Barkley's theoretical model of executive functioning, which was employed to design the BDEFS for adults. Barkley's publications on attention-deficit/hyperactivity disorder (ADHD), executive functioning, and noncooperation among children include numerous books and book chapters as well as more than 260 scientific articles. Items were selected for the BDEFS-CA based on Barkley's theory of EF and upon a review of the literature on EF. The BDEFS-CA is a "downward extension of the BDEFS for adults" (manual, p. 38) that also relied on factor analytic methods to select items. Selected items reflect issues in EF such as inhibition, verbal working memory, nonverbal working memory, organization of behavior across time, motivational self-regulation, and fluency. A factor analysis of the prototype of the BDEFS yielded five factors that Barkley identified as central to EF: self-management to time, self-organization/problem solving, self-discipline or inhibition, self-motivation, and self-activation/concentration. Barkley's theory of EF illustrated the problem with executive functioning tests and the dangers of relying on traditional executive functioning tests as the gold standard for evaluating EF because traditional tests appear to measure a different construct from the functional scales of EF. Barkley noted that the majority of tests designed to assess executive functioning were not developed to gauge EF. He argues that his scales more accurately reflect how EF deficits affect one's ability to plan, organize, set goals, and attain desired goals.

TECHNICAL. The BDEFS was based on more than 16 years of research on a prototype of the scale. The author of the BDEFS-CA compared it to other assessments of executive functioning such as the Behavior Rating Inventory of Executive Function (BRIEF; 15:32) and traditional EF measures.

Standardization. The original sample for the BDEFS-CA included 1,922 parents of children and adolescents; the final normative sample included 1,800 parents of children ages 6–17 (n = 451 males

ages 6–11, n = 450 males ages 12–17, n = 451 females ages 6–11, and n = 448 females ages 12–17). Because the normative sample contained a higher proportion of White individuals, college educated persons, and males than the 2000 U.S. Census, the test author reduced the original sample by 6% by removing at random some White males with a bachelor's degree or higher. According to the test author, the BDEFS-CA normative sample is more extensive than samples used in other similar scales in that participants were drawn from all regions of the United States and represent the geographic distribution of residents found in the 2000 Census. It should be noted that the sample had fewer individuals with less than a high school education than occurred in the 2000 U.S. Census. The test author suggests that parents with less education tended to report more executive deficit issues with their children. The normative sample also contained fewer Blacks, and participants had a much higher median income than the U.S. Census average. The test author notes that the U.S. Census does not separate parents from nonparents in terms of income and that it is possible that parents have a higher income compared to nonparents. Finally, the normative sample for the BDEFS-CA contained more married and more working individuals than the proportion found in the U.S. Census; however, the U.S. Census does not specify whether the married and working persons are parents.

Reliability. The subscales of the BDEFS-CA are significantly and moderately to highly intercorrelated. Internal consistency of the subscales was adequate with alpha coefficients that were all .96 or .97. Internal consistency estimates were .99 for the long form and .95 for the short form. These results are similar to other rating scales of EF in children and to the BDEFS. Test-retest reliability (n = 86) over a 3- to 5-week period was satisfactory with reported coefficients that ranged from .73 (Self-Management to Time) to .82 (Total EF Summary Score and Self-Regulation of Emotion). Test-retest reliability for the short form was estimated with a coefficient of .79. All coefficients were significant at $p < .001$. The results are similar to other measures of EF in children such as the BRIEF, which used a 2-week interval. Further estimates of the reliability of the BDEFS-CA with large samples should continue to assess more completely the psychometric properties of this instrument.

Validity. Because the BDEFS-CA was developed from Barkley's theory of executive deficits among individuals, construct validation procedures were relevant to the evaluation of the validity of this scale. The test authors examined the convergent validity of the BDEFS-CA and other rating scales such as the BRIEF. The correlations between the BDEFS-CA and the BRIEF were significant and revealed a very high coefficient for the total scores of each scale (r = .92). Studies of discriminant validity demonstrated low correlation coefficients between the adult version of the BDEFS and IQ and academic achievement, but a study of the BDEFS-CA and IQ/Academic achievement has not been conducted. In terms of criterion validity evidence, the correlations between BDEFS-CA scores and ADHD ratings according to *DSM-IV* symptoms were satisfactory with coefficients that ranged from .60 (Time Management and ADHD scale hyperactive/impulsive) to .88 (Self-Motivation and ADHD scale inattention). The criterion validity of the BDEFS-CA was assessed by differentiating EF disorders from other disorders such as speech and language disorders, motor coordination disorders, developmental disorders, seizure and tic disorders, autism spectrum disorders, learning disabilities, and psychiatric disorders. The results showed that ADHD impacts EF in terms of daily living activities more so than the other disorders. The test author suggests that the scale demonstrates how EF deficits appear in functional behavior in a variety of disorders. Future research should investigate the impact of psychiatric and neurological disorders on the BDEFS-CA and comorbid ADHD.

COMMENTARY. The BDEFS-CA is a rather valid and reliable instrument to gauge how executive functioning deficits affect a child or adolescent's ability to regulate him or herself over time in order to attain future goals. The advantages of the instrument are that it yields important information about how executive functioning deficits are exhibited in the daily living activities of children and adolescents and it is cost effective and efficient. However, elevated scores may be obtained by persons with psychiatric conditions rather than frontal lobe dysfunctions. The subscales of the BDEFS-CA are highly intercorrelated so that an elevated score in only one area of EF is uncommon unless a highly localized brain injury is present or the parent or child is malingering. In addition, rating scales assume that the parent and the examiner interpret the questions in the same manner, whereas parents may perceive an item to be different than the test developer intended. Therefore, it is advisable to supplement rating scales with other measures of EF and interviews to fully assess parental factors and possible environmental and physical influences on the executive functioning of children and adolescents.

SUMMARY. The BDEFS-CA is an adequately reliable and valid scale to evaluate EF deficits in children and adolescents ages 6–17. The scale provides important information about how executive functioning deficits affect the behavior of children and adolescents, and it can be used for research, clinical, and educational purposes. Scores on the BDEFS-CA may reflect important changes in functioning that would suggest an alteration in treatment. Future research should continue to investigate the reliability and validity of the scale as well as possible cultural differences in EF among children and adolescents.

REVIEWER'S REFERENCES
Barkley, R. A. (2011). Barkley Deficits in Executive Functioning Scale (BDEFS). New York, NY: Guilford Press.
Biederman, J., Petty, C. R., Fired, R., Fontanella, J., Doyle, A. E., Seidman, L. J., & Faraone, S. V. (2007). Can self-reported behavioral scales assess executive function deficits? A controlled study of adults with ADHD. *Journal of Nervous and Mental Disease, 195*, 240–246.

[12]

Barkley Functional Impairment Scale.

Purpose: A self-report assessment "intended for clinical purposes—specifically, to be used to evaluate the range of functional impairment in clinic-referred or high-risk adults."

Population: Ages 18-89.

Publication Date: 2011.

Acronym: BFIS.

Scores, 2: Mean Impairment, Percent Domains Impaired; 15 domains: Home-Family, Home-Chores, Work, Social-Strangers, Social-Friends, Community Activities, Education, Marriage/Cohabitation/Dating, Money Management, Driving, Sexual Relations, Daily Responsibilities, Self-Care Routines, Health Maintenance, Childrearing.

Administration: Individual.

Forms, 4: Long Form: Self-Report, Quick Screen: Self-Report, Long Form: Other-Report, Quick Screen: Other-Report.

Price Data, 2011: $149 per manual, including all forms and score sheets (including permission to photocopy).

Time: (5-7) minutes for Long Form; (3-5) minutes for Quick Screen.

Author: Russell A. Barkley.

Publisher: Guilford Publications, Inc.

Review of the Barkley Functional Impairment Scale by MERITH COSDEN, Professor, Department of Counseling, Clinical, & School Psychology, University of California, Santa Barbara, Santa Barbara, CA:

DESCRIPTION. The Barkley Functional Impairment Scale (BFIS) is a 15-domain self-report instrument that assesses functional impairment in major psychosocial domains. Functional impairment is differentiated from clinical symptoms associated with specific disorders. That is, functional impairment is viewed as an inability to perform effectively in major life domains, which the test author argues is separate from clinical symptom severity. Although functional impairment is viewed as dimensional (i.e., respondents are asked to rate their level of functioning in specific activities), respondents are considered to have an impairment if they score similarly to the respondents in the top percentiles of the normative standardization sample.

The BFIS Long Form (BFIS-LF) asks adults to indicate how much difficulty they have in their personal functioning in each of 15 areas: (1) home life with immediate family; (2) chores/managing household activities; (3) work; (4) social interactions with strangers; (5) relationships with friends; (6) community activities; (7) educational activities; (8) marital, cohabitating, or dating relationships; (9) money management; (10) driving; (11) sexual relations; (12) organizing/managing daily responsibilities; (13) daily self-care routines; (14) health maintenance; and (15) childrearing. Each item is rated on a 0 to 9 scale anchored by *not at all* at one end and *severe* at the other. Respondents can also select *does not apply* as an option.

In addition to domain-specific scores, a Mean Impairment score is obtained by adding the responses for each item and dividing by the number of items to which the individual has responded. Responses are transferred to score sheets that differ by age group, with 18–39-, 40–59-, and 60–89-year-olds clustered based on normative differences for functional impairment found across these groups. The BFIS-LF yields 17 scores: 15 domain-specific scores, a Mean Impairment score, and the percent of domains falling in the impairment range. Domain scores that fall in the 93rd to 95th percentile relative to the normative group are boldfaced on the score sheet and are considered to reflect functional impairment, as are Mean Impairment scores above the 93rd–95th percentile.

There are three forms associated with the BFIS-LF. The Self-Report is the one for which there are norms. There is also an Other-Report form that has the same items as the Self-Report form and is intended for use by someone who knows the subject well. This form is not scored, but instead used clinically to determine similarities between self and other perceptions of the impairment. Finally, there is an Impairment Interview form. This form lists each domain followed by space with instructions for how to interview the client to allow for affirming and describing the impairments noted on the Self-Report.

There is also a short form of the BSIF called the Quick Screen. It contains six of the BSIF-LF domains: Home Life-Family, Home-Chores, Self-Care, Social-Friends, Education, and Work. The test creator indicates that these are the most important areas for basic functioning, particularly from the perspective of government agencies that require assessments to determine level of impairment. The Quick Screen also has Self-Report, Other-Report, and Impairment Interview forms.

The BFIS has multiple purposes. It can be used clinically to identify client needs and develop treatment plans; it can be used in research as a measure of change; and it can be used as a measure for assessing disability or impairment for legal purposes. The target population is adults who have disorders that might impair their life functioning, or who might need evaluation to qualify for disability services or compensation. The BFIS is not intended to be the sole determinant of impairment, however. Triangulation is important, either with the Other-Report and Impairment Interview, or other measures of impairment.

DEVELOPMENT. The test author began development of the BFIS in a study involving adults with attention deficit hyperactivity disorder (ADHD) for which he created an Impairment Rating Scale (IRS). IRS respondents were given a 4-point Likert scale to rate the frequency of problems in 10 areas: home life, work, social interactions, community activities, educational activities, marriage and dating, money management, driving, leisure activities, and handling daily activities. These domains were derived from guidelines developed by groups such as the Social Security Administration and the American Medical Association. The test author adapted this scale to better understand functioning and functional impairment within a broader normative sample. Thus, the scale was expanded to include 10 additional domains. Five of these were maintained in the final BFIS (i.e., home life was separated into completing chores/managing a household, self-care, and home life with family; social interactions was separated into social relationships with friends and social interactions with strangers; and sexual activities and health maintenance were added). Five other domains (caring for property, obeying the law, avoiding use of illegal substances, and controlling use of legal substances) were initially added, but as a result of both statistical and conceptual concerns were later discarded, leaving the current 15 domains. In addition, the rating scale was expanded to a 10-point scale reflecting severity rather than frequency of impairment, and the marriage scale was updated to be inclusive of close cohabiting relationships.

TECHNICAL.

Standardization. A nationally based normative sample of 1,249 adults was obtained in 2010 though a scientifically determined random selection process. Respondents represented six age groups (18–29, 30–39, 40–49, 50–59, 60–69, and 70 plus) in nine regions across the country, with at least 100 men and 100 women in each age group. Once selected for the sample, there were no exclusion criteria. Thus, respondents represent a wide range of ethnicities, economic strata, educational levels, and employment circumstances, which are delineated in the test manual.

Reliability. With regard to reliability, the test manual presents data on the internal consistency of the BFIS-LF for the normative sample and test-retest correlations for a subsample of this group. Internal consistency of the domain ratings was high for both the full BFIS-LF (alpha coefficient was .97) and the Quick Screen (alpha coefficient was .92). Test-retest reliability over a 2- to 3-week period was calculated for 62 adults in the normative sample; although this is a relatively small subsample, participants were selected to equally represent men and women from each age group. Correlation coefficients for domain scores ranged from moderate to high. At the lower end were coefficients for education and health maintenance at .40 and .41, respectively; higher correlation coefficients were obtained for social interactions with strangers (.72), social interactions with friends, and driving (.71 each). Reliability for the Mean Impairment Score was also high demonstrating a correlation coefficient of .72.

Validity. The test manual presents evidence for the construct validity of the measure as a whole and for some of the specific domains based on additional assessments conducted with the normative sample. For example, disability status of the normative sample was associated with impairment on the work domain, educational level with scores on the education domain, and annual income with impairment in the money domain, while all three characteristics were also associated with Mean Impairment scores. Somewhat weaker construct validity data were reported for driving, daily responsibilities, and health maintenance. Validity data for childrearing, sexual relations, community activities, social relationships with friends, and social relationships with strangers were not presented in the test manual, which suggests that further research should be conducted in those domains.

COMMENTARY. Functional impairment is an important yet often overlooked area for assessment. The BFIS provides a self-perspective on functional problems across many major life activities. The test manual provides the strongest evidence for its validity as a global measure of functioning. Both the national norms, which provide a basis for comparing behavior, and the clinical information provided by the domain-specific scores, are particularly useful. Concern is raised regarding the utility of some of the domain-specific ratings given their moderate test-retest reliability over a short period of time. There are several possible reasons for this outcome. For example, only one item is used for each domain score and some domains may be malleable even over short periods of time. Further, the definition of functional impairment is vague; thus, respondents may vary in the behavioral referents they use to respond from one time to the next. A positive note is that the instrument is quick and easy to administer. Although the Quick Screen provides an abbreviated measure, the BFIS-LF itself is relatively short, so it is not clear when the shorter version would be needed. As indicated in the test manual, the BFIS is not intended to be used as the sole determinant of impairment, but requires triangulation from multiple sources. The test manual provides means for triangulation through the Other Report and the Impairment Interview. Although interesting, additional research is needed to determine the full utility of the BFIS in determining functional impairment for both clinical and legal purposes.

SUMMARY. The BFIS is a short, easily administered self-assessment of functional problems. The normative sample provides a standardized manner for interpreting findings. The high correlations among domain scores, coupled with the reliability and validity of the Mean Impairment score, suggests that this is the best score for use in research and evaluation. The domain scores, however, can provide clinically useful information, particularly in conjunction with the Other Report and Impairment Interview.

Review of the Barkley Functional Impairment Scale by ROBERT WRIGHT, Professor Emeritus, Measurement & Statistics, Widener University, Chester, PA:

DESCRIPTION. The BFIS provides a norm-referenced measure of psychosocial impairment within the population of adult Americans. The approach employed by the BFIS involves a brief self-report by an individual about his or her perceptions of specific areas of psychosocial impairment.

The BFIS provides two versions, a long form (BFIS-LF) consisting of what the test author describes as 15 Likert-type scale items (10 levels each), and a short form the BFIS-Quick Screen. The quick screen is composed of 6 of the 15 items of the BFIS-LF. When either form is used in the assessment process for an individual, a second BFIS should be independently completed by a person knowing the patient (spouse, care giver, housemate, etc.) to provide a second assessment perspective.

BFIS scores can be used prior to, and following an intervention for an individual receiving therapy, to evaluate the intervention's efficaciousness. Although use of the BFIS is not restricted to individuals with neurological involvement, it may be completed by individuals following a neurological incident (e.g., brain lesion, head injury, cerebrovascular accident, transient ischemic attack, dementia, or a neurological infection such as encephalitis myelitis, meningitis, and other neural-tube infections [arachnoiditis], and human immunodeficiency virus [HIV] to examine premorbid functioning. This retrospective approach involves asking the patient to respond (from memory) how he or she functioned prior to the neurological insult. A second form is then completed by the individual describing his or her current level of functioning.

In these applications of the BFIS another assessment form is also to be completed by an individual close to, and very familiar with the patient being evaluated. Discrepancies are to be anticipated, but large differences between the evaluation by another person and the self-evaluation should be explored.

The BFIS provides a form for taking clinical notes during subsequent follow-up questioning. This form, the BFIS Impairment Interview, is used to probe the patient's perception when the response to the BFIS indicates a high degree of functional impairment. A high degree of functional impairment is defined as having a BFIS score more severe than is reported by 93% (+ 1.5 *SD*) or 98% (+ 2.0 *SD*) of the normative population.

To reduce the likelihood of self-report bias threatening the validity of the data, the test author suggests that scores indicating a significant level of perceived functional impairment be subjected to a third level of assessment. This is in addition to the BFIS (both Self and Other) and the clinical interview. The third step involves gathering supporting artifacts and documentation related to the impairment. Prior to presenting a conclusive diagnostic statement, there should be a full analysis (triangulation) including three forms of evidence supporting the BFIS data.

DEVELOPMENT. The concept of mental deficits was introduced by the Americans with Disabilities Act of 1990 (ADA). Prior to the ADA, the term handicapped was used to describe all forms of functional disadvantage experienced by individuals. Mental deficiencies were further divided into three levels: physical (organic), cognitive-behavioral, and psychosocial.

ADA rule-making is the responsibility of the Equal Employment Opportunity Commission (EEOC). They further clarified the interpretation of the term "mental disability" by requiring it be based on a normative comparison to the population. Currently, identification of an individual with a disability requires documentation of a significant restriction in a major life activity of the individual compared with abilities of average individuals. Similar guidelines are also used for evaluating individuals applying for workers compensation and/ or Social Security Disability Insurance from the Social Security Administration.

The BFIS was developed as part of ongoing longitudinal research into the comorbidity factors seen in adults originally diagnosed during their childhoods as having Attention Deficit/Hyperactivity Disorder (ADHD), Hyperactive Type. A 10-item problem intensity scale (four levels per item) measuring psychosocial impairment was developed and included in a larger prototype instrument, assessing risk factors among adults with ADHD. This instrument, the Impairment Rating Scale (IRS), asked respondents to consider the last 6 months of their lives and answer 10 items related to their capacity to deal with 10 different domains of major life activities.

As part of ongoing research the original IRS was expanded to include the measurement of 20 independent domains using 20 problem-intensity questions. Each of these 20 items was developed with 10 ordinal sequenced choices assessing the level of severity of the perceived impairment. This revised instrument, the BFIS-LF, retained the 10 original item stems (stimulus statements) from the IRS. Following factor analysis, 3 of the 20 items were removed because they failed to align with the principal factor of psychosocial impairment. Two other items were removed due to low factor loadings and because they seemed "trivial" (manual, p. 23). The final BFIS-LF includes questions assessing impairment in the following domains: Home-Family, Home-Chores, Work, Social-Strangers, Social-Friends, Community Activities, Education, Marriage/Cohabiting/Dating, Money Management, Driving, Sexual Relations, Daily Responsibilities, Self-Care Routines, Health Maintenance, and Childrearing.

A shorter form of the BFIS, known as the Barkley Functional Impairment Scale Quick Screen, was also developed and included in the test manual. This measure includes only six items identified as being of most interest by governmental agencies making decisions related to the disability of individuals. These items focus on Home-Family, Home-Chores, Self-Care Routines, Social-Friends, Education, and Work.

TECHNICAL. The BFIS was standardized with a national sample designed to represent the adult population of the United States. The sample was established by a random selection of telephone numbers and residential addresses, and stratified by 6 age groups, gender, and 9 geographical regions of the United States. It matched the U.S. Census data on a number of other demographic variables as well.

Data from the 15 problem-intensity items of the BFIS were treated as parametric values and analyzed with unrotated principal component factor analysis. The result was the delineation of a single factor for psychosocial impairment that accounted for 52.9% of the variance. The median factor loading was .75 and the range was from .58 to .84.

Two different severity ratings (cut scores) were determined for each of the 15 impairment domain scores. These were defined by the frequency of occurrence of item ratings in the normative sample. The distribution of impairment scores tends to be positively skewed, as most individuals in a normal population report they experience few if any impairments, and those are usually of low severity. The test author selected the score point where only 7% (93rd percentile) or fewer of the population reported an equivalent level of impairment severity. For a more conservative interpretation, the test author also identified BFIS scores at the 98th percentile. These high-severity levels are triggers for the treating clinician to use the BFIS Impairment Interview to explore the nature of the psychosocial impairment.

Internal consistency reliability of the BFIS-LF appears high with a reported alpha coefficient of .97, and a BFIS Quick Screen alpha coefficient of .92. A random sample ($N = 62$) of the normative group was posttested 2 or 3 weeks following initial testing. Pearson product moment correlations were used to establish test-retest reliability for the 15 domains measured by the problem intensity items. Correlation coefficients ranged .40 for Education to .72 for the Social-Strangers. Test-retest reliability estimates were .72 for the combined score and .71 for the 6-item BSIF Quick Screen. Correlation coefficients for the 15 problem intensity items ranged from .40 (Education) to .72 (Social-Strangers), with the majority of values exceeding .50. Reliability coefficients for stability lower than .70 may be considered below the threshold required for meaningful psychological measurement (Nunnally & Bernstein, 1994). By classical test theory these levels of reliability indicate that more than half of the variation of the total BFIS-LF and the BFIS Quick Screen is composed of error variance. Because the 15 individual questions have lower reliability coefficients than the full scale, this problem is compounded for the problem-intensity items.

Missing from the test manual for the BFIS are standard errors of measurement for the total scale and the 15 individual items.

To be valid, a new measurement must first be reliable (Anastasi & Urbina, 1997). Validity also requires the measurement instrument assess a well-defined construct. This requirement for construct definition is well met by the BFIS author. The test author used older research with the IRS scale (10 items with 4 levels per answer) to support the construct validity of the BFIS and its 15 items each scaled with 10 levels of severity. The test author also employed other data (an "early version" of the BFIS) from a study of executive functioning with adults diagnosed with ADHD to document the interrater reliability of two ratings (Self and Other).

These data demonstrated a moderate correlation coefficient (.68) between self-reported and other-reported scores. There were a number of validation studies reported for the 10 items of the IRS, but their usefulness in establishing the *bona fides* of the BFIS is open to question.

Confirmatory factor analysis has provided clear evidence that the BFIS is composed of a single core factor measuring psychosocial impairment. The confirmatory factor analysis involved adding variables from other assessments with the 15 BFIS domain items into a matrix of variables, and conducting a factor analysis with the expanded matrix of variables using Varimax rotation. The result was the identification of one clear factor for the BFIS items, and a second factor consisting of variables from the other assessments. This analysis would have benefited from the reporting of one of the appropriate comparison of fit models for matching the rotated factor structure for the BFIS with the original structure from the unrotated principal component factor analysis.

COMMENTARY. The Barkley Functional Impairment Scale (BFIS) must be viewed as a work in progress. The test author acknowledges the need for further data documenting item stability for the BFIS and evidence of the instrument's ability to discriminate specific areas (domains) of psychosocial activity reported to be problematic by respondents. The BFIS provides a solid framework for making clinical assessments of the level of psychosocial impairment being experienced by an individual. The BFIS assessment is normed using a well-established national sample that provides a representative model of adults in the U.S.

The recommended administration process for the BFIS increases its reliability by having another person who is very familiar with the individual (client or patient) complete the same measurement about that individual. A high degree of concordance between the two scores indicates a potentially valid assessment. Low agreement between self and another evaluator on the BFIS items presents a problem requiring clinical interviews and further analysis.

There is a problem with the stability (reliability over time) of the BFIS. This is especially evident when the 15 individual items are used as separate assessments of domains of psychosocial impairment. The test manual needs to provide the instrument's standard error of measurement data so readers can accurately interpret score data.

SUMMARY. The BFIS makes an important contribution to the field of assessment of adult psychosocial impairment resulting from psychiatric disorders, neuropsychological problems, and disturbances in medical neurology. The BFIS can fit into an assessment plan that may also include a neuropsychological assessment such as the Luria-Nebraska Neuropsychological Battery (Golden, Purisch, & Hammeke, 1985) and measures of adult cognition such as the Wechsler Adult Intelligence Scale–Fourth Edition (Wechsler, 2008).

The low to moderate reliability of the BFIS calls for caution with interpreting both the total assessment score and also the 15 domain scores. Those domain scores are measured as 10-point problem intensity self-assessments. Future editions of the BFIS may be able to improve stability (reliability) by developing several new items for assessing each of the domains. A second way to improve reliability would involve reducing the number of answer options for the problem intensity questions to seven.

The major contribution of the BFIS is its national normative group that provides a statistical basis for diagnostic conclusions about the degree of adult psychosocial impairment.

REVIEWER'S REFERENCES

Anastasi, A., & Urbina, S. (1997). *Psychological testing* (7th ed.). Englewood Cliffs, NJ: Prentice Hall.
Golden, C. J., Purisch, A. D., & Hammeke, T. A. (1985). Luria-Nebraska Neuropsychological Battery, Form II. Torrance, CA: Western Psychological Services.
Nunnally, J. C., & Bernstein, I. H. (1994). *Psychometric theory* (3rd ed.). New York, NY: McGraw-Hill.
Wechsler, D. (2008). Wechsler Adult Intelligence Scale–Fourth Edition. San Antonio, TX: Pearson Assessment.

[13]

Barkley Functional Impairment Scale–Children and Adolescents.

Purpose: Designed to "[assess] psychosocial impairments in 15 domains of major life activities."
Population: Parents of children ages 6–17.
Publication Date: 2012.
Acronym: BFIS-CA.
Scores, 18: With Mother, With Father, School Performance, With Siblings, Playing in Neighborhood, Community Activities, Visiting Others, Playing at School, Managing Money, Self-Care, Doing Chores, School Homework, Following Rules, With Other Adults, Playing Sports, Home–School Mean Impairment Score, Community–Leisure Mean Impairment Score, Number of Impaired Domains.
Administration: Individual.
Forms, 2: Parent Rating Scale, Parent Interview.
Price Data, 2013: $126.65 per manual (176 pages), includes permission to reproduce forms and score sheets for personal use.
Time: (5–7) minutes.
Author: Russell A. Barkley.
Publisher: Guilford Publications, Inc.

Review of the Barkley Functional Impairment Scale–Children and Adolescents by JUSTIN LOW, Assistant Professor of Educational and School Psychology, University of the Pacific, Stockton, CA:

DESCRIPTION. The Barkley Functional Impairment Scale–Children and Adolescents (BFIS-CA) consists of a rating scale and an interview form to assess impairment in various domains of psychosocial functioning in children and adolescents ages 6 to 17 in the United States. According to the test author, impairment refers to both the individual's inability to meet the demands of daily life and the resulting harm that the individual suffers. Accordingly, the test was developed to assess parent-rated child impairment, rather than a child's symptoms, which approach results in a non-normal distribution of scores. The rating scale, interview form, administration instructions, and technical information are provided in a single book, and clinicians are allowed to photocopy the scale for parents to complete.

Parents rate their children on 15 Likert-scaled (0–9 point) questions to assess areas of primary functional impairment following which they complete eight additional items that assess secondary areas of impairment. The form takes 5–7 minutes for a parent to complete, following which the clinician encourages the parent to complete any skipped items. Raw scores from all 23 items can be converted to percentile ranks based on sex and age range (6–11 and 12–17). Additionally, scores from the primary 15 domains of functioning can be compared to the entire normative sample to determine whether a score indicates significant impairment in its respective domain. Normative information is also available for the number of domains on which a child is rated as significantly impaired and for home-school and community impairment composites. The clinician can then use the interview form to gather supplementary information regarding any domain scores rated as significantly impaired.

The test author reports that the BFIS-CA can be used to assess a client's response to treatment or to evaluate change in impairment due to injury. To this end the authors provide a table with the differences needed between pre- and post-test scores to be considered not due to chance. Threshold scores are also available to determine whether a child's impairment score falls within the normal range of scores.

DEVELOPMENT. The BFIS-CA is based on the Home Situations Questionnaire (HSQ; Barkley, 1981), which was developed to determine the degree to which externalizing problems interfered with common daily situations. However, the BFIS-CA is different from the HSQ in several important ways. Instructions for the BFIS-CA are independent of any types of disorders or symptoms, whereas the HSQ was specific to externalizing behavior problems. Thus, the BFIS-CA is a more general measure of impairment. Items were revised to reflect a greater number of important areas of daily functioning, and descriptors were added to the 0–9 point scale. Additionally, the normative sample for the BFIS-CA is a nationally representative sample, as opposed to the two-state normative sample of the HSQ.

Parents were selected at random and invited to participate in the normative sample. Parents who agreed to participate took the survey on an Internet site using unique log-in information; individuals without Internet access were provided with a computer and Internet access. The sample initially included 1,922 respondents but was pared down to 1,800 participants resulting in a more nationally representative sample (the 122 participants who were excluded from the study were male, ethnically White, or college-educated). Scores from the BFIS-CA were also studied in a principal components factor analysis with varimax and promax rotations. Both rotated solutions yielded the same two-factor (i.e., home-school and community) results.

TECHNICAL. The normative sample consisted of 1,800 parent raters (ages 18–68) whose children were equally distributed among each of the 12 age groups (6–17) with at least 75 boys and 75 girls in each group. The normative sample is nationally representative and approximates many key demographics with some caveats. Compared to the 2000 U.S. Census, those in the normative sample had more education, consisted of more Midwesterners and fewer Southerners, were less likely to identify as Black, had a higher income, and were more likely to be married. Because not all respondents in the normative sample provided ratings on all 15 primary domains, data from the normative sample were analyzed with analysis of variance to determine whether the completeness of a respondent's answers were dependent on sex or age. Results indicated that participants in the normative sample responded to items independent of the child's sex or age. It is also important to note that the normative sample is used only for the rating scale and not the interview form because the interview form is used solely to clarify and provide supporting information for items rated as functionally impaired on the rating scale.

Internal consistency estimates for the overall test and for the two composite scores were very strong (overall alpha coefficient was .97; Home-School alpha coefficient was .95; Community-Leisure alpha coefficient was .96). Test-retest reliability was evaluated using 86 parents who agreed to take the test a second time, 3–5 weeks after the first administration. Most test-retest reliability coefficients for the 15 primary domains of functional impairment demonstrated at least moderate reliability (.73 to .89), but five test-retest reliabilities of these domains were below .70 (.56 to .69). Composite test-retest reliability coefficients were adequate (i.e., .83 and .86). Test-retest reliability coefficients for the secondary domains also were in the moderate range (.66 to .83 for scaled items; kappa = .73 to .88 for categorical items). *T*-tests did not reveal any significant differences on the 15 primary domains, composites, or scaled items of the secondary domain questions.

Distinguishing between impaired and non-impaired children and adolescents appears to be a valid use of the BFIS-CA. To provide this evidence of validity, scores of children who had been professionally diagnosed, as reported by parents, with neurodevelopmental disorders, specific learning disabilities, or psychiatric disorders were compared with the scores of children who had not received these diagnoses. In general, children who were diagnosed with these disorders were rated as more functionally impaired. Children who received psychiatric, psychological, or educational interventions were also generally rated as more functionally impaired than children in the rest of the normative sample. The BFIS-CA correlated moderately with measures of executive functions and ratings on a 4-point Likert scale of attention-deficit/hyperactivity disorder (ADHD) symptoms such that individuals rated as functionally impaired were more likely to have executive function deficits and higher ADHD ratings. No correlations were calculated between BFIS-CA scores and scores from measures of adaptive behavior or commonly used measures of functional impairment, such as the Children's Global Assessment Scale (CGAS; Shaffer et al., 1983). The test author also provided correlation coefficients using scores from primary and secondary domains of functional impairment (e.g.,

whether a respondent's child had been suspended from school, which is a secondary domain, correlated with various primary domains related to school impairment) as evidence of validity; however, these correlation coefficients may be evidence of consistency between primary and secondary domains of impairment as much as they are evidence of validity. Notably, the test author did not provide a correlation matrix of scores.

COMMENTARY. The BFIS-CA appears to be a helpful tool in determining the degree of impairment resulting from a mental health problem, and it has several strengths. First, it differentiates itself from other measures of functional impairment in that it is a multidimensional, as opposed to a unidimensional, measure of functional impairment, such as the CGAS (Shaffer et al., 1983). Additionally, it has a large nationally representative normative sample so clinicians can determine percentile ranks associated with the severity of parent-rated impairment. Another helpful aspect of the measure is that the rating scale and interview form are provided in the test manual so that clinicians can use photocopies of the rating scale instead of continually paying for new protocols. The reliability of scores for some of the primary domains may be considered somewhat low; however, composite scores demonstrate adequate reliability. Evidence of validity is adequate, yet could be improved by providing correlations with measures that more closely approximate functional impairment rather than executive functions. Finally, correlation matrices of domain scores are missing, and future versions of the test manual would benefit from their inclusion.

SUMMARY. The BFIS-CA is distinguishable from other rating scales in that it is not a diagnostic schedule or a questionnaire of symptoms; rather, it assesses impairments in functioning that result from the symptoms of mental health problems. Parents' ratings of their children can be compared to a nationally representative normative sample on 15 primary domains of functional impairment, which yield three summary scores, and eight secondary domains. Reliability estimates for composite scores are adequate as is evidence of the validity of the measure for distinguishing impaired from nonimpaired children and adolescents. Accordingly, the test is recommended for clinicians seeking to determine whether the parent-rated, functional impairment associated with a mental health problem is significant.

REVIEWER'S REFERENCES
Barkley, R. A. (1981). *Hyperactive children: A handbook for diagnosis and treatment.* New York, NY: Guilford Press.
Shaffer, D., Gould, M. S., Brasic, J., Ambrosini, P., Fisher, P., Bird, H., & Aluwahlia, S. (1983). A Children's Global Assessment Scale (CGAS). *Archives of General Psychiatry, 40,* 1228–1231. doi:10.1001/archpsyc.1983.01790100074010

Review of the Barkley Functional Impairment Scale–Children and Adolescents by CYNTHIA A. ROHRBECK, Associate Professor of Psychology, The George Washington University, Washington, DC:

DESCRIPTION. The Barkley Functional Impairment Scale–Children and Adolescents (BFIS-CA) is a parent rating of child/adolescent impairment in major areas of daily life. Measuring impairment is important in several types of evaluations, including mental disorder diagnoses (e.g., *Diagnostic and Statistical Manual of Mental Disorders*; DSM-IV-TR; American Psychiatric Association, 2000) and in determination of disabilities under the Individuals with Disabilities Education Act (IDEA, 2004). However, the definition of "functional impairment" in such evaluations has not been operationalized. The BFIS-CA was designed to fill this gap. It provides scores indicating the degree of impairment on multiple domains of functioning and norms for comparison purposes.

The BFIS-CA includes 15 items, with each item measuring impairment in one of 15 domains (e.g., interactions with mother, school performance, activities in the community, self-care, completing chores, playing sports). Item responses are on a Likert scale from 0 (*not at all*) to 9 (*severe*). (There is also an option of *does not apply*.) The second part of the questionnaire contains eight questions about the child's current activities, including information about social interactions and school performance. After the questionnaire is completed, the BFIS-CA Parent Interview can be used to provide additional details for those domains in which the child was rated as impaired (defined as above the 93rd percentile). A professional can use responses to these questions to evaluate the credibility or appropriateness of the parent ratings in that domain–for example, a parent who views a grade of B, instead of an A, as evidence of impairment.

The 15 items, or domains, can be combined into two broader categories: Home-School Mean Impairment (9 domains) and Community-Leisure Mean Impairment (6 domains). A total score for impairment also can be computed. Scores can be compared to the overall norm group and/or compared to different scoring profiles for males and females in two age groups, 6–11 and 12–17. The

appendix to the BFIS-CA manual includes the BFIS-CA rating scale, the parent interview, and four scoring profiles by gender and age groups (that also include the overall group scores).

The BFIS-CA questions appear straightforward, and the test author notes that the BFIS-CA can be completed in 5–7 minutes. Scoring is straightforward; percentile ranks are easy to compute using the included profiles. Deciding how to interpret ratings based on answers to the parent interview is more subjective and based largely on professional judgment. No information is provided about how long it takes for the administrator to score the BFIS-CA. The purchaser of the BFIS-CA manual has the right to reproduce scales and scoring sheets for his or her personal clinical or research use.

DEVELOPMENT. In developing the BFIS-CA, the author wanted a quick and easily administered instrument that would (a) measure functional impairment, (b) be applicable to children with a variety of problems and disabilities, and (c) provide norms against which to compare scores. The BFIS-CA was based on Barkley's Home Situations Questionnaire (HSQ; Barkley & Edelbrock, 1987) and the Barkley Functional Impairment Scale (BFIS; Barkley, 2011), a similar impairment scale for adults. Unlike the HSQ, the BFIS-CA explicitly asks about "impairment" (as opposed to "behavior problems"), is designed for children and adolescents with many different disorders and disabilities (not primarily for those with disruptive behavior disorders), measures a wider range of domains, and provides nationally representative norms.

TECHNICAL. Norms for the BFIS-CA are based on a nationally representative sample ($N = 1,800$) with regard to region, ethnicity, gender, and employment status (based on the 2000 U.S. Census). The sample was obtained through Knowledge Networks (see www.knowledgenetworks.com), an online survey company. Parents with children ages 6–17 completed the questionnaire portion of the measure online, but did not complete the parent interview. The test author provides information about how the normative sample differs from the 2000 Census data on several dimensions, including education (slightly more college degrees), inclusion of African Americans (slightly fewer), household income (slightly higher), marital status (slightly more married parents), and psychiatric diagnoses (children may have been underrepresented on some specific disorders). The sample appears comparable to Census data on other available characteristics (geographic region, other ethnicities, employment status, and overall rates of child psychiatric disorders).

The internal consistency of the total score and the two broad impairment scales (Home-School and Community-Leisure) is quite high; all alpha coefficients were well above .90. Test-retest reliabilities for each domain varied from moderate to high (.56 to .89).

The BFIS-CA is designed to measure psychosocial impairment. Impairment was defined as "the extent of difficulty a child or adolescent experiences in functioning effectively in a major domain of life activity relative to others of the same age (and often, sex)" (manual, p. 51). There was no evidence provided for the choice of 15 domains as representing the most important, or all, potential areas of impairment.

Rotational factor analyses resulted in two factors, each accounting for more than 30% of the variance. These results led to the creation of two broad scores: Home-School (impairment) and Community-Leisure (impairment). Age and gender differences were apparent on some individual domains, suggesting the potential importance of norms presented separately by gender and age groupings. Evidence of convergent validity–relationships of the BFIS-CA to other measures that also assess impairment such as the Child Behavior Checklist (CBCL; Achenbach, 2001) or the Behavior Assessment System for Children-2 (BASC-2; Reynolds & Kamphaus, 2004)–is not yet available. On the other hand, the test author provides a comprehensive chapter showing the relationships between BFIS-CA scores and parent reports of developmental disabilities and psychiatric disorders collected in the normative sample. Children and adolescents with attention-deficit/hyperactivity disorder (ADHD) diagnoses had higher ratings on impairment than those without; there was such a difference that those children with comorbid ADHD diagnoses were removed when examining potential differences in impairment for children with other disorders. In some cases, this resulted in small groups of children with disorders, so such findings need to be replicated. Children diagnosed with oppositional defiant disorder and bipolar disorder also showed higher impairment scores than those without such diagnoses. Differences in impairment scores between children with diagnoses of other disorders and those without were less pronounced, and in some cases

varied in degree (for example, among developmental or internalizing disorders). Those differences may be better understood if replicated in future research.

Evidence of criterion validity was obtained by comparing children/teens who were rated as above the 93rd percentile on impairment with those who were not. The more impaired subgroup was significantly more likely than the other children and adolescents to have received psychiatric medications, academic tutoring, special education, speech and language therapy, and psychological therapy.

COMMENTARY. The BFIS-CA is a brief and easy test to administer that shows promise for assessing impairment in children and adolescents. Its strengths include a multidimensional assessment of impairment and a nationally representative normative group. In contrast to single-dimension ratings of functioning, or impairment (e.g., the Global Assessment of Functioning Scale in the DSM-IV-TR [APA, 2000]), the BFIS-CA provides a multidimensional measure of impairment. In contrast to other widely used parent ratings of children that also provide norms (e.g., the CBCL or the BASC-2), the BFIS-CA provides a broader assessment of impairment across more domains. Indeed, the BFIS-CA may provide an additional, and complementary, measure of impairment when using the rating sections of psychological symptoms on the CBCL and BASC-2.

Given the newness of the BFIS-CA there remain questions to be answered in future clinical use and research. The high internal consistencies in the two broader subscales and the overall measure suggest the possibility that impairment could be measured with fewer items or that the measure may be less multidimensional than expected. It will be important to show that the BFIS-CA is a more reliable and valid measure of the functional impairment construct than other measures that are shorter or unidimensional. It is also possible that the BFIS-CA norm group provides overestimates of impairment because parents did not complete the follow-up questions (explaining the basis for their ratings) on the parent interview. Therefore, it would be helpful to have a subgroup of respondents with interview data to know whether impairment scores were higher than justified. The test author notes the need to include other sources of information when determining impairment in addition to the BFIS-CA. A complementary teacher rating of impairment is in development, which could help buttress ratings on the BFIS-CA. Additional perspectives or ratings of impairment also could help with assessing possible misrepresentation of impairment, such as malingering. It should be noted that use of the BFIS-CA with populations outside of the U.S. might not be appropriate, given the normative sample.

Future use of the BFIS-CA will provide additional information on its construct validity and its utility. For example, in addition to measuring impairment, the BFIS-CA might be sensitive in showing pre-post injury status or pre-post treatment change.

SUMMARY. The BFIS-CA was designed to be a multidimensional parent rating of child/adolescent impairment that would be of particular use to individuals diagnosing disorders or involved in disability determinations. The BFIS-CA meets its goals of ease of administration, broad applicability, and ability to compare scores to a normative sample. It appears to provide a broader assessment of impairment than prior measures. Initial evidence of reliability and validity suggests promise for measuring impairment, albeit from only a parental perspective.

REVIEWER'S REFERENCES

Achenbach, T. M. (2001). *Manual for the Child Behavior Checklist/4-18 and 1991 Profile.* Burlington, VT: Author.
American Psychiatric Association. (2000). *Diagnostic and statistical manual of mental disorders* (4th ed., text rev.). Washington, DC: Author.
Individuals with Disabilities Education Act, 20 U. S. C. § 1400 (2004).
Barkley, R. A. (2011). Barkley Functional Impairment Scale (BFIS). New York, NY: Guilford Press.
Barkley, R. A., & Edelbrock, C. S. (1987). Assessing situational variation in children's problem behaviors: The Home and School Situations Questionnaire. In R. J. Prinz (Ed.), *Advances in behavioral assessment of children and families* (Vol. 3, pp. 157–176). Greenwich, CT: JAI Press.
Reynolds, C. R., & Kamphaus, R. W. (2004). Behavior Assessment System for Children-2. Circle Pines, MN: American Guidance Service.

[14]

The Beery-Buktenica Developmental Test of Visual-Motor Integration, Sixth Edition (Beery VMI).

Purpose: "Designed to assess the extent to which individuals can integrate their visual and motor abilities (eye-hand coordination)."

Publication Dates: 1967-2010.

Acronym: Beery VMI.

Scores, 3: Beery VMI, Visual Perception (optional), Motor Coordination (optional).

Administration: Individual or group.

Forms, 2: Full, Short.

Price Data, 2013: $135 per starter kit including manual, 10 full forms, 10 short forms, 10 Visual Perception forms, and 10 Motor Coordination forms; $65 per manual; $104 per 25 full forms; $78 per 25 short forms; $18 per 25 Visual Perception forms; $18 per 25 Motor Coordination forms (bulk discounts available

for forms); $163.50 per Teaching Materials starter kit including My Book of Shapes, My Book of Letters and Numbers, Developmental Teaching Activities, Developmental Wall Chart, Stepping Stones Parent Checklist, and materials on CD; $43.50 per My Book of Shapes; $43.50 per My Book of Letters and Numbers; $55 per Developmental Teaching Activities; $30.75 per Stepping Stones Parent Checklist; $25 per Developmental Wall Chart for Visual-Motor Integration.

Comments: Includes updated norms for ages 2 through 18; subtests must be administered in the appropriate sequence.

Authors: Keith A. Beery, Natasha A. Beery, and Norman A. Buktenica (full and short forms).

Publisher: Pearson.

    a) BEERY VMI.

       1) *Full form.*

       Population: Ages 2-100.

       Time: (10-15) minutes.

       2) *Short form.*

       Population: Ages 2-7.

       Time: (5-15) minutes.

    b) VISUAL PERCEPTION [OPTIONAL].

    Population: Ages 2-100.

    Time: (3-7) minutes.

    c) MOTOR COORDINATION [OPTIONAL].

    Population: Ages 2-100.

    Time: (3-7) minutes.

Cross References: For reviews by Theresa Graham and by Thomas McKnight and Tiffany Chandler of the 5th Edition, see 17:20; for a review by Jan Visser of the 4th Edition, Revised, see 14:119; see also T5:815 (52 references); for reviews by Darrell L. Sabers and James E. Ysseldyke of the Third Revision, see 12:111 (25 references); see also T4:768 (42 references), 9:329 (15 references), and T3:701 (57 references; for reviews by Donald A. Leton and James A. Rice of an earlier edition, see 8:870 (24 references); see also T2:1875 (6 references); for a review by Brad S. Chissom of an earlier edition, see 7:867 (5 references).

Review of The Beery-Buktenica Developmental Test of Visual-Motor Integration, Sixth Edition by G. MICHAEL POTEAT, Associate Professor, Department of Psychology, East Carolina University, Greenville, NC:

DESCRIPTION. The Beery-Buktenica Developmental Test of Visual-Motor Integration, Sixth Edition, typically referred to as the Beery VMI, is the most recent version of an instrument first published in 1967. The sixth edition of the Beery VMI consists of a 209 page manual and four test forms. Two of the forms are for the Beery VMI and are identical except the short form (21 items) is designed for use with children age 2 to 7 years and the full form (30 items) for use with individuals up to 100 years of age. The first 21 items, or geometric figures, on the two forms are identical, and the short form is used to reduce cost. The Beery VMI (to distinguish the instrument from other tests using the abbreviation VMI) is typically very simple to administer to children older than 5 years unless the examinee has some form of neurological or developmental impairment. The other two supplemental forms included with the Beery VMI are Motor Coordination and Visual Perception. Both supplemental tests use the same geometric shapes as the Beery VMI; they are administered only when perception and coordination need to be evaluated separately.

The authors recommend that the Beery VMI be administered by two or more adults to 20 or more children simultaneously to maximize efficiency. For young children and individuals with suspected developmental delays or neurological impairments, individual administration is typical. The method of administration is determined by the purpose of the evaluation. Group testing is designed for screening (e.g., kindergarten children), and individual testing is intended for diagnostic purposes, such as assessment to determine eligibility for special education.

Regardless of the administration strategy selected, the administration of the Beery VMI will for most evaluations consist simply of providing a No. 2 pencil (no eraser) or a ballpoint pen, presenting the test booklet with the reverse side up, and instructing the individual(s) to copy the shapes starting with Item 7. Separate instructions are provided for group and individual administration, but the procedure is relatively simple either way except with individuals younger than 5 years of age or those with developmental delays. For individual assessment, the examiner should have sufficient knowledge of the test taker to estimate the examinee's level of functioning. For group administration, it is possible that some children might not be able to complete even the easiest items, and a follow-up assessment would be indicated. In either case, if the examinee cannot complete Item 7 correctly then it is necessary to administer Items 1 through 6. Items 4 through 6 involve having the examinee attempt to imitate the examiner's drawings. Examinees who do not successfully imitate any of the drawings are asked to imitate scribbling. If the examinee does not scribble, then the Visual Perception items are administered. These items involve asking the child to point to her own specific body parts and to point to animals and body parts presented on a laminated

card. The typical examinee who starts at Item 7 is asked to copy simple geometric forms that become increasingly complex. Scoring is discontinued after the examinee has failed three consecutive items (ceiling), but procedures for testing the limits are also provided. There are no time limits for the Beery VMI. The supplemental Motor Coordination and Visual Perception tests are timed.

DEVELOPMENT. A detailed history of the development of the Beery VMI is provided by the test authors. It is sufficient to state that the Beery VMI is based on the concept that the integration of visual (sensory) and motor functions are indicative of development and have value in the diagnosis of various developmental and learning disorders. The Beery VMI has a long history and is an instrument with generally excellent psychometric properties, but the theory needs to be updated. The current level of knowledge about sensory and motor development based on research in neuroscience (for a summary see Breedlove, Watson, & Rosenzweig, 2010) demonstrates how limited knowledge of "visual-motor integration" was when Keith Beery developed the VMI. That these advances were impossible to imagine in 1967 does not invalidate the usefulness of the Beery VMI, but the theory should be integrated with more recent research. To a certain extent, the authors do acknowledge the idea that the remediation of sensory-motor integration and sensory-integration modalities has not resulted in the success popularized by many "sensory-integration" proponents four decades earlier. This lack is also reflected by the strategies in the Beery VMI manual provided for planning educational services or remediation.

TECHNICAL. The technical characteristics of the Beery VMI are good. Reliability has been established through measures of internal consistency, test-retest, and across multiple scorers. The internal consistency varies depending upon the method used, but all coefficients are above .80 and most are above .90. Reliability across time (test-retest) is lower depending upon time between assessments and the sample used in the studies, but the average across 2 weeks for a sample of children between 5 and 12 years of age was .88. The lowest measure of stability was found over a 2-week period with a group of institutionalized emotionally disturbed children ($r = .59$), but the lower value probably is due to subject variables. Interscorer reliability is generally excellent, and research is presented suggesting that teachers can be trained in 2 to 3 hours to score the Beery VMI reliably. Most of the interscorer reliability coefficients were above .90, and some were as high as .99. These values reflect the excellent directions provided for scoring the test.

The validity of the Beery VMI has also been examined using a variety of techniques. The content validity is largely based on the relationship between the tasks required by the test and the authors' definition of visual-motor integration as "the degree to which visual perception and finger-hand movements are well coordinated" (manual, p. 13). Other evidence of validity is provided through research demonstrating that scores on the Beery VMI are generally moderately correlated with other instruments purported to measure visual motor integration (e.g., the Bender-Gestalt). Construct validity is demonstrated by the relationship between the Beery VMI and chronological age, Wechsler Intelligence Scale for Children–Revised Performance IQ, and various developmental tests of basic skills. Children identified as having attention deficits, brain injury, and similar impairments do less well on the Beery VMI than do control subjects. However, few delays are found with children identified with language disorders. Considerable evidence also exists that the Beery VMI is at least moderately correlated with future academic achievement. Most research has suggested that performance on the Beery VMI is similar across gender and ethnic groups in the U.S. Some evidence also is presented to support the use of the Beery VMI in the neurological assessment of older adults.

Factor analysis has been employed in some research with the results suggesting that the Beery VMI measures multiple factors and in other research suggesting that it is a single factor measure. Because the results of factor analysis are to a large degree dependent on the methodology employed, it is hard to evaluate the findings without reading the original research. Based on the information provided in the test manual, it appears that the Beery VMI primarily loads on one dimension, but this reviewer believes that there may also be a factor that is influenced by developmental age.

The normative data provided for the Beery VMI are certainly adequate. The characteristics of the sample of more than 1,700 participants used for the 2010 norms closely match the U.S. Census data. In addition, the authors report that unlike aptitude test scores (e.g., IQ measures), there has been little change in the performance of normative samples over time. This observation suggests that

the instrument is measuring some basic developmental variable not strongly influenced by cultural changes. Standard scores for the Beery VMI are provided in 2-month intervals from ages 2 to 13. The supplemental Visual Perception and Motor Coordination instruments have norms by 3-month intervals for the same age range. From ages 13 to 19, the Beery VMI norms are by age in years, and the norms for the supplemental tests cover 2-year periods (e.g., from 13:0 through 14:11). The normative intervals for adults are by decade. All of the norms provide standard scores with a mean of 100 and a standard deviation of 15. The standard error of measurement is approximately 5 but varies by age. Standard scores can be converted to other scales (e.g., percentiles and scaled scores).

Overall, the Beery VMI can be characterized as having very good reliability and good evidence of validity as a measure of visual-motor integration as defined by the test authors.

COMMENTARY. The Beery VMI is an instrument with a long history. It is in many ways unchanged over a period of 40 years. Some additional materials are now provided with the measure, but overall, the current version is remarkably like the instrument that this reviewer first used in the 1970s. It is easy to administer and has good reliability and adequate validity. For its primary intended purpose as a screening instrument to identify children with visual-motor integration deficits, the Beery VMI may be the best choice of instruments currently available. The Beery VMI is also frequently used by professionals (especially school psychologists, but also occupational therapists and others) in the individual assessment of children referred for special education. The cost to screen large numbers of children would be a consideration before adopting the instrument for that purpose. For the individual assessment of children (especially young children) referred for special education and related services, it is highly recommended. This reviewer is less certain about recommending the Beery VMI in the assessment of older adults with suspected neurological and cognitive problems. Further research is needed to demonstrate the validity of using the Beery VMI for this purpose.

SUMMARY. The Beery VMI remains a useful instrument some 40-plus years after it was first published. In addition to providing normative information about the visual-motor integration of children, it also provides an opportunity for the examiner to observe certain important behaviors.

Some examples include the pencil grasp employed, the reaction to more difficult forms, perseverance and perseveration, and attention to detail. School psychologists frequently note observations such as crossing the midline when drawing a vertical-horizontal cross and other developmental observations that are covered in the Beery VMI manual. Anomalies such as significantly stronger performance on the Beery VMI than on intelligence or achievement measures may be indicative of a cultural or language issue that needs to be investigated. Determining whether deficits are primarily a function of perception or motor coordination is also important, and the supplemental forms would be helpful for that purpose. The Beery VMI is also useful for evaluating individuals who have suffered a head injury and are suspected of having a traumatic brain injury (although a diagnosis would certainly not be made solely on the basis of performance on the Beery).

The popularity of the Beery VMI is difficult to overstate. A quick electronic review of the research showed that the Beery VMI was used or referenced in more than 100 research articles or books published in 2012 alone. The variety of research topics using the Beery VMI as a measurement variable is staggering. It must be considered the standard for measuring visual-motor integration. The conception of visual-motor integration is simplistic, but like the concept of intelligence, it is a construct that provides a useful index of development.

REVIEWER'S REFERENCE

Breedlove, S. M., Watson, N. V., & Rosenzweig, M. R. (2010). *Biological psychology: An introduction to behavioral, cognitive, and clinical neuroscience.* Sunderland, MA: Sinauer Associates.

[15]

Behavior Intervention Monitoring Assessment System.

Purpose: Designed to "monitor children/youth's progress in behavioral and psychosocial intervention."
Population: Ages 5-18.
Publication Date: 2011.
Acronym: BIMAS.
Scores, 5 Scales: Conduct, Negative Affect, Cognitive/Attention, Social, Academic Functioning.
Administration: Individual or Group.
Parts, 2: BIMAS Standard, BIMAS Flex.
Forms, 4: Self-Report (ages 12–18), Teacher, Parent, Clinician.
Price Data, 2013: $99 per manual; $4 per annual site license (minimum 25, volume discounts available).
Time: (5–10) minutes.
Comments: Following administration of BIMAS Standard form, "assessors can custom-design Flex items

... one- to five-item mini-assessments [used] for frequent progress monitoring." Online and paper-and-pencil administration available.
Authors: James L. McDougal, Achilles N. Bardos, and Scott T. Meier.
Publisher: Multi-Health Systems, Inc.

Review of the Behavior Intervention Monitoring Assessment System by KATHY J. BOHAN, Associate Professor of Educational Psychology-School Psychology, Northern Arizona University, Flagstaff, AZ:

DESCRIPTION. The Behavior Intervention Monitoring Assessment System (BIMAS) is a progress-monitoring tool designed to measure change in school-aged children's behavioral and psychosocial behaviors in response to intervention or treatment. The empirically based rating system can be used in screening, progress monitoring, outcome assessment, and program evaluation. The test authors promote the use of a new test construction approach highly sensitive to change. Rating forms consisting of 34 items are used to collect information from teachers, parents, and youth (aged 12–18 years). An additional 31-item form is available for use by clinicians. Items are rated on a 5-point scale indicating whether the behavior has been observed from *never* (not observed) to *very often* (observed 7 or more times or to an extreme extent) during the past week. The items have parallel content designed to measure both problems and strengths.

The Behavioral Concern Scales include Conduct (9 items), Negative Affect (7 items), and Cognitive/Attention (7 items). The Conduct scale is a measure of anger management, bullying behaviors, substance abuse, and deviance. The Negative Affect scale identifies symptoms of depression and anxiety. The Cognitive/Attention scale considers attention, organization, focus, memory, and planning. The Adaptive scales consist of Social (6 items) and Academic Functioning (5 items). The Social scale assesses communication, interpersonal skills, and sustained friendships. The Academic Functioning scale addresses academic performance, attitudes towards learning, and attendance.

The BIMAS provides secure online administration and scoring. Administration time for the standard forms is estimated to take 5 to 10 minutes. Paper-and-pencil forms also can be created, scanned, and uploaded into the web-based data management system. Hand-scoring is not available. The system produces four categories of reports: (a) Assessment reports (i.e., single point in time results for a district, school, grade, class, intervention group, or individual student), (b) Progress reports (i.e., over time at the multistudent or individual student level), (c) Comparative reports (i.e., compare groups or different raters' ratings on individual students), and (d) Demographic reports to target group risk factors during universal screening or intervention design.

An additional feature of the system is the BIMAS Flex option. This option allows examiners to target specific concern behaviors and/or adaptive skills for routine progress monitoring. For each of the standard 34 items, an assessor can select from a pool of additional items to create forms for frequent, targeted progress monitoring. Individualized scoring criteria and goal lines can be established, as well as scheduled reminders that can be emailed to raters. Depending upon how many behaviors or skills are targeted, the administration time is usually less than 5 minutes. This option provides a brief, efficient, and time-sensitive way to measure progress on individualized intervention or treatment goals.

DEVELOPMENT. The test authors' intent was to develop a multiple informant system that uses brief, repeatable, and psychometrically sound measures of behavior problems, social-emotional concerns, and adaptive behaviors for use in a response to intervention framework. A key feature of the system is to create items that are change-sensitive. To accomplish this goal, Meier (2008) proposed a set of Intervention Item Selection Rules (IISRs) to guide test construction. The rules were established as a result of several studies conducted by the BIMAS authors. IISRs specify that the selected items must be theoretically grounded. Unlike trait-based rating scales, the state-based items–termed intervention-based items–are aggregated across individuals. This approach is designed to reduce random error and to increase responsiveness to treatment effects. The rules address removal of items with ceiling or floor effects, ensure measured change is in the expected direction, and require the measure to be sensitive to showing no change with non-treatment comparison groups. Item development for the BIMAS followed these rules to create an initial item pool. Data from normative and clinical samples were collected to identify the factor structure of the measures.

TECHNICAL. The normative sample was collected between March 2007 and May 2009. The sample consisted of ratings from 1,400 teachers (BIMAS-T), 1,400 parents (BIMAS-P), and 700 adolescents (BIMAS-SR). The sample participants were identified through 25 site coordinators at various locations throughout the United States. Coordinators were recruited through test author and publisher contacts and publisher recruitment efforts. The sample was generally representative of the race/ethnicity, gender, geographical regions, and parental education levels of the U.S. population based on the 2000 U.S. Census report. When discrepancies were found, the test authors used weighted adjustments to improve representation. Various age groups were represented, with 100 children (50 males, 50 females) in each age group. Data about the specific locations of participating sites, type of communities (urban, suburban, rural), types of schools (public, private, charter), or types of clinics represented in the sample were not presented, although the test manual does provide a list of data collection sites.

Multivariate analyses of variance (MANOVAs) were used to examine age and gender relationships. Significant main effects for age (small to moderate effect sizes) were identified. On the teacher and parent forms, behavioral concerns decreased from ages 5 to 12, and then increased until age 18. Adaptive behaviors showed the opposite pattern, as might be expected. On the self-report, adolescents tended to show a slight increase in behavioral concerns between age 12 and age 15, but those concerns then decreased until age 18. Gender effects suggested boys were rated slightly higher on the Behavioral Concerns scales than girls, and girls were rated somewhat higher than boys on Adaptive scales. Age X Gender interactions suggested significant gender effects at certain ages. The default setting for report generation is combined gender norms; however, gender-specific norms are a scoring option.

The final version of the BIMAS used a cumulative frequency distribution of raw scores across the five scales for the various age groups. Consistent with other behavioral rating scales, the distribution was skewed. The test authors used regression analysis to mitigate effects of sampling variability, producing smoothed percentiles. These smoothed percentiles were used in combination with the original unsmoothed percentiles to establish the final percentile ranks. These percentile ranks were then converted to non-linear T-scores with a mean of 50 and a standard deviation of 10.

The test manual provides evidence of good levels of internal consistency across rating scales. Alpha coefficients ranged from .81 to .91 on the BIMAS-T, .77 to .90 on the BIMAS-P, and .75 to .88 on the BIMAS-SR. Test-retest reliability was established from two administrations in a 2- to 4-week period without interventions. Reported correlation coefficients ranged from .85 to .91 on the BIMAS-T, .79 to .96 on the BIMAS-P, and .81 to .90 on the BIMAS-SR. The test authors provide evidence of the validity of test score use through moderate to high correlation coefficients when BIMAS scales were compared with comparable scales on the Conners Comprehensive Behavior Rating Scales (CBRS). The test authors provided evidence of content validity by addressing the structure and alignment of items with BIMAS components.

COMMENTARY. The test manual is well organized and includes step-by-step guidelines for administration, scoring, and interpretation. A case study is provided as well as color-coded charts and sample reports. The automated reports include graphic displays for ease of interpretation for varied purposes. The test authors provide preliminary evidence to support the use of the BIMAS as a progress-monitoring tool. Although additional studies are needed to establish the utility of the measures, the BIMAS shows promise in attaining its purpose as a measure sensitive to change and as a tool to assist with sound decision-making.

SUMMARY. The BIMAS is a multirater system using brief rating scales for universal screening, progress monitoring, and program evaluation. In designing the system, the developers used a unique approach for assessing change in problem behaviors and adaptive skills. The additional BIMAS Flex items provide a useful way for teachers to set individual goals, monitor progress, and make informed decisions about intervention. As the test authors highlight, the Response to Intervention framework adopted by schools today, as well as the managed behavioral health care system demands valid and reliable measures of impact of interventions and treatment to reduce problem behaviors and improve adaptive functioning for children and youth. The BIMAS, developed using the Intervention Item Selection Rules (IISRs), shows strong promise to fill this niche in schools and clinics.

REVIEWER'S REFERENCE

Meier, S. T. (2008). *Measuring change in counseling and psychotherapy*. New York, NY: Guilford Press.

Review of the Behavior Intervention Monitoring Assessment System by FELICIA CASTRO-VILLARREAL, Assistant Professor of Educational Psychology, University of Texas at San Antonio, San Antonio, TX:

DESCRIPTION. The Behavior Intervention Monitoring Assessment System (BIMAS) is an individually or group administered rating scale designed to monitor school-aged students' responses to behavioral and psychosocial intervention within Response to Intervention (RTI) frameworks. As such, the BIMAS can be used for screening, progress monitoring, outcome assessment, and program evaluation for students ages 5–18. The BIMAS yields *T*-scores for five scales including three Behavioral Concern scales measuring Conduct, Negative Affect, and Cognitive/Attention, and two Adaptive Behavior scales evaluating Social and Academic Functioning.

The BIMAS has teacher, parent, clinician, and self-report rating form options. Test materials include the test manual and rating forms. The test manual opens with discussion of the main features, components, and uses of the BIMAS followed by a brief literature review on RTI and scale development utilizing Intervention Item Selection Rules (IISRs; Meier, 2004), thereby making the case for another behavior rating scale, clinical/school utility, and innovation in test construction.

The BIMAS includes standard and Flex form options. The standard form includes teacher, parent, and self-report rating forms and is composed of change sensitive items that can be used for screening and progress monitoring. The teacher, parent, and self-report standard forms include 34 items, each of which represents behavior during the past week. Raters respond using a 5-point Likert scale (0 = *never* [observed 0 times or not observed], 1 = *rarely* [observed 1–2 times or to a minimum extent], 2 = *sometimes* [observed 3–4 times or to a moderate extent], 3 = *often* [observed 5–6 times or to a significant extent], and 4 = *very often* [observed 7 or more times or to an extreme extent]). The clinician standard form includes 31 items rated on the same 5-point scale, with one item on therapy appointment attendance replacing the items on academic functioning. Rating forms are usually completed and scored online but can be administered via paper-and-pencil format at the beginning of a school year for screening purposes and subsequently in the winter, spring, and summer for benchmark assessment and/or for periodic (e.g., 6 to 10 weeks) progress monitoring.

Individualized Flex forms are constructed from a bank of positively and negatively worded items to enable monitoring of both behavioral concerns and adaptive behavior. Flex forms consist of one to five items ideal for brief and repeated assessment. Designed exclusively for frequent progress monitoring, the Flex form can be administered hourly, daily, and weekly. Additionally, scoring criteria using item descriptors can be set for any Flex item where any of the 5-point item responses can be labeled desirable or concerning. Because items are individualized and predetermined, goals, increases or decreases in behavior, targeted intervention behaviors, and item responses can be frequently monitored for alignment.

The standard form takes between 5 and 10 minutes to complete whereas the Flex form typically can be completed in 5 minutes or less. Flesch-Kincaid readability estimates found the standard teacher and parent forms require a 5.7 reading level to complete and the standard self-report form requires a 4.6 level. Raters familiar with the youth in question can complete the BIMAS according to the current week's behavior.

The BIMAS renders T-scores, with scores below 60 indicating low risk, scores between 60 and 69 indicating some risk, and scores of 70 or greater indicating high risk. The three Behavioral Concern scales (Conduct, Negative Affect, and Cognitive/Attention) are interpreted according to the aforementioned descriptors. Adaptive scales are strength-based and therefore warrant different qualitative descriptors. High scores indicate the presence of positive behaviors that merit a strength descriptor whereas low scores suggest desired behaviors are infrequent and thus warrant a concern descriptor. BIMAS scores also are presented as percentile ranks, and both 90% and 95% confidence intervals are provided for each scale. Additionally, in order to facilitate item level interpretation, item level scores are matched with item descriptors that coincide with score placement in the normative group. Item descriptors for Behavioral Concern scales range from concern to no concern, an indication of frequency of behavior in the norm group. Item descriptors for Adaptive Scales include positive, fair, mild concern, and concern, and also align with frequency of behavior relative to the norm group.

Because the BIMAS allows for repeated measurement, change over time is measured with time series graphs, the Reliable Change Index (RCI), and effect size estimates (ES). The RCI denotes statistically significant change from Time 1 to Time 2 and is calculated at the $p < .10$ level of significance. ES estimates are also provided to indicate the strength of change over time. As an additional option, the BIMAS compares scores between raters

and groups. Therefore, when T-scores are similar they should be interpreted as similar regardless of scale descriptor ranges, and when T-scores are significantly different, they should be interpreted as different despite parallel scale descriptor ranges.

The BIMAS generates four types of reports: Assessment, Progress, and Comparative reports—which are available at the individual and group level—and Demographic reports, which are available at the group level. Additionally, a Risk Level Pyramids report can be generated to depict Universal Assessment results for an entire class. Multilevel assessment reports for district, school, and grade level enable assessors to estimate risk and adaptive functioning across behavioral and adaptive functioning areas to aid in needs assessment and in the identification of children and youth at highest risk. Individual level assessment reports are used primarily to identify target student concerns and strengths at a static point in time. Progress reports, by contrast, depict behavior and response to intervention over time, thereby demonstrating student response to district programming. In the same vein, progress reports at the group level are useful for program evaluation and measurement of program efficacy. Reports show changes in percentage of students at various levels of risk and changes in group averages in behavioral domains. Individual progress reports come in the form of time series scores or statistically significant change in T-scores based on the RCI. For examination of local norms, Comparative reports depict district performance, which facilitates comparison of individual schools to overall district averages. Similarly, school and grade level reports enable school-by-school and class-by-class comparisons. Finally, individual comparison reports enable examination of interrater consistency.

DEVELOPMENT. The BIMAS Standard was developed based on the empirical study of thousands of teacher, parent, and self-report ratings collected over 3 years designed to extract items sensitive to change. The rationale for test development was based on a need for screening and progress-monitoring measures for data-based decision-making in behavioral RTI frameworks. To accomplish this task, the test authors developed a change sensitive measure based on IISRs, an empirically supported technique for selecting change sensitive items. Item selection was based on preliminary and rational analysis including the utilization of change sensitive items derived from

Meier's (2004) research and a three-step process involving determining face validity, screening for parallel content across rater forms, and item analysis for age appropriateness. Normative and clinical data were analyzed to confirm item content, and confirmatory factor analysis was used to confirm final scale structure. Results indicated adequate model fit.

Final scale structure resulted in Behavioral Concern and Adaptive scales. The Behavioral Concern scales include the Conduct scale (9 items), items that relate to physical and verbal aggression, substance abuse, and deviant behaviors; the Negative Affect scale (7 items), items that relate to anxious and depressive symptomology; and the Cognitive/Attention scale (7 items), items related to attention, planning, and memory. The Adaptive scales include the Social scale (6 items), items related to social and interpersonal skills; and the Academic Functioning scale (5 items), items that relate to academic achievement.

The BIMAS Flex was constructed to address specific intervention targets to assess response to intervention. Each BIMAS scale has about 10 to 15 positively or negatively worded items that combine to create a pool of 655 Flex items for the teacher, parent, and self-report forms and 586 items for the clinician form. Scoring criteria for item descriptors were based on means, standard deviations, cumulative frequency, and percentile ranks for each normative group for each of the 34 items on the standard form. Percentile ranks were derived for each age group by gender and for males and females combined. As with item selection, rational rules were also used in final scoring criteria for item descriptors. A concern item score indicates a behavior reportedly occurs more frequently than for others in the norm group, a mild concern score indicates behavior reportedly occurs only slightly more frequently, and a no concern score means the behavior occurs no more frequently than those in the norm group. Considering higher scores on the adaptive scales indicate fewer concerns, the adaptive scales correspond with positive, concern, mild concern, and fair scale descriptors. Concern and mild concern scores differ in terms of frequency of observed behavior, with mild concern indicating a youth's adaptive behavior was rated as occurring slightly less frequently than for those in the normative group. Fair items suggest the youth engages in the behavior at a frequency similar to that of the normative group. A positive score suggests the

youth exhibits the behavior more frequently than it occurs in the normative sample.

TECHNICAL.

Standardization. During standardization, teachers and parents completed standard forms for 1,400 students, 50 males and 50 females at each age level representing ages 5 to 18. The self-report normative sample comprised 700 youth, 350 males and 350 females ages 12 to 18, with 100 youth in each age group. Demographic data including age, gender, parental education level, race/ethnicity, and geographic region were collected using stratified sampling procedures. To account for disproportionality, each sample was weighted through statistical procedures resulting in a sample that closely resembled race/ethnicity and geographic region statistics from the 2000 U.S. Census. Demographic data also are provided for 538 teacher ratings, 467 parent ratings, and 350 youth self-reports from youth with a confirmed clinical diagnosis.

Norms were divided into six age groups for the teacher and parent forms (5–6, 7–9, 10–11, 12–13, 14–16, and 17–18) and three age groups for the self-report form (12–13, 14–16, and 17–18) based on multivariate analyses of variance (MANOVAs) age and gender interaction effects. Although the combined sample reflects general population gender differences, gender specific norms are also available.

Reliability. Score reliability was assessed with internal consistency and test-retest reliability analyses. With regard to internal consistency, alpha coefficients are provided for all scales for the various forms but were computed on a weighted sample composed of 85% of the normative group and the remaining composed of the clinical sample to reflect real world estimates. Coefficient alpha values for the teacher form demonstrated high levels of internal consistency for the majority of scales with values ranging from .81 to .91. Coefficient alpha values for the parent form ranged from .77 to .90, and values for the self-report form ranged from .75 to .88. Adequate to excellent levels of internal consistency were found across age and gender.

Test-retest analyses based on intervals ranging from 2 to 4 weeks were conducted with 112 teachers, 83 parents, and 53 youth. All coefficients were statistically significant at $p < .001$ and ranged from .79 to .96, suggesting a high degree of score stability over time. Consistency between raters was also assessed using a sample of 162 youth self-reports. Correlation coefficients were moderate but significant ($p < .001$) for teacher and parent to self-report comparisons (.54 to .69 and .59 to .69, respectively). Teacher to parent comparisons showed higher correlation coefficients with values ranging from .79 to .86.

Validity. The test manual provides an abundance of evidence related to validity. Due to space limitations this description will be limited to a summary of content and construct validity. Content validity was based on the relation between specific items and external criteria and expert reviews. Confirmatory factor analysis fit indicators provided support for the scale structure as models approached adequate fit for all three forms. Fit indices for the teacher form were reported as follows: NFI = .91, NNFI = .87, CFI = .91, and RMSEA = .13. Parent form fit indices were reported as follows: NFI = .89, NNFI = .85, CFI = .90, and RMSEA = .13. Fit indices for the self-report form were reported as follows: NFI = .92, NNFI = .90, CFI = .93, and RMSEA = .10. The BIMAS scale structure was further validated with significant yet moderate correlation coefficients observed between the scales for all three rater types.

Construct validity was assessed with convergent and discriminant analyses to determine whether scores on the BIMAS correlated with scores on similar and dissimilar measures in theoretically expected ways. BIMAS scores were compared to Conners Comprehensive Behavior Rating Scales scores (Conners CBRS; Conners, 2008; 18:33). All Conners CBRS scales that assess similar constructs were moderately to strongly correlated at the $p <$ .001 level. Correlations between BIMAS Conduct scale scores and two Conners CBRS scales that measure physical and verbal aggression and violence potential produced coefficients that ranged from .49 to .78. Correlations between BIMAS Negative Affect scores and two Conners CBRS scales that assess negative mood produced coefficients that ranged from .38 to .70. Correlations between BIMAS Cognitive/Attention values and scores on three Conners CBRS scales produced coefficients that ranged from .46 to .69. Correlations between BIMAS Social scores and Academic Functioning scores and the Conners CBRS DSM-IV-TR Autistic Disorder and Asperger's Disorder scales yielded coefficients between −.47 and −.71 and between −.31 and −.49, respectively.

COMMENTARY. Strengths of the BIMAS include its utility as a screening and progress monitoring for RTI tool, development based on IISRs, the abundance of validity information presented,

and the test manual's dual function as a technical guide and resource for RTI, screening, and progress monitoring. Computer-based administration, scoring, and graphic data depiction are also advantages for the user, particularly with regard to screening and progress monitoring.

Perhaps the greatest strength of the BIMAS is the empiricism underlying item selection and scale development and the detail with which test psychometrics were established and presented. For example, detailed information on the utility of the BIMAS as a progress-monitoring tool (e.g., ES estimates, RCI, CFA, and classification statistics such as Sensitivity and Specificity) is provided where users are able to examine indicators and reference tables to make informed decisions as to whether the BIMAS fits their needs as a screening and progress monitoring tool. This is especially important given the expansion of RTI models and increased emphasis on data-based decision-making.

SUMMARY. The BIMAS is a brief and repeatable screening and progress-monitoring tool developed for use in RTI frameworks and is designed to assess behavioral, emotional, social, and academic functioning of school-aged youth. Because of the widespread implementation of RTI models in schools, tools of this type have gained popularity, yet most screening and progress-monitoring tools measure academic skills alone. Moreover, the BIMAS is the first of its kind to be developed based on IISRs. As such, the BIMAS offers unique value in its utility as a screening and progress-monitoring tool. The psychometric evidence provided in the test manual is comprehensive, and supports use of the BIMAS as a screening, progress-monitoring, outcome assessment, and program evaluation tool. It will be especially important to examine how the BIMAS can be used with other data and in RTI frameworks to enhance decision validity for measuring response to intervention and high-stakes decisions.

REVIEWER'S REFERENCES
Conners, C. K. (2008). *Conners Comprehensive Behavior Rating Scales manual.* Toronto, Canada: Multi-Health Systems.
Meier, S. T. (2004). Improving design sensitivity through intervention-sensitive measures. *American Journal of Evaluation, 25,* 321–334.

[16]

Behavioral Assessment of Pain-2 Questionnaire.

Purpose: An assessment tool to understand "factors which may be working to exacerbate and/or maintain subacute and chronic nonmalignant pain."

Population: Subacute and chronic pain patients.

Publication Dates: 1990-2009.

Acronyms: BAP-2, Post BAP-2.

Scores, 51: 15 scales, 35 subscales, plus Disability Index: Pain Behavior Scale (Affective/Behavioral, Audible/Visible), Pain Descriptor Scale (Pulling, Tight and Dull [PTD], Sore, Aching, and Tender [SAT], Throbbing and Sharp [TS]), Activity Interference Scale (Domestic/Household Activities, Heavy Activities, Social Activities, Personal Care Activities, Personal Hygiene Activities), Avoidance Scale, Spouse/Partner Influence Scale (Reinforcement of Pain, Discouragement/Criticism of Pain, Reinforcement of Wellness, Discouragement/Criticism of Wellness), Physician Influence Scale (Physician Discouragement/Criticism of Pain, Physician Reinforcement of Wellness, Physician Discouragement/Criticism of Wellness, Physician Reinforcement of Pain), Pain Beliefs Scale (Catastrophizing, Fear of Reinjury, Expectation for Cure, Blaming Self, Entitlement, Future Despair, Social Disbelief, Lack of Medical Comprehensiveness), Perceived Consequences Scale (Social Interference, Physical Harm, Psychological Harm, Pain Exacerbation, Productivity Interference), Mood Scale (Depression, Muscular Discomfort, Anxiety, Change in Weight), 6 validity scales.

Administration: Individual.

Forms, 2: Behavioral Assessment of Pain-2 Questionnaire, Post Behavioral Assessment of Pain-2 Questionnaire.

Price Data, 2012: $21 per computer-generated clinical report from BAPTrax Software (volume discounts available); $25 per prepaid mail-in answer premium full-service reports (volume discounts available).

Foreign Language Edition: Spanish and French editions (unnormed) available.

Time: (30) minutes or less per test.

Comments: Self-report instrument; two options for generating a clinical profile: via BAP-2 software or mail/fax service; Post BAP-2 analyzes the changes over the course of treatment providing outcome data for the pain program.

Authors: Michael J. Lewandowski and Blake H. Tearnan.

Publisher: Pain Assessment Resources.

Cross References: For reviews by Gerald E. De-Mauro and Ronald J. Ganellen of an earlier edition, see 12:49.

Review of Behavioral Assessment of Pain-2 Questionnaire by BRIAN F. FRENCH, Professor of Educational Psychology, and CHAD M. GOTCH, Clinical Assistant Professor of Educational Psychology, Washington State University, Pullman, WA:

DESCRIPTION. The Behavioral Assessment of Pain-2 Questionnaire (BAP-2) is an individually administered self-report questionnaire to be used by a pain management clinician to assess chronic pain comprehensively when working with patients.

The test authors state that the main purpose of the BAP-2 is to measure pain characteristics, levels of activity, mood, attitudes about pain, coping strategies, and behavioral responses to pain, primarily with an adult population. The multidimensional questionnaire is composed of 223 questions with a variety of response formats from dichotomous items to rating scale items with various response options (e.g., 7, 10 point scale). Up to 42 scores are generated across eight domains, such as Pain Behavior and Mood. These scores provide a comprehensive, accurate, and clinically useful objective pain assessment, including factors exacerbating or maintaining pain, to assist decisions about appropriate treatment for adults suffering from subacute and chronic benign pain. Two forms, one for pre- and one for post-assessment, are available and may be obtained in Spanish and French translations.

Administration generally occurs in the physician's office and requires approximately 30 minutes. The BAP-2 is said to save time compared to a health care professional collecting the information by other means. Forms are scored via computer or via mailing to a central location for processing. The resulting outcome is a 23-page clinical profile report, based on scores in the areas of Activity Interference, Activity Avoidance, Spouse/Partner Influence, Physician Influence, Pain Beliefs, Perceived Consequences, Mood, Disability, Pain Behavior, Pain Descriptors, and validity judgments regarding patient responses. The report also addresses medication, stimulant, and depressant usage; health care usage; and pain ratings. No special professional testing qualifications are required to administer the test or interpret the results.

DEVELOPMENT. The BAP-2 was constructed based on the assumption that pain, as a construct, is best understood by considering the interaction of environmental, psychological, and biological causes. As such, the BAP-2 rests on the domains of a biopsychosocial model of pain. The BAP-2 is based on its predecessor, the Behavioral Assessment of Pain (BAP). BAP items were constructed using a two-phase process. In Phase 1, 411 items across eight scales and numerous subscales were written and administered to 307 patients. Items were eliminated if they (a) did not support a simple structure in exploratory factor analysis, (b) demonstrated lowered internal consistency reliability estimates, or (c) were poorly written. No documentation was provided in the test materials for these judgments. In Phase 2, a more extensive demographic section was developed, the response scale was changed for the Coping scale, and the Perceived Consequences scale was added. The revised scales were administered to a second sample ($N = 326$ patients). The test structure was examined via factor analyses.

To make the assessment resource more user friendly, the BAP-2 was shortened to 223 items from the original BAP length of 390 items. This reduction was not documented, particularly with regard to the maintenance of content representation. According to promotional materials about the BAP-2, the items, written at an eighth-grade reading level, comprise the domains of Demographic Information (55 items), Pain Behavior (8 items), Activity Interference (34 items), Activity Avoidance (34 items), Spouse/Partner Influence (27 items), Physician Influence (25 items), Pain Beliefs (26 items), Perceived Consequences (24 items), and Mood (34 items). There is misalignment between the total number of items reported in these promotional materials, the numbers of items reported for each subscale by the test authors, and the actual numbers of items by subscale on the questionnaire form.

TECHNICAL. The standardization of the BAP-2 was based on a sample of subacute and chronic pain patients ($N = 1,012$) from across the United States. No information was given about the representation of this sample to the larger population of interest or for various demographic groups. The sample profile report includes norm averages. There was no information available about the translation and adaptation processes for the BAP-2 into Spanish and French languages.

Reliability evidence is not presented specifically for the BAP-2 in the material reviewed. However, the material introducing the BAP-2 claims a high degree of internal consistency and stability reliability, based on evidence gleaned during the development of the parent instrument. Internal consistency reliability (coefficient alpha) for the BAP was reported to be above .80 for all but three subscale scores (Personal Hygiene Activities, .43; Personal Care Activities-past, .44; and Personal Care Activities-current, .37). Test-retest reliability was also assessed in the development phases with 35 patients retested 10 to 14 days after initial testing. Coefficient values were reported to be above .80 except on two subscales (Spousal Reinforcement of Wellness, .58; Personal Hygiene Activities, .45).

Limited validity evidence is presented to support the use and inferences of the BAP-2 scores in the manner advocated in the literature provided. It appears that all evidence for the BAP-2 is based on evidence established for the original version, the BAP (Tearnan & Lewandowski, 1992). Evidence of content representation established for the BAP was based on a survey of the pain literature, matching domains to the biopsychosocial model of pain, and interviewing hundreds of chronic pain patients to capture areas common to clinical inquiry. Internal structure validity evidence is provided both from exploratory and confirmatory factor analyses on each subscale during both phases of the development of the BAP. Validity evidence derived from associations with other variables showed moderate to strong positive relationships between BAP and Depression, Anxiety, Spouse/Partner Influence, and Current Activity Level scales with like scales on other instruments such as the Beck Depression Inventory ($r = .76$), Minnesota Multiphasic Personality Inventory Dysthymia Scale ($r = .61$), West Haven-Yale Multidimensional Pain Inventory (WHYMPI) Spousal Solicitousness Scale ($r = .75$), and the WHYMPI Household Chores Subscale ($r = .72$). Classification of level of functional impairment (high/low) was reported with a rate of 97% accuracy. There was no mention of prediction or response to treatment or response processes validity evidence.

COMMENTARY. The BAP-2 holds some promise as a tool that clinicians may use in a battery of assessments to evaluate an adult's pain. The test authors are commended for developing the assessment grounded in a theory that is documented in the pain literature. The authors have stated that the BAP-2's primary purpose is to provide reliable and valid information for assessing the various factors contributing to chronic pain and developing a patient profile in comparison to national norms. At this time, this reviewer would not recommend the BAP-2 for these stated purposes in the absence of the necessary reliability and validity information.

The publication material advocates for scores to be used at the individual level to develop patient profiles documented in a 23-page profile report based on patient responses. Such use is not supported by the evidence presented in the materials reviewed. Furthermore, the claim is made that the internal consistency reliability estimates are adequate for the stated purposes. The test authors (and interested readers) are encouraged to read Nunnally and Bernstein (1994) as one source for reliability standards when making decisions at the individual level. The values reported for the BAP are not adequate for individual decisions, and no evidence is provided for BAP-2 scores. Work to improve internal consistency reliability and to report values on the BAP-2 is encouraged.

Information about the samples used to provide normative scores (*T*-scores) for the profiles is lacking. The samples are said to be sufficient in size and to match the target population in terms of the experience of pain. Demographics of the samples are provided (sex, age, duration of pain, type of pain, employment, and marital status), but no information is provided about the target population along these variables. There was difficulty in assessing whom these normative scores represent across the subscales and how to interpret an individual profile. This reviewer questions how useful the profiles are in absence of such information.

A clear weakness of the BAP-2 is a lack of psychometric evidence to support the instrument's use for the stated purposes. Various forms of evidence are provided on the BAP from 1992 (Tearnan & Lewandowski), but there appears to be no such information for the BAP-2. With major content alterations (e.g., substantial reduction in the number of items), one cannot rely on past psychometric evidence to support score inferences on the revised version. Providing more technical information on the development and functioning of the BAP-2, including the translated versions, and referencing how its development comports with the *Standards for Educational and Psychological Testing* (AERA, APA, & NCME, 1999) in the materials used to promote the questionnaire would be beneficial (Downing, 2006).

SUMMARY. The BAP-2 is designed to be an individually administered self-report questionnaire to assess chronic pain comprehensively, and to be used by the pain management clinician when working with patients. With the appropriate psychometric information, such a measure could be used in a variety of ways (evaluation, supplement to patient planning) as stated in the test materials. Unfortunately, limited score reliability and validity information is provided on the BAP-2 to support the inferences from the BAP-2 scores advocated by the developer. The test authors are encouraged to gather the necessary data to support the use of the BAP-2 for individual decision-making purposes.

REVIEWERS' REFERENCES

American Educational Research Association, American Psychological Association, & National Council on Measurement in Education. (1999). *Standards for educational and psychological testing.* Washington, DC: American Educational Research Association.

Downing, S. M. (2006). Twelve steps for effective test development. In S. M. Downing & T. M. Haladyna (Eds.), *Handbook for test development* (pp. 3–26). Mahwah, NJ: Erlbaum.

Nunnally, J. C., & Bernstein, I. H. (1994). *Psychometric theory.* (3rd ed.) New York, NY: McGraw-Hill.

Tearnan, B. H., & Lewandowski, M. J., (1992). The behavioral assessment of pain questionnaire: The development and validation of a comprehensive self-report instrument. *American Journal of Pain Management, 2,* 181–191.

Review of the Behavioral Assessment of Pain-2 Questionnaire by ASHRAF KAGEE, Professor, Department of Psychology, Stellenbosch University, Stellenbosch, South Africa:

DESCRIPTION. The Behavioral Assessment of Pain-2 Questionnaire (BAP-2) is a self-report assessment instrument that is used, according to the test publisher, to identify the factors that may "exacerbate and/or maintain subacute and chronic non-malignant pain." The BAP-2 contains 223 test items that are presented at an eighth-grade reading level. The scale is an updated version of the Behavioral Assessment of Pain Questionnaire (BAP).

The test authors indicate that the BAP-2 takes less than 30 minutes to complete. It may be administered by an untrained assistant or secretary. There are two ways to generate a clinical profile using the BAP-2. A software package is available, and scores may be entered manually. A 23-page profile report may then be printed on site. Alternatively, answer sheets may be mailed or faxed to Pain Assessment Resources for scoring. The clinical profiles are then mailed back on the same day. The latter option may save considerable time in a busy clinical practice. A Post BAP-2 also is available so that comparisons may be made between the patient's profile before and after treatment.

The summary page of the profile report provides both raw and uniform *T*-scores for each scale, information that assists the clinician in interpreting the test results. This standardization is useful information as the *T*-scores permit comparisons of the scores of each scale with one another, which would not be possible if only raw scores were used. The BAP-2 has been normed on samples of subacute and chronic patients; thus, a *T*-score of 50 represents the average of patients who experience some level of pain and significant levels of impairment. *T*-scores above 50 should be regarded as highly significant according to the test materials. In the clinical profile generated from the scores, the respondent's mean scores may be compared with normative sample means.

DEVELOPMENT. The development of the original version of the BAP was reported by Tearnan and Lewandowski in 1992. Scale development occurred in two phases. In Phase 1 the questionnaire was developed and administered to a large number of patients experiencing chronic pain. Item and factor analysis followed, and items with low internal consistency with other items or low factor loadings were omitted. In Phase 2, the revised questionnaire was administered to a separate sample of 326 chronic pain patients, and the psychometric properties were calculated. The BAP-2 is shorter than the original BAP, which contained 390 items. Most of the original scales (e.g., Activity Interference, Activity Avoidance, Spouse/Partner Influence, Pain Beliefs, Perceived Consequences) have been retained, and six validity scales and a medication scale have been added.

The BAP-2 is rooted in the biopsychosocial model and, to this extent, the scales represent all three domains of the model, with an emphasis on the environmental and psychological dimensions. The model acknowledges that a mechanistic and linear conceptualization of pain is inherently limited and as such emphasizes the interaction and synthesis of a multitude of factors that result in the subjective experience of pain. With patients reporting chronic pain, environmental and psychological factors play a prominent role in the person's subjective experience, and the BAP-2 sets out to assess these various dimensions. The scale also was designed as an extension of the clinical interview so as to increase its utility.

TECHNICAL. Information describing the development and norming of the original version of the BAP is described in a scholarly article (Tearnan & Lewandowski, 1992), which appears to be the only published article about the measure. Data from Lewandowski's dissertation in 1990 formed the basis of the factor analysis that led to the BAP-2. There appears to be no manual accompanying the instrument. However, an introductory document describes its various subscales, along with the rationale for its use.

Of the sample of 633 participants on which the BAP was validated, 414 (65.4%) indicated low back pain and 219 (34.6) indicated pain at other body sites, such as leg, head, neck, and so forth. As reported by Tearnan and Lewandowski (1992), the BAP scales demonstrated discriminant and concurrent validity with the West Haven-Yale Multidimensional Pain Inventory and the Sickness Impact Profile among the sample.

In Phase 1 of the validation study, most of the subscale alpha coefficients were above .75,

although three subscales demonstrated modest reliabilities, namely Reinforcement of Pain (.62); Personal Care (.55) and Blaming Doctors (.65). Correlations between subscales ranged from .00 to .67, with the majority of coefficients being low to moderate. Of the 34 subscales, eight demonstrated intercorrelations above .50.

In the confirmatory factor analysis conducted in Phase 2 of the validation study, the goodness of fit between the a priori model and the observed data was acceptable. Most subscales had alpha reliability coefficients above .80 in the second phase of the study, although three had values below .50, namely, Personal Care for past activities (.44); Personal Hygiene for past activities (.43), and Personal Care for current activities (.37). In a test-retest reliability study with a 10- to 14-day readministration period, the coefficients for the majority of scales exceeded .80.

COMMENTARY. The BAP-2 is a lesser known and much less vigorously researched measure of chronic pain than instruments such as the McGill Pain Questionnaire or the West Haven Pain Inventory; its strength lies in its multidimensionality and comprehensiveness. It assesses pain behavior and pain description in considerable detail and thus provides the clinician with finely detailed information about the patient. The Post BAP-2 also offers the opportunity for clinicians to assess the outcome of treatment and its effects on the patient's experience of pain. This instrument is intended for use among a very specific group, namely, persons reporting chronic pain. To this extent its use is likely to be limited to medically related contexts. It does not seem to address other dimensions of the psychological experience of pain such as malingering and phantom pain, although consistency of item endorsement may be inferred by examining the validity scales.

SUMMARY. The BAP-2 is a thoughtfully designed measure of pain behavior and description, intended for use among medical patients for whom chronic pain is a presenting problem. The development of the scale, including exploratory and factor analysis, is reported in detail. Its strength lies in its ease of administration and parsimonious scoring procedures, as well as in the validity scales that assess response style.

REVIEWER'S REFERENCE

Tearnan, B. H., & Lewandowski, M. J. (1992). The behavioral assessment of pain questionnaire: The development and validation of a comprehensive self-report instrument. *American Journal of Pain Management, 2*, 181–191.

[17]

Behavioral Summary.

Purpose: Provides "screening of behavioral adjustment problems in children and adolescents."

Population: Grades K-12.

Publication Date: 2009.

Administration: Group.

Price Data, 2013: $63 per hand scoring kit including 10 Parent Report AutoScore forms, 10 Teacher Report AutoScore forms, 10 Student Report AutoScore forms, and manual (134 pages); $314 per computer scoring kit including 10 Parent Report AutoScore forms, 10 Teacher Report AutoScore forms, 10 Student Report AutoScore forms, manual, and Unlimited-Use CD for computer scoring; $19.50 per 25 AutoScore forms; $45 per manual; $289 per Unlimited-Use CD for computer scoring and interpretation.

Comments: Ratings by parents, teachers, and self-report; scoring on PC with Windows 98, ME, 2000, XP, or Vista.

Authors: David Lachar and Christian P. Gruber (all forms and manual), Sabine A. Wingenfeld and Rex B. Kline (teacher report form).

Publisher: Western Psychological Services.

   a) PARENT REPORT.

   Population: Grades K-12.

   Scores, 14: 2 Validity scales (Inconsistent Responding, Exaggeration), 8 Adjustment scales (Impulsivity & Distractibility, Defiance, Family Problems, Atypical Behavior, Somatic Concern, Emotional Problems, Social Withdrawal, Social Skill Deficits), 3 Composite scales (Externalization, Internalization, Social Adjustment), Total score.

   Time: (15) minutes.

   b) STUDENT REPORT.

   Population: Same as *a* above.

   Scores: Same as *a* above.

   Time: Same as *a* above.

   c) TEACHER REPORT.

   Population: Grades 4-12.

   Scores, 15: 4 Academic Resources scales (Academic Performance, Academic Habits, Social Skills, Parent Participation), 7 Adjustment Problems scales (Health Concerns, Emotional Distress, Unusual Behavior, Social Problems, Verbal Aggression, Physical Aggression, Behavior Problems), 3 Disruptive Behavior scales (Attention-Deficit/Hyperactivity, Oppositional Defiant, Conduct Problems), Total score.

   Time: (20) minutes.

Review of the Behavioral Summary by JOHN S. GEISLER, Professor Emeritus, Western Michigan University, Kalamazoo, MI:

DESCRIPTION. The Behavioral Summary is a multidimensional assessment of behavioral adjustment issues facing children and adolescents, 5 to 19 years of age. It consists of three instruments (called "forms" by the test authors): A Parent Report, a Student Report (both of these instruments consist of 96 parallel items), and a Teacher Report (102 items). Most of these items are in a statement format. The parent and student statements are parallel in nature and the responses are either true (T) or false (F) to all statements. The Teacher Report uses two graduated response systems, either Never, Seldom, Sometimes, Usually (1–4), or Deficient, Below Average, Average, Above Average, Superior (1–5), depending on the scale. The test authors state that the item statements are written at the fourth grade level. The Behavioral Summary is hand scored (an accessory computer program is available for reporting the results, but responses must be entered from the answer sheets). Raw scores are converted to *T*-scores. The test authors stress that the Behavioral Summary should not be used in isolation but should be part of a complete evaluation system including interviews, observations, and the administration of other appropriate instruments. The developers contend that as many people as possible should be part of the assessment process.

The Parent Report and the Student Report include 14 scales organized under four groupings (A, B, C, & D):

   A. Two Validity scales: Inconsistent Response Index (INC–14 paired items) and Exaggeration (EXG–18 items);

   B. Eight Adjustment scales: Impulsivity & Distractibility (ADH), Defiance (DEFY), Atypical Behavior (ATYP), Somatic Concerns (SOM), Emotional Problems (EMOT), Social Withdrawal (WDL), Social Skill Deficits (SSK), and Family Problems (FAM);

   C. Three Composite scales: Externalization (EXT, a sum of the ADH and DEFY scores), Internalization (INT, a sum of the ATYP, EMOT, and SOM scores), and Social Adjustment (SOC, a sum of the WDL and SSK scores); and

   D. Total Score (a sum of the raw scores for the three composite scores as well as the FAM adjustment scale raw score).

All individual scales (except INC and EXG) are composed of 12 items each.

The Student Report and the Parent Report scales are reported to assess the following dimensions and are scored for both students and parents: ADH–Impulsivity & Distractibility (inattentive, overactive, impulsive); DEFY–Defiance (disruptive, disobedient, confrontational); FAM–Family

Problems; ATYP–Atypical Behavior (below average estimates of academic achievement and adaptive behavior); SOM–Somatic Concern (headaches, pain, dizzy complaints); EMOT–Emotional Problems (irritability, moody, oppositional); WDL–Social Withdrawal (socially withdrawn); and SSK–Social Skills Deficits (isolated, rejected, ignored).

The Teacher Report consists of items in three groupings (A, B, C):

A. Academic Resources is composed of four scales (the number of items is given in parentheses) and, except for the Academic Performance scale, the range of the graduated responses is 1–4: (1) Academic Performance (AP–8), (2) Academic Habits (AH–13), (3) Social Skills (SS–8), and (4) Parent Participation (PP–6);

B. Adjustment Problems: (1) Health Concerns (HC–6), Emotional Distress (ED–15), Unusual Behavior (UB–7), Social Problems (SP–12), Verbal Aggression (VA–7), Physical Aggression (PA–5), Behavior Problems (BP–15); and

C. Disruptive Behavior: (1) Attention-Deficit/Hyperactivity (ADH–16), (2) Oppositional Defiant (OPD–16), and (3) Conduct Problems (CNP–16).

The test authors provide descriptions of elevated scores and the issues that face children who produce T-scores that are 1, 2, 3, or 4 standard deviations above the mean. Suggestions are provided for remediation and intervention. The language in this section is tentative in nature and the test authors strongly suggest that supportive and additional verifiable information is needed before engaging in a program for intervention. Six case studies are reported in the test manual. The items, item response choices, score reports, scoring worksheet, and profile report (consisting of raw and T-scores) are all contained in a single booklet that requires respondents to mark choices on an answer sheet. The 14 raw scores are reported on the profile report, and using the T-score columns on the extreme edges of the page, the corresponding T-scores are computed and the circled raw scores are connected to each other.

DEVELOPMENT. The Behavioral Summary content is drawn from previous instruments (most of them developed by the current authors of the Behavioral Summary) and may be considered a consolidation and shortened form of the Personality Inventory for Children (2001), the Personality Inventory for Youth (1995), and the Student Behavior Survey (2000). The test authors repeatedly refer

readers to the manuals of these precursor instruments for validation, history, conceptualization, and justification. There is little discussion of the development of the Behavioral Summary provided in the 2009 manual.

TECHNICAL. Reliability data are reported in three tables corresponding to the three groups in the standardization samples: parents, students, and teachers. Alpha coefficients for parent samples ranged from .63 to .93 across all scales with medians of .72 and .86 for the Adjustment and Composite scales (N = 2,306). Test-retest coefficients ranged from .58 to .85 across all scales. The median Adjustment and Composite scales test-retest coefficients were .78 and .80, respectively (N = 38, 1 week interval). Standard errors of measurement (*SEM*) data are provided, but it is not known whether or not the *SEM*s reported refer to the raw scores or the T-scores.

The standardization samples were drawn from groups throughout the United States and consisted of parents (approximately 2,300) and a like number of students. The table containing the student data reported the numbers of students in the age range from 9 or less to 18 or greater. The number of Teacher Reports was approximately 2,600. The ethnic background, geographic region, parents' education levels, and ages of the children/adolescents were reported. Of special note is the fact that the geographic distribution of students included students from the Midwest (N = 1,371), South (N = 561), and West (N = 395), but none from the East. The corresponding reliability data for the student samples were: .65 to .92 across scales with median coefficients of .70 and .83 (coefficient alpha, N = 2,327). The test-retest correlation coefficients ranged from .74 to .90 across scales. The median coefficients were .80 and .78 for the Adjustment and Composite scales (N = 89, 1 week interval). For the Teacher Report, the alpha coefficients ranged from .86 to .95 across the individual scales (median range .90 to .94 across the Academic Resources, Adjustment Problems, and Disruptive Behavior Scales, N = 2,612). Test-retest coefficients ranged from .76 to .94 (across scales) with median coefficient ranges from .85 to .91 (N = 52, no interval provided). No reliability evidence was reported for the validity scales (INC and EXG) for any of the three groups. Also, no probability levels accompanied any of the reported coefficients. The test-retest data were reported on three samples: N = 110, 129, and 52.

The test authors reported validity correlation coefficients among a few scales using parent, student, and teacher data. The highest range of coefficients were associated with scales that measured similar constructs (e.g., Physical Aggression–Verbal Aggression reported by teachers = .81). Comparisons were made between the standardization group scores (N approximately 2,500) and scores on the same scales reported by samples of students (N approximately 1,300) who were referred to clinicians and school personnel for behavioral issues. Very little additional validity data were reported. The test authors did say that additional validity data are available in the manuals for the predecessor instruments.

COMMENTARY. The test authors are to be commended for condensing three longer behavioral assessment instruments into a shorter, more manageable instrument (although it is really three different instruments). Most of the items are clearly stated and unambiguous. Also of note is the fact that the test authors clearly state that the Behavioral Summary is not to be used as a single, isolated instrument for reporting and analyzing behaviors. Rather, the test should be used as a supplement to other assessment procedures and instruments.

Procedures for scoring and profiling scores is very problematic and in need of modification. The instrument can be hand scored. If it is hand scored, raw scores must then be plotted on the profile sheet. If two parents, three teachers, and one child were to complete the Behavioral Summary then 732 (some are double scored) items would be tallied resulting in 156 raw and 156 T-scores and resulting profiles. The chance for human error is very high. The INC scores require test givers to search out the responses to 28 different items, record the responses, determine 14 item pair difference raw scores, and convert raw scores to T-scores. Even if computers were used to report scores, the items and item responses are not on answer sheets that can be processed by computers. Mark sense answer sheets or direct computer answered items would resolve this serious problem. The computer scoring (additional service) does generate additional scoring services that can be helpful (e.g., parent/parent, student/parent differences). Also nearly half of the 96 items on the Parent Report and Student Report (46 items) are double scored, the responses being included on the scores of the INC and EXG and various other scales. It is questionable whether or not items can be scored for more than one scale, especially in the absence of analyses, data, rationale, or justification for the choice of the scales and scale items.

Validity evidence is very scant–almost nonexistent. The test authors refer readers back to the original instruments' manuals for validity reports. The validity data for the Behavioral Summary need to be in the current manual, not in secondary sources. This is a major drawback. The comments regarding high scores on the EXG scale are unwarranted. The test authors do more than suggest that high EXG scores are a reflection of psychopathology. Evidence for these types of statements are not provided. The reliability data appear adequate for this type of instrument despite modest sample sizes.

The standardization sample size is adequate; however, several caveats are warranted. The test authors report the parent sample data for the ages of children whose parents completed the Parent Report (5–19 years of age). However, the ages of the children who completed the Student Report is wanting. The age range for the children is not the same as the parents. The exact number of 5, 6, 7, 8, and 9-year-olds in the standardization was not reported. Some age ranges were collapsed into categories. If the Behavioral Summary is designed to be used by various age groups, then all age groups need to be included in the standardization sample. T-scores may not be the best type of scores to be used with this type of instrument. An examination of the T-score conversion table shows that many of the raw scores are skewed. For example, a score of 1 on the FAM scale (Parent Report–Female) converts to a T-score of 47. All the other 11 scores on this scale are above a T-score of 50. A raw score of 22 (of a possible 24) on the Teacher Report (males aged 12–18, Parent Participation scale) has a converted T-score of 50, which means that 21 of the 24 scores are below that point. Perhaps percentile ranks would be more helpful and understandable. More people, including professionals, have a better understanding of percentile ranks than T-scores. A more informative type of data would be criterion-related difference scores (e.g., between clinical samples and standardization samples). Also, the inclusion of the Parent Participation scale is questionable. The statements made in the manual regarding lower scores on this scale appear highly subjective (uncooperative parents, nonrealistic expectations of school and student potential).

It is interesting to note that the T-scores on the Teacher Report are not only dependent on gender, but also the age of the children being evaluated. There are two age groupings, 5–11 years and 12–18 years. They have separate raw score/*T*-score conversions. If there is a difference between age grouping scores for the Teacher Forms is it possible that there are also age grouping differences on the Parent and Student Reports? Is it possible that 10-year-old students respond differently than 19-year-old students? The Parent Report and Student Report students, despite a 15-year age span are all scored on the same raw and *T*-score systems.

SUMMARY. The Behavioral Summary is designed to assess the behavior patterns of students from age 5 to 19. The assessments are performed by three different groups: student's self-assessment, parent's assessment of their children's behaviors, and teacher's assessments. The Student and Parent Reports are parallel in nature and attempt to assess many of the behaviors as well as additional academic performance-related scales.

The Behavioral Summary demonstrates adequate reliability as evidenced by correlation coefficients. However, the validity data are very much lacking, the dearth of which cannot be justified. Item selection, choice, and justification are not provided. The test authors report that three predecessor instruments provided the foundation for the Behavioral Summary, but they failed to provide the rationale for the item selection and the data that led to the newly formed instrument. The scoring of the instrument is cumbersome and antiquated and leaves ample room for serious human error in hand scoring, transcribing scores, converting raw scores to *T*-scores, and plotting scores.

The developers are to be commended for informing consumers that the Behavioral Summary should never be used as a single measure of behavior assessment. Rather, it should be combined with various sources of information in order to make informed decisions about children and adolescents. It can be marginally useful in this regard, but needs improvement in order to make a significant contribution to behavior assessment.

Review of the Behavioral Summary by STEPHANIE STEIN, Professor and Chair, Department of Psychology, Central Washington University, Ellensburg, WA:

The Behavioral Summary is a compilation of three separate rating forms, designed to be used as a screening measure for identifying behavior problems in children in Grades K–12. These brief rating forms are adapted from three prior published instruments

by the same authors – the Personality Inventory for Children, Second Edition (PIC-2; 16:183), the Personality Inventory for Youth (PIY; 13:231), and the Student Behavior Survey (SBS; 15:250).

DESCRIPTION. The Behavioral Summary is administered individually to children, parents, and/or teachers using multiple-sheet carbon-copy forms that provide the questions on the top sheets (both sides) and a scoring worksheet on the second sheet. Because of the multiple pages, it requires the respondents to press hard when they mark their answers. The form also includes a removable two-sided Behavioral Summary profile for converting the obtained raw scores to *T*-scores and transferring them to a visual profile graph. The parent and child forms each have 96 true/false items and the teacher form has 102 Likert-type items, some on a scale of 1–5 and the majority on a scale of 1–4. Completion of the report forms by the respondent is fairly straightforward and predicted to take no more than 15 to 20 minutes, depending on the form. Though none of the forms instruct the respondent about a time frame in which to consider the child's behavior, the teacher form is likely to reflect ratings of the child within the past year, given that teachers usually only have students in class for one year. However, because the parent and student forms also do not delineate a time frame (i.e., within the past month, past 6 months, etc.), each respondent could potentially use very different time frames in making the ratings. In addition, the wording on items within the parent form is inconsistent. Most of the items say "My child" or "I," but others say "The child's parents…"

All forms can be hand scored using the carbon forms, though computer scoring is also an option. The forms include all the directions theoretically needed to accurately score the instrument. However, the scoring of the completed forms is very confusing, especially for first-time users. The person scoring the forms has to follow a series of tiny dotted lines, solid lines, and/or dot-dash lines to sum up the different scales and look for circled/not circled boxes, as well as flip back and forth between the pages. Even individuals who are well trained in assessment are likely to make scoring errors on these forms until they adapt to following the convoluted lines. After the raw scores for each scale are obtained, the person scoring the form turns to the attached Behavioral Summary Profile (separate for males and females), enters the raw scores at the bottom of the profile, and uses the profile to find and plot the corresponding T-score for each raw score. Finally, the scale raw scores, which are entered into one of three shaped boxes (circle, diamond, or triangle), are then summed and entered into the corresponding shaped boxes for each of the composite scores and total score. Though it is convenient to have all of the scoring and scale profiles on the same form as the questionnaire, the complexity of the scoring process leaves one wondering whether the convenience of all-in-one forms is worth the resulting confusion. Because of this potential confusion, the inexperienced scorer should probably be referred to the test manual, which provides visual examples of a completed form, scoring worksheet, and behavioral profile.

The responses on the parent and child forms are scored on eight adjustment scales, three composite scales, two validity scales (Exaggeration and Inconsistent Responding), and a total score. The teacher form provides scores on four academic resources scales, seven adjustment problem scales, three disruptive behavior scales, and one validity scale. All three forms provide separate scoring profiles for males and females and the teacher form further divides the profiles by age of the student (5–11 years and 12–18 years). Once the instruments have been scored, the examiner can refer to the test manual for guidelines on interpretation of the individual scales and composites. T-scores one standard deviation (SD) above the mean are used to indicate that a behavioral problem exists, though two SDs above the mean are also used for specific scale interpretations. Most scales on the parent form have separate levels of interpretation for T-scores 60–69 and another for T-scores 70–79.

DEVELOPMENT. The items for the Behavioral Summary were drawn from three separate instruments by the same authors: Personality Inventory for Children (PIC-2; Second Edition; 2001), Personality Inventory for Youth (PIY; 1995), and Student Behavior Survey (SBS; 2000). The test authors' rationale for developing the Behavioral Summary rather than relying on the original three instruments was the need for a shorter instrument that could be used to screen for behavioral concerns in children and adolescents. It is not exactly clear how specific items for the Behavioral Summary were selected from the larger pool of items on these prior instruments. It appears that clinical or expert judgment was the main strategy for selecting items, particularly for the Teacher Report Form. The test authors apparently selected items from the original

three instruments that were primarily focused on behavior and used that narrower collection of items to develop the current Behavioral Summary.

The various scales on the Behavioral Summary were developed initially through a process of clinical judgment, where items that appeared to be measuring similar behavioral constructs were grouped together. Following the initial grouping, the individual scales were administered to the clinical samples and assessed for internal consistency as well as correlational strength between individual items and the scale as a whole. The two validity scales were developed through the pairing of similar items (Inconsistent Responding scale) and examination of items that were infrequently endorsed by the individuals in the standardization and clinical populations (Exaggeration scale). The development of the composite scales is not described in the test manual.

TECHNICAL.

Standardization. The standardization samples for the Behavioral Summary were as follows: Parent Report (n = 2,306), Student Report (n = 2,327), and Teacher Report (n = 2,612). On all forms, the standardization samples consisted of approximately balanced numbers of males and females, with females always slightly more represented. Ethnicity and SES were fairly represented for each form, based on U.S. Census data, with geographical representation more clustered in certain regions (heaviest in the south for Parent and Teacher Reports, mostly in the Midwest for Student Report). The respondents on the Parent Report were primarily mothers.

The participants in the clinical samples were as follows: Parent Report (n = 1,551; 68% male), Student Report (n = 1,178; 50.8% male), and Teacher Report (n = 1,315; 72.4% male). On all report forms, the clinical samples were primarily white, though ethnic diversity was represented in all three forms. No information about SES was given for any of the clinical samples, nor were the respondents (mother or father) specified on the Parent Report. Referral sources included clinics, schools, and juvenile justice for the Parent and Teacher Reports and inpatient/outpatient for the Student Report.

Reliability. The test authors report internal consistency and retest reliability data for both the standardization and clinical samples on all three forms. On the Parent Report form, the internal consistency coefficients for the standardization sample range from .63 to .82 on the Adjustment scales (median = .72), .78 to .89 on the Composite scales (median = .86), and .93 on Total score. Similar but slightly higher internal consistency coefficients were found for the clinical sample on the Parent Report form. Retest reliability coefficients (1 week) for the standardization sample (n = 110) range from .58 to .85 on the Adjustment scales (median = .78), .71 to .85 on the Composite scales (median = .80), and .77 for Total score. The retest reliability coefficients (retest interval of 1 week) for the clinical sample (n = 38) were consistently strong, ranging from .85 to .89 for the Adjustment scales (median = .87), .89 on all the Composite scales, and .89 for the Total score.

On the Student Report form, the internal consistency coefficients for the standardization sample range from .65 to .79 on the Adjustment scales (median = .70), .79 to .84 on the Composite scales (median = .83), and .92 on Total score. Again, very similar but slightly higher internal consistency coefficients were found for the clinical sample on the Student Report form. Retest reliability coefficients (1 week) for the standardization sample (n = 129) range from .77 to .90 on the Adjustment scales (median = .80), .83 to .88 on the Composite scales (median = .87), and .90 for Total score. The retest reliability coefficients (retest interval of 1 week) for the clinical sample (n = 89) range from .69 to .82 for the Adjustment scales (median = .78), .79 to .86 on the Composite scales (median = .85), and .89 for the Total score.

Finally, on the Teacher Report form, internal consistency coefficients for the standardization sample range from .86 to .94 on the Academic Resources scales (median = .90), .86 to .93 on the Adjustment Problem scales (median = .89), and .92 to .95 on the Disruptive Behavior scales (median = .94). Very similar internal consistency coefficients were also found for the clinical sample on the Teacher Report form. The retest reliability coefficients (interval not specified) for the standardization sample (n = 52) on the Teacher Report form range from .78 to .88 for Academic Resources scales (median = .85), .76 to .92 for the Adjustment Problem scales (median = .88), and .90 to .94 (median = .91) on the Disruptive Behavior scales. The clinical sample (n = 31) on the Teacher Report form had retest reliability coefficients (interval not specified) ranging from .77 to .97 for Academic Resources scales (median = .89), .66 to .86 on Adjustment Problem scales (median = .81), and .69 to .90 (median = .86) on the Disruptive Behavior scales.

Validity. The Behavioral Summary manual addresses concurrent validity, convergent/divergent validity, and contrasted group validity. With regard to evidence that supports concurrent validity, the manual refers to a variety of rating scales and expert clinician ratings that have been compared against one or more of the "instruments underlying the Behavioral Summary" (p. 57), but no correlation coefficients or other quantitative data are provided in the test manual to support the claim for concurrent validity.

In the discussion of evidence pertaining to convergent and divergent validity, the test authors do provide an intercorrelation table between select scales on the three report forms that supposedly assess the constructs of externalizing and internalizing symptoms. No information is provided on how these specific scales were selected as representing one of these two constructs, though the presumption is that this was done through expert judgment. The table differentiates between the following comparisons: similar constructs within the same report form, similar constructs on different report forms, dissimilar constructs within the same report form, and dissimilar constructs on different report forms. Though some of the resulting correlations are strong (coefficients range from .79 to .87), primarily on the similar scales on the Teacher Report form, the rest of the correlations intended to illustrate convergent validity are weak to moderate (coefficients range from .14 to .55). The correlations supporting divergent validity (i.e., different constructs, different instruments) were primarily weak (.06 to .37), as predicted.

Finally, the test authors make a case for contrasted group validity. They compared the obtained means from the standardization (not referred) sample and the referred sample and found that there were significant differences (p < .001) between the two groups on every individual and composite scale on all three forms. Similarly, they found large effect sizes between the two groups on the Parent and Teacher forms and medium effect sizes on the Student form.

COMMENTARY. The Behavioral Summary has several strengths as a tool for assessing children and adolescents. The three separate forms allow the evaluator to gather behavioral information from a variety of sources (parent, teacher, child) and look for both convergence and divergence in the ratings. The test manual provides detailed information on scoring and interpretation, as well as several case examples. The standardization sample is substantial in size with reasonably good representation of ethnic and SES diversity. Geographic diversity is more limited, though. The coefficients for internal consistency and retest reliability suggest that all three forms have moderate to high reliability, especially on the composite scores and total score. In contrast, evidence in support of validity is much more sketchy. In particular, the test authors could do a better job of providing evidence for concurrent validity rather than just claiming it exists. Hand scoring of the surveys is awkward and confusing, so computer scoring may be a better option. Other minor issues with the instruments themselves are inconsistent wording and lack of guidelines for a time frame in which to consider the child's behavior. More importantly, the decisions regarding selection of items are vague, with too much conveniently explained by "clinical judgment." In addition, though the test manual provides detailed interpretations for elevated scores, the evidence needed to back the validity of these interpretations is absent.

SUMMARY. At first glance, the Behavioral Summary looks like a quick and easy way to screen for behavioral concerns in children and adolescents. However, the test authors have relied too much on the presumption that if their prior instruments are well-respected, then this one will be, too. Unfortunately, they do not provide sufficient evidence for the validity of this measure as a screening tool. One can hope that further research with the Behavioral Summary will provide the evidence for criterion-related validity necessary to give evaluators confidence in the measure. In the meantime, evaluators may want to consider using the Behavior Assessment System for Children [Second Edition] (BASC-2; 17:21; Reynolds & Kamphaus, 2004) for a comprehensive, reliable, and valid measure of behavior in children and adolescents.

REVIEWER'S REFERENCE

Reynolds, C. R., & Kamphaus, R. W. (2004). Behavior Assessment System for Children [Second Edition]. San Antonio, TX: Pearson.

[18]

Bell Relationship Inventory for Adolescents.
Purpose: Designed for use "in schools and clinical settings for quickly and accurately assessing object relations ego functioning in children and adolescents."
Population: Ages 11-17.
Publication Date: 2005.
Acronym: BRIA.
Scores, 6: Alienation, Insecure Attachment, Egocentricity, Social Incompetence, Positive Attachment, Response Bias.

Administration: Group.
Price Data, 2010: $99 per kit including Autoscore forms, 1 manual for the Bell Object Relations and Reality Testing Inventory (1995, 82 pages), and 1 manual supplement for the BRIA (2005, 27 pages); $37 per 25 Autoscore forms; $55 per manual for the Bell Object Relations and Reality Testing Inventory; $22 per manual supplement for the BRIA.
Time: (10-15) minutes.
Comments: The BRIA is a version of the Bell Object Relations and Reality Testing Inventory, Form O (14:45) adapted for use with adolescents ages 11-17; self-report format.
Author: Morris D. Bell.
Publisher: Western Psychological Services.
Cross References: For reviews by Glen Fox and Steven I. Pfeiffer of the Bell Object Relations and Reality Testing Inventory, see 14:45; see also T5:297 (2 references).

Review of the Bell Relationship Inventory for Adolescents by GENE N. BERG, Adjunct Instructor Psychology, Chapman University, Riverside, CA:

DESCRIPTION. The Bell Relationship Inventory for Adolescents (BRIA) is a 50-item True/False inventory that is administered to a child or adolescent. The test publisher suggests that the test is appropriately used in schools and clinical settings to quickly and accurately assess object relations and ego functioning in children and adolescents from the ages of 11 through 17. The test is designed to assess attachment, social functioning, and emotional bonds. The test publisher indicated that the test takes only 10 to 15 minutes to administer, can be administered individually or in a group, and requires a sixth grade reading comprehension ability.

The BRIA test kit includes the Bell Object Relations and Reality Testing Inventory (BORRTI; 14:45) manual, the BRIA manual, and test packets (with attached profile sheets). The BORRTI manual provides information on the development of the BORRTI for adults.

The BRIA is based on the original research development of the BORRTI. The BORRTI was developed as a test for adults and its shortened version, Form O, was used as a starting point in the development of a form appropriate to use with children and adolescents. Items for the BRIA were taken from the BORRTI and revised for use with children and adolescents. Additional items were added and the BRIA was developed.

The inventory is self-scoring, thanks to an attached scoring and profile sheet. Scoring directions are included in the testing packet. Once the test is completed, the examiner can score the test, complete the scoring computations on the factor variables, and graph the resulting factor areas using the respective raw scores, *T*-scores, and percentile ranks. The resulting test scores and profile can be interpreted through norms for the reference group and review of the BRIA and the BORRTI manuals.

DEVELOPMENT. The BRIA was developed through revisions of items on the BORRTI with additional test items added. The BRIA focuses on the assessment of psychoanalytic constructs relating to relationships, attachment, security, ego development, and affective and emotional qualities in relationships. The BRIA is based upon the theoretical thinking that influenced the development of the BORRTI–specifically, the theoretical work of Bellak, Hurvich, and Gediman on the assessment of ego functioning (1973). In theory, object relations and reality testing are ego functions at the center of a healthy psychological life; they are compromised in psychopathology. The BORRTI was originally developed as a standardized measure of ego functioning.

The BRIA provides scale scores on the following subscales: (ALN) Alienation/Lack of Trust relating to difficulty with intimacy and feelings of alienation, (IA) Insecure Attachment/Sensitivity relating to rejection, fears of separation and abandonment, (EGC) Egocentricity/Lack of Empathy relating to self-protectiveness and tendency to control and exploit, (SI) Social Incompetence/Social Discomfort relating to shyness and difficulty making friends, (POSAT) Positive Attachment/Satisfaction with Current Relationships with Peers and Parents, and (RBIAS) Response Bias. Scale scores can be reviewed in terms of level of clinical significance, compared to norms, and graphically presented on the scale profile. Interpretative hypotheses can be developed in relationship to the profile configurations. The BRIA manual provides a number of profile examples that provide assistance for interpretation of results. In addition, the BORRTI manual provides interpretive guidance relating to the ALN, IA, EGC, and SI subscales.

TECHNICAL. The BRIA was standardized and normed on a sample of 815 children and teenagers, 705 of whom were from public schools and 110 of whom were from clinics and residential treatment centers with an almost equal number of boys and girls between the ages of 11 to 17. Standard scores were developed using 625 public school students for whom complete data existed.

The test manual gives a listing of the demographic characteristics of the nonclinical reference group, which came from the Northeastern region of the United States. There is somewhat limited research on the BRIA, but much of the original thinking and research for the development of the BRIA is based on the BORRTI. The BRIA manual includes some clinical case examples of profile configurations for the BRIA. The examples give some insights with respect to interpretation of testing profiles, yet it is apparent that there has been considerably less research and application of the BRIA than with the BORRTI.

Although many of the content areas originally studied in the BORRTI are appropriate for children and adolescents, the test was originally developed for use with adults. The BRIA will require further research with respect to the appropriateness of the norms developed for children and adolescents. It would be helpful if there was research on larger populations of children and adolescents with cutoff scores for normal children as well as children with psychopathology and defective ego functioning.

Various measures have been utilized to estimate the reliability of the BRIA. Internal consistency estimates listed in the manual are moderate to high. Coefficient alpha was utilized as a measure of internal consistency for each scale.

Regarding validity, a principal component factor analysis was conducted in the early development of the test. An oblique rotated factor solution yielded five factors that accounted for 16% of the variance. Evidence supporting divergent, concurrent, and discriminant validity was reviewed. Coefficients were generally in the low to moderate range for the full development sample and moderate to high for the reference sample suggesting that there is sufficient independence among the scores to justify separate scoring and interpretation. The single scale of Positive Attachment (POSAT) was significantly negatively correlated with the other scales on the BRIA. As expected, there is an inverse relationship between the scores reflective of deficiencies (in object relationships and ego functioning) and scores relating to positive relationships (reflected in POSAT scores). Some of the individual scale scores relating to object relationships and ego functioning share some degree of variance and may not be fully differentiated.

COMMENTARY. The BRIA is a very brief inventory that can be easily utilized in the assessment of children and adolescents. Test materials are relatively straightforward and easy to understand for administration and scoring. The test would be an excellent resource in a setting where there are limited time and resources for the assessment of children and adolescents. The self-scoring feature makes the test convenient to use and readily provides a graphic presentation of object relations and ego functioning.

A key weakness of the BRIA is that the majority of research available relates to the BORRTI, which is based primarily on adult norms. The BORRTI manual norms are utilized for the interpretation of four of the six scales on the BRIA (ALN, IA, EGC, and the SI). There is considerable research and review on the BORRTI, but considerably less research on the BRIA.

The BRIA examines a number of object relations and ego functioning constructs frequently referred to in the psychoanalytic research addressed in the individual scales. However, there are some distinct differences with respect to children and teens and adults that may not be readily addressed in the test. This is noted in the test manual in reference to limitations of the test. The test should be used with some degree of caution and care. Assessment with the BRIA should be made in the context of other tests, clinical observations, and available background information. Research with larger samples may further refine and develop the BRIA as an important measure for adolescents and children. The norms for the test should be strengthened through further research with larger, more representative, clinical samples.

SUMMARY. The BRIA is a 50-item measure of object relations and ego functioning for children and adolescents designed to be individually or group administered. The BRIA was developed through revisions of the BORRTI with new additional items. The test was standardized on 815 children and adolescents. The test provides some preliminary assessment for children and adolescents, yet has somewhat limited research and standardized norms. Further research with larger more representative samples would improve the norms for the test.

REVIEWER'S REFERENCE

Bellak, L., Hurvich, M., & Gediman, H. (1973). *Ego functions in schizophrenics, neurotics, and normals.* New York, NY: Wiley.

Review of the Bell Relationship Inventory for Adolescents by GLEN E. RAY, Professor of Psychology, Auburn University Montgomery, Montgomery, AL:

DESCRIPTION. The Bell Relationship Inventory for Adolescents (BRIA) is based on the original Form O (Object Relations subscales) of the larger Bell Object Relations and Reality Testing Inventory (BORRTI; 14:45). The BRIA was created to assess ego functioning with regard to object relations in preadolescent and adolescent children ages 11–17. That is, identification of children "at high risk for experiencing psychological disturbances and difficulties with interpersonal relationships" (manual, p. 1) is the core purpose of the BRIA. Four negative dimensions of object relations are assessed: Alienation (ALN), Insecure Attachment (IA), Egocentricity (EGC), and Social Incompetence (SI). One positive dimension of object relations is assessed: Positive Attachment (POSAT). In addition, a validity measure labeled Response Bias (RBIAS) is also included.

The BRIA is in a self-report format with True-False response options. The test is administratively flexible and may be administered in a large classroom setting, in a small group, or to an individual. All that is needed is a pen/pencil and the "Autoscore form" to record responses. The answer form contains three parts: 50 test items, a scoring worksheet, and a graphic profile sheet. Directions are provided on the answer form and are very straightforward with regard to the True-False response set that is required. Ensuring that all responses are obtained and free of double-marked responses appears to be the only major concern for successful administration.

Scoring of the BRIA is completed manually using the instructions located on the scoring worksheet. The scoring worksheet is composed of 2 pages (25 items each) with each object relations dimension having a separate column plus a column for the validity scale. There are three steps to scoring the BRIA: calculating raw scores for each dimension, converting each dimension raw score into a standardized T-score, and then graphically creating the profile. Specifically, to score the BRIA, one first calculates raw scores by adding up the scoring weights circled for each column for each separate dimension. Raw score totals are then entered at the bottom of each respective column on the second page of the scoring sheet. On the profile sheet each raw score total is transferred to the bottom of each respective column and the raw score total is circled within each column. Each raw score total is transformed into a T-score by simply following the row to the right or left from where the raw score value (circled) appears. Last, one simply connects the circled raw score values to create an interpretive profile.

DEVELOPMENT. The BRIA was created as a self-report measure to capture the phenomenological nature of object relations in children. Item development began with the original 45 items of the BORRTI Form O. Given that the BORRTI was developed for adults, the original items were modified and rewritten to be age appropriate for use with preadolescents and adolescents. Further, new items were added to "capture unique features of adolescent experiences in relationships" (manual, p. 13). The new test items were developed and refined by utilizing age-appropriate focus groups. All test items were written in a manner that reflects "an individual's personal experience rather than a clinical description of the phenomenon in question" (manual, p. 25). To ensure readability, all items were assessed for reading ease using the Flesch Reading Ease score (88.2%) and for grade level using the Flesch-Kincaid Grade Level (3.5) as reported in the BRIA manual (p. 13).

TECHNICAL. The total sample for the BRIA was composed of 705 children from public schools and 110 children from clinics and residential treatment facilities (N = 815). The sample was 53.9% female and 46.1% male. Ages ranged from 11 to 17, with an average age of 14.4. School grades ranged from 6th to 11th, with the average being 8th grade. The sample was composed of 64.5% White, 19.4% African American, 8.8% Hispanic, 3.1% Asian, and 4.2% Other. There were 625 children from public school with completed BRIAs that served as the nonclinical reference group from which standard scores were then created.

The factor structure of the BRIA appears to be quite strong with congruence coefficients for the five factors ranging from .76 to .91. Further, internal consistency (coefficient alphas) of the BRIA items for the entire sample are ".76 for POSAT, .69 for ALN, .76 for IA, .69 for EGC, and .76 for SI" (manual, p. 15). Thus, items are clustering together demonstrating similarity with regard to children's understanding and evaluation of the various items that compose the different dimensions. The BRIA manual presents data for both the full development sample and for the nonclinical reference sample.

The intercorrelations between the five BRIA dimensions ranged from .30 to .58 for the nonclinical reference sample. This reflects adequate nonshared variation among dimensions to warrant having and interpreting the various dimensions separately. It is important to note that some degree of shared variance is expected given that these are all dimensions, of the larger construct of object relations. It is further validating that POSAT, the positive dimension, is negatively related with the other four negative dimensions ALN, IA, EGC, and SI. Concurrent validity evidence has been demonstrated for the BRIA by comparing scores on the BRIA scales with scores on BORRTI scales with the same name. This comparison revealed correlations ranging from .43 to .83 (p < .001). Additionally, concurrent validity evidence was demonstrated by investigating the relationship between BRIA scores and scores on established personality inventories. The BRIA was also very good at discriminating between the clinical and nonclinical sample and at discriminating among different subgroups of the clinical sample (residential psychiatric vs. residential family). This discrimination among groups was especially salient for the ALN dimension.

COMMENTARY. The BRIA is a well-developed self-report measure of object relations for use with preadolescents and adolescents. Both positive and negative dimensions of object relations are accounted for, and the simplicity and flexibility of administration and scoring make the BRIA a valuable tool in clinical and research settings. The BRIA benefits from being created out of a well-established measure of ego functioning (the BORRTI). As such, many of the theoretical, rational, and practical concerns have been identified and well-addressed. A potential weakness that must be levied against all tests delivered in a self-report format and not just the test reviewed here centers around the independence of the response behaviors. That is, responses are valid to the extent that the administrator is confident that the responses reflect the behavior of the person taking the test and nothing else. This concern is magnified with large group administrations and in other situations where distractions to the test taker are more likely to occur. This issue is addressed in the administration section of the test manual. Further, some measurement experts may consider reliability coefficients less than .70 to be unreliable in certain research or clinical contexts. Finally, and as mentioned in the test manual, the dimensions of the BRIA do not represent an exhaustive number of object relations dimensions that may exist.

SUMMARY. The BRIA offers a well-designed, relatively quick (50 True-False items) assessment of a core aspect of ego functioning in preadolescents and adolescents. The reliability and validity of the use of BRIA test scores has been established. It is administratively flexible and can be used in multiple settings. Scoring and interpretation are straightforward. As such, this is a worthy measure of object relations in children.

[19]

BEST Literacy.

Purpose: Designed to "measure adult English language learners' ability to read and write in English in authentic situations in the United States."
Population: Ages 16 and over.
Publication Date: 2008.
Scores, 3: Reading, Writing, Final Scale Score.
Administration: Group or individual.
Forms, 3: Form B, Form C, Form D.
Price Data, 2012: $36-50 per Form B (including 20 booklets with corresponding scoring sheets); $36-50 per Form C (including 20 booklets with corresponding scoring sheets); $36-50 per Form D (including 20 booklets with corresponding scoring sheets); $26 per test manual (64 pages); $25 per printed technical report (130 pages) or $10 per electronic PDF of technical report.
Time: (60) minutes.
Comments: May be used as a pretest and posttest using the different forms available.
Author: Center for Applied Linguistics.
Publisher: Center for Applied Linguistics.

Review of BEST Literacy by GEORGE ENGELHARD, JR., Professor of Educational Measurement and Policy, and AMINAH PERKINS, PhD candidate, Educational Studies, Emory University, Atlanta, GA:

DESCRIPTION. BEST Literacy is a competency-based assessment that is designed to assess English language proficiency for adults in authentic situations within the United States. The assessment is intended for English language learners (16 years of age and older), who are currently enrolled as students in a U.S. educational program. BEST Literacy is a measure of adult English language proficiency that focuses on functional literacy tasks to assess reading and writing ability in English. The BEST Literacy is recommended for use in making placement decisions, assessment of student progress, instructional planning, program evaluation, and accountability reporting.

BEST Literacy consists of three parallel forms (Forms B, C, and D) with 11 parts in each form: 7 parts assess Reading (49 items) and 4 parts assess Writing (19 items). There are some overlapping items across forms. Each part addresses a different topic area (personal information; calendar; food labels; clothing labels; rent check; envelope;

telephone directory; train schedule; reading passages; ads, signs, notices, etc.; and personal notes). Examinees indicate all of their responses directly in the test booklet.

Raw scores for each section are converted into scale scores. There are a total of 78 points on the assessment with 49 points for Reading and 29 points for Writing. Performance on Best Literacy can be interpreted using the Student Performance Levels (SPLs) and National Reporting System (NRS). The SPLs are descriptors of English language ability across three areas, general language ability, listening comprehension, and oral communication, for non-native adult English language learners. SPLs were initially created by the U.S. Department of Health and Human Services in the mid-1980s and later revised by the Spring Institute in 1998. NRS is a reporting system that provides learning outcomes for federally funded adult education programs in the U.S. developed by the Department of Education in the 1990s.

DEVELOPMENT. The test developers describe BEST Literacy as an update to the Basic English Skills Tests (BEST) that was originally developed in the early 1980s (BEST Literacy technical manual, 2008). The BEST was also developed by the Center for Applied Linguistics, and it consists of two sections (oral interview and literacy skills) that are recommended for use with adults in language education programs in the United States. Specifically, BEST Literacy serves as an update to the literacy section of the BEST. Previous reviews of the BEST suggest that the assessment is "technically strong, normed to an appropriate group, and addresses the typology of situations students will encounter" (Jaynes, 1992, p. 61). The goal of the developers of BEST Literacy was to bring up to date the literacy section of the BEST, while not compromising its psychometric properties.

TECHNICAL. Norms for the test were based on a relatively small sample ($N = 407$) tested at institutions from seven different states across the U.S. Students were mainly native Spanish speakers. In the future, the size of the normative sample should be increased, and the representativeness of the sample should be improved to more closely match the intended population of test takers. One specific technical concern is that the small norm group yields sample sizes for each individual form with fewer than 100 examinees within each form with the exception of Form D. Even though a very robust measurement theory (Rasch model) was used to calibrate and equate the forms, a larger sample would provide more precise information regarding the psychometric quality of the BEST Literacy. Future editions of the technical manual should include information regarding age and gender for the normative group.

Internal consistency estimates of reliability for each of the three forms are high with values of .92 for Form B, .94 for Form C, and .94 for Form D. Interrater reliability estimates for the forms that were double scored (30% of the total) are high for the Reading and Writing sections of the test with estimates ranging from .97 to above .99. Estimates for decision consistency and accuracy support the inference that BEST Literacy does a good job of placing students into the NRS and SPL categories. No information is provided on test-retest reliability and equivalent forms reliability.

The test authors have provided a variety of support from an array of sources to justify the validity of the scores obtained from BEST Literacy. Evidence was provided to support the fact that the test content encompasses the intended topics for assessing adult English language learners' ability to read and write in English.

The test authors indicate that 7 Reading items (3.8% of the total Reading items) were misfitting using the requirements set forth by Linacre (2011). Also, 2 of the 58 Writing items (3.4% of the total Writing items) were found to be misfitting. The revised technical manual should include additional tables summarizing model-data fit to the Rasch model. It would be helpful for potential users to have information on the unstandardized Infit and Outfit statistics, reliability of separation indices, and other commonly reported Rasch-based statistics.

One of the strong advantages of using Rasch measurement is that it provides variable maps that can be used to visually represent the latent variable of English language proficiency. A variable map displays both person and item locations on the latent variable, and the performance standards based on NRS and SPL categories can also be added to increase the interpretive value of the variable maps. The test authors should consider taking full advantage of variable maps in the next version of the test manual. Factor analysis could have also been used to provide additional evidence to support the inferences that there are two constructs (Reading and Writing) in the assessment.

Scale scores are calculated based on a concurrent calibration across the three forms of the BEST Literacy. The test authors should consider using different units for the scaled scores because the current equated scores appear to be indistinguishable to users. This may lead users to simply use the raw scores instead of the equated scale scores.

Teacher judgments of student placements into NRS levels were compared to actual student placements given their scores. The validity coefficients (correlations) were reasonable with values of .62, .64, and .67 for Reading, Writing, and Total scale scores, respectively.

COMMENTARY. The test authors suggest that individuals with very limited English proficiency, and those primarily interested in oral competency, use one of their other products (e.g., BEST Plus). The test authors do not say if BEST Literacy is an ineffective measure for these groups.

The norm group was mainly composed of native Spanish speakers. It is not clear that BEST Literacy provides adequate information for use of the scores with English language learners from other language backgrounds. The test developers claim that the assessment can be used for "English Language Learners," even though insufficient evidence is provided to justify the use of the assessment for nonnative Spanish speakers. Caution should be used when this assessment is administered to nonnative Spanish speakers.

SUMMARY. Overall, it appears that the test authors have accomplished their major goal of updating the literacy section of the BEST with BEST Literacy without negatively impacting its psychometric soundness. The reliability and validity information could be expanded upon to supply potential users with additional information to utilize the assessment for the intended purposes.

REVIEWERS' REFERENCES

Center for Applied Linguistics. (2008). *BEST Literacy: Technical report*. Washington, DC: Authors.

Center for Applied Linguistics, Kenyon, D., Stansfield, C. W., Johnson, D., Grognet, A., & Dreyfus, D. (1988). Basic English Skills Test. Washington, DC: Center for Applied Linguistics.

Jaynes, P. A. (1992). [Review of the Basic English Skills Test.] In J. J. Kramer & J. C. Conoley (Eds.), *The eleventh mental measurements yearbook* (pp. 60-61). Lincoln, NE: Buros Institute of Mental Measurements.

Linacre, J. M. (2011). A user's guide to WINSTEPS MINISTEP Rasch-model computer programs. Chicago, IL: MESA Press.

Review of BEST Literacy by YUANZHONG ZHANG, Faculty, Miami-Dade College, Miami, FL:

DESCRIPTION. Designed by the Center for Applied Linguistics (CAL), a leading professional organization based in Washington, DC, which presumably provides "the single most important source of information on second-and-foreign-language teaching and learning" (Garfinkel, 1992),

BEST Literacy is a competency-based instrument of assessment for adult learners with emerging knowledge of the English language. With three parallel forms labeled as B, C, and D, BEST Literacy focuses on measuring test takers' functional aspects of literacy in authentic, everyday contexts of communication commonly encountered in the U.S.

The current version of the test published in 2008 is composed of 11 language tasks with 7 related to Reading and 4 related to Writing, with a total number of 49 Reading test items, and 29 Writing test items. The test is administered on a group basis, and examinees are required to complete the test within an hour.

DEVELOPMENT. BEST, an acronym that stands for Basic English Skills Test, has a history of almost three decades of application in adult ESL assessment. The older version, released first in 1982, consisted of two sections: the oral interview section that included 49 listening comprehension and speaking items and the literacy skills section that contained 68 items of reading and writing activities (Clark & Grognet, 1985; Eakin & Illyin, 1987). With the goal of retaining "the essential psychometric qualities of the BEST Literacy Skills Section" (manual, p. 43), the current version was field trialed in seven states in the U.S. including AZ, CO, IL, NM, OH, TN, and TX, including the participation of 407 students in the field test. The sample of the field test populations, which represent 30 different native languages with Spanish as the most widely used mother tongue, exemplifies the demographic characteristics of adult learners of English in the U.S.

One of the distinguishing features of BEST Literacy is its accentuation on authenticity in content. The situations and contexts on which BEST draws are of interest and relevance to adults. The Reading tasks, for example, are built on real-life scenarios such as finding a date in the calendar, reading food labels, looking up a phone number in a telephone directory, and so forth. Similarly, the Writing tasks are developed from tapestries that are likely to come across in daily life including filling out a form, writing a personal check, addressing an envelope, and composing notes. Instead of utilizing the discrete-point form, the test items in BEST Literacy are grounded on literacy events in connected contexts. For instance, the Writing task of "filling in personal background form" (manual, p. 18) holds 10 blanks covering various kinds of information. Such a feature of BEST Literacy reveals a constructivist view of literacy as an act of meaning-making rather than decoding, and provides useful guidance for developing ways to teach literacy in meaningful contexts.

TECHNICAL.

Standardization. As a standardized survey test (Dubin, Eskey, & Grabe, 1986) designed to measure the general proficiency of English reading and writing in adults above the age of 16, the technical features of the BEST Literacy include the following four interrelated aspects:

First, the content of the test is standard in all three forms, applying the same format and task types to ensure content equivalence. Utilizing a combination of objective and subject test items, the response formats of BEST Literacy include source-based responses and constructed responses. The source-based responses require test takers to identify the correct answer from given alternatives or clues. The constructed responses include formulaic responses such as provision of personal information in filling out a form, and open-ended free responses such as the writing of a brief note. Second, a detailed procedure of field testing is present including the description of the sampling frame, the definition of measurement scales, the development of norms based on the distribution of scores, and the equating of all forms of the test. Third, the scoring rubrics for each test item are developed. Although the reading tasks are scored either as right or wrong, the writing tasks are graded according to a rubric wherein measurement is based on the quality of response. Fourth, for each individual form of the test, information about the conversion of raw scores into scale scores is provided.

Reliability. The field test shows that internal consistency of BEST Literacy is strikingly high (.92, .94, and .94, for Forms B, C, and D, respectively), and that the interrater reliabilities for the Writing part of the test are extraordinarily strong as well (.97, .97, and .99 for Forms B, C, and D, respectively).

Moreover, the current version of the test has retained the essential traits of its previous version even though they are more than two and a half decades apart from each other in age. The consistency in student performances between the old and new versions of the BEST can be identified from the reported data in the BEST Literacy technical report (2008, pp. 13-22). Based on the comparison of the two sets of the mean (M) scores and the standard deviations (SD) between Reading Old Form B ($M = 32.87$; $SD = 9.36$) and Reading

New Form B (M = 34.88; SD = 9.44), an effect size (d) of .21 is obtained. Similarly, an effect size (d) of .15 is yielded from comparing the two sets of mean scores and the standard deviations between Reading Old Form C (M = 34.54; SD = 10.39) and Reading New Form C (M = 32.96; SD = 11.22). For the writing section, the comparison of Writing Old Form B (M = 19.48; SD = 6.49), and Writing New Form B (M = 21.49; SD = 6.60) results in an effect size (d) of .31. Finally, the comparison of Writing Old Form C (M = 19.93; SD = 6.55) and Writing New Form C (M = 20.57; SD = 6.05) produces an effect size (d) of .10. It is worthy to note that the small values of the effect size emanating from the sets of data sources provided in the Technical Report of BEST Literacy (2008) corroborate the high degree of comparability between the old and new version of the test instrument.

Another significant pattern of reliability is manifested in the statistically negligible variance of students' performance across different forms of the test within the same version. In the old version of BEST, the variance ($F_{(1, 136)}$ = .98) between Reading Form Old B (M = 32.87; SD = 9.36; N = 67) and Reading Form Old C (M = 34.54; SD = 10.39; N = 71) is statistically nonsignificant (p > .05). So is the variance ($F_{(1, 136)}$ = .16) between Writing Form Old B (M = 19.48; SD = 6.49; N = 67), and Writing Form Old C (M = 19.93; SD = 6.55; N = 71). In the current version, the variance ($F_{(2, 226)}$ = 1.01) among Reading New Form B (M = 34.88; SD = 9.44; N = 69), Reading New Form C (M = 32.96; SD = 11.22; N = 71), and Reading New Form D (M = 32.63; SD = 11.22; N = 129) is also statistically nonsignificant (p > .05). Such is also true for the variance ($F_{(2, 226)}$ = 2.26) among Writing New Form B (M = 21.49; SD = 6.60; N = 69), Writing New Form C (M = 20.57; SD = 6.05; N = 70), and Writing New Form D (M = 19.43; SD = 6.94, N = 130).

Validity. Evidence supporting criterion-related validities of BEST test scores is illustrated by a number of measures reported in the BEST Literacy test manual (2008, pp. 44-45) including the moderately strong correlations between scores and teacher ratings ($r_{(New\ Form\ B)}$ = .64, $r_{(New\ Form\ C)}$ = .62; $r_{(New\ Form\ D)}$ = .67), the correlations between scores in the Reading section and those in the Writing section, which range from moderately strong ($r_{(New\ Form\ B)}$ = .66) to strong ($r_{(New\ Form\ C)}$ =.79; $r_{(New\ Form\ D)}$ = .80), and the interscale cross-validation through alignment with the performance descriptors of the ESL Educational Functioning Levels of the National Reporting System (NRS), and with those of the Reading and Writing Student Performance Levels (SPLs). Using the cutoff score approach to designate the performance levels described in the NRS and SPL, the researchers of BEST Literacy have provided a concrete guide for interpreting the scores.

Of course, there are many factors that can affect the reliability and validity of the test. The choice of tasks could be the one major factor that has impacts on the outcomes of students' performance. As noted in the BEST Literacy Technical Report (2008), "only the note-writing tasks on *BEST* Literacy allow students to display the ability to 'write some simple sentences'" (p. 89). Despite the limitations in judging learners' ability to compose extended texts in written communication, the test is overall a useful tool for evaluating adult learners' proficiency of functional literacy in English.

COMMENTARY. The most noticeable strength of BEST Literacy is illuminated in its comprehensible content and practical tasks that motivate learners' purposeful use of written language. As language is acquired primarily through absorption of comprehensible input, which is slightly higher than the learners' current level, and can be understood through the context (Krashen, 1985), the tasks in BEST Literacy offer rich, meaningful sources of comprehensible input by integrating texts and graphics. The friendly personalized contexts of testing help learners to perform at their best possible level by alleviating test anxiety. By focusing on practical, everyday funds of knowledge (Moll & Gonzalez, 2004) of communication, BEST Literacy recognizes that adults' attainment of L2 proficiency is influenced by their L1 proficiency, and capitalizes not only on learners' knowledge about the target language, but also on their knowledge about the culture and experiences including those learned through the first language.

SUMMARY. Like any other standardized test, BEST Literacy relies mainly on objective test items rather than subjective test items such as essay questions that require elaborate thinking and organization. Although it helps to minimize the interference from the influence of the scorers, it constrains, on the other hand, the exposure to dynamic cycles of literacy use and may, therefore, leave out important insights about the attributes it purports to assess. Although the information in some of the test items appears to be dated

(Wigglesworth, 2005), BEST, as its name suggests, is undoubtedly a thoughtfully designed test that assesses adults' ESL literacy at the survival level in the best possible way.

REVIEWER'S REFERENCES

Center for Applied Linguistics. (2008). *BEST Literacy technical report*. Washington, DC: Author.

Center for Applied Linguistics. (2008). *BEST Literacy test manual*. Washington, DC: Author.

Clark, J. D., & Grognet, A. G. (1985). Development and validation of a performance-based test of ESL "survival" skills. In P. C. Hauptman, R. LeBlanc, & M. B. Wesche (Eds.), *Second language performance testing* (pp. 89-110). Ottawa, Canada: University of Ottawa.

Dubin, F., Eskey, D. E., & Grabe, W. (1986). *Teaching second language reading for academic purposes*. Reading, MA: Addison-Wesley.

Eakin, E., & Illyin, D. (1987). Basic English Skills Test. In J. Alderson, K. J. Krahnke, & C. W. Stansfield (Eds.), *Reviews of English language proficiency tests* (pp. 9-10). Washington, DC: Teachers of English to Speakers of Other Languages.

Garfinkel, A. (1992). [Review of the Basic English Skills Test.] In J. J. Kramer & J. C. Conoley (Eds.), *The eleventh mental measurements yearbook* (pp. 59-69). Lincoln, NE: Buros Institute of Mental Measurements.

Krashen, S. D. (1985). *The input hypothesis: Issues and implications*. London, England: Longman.

Moll, L., & Gonzalez, N. (2004). Engaging life: A funds-of-knowledge approach to multicultural education. In J. Banks & C. A. M. Banks (Eds.), *Handbook of research on multicultural education* (2nd ed., pp. 699-715). New York, NY: Jossey-Bass.

Wigglesworth, G. (2005). Basic English Skills Test (BEST). In S. Stoynoff & C. Chapelle (Eds.), *ESOL tests and testing: A resource for teachers and administrators* (pp. 35-37). Alexandria, VA: Teachers of English to Speakers of Other Languages.

[20]

The Brain Injury Rehabilitation Trust Memory and Information Processing Battery.

Purpose: Designed to "assess memory and information processing skills or to detect and/or assess impairments in these skills for either clinical, educational, occupational or research purposes."

Population: Adults.

Publication Date: 2007.

Acronym: BMIPB.

Administration: Individual.

Forms, 4: 1, 2, 3, 4.

Price Data, 2007: £445 per complete battery; £44 per 25 Memory and Learning forms and 25 Speed of Information Processing forms Form 1; £44 per 25 Memory and Learning forms and 25 Speed of Information Processing forms Form 2; £44 per 25 Memory and Learning Forms and 25 Speed of Information Processing forms Form 3; £44 per 25 Memory and Learning forms and 25 Speed of Information Processing forms Form 4.

Time: (45-60) minutes.

Comments: Test authors suggest the assessment be administered by "chartered psychologists with post qualification experience and knowledge of neuropsychology or the psychology of aging."

Authors: Anthony K. Coughlan, Michael Oddy, and John R. Crawford.

Publisher: The Brain Injury Rehabilitation Trust [England].

  a) STORY RECALL.
    Scores, 3: Immediate, Delayed, Retained%.
  b) FIGURE RECALL.
    Scores, 4: Copy%, Immediate%, Delayed%, Retained%.

  c) LIST LEARNING.
    Scores, 4: A1-A5 Total, A6, B, Intrusions.
  d) WORD RECOGNITION.
    Scores, 6: A Words, B Words, Total Word Recognition, List A, List B, Total List Recognition.
  e) DESIGN LEARNING.
    Scores, 4: A1-A5 Total, A6, B, Intrusions.
  f) DESIGN RECOGNITION.
    Scores, 6: Correct Positive, Correct Negative, Recognition Total, Design A Correct, Design B Correct, Identification Total.
  g) SPEED OF INFORMATION PROCESSING.
    Scores, 4: Total, Errors%, Speed, Adjusted Total.

Review of the Brain Injury Rehabilitation Trust Memory and Information Processing Battery by ANDREW S. DAVIS, Associate Professor, and W. HOLMES FINCH, Assistant Professor, Department of Educational Psychology, Ball State University, Muncie, IN:

DESCRIPTION. The Brain Injury Rehabilitation Trust Memory and Information Processing Battery (BMIPB) is a norm-referenced standardized measure of memory and information processing. The tests in the BMIPB are largely derivations of classical measures, but the test authors indicate the test materials are new. The BMIPB has four different forms that are very useful for serial assessments. The test authors note that the BMIPB should take about 45–60 minutes to administer and should be used in the United Kingdom by "chartered psychologists with post qualification experience and knowledge of neuropsychology or the psychology of ageing" (manual, p. 4). The test authors also suggest a similar level of expertise for psychologists outside the United Kingdom.

The BMIPB consists of seven tests: Story Recall, List Learning, Word Recognition, Figure Recall, Design Learning, Design Recognition, and Speed of Information Processing. Experienced practitioners will recognize the format of most of these measures, and the similarity between these tests and other widely used measures helps provide evidence of validity. The second, third, and fourth forms of the test were standardized sequentially using subsamples of the Form 1 sample, and as such, serial administration of the forms should follow their numbered ordering. All four forms provide age-based norms that are derived from the entire sample and Form 1 provides an additional six sets of norms based on age ranges, and Forms 2, 3, and 4 each provide an additional three sets of norms based on age ranges. An interesting component is a computer-scoring program that uses regression-based continuous norms to compare a patient's obtained score with a predicted score based on age and education, with a resulting discrepancy score that is expressed as a T-Score. The computer program assists in measuring changes between administrations by using regression equations to predict the retest score using the patient's initial score and the standardization sample; the difference between the obtained and predicted score is expressed as a T-Score. One issue for consideration when using this program is that the test authors do not provide information regarding the relative accuracy of this regression equation (i.e., percent of variance accounted for by the predictors, age, and education). Thus, although this feature is intriguing, it must be used with some caution.

DEVELOPMENT. The BMIPB was standardized in the United Kingdom and was developed from the Adult Memory and Information Processing Battery (AMIPB; Coughlan & Hollows, 1985), which is the most commonly used memory battery by clinical neuropsychologists in the United Kingdom (Warburg, 2001 as cited in BMIPB test manual). The test authors report that the BMIPB differs in several ways from the AMIPB in that the test materials in the BMIPB are new, the BMIPB has four versions compared to the two in the AMIPB, the BMIPB includes tests of recognition memory, and the BMIPB has one processing speed test whereas the AMIPB has two.

The normative sample consisted of healthy individuals between 16 and 89 years of age. Participants were excluded if they had sensory impairment, drug dependence, or a precluding medical condition, as well as other factors. The sample was also selected based upon educational level in the general population by using U.K. Census data from 2001 and the Labour Force Survey from 2005; the highest age band (75–89) was inferred from the age band of 65–75 years due to "census limitations." The test authors report chi square results that suggest the educational level of the sample did not differ from the Labour Force Survey Data. The normative sample was matched for gender according to the 2001 Census, and chi square data indicated the differences between the normative sample and United Kingdom population did not differ significantly.

The test authors also compared the occupational status of their sample to the general population and found that overall differences were present between the sample and the general population using 11 categories, although when 2 categories

were removed the difference was no longer significant. Estimated IQs were calculated for the sample using the Wechsler Test of Adult Reading (WTAR; Psychological Corporation, 2001) and the National Adult Reading Test (NART; Nelson & Willison, 1991) and the estimated IQs of the sample were close to the population mean. The ethnicity of the sample did not closely match the 2001 Census data, which the test authors attribute to attempting to match the normative sample to the general population for age, educational level, and gender as the "main variables." More specifically, the sample overrepresented the White group and underrepresented others.

Interestingly, the test authors also administered measures of anxiety and depression to the sample and results suggest "there is no good reason to suspect that the normative data for the BMIPB measures are distorted by anxiety or depression" (manual, p. 24). The normative sample for Form 1 consisted of 300 participants divided into four age bands that closely matched the demographics of the general population of the United Kingdom. The normative data for Form 2 were obtained by retesting 100 of the participants from the Form 1 sample 4–12 weeks after they took the Form 1 version. Normative data for Form 3 came from retesting 50 of the participants who took the Form 2 version 4–8 weeks after they took the Form 2 version. Normative data for Form 4 were from the same 50 participants who took the Form 3 version, collected 4–8 weeks later. Appendices in the test manual provide demographic data for the normative samples.

TECHNICAL. The test authors report a series of studies examining the demographics of the sample as they relate to the BMIPB scores. A study using hierarchical multiple regression showed that there was an inverse linear relationship between age and each of the BMIPB subtests. In addition, the test authors found a quadratic relationship between age and several of the BMIPB scores. The nature of this quadratic effect was not explained further, leaving the reader with the knowledge that the relationship was nonlinear but not precisely how the nonlinearity was manifested. They also report that correlations between BMIPB scores and educational level were small (.13 to .36) but significant at the .001 level for all the scores except for Story Recall Retained%, which was significant at the .05 level. Gender differences were not found for the BMIPB scores aside from a small difference on List Learning A1-A5 with females performing slightly better than males. Occupational status was ranked and correlated with BMIPB scores using Spearman's rho, revealing significant correlation coefficients for 9 of the 10 scores at the .05 level. Correlation coefficients were obtained between the two measures of estimated IQ and BMIPB scores, and none were above .30; this finding led the test authors to suggest that estimated premorbid IQs may not be useful for measures of memory and information processing.

In addition to examining relationships between the BMIPB and several demographic factors, the test authors also reported reliability estimates. They first assessed the interrater reliability of Form 1 for components of the instrument that must be scored subjectively. They selected a sample of 30 individuals whose verbal responses were audiotaped from the Story Recall, List Learning, and List Recognition tests. The examiner and a research assistant subsequently scored the entire test independently of one another, including these verbal components. A Pearson's correlation coefficient was then calculated between the two sets of ratings for each of the subtest scores, with values of .90 for the subjective measures and 1.0 for the objective scoring. The test authors report that differences in ratings on the Story Recall task were due to the recordings and not due to interpretation, whereas variations on Figure Recall were due to differences in interpretation by the raters. It should be noted that no elaboration regarding difficulties with the recordings was provided.

The test authors also estimated test-retest reliability using two different samples. First, data were compared from 22 individuals who were given Form 1 twice with a 1-month separation between administrations. The test authors found correlation coefficients between the scores ranging from -.14 to .94. The majority of these correlations were positive and larger than .50, while the correlation of -.14 was for the Story Recall Retained%. In addition, data from the norming sample of 100 individuals who took Form 1 first and then were retested with Form 2 were also used to estimate test-retest reliability. The correlation coefficients for this second study were higher, ranging in value from .13 to .89, with only that of Story Recall Retained% (.13) below .50.

In addition to assessing the reliability of the instrument, the test authors were concerned with quantifying potential practice effects for the BMIPB, as four forms were designed to allow for repeated use with the same individuals over time. The test authors report on five different studies that were used to assess the impact of practice effects. These studies were designed as follows: (a) Individuals were tested on Form 1 twice (1 to 3 months apart) to quantify the size of retest effects using the same form; (b) One group was given only Form 2 at one point in time, while the other group was given both Forms 1 and 2 taken 1 to 3 months apart. The purpose of this study was to ascertain whether practice effects occur as the result of taking different forms of the BMIPB; (c) One group of examinees was given Form 1 while another matched group was given Form 2 and the results were compared. This study was designed to help ascertain the degree to which the two forms were equivalent without introducing practice effects; (d) One group of individuals were given Forms 1 and 2, 3 months apart, with scores compared against a second group who were given the two forms 6 months apart, in order to quantify the length of practice effects; (e) Performance on Forms 1 and 2 was compared for the 100 individuals in the norming sample.

Results of these studies demonstrated that (a) there were strong practice effects when the same form was given with a 1-month separation, (b) the use of different forms largely eliminates this practice effect, (c) Forms 1 and 2 did not yield significantly different mean scores for the matched groups of individuals, (d) there were no significant differences in change scores between the 3-month and 6-month delay groups, suggesting that practice effects are not greater for the shorter intervals, and (e) there were no significant differences in mean scores between Forms 1 and 2 for individuals both given with a 3-month gap between administrations, suggesting the absence of practice effects.

COMMENTARY. The BMIPB is a well-designed measure of memory and information processing. A strength of the test is that it was designed with serial assessment in mind, using four separate forms of the test to help cope with practice effects and it will be prudent to use these multiple forms in sequential order. The test authors provide evidence from empirical studies, described above, that was able to quantify the practice effects. The test authors also provide good details of their normative sample including age, gender, educational level, and occupational status that by and large appears representative of the United Kingdom general population.

The test manual does a nice job explaining how to administer and score the tests. Examiners familiar with memory assessments will be able to use the BMIPB easily. Examiners will appreciate the detailed scoring instructions and rubric for Story Recall and Figure Recall. The test manual does not provide an interpretation section, but this should not be a problem for experienced practitioners as the tests should be familiar to those who are used to memory and processing speed tests. Norm-referenced scores are available for all four forms via cutoffs associated with seven specific percentile ranks (2, 5, 10, 25, 50, 75, and 90). Multiple scores are available for each of the seven tests that results in a total of 31 scores. Overall composite scores are not included and interpretation is done at the subtest level. Standard scores are not provided and no explanation was given regarding why they are absent.

In terms of the technical qualities of the instrument, what is reported is quite good. Reliability estimates for the samples included in the various studies were generally high. The test authors offer a convincing argument with regard to the absence of practice effects when the instrument is administered as intended. It would have been helpful had interrater reliability been investigated through the use of Generalizability Theory, although certainly the correlations were informative. Perhaps the only troubling aspect of the technical reporting for the BMIPB was that limited evidence supporting the validity of test score use was presented. Although it seems clear that the instrument provides consistent scores across raters and time, there is little information regarding how well the BMIPB measures what is intended. Indeed, there was a dearth not only of technical validity evidence, but even of information regarding content validity.

SUMMARY. The BMIPB represents a good addition to the lexicon of memory tests and provides updated norms for classic well-validated memory and information processing speed tests. The test authors were quite diligent in crafting their normative sample by considering age, gender, educational level, and occupational status; unfortunately, the normative sample was not quite representative of the United Kingdom population in terms of ethnicity. A primary strength of the BMIPB is inclusion of three additional forms that will be useful in serial assessment with the test authors considering the implications of practice effects. At this point there do not seem to be any validity studies that have

been conducted with the BMIPB. Although many of the scores will have some inherent validity as the tests are adaptations of well-validated measures, users may like to see that the new materials on the BMIPB follow the pattern of sound psychometrics present on other frequently used memory and processing speed tests.

REVIEWERS' REFERENCES
Coughlan, A. K., & Hollows, S. E. (1985). The Adult Memory and Information Processing Battery (AMIPB). Leeds, UK: St. James's University Hospital.
Nelson, H. E., & Willison, J. (1991). The National Adult Reading Test (NART): Test manual (2nd ed.). Windsor, UK: NFER Nelson.
Psychological Corporation. (2001). Wechsler Test of Adult Reading (WTAR). San Antonio, TX: Psychological Corporation.
Warburg, R. (2001). Assessment of memory problems by clinical neuropsychologists. Thesis submitted in partial fulfillment of degree of Doctorate in Clinical Psychology, University of Wales.

Review of the Brain Injury Rehabilitation Trust Memory and Information Processing Battery by STEPHEN J. FREEMAN, Professor, Department of Psychology, Counseling, & Special Education, Texas A&M University-Commerce, Commerce, TX:

DESCRIPTION AND DEVELOPMENT. The Brain Injury Rehabilitation Trust Memory and Information Processing Battery (BMIPB) is an individually administered measure of memory and information processing skills (individuals ages 16–89) that may be used to assess impairments in these skills for clinical, educational, occupational, or research purposes. The BMIPB was developed from the Adult Memory and Information Processing Battery (AMIBP; Coughlan & Hollows, 1985). According to the BMIPB authors, "the goal of the test is to provide a new test which retains but extends the popular format of the AMIPB, which has up-to-date and more extensive normative data, and which makes use of developments in psychometric methods" (manual, p. 5).

There are four parallel forms of the BMIPB each comprising seven subtests: Immediate and Delayed Story Recall, which is structured similarly to the Wechsler Memory Scale-IV Logical Memory Test; List Learning A and B, where List A is a 15-word list read to the examinee and recalled from memory with a discontinuation rule of 5; it is followed by List B, an interference trial. List B is a 15-word List with only one administration followed by a final recall attempt of list A; Word Recognition is a two-item forced-choice task of visual recognition of the 30 words comprising the list learning task; Immediate and Delayed Figure Recall; Design Learning A and B, where Design A is a 9-line design to be reproduced from memory, repeating the procedure until the design is reproduced accurately or five attempts have been made, followed by one attempt to reproduce Design B and then another attempt to reproduce Design A; Design Recognition requires recognition of the two previous designs (A & B) in a group of 40 designs; Speed of Information Processing requires the performance of cancellation tasks and a motor speed cancellation task.

The administration and scoring manual provides instructions that are clear and easy to follow. Directions for administration and scoring include examples of allowable prompts and scoring. For examinee clarification, demonstration, or sample items are provided prior to the start of several subtests. Percentile ranks are reported for each measure and age group on each form.

TECHNICAL. The norming sample for the BMIPB consisted of 300 male and female participants from the U.K. ranging in age from 16 to 89 years. A list of exclusion criteria included in the test manual (e.g., medical and/or psychological issues) was used to disqualify participants from the normative sample. The test manual describes attempts to ensure normative sample representativeness to the U.K. Census report matched on age, education, gender, and ethnicity (97.3% of participants were white). Geographic representation was reported as not important and limited to the South East of England. The test manual reports normative data for Form 1 was obtained from 300 participants. Normative data for Forms 2, 3, and 4 were obtained by sequential retesting of a subset of participants from the original 300 participants (Form 2 $N = 100$ selected from Form 1 participants, Form 3 $N = 50$ selected from Form 2 participants, Form 4 $N = 50$ retested participants from Form 3). The sample was subdivided into six age bands for Form 1: 16–29, 30–44, 45–60, 60–70, 61–89, and 71–89. The rationale for overlap in age bands was not explained. Age bands for Forms 2, 3, and 4 were 16–40, 41–60, and 61–79. The different age bands are reportedly due to the number of participants assessed on each form. A CD accompanying the test material is reported "as an alternative to, and extension of, the norm tables a program, BMIPB_Score.exe, is available that provides continuous regression based norms" (manual, p. 11).

The test manual reports three measures of reliability: interrater, test-retest, and parallel or alternate forms. The reliability coefficient for interrater reliability for subjective scoring was reported as .90. Test-retest reliability coefficients were reported for Story Recall, Figure Recall, List Learning, Design Learning and Speed of Information Processing (SoIP) on Forms 1 ($N = 22$, time interval 1 month). Coefficients for Form 1 ranged from .94 (SoIP) to Story Recall Immediate .44, Delayed .37, and -.14 Retained%. Test-retest (alternate form) coefficients for Form 1 and 2 ($N = 100$, time interval 1 to 3 months) ranged from .89 (SoLP) to Story Recall Immediate .67, Delayed .74, and .13 Retained%. The test authors acknowledge Story Recall Retained% is not a useful indicator and recommend it not be used. Similar caution is offered for Figure Recall Retained%. Equivalency of Forms 1 and 2 was reported using 33 participants from the Form 1 sample with 33 graphically matched participants taking Form 2 without prior testing on Form 1. No significant differences in difficulty were reported. The test authors report a potential for small but practically insignificant practice effect simply due to the experience of the examinee taking the instrument a second time. No estimates of internal consistency were reported. The test manual was mute regarding validity of BMIPB test score use with no evidence reported or discussed.

COMMENTARY. According to the test manual, the BMIPB "provides normative data for a sample of adults within the U.K. on various tests of memory and information processing" (manual, p. 4). The percentages of the U.K. population according to the 2001 Census and the normative sample according to age, gender, and educational level were proportional. The normative sample was small and spuriously skewed with white participants being overrepresented (> 97%) and sampling was geographically limited. Estimates of reliability included interrater, test-retest, and alternate forms reliability. Equivalence of Form 1 and 2 was reported using two groups of matched pairs. Oddly, data related to internal consistency reliability were conspicuously absent from the test manual. Similarly, data supporting the validity of test score use were in short supply.

SUMMARY. The BMIPB is an attractive, physically well-constructed test battery with very good face validity. However, significant criticism can be made regarding the demographic information presented on the normative sample as well as its size. The concept of unitary validity is defined as "the degree to which evidence and theory supports the interpretation of test scores" (American Educational Research Association, American Psychological Association, & National Council on Measurement in Education, 1999). Impara (2010), writing in *The*

Eighteenth Mental Measurements Yearbook, posited "validity evidence is the sine qua non required for the use of any test" (p. 818). The lack of validity evidence for BMIPB scores–essential to evaluate the appropriateness of the intended score interpretations–makes it impossible to support its use.

The test manual reports that the BMIPB's predecessor, the AMIPB, is the most frequently used memory battery by neuropsychologists in the U.K. and the goal of the test authors was to provide an updated instrument making use of developments in psychometric methods (manual, p. 5). With this in mind, the BMIPB does warrant further research in order to continue its development and to establish its validity as a clinical diagnostic tool consistent with the standards set forth in the 1999 *Standards for Educational and Psychological Testing* (AERA, APA, & NCME). The potential usefulness of the BMIPB will be contingent on the outcome of this research. Until such supportive research is forthcoming, use of the BMIPB cannot be recommended.

REVIEWER'S REFERENCES

American Educational Research Association, American Psychological Association, & National Council on Measurement in Education. (1999). *Standards for educational and psychological testing.* Washington, DC: American Educational Research Association.

Coughlin, A. K., & Hollows, S. E. (1985). The Adult Memory and Information Processing Battery (AMIPB). Leeds, U.K.: St. James's University Hospital.

Impara, J. C. (2010). Assessing the validity of test scores. In R. A. Spies, J. F. Carlson, & K. F. Geisinger (Eds.), *The eighteenth mental measurements yearbook* (pp. 817-823). Lincoln, NE: Buros Institute of Mental Measurements.

[21]

BRIGANCE® Comprehensive Inventory of Basic Skills II.

Purpose: Designed to compare "a student's mastery of various skills to those of other students around the country" and can be completed "as part of a battery to determine eligibility for special education services."

Publication Dates: 1976-2010.

Acronym: CIBS-II.

Administration: Individual.

Price Data, 2010: $339 per classroom kit including Reading/ELA and Math Inventory, 20 record books, and 1 canvas tote; $249 per Standardized Inventory including assessments, Standardization and Validation manual (2010, 152 pages), and 20 record books; $49 per Standardization and Validation manual; $35 per 10 record books; $329 per 100 record books.

Authors: Brian F. French and Frances Page Glascoe.

Publisher: Curriculum Associates.

Cross References: For reviews by Gregory J. Cizek and Mary J. McLellan of an earlier edition, see 14:51; see also T5:340 (1 reference); for reviews by Craig N. Mills and Mark E. Swerdlik of the original edition, see 9:162.

a) READINESS ASSESSMENTS.

Population: Ages 5-0 to 6-11.

Scores, 40: 21 Task Scores (Personal Data Response, Identifies Body Parts, Understands Directional and Positional Concepts, Standing Gross-Motor Skills, Walking Gross-Motor Skills, Prints Uppercase Letters in Sequence, Prints Personal Data, Writes Numerals in Sequence, Readiness for Reading, Knows Common Signs, Oral Expression, Reads Lowercase Letters, Rote Counting, Understands Quantitative Concepts, Counts Objects, Reads Numerals, Articulation–Initial Sounds of Words, Articulation–Final Sounds of Words, Auditory Discrimination, Identifies Initial Consonants in Spoken Words, Sounds of Letters), 13 Supplemental Task Scores (Recognizes Colors, Self-Help Skills, Running and Skipping Gross-Motor Skills, Draws a Person, Visual Motor Skills–Forms, Prints Lowercase Letters in Sequence, Prints Uppercase Letters Dictated, Prints Lowercase Letters Dictated, Reads Lowercase Letters, Visual Discrimination–Forms/ Letters/and Words, Recites Alphabet, Joins Sets, Numeral Comprehension), and 6 Composite Scores (General Knowledge and Language, Gross-Motor Skills, Graphomotor and Writing Skills, Reading, Math, Phonemic Awareness.

Time: (60) minutes.

b) FIRST-GRADE THROUGH SIXTH-GRADE ASSESSMENTS.

Forms, 2: Form A (Pretest), Form B (Post Test).

Population: Ages 7-0 to 12-0.

Scores, 16: 9 Task Scores (Word Recognition Grade-Placement Test, Word Analysis Survey, Reading Vocabulary Comprehension Grade-Placement Test, Comprehends Passages, Computational Skills Grade-Placement Test, Problem Solving Grade-Placement Test, Spelling Grade-Placement Test, Sentence- Writing Grade-Placement Test, Listening Vocabulary Comprehension Grade-Placement Test), 2 Supplemental Task Scores (Warning and Safety Signs, Warning Labels), and 5 Composite Scores (Basic Reading, Reading Comprehension, Math, Written Expression, Listening Comprehension).

Time: (45-60) minutes.

Review of the BRIGANCE® Comprehensive Inventory of Basic Skills II by JENNIFER N. MAHDAVI, Associate Professor of Special Education, Sonoma State University, Rohnert Park, CA:

DESCRIPTION. Now in its third version, the BRIGANCE Comprehensive Inventory of Basic Skills II (CIBS-II) has long been a popular tool for special educators for use as a criterion-referenced assessment of fundamental academic skills. With the previous version, the CIBS-R, standardization and norm-referencing were added to better compare an individual student's performance with same-age peers. The CIBS-II updates the previous norms and adds new assessments.

The CIBS-II consists of two large binders of assessments covering Reading, English/Language Arts (ELA), Mathematics, and Academic Readiness. Administering prescribed subscales yields norm-referenced composite scores in Phonemic Awareness, Mathematics Readiness, Basic Reading, Reading Comprehension, Mathematics, Written Expression, and Listening Comprehension. There are also timed measures in Math, Writing, and Reading that may be used to determine whether students use an appropriate amount of time to complete basic tasks. In addition, there are two different record books to use, one for administering the CIBS-II in a standardized way and one for evaluating a larger number of basic skills.

For those who wish to use the CIBS-II as a purely criterion-referenced measure, directions for grade-based starting points and administration of each probe are offered in the binders. The CIBS-II is standardized, with two forms available, and is estimated to require 45–60 minutes to administer. There are 34 probes in the standardized readiness battery and 11 in the first through sixth grade battery; however, the test administrator may choose to give fewer measures. Basal (2 to 5 consecutive correct items) and ceiling (3 to 5 consecutive correct items) rules are described in the manual. These rules seem to be an improvement over the ones in the CIBS-R (Cizek, 2001), although the authors still do not describe how the basal and ceiling rules were established.

Raw scores can be converted to scaled scores (mean = 10, SD = 3) with confidence intervals, percentile ranges, and age and grade equivalents; scaled scores for some measures can be combined to create composite scores. For some broad measures, standard scores (mean = 100, SD = 15) are available. Conversions from raw to derived scores can be made by using the tables in the appendix of the manual or by entering the raw scores into a free online calculator. The manual describes how to interpret these scores, as well as provides cautions about using grade or age equivalents. Brigance also offers a fee-based online management system in which teachers may store scores for analysis and progress monitoring.

DEVELOPMENT. French and Glascoe write that Albert Brigance, the developer of the original CIBS in the 1970s, "thought it best for educators to know exactly which letters of the alphabet a child could name or decode, because such information is essential for effective teaching"

(2010, p. iv). This focus on criterion-referenced assessments, which can be used to determine the depth and breadth of students' skills, is maintained in the CIBS-II. The assumption is that the different subscales can be selectively used to assess student skill levels and plan individualized instruction based on that information.

There have been several additions to this version of the assessment. Measures that assess processing speed are included so that problems with skill mastery can be differentiated from problems with fact retrieval. Reading comprehension measures have been made longer and items have been added to assess more complex skills, such as inference and figurative language. The Writing section now includes prompts for different genres of compositions.

Little information is provided in the manual or binder about construct definitions or item development. The Reading/ELA assessments are said to reflect state standards and the Math assessments to be keyed to the National Council of Teachers of Mathematics strands. These assertions are not substantiated. Pilot testing of new items does not appear to have been conducted.

TECHNICAL.

Standardization. The norm sample was selected to represent U.S. Census data from 2007 as well as National Center for Education Statistics Core of Common Data from 2006-2007. Teachers in 97 schools in 22 U.S. states were asked to select students that fit various criteria. The participants were stratified by region, socioeconomic status, parental education level, gender, and ethnicity. The samples appear to be adequate, with 383 children 5-7 years old participating in the readiness assessments and 1,411 in the first-sixth grade ones. Young children with more educated parents were intentionally overrepresented due to projections that U.S. adults will be attaining higher levels of education over the next 15 years. However, the age categories were not evenly distributed, with 149 participants 12 years of age as a low number, to 270 participants 11 years of age. There is no reason offered for these differences.

Although the CIBS-II is very commonly used by special education teachers to monitor the progress of children with disabilities, there is no information in the manual about how many children with disabilities participated in the norming process, nor about the general ability stratification of the sample.

Reliability. For standardization and reliability purposes, teachers assessed their own students in their own classrooms, a practice that reflects the way the CIBS-II is designed to be used. The reliability of internal scaled and composite scores was measured using the Cronbach's alpha statistic, where this reviewer might consider .80 acceptable. On the CIBS-II, alpha coefficients range between .58 and .97. Generally, as expected, internal consistency reliability is higher on composites obtained by older children. Standard errors of measurement (*SEM*) were also calculated, based on the Cronbach's alpha coefficients, and the *SEM*s are relatively small. This indicates that a child's "true" test score is likely to be near the score obtained on a measure on a particular day.

Test-retest reliability measures were not conducted for the CIBS-II because this version of the test "was not altered in a sufficient manner to require stability to be examined again" (French & Glascoe, 2010, p. 62). Test-retest reliability statistics from the CIBS-R are reported; a critique of these was offered in the *Mental Measurements Yearbook* review of this test (Cizek, 2001). Alternate-forms score reliability was tested with the original CIBS-II and appeared to be adequate, but these reliabilities have not been updated.

Validity. To determine whether CIBS-II standardized composites had construct validity, several types of analyses were conducted. Confirmatory factor analyses indicated that the composites were valid; however, some scales had higher than expected intercorrelations with others (such as Phoneme Awareness with Math), which may indicate that there is greater overlap among subscales than intended. Correlations among subscales within composites were statistically significant. Differential item functioning analyses concluded that students from different demographic groups had similar performance on the CIBS-II measures.

In terms of concurrent validity with other commonly used assessments, the CIBS-II for elementary grades is moderately correlated with achievement tests such as the Nevada Criterion-Referenced Test, Michigan Education Assessment Program (MEAP), and the TerraNova. The readiness assessments are moderately correlated with the Dynamic Indicators of Basic Early Literacy Skills (DIBELS). The aptitude test Wechsler Intelligence Scale for Children-IV (WISC-IV) also has low to moderate correlations with the elementary composite scores.

Although the manual for the CIBS-II reports on several kinds of validity, most of the validation studies were small (44 students on the DIBELS, 55 on the MEAP, and 104 on the WISC-IV). Content validity is discussed in the manual in one paragraph that refers the reader back to previous versions of the test.

COMMENTARY AND SUMMARY. The CIBS-II is most useful in determining areas of relative strength or weakness in basic academic skills for children in Grades K-9, in discovering specific skills that a child has mastered, and in comparing a child's progress to a normative sample. Results from the CIBS-II may be used to write Individualized Education Plan goals, plan instruction specifically targeted to a child's needs, and monitor progress toward skill mastery.

As a norm-referenced, standardized measure, the CIBS-II offers questionable technical adequacy. Although the norming group is adequate, the level of statistical analysis regarding internal relations among test components is extreme in the face of limited examination of basic validity and reliability statistics. There is little discussion of a theoretical model or of current research considered in revising items or about test construction. Although there are claims in the manual that content in this version of this measure were updated, the precise nature of these updates is not clear. Using the CIBS-II to compare students to same-aged peers is possible; however, there are other individualized measures, such as the Woodcock-Johnson III and the Wechsler Individualized Achievement Tests–Revised, that provide more information and more rigorous psychometrics.

The strength of the CIBS-II is its utility as a criterion-referenced measure, which is user-friendly, flexible, and instructionally relevant. Its many short, sharply focused probes can measure progress over time in areas such as "reads words with common endings" and "addition of fractions and mixed numbers." As a Comprehensive Inventory of Basic Skills, this test lives up to its name and will continue to be a welcome tool for teachers, especially special educators.

REVIEWER'S REFERENCES

Cizek, G. J. (2001). [Review of the BRIGANCE® Diagnostic Comprehensive Inventory of Basic Skills, Revised.] In B. S. Plake & J. C. Impara (Eds.), *The fourteenth mental measurements yearbook.* Retrieved from the Buros Institute's Test Reviews Online website: http://www.unl.edu/buros.

French, B. F., & Glascoe, F. P. (2010). *Brigance: Comprehensive Inventory of Basic Skills II: Standardization and validation manual.* North Billerica, MA: Curriculum Associates, Inc.

Review of the BRIGANCE® Comprehensive Inventory of Basic Skills II by CONNIE T. ENGLAND, Professor, Graduate Counseling & Guidance, Lincoln Memorial University, Knoxville, TN:

DESCRIPTION. The examiner manual states that the BRIGANCE® Comprehensive Inventory of Basic Skills-II (CIBS-II) is designed to compare "a student's mastery of various skills to those of other students around the country" (p. 1) and can be completed "as part of a battery to determine eligibility for special education services" (p. 2). The CIBS-II provides a 152-page standardization and validation manual, 20 student record books (student record book for the CIBS-II and student record book for the CIBS-II Standardized), and two binders containing all assessment stimuli. The binders' easel design allows for convenient test administration with testing procedures located on the examiner side of each page. Classroom teachers, special education teachers, psychologists, occupational and physical therapists, and speech-language pathologists are listed as potential users of the CIBS-II. Special examiner qualifications include: familiarity with directions and scoring procedures, practiced administration prior to testing a student, and if planning to use the standardized scoring, ability to strictly adhere to directions accompanying each assessment. The authors note that nonstandardized versions of assessments should be used only for probing of prerequisite skills and, therefore, invalidate normative comparisons.

DEVELOPMENT. The authors support the normative structure of the CIBS-II by identifying the following important changes to the CIBS-R. The CIBS-II Standardized uses individual assessment raw scores to create cumulative frequencies (with 6-month intervals for ages 5 to 11 years, and a 1-year interval for age 12), with subtests producing smoothed normalized scaled scores having a mean of 10 and a standard deviation of 3. Broad areas are created by totaling subtest scores to produce composite quotient scores (for composites with more than one subtest) that are converted to sums yielding quotients with a mean of 100 and a standard deviation of 15. Appendices A and B equate raw scores for first through sixth grade assessments eliminating separate norms for each form; and, although no direct conversions between the CIBS-II and earlier versions were conducted, the authors maintain the CIBS-II may provide "approximate improvement" information for use with earlier versions. Basal, ceiling, and entry points

are indicated on student record forms. For answers provided by parents' or guardians' responses, only "yes" responses are indicated in the record book. Standardized scores are provided for the Readiness and first through sixth grade assessments. Raw scores are used to compute composites and derived scores are reported for scaled scores, percentiles, and grade/age equivalents.

The CIBS-II record book is divided into two broad categories: Reading/ELA and Mathematics. The Reading subgroups include Readiness, Speech, Listening, Word Recognition (used for grade placement), Oral Reading, Reading Comprehension (short passages), Reading Comprehension (long passages), Word Analysis for Forms A & B (that include auditory discrimination of long/short vowels and final consonants, blends, common endings, digraphs and diphthongs, phonetic irregularities, suffixes, prefixes and syllabication), Functional Word Recognition, Spelling, Writing, and Responding to Writing Prompts. The Mathematics subtests include Math Grade Placement tests, Numbers and Operations, Algebra, Geometry, Measurement, and Data Collection and Probability.

The CIBS-II manual states that bilingual students were included in the standardization process and outlines adaptations for bilingual or non-English-speaking students. Adaptations are also given for students with the following exceptionalities: motor impairment, hearing impairment or deafness, visual impairment or blindness, severe speech impairment, emotional disturbance and behavior problems, significant health problems, autism and other developmental delays, traumatic brain injury, intellectual difficulties, and possible giftedness and academic talent.

Guidelines for extrapolating scores for students substantially above or below age norms for the CIBS-II Standardized are also provided. Examiners are cautioned that although quotients and scaled scores can be computed, the use of derived score tables in the Appendices tends to produce extreme results at the highest and lowest ends of the quotient range. The manual also provides guidance on interpreting CIBS-II Standardized scores and outlines the use of the record book in pre/posttesting and in program evaluation. Record books are designed to be reused with each student to track progress and to monitor the effectiveness of instruction or to detect sensory deficits, emergence of health problems, or adverse changes in psychosocial risk status.

Standardization of the CIBS-II included 383 students for the Readiness subtests and 1,411 for first through sixth grade subtests. Students from across the country were tested by teachers assessing their own pupils and by school psychologists. The authors suggest that the equivalency of Forms A and B reflects favorably on the clarity of administration guidelines and provides certainty that different examiners using the standardized procedures will provide similar assessment results.

TECHNICAL. Earlier reviews of the CIBS and CIBS-R (Cizek, 2001; McKellan, 2001; Mills, 1985; and Swerdlik, 1985) recommend using these instruments for skill acquisition measurement, not for normative comparisons. French and Glascoe (the authors of the CIBS-II standardization and validation manual) counter these earlier criticisms by providing revised normative sampling data, and additional reliability and validity evidence to support the normative capabilities of the CIBS-II Standardized.

Reliability estimates for the CIBS-II Standardized reveal what this reviewer considers low internal consistency alpha coefficients. The authors assert that the CIBS-II's orientation toward measurement of skill sets based on criterion referencing rather than on their degree of discriminating power account for the lower internal consistency values. Of the total sample, 41 students in kindergarten through sixth grade were examined to provide test-retest reliability estimates. The manual also includes CIBS-R test-retest correlations asserting that the CIBS-II was not substantially altered from previous standardization sampling making extensive reassessment of test stability unwarranted. Although alternate-form reliabilities for the CIBS-II are reported as high, only 10% of the sampling population was tested using both versions.

Criterion-referenced validity studies with other achievement measures (i.e., Dynamic Indicators of Basic Early Literacy Skills [DIBELS], Nevada CRT, Michigan Educational Assessment Program [MEAP], TerraNova, and with one ability measure, the Wechsler Intelligence Scale for Children-IV) revealed moderate to weak correlations, with strongest correlations found between the TerraNova and CIBS-II Reading scores (.63) and weakest relationships found across Mathematics assessments (.28). Despite high interfactor correlations on certain subscales the authors support their five-factor test structure (Basic Reading, Reading Comprehension, Math, Written Expression, and Listening Comprehension) as providing the best fit for the standardization sample.

COMMENTARY. Overall, a credit of the CIBS-II is its continuing efforts to provide guidance with sequencing of skill sets suitable for classroom implementation or IEP development. Unfortunately, as a norm-referenced measure, it fails. Exploratory factor analysis of all nine subtests reveals high intercorrelations among five subtests implying a lack of a particular dimensional structure, making normative comparisons of factor quotients questionable.

Composite scores from the CIBS-II appear to be suitable for such low stakes uses as monitoring student progress, identifying strengths and weaknesses, or setting learning goals. However, questions about the plausible existence of more complex interpretations of subtest scores render the composite score structure unsuitable for such high stakes uses as qualifying students for placement in special education courses or for accountability reporting (Breidenbach, 2009, p. 88).

SUMMARY. The overarching criticism of the CIBS, and the CIBS–R, continues to plague the current CIBS-II Standardized version. Without overwhelming empirical support for the five-factor composite score structure, the CIBS-II Standardized lacks sufficient evidence to support its norm-referencing ability or for use in determining eligibility for special education services.

REVIEWER'S REFERENCES

Breidenbach, D. H. (2009). *A factor analytic study of the internal structure of the Brigance Comprehensive Inventory of Basic Skills–II.* Retrieved from ProQuest Digital Dissertations (UMI 3382079)

Cizek, G. J. (2001). [Review of the BRIGANCE® Diagnostic Comprehensive Inventory of Basic Skills, Revised.] In B. S. Plake & J. C. Impara (Eds.), *The fourteenth mental measurement yearbook* [Electronic version]. Retrieved June 1, 2011, from Buros Institute's Test Reviews Online website: http://www.unl.edu/buros.

McLellan, M. J. (2001). [Review of the BRIGANCE® Diagnostic Comprehensive Inventory of Basic Skills, Revised.] In B. S. Plake & J. C. Impara (Eds.), *The fourteenth mental measurement yearbook* [Electronic version]. Retrieved June 1, 2011, from Buros Institute's Test Reviews Online website: http://www.unl.edu/buros.

Mills, C. N. (1985). [Review of the BRIGANCE® Diagnostic Comprehensive Inventory of Basic Skills.] In J. V. Mitchell, Jr. (Ed.), *The ninth mental measurements yearbook* [Electronic version]. Retrieved June 1, 2011, from Buros Institute's Test Reviews Online website: http://www.unl.edu/buros.

Swerdlik, M. E. (1985). [Review of the BRIGANCE® Diagnostic Comprehensive Inventory of Basic Skills.] In J. V. Mitchell, Jr. (Ed.), *The ninth mental measurements yearbook* [Electronic version]. Retrieved June 1, 2011, from Buros Institute's Test Reviews Online website: http://www.unl.edu/buros.

[22]

BRIGANCE® Inventory of Early Development II.

Purpose: Designed to "determine readiness for school; track developmental progress; provide a range of scores needed for documenting eligiblity for special education services; enable a comparison of children's skills within and across developmental domains/skill areas in order to view strengths and weaknesses; determine entry points for instruction;[and]assist with program evaluation."

Population: Developmental ages birth to age 7.
Publication Dates: 1978-2010.
Acronym: IED II.
Scores, 22: Physical Development: Fine-Motor Subdomain (Drawing/Visual Motor, Writing, Total), Physical Development: Gross-Motor Subdomain (Nonlocomotor, Locomotor, Total), Total Physical Development Domain/Skill Area, Language Development: Receptive Subdomain (Nouns and Early Listening, Actions, Total), Language Development: Expressive Subdomain (Isolated Skills, Contextual Skills, Total), Total Language Development Domain/Skill Area, Academic/Cognitive: Mathematical/General Concepts Subdomain (Mathematical/General Concepts), Academic/ Cognitive: Literacy Subdomain (Literacy), Total Academic/Cognitive Domain/Skill Area, Daily Living Domain/Skill Area (Self-Help, Prevocational, Total), Total Social and Emotional Development Domain/Skill Area, Total Adaptive Behavior.
Administration: Individual.
Price Data, 2012: $299 per classroom kit including Inventory of Early Development II, 20 record books, testing accessories kit (blocks, scissors, and other manipulatives), canvas tote; $299 per standardized kit including standardized assessments, 20 standardized record books, testing accessories kit (blocks, scissors, and other manipulatives), standardization and validation manual (2010, 250 pages), and canvas tote; $329 per 100 record books; $35 per per 10 record books.
Time: (20-25) minutes.
Comments: Previous edition was entitled BRIGANCE Diagnostic Inventory of Early Development-II.
Author: Frances Page Glascoe.
Publisher: Curriculum Associates, Inc.
Cross References: For reviews by Andrew S. Davis and W. Holmes Finch and by Lauren R. Barton and Donna Spiker of the previous edition, see 17:31; for reviews by C. Dale Carpenter and Douglas A. Penfield of an earlier edition, see 12:326; see also T4:2256 (3 references); for reviews by Stephen J. Bagnato and Elliot L. Gory of an earlier edition, see 9:164.

Review of the BRIGANCE® Inventory of Early Development II by ABIGAIL BAXTER, Associate Professor of Special Education, University of South Alabama, Mobile, AL:

DESCRIPTION. The BRIGANCE® Inventory of Early Development is composed of two instruments: the BRIGANCE Inventory of Early Development II (IED II) and the BRIGANCE Inventory of Early Development II Standardized (IED IIS). Both are for use with children under the age of 7 years. The IED II, a criterion-referenced measure, assesses children's physical, language, and social-emotional development, literacy, mathematical understanding, and daily living skills. The

individual items are arranged within a large binder into "key skill areas": Preambulatory Motor Skills, Gross-Motor Skills, Fine-Motor Skills, Language Development, Academic/Cognitive: Literacy, Academic/Cognitive: Mathematical Concepts, Daily Living, and Social and Emotional Development. Within each of these areas there are skill sequences. For each skill sequence there is an overview of the skill, assessment methods, and a listing of needed assessment materials. Comprehensive and supplemental skill sequences are available for each key skill area. Comprehensive Skill Sequences provide a more fine-grained skill sequence and include intermediate skills that may be useful for students who have difficulty making progress using the general skill sequences or for task analyses. Supplemental Skill Sequences include additional skill practice in naturalistic settings. The binder also includes Milestone Skills by Developmental Age Level, a re-arrangement of the skills based upon developmental age levels. Assessment results are recorded in the record book. Color coding and different notation systems allow for using the same record book for six separate administrations, thus providing longitudinal information on objectives and progress.

The IED IIS is a norm-referenced assessment made up of 44 of the IED II key skill assessments that were standardized and validated. The IED IIS provides norm-referenced scores (e.g., developmental quotients [$M = 100$, $SD = 15$], percentile ranks, and age equivalents) that can be used for diagnostic and special educational eligibility purposes. The skill areas are divided into composite areas, subdomains, and domains (i.e., Physical Development, Language Development, Academic/Cognitive, Daily Living, and Social and Emotional). Scores are available for subdomains, domains, and for Total Adaptive Behavior. However, composite, subdomain, domain, and skill area scores are not available at all ages. Scores allow for comparisons within and across subdomains and domains. Some items can be tested directly or completed by parental or teacher report, as specified in the administration manual. Basal and ceiling rules are presented in the manual and in the record form. Basal and ceiling rules differ for the different items so having them listed with the items is helpful.

DEVELOPMENT. There is relatively little information about the development of these two tools. The BRIGANCE Inventory of Early Development II is a revision of the BRIGANCE

Inventory of Early Development. In 2001, validation procedures began to create the IED IIS. In addition, modifications were made to skill sequences and ages associated with items based on contemporary developmental expectations; however, these modifications are not described. Field testing and reviews were completed by people in 23 states and one Canadian province. In 2010, new assessment items were also added to the Academic/Cognitive Literacy portion of the assessment. Again, these new items and their development are not detailed. The format and organization of the IED II was also adjusted to improve the user-friendliness of the tool.

The 44 items on the IED IIS were selected from the IED II by a panel of professionals who evaluated the items in terms of their appropriateness and the standardized instructions. These panel members also field tested the items. The final set of items were "predictive of important aspects of development and that directions were sufficiently clear and replicable" (technical manual, p. 68).

TECHNICAL. There is no technical information presented about the IED II. What information there is concerns the IED IIS.

Standardization and validation of the IED IIS began in 2001 at 24 sites. The sites represented all four regions of the United States but only 15.7% of them were in the "North" and 32.1% of them were in the "West" (technical manual, p. 68) suggesting that the West may have been overrepresented in the standardization sample and the North underrepresented. A total of 1,171 children were in the standardization sample but the majority of them (93%) were younger than 5 years old. Additionally, there was a higher percentage of children whose parents' educations were college or higher (31.5%) than in the general population (23.2%). The sample was more urban/suburban and had slightly more children from two-parent homes than U.S. Census figures. Finally, 51% of the children were recruited from medical settings and 18% from special education sources; no information is provided about disabilities or level of developmental delay in the standardization sample.

Information on the reliability of the IED IIS is presented in the test's technical manual. Information from the current and the original validation in 1991 are included. Guttman lambdas provide evidence of internal consistency of the subdomains and domains. Values range from .86 to .99. Test-retest reliability data are presented from both validation studies. The test-retest interval for the original validation study is not reported but the interval for the most recent validation effort was 1 week. The data, however, show evidence of test-retest reliability. For the 2003 validation, evidence of interrater reliability is linked to the observed agreement between two observers who tested 36 children "with select assessments from the IED II … within one week" (technical manual, p. 79). It is unclear whether the entire IED IIS was used or just parts of it. These data are combined with results from a 1988 study by Brulle and Ivarie with 5- and 6-year-olds and presented as evidence of interrater reliability. Although the percent agreements range between .80 and .98, percent agreement is not a robust indicator of reliability.

Validity of the IED IIS test scores is supported in many ways. For content evidence, in addition to comparing IED IIS items to the developmental literature, scores on the IED IIS were compared across different ages. Although there was some overlap in the range of raw scores at some ages, the median scores differed with age. Construct evidence was offered in the form of the patterns of correlations between scores on the subdomains, domains, skill areas, and composites. Evidence of concurrent validity was provided by comparing scores from the IED IIS to test scores for 484 children who were also assessed by another battery of tests that included other measures of skills assessed by the IED IIS. Examiners of infants and toddlers rated the children's performance in terms of being below average, average, or above average. Teachers of school-age children rated how easily students handled school work. All correlations between the IED IIS and other measures of similar developmental skills were significant; some of the correlations involving examiner ratings were not significant. In terms of discriminant validity, members of different racial/ethnic groups did not differ in their performance on the IED IIS; however, children whose parents had completed high school scored higher on the IED IIS and children on Medicaid or who received assistance with lunches at school scored lower on the IED IIS.

COMMENTARY. Together the IED II and IED IIS have the potential to be the one assessment system used for young children. The IED IIS provides norm-referenced scores that are needed for special education eligibility decisions. The IED II, as a criterion-referenced assessment linked to the IED IIS, provides the structure for IFSP and IEP development, implementation, and progress monitoring. These types of authentic assessments are valued in the field of early childhood special education (Bagnato, Neisworth, & Pretti-Frontczak, 2010).

The IED II should follow in the footsteps of its predecessors as a useful criterion-referenced tool in early childhood settings. It is easy to use and provides a great deal of support and additional information for teachers to use when working with young children. In addition, there are BRIGANCE materials that can be used with older children, especially those eligible for special education services, so there is some degree of consistency in assessment across the age span. The ability of teachers to use BRIGANCE materials rather than multiple curricula and assessments seems to be an asset.

The IED IIS, however, has a large limitation in terms of its use with young children. Federal regulations require an assessment of motor, communication, cognitive, adaptive, and social-emotional development for all infants and toddlers referred for early intervention. This assessment is to be used for both eligibility determination and program planning. However, the IED IIS does not provide Academic/Cognitive subtests or domain scores for infants under the age of 1 year. In addition, it is possible that toddlers with delays may not be able to receive a score in this domain. Additionally, social-emotional development scores are not available for children older than 3 years. These scores would be very useful for those trying to work with young children and trying to understand their atypical behavior in school. Additional problems with the IED IIS include a lack of clarity about its psychometric properties as separate from previous validation studies and some potential problems with the representativeness of its norm group.

SUMMARY. The IED II and IED IIS are the newest tools in the BRIGANCE series of assessments. The IED II and IED IIS provide different types of assessment information about the skills of children under the age of 7. The IED II provides criterion-referenced information that is useful to parents, child care workers, early interventionists, and teachers. The IED IIS provides norm-referenced information that is useful in helping children access services and obtain the services they need.

REVIEWER'S REFERENCES

Bagnato, S. J., Neisworth, J. T., & Pretti-Frontczak, K. (2010). *Linking authentic assessment and early childhood intervention: Best measures for best practices* (2nd ed.). Baltimore, MD: Brookes.

Brulle, A. R., & Ivarie, J. (1988). Teacher checklists: A reliability analysis. *Special Services in the Schools*, 5(1-2), 67-75. doi: 10.1300/J008v05n01_04

Review of the BRIGANCE® Inventory of Early Development II by LISA F. SMITH, Professor of Education and Dean, University of Otago College of Education, Dunedin, New Zealand:

DESCRIPTION. The BRIGANCE® Inventory of Early Development II (IED II) is used to evaluate children from birth to age 7 for school readiness; developmental progress, strengths, and weaknesses; eligibility for special education services; instructional entry points and progressions; and program evaluation. The IED II comprises a criterion-referenced battery along with a standardized and validated (i.e., norm-referenced) revision of the BRIGANCE Inventory of Early Development, with considerable overlap between the two assessments. Both the IED II and the IED II Standardized can be administered by a variety of early childhood professionals, although specialized training is required to interpret the statistics obtained from the standardized assessment. Selected assessments may be administered as determined by the needs and age of the child to be tested. Required accessories can be assembled or purchased from the test publisher.

The IED II includes assessments for Physical Development (Preambulatory, Gross-, and Fine-Motor), Language Development, Academic/Cognitive (Literacy and Mathematical Concepts), Daily Living, and Social and Emotional Development. It provides clear support for monitoring individual student progress; conducting program evaluations, including special education programs needing to meet IDEA requirements; and developing IEPs.

The IED II Standardized is composed of assessments in five domains, each of which have two subdomains: Physical Development (Fine- and Gross-Motor Skills), Language Development (Receptive and Expressive Language), Academic/Cognitive (Mathematical/General Concepts and Literacy), Daily Living (Self-Help and Prevocational), and Social and Emotional Development (Play Skills and Behaviors, and Engagement and Initiative Skills). These sum to an indication of Total Adaptive Behavior performance.

The standardization and validation manual is particularly well-written. The introduction sets out eight principles for measurement in child development, and argues for regular monitoring of children's development in terms of their skills and progress. The introduction is followed by a comprehensive chapter that describes procedures for the standardized administration of the IED II. Modifications for children with special needs are explained in a clear and easy-to-follow fashion. Moreover, the assessment procedures, instructions for evaluating students with special needs, and milestone skills by age level would be a welcome reference for use in a child development course. Chapter 5, "Using the IED II in Teaching and Learning," is equally valuable beyond its intended use with the battery. However, the literature in the section on Making Retention Decisions (p. 21) is at least two decades old and, in general, the references throughout could use updating (e.g., Examples from the Research Literature, p. 66).

Scoring is clearly explained and supported by well-designed tables, illustrations, and recording sheets. Suggested entry points, basal, and ceiling criteria are provided; these might need to be adjusted for children with special needs. Detailed instructions with examples are provided for deriving raw scores, quotients, percentile ranks, age equivalents, instructional ranges, and total adaptive behavior scores. For deriving a raw score range, the 68% confidence level for the standard error of measurement is provided. Multipliers to find the 90% and 95% confidence levels are given; however, it would be helpful to provide these confidence intervals rather than requiring additional calculations. A well-written guide for interpreting scores is also provided, followed by a completed sample report.

DEVELOPMENT. The majority of the information regarding the development of the IED II is contained in the standardization and validation manual. The test authors credit professionals from 23 states for assisting with the validation of the IED II. The Northeast and the Mountain States are underrepresented. The IED II and the IED II Standardized align with U.S.A. state and federal standards for the skill areas assessed, as well as with requirements for Head Start assessments.

TECHNICAL. It should be noted that all technical information refers to the IED II Standardized.

Standardization. The standardization and validation study was done in 2003 with 1,171 children participating. U.S. Census Bureau statistics (mainly from 2003) are reported for that sample. A panel of seven child development professionals chose the assessments for the standardization study; details of the selection processes and pilot work are not provided. An online search of recent Census data showed that the age range, gender, and ethnic background of the 2003 sample are repre-

sentative of the current U.S. population, except for having somewhat lower numbers of children over 5 years of age in the sample. In terms of regional representation, the North is somewhat underrepresented in favor of the West. Family and parental demographics are also representative for education level, income as indicated by federal school lunch program participation, rural and urban residency, and marital status. Parental education at the college+ level is somewhat underrepresented in the sample. Participation is overrepresented by medical settings; no information is provided for participants from settings regarding disorders or special needs.

By way of demonstrating that the IED II can be administered by a variety of professionals in a wide range of settings, the author of the technical manual stated, "Potential performance differences across sites were assessed via *t*-tests" (p. 71). Complete data are not provided. Analysis of variance would have been more appropriate for several of the comparisons; if multiple *t*-tests were used, no adjustments are reported. A large number of normative and conversion tables are provided for composite scores, subdomains, and domains, graduated by appropriate month/year levels to produce quotients, percentile ranks, age equivalents, and instructional ranges.

Reference is made to a translation of the assessments into Spanish. However, no validation information is provided for the Spanish norming study other than the percentage (8.6%) of families and children participating.

Reliability. As far as can be determined, all reliability data are from the 2003 standardization study. Original alpha coefficients from the standardization study done in 1991 are given for those assessments that are also in the IED II. Not all assessments were administered; large blocks of skills are not shown, in particular related to basic number and word skills. The data that are shown have good to very good reliabilities. To compensate for concerns regarding estimating lower bounds, Guttman lambda coefficients were used for composites, subdomains, and domains. Scores ranged from .86 for Drawing/Visual Motor to .98 for Receptive Language. Test-retest reliability was calculated for a sample of 36 children from birth to 12 months of age, for new test items pertaining to that age range. Those reliabilities are mostly above .80. Interrater reliability was based on 36 children taking selected assessments from the IED II within one week. Information about the raters, the children, or the assessments used is not provided. A table presents results combined from this study and a previous study done in 1988 by Brulle and Ivarie. It is not clear how the data were combined. Given that, the interrater reliabilities–reported as percent agreement–range from .80 for Social and Emotional Development to .98 for Receptive Language.

Validity. Evidence supporting content validity is offered by way of the child development professionals who participated in the development and testing of the IED II, although individual credentials are not provided. Increased achievement with age is also provided as evidence of content validity. This is not particularly strong evidence, especially given that no distinction is shown for children with different types of special needs. Favorable commentary from previous reviews of the battery provides additional evidence of content validity but does not speak directly to this revision.

Some evidence of construct validity is provided through tables of intercorrelations between scores on the standardized assessments in the IED II domains, subdomains, and skills. Although the correlations are largely adequate, little interpretation is offered to assess whether convincing evidence of construct validity has been demonstrated. A factor analysis using a varimax rotation and controlling for age yielded a three-factor solution (Understanding and Expressing, Movement and Social Activity, and Academic/Preacademic) that accounted for 84% of the variance for the subdomains. The subdomains that loaded on the three factors are not always aligned with the label for the factor. For example, the subdomain Mathematical/General Concepts loads on the factor Understanding and Expressing and not Academic/Preacademic. The subdomains Prevocational and Engagement and Initiative load on the factor Movement and Social Activity. It would be helpful to know more about this analysis to better interpret its results.

Evidence supporting concurrent criterion validity also comes from the 2003 standardization sample of the IED II. A subset of 484 children from that group was assessed using appropriate measures for cognitive assessment (e.g., Bayley Scales of Infant Development, Stanford-Binet), achievement (e.g., Woodcock-Johnson Psycho-Educational Battery–Revised: Tests of Achievement, Kaufman Test of Educational Achievement), language and adaptive measures (e.g., Rosetti Infant Toddler Language Scale, Vineland Adaptive Behavior Scale),

physical development (e.g., Bayley Scales, Battelle Developmental Inventory), social and emotional development (e.g., Bayley Scales, Vineland Adaptive Behavior Scale), and teacher/examiner ratings for children in kindergarten and first grade. Parents of children over age 2 completed the Child Development Inventory. A table of correlations is provided for the IED II domains and subdomains with the diagnostic measures; it is not clear which diagnostic measures are reported or how the results vary by age groups or children with special needs. Correlations for examiner ratings were not significant for expressive language, daily living, or social and emotional development. Given the large number of assessments included, more information is needed to evaluate the data.

Discriminant function analyses were performed for four groups: with/without prematurity, with/without psychosocial risk, with/without known developmental disabilities, and with/without highly advanced development. The selection process, ages, or number of participants in each group are not provided. Three analyses of covariance also were implemented to compare Caucasian children/other ethnicities, children whose parents did/did not complete high school, and children who did/did not qualify for Medicaid or federal free/reduced lunch. The ethnicity analysis was not significant; the other two analyses showed significant differences between the groups. Given the lack of information about the sample, it is difficult to interpret how these findings should be applied.

Evidence of predictive validity is briefly summarized. The technical manual refers the reader to prior research dating from 1984–1999 for further detail.

COMMENTARY. The IED II will have wide appeal for a variety of professionals who work with children. Strengths of the IED II include the flexibility of the two assessment batteries, well-written test manuals, well-designed and researched test materials that permit normative comparisons, ease of administration and scoring, and the ability to use the assessments either for groups or individual children with diverse needs. Teachers will find the support materials helpful in designing instructional groups and interventions, and will find it easy to use the developmental record book, which permits tracking a child's progress over time through using pens of different colors to record scores. School psychologists and medical professionals will find the IED II a valuable diagnostic tool.

The IED II could use a technical update for establishing current evidence of reliability and validity. Updated information could be placed online, given how many tables could be generated.

SUMMARY. Even taking into account the lack of current, comprehensive psychometrics, the IED II is a valuable assessment that meets its stated purposes. It can be used with confidence, either on its own for classroom use or as part of a battery for diagnostic testing.

[23]

Bruininks Motor Ability Test.

Purpose: Designed to assess "an adult's motor abilities related to improvement in physical functioning and/or requirements for activities of daily living ... to guide treatment, set treatment goals, and monitor progress toward those goals."

Population: Ages 40 and older.

Publication Date: 2012.

Acronym: BMAT.

Scores, 8: Fine Motor Composite (Fine Motor Integration, Manual Dexterity, Total), Gross Motor Composite (Balance and Mobility, Strength and Flexibility, Total), Coordination, Total Motor Composite.

Subtests, 5: Fine Motor Integration, Manual Dexterity, Coordination, Balance and Mobility, Strength and Flexibility.

Administration: Individual.

Forms, 2: Full, Short.

Price Data, 2013: $580 per complete kit including manual (227 pages), administration easel, comprehensive record form (25), comprehensive form examinee booklet (25), short form (25), short form examinee booklet (25), scoring transparency, blocks with string, penny pad, penny box, plastic pennies (50), elbow pad, tennis ball, stopwatch, red pen, black marker, adult scissors, hand gripper–blue, hand gripper–green, envelope, numbered half cones (4), sewing board with string; $90 per manual.

Time: (8–16) minutes per subtest, (60–75) minutes complete battery, (15–25) minutes short form.

Comments: Test is an adult adaptation of the Bruininks-Oseretsky Test of Motor Proficiency, Second Edition. Subtests may be administered individually.

Authors: Brett D. Bruininks and Robert H. Bruininks.

Publisher: Pearson.

Review of the Bruininks Motor Ability Test by KENNETH M. HANIG, Staff Psychologist, Logansport Joint Special Services, South Bend, IN:

DESCRIPTION. As noted by the test authors, the Bruininks Motor Ability Test (BMAT) is an individually administered, standardized test of gross and fine motor skills for adults ages 40 and older. It is the adult adaptation of the Bruininks-Oseretsky Test of Motor Proficiency–Second Edition (BOT-2, 2005; 18:15), which is used for individuals ages 4–21. The BMAT can be used by professionals in occupational therapy, physical therapy, nursing, human performance assessment, physical rehabilitation, psychology, and related disciplines. According to the test authors, the BMAT assesses an adult's motor abilities related to improvement in physical functioning and/or requirements for activities of daily living (ADLs), and it can help guide treatment goals and monitor progress toward those goals.

The test can be given in total or in individual sections, depending on the physical condition of the test taker, the setting, any localized impairments that the individual may have, and so forth. Five subtests are included in the measure: Fine Motor Integration, Manual Dexterity, Coordination, Balance and Mobility, and Strength and Flexibility. There is also a short form that provides an estimate of overall motor ability after a 15- to 25-minute administration.

According to the test authors, the measure yields standard scores relative to a large, nationally representative sample of motorically healthy adults. Scores that were derived from a sample of adults with motor impairments are included and can be used for additional interpretive analysis. The test can be scored either by hand or with computer software from the publisher.

One attractive feature that is included by the test authors is an administration easel that guides the examiner through specific details of test administration and includes photographs depicting what the test taker and test administrator are required to do. Scoring guidelines also are noted on the easel. For each item, the easel provides an at-a-glance dashboard with key information, including verbatim instructions.

A test manual is included with more detailed information, including norms, technical information about test development, reliability and validity information, and information regarding interpretation of results.

The BMAT is composed of five subtests. Subtest 1 covers Fine Motor Integration, with 7 items administered. This subtest measures precise control of finger and hand movements that must be combined with visual stimuli. The second subtest, Manual Dexterity, includes 5 items. The measure uses goal-directed tasks that involve reaching, grasping, and bimanual coordination with small objects. Subtest 3, Coordination, includes 6 items. This subtest assesses the examinee's ability to coordinate movements of the hands, arms, and feet. The fourth subtest, Balance and Mobility, measures performance on 7 items, evaluating motor control skills that are integral for standing, walking, and using stairs. Subtest 5, Strength and Flexibility, combines 6 items that measure the strength and endurance of muscle groups in the legs, torso, arms, and hands with one item measuring flexibility of the lower back.

The test manual provides comprehensive information regarding assessing an examinee's ability to perform skill items on the BMAT. Minimum motor ability requirements by subtest are described, such as on subtests 1 and 2, where the examinee needs to have the ability to sit at a table and use both hands. The test authors also indicate that the clinician may need to use his/her judgment in deciding whether the examinee is capable of giving adequate responses to the items. Test materials and equipment requirements are also described. The test manual includes gender specific and combined gender norms. The test authors state that the combined gender norms are recommended when the BMAT is used as part of an evaluation of the amount of assistance that an individual requires to perform ADLs. Because the motor requirements for performing ADLs are the same for men and women, the combined gender norm sample is the more relevant reference group. The test authors emphasize that there is no right or wrong choice of norms in an absolute sense.

Test authors sometimes seem to assume that completing test record forms is an intuitive process for examiners, but the BMAT authors devote an entire chapter to that process. The manual provides detailed examples of how the examiner is to convert raw scores to point scores, make notes during observations, obtain norm-referenced scores, convert scores to standard scores and percentile ranks, as well as to determine confidence intervals, complete the score profile page, and conduct pairwise comparisons. Examples regarding the short form are provided as well.

BMAT standard scores have a mean of 500 and a standard deviation (SD) of 20. The test authors note that traditional standard scores such as T scores and IQ standard scores cannot express scores that are more than 5 or 6 SDs below the normative mean and thus would not be sensitive to performance differences or changes below that

range. The BMAT standard scores extend downward to 200, or 15 SDs below the normative mean, allowing them to reflect ability differences and changes among highly impaired individuals on all subtests and for all age groups.

The authors also devote a chapter to score interpretation. One issue that may be of initial confusion to a new test user is the authors' use of a point score. As the test authors explain, the size and spread of raw scores differ greatly from item to item. Raw scores from two items may differ in size and spread, as well as whether high scores are better or worse. To solve the potential issues posed by the lack of compatibility of item raw scores, BMAT raw scores are converted to point scores. BMAT point scores have roughly comparable sizes and spreads across the various items within a subtest, and all point scores are scaled so that higher scores represent better performance. When item point scores are summed to a total point score to represent performance on the subtest as a whole, each item counts roughly the same toward that sum. A more technical example of how point scores are derived is included in another chapter. Basically, the number of point score categories had to be decided for each subtest. Some subtests had seven possible raw scores (0 to 6) and some had eight (0 to 7). Hence, eight score point categories were used. Then, raw score to point score conversions were developed by inspecting the raw score frequency distributions in the norm sample and in a motor-impaired comparison group.

DEVELOPMENT. The test authors indicated that the BMAT was developed after listening to the concerns of professionals who conduct motor assessments with adult populations. Practitioner input was solicited during the early stages of development. Four developmental goals were noted during that time. One was for maximum flexibility. The BMAT can be customized to focus on one or two specific motor skill areas, or the administration can be more comprehensive. A second consideration was for national norms. The large sample was selected to represent the U.S. adult population. A third consideration was for sensitivity within the impaired range; hence, test items were developed to be sensitive to differences in ability among impaired adults. The tables that convert raw scores to point scores were designed to provide greater score differentiation in the impaired range, and the use of a scale with a mean of 500 and a standard deviation of 20 reflects sensitivity to ability differences among highly impaired individuals. Finally, there was a goal of functional relevance. Test developers wanted the measure to assess the behaviors and component motor skills that enable or prevent the performance of ADLs.

During the pilot phase, examiners, all of whom were physical therapists, completed a feedback form that asked questions about each test item. One question asked examiners to rate the extent to which performance on the test item appeared to be related to the ability to perform ADLs. Another question asked examiners to nominate, for each item, specific ADLs they thought were related to performance on the item. A number of tables are provided to indicate how the skills are reflected on the measured items.

The test authors describe content development in a detailed chapter of the test manual. The 32 BMAT items include motor performance tasks taken directly from the BOT-2, tasks adapted from the BOT-2, and newly developed tasks. Several rounds of piloting were conducted to gather feedback and shape the item pool. In one round, 10 examiners administered 43 items to 37 test takers, all without motor impairments. Afterward, seven of those items were eliminated, and some were modified. Twelve new examiners then administered the test to 44 impaired and 28 unimpaired participants. After modifications that resulted from examinees' feedback and item data analyses between the two groups, 34 items were left for the standardization version. Two items were removed after standardization, resulting in the current 32-item test. A total of 1,058 adults met the criteria for the norm sample. Of those, 58 were eliminated to improve the match to the demographic targets, leaving a final norm sample of 1,000. The test authors note that Hispanic and Whites were somewhat overrepresented and African-Americans and others were underrepresented. In terms of educational level, the test authors state that the lowest education category was somewhat underrepresented and the highest category was overrepresented. A detailed chart describing the characteristics of the motor-impaired comparison group (N = 82) is presented in the test manual.

TECHNICAL. The reliability of the BMAT indicates the extent to which test results are dependable and repeatable. Test-retest studies were used to evaluate temporal stability. During a 6- to 12-day interval, 69 individuals from the norm sample were tested twice. The sample consisted

entirely of examinees ages 65 and older in order to ensure adequate variation in the test scores. The resulting correlation coefficients ranged from a low of .77 for Fine Motor Integration to a high of .92 for Strength and Flexibility, with a median of .86 across the five subtests. Interscorer reliability was evaluated using a design in which examinees were tested by one examiner while a second examiner observed and independently recorded item scores. Intraclass correlations were computed, and all of the adjusted coefficients approached a perfect 1.00. The lowest reliability estimate, for Fine Motor Integration, was .95. As a measure of internal consistency, split-half reliability coefficients were reported for separate age groups. Some of the Fine Motor Integration, Coordination, and Balance and Mobility coefficients for the younger age groups in the normative sample were below .50 but all coefficients for the motor-impaired comparison group were above .80.

Validity of the BMAT was described as the extent to which the test scores measure what they purport to measure. Validity evidence addressed test content validity, demographic trends, clinical utility, and relationships with other tests of motor performance.

In terms of test content, the BMAT borrowed heavily from the BOT-2. The test authors concluded that the considerable evidence for validity and user acceptance of the BOT-2 provided the foundation for content validity of the BMAT. The test was honed over multiple rounds of data collection. Mean subtest total point scores were noted on various tables as a function of age and gender. Various tables also provide evidence for the BMAT reflecting that motor proficiency declines with age. Regarding clinical utility, differences in two groups (the motor-impaired comparison group and a matched sample from the normative group) were compared in terms of standard deviation units, a measure of effect size (i.e., the effect of being in one group versus the other). Effect sizes of .80 are considered large. By that criterion, the BMAT effect sizes are large, indicting strong clinical utility. Finally, performance on the BMAT was compared to performance on the Beery VMI, the Nine-Hole Peg Test (NHPT), Berg Balance Scale (BBS), and the Modified Barthel Index (MBI). Correlation coefficients were statistically significant, though not high. The correlation coefficient for the Beery VMI was .34. The BMAT Manual Dexterity subtest and the NHPT reflected coefficients in the .70s.

The Berg Balance Scale and the BMAT Balance and Mobility subtest correlation coefficient was .86. The MBI did not correlate highly with the BMAT because it is not a motor performance test like the NHPT or BBS. However, the Gross Motor Composite of the BMAT and 5 of the 7 MBI items yielded values as high as .40 and above. Intercorrelations among BMAT subtest, composite, and short form scores are provided as well.

COMMENTARY. This reviewer was impressed with this test. Professionals in clinical positions, such as those working in a nursing home facility or even hospital or rehabilitation setting, likely would find the BMAT to be a valuable tool for assessing individuals' treatment needs and progress in that treatment. Also, patients who have had strokes or paralytic conditions secondary to injuries, among others, could also be assessed using this measure, and treatment providers would get valuable information for that patient's treatment needs. In short, the test seems to have a wide range of clinical utility for adult populations. The test manual is well done, easy to read and follow, and provides good interpretive guidelines. The test authors thoroughly describe administration issues, such as establishing rapport, maintaining rapport, preparing for administration, and so forth. Especially impressive is the description under preparing the testing area, which covers exact measurements to be used, taping lines, placement of numbered cones (included in the kit), and determining hand and foot preferences. The use of the easel will enable the examiner to test specifically and score reliably the items that are administered. The test authors do a very good job describing how the test is to be scored and offer numerous examples to aid the examiner in scoring.

SUMMARY. The BMAT is a measure that assesses adult motor abilities related to improvement in physical functioning and/or requirements for activities of daily living, to guide treatment, set treatment goals, and monitor progress toward those goals. The test borrows heavily from the BOT-2, although new items and norms were developed for the BMAT. Pilot studies addressed the use of the items as well as their ability to reflect the content being evaluated. Reliability and validity studies were well done, although for various reasons, some of the resulting correlation coefficients were a bit low. In those cases, which involved validity studies more than reliability studies, the test authors gave detailed explanations for their results. The

test manual and materials are well organized and informative, as well as useful for administration, scoring, and interpretation.

Review of the Bruininks Motor Ability Test by MARTIN J. WIESE, School Psychologist, Lincoln Public Schools, Lincoln, NE:

DESCRIPTION. The Bruininks Motor Ability Test (BMAT) is an individually administered, standardized test of gross and fine motor skills for adults ages 40 and older. It is an adult adaptation of the Bruininks-Oseretsky Test of Motor Proficiency-Second Edition (BOT-2; 18:15), which is used with younger individuals, ages 4 to 21 years. The BMAT is designed to assess an individual's motor abilities and activities required for everyday life. It also can be used to detect improvement in physical functioning, set treatment goals, and monitor progress. The comprehensive form has 32 functional test items or tasks that comprise five subtests: Fine Motor Integration, Manual Dexterity, Coordination, Balance and Mobility, and Strength and Flexibility. Administration is designed to be flexible; examiners can selectively administer any or all of the subtests depending on assessment needs. If time restrictions or client limitations do not allow administration of the comprehensive test, there is also a short form that provides an estimate of overall motor ability. The BMAT includes an administration easel that is used to present photo illustrations of required tasks and contains verbatim instructions for the examiner.

Each subtest takes about 8 to 16 minutes to administer. Total administration time for the full test battery ranges from 39–73 minutes for motorically healthy individuals and 39–87 minutes for motor-impaired individuals. The five areas assessed with the comprehensive form (32 items) include (a) Fine Motor Integration, which requires precise control of finger and hand movements. These abilities are measured with three drawing tasks, shape recognition, use of scissors and folding paper; (b) Manual Dexterity, which requires reaching, grasping, and manual manipulation with small items. These timed tasks require picking up and transferring small objects, stringing blocks, and completing a sewing-like activity; (c) Coordination, which measures coordination of hands, arms, and feet and involves touching and moving various body parts in specified manners and catching/throwing a tennis ball; (d) Balance and Mobility, which measures motor control skills necessary for standing, walking, and using stairs; and (e) Strength and Flexibility, which measures strength and endurance of the legs, torso, arms, and hands, as well as flexibility of the lower back. The short form (10 items) contains two items from each of the five areas.

Most of the materials are provided with the test kit, but the examiner will need to provide additional items to administer the complete assessment. These items include a tape measure, masking tape or similar, an armless chair, a stair step or exercise step, and several dumbbells of various weights.

Administration instructions are located in the administration easel and are accompanied by photo illustrations making the directions clear and easy to follow. Each subtest begins with an introductory page to give the examiner an overview of the subtest, the number of items, and general directions. The introduction is followed by item pages that contain detailed instructions for administering and scoring each item. Four of the subtests include helpful photos to supplement the examiner's verbal instructions. Depending on the subtests selected, some preparation of the testing area may be necessary prior to administration. For example, two subtests (Coordination, Balance and Mobility) require measured lines to be taped to the floor.

Client information, hand preference, and subtest raw scores are recorded on the record form. It is recommended that subtests be presented in the order they appear and that raw scores be recorded as soon as the examinee finishes each item trial. Space is provided on the record form to record notes and observations during administration. Subtest raw scores are converted to points via tables located in the record form. Total subtest points are then used to obtain norm-referenced scores (standard scores and percentile ranks).

The BMAT is standardized to use an atypical scale with a mean of 500 and standard deviation of 20. This scale was selected to provide scores many standard deviations below the normative mean to differentiate levels of performance and detect changes among highly impaired individuals. Standard scores are available for each of the five subtests, as well as a Fine Motor summative score, Gross Motor summative score, and Total Motor Composite Score.

DEVELOPMENT. The test authors indicate that the BMAT was developed in response to re-

quests from users of the Bruininks-Oseretsky Test of Motor Proficiency-Second Edition (BOT-2) who desired a nationally normed test of adult motor skills. Hence, many of the BMAT items are taken directly from the BOT-2. Development included several rounds of pilot testing (during which examinee performance and examiner feedback was used to modify items, clarify instructions, and address safety concerns) followed by standardization testing with a nationally representative sample.

TECHNICAL. The final standardization sample included 1,000 English-speaking individuals, living independently, with no known motor impairments, and representative of the U.S. population in terms of race/ethnicity and education level. All norm sample participants also had normal vision (with or without corrective lenses) and did not take medications known to affect motor skills. Three sets of norms were developed including females only, males only, and females and males combined, separated into nine different age groups (40–85+). Equal numbers of females and males are included in each age group.

In addition to the standardization norm group, data from a sample of 82 individuals with motor impairments who were unable to live independently were collected to provide another reference group to use when interpreting BMAT performance. Data were also collected to establish the reliability and validity of the BMAT.

Scores were standardized with a mean of 500 and a standard deviation (*SD*) of 20. This scale was used to provide examiners with a scale that is sensitive to small changes in motor skills. Unlike most other standardized assessments that are normed with scores ranging plus or minus 4 standard deviations around the mean, the BMAT allows for scores that extend many standard deviations below the normative mean. For examples, the Total Motor Composite scores range from a high of 550 (2.5 *SD* above the mean) to a low of 200 (15 *SD* below the mean).

Test-retest reliability estimates are provided. Sixty-nine participants, ages 65 and older, were administered the BMAT twice within a 6- to 12-day interval. Both Pearson correlation coefficients and adjusted correlation coefficients are presented. For the five BMAT subtests, correlation coefficients range from .77 (Fine Motor Integration) to .92 (Strength and Flexibility). The reliability coefficients for the three composite scores range from good to excellent: .88 for Fine Motor, .93 for

Gross Motor, and .94 for Total Motor. Interscorer reliability study results are presented and indicate excellent interscorer agreement (coefficients range from .95 to .99). Split-half correlations are reported separately by age group and range from fair to excellent.

Support for the validity of the use of BMAT test scores includes face validity, correspondence with expected demographic trends, clinical utility, and relationships with other measures of motor ability. Face validity was established through review of items by professional examiners; the test items appear to measure what they purport to measure (fine and gross motor skills). BMAT performance reflects expected declines in motor skills as a function of age and gender. Mean scores for each of the five subtests show a decline as the age of the subject increases. Clinical utility is indicated by comparing motor-impaired individuals' BMAT scores with scores from an independent-living reference group. As predicted, scores from the impaired sample are significantly lower than scores from the unimpaired reference group. All mean differences between the two groups are statistically significant with large effect sizes (> .80).

Overall, the test authors present strong evidence of reliability and validity of the BMAT. Scores reflect anticipated age-related declines in fine motor skills, manual dexterity, coordination, balance, and flexibility; differentiate between unimpaired and motor-impaired individuals; and correlate significantly with other measures of motor ability.

COMMENTARY AND SUMMARY. The BMAT appears to be an effective means to assess older individuals' motor abilities, detect improvement in physical functioning, and monitor progress. Developed as an adult adaptation of the BOT-2, items are functionally relevant to daily living skills, and administration instructions are clear and easy to understand for the examiner. In addition, the easel format simplifies administration by presenting photo illustrations of required tasks to the examinee. The record form allows for easy recording of responses and item scoring. The test authors provide strong evidence of reliability and validity. The reliability of the three composite scores ranges from good to excellent. The BMAT correlates significantly with other measures of motor ability and differentiates between unimpaired and impaired individuals. The BMAT should be useful in assessing adult motor functioning, designing interventions, and monitoring progress.

[24]
Calibrated Ideational Fluency Assessment.

Purpose: Designed "to characterize a respondent's verbal, nonverbal, and overall generativity."
Population: Ages 18 to 92.
Publication Date: 2010.
Acronym: CIFA.
Scores, 11: Acceptable Designs, Unacceptable Designs, Percent Unacceptable Designs, S Words, P Words, Letter Word Fluency, Animals, Supermarket Items, Category Word Fluency, Verbal Fluency Total, Ideational Fluency Composite.
Subtests, 2: Design Fluency, Verbal Fluency.
Administration: Individual.
Price Data, 2014: $225 per introductory kit, including professional manual (108 pages) and 50 record booklets; $65 per 25 record booklets; $94 per professional manual.
Time: (10) minutes.
Authors: David J. Schretlen and Tracy D. Vannorsdall.
Publisher: Psychological Assessment Resources, Inc.

Review of the Calibrated Ideational Fluency Assessment by MARTA J. COLEMAN, Teacher and Researcher, Gunnison High School, Gunnison, CO:

DESCRIPTION. The Calibrated Ideational Fluency Assessment (CIFA) was designed as an individually administered cognitive test to rate design and verbal fluency in adults in order to assist in diagnosis of neuropsychological disorders such as early stages of Alzheimer's disease, schizophrenia, bipolar disorder, subcortical dementias, Parkinson's disease, and traumatic brain injury. The test authors report that diagnostic criterion validity was established for adults with Parkinson's disease, schizophrenia, bipolar disorder, and probable dementia. Because some neuropsychiatric and neurological disorders may be associated with deficits in ideational fluency, the CIFA may be appropriate for use in characterizing such deficits. English-speaking men and women ages 18–92 years are the targeted population for use of this test. The test authors warn against use of the CIFA for people who speak English as a second language and for individuals who have visual or physical impairments that would preclude them from completing test tasks. The CIFA consists of two 4-minute subtests, Design Fluency and Verbal Fluency; performance on these subtests likely involves different cognitive processes regarding lexical retrieval, speed, working memory, strategy generation, self-monitoring, and creative thinking. The examinee is required to generate visual or visuoconstruction formations as quickly as possible while attending to specific rules. For example, in the Design Fluency task, the examinee is asked to make drawings that consist of four parts, any of which may be an arc, a circle, or a straight line. The examiner should be well trained in psychological testing to administer and interpret test results, which can be tallied within 5 minutes of the administration. The examiner should also be skilled in noting the design creation possibilities that involve any combination of four parts consisting of a circle, an arc, or a straight line. During the Verbal Fluency subtest, the examiner should be able to quickly discern acceptable oral responses in both Letter Word Fluency and Category Word Fluency tasks to obtain scores. The examinee is asked to recite words and names of objects as rapidly as possible in 60 seconds and within certain other constraints. The examiner must familiarize himself or herself with all types of errors possible on the subtests prior to testing because the examiner is required to correct the first instance of each type of error during the administration and to record the examinee's responses verbatim. Very clear instructions for administration are provided in the test manual. An actual script details how the examiner is to conduct the test. Test administrators must provide a pencil without an eraser, a stopwatch, and sheets of blank paper for the Design Fluency subtest.

In the Design Fluency subtest, the Acceptable Designs raw score is calculated by subtracting the number of unacceptable designs from the number of total designs during the 4-minute testing period. Raw scores can be converted to scaled scores, T scores and percentile ranks by using the varied appendices in the test manual or an electronic version (purchased separately) of the Calibrated Neuropsychological Normative System Software Portfolio. Age-, sex-, and education-calibrated norms are presented in the test manual for the examiner to use in interpreting results. Scores are classified as follows: Normal: extremely superior, very superior, superior, high average, average, low average; Borderline: borderline; Abnormal: mildly abnormal, moderately abnormal, and extremely abnormal. Two sample reports are provided in the test manual describing two patients, their histories, scores on the test, interpretation of the results, and recommendations.

DEVELOPMENT. The test authors report that tests of ideational fluency have proven useful for the differential diagnosis of many neuropsychiatric and neurological disorders. The authors trace the origins of the CIFA to the fixed condition of Jones-Gotman and Milner's Design Fluency Test (1977), which was conceived as a visuospatial analogue of Thurstone's written word fluency test (1938). Clear explanation is provided for the exclusion of the original free condition of Jones-Gotman and Milner's Design Fluency Test. This revised ideational fluency assessment was developed to provide more consistent administration procedures and to establish stronger interrater and test-retest reliability.

TECHNICAL. Normative sampling is described through an explanation of the Johns Hopkins University Aging, Brain Imaging, and Cognition (ABC) study, though no date for this study is provided. In Phase I of the ABC study, 215 adults were recruited via random-digit dialing of households in the Baltimore, MD, area. Another 179 adults in the Baltimore, MD, and Hartford, CT, areas were recruited for Phase II. All 394 participants were given physical and neurological examinations, psychiatric interviews, laboratory blood tests, brain MRI scans and cognitive testing. Based on exclusion criteria such as brain injury, bipolar disorder, substance abuse, or the presence of Parkinson's disease or Alzheimer's disease, 67 participants were excluded from the study. The remaining 327 participants established the standardization sample for the Calibrated Neuropsychological Normative System (CNNS; 19:25) and were administered the CIFA and other neuropsychological assessments. The test manual reports variations between the samples for the CIFA subtests because not all participants took every test; 319 participants took the Design Fluency subtest, and 326 participants took the Verbal Fluency subtest.

No explanation was given about why the specific time limits (60 seconds for the Verbal Fluency tasks and 4 minutes for the Design Fluency subtest) were selected. No information regarding the appropriate time between test and retest is given.

Multiple regression analysis was used to establish scaled scores on specific predictor variables. Test performance predictor models were developed: (a) age; (b) age, sex, and education; (c) age, sex, and race; (d) age, sex, education, and race; (e) age, sex, education, and Hopkins Adult Reading Test (HART A/B) score; (f) age, sex, education, race, and HART A/B score; (g) age, sex, and HART A/B score; (h) age, sex, race, and HART A/B score. A composite score is calculated by summing T scores and converting them to standard scores for each of the eight predictor models. The test authors report that analyses of scores show they approximate the normal distribution.

Interrater reliability for the Design Fluency subtest was examined using intraclass correlation coefficients (ICCs): two-way, random, and absolute agreement among five raters who scored 50 Design Fluency subtests. Reliability coefficients averaged .97 for Acceptable Designs and .94 for Unacceptable Designs. Repeated measures ANOVA with Bonferroni-corrected post-hoc tests were used to determine variation among the five raters. The test authors report test-retest reliability data from Kingery et al. (2006), who tested 87 healthy adults twice over an average of 5.5 years and found ICCs of .67 for Acceptable Designs and .37 for Unacceptable Designs. Interrater reliability is reported from other studies regarding the scoring of Verbal Fluency by other raters who achieved an average ICC of .99; the test authors report a similar finding. The test-retest correlation coefficients for Letter Word Fluency and Category Word Fluency tasks from the Verbal Fluency subtest are reported at or exceeding .70 for intervals ranging from weeks to years. The test authors report demonstrating long-term (average interval was 5.5 years) test-retest stability with ICCs of .88, .78, and .87 for Category Word Fluency, Letter Word Fluency, and Verbal Fluency Total, respectively. Coefficient alpha was used as an internal consistency estimate of the reliability of test scores. The test authors examined the total number of words generated for Category Word Fluency (alpha = .73) and Letter Word Fluency (alpha = .82). Internal consistency for the Design Fluency subtest was not estimated because the Acceptable Designs score does not assess the same ability as the Unacceptable Designs score. The reliability of a test also may be expressed in terms of the standard error of measurement (*SEM*), which is well suited to the interpretation of individual scores (Anastasi & Urbina, 1997); no *SEM* is reported in the test manual.

Validity, a unitary concept, regards test scores and how they are interpreted (Impara, 2010). The discussion of validity evidence in the test manual lacks a thorough presentation; only brief mention is made of validity evidence in the testing process, test construction, and the fairness of the testing process and score interpretation. Positive correlations are noted between Acceptable Designs scores and Letter Word Fluency (r = .49, p < .001), Category Word Fluency (r = .51, p < .001), and Verbal Fluency Total (r = .57, p < .001) scores. Factor analyses

of 13 cognitive measures are reported yielding a four-factor solution that accounted for nearly 77% of the total variance in 283 healthy adults and a three-factor solution that accounted for 69% of the total variance in 260 adults with severe psychiatric or medical conditions. In both models, three CIFA scores had loadings greater than .6 on a single factor the authors labeled *ideational generativity*. Construct evidence of validity for both subtests is discussed as divergent thinking, processing speed, and the ability to monitor output for rule breaks and repetitions. In addition, visual-perceptual accuracy, visual-constructional skills, and visuospatial working memory constructs are measured in the Design Fluency subtest, and lexical retrieval processes are measured in the Verbal Fluency subtest. Finally, correlations between CIFA scores and other cognitive ability measures are presented for the normative sample of 327 healthy adults and for a pooled sample that also included 324 adults with significant medical or psychiatric conditions. Of the subtests of the CIFA, the Verbal Fluency and Design Fluency scores correlate with each other (Pearson rs = .57 to .59) in the normative and pooled samples.

COMMENTARY. The CIFA is a brief and easy test to administer with strengths in ease of use and interpretation for the skilled examiner. Scoring is relatively simple. Normative data need to be based on a more ethnically and geographically diverse sample. In future editions of the test manual, the authors would do well to consider a more thorough discussion of the evidence that bears on the validity of test score use as validity evidence presented is somewhat limited. Additional case examples beyond the two that are currently presented would also be welcome.

SUMMARY. The CIFA is designed as an individually and quickly administered measure of design and verbal fluency in English-speaking adults to assist professionals in identifying neuropsychological disorders. The administrative guidelines are well written and clearly articulated. The CIFA achieves its stated purpose, admitting an interplay of possible factors with some scores showing very different patterns of correlation with other cognitive measures in CIFA normative data. The theoretical framework discussed for this instrument is documented and clearly presented.

REVIEWER'S REFERENCES
Anastasi, A., & Urbina, S. (1997). *Psychological testing* (7th ed.). Upper Saddle River, NJ: Prentice Hall.

Impara, J. C. (2010). Assessing the validity of test scores. In R. A. Spies, J. F. Carlson, & K. F. Geisinger (Eds.), *The eighteenth mental measurements yearbook* (pp. 817–823). Lincoln, NE: Buros Institute of Mental Measurements.

Kingery, L. R., Schretlen, D. J., Sateri, S., Langley, L. K., Marano, N. C., & Meyers, S. M. (2006). Interrater and test-retest reliability of a fixed condition design fluency test. *The Clinical Neuropsychologist, 20,* 729–740.

Review of the Calibrated Ideational Fluency Assessment by ANTHONY T. DUGBARTEY, Adjunct Associate Professor, Department of Psychology, University of Victoria, Victoria, British Columbia:

DESCRIPTION. The Calibrated Ideational Fluency Assessment (CIFA) is an individually administered instrument for measuring unstructured production of words and designs under circumscribed conditions. Verbal fluency tasks have long been included in the traditional inventory of neuropsychological tests of language functions and, together with nonverbal generation analogues, used to tap executive control functions. The CIFA follows this tradition as an instrument developed for use with adults with neuropsychiatric disorders. The instrument developers note, however, that the CIFA may not be an appropriate tool for use with individuals with less than 3 years of formal education or with non-native English speakers, because there are no norms for these subgroups. As well, it would not be appropriate to administer the Design Fluency subtest to individuals with severe vision impairments or individuals who are unable to use a pencil because of neurological motor abnormalities.

The CIFA contains two subtests: Design Fluency and Verbal Fluency. For each of the Verbal Fluency tasks, examinees are asked to name as many words as they can think of that meet certain criteria within a specified time period. For the Design Fluency subtest, examinees draw as many designs as possible. Administration of the Design Fluency subtest yields three types of scores (i.e., Acceptable Designs, Unacceptable Designs, and Percent Unacceptable Designs). Although the Verbal Fluency subtest yields seven types of scores, the subtest nevertheless retains the traditional distinction of phonemic and semantic fluency, in addition to an aggregated verbal fluency score. Finally, an Ideational Fluency Composite score (from the sum of the normed scores for Acceptable Designs, Letter Word Fluency, and Category Word Fluency) is derived. In addition to the CIFA record booklet, all that the examiner needs to administer the test is a writing instrument, blank sheets of paper, and a stopwatch. The CIFA professional manual includes a very detailed scoring guide, with well laid out illustrative examples of acceptable and unaccept-

able designs. Scoring of the Verbal Fluency tasks is uncomplicated.

The test manual provides detailed appendices from which the examinee's obtained scores can be converted using appropriate demographic (age-, education-, and sex-based) norms.

DEVELOPMENT. The CIFA was essentially adapted from extant standardized psychometric tests (see, for example, Goodglass & Kaplan, 1972; Ruff, 1996). As such, although the CIFA has some unique attributes, the subtests that comprise it were not originally conceived of and developed by the test authors. The test authors make no such claims. Instead, they describe the CIFA in the test manual as a speeded test of generativity that was developed primarily "to provide consistent administration and scoring for commonly used tests of ideational fluency" (manual, p. 21). Although the authors provided no rationale in the professional manual for their decision to use the specific letters chosen for the phonemic fluency subtest, these letters nevertheless are among the most commonly used for this test (Strauss, Sherman, & Spreen, 2006). Very brief information is provided in the test manual about the multiple regression analysis (MRA) procedures that were used in calibrating the normative sample for the CIFA. In contrast, considerable detail, including what appears to be the test authors' rationale for using MRA, is laid out in a journal article (Testa, Winicki, Pearlson, Gordon, & Schretlen, 2009) that should be considered an essential accompaniment to the manual, because it includes considerable detail about the norming technique.

TECHNICAL. The normative sample included 327 healthy community residents in Baltimore, MD, and Hartford, CT, who were contacted through random-digit telephone calls to their residences. Their ages ranged from 18 to 92 years, 57% were women, and 80% self-identified as Caucasians. The CIFA was only one of the 17 psychometric tests administered to each participant. Participant recruitment was conducted in two phases, but no explanation is provided in the test manual as to why this was done. The normative data were derived first by converting raw scores to scaled scores, and then to T-scores using various combinations of age, sex, education, race, and premorbid IQ estimates.

Reliability studies were performed using measures of interrater reliability and test-retest reliability. Interrater reliability scores ranged from .94 (for Unacceptable Designs) to .99 (for the Verbal Fluency tasks). Test-retest reliability analyses over an average period of 5.5 years was appreciably good for Design Fluency (intraclass correlation of .67 for Acceptable Designs, *n* = 87) and Verbal Fluency (intraclass correlation of .87 for Verbal Fluency Total, *n* = 100) subtests. Internal consistency of the standardization sample, estimated with coefficient alpha, was an acceptable .82 for the Letter Word Fluency task, but rather low (.73) for the Category Word Fluency task.

Construct validity was assessed by comparing three CIFA scores and scores from an assortment of other neuropsychological tests. Test developers interpreted the resulting findings, using exploratory factor analyses, to conclude that the CIFA scores loaded quite highly on a factor they called ideational generativity.

COMMENTARY. The CIFA appears to be a quite satisfactory measure of oral word productivity and visual design fluency. Although the psychometric evidence appears sound enough to interpret results with a fair degree of reliability, construct validity of the CIFA is best considered a work in progress. In particular, what is lacking is empirical evidence of the instrument's validity from independent researchers who are not affiliated with the authors of the CIFA.

The main strength of the CIFA is that the Verbal and Design Fluency subtests are co-normed. As such, there is increased precision in the examination of divergent thinking because of the direct comparison one can make between an examinee's verbal and visual generativity skills. A second strength of this measure is the streamlined, clear, and well-defined scoring criteria for the Design Fluency subtest. And a third advantage of the CIFA is its very short administration time.

There are several potential problems with the CIFA. First, the name of the test may be misleading: There is more to ideational fluency than the verbal and figural fluency stimuli that this test utilizes. Motor (or movement sequence) fluency and olfactory fluency, for example, are not included in the CIFA.

A second criticism of the CIFA pertains to the scope of coverage of the professional manual, which is thin on many details. For example, not much is provided by way of historical account of the origins of verbal and design fluency measures. Although the CIFA developers fittingly mention Louis Leon Thurstone as the originator of the written word fluency test and contend that the visuospatial analogue was developed by Marilyn

Jones-Gotman and Brenda Milner (1977), this is only partially accurate. The origins of the verbal fluency procedure can be traced to the classical clinical neurologists of the late 19th Century. For example, the celebrated case study by Paul Broca, which culminated in the aphasic syndrome that bears his name, marked the beginnings of careful delineation of impaired oral verbal fluency following anterior cerebral lesions. This path was further refined by John Hughlings Jackson, who differentiated between nonfluent and fluent aphasia, the latter with spontaneous word productivity being less than 50 words per minute. As well, the work of Guilford (1967), whose structure of intellect model includes a test of divergent production, precedes Jones-Gotman and Milner's work on design fluency by at least a decade.

Third, the CIFA developers are silent on the issue of the appropriateness of using ideational fluency measures to assess creativity. A caveat ought to have been provided in the test manual about this, because the instrument was not validated specifically for measuring the construct of creativity, or for that matter, intelligence. There is a wealth of empirical information on ideational fluency as a measure of creativity (Bossomaier, Harré, Knittel, & Snyder, 2009; Chan et al., 2001; Snyder, Mitchell, Bossomaier, & Pallier, 2004). Moreover, the work of Guilford (1967), which paved the way for the development of such divergent thinking measures as the CIFA, was originally designed to appraise intelligence.

Fourth, CIFA was validated and normed with a geographically restricted sample of adults in two U.S. cities (i.e., Baltimore, MD, and Hartford, CT). The extent to which the norms are applicable to other regions in the United States is simply unknown. Furthermore, there is little by way of applicability of the CIFA in cross-cultural settings or with immigrant populations. A related problem is that some of the designs that are not readily nameable in mainstream United States culture may be nameable in other cultures. It would be prudent to advocate that examiners exercise caution when scoring acceptable designs for the Design Fluency subtest. One strategy to reduce confounds might be to ask examinees after they complete the subtest whether they can name any of the designs they generated.

SUMMARY. The CIFA represents a brave refinement in existing tests that assess verbal fluency and design fluency. Those who are familiar with such extant tests as the Controlled Oral Word

Association Test and the Ruff Figural Fluency Test (15: 209) would have very little difficulty using the CIFA, which would perhaps be a useful addition if one wishes to take advantage of the co-norming the CIFA affords. Perhaps with additional empirical research aimed at corroborating the construct validity of the CIFA, as well as extension of the norms to include cultural, linguistic, and geographically diverse populations, this instrument may see increased prominence in applied clinical neuropsychological circles.

REVIEWER'S REFERENCES

Bossomaier, T., Harré, M., Knittel, A., & Snyder, A. (2009). A semantic network approach to the creativity quotient (CQ). *Creativity Research Journal, 21*, 64–71.

Chan, D. W., Cheung, P., Lau, S., Wu, W. Y. H., Kwong, J. M. L., & Li, W. (2001). Assessing ideational fluency in primary students in Hong Kong. *Creativity Research Journal, 13*, 359–365.

Goodglass, H., & Kaplan, E. (1972). Boston Diagnostic Aphasia Examination. Philadelphia, PA: Lea & Febiger.

Guilford, J. P. (1967). *The nature of intelligence*. New York, NY: McGraw Hill.

Jones-Gottman, M., & Milner, B. (1977). Design fluency: The invention of nonsense drawings after focal cortical lesions. *Neuropsychologia, 15*, 653–674.

Ruff, R. (1996). Ruff Figural Fluency Test. Odessa, FL: PAR.

Snyder, A., Mitchell, J., Bossomaier, T., & Pallier, G. (2004). The creativity quotient: An objective scoring of ideational fluency. *Creativity Research Journal, 16*, 415–420.

Strauss, E., Sherman, E. M. S., & Spreen, O. (2006). *A compendium of neuropsychological tests: Administration, norms and commentary* (3rd ed.). New York, NY: Oxford University Press.

Testa, S. M., Winicki, J. M., Pearlson, G. D., Gordon, B., & Schretlen, D. J. (2009). Accounting for estimated IQ in neuropsychological test performance with regression-based techniques. *Journal of the International Neuropsychological Society, 15*, 1012–1022.

[25]

Calibrated Neuropsychological Normative System.

Purpose: "Designed to assist clinicians and researchers in their interpretation of the tests that make up the system…by accounting for variation in test performance in demographic background and estimated premorbid IQ."

Population: Ages 18 to 92.

Publication Date: 2010.

Acronym: CNNS.

Scores, 95: 67 measure scores and 6 factor scores (Processing Speed, Attention/Working Memory, Verbal Learning and Memory, Visual Learning and Memory, Ideational Fluency, Executive Functioning) derived from 25 tests; 22 Discrepancy Scores.

Administration: Individual.

Price Data, 2013: $160 per introductory kit, including professional manual (175 pages) and 50 record forms; $739 per introductory kit with CNNS-SP scoring CD-ROM; $625 per CNNS-SP scoring CD-ROM; $50 per 52 record forms; $120 per professional manual.

Time: Administration time not reported.

Comments: The system "consists of widely used neuropsychological measures that are co-normed." Scores are derived from the following tests, which are not included in the price of the system: Hopkins Adult Reading Test, Mini-Mental State Examination, Mental Status Examination-Telephone, Right-Left Orientation, Grooved Pegboard Test, Salthouse Perceptual Comparison Test, Trail Making Test, Digit Span, Brief Test

of Attention, Modified Wisconsin Card Sorting Task, Cognitive Estimation Task, Iowa Gambling Task, Calibrated Ideational Fluency Assessment, Boston Naming Test, Benton Facial Recognition Test, Career Abilities Placement Survey, Clock Drawing, Rey Complex Figure Test, Hopkins Verbal Learning Test-Revised, Brief Visuospatial Memory Test-Revised, Wechsler Memory Scale-Revised, Prospective Memory Test, Recency Discrimination Test, Lawton Activities of Daily Living Questionnaire, Geriatric Depression Scale-15. Professional manual provides age-based norms; CNNS-SP computerized scoring program provides norms based on eight different combinations of demographic and premorbid variables.

Authors: David J. Schretlen, S. Marc Testa, and Godfrey D. Pearlson.

Publisher: Psychological Assessment Resources, Inc.

Review of the Calibrated Neuropsychological Normative System by RIK CARL D'AMATO, Editor-in-Chief of the International Journal of School and Educational Psychology, Professor of School Psychology, Chicago School of Professional Psychology, Chicago, IL, and YUAN YUAN WANG, completing her PhD in Psychology in the Faculty of Social Sciences and Humanities, University of Macau, Macau SAR, China:

DESCRIPTION. The authors indicate that the Calibrated Neuropsychological Normative System (CNNS) is designed to assist practitioners and researchers in interpreting 25 neuropsychological tests (including some that are widely used) that compose the CNNS system. This system accounts for variation in test performance based on demographic background and estimated premorbid IQ. Scores from the 25 tests can be combined to form six factors including Processing Speed, Attention/Working Memory, Verbal Learning and Memory, Visual Learning and Memory, Ideational Fluency, and Executive Functioning. These factors are among the most unique features of the system that will be discussed more fully later. A few individual tests are included as part of the system and can be used clinically. The first test that is available in the manual is the Hopkins Adult Reading Test (HART), which contains two parallel forms (A and B), each consisting of one letter and 34 words that the client is asked to pronounce. Unlike other tests in the system, the HART score is used as a predictor variable. Although some tests are included as part of the measure, the majority of tests must be purchased separately.

The following tests are used as subcomponents of the overall measure: the Mini-Mental State Examination is widely used for the screening of dementia and can quickly assess a range of cognitive functions using 11 different tasks. The Mental Status Examination–Telephone Version is a cognitive screening test consisting of eight subtests that can be administered in person or by telephone in 7 to 10 minutes. The Right–Left Orientation test requires clients to point to right- and left-side body parts upon the examiner's verbal request. The Grooved Pegboard Test consists of a board that contains holes, each with a uniquely positioned groove. The examinee is instructed to insert 25 pegs into the board, and the completion time for each hand is recorded. The Salthouse Perceptual Comparison Test is a letter and pattern comparison task consisting of pairs of letter strings or line-drawn patterns, and the examinee is required to classify the letters or patterns as same or different as quickly as possible. The Trail Making Test evaluates speeded scanning and visuomotor tracking, divided attention, and cognitive flexibility. The Digit Span test is used to assess immediate auditory attention and working memory. The Brief Test of Attention requires the examinee to count how many letters are read, while disregarding numbers, using an audio recording of 10 increasingly longer lists of letters and numbers. The Modified Wisconsin Card Sorting Task is a variation of the original test, requiring clients to sort cards according to specific directions. The Cognitive Estimation Task consists of 10 items that require clients to respond to questions that do not have readily apparent answers in order to assess reasoning, self-monitoring, and executive functioning. The Iowa Gambling Task is designed to assess decision making derived from a computerized card test. The Calibrated Ideational Fluency Assessment evaluates the spontaneous production of words under restricted conditions, which consists of verbal and design fluency tasks. The Boston Naming Test uses 30 items to assess confrontational naming using stimuli from the 85-item experimental version. The Benton Facial Recognition Test assesses a client's ability to match unfamiliar faces pictured under varied lighting conditions and angles of exposure. The Career Abilities Placement Survey is designed to assess vocationally relevant abilities, but for the CNNS, only the spatial relations subtest was used. On the Clock Drawing test, the client is asked to draw the face of a clock. The CNNS manual offers a great deal of information about this test including directions, clock drawing scoring criteria, and clock drawing scoring examples. The Rey Complex Figure Test requires the client to copy a complex, two-dimensional line drawing. The total copy score and total copy time are recorded. The Hopkins Verbal Learning Test–Revised examines verbal learning and memory. The Brief Visuospatial Memory Test–Revised measures nonverbal learning and memory. The CNNS uses two Wechsler Memory Scale–Revised subtests, Logical Memory and Visual Reproduction. Both assess immediate recall and delayed recall. The Prospective Memory Test assesses the client's ability to perform an intended action at a particular time in the future. The Recency Discrimination Test assesses memory for temporal order. On this measure, the client is shown 15 pairs of drawings used earlier in the Boston Naming Test and asked to identify which drawing from each pair appeared first. The Lawton Activities of Daily Living Questionnaire estimates the independent living skills of the client for physical activities such as eating, dressing, grooming, and home ambulation. The Geriatric Depression Scale–15 evaluates behaviors related to depression.

The Calibrated Neuropsychological Normative System Software Portfolio (CNNS-SP) is an unlimited-use computer program that facilitates the scoring of the tasks and tests included in the CNNS. The CNNS-SP appears user-friendly and would seem necessary when dealing with this long list of tests and their scores. However, the CNNS-SP program was not available for review. A positive aspect of this system is that it offers the examiner the ability to classify clients into qualitative categories based on their standard scores (e.g., extremely superior, very superior, average, low average, mildly abnormal). The target population for CNNS is clients between the ages of 18 and 92. No administration time information was provided for the CNNS.

DEVELOPMENT. This system grew out of the Johns Hopkins Aging, Brain Imaging, and Cognition (ABC) study, for which 215 adults were recruited in the first phase. An additional phase added another 179 adults to the sample. A total of 67 participants were excluded based on a number of criteria (e.g., history of specific diseases and disorders). This left a total of 327 participants in the standardization sample.

The initial step in developing the CNNS was to convert raw scores of each separate test into scaled scores (M = 10; SD = 3), a process that normalized the distribution of each test score. Higher scores indicate better test performance. The entire standardization sample (N = 327) was used in the raw score to scaled score conversion. Test performance was then calibrated using a multiple regression analysis. Eight different predictor models were developed: (a) age; (b) age, sex, and education; (c) age, sex, and race; (d) age, sex, education, and race; (e) age, sex, education, and HART A/B score; (f) age, sex, education, race, and HART A/B score; (g) age, sex, and HART A/B score; and (h) age, sex, race, and HART A/B score. The scaled scores were converted to T scores, and the accuracy of the T scores was assessed for all eight predictors. As previously mentioned, six factor scores were established. These factors could be quite helpful in understanding clients' skills and disabilities. The authors report a six-factor solution is most appropriate, but no data were provided. The authors provide additional statistical information related to development of the CNNS in 11 appendices in the manual.

TECHNICAL.

Standardization. The standardization of the CNNS includes 327 participants from Baltimore and Hartford who were recruited from random-digit dialing of households as part of the ABC study. The authors initially developed T scores and assessed them in several ways. Next, the authors developed factor scores. Finally, the authors developed discrepancy scores that can be used to help understand a client's abilities and disabilities. The sample included participants from 18 to 92 years of age ($M = 54.8$; $SD = 18.8$), with slightly more women (56.6%) than men (43.4%). The majority of the CNNS sample was Caucasian (80.1%), with 18% African Americans and 1.8% persons of other racial/ethnic backgrounds. It is questionable whether the test scores are able to reflect the neuropsychological functioning of individuals from populations other than Caucasian or African American (e.g., see Davis & D'Amato, in press). Many current psychological and neuropsychological measures are based on a standardization sample that better reflects the current makeup of the U.S.

Reliability. The test-retest reliability of the six factor scores ranges from .50 to .80. Although the test authors claim the CNNS shows good to excellent internal factor score reliabilities, some of the lower reported scores associated with test-retest reliabilities are obviously of great concern.

Validity. Traditional validity evidence is not reported for the CNNS, which is not an instrument, per se, but a collection of instruments from which a system of norms was developed. [Editor's note: Validity evidence for some of the tests comprising

the CNNS is available in the technical manual/ section of the individual tests.] Given the uniqueness of the system, the authors chose to focus on clinical validity. Evidence of validity is provided in the form of several investigations, including clinical groups of individuals with Parkinson's disease, schizophrenia, bipolar disorder, and probable/possible dementia as well as a mixed clinical sample. Scores obtained from respondents in the clinical groups were compared to scores obtained by individuals in the standardization sample.

COMMENTARY. The CNNS ties together the norms of a great variety of neuropsychological tests that assess neurocognitive and life domains. This attribute would seem to offer uninitiated neuropsychologists support in understanding client factor-based domains and related functions. Because the CNNS involves a large number of tests, the administration process is very time-consuming. Although it is improbable that a clinical neuropsychologist would administer all the tests comprising the system to a single client, the system allows practitioners to use selected tests from the system's collection, which is a strength. Moreover, the authors do not adequately explain the reason why certain tests were selected whereas others were excluded. Indeed, the potential overlap among different tests would seem to be problematic. The authors provide incomplete psychometric information about the CNNS, such as the validity of test score use.

The authors claim that one major advantage is that the CNNS provides corrections for demographic variables and estimated premorbid IQs based on the HART. The CNNS allows users to interpret test performance based on an individual's demographic background and estimated premorbid IQ, which may increase the precision by accounting for variation caused by individual differences. So too, the CNNS-SP claims the practitioners may choose which set of prediction equations to use for report generation. Although this feature would seem to be useful, it could not be viewed or evaluated. Finally, the standardization sample is small and not representative of the U.S. population.

SUMMARY. The CNNS is designed to assess a wide range of neuropsychological abilities of individuals ages 18 to 92. This measure represents a complicated system that provides a set of norms based on the authors' selection of 25 tests that they suggest are widely used in neuropsychological assessment. The majority of these tests must be purchased separately. Additionally, the neuropsychological system did not meet its goal of appropriately assessing neuropsychological functions given the small number of participants who comprised the standardization sample and the myriad set of neuropsychological variables. In the opinion of these reviewers, the technical features (i.e., reliability and evidence of validity of test score use) have not been adequately addressed. Given these concerns, the current neuropsychological system is not recommended for clinical use at the current time.

REVIEWERS' REFERENCE

Davis, J. M., & D'Amato, R. C. (Eds.). (in press). *Neuropsychology with Asian-Americans. Issues of diversity in clinical neuropsychology series*. New York, NY: Springer.

Review of the Calibrated Neuropsychological Normative System by JENNIFER M. STRANG, Traumatic Brain Injury Program Manager, Northern Regional Medical Command, Fort Belvoir, Virginia:

DESCRIPTION. The Calibrated Neuropsychological Normative System (CNNS) is a set of norms designed to "assist clinicians and researchers in their interpretation of the tests that make up the system" (manual, p. 1). The system provides corrections for demographic variables (i.e., age, sex, education, race) as well as estimated premorbid IQ, based on the Hopkins Adult Reading Test (HART A/B). The authors indicate that these calibrated norms improve the clinician's ability to provide more precise test interpretations by accounting for individual differences. They further assert that the system is advantageous in that it "consists of widely used neuropsychological measures that are co-normed" (manual, p. 1).

The manual provides clear and concise descriptions of all of the tests that are included in the system; there are a total of 25 measures. Although the authors claim that the measures are "widely used," there are several tests that, in this reviewer's experience, are somewhat uncommon (e.g., Salthouse Perceptual Comparison Test, Cognitive Estimation Task). However, given that some clinicians may be unfamiliar with these tests, they are available free of charge on the publisher's website. The website includes the instructions, scoring forms, and guidelines, stimuli, and references for these tests; interpretive guidelines are provided in the manual. The following measures are available on the website: Hopkins Adult Reading Test (HART A/B), Salthouse Perceptual Comparison Test (PCT), Grooved Pegboard Test (scoring sheet only), Clock Drawing Test (CDT), Boston Naming Test-30 (BNT-30), Recency Discrimination Test (RDT), Cognitive Estimation Test (CET),

Prospective Memory Test (PMT), Lawton ADL/IADL Questionnaire (ADL/IADL), Geriatric Depression Scale-15 (GDS-15), and Mental Status Examination-Telephone Version (MSE-TV). The other measures included in the system are administered and scored according to standard procedures. It should be noted that the CNNS also includes subtests from the Wechsler Adult Intelligence Scale–Revised (WAIS-R) and the Wechsler Memory Scale–Revised (WMS-R). The authors describe their rationale for using the older versions of the Wechsler tests, stating that "first, the CNNS provides updated normative data for these subtests...second, a great deal of research has been conducted using these measures" (manual, p. 11). Although this rationale is sound, from a practical perspective, many clinicians may no longer have access to these measures.

Recording raw scores on the record form is quick and easy. Conversion of raw scores to scaled scores and T scores also is straightforward. In addition to individual subtest scores, factor scores may be obtained (i.e., Processing Speed, Attention/Working Memory, Verbal Learning and Memory, Visual Learning and Memory, Ideational Fluency, Executive Functioning), although certain tests must be administered to compute the summary scores. Of note, the conversions presented in the Professional Manual are based on age only. Therefore, in order to obtain corrections for the other demographic variables and premorbid IQ, the scoring software package is required (Calibrated Neuropsychological Normative System Software Portfolio, CNNS-SP). In addition to eight different prediction models, the computerized scoring system also computes discrepancy scores, statistical significance (if applicable), and cumulative percentile for each discrepancy.

DEVELOPMENT. In developing the CNNS, the authors endeavored to create a normative system that enables the user to interpret raw test data based on demographic background and premorbid ability. All of the tests included in the CNNS were administered to adults participating in a study of normal aging. Following test administration, each test score distribution was normalized by converting raw scores to scaled scores, such that higher scaled scores reflected better test performance. Scaled scores were then converted to T scores, and multiple regression analysis was used to predict test performance based on an individual's demographic background and premorbid ability. Eight different predictor models were derived using different combinations of the predictor variables (i.e., age, sex, education, race, premorbid IQ). The authors include considerable detail about the processes used to evaluate the accuracy of the calibrated T scores. Following T score conversion, six factor scores were constructed using confirmatory factor analyses. The statistical significance of score discrepancies and the base rates of factor score discrepancies also were calculated. Finally, estimated premorbid WAIS-III IQ scores based on HART A/B scores were derived using linear regression. Overall, the authors provide substantial detail regarding the development of the CNNS.

TECHNICAL. The standardization sample was composed of 327 neurologically normal participants who were recruited as part of the Johns Hopkins Aging, Brain Imaging, and Cognition (ABC) study. Recruitment occurred through random-digit dialing of households from the Baltimore, MD, and Hartford, CT, areas. The participants ranged in age from 18 to 92 years, and detailed data on the other demographic characteristics and test performance are summarized in the manual. Although the sample size seems relatively small, according to Testa, Winicki, Pearlson, Gordon, and Schretlen (2009), the multiple regression approach avoids certain limitations of the conventional approach to stratifying participants; namely, "sample size criteria are more forgiving for the RBN [regression-based norms] approach" (p. 1013).

Clinical validity also was investigated and included ABC study participants who were excluded from the standardization sample due to medical or psychiatric conditions. The clinical sample sizes range from a low of 24 in the Parkinson's disease group to a high of 176 in the probable/possible dementia group. Again, the demographic and test performance data are summarized in the manual, though not at the same level of detail as for the normative sample. For additional information on the reliability and validity of the individual tests that constitute the CNNS, the authors refer the reader to the original sources of data on the psychometric properties of the measures.

COMMENTARY. The developers of the CNNS appear to have achieved the goals they intended to reach. The scoring system is easy to navigate, and the manual provides helpful guidelines for interpreting the scores, including case examples with different performance profiles. As stated by the authors, the two major advantages of the system include the provision of corrections for several de-

mographic variables and premorbid ability, as well as the inclusion of 25 "widely used" neuropsychological tests that are co-normed. Such features assist the user in providing more precise test interpretations by accounting for individual differences. Regarding the first advantage, it is important to note that the score conversions presented in the Professional Manual are based on age only. Therefore, in order to obtain corrections for the other demographic variables and premorbid IQ, the scoring software is required, which is a significant expense. With regard to the second advantage, there are several tests that, in this reviewer's experience, are somewhat uncommon. Perhaps anticipating this issue, certain tests are available free of charge on the publisher's website. The website also includes the instructions, scoring forms, and guidelines, stimuli, and references for these tests. Another possible limitation, for some clinicians, is the inclusion of subtests from the WAIS-R and WMS-R. Although it is true that newer versions have less validation evidence, from a practical perspective, many clinicians may no longer have access to the older versions of these scales. The authors provide sufficient detail regarding the development and standardization of the CNNS. Continued research with special clinical groups would strengthen the clinical applicability of the CNNS as, compared to the normative sample, the clinical group sample sizes are small.

SUMMARY. The CNNS meets its goal of creating a normative system that enables the user to provide more precise test interpretations by accounting for individual differences. A total of 25 co-normed measures constitute the CNNS, and several tests are available free of charge on the publisher's website. The scoring system is easy to navigate, and the manual provides helpful guidelines for interpreting the scores. However, importantly, it is necessary to purchase the accompanying scoring software in order to obtain full benefit of the CNNS. Overall, the authors provide sufficient detail regarding the development and standardization of the CNNS. Although there is limited information on the psychometric properties of the individual tests that comprise the CNNS, references are provided. Continued research with special clinical groups would strengthen the clinical applicability of the CNNS. In sum, the CNNS is a viable alternative to other commonly used normative systems.

REVIEWER'S REFERENCE

Testa, S. M., Winicki, J. M., Pearlson, G. D., Gordon, B., & Schretlen, D. J. (2009). Accounting for estimated IQ in neuropsychological test performance with regression-based techniques. *Journal of the International Neuropsychological Society, 15*, 1012-1022.

[26]

The Capute Scales.

Purpose: "Designed to help the clinician determine the presence of atypical development in the two streams of cognitive development: language and visual motor skills."

Population: Ages 1 month to 36 months.

Publication Date: 2005.

Acronyms: CAT; CLAMS.

Scores, 3: Cognitive Adaptive Test Developmental Quotient, Clinical Linguistic & Auditory Milestone Scale Developmental Quotient, Full Scale Developmental Quotient.

Administration: Individual.

Price Data, 2010: $375 per complete test system including manual (115 pages), scoring sheets, and test kit; $25 per 20 scoring sheets; $325 per test kit including laminated card of images, notepad, crayons, cloth, form board, plexiglass pane, pegboard, dowel, cup, plastic jar, 10 blocks, plastic ring, bell, and tote bag; $55 per manual.

Foreign Language Editions: Spanish and Russian editions available.

Time: (6–20) minutes for both scales.

Comments: Developmental quotients are provided for the Cognitive Adaptive Test and Clinical Linguistic and Auditory Milestone Scale. These are summed to yield a Full Scale Developmental Quotient for the entire scale.

Authors: Pasquale J. Accardo and Arnold J. Capute.

Publisher: Paul H. Brookes Publishing, Co., Inc.

Review of The Capute Scales by STEFAN C. DOMBROWSKI, Professor and Director, School Psychology Program, and WILLIAM TANGUAY, Professor, School Psychology Program, Rider University, Lawrenceville, NJ:

DESCRIPTION AND DEVELOPMENT. Developed for physicians and nurses working with pediatric populations, The Capute Scales were designed to assess the cognitive development of children ages 36 months or younger in two areas: language and visual-motor. The test manual indicates that the scales were developed out of a critical clinical, research, and developmental need for a measure that could quantify developmental rates and facilitate the determination of the presence of delay. The Capute Scales comprise two test batteries. The language battery (Clinical Linguistic & Auditory Milestone Scale [CLAMS]) relies on parental history in the first 18 months of life and a combination of parental history and clinical observation from 18 to 36 months. The visual-motor problem-solving battery (Cognitive Adaptive Test [CAT]) requires direct observation of a child engaged in specific test item tasks during the administration. The Capute Scales require adherence to standardized administration procedures and assist the pediatric practitioner in screening for the presence of several common developmental disabilities of childhood including intellectual disability, autism, cerebral palsy, and communication delays. The Capute Scales test kit contains a manual, scoring sheets, and several manipulatives. The manual is clearly written and easy to follow. Illustrations assist the clinician in administering and scoring items. Scoring of The Capute Scales is straightforward and yields a developmental quotient that is scaled to a commonly used metric (mean = 100; SD = 15). The Capute Scales have been translated into Spanish and Russian.

TECHNICAL. The Capute Scales were normed based on five clinical sites across the Eastern and Central United States: Baltimore, Providence, Buffalo, Rochester, and St. Louis. A total of 1,239 individuals were initially included in the normative sample. Individuals were excluded from the normative sample if they experienced a known, preexisting developmental condition (e.g., prematurity, pregnancy-related complications including drug use) resulting in a final sample size of 1,055 participants. They were also excluded if English was not the primary language used in the home. Later studies extended norms to Spanish- and Russian-speaking populations. Enrollment targets were established to yield an even distribution of children by sex, race, and age (10 strata from 2 months to 36 months). Actual enrollment was generally evenly distributed across the 10 strata although age 30 months contained only 6.6% of the sample. There was a higher percentage of males (53.2%) than females (46.8%). The ethnic composition was distributed as follows: Caucasian (56.7%), African American (32.3%), and Other (11.0%). Intraclass correlations (ICC) were computed for Total CAT (.98), Total CLAMS (.97) and for each race and sex demographic (.97 to .98). Results suggested strong agreement between CAT/CLAMS scores and chronological age. The test manual reports that low variation in race/sex ICC values suggests the influence of demographics to be trivial on total scores. The test manual indicates that The Capute Scales were studied for their validity relationship with the first two editions of the Bayley Scales of Infant Development (BSID; Hoon, Pulsifer, Gopalan, Palmer, & Capute, 1993; BSID-II, Leppert, Shank, Shaper, & Capute, 1998), but failed to furnish concurrent validity evidence in the test manual. Protocols to establish interrater reliability were introduced prior to test administration. Examiners were compared with a single, "gold standard" expert rater on three video-recorded administrations. Training was continued until future raters achieved 80% or higher agreement on these sample exercises. Additional reliability evidence was not provided. *Z*-scores were computed (mean = 100, *SD* = 15) from CAT/CLAMS raw scores and converted into Developmental Quotient scores (DQ = Age-Equivalent Score / Chronological Age x 100) utilized to assess a child's overall developmental progression. Of the participants in the standardization sample, 0% to 5% of participants (DQ, Total CAT, and Total CLAMS) in each age stratum fell below 2 standard deviations (*z* = 70) from the mean with one exception: 12.5% of CAT scores for participants in the 2-month age stratum fell below 70. The test manual states that this age group also exhibits the highest score variability across participants (*SD* = 25.9). In comparison, participant CAT scores in the 36-month age stratum exhibited the lowest variation (*SD* = 7.0). Overall, total score variability was greatest on CLAMS and less pronounced on both CAT and DQ across age strata.

COMMENTARY. Created to support medical and nursing practitioners in conducting pediatric assessments, The Capute Scales serves as a brief, yet informative measure of developmental progress. With strengths suited to quick evaluation (6–15-minute administration time with limited up-front training required), The Capute Scales function as an evolution of similar previous instruments when utilized in primary care settings. However, the underlying psychometric properties of the scales could be improved upon. The normative data are not representative of U.S. Census population demographics. Of particular concern, the normative sample excluded the entirety of the Western and Southern United States and was constrained to only five clinical locations located in the Midwest and Northeast regions. All races other than Caucasian and African American are grouped in the "Other" category. With such a broad and nonrepresentative demographic category, the use of The Capute Scales with additional racial/cultural groups may be problematic. Also, validity evidence is lacking including concurrent validity studies with other measures of infant and toddler development and predictive validity evidence with measures that assess for developmental delay. Reliability evidence is similarly unavailable omitting critical test-retest studies and examination of internal consistency indices. Although these limitations exist, the test

manual's recommendation of pairing The Capute Scales with developmental history and clinical judgment is sound. This "combined approach" to developmental assessment can serve to indicate the need for further developmental and cognitive evaluation with measures that have more robust technical properties.

SUMMARY. The Capute Scales attempt to provide clinicians with a rapid "litmus test" for the identification of developmental delay. Grounded in a rich foundation of developmental research, The Capute Scales can serve as an important tool in screening for developmental delays. The administration and scoring of The Capute Scales is brief and straightforward, critical assets for time-constrained clinical environments. Due to several psychometric limitations including a nonrepresentative normative sample and limited validity and reliability evidence, drawing definitive, quantitative conclusions from The Capute Scales is not advised. As a structured interview, however, The Capute Scales can function as a valuable component in a comprehensive assessment of developmental progress.

REVIEWERS' REFERENCES

Hoon, A. H., Pulsifer, M. B., Gopalan, R., Palmer, F. B., & Capute, A. J. (1993). Clinical adaptive test/clinical linguistic and auditory milestone scale in early cognitive assessment. *Journal of Pediatrics, 123*, S1-S8. PMID: 7686574

Leppert, M. L., Shank, T. P., Shaper, B. K., & Capute, A. J. (1998). The Capute Scales: CAT/CLAMS—A pediatric assessment tool for the early detection of mental retardation and communicative disorders. *Mental Retardation and Developmental Disabilities Research Reviews, 4*, 14–19.

Review of The Capute Scales by CARLEN HENINGTON, Associate Professor of School Psychology, and CARMEN D. REISENER, Assistant Professor of School Psychology, Mississippi State University, Mississippi State, MS:

DESCRIPTION. The Capute Scales, designed to assess atypical development across two domains (language, visual-motor) in children (cognitive age of less than or equal to 36 months), includes two measures: (a) Cognitive Adaptive Test (CAT), a test of visual-motor skills with 57 items; and (b) Clinical Linguistic & Auditory Milestones Scale (CLAMS), a test of 26 expressive and 17 receptive milestones (both across 19 test ages). This version is based upon norms obtained in a multicenter standardization study conducted with typically developing children.

The Capute Scales includes the manual, 4-page scoring sheets, and test items used during administration (i.e., laminated images card, cup, plastic jar, transparent panel, 10 cubes, notepad, crayons, cloth, shape formboard, pegboard with 6 pegs, 8-inch stick, ring, bell, tote bag), all available separately. Close supervision is necessary as some items may pose a choking hazard.

Instructions for administration, requiring 6-15 minutes, for both components are clear and easy to follow. To minimize transition from one test object to another and reduce child frustration, all items using a specific test object (e.g., ring) should be administered before moving to the next object (e.g., blocks). The test authors caution that for reliability, standardized administration is imperative and indicate that parents present (recommended and often holding the child) must not direct the child during the assessment. The CAT predominantly requires direct observation of responses to various stimuli and tasks. For much of the CLAMS, administration involves a parent/caretaker interview. To facilitate child success, evaluators begin administration two age levels below the parent's estimation of the child's functional age. Basal is obtained when all items within two successive age levels, or age sets, are completed successfully. Ceiling is reached when no items in an age set are completed successfully. Age sets begin at 1 month, occur in monthly increments through 12 months of age, and then graduate in larger increments (i.e., 2-month increments through 18 months, 3-month increments through 24 months, 6-month increments through 36 months) on both measures.

All items are scored as "yes" or "no" (e.g., "understands no"). Items have varying weights depending upon the number of items in an age set and the number of months in the increment. For example, two items in a monthly age set would each have a weighted value of .5; conversely, three items in a 3-month age set would have a weighted value of 1.0. Obtaining the scale score is straightforward (i.e., age equivalent scores are the basal age plus total of weighted items through ceiling age). These scores can be converted to a rate of development, or developmental quotient (DQ), using the formula: Age Equivalent (months) / Chronological Age (months) x 100. A full-scale developmental quotient (FSDQ) is a composite of the CAT and CLAMS calculated by obtaining the arithmetic mean of both DQ scores. All scores are calculated directly on the scoring protocol. Receptive and expressive language age equivalents can be noted for comparison.

The test authors claim The Capute Scales are a valuable clinical tool for pediatric practitioners because they provide differentiated diagnosis of a number of development disorders and delays (e.g., intellectual disability, autism, communication disorders, language delay). Notably, the test authors also indicate this measure is intended to be only a "component of a general assessment of development" (p. 29, Accardo & Capute, 2005). Additionally, the authors report that The Capute Scales are a research tool comparable to the Bayley Scales of Infant Development (BSID; Bayley, 1993), with strong concurrent validity between the two scales. Cited advantages of this measure over the BSID include: (a) reduced dependence upon certified individuals for administration, (b) less formal training required for accurate administration, (c) reduced administration time, and (d) lower materials cost.

DEVELOPMENT. The Capute Scales are based upon a history of criterion-referenced assessment of infants and children (Accardo & Capute, 2005). The CAT, visual-motor skills measure, is purported to be based upon the original Cattell test of development (Cattell, 1940) and concepts developed by Arnold Gesell (see Gesell & Amatruda, 1947). The CLAMS, originally developed in 1973 as a language battery to identify children's developmental progress in 29 sequential milestones, was later refined to include 25 linguistic and auditory milestones for children up to 24 months. The CAT and CLAMS were combined to form the CAT/CLAMS in 1996 (Capute, 1996).

TECHNICAL. In 1998, the process of standardization and collection of norming data began with trained individuals who mastered (80% reliability) standardization protocols. Five sites were selected in the northeast and central U.S. for norming activities, and a total of 1,239 children ages 1–36 months participated. These children were selected to reflect sex (male = 53.2%), race (White = 56.7%, Black = 32.3%, other = 11.0%), and 10 age strata. Age strata were controlled such that the child was within a prescribed (based upon age) timeframe of that age (e.g., within 1 week of the 2-month age, within 4 weeks of the 18-month age) with no fewer than 82 children participating at each age. Criteria for inclusion (e.g., primary home language is English) and exclusion (e.g., no noted risk such as prematurity, abnormal growth parameters, documented pregnancy difficulties) were controlled to include only children with no known developmental conditions. Parental demographic data were also collected. Interclass correlations for CAT and CLAMS across sex and race are high (r = .97 to .98). Raw scores were converted such that standardized scores (M = 100, SD = 15) and z-scores were evaluated using regression analysis to determine linear relationships. These converted scores are presented in a table with corresponding percentile ranks such that a child's raw score can be converted to any of the scores (e.g., percentile, standardized, z-score) across each age set. Additionally, tables of expected achievement of milestones based upon the normative data are also presented for the CAT and CLAMS.

To support test score validity of The Capute Scales, two previous studies (i.e., Hoon, Pulsifer, Gopalan, Palmer, & Capute, 1993; Leppert, Shank, Shaper, & Capute, 1998) are cited comparing the CAT/CLAMS to the BSID with acceptable correlations (no statistics provided). However, two independent studies were located. One examined the CAT/CLAMS as a screener for preterm infants and predictor of BSID scores (Vincer et al., 2005), and indicated sufficient sensitivity and specificity for a screening tool. The second study examined concurrent and predictive validity of the CAT/CLAMS with BSID (Voight et al., 2003), and showed a moderate to strong correlation (r = .39 and .74, respectively) to BSID Mental Development Index (MDI) scores at ages 12 and 30 months, and a modest correlation of 12-month CAT/CLAMS DQ scores to 30-month BSID MDI scores (r = .18).

The manual also provides information regarding administration of The Capute Scales to children who are Spanish speakers and who are from Russia. However, information provided on these populations is preliminary with noted limitations. The translated protocols are provided.

COMMENTARY. Pediatric health care providers and researchers may find The Capute Scales useful as a screening measure. Although the test authors indicate it can be used as a diagnostic tool and allows for differential diagnosis of a number of disorders and delays in young children, given the moderate concurrent validity with other more effective measures, The Capute Scales are unlikely to provide sufficient evidence for psychological and psychiatric diagnosis. The predictive relationship between The Capute Scales and the BSID indicates that diagnosis using this measure should be viewed with caution.

With two to four items within each age set and some age sets comprising 6-month increments, there is concern for the sensitivity and specificity of the measures. The test authors indicate a start point of two age sets below expected functional age and also recommend all items related to a specific assessment object (e.g., ring) be administered together. However, not all test items involve demonstration and the directions do not indicate how to address items that are considered more advanced when the child performs them without demonstration and while presenting easier items first to allow child success. As stated by the test authors, many of the language items are scored according to parent report leading to concerns of accurate measurement. The test authors suggest looking for consistency within the reported abilities (e.g., "mature jargoning is coincident with a vocabulary of approximately 7–10 words," manual, p. 11) to valid responses. In summary, the manual would benefit from inclusion of recent concurrent and predictive validity studies, additional administration information for spontaneous and "from demonstration" tasks, and new research provided for the translated protocols.

SUMMARY. The Capute Scales are a norm-referenced instrument with adequately established norms–easy to administer, score, and interpret as a measure of visual-motor and language development in children (1–36 months). It yields raw scores translated into developmental quotients (DQ), standard scores (M = 100, SD = 15), percentile ranks, and z-scores across three scales: the CAT, CLAMS, and Full-scale (FSDQ). The measure is best considered as a screener.

REVIEWERS' REFERENCES

Accardo, P. J., & Capute, A. J. (2005). *The Capute Scales: Cognitive Adaptive Test/Clinic Linguistic & Auditory Milestone Scale manual.* Baltimore, MD: Brookes Publishing.

Bayley, N. (1993). *Bayley Scales of Infant Development-Second Edition.* San Antonio, TX: Harcourt Assessment.

Capute, A. J. (1996). *The Capute Scales: CAT/CLAMS instruction manual.* Baltimore, MD: Kennedy Fellows Association.

Cattell, P. (1940). *The measurement of intelligence of infants and young children.* New York, NY: Harcourt Assessment.

Gesell, A., & Amatruda, C. S. (1947). *Developmental diagnosis: Normal and abnormal development.* New York, NY: Paul B. Hoeber.

Hoon, A. H., Pulsifer, M. B., Gopalan, R., Palmer, F. B., & Capute, A. J. (1993). Clinical adaptive test/clinical linguistic and auditory milestone scale in early cognitive assessment. *Journal of Pediatrics, 123,* S1-S8. PMID: 7686574

Leppert, M. L., Shank, T. P., Shaper, B. K., & Capute, A. J. (1998). The Capute Scales: CAT/CLAMS—A pediatric assessment tool for the early detection of mental retardation and communicative disorders. *Mental Retardation and Developmental Disabilities Research Reviews, 4,* 14–19.

Vincer, M. J., Cake, H., Graven, M., Dodds, L., McHugh, S., & Fraboni, T. (2005). A population-based study to determine the performance of the Cognitive Adaptive Test/Clinical Linguistic and Auditory Milestone Scale to predict the Mental Developmental Index at 18 months on the Bayley Scales of Infant Development-II in very preterm infants. *Pediatrics, 116,* e864-e867. DOI: 10.1542/peds.2005-0447

Voight, R. G., Brown, F. R., III, Fraley, J. K., Liorente, A. M., Rozelle, J., Turcich, M., Jensen, C. L., & Heird, W. C. (2003). Concurrent and predictive validity of the Cognitive Adaptive Test/Clinical Linguistic and Auditory Milestone Scale (CAT/CLAMS) and the Mental Developmental Index of the Bayley Scales of Infant Development. *Clinical Pediatrics, 42,* 427-432. doi: 10.1177/000992280304200507

[27]
Career Motivation Profile.

Purpose: "Designed to determine which components, out of 17 identified motivators, one values as essential to his/her career fulfillment."

Population: Under age 17 through adult.

Publication Date: 2011.

Acronym: CAMOP.

Scores: 17 motivators: Achievement, Balanced Lifestyle, Change and Variety, Creativity, Financial Reward, Identity and Purpose, Improvement, Independence, Inspiration, Learning, Mobility, Power, Recognition and Appreciation, Social Factors, Stability, Status, Fun and Enjoyment.

Administration: Individual.

Price Data: Available from publisher.

Time: (20) minutes.

Comments: Self-administered online assessment. The test publisher advises that the test manual is being updated to include more information about methodology and theoretical background used in the development of the test. The test publisher also advises that this information is available to clients, as are benchmarks for relevant industries and racial/ethnic group comparison data. However, this information was not provided to Buros or the reviewers.

Author: PsychTests AIM, Inc.

Publisher: PsychTests AIM, Inc. [Canada].

Review of the Career Motivation Profile by CAROLINE M. ADKINS, Professor Emeritus, School of Education, Hunter College, City University of New York, New York, NY:

DESCRIPTION. The Career Motivation Profile (CAMOP) is a self-administered 40-item computer-based assessment tool that is purported to evaluate certain personality characteristics and/or specific skill sets that provide information about work-related values and motivations. Individuals are asked to respond to questions about the importance to them of a variety of work-related factors or situations. The majority of items have a four or five multiple-choice format option that reflects varying degrees of importance or significance. The last 3 items in the inventory are different in that respondents are asked to select up to 5 factors out of a list of 17 about which they feel most strongly.

Scoring is done automatically after the test is completed. The results are organized in three ways. The first way is in the form of a graph listing each of the 17 motivators the test assesses: Achievement, Balanced Lifestyle, Change and Variety, Creativity, Financial Reward, Identity and Purpose, Improvement, Independence, Inspiration, Learning, Mobility, Power, Recognition and Appreciation, Social Factors, Stability, Status, and Fun and Enjoyment. On a line accompanying each factor is the score achieved out of a possible 100. The second score is a verbal description of each factor, which includes its definition, meaning and application to career choice, employment setting, personality characteristics, work-related values, and specific career behaviors. This description again is accompanied by a numerical score that reflects the score the person achieved on each factor. The third score organizes the results by grouping and categorizing the individual's major, minor, and insignificant motivators.

Linked to the interpretation of scores on the CAMOP is another section entitled "Advice." This section offers suggestions for "increasing one's motivation at work." This section is organized according to each of the individual's motivators/factors. Each factor is accompanied by a number of suggestions related to actions a person can take to help satisfy a given motivator or value. For example, under the value Achievement, the advice is to "look for or create the opportunity to take on tasks you find personally challenging." Suggestions are also offered that relate to obstacles that "can hinder or sidetrack" achievement-oriented people. This section appears to be related to helping the test-taker to interpret their scores and to extend their meaning to actual work choices or behaviors.

DEVELOPMENT. The procedures used to develop the CAMOP are not described in the manual. Thus, there is no information about the theory or constructs underlying its design, such as how questions or items were developed and selected (or deselected) for inclusion in the measure or how items were grouped into factors or scales. There is also no information about the reasons or need for its development, who it was intended for, or what uses and applications the authors envisioned for it.

TECHNICAL.

Standardization. The CAMOP was standardized on a large volunteer sample of 6,165 people. Descriptive statistics, graphical scores, and results for ANOVA comparisons are reported in the manual for the entire sample and for an analysis of scoring differences according to gender, age, level of education, amount of income, occupational position, and satisfaction with current field. The number of respondents in each of these categories appears balanced and well-represented. No information is provided regarding racial or ethnic differences.

The size of the sample is robust for standardization purposes and the analysis of comparison variables is detailed and comprehensive. Using the standardization sample for test interpretation is somewhat problematic in that little demographic information is provided about the sample, for example, what geographic area they represent, whether they are from urban or rural settings, in what type of occupations they were, or how was satisfaction with their jobs defined? In other words, the question of how representative the sample is for populations who may use the CAMOP is not addressed.

Also, if a test user wants to understand how an individual's score compares to scores achieved by the standardization sample, the user has to sort through many pages of graphs and statements of ANOVA comparisons. There is a real need to synthesize this data, to interpret it for the test user, and to suggest what score differences might mean for different age groups or for people from different socioeconomic groups as reported by varying income levels.

Reliability. Reliability is reported in the manual only by internal consistency coefficients. Reliability coefficients (coefficient alphas) range from .37 for the Fun and Enjoyment Scale to .73 for the Improvement Scale. The mean alpha across all 17 scales is .79. These analyses suggest that internal consistency within the different scales is fairly moderate but not high. Test-retest or parallel test form reliability information was not provided.

Validity. With respect to validity, the CAMOP appears to have good face validity because each motivator (scale) is well-defined, seems to include relevant work-related behavior, and emphasizes both intrinsic and extrinsic values. So on the "face" of it, the CAMOP appears relevant for assessing one's work-related motivations. Although there is some face validity, there is no evidence that the items or scales were empirically derived with item, factor, or scale analyses.

Each of the motivators in the CAMOP is presumed to be measuring different factors. Items in the factors or scales are grouped together with varying numbers of items but one does not know if these scales are measuring separate factors or measuring similar or overlapping constructs. The very least we need to see are intercorrelation analyses of scale scores to demonstrate how much confidence can be placed in differences between subscale scores.

A major problem with the CAMOP is the fact that there is no information about the theoretical underpinnings of the measure. There is no reference to achievement theory or motivation theory as in

Murray's (1938) or McClelland's (1953) work on Need Achievement or to Super's (1957) Career Development and Counseling theory. It also appears that little attention was paid to differences between relevant career variables such as interests, abilities, values, and personality characteristics. These constructs appear to be all mixed together in the scale definitions.

To address the issue of how meaningful scores attained on the CAMOP are in assessing the career motivations of the individual test-taker, some information about how scores on the CAMOP correlate with other relevant indices of career behavior is needed. For example, are age differences on scores on the CAMOP related to developmental stages or stages of career development? Is there any evidence that scores on individual scales such as Achievement correlate with grade-point average, occupational level, or socioeconomic status? Of great importance is how other measures of job satisfaction correlate with CAMOP difference scores on satisfaction with current field.

COMMENTARY. The CAMOP is an inherently interesting measure for people who wonder what career direction they should take or what changes they need to make. There are many people who would benefit from a systematic assessment of their work-related values and motivations. The major problem with the CAMOP is that there is little here to indicate it has any predictive value. The user has to have a level of trust, not supported by any data, that a given scale really indicates a higher or lower level of motivation that is relevant to real life career behavior and choices.

One questions the degree to which this instrument relates to career development theory and behavior. The lack of test development and validity information leaves significant questions in the mind of this reviewer. The test constructors clearly worked with competent statisticians, given the abundance of statistical graphs and tables in the manual. These statistics describe the standardization sample's performance on the CAMOP but do not appear to be guided by other principles of test construction.

The CAMOP manual is also not very useful to the test user. As noted above, information on test development and validity studies is missing, thus it is difficult to use the CAMOP for test interpretation. Specific sections on interpretation of test scores need to be included in the manual with examples of how client profiles relate to different types of career behavior and choices. The developers would be well-advised to consult the manuals of a well-regarded vocational instrument such as the Strong Interest Inventory (18:128).

It is possible that the test developers never intended that the manual be used for test interpretation, relying instead on computer-generated scoring with direct feedback to the individual test-taker, bypassing any professional administration or interpretation of scores. Eliminating the professional who administers and interprets a test is, of course, an intrinsic part of direct, self-administered online assessment tools. In many respects this form of assessment could be very beneficial to people. They can respond to an assessment measure and obtain immediate results in the privacy of their home or office. The danger, as is true of the CAMOP and other online assessment tools, is that the developers have bypassed and ignored the foundations of relevant theory, constructs, and principles of test construction.

SUMMARY. The CAMOP does not appear to be a psychometrically sound instrument. To establish its usefulness as a career assessment and career counseling tool, more extensive reliability and validity studies and analyses are very much needed. More importantly, there is very little evidence that the developers were guided by any theories of career development, behavior, or motivation. This is an important conceptual and empirical limitation and one that is too often found in many other computer-based assessment measures. Before the test-user can have any confidence in using this instrument to assess career motivation, much more information is needed about its development, intended use, and theoretical underpinnings.

REVIEWER'S REFERENCES

McClelland, D. C., Atkinson, J. W., Clark, R. A., and Lowell, E. L. (1953). *The achievement motive.* New York, NY: Appleton-Century.
Murray, H. A. (1938). *Explorations in personality.* New York, NY: Oxford University Press.
Super, D. E. (1957). *The psychology of careers.* New York, NY: Harper & Row.

Review of the Career Motivation Profile by BRUCE BISKIN, Senior Associate, Delaware Valley Career Solutions, Newtown, PA, and Adjunct Assistant Professor of Graduate Education, Leadership, and Counseling, Rider University, Lawrenceville, NJ:

DESCRIPTION. The Career Motivation Profile (CAMOP) is a 40-item inventory designed "to evaluate certain personality characteristics and/or specific skill sets. This information will be used to provide insight about what is important to the test-taker and/or in which settings he/she would

most likely thrive" (manual, p. 11). The test manual further reports, "The Career Motivation Test [*sic*] was designed to determine which components, out of 17 identified motivators, one values as essential to his/her career fulfillment. It pinpoints all a person's major, minor and insignificant motivators, along with a detailed breakdown on what that means" (p. 1). The manual lists the intended application of CAMOP as "pre-employment," suggesting it can be used in making hiring or placement decisions.

The CAMOP is available online to corporate clients through Psychtest's ARCH Profile assessment system (www.archprofile.com/corporate). The CAMOP–or a version of it–seems to be available to take by anyone under the name of "The Career Motivation Test" at a companion site, http://testyourself.psychtests.com.

The CAMOP comprises 40 objectively scored items in several formats. Most of the scales comprise responses to 5 items (one comprises responses to 6). That there are 17 scales suggests that each item contributes to the score on more than one scale. The manual states that the CAMOP can be completed in about 20 minutes. On completion of the final item, the respondent receives a detailed report comprising six sections: Summary (top motivator with its description); Introduction (what are motivators and why are they important); Graphics (graphic summary of scores, showing absolute and relative strength of motivators); Details (detailed description of the meaning of each motivator and the associated score earned); Major and Minor Motivators (motivators classified as major, minor, and insignificant); and Advice (suggestions for increasing one's motivation at work for each of the 17 motivators). The report has a professional appearance and is easy to read.

This reviewer received access to a demonstration administration of the CAMOP through the publisher's website and a psychometric report that included over 90 pages of tables and analyses with no narrative explanation. Although additional information was requested from the publisher, it was not received. Therefore, this review is based only on the information provided.

DEVELOPMENT. The information package received contained no information about the development of the CAMOP scales or items, including the selection of the 17 motivators to be measured or the measurement model used to create the scales.

TECHNICAL. The psychometric report contains some data that would normally be included in a technical manual. The review includes this information where available.

Administration and scoring. The ARCH Profile interface was easy to use. This reviewer completed the CAMOP within the expected time. It is not clear whether the noncorporate interface is comparable to that of the ARCH Profile system.

Scores for each of the 17 motivators seem to be reported on a scale from zero to 100, though the documentation provided does not state this explicitly nor does it describe the meaning of scale scores (e.g., percentages, standard scores) other than higher scores represent higher levels of motivation. The measurement model used to generate raw scores (classical test or item response theory) is also unknown. Given the relatively small number of responses included on each scale, a change in a single response may potentially have a substantial impact on scores that range from zero to 100. Including error bands in the Graphics section would go a long way to addressing this issue–particularly for test takers who may not be discussing the results with a professional.

Typically, when the number of items is substantially less than the number of total score points among scales, the scales are ipsatively scored. With ipsative scoring, scale scores are correlated with each other because choosing one option is scored positively for one scale and negatively for another, for example. As a result, it is impossible to score high or low on all scales. To the extent the CAMOP scales are ipsative, it may be appropriate to rank them for a single respondent (e.g., "financial needs" are more motivating than "achievement needs"), but without additional information the test user does not know whether the scales with the highest scores represent strong motivators–or just the strongest ones, which may actually be moderate or weak. A similar interpretation can be made for scales with the lowest scores. The CAMOP report does not explain how the scale scores are obtained.

Time limits. The ARCHProfiles manual suggests that test takers can complete the CAMOP in about 20 minutes; however, administration is untimed.

Norms. The CAMOP psychometric report data are based primarily on a self-selected, uncontrolled sample who took the CAMOP on two websites—queendom.com and psychtests.com—where anyone can take a variety of types of assessments. The period during which the sample data were collected was not reported. The sample included 6,165 respondents who agreed to participate in a validation study. The psychometric report describes some of the demographic characteristics of the sample, including gender and age. In this unselected group, 14% did not report gender and 17% did not report age. As a result, it is unclear how representative the core sample is for any particular respondent or purpose. (Analyses reported later in the psychometric report also describe portions of the sample broken down by educational attainment, job level, socioeconomic status, and job satisfaction. For each of these variables, subgroups are equal in number; however, it is not clear how these subsamples were selected.)

Means and standard deviations are reported for scores in all subgroups on each CAMOP scale in the psychometric report, but percentile/score conversion tables often associated with norms are not. The psychometric report does show histograms and bar graphs for scores on each scale in the total sample of 6,165 respondents. Because many of the distributions appear either skewed negatively (i.e., more high scores than low scores) or bimodal, percentile tables would be especially helpful when interpreting scores.

Reliability. The psychometric report includes internal consistency reliability estimates (coefficient alpha) for scores related to each of the 17 scales and for the total of all 37 items. Because there is no reason to believe that the motivators as a group would be related to each other, this reviewer was puzzled by inclusion of the latter coefficient alpha, which was .79. Estimates for the 17 scales range from a high of .79 (Mobility) to a low of .37 (Fun and Enjoyment). The median reliability estimate is .62. On one hand, these reliability estimates are reasonably good for such short scales (5–6 items); however, that does not mean they are substantial enough upon which to base impartial decisions, particularly if the CAMOP scores constitute a critical part of a pre-employment decision process. Again, error bands around CAMOP scores in the Graphics section of the report representing the typical error (e.g., one standard error of measurement or the interquartile range of the scores) would be helpful in interpreting the scores reported. The psychometric report does not include test-retest reliability estimates, so estimates of the stability of CAMOP scores are unavailable.

Validity. Validity refers to the accuracy of interpretations and decisions made from test scores. Typically, a standard test manual will include, or refer to, evidence to support the validity of test scores for each recommended use. The type of evidence presented is described and an explanation for how it supports the validity of score interpretations—and any resulting decisions—is given. Although the CAMOP psychometric report contains a wealth of statistical data identified as "Validity Analysis," there is no narrative explanation of how these data support the validity of the CAMOP for any particular purpose. Bar graphs representing mean scores on each scale broken down by a variety of demographic factors (e.g., gender, age, education) are included, but these do not include error bands. Even if they did, there is no explanation of how these results support the validity of CAMOP scores. For example, data are presented for mean scores on each CAMOP scale for over 1,900 men and 1,900 women. The data, however, are unaccompanied by a discussion of how the level and pattern of scores for men and women are consistent with expectations that support the validity of score interpretations. The psychometric report contains over 60 pages of detailed statistical reporting labeled as "validity analysis," but they are not explicitly–or implicitly–linked to use of the CAMOP scores for any particular purpose. As a result, it is inappropriate to label this section of the report as "Validity Analysis" without supporting explanations. In short, the material available to review contained little or no information supporting the validity of interpretations and decisions made from the CAMOP's scores.

COMMENTARY. The CAMOP comprises scales to assess 17 motivators for work. Work environments that are not compatible with an individual's most significant work motivators are likely to result in low job motivation. Unfortunately, the limited information available on which to evaluate the CAMOP as a measure of work motivations was disappointing. The publisher failed to include an actual technical/user manual. As a result, little or no information was available about the conceptual basis and technical development of the CAMOP or whether score interpretations based on the CAMOP are likely to be valid. The section in the psychometric report labeled, "Validity Analysis" was simply a long series of statistical analyses with no explanation of how they supported inferences from CAMOP scores. Internal consistency reliability estimates were provided but, at best, one can conclude they are reasonable—for scores based on short scales of 5–6 items that are assessing useful constructs. Regardless of scale length, reliability estimates in the range

reported are far too low for making high-stakes decisions in pre-employment screening.

Given the limited information available and the limitations of short, ipsatively scored scales, this reviewer cannot recommend using the CAMOP to assess work motivators as part of any pre-employment decision making. Any value for using the CAMOP in making high-stakes decisions may lie in additional technical documentation, including development information and validity support presently unavailable. As a companion to a technical manual, the psychometric report might serve as an outstanding statistical appendix; on its own, it contains little interpretive information of use to a test user.

SUMMARY. Based on the limited information provided and the convenience nature of the validation sample, there is little to recommend the CAMOP as a useful, reliable measure of work motivators on which to base decisions. If the publisher has technical documentation for the CAMOP that would satisfy the needs of a future reviewer to provide a more accurate evaluation, that information should be provided. Based on the paucity of information available, use of the CAMOP for pre-employment decisions should be avoided.

[28]
Careprovider Aptitude Personality & Attitude Profile.

Purpose: Designed to examine "whether the personality traits and skills a person possesses match those required to excel in the caregiving field."

Population: Potential caregivers.

Publication Date: 2011.

Acronym: CAPAP.

Scores, 29: Overall Results, Emotional Strength, Fortitude, Impression Management, Interpersonal Skills, Work Abilities, Work Attitudes, Helpfulness, Empathy, Reaction to Stress, Discretion, Social Insight, Communication Skills, Assertive Communication, Diligence, Organization, Dependability, Attention to Detail, Efficiency, Self-Discipline, Comfort with Decision-Making, Physical Hardiness, Patience, Attitude Towards Honesty, Attitude Towards Safety, Attitude Towards Teamwork, Optimism, Social at Work, Acquiescence.

Administration: Individual.

Price Data: Available from publisher.

Time: (30) minutes.

Comments: Self-administered online assessment. The test publisher advises that the test manual is being updated to include more information about methodology and theoretical background used in the development of the test. The test publisher also advises that this information is available to clients, as are benchmarks for relevant industries and racial/ethnic group comparison data. However, this information was not provided to Buros or the reviewers.

Author: PsychTests AIM, Inc.
Publisher: PsychTests AIM, Inc. [Canada].

Review of the Careprovider Aptitude Personality & Attitude Profile by RICHARD REILLY, Professor Emeritus, Stevens Institute of Technology, Hoboken, NJ:

DESCRIPTION. The Careprovider Aptitude Personality & Attitude Profile (CAPAP) is an individually administered online measure that purports to assess suitability for a career as a caregiver. The estimated time for the test is 30 minutes. The manual states that the purpose of the test is to assess "whether the personality traits and skills a person possesses match those required to excel in the caregiving field" (p. 1). The manual also states that the application of CAPAP is for pre-employment testing. According to the authors the CAPAP includes "114 [items] plus additional questions" (manual, p. 1). The total number of items for the version reviewed was 144 items. Respondents are advised that they should be in a quiet place and have enough time to complete the test in one sitting. Respondents are told that the purpose of the CAPAP is to "evaluate certain personality characteristics and/or specific skill sets" and that this information "will be used to provide insight about what is important to you and/or in which settings you would most likely thrive" (online test instructions). Respondents are advised to "answer choices that reflect how you usually feel or act–those that most accurately describe your general feelings or behaviors." Respondents are warned "that there are measures in place that are intended to pick up attempts at self-misrepresentation. If there is an indication that you are not being truthful or taking the test carelessly, the results might be considered invalid" (online test instructions).

The instructions are clear and easy to follow. A progress indicator is shown at the top of each page, which indicates percentage of the test completed. Respondents must complete all items in order to advance to the next screen. Throughout the test, respondents are presented with a variety of different item types. These include personality items, attitudinal items, and scenario-based items. The test includes a variety of item-response scales, most of which are 5-point scales that assess attitudes or frequency of behavior. The exceptions are the

scenario-based questions that present work-related scenarios and ask the respondents to choose one of several alternatives presented. The alternatives are not arranged on a continuous scale and range from three to six alternatives. A radio button format is used for all responses.

Upon completion of the test, a report is automatically generated that includes 28 different scores. An overall score purports to assess the likelihood that the respondent would "do well in a career as a caregiver" (online test report). This score, like all other scores on the CAPAP, is reported on a 0 to 100 scale, where higher scores reflect better suitability for a caregiver career. Three summary scores, as well as their subscores, are also reported. The summary score for Interpersonal Skills is based on the subscores Helpfulness, Empathy, Emotional Strength, Reaction to Stress, Discretion, Social Insight, Communication Skills, and Assertive Communication. The summary score for Work Abilities is based on the subscores Diligence, Organization, Dependability, Attention to Detail, Efficiency, Self-Discipline, Comfort with Decision-Making, Patience, and Fortitude. The summary score for Work Attitudes is based on the subscores Attitude Towards Dishonesty, Attitude Towards Safety, Attitude Towards Teamwork, Optimism, and Social Values. The final two scores purport to assess Impression Management–"the degree to which the results on this test are distorted or manipulated" and Acquiescence–which "assesses whether you responded to the questions in a careless manner" (online test report). The report provides a graphic summary of all scores as well as definitions of the construct that each score purportedly reflects. Feedback to the respondent includes an overall recommendation (e.g., recommended for a position as a caregiver) as well as more specific feedback for each construct. An additional section of the report lists key strengths and limitations of the respondents.

DEVELOPMENT. The test manual presents very little information on the development of the items or scores included in the CAPAP. No theory or rationale for the selection of items, subscales, or summary scores is presented. No evidence is given to support content validity, nor how items were developed or selected, whether item analysis was used to remove items, or whether items were reviewed by content experts.

TECHNICAL. The test manual indicates that the overall score is based on 120 items with an alpha of .94. The three summary scores are Interpersonal Skills (40 items, alpha of .85), Work Abilities (54 items, alpha of .90), and Work Attitudes (22 items, alpha of .79). The numbers of items making up the subscores within each summary area are not reported. No reliability coefficients were reported for the 22 subscales or for the Impression Management and Acquiescence scales. The discrepancy between the 116 items making up the summary scores and the 120 items making up the total score is not explained. Although the range of the scores appears to be 0–100, the manual does not explain how the scores were scaled, or how any of the scores were derived.

The manual reports a sample size of 5,271 individuals (2,803 women, 704 men, and 1,764 unknown) and notes that they all took the CAPAP on-line at one of three sites. They further note that the sample was uncontrolled and self-selected and that all "validation items were self-report" (manual, p. 2). The manual reports sample sizes, minimum and maximum scores, and means and standard deviations for all 28 scores listed above. In addition to the 28 scores discussed above the manual includes data for a 29th scale, Physical Hardiness, which is not mentioned in the feedback report. The manual reports the age distribution on two separate pages in the manual with slightly different breakdowns for age categories. It should be noted that 16% of those reporting age were below 18 years old, which would seem to be outside the range for viable candidates for caregiver jobs. The manual also includes a series of frequency charts for the various scores. Although most of the subscores appear to be negatively skewed there is no report of skewness indices for the scales. The distribution of the overall scales appears to be fairly normal although no statistics are given to support normality.

The section labeled Validity Analysis presents a series of comparative analyses. First, a series of t-tests with accompanying bar charts are reported for males versus females on all of the scores, with results showing consistently higher scores for females. It should be noted that the subsamples of males and females in this set of analyses was reported as 704 for each group (df = 1,406) although the total number of females reported elsewhere was 2,803. The manual does not explain why or how the 704 females were selected for this analysis. The next section includes a series of analyses of variance (ANOVA) using age as an independent variable and each of the CAPAP scores as dependent variables. Post hoc analyses generally showed that the 14–17-year age group scored lower than other age groups. This section also includes a series of bar charts showing the distribution of each construct by age. The next section reports a series of ANOVAs with education as the independent variable and the various CAPAP scores as dependent variables. The total sample was divided into seven categories based on education (below high school to master's/PhD). The within-group sample size for each of these seven groups was 204 (df = 6; 1,421), but it is not explained how or why the individuals within the subsamples were selected. A variety of significant results were reported with more educated individuals generally scoring higher than less educated individuals (it should be noted that education would logically be confounded with age, given the distribution of age reported). The final section includes a series of ANOVAs with experience as a caregiver as the independent variable and CAPAP as the dependent variable. These analyses divided experience into four categories based on responses to the question, "Have you ever worked in the caregiver field?" Alternatives included, "No desire to do so," "Yes, but will/have changed careers," "No, but I would like to," "Yes, and I will continue" (manual, p. 75). The sample size for each category was 297 but again it was not explained why or how these subsamples were selected. Scores were generally higher for those who work in the caregiver field and plan to continue and those who would like to work in the caregiver field. Significance levels for each ANOVA are reported but no post hoc tests are reported. The manual provides a series of bar charts showing score distributions by experience. The remainder of the manual consists of appendices with means and standard deviations for the various comparisons.

In sum, there is limited evidence provided for the validity of the CAPAP and the various subscales on which feedback is provided. There is no discussion of item analyses, subscale reliabilities, correlations between subscores, or factor analytic results that might support the constructs included in the test. The primary evidence for validity of the CAPAP is the series of ANOVAs showing differences for responses to the "Experience" item. However, the persuasiveness of this evidence is mitigated by the uncontrolled nature of the sample, the self-report nature of the items, and potential response bias. In addition, the sample for the experience analysis has a number of potential confounds (age, gender, education), which are not controlled and which, as the manual reports, have significant relationships with the CAPAP scores.

COMMENTARY. The CAPAP includes a mix of personality, attitudinal, and situational items that could potentially predict satisfaction and/or performance in caregiver fields. Unfortunately, little evidence is provided to support the validity of CAPAP for this purpose. In addition, the extensive detailed report that provides feedback to candidates on 28 different scores requires that these scores have some evidence of construct validity. The manual provides no evidence for the validity of these constructs either with respect to the content of the various measures or with respect to empirical evidence that these constructs are distinct. The manual would benefit from a narrative that explains how the CAPAP was developed with a complete description of how the items and scales were selected or developed as well as a thorough psychometric analysis of the various subscores/constructs.

SUMMARY. The CAPAP is designed to assess the personality traits and skills required for success/satisfaction in the caregiver field. The test provides an overall recommendation for suitability as a caregiver and detailed feedback on 28 different scores. The manual provides little substantive evidence for the validity of the various scores reported. All data were collected from an uncontrolled sample and the limited validity evidence provided is of dubious quality. The use of the CAPAP for selection or guidance in caregiver fields cannot be recommended as the evidence does not meet the minimum scientific/professional requirements for validity.

Review of the Careprovider Aptitude Personality & Attitude Profile by KEITH F. WIDAMAN, Professor of Psychology, University of California, Davis, CA:

DESCRIPTION. The Careprovider Aptitude Personality & Attitude Profile (CAPAP) is a relatively short, self-report measure designed to provide information regarding the suitability of a person for a position as a careprovider. As the aging population of the United States and other countries continues to grow in size, the need for caregivers is also growing. Thus, the CAPAP was developed to provide a quick screening device to determine whether a person has the aptitude, personality, and attitudes that would provide a good fit for a position as a careprovider.

The manual states that the CAPAP consists of 114 questions, plus a number of additional

items (not described in the manual). The assessment takes about 30 minutes to complete and is self-administered through an online website. Major scale scores are provided on three broad content domains of Interpersonal Skills, Work Abilities, and Work Attitudes. Within each of these broad areas, narrower scales are available. For example, the Interpersonal Skills domain contains eight narrower scales including Helpfulness, Empathy, and Emotional Strength. The nine narrower dimensions within the Work Abilities domain include Organization, Attention to Detail, and Dependability. Under Work Attitudes, the five narrower scales include Attitude Towards Safety and Attitude Towards Teamwork. In addition to the multiple content scales, scores are provided on two validity scales that assess Impression Management and Acquiescence.

The CAPAP was developed to be administered to persons across a wide range of ages. Indeed, the sample on which statistical indices for scale scores were computed consisted of over 5,000 individuals spanning the age range from 13 years or younger to 45 years or older. Scores for each scale are reported on a scale that ranges from 0 to 100, and average scores on each major domain tend to fall near 70, with SDs between 9 and 11 points.

DEVELOPMENT. The CAPAP was first published in 2011, so this review covers the first edition of this measure. Little information was provided in the manual with regard to the way in which the CAPAP items and scales were developed. The manual stated that the Interpersonal Skills domain contains 40 items, the Work Abilities domain has 54 items, and the Work Attitudes domain consists of 22 items—a total of 116 items across these three domains. The overall score on the CAPAP is reported to be calculated across 120 items, and the source of the additional items is unclear. In addition to the lack of precision with regard to the total number of items, no information was provided in the manual regarding the number of items for each of the narrower scales or the rating scale on which item responses were obtained.

One positive feature of the CAPAP is the online web interface on which the instrument is administered and scores are reported. After completing the CAPAP, a detailed report is provided. An overall score is reported with a recommendation regarding whether a person would be a good candidate to be a caregiver. Then scores are reported for each of the three major domains—Interpersonal

Skills, Work Abilities, and Work Attitudes–and for each of the narrower dimensions within each of these domains. Accompanying the score is an interpretive summary that notes strengths and weaknesses within each domain.

TECHNICAL. Little detailed information was provided regarding the sample on which CAPAP statistics are based. The manual states that the sample of 5,271 respondents was not controlled, having filled out the CAPAP on one of three websites. In addition to completing the CAPAP, respondents provided information on their age, sex, highest level of education completed, and whether they had ever worked in the caregiver field. Of the 5,271 respondents, 2,803 self-identified as women, 704 as men, and 1,764 declined to state their gender. A total of 3,619 persons fell in nine age categories, varying between 13 years and below through 45 years and above; presumably, the remaining 1,652 respondents declined to state their age. More detailed breakdowns of respondents with regard to highest education completed and caregiver experience were also provided.

For each of the 27 content scores and the two validity scales, the mean, *SD*, and minimum and maximum values across the entire sample of 5,271 respondents were reported. Additionally, the univariate distribution, with a normal curve overlay, was provided graphically for each scale. Many of the scales appeared to have negative skew, although a minority appeared to be fairly normally distributed. No norming tables were provided for converting raw scores to a standardized metric, so only raw scores, with means and *SD*s that vary across scales, are available for use.

As for reliability, the manual listed coefficient alpha estimates of reliability of .94 for the CAPAP overall score and .85, .90, and .79 for Interpersonal Skills, Work Abilities, and Work Attitudes, respectively. No reliability estimates were provided for the narrower dimensions within each domain, so the reliability of these scales is unknown. No other forms of reliability were reported.

The validity information for the CAPAP consisted of analyses of mean differences across categorical groups based on the supplementary questions asked of respondents. In a sample of 704 women and 704 men, women had higher scores than men on 20 of the 22 scales for which significance test values were reported, with men having higher scores on only the Physical Hardiness and Optimism scales. Presumably, males

and females did not differ on the remaining 5 scales shown in a table listed as Annex 1, but no statement to this effect was provided. No indices of effect size were provided, standardized or otherwise, so the magnitude of effects of gender on scores must be computed. Using a Cohen's *d* metric, mean sex differences appeared to vary between .05 and .40 *SD* units, with most falling below .25. As a result, the mean gender differences were of relatively small magnitude, despite their statistical significance.

Similar analyses portrayed as indicators of validity were reported for mean differences for the remaining background variables on each of the 27 CAPAP scores. Significant mean differences across the nine age groups were reported on all 27 content scores (shown in Annex 2), across the seven education groups on 26 of the 27 scores (shown in Annex 3), and across the four careprovider experience groups on 26 of the 27 scores (shown in Annex 4). Significant overall main effects were followed up by post hoc testing of mean differences, although the post hoc test used was not specified. As with sex differences, no indicators of effect size were provided to aid in evaluating the magnitude of effects in these analyses.

No standard evidence supporting validity was provided in the manual. For example, common forms of construct validity–such as correlations with other instruments that purportedly assess the same underlying constructs or factor analyses to justify the provision of scores on multiple dimensions–were not discussed. Content validity could have been discussed, but was not. No forms of criterion-related validity were reported, at least under this rubric. In the analyses of careprovider experience groups, two groups–persons who currently are careproviders and persons who are not careproviders but would like to be–tended to score higher on all or most scales than the remaining two groups–persons who are careproviders but intend to change jobs and persons with no desire to be caregivers. Whether such evidence supports criterion-related validity is left to the reader. Finally, no information regarding test fairness or ability to fake-bad or fake-good on the CAPAP was provided.

COMMENTARY. The CAPAP appears to be a well-formatted, easy-to-complete self-report measure of qualities one would seek in a caregiver. But considerable concerns attend its use. The primary concern of this reviewer is the lack of detailed, psychometrically sophisticated evaluation of the reliability and validity of CAPAP scores. Preceding sections of this review indicate the kinds of investigations that would yield useful information on reliability and validity; no additional detail is needed here. At present, technical data for the CAPAP on reliability are in short supply, and on validity virtually nil. Although CAPAP scores may have substantial validity, little information documenting this validity has been presented.

SUMMARY. The developers of the CAPAP have produced a measure of optimal caregiver attitudes and abilities that can be administered and scored in an efficient manner. Unfortunately, almost no information is currently available about how scale scores were calculated or about the reliability and validity of CAPAP scores. Without further information on these matters, no firm recommendation in favor of the CAPAP can be made.

[29]

CASAS Life and Work Listening Assessments.

Purpose: Designed "to measure English language learners' listening comprehension skills" for progress monitoring and evaluation.
Population: Adult English language learners.
Publication Date: 2012.
Scores, 3: Appraisal (optional), Pre-Test, Post-Test.
Administration: Group.
Levels, 3: A, B, C.
Forms, 6: 981L, 982L, 983L, 984L, 985L, 986L.
Restricted Distribution: Distribution restricted to agencies completing the CASAS Implementation Training.
Price Data, 2012: $475 per Testing Package with Appraisal, including Form 980 Appraisal Listening Test CD, 25 Form 980 Appraisal Reading Test Booklets, Form 980 Appraisal Test Administration Manual, Level A Form 981 CD, Level A Form 982 CD, Level A Forms 981 and 982 test booklets (25 each), Level B Form 983 CD, Level B Form 984 CD, Level C Form 985 CD, Level C Form 986 CD; $350 per package without Appraisal material; $50 per CD (Appraisal, Form 981, Form 982, Form 983, Form 984, Form 985, or Form 986); $35 per 25 Appraisal Form 980 answer sheets; $70 per 25 Appraisal Form 980 Reading Test Booklets; $75 per Level A CD and 25 Test Booklets (Form 981 or Form 982); $25 per 25 Level A test booklets (Form 981 or Form 982); $22 per Test Administration Manual (41 pages).
Time: (50) minutes.
Comments: May be administered via paper and audio CD or via computer.
Author: CASAS.
Publisher: CASAS.

Review of the CASAS Life and Work Listening Assessments by JORGE GONZALEZ, Associate Professor, School Psychology Program, and HEATHER DAVIS, Doctoral Student, Special Education Program, Texas A&M University, College Station, TX:

DESCRIPTION. The CASAS (Comprehensive Adult Student Assessment Systems) Life and Work Listening Assessments (LWL) is an individually and/or group administered measure of adult English language learner (ELL) listening comprehension skills for use within adult education English as a second language (ESL) classes or training programs to assess progress in meeting educational goals. It was specifically designed to assess listening skills as outlined by the National Reporting System (NRS) six Educational Functional Levels (EFLs) for the adult education ESL population. The test is described as a "substantial revision of the CASAS listening assessment series" (technical manual, p. 2). The test consists of two parallel forms each with 38 items varying across six item types. The test can be administered on paper or via computer.

Two parallel forms were developed at each of three test levels (A, B, C; three item types per level) to measure ESL adult learners' progress across the six NRS functional levels ranging from Level 1: Beginning ESL Literacy (LWL Level A) to Level 6+: Exit from Advanced ESL (LWL Level C). According to the test manual, the parallel forms were designed to demonstrate gains across an array of listening skills required in daily living and work. Examiners can use CASAS Form 80 to determine the appropriate LWL Level to begin assessment and instruction using the LWL series.

DEVELOPMENT. The LWL test blueprint and item development processes were designed to evaluate the listening comprehension construct across diverse ELL/ESL examinees. Item development followed a standard protocol using best practices and generally accepted industry standards including expert item writers, rigorous item review, clinical tryout for feasibility, pilot testing to ensure usability, and field testing on a representative sample of the ESL adult learner population. Items were created following national needs assessment surveys and recommendations from the CASAS National Consortium. Item revision included both classical item statistics and preliminary item calibration. As noted in the test manual the extra stage of pilot testing prior to field testing allowed for further item refinement. Item types included *photo prompt*, *comprehension*, *next line*, and *which is correct*. Both parallel forms allow for item repetition at the lower levels of proficiency and also include preview questions (i.e., practice items). The test authors also note the use of universal design principles to ensure the test is appropriate for general use across populations with a wide range of functional capability.

Items under consideration for field testing were subsequently subjected to fairness and sensitivity panel review. Field testing occurred in two phases: Phase 1 (2006-2008) and Phase 2 (2010-2011). Items from both phases were used in the construction of the 2011 assessment. In Phase 1, four sets of field-test forms were developed (A, B1, B2, and C) with four anchor sets of common items to link between levels. This process established the initial scaling of the LWL with a mean of 200 and a standard deviation of 10 scale points. Rasch item calibration was used to put all items on a common scale. In Phase 2, two sets of field-test forms were constructed (A, C) with two anchor sets of common items to link between levels. Following field testing, items were subjected to classical item analyses including p-values, point-biserial correlations, discrimination indices, and a breakdown of examinee performance. For Level A, the range of p-values was .36 to .92; for Level B, .41 to .84; and for Level C, .38 to .76. Point-biserial correlation coefficients ranged from .31 to .63 for Level A, .25 to .67 for Level B, and .29 to .55 for Level C. Items meeting acceptable criteria were calibrated and linked to the IRT scale. Differential item functioning analyses were conducted following field-test trials and with ongoing psychometric analyses. No items with a Delta statistic of 1.5 or greater were used in the final test forms.

TECHNICAL. Field-test sites receiving federal funding for the target population, programs using CASAS assessments, or sites interested in using the assessments were identified across 20 states from different geographical regions and the District of Columbia. Subgroup demographic analyses evaluated through consistent classical item statistics and internal reliability estimates provided adequate evidence in the development of nonbiased test items across subgroup populations.

Reliability. Internal consistency of each of the LWL test forms resulted in adequate alpha coefficients, ranging from .85 to .89. Parallel assessments across all three developed forms demonstrated high Pearson correlation coefficients ranging from .83 to .89. Additional analyses using test characteristic curves indicated developed test forms performed as intended with Level A forms functioning similarly among lower level examinees and Level C forms functioning similarly among higher level examinees. Identical slopes indicate how each form discriminates between lower- and higher-level examinees. No differences were found between paper-and-pencil and computer-based test formats. All forms of the LWL show strong evidence of reliability.

Validity. Construct validity evidence was provided through a subject matter expert theoretical construct validity study. Experts were asked whether the LWL adequately measured the theoretical constructs of listening comprehension. Five reviewers endorsed the LWL Assessments as appropriately measuring listening skills and providing a valid measure of listening comprehension through written responses regarding test items they reviewed. Convergent validity evidence based on the criterion of the LWL constructs provided moderate evidence of convergence with the TABE CLAS-E, another NRS-approved listening comprehension assessment for adult ESL students. Correlation coefficients ranged from .61 to .73 across the ability levels of the listening assessment. Further evidence of construct validity included moderate correlation coefficients confirming appropriately developed constructs in listening comprehension as intended for assessing and monitoring adult ELLs.

COMMENTARY. The LWL Assessments provide a progress-monitoring tool for agencies providing services to adult ELLs. With recruitment and support of NRS and the CASAS Consortium ESL committee, an effective assessment measuring listening comprehension skills of adult ELLs provides a tool to federal agencies in need of appropriately placing and monitoring the progress of these learners. Because this is a newly developed measure within the CASAS assessment tools, only field testing has been conducted to provide evidence in the measurement of listening comprehension constructs. Further test administrations and data collection on measurement outcomes will provide stakeholders with valuable information for improving test items and ensuring sustainability of the assessment. Although the test manual provides sufficient information about test user qualifications and training, further information about specific reliability and validity coefficients should be provided in the administration manual to better inform test users about delivering the LWL with precise accuracy to correct ELL populations.

SUMMARY. The CASAS LWL Assessments were designed to measure listening comprehension in adult ELLs through agencies working to improve literacy skills within this population. Through rigorous test development procedures and the creation of a supporting test manual, the LWL demonstrates adequacy in measuring progress of adult ELLs in acquiring English. Although further developments to the test manual are warranted to include additional information on the psychometric properties of the LWL, test users are given sufficient information on identifying the level of the ELL and correctly linking the level of each learner to appropriate assessment and instruction tools. In a world of increasing accountability, future resources could depend on the use of the LWL as a progress-monitoring tool when considering future funding resources and improvements in the education of adult ELLs. Further administration and use of the CASAS LWL will help to ensure the sustainability of this listening comprehension measure.

Review of the CASAS Life and Work Listening Assessments by STEPHEN T. SCHROTH, Assistant Professor of Educational Studies, Knox College, Galesburg, IL:

DESCRIPTION. The CASAS (Comprehensive Adult Student Assessment Systems) Life and Work Listening Assessments (LWL) consists of a series of tests that evaluate the listening comprehension skills of English language learners (ELLs) enrolled in English as a second language (ESL) courses. Seeking to measure ELL's educational gains in listening comprehension skills, the LWL comprises six parallel test forms. The LWL is used to assess ELL's listening comprehension skills from a beginning to an advanced level and determines which of six Educational Functional Levels (EFLs) an ELL has attained. The six EFLs are 1—beginning ESL literacy, 2—low beginning ESL, 3—high beginning ESL, 4–low intermediate ESL, 5—high intermediate ESL, and 6—advanced ESL. The EFLs are identical to those devised by the National Reporting System. As a result, the LWL can be used for the purposes of local and state agency monitoring and accountability reports submitted to the National Reporting System for federally funded adult education programs. LWL scores and score gains can be aggregated to provide meaningful summative assessments regarding program effectiveness.

The LWL assesses EFLs through a series of items that balance general life skills and employment-related content. The items are presented in real life, functional contexts that are relevant to adult learners. The LWL consists of six test forms designed to be used with three levels of ability that align with specific EFLs: A, B, and C. Level A is aligned with the content of EFLs 1 through 3 and assists with placement into EFL 4, Level B assesses EFLs 3 and 4 and placement into EFL 5, and Level C measures EFLs 5 and 6 and exit from the system. Pretests and posttests are provided at each level in two parallel forms. Items on the test use simple conversations, statements, telephone calls, voice mail, and other recordings made using natural intonation, speech, and speed to assess listening comprehension. Available either as paper-delivered assessments with audio CDs or as computer-based tests, the LWL may be either individually or group administered.

The LWL is primarily designed as an evaluation tool. Although the measure assesses adult ELLs' listening comprehension, it is not designed to diagnose learners' specific strengths and weaknesses with regard to listening tasks. The test authors suggest the LWL may be used to provide a useful piece of information regarding a learner's strengths and weaknesses; however, a more comprehensive assessment would include classroom performance, homework assignments, observations, and other formative assessments.

DEVELOPMENT. The LWL is a new assessment, first introduced in 2011, that measures gains in student listening comprehension rates for individuals enrolled in adult ESL classes. Specifically developed to assess the National Reporting System's six EFLs, the LWL went through a process of test development that included several steps. Initially, the test specification process involved a needs assessment, defining the target population, purpose, and construct. Priority content standards were identified and aligned with the EFLs, after which item specification began, including types, format, and difficulty distribution. A test blueprint was devised, and item drafting, review, content alignment, and fairness and sensitivity examination began. Next, item evaluation commenced through a clinical tryout and pilot testing, with item revision based upon the results. Field testing next considered form construction, devising guidelines, sampling, administration, and an examination of the technical design.

Item evaluation considered classical item statistics and bias differentials, IRT calibration, and evaluation of fit. Form construction, which sought to produce parallel forms for each level, examined content and difficulty distributions, standard setting, linking/equating, mode considerations, and testing and scoring guidelines. Form evaluation examined form performance, the parallel forms, classification consistency, comparability studies, examinations of content and construct validity, and a speededness study. After this, an operational administration and reporting technical manual was prepared, and periodic reviews were scheduled.

TECHNICAL. The standardization sample for the LWL was drawn from populations served by 123 field test agencies based in 20 of the United States and representing all regions of the country. Of the 123 field test agencies, 52 were in California, 20 were in Florida, 8 were in Maryland, and 7 were in Kansas. No other state had more than 5 field agencies represented, and the District of Columbia, Illinois, Iowa, Michigan, and New York (among others) had one apiece. In total, field tests were administered to 7,183 individuals. The sample was largely representative of the adult education ESL population in the United States with regard to age and gender and "to a lesser degree, race/ethnicity" (manual, p. 35). The sample was overrepresentative of Haitian immigrants and ESL programs in California. The LWL also included few samples from programs in some states with large immigrant populations, such as Illinois, Iowa, and New York, which is unfortunate.

Content validity of the test items was reviewed by a group of subject matter experts who assisted both in judging the standards and competencies contained on the LWL as appropriate and in seeing that those standards and competencies were assigned to the correct EFL. Very little other evidence is provided to support validity inferences. Reliability coefficients for all three levels of the LWL are reported to meet or exceed .95. Parallel forms correlation coefficients indicate that the test/retest Pearson correlation is .89 for Level A forms, .85 for Level B forms, and .83 for Level C forms. Construct validity evidence was also provided through analyses by subject matter experts. In addition, a criterion-related validity study was conducted that compared the LWL to another test approved by the National Reporting System to measure listening compre-hension, the TABE CLAS-E. Pearson correlation coefficients between the LWL and the CLAS-E scores were .71 for Level A, .73 for Level B, and .61 for Level C.

The interval needed to achieve a significant gain appears to be approximately 60 days, or two months, after which a statistically significant gain is made by the group as a whole. These data could be helpful for administrators in determining the schedule needed for effective courses, although CASAS recommends 70 to 100 hours of instruction be provided between pretesting and posttesting.

COMMENTARY. The LWL is a convenient and easy assessment to administer and one that shows a great deal of promise. The LWL's major strengths are its ability to be administered in either individual or group settings and its exploration of listening skills as defined by the National Reporting System's EFLs. Further work needs to be done to increase the representativeness of the sample used. The development plan for the LWL is strong, and multiple opportunities were taken to examine content validity, construct validity, and the reliability of the test. Expanding the examination of validity beyond subject matter experts, however, would increase confidence in this process.

Using the LWL may provide administrators of adult ESL programs information regarding the optimal duration of such a class, the number of days and hours per week that the class should meet, and the most effective class sizes. Further research regarding this aspect of the LWL would be welcome.

SUMMARY. The LWL is designed as an individually or group administered measure of listening comprehension for adults who participate in ESL programs. This test meets its goal of providing an inexpensive and easy way of monitoring performance of adult ESL programs in a manner that is responsive to federal, state, and local agencies. The LWL also provides some information regarding the progress of individual students within an adult ESL program, but those seeking information related to this feature might also consider the BEST Plus or the TABE CLAS-E. The instrument also provides an inexpensive and convenient way to monitor pretest and posttest performance of adults in such classes, although multiple measures should be considered in making programming decisions regarding individuals.

[30]

CASAS Life and Work Reading Assessments.

Purpose: Designed to "measure learning progress of members of the youth and adult education population in the content domain of reading."

Population: Youth and adult learners.

Publication Dates: 2005-2010.

Scores, 3: Appraisal, Pre-Test, Post-Test.

Administration: Group.

Levels, 4: A, B, C, D.

Forms, 12: 81, 82, 81X, 82X, 83, 84, 185, 186, 85, 86, 187, 188.

Restricted Distribution: Distribution restricted to agencies completing the CASAS Implementation Training.

Price Data, 2011: $70 per 25 Level A, Form 81; $70 per 25 Level A, Form 82; $70 per 25 Level A, Form 81X; $70 per 25 Level A, Form 82X; $70 per 25 Level B, Form 83; $70 per 25 Level B, Form 84; $70 per 25 Level C, Form 85; $70 per 25 Level C, Form 86; $70 per 25 Level C, Form 185; $70 per 25 Level C, Form 186; $70 per 25 Level D, Form 187; $70 per 25 Level D, Form 188; $22 per Test Administration Manual (2005, 22 pages); price information for technical manual (2010, 274 pages) available from publisher.

Time: (60) minutes.

Comments: An appraisal test is administered first to identify the appropriate level of pretest. The pretest is administered and the score from the pretest guides the choice of posttest. A chart for guiding pretest/posttest choice is provided in the administration manual. Students move up through the levels of testing as their skills develop. Includes test items based on the application of functional reading skills as found in realistic life-skill or workplace contexts. Available via both paper-and-pencil tests and computer-based delivery.

Author: CASAS.

Publisher: CASAS.

Review of the CASAS Life and Work Reading Assessments by ZANDRA S. GRATZ, Professor of Psychology, Kean University, Union, NJ:

DESCRIPTION. The CASAS (Comprehensive Adult Student Assessment System) Life and Work Reading Assessments are a series of tests focused on measuring reading skills as related to everyday life and employment. The series is part of a broader system of assessments that include measures of math, listening comprehension, writing, speaking, and critical thinking. The 12 reading assessment forms span four levels (A to D) from beginning literacy to high school level. In addition, four Reading for Citizenship and two Secondary Language Arts assessment test forms are available. As noted in the test administration manual, the CASAS reading assessments may be used to place and diagnose students and to monitor their progress. To enable multiple testing at the same level, at each level an alternate form exists. Tests may be administered in paper-and-pencil format or via computer. Although there is no time limit for the tests, the administration manual reports that most test takers finish within one hour.

The CASAS levels correspond to the National Reporting System for Adult Education (NRS) levels, and, as noted by the Federal Information & News Dispatch, CASAS reading assessments, Reading for Citizenship, and Secondary Language Arts assessments have been found acceptable for use with adult education programs including adult basic education (ABE), adult secondary education (ASE), and English as a second language (ESL). As noted in the test manual and recent publications, forms for persons with visual disabilities have been developed (Posey & Henderson, 2012); beyond this, the technical manual details accommodations for persons with specific disabilities.

Each item is labeled by content, competency, and task, and the nature of student performance measured by the item is indicated. CASAS provides lists of items and competencies for use in summarizing individual student performance as well as forms on which group data can be summarized. For each test form, the administration manual provides an answer key and a chart for correcting raw scores to scale scores. The manual also indicates score ranges for which scores should not be used due to lack of precision (high conditional standard errors of measurement). Scale scores are reported separately for both ESL and ABE cohorts. Training (in person or by video) is required of test users.

DEVELOPMENT. As noted in the technical manual, the first CASAS test forms were created in 1981. During the 1980s, the test publisher created item banks, calibrated via item response theory, in the areas of reading and math. During the late 1980s the item bank was expanded by adding employment-oriented items in reading and math as well as high school level items.

The development of new items and test forms stemmed from needs expressed by those working in the field of ABE and ESL. New forms have extended the beginning level, and an extended level to bridge levels B and C are being tested. This responsiveness to requests may explain the somewhat confusing labeling of test forms. Although the administration manual indicates the level of each form, the numbering system is not transparent.

The item development process used by CASAS is extensive and follows current standards and thinking within psychometrics. Test items go through several reviews and pilot testing prior to being considered for the item bank. Test forms were developed with consideration of item difficulty, content area, and task. Using Rasch methodology, CASAS has linked all forms onto a uniform score scale. Specifically, the logit metric was translated to a 3-digit scale with a mean across all tests of 200 ($SD = 10$).

Reviews for bias involved expert review panels and statistical analyses. After panels reviewed items for possible bias, differential item functioning (DIF) analyses were conducted focusing on comparisons by gender, Hispanic/Anglo, African American/Anglo, and English/other than English. Additional review was afforded those items that were statistically identified for possible bias (delta greater than 1.5). Although specifics were not disclosed, the technical manual indicates that items identified for potential bias were used only if necessary for the content of the test when no other content-specific item existed.

TECHNICAL.

Reliability. Alpha coefficients were used to estimate internal reliability. Coefficients ranged from .82 to 91 across forms. Similar results were obtained when reliability was computed by subgroups defined by gender, ethnicity, and language (English vs. non-English). Mean point-biserial coefficients by form ranged from .52 to .75.

Alternate form reliability, with a maximum interval of 15 days, ranged from .72 to .86, with an average across levels of .81. With outliers removed, alternate form reliability coefficients increased to .81 to .92, with an average estimate across levels of .89. As might be expected, the removal of outliers increased the correlation observed; what is not known is the definition of outliers, who comprised 9.3 percent of the sample. Also examined was the consistency between administration modes (computer vs. paper and pencil). For the six forms for which data were reported, the correlations between methods administered one day apart ranged from .83 to .94. DIF analyses across modes by item were conducted; items on which a difference in difficulty by mode was observed were identified for further review. The nature and outcome of the review is not shared in the technical manual. Reliability of classification across forms was also explored. Significant differences across forms were not found for all levels except those that involved forms for level D (adult secondary). Raw score to scale score conversions across parallel forms yielded a correlation coefficient of .88.

Validity. CASAS built in content validity in the item writing process. Item writers were given blueprints indicating competencies, basic skills, and/or content standards at a particular instructional level. As already noted, the blueprints for new tests were developed based on needs and input from practitioners. Draft items were then reviewed by master item writers followed by clinical tryouts.

CASAS National Consortium, representing 30 states, developed reading basic skills content standards. Cut scores between levels were developed operationally in 1980 and revised in 1996 through borderline group methods. In 2008, a test-centered judgment-based standard setting procedure was used to provide evidence of the link between CASAS and NRS levels. The bookmark standard setting method was used to identify the performance level descriptors and cut scores that separate each NRS educational functioning level. Panels were provided data from three states relative to the numbers of students placed in each NRS level; these data supported refinement of cut scores. Results relative to the earlier version were consistent with the revised version for all levels except Advanced ESL and Exit from Advanced ESL. As will be noted later, issues relative to discrimination at the upper levels may have limited the consistency in level designations. The technical manual indicates more studies at the upper levels are planned. Standards were found to be correlated to the Workforce Investment Act Title II NRS levels and aligned to CASAS assessments. Several states field tested the content standards to ensure they were complete and aligned to CASAS and NRS levels.

Original version CASAS scores were linked to the Center for Applied Linguistics behavioral objectives, Mainstream English Language Training levels. Linkages to the Basic English Skills Test were reported with regard to corresponding ranges; correlation coefficients between the measures were not offered in the technical manual. Similarly, ranges on CASAS levels were linked to NRS levels, ESL functioning levels, National Adult Literacy Survey levels, Student Performance Levels, and years of school completed. Although linkages were delineated, the manner in which they were generated and the extent to which they were based on empirical data are not evident.

In 2002, CASAS and GED scores were compared. As CASAS scores increased, so did GED scores. However, more precise statistical data were not reported.

Concurrent validity evidence was provided by a midyear study in which teachers were asked to place students in one of the NRS educational functioning levels. Completed separately for ESL and ABE, CASAS scores increased as NRS level increased. When compared to grade level, CASAS scores differed between grades for all levels except Grade 12 to 13+. Across all forms, participants with 6 or fewer years of education scored lower on CASAS than those with 7 or more years of school. Change in CASAS test performance was compared to hours of instruction. For those with pretest hours of instruction less than 236, a clear pattern of increased CASAS scores with additional hours of instruction was evident; this finding was not observed for those who began with 236 or more hours.

The technical manual reports ongoing examination of item functioning to ensure items continue to demonstrate suitable reliability and validity. However, details of changes observed, if any, were not provided. Also, it might be prudent to link CASAS test performance on the citizenship test forms to performance on citizenship exams.

COMMENTARY. CASAS employs extensive psychometric means, including both classical test theory and item response theory to ensure test efficacy. At times, items are referred for further review (e.g., due to bias concern, differences between computer and paper/pencil administration modes); the outcomes of these reviews are not evident in the technical manual. In addition, questions as to the usefulness of CASAS to measure growth at the high end of the performance spectrum are evident in the data reported (e.g., ability to demonstrate change). These concerns may be linked to those of Flowerday (2005), who noted an issue relative to the limited numbers of items measuring higher order processes. Also, uniqueness and usefulness of scores from the Reading for Citizenship tests need to be explored.

Overall, evidence from multiple sources and studies are available to support the reliability and validity of CASAS. Data support the use of CASAS to identify NRS level and to measure progress of ABE and ESL students. The only caveat may be at the upper levels of ability assessed by CASAS.

SUMMARY. CASAS is well known in the discipline and recognized by practitioners in ESL, ABE, and ASE programs; between 2005 and 2008, 37 states used one or more levels of CASAS. This reviewer agrees with earlier reviewers (Gorman & Ernst, 2004; Flowerday, 2005; Parke, 2005) who indicated that the CASAS is a suitable measure for placing students and measuring growth within ABE and ESL programs. The CASAS Life and Work Reading Assessments follow in this tradition.

REVIEWER'S REFERENCES

Flowerday, T. (2005). [Review of the Comprehensive Adult Student Assessment System (CASAS-Third Edition)]. In R. A. Spies & B. S. Plake (Eds.), *The sixteenth mental measurements yearbook* (pp. 256–258), Lincoln, NE: Buros Institute of Mental Measurements.
Gorman, D., & Ernst, M. L. (2004). Test review: The Comprehensive Adult Student Assessment System (CASAS) Life Skills Reading Tests. *Language Assessment Quarterly, 1,* 73–84.
Parke, C. S. (2005). [Review of the Comprehensive Adult Student Assessment System (CASAS-Third Edition)]. In R. A. Spies & B. S. Plake (Eds.), *The sixteenth mental measurements yearbook* (pp. 258–261), Lincoln, NE: Buros Institute of Mental Measurements.
Posey, V. K., & Henderson, B. W. (2012). Comprehensive Adult Student Assessment Systems Braille Reading Assessment: An exploratory study. *Journal of Visual Impairment & Blindness, 106,* 488–499.

Review of the CASAS Life and Work Reading Assessments by DARRELL L. SABERS, Professor Emeritus of Educational Psychology, and CHRISTINE CALDERON VRIESEMA, Doctoral Student, University of Arizona, Tucson, AZ:

DESCRIPTION. The pretests and posttests in the CASAS Life and Work Reading series are intended for native or non-native English-speaking youth and adults who participate in the CASAS program. The Life and Work Reading tests measure reading comprehension across a variety of life contexts. The tests contain both reading and employment content, with the assessments addressing employability through the Workforce Skills Certification System. There are four exam levels in the series (A, B, C, and D), with Level D being the most difficult. Tests are multiple choice, and the number of items varies depending on the level of the exam. Examinees are given approximately one hour to complete an exam. Tests are administered via computer or paper and pencil; these reviewers only reviewed the paper-and-pencil tests. Exams are level-appropriate in that examinees are administered an appraisal test that determines the exam level of the pretest. The posttest exam level is determined by the examinee's score on the pretest. The appraisal tests were not provided for review, nor were the certification tests.

Reading exams are scored using a scanner, CASAS TOPSpro software, or by hand. The examinee's raw score is obtained by determining the number of items answered correctly. After the raw score is determined, it is converted to a scale score. Scale scores relate to CASAS basic skills levels and are used to make comparisons across other CASAS tests or the National Reporting System for Adult Education (NRS) educational functioning levels. Of note, scale scores cannot be generalized outside of the CASAS program.

DEVELOPMENT. The CASAS test development procedure is an excellent demonstration of how curriculum should define what is taught and what is tested. The development of the tests follows the instructional mission of the program. The items in the item bank from which all tests are constructed were pilot tested and field tested with adult basic education and English as a second language learners. The Educational Testing Service guidelines for fairness and sensitivity were followed closely in producing the item bank. The NRS was the "curriculum" for instruction and test development, and the NRS adult education population was the target population for instruction and test development.

TECHNICAL. Because the tests are not intended to be used with any nationally representative population, there is no attempt to address a national census population. However, the NRS adult education population was used as the target population for the preparation of the item bank. This population is well described in the technical manual. The tests approximate this population with regard to gender and ethnicity/race only. The use of the tests is intended to be based on level of reading ability rather than age of participants.

Rather than typical standardization data such as standard scores and percentile ranks for individuals, the technical manual presents information on the match of scores to the NRS educational functioning levels. There is an adequate description of the standard-setting procedures used to establish cut scores for transforming scale scores on tests to estimates of examinees' NRS educational functioning levels.

At every level, the objectives of instruction are the objectives for the tests. There are alternate forms of the tests for every instructional program in the series, and every item in each test assesses an objective in the curriculum. An examination of the reading assessments' content validity suggests that evidence of relevance is well demonstrated. Although each item is relevant for the curriculum, however, representativeness of content validity is not as well established.

Reliability data are presented for alternate forms of the assessments. The overall correlation coefficient between exams was .81 for a combined sample of more than 2,000 pairs of scores for examinees across eight different pairs of forms representing all CASAS levels. There is no information to help a reader interpret what such a coefficient indicates with regard to reliability of any form that an instructor might use. Alternate forms reliability was also calculated between the pairs of exams for each test level. The correlations between the two forms for each reading level are acceptable, but the numbers of participants in the separate analyses were not presented in the CASAS technical manual.

It should be noted that the correlational statistics describing the relationships between alternate forms may be inflated. The CASAS program has many agencies contributing to the data collection for the many tests within the Life and Work series, and the resulting composite data contain between-agency variability in addition to the desired within-agency variance. The reported coefficients may be spurious compared to what would be found within any one agency. However, these reported alternate forms reliability estimates are not necessary given that there are conditional standard errors of measurement (CSEMs) available for the cut scores that the users will have to represent the level of learning for the examinees. If CSEMs were available for all scores, users could construct confidence intervals for each score to enhance proper interpretation of the performance of every examinee.

COMMENTARY. The program is unusual in that the tests cannot be administered or scored by anyone who has not completed CASAS implementation training. With required training that includes interpretation and use of scores, misuse of the tests should be minimized. It is understandable that there is no test interpretation section in the manual for instructors who have had that training, but there is information in the technical manual that further emphasizes aspects of test interpretation that should be remembered. For example, the grade level scores are not typical grade equivalent scores, and the manual emphasizes that the scores should only be used to comply with regulations. The grade level scores represent the reported level of school attendance rather than actual or estimated grade placement of students achieving the median score as represented by traditional grade equivalent scores. Because the examiners and the teachers have all been trained by CASAS, no third parties should see CASAS tests or results.

There are differences in the number of items that address an objective across the two forms. When a major purpose of the testing is to determine the amount of learning between pretest and posttest, it would be more effective if the tests were perfectly parallel in content representativeness. As the opportunity for further test development is available (as indicated by reference in the technical manual to additional tests to be developed), it is recommended that the future tests be made more parallel in content (the present forms are already equivalent in difficulty). To emphasize the importance of the content representativeness issue, these reviewers would prefer that the two forms of each test be identified as "alternate" forms rather than "parallel" forms, the term that is used in the technical manual.

There is a great opportunity for gathering data for the tests in the CASAS program because at every level of instruction students take pretests and posttests. Also, with assessments so well tied to instruction, there are opportunities to test students more than twice per instructional period. This can help teachers assess what the students know in order to determine what should be taught. This is a great advantage over other testing programs that do not share test results with instructors for a within-class analysis. The technical manual encourages agencies to obtain posttest scores for participants leaving a program early; this practice supports the gathering of additional data for test analysis and development. Additional data can be gathered in several ways to increase the size of the test bank from which the tests can be developed. One option is to give a separate section of a test during regular testing, with new items included in that separate section. Another option is to include some new items within a test form, and use the data from these items for item tryout purposes rather than being scored as part of the test. A third option would be to give an entire test in addition to the pretests and posttests of the program, similar to having a midterm exam that is parallel in content to the pretests and posttests. These exams would fill a need users have requested for an additional exam for the courses of instruction, as well as to provide information with which to construct a third exam that is truly parallel to the others.

SUMMARY. There is much to recommend in the CASAS program, especially the good model of test development, extensive training of examiners with practice in test interpretation, and test security with restricted access to the tests. The technical manual is clear that additional test development is forthcoming, and there will be adequate opportunity to address the few shortcomings noted in the present version. The NRS suggests that an important use of the tests is to "measure learning gains" (technical manual, p. 2). The comments on the current status of the CASAS tests offered here are intended to improve that measurement.

[31]
ChemTest (Form AR-C).

Purpose: Designed for selecting candidates with basic chemical knowledge.
Population: Applicants and incumbents for jobs requiring knowledge of chemical principles.
Publication Dates: 2001-2008.
Scores, 9: Physical Knowledge, Acids/Bases & Salts, Compounds, Elements, Miscellaneous, Chemical Knowledge, Mechanical Principles, Gases & Fluids, Total.
Administration: Group.
Price Data, 2012: $23 per consumable self-scoring test booklet or $25 per online test administration (minimum order of 20); $24.95 per manual (2008, 16 pages).
Time: Untimed, no longer than 60 minutes.
Comments: Self-scoring instrument; available for online test administration.
Author: Roland T. Ramsay.
Publisher: Ramsay Corporation.
Cross References: For a review by John Tivendell of an earlier edition, see 17:39.

Review of the ChemTest (Form AR-C) by RONALD S. LANDIS, Nambury S. Raju Chair of Psychology, Illinois Institute of Technology, Chicago, IL:

DESCRIPTION. The Ramsay Corporation Job Skills ChemTest (Form AR-C) is designed for use in organizational settings in which an assessment of applicant and/or employee knowledge of chemical properties is desired. This test is likely to be of interest to those interested in using this instrument as a pre-employment (i.e., selection) test or those interested in assessing incumbent knowledge (e.g., following a training intervention). The ChemTest (Form AR-C) is composed of 43, four-alternative, multiple-choice items and is available in a self-scored, paper-and-pencil format and online through the test publisher's website. The test comprises eight specific, content areas with the assessment of a ninth area (Safety) embedded throughout the test. The first content area (Physical Knowledge) contains 6 items that assess basic principles such as heat, sound, and energy. The second content area comprises 6 items that measure knowledge of Acids, Bases, and Salts. Another set of

6 items (Compounds) generally address knowledge of chemical formulas and properties of particular compounds, though at least one of the items appears to be related to the prior item set (Acids, Bases, and Salts). A fourth content area (Elements) contains 6 items, 5 of which focus on knowledge of properties and chemical symbols of metals. A set of 3 items (Miscellaneous) are included that assess general measurement in chemistry followed by a set of 4 items that measure general Chemical Knowledge such as evaporation. Mechanical Principles are assessed with a set of 8 items that assess general physics knowledge. Several of the items in this section involve torque, fulcrums, etc., and require interpretation of diagrams and figures. The final content area (Gases and Fluids) includes 4 items that measure knowledge of how gases react under common environmental conditions, safety practices in combining different fluids, and how moisture content can be controlled.

The test booklet is visually appealing and professionally produced. The inside front page includes spaces for test taker name, social security number, job title, date, time, and obtained test score. In addition, this page provides a brief set of instructions for completing the test along with two practice exercises. These are not truly practice exercises/items, but rather are already completed examples that illustrate how test takers are to record and/or change answers on the test. The 43 items are then presented on seven pages with descending widths. This formatting is necessary given that the back page serves as the answer sheet for the exam. Overall, the test formatting and instructions should prove relatively straightforward for most test takers.

Of the 16-page "Manual for Administration and Scoring," only 4 pages are specifically devoted to administration and scoring of the test. The remaining pages describe the primary application of this test, a brief, bulleted list of the content areas on the test, development of the measure, a somewhat sparse presentation of the psychometric properties of the test, and a summary of normative data. Applications of this test may potentially reach beyond the *Dictionary of Occupational Titles* (DOT) and O*NET categories identified in the manual; however, care should be taken to demonstrate that the knowledge assessed by the ChemTest (Form AR-C) is required by test takers for the focal job at the time of hire.

DEVELOPMENT. The test manual indicates that two industrial and organizational (I/O) psychologists originally drafted a set of 60 items to measure the content areas of interest. Although the test is purported to measure knowledge and skill in the area of chemistry, the manual does not provide any supporting references or logic regarding why the particular content areas were chosen or what defines the construct space. On the basis of feedback provided by 10 job experts, 17 of the original items were removed. The remaining 43 items were then administered to a sample of 169 applicants for jobs in the chemical industry. On the basis of this pilot testing, 18 items were revised with the goal of improving simplification, readability, and validity. These refinements produced an earlier version of the ChemTest (Form AC) that was used until the most recent revisions were made to the exam. As reported in the manual, the earlier version of the test had been administered 790 times. The manual indicates that 2 items were replaced in 2008. No additional information is provided regarding why the items were replaced and no item-level information (i.e., item difficulty or point-biserial correlations) is presented for these items.

TECHNICAL. Minimal normative data are provided for the ChemTest (Form AR-C) and are based on a group of 790 male and female test takers. The normative data indicate percentile ranks for raw scores ranging from 10 to 39 on the test. Although scores greater than 39 and less than 10 are possible, these correspond to the 99th and 1st percentiles, respectively.

The test developers report observed reliability for the previous version of the ChemTest (RCJS ChemTest) as KR-20 = .78 for the sample of 790 test takers. Although this value is perhaps somewhat lower than desirable, the likely heterogeneous nature of the items (e.g., eight different content areas) suggests that internal consistency measures such as KR-20 may reflect conservative estimates of reliability. Item difficulty values provided in the test manual appear reasonable (ranging between .15–.92) as do the reported point-biserial correlations (ranging between .36–.67). Although the two new items were not included in the calculation of KR-20, test length (i.e., 43 items) would suggest that these items would not have an appreciable impact on internal consistency.

Limited validity evidence is presented in the manual. Content-related evidence of validity is drawn from three studies. Of note, none of these studies was conducted with the latest version of the test, two of the three reported a different number of items (37 and 38), and all three studies appear to focus on different jobs. These inconsistencies create some ambiguity in drawing strong inferences about the content validity evidence supporting the test.

Criterion-related validity evidence is limited to three reported correlations with different job performance criteria in a sample of 151 employed chemical workers. Unfortunately, the observed correlations (.20, .21, and .25) are not accompanied by any specific tests of statistical significance nor are they linked to the specific job performance criteria that were used. Therefore, as was the case with the content validity evidence, it is difficult to draw inferences about the criterion-related evidence of validity supporting this test. Given that this test may be used as a selection tool, users will likely be interested in knowing whether the ChemTest produces differential validity and/or differential item functioning across protected subgroups (e.g., race, gender). Unfortunately, no information is provided with respect to these issues. As the test manual states, no formal studies of construct validity for the ChemTest (Form AR-C) have been conducted to date.

COMMENTARY. The ChemTest (Form AR-C) is easy to administer and score. Psychometric evidence is limited and should be strengthened through additional studies. At a minimum, the test manual should provide a much clearer explanation of the focal construct measured by this test. Content and construct evidence of validity may be questioned insofar as almost 20% of the items (i.e., 8 of 43) explicitly measure a dimension (i.e., Mechanical Principles) that does not, on its face, appear to assess the construct of interest. Evidence regarding the extent to which this test produces mean differences across race or gender subgroups, differential prediction or validity, and/or differential item functioning would be valuable for those users interested in applying this test in selection contexts. Additional criterion-related evidence of validity would also be important.

SUMMARY. The ChemTest (Form AR-C) was designed to be a simple, efficient measure of basic chemistry knowledge that could be used by organizations for purposes of pre-hire testing and/or an assessment of learning of such topics as part of training. Although the test is relatively easy to read and could be easily administered to individuals and large groups, several aspects of the test may limit its utility. First, a substantial number of items (8 of 43) appear to assess basic physics knowledge

more than chemistry. Such knowledge may be valuable for some occupations or jobs, but the test is not likely a pure measure of chemistry knowledge. The reported psychometric evidence is limited and critical information (e.g., extent to which there are mean differences across race or gender subgroups, differential prediction or validity, differential item functioning) is simply not provided. Clearly more information is needed in relation to these questions and the authors ask users to share data collected through this tool. Given the potential legal ramifications associated with using tests as selection tools, potential users of the ChemTest should ensure that the content of this test can be clearly mapped onto the requirements of the particular job at hand.

Review of the ChemTest (Form AR-C) by STEPHEN STARK, Associate Professor, I/O Psychology & Quantitative Methods, University of South Florida, Tampa, FL:

DESCRIPTION. The ChemTest (Form AR-C) is a 43-item, four-option multiple-choice assessment measuring knowledge and skill in the area of chemistry. It is currently available in both online and paper-and-pencil forms. According to the test administration and scoring manual (test manual), the test is "intended for use for pre-employment selection or for assessing incumbents in jobs where the knowledge of chemical principles is a required part of training or job activity" (p. 1). In the *Dictionary of Occupational Titles* framework, the job title most closely connected to the intended examinee population is Chemical Operator III or, alternatively, reactor operator. In the O*NET framework, the category classification is Chemical Equipment Operators and Tenders (51-9011.00). The job definitions and relevant tasks for related positions are provided.

The test is designed to measure basic knowledge in eight content areas with the numbers of items in each area shown in parentheses as follows: Physical Knowledge (6), Acids, Bases, and Salts (6), Compounds (6), Elements (6), Miscellaneous (3), Chemical Knowledge (4), Mechanical Principles (8), and Gases and Fluids (4). According to the manual, safety is a "pervasive" theme.

According to the test manual, the test should be administered under close supervision in a secure, quiet, and comfortable environment, but without time limits. General guidelines are provided to proctors for interacting with examinees, distributing and collecting materials, answering questions before and during the assessment, and monitoring examinee behavior. Scripts are provided under the heading "Specific Directions," which are to be read aloud when initiating testing sessions and delivering test instructions. Proctors are directed to record the elapsed time to completion on each examinee's test booklet, and information is provided in a subsequent section of the test manual concerning use of the self-scoring feature of the paper-and-pencil form. The test manual encourages proctors to take the test to gain familiarity with the materials before administering it to examinees.

DEVELOPMENT. The 43-item instrument contains items written by industrial/organizational psychologists who were deemed suitable after reviews by a combination of job experts and PhD-level trainers. All but 2 items were also evaluated empirically using data collected from a sample of 790 male and female applicants and incumbents at a chemical company in the U.S. mid-Atlantic region. The test manual shows item difficulty and discrimination statistics, summary information concerning reliability, content validity, and three criterion-related validity coefficients for job performance that were subsequently obtained using a concurrent research design involving 151 employed chemical workers. The test manual states that the construct measured by the ChemTest (Form AR-C) is "knowledge of chemical facts and principles… No formal studies of construct validity have been conducted, but construct validity is attained by the procedures of development" (p. 13).

TECHNICAL. For the sample of 790 applicants and incumbents utilized for test development, the mean score on the 43-item assessment was 23 with a standard deviation of 6.21. The KR-20 reliability of the measure was .78. Proportion correct scores for individual items ranged from a high of .92 to a low of .15, with most values lying between .40 and .70. Item-total correlations were generally around .50. The three reported criterion-related validity coefficients for job performance ranged from .20 to .25. A table of percentile ranks is provided in the test manual to facilitate the interpretation of raw scores, with the mean of 23 in the development sample coinciding with the 52nd percentile rank. No information is provided in the test manual concerning test dimensionality, correlations of ChemTest scores with other measures of general cognitive ability, job knowledge measures,

counterproductive performance, or organizational citizenship performance outcomes. In addition, no information is provided regarding means and validities for different examinee subgroups.

COMMENTARY.

Test manual. The test administration and scoring manual provides a bare minimum of information about the process of test development and validation. As such, this reviewer suggests that interested organizations seek additional technical information from the test publisher and, in the absence of more detail, the organizations should conduct local validation studies prior to using the test for high stakes decision making. Perhaps a separate technical manual is available that can provide the type of detailed psychometric information that is recommended, for example, in the *Standards for Educational and Psychological Testing* (American Educational Research Association, American Psychological Association, & National Council on Measurement in Education, 1999), but such information was not included in the packet provided for this review.

Nonetheless, the reviewer suggests that the publisher include additional information in the packets provided to industry professionals charged with evaluating the potential usefulness of the assessment. Information concerning the composition of the development and validation samples, means and possibly validities for applicant and incumbent subgroups, and validity results for an array of specific job performance criteria should be made available to potential consumers. Because the test measures knowledge of basic chemistry, congruent perhaps with a high school or introductory two-year college course, this reviewer believes there is a strong possibility of adverse impact against protected group members. Consequently, differential prediction analyses, as well as differential item and test functioning analyses, should be conducted and the results reported in a nontechnical way along with the very basic content validity information, KR-20 reliability, and concurrent validity coefficients that are already included.

Test forms. Table 3 (p. 10) in the test manual lists "Various" under the column entitled "Form." The reviewer is uncertain as to the meaning of Various. One critical concern with a 43-item test that allows for "self-scoring" is the security of the items. With paper-and-pencil and online testing options, it is only a matter of time before the content of the 43-item assessment is exposed sufficiently to inflate scores and undermine test validity. A large pool of items combined with alternative forms that have been equated is clearly needed for high stakes, high volume applications.

SUMMARY. The ChemTest (Form AR-C) (2001, 2008) assesses knowledge of basic chemistry in eight related areas using four-option, multiple-choice items. The test is designed for jobs related to Chemical Operator as defined in the *Dictionary of Occupational Titles*, O*NET, and sample tasks listed in the test manual. The paper-and-pencil self-scoring test booklet is straightforward and easy to use, and the availability of an online form provides another option for assessment in computerized, possibly high volume testing sites.

REVIEWER'S REFERENCE

American Educational Research Association, American Psychological Association, & National Council on Measurement in Education. (1999). *Standards for educational and psychological testing*. Washington, DC: American Educational Research Association.

[32]

Childhood Autism Rating Scale, Second Edition.

Purpose: "For identifying the presence of behavioral symptoms of autism to support the diagnostic process and also for research and classification purposes."

Publication Dates: 1986-2010.

Administration: Group.

Price Data, 2012: $158 per complete test kit including 25 Standard Version rating booklets, 25 High-Functioning rating booklets, 25 Questionnaires for Parents or Caregivers, and manual (2010, 109 pages); $37 per 25 Standard Version rating booklets; $37 per 25 High-Functioning rating booklets; $26 per 25 Questionnaires for Parents or Caregivers; $74 per manual.

Time: (5-10) minutes.

Comments: Questionnaires for Parents or Caregivers are included to aid in diagnostic decision-making and supplement data-gathering but are not scored.

Authors: Eric Schopler, Mary. E. Van Bourgondien, G. Janette Wellman, and Steven R. Love.

Publisher: Western Psychological Services.

a) CHILDHOOD AUTISM RATING SCALE, SECOND EDITION–STANDARD VERSION.

Acronym: CARS2-ST.

Population: Ages 2 through 5 (or older if estimated IQ below 79).

Scores, 16: Relating to People, Imitation, Emotional Response, Body Use, Object Use, Adaptation to Change, Visual Response, Listening Response, Taste, Smell, and Touch Response and Use, Fear or Nervousness, Verbal Communication, Nonverbal Communication, Activity Level, Level and Consistency of Intellectual Response, General Impressions, Total.

b) CHILDHOOD AUTISM RATING SCALE, SECOND EDITION–HIGH-FUNCTIONING VERSION.

Acronym: CARS2-HF.

Population: Ages 6 and over (with estimated IQ above 80).

Scores, 16: Social-Emotional Understanding, Emotional Expression and Regulation of Emotions, Relating to People, Body Use, Object Use in Play, Adaptation to Change/Restricted Interests, Visual Response, Listening Response, Taste, Smell, and Touch Response and Use, Fear or Anxiety, Verbal Communication, Nonverbal Communication, Thinking/Cognitive Integration Skills, Level and Consistency of Intellectual Response, General Impressions, Total.

Cross References: See T5:459 (40 references) and T4:439 (6 references); for reviews by Barry M. Prizant and J. Steven Welsh, see 11:65 (4 references).

Review of the Childhood Autism Rating Scale, Second Edition by KORESSA KUTSICK MAL-COLM, School Psychologist, The Virginia School for the Deaf and Blind, Staunton, VA:

DESCRIPTION. With the second edition of the Childhood Autism Rating Scale (CARS2) the authors attempted to accomplish several goals. The first of these was to extend the utility of the CARS for a wider variety of professionals who work with individuals who are suspected of having autism. The second was to expand item coverage to address characteristics of autism in individuals whose intellectual abilities are above average levels, who are older than age 6 years, or who have fairly well-developed language functioning. The third was to refine the format of the CARS rating booklet.

The CARS2 includes three forms: The Childhood Autism Rating Scale, Second Edition–Standard Version (CARS2-ST), the Childhood Autism Rating Scale, Second Edition–High-Functioning Version (CARS2-HF), and the Childhood Autism Rating Scale, Second Edition–Questionnaire for Parents or Caregivers (CARS2-QPC). The structure and items of the CARS were not significantly altered in the CARS2-ST. The test authors noted that researchers and others who want to continue with longitudinal studies can still make direct comparisons between the CARS and CARS2-ST scores because items comprising the scales are the same. The major changes in the second edition are found in the creation of the CARS2-HF. This scale is composed of items similar to those of the CARS2-ST but reflects diagnostic information available for individuals 6 years of age and older who are higher functioning in terms of intellectual and verbal abilities. The CARS2-QPC is a questionnaire that can be used to gather additional information about an individual's functional status as noted by those who provide care for the individual. This questionnaire is not scored, but is used to gather information to complete the CARS2-ST and CARS2-HF.

The main purpose of the CARS2-ST and CARS2-HF has not changed from that of the original CARS. The scales were designed to identify those behaviors that an examinee may be exhibiting that are characteristic of autism and to help formulate diagnostic hypotheses regarding causes of the behaviors. The obtained total score reflects the degree to which an examinee's score is similar to those with autism rather than to a general nonclinical population. The scale may be used by professionals such as psychologists, physicians, special education teachers, and speech pathologists who have training in the characteristics of autism as well as experience in working with individuals with autism spectrum disorders. The CARS2 forms may be used in settings such as schools, treatment centers, and diagnostic clinics.

To complete either of the CARS2-ST or the CARS2-HF, professionals gather information about the examinee's functioning from their own observations made during formal assessment sessions using other instruments and from observations of individuals in their learning or living environments. Raters also should review relevant client information from school or medical records and interview teachers and parents or caregivers prior to completing the CARS2-HF. Raters then review 15 different categories of behaviors associated with autism presented in the scales. For each of these items a rating of 1–4 is given. Raw scores are then added and converted to a T-score using a chart presented on the rating booklet.

DEVELOPMENT. The content of the CARS2-ST was not significantly altered from the 1988 edition of the CARS. The CARS2-ST contains the same 15 behavioral categories of autism as did the CARS. The test authors noted that these categories were based on diagnostic criteria presented by the American Psychiatric Association and the World Health Organization. A comprehensive review of autism research and literature as well as work with populations with autism at the TEACCH Program in North Carolina where the scales originated were used as the basis for item development on all forms of the CARS. Clarification to the ratings for some items of the CARS2-ST was

added based on feedback from users of the original CARS. The format of the record form was changed to allow for more notetaking to provide examples of the items that were noted during observations of the individual being evaluated.

The creation of the CARS2-HF comprised most of the work in the redevelopment of the CARS2. Items for this form were amended from the original CARS to reflect the original 15 items, but included current research and diagnostic criteria for conditions such as Asperger's Disorder and high-functioning autism. A detailed review of research and issues related to these characteristics of autism for individuals who are higher functioning is presented in the manual as a basis for the refined 15 items and their corresponding 4-point ratings.

TECHNICAL. The test authors note previous work on the CARS as a basis for the technical support of the revised scales. The original CARS was standardized on 1,606 individuals. That sample was composed mostly of white males and was noted to be reflective of the population served by the TEACCH Center where the scales were developed rather than general U.S. demographic characteristics. The CARS2-ST was standardized on 1,034 individuals with autism. Again, this sample was noted to reflect demographic characteristics of individuals diagnosed with autism rather than general U.S. demographic features. The CARS2-ST standardization sample continued to be primarily composed of white males (78% males and 60% white) although other races/ethnic groups were represented as well. The age distributions primarily represented the 2–15-year-olds with only 7% of the sample being age 16 years or older.

A separate standardization sample was reported for the CARS2-HF. This sample was composed of 994 individuals of whom 248 were diagnosed with high-functioning autism; 231 with Asperger's Disorder; 95 with Pervasive Developmental Disorder; 179 with Attention Deficit/Hyperactivity Disorder; 111 with Learning Disorder; and 69 with "other clinical diagnoses." In addition, 40 nonautistic students from special education programs and 21 from general education programs were included in this scale's standardization sample. Again, this sample was composed primarily of males (78%). Racial identity and other demographic characteristics of this sample more closely reflected the U.S. population. Participants ranged in age from 6 to 57 years, again with a greater percentage falling in the age ranges of 6 to 15 years.

Reliability. The test authors present a review of reliability evidence for the CARS as a basis for the reliability of the CARS2-ST. No current information regarding test-retest reliability or inter-rater reliability is presented for the CARS2-ST. An internal consistency estimate of .93 was obtained. Item-to-total correlations for the CARS2-ST ranged from .43 to .81. The standard error of measurement (*SEM*) for the total raw score was noted to be .68, which was rounded to 1 point above or below the raw score at the 68% confidence level. With so few items on the scale, a low *SEM* would be expected.

For the CARS2-HF, item-to-total correlations ranged from .53 to .88, offering support for internal consistency. Interrater reliability was explored by having two trained raters independently complete CARS2-HF forms for 239 individuals from the standardization sample. For the total scores a correlation of .95 was obtained. Weighted kappa estimates indicated a median level of .73 for agreement on ratings of each individual item. The raw score *SEM* was found to be .73, which was rounded to 1 point above and below the total raw score at the 68% confidence level for a true score range.

Validity. Several studies that support the use of test scores from the CARS2-ST and CARS2-HF are presented in the manual. Initial analysis of the factor structures of the CARS2-ST identified two factors. One factor structure was noted to be related to communication and sensory issues. The second was related to emotional issues. For the CARS2-HF, a three-factor structure was identified, with the first being related to social and emotional issues, the second to cognitive functioning and verbal abilities, and the third to sensory issues. Convergent and divergent evidence that supports both forms was also provided. When CARS2-ST and CARS2-HF total scores were compared to the Autism Diagnostic Observation Schedule (Lord, Rutter, DiLavore, & Risi, 1999), which is a very structured direct assessment for behaviors associated with autism, obtained correlations were .79 for the CARS2-ST and .77 for the CARS2-HF. These results suggest that both scales tap similar characteristics of autism, but in different ways. When compared to the Social Responsiveness Scale (Constantino & Gruber, 2005) completed by parents, correlations of .38 for the CARS2-ST and .47 for the CARS2-HF were found. These lower to moderate correlations are typical of scales comparing parent and professional ratings of individuals.

COMMENTARY. The current edition of the CARS fulfilled the test authors' goal to expand the utility of the scales. Several years of research with the CARS supported reliability and validity of its scores and suggested the CARS as an instrument that could be used as one part of an assessment battery to identify behaviors associated with autism spectrum disorders in referred populations. The strength of the CARS2-ST and CARS2-HF scales is the adherence to diagnostic criteria and research findings related to autism that are reflected in the items. The brevity of the test and the relative ease of examiner training and administration are also positive features of the CARS2. Additional research into the reliability and validity of both scales should be continued. The test authors note the history of research to support the reliability of the original CARS, but should have included more specific information regarding the statistical properties of the CARS2 as populations and research groups change over time. It would be interesting to note further studies on the differential power of the CARS2 forms when used with nonclinical groups to ascertain whether the scales are sampling behaviors associated with autism or other behaviors demonstrated in the general population. Although efforts to expand the geographical representation of the sample were mentioned, it would have been helpful if specific details were provided rather than referring users to other research for these data. The addition of the CARS2-HF scale was a positive aspect of the CARS revision. This form could prove a valuable instrument for use with higher functioning individuals with autistic traits, as few scales are available for this population. The CARS2 might be most applicable to younger clients (less than age 15 years) as few older subjects were included in the standardization samples. Some caution also might be warranted when the scales are used with clients other than white males as there were fewer numbers of others in the standardization samples.

SUMMARY. The three forms of the CARS2 were developed to provide measures of the extent to which an individual demonstrates 15 different behaviors characteristic of autism. These scales represent a continuation of the test authors' efforts to refine assessment procedures that reflect current research and diagnostic criteria related to autism spectrum disorders. Additional research is still needed to strengthen the technical properties of the forms of the CARS2. The CARS2-ST and CARS2-HF have value in being included in a comprehensive evaluation process of clients who appear to demonstrate characteristics of autism. The CARS2-QPC can be used to gain information from a variety of sources that can be incorporated into the ratings of the formal CARS2 scales.

REVIEWER'S REFERENCES

Constantino, J. N., & Gruber, C. P. (2005). *Social Responsiveness Scale (SRS): Manual*. Los Angeles, CA: Western Psychological Services.

Lord, C., Rutter, M., DiLavore, P. C., & Risi, S. (1999). *Autism Diagnostic Observation Schedule (ADOS): Manual*. Los Angeles, CA: Western Psychological Services.

Review of the Childhood Autism Rating Scale, Second Edition by MARY J. McLELLAN, Department of Educational Psychology, Northern Arizona University, Flagstaff, AZ:

DESCRIPTION. All professionals who work with children across the country know there is a huge growth in the numbers of children suspected of being on the Autism Spectrum. Professionals must have good assessment measures to help guide their diagnostic decisions. The Childhood Autism Rating Scale, Second Edition (CARS2) is an instrument to assist in making an accurate diagnosis. The CARS2 was published in 2010 by Western Psychological Services. The test authors, Schopler, Van Bourgondien, Wellman, and Love, collaborated to update the original version of the CARS. The original CARS, by Schopler, Reichler, and Renner, was formally published in 1988 as an adaptation to the 1971 form. The 1988 version has been used widely within the professional community to assist in the diagnosis of children with autism. The CARS2 includes the Standard Version, High-Functioning Version, and Questionnaire for Parents or Caregivers. The two new questionnaires, the High-Functioning Version and the Questionnaire for Parents or Caregivers, are designed to expand the utility of the Standard Version. The Standard Version has not changed from the original version, but a new standardization sample was employed. The manual for the CARS2 provides a chapter on Intervention Planning and Resources. This chapter includes information about structured teaching and specific examples of methods to teach individuals on the autism spectrum. The resources offered in this chapter come from TEACCH strategies (Mesibov, Shea, & Schopler, 2005).

The CARS2 provides test users with the opportunity to rate an examinee on 15 items that relate to characteristics of individuals with Autism or Autism Spectrum Disorders. The Standard Version and High-Functioning Version both have 15 items, but there is some difference in the content of the items. The test manual emphasizes observation and multiple sources of data to complete the ratings. Examples of the ratings are provided in the manual in addition to detailed descriptions of specific behaviors related to items.

DEVELOPMENT. The CARS2 comes from a long history of over 40 years of development. The original research forms were revised to accommodate different classification systems and diagnostic ratings over the years. The 15 items comprising the Standard Version of the CARS2 are the same as the 1988 edition. The High-Functioning Version of the CARS2 provides an opportunity to rate individuals at the higher end of the autism spectrum and is also constructed as a 15-item scale. The High-Functioning Version is similar to the Standard Version, but includes items of Social-Emotional Understanding, Emotional Expression and Regulation of Emotions, Relating to People, and Thinking/Cognitive Integration Skills. The Questionnaire for Parents or Caregivers is designed to provide information for the examiner to complete the Standard or High-Functioning Version but does not have specific scores.

TECHNICAL.

Standardization. The standardization sample for the Standard Version of the CARS2 consisted of 1,034 individuals with age ranges between 2 and 36 years. The individuals in the sample had previous diagnoses of autism from various clinics around the United States. The demographics of the sample were roughly equivalent to the U.S. population, except for an overrepresentation of males. The higher male population is consistent with a higher proportion of males having a diagnosis of autism. The High-Functioning version of the CARS2 was developed using a sample that consisted of 994 individuals with a range of diagnoses, including high functioning autism, Asperger's Disorder, Pervasive Developmental Disorder-Not Otherwise Specified, Attention Deficit/Hyperactivity Disorder, learning disorder, and other clinical diagnoses. A small number (21) of nonautistic general education students were also included. The sample characteristics show some variation from population statistics, but are considered appropriate by this reviewer.

Reliability. The reliability of the CARS2 is reported to be satisfactory. Internal consistency and interrater reliability estimates for both the

CARS2 Standard Version and the CARS2 High-Functioning Version were considered to be within acceptable ranges. Internal consistency estimates for the CARS2 Standard Version were reported to be .93 and .96 for the High-Functioning Version. The description of reliability in the test manual references the original sample of the CARS often and it is sometimes difficult to find the coefficients for the current versions. The values do appear to be adequate.

Validity. Validity evidence for the CARS2 test scores appears adequate to support the use of test scores for the stated purpose. Specifically, the internal validity of the measures (Standard and High-Functioning Versions) is high. The test manual reports various research studies that support the use of CARS test scores to identify individuals with autism. There is a vast body of research utilizing the CARS and there appears to be adequate evidence that the CARS2 is an effective tool for making a differential diagnosis for individuals with autism and high-functioning autism.

COMMENTARY. The CARS2 provides a comprehensive rating system for individuals who are being evaluated for autism. The examiner relies on observation, information gained from others, and parent report. The rating system for the Standard Version is well developed and provides ample opportunity to identify characteristics related to autism. When compared to the Autism Diagnostic Observation Schedule (Lord, Rutter, DiLavore, & Risi, 1999), the CARS2's main weakness is the lack of structured activities that can elicit responses from a child for comparison to other children who have been exposed to the same structured activities. The situations in which children are observed are, by nature, complex, and the examiner is required to analyze the support given in addition to anticipating how the child might function with or without the support observed. The High-Functioning Version has less information regarding the efficacy of the rating system, but it appears to have promise. Similar concerns regarding lack of structured activities are noted with the High-Functioning Version.

SUMMARY. The CARS2 provides a well-researched instrument, as the Standard Version is identical to the CARS. The CARS2 has added a High-Functioning Version and a Questionnaire for Parents or Caregivers that adds to the examiner's ability to rate accurately. This instrument provides a rich guide for professionals who are required to make diagnoses of or related to autism. The CARS2 is completed exclusively through observation, and the examiner should be careful to understand the context of the situation the examinee is experiencing and the strengths (or weaknesses) of the supports present. The context can drastically impact the functioning level of the examinee.

REVIEWER'S REFERENCES

Lord, C., Rutter, M., DiLavore, P. C., & Risi, S. (1999). *Autism Diagnostic Observation Schedule (ADOS): Manual.* Los Angeles, CA: Western Psychological Services.
Mesibov, G. B., Shea, V., & Schopler, E. (2005). *The TEACCH approach to autism spectrum disorders.* New York, NY: Spring Science + Business Media.

[33]

Children's Depression Inventory 2nd Edition.

Purpose: Designed to provide "comprehensive multi-rater assessment of depressive symptoms in children."

Population: Ages 7-17.

Publication Dates: 1977–2011.

Acronym: CDI 2.

Scores, 14: Self-Report Full-Length-7: Total Score, Emotional Problems Scale Score, Functional Problems Scale Score, Negative Mood/Physical Symptoms Subscale Score, Negative Self-Esteem Subscale Score, Ineffectiveness Subscale Score, Interpersonal Problems Subscale Score; Self-Report Short-1: Total Score; Parent Report-3: Total Score, Emotional Problems Scale Score, Functional Problems Scale Score; Teacher Report-3: Total Score, Emotional Problems Scale Score, Functional Problems Scale Score.

Administration: Individual or group.

Forms, 4: Self-Report Full-Length, Self-Report Short, Parent Report, Teacher Report.

Price Data, 2013: $399 per complete software kit including manual, Software Scoring Installation (USB key), 25 self-report response forms, 25 self-report short response forms, 25 parent response forms, and 25 teacher response forms; $88 per manual; $289 per handscored kit including manual, 25 self-report QuikScore forms, 25 self-report short QuikScore forms, 25 parent QuikScore forms, and 25 teacher QuikScore forms.

Foreign Language Edition: Available in Spanish online.

Time: (15) minutes for Self-Report Full-Length; (5) minutes for Self-Report Short; (10) minutes for Parent Report; (5) minutes for Teacher Report.

Comments: This is a multi-rater assessment; available in paper-and-pencil and online administration and scoring.

Authors: Maria Kovacs and MHS Staff.

Publisher: Multi-Health Systems, Inc.

Cross References: For reviews by Janet F. Carlson and Stephen J. Freeman of the 2003 Update, see 17:41; see also T5:472 (235 references) and T4:450 (71 references); for reviews by Michael G. Kavan and Howard M. Knoff of an earlier edition, see 11:66 (63 references).

Review of the Children's Depression Inventory 2nd Edition by JEFFREY A. ATLAS, Director, Mental Health Services, SCO Family of Services, Queens, NY:

DESCRIPTION. The Children's Depression Inventory 2nd Edition (CDI 2) is a multifaceted and multidimensional inventory of depressive symptoms in children aged 7 to 17. It is composed of youth, short-form youth, parent, and teacher forms that offer increasing vantage points for assessing the content and severity of symptoms within different milieus and social contexts. Given the prevalence and co-morbidity of depression in problems facing children, the CDI 2 may be a useful tool to consider as part of a fuller evaluation of normal and clinical populations. The instrument provided the present reviewer was the hand-scored kit including one technical manual and tear-away forms featuring underlying scoring templates and summary data sheets utilizing T-score values for total scores and subscales in the extended forms.

The CDI 2 is most likely to be used as part of a comprehensive, individually administered psychological evaluation, particularly in cases where there is a differential diagnostic question concerning the presence of depression. The short self-report version may be the more likely to be applied in epidemiological research or program evaluation group contexts, or as a preliminary scale one might consider prior to embarking on a comprehensive psychodiagnostic evaluation where depression is one of the presenting rule-outs.

DEVELOPMENT. "The starting point for the CDI was the Beck Depression Inventory" (p. 11), which earlier demonstrated utility in many studies of children as well as adults, for instance in showing greater sensitivity than a comparable (adolescent) depression scale in identifying moderate to severe depression in a group having a primary diagnosis of Posttraumatic Stress Disorder (Atlas & DiScipio, 1992).

The CDI 2 manual provides a succinct overview of the history of applying the descriptor of depression to children, the basis of the original CDI in the Beck Depression Inventory (Kovacs, 1992), and updating of items and development of new norms for the CDI 2.

The items of the Beck Depression Inventory (BDI) were reworded by enlisting the help of a convenience sample of inpatient and partially hospitalized 10–15-year-old youth.

As described in the manual, the BDI item concerning changes in sexual interest was omitted and a number of items concerning school and peer relations were added. A second development phase entailed further piloting with youth under psychiatric and psychological care, semantic-conceptual item analysis, and applications of the revised inventory with psychiatrically hospitalized, unspecified control youth, and a public school sample, all within age ranges comprising 8 to 13 years. Based upon analyses of these results, two items were deleted and four items having face validity in their substance and age-appropriateness were added. A third phase is described as pilot-testing and consultation with colleagues to improve item comprehensibility. A fourth phase yielded the scoring templates used in the final version of the CDI.

The CDI 2 features 3 new items covering excessive sleep, overeating, and memory difficulties. Three items were rewritten and 2 were removed, yielding a 28-item revised forced-choice descriptor checklist featuring absence, evidence, or appearance of disabling depressive symptoms mapping onto the *Diagnostic and Statistical Manual of Mental Disorders, Fourth Edition* (American Psychiatric Association, 2000) delineation of Major Depressive Disorder and Dysthymic Disorder. The teacher and parent rating forms were unchanged from the earlier CDI and are rated along a 4-point frequency scale, with some items reverse-scored in terms of severity, a more nuanced format that may circumvent response bias.

TECHNICAL.

Standardization. The CDI 2 self-report forms were restandardized on a new sample of 1,100 students aged 7-17 years, while new parent form ($N = 800$) and teacher form ($N = 600$) standardization data were collected as well. The student participants were drawn from a larger sample of 1,597 to conform to set age, sex, and demographic stratification variables. Each boy and girl cell from ages 7–17 years contained 50 individuals. Percentages of Asian (3.3), African American (16.1), Hispanic (14.5), and White (62.0) individuals align closely with U.S. Census 2000 figures. The regional distributions of sample participation are reasonable, despite a moderate overrepresentation of Northeast (40.5%) areas.

The test authors added teacher- and parent-rated form standardization data to the original CDI to more closely match census ethnic categories. These figures and the age-group and sex stratification are representative; a minor flaw may reside in the parent's rating comprising 86.8% biological mothers, but this would not appear to prejudice the standardization data on depression in a predictable way and may also reflect likely future parent respondent composite figures as the scales are employed.

A CDI 2 clinical sample included 319 children aged 7–17, 61% of whom were male. The sample was drawn from "professionals in private clinics or school psychologists working in schools" (technical manual, p. 57). Inspection of the summary demographic data pertaining to this group (technical manual, p. 60) suggests adequate sex, ethnic, and diagnostic representation, the latter comprising Major Depressive Disorder (33.86%), Attention-Deficit Hyperactivity Disorder (28.21%), Conduct Disorder/Oppositional Defiant Disorder (24.14%), and Generalized Anxiety Disorder (13.79%) categories. Asians are underrepresented in the clinical sample, listed as contributing three cases of Major Depressive Disorder and one of Conduct Disorder/Oppositional Defiant Disorder.

New clinical data were not collected for the teacher- and parent-rater forms, which featured CDI data from 167 parents and 114 teachers, with overrepresentation of Whites (77.9%). The original data were collected through psychologists in outpatient settings only, posing some limits to generalizability. The paucity of data in this area is somewhat puzzling, given the ease of use of the CDI 2 and its predecessor instruments. One study alone, in which the present reviewer was involved, analyzed the BDI in 42 adolescent inpatients (Atlas, DiScipio, Schwartz, & Sessoms, 1991), which in number constitutes over a third of the teacher-rated forms described in the test manual's clinical standardization data.

Confirmatory factor analysis utilizing self-report data from the total (normal and clinical) sample of the CDI 2 demonstrated goodness-of-fit of the scale with a model of depression representing higher order domains of emotional and functional problems, each subsuming respectively Negative Mood/Physical Symptoms and Negative Self-Esteem, and Interpersonal Problems and Ineffectiveness. The Emotional Problems scale correlated with the Functional Problems scale at $r = .77$; moderate to high intercorrelations of the four subscales suggested collective and independent significance of these areas in defining the construct of depression.

The short form CDI 2 was refined by choosing 12 items having the greatest effect size in differentiating a Major Depressive Disorder group ($N = 108$) with a control group ($N = 108$) drawn from the standardization group, matched on sex, age, and ethnicity. Some items from the original CDI were reallocated to the subdomains of Emotional and Functional problems, and resulting correlations evaluated. The intercorrelations of the Emotional and Functional problem domains, .65 for the teacher form and .61 for the parent form, were significant at the .001 level.

Analyses of the age-by-sex interaction showed significance, with the higher scores of girls aged 13–17 contributing to much of the effect. Separate norms are provided for the sexes by 7–12- and 13–17-year-old categories; combined norms are offered as well, which may be of use in research and program evaluation endeavors.

Validity. Discriminant validity was assessed by comparing standardization sample Major Depressive Disorder children with those bearing diagnoses of Generalized Anxiety Disorder, Conduct Disorder/Oppositional Defiant Disorder, and Attention-Deficit Hyperactivity Disorder. Analyses of covariance yielded Fs significant at less than .001, with Major Depressive Disorder showing higher T scores across Total Scores, domains, and subscales in all pairwise comparisons except for Generalized Anxiety Disorder in the functional (social) domains and for the Interpersonal Problems subscale comparison to Conduct Disordered/Oppositional/Defiant youth.

Comparisons of a standardization group comprising normal and clinical samples who completed both the CDI 2 and the Conners CBRS (Conners, 2008) yielded correlation coefficients across domains and subscales ranging from .38 (Negative Self-Esteem) to .59 (Negative Mood/Physical Symptoms), demonstrating moderate convergent validity.

Reliability. Internal consistency of the CDI 2 was assessed through coefficient alpha statistics. The alpha coefficients for the total sample ($N = 1,351$) subdomains and subscales ranged from .67 (Interpersonal Problems in the 7–12-year-old female group) to .91 for the overall group Total Score; the Total Score alpha coefficient for the short form was .82, all acceptable estimates of internal consistency.

For the updated teacher form, alpha coefficients for the subdomains ranged from .79 for 7–12-year-old females in Emotional Problems to .89 for the Total Score. The updated parent form featured subdomain alpha values ranging from .69 for 13–17-year-old females in Functional Problems to .88 for the Total Score, again reflecting acceptable internal consistency.

A small subsample of 79 children were retested at 2- to 4-week intervals using the self-report measures, with correlation coefficients of .74 for the Total Score of the full-length CDI 2, and .77 for the short from. No new test-retest data were collected for the teacher and parent forms. At this juncture, given the ambiguity of the collection periods, small sample size, and absence of teacher and parent data, temporal stability of CDI 2 test scores requires further research.

COMMENTARY. There is much to like about this test. It is based upon a seminal volume and assessment instrument on depression, built from a youth-age adaptation that demonstrated very good predictive validity, and has many practical and psychometric features that testing professionals have come to expect from current well-researched measurements. The compact test manual contains a brief history of the construct of depression from one of the leading experts in the field. There are useful reminders of principles of informed consent and assent in testing. Empirical data are provided to use in contexts of specified missing items, prorating of scores, comparisons of the present and earlier incarnation of the CDI, and in comparing the significance of agreement/disagreement between raters.

There are some lacunae. The sample evaluation of "Jennifer" in the test manual leaves unexplained how a disturbance in appetite can bring about endorsements of items indicating both a reluctance to eat and a characterization of her eating as "OK." The addition of an overeating item in the CDI 2 leads to this potential incongruity.

The CDI may have been translated successfully into 43 languages but one may question the posited "universality" of features of childhood depression if the identifying instrument mines several items related to feelings about school, which are not obviously culturally congruent across English, Oshindongan, and Xhosa populations. (There is a difference between language and cultural translation, between words and norms.) These are minor quibbles concerning an instrument that holds much continued promise.

SUMMARY. The CDI 2 is a comprehensively normed instrument suitable for use in English-speaking youth ages 7–17 possessing a second-grade reading level. As pointed out by the test authors, it does not replace a diagnostic battery but may serve as an integral part of certain assessments, particularly those in which depression may be a referral question or presenting feature. Further research with inpatient psychiatric populations may expand the generalizability of the CDI 2. As it stands, the instrument will be of good use to psychologists working in school, outpatient, and social service settings.

REVIEWER'S REFERENCES

American Psychiatric Association. (2000). *Diagnostic and statistical manual of mental disorders* (4th ed., Text Revision). Washington, DC: American Psychiatric Association.
Atlas, J. A., DiScipio, W. J., Schwartz, R., & Sessoms, L. (1991). Symptom correlates among adolescents showing posttraumatic stress disorder versus conduct disorder. *Psychological Reports, 69,* 920-922.
Atlas, J. A., & DiScipio, W. J. (1992). Correlations of Beck Depression Inventory and Reynolds Adolescent Depression Scale. *Psychological Reports, 70,* 621-622.
Beck, A. T. (1967). *Depression: Clinical, experimental and theoretical aspects.* New York, NY: Harper & Row.
Conners, C. K. (2008). *Conners Comprehensive Behavior Rating Scales manual.* Toronto, Canada: Multi-Health Systems.
Kovacs, M. (1992). *Children's Depression Inventory (CDI) manual.* Toronto, Canada: Multi-Health Systems.

Review of the Children's Depression Inventory 2nd Edition by RENÉE M. TOBIN, Professor of Psychology, and THOMAS D. MULDERINK, Doctoral Student, Illinois State University, Normal, IL:

DESCRIPTION. The Children's Depression Inventory 2nd Edition (CDI 2) is a multirater instrument designed to assess depressive symptoms in children from 7 to 17 years old. The tools come in four forms: the long and short self-report forms, the parent form, and the teacher form. The CDI 2 is intended for use as a screening instrument or as a part of a comprehensive evaluation, rather than a stand-alone diagnostic tool. The CDI 2 builds on previous versions of the test by adding, updating, and removing a few items on the self-report forms. The self-report long form (CDI 2:SR) contains 28 items, whereas the self-report short form (CDI 2:SR[S]) contains 12, as does the teacher form (CDI 2:T). The parent form (CDI 2:P) contains 17 items. All four forms of the CDI 2 produce a single Total Score for each individual. The teacher, parent, and self-report long form also provide two additional scales: the Emotional Problems and the Functional Problems scales. The self-report long form provides four additional subscales, previously seen on the original CDI (Ineffectiveness, Interpersonal Problems, Negative Mood/Physical Symptoms, and Negative Self-Esteem). The time frame for ratings on all versions is the past 2 weeks.

DEVELOPMENT. When the CDI was developed in 1977, the main goal was to establish a measure of depressive symptoms in children and adolescents. At the time, the test author turned to the Beck Depression Inventory as the prototype for developing a comparable measure for assessing youth. With the present version, the test developers have maintained this objective and have only made minor modifications to the instrument to account for changes in the diagnostic criteria in the *Diagnostic and Statistical Manual of Mental Disorders, Fourth Edition, Text Revision* (DSM-IV-TR; American Psychiatric Association, 2000) and in the research literature. The CDI 2 also has maintained or improved on the physical presentation of items and on the psychometric properties of previous editions. Accordingly, the test author updated the norms based on the 2000 U.S. Census.

Three new items were added to the CDI 2:SR that assess symptoms of hypersomnia, hyperphagia, and cognitive difficulties (i.e., impaired thinking and concentration), which were underrepresented in the previous edition of the CDI. Five other items were either removed or edited to keep the instrument's length down and to insure the questions were understood as intended. The time to administer each form is reasonable. The longest form (CDI 2:SR) takes an estimated 15 minutes to complete. Similarly, both the CDI 2:T and the CDI 2:SR(S) take approximately 5 minutes to complete, which is useful for repeated administrations and in school contexts.

TECHNICAL. In general, the psychometric properties of the CDI 2 far exceed the recommendations offered by the American Educational Research Association, American Psychological Association, and National Council on Measurement in Education (1999). The test authors provide thorough and compelling data about the reliability and validity of this instrument.

The normative sample for the self-report forms (long and short) consists of 1,100 children ranging from 7 to 17 years. The normative sample was stratified by race/ethnicity, age, and sex. The test developers report that the racial/ethnic composition closely matches data in the 2000 U.S. Census Report. When more than the required number of cases was available, the test developers made an effort to include respondents from all geographic regions. The test manual does not provide a breakdown of recruitment strategies.

The normative sample for the parent and teacher forms consists of 800 and 600 cases, respectively. The test developers used the data from the original CDI as well as new data to create the current normative sample. As noted in the test manual, the original CDI data set was over-representative of Whites and underrepresentative of minorities. These issues have been addressed in the updated sample. As with the self-report form, an equal number of boys and girls were represented for each age range. The test developers provide percentages regarding the parents' relationship to the children they rated. For both forms, the racial/ethnic composition of the sample represents that of the 2000 U.S. Census within 5%. Information on geographic region is not provided for either form, nor is information on the sex or the race/ethnicity of the teacher raters. Similarly, parent education levels are not specified.

Clinical samples for the self-report forms consisted of 319 children between 7 and 17 years. The test manual provides a breakdown of the racial/ethnic composition of the sample. Diagnoses of the children in this sample include major depressive disorder (MDD), attention-deficit/hyperactivity disorder (ADHD), conduct disorder/ oppositional defiant disorder (CD/ODD), and generalized anxiety disorder (GAD). Many of the cases of MDD had comorbid diagnoses. New clinical cases were not collected for the new edition of the CDI 2 parent and teacher forms. Children recruited for the clinical sample were selected based on the results of the Clinical Diagnostic Form, which was used to determine whether each child's diagnosis reflected the DSM-IV criteria. The test manual provides limited information regarding how participants or data collectors were selected for the sample.

Internal consistency estimates, as measured by coefficient alpha, for the scores from the total sample of the CDI 2:SR range from .73 (Interpersonal Problems) to .91 (Total Score). A correspondingly high alpha coefficient of .82 was obtained with the normative sample for the CDI 2:SR(S) (range was from .77 to .85). Similarly high levels of internal consistency were found for the CDI 2:T (range was from .82 to .89) and CDI 2:P (range was from .79 to .88). Overall, these results suggest strong internal consistency for all four measures. The test manual also provides *SEM* values based on the *T*-scores of the CDI 2 for all four test forms.

Test-retest reliability for the self-report forms was computed based on a subset of 79 children from the standardization sample. Corrected reliability estimates ranged from .76 to .92, indicating that the scores of the CDI 2:SR and SR(S) have strong stability over time (the inventory was completed twice for these children within 2 to 4 weeks). Due to practical constraints, the test authors did not conduct new analyses of test-retest reliability for the CDI 2:T and CDI 2:P.

The test manual also provides information on the validity of the CDI 2. Discriminant validity was assessed in two ways. First, MANOVA and ANCOVA analyses were used to assess pair-wise differences between the following groups: MDD vs. Matched Controls, MDD vs. GAD, MDD vs. CD/ODD, and MDD vs. ADHD. The results of these analyses provide evidence of discriminant validity for both self-report forms, with one notable exception (i.e., comparisons with GAD on the ineffectiveness, interpersonal problems, and functional problems subscales of the long form). Second, discriminant function analysis revealed that when classifying MDD versus matched control cases the overall correct classification total score was accurate 78.3% for the long form and 80.8% for the short form. When classifying MDD versus other diagnoses the overall correct classification of the total score was 72.6% for the long form and 70.3% for the short form. Information regarding the parent- and teacher-rater forms was not provided in the test manual.

Convergent validity was examined using a sample of 266 youth who completed the CDI 2 and either the Beck Depression Inventory–Youth version (BDI-Y; Beck, Beck, & Jolly, 2001) or the Conners Comprehensive Behavior Rating Scales (Conners CBRS; Conners, 2008). Correlation coefficients for the CDI 2:SR with the BDI-Y range from .28 (Negative Mood/Physical Symptoms) to .37 (Negative Self-Esteem, Functional Problems, and Total Score). Correlation coefficients with the Conners CBRS range from .38 (Negative Self-Esteem) to .59 (Negative Mood/Physical Symptoms).

COMMENTARY. The technical manual for the CDI 2 is well-written and easy to follow. The forms are also well-formatted, concise, and easy to read. Like its predecessor, administering any of the four CDI 2 forms is simple. All forms were written at or below the 2.2 grade level and were designed to be completed independently. Conveniently, the test manual provides detailed instructions for verbal administration of the CDI 2 by the assessment professional when necessary (e.g., when reading ability is a concern). The test developer's detailed explanation for hand scoring the CDI 2 also makes this task minimal. The CDI 2 can also be scored electronically. Similarly, interpretation of the CDI 2 scores is straightforward because of the detailed instructions provided in the technical manual.

Although issues of psychomotor retardation and endorsements of suicidality are not fully covered in the CDI 2, the test developers provide adequate justification for these omissions. The CDI 2 is well-designed for repeated administration to allow for progress monitoring of a single individual across time. The CDI 2 was clearly designed to maintain the quality of the previous edition of the instrument, but also to increase its utility in both clinical and research situations. Although great attention was paid to aligning the normative sample with the current U.S. Census Report, information regarding parent education level and socioeconomic status was missing, consistent with the previous edition of the CDI.

SUMMARY. The Children's Depression Inventory, 2nd Edition (CDI 2) is an individually administered, multi-rater set of instruments designed to assess depressive symptomatology in youth between 7 and 17 years. The self-report long form (CDI 2:SR) produces 3 scale scores (Total Score, Emotional Problems, and Functional Problems) with 4 subscale scores (Ineffectiveness, Interpersonal Problems, Negative Mood/Physical Symptoms, and Negative Self-Esteem). Both the teacher and parent versions produce three scales as well (Total Score, Emotional Problems, and Functional Problems), whereas the self-report short form (CDI 2:SR[S]) produces a single total score. The minor changes from the previous version include the addition of three new items, some minor editing of existing items, and the removal of two items. All versions of the CDI 2 have new or updated normative samples that better represent the intended population. The psychometric properties of the CDI 2 are solid with evidence of strong reliability and both convergent and discriminant validity. Administration, scoring, and interpretation are straightforward with help from an easy-to-follow and well-organized technical manual. More attention to technical aspects for both the parent and teacher versions (CDI 2:T and CDI 2:P) would have been beneficial, though the information provided is adequate. In general, this instrument is strongly recommended.

REVIEWERS' REFERENCES

American Educational Research Association, American Psychological Association, & National Council on Measurement in Education. (1999). *Standards for educational and psychological testing.* Washington, DC: American Educational Research Association.

American Psychiatric Association. (2000). *Diagnostic and statistical manual of mental disorders* (4th ed.-text revision). Washington, DC: APA.

Beck, J. S., Beck, A. T., & Jolly, J. B. (2001). *The Beck Depression Inventories—Youth manual.* San Antonio, TX: The Psychological Corporation.

Conners, C. K. (2008). *Conners Comprehensive Behavior Rating Scales manual.* Toronto, Canada: Multi-Health Systems.

[34]

Children's Measure of Obsessive-Compulsive Symptoms.

Purpose: Designed to provide an "objective assessment and quantification of the subjective experience of children and adolescents with both overt and covert behavior problems related to obsessions or compulsions at either a subclinical or clinical level."

Population: Ages 8-19.

Publication Date: 2010.

Acronym: CMOCS.

Scores, 10: Defensiveness, Inconsistent Responding, Fear of Contamination, Rituals, Intrusive Thoughts, Checking, Fear of Mistakes and Harm, Picking/Slowing, Impact, Total.

Administration: Group.

Price Data, 2013: $109 per complete kit including 25 AutoScore forms and manual (62 pages); $49 per 25 AutoScore forms; $68.50 per manual.

Time: (10-15) minutes.

Authors: Cecil R. Reynolds and Ronald B. Livingston.

Publisher: Western Psychological Services.

Review of the Children's Measure of Obsessive-Compulsive Symptoms by ANNETTE S. KLUCK, Associate Professor, Auburn University, Auburn, AL:

DESCRIPTION. The Children's Measure of Obsessive-Compulsive Symptoms (CMOCS) is a self-report measure designed for use by mental health professionals working with children and adolescents ages 8 to 19 (hereafter referred to as minors) who experience obsessive or compulsive symptoms (OCS), including those with Obsessive-Compulsive Disorder (OCD). The CMOCS can be administered in individual or group format and is available in English. Completing test items requires a second grade reading ability, but test administrators can read items to minors who lack adequate reading skills.

Administration of the CMOCS is simple, and the directions are generally clear. The evaluator is directed to provide a distraction-free location for the minor to complete the test. Directions in the test manual emphasize the need to explain to respondents that missing items make the test-results inaccurate, and test administrators are encouraged to answer questions about the test directions and be available to clarify items during testing. Test users are discouraged from engaging in long discussions about items and should encourage minors to respond as best they can if brief explanations appear insufficient. Test takers use the AutoScore Form, which contains directions and all items, to respond to test questions. Administration takes 10 to 15 minutes.

Scoring is completed by hand using the AutoScore Form, which contains most information needed to compute the standard scores. The test manual contains additional scoring directions and a sample scored profile. Because the manual does not contain all required information to score the responses, users will need to review the directions on the AutoScore Form, which is reproduced in the test manual. According to the test manual, scoring usually takes 10 minutes or less. In addition to a Total score (sum of all items), the CMOCS yields an Impact summary score (a measure of functional impairment that results from the OCS reported by the test taker) and six problem area scores (Fear of Contamination, Rituals, Intrusive Thoughts, Checking, Fear of Mistakes and Harm, and Picking/Slowing). Finally, the CMOCS contains two validity scales to help identify profiles that are likely to be invalid and should not be interpreted due to inconsistent or defensive responding.

DEVELOPMENT. The test authors sought to create a brief objective assessment tool that would (a) be appropriate for use as a self-report measure with minors, (b) provide a specific measure of symptoms associated with OCD, and (c) provide an evaluation of OCS that can occur in the absence of OCD. Specifically, the test authors described a goal of creating a test that is efficient for assessing symptoms associated with OCD in minors as well as assessing OCS that may be of clinical interest, such as those that occur with other psychiatric disorders like depression (e.g., rumination) or eating disorders (e.g., counting calories, rituals as part of weight control). A panel of three professionals with expertise in OCD, child and adolescent assessment, and measurement reduced an initial item pool of 168 to 119. No specific information about the process of generating items or the elimination of items by the experts is provided. The test authors conducted a pilot study on the 119 items using an ethnically diverse sample of 338 children ages 8-19 to select preferred language for test items and to identify for elimination those items with low item-to-total correlations. The pilot study resulted in 56 items being retained with item-to-total score correlation coefficients ranging from .25 to .60. The construction of the problem area scales is not specifically outlined in the test manual. However, the test authors indicate that with regard to the development of these scales, "Paramount were an awareness of the essential behavioral elements of various problematic obsessions and compulsions and practical considerations regarding the use of the final instrument in the daily work of professionals" (manual, p. 34).

TECHNICAL. A total of 2,325 minors ages 8–19 from community and school settings comprised the reference sample from which the standardization sample was drawn. The standardization sample included 1,644 minors selected to approximate the 2000 U.S. Census data. No individuals from clinical settings were included as part of the reference group or standardization sample. The standardization sample contained fewer older adolescents relative to other ages, and slightly more females (n = 854) than males (n = 790). Race/ethnicity for this sample closely approximated that of the U.S. population for individuals under age 17. The standardization sample also had an overrepresentation of individuals from the Northeast region of the U.S. (45%) and an underrepresentation of individuals from the South (18%) relative to Census data. Children whose parents have some college or a college degree were underrepresented in the standardization sample. A consistent significant gender effect was found in the full reference sample with girls scoring above and boys below the standardized mean on all scales. Although not consistent with the OCD prevalence rate, gender differences in the prevalence of externalizing and other internalizing disorders, the latter of which showed more OCS (e.g., Leadbeater, Kuperminc, Blatt, & Hertzog, 1999), may explain this finding. Some significant deviations from the mean emerged across age groups on various scales, but there was no obvious pattern. In contrast, African American minors from the full reference group consistently scored significantly higher than the mean across all scales. This pattern was not found for Asian or Hispanic/Latino minors (scores for Caucasian minors were not reported). Despite these findings, a single set of norms is used for all test respondents.

Studies on the reliability of the CMOCS provide support for its use. Internal consistency in the full reference sample ranged from adequate to excellent (rs between .70 and .94) with better internal consistency estimates for the Total scale. Slightly lower estimates were obtained for some age groups and for African American minors within the full reference sample. Test-retest reliability coefficients (N = 51) for a 1- to 2-week interval were adequate (.78 to .95).

Construct and criterion-related evidence of validity provided in the test manual offers some support for the use of the CMOCS in examining the extent to which minors experience unusual levels of OCS. In a factor analysis of the CMOCS, many, though not all (particularly for the Checking and Picking/Slowing scales), items loaded onto factors representing their assigned scales, and many items loaded onto multiple factors. Children with OCD had higher mean scores for both summary scales (Total and Impact) and all but one (Checking) problem area scales than children with other diagnoses, and internalizing diagnoses were associated with higher scores than externalizing diagnoses (note, not tested statistically). Correlations between CMOCS summary scale scores with scores on a measure of anxiety (the Revised Children's Manifest Anxiety Scale: Second Edition [RCMAS-2; 18:108]) yielded moderate to high coefficients (rs = .56 to .72) for the full reference group, with problem area scales showing lower coefficients (rs = .33 to .69), and support the criterion-related validity of the CMOCS. Correlations between the CMOCS Total Score with parent and teacher ratings were weaker for externalizing problems (rs = -.22 to .29), but also anxiety/shyness (rs = .17 and .26), on the Conners' Rating Scales for 75 individuals with suspected attention deficit/hyperactivity disorder. In that same sample, the correlation between the CMOCS Total score and a self-report measure of depression (Children's Depression Inventory) was moderate (r = .43).

COMMENTARY. The CMOCS is easy to administer and can aid in the evaluation of developmentally excessive OCS that may be experienced by children with a variety of psychological problems. The use of a nonclinical standardization sample is a strength that allows for meaningful interpretation of elevations on subscales. Additional strengths include use of a relatively representative standardization sample, inclusion of measures of valid responding, and psychometric studies lending support for the reliable (and, to a lesser extent, valid) use of the measure.

The test manual would benefit from more detail in multiple areas (e.g., item selection process, mean T-scores for Caucasian individuals, fit indices in validity studies on model equivalence). Lack of treatment studies and longer test-retest intervals make it premature to use the measure to monitor treatment progress. The average Total score for the small group of children with OCD fell within 1 standard deviation of the mean, which is problematic for using the CMOCS to screen for OCD. Research to identify cut scores with adequate sensitivity and specificity is needed to support this use. Finally, research on prevalence rates of OCD and internalizing disorders (e.g., Breslau, Aguilar-Gaxiola, Kendler, Su, Williams, & Kessler, 2006) do not support the reported disparities for African American individuals on the CMOCS. Caution is required in the use of this measure with African American minors because it may overpathologize them.

SUMMARY. The CMOCS is designed as a self-report assessment of OCS that may bear on diagnosis and treatment of minors receiving mental health services. There is not yet sufficient information to use the test for screening for OCD. Although there is some initial evidence to support the reliable and valid use of the CMOCS, clinicians should confine use of the measure to supplementing clinical interviews with the child and adult informants to aid in identifying unusual levels of OCS (and related impairment) in minors receiving mental health care.

REVIEWER'S REFERENCES

Breslau, J., Aguilar-Gaxiola, S., Kendler, K. S., Su, M., Williams, D., & Kessler R. C. (2006). Specifying race-ethnic differences in risk for psychiatric disorder in a USA national sample. *Psychological Medicine, 36*, 57–68. doi:10.1017/S0033291705006161
Leadbeater, B. J., Kuperminc, G. P., Blatt, S. J., & Hertzog, C. (1999). A multivariate model of gender differences in adolescents' internalizing and externalizing problems. *Developmental Psychology, 35*, 1268–1282. doi:10.1037/0012-1649.35.5.1268

Review of the Children's Measure of Obsessive-Compulsive Symptoms by KELLY BREY LOVE, Faculty Psychologist, Lincoln Family Medicine Program/ Lincoln Behavioral Health Program, Lincoln, NE:

DESCRIPTION. The Children's Measure of Obsessive-Compulsive Symptoms (CMOCS) is a 56-item self-report measure designed to evaluate obsessive and compulsive behaviors as well as their effect on youth 8–19 years of age. The CMOCS is purported to evaluate obsessions and compulsions at the clinical and subclinical level; however, the test authors caution that it is not to be used alone as a diagnostic measure for Obsessive-Compulsive Disorder (OCD). The CMOCS may be administered individually or in groups. The measure is designed in Likert-scale format (*never* = 0, *sometimes* = 1, *often* = 2, *almost always* = 3), with a reported reading level of mid-second grade. Administration is estimated to take 10–15 minutes, likely dependent on reading ability. Overall scores from the CMOCS produce a Total score and an Impact score. Responses are separated into six problem area scores: Fear of Contamination, Rituals, Intrusive Thoughts, Checking, Fear of Mistakes and Harm, and Picking/Slowing. These problem area scores combine to form the Total score. The measure also contains an Inconsistent

response index and a Defensiveness score to assess response validity. The Inconsistent response index is calculated by examining the difference between items that are highly correlated. The Defensiveness score is calculated by counting the number of zeros (*never* responses) chosen by the respondent. Scoring, which is completed by hand, is estimated to take 10 minutes or less.

Uses reported by the test authors include administering the CMOCS as part of a comprehensive assessment for OCD, for improved intervention planning, and multiple uses in school settings (e.g., determination as to whether a student may meet criteria for emotional disturbance, Individualized Education Program planning, assistance with a manifestation determination, and objective evaluation of intervention efficacy–specifically response to intervention). The CMOCS is reportedly appropriate for use in a variety of settings: school, clinical, forensic, and research. Trained clinic staff are allowed to administer and score the CMOCS; however, it is recommended that individuals with graduate-level instruction (including formal academic training and supervised experience) with like instruments interpret results.

DEVELOPMENT. The primary goal for development of the CMOCS appears to be identification and evaluation of obsessive and compulsive symptoms through a brief, self-report measure. The test authors believe the specific information gained from this assessment can assist in treatment planning and evaluation of treatment efficacy, if needed. The pilot study for the CMOCS was completed using an initial 168 items related to obsessions and compulsions. These questions were then narrowed to 119 items, by "three doctoral-level experts" (manual, p. 33) in OCD, child and adolescent assessment, and psychological test development; however, the qualifications/specific expertise is never defined. Items were chosen using extant literature review, including DSM-IV-TR (American Psychiatric Association, 2000) criteria. The pilot study included 338 youth 8–19, gender relatively equal, with overrepresentation of ethnic minorities. Statistical analyses narrowed the pool to the final 56 items.

TECHNICAL. The reference sample included 2,325 children and adolescents, drawn from nonclinical school and community settings in the U.S. The standardization sample ($N = 1,644$) was drawn from the reference sample. Relatively even gender distribution (48% male, 52% male), and age (8–19) were noted; however, those comprising the age group of 18–19 were significantly fewer. Minorities were deliberately overrepresented. Geographically, the Northeast was significantly overrepresented and the South underrepresented based on 2000 U.S. Census figures.

The CMOCS demonstrated strong internal consistency (Total score alpha coefficient was .94), as well as adequate consistency across problem area scales (alpha coefficients ranged from .70 to .81). The problem areas of Picking/Slowing and Checking demonstrated relatively lower internal consistency, but they still were in the acceptable range for the full reference sample (coefficients of .70 and .71, respectively). One- to two-week test-retest reliability was also good ($n = 51$; $r = .78–.95$). Internal consistency for African Americans was lower than for other ethnic/racial groups and for the reference sample as a whole.

The CMOCS appeared to have adequate content evidence of validity, as items were created by reported experts in this subject area. The test authors also report moderate to strong interscale correlation coefficients for the problem area scales (.51–.75). African Americans again had lower interscale correlations than the sample as a whole ($r = .41–.68$).

The test authors identified and described three other measures that are often used to evaluate obsessions and/or compulsions, but they reported these measures are most accurately described as "research instruments" (manual, p. 8) because of limited information regarding normative data and psychometric properties. The test authors did not report correlations between CMOCS scores and scores from any of these measures. The authors, however, did evaluate the CMOCS against the Revised Children's Manifest Anxiety Scale: Second Edition (RCMAS-2; Reynolds & Richmond, 2008; 18:108) and the Children's Depression Inventory (CDI; Kovacs & Multi-Health Systems, 2003). Correlation coefficients between the CMOCS and the RCMAS-2 were positive and strong (.56–.72). Positive correlation coefficients also were reported between the CMOCS and the CDI (.18–.47), adding additional validity evidence that the CMOCS is indeed evaluating internalizing problems. The test authors repeatedly state that the CMOCS should not be used as a stand alone assessment of OCD, but rather as part of a comprehensive five-step process, including the final step of considering CMOCS scores along with clinical interviews, proxy reports, and reviews of any additional assessment scores.

COMMENTARY. The CMOCS has a comprehensive, well-written manual that provides a significant amount of information regarding all aspects of the measure. The measure itself is easy to administer and score, and the psychometric evidence supports the stated goal of the test authors "to assess obsessive and compulsive behaviors (actions as well as thoughts) and their impact on children and adolescents between the ages of 8–19 years" (manual, p. 3). The inclusion of the Impact scale is beneficial in identifying the negative effect of symptoms/behaviors. However, there are several weaknesses that need to be mentioned. The size of the OCD clinical subsample was extremely small ($n = 30$), thus limiting comparisons. Computer administration and scoring would improve accuracy and efficiency, especially in group administrations. Another weakness is that the measure is only available in self-report format. The addition of a parent/teacher evaluation form would provide additional (objective) important information regarding observations of compulsions/obsessions. The lower reliability coefficients for African Americans are also a concern. The sample consists of fewer adolescents ages 18–19 compared with other age groups, which might reduce the ability to accurately assess individuals in the upper end of the age range.

SUMMARY. The CMOCS was designed to be a brief self-report measure used to evaluate obsessive and compulsive behaviors as well as impact on youth 8–19 years of age. The measure fills a demonstrated void, as there is a dearth of well-researched clinical self-report measures of obsessive and/or compulsive behaviors. The CMOCS appears to have sound psychometric data to support its use in a variety of settings and geographic locations. However, as reported above, caution should be used for administration/interpretation with African American youth due to lower reliability and validity estimates, as well as with youth 18–19 years of age.

REVIEWER'S REFERENCES

American Psychiatric Association. (2000). Diagnostic and statistical manual of mental disorders (4th ed., text rev.). Washington, DC: Author.

Kovacs, M., & Multi-Health Systems. (2003). Children's Depression Inventory: Technical manual update. North Tonawanda, NY: Multi-Health Systems.

Reynolds, C. R., & Richmond, B. O. (2008). Revised Children's Manifest Anxiety Scale, Second Edition (RCMAS-2): Manual. Los Angeles, CA: Western Psychological Services.

[35]

Children's Psychological Processes Scale.

Purpose: An internet-based teacher rating scale designed "to facilitate the identification of psychological processing deficits in children referred for a learning disability evaluation."

Population: Ages 5-0 to 12-11.
Publication Date: 2012.
Acronym: CPPS.
Scores, 12: Attention, Auditory Processing, Executive Functions, Fine Motor, Fluid Reasoning, Long-Term Recall, Oral Language, Phonological Processing, Processing Speed, Visual-Spatial Processing, Working Memory, General Processing Ability.
Administration: Individual.
Price Data, 2012: $169 per introductory kit, including printed manual (87 pages) and 50 online reports and rating forms; $149 per introductory kit, including downloadable PDF manual and 50 online reports and rating forms; $56.25 per 25 online reports and rating forms; $195 per 100 online reports and rating forms; $39 per downloadable PDF manual; $59 per printed manual.
Time: (12-15) minutes.
Author: Milton J. Dehn.
Publisher: Schoolhouse Educational Services, LLC.

Review of the Children's Psychological Processes Scale by RONALD A. MADLE, Licensed Psychologist, Mifflinburg, PA, and Adjunct Associate Professor of School Psychology, The Pennsylvania State University, University Park, PA:

DESCRIPTION. The Children's Psychological Processes Scale (CPPS), a web-based teacher rating scale completed and scored online, is intended to measure psychological processes (hereafter referred to as "processes") that impact on academic learning in children 5 to 12 years of age. The primary purpose of the CPPS is the identification of processing deficits in learning disability evaluations; secondary uses include screening, intervention planning, and measuring response to interventions.

The CPPS introductory kit comes with a test manual (either printed or downloadable pdf) and 50 online reports and administrations. Additional administrations are available in packages of 25 or 100, which include all materials needed to administer the scale and to generate a printed report. The examiner's manual describes administration procedures, research related to the various types of academic learning and psychological processes as well as the relationships among them, standardization procedures, and information on reliability and validity of the scale. The final manual section provides interpretive guidelines as well as a sample case study illustrating their use.

The CPPS has 121 items divided among 11 process scales (Attention, Auditory Processing, Executive Functions, Fine Motor, Fluid Reasoning, Long-Term Recall, Oral Language, Phonological Processing, Processing Speed, Visual-Spatial Pro-

cessing, and Working Memory). An overall composite, General Processing Ability (GPA), is based on all items.

The rater for the CPPS is typically the student's regular classroom teacher but can be any academic skills teacher who has had at least 6 weeks of contact with the student. After the administrator adds the rater to the CPPS account, an e-mail is sent that provides an online link, user name, and password for the designated rater. The rater can complete the scale online or print a hard copy and send the completed form to the administrator for entry into the computer.

Each item on the scale depicts an academically related processing difficulty that is readily observable by classroom teachers. Items are rated based upon the frequency with which the behavior occurs (*never, sometimes, often, almost always*). New raters will typically need 12–15 minutes to complete the CPPS. The computer program will accept the rating form only after all items are completed.

When ratings have been completed, the administrator, who can review but not change rater responses, accesses the record and generates a report. In addition to identifying information, the report includes a brief narrative; a table of *T*-scores with confidence intervals, percentile ranks and change sensitive *W*-scores; a graph of banded *T*-scores; a strengths and weaknesses table; and an optional *T*-score to standard score ($M = 100$, $SD = 15$) conversion table. Although higher *T*-scores indicate greater processing difficulties, the standard scores use lower scores to represent weaker processing abilities to facilitate comparison with ability and achievement measures. Report options include setting the standard error of measurement confidence intervals (68%, 90%, or 95%) and displaying responses to each item grouped by scale and presented in developmental sequence. The reports are stored alphabetically and can be printed or downloaded at any time.

DEVELOPMENT. The test manual indicates the primary goal was to develop a set of items that, using observable behaviors requiring no inferences about internal states, would differentiate between students with and without learning disabilities.

After developing an initial set of 75 items across 10 subscales, a pilot study was completed using 37 regular education teachers. Each rated three students—one each with average, low average, and high average academic abilities. Statistical analyses showed most items had desirable item characteristics, but there were uneven item difficulty gradients and ranges. This prompted an expansion to 147 items. In the item tryout phase, 27 raters in an urban Minnesota school district rated either three or six students (N = 96) using a similar methodology to the pilot. Analysis of the combined data to this point resulted in several changes: (a) changing all items to negative wording (i.e., cannot do …) to improve item characteristics, (b) eliminating 24 problematic items, and (c) adding 15 items to create an 11th subscale. These changes resulted in a 138-item standardization version. Final item selection occurred after norming and factor analysis, when 17 additional items were eliminated from the scale.

TECHNICAL.

Standardization. The CPPS standardization sample consisted of 1,121 subjects from 30 states and the District of Columbia. Stratification was based on the most current population statistics available from the U.S. Census Bureau (as of January 7 and July 7, 2011).

For norm development, weights were calculated based on deviations from the current population data for geographic region, urban versus rural residence, gender, race, and Hispanic status. This process statistically adjusted the obtained data to closely approximate the U.S. population statistics. With the exception of having more subjects from the West and fewer from the South, most variables were reasonable approximations of the population statistics. Parental education and free and reduced lunch status were also compared to the Census data but were not weighted. Academic skills rankings indicated 63.5% of the sample had average skills, 18.6% had above average skills, and 17.9% had below average skills. About 8.5% of the sample had educational disabilities. Norms tables are not presented in the test manual but are embedded in the online scoring program.

Reliability. Internal consistency reliability estimates (coefficient alpha) computed by normative age groups for the subscales ranged from .88 to .98 with the majority of the coefficients in the mid-90s. Only 2 of the 11 scales (Auditory Processing and Visual-Spatial Processing) had more than one coefficient below .90. The GPA reliability estimate was .99 across all age groups. The test authors do note, however, that the alpha coefficients may overestimate true population reliabilities due to the scaling characteristics of the item responses.

A study using 22 teachers rating 22 students was used to examine interrater reliability. Each teacher rated 1 to 7 students over intervals ranging from the same day to 42 days. Correlation coefficients for rater pairs for the 11 subscales ranged from .21 to .90. Only two of the pairs, however, had particularly low correlations (.21 and .38). Overall, the median interrater reliability coefficient was a respectable .77.

Validity. Various types of evidence are presented to explore different aspects of validity of test score use. Expert review of the item content, the developmental sequencing of items by difficulty, and the high internal consistency found in the reliability studies provided support for construct validity through the examination of test content. Additional studies using external data also supported construct validity as well as concurrent and predictive validity evidence. These studies generally examined the relationship of CPPS to other measures of psychological processing and academic outcomes.

The primary study involved the collection of CPPS ratings on 40 children (mean age = 9-6). Each child then was tested using the Woodcock-Johnson III Tests of Cognitive Ability (WJ III COG) and Tests of Achievement (WJ III ACH) (Woodcock, McGrew, & Mather, 2001; 15:281). The sample included 6 children with a documented disability and 6 with below average academic ratings. As expected, moderate to strong (.30 to .70) correlation coefficients were found for the majority of pairings of WJ III ACH cluster scores and the CPPS GPA. (The actual correlations were negative because of the CPPS reverse scoring.) Two particular findings noted were that (a) clusters including multiple academic skills (e.g., reading, written language, and math) correlated significantly with every CPPS scale, and (b) Academic Fluency cluster correlations with every CPPS scale and the GPA were among the strongest (.55 to .81). The latter was thought to reflect the greater demands placed on psychological processes by timed tests. Finally, although Mathematics Calculation showed fewer significant correlations with the process scales, those present were consistent with expectations based on prior research.

Correlation of the WJ III COG scales–with more direct correspondence with the CPPS subscale constructs–provided additional evidence for both convergent and discriminant validity. That is, WJ III COG and CPPS scales that purport to measure the same processes typically correlated significantly while correlations of dissimilar scales were not significant. Although this pattern was not uniformly evident, it was persuasive. Similar to the finding with the WJ III ACH, the WJ III COG Cognitive Fluency cluster was strongly related to all CPPS subscales. Additional fine grain relationships of data, which are beyond the scope of this summary, were presented to further support CPPS validity.

A similar study (N = 33) was reported using relevant scores from the Behavior Rating Inventory of Executive Function (BRIEF; Gioia et al., 2000; 15:32). As anticipated, relevant CPPS subscales correlated significantly with the BRIEF composite score and subscales, with the strongest correlations observed for Attention, Executive Functions, and Working Memory.

Analyses of the correlations between CPPS GPA and teachers' ratings of academic skills, as well as teachers' estimates of parent education levels, also showed the presence of significant relationships.

Finally, a sample of 37 children with various learning disabilities was matched to 37 children from the standardization sample based on gender, age, and grade placement. A paired-sample t-test confirmed that the learning disabilities group mean showed significantly greater processing difficulties on each subscale and the GPA. Based on statistical analysis of these data, the ability of the CPPS GPA to correctly classify children with and without learning disabilities was examined by determining the optimal cut score for classification. This T-score (57) correctly classified 85% of participants, although this value may have been inflated because an independent sample was not used for confirmation.

Internal structural validity. Analyses of the CPPS internal structure were conducted across four age groups to identify dimensions that might help in clinical interpretation of the CPPS subscale scores. An initial principal component factor analysis revealed one broad general dimension that was interpreted as general psychological processing ability. Subsequently, maximum-likelihood factor analysis was completed for both two- and three-factor models. Although there was some variation across age groups, the results generally were supportive of both models. The two-factor solution showed general processing ability and self-regulatory processes factors, with the addition of a visual-motor processes factor in the three-factor model. Cluster analysis using Ward's method showed similar clusters with occasional addition of minor subgroups, such as a fourth cluster of oral language and auditory processing in the two older age groups.

COMMENTARY AND SUMMARY. With the changes in operational definitions in the most recent iteration of the Individuals with Disabilities Education Act (2004) there have been a number of attempts to develop and validate new instruments and methods that go beyond aptitude-achievement discrepancies as being indicative of learning disabilities. The CPPS provides an innovative, easily administered and scored, and potentially useful instrument in this endeavor.

Standardization was well planned and executed, with statistical weighting being used to adjust for relatively small deviations from current population demographics. Internal consistency estimates for both the GPA and the individual scales are good, especially for a rating scale. Interrater reliability estimates were generally, but not always, acceptable. Validity evidence provided offers considerable support for using CPPS scores both as a measure of psychological processes and as a predictor of academic problems. Evidence of convergent and discriminant validity is impressive for such a new scale.

Although factor and cluster analyses generally supported two- and three-factor models, at this stage in development the CPPS appears most appropriately interpreted at a global level using the composite (GPA) score. That is, the greatest support is for using the GPA to determine whether one or more processing deficits are present in a child having substantial academic problems. It provides a method of estimating the likelihood that some type of processing deficit may be present and, based on the reported validation study, may provide a viable cut score for this aspect of learning disability determination.

Although there is some support for the validity of the subscales, it is more limited because the majority of scale variance is at the global level. Until more research is available, subscale scores are more appropriately used in planning decisions than in high stakes decision making. For example, they could be used in planning areas to be assessed with more direct process testing or planning types of interventions (based on apparent processing problems) that might be most likely to succeed with academic performance remediation programs.

A few areas were noted where improvements might be made in future editions. One relates to the scores provided. The use of negatively scored T-scores may be confusing to many audiences, making the use of standard scores preferable for reporting. If this is the case it would be useful to also print percentile ranks and confidence intervals for these scores in the optional score conversion table. A second desirable enhancement would be to add the ability to compare or otherwise consolidate information from multiple raters.

REVIEWER'S REFERENCES

Gioia, G. A., Isquith, P. K., Guy, S. C., & Kenworthy, L. (2000). Behavior Rating Inventory of Executive Function. Lutz, FL: Psychological Assessment Resources, Inc.

Individuals with Disabilities Education Act, 20 U.S.C. § 1400 (2004).

Woodcock, R. W., McGrew, K. S., & Mather, N. (2001). Woodcock-Johnson III. Itasca, IL: Riverside.

[36]

Classroom Assessment Scoring System.

Purpose: Designed to "assess classroom quality in preschool through third-grade classrooms."

Population: Preschool through third-grade students.

Publication Dates: 2008-2009.

Acronym: CLASS.

Scores, 13: (10 dimension scores) Positive Climate, Negative Climate, Teacher Sensitivity, Regard for Student Perspectives, Behavior Management, Productivity, Instructional Learning Formats, Concept Development, Quality of Feedback, Language Modeling; (3 composite domain scores) Emotional Support, Classroom Organization, Instructional Support.

Administration: Group.

Price Data, 2009: $49.95 per CLASS Manual Pre-K (2008, 108 pages); $49.95 per CLASS Manual K-3 (2008, 112 pages); $28 per 60 CLASS pre-K and K-3 observation and scoring sheets.

Time: (120-180) minutes.

Comments: The CLASS is a comprehensive observation system; researchers, teachers, principals, school psychologists, educational consultants, or other potential users must receive training to use the test. See the CLASS web site (http://www.classobservation.com) for more information on training.

Authors: Robert C. Pianta, Karen M. La Paro, and Bridget K. Hamre.

Publisher: Paul H. Brookes Publishing Co., Inc.

Review of the Classroom Assessment Scoring System by SARAH M. BONNER, Associate Professor, Department of Educational Foundations and Counseling Programs, Hunter College, City University of New York, New York, NY:

DESCRIPTION. The Classroom Assessment Scoring System (CLASS) is an observation-based instrument intended to measure the quality of prekindergarten through third grade classrooms. Classroom quality is rated in 10 dimensions with a single holistic rating per dimension, using a 7-point Likert-type scale. Observations are conducted in 30-minute cycles consisting of a 20-minute observation and a 10-minute scoring period. Four to six cycles are recommended, totaling a 2- to 3-hour observation and scoring period. Detailed descriptors and rating guidelines at both the K-3 and the Pre-K levels are provided, and professional training is available and recommended.

To obtain scores on the CLASS, an average score for each of the 10 dimensions is calculated over the number of cycles. These dimension scores are then averaged into 3 broad domain scores: Emotional Support (Positive Climate, Negative Climate, Teacher Sensitivity, Regard for Student Perspectives); Classroom Organization (Behavior Management, Productivity, Instructional Learning Formats); and Instructional Support (Concept Development, Quality of Feedback, and Language Modeling). Calculations can be done with a hand calculator.

The authors of the test recommend the following uses for the CLASS: research, accountability, program planning and evaluation, and teacher professional development. According to the manual, the CLASS can be used to rate overall classroom or individual teacher or student teacher quality, and observations can be rated based on live or videotaped performance.

DEVELOPMENT. The CLASS was under development for a decade and is based on a theory that social interactions between children and adults are the main mechanisms for children's social and cognitive growth. Little information about the processes leading from previous versions of the CLASS to the current one is provided. Although the manual states that the dimensions on the CLASS were developed through empirical investigations that included focus groups and pilot testing, no detail is given about these investigations. The manual names the Classroom Observation System (COS) as a precursor to the CLASS, and data from the COS are included as evidence about CLASS quality; however, little information is provided about how or why the COS was changed into the CLASS. The manual also reports data on dimensions not found in the current CLASS (Overcontrol and Student Engagement), and research cited includes data based on a different factor structure (La Paro, Pianta, & Stuhlman, 2004).

TECHNICAL. Neither norms tables nor performance standards are provided; rather, scores in the three domains may be compared within one classroom or across an organization. Little information is reported about the economic or cultural diversity of the samples in studies from which technical data were gathered. Several of those studies use previous versions of the CLASS and/or time-sampling frameworks for observations that differ from those currently recommended. The largest and most geographically diverse samples are from 694 preschool classrooms in 11 states, and 730 kindergarten classrooms in 6 states; the data from these samples are based on a configuration of dimensions and domains for the CLASS different from the current version.

For interrater reliability evidence, the manual reports that two trained raters independently double-coded 33 videotaped segments and obtained agreement rates (defined as within 1 point) ranging from 78.8% to 96.9% agreement on the 10 dimensions, and that similar results have been obtained in previously published studies. This reviewer does not consider this convincing evidence that high interrater agreement is likely in ordinary field settings. Stability of scores over time is estimated using classroom-level data from preschool (n = 240) and third grade (n = 68). Evidence about the stability of scores over multiple scoring cycles is provided in the form of correlations between dimension scores over one to three observational cycles with total dimension scores averaged over four cycles. These part-whole correlations are necessarily inflated, as is acknowledged in the manual. It would have been more appropriate to report the simple intercorrelations between cycles one through four for each dimension. The manual also reports statistically significant trends in scores for some domains related to time of day, day of observation, and time of school year. In the preschool sample, for instance, scores for Emotional Support significantly decreased over the course of the school day. Also, correlations between scores obtained on the same preschool classrooms in spring and fall ranged from .64 (Behavior Management) to .25 (Quality of Feedback), indicating relatively low stability over an extended time period in the latter dimension of classroom quality. The manual reports significant changes in means on Quality of Feedback and Concept Development over the course of the school year as a result of paired sample t-tests; it would have been helpful to know effect sizes.

Claims about face and construct validity are based on review of literature, piloting, and opinions of experts, but no specific detail is provided about the results of piloting or expert panels. Confirmatory factor analyses of the three-factor structure of the CLASS do not show optimal fit indices, and the Classroom Organization dimension appears weakly substantiated by data, with relatively low factor loadings and internal consistency estimates across several studies.

The manual reports evidence of criterion-related validity through correlations between CLASS dimensions and two other established measures of classroom quality: the Early Childhood Environment Rating Scale–Revised (ECERS-R; Harms, Clifford, & Cryer, 1998) and the Emerging Academics Snapshot (EAS; Ritchie, Howes, Kraft-Sayre, & Weiser, 2001). CLASS scores correlate moderately with the ECERS-R, with correlations ranging from .63 between CLASS Emotional Support and ECERS-R Interactions, to .33 between CLASS Emotional Support and ECERS-R Provisions. Correlations between CLASS domains and percent of time in specific instructional activities as measured by EAS are much smaller. CLASS Instructional Support domain correlated .12 with percent of time in literacy and language, and .03 with percent of time in math. No sample sizes are provided for these data.

The manual asserts that the CLASS predicts children's academic and social outcomes. The assertion is based on published studies using the COS, the precursor to the CLASS, and more relevantly, several recently published studies. For example, Mashburn et al. (2008) found that the CLASS Instructional Support domain was a more robust predictor of various established measures of preschoolers' academic performance than the total ECERS-R score, and that CLASS Emotional Support was a predictor of teacher ratings of children's social competence and problem behaviors. However, the version of CLASS in this study differed considerably from the current published version. Downer et al. (2012) found that the measured CLASS domains of Emotional Support, Classroom Organization, and Instructional Support were correlated with improvements in early childhood developmental outcomes. Rimm-Kaufman, Curby, Grimm, Nathanson, and Brock (2009) found that the domain of Classroom Organization (which the authors referred to as classroom management) was a strong predictor of children's self-regulatory adaptive behavior, whereas the Instructional Support domain had a negative relationship with the same dependent variable. These results suggest that CLASS is a useful instrument for prediction of student outcomes in early childhood.

COMMENTARY. A strength of the CLASS is that it is associated with a general trend away from measuring quantity of materials to quality of interactions in early childhood classrooms. Other strengths are clarity in guidelines for rating observations and reasonable ease of use. One weakness of the instrument is that it provides only a broad assessment of instructional quality. The Instructional Support domain is insensitive to content; for instance, a classroom could receive consistently high scores on Instructional Support in the complete absence of mathematics instruction. Also, the Classroom Organization domain is problematic. The construct measured by Classroom Organization is ill-defined, the relative structural weakness of the domain suggests psychometric problems, and valid uses for the domain score are not shown. Finally, the reviewer considers that test users should consider possible time of day, day of observation, and time of year effects when interpreting scores, especially if scores are to be used as part of teacher evaluations or for accountability purposes. Development of norms (both for fall and spring) would strengthen interpretability of results from the CLASS for such uses.

SUMMARY. The CLASS is a very promising instrument for measuring quality in early childhood education at the classroom level. Its use as a research instrument is adequately supported in the manual and by more recent evidence in the field. Because it does not provide a detailed assessment of instructional content, in cases where relationships with specific academic outcomes are of interest, it may be best used in combination with other instruments such as the Early Childhood Environment Rating Scale-Extension (ECERS-E; Sylva, Siraj-Blatchford, & Taggart, 2003) or the EAS. More data relating to reliability of the instrument in its current version need to be gathered, the factor structure of the CLASS needs to be confirmed, and validity of the Classroom Organization domain needs to be established. Finally, to support use of this instrument for accountability or program evaluation purposes, norms or standards should be developed.

REVIEWER'S REFERENCES

Downer, J. T., López, M. L., Grimm, K. J., Hamagami, A., Pianta, R. C., & Howes, C. (2012). Observations of teacher-child interactions in classrooms serving Latinos and dual language learners: Applicability of the Classroom Assessment Scoring System in diverse settings. *Early Childhood Research Quarterly, 27,* 21–32.

Harms, T., Clifford, R. M., & Cryer, D. (1998). Early Childhood Environment Rating Scale–Revised Edition (ECERS-R). New York, NY: Teachers College Press.

La Paro, K. M., Pianta, R. C., & Stuhlman, M. (2004). The Classroom Assessment Scoring System: Findings from the prekindergarten year. *Elementary School Journal, 104*(5), 409-426.

Mashburn, A. J., Pianta, R. C., Hamre, B. K., Downer, J. T., Barbarin, O. A., Bryant, D., ... Early, D. M. (2008). Measures of classroom quality in prekindergarten

and children's development of academic, language, and social skills. *Child Development, 79*(3), 732-749.

Rimm-Kaufman, S. E., Curby, T. W., Grimm, K. J., Nathanson, L., & Brock, L. L. (2009). The contribution of children's self-regulation and classroom quality to children's adaptive behaviors in the kindergarten classroom. *Developmental Psychology, 45*(4), 958–972.

Ritchie, S., Howes, C., Kraft-Sayre, M., & Weiser, B. (2001). *Emerging academics snapshot.* Los Angeles: University of California at Los Angeles.

Sylva, K., Siraj-Blatchford, I., & Taggart, B. (2003). *Assessing quality in the early years: Early Childhood Environment Rating Scale-Extension (ECERS-E): Four curricular subscales.* Stoke-on Trent, England: Trentham Books.

Review of the Classroom Assessment Scoring System by MARY (RINA) M. CHITTOORAN, Associate Professor, Department of Education, Saint Louis University, St. Louis, MO:

DESCRIPTION. The Classroom Assessment Scoring System (conveniently abbreviated CLASS) is an observational measure developed to "assess classroom quality in preschool through third-grade classrooms" (manual, p. 1). The domains assessed by the CLASS, with associated dimensions in parentheses, are Emotional Support (Positive Climate, Negative Climate, Teacher Sensitivity, and Regard for Student Perspectives), Classroom Organization (Behavior Management, Productivity, and Instructional Learning Formats), and Instructional Support (Concept Development, Quality of Feedback, and Language Modeling).

The CLASS may be used by researchers, school faculty and administrators, and other support staff to enhance research, accountability, program planning and evaluation, and professional development and supervision. Training needs for administration, scoring, and interpretation are minimal. Generally, the CLASS is designed to be used in blocks of at least 2 hours with each observation cycle taking approximately 30 minutes. Twenty of those minutes are used for observation of behaviors and taking notes, followed by a 10-minute period for recording codes. Finally, the observer makes judgments based on the "range, frequency, intention, and tone of interpersonal and individual behavior during the observation time" (manual, p. 9). This cycle can be repeated if necessary, up to six times over 3 hours and allows observers to gain a complete picture of the behaviors and interactions occurring within the classroom during both structured and unstructured times. Observations using the CLASS are recorded as Occurring or Not Occurring, whereas additional informal observations can help in the gathering of data that may be unique or of particular relevance to the observer and that can lend depth and context to other information. The observer derives one score for each dimension per observation cycle based on the extent to which certain behavioral markers are evident. Behaviors are rated along a 7-point range (Low = 1 & 2; Mid = 3, 4, & 5, and High = 6 & 7); ratings are averaged across cycles within each dimension and then converted to composite domain scores for each of the three domains.

DEVELOPMENT. The CLASS has its roots in the "developmental theory and research suggesting that interactions between students and adults are the primary mechanism of student development and learning" (manual, p. 1). The measure focuses primarily on ways in which teachers actively use classroom materials and resources and engage with students. "The CLASS was developed based on an extensive literature review as well as on scales used in large-scale classroom observation studies in the National Institute of Child Health and Human Development (NICHD) Study of Early Care and the National Center for Early Development and Learning (NCEDL) Multi-State Pre-K Study" (manual, p. 1). The three dimensions assessed by the CLASS were derived from a review of other classroom observation measures, a literature review, focus groups with classroom teachers, and pilot studies. The CLASS is based on the assumption that domains and dimensions evaluated across the grades are similar, but that they manifest differently based on the particular age or group under consideration.

TECHNICAL. The bulk of technical information about the CLASS comes from six major studies involving nearly 2,000 early childhood and elementary classrooms around the United States over a period of 10 years. The manual includes descriptive statistics showing means, standard deviations, and ranges across all six studies. After the initial submission of this review, the publisher of the CLASS provided information about four relatively recent studies utilizing the measure; information from these articles has been incorporated into this review.

The CLASS dimensions were found to be moderately to highly correlated with one another in two studies involving 776 classrooms across the country; related dimensions showed higher correlations than unrelated dimensions. Confirmatory factor analyses using five of the six studies revealed that a three-factor model (as described by the domains) provided the best fit. Factor loadings are in the moderate to high range and each domain has moderate internal consistency across the studies, with the Emotional and Instructional Support Domains having the highest loadings and

the highest levels of internal consistency. A study of 2,884 pre-K Latino as well as dual language learner (DLL) students (Downer, López, Grimm, Hamagami, Pianta, & Howes, 2012) showed that the CLASS factor structure was invariant across both populations.

Studies of reliability, as one would expect, given an observational measure, focused heavily on interrater reliability. A moderately high interrater reliability coefficient of .87 was obtained when the evaluations made by three experienced coders were compared to those of trainees on the CLASS and when they independently but simultaneously coded several videotaped segments of behavior. Interrater agreement across all 10 dimensions was examined using two observers who coded a total of 33 tapes; the percentage of agreement ranged from a low of 78.8 to a high of 96.9 with a mean of 87.1. Stability of scores was examined by assessing preschool and third grade classrooms. Moderate to moderately high reliability coefficients were obtained across the following: observational cycles, days in a week, the school year, and children and/or days.

Construct validity and face validity were assessed by soliciting input from content experts in teaching effectiveness and classroom quality. Evidence of criterion-related validity was provided in two ways. Concurrent validity was determined by comparing the CLASS with other measures of classroom quality (e.g., the Early Childhood Environment Rating Scale–Revised Edition and the Emerging Academics Snapshot) and related constructs such as teacher depression and adult-centered attitudes; results suggested low to moderate correlations among measures and factors. In addition, classroom quality, as measured by the CLASS, in a study involving 172 kindergartners was linked to improvements in students' behavioral control (Rimm-Kaufman, Curby, Grimm, Nathanson, & Brock, 2009). At the fifth- and sixth-grade levels, in a sample of 1,399 children, the positive relationship between students' grades and the emotional climate of their classrooms as measured by the CLASS, was found to be mediated by student engagement (Reyes et al., 2012). Predictive validity was assessed by comparing CLASS results to those obtained in the NCEDL Multi-State Study; findings suggested that classroom quality, as measured by the CLASS, was associated with children's performance at the end of preschool as well as gains in their performance across the preschool years. In a large-scale study of 2,439 prekindergartners across 11 states, Mashburn et al. (2008) found that teachers' instructional interactions and emotional interactions, as measured by the CLASS, predicted their students' academic and language, and social skills respectively. The Downer et al. (2012) study further showed that the CLASS predicted school readiness in both Latino and DLL prekindergarten students.

COMMENTARY. As an observational, multidimensional measure of the use of classroom resources and student-teacher interactions, the CLASS is one of the few measures of its kind and one of the most widely used. It is particularly useful in today's climate, given the decrease in the use of formal, standardized assessment and the increase in informal measures. The lead author, Robert C. Pianta, has built a reputation as a scholar and early childhood expert and as such, lends credibility to the CLASS. It is portable and lightweight, easy to use, and provides useful information in a number of important dimensions and domains found to be relevant to classrooms. It has been extensively tested in classrooms across the United States and appears to have been successfully used in a number of settings and across various age groups. The manual has a great deal of general information about how to conduct observations as well as specific information about how to use the CLASS to conduct classroom observations. The exemplars are detailed, and the sample conversations illustrating particular behavioral interactions are useful and leave little room for misinterpretation. The manual appears well-written. The scoring sheets are easy to use, and the Dimensions Overview foldouts provide quick and easy access to important information both for training and scoring purposes. The CLASS appears to have adequate internal consistency. Construct and face validity are adequate as are concurrent and predictive validity; both interrater reliability and stability of scores appear acceptable.

Despite its positive features, the CLASS is not without some minor problems. To begin with, it seems oddly named. The title, Classroom Assessment Scoring System, simply does not capture the essence of the measure or describe it fully. This is particularly odd, given the authors' insistence that the CLASS does not so much assess classrooms as it does what occurs *within* those classrooms.

The manual glosses over the actual development of the CLASS without providing details about the process of planning, development, refinement, and piloting. Further, information about development appears to be sprinkled throughout

the manual in no logical order; this makes for difficult reading. There are a number of references to other studies and websites for more information; however, readers will want all of this background in one place and not want to have to hunt for it. The manual includes information about six large-scale studies using the CLASS; however, as the authors indicate, these studies do not comprise a nationally representative sample. There is no information about race, ethnicity, language, socioeconomic status, gender, or exceptionality in the classrooms that were studied. And certainly, we know that these factors influence teacher behaviors and interactions in the classroom. Criterion validity–which really should be criterion-related evidence of validity–is defined incompletely on page 107 of the manual as "the extent to which a measure is associated empirically with other measures of similar constructs." Concurrent validity (which the authors refer to, incorrectly, as criterion validity) has been examined but should be studied more fully.

SUMMARY. The CLASS is a unique addition to the collection of measures available to assess classroom behaviors and interactions. It allows for the gathering of multidimensional information in an organized, systematic, and comprehensive way. It could be very useful as part of a comprehensive assessment battery in early childhood settings; however, the lack of information about development and the need for more studies regarding its technical merits warrant a careful interpretation of findings, at least until further information is forthcoming.

REVIEWER'S REFERENCES

Downer, J. T., López, M. L., Grimm, K. J., Hamagami, A., Pianta, R. C., & Howes, C. (2012). Observations of teacher-child interactions in classrooms serving Latinos and dual language learners: Applicability of the Classroom Assessment Scoring System in diverse settings. *Early Childhood Research Quarterly, 27*, 21–32.

Mashburn, A. J., Pianta, R. C., Hamre, B. K., Downer, J. T., Barbarin, O. A., Bryant, D., ... Early, D. M. (2008). Measures of classroom quality in prekindergarten and children's development of academic, language, and social skills. *Child Development, 79*(3), 732–749.

Reyes, M. R., Brackett, M. A., Rivers, S. E., White, M., & Salovey, P. (2012). Classroom emotional climate, student engagement, and academic achievement. *Journal of Educational Psychology.* Advance online publication. doi: 10.1037/a0027268.

Rimm-Kaufman, S. E., Curby, T. W., Grimm, K. J., Nathanson, L., & Brock, L. L. (2009). The contribution of children's self-regulation and classroom quality to children's adaptive behaviors in the kindergarten classroom. *Developmental Psychology, 45*(4), 958–972.

[37]

Clerical Aptitude Assessment.

Purpose: Designed to "examine how well the test-taker is suited for a career in the clerical field."

Population: Potential clerical workers.

Publication Date: 2011.

Acronym: CLAA.

Scores, 34: Work Habits (Diligence, Organization, Time Management, Dependability, Attention to Detail, Efficiency, Self-Discipline, Concentration, Initiative,

Adaptability/Trainability, Tolerance for Routine Work), Interpersonal Skills (Communication Skills, Conflict Resolutions Skills, Willingness to Compromise, Desire for Control, Likeability, Emotional Strength, Helpfulness, Discretion, Reaction to Criticism), Office Skills (Arithmetic, Filing, Reading Comprehension, Graph and Chart Reading, Proofreading Skills, Data Entry Skills, Typing Skills, Short-Term Memory Skills), Impression Management, Acquiescence, Overall Score.

Administration: Individual.

Price Data: Available from publisher.

Time: (40) minutes.

Comments: Self-administered online assessment. The test publisher advises that the test manual is being updated to include more information about methodology and theoretical background used in the development of the test. The test publisher also advises that this information is available to clients, as are benchmarks for relevant industries and racial/ethnic group comparison data. However, this information was not provided to Buros or the reviewers.

Author: PsychTests AIM, Inc.

Publisher: PsychTests AIM, Inc. [Canada].

Review of Clerical Aptitude Assessment by JAMES T. AUSTIN, Senior Research Specialist and Director of Assessment Services, Center on Education and Training for Employment, The Ohio State University, Columbus, OH:

DESCRIPTION. This online-only assessment consists of multiple-choice cognitive and noncognitive items. Test purpose is defined on the website of the developer-publisher, PsychTests AIM, Inc., as "Assesses whether the personality traits and skills a person possesses match those required to excel in the Clerical field." A related statement is found in the print manual and it seems possible to use test scores in vocational-career counseling. A related website offers a sample report that claims that the scores "help human resource managers and employers assess a candidate's potential for being a competent Administrative Assistant." This assessment should be understood within the long tradition of tests of clerical ability and aptitude dating back to work by Andrew and Paterson (1934). Vocational interests in clerical work and occupations were part of such early instruments as the Strong Vocational Interest Blank and its successors, as well as the Kuder scales. The statement of purpose implies that the construct assessed by the overall test score would be used primarily to predict future behavior and performance in clerical occupations. The combination of noncognitive and cognitive items in the Clerical Aptitude Assess-

ment (CLAA) is intuitively appealing. This writer reviewed test administration at the Arch Profile website (www.archprofile.com). This review is based on review of the 2011 manual, accessing a log-in account provided by the publisher to the reviewer, and investigation of the website of the test publisher and several related websites.

DEVELOPMENT. The manual provides little detail about how the test was constructed (e.g., construct definition, test specification, item writers, and other details). Such details, for this reviewer but more importantly for potential users, support decision making about whether to use this test for selection or achievement purposes. The manual opens with a list of "Vitals" that includes the number of items (196) but also indicates that there are "additional questions" without clarification of the purpose of these latter items (e.g., pretest items are a possible explanation). The next feature is item type: self-assessment, scenarios, interactive, timed exercises, mathematical, and memorization. Estimated completion time is 40 minutes. No short form is offered. Purpose is stated as given above, and two proposed interpretations of test scores are for pre-employment testing and job analysis. In the United States and Canada, pre-employment testing requires careful attention to design-development of the test and validation of test scores for this purpose. A second section on "Features" follows with a focus on the score report with an introduction, overall suitability for a clerical career, and scores on scales of Work Habits, Interpersonal Skills, and Office Skills. These scales are themselves composed of numerous smaller scales, which are defined in the text and also reported in the manual as described below in the Technical section. The report is rounded out with scales measuring Impression Management and Acquiescence, together with Advice (to test-takers). There is no mention in the manual of whether the scores can be archived at the website for the test-taker or the test user organization; this could enhance the usefulness of the test scores for test-takers and test users.

TECHNICAL. A statement at an associated website speaks to standards followed in test development by the publisher (www.queendom.com/about/media/credibility_popup.html). Technical information is presented in the print manual, beginning with statistical information on gender and age for a self-selected sample of 691 individuals who participated in a field test (518/588 persons who reported their gender were female; the distribution for 637 individuals reporting their age category ranged from 10%–19% across six categories). Descriptive statistics are provided in a table with columns headed Scale Name, N, Minimum, Maximum, Mean, and Standard Deviation. Possible ranges for the scores are not provided; therefore, it is difficult to interpret the average score of 49.48 given the heterogeneous item types. Reliability evidence presented includes scale names, the number of items (out of 196+ total items), and an estimate of coefficient alpha. Reliability estimates (internal consistency) for the overall and three subscores range from .88 (Office Skills; 43 items) to .94 (Overall Score; 146 items). Subscores for Impression Management (9 items) and Acquiescence (10 items) are much shorter and the corresponding reliability estimates reflect their length (.74 and .61, respectively). Not all of the components listed as part of the Office Skills scale were included in the reliability table; missing were Proofreading Skills, Data Entry Skills, Typing Skills, and Short-Term Memory Skills (although values were provided in the descriptive statistics section of the psychometric report).

The manual authors next present a second section, the psychometric report (total length of the manual, given by the footers, is 163 pages). The beginning repeats selected prior pages. This section consists of well over 100 pages of analysis of variance results pertaining to various background characteristics reported by the self-selected sample and filtered by respective subgroups formed on self-reported gender, age, education, socioeconomic status, clerical/administrative experience, and supervisor rating of performance in the clerical/administrative field. Each section begins with a very brief summary of the results, but not the meaning of the tests. Graphic plots for the subscales and their components are presented with statistical test results and very little text to explain the meaning of the statistical result. A summary table would have been very helpful in understanding the pattern and significance of the results. In addition, a section entitled validity analysis indicates that gender was restructured to have equal groups ($n = 73$ males and females). This restructuring is not explained, but it could be inferred that it means sampling randomly among the female respondents to match the number of males.

COMMENTARY. What was revealed by a review of the materials and test publisher websites is an instrument that is not ready for high-stakes use due to incomplete specification and inadequate

documentation. Scores are reported to test-takers that may not be based on adequate numbers of items, when the requirements for valid and interpretable subscores are available (Haladyna & Kramer, 2004). An internet self-selected sample of the size reported (nearly 700 respondents) can be helpful, but as the sole source of evidence it is lacking. No questions that dealt with one's motivation or one's current position in clerical work were included, which means that the appropriateness of the sample for the intended score interpretation cannot be evaluated easily if at all. If one views validation as a joint responsibility of the developer and the user of the test scores, a large burden is placed on the user of this measure. Additionally, given the existence of well-developed tests and scales for clerical knowledge and skill that provide interpretable scores for large corporations and the public sector (two of the largest categories of users of such information in hiring), the CLAA faces a formidable challenge to present a suitable tool. Still, there are multiple sources that describe the development of such tools–this reviewer located a comprehensive description by Hicks (2000) at the archives of the International Personnel Assessment Council (IPAC) website. Her presentation covers development of a General Clerical Test Battery for San Diego County, and includes the steps one would expect in a competent process with documentation. The *Handbook of Test Development* (Downing & Haladyna, 2006) is a general source of information about methods to evaluate educational and credentialing measures.

SUMMARY. The Clerical Aptitude Assessment, as presently constituted, should not be used for a stated purpose of hiring decisions because of a lack of evidence pertaining to content and relationships with valued outcomes. In order to support the use of this measure in higher stakes environments, what is required includes (a) construct definition, (b) provision of additional technical details (test specification, item bank features, etc.), (c) investigations into uses of scores with samples of clerical workers in work organizations, applicants for such positions, or individuals in training, and (d) additional investigations into score usage argument elements provided by the 1999 *Standards for Educational and Psychological Testing* (AERA, APA, & NCME, 1999) or the 2003 *Principles for the Validation and Use of Personnel Selection Procedures, Fourth Edition* (Society for Individual and Organizational Psychology, Inc., 2003). For example, on the basis of what occupational information was this item bank developed? Further, what is the relationship between scores on this measure and training or credentials? Those who must test clerical knowledge-skill and ability for personnel selection or certification have a responsibility to develop or use tests that possess and can demonstrate this evidence. SHL, a talent management consulting firm that includes Previsor, is one vendor with substantial evidence on the use of its tools in actual selection situations and their research basis. Also, Psychological Services, Inc. (PSI) includes clerical constructs as part of two test batteries, the Employee Aptitude Survey (Grimsley, Ruch, Warren, & Ford, 2000; T8:989) and the Basic Skills Tests (Ruch, Shub, Moinat, & Dye, 1984; T8:2175). Extensive reliability and validity evidence is presented supporting these tests.

In conclusion, the CLAA appears to combine in one tool both knowledge-skill-ability cognitive constructs and noncognitive measures that may be related to job motivation. It is impossible, however, to determine exactly what is being measured from the materials provided. This tool cannot be recommended for the purposes stated, which may be high stakes in nature for test users and test takers located in Canada and the United States. Still, steps can be taken to provide the types of evidence and documentation deemed necessary for use of this test as stated in its intended uses.

REVIEWER'S REFERENCES

American Educational Research Association, American Psychological Association, & National Council on Measurement in Education. (1999). *Standards for educational and psychological testing.* Washington, DC: American Educational Research Association.

Andrew, D. M., & Paterson, D. G. (1934). *Measured characteristics of clerical workers.* Minneapolis, MN: University of Minnesota Press.

Downing, S. M., & Haladyna, T. M. (Eds.). (2006). *Handbook of test development.* Mahwah, NJ: Lawrence Erlbaum.

Grimsley, G., Ruch, F. L., Warren, N. D., & Ford, J. S. (2000). Employee Aptitude Survey, Second Edition. Burbank, CA: Psychological Services, Inc.

Haladyna, T. M., & Kramer, G. A. (2004). The validity of subscores for a credentialing test. *Evaluation & The Health Professions, 27,* 349-368.

Hicks, R. (2000, June). *Development of the General Clerical Test Battery.* Presentation at the International Personnel Assessment Council annual conference, Washington, DC.

Ruch, W. W., Shub, A. N., Moinat, S. M., & Dye, D. A. (1984). *PSI Basic Skills Tests for Business, Industry, and Government.* Burbank, CA: Psychological Services, Inc.

Society for Industrial and Organizational Psychology, Inc. (2003). *Principles for the validation and use of personnel selection procedures* (4th ed.). Bowling Green, OH: Author.

Review of the Clerical Aptitude Assessment by SHELDON ZEDECK, *Professor of the Graduate School, University of California at Berkeley, Berkeley, CA:*

DESCRIPTION. This review is based on material presented in (a) a document entitled "*pt/psychtests*: CLAA (Clerical Aptitude Assessment)," provided by the publisher (2011), that contains a 5-page overview and 163-page psychometric report (referred to as a "manual" in this review); (b) a 1-page description provided in the test publisher's catalogue (PsychTests AIM, 2012, p. 17); (c) a review of a sample report; and (d) examination of an online demo of the actual test. The test is purported to measure how well a test-taker is suited for a career in the clerical field; and to measure certain personality characteristics and/or specific skill sets that will provide insight to the test-taker with respect to what is important to the test-taker and/or the settings in which the test-taker might work.

The Clerical Aptitude Test (CLAA) is described in the reviewed documents as a test with "196, plus additional questions" (manual, p. 1), which can be administered online in an estimated 40-minute completion time. The question types include self-assessments, responding to situations, interactive timed exercises for memory assessment, and solving arithmetic problems. The documentation indicates that results are reported on the following three general dimensions (subfactors) and 28 subscales: Work Habits (Diligence, Organization, Time Management, Dependability, Attention to Detail, Efficiency, Self-Discipline, Concentration, Initiative, Adaptability/Trainability, and Tolerance for Routine); Interpersonal Skills (Communication Skills, Conflict Resolution Skills, Willingness to Compromise, Desire for Control, Likeability, Emotional Strength, Helpfulness, Discretion, and Reaction to Criticism); Office Skills (Arithmetic, Filing, Reading Comprehension, Graph and Chart Reading, Proofreading Skills, Data Entry Skills, Typing Skills, and Short-Term Memory Skills); in addition, results are presented for Impression Management; and Acquiescence. There are common, and straightforward definitions provided for each of the subscales and subfactors. The number of items for each of the subfactors and subscales ranges from 4 to 15. The documentation also indicates that "Advice" is provided to the test-taker to facilitate his or her improvement and increase suitability for the clerical career.

DEVELOPMENT. There is no information provided on how the subfactors, subscales, or items were identified and generated nor is there any hypothesizing or literature base for the relevance of the subfactors and subscales to clerical and administrative work.

TECHNICAL. The statistical information and technical documentation provided for the test is based on 691 participants who took the online test. The sample was uncontrolled such that participants self-selected to take the assessment and opted to participate in the validation study. All validation items were gathered through self-report.

The sample of 691 is composed predominantly of females (75%), ranging in age from below 17 (19%) to 50+ (10%), relatively evenly distributed in terms of education levels (ranging from "some high school" to "Master's/PhD degree") and with the mode salary, used as a proxy measure for "socio-economic status," in the range of $25,000 to $50,000. Frequency distributions, minimum and maximum scores, and means and standard deviations are reported for the various subfactors and subscales, and by demographic characteristic. In addition, results of analysis of variance (ANOVA) are presented for subfactors and subscales as a function of the particular variable (e.g., differences among the age groups or differences among salary levels).

With regard to the ANOVAs, there is a limitation in what is reported. In particular, page 3 of the psychometric report indicates that the "T-test and ANOVA analyses are dependent on sample size. Therefore, a seemingly large difference between two groups may not show statistical significance because of a group's small sample size. By the same token, with very large groups, small but systematic differences between groups may be statistically significant without having any noticeable practical impact." This is an appropriate evaluation and conclusion regarding statistical analyses. Unfortunately, the issue is not addressed completely appropriately in the data presentation. The report identifies differences that are significant at the conventional level of $p < .05$, but also reports "marginal" significant results and "trends" based on significant differences at the $p < .1$ level. Adopting less conventional p levels does not address the sample size/statistical significance issue. Effect size measures such as correlations, eta-squares, or d statistics would be preferable to indicate the degree of relationship between the variables of interest or the amount of test score variance explained by the characteristic. In addition, for those post hoc comparisons of differences between particular levels of a variable that are reported in the "manual" (e.g., between age groups of 18–24 vs. 25–29), there is no indication of whether the test of significance was adjusted for multiple comparisons. These omissions severely limit the interpretation and value of the analyses.

An additional concern is that for the gender variable, the analyses of subfactor and subscale differences are based on sample sizes of 73 women and 73 men. Whereas the total sample was composed of 518 women and 80 men, the reduction for ANOVA analysis was accomplished by a "gender variable [that] was restructured in order to create equal groups" (see p. 24 of the psychometric report in the manual). This rationale for the creation of equal sample sizes for the purpose of the ANOVA is unclear and unnecessary. Accordingly, the results reported for male-female differences are limited.

Another piece of demographic/background data reported in the psychometric report, which is critical to the test's evaluation, is the "clerical/administrative experience" (manual, p. 104) level of the participants. The issue for a test developer is whether the developmental sample for the test represents the sample to which the test will be administered and to whom inferences will be made. For the "experience" variable used in CLAA analyses, the question for the participant was "are you currently working in the Administrative or Clerical field?" and the response data are reported in terms of (a) "Yes, and I plan to continue in this line of work" or (b) "No, and I have no desire to work in this field." The sample sizes reported for these two response categories are 51 and 71, respectively. The question, coding, and analysis for this experience characteristic is confusing and troubling for several reasons. First, there is potential confounding in terms of whether one is currently working in the field AND his or her desire to continue to work in the field. Second, why are there responses from only 122 of the 691 participants? Omission of such a high percentage of respondents (approximately 82%) limits interpretation and generalizability. Third, and most critically, the data suggest that only 51 out of the 691 are currently working in or have a desire to work in the administrative or clerical field; consequently, approximately 92% of the sample on whom data were collected and reported are not in or interested in administrative or clerical work. This outcome raises serious doubts about the appropriateness of the sample for generating any norms or for being representative of applicants who would take the test for purposes of gaining entry into the field.

A final demographic issue is the fact that no information is presented with regard to race and ethnicity composition and differences. And, it would be informative to have cross-tabs of demographics, such as how males in the "below 17 age group" compared to the females in the "below 17 age group."

With regard to reliability, the overview in the "manual" (p. 5) presents coefficient alpha for the 3 subfactors and for 26 of the subscales (no reliability result is reported for the subscales of "data entry skills" and "typing skills"). The reliabilities for the 3 subfactors range from .88 to .93, with a reliability of .94 for the "overall score." These are reasonable reliability results. However, examination of the reliabilities for the 26 subscales shows a range from .58 to .82, with 15 of the reliabilities being less than .70. Recognizing that the subscale reliabilities are based on a small subset of items, these results still indicate limitations in the test and the accuracy of the subscale scores given that subscale scores are used for the construction of advice and feedback to the test taker.

Validity analysis and evidence can be deduced from the data presented in the psychometric report, in the manual, regarding relationships between test scores and some criterion of performance. The manual presents data and results for the relationship between the subfactors and subscales with a "supervisor rating of performance in clerical/administrative field" (manual, p. 123). The latter criterion was assessed via a self-report from the test-taker with regard to the question of "How did/do your supervisors rate your performance?" and with the potential response categories being "excellent" (n = 50), "above average" (n = 50), and "average" (n = 50). There are a number of concerns and questions regarding this measurement and validation strategy. One, why are data reported for only 150 out of the 691 participants? Again, limited sample sizes impact generalizability, interpretability, and applicability to the clerical field. Two, was there a constraint to have equal sample sizes in each of the response categories? Three, why wasn't there a response category or two that reflected "below average" performance or "very poor performance"? Four, performance data are reported for 150 participants, yet other information presented in the "manual" indicates that only 51 are working in or desire to be in an administrative or clerical field. Do 51 participants provide an adequate representation of those in the clerical or administrative field? Five, what was the "performance" that was being evaluated—performance in and on what? How did the test-taker define "performance"? And, six, and perhaps most important, how much value and accuracy is there when the measurement of the key criterion variable is based on a *self-report* of another's (supervisor's) evaluation of that test-taker? Issues of bias and impression management need to be taken into account with such data.

Regarding specific validity results, the data and results (p values and mean scores) are presented in terms of ANOVA differences on subfactor and subscale scores for the three levels of performance. No effect size measures or correlations are presented. Issues noted above regarding use of trends, marginal results, and no adjustment for post hoc comparisons pertain to the validity results, too.

Regarding the test itself, the online presentation and administration was reasonable, many of the items have face validity and are similar to other personality, judgment, arithmetic, filing, data entry test items, and the like. There are, however, some issues and concerns with particular specifics pertaining to instructions, context, and content. First, on the opening screen, the test-taker is presented with a statement that there are "196 + questions." The "+ questions" part of the statement can raise concerns for the test-taker, such as what does "+ questions" mean; which ones are the "+ questions;" and how are responses to them to be used in scoring the test? Second, during one portion of the test, the test-taker is asked to provide responses to arithmetical problems (to do calculations) and, in another portion, to memorize and record information presented on prior screens. There is no instruction as to whether a test-taker can use paper and pencil or a calculator to respond to the questions or whether notes can be taken–if the test-taker is taking the exam on his or her own computer, there is no control as to how he or she takes the test. Accordingly, the accuracy of the results for the test-taker is questionable. Third, for the arithmetic questions, five specific possible numerical solution options are presented for each question, but in addition, each question has another alternative response category of "I don't know." Does a response to this latter option indicate that the test-taker did not attempt to answer the question or derived a solution that did not match one of the alternatives? My sense is that if a test-taker tried to solve an arithmetical problem and generated an answer that was not one of the first five options, he or she would guess at the response rather than state "I don't know." In essence, I am not sure of the value or purpose of the "I don't know" option–how does it fit into the scoring and interpretation of the results? (Also, there is no indication of whether there is a penalty for guessing.)

There is also concern about some of the item content and format. There are questions asking the test-taker to attend to a series of phone numbers from different areas of the world, presented one series at a time on a screen, and then requesting the test-taker to "type in the form as many numbers as you can recall." First, if this is to simulate memory tasks, does the "phone number" context make it more relevant to a clerical task? Is the concern with "face validity" or with tapping questions that are critical and important for clerical and administrative work? Also, if the test-taker needs to type in "as many numbers" as can be recalled, is there partial credit if some of the numbers are correct and others are not? The same concerns expressed here also pertain to the section of the test dealing with memorizing a more complicated set of information–person's title, address, company name, or phone number. On the job, such information might be written down by a clerical staff person, with the written notes then used to complete work tasks requiring the use of such information. There is also a proofreading set of questions. With respect to its relevance in today's word-processing world, where almost all software has spelling and grammatical checks, is this portion of the test necessary? In essence, the point of the concerns expressed here is that it would have been informative to have information about the item generation and the items' links to job tasks as identified in job analyses.

The section on data entry skills can also present a problem. For this part, the test-taker is asked to print out a form that is linked on the screen. Upon coming to this part of the exam, this was the first time one becomes aware of the fact that one would need to be linked to a printer to take or complete the test. This can cause a problem and stress for a test-taker who might be on a laptop or tablet when taking the test.

Questions pertaining to the test items dealing with filing also may present unintended consequences. For example, the test-taker is presented with a country in the stem of the question and asked to file it under one of several folder labels, where the possible folders are the continents. Thus, for example, if an item asked the test-taker to file the country of Turkey in its appropriate folder, the test taker would need to know whether Turkey is in Europe or Asia–thus, this portion of the CLAA is not only a test of filing, but also is assessing a knowledge of geography (which,

by the way, is something that can be looked up if one is actually asked to file a country under a continent as opposed to answering based on memory or knowledge).

A final product reviewed is a sample report. This report presents information in terms of (a) a summary, (b) introduction to the test and what it measures, (c) graphs of each score on a 100-point scale, (d) detailed results, (e) strengths and limitations, and (f) advice. In general, this report format and content is similar to these produced by many personality and skills tests. Unfortunately, for the score points presented in the report, there are no norm tables that the test-taker can use to compare his or her performance relative to others of the same gender, age, experience, etc. Finally, it would be useful for a potential adopter or user of the test if the manual contained a sample report.

COMMENTARY AND SUMMARY. The CLAA is not ready for "prime time" use for several reasons. One, the developmental data are limited to a self-selected group of respondents, very few of whom have or are interested in clerical or administrative work. Two, the information needed to evaluate the psychometric properties of the test is based on some equivocal decisions (e.g., to eliminate data in order to create equal sample sizes), lack of full information needed for evaluation (e.g., effect sizes such as correlations), a questionable operationalization of the criterion of performance, and lack of normative data. With regard to the test, there are concerns about particular types of content and requests for test-taker responses that pertain to the applicability to today's clerical and administrative work. The bottom line is that more information, analyses, results, and documentation are needed as well as refinement of the test itself. One place to start would be to define more appropriately what is meant by "suited" that is found in the statement that "The test purports to measure how well a test taker is suited for a career in the clerical field." Does "suitability" mean effective performance, success in likely advancement within the clerical/administrative field, satisfaction, or some other outcome measure? Accordingly, more data and research are necessary before the test can be appropriately evaluated for use in the field.

REVIEWER'S REFERENCES

pt/psychtests: CLAA (Clerical Aptitude Assessment). (2011). PsychTests AIM: Canada.

PsychTests AIM. (2012). *Assessment solutions*. Montreal, Canada: PsychTests AIM.

[38]

Clinical Evaluation of Language Fundamentals Preschool–Second Edition–Spanish Edition.

Purpose: Designed to provide "comprehensive language evaluation for Spanish-speaking preschool children."

Population: Ages 3-0 to 6-11.

Publication Dates: 2004–2009.

Acronym: CELF Preschool-2 Spanish.

Scores, 15: Basic Concepts, Word Structure, Recalling Sentences, Concepts and Following Directions, Expressive Vocabulary, Sentence Structure, Word Classes, Phonological Awareness, Early Literacy Rating Scale, Descriptive Pragmatics Profile, Core Language Score, Receptive and Expressive Language Index Score, Expressive Language, Language Content, Language Structure Index Score.

Subtests, 10: Basic Concepts, Word Structure, Recalling Sentences, Concepts and Following Directions, Expressive Vocabulary, Sentence Structure, Word Classes, Phonological Awareness, Early Literacy Rating Scale, Descriptive Pragmatics Profile.

Administration: Individual.

Levels, 4: Level 1: Identify whether or not there is a language disorder; Level 2: Describe the nature of the disorder; Level 3: Evaluate early classroom and literacy fundamentals; Level 4: Evaluate language and communication in context.

Price Data, 2010: $379 per CELF Preschool-2 Spanish Kit including manual (2009, 310 pages), 25 record forms, Spanish stimulus manual, and 25 rating scale forms; $105 per manual; $325 per Spanish stimulus manual.

Foreign Language Edition: English-language edition is Clinical Evaluation of Language Fundamentals Preschool-Second Edition (17:49).

Time: (15-20) minutes for Level 1; remaining subtest time varies.

Comments: This is a parallel edition to the CELF Preschool 2 (17:49), not a translation; subtests can be used individually.

Authors: Elisabeth H. Wiig, Wayne A. Secord, and Eleanor Semel.

Publisher: Pearson.

Review of the Clinical Evaluation of Language Fundamentals Preschool-Second Edition-Spanish Edition by JAMES DEAN BROWN, Professor of Second Language Studies, and MARTA GONZALEZ-LLORET, Professor in Spanish, University of Hawai'i at Manoa, Honolulu, HI:

DESCRIPTION. The Clinical Evaluation of Language Fundamentals Preschool-Second Edition -Spanish Edition (CELF Preschool-2 Spanish) "is an individually administered clinical tool for the identification, diagnosis, and follow-up evaluation of language and communication disorders in Spanish-speaking children" (manual del examinador, p. 1) designed to assess receptive language, expressive language, language content, and language structure. It includes seven subtests (Conceptos Básicos, Estructura de Palabras, Recordando Oraciones, Conceptos y Siguiendo Direcciones, Estructura de Oraciones, Vocabulario Expresivo, and Clases de Palabras); one supplementary subtest that produces criterion scores (Conocimiento Fonológica); and two rating scales that produce criterion scores about the child's skills outside of the testing situation (Escala de Valoración de Alfabetización Temprana, and Clasificación Pragmatica). Four decision levels are described: Level 1–Determine if a language disorder exists, Level 2–Describe the disorder, Level 3–Evaluate early classroom and literacy fundamentals, and Level 4–Evaluate language and communication in context.

An examiner's manual (manual del examinador) provides guidelines for administration, scoring, and interpreting test performances; descriptions of the purpose, design, and development of the test; and technical information about the normative data, reliability statistics, and validity analyses. A stimulus manual (manual de estímulos) contains the colored drawings that serve as testing stimuli. A record form (folleto de registro) for each child contains directions, test items and response choices, space for recording answers, and several checklists. The rating scales (escalas de valoración) for each child includes the Early Literacy and Descriptive Pragmatics Profile rating scales in English and Spanish (to be filled out by a caregiver, teacher, etc.).

The test authors stress that examiners must be fluent Spanish speakers trained in school psychology, special education, speech/language pathology, or another closely allied profession. Under some conditions, a person with one of those backgrounds can do the testing with an interpreter.

DEVELOPMENT. The examiner's manual provides a clear explanation of the test's goals and relationships to the parallel English version of the Clinical Evaluation of Language Fundamentals Preschool–Second Edition (CELF Preschool-2; 17:49) and higher level Clinical Evaluation of Language Fundamentals–Spanish–Fourth Edition (CELF-4 Spanish). The test authors explain the CELF Preschool-2 assessment model and how the CELF Preschool-2 Spanish was developed including content and bias reviews (involving seven experts), pilot research (with feedback from

28 speech-language pathologists), and piloting of the test (n = 89).

TECHNICAL. The standardization research sample (n = 464) is described in terms of age, sex, place of origin, primary caregiver education, geographical region, time in U.S., Spanish dialect, and Spanish use/exposure. The test authors then report on a study of the appropriateness of separate percentiles for monolingual and bilingual children, and studies of the adequacy of the norms and the effects of the discontinue rules. They provide substantial normative data in Appendices A–G and discuss at length the standard scores, age equivalents, and criterion scores. In addition, they describe Growth Scores and Index Score differences for the receptive and expressive language index score differences, and for the language content and structure index score differences.

The test authors provide considerable evidence of the reliability of the test scores including test-retest reliability and standard error of measurement (*SEM*) estimates for all subtests and composites for different ages separately and combined. Decision consistency estimates are provided for the four sets of criterion-referenced scores for different ages separately and combined. Cronbach alpha and split-half reliabilities (and corresponding *SEM*s) are also reported for all subtests and composites for half grades separately and combined across all ages (also separately for children diagnosed with a language disorder). In addition, average inter-scorer agreement statistics are provided for the four ratings-based subtests. Generally, these reliability and agreement estimates indicate moderate to high degrees of score consistency.

The test authors also provide evidence of the validity of scores based on evidence derived from: content, response process, internal structure, relations to other variables (e.g., between CELF Preschool-2 English and Spanish versions and with CELF Preschool-4 Spanish), and a study of 90 Spanish speakers with language disorders matched with 90 children with no such disorders for the diagnostic accuracy of the Core Language Scores.

COMMENTARY. Generally, this test was carefully and competently developed, validated, and explained. However, as with any test, it could be improved. We noticed several small problems:

1. Some examiners may find the scoring directions, administration procedures, and interpretations rather complex (e.g., the chapters on these topics

are 106 pages long), especially those examiners who do not have the time to thoroughly absorb the examiner's manual or who do not administer the test often.

2. The test authors do say that examiners can save time by using discontinue rules (i.e., stopping when students have missed a certain number of items). This practice can cause two problems: It does not allow all children to show what they can do on all items and it may tend to inflate any internal consistency reliability estimates.

3. The test authors include criterion-referenced scores (examiner's manual, p. 101) for norm-referenced tests. This confused us until we realized that the authors were referring only to a cut-point criterion; this should not be confused with the sort of criterion-referenced testing that is carefully designed to measure and provide separate scores for individual learning outcomes.

4. The test authors are uncharacteristically vague about growth scores. They use an agentless passive in describing them (i.e., "Growth scores were derived…," examiner's manual, p. 163) and then never explain how these scores "were derived" (aside from saying that item response theory analysis was performed using Winsteps 3.31 and the resulting theta ability scores "were then rescaled to form the growth scores").

5. With regard to Hispanic culture, two problems occurred to us:

a. The test authors advise examiners that it is "more professional and respectful" to "address the primary caregiver directly and maintain eye contact" (examiner's manual, p. 20). This does not ring true to us. It is likely that many Hispanics will interpret direct eye contact as intimidating.

b. The picture of the calendar (stimulus manual, p. VE 17) shows the week starting on Sunday instead of Monday, which may be confusing for children accustomed to seeing Spanish calendars where Monday is the first day of the week.

6. With regard to the Spanish language, three types of problems surfaced in about a dozen places:

a. Typographical errors (e.g., *quiere dormer* should be *quiere dormir*, and *va a dormer* should be *va a dormir* in Item 4 of the *estructura de palabras*) (examiner's manual, p. 257).

b. Missing acceptable answers (e.g., the verb *mirar* should be included as an alternate to *ver* as in *se está mirando* or *está mirándose* in Item 12 of the estructura de palabras) (examiner's manual, p. 259 & record form, p. 7).

c. Syntactic structures closer to English than Spanish (e.g., *Aquí está un gato* should be *Esto es un gato* when used for identification and *Aquí hay un gato* when used for location) (folleto de registro, p. 6).

However, to give the test authors due credit, they do go well beyond the call of duty in a number of other ways:

1. In chapter 4, they clearly explain how to interpret confidence intervals, percentile ranks, and growth scores; how the decision making process should proceed; and how these scores and decisions are related to federal law.

2. In the same chapter, they present four case studies that are quite illuminating.

3. The test authors take care to discuss relevant language learning issues such as simultaneous versus sequential bilinguals, additive language versus subtractive environments, basic interpersonal communication skills versus cognitive academic language proficiency, and Spanish proficiency issues that could create bias in interpreting scores.

4. The test authors include a laudable paragraph on the "user's responsibilities" (examiner's manual, p. 9), and explain how to handle dialectal variations, Anglicisms and code switching, out-of-age-range testing, self-correction, as well as slow, undermotivated, culturally different, and linguistically different learners. They also warn that test scores are not diagnoses.

5. The test authors caution examiners to take into account the existing body of knowledge in fields such as intercultural differences, second language acquisition, bilingual language development, retention/loss of first languages, language disorders, code switching, nonstandard assessment practices, test modification/adaptation, and use of interpreters.

6. The test authors provide excellent information on special concerns in assessing Hispanic children: They discuss how interactions with adults are different in Hispanic and Anglo cultures, and observe that Hispanic parents who do not visit their children's schools may not be doing so because they lack interest in their children's education, but rather because they are ashamed of their own lack of education.

SUMMARY. The CELF Preschool-2 Spanish provides a Spanish language version of the CELF Preschool-2 in English and serves as a downward extension of the higher level CELF-4 Spanish. It can be appropriately used for identifying, diagnosing, and further evaluating Spanish language and communication disorders in Spanish-speaking

children. The standardization procedures are clearly explained, and the arguments made for the reliability and validity of the scores are comprehensive and convincing. In addition, the test authors carefully explain the issues involved in decision making based on the various scores of this test and carefully caution users to be judicious in using the test scores.

Review of The Clinical Evaluation of Language Fundamentals-Preschool-Second Edition-Spanish Edition by GERALD TINDAL, Castle-McIntosh-Knight Professor of Education, College of Education, University of Oregon, Eugene, OR:

The Clinical Evaluation of Language Fundamentals-Preschool-Second Edition-Spanish Edition (CELF Preschool-2 Spanish) is designed for clinicians to diagnose and classify language disorders in young Spanish-speaking children. It is subtitled as a clinical evaluation of language fundamentals. The test is bundled with the following materials: (a) an administration manual for the examiner that includes extensive information on its purpose and use, development of items, directions for administration, scoring, reporting, and interpretation of subtests; (b) stimulus materials for the student that are primarily colorful drawings of people and animals that can be displayed in a flip-over triangular stand; (c) two sets of recording forms for rating students on skills and interactive proficiencies, as well as summarizing performance on the subtests with a cover sheet to report subtest scaled scores, core language scores and indexes, and, finally, discrepancy comparisons.

DESCRIPTION. "Subtests are designed to measure the child's ability to access semantic and syntactic knowledge in a variety of conceptual contexts. This enables you to understand whether the child's linguistic ability relate to specific or global difficulties with language structure and meaning. CELF Preschool–2 Spanish also was developed to measure the ability to generate spoken language" (manual del examinador, p. 180).

The test is packaged in two age levels. For ages 3 to 4 years, seven subtests are presented: (a) Conceptos Básicos, (b) Estructura de Palabras, (c) Recordando Oraciones, (d) Conceptos y Siguiendo Direcciones, (e) Vocabulario Expresivo, (f) Estructura de Oraciones, and (g) Clases de Palabras. For ages 5–6, four subtests are presented: (a) Conceptos Básicos, (b) Conocimiento Fonológico, (c) Escala de Valoración de Alfabetizacion Temprana, and (d) Clasificación Pragmatica.

Because the test is written and administered in Spanish, an important chapter describes how to collaborate with an interpreter (for monolingual test administrators). Otherwise, the directions are clear in how to administer the test, including specific wording and presenting test materials; most subtests include teaching items, which help ensure performance is not confounded with misunderstanding how to perform. Although most of the items (and subtests) are objectively scored, some constructed responses are used, in which case extensive directions and training are presented. The final chapter in subtest administration focuses on completing the score summary and analysis pages. Directions are presented for converting raw to scaled scores, determining subtest confidence intervals, percentile ranks, age equivalents, composite scores, discrepancy comparisons, index and subtest profiles, and finally completing a criterion score chart as well as recording growth scores and plotting them on a growth chart.

In Levels 1 and 2, CELF Preschool–2 Spanish provides a number of subtest scale scores, a core language score, and several index scores (receptive language, expressive language, language content, and language structure). In addition, norm-referenced scores can be determined and reported as percentile ranks, age equivalents, or growth scores. In the end, test scores may be interpreted for the following four purposes: (a) determination of a disorder, (b) description of the disorder, (c) evaluation of early classroom and literacy fundamentals, and (d) evaluation of language in context.

DEVELOPMENT. The CELF Preschool–2 Spanish is a derivative of the CELF–Fourth Edition and designed to be parallel with, and have the same subtests as, the CELF Preschool. The test manual describes 13 principles in its design that reflect attention to subtest functioning (floors and ceilings), best practices in language assessment, and development of technical adequacy. Primary attention is given to development of three core scores for children ages 3:0–4:11 and three other core subtest scores for children ages 5:0–6:11: "The core subtests chosen for each age group demonstrated the greatest discrimination in identifying language disorders and proved to be the most clinically sensitive" (manual del examinador, p. 134).

Index scores (composite scores from two or three subtest scaled scores) are designed to reflect a child's strengths and weaknesses. For example, a Receptive Language Index (RLI) and an Expressive Language Index (ELI) can be derived. In addition, "during the early phases of development of CELF Preschool–2 Spanish, the subtests that were used in the index scores were expanded to include additional aspects of early developing language and literacy skills. The subtests were grouped to form one composite with primarily semantic content (Language Content Index) and a second composite with primarily morphological and syntactic content (Language Structure Index)" (manual del examinador, p. 134).

The test design is described by addressing specific difficulties for children with language disorders. For example, this population frequently has difficulty with basic concepts, mastering word structure rules, remembering and repeating spoken sentences, following oral directions, delayed acquiring of expressive language and vocabulary, mastering syntactic structures, categorizing words, being aware of the sound system (including words, syllables, and phonemes), unevenly developing skills in early reading, and verbally interacting within specific social contexts. Each of these difficulties forms a conceptual basis for the development of a subtest.

Specific steps are described in test development that included bias and content reviews from experts, pilot testing of seven measures by speech-language pathologists for a sample of 89 children from across the U.S., and pilot scoring of three subtests that use constructed responses (and therefore require a judgment of accuracy). Items were analyzed for percentage of children passing, analysis of discrimination, and length of testing time.

The standardization version of the CELF Preschool–2 Spanish was completed with 85 qualified examiners testing a total sample of over 700 children who were stratified into eight 6-month age groups (from 3 years 0 months to 6 years 11 months). Data also are reported on sampling distributions for sex, place of origin, primary caregiver education level, geographic region, length of time living in the U.S., Spanish dialect spoken, and frequency and context of Spanish usage and exposure (as reported by the primary caregiver). These variables were not controlled but simply used to describe various breakdowns and cross-tabulations. Finally, the three subtests using constructed responses were compared using two scoring systems. Two dimensions are used to compare students in the normative sample across the entire distribution of ages: monolingual versus bilingual students and use of comprehensive and expressive language.

The final normative scores are presented after analyzing test items for difficulty, differential item functioning, and ease and reliability of scoring; these data are used to adjust or select specific items. In the end, normative data are reported in the 6-month age groups with at least 50 children in all but the youngest age group. In a series of appendices, normative data are reported in tables for the following: subtest scaled scores, composite standard scores, percentile ranks, normal curve equivalents and stanines, age equivalents, discrepancy comparisons, criterion scores (comparing students with and without language disorders), and growth scores (using item response theory).

TECHNICAL. The manual del examinador includes a chapter on evidence of reliability and validity. Several studies are presented concerning reliability, including the following:

Evidence of test-retest stability is provided based on 66 students from the standardization sample who were retested within 2 to 29 days, with both tests administered by the same examiner. Children in the sample were distributed in age, sex, place of origin, geographic region, and primary caregiver education level. Average (and variance) values are reported (with the second test usually higher than the first, which is not surprising given practice effects and the developmental nature of language acquisition). Corrected correlations range form the upper .60s to the mid .90s.

Evidence of internal consistency is presented for both the normative sample and a population of students identified with a language disability. Coefficient alpha ranges from .71 to .96 across the various subtests and rating scale composites.

Evidence of reliability based on the split-half method (odd-even) for subtests, ratings, and composite scores are calculated with coefficients across the normative age groups ranging from .67 to .98.

Interscorer reliability for the constructed response subtests is presented for five scorers (using pairs of scorers and a third independent reviewer to resolve differences). Agreement ranges from .93 to .98.

Based on the reliability data, the standard error of measurement and confidence intervals are depicted. Finally, a number of index score differences are presented for receptive and expressive language as well as language content and language structure. The tables present percentage of discrepancies in the normative sample and for a language disorder sample.

Several types of validity evidence are reported using the *Standards for Educational and Psychological Testing* (American Educational Research Association, American Psychological Association, & National Council on Measurement in Education, 1999):

Evidence based on content cites a review by a group of experts "recruited for their understanding of language usage among Hispanic populations" (manual del examinador, p. 180).

Evidence based on response process is presented in the form of access and associated skills (student ability to understand oral and spoken language, generate spoken language, and have intact cognitive abilities), all of which are required to perform on the subtests.

Evidence based on internal structure is presented through intercorrelational studies and factor analytic studies. Moderate correlations are depicted among the subtests (not only because they measure similar constructs but some composites are composed of nested subtests). The correlations range from the low .50s to low .90s across the subtests and composite summaries. The factor analytic study uses structural equation modeling to organize the reporting categories for receptive and expressive language as well as language content and structure. Loadings of subtests on these constructs is confirmed with the "proposed theoretical model fit[ting] the normative data adequately" (manual del examinador, p. 185).

Finally, evidence based on other variables was organized primarily on the related CELF measures (Preschool 2 and CELF–4 Spanish). For a group of 30 students taking the various measures, low to moderate correlations are presented. A special group study is described that distinguishes children diagnosed with a language disorder and a matched control sample. Significant differences are apparent between these two populations. As part of this study, a receiver operator characteristics (ROC) analysis is used to document the positive predictive power and negative predictive power. Results indicate that a core language score of 85 or less has sensitivity values of .86 and a specificity value of .89. "This indicates that 86% of the children previously identified with a language disorder were identified by CELF Preschool–2 Spanish and that 89% of the children in the typically developing matched population were identified as not having a language disorder" (manual del examinador, p. 194).

COMMENTARY. The CELF Preschool–2 Spanish is a well-organized test for language clinicians to document a number of disorders present in young Spanish-speaking children. The stimulus items are appealing and administration directions clearly organized to elicit language for this population. The test is bundled in a very orderly fashion for the test administrator to use with the recording forms, providing a variety of essential information for many different language behaviors that can be aggregated into two primary indexes: Receptive-Expressive and Language Content-Structure.

SUMMARY. The test can provide very useful information for a population of young Spanish-speaking children that may well disentangle developmental inferences about language, disability, and context. The subtests are well structured around critical basic language functions; the scores for subtests, composites, and indexes are likely to reveal meaningful differences between children with a disability from those developing normally; and the behavioral ratings enhance interpretation of test performance with contextual issues.

REVIEWER'S REFERENCE

American Educational Research Association, American Psychological Association, & National Council on Measurement in Education. (1999). *Standards for educational and psychological testing.* Washington, DC: American Educational Research Association.

[39]

College-to-Career Transition Inventory.

Purpose: Designed to "help students pinpoint the false beliefs and potential gaps in knowledge and skills that might prevent them from finding a job, further advancing their education, and succeeding in their career."

Population: Individuals transitioning to the workplace from high school, college, vocational, technical, and training programs.

Publication Date: 2010.

Acronym: CCTI; C2C.

Scores, 5: Life Management, Emotional Intelligence, Job Search, Transition to Work, Career Management.

Administration: Group.

Price Data, 2011: $41.95 per 25 assessment booklets.

Time: (20-25) minutes.

Comments: The administrator's guide (14 pages) is available for download on the publisher's web site.

Author: John J. Liptak.

Publisher: JIST Publishing, Inc.

Review of the College-to-Career Transition Inventory by MICHAEL BUNCH, Senior Vice President, Measurement Incorporated, Durham, NC:

DESCRIPTION. The College-to-Career Transition Inventory (CCTI), developed by John J. Liptak, consists of a set of 60 statements addressing five dimensions (scales) of college-to-work transition: Life Management, Emotional Intelligence, Job Search, Transition to Work, and Career Management. The instrument comes in a tri-fold booklet (25.5 inches x 11 inches, or three 8.5-inch x 11-inch pages side by side) with all 60 statements printed in color-coded sections on one side of the form and instructions for interpretation on the other. It can be self-administered and scored or administered and scored by a professional.

The 60 statements are in 10 blocks of 6 with alternating shades to make it easy to move from section to section. Each statement is a self-description to which the examinee responds on a 4-point Likert scale: *A Lot Like Me*, *Somewhat Like Me*, *A Little Like Me*, and *Not Like Me*. Instructions guide the examinee through five steps: Completing the inventory, totaling the scores, profiling the scores, interpreting the profile, and developing a college-to-career success plan. The instructions for interpreting the profile describe each scale in terms of people who score low on it and provide suggestions for success on that scale. For example, the explanation of Emotional Intelligence states that "People scoring low on this scale need assistance in developing emotional intelligence skills. Emotional intelligence skills are highly valued in the workplace and include communicating effectively with others, resolving conflicts, being assertive, and controlling one's emotions" (inventory form, p. 6). Suggestions for success include seven statements, such as the following, "Become a great problem solver and decision maker. Employers want workers who make logical, informed decisions and stick with them" (inventory form, p. 4). The other scales have similarly worded descriptions and five to nine suggestions each. The final step encourages examinees to make a list of things they will do to ensure their success.

The 14-page manual explains how to administer and interpret results of the CCTI. It provides background information and a rationale for the creation of the inventory. Contents include an overview of the problems confronting graduates entering the workforce, a theory of college-to-career transitions, directions for administering the CCTI, interpretation of scores, and a summary of research and development efforts. Scores on each scale are interpreted as Low, Average, or High. These designations are associated with score ranges as well as narrative descriptions. The author offers an illustrative case with sample scores on each of the five scales to drive the point home.

DEVELOPMENT. The manual sets forth four guidelines, based on the theory of transition:

1. The instrument should measure a wide range of career transition characteristics.

2. The instrument should be easy to administer, score, and interpret.

3. The instrument should apply to both men and women.

4. The instrument should contain items that are applicable to people of all ages.

Within this framework and an extensive review of the literature, the author created a large pool of items to measure the five scales and then winnowed that pool to the final 60. The details of this process are not offered.

TECHNICAL.

Standardization. The manual indicates that data from 30 college students were used in the calculation of reliability coefficients and that data from 20 college students were used in the calculation of interscale correlations. Score means are based on data from 229 college students.

Reliability. The manual reports both internal consistency and temporal stability reliability estimates. Raw split-half correlations for the five scales range from .55 to .77, which would translate into split-half reliability coefficients of .71 to .87. The test-retest reliability coefficients (with 1 month between administrations) range from .83 to .91.

Validity. The manual presents scale intercorrelations and differences in mean score by gender as evidence of scale validity. Scale intercorrelations range from about -.38 to +.43. Male-female scale score differences are generally less than half a standard deviation.

COMMENTARY. The instrument appears well-constructed, and the manual starts out well. The case for the need for such an instrument is forcefully presented, the literature review is concise and focused, and the theory behind the development of the instrument is well-developed. But the psychometric support just is not present. Although the items seem reasonable and clearly aligned to their respective scales, there is scant information in the manual to support such a claim. For example, although Dr. Liptak is the apparent author of the items, there is no discussion of how he (or someone else) created the items or evaluated them, other than the vaguely referenced split-half statistical study. There is no mention of factor analyses leading to elimination of items that loaded on the wrong scales or of removal of individual items with low point-biserial correlations with scale total. Nor is there any discussion of any type of iterative process of item tryout and improvement over time or review by a disinterested third party.

The discussion of reliability and validity is similarly lacking. Samples of 20–30 college seniors provided all the correlation data. The male and female mean scores were based on much larger samples (109 males and 120 females). Yet, even here, the discussion in the manual focuses on those scales on which each group scored high or low, rather than on which scales they differed most.

The scale score intercorrelations are also puzzling. Several are negative. Although it is not unusual for individuals to score high on one scale and low on another, the theory expounded in the first third of the manual would have suggested at least moderately positive intercorrelations. Nor is there any explanation for correlations such as -.38 between Job Search and Career Management. Of course, these correlations are based on a sample of 20 college students; therefore, given the size of the standard error of correlations based on samples of this size, only 2 of the 10 reported correlation coefficients are effectively nonzero. Yet, there is no advisory in the manual to interpret the correlation coefficients with caution due to the small sample sizes.

The most disappointing feature of the manual is the arbitrary designation of score ranges. The 12 items in each scale yield scores of 1 to 4, for a possible total score of 12–48. The manual reports a raw-score range for Low, Average, and High, without reference to any validation of these ranges. Moreover, the three score ranges are identical across the five scales. A score of 24 to 36 is considered Average for each scale. Scores below 24 are Low, and scores above 36 are High. Although one might reasonably expect the mean score on each scale to be around 30, the total-group ($N = 229$) mean scores are all around 36 points, indicating that most of the students in the norming group scored High.

SUMMARY. Dr. Liptak has made a good start. He has created 60 items that are probably as good as any constructed for the purpose of helping young people make the transition from college to career. This reviewer would consider the CCTI a potentially good research tool. It needs to be validated, and no doubt will be in the future. In the meantime, however, this reviewer would caution college and career counselors to seek other instruments or use this one primarily in the context of research studies. The items themselves could also serve as conversation starters for counseling sessions. But to use the scores to build profiles and label anyone Low, Average, or High would be problematic.

Review of the College-to-Career Transition Inventory by TRACEY WYATT, Academic Dean and Associate Professor of Psychology at York College, York, NE:

DESCRIPTION. The College-to-Career Transition Inventory (CCTI) is a gender-neutral inventory that can be administered individually or in a group. Apparently designed for test-takers age 15–24, though the norms developed for the measure range from 19 to 35, the inventory is appropriate for people at or above the seventh grade. The authors claim the inventory is designed to help students "pinpoint the false beliefs and potential gaps in knowledge and skills that might prevent them from finding a job, further advancing their education, and succeeding in their career" (administration guide, p. 1).

The CCTI is a self-scored and self-interpreted inventory administered over a 20- to 25-minute time period and covering five scale areas associated with career choice: Life Management, Emotional Intelligence, Job Search, Transition-to-Work, and Career Management. The CCTI provides test-takers with a graphic presentation, through the self-scoring profile, of their knowledge of self, the world of work, and their skill level in job search and career management. The CCTI does not require any other materials or special equipment, thus providing immediate results for test-taker and counselor. Scoring is simple and follows a four-step process from writing answers, scoring, profiling scores, and creating a success plan. Interpreting scores uses a simple content-referenced format in the form of raw scores. The inventory booklets are consumable and provide a take-home profile and action plan for the test-taker to utilize.

The author suggests the CCTI can assist job seekers in not making costly mistakes in career choice through a more informed transition from the academic mind-set of freedom and autonomy to one found in the work place of structure and teamwork. The author was influenced by the work of Levinson (transition from college to the world of work), Erikson (ego identity), and Super (career choice over the lifespan), all of whom focus on critical turning points in one's life. The author believes the CCTI is a relevant measure of the very "hard" job-related knowledge and skills and "soft" social skills many universities, colleges, and vocational schools are attempting to include within their curriculum.

DEVELOPMENT. The author sought to develop an instrument that met four goals: to measure a wide range of career transition characteristics; to be easy to administer, score, and interpret; to apply to both men and women; and to be applicable to people of all ages. The CCTI is designed to assist test-takers in exploring their readiness, enhance strengths, and overcome weaknesses to successfully manage and execute the transition from college to the world of work. The development of the scales: Life Management, Emotional Intelligence, Job Search, Transition to Work, and Career Management, was based upon the content domain of a review of developmental career theory literature and research of college graduates' management of critical turning points as applied to transitions, career choice, and maturation. The inventory is composed of 60 total statements of which 12 statements are assigned to each of the five scales. The test-taker self-scores each scale and plots the total raw score onto a profile grid. From the profile, the CCTI provides information in the form of a self-feedback loop through a creation of an action plan, which they are then challenged to complete. Test-takers rate each statement on a 4-point scale. Included in the CCTI is a scoring profile, interpretive guide, and a College-to-Career Success Plan.

TECHNICAL. The CCTI was developed having made use of research questions previously assessed in studies reviewed by the authors. From this body of research questions were selected and subjected to a split-half analysis to assess the reliability of each question.

Reliability. The pilot study was composed of college seniors and others in transition ($N = 20$). For each of the five scales of interest, test-retest, split-half, and interscale correlations were found to be significant at the .01 and .05 levels. Significant results for split-half correlations at the .05 level ranged from $r = .55$ (Job Search scale); at the .01 level, split-half correlations were $r = .77$ (Emotional Intelligence scale), $r = .76$ (Life Management), $r = .66$ (Transition to Work), and $r = .75$ (Career Management). In a follow-up assessment of the sample population using the test-retest method, 30 people were measured. The correlation was found to be significant at the .01 level; $r = .89$ (Job Search scale); $r = .90$ (Emotional Intelligence scale); $r = .89$ (Life Management); $r = .83$ (Transition to Work); and $r = .91$ (Career Management).

Validity. An analysis of the mean and standard deviation scale differences between men and women suggests that men and women equally seem to have trouble in using job search skills to find a job (M = 34.51) and transitioning into the workplace (M = 35.79). Relative to the remaining scales, women scored higher than men on Emotional Intelligence (M = 39.02), Career Management (M = 37.95), and Job Search (M = 35.33). Men scored higher than women on Life Management (M = 38.32) and Transition to Work (M = 36.46).

COMMENTARY. The CCTI provides colleges, vocational schools, and universities with a simple-to-use tool by which students, preparing to enter the world of work, can assess their career decision-making readiness. Using the theoretical research of critical turning points, emotional intelligence, and transitional moments, the authors have designed an inventory easy to use, inexpensive, and portable. It is more than just exploratory as test-takers develop a college-to-career action plan. Ideal for individual or group administration, the career counselor, career center, or senior seminar class would find the CCTI an attractive, easy-to-navigate, and conversation-invocative measure.

SUMMARY. The College-to-Career Transition Inventory (CCTI) is designed to assist graduating students and others in career transition to identify deficits in knowledge and skills that might prevent them from finding a job, further advancing their education, and succeeding in their career. The CCTI makes use of extensive research in its presentation of five scales whereby the test-taker can derive, through a series of 60 self-scored statements, a graphic presentation of their knowledge of self, the world of work, and their skill level in job search and career management.

The inventory is particularly helpful to test-takers through its scoring profile, interpretive guide, and action plan. The author suggests the CCTI can assist job seekers in not making costly mistakes in career choice through a more informed transition from the academic mind-set of freedom and autonomy to one found in the work place of based more on structure and teamwork. The value of any measure is the follow-through by the test-taker. Like any self-administered inventory, the CCTI should stress the importance of using the results in concert with some form of decision accountability in following through with the profile and College-to-Career success plan.

[40]
Communication Skills Assessment.

Purpose: Designed to assess "how well a person communicates with others" and "whether he or she has any problem areas that can potentially inhibit the communication process."
Population: Under age 17 through adult.
Publication Date: 2011.
Acronym: COMSA-R2.
Scores, 5: Overall Score, Insightfulness, Verbal Expression, Assertiveness, Listening Skills, Emotional Management.
Administration: Individual.
Price Data: Available from publisher.
Time: (15) minutes.
Comments: Self-administered online assessment. The test publisher advises that the test manual is being updated to include more information about methodology and theoretical background used in the development of the test. The test publisher also advises that this information is available to clients, as are benchmarks for relevant industries and racial/ethnic group comparison data. However, this information was not provided to Buros or the reviewers.
Author: PsychTests AIM, Inc.
Publisher: PsychTests AIM, Inc. [Canada].

Review of the Communication Skills Assessment by RIC BROWN, Adjunct Faculty, Statistics and Higher Education, Northern Arizona University, Flagstaff, AZ:

DESCRIPTION. As described in the introduction to the online test, the purpose of the Communication Skills Assessment (COMSA-R2) is to "evaluate certain personality characteristics and/or specific skill sets." The purpose statement indicates that the scale evaluates how well an individual communicates with others and identifies areas that might inhibit the communication process. Its stated application is for pre-employment testing.

The test taker is to read the questions and choose a response on a 5-point scale that indicates the degree to which the statement applies. The directions are very clear and tell test takers to respond with respect to how they usually feel or act, the degree to which the statement most accurately describes them and their general feelings or behaviors. The instructions go on to say that there are no right or wrong answers and that respondents must be candid and serious for the results to be meaningful.

The test is to be completed in one sitting. In a practice test taken, the 15 minutes allotted was an appropriate amount of time. The questions are straightforward and clear. The response selection varies with the prompt (e.g., 5 = *mostly true* or 5 = *quite often*). All responses use a 5-point descending scale with the numbers appearing below each response option.

The test contains 38 questions. When finished, the respondent is given a prompt to score the test. For purposes of this review, the test was taken on two separate occasions with responses manipulated to examine how the summary report might differ.

The report appears with six areas of results shown: Summary, Introduction, Graphs, Detailed Results, Strengths and Limitations and Advice. In the Summary section, a score from 1-100 is provided, as well as an overall statement using adjectives such as excellent, good, and so on. The Introduction is a general statement indicating that the goal of the test is to demonstrate how effectively one communicates with others and to offer advice to improve any problem areas that could inhibit the communication process. The report goes on to say that effective communication is integral for work relationships and that an important consideration is not only what is said but also how it is said. The Graphs section provides a score for each of five subareas: Insight-fulness (ability to see other points of view), Verbal Expression (ability to deliver a clear message), Assertiveness (ability to express differing opinions), Listening Skills (ability to actively listen), and Emotional Management (ability to deal with self and other's emotions). Detailed Results provides a specific written description of the meanings of the subareas for the respondent's score using descriptors, such as excellent, generally able, good, fairly adept, quite proficient, moderate, and so on. Strengths and Limitations are then given in list form (strengths, potential strengths, and limitations). Advice comes in the form of statements that suggest specific behaviors.

DEVELOPMENT. Although there is no specific information included in the technical manual regarding the development of the test's dimensions or questions, the test publisher offers a document regarding the company's normal test development procedures. Examination of that document reveals a standard psychometric design protocol that includes defining of concepts, review of relevant literature, question and respondent prompt development and refinement, and scoring and interpretation of results. Once developed, an instrument goes through preliminary statistical analysis and revision, followed by large-scale statistical analysis. It is this large-scale analysis that is provided in the COMSA-R2 psychometric report.

A perusal of the effective communication literature indicates that the subscales are consistent with current thinking in the field. As well, the interpretation of results makes suggestions with regard to communication style that reflect contemporary literature.

TECHNICAL. The psychometric report includes data from more than 22,000 respondents who took the online assessment at Queendom.com, Psychtests.com, or PsychologyToday.com. The test publisher notes that all data are self-report from respondents who volunteered to participate in the validation study.

As evidence of reliability, alpha coefficients are presented. The coefficients range from .68 (Assertiveness, a 6-item scale) to .87 (Verbal Expression, a 7-item scale). The other three scales include 9 items each. The Overall Score (38 items) has an alpha coefficient of .91. The coefficients are certainly appropriate for a test of this type.

Means, standard deviations, and bar graphs are provided for the total score and each subscale score across a variety of demographics, including age, gender, education level completed, current position, socioeconomic status (income ranges), satisfaction with current field of employment, and self-rating of job performance. Although analysis of variance results are presented for subscale and total scores on each demographic variable, the categories of the demographic variables have sample sizes ranging from 300 to 3,600. Thus, small differences are statistically significant (also noted by the test publisher). However, the means across groups do reflect useful variability.

COMMENTARY. Taking the test was generally easy with clear instructions provided. Particularly appealing in the administration was the varying of response prompts to match the tenor of the statements made. Assuming participants are honest in their responses, the explanations of the results are detailed and useful. Acquiescence is always a concern for assessments such as this one. However, the phrasing of the statements and response prompts would seem to lessen such acquiescence.

The results section of the test report was quite extensive and clear. The strengths and weaknesses section provided useful information, and the advice seemed appropriate.

SUMMARY. As a self-help tool or a professional development exercise, the COMSA-R2 seems quite appropriate. The internal consistency meets the standards for reliability. Although the stated purpose of the instrument is in pre-employment testing, there are no data presented to justify any decision-making use for employment (e.g., no data suggesting one skill or lack thereof affects job performance). The self-rating of job performance, although interesting, is not a substitute for a workplace performance validity study. The demographic data presented might be useful for personnel or professional development officers in helping individual test takers interpret their responses and improve workplace communication effectiveness.

Review of the Communication Skills Assessment by MONICA GORDON PERSHEY, Associate Professor, Speech and Hearing Program, School of Health Sciences, Cleveland State University, Cleveland, OH:

DESCRIPTION. The Communication Skills Assessment (COMSA-R2) is a self-report inventory designed to determine how effectively an individual communicates with others. Upon completion of this online questionnaire, examinees obtain detailed computerized profiles of strengths and weaknesses as communicators. The profile offers advice for altering some underlying traits, attitudes, beliefs, skills, or behaviors that could inhibit the process of communicating with others.

The COMSA-R2 is a 38-item inventory that takes about 15 minutes to complete. The test is four pages long with 9 to 11 questions per page. Self-administration involves reading each one-sentence I-statement (e.g., "I tend to…") and selecting one of five levels of agreement with the statement. The pages on screen will not advance if every item is not answered. Testing must be completed in one sitting, and the examinee can only move forward through the test–there is no way to return to previously completed pages. Responses are scored by the software, and results are obtained immediately.

The examinee's results report features six tabs: Introduction, Summary, Graphs, Detailed Results, Strengths and Limitations, and Advice. The Introduction is a general description of the purpose of the test. It reads, in part, "Communication is integral for any work relationship … Communication involves more than just talking and listening; it's a matter of knowing how to send a clear and concise message to others, being able to read others and empathize, being comfortable expressing one's emotions, and communicating in an assertive manner when necessary." The Summary provides a one-paragraph description of the test taker's overall communication skills. The content reinforces the strengths that are reported and points out weaknesses via constructive remarks directed toward the test taker.

The Detailed Results section identifies how the examinee scored on five subscales: Insightfulness, Verbal Expression, Assertiveness, Listening Skills, and Emotional Management. This section defines the purpose of each subscale and displays a numerical score between 0 and 100 for the Overall Score and for each subscale. A paragraph or two of explanation about the examinee's performance on each subscale helps the examinee understand how his/her responses have contributed to the scores. The graphs section represents the scores as points from 0 to 100 on a horizontal line. The Strengths and Limitations section lists strengths, potential strengths, and limitations. The Advice section provides bullet-point suggestions for improving communication, grouped under three headings: being understood, understanding others, and body talk.

The test manual states that the intended application of the assessment is pre-employment testing. The online instructions inform test takers that managers can review subscale scores, overall scores, and interpretations, but not individual item responses.

DEVELOPMENT. Neither the test manual nor the online test include discussions of the constructs that the COMSA-R2 is designed to assess, nor do these materials offer any description of the underlying theories or assumptions that guided test development. No definitions of the properties being assessed appear, and there are no citations to relevant literature. Rationales for item development and selection are not described. In the absence of information about the test's conceptual intent, it is not possible to determine whether the test items measure an intended construct. The test materials also do not descibe how the test guards against misrepresentation by an examinee.

TECHNICAL. The COMSA-R2 was piloted on Queendom.com, Psychtests.com, and PsychologyToday.com. Participation was self-selected. Sampling was uncontrolled. A total of 22,721 respondents included 51% women, 29% men, and 20% of unknown gender. Age groups ranged from below 17 (18%) to 50 or older (6%). Thirty-two percent of the sample was 18–24 years of age, suggesting that college students participated heavily. Only 15% of the sample was age 40 or over, and age is unknown for 8% of participants. Descriptive statistics provide mean scores for the Overall Score and for each of the five subscales. Graphical results show essentially normal distributions of means for the test and the subscales.

The test manual provides reliability analyses for the overall test and each of the five subscales. Coefficient alpha for the Overall Score is .91; subscale alpha coefficients are Insightfulness, .70; Verbal Expression, .87; Assertiveness, .68; Listening Skills, .80; and Emotional Management, .75.

Participants opted to self-report validity comparison variables including gender, age, education level completed (grade school through doctorate), academic achievement (grades earned: top, good, average, below average), position (employment as an entrepreneur, manager, non-manager, or not employed), socioeconomic status (four levels of reported income), satisfaction with current field (satisfied, somewhat satisfied, unsatisfied), and performance in current field (good, acceptable, unsatisfactory). The test manual reports results of ANOVAs and post-hoc analyses of total test and subscale scores in narrative and graphic form. A sample of 1,000 women significantly outscored a sample of 1,000 men on the Overall Score and all subscales. Comparisons of approximately 1,400 individuals per age bracket yielded the significant finding that scores increased with age. For education ($n = 3,067$), negligible upward trends were revealed. The trend for academic achievement (approximately 800 respondents per descriptor) suggested that persons with better grades had higher scores. Regarding position, responses for approximately 750 participants per employment category showed that managers consistently obtained the highest scores, significantly higher than scores obtained by the other groups. Individuals with higher socioeconomic status had higher scores for the total test and all subscales except Listening Skills compared to lower SES respondents. Respondents who were satisfied with their current position scored consistently and significantly higher on subscales and the total test compared to respondents who were less satisfied in their current positions. Similarly, the somewhat satisfied group scores were consistently and significantly higher than the unsatisfied group scores. Respondents who reported good performance in their current field scored consistently and significantly higher on subscales and the total test compared

to respondents who reported lower levels of job performance. Similarly, those reporting acceptable performance had scores that were consistently and significantly higher than those reporting unsatisfactory performance.

COMMENTARY. The test manual states that the intended application of the assessment is pre-employment testing, but there is no explanation of how the results can guide hiring decisions, other than to imply that higher scores are preferred. It is not stated in the test manual or online whether employers who purchase the test receive a copy of the test manual. Even if they do, a main flaw of the COMSA-R2 is that the manual omits construct information and instructions to guide interpretations of results. In the absence of explicit instructions concerning the meaning of test scores, an employer apparently would review an applicant's results and then make a subjective interpretation, presumably at face value. It seems that the test authors could have used the validation data to offer guidance in this area. For example, the validation study showed that unsatisfied employees tend to have lower scores than satisfied employees. Perhaps an applicant with a lower score could turn out to be an unsatisfied employee; however, no interpretations of this nature are offered. An employer might not be able to apply the validation statistics to arrive at this or other interpretations.

Another consideration is whether the COMSA-R2 would be sensitive to the responses of test takers over the age of 50. Many fewer persons of this age bracket participated in the validation study and their scores were consistently higher than those of younger respondents. Perhaps this test might not reveal that much about the relative strengths and weaknesses of an older applicant; on the other hand, an older applicant who scores poorly could be subjectively judged to be quite different from his/her age peers.

Although women outscored men by a statistically significant margin, mean scores do not suggest a need for separate score interpretations for women and men. But subjective expectations for female and male applicants might differ.

There is no information on the ethnicity of validation study participants, so it is not possible to determine whether the test is sensitive to cultural differences.

One strength of the COMSA-R2 is its simplicity. A quick check of the readability level of a sample portion of the test placed it at Grade 8, 9 months (obtained via the Microsoft Word 2003 spell-check function). Furthermore, the results are written in language that feels personalized.

SUMMARY. The COMSA-R2 is a self-report measure designed to reveal some of the underlying traits, attitudes, beliefs, skills, or behaviors that could affect how well an individual communicates interpersonally. The test is easily administered online, simple to read and understand, and results are available immediately.

[41]
Comprehensive Executive Function Inventory.

Purpose: Designed to "measure behaviors that are associated with Executive Function in children and youths."
Population: Ages 5–18.
Publication Date: 2013.
Acronym: CEFI.
Scores, 13: Attention, Emotion Regulation, Flexibility, Inhibitory Control, Initiation, Organization, Planning, Self-Monitoring, Working Memory, Full Scale, Consistency Index, Negative Impression, Positive Impression.
Administration: Individual or group.
Forms, 3: Self-Report (ages 12–18), Parent, Teacher.
Price Data, 2014: $92 per technical manual (195 pages); $329 per complete online kit, including manual and 25 Self-Report/Parent/Teacher online forms; $549 per complete scoring software kit, including manual, scoring software program (USB key), and 25 Self-Report/Parent/Teacher response forms; $269 per complete handscored kit, including manual and 25 Self-Report/Parent/Teacher QuikScore forms.
Foreign Language Edition: Spanish edition available.
Time: (15) minutes.
Comments: Online and paper-and-pencil administration available.
Authors: Jack A. Naglieri and Sam Goldstein.
Publisher: Multi-Health Systems, Inc.

Review of the Comprehensive Executive Function Inventory by JOE W. DIXON, Licensed Psychologist, Private Practice, Tuscaloosa, AL:

DESCRIPTION. The Comprehensive Executive Function Inventory (CEFI) developed by Naglieri and Goldstein is a 100-item rating scale designed to assess behaviors frequently associated with executive function (EF) in children and adolescents ages 5 through 18 years. This new instrument can be completed on a 5- to 18-year-old by parents and teachers, and the self-report form can be completed by a 12- to 18-year-old. The rating scales can be completed via paper and pencil or online. The 100 items were selected for their clinical usefulness following statistical analysis, and they assess the following nine dimensions: Attention, Emotion Regulation, Flexibility, Inhibitory Control, Initiation, Organization, Planning, Self-Monitoring, and Working Memory. The test authors envision use of the CEFI to assist in diagnostics and treatment planning for individuals, to screen groups of individuals, to evaluate the effectiveness of intervention programs, and as a research instrument. Available are separate parent (5 to 18 years), teacher (5 to 18 years), and self-report (12 to 18 years) forms. All forms are available in English and Spanish. Norms are set to have a mean of 100 and a standard deviation of 15. All forms are available in the Multi-Health Systems QuikScore™ format. The scoring forms are multilayered, and writing transfers through to a hidden grid on the lower layers. The forms include conversion tables easily allowing transformation to standard scores and percentile ranks. Scoring software also is available. CEFI reports can be generated through the online scoring system or by using the scoring software.

The test authors readily acknowledge that there is a diversity of opinion about how executive function is defined. The test manual provides a good discussion of EF and points out that three widely accepted global components include inhibitory control, set shifting, and working memory. There is theoretical and empirical support for these components in the literature as well as for the idea that EF is not solely a function of frontal lobe development. EF is also linked with temperament, social–emotional functioning, academic abilities, and general intelligence. The test authors point out that most executive function tasks make integrative demands of all these abilities. Regardless of one's theoretical orientation or definition of EF, the test authors argue that it is appropriate to focus on these widely accepted cognitive concepts when measuring strengths and weaknesses in a child or adolescent's EF.

DEVELOPMENT. The test authors report that the CEFI, designed as a scale to assess strengths and weaknesses in EF, was in development for a period of 3 years (2009–2012). The test authors, who have numerous publications and experience in working with children and adolescents with cognitive disorders, conducted an extensive review of the literature to narrow down the dimensions to be assessed. The dimensions fall generally into two domains: cognitive and behavioral. Cognitive items targeted time management, working memory, decision-making, goal-directed behavior, planning, resistance to distraction, persistence, attention to detail, and perspective taking. Behavioral items targeted sustained attention, cueing, shifting, stopping and starting, motor inhibition, and verbal inhibition. Also considered was an emotional domain targeting motivation, flexibility, regulation, and stress tolerance. In order to assess rater bias, Negative Impression and Positive Impression scales were specifically developed. Once the normative data were compiled and analyzed using exploratory factor analysis, it was possible to then develop a Consistency Index, which assists in detecting inconsistent responding by a rater. Thus, several useful validity indicators are embedded within the 100-item CEFI scale. Note there are 90 clinical items and 10 items that assess negative and positive impressions.

The initial developmental process generated 165 items for a pilot study that included a sample of 270 parents, 253 teachers, and 271 children and adolescents. Participants included both males and females; Hispanics, Asians, Blacks, Whites, and others; residents of all four major regions of the United States; and a cross-section of parental educational attainment from high school diploma or less to some college or bachelor's degrees and higher. Children and adolescents were selected from the general population and from clinical subsets of the general population including those diagnosed with attention-deficit/hyperactivity disorder (ADHD), mood disorder, and learning disabilities (LD). Several levels of review were included with experts in child psychiatry and child clinical psychology.

TECHNICAL. Once the pilot study data were analyzed, construction of the final scale resulted in a CEFI with 100 items. The published norms in the user's manual were derived from a sample of 3,500 participants, including 50 males and 50 females in each age bracket. Several clinical groups were included: ADHD, LD, autism spectrum disorder, mood disorder, anxiety disorders, oppositional defiant disorder, and traumatic brain injury. The standardization sample as reported in the test manual appears to be representative of the U.S. population of children and adolescents.

Exploratory factor analysis resulted in a single-factor solution. Despite that result, nine CEFI scales were created, based in part on the original key concepts developed by the test authors, revisions made during the pilot stage, and research on EF found in the literature supporting these nine dimensions of

EF. Assignment of individual items to one of the final nine dimensions was based on the item content, clinical experience, and judgment. The one-factor solution, which was found at both the item-level and the scale-level, strongly indicates that the CEFI items are all describing one dimension: executive function. Thus, although nine subdimensions are in the overall CEFI scale for clinical utility, the totality of the CEFI can be said to measure EF.

The CEFI manual reports in detail the final statistical analysis complete with numerous correlation tables. The test authors provide a good discussion of internal consistency and present a table of alpha coefficients for the CEFI normative and clinical/educational sample. The Full Scale coefficients were all .97 or higher. Alpha coefficients for separate CEFI scales were also high. The median CEFI reliability coefficients for the normative sample were .89 for parents, .93 for teachers, and .80 for self-reports. Test-retest reliability results were excellent with all three rater forms yielding r values ranging from .77 to .91 for the Full Scale and .74 to .91 for the individual scales. Cohen's d statistic was also computed (.02, .11, and .06 for parent, teacher, and self-reports, respectively), with results suggesting that the effect of time across administrations was negligible. Thus, these measures are stable across time and can be used to chart a child's progress, or lack thereof.

Content validity, construct validity, and criterion-related validity were all examined, and results are reported in the user's manual. Individual items making up the nine scales were based upon the test authors' professional knowledge and experiences and a thorough review of the literature. Even a cursory review of the items on the CEFI clearly indicates strong face validity for the items that were finally selected. Construct validity evidence was collected in part through the exploratory factor analyses, and the results revealed strong evidence of the unitary dimension of the CEFI at the scale level. This result was found to be consistent across gender, age group, race, ethnicity, and clinical/educational status. Findings such as this provide strong evidence related to construct validity. Further, another means of evaluating construct validity is to show comparable measurement performance for participants in disparate groups. This analysis was conducted utilizing the accepted four-fifths rule, a measure of ratios between minority groups and majority groups, to assess for meaningful differences between subgroups. Employing the four-fifths rule, disparate impact was not detected on any of the three forms for either the Black or the Hispanic groups relative to the White group. An additional analysis was conducted on data collected using the CEFI with Canadian populations and U.S. populations. There were no significant differences between these two groups, again indicating good construct validity. Lastly, criterion validity was evaluated through analysis of variance (ANOVA) results examining differences between the general population (matched on age, gender, race/ethnicity, and parent's education level) and children and adolescents independently and previously diagnosed with specific clinical disorders. Results from these analyses provided strong evidence for criterion validity. The test manual goes on to provide data in table format discussing independent studies that were conducted comparing results to those from CEFI the Behavior Rating Inventory of Executive Function (BRIEF; 15:32) The Das-Naglieri Cognitive Assessment System (CAS; 14:109), the Woodcock-Johnson III Tests of Achievement (WJIII; 15:281), and the Wechsler Intelligence Scale for Children-Fourth Edition (WISC-IV; 16:262). The CEFI user's manual is rich with data for the statistically curious.

COMMENTARY. A significant strength of the CEFI is the extensive amount of validating research that went into not only selecting the items, but also the statistical analysis conducted on the large sample size resulting in a reliable and valid instrument suitable for clinical use. The CEFI also has great utility in that it can be used by a clinician with a single child, it can be group administered, it can be used to assess intervention effects on a school-wide or hospital-wide basis, and it can be used as a research instrument. This range of applications is possible because of its simple design and its administration and scoring options (i.e., traditional paper and pencil, online, scoring software).

The only real weakness of the CEFI is the same weakness that exists for all teacher, parent, and self-report inventories: The accuracy of the scores depends upon the accuracy of the ratings. However, many years of research have shown that, on the whole, most people will provide valid information through the use of such instruments that can be clinically applied to better understand children and adolescents.

SUMMARY. Of all the self-report inventories available today, the CEFI certainly stands out as a state-of-the-art measure of EF. The CEFI's theoretical and conceptual underpinnings, its thoughtful and careful development, and its functional utility for the clinician and the researcher alike make it a first choice when there is a question about a child's or an adolescent's executive functioning.

Review of the Comprehensive Executive Function Inventory by TAWNYA MEADOWS, Pediatric Psychologist, Geisinger Health System, Danville, PA:

DESCRIPTION. The Comprehensive Executive Function Inventory (CEFI) is a parent, teacher, or self-report rating scale designed to measure executive functioning in children 5–18 years old. Parent and teacher forms are for rating children ages 5–18 years; the self-report form is for youth ages 12–18 years. Raters should have adequate reading skills (fifth-grade level for rating items, seventh-grade level for directions) and proficiency in English (or Spanish for Spanish forms). Raters also need to be familiar with the individual they are observing and rating. Ratings are to be based on observations from the previous 4 weeks. Time to complete the rating scale is approximately 15 minutes.

The intended uses of the instrument are (a) assisting in an individual's diagnostic decisions, treatment planning, treatment effectiveness, and monitoring ongoing treatment; (b) screening a group of children to determine who needs a full evaluation or to identify those who may need additional support; (c) evaluating an intervention program; and (d) as a tool in a research context.

Rating scales may be administered and scored using MHS QuikScore™ forms, via online administration and scoring, or with a software scoring program. If electronic scoring is used, reports may be generated in one of three forms: Interpretive Report, Progress Monitoring and Treatment Effectiveness Report, and Comparative Report. B-level qualifications (described on the test publisher's website) are required for interpretation of the results. In addition to a Full Scale score, there are nine scale scores, a Consistency Index, a Positive Impression scale, and a Negative Impression scale. The nine scale scores are Attention, Emotion Regulation, Flexibility, Inhibitory Control, Initiation, Organization, Planning, Self-Monitoring, and Working Memory. All scales have a mean score of 100 and standard deviation of 15. Interpretive reports are purported to provide guidance in selection of intervention strategies. However, the test authors do not provide any statistical support for this claim.

DEVELOPMENT. The test authors report interest in measuring if and how a person reaches a goal, which they describe as "the essence of executive function" (manual, p. 8). They view executive function as encompassing several neuropsychological processes such as planning, monitoring actions, initiation, multi-tasking, verbal reasoning, inhibition, mental flexibility, working memory, attention, and problem solving. The test authors attempted to measure the construct of executive functioning via a rating scale as such instruments can easily reflect if and how a person achieves goals in a variety of natural environments. Item content was derived from a comprehensive review of theory and research conceptualized as either behavioral or cognitive. In addition, there was an emotional domain, and Negative and Positive Impression scales and a Consistency Index were developed. Items on the impression scales are infrequently endorsed (less than 5% of the time in the normative sample).

A sample of 270 parents, 253 teachers, and 271 youths comprised the pilot study. Youths were between the ages of 5 and 18 years and were identified as coming from either a general population or clinical/educational group diagnosed with attention-deficit/hyperactivity disorder (ADHD), mood disorder, or learning disability. Only youth ages 12–18 years were asked to complete the self-report form due to developmental considerations. Pilot items were reviewed by experts in child psychiatry and clinical child psychology, and data were used to select, revise, and add items for the normative data collection. Based upon this expert review and statistical analysis of pilot data, 112 items were selected for use in the normative study.

TECHNICAL. The normative sample consisted of 3,500 ratings that included ratings of 50 males and 50 females at each age who were representative of the U.S. population across several demographic variables. The clinical/educational group consisted of 872 youths. The percentage of the sample that met eligibility for special education services was slightly lower in the sample than that found in the U.S. population. However, the difference between the proportion of demographic variables in the U.S. population to the normative sample is acceptable at less than 1%. The test authors included extensive tables to support their claims of representativeness. In addition, the test authors conducted several relevant statistical analyses to evaluate potential age or gender effects. Further-

more, the test authors concluded that there were no disparate impacts based upon race or ethnicity.

Eight consistency items were created based upon items found to be highly correlated. The raw scores on the normative sample's responses were transformed to standard scores with a mean of 100 and a standard deviation of 15. A standard score of 75 served as a cutoff. The Negative and Positive Impression scales were formed by a process similar to that used for the Consistency Index and appear to be satisfactory.

Finally, factor analysis reduced the total number of items from 112 to 100, 10 of which form the Negative and Positive Impression scales. Subsequently, exploratory factor analysis was run on half of the normative data. The data appeared to be explained best by one factor. Procedures appeared standard and comprehensive. However, the test author created nine scales based upon a review of the literature, item content, and clinical experience and judgment. Then, a second level of exploratory factor analysis revealed that the nine scales clustered into one factor.

Once the final version was completed, all items, demographic data, and instructions were translated into Spanish. However, no attempt to establish validity or reliability of this version is mentioned in the test manual.

The test authors appropriately demonstrate criterion-related validity evidence through an examination of statistical relationships with the Behavior Rating Inventory of Executive Function (BRIEF; 15:32), the Das-Naglieri Cognitive Assessment System (CAS; 14:109), the Wechsler Intelligence Scale for Children-Fourth Edition (WISC-IV; 16:262), and the Woodcock-Johnson III Tests of Achievement (WJIII; 15:281).

Reliability was adequately demonstrated through the calculation of alpha coefficients. For both samples, clinical/educational and normative, Full Scale coefficients were all .97 or higher. In addition, test-retest reliability and stability were adequately demonstrated by the test authors through valid means.

COMMENTARY AND SUMMARY. The Comprehensive Executive Function Inventory (CEFI) is a promising measure of executive functioning. Until now, there have been only a few measures of executive functioning with only one standing out as a leader, the BRIEF (Baron, 2000). The CEFI's advantages include its larger, more representative normative sample and its validated self-report version for adolescents. However, because the CEFI is a new measure in a limited market of comprehensive assessments of executive functioning, there is a paucity of research beyond that conducted by the test authors for the purpose of test development. The instrument appears user-friendly such that it can be completed and scored in a few minutes. The instrument appears to have adequate evidence of reliability and validity of test score use. One limitation is the lack of evidence of validity surrounding the claim that test scores can be used for treatment planning.

REVIEWER'S REFERENCE

Baron, I. S. (2000). Test review: Behavior Rating Inventory of Executive Function. *Child Neuropsychology, 6*, 235–238.

[42]

Computerized Oral Proficiency Instrument.

Purpose: Designed to assess "students' oral language proficiency in Arabic or Spanish."

Population: Native English speaking upper high school students, college students, and professionals who are learning the target language.

Publication Date: 2008.

Acronym: COPI.

Scores: 10 ratings: Novice Low, Novice Mid, Novice High, Intermediate Low, Intermediate Mid, Intermediate High, Advanced Low, Advanced Mid, Advanced High, Superior.

Administration: Group.

Editions, 2: Spanish, Arabic.

Levels: 4 proficiency levels: Novice, Intermediate, Advanced, Superior.

Price Data, 2011: $125 per test kit including Test Administration Program on CD-ROM, Training and Rating CD-ROM, and manual (51 pages).

Time: (45-60) minutes.

Comments: Computer-based, semi-adaptive test; technology requirements include a personal computer (not a Macintosh) with a sound card, CD-ROM drive, headset or speakers, microphone, monitor, keyboard, and mouse; publisher recommends using with the Spanish Multimedia Rater Training Program or the Arabic Rater Training Kit, both available separately.

Author: Center for Applied Linguistics.

Publisher: Center for Applied Linguistics.

Review of the Computerized Oral Proficiency Instrument by SANDRA T. ACOSTA, Assistant Professor of Bilingual Education, Educational Psychology, Texas A&M University, College Station, TX:

DESCRIPTION. The Computerized Oral Proficiency Instrument (COPI) is a computer-based oral language proficiency test developed by the Center for Applied Linguistics (CAL) and published in 2008. The purpose of the COPI is to assess examinees' speaking and communication ability in Arabic or Spanish via recorded speech samples elicited using authentic tasks, that is, situations or scenarios (e.g., making a complaint) encountered in real-life. A Multimedia Rater Training Program and accompanying workbook (Center for Applied Linguistics, 2005) for evaluating examinees' speech samples are sold separately. Examinees' responses are rated using the 1999 American Council on the Teaching of Foreign Languages (ACTFL) Proficiency Guidelines (see Breiner-Sanders, Lowe, Miles, & Swender, 2008). The four ACTFL oral proficiency levels for speaking are novice, intermediate, advanced, and superior. When rating and reporting examinees' responses, all levels below superior are further divided into the following sub-levels: low, mid, and high (e.g., intermediate mid [IM]). Examinees' overall oral proficiency score calculated by the computer algorithm is a global rating consisting of the examinees' highest and most consistent performance across all test items (i.e., tasks). The COPI target population is English speakers ranging in age from adolescents to post-secondary adults. This review addresses only the COPI Spanish version.

Test administration for the COPI takes approximately one hour. The number of test items ranges from a minimum of 7 to a maximum of 11. Test administration is straightforward; however, program installation, hardware support, and rater training are the responsibility of the purchaser. The following overview presents three facets of administering the COPI: test directions, examinee choice, and test items or task prompts.

The first facet—test directions—comprises the tutorial for using the software (e.g., how to record speech samples) and directions for responding to tasks. With the exception of task prompts, all directions appear in oral and print formats, thus allowing the examinee to read as well as listen to the directions in English. For advanced and superior levels, examinees may choose either English or Spanish test directions.

The second facet—examinee choice—includes initial self-assessment, item difficulty levels, and task scenario. Examinees begin the test by selecting their estimated oral proficiency level from one of the four proficiency levels (e.g., novice). Each level contains descriptors of the oral language skills associated with that level. Then, at specific time-points during the test, examinees may choose to continue responding to test items in the same proficiency level or change proficiency levels (one level higher or lower). In addition to examinees' selection of item difficulty level (i.e., proficiency level), the computer algorithm (self-adaptive strategy) ensures that items of varying difficulty levels are included in the test. During the test, examinees may choose one of three different scenarios when responding to each task prompt/test item. In the third facet—task prompts—native speakers representing different Spanish-speaking countries deliver the prompts orally; thus, the examinee hears but does not read task prompts. Color-coded timer dots signal response planning and response delivery times. Response times range approximately from two to four minutes.

DEVELOPMENT AND TECHNICAL. The test administrator manual and the rater training workbook do not provide technical information about the COPI (e.g., validity, interrater reliability) or details about test development. Despite requests for clarifications about test development and reliability evidence, CAL personnel have not responded to this reviewer. Nonetheless, in a *CALdigest* report brief, Malone (2007, October) provided an overview of the development of the COPI. The author reported that the design originated from two oral proficiency tests: (a) the ACTFL Oral Proficiency Interview (OPI), a speaking ability assessment administered by a certified rater using a conversation format; and (b) the CAL Simulated Oral Proficiency Interview (SOPI), a tape-mediated assessment of speaking ability. In addition, Malone (2007, October) indicated that the COPI would be field-tested in 2007 and that field-test results would provide reliability evidence for the COPI. A search of *CALdigest* reports and the references section of the COPI Test Administrator Manual produced no reports on the COPI field-test results.

Malone (2007, October) also mentioned a feasibility study for developing the COPI conducted by Kenyon and Malabonga (2001). In their study, Kenyon and Malabonga (2001) recruited 55 university students consisting of one graduate student from a linguistics course and 50 undergraduate and four graduate students from language classes in Chinese, Arabic, and Spanish. Only the Spanish language students ($N = 24$) were administered the OPI, SOPI, and COPI. Because of the small sample of Spanish language students, Kenyon and Malabonga (2001) used the nonparametric Friedman test for analyzing the data gleaned from the OPI, SOPI, and COPI. Correlations between the

tests ranged from .92 to .95. The authors noted that the COPI consisted of a pool of 100 items drawn from the SOPI. Employing the same sample of 55 university students, Malabonga, Kenyon, and Carpenter (2005) found that 92% of examinees taking the COPI correctly identified their oral proficiency level in the initial self-assessment.

COMMENTARY. The COPI has several strengths. These include the format and organization of the computer-based assessment program and the interactive software for training raters. Test directions are clear; sample items provide authentic examples of examinees' responses to task prompts from each oral proficiency level. The rater-training program is self-paced and allows raters to compare their ratings of speech samples to the scores of experienced raters. Raters may also listen to task prompts and directions for each response as needed. However, two weaknesses limit the COPI's utility.

First, the ACTFL oral proficiency standards/guidelines have changed. The COPI is no longer aligned to current ACTFL oral proficiency guidelines. In 2012, ACTFL published revised guidelines (American Council on the Teaching of Foreign Languages, 2012). Changes to the ACTFL speaking guidelines included the addition of a fifth proficiency level, distinguished. Although descriptors (i.e., criteria) were added for the distinguished level, descriptors for the other four oral proficiency levels remained the same.

A second and more critical issue is the gaps and omissions related to item development and the psychometric properties of the COPI. Although the COPI is a criterion-referenced test based on ACTFL oral proficiency guidelines or standards, validity evidence should be presented to support the interpretation of the test results. Similarly, little substantive information is provided about item development, field-testing, construct operationalization, test assumptions, and measurement error. Further, there appears to be a test score ceiling effect at the superior oral proficiency level that is not addressed in the testing materials. (The superior level is the only level with no sublevels). How informative are test results when evaluating examinees' test-score gains at the upper proficiency levels of COPI?

SUMMARY. The COPI (Spanish version) is a computer-based Spanish oral language proficiency assessment of English-speaking adolescents and post-secondary adults. Raters, trained on an interactive software program for rating oral language proficiency, evaluate the speech samples elicited by the COPI using the ACTFL 1999 Proficiency Guidelines–Speaking. The COPI is described as a "low- to medium-stakes test" for formative assessments, that is for measuring student progress (manual, p. 2). Potential users should be advised that the COPI, which was published in 2008, is not fully aligned with current ACTFL proficiency guidelines for speaking because it does not include the "distinguished" level that was added in the 2012 revision (cf. ACTFL, 2012). Further, research evidence that supports the validity and reliability of COPI scores, including interrater reliability, is inadequate. These issues raise the question of the relevance and the usefulness of the COPI as a measure of oral language proficiency in Spanish.

REVIEWER'S REFERENCES

American Council on the Teaching of Foreign Languages. (2012). *ACTFL Proficiency Guidelines 2012*. Alexandria, VA: Author. Retrieved from http://actflproficiencyguidelines2012.org/

Breiner-Sanders, K. E., Lowe, P., Jr., Miles, J., & Swender, E. (2000). ACTFL Proficiency Guidelines—Speaking: Revised 1999. *Foreign Language Annals, 33*(1), 13–18. doi: 10.1111/j.1944-9720.2000.tb00885.x

Center for Applied Linguistics. (2005). *Multimedia rater training program workbook*. Washington, DC: Author.

Kenyon, D. M., & Malabonga, V. (2001). Comparing examinee attitudes toward computer-assisted and other oral proficiency assessments. *Language Learning & Technology, 5*(2), 60–83. Retrieved from http://llt.msu.edu/vol5num2/kenyon/default.html

Malabonga, V., Kenyon, D. M., & Carpenter, H. (2005). Self-assessment, preparation and response time on a computerized oral proficiency test. *Language Testing, 22*(1), 59–92. doi: 10.1191/0265532205lt297oa

Malone, M. E. (2007, October). Oral proficiency assessment: The use of technology in test development and rater training. *CALdigest*. Retrieved from http://www.cal.org/resources/digest/oralprof.html

Review of the Computerized Oral Proficiency Instrument (Spanish or Arabic) by ELVIS WAGNER, Assistant Professor, Temple University, Philadelphia, PA, and ANTONY JOHN KUNNAN, Professor, California State University, Los Angeles, CA:

DESCRIPTION. The Computerized Oral Proficiency Instrument (COPI) is an individually administered, semi-adaptive, low- to medium-stakes test of oral proficiency. It is offered in Spanish or Modern Standard Arabic. It was designed to assess adult native-English speakers (including high school students) and provides score reports using the American Council on the Teaching of Foreign Languages (ACTFL) proficiency levels (Novice, Intermediate, Advanced, or Superior). An institution or language program can purchase the COPI from the test developer, the Center for Applied Linguistics (CAL), for $125, which allows for the testing of up to 25 students. Purchasers install the testing program on their computers, and test takers individually take the test on a computer, with no need for an interlocutor, except for an introduction and initial instructions on how to use the computer and the test program.

The test begins with a self-assessment in which test takers choose a can-do statement about their target language oral ability. Based on this self-assessment response, the computer program presents a sample task at the level appropriate for the test taker. The test taker responds to the sample task and then has a chance to change the starting level of the test if he or she thinks the sample task level was too difficult or too easy. Test takers then complete between 7 and 11 tasks based on choices made by both the test taker and the computer algorithm.

The tasks require the test taker to speak in simulated real-life situations. Each task specifies the setting, the situation, and the interlocutor. The lower-level tasks include pictures that provide contextual information. Topics are based on daily life, school, or work contexts. Each task seeks to elicit a certain language function, such as apologizing, and each task is written to elicit language functions at the different ACTFL proficiency levels. The tasks for the Arabic version of the COPI have two versions based on the gender of the test taker; the versions differ with regard to topic and how the test taker is addressed.

For each task, the test taker hears and reads the task directions and then is given from 2 to 4 minutes of thinking time. When the test taker hears the prompt, he or she has 1.5 to 3.5 minutes to speak the response into the computer microphone. Test takers have some control over the difficulty level of the test tasks presented, the choice of topic, and the choice of the language of the directions (in English, or in the target language). The COPI has more than 100 tasks per language, from which the computer algorithm chooses (in conjunction with the preferences of the test taker) the 7 to 11 tasks for each test taker. Once the test is completed, which takes from 45 to 60 minutes, the computer generates a summary showing how many tasks were completed at each difficulty level.

The oral responses are rated by trained human raters. Test takers receive a score following the criteria of the ACTFL Speaking Proficiency Guidelines. The ACTFL Guidelines have 10 possible ratings: Novice Low, Novice Mid, Novice High, Intermediate Low, Intermediate Mid, Intermediate High, Advanced Low, Advanced Mid, Advanced High, and Superior.

DEVELOPMENT. In developing the COPI, the developers report having sought to create a test of oral proficiency based on the ACTFL Speaking

Proficiency Guidelines, which are widely used in academia, government, and language programs, and are recognized as de facto national foreign language proficiency standards. The test developers claim that by using the ACTFL Guidelines, rather than criteria developed specifically for the test, the interpretation of the scores is easier and more transparent for test users.

The COPI is an adaptation of the Simulated Oral Proficiency Interview (SOPI), which is itself an adaptation of the Oral Proficiency Interview (OPI). The OPI was developed to create a performance-based assessment of oral proficiency. The rationale for creating a computer-based version of the OPI was to be able to utilize multimedia computer technology to give test takers more control over the testing situation, while still preserving the standardization of the testing procedure, as well as to increase efficiency and reliability in scoring.

TECHNICAL.

Standardization. Because the COPI scores are based on the ACTFL Guidelines, in which proficiency is defined in terms of the language tasks or functions that a test taker can perform, the test is not a norm-referenced test, and thus it is argued that a standardization/norm sample is not applicable.

Reliability. It is difficult to estimate how reliably the COPI assesses test takers' oral proficiency because of the semi-adaptive nature of the exam. The computer algorithm is designed to choose tasks based in part on the ability level of the test taker as well as the need to assess a variety of language functions, and there are more than 100 possible tasks from which the seven to 11 tasks are selected. In addition, the test taker has some control over the tasks that are selected. Therefore, it is not possible to estimate reliability using a simple parallel forms measure. In addition, because the tasks are designed to measure different language functions, in which a particular test taker will likely have varying ability levels, it is not possible to estimate the internal consistency reliability of the test.

Oral performance tests also present difficulties in the reliability of the scoring. Raters are trained using rater training materials provided with the COPI. The potential raters listen to and rate more than 200 authentic examinee responses. After a potential rater completes the CD training, CAL provides a calibration tape with responses that have to be scored. These scores are submit-

ted to CAL for evaluation, and a rater has to achieve a certain accuracy level to become certified. Nevertheless, because the scoring is done "in house," rather than by a central entity, there is no guarantee that test users will measure or assess the performance of individual raters. The test developers recommend double-rating the responses, but ultimately this decision is up to the users of the COPI.

Validity. Numerous validity studies have been conducted to support inferences made from the COPI. Kenyon and Malabonga (2001) reported a rank order correlation of .95 between ratings on the COPI and the SOPI. Malabonga, Kenyon, and Carpenter (2005), examining the effectiveness of the self-assessment component of the COPI, found a moderate to high correlation with actual performance on the COPI and reported 92% of the test takers chose a task at the level recommended by the self-assessment instrument. Malabonga, Kenyon, and Carpenter (2005) also examined the appropriateness of the length of thinking and speaking time of the tasks.

One of the difficulties in using a semi-direct measure of speaking ability (where the test taker speaks into a computer) is the inherent artificiality of the context in that there is no human interaction. Kenyon and Malabonga (2001) examined COPI test takers' attitudes and found that for the most part, test takers had positive views toward the instrument, especially the fact that they had some control over the choice of tasks, difficulty levels, and thinking and response time.

Fairness. An additional area of investigation that complements reliability and validity is fairness: whether the COPI is fair to test takers based on differences such as gender, age, and presence of disability. Gender is an important variable in the Arabic version of the test because male and female test takers receive different topics for speaking. In this case it would be necessary to know whether the tasks of the two versions are of comparable difficulty. Similarly, because test takers from different age groups take both tests, it would be necessary to know whether the test tasks are of comparable difficulty to the different age groups of test takers. Finally, as more test takers with disabilities are taking such tests, it would be necessary to know what accommodations are provided to test takers with disabilities and whether any studies have been conducted to verify whether the accommodations provided are not biased in favor of test takers with disabilities. These studies would enhance the beneficial value of the COPI.

COMMENTARY. The COPI is a practical and useful test for the assessment of oral proficiency in Spanish and Arabic. This is very important because there are few other measures of oral proficiency in these languages that are accessible and reasonably priced. The fact that test takers have to speak to a computer, rather than interacting with a human interlocutor, is potentially problematic. Nevertheless, although the COPI is a semi-direct measure, it still is a performance assessment in which test takers actually demonstrate their oral ability. Using human interlocutors for each individual test taker would dramatically increase the cost of the assessment and would also negatively affect the standardization and reliability of the assessment. The COPI seeks to avoid these problems by providing standardized testing procedures while using computer technology to provide important contextual information. Perhaps the key strength of the COPI is the fact that it is semi-adaptive. Using computer technology allows for the individual test taker to have some control over the difficulty level of the tasks and the topics chosen, which should lower negative test-taker affect. The technology also makes it possible to create an algorithm that chooses tasks based on ability level in order to best assess the test taker's proficiency according to the ACTFL guidelines.

Although a number of validity studies have been carried out, more studies (such as fairness) are needed to examine whether the test is fair to all test takers, how the test results are actually used by test users, and how the test results compare with independent measures of oral proficiency.

SUMMARY. The COPI is designed to be an individually administered measure of oral proficiency in Spanish or Arabic. It is designed as a semi-adaptive measure so that test takers would be comfortable taking the test, but also so that it would be best able to provide scores within the context of the ACTFL Proficiency Guidelines. The test meets its goal of assessing oral language proficiency in a practical and useful manner.

REVIEWERS' REFERENCES
Kenyon, D. M., & Malabonga, V. (2001) Comparing examinee attitudes toward computer-assisted and other oral proficiency assessments. *Language Learning & Technology, 5*, 60–83.
Malabonga, V., Kenyon, D. M., & Carpenter, H. (2005). Self-assessment, preparation and response time on a computerized oral proficiency test. *Language Testing, 22*, 59–92.

Conflict Tactics Scales.
Purpose: Designed to obtain reports of domestic violence among abusive adult partners and "physical maltreatment and neglect of children by parents, as well as nonviolent modes of discipline."
Population: Adults.
Publication Date: 2003.
Administration: Individual.
Price Data, 2012: $87.50 per complete test kit including Handbook (146 pages), 10 CTS2 AutoScore forms, and 10 CTSPC AutoScore forms; $45 per 25 CTS2 AutoScore forms; $45 per 25 CTSPC AutoScore forms; $60 per Handbook; $60 per continuing education questionnaire and evaluation form.
Authors: Murray A. Straus, Sherry L. Hamby, and W. Louise Warren.
Publisher: Western Psychological Services.
a) REVISED CONFLICT TACTICS SCALES.
Acronym: CTS2.
Scores, 5: Negotiation, Psychological Aggression, Physical Assault, Injury, Sexual Coercion.
Time: (10-15) minutes.
b) CONFLICT TACTICS SCALES: PARENT-CHILD VERSION.
Acronym: CTSPC.
Scores, 6: Nonviolent Discipline, Psychological Aggression, Physical Assault, Weekly Discipline, Neglect, Sexual Abuse.
Time: (10) minutes.

Review of the Conflict Tactics Scales by M. MEGHAN DAVIDSON, Assistant Professor of Counseling Psychology, University of Nebraska-Lincoln, Lincoln, NE:

DESCRIPTION. The Conflict Tactics Scales (CTS) are composed of the Revised Conflict Tactics Scales (CTS2) and the Conflict Tactics Scales: Parent-Child Version (CTSPC). These scales are based on the original CTS first published in the early 1970s (Straus, 1973) and developed for epidemiological studies. Both the CTS2 and the CTSPC are self-report inventories, intended to measure the use of specific tactics employed by an intimate couple during a conflict and current maltreatment from parents, respectively. The test authors note that neither the CTS2 nor the CTSPC is intended to measure attitudes, causes, or consequences of conflict or violence. The CTS2 was designed to have symmetry of measurement such that the behavior of both the respondent and the respondent's partner is assessed. The CTSPC was developed as an alternative to retrospective accounts by adults regarding experiences during childhood with their parents, and directs attention towards behaviors utilized by parents during a conflict with a child.

The test authors state the CTS2 and the CTSPC are appropriate for individuals 18 years of age or older, and may be used with a wide range of individuals including clinical (i.e., inpatient and outpatient clients) and nonclinical (i.e., people from the general population) samples, incarcerated offenders, and parolees. The CTS2 and the CTSPC can be utilized as (a) an indicator of conflict and violence in an intimate partnership, (b) an indicator of severity of violence in an intimate relationship, (c) an indicator of maltreatment toward children, and (d) an inventory to monitor client progress and change. A total of 10–15 minutes is required to complete the CTS2 and an additional 10–15 minutes is needed to complete the CTSPC.

The CTS2 is composed of 39 items with an 8-point response scale indicating frequency of behaviors during the past year. Each item is asked twice, once about the respondent and once about the respondent's partner, yielding a total of 78 items; thus, behaviors or tactics are assessed in terms of being both used and received by the respondent. These items are scored by summing the midpoints for the response categories to yield the following five subscale scores for both Self and Partner: Negotiation, Psychological Aggression, Physical Assault, Injury, and Sexual Coercion. Additional indicators within each subscale are also scored such that Negotiation includes emotional and cognitive components, whereas Psychological Aggression items address verbal and symbolic actions that bring about psychological distress. Physical Assault, Injury, and Sexual Coercion include minor and severe components. As well, tactics occurring previously but not in the past year are also noted in each of the five areas. An overall score is not computed, nor is a total score computed for Self or Partner. The CTS2 AutoScore Form is a perforated booklet composed of an answer sheet for responding to items, a carbon transfer sheet, a scoring worksheet, and a summary sheet. The CTS2 summary sheet includes data to make comparisons to college student average scores.

The CTSPC is composed of 22 core items and 13 optional items. The 22 core items have an 8-point response scale indicating frequency of parent-child interactions during the past year. These items are scored by summing the midpoints for the response categories to yield the following three subscale scores: Nonviolent Discipline, Psychological Aggression, and Physical Assault. Additional indicators within the Physical Assault subscale are scored with minor, severe, and extreme ratings. The 13 optional items are scored into subscales of Weekly Discipline, Neglect, and Sexual Abuse. As well, tactics occurring previously but not in the past year are also noted in each of five of the six areas with the exception being Weekly Discipline. An overall score is not computed. The CTSPC AutoScore Form is a perforated booklet composed of an answer sheet for responding to items, a carbon transfer sheet, a scoring worksheet, and a summary sheet. The CTSPC summary sheet includes data to make comparisons to a normative sample.

DEVELOPMENT. Both the CTS2 and the CTSPC are rooted in Conflict Theory (Adams, 1965; Coser, 1956; Dahrendorf, 1959; Scanzoni, 1972; Simmel, 1955; Straus, 1979), predicated on the assumption that although conflict is an unavoidable aspect of all human relationships, violence as a tactic to manage such conflict is not. These two measures were born from the original CTS in which items included conflict tactics that honed in on three areas: using (a) rational conversation, (b) harmful verbal and nonverbal methods that threaten or hurt the recipient, and (c) physical force against the recipient. The test authors note that the CTS items were developed to incorporate the continuum of coercive behavior, from rational discussion to assaults using weapons.

The test authors revised the CTS to develop the CTS2, which includes many of the original CTS items as well as revised and new items. More specifically, all three of the CTS subscales were revised and two were renamed for the CTS2: Reasoning became Negotiation whereas Verbal Aggression became Psychological Aggression. Additionally, two new subscales were created: Injury and Sexual Coercion. Theory, previous experience utilizing the CTS in a variety of settings, and critiques of the CTS directed the item revisions and additions for the CTS2. A pilot version of the CTS2 with 60 items was administered to an undergraduate college student sample of 317 students. These students were at least 18 years of age and reported being in a heterosexual dating, cohabitating, or marital relationship lasting at least 1 month during the preceding year. These 60 items were then reviewed using frequency distributions and internal consistency estimates (i.e., coefficient alpha). Additionally, chi-square analyses were used to investigate the Psychological Aggression items. From these statistical reviews, a 39-item measure (with each item being asked twice) with five subscales was created.

The CTSPC was developed by modifying items from the CTS as well as generating new items. More specifically, the Reasoning subscale of the CTS was modified to create the CTSPC Nonviolent Discipline subscale, the CTS Verbal Aggression subscale was adapted to develop the CTSPC Psychological Aggression subscale, and the CTS Physical Assault subscale was modified to create the CTSPC Physical Assault subscale. Additionally, three wholly new (optional) subscales were created: Weekly Discipline, Neglect, and Sexual Abuse. Previous adaptations of the CTS for use in measuring child maltreatment, as well as reviews of various methods used to document child abuse, directed the item revisions and additions for the CTSPC. No pilot testing was conducted to statistically examine the generated items of the CTSPC.

TECHNICAL. A standardization sample to test the CTS2 was not obtained per se; rather, the pilot sample of undergraduate students (N = 317) was used to provide normative data. This sample was primarily female (64%) and had a mean age of 21.7 years (SD = 5.1). No information regarding race, ethnicity, or geography was provided. Additionally, scant data are reported for a group of incarcerated female substance abusers (N = 359) and two groups of "high-risk" postpartum mothers in San Diego (N = 295) and Hawaii (N = 472).

Estimates of internal consistency for the CTS2 perpetration items based on the normative college sample are as follows: alpha = .86 for Negotiation, alpha = .79 for Psychological Aggression, alpha = .86 for Physical Assault, alpha = .95 for Injury, and alpha = .87 for Sexual Coercion. Internal consistency estimates for this sample regarding the victimization items were not provided. Regarding the sample of incarcerated women, internal consistency estimates were provided for both the perpetration and victimization items and these ranged from .34 (Sexual Coercion) to .87 (Physical Assault) and from .74 (Sexual Coercion) to .94 (Physical Assault), respectively. In terms of the postpartum mothers from San Diego, internal consistency estimates are provided only for perpetration items on the Negotiation, Psychological Aggression, and Physical Assault subscales, and these ranged from .43 to .84. Finally, internal consistency estimates are provided for only two subscales for the postpartum

mothers from Hawaii; however, both perpetration and victimization items were analyzed revealing alpha = .86 and .75 for perpetration on the Physical Assault and Injury subscales, and alpha = .93 and .84 for victimization on the Physical Assault and Injury subscales. No test-retest reliability estimates are reported for any of these three samples.

The test authors note that accumulating validity evidence for the CTS2 is in "its initial stages" (handbook, p. 46). Regarding construct evidence, the CTS2 Physical Assault subscale has been compared to scores on the Personal and Relationships Profile (Straus & Hamby, in press) for a sample of 391 undergraduate students (255 female, 136 male), demonstrating adequate construct validity of this subscale. Other attempts at evidencing validity are offered including average scores for males and females, intercorrelations between the subscales, and a factor analysis among a sample of incarcerated female substance abusers. Criterion-related evidence and predictive evidence are not provided.

Psychometric information for the CTSPC was obtained from a 1995 Gallup telephone interview with a random probability sample (N = 1,000) of telephone households in the contiguous United States. The mean age of parent interviewees was 36.8 years (no SD reported), and 66% were female. The data for the referent children identified in this sample mirrored 1990 U.S. Census data for demographics of children under the age of 18 years. The mean age of the referent children was 8.4 years (no SD reported). Estimates of internal consistency for the CTSPC based on this Gallup sample of parents are as follows: alpha = .70 for Nonviolent Discipline, alpha = .60 for Psychological Aggression, and alpha = .55 for Physical Assault. Internal consistency estimates for this sample regarding the optional Weekly Discipline, Neglect, and Sexual Abuse subscales were not provided. The test authors note that no test-retest reliability estimates are available for the CTSPC.

The test authors do not provide any of their own validity evidence for the CTSPC, stating that such evidence can be found in previously published studies. Regarding construct validity, studies utilizing prior versions of the CTSPC are cited. Other attempts at evidencing validity are offered including references to research examining correlations between the CTSPC and various demographic variables, and intercorrelations among the CTSPC subscales. Criterion-related evidence and predictive evidence are not provided.

COMMENTARY. The CTS2 and the CT-SPC are brief and easy-to-administer measures that have tremendous potential in the field of intimate partner violence and child maltreatment assessment. Indeed, the CTS has been one of the most widely used assessments in the respective field. The primary strength of the CTS2 is its attention to measuring both perpetration and victimization, whereas the primary strength of the CTSPC is its attention to current maltreatment from parents rather than retrospective reports from adults. Another strength is the large research base and published literature utilizing these scales, particularly the CTS2. Despite these strengths, the psychometric evidence for both the CTS2 and the CTSPC needs further empirical support, specifically in regard to construct, criterion, and predictive evidence of validity, as well as with respect to test-retest reliability. Additionally, the normative sample for the CTS2 raises a number of concerns regarding generalizability to the population at large. More specifically, the representativeness of the undergraduate sample is unclear as this group seems skewed to a more educated and perhaps higher socioeconomic demographic of people, and the lack of racial and ethnic demographic information for this normative sample is problematic. As well, the inclusion of individuals only involved in heterosexual intimate relationships severely limits the utility of the CTS2 to heteronormative populations, and may well foster the false belief that coercion and violence occur only in heterosexual relationships. The CTS2 and CTSPC also seem limited to individuals born and raised in the United States as the test authors note that these measures help understand "violence in American culture as it occurs in families and intimate relationships" (handbook, p. 1). Finally, there are concerns regarding the CTS2 measuring tactics out of context, and the ways that the information gleaned from the scale may not fully capture the realities of intimate partner violence (e.g., women scoring equal to men may be reflective of retaliation of intimate partner violence being first perpetrated upon them rather than being the initiator of violence).

SUMMARY. The Conflict Tactics Scales (CTS), composed of the Revised Conflict Tactics Scales (CTS2) and the Conflict Tactics Scales: Parent-Child Version (CTSPC), are self-report measures of specific tactics employed by an intimate couple during a conflict and current child maltreatment from parents, respectively. The assessments meet these intended goals and both have begun to demonstrate adequate empirical evidence supporting their psychometric properties. The CTS2 and the CTSPC are likely to be useful in a variety of settings including clinical and nonclinical settings. Professionals seeking ways to assess intimate partner violence, child abuse, and change via clinical intervention and treatment would likely find the CTS2 and CTSPC useful measures. Further investigation and psychometric evidence including more diverse samples with regard to age, education level, race, and ethnicity would greatly enhance the validity of the CTS2 and CTSPC.

REVIEWER'S REFERENCES

Adams, B. N. (1965). Coercion and consensus theories: Some unresolved issues. *American Journal of Sociology, 71*, 714-716.

Coser, L. (1956). *The functions of social conflict.* New York, NY: Free Press.

Dahrendorf, R. (1959). *Class and class conflict in industrial society.* London, England: Routledge and Kegan Paul.

Scanzoni, J. (1972). Marital conflict as a positive force. In J. Scanzoni (Ed.), *Sexual bargaining* (pp. 61-102). Englewood Cliffs, NJ: Prentice-Hall.

Simmel, G. (1955). *Conflict and the web of group affiliations.* Glencoe, IL: Free Press.

Straus, M. A. (1973). A general systems theory approach to a theory of violence between family members. *Social Science Information, 12*, 105-125.

Straus, M. A. (1979). Measuring intrafamily conflict and violence: The Conflict Tactics (CT) Scales. *Journal of Marriage and Family, 41*, 75-88.

Straus, M. A., & Hamby, S. L. (in press). *The Personal Relationship Profile (PRP): Manual.* Los Angeles, CA: Western Psychological Services.

Review of the Conflict Tactics Scales by JOHN J. VACCA, Associate Professor of Education, Saint Joseph's University, Philadelphia, PA:

DESCRIPTION. According to the information provided for the Conflict Tactics Scales (CTS), it is an individually administered assessment tool designed to obtain reports of domestic violence among abusive adult partners and "physical maltreatment and neglect of children by parents, as well as nonviolent modes of discipline" (handbook, p. 75). Further, the primary purpose of the CTS is to identify incidence of physically aggressive acts of intimidation and coercion that are present in an intimate relationship either between two partners and/or their children. The test authors identify a potential adaptation for use in other relationships beyond that of intimate partners. The wording of items can be adapted, for example to allow an adolescent to answer questions about parent to parent behaviors and interactions, behaviors between siblings, or interactions with same sex peers. There are two versions of the CTS that are available currently for use: the CTS2 (revised CTS) and the CTSPC (Parent-Child). The test authors state that the intended use and application of the CTS2 and CTSPC are primarily seen in family therapy, law enforcement and correctional facilities, and research. Information from the CTS also may be used in the coding of archival data from police records, orders of protection, and psychiatric intake/interviews.

Total average administration time is no longer than 20 minutes for each version. A test kit accompanies both the CTS2 and CTSPC that includes a handbook and autoscore forms. The test authors provide both samples of completed tests with calculated raw scores and instructions for interpretation of resultant score to the examiner. There are 78 items on the CTS2 (39-Self, 39-Partner), and there are 22 core items (and 13 optional items) on the CTSPC. Composite raw scores for both versions are provided after analysis of the completed form. On the CTS2, five composite scores are derived that address the following: Negotiation, Psychological Aggression, Physical Assault, Injury, and Sexual Coercion. For the CTSPC, six composite scores are derived that address the following: Nonviolent Discipline, Psychological Aggression, Physical Assault, Weekly Discipline, Neglect, and Sexual Abuse. The ratings of each question by the respondent range from 0 (*Never*) to 7 (*Not in the past year, but it happened before*). Ratings between 1 and 6 are aligned with the frequency of occurrence (i.e., 1 = *Once*, 2 = *Twice*, 3 = *3-5 times*, 4 = *6-10 times*, 5 = *11-20 times*, 6 = *More than 20 times*). Following completion of the instrument, the test authors indicate that the "midpoints" of each of the ratings are added together to provide total raw scores for each of the composites mentioned previously. The carbon response form provides for easy tallying and transferring of raw scores. Once the composite raw scores are completed, the examiner can see the frequency of behaviors identified by the respondent that their partner did to them and that they identified for what they did to their partner.

The administration of the CTS2 and CTSPC follows a standard, self-report format. The test authors identify that the questions on the form can be delivered in an interview, although they caution that any departure from the original design of the instrument may restrict the ability to generalize findings. The test authors provide clear instructions for administration. The evaluator provides a quiet and distraction-free environment for the individual completing the form. The individual is instructed to provide only one answer for each question. In the CTS2, questions are presented in pairs (what the participant did and what their partner did). The literacy level/readability of the content of the questions on the form was determined to be at the fourth grade level (determination made through completion of the Flesch-Kincaid method). Average scores and percent of occurrences among the respondents in the test sample are provided to allow the examiner to assess relative significance of the information provided by the respondent.

DEVELOPMENT. The pedagogical framework for the CTS is based on Conflict Theory. The paradigmatic assertion that follows this theory highlights that the inevitable occurrence of conflict in relationships is a natural component of any association; yet it stipulates that use of violence as a "tactic" to deal with conflict is not natural. The test authors state that "without the change that can be achieved through conflict, a social unit–be it a nation or a family–runs a high risk of collapse" (handbook, p. 5). The use of violence, however, as a tactic to handle conflict seems futile. The focus of the original CTS and its revised version is the occurrence and incidence of specific acts or events, not on attitudes about conflict or violence nor is it on causes or consequences of different tactics. The test authors see this as a strength when compared with other instruments. This is because the identification of specific tactics and their corresponding incidence is paramount in assembling a comprehensive assessment battery that will thoroughly investigate etiology. Revisions leading to the current versions consisted mainly of formatting, hierarchical ordering of items, attending to the sensitivity of vocabulary with respect to gender and severity of violence, and specifying composites. The test authors identify that the CTS2 was the result of a pilot study conducted with college students (*n* = 317), yet information about how the study was conducted and how the results were used to shape the revisions of the CTS is lacking.

TECHNICAL. Overall, the test authors clearly identify limitations in the use of scores from the CTS or CTSPC given limited evidence of test reliability. As a result, they recommend that clinicians regard use of the tool as supplementary to any battery of assessment measures that have better established psychometric properties. The ability of the clinician to assess the incidence of violent behavior and maladaptive tactics for conflict serves as an important starting point to the design and implementation of a therapeutic intervention plan. Furthermore, the test authors endorse its use as "interview guides, as checklists to document the categorical presence and frequency of each specific behavior in a given relationship, and as tools to focus therapeutic discussion and interpartner communication" (handbook, p. 43).

In terms of reliability, well-established values of internal consistency for the CTS2 are provided as a result of pilot testing with a sample of college students ($n = 317$). Coefficient alpha estimates range from .79 to .95 for the five scales. Similar ranges were documented from three follow-up studies with large samples ($n = 359$, $n = 295$, $n = 472$) representing incarcerated female substance abusers and high-risk postpartum mothers; however, lower alpha coefficients were determined for the Sexual Coercion scale. The test authors concluded that this could have been the result of limits in the array of behaviors that were reported by the respondents in the sample. Review of the CTSPC provides lower values for reliability when compared against the CTS2 with coefficients ranging from .55 to .72, with stronger values for Nonviolent Discipline and Psychological Aggression. Lower values are also reported for validity, with coefficients in the low moderate range (i.e., .42 to .53).

For measures of validity, adequate correlation coefficients are reported for the CTS2 when compared against a reportedly similar instrument (The Personal and Relationships Profile; Straus & Hamby, in press). The data were collected from a sample of college students ($n = 391$). The test authors state that adequate construct evidence emerged from an examination of the factor loading of each of the composite areas assessed when compared against the original CTS. Furthermore, use of the CTS and the revised versions have documented the relationships between high incidence of violent tactics present in households and corresponding results of interpersonal problems, delinquency, and excessive aggression. Correlation coefficients are also reported distinguishing profiles for gender within moderately acceptable levels (.41 to .91).

COMMENTARY. The CTS2 and CTSPC are valuable inventories to incorporate into any data collection regimen focusing on individuals experiencing negative sequelae from violent interactions with significant partners. The inventories provide a nonthreatening forum for clients to identify their involvement and their partners' involvement in aggressive acts with each other. Both versions are also helpful for adolescents to identify such acts that are present in their nuclear family. Although the psychometric data provided by the test authors are generally acceptable, they are based on small restricted samples focusing only on college students and women with preexisting conditions (i.e., substance abuse history, postpartum depression).

The data reported for the CTSPC are particularly concerning not only because of the small sample sizes that were used but also because there does not appear to be a well-established alignment with conflict theory and family systems theory. Therefore, test users are urged to consider this lapse with respect to generalizability. Further, sole use of the CTS versions to guide decision making whether diagnostically or for treatment should not be implemented. Rather, clinicians should regard the information collected as an augment to a complete assessment battery in order to avoid any false assumptions about given relationships.

SUMMARY. Two revised versions of the CTS are available to mental health and related professionals involved in working with individuals exposed to violent tactics used in intimate relationships. Both inventories are aligned with the intent of the test authors to identify incidence of maladaptive behaviors and interactions. Unfortunately, the test authors fall short in providing a solid psychometric foundation, which significantly restricts efforts for generalizability and sustained treatment utility. Professionals interested in using the CTS are recommended to consider the information collected as baseline in the standard intake process. Therefore, the data generated should not form the sole foundation for diagnosis and/or treatment.

REVIEWER'S REFERENCE

Straus, M. A., & Hamby, S. L. (in press). The Personal Relationship Profile: Manual. Los Angeles: Western Psychological Services.

[44]

Coping Skills Assessment.

Purpose: Designed to "evaluate whether an individual uses healthy or unhealthy coping mechanisms to deal with stress."

Population: Below 17 through adulthood.

Publication Date: 2011.

Acronym: COSA.

Scores, 16: Overall Score, Problem-Focused Coping, Emotion-Focused Coping, Hang-Ups, Problem Solving, Information Seeking, Negotiation, Social Support, Positive Cognitive Restructuring, Emotional Regulation, Distraction, Rumination, Avoidance, Helplessness, Social Withdrawal, Opposition.

Administration: Individual.

Price Data: Available from publisher.

Time: (20) minutes.

Comments: Self-administered online assessment. The test publisher advises that the test manual is being updated to include more information about methodology and theoretical background used in the development of the test. The test publisher also advises that this information is available to clients, as are benchmarks for relevant industries and racial/ethnic group comparison data. However, this information was not provided to Buros or the reviewers.

Author: PsychTests AIM, Inc.

Publisher: PsychTests AIM, Inc. [Canada].

Review of the Coping Skills Assessment by SUSAN N. KUSHNER BENSON, Associate Professor of Educational Research, Assessment, and Evaluation, University of Akron, Akron, OH:

DESCRIPTION. The purpose of the Coping Skills Assessment (COSA) is to evaluate whether an individual uses healthy or unhealthy coping mechanisms to deal with stress. The 64-item scale is intended to be used in preemployment testing and for counseling purposes, and the test authors estimate that the scale can be completed in 20 minutes. The test authors state that COSA can be used with individuals ranging in age from below 17 through adulthood. The test authors should consider providing a more precise lower age limit as "below 17" is too vague.

The COSA is composed of three primary subscales: Problem-Focused Coping, Emotion-Focused Coping, and Hang-Ups. The subscales address ways of handling stress that deal with (a) taking action to improve the stressor, (b) learning how to deal with stressful situations emotionally, and (c) "empty" coping strategies that are not likely to be helpful. Each of the three primary subscales is further defined by three to five secondary subscales. For example, the primary subscale Problem-Focused Coping includes the secondary subscales Problem Solving, Information Seeking, and Negotiation. Thus, 16 scores are available: total score, scores on three primary subscales, and scores on 12 secondary subscales. The same 5-point response scale is used for all items, ranging from 1 = *most of the time* to 5 = *almost never*.

DEVELOPMENT. The test authors did not provide specific information about the developmental process of the COSA. Typically such a description would include a discussion of the theory and research that defines the construct of interest, the process used to generate and evaluate the initial item pool, and the iterative process used to cull the initial pool of items—which tends to be quite large—to more manageable numbers. This process typically entails a blend of logical evaluation in the form of expert judgment combined with statistical procedures such as factor analysis. This information is instrumental in establishing the rigor of the instrument development process. Without this information, one is left to question whether the items were generated based on sound psychometric principles.

TECHNICAL.

Standardization. The standardization sample for the COSA consisted of 8,998 participants, 60% women, 27% men, and 13% unknown. Half of the standardization sample fell within the "below 17" and "18 to 24" age ranges with the smallest percentage (6%) classified as "50 and older." All participants completed the measure online at one of three different "pop-psychology" websites that the general public would be likely to visit for self-help needs. Because of convenience sampling and a sample that is heavily based on young females, the norms provided are not likely to be appropriate for all age ranges and for men. Data are not provided separately by ethnic groups.

Reliability. The test authors estimate internal consistency reliability and report alpha coefficients for the 16 available scores. The alpha coefficient for the total score was .94. Alpha coefficients for the three primary subscales were .89, .88, and .93, respectively, for Problem-Focused Coping, Emotion-Focused Coping, and Hang-Ups. Thus, the overall scale and three subscales demonstrate high internal consistency. Alpha values for the 12 secondary subscales ranged from .64 to .87. The lower alpha values could be explained by the smaller number of items on the secondary subscales, but the test authors could have used the Spearman-Brown prophecy formula to estimate reliability with additional items. No estimates of stability (test-retest) are reported, and this is a major shortcoming of the instrument. Although internal consistency and stability are both estimates of reliability, they are not interchangeable.

Validity. The *Standards for Educational and Psychological Testing* (1999) were developed by the American Educational Research Association (AERA), the American Psychological Association (APA), and the National Council on Measurement in Education (NCME), and within the psychometric community these criteria are considered the framework against which instruments should be developed and evaluated. Five sources of validity evidence are identified and discussed in the *Standards*: evidence based on test content, evidence based on response processes, evidence based on internal structure, evidence based on relations to other variables, and evidence based on consequences of testing. Although the test authors include a large section in the COSA technical report titled "Validity Analysis," they do not actually provide any evidence to support the validity of the COSA. What the test authors provide in this section are: (a) descriptive data (bar charts, means, and standard deviations) for men and women and for the different age categories on the various subscales, and (b) tests of statistical significance (t-test and ANOVA) to demonstrate whether the differences between males and females and the differences between age groups were statistically significant. Had the test authors provided a cogent, scholarly discussion of known (substantiated) differences in stress coping skills between gender and age groups, then the data reported could have been used as sources of evidence of relationship to other variables. No such discussion was provided; thus, the copious graphs and data in this section are ineffective for judging validity. In a second section of the technical report, the test authors compare subscale scores to comparison variables. For example, scores on the overall scale and subscales were compared to four variables that one would expect to be correlates of coping skills: frequency of conflict, life satisfaction, work satisfaction, and ability to cope with stress. As evidence of relationship to other variables, however, the test authors should have reported correlation statistics between the COSA subscales and these four variables. The meaning of the correlations, previously referred to as evidence of concurrent validity, is dependent upon the validity and reliability of the comparison measures. In other words, the test authors would need to address the validity and reliability of the measures of frequency of conflict, life satisfaction, work satisfaction, and ability to cope with stress, but they did not.

COMMENTARY. To facilitate this review process, the test publisher provided an online link and temporary login information for the COSA. Based on personal experience completing the COSA, a few additional observations are warranted. First, the COSA appears to have strong face validity. The individual items certainly would be interpreted by the test taker as measures of stress, and suggestions for stress management that are offered in the test score report are those that are recognized as stress reduction strategies. For example, keeping a journal or learning to say "no" are common sense suggestions. Second, PsychTests AIM, Inc. has authored a similar measure called the Coping & Stress Management Skills Test (CSMST). Items on the CSMST and the COSA are strikingly similar. No explanation is provided in the technical manual about the similarities and differences between the two. One would expect that scores on the CSMST would be used as criterion-related validity evidence for the COSA. Finally, the test authors provide the following disclaimer for the CSMST: "Tests available on Psychtests.com are intended for personal use only. Using them for professional purposes constitutes a violation of Psychtest's Terms of Use and will result in suspension of your account" (publisher's website). If this disclaimer will apply to the COSA, the test authors' claim that COSA scores can be used in preemployment and counseling situations would be suspect.

SUMMARY. The claim that the COSA can be used in preemployment and counseling situations is not substantiated by the evidence and documentation provided by the test authors. Although the COSA may have potential, a thorough description of the developmental process, compelling and appropriate evidence to support validity, and test-retest estimates of reliability need to be reported. As is, the COSA is appropriately situated within the realm of self-help websites and pop-psychology. Professionals who are in need of an instrument to measure coping skills would be better advised to consider the Coping Inventory for Stressful Situations, Second Edition (CISS; Endler & Parker, 1990; 1994; 1999; 15:69) which has been critically reviewed and documented in the scholarly literature.

REVIEWER'S REFERENCES

American Educational Research Association, American Psychological Association, & National Council on Measurement in Education. (1999). *Standards for educational and psychological testing.* Washington, DC: American Educational Research Association.

Endler, N. S., & Parker, J. D. A. (1990). Multidimensional assessment of coping: A critical evaluation. *Journal of Personality and Social Psychology, 58,* 844-854.

Endler, N. S., & Parker, J. D. A. (1994). Assessment of multidimensional coping: Task, emotion and avoidance strategies. *Psychological Assessment, 6,* 50-60.

Endler, N. S., & Parker J. D. A. (1999). Coping Inventory for Stressful Situations: Manual. Toronto, Canada: MHS.

Review of the Coping Skills Assessment by ROMEO VITELLI, Psychologist, private practice, Hamilton, Ontario, Canada:

DESCRIPTION. The Coping Skills Assessment (COSA) is a 64-item online self-assessment measure developed by PsychTests for the assessment of potential employees and the types of coping mechanisms–whether healthy or unhealthy–that they use in stressful situations. Designed to be completed in 20 minutes, the test items are scored along a 5-point scale ranging from *most of the time* to *almost never.* The computerized scoring report provides test scores along the following dimensions:

Problem-Focused Coping. Dealing with stress by taking action to improve the stressful situation. Problem-focused coping strategies include problem-solving, information-seeking, and compromise negotiations.

Emotion-Focused Coping. Dealing with the emotional aspects of stress. Methods of handling stressful situations through emotion-focused coping can include seeking social support, positive cognitive restructuring of the stressful situation, emotional regulation (such as relaxation techniques or seeking positive emotional outlets), and distraction from the stressful situation.

Use of "Hang-Ups." Empty coping strategies that fail to resolve the stressful situation in a positive way. These approaches may include obsessive rumination about the stressor, avoidance of the stressful situation, learned helplessness, social withdrawal, and becoming oppositional.

The COSA computerized scoring report provides an individualized profile that presents scores along a scale from 0 to 100 on each of the test dimensions and provides feedback on strengths and limitations. The report also gives detailed advice about more positive ways of handling stress that draws on existing stress research to warn test takers of potentially unhealthy stress management strategies that might interfere with the test taker's ability to function in the workplace.

DEVELOPMENT. Because of the role of stress in various psychological and physical ailments, workplace stress is a significant concern for organizations; it is also a financial drain. The impact of workplace stress is reflected in time lost due to illness, poor work motivation, and impairments in the overall organizational culture. According to an American Psychological Association survey on workplace stress (American Psychological Association, 2011), more than one-third of workers (36% of the survey sample) reported feeling tensed or stressed during their workday. Of those, 20% rated their average daily stress as 8, 9, or 10 on a 10-point scale. The reasons for workplace stress may vary from inadequate financial and nonfinancial recognition to poor relationships with supervisors or other employees.

Although employers cannot protect workers from stress that arises outside the work environment (except through providing employee assistance counseling), identifying potential stressors in the workplace and assessing the ability of prospective employees to cope with stress in an effective manner becomes critical in the hiring process.

In examining the relationship between stress and coping, psychological models have focused on specific areas of coping including problem-focused coping, emotion-focused coping, cognitive reappraisal, and symptom management. In the model conceptualized by Susan Folkman and Richard Lazarus (Folkman & Lazarus, 1980), coping strategies are essentially situation based and come into play in specific stressful situations. As coping with stress and avoiding worker burnout has become an important field of industrial psychological research, psychometric measures of healthy and unhealthy coping strategies have become more important in the employment process.

In developing the COSA, a standardization sample of 8,998 participants was used (60% female, 27% male, 13% unreported) ranging in age from under 17 to over 50. The validation study was carried out online using the websites Queendom.com, Psychtests.com, and Psychologytoday.com. The sample was self-selected, and validation analyses were conducted using completed test responses only.

TECHNICAL. The COSA psychometric report provides extensive information on reliability data obtained for the COSA. Coefficient alpha values ranged from .64 to .93 across all COSA subscales, with a .94 coefficient for the Overall Score. No test-retest reliability evidence is provided.

Psychometric data on the COSA items showed significant age and gender differences. Women outscored men on scales of Social Support, Information Seeking, Rumination, Helplessness, Opposition, Problem-Focused Coping, and Hang-Ups. Men significantly outscored women on Negotiation, Emotional Regulation, Distraction, and on the Overall Score. All differences were significant at the .001 level.

ANOVA analyses and post-hoc comparisons also showed significant differences by age group, although the effect sizes were less pronounced than for gender. As expected, older workers scored higher than younger workers on most COSA scales including Problem Solving, Information Seeking, Negotiation, and Social Support. Younger workers tended to outscore older workers on negative coping strategies such as Distraction, Rumination, Avoidance, and Helplessness, although the trends were not entirely consistent. Overall, older workers scored higher on both Problem-Focused and Emotion-Focused Coping as well as on the Overall Score.

ANOVAs and post-hoc comparisons were used to examine scores across groups of responders who were not very satisfied, somewhat satisfied, or very satisfied in their (a) overall life, (b) work, and (c) ability to cope. Scores were in the predicted directions for the COSA subscales (e.g., Problem Solving, Information Seeking, Negotiation, Social Support, and Positive Cognitive Restructuring), and differences among the groups were significant ($p < .001$).

Validation data appear limited to evidence collected from sources within the test, such as that presented in the previous paragraphs. Further research is needed to link COSA scores to real-world measures of worker effectiveness such as lost sick days, employer ratings, or other indicators of healthy or unhealthy workplace functioning.

COMMENTARY. Although the COSA fills an important niche with respect to measuring potential workers' ability to cope with stressful situations and the nature of their preferred coping strategies, further research is needed to establish the measure's value in employee selection and retention. The lack of a manual prevents a more complete evaluation of potential uses for the COSA and how the test profile can be used by human resource departments and employee assistance programs in dealing with worker stress. As well, the lack of sufficient validation research limits potential uses of the COSA in many testing situations and also limits the recommendations that can be made based on COSA scores.

SUMMARY. The Coping Skills Assessment (COSA) is an online measure of potential employees and the types of coping mechanisms—whether healthy or unhealthy—that they use in stressful situations. The online administration and scoring format make it easy to use, and the constructive feedback it provides allows for employee self-evaluation. Although the reliability data provided are quite extensive, validity data remain limited at this time. The lack of a COSA manual is also a drawback.

REVIEWER'S REFERENCES
American Psychological Association. (2011). *Stress in the workplace.* Washington, DC: Author.
Folkman, S., & Lazarus, R. S. (1980). An analysis of coping in a middle-aged community sample. *Journal of Health and Social Behavior, 21,* 219-239.

[45]

Creativity and Problem-Solving Aptitude Test.

Purpose: "Designed to evaluate a person's creative problem-solving potential based on pertinent personality traits."

Population: Under age 17 through adult.
Publication Date: 2011.
Acronym: CAPSAT.
Scores, 5: Comfort with Decision Making, Flexibility, Openness to Creativity, Sense of Self-Efficacy, Overall Score.
Administration: Individual.
Price Data: Available from publisher.
Time: (15) minutes.
Comments: Self-administered online assessment. The test publisher advises that the test manual is being updated to include more information about methodology and theoretical background used in the development of the test. The test publisher also advises that this information is available to clients, as are benchmarks for relevant industries and racial/ethnic group comparison data. However, this information was not provided to Buros or the reviewers.
Author: PsychTests AIM, Inc.
Publisher: PsychTests AIM, Inc. [Canada].

Review of the Creativity and Problem-Solving Aptitude Test by MERITH COSDEN, Professor, Department of Counseling, Clinical, & School Psychology, University of California, Santa Barbara, Santa Barbara, CA:

DESCRIPTION. The Creativity and Problem-Solving Aptitude Test (CAPSAT) is a 36-item measure that purports to assess Comfort with Decision Making, Flexibility, Openness to Creativity, and Sense of Self-Efficacy. The assessment is available online and is self-administered. After taking the assessment, one can print a report that indicates where one's score falls relative to the sample described in the manual, and what the scores mean. The report also lists strengths, potential strengths, and limitations and presents advice on how to increase one's creativity. Although written feedback varies based on the respondent's test scores, it is not clear how many variations in feedback are available and provided.

The manual provides descriptive information about the measure overall and its subscales. The manual also provides analyses of test score differences as a function of gender, age, educational level, grades, and self-rated problem-solving ability. Significant findings are described in the text and displayed in corresponding figures. However, understanding the meaning of the scale scores is limited by what is not provided in the manual; that is, the manual does *not* present a description of the theory behind the test, how it was developed, clear description and definition of subtest domains, or appropriate assessment of its validity.

DEVELOPMENT. No information is available on the development of the scale. How test items were developed or selected for inclusion on the measure is not described.

TECHNICAL.

Standardization. Assessment data on 24,994 participants are presented in the manual. All participants self-selected to take the measure, responding to a request to take the survey electronically on one of several websites. The manual does not indicate whether participants were fiscally compensated for their time. Of these participants, 50% reported they were women, 34% reported they were men, and a relatively large proportion (16%) did not indicate their gender. It does not appear that there were age restrictions put on test-takers, as the age groups are listed as below 17 (no minimum noted), 18–24, 25–29, 30–39, and 40 and over (no top age noted); 11% of the sample did not report age. Participants were asked about their education; the manual reports that approximately 400 respondents fit into each of the following categories: grade school, some high school, graduated from high school, junior college, college, having an Associate's degree, Bachelor's degree, or Master's degree. It appears that random samples of each group were drawn so that the groups were relatively equal in size. A higher number reported technical/trade school (N = 511) or a Ph.D. (N = 493). Participants were also asked about their employment. The manual does not clarify how this question was asked, or recoded, as: Entrepreneur, Managerial, Non-managerial, and Not Employed. The manual states that there were exactly 1,015 respondents in each category. The manual also indicates that respondents were asked about their school grades; although details are not provided on how grades were reported, they are recoded as Top Grades, Good Grades, Average Grades, and Below Average grades. Again, no information is provided as to what these categories represent, although exactly 450 respondents are reported in each group. Finally, respondents are categorized on the basis of self-reported problem-solving ability. Categories of Excellent, Good, Satisfactory, and Poor were created, with exactly 450 respondents reported in each category.

Reliability. Coefficient alpha was calculated for each subscale and for the assessment overall. Although the manual does not specifically state this, it is assumed that these measures are based on the full sample of 24,994 participants. Alphas range from .72 to .87 for the scales, with an alpha of .90 for the overall score.

Validity. Although the manual has a section labeled Validity Analysis, the analyses presented look at differences as a function of client characteristics, such as age, gender, educational level, grades, vocational position, and self-rated problem-solving ability, without clarifying how these are related to the validity of the scales. That is, although the manual indicates that there are statistically significant differences between women and men, age groups, and respondents with different educational levels, grades in school, vocational positions, and problem-solving abilities, it does not indicate why these differences would be predicted or how they might "validate" the scales. Further, no effect sizes are presented. Given the large number of participants on which the analyses are based, many small differences are statistically significant, although they may not be clinically important. The statistical analyses are followed by graphs that represent group differences; however, these can be misleading in that the scaling of the axes is not standardized across figures, and small numeric differences appear large based on their scale. Finally, the constructs themselves are not defined. For example, it is not clear whether "Openness to Creativity" is the same as or different from the construct typically labeled as "Creativity." Other constructs, such as "Comfort with Decision Making" also would benefit from further description as this could be defined in different ways. No studies are presented that compare these subscales to other measures of similar constructs (e.g., creativity or self-efficacy) that are already in the literature. It must also be noted that because all of the responses were obtained anonymously online, the validity of participants' self-descriptions is itself in question.

COMMENTARY. The CAPSAT is easy to complete as a short, self-administered survey. However, although the questions are interesting, what they measure remains a question. Without information on test development or studies of construct validity it is not evident what skills or abilities the test is actually measuring. Unfortunately, users who accept the titles of the scales (Comfort with Decision Making, Flexibility, Openness to Creativity, and Sense of Self-Efficacy) as reflecting the skills they name may be misled as these tests have not been validated. The purpose of this assessment as a whole is unclear.

SUMMARY. The CAPSAT is a electronic survey that purports to measure four areas related to creativity and problem solving: Comfort with Decision Making, Flexibility, Openness to Creativity, and Sense of Self-Efficacy. Although these are potentially important areas of functioning, the manual does not provide evidence of the validity of this measure. Although easy to self-administer, the lack of theory behind development of the scale, poor definition of subscales, and reliance on a convenience sample for its standardization sample, make interpretation of findings a challenge. Given the availability of other measures of similar constructs, recommended uses of the CAPSAT are not evident.

Review of the Creativity and Problem-Solving Aptitude Test by ALLEN I. HUFFCUTT, Caterpillar Professor of Psychology, Bradley University, Peoria, IL:

DESCRIPTION. The Creativity and Problem-Solving Aptitude Test (CAPSAT) is a self-report measure of creativity. It is not demonstrative in that test-takers do not actually solve a problem using creativity, but rather this measure is based on self-reports of various attitudes and strategies involved in problem solving. Two things are worthy of note about this test. The first is the focus on creativity, which is traditionally a somewhat difficult construct to assess. The second is that, although creativity is generally considered to be a cognitive construct, the test developers approach it from a personality/social perspective.

DEVELOPMENT. Very little information is provided about the development of this test. A detailed overview of its development would be helpful.

TECHNICAL. The questions that comprise the CAPSAT seem reasonable and well thought out. However, without the reporting of item analyses and factor analyses, it is difficult to get a sense of the measure's psychometric properties. The scaling (which varies by section) is Likert format and seems well done. For example, the opposite of "Almost Never" was "Most of the Time," a variation this reviewer thought was creative and better than "Almost Always."

The test manual is commendable in several respects, particularly in regard to data reporting. Descriptive data are provided in great detail on all measures, and the charts that illustrate these findings are well done and informative. There are extensive analyses of group difference variables, including gender, age, education, and grades. Finally, the sample size of the normative group is around 25,000, which is also commendable.

There are, however, several aspects of the test manual that are lacking. Perhaps the most prominent is the lack of statements describing the conceptual development of the measure. The authors provide no rationale as to why Comfort with Decision Making, Flexibility, Openness to Creativity, and Sense of Self-Efficacy are the main facets of creativity. Development of the creativity construct, along with citation of relevant literature, would greatly enhance the status of the CAPSAT. Further, the measurement side should be addressed as well, in particular why the authors choose to assess a cognitive construct via personality (which is not necessarily bad, but it would be informative to know why they have chosen this approach).

In addition, there is a lack of construct validity evidence. The only construct-related analysis provided appears to be self-rated problem-solving ability. Although it would take time and effort, the test developers really should find external avenues for evidence of construct validity, which could include ratings of creativity by employers, correlation with other creativity measures, etc. In regard to the latter point, one of the analyses this reviewer would have found interesting is the degree to which CAPSAT scores correlate with measures of general intelligence.

Finally, although the test developers noted the extensive moderating influence of variables such as gender and age, they did not provide advice to potential test users about what to do with these differences. For instance, should test-takers be scored relative to their own demographic group or in an absolute sense relative to all test-takers?

A few last observations follow, none of which are as major as those listed above. First, the reliability (alpha) analyses show a wide range, from what this reviewer considers to be exceptional (.90 for the Overall Score) to barely acceptable for Flexibility (.73) and Openness to Creativity (.72). The test developers are encouraged to work on raising the alpha values for these latter two indices, whether that is done through careful item analysis or through the addition of more test items.

Second, the frequency graphs provided show some degree of negative skew in all five indices, although none are severe enough to cause any real problems. That said, the test developers are encouraged in future versions to consider ways to normalize all five distributions. Doing so might involve the addition of a small number of questions that only people at the highest level on these indices would endorse.

COMMENTARY. The limitations noted above do not necessarily imply that the CAPSAT is a deficient measure. Rather, they leave this reviewer looking at this test with a sense of uncertainty. If these limitations can be addressed, the CAPSAT has the potential to fill a potentially valuable and somewhat underdeveloped spot in the assessment arena, namely measurement of creativity in the context of problem solving.

As to the report generated when one takes the CAPSAT, there is both a positive and a negative aspect. On the positive side, the report itself seemed detailed, meaningful, and reasonably accurate. One could easily see a report such as this providing useful feedback for people in the workplace. On the negative side, the report prints in small text and uses only one side of the pages. Whether such formatting is a product of internet printing is uncertain. The authors are encouraged to make the report format more user-friendly, including the possibility of generating a pdf file.

SUMMARY. It is encouraging to see measures of creativity being developed. The CAPSAT has the potential to be a meaningful test of creativity, but considerably more development (and reporting) is needed before it can achieve that status.

[46]
Customer Service Aptitude Profile.

Purpose: Designed to "assist in the selection, placement, and development of people to work in customer service roles."
Population: Ages 15 and over.
Publication Date: 2002.
Acronym: Customer Service AP.
Scores, 21: Self-Enhancement, Self-Criticism, Inconsistent Responding Index, Sales Disposition, Initiative-Cold Calling, Sales Closing, Achievement, Motivation, Competitiveness, Goal Orientation, Planning, Initiative-General, Team Player, Managerial, Assertiveness, Personal Diplomacy, Extroversion, Cooperativeness, Relaxed Style, Patience, Self-Confidence.
Administration: Group.
Price Data, 2010: $137 per CD good for 10 uses; $21.50 per Employers Guide (24 pages); $16.50 per 100 PC answer sheets.
Time: (20) minutes.
Comments: Self-report format; may be taken online or with paper-and-pencil.
Authors: Sander I. Marcus, Jotham G. Friedland, and Harvey P. Mandel.
Publisher: Western Psychological Services.

Review of the Customer Service Aptitude Profile by MICHAEL BUNCH, Senior Vice President, Measurement Incorporated, Durham, NC:

DESCRIPTION. The Customer Service Aptitude Profile (Customer Service AP), published by Western Psychological Services, consists of 140 statements to which examinees respond on a 5-point scale (*Always True, Mostly True, Sometimes True/Sometimes False, Mostly False, Always False*). The statements, all quite short and written at a sixth-grade reading level, refer to personal characteristics or habits that cluster into five domains: Sales Success, Motivation & Achievement, Work Strengths, Interpersonal Strengths, and Inner Resources. Within each domain, there are three or four scales; for example, Sales Success includes the scales Sales Disposition, Initiative-Cold Calling, and Sales Closing. The manual (called the employers' guide and written in 2002) contains 18 such scales; however, the publisher's website now shows only 17, the scale for Managerial having been dropped. [Editor's Note: The publisher advises this error is being corrected.] The statements and response options are on a scannable two-sided sheet that examinees complete, along with minimal personal information. The test may also be administered and scored via computer administration.

The test is accompanied by the employers' guide, which contains directions for administration, a description of the test, and an extensive discussion of various score report scenarios. The employers' guide contains the basic technical information about the test and refers to another document, the SalesAP manual, which contains additional technical information.

Examinees take the test under the direction of a test administrator. The employers' guide provides general directions for individual and group administrations, along with a guide to interpretation. This guide relates 42 sample items to a specific domain and scale.

The score report includes raw and adjusted percentile ranks on all 18 of the scales, along with a graphic representation of these scores showing whether the examinee scored *Very Low, Low, Average, High,* or *Very High* on each scale. The most intriguing aspect of the report is the lengthy narrative for each of the five domains and 18 scales. The sample report included 4 pages of very specific narrative keyed to precise percentile rank scores. Raw responses to all 140 items are included at the end of the report. In all, the sample individual score report reviewed was 6 pages long, most of which was narrative.

DEVELOPMENT. The Customer Service AP seems to be identical to the Sales Achievement Predictor (SalesAP; Friedland, Marcus, & Mandel, 1995). Indeed, not only are the 140 items on the Customer Service AP the same items found on the SalesAP, they are in exactly the same order. These 140 items were selected by the authors from an initial pool of over 600 items generated from the authors' model of performance in the workplace. Their model involved a developmental perspective. For additional insights into the development of the initial instrument (and therefore this one), the reader is referred to reviews of the SalesAP in *The Fourteenth Mental Measurements Yearbook* (Bruner, 2001; Roberts, 2001).

TECHNICAL.

Standardization. The Customer Service AP was standardized on a sample of 1,375 individuals (660 male and 715 female), aged 15 and older. About one-third were students, many of whom had been referred for low performance.

Reliability. The employers' guide reports both internal consistency and test-retest (1 year) reliability coefficients. Internal consistency measures, based on 745 examinees, range from .66 to .88, with a median of .81. Test-retest estimates, based on 36 examinees range from .67 to .90, with a median of .80. Self-Confidence ($r = .88$) and Managerial ($r = .87$) are the most internally consistent scales, whereas Intuitive General ($r_{tt} = .90$) and Initiative-Cold Calling ($r_{tt} = .88$) are the most stable.

Validity. Validity arguments are based on two sets of correlations between the Customer Service AP and other measures. The authors present correlations between the 18 scale scores and scores on the 16 Personality Factor (16PF) test (Cattell, 1986) for 377 examinees. The 288 correlations range from -.58 to +.60 and are mostly in expected direction and size. For example, the correlation between the Customer Service AP scale Initiative-Cold Calling and 16PF factor Venturesome is +.60. The correlation between the same Customer Service AP scale and 16PF Factor Self-Doubting is -.31. Both correlations are significantly different from 0.

The authors also provide a table of correlations between Customer Service AP scales and supervisor ratings for 52 new hires. Supervisors rated new hires on seven dimensions of performance after 2 months on the job. Correlations ranged from -.46 to +.62, and out of 126, 50 were nonsignificant. Of the remaining 76 correlations, most were predictable, but there were a few surprises. For example, the correlation between the Customer Service AP scale Cooperativeness and employer ratings on Initiative was -.45. The employer rating for Cold Calling also had a negative correlation with Cooperativeness ($r = -.46$). Other surprises were not so much related to the absolute magnitude of the correlation but to the relative magnitude. For example, the best predictor of employer ratings of Diplomacy was not Personal Diplomacy ($r = .35$) but Achievement ($r = .47$), followed by Sales Disposition and Initiative-General ($r = .43$), followed by Initiative-Cold Calling ($r = .42$), Competitiveness ($r = .40$), and Managerial ($r = .39$). Customer Service Personal Diplomacy tied for seventh place with Sales Closing as a predictor of Diplomacy. Thirteen of the 18 scales correlated significantly and positively with Overall Sales Performance, 4 had insignificant correlations, and 1 (Cooperativeness) correlated negatively. Interestingly, this scale correlated negatively with every dimension of supervisor ratings.

COMMENTARY. The 140 statements, although reasonable looking, are a bit of a mystery. Specifically, although the authors are no doubt experts in their field, they do not discuss in any detail in the Customer Service AP employers' guide their development and selection of the statements on which scores are based. The discussion in the SalesAP manual is quite brief, and although it mentions factor analyses and other analyses of a pool of over 600 items, no factor-analytic results or other psychometric data pertaining to item selection are presented. Beyond those omissions, reliability is fairly good to good, with most scales falling into the "good" range. Standardization involved a reasonable number of examinees, but their representativeness is not established.

Correlations with external criteria are fairly impressive, however. In general, scores on the Customer Service AP (or SalesAP) correlate well with supervisory ratings of sales performance. Apart from a few surprises, correlations were significant and in the expected direction. Nearly every scale predicted overall sales performance, which may be the primary goal of such an instrument.

SUMMARY. As noted above, the items of the Customer Service AP are identical to the items of the Sales AP. Moreover, the psychometric information contained in the Customer Service AP manual is also identical to the psychometric information contained in the manual for the SalesAP.

The scales are identical, the standardization sample was the same, and the tables are lifted directly from the SalesAP manual. Nowhere in the Customer Service employers' guide is there any acknowledgement that this test is identical to the SalesAP test, nor is there any attempt to differentiate between customer service and sales achievement. Given the differences between sales and customer service, did the authors empirically or otherwise derive scoring algorithms for the Customer Service AP that would be different from those for the SalesAP? The manual does not say. Given that no new validity studies are reported in the Customer Service AP employers' guide (indeed, there are actually fewer studies reported in the Customer Service AP manual than in the SalesAP manual), it seems unlikely that the scores for customer service are any different from the scores for sales performance. Thus, one is forced to ask, "Why does this instrument exist?" If there is a valid reason for having a customer service test, should it not be at least a little different from the sales achievement test? And if it is at least a little different, should there not be some documentation of those differences? The documentation for the Customer Service AP leaves a great many open questions as to the differential validity of the instrument.

REVIEWER'S REFERENCES

Bruner, G. C. (2001). [Review of the Sales Achievement Predictor]. In B. S. Plake & J. C. Impara (Eds.), *The fourteenth mental measurements yearbook* (pp. 1048–1049). Lincoln, NE: Buros Institute of Mental Measurements.

Cattell, R. B. (1986). The 16 Personality Factor Questionnaire (16PF). Champaign, IL: Institute for Personality and Ability Testing.

Friedland, J. G., Marcus, S. I., & Mandel, H. P. (1995). Sales Achievement Predictor (SalesAP). Los Angeles, CA: Western Psychological Services.

Roberts, B. W. (2001). [Review of the Sales Achievement Predictor]. In B. S. Plake & J. C. Impara (Eds.), *The fourteenth mental measurements yearbook* (pp. 1049–1051). Lincoln, NE: Buros Institute of Mental Measurements.

Review of the Customer Service Aptitude Profile by CLEBORNE D. MADDUX, Foundation Professor of Counseling and Educational Psychology, University of Nevada, Reno, Reno, NV:

DESCRIPTION. The Customer Service Aptitude Profile (Customer Service AP) is an adaptation of the Sales Achievement Predictor (SalesAP; Friedland, Marcus, & Mandel, 1995). It is intended to help employers make better decisions about the hiring, training, and placement of personnel in customer service and customer service-related jobs. The instrument is intended for use with both applicants and existing employees, although the employers' guide (p. 2) cautions that results of the instrument should never be the sole source of information used in making personnel decisions. The guide suggests that results can be useful in creating development programs for customer service employees as well as for providing additional information to assist in hiring decisions.

The Customer Service AP is untimed, usually requires 20 to 25 minutes for administration, and "should be used by human resource specialists, psychologists, or trained individuals under their direct supervision" (employees' guide, p. 2). The instrument is group administered in paper-and-pencil format or it can be computer administered through use of a furnished CD and USB key good for 10 administrations. The Customer Service AP is intended for use with individuals 15 years of age or older.

The instrument consists of 140 brief, self-descriptive statements with a 5-point Likert-style response format (1 = *always true*, 2 = *mostly true*, 3 = *sometimes true and sometimes false*, 4 = *mostly false*, 5 = *always false*). Items are written at a sixth-grade reading level and may be read to individuals with visual impairments. Assistance in marking responses can be provided to individuals with motor impairments.

Manual scoring is not an option. Automatic scoring is carried out by software on the CD, although FAX answer sheets and a FAX service account can also be obtained from the publisher for remote scoring. [Editor's Note: The publisher advises the FAX service account will be phased out as of April 2013.]

An individual, multipage profile called a Customer Service AP Test Report is generated by the software found on the CD. Responses to individual items and demographic data are either typed in by the administrator after a paper-and-pencil administration, or imported automatically from a computer administration.

At the top of the Test Report, the computer software generates a specific recommendation about the individual's suitability for customer service. The respondent is identified as "highly recommended for a customer service role," "basically recommended for a customer service role," or "not recommended for a customer service role" (employers' guide, p. 13).

The Customer Service AP provides 21 scaled scores, 18 of which are grouped into five Response Style Indexes (Sales Success, Motivation and Achievement, Work Strengths, Interpersonal Strengths, and Inner Resources). The other 3 scaled scores are Validity and Response Style scales that "represent the individual's level of attention to the meaning of Customer Service AP statements (Inconsistent Responding) and tendency toward positive (Self-Enhancing) or negative (Self-Critical) self-presentation" (employers' guide, p. 4). The Self-Enhancing and Self-Critical scores are used to adjust percentile ranks for those individuals who present themselves in an overly positive or negative light, although no information is provided on exactly how these items are used to adjust scores. The employers' guide simply states that "Hundreds of rules are used to determine whether to adjust percentile scores, and by how much, based on a person's response style" (p. 1). The Inconsistent Responding score is used to inform administrators either that the person has responded (a) in a haphazard or inconsistent manner or without attending to item content, or (b) consistently and without unusual emphasis on positive or negative responses.

The 18 scaled scores are presented on the Test Report as both adjusted and unadjusted percentile ranks. There is no information on the scores from which these percentile ranks were generated. The manual states that "The technical characteristics of the scores used to generate the Customer Service AP TEST REPORT™ are fully presented in the SalesAP Manual" (employers' guide, p. 17). The SalesAP is the Sales Achievement Predictor (Friedland, Marcus, & Mandel, 1995) from which the Customer Service AP was developed. The manual for this latter instrument is available from the same publisher at an additional cost of $60.50.

Scores in the form of percentile ranks are presented on the Test Report in bar graph format with each of the 18 bars color coded as (a) low or very low, (b) average, or (c) high or very high. It is important to note that although both adjusted and unadjusted percentile ranks are listed on the report, the bar graph is a visual display only of the adjusted percentile ranks.

The profile then presents a computer-generated interpretive narrative with the following headings, each of which includes three to five paragraphs tailored to the individual's performance: (a) Validity and Response Style, (b) Customer Service and Inside Sales Characteristics, (c) Sales Success Characteristics, (d) Motivation and Achievement Characteristics, (e) Work Strengths, (f) Interpersonal Strengths, (g) Inner Resources, (h) Additional Profile Characteristics, and (i) Career Interest Areas. No information is provided on how the interpretive comments are generated.

The profile also provides a list of the respondent's Likert-style answers to each of the 140 questions. After this section, the Test Report contains several pages devoted to Customer Service Achievement Recommendations. This is a computer-generated list of practical suggestions in narrative format to help the individual improve his or her customer performance, and this section of the report can be removed and given to the respondent, if desired.

The instrument is furnished with the CD, an employers' guide booklet, and 100 PC answer sheets. The CD contains the software needed for computer administration and a user's guide, which contains information on how to use the CD.

DEVELOPMENT. The Customer Service AP is an adaptation of the Sales Achievement Predictor (SalesAP; Friedland, Marcus, & Mandel, 1995). No information is provided on the specifics of development.

TECHNICAL.

Standardization. Very little technical information is provided, and readers interested in technical information are referred to the manual for another instrument (at additional cost), from which the Customer Service AP was developed. The Customer Service AP employers' guide contains only six paragraphs of text and several tables related to psychometric background. The guide states that the reference sample included 1,375 male and female working adults and job applicants who were 15 years of age and older. No further information is provided about how they were selected and very little demographic information is provided.

Reliability. Internal consistencies for the 18 scales and test-retest reliabilities for 20 of the scales are presented in table format. No information is presented on how these were calculated except to assert they were based on scores of a subgroup of 745 individuals from the reference sample. Internal consistency coefficients are acceptable and in the range from .66 to .88. Test-retest reliability estimates are for 36 individuals who were retested after 1 year and range from .67 to .90. No information is given on how these individuals were selected and no demographics are provided.

Validity. The guide also presents a table of correlations between the scale scores and the 16 Personality Factor Questionnaire (16PF; Cattell, 1986) based upon a sample of 377 individuals. These correlations provide some limited evidence for criterion-related validation. Evidence for predictive validity is in the form of a table of correlations among the 18 scaled scores of the Customer Service AP for 52 job applicants and the performance ratings of their supervisors made 2 months after they were hired. It is difficult to interpret these correlations because insufficient details are supplied.

COMMENTARY. The Customer Service AP is a brief instrument that can be administered in paper-and-pencil format or administered by computer using the software on the supplied CD. It is intended for use with individuals 15 years of age or older to measure "characteristics related to customer service potential and performance, such as diplomacy, cooperativeness, patience, and assertiveness" (employers' guide, p. 1). The instrument consists of 140 brief, self-descriptive statements, each of which is responded to by means of a 5-point, Likert-style scale. Scoring is automatic through use of the computer software or, alternatively, through use of optional FAX answer sheets.

The instrument is quick and easy to administer and the software is intuitive and easy to use. The computer-generated profile is detailed and written in easy-to-understand language that can be shared with respondents. Scores furnished are adjusted and unadjusted percentile ranks and both are shown on the profile. Unfortunately, only the adjusted percentile ranks are shown in bar graph format. This is a problem because no details are available on which information is used or how it is used in adjusting these percentile ranks.

The major problem with the instrument is the absence of technical details. No standardization data are given with the exception of the number of cases in the reference sample (1,375). No details are given concerning how the percentile ranks are derived and readers who want additional technical data about the items or scores are instructed to purchase the manual of another test, available for an additional $60.50. Although percentile ranks are easy for lay people to understand, they are statistical dead ends and standard scores should also be made available. Reliability and validity data are scanty and difficult to evaluate because scant demographics or other details are presented concerning the samples used to produce reliability and validity data. The incomplete data on predictive validity in which Customer Service AP scores were correlated with the ratings of supervisors given 2 months after hiring of applicants is potentially useful, but is rendered uninterpretable due to the absence of details about these applicants and supervisors including who they were, how they were chosen, and how the ratings were done.

SUMMARY. The Customer Service AP was developed to provide employers with information about applicants' and current employees' characteristics related to customer service potential and performance. It is a promising instrument that is quick and easy to administer and comes with software that is intuitive and easy to use. The computer-generated Test Report is detailed and written in text that lay people can understand. Weaknesses include the fact that the only scores produced are adjusted and unadjusted percentile ranks, the bar graphs are visual representations of only the adjusted percentile ranks, no details are made available on how the adjustments are made, and technical data on instrument standardization, reliability, and validity are missing or incomplete. The technical basis of the instrument may be sound, but cannot be fairly evaluated by reference to the data provided. Because of these weaknesses, the Customer Service AP must be considered an experimental instrument with mostly unknown reliability and validity.

REVIEWER'S REFERENCES
Cattell, R. B. (1986). The 16 Personality Factor Questionnaire (16PF). Champaign, IL: Institute for Personality and Ability Testing.
Friedland, J. G., Marcus, S. I., & Mandel, H. P. (1995). Sales Achievement Predictor (SalesAP). Los Angeles, CA: Western Psychological Services.

[47]

Customer Service Profile.

Purpose: Designed to "assess whether a test-taker's skills and personality traits match those required to work in the customer service field."

Population: Under age 17 through adult.

Publication Date: 2011.

Acronym: CSP.

Scores, 20: Soft Skills (Communication Skills, Conflict Resolution, Social Skills, Patience, Self-Control, Hostility, Negative Reaction to Intimidation, Negative Reaction to Criticism), Psychological Strength (Coping Skills, Positive Attitude, Mental Toughness, Perspective), Work Habits (Organizational Skills, Conscientiousness, Self-Motivation), Impression Management, Overall Score.

Administration: Individual.

Price Data: Available from publisher.

Time: (30) minutes.

Comments: Self-administered online assessment. The test publisher advises that the test manual is being updated to include more information about methodology and theoretical background used in the development of the test. The test publisher also advises that this information is available to clients, as are benchmarks for relevant industries and racial/ethnic group comparison data. However, this information was not provided to Buros or the reviewers.

Author: PsychTests AIM, Inc.

Publisher: PsychTests AIM, Inc. [Canada].

Review of the Customer Service Profile by
*NEETA KANTAMNENI, Assistant Professor, and
TARA LAYMON, Doctoral Student, Counseling
Psychology Program, Department of Educational Psychology, University of Nebraska-Lincoln, Lincoln, NE:*

DESCRIPTION. The Customer Service
Profile is a 74-item self-report instrument designed
to screen applicants for work in customer service.
The purpose of this instrument is to "assess whether
a test taker's skills and personality traits match those
required to work in the Customer Service field"
(manual, p. 1). The CSP is administered online and
takes approximately 30 minutes to complete. Items
are either situational, requiring the test taker to
select from a variety of responses to a scenario, or
self-assessment, requiring the test-taker to rate how
well statements align with their self-perceptions.

The CSP includes three scales, 15 subscales,
an Impression Management Score, and an Overall
Score. The description of the scales are as follows:
Soft Skills assesses how an individual handles
social situations, Psychological Strength measures
an individual's ability to cope with common work
stressors, and Work Habits assesses an individual's
work ethics and ability to work efficiently. The Soft
Skills scale is composed of eight subscales including Communication Skills, Conflict Resolution,
Social Skills, Patience, Self-Control, Hostility,
Negative Reaction to Intimidation, and Negative
Reaction to Criticism. The Psychological Strength
scale comprises four subscales including Coping
Skills, Positive Attitude, Mental Toughness, and
Perspective. The Work Habits scale is composed
of three subscales including Organizational Skills,
Conscientiousness, and Self-Motivation. Finally,
an Impression Management score is provided to
assess whether items are responded to in a socially
desirable manner.

Once a test is completed, a report provides
scores on the overall test and on each scale and
subscale. Scores appear to range from 0 to 100,
with higher scores corresponding to greater skills
and/or abilities in each specific area. The test report provides an introduction to the test results,
an overall recommendation of suitability for a
career in customer service, brief descriptions of the
results for each of the scales and subscales, a list
of strengths and limitations based on scores, and
generic advice and tips to improve customer service
skills. It is important to note that not all scales and
subscales described above were clearly identified in
the manual. The Work Habits construct was not

defined in the manual, the Work Habits scale and
Organizational Skills subscale were omitted from
the description of scales, and no rationale was
provided for assessing Impression Management.

DEVELOPMENT. The CSP manual did
not provide information about test development or
construction, and the assessment does not appear
to be grounded within a theoretical framework.
Considering that no information was provided
about item construction, it is not apparent how
constructs were defined, how scales and subscales
were formed, and how items were developed to
measure constructs. Although the test report and
manual define scales and subscales, these definitions are not presented within a theory of customer
service. Further, many of the skills assessed within
the CSP are useful and necessary in a broad range
of employment fields.

TECHNICAL. The standardization sample
for the CSP consisted of 1,397 participants (58%
women, 27% men, and 15% of unknown gender)
who self-selected to take the instrument online. The
sample is described as uncontrolled. Participants
ranged from below 17 to over 50. The mean score
for each scale for the standardization sample was as
follows: 71.43 (*SD* = 13.61) for the Overall Score,
71.13 (*SD* = 15.04) for the Soft Skills scale, 75.10
(*SD* = 14.11) for the Psychological Strength scale,
and 72.65 (*SD* = 15.63) for the Work Habits scale.
Graphical representations of frequency distributions showed a positive skew for all of the scales.
Frequency distributions also displayed a positive
skew for each of the subscales with the exception
of Hostility, Negative Reaction to Intimidation,
Negative Reaction to Criticism, and Impression
Management, which displayed negative skews.

Reliability. The coefficient alpha values for the
standardization sample for the Overall Score and
the three primary scales ranged from .84 (Work
Habits) to .96 (Overall Score), representing high
internal consistency. Five of the subscales and the
Impression Management scale achieved coefficient
alpha values of .70 or higher; nine of the remaining 10 subscales were above .60. The Self-Control
subscale had the lowest coefficient alpha value at
.57. Other tests of reliability (i.e. split-half reliability,
test-retest) were not included in the manual.

Validity. Evidence for validity of the CSP
consisted of examining differences on scales and
subscales across gender, age, education, academic
grades, satisfaction with current field, performance
in current field, and experience in customer service

fields. Women scored significantly higher than men on the Work Habits scale and the Perspective and Organizational Skills subscales whereas men scored significantly higher on the Mental Toughness subscale. However, some of the *p*-values were reported simply as "less than 0.05"; it is questionable to use this level for hypothesis testing because of the large size of the data set.

Younger examinees (below 17 and 18 to 24 years) generally scored significantly lower than older examinees on the Soft Skills scale, the Psychological Strength scale, and the Work Habits scale as well as on many of the subscales. Individuals with the lowest level of education (some high school) scored significantly lower on the Overall Score and the three scales when compared with individuals with higher education levels. Participants who reported below average to average grades were outscored in several areas by the higher academic achievement groups. Similar results were found with participants who rated themselves as "average" in their current field when compared with those who rated themselves as "above average." Additionally, participants who rated themselves as "not very satisfied" with their current field scored significantly lower on the three scales and several subscales than those who identified themselves as "somewhat satisfied" and "very satisfied." Finally, participants who did not have previous experience in customer service were outscored on the overall test, the three scales, and many of the subscales by participants who had experience.

COMMENTARY. The purpose of the CSP is to measure 15 different dimensions of customer service skills. The assessment ambitiously tries to examine skills required to be successful in the customer service field, but several concerns arose when examining this test. First, it is unclear how the test items were developed and whether there is any theoretical framework grounding the test. This information is critical to ensuring that the test is measuring skills specifically necessary to be successful in the customer service field. Additionally, it does not appear that many of the scales and items differentiate between success in customer service and success in other types of employment. This combined with the fact that no information is provided on test construction and item development makes it difficult to establish content and construct evidence of validity for this test.

Validity was examined solely by comparing scales and subscales across gender, age, education, academic grades, job satisfaction, work performance, and customer service experience. This research was conducted perhaps to establish criterion-based evidence of validity; however, the authors do not provide a rationale for why these variables are expected to be related to customer service skills. It is unclear why performance in and satisfaction with an individual's current employment is related to customer service skills, particularly if an individual is employed in work that requires little to no customer interaction. Further, the gender differences found on some of the subscales may provide evidence that the test may contain some gender bias. Additionally, a clear rationale was not provided as to why Impression Management is measured within this test.

Information is missing regarding how participants included in the standardization sample were recruited, leaving open the possibility of sampling bias. Further, more demographic information is needed on this sample such as participants' race/ethnicity. Reliability estimates for the overall test and the three primary scales appear to be very high, suggesting that items on these scales are internally consistent. However, the internal consistency reliability estimates for some of the subscales are low, bringing into question whether these subscales are consistently examining the construct of interest. This finding would not be problematic if the test focused solely on the overall test score and the three primary scales. However, detailed explanations of a test taker's results on each of the subscales are provided in the test report, despite the low reliability of some subscales. Further, test-retest reliability was not examined. This lack is a shortcoming, because consistency over time is both necessary and relevant when assessing for customer service skills. Finally, no information was provided in the manual about how test scores are evaluated and how the test report is compiled. It is imperative that the manual discuss how responses are scored and what means are being used to evaluate a test taker's responses.

SUMMARY. The CSP is a multidimensional assessment intended to measure effective customer service skills and traits. The instrument is user-friendly and administered online. Test takers completing the CSP are provided with a detailed overview of their skills in these 15 areas along with a description of their suitability for employment within the customer service field. More research is needed to determine clearly the validity of the measure as detailed information about a theoretical framework, test development, and the standardization sample is not provided. Further validation studies also are needed to ensure that the CSP is comprehensively measuring customer service skills.

Review of the Customer Service Profile by M. DAVID MILLER, Professor of Research and Evaluation Methods, University of Florida, Gainesville, FL:

DESCRIPTION. The Customer Service Profile (CSP) is an online measure of skills and personality traits needed to work in the field of customer service. In assessing the match between job requirements and the skills and personality traits of an examinee, the assessment is designed to assist human resource testing for screening and training. The assessment consists of 96 situational and self-assessment items (the Psychometric Report says "74, plus additional questions" [p. 1]). The items use a mixture of multiple-choice and Likert formats.

The CSP reports a general score, three subfactors, and 15 subscales. The three subfactors are Soft Skills, Psychological Strength, and Work Habits. Soft Skills measures the ability of the examinee to handle social situations and includes the following skills (subscales): Communication Skills, Conflict Resolution, Social Skills, Patience, Self-Control, Hostility, Negative Reaction to Intimidation, and Negative Reaction to Criticism. Psychological Strength measures the ability of the examinee to cope with the daily hassles of a job and includes the following skills (subscales): Coping Skills, Positive Attitude, Mental Toughness, and Perspective. Work Habits measures the ability of examinees to comport themselves in the workplace and to complete tasks in a productive, thorough, and efficient manner, and includes the following skills (subscales): Organizational Skills, Conscientiousness, and Self-Motivation. In addition, Impression Management assesses the tendency of an examinee to provide socially desirable responses on the assessment.

DEVELOPMENT. No information is provided in the Psychometric Report nor on the website about the development of the CSP. The basis for content selection does not appear to be linked to any specific theories or underlying assumptions. No pilot testing is reported.

TECHNICAL. Limited information is reported about the technical properties of the assessment. The Psychometric Report includes descriptive statistics for the sample characteristics, descriptive statistics for the assessment, descriptive statistics for the assessment by selected grouping variables, and coefficient alpha indices of reliability.

Norms are not provided, and the population of examinees is not defined. However, descriptive statistics for the general score, three subfactors, and 15 subscales are provided. The sample is based on 1,397 examinees who have taken the CSP at one of three websites. As described in the Psychometric Report, the sample was "uncontrolled" and based on self-selection. Thus, the data are based on a convenience sample that may not represent any known population. The sample was 58% female, 27% male, and 15% of unknown gender. The age distribution was reported in categories from "below 17" to "50+" with the 18–24-year age group representing the mode (24.0%). Means and standard deviations are reported for each of the scores. The full distributions are not reported nor are any standards reported for making decisions about screening or training. Thus, the descriptive data do not provide a basis for making decisions or for using the assessment in screening or training.

Coefficient alpha values are reported for the Overall Score (.96), the three subfactors, the 15 subscales, and Impression Management. The internal consistency is high for the Overall Score and the three subfactors (.84–.94). However, there is a wide range in the reliability estimates for the 15 subscales (.57–.83). Ten of the 15 subscales had internal consistency estimates below .70 suggesting that, with a few exceptions, score uses and interpretations should be limited to the Overall Score and the subfactors.

Because the intent of the CSP is to examine the match between job requirements and the skills and personality traits of examinees, validity evidence should focus on interpretations and uses linked to the match of the job and the person's skills and traits. Thus, one should provide content evidence that shows the assessment matches job requirements for specific jobs and provide empirical evidence of the relationship between job performance and the assessment. Neither type of evidence is reported for the CSP. No description of the content of the CSP is provided regarding test development, including test specifications, nor is evidence provided through expert review of the content. Thus, potential test users do not have validity evidence based on the content of the CSP that supports the uses and interpretations described for the assessment.

The limited validity evidence reported examines the relationship between test scores and performance in the field and experience in the field. Performance in the current field is based on a self-report, and significance tests were conducted to compare examinees who rated their own performance as good ($n = 310$) with those who rated their performance as average ($n = 310$). The actual employment fields for the examinees are not reported. Examinees who rated their performance as good scored significantly higher on the Overall Score, the three subfactors, and 12 of the 15 subscales than examinees who rated their performance as average. Experience in the customer service field compared 75 examinees with experience with 75 examinees without experience. Similar to the performance results, examinees with experience in the customer service field scored significantly higher than examinees without experience on the Overall Score, the three subfactors, and 12 of the 15 subscales. Similar analyses and results are reported for examinees' level of general satisfaction with their current field.

In addition, significance tests were conducted to compare test results by gender, age, education, and grades. Although the results are reported, no interpretation of the results is provided. Consequently, it is difficult to understand whether a significant difference is expected and provides additional validity evidence or is a potential source of bias. For example, the only significant gender differences were on the Work Habits subfactor and three of the subscales. It is not clear whether the difference is expected (i.e., Work Habits should be higher for women) or is a potential source of bias (i.e., use of the Work Habits subfactor favors females unfairly). This finding is further confounded by the use of an uncontrolled sample that selected to complete the assessment and the extra items.

COMMENTARY. The CSP was developed to provide an assessment that shows the match between skills and personality traits of examinees and the job requirements in the field of customer service. The Psychometric Report and the publisher's website fail to provide a description of the process that was used to develop the instrument. Consequently, the validity of the assessment for screening or training is questionable. A solid foundation needs to be established (i.e., developed or reported) that includes a theoretical basis for the constructs being measured, content specifications, and their links to specific job requirements. The *Standards for Educational and Psychological Testing* (AERA, APA, & NCME, 1999) recognize validity as the most important issue in test use. Two primary types of evidence that should be reported with a screening assessment are evidence based on content and evidence based on relationships with job performance. The CSP does not provide any evidence based on content, and the evidence based on relationships with job performance is quite weak. Other instruments have used measures of job performance that are not self-report. The validity of the self-report measures for this use is questionable, and the range of options (good or average) does not show the full range of possible job performance. In addition, it is unknown what jobs are being included for those participating in the ratings for the job performance item. Thus, the validity evidence needs to be strengthened before any uses or interpretations could be justified for the assessment.

Decisions about screening and training also require a clearly defined standard. No standard-setting procedure has been reported for the CSP. Thus, the cutoffs for any decisions are questionable. The cutoffs also are not based on estimates from the population distribution because norms have not been established. The distributions that have been reported for the CSP are presented as graphs only and are not based on a defined population nor any rigorous sampling framework. The sample is clearly problematic for interpreting scores because it is self-selected.

SUMMARY. The CSP was developed to measure skills and personality traits of examinees for their match to job requirements in the field of customer service. Although the content of the CSP appears to measure the constructs defined for the assessment, there is not documented or rigorous evidence regarding the content of the assessment. Reliability is high for the Overall Score and the three subfactors: Soft Skills, Psychological Strength, and Work Habits. Reliability is not as high for the shorter subscales, and caution should be exercised in their use. Validity evidence showing the relationship between the CSP and job performance is based on self-report. Consequently, the validity evidence for the CSP is not sufficient for any use or interpretation with stakes as high as job screening.

REVIEWER'S REFERENCE

American Educational Research Association, American Psychological Association, & National Council on Measurement in Education. (1999). *Standards for educational and psychological testing.* Washington, DC: American Educational Research Association.

[48]

Decoding and Spelling Proficiency Test-Revised.

Purpose: Designed to provide "a detailed profile of crucial literacy skills that underlie reading and spelling."

Population: Ages 6-25.
Publication Dates: 1982-2010.
Acronym: DSPT-R.
Scores, 4: Decoding, Visual Recognition, Auditory-Visual Recognition, Spelling.
Administration: Group.
Forms, 2: Parallel Forms A and B.
Price Data, 2010: $139 per test kit including manual (2010, 219 pages), 25 record Forms A, 25 record Forms B, 25 test booklets Form A, and 25 test booklets Form B; $49 per manual.
Time: (25-40) minutes.
Comments: "The current version…is a revision of the Diagnostic Spelling Potential test"; the four parts can be administered separately or in conjunction with one another.
Authors: Michael Milone and John Arena.
Publisher: Academic Therapy Publications.
Cross References: For information regarding the Diagnostic Spelling Potential Test, see T4:790 (1 reference); for reviews by Marcee J. Meyers and Ruth Noyce of the Diagnostic Spelling Potential Test, see 9:345 (1 reference).

Review of the Decoding and Spelling Proficiency Test– Revised by TIMOTHY SHANAHAN, Professor of Urban Education, University of Illinois at Chicago, Chicago, IL:

DESCRIPTION. The Decoding and Spelling Proficiency Test–Revised (DSPT-R) includes an individually administered test of oral word reading or decoding, and an individually or group-administered test of printed word recognition and spelling for use with children and young adults, ages 6-6 to 25. There are two forms of the test, and each includes four parts: Decoding, Visual Recognition, Auditory-Visual Recognition, and Spelling from Dictation. Each section includes 90 items, and students are routed through these on the basis of their ability level; administration of the four-test battery usually takes between 25–40 minutes.

The decoding test provides a list of 90 printed words arranged in order of difficulty, and students are asked to read these words aloud. Words the examinee can name correctly within 2 seconds are designated as sight words, and those that take longer or with which the examinee has some difficulty are classified as having been decoded phonetically. Because the words are read in a list, and thus, without context, they represent students' ability to either read words from memory or through decoding. Students begin the test at a point determined by grade level and continue until they get 5 consecutive items incorrect.

The Visual Recognition section of the DSPT-R is a measure of how well students recognize the correct spelling of words; the words are not read to the students. Again, there are 90 items–arrayed in order of difficulty, and each item includes four versions of a word's spelling; one spelling is correct, and the other three usually include misspellings that if sounded out would lead to a correct pronunciation (thus, for a word like *greet*, the distractors might be *grete, greit, gret*). Again, there are grade-level-determined starting points, and for this test examinees are given 15 minutes to find as many correct spellings as they can.

The Auditory-Visual Recognition test examines the ability to find the correctly spelled version of a word that has been named by the examiner. The items are the same as those included in the Visual Recognition test. Finally, the Spelling test includes a series of lines on which the examinees are to write words that are dictated to them by the examiner.

The test administration is scripted, and the examiner must monitor student performance along the way to determine basal and ceiling levels, and to know when to discontinue testing. For group administration, all students begin and end at the same level, with starting point determined by grade level. All instructions are given orally. There is no overall test score, but scores are derived from each of the four tests that are included in the battery. Each test results in a raw score, standard score, and percentile rank. Some further analysis is possible, such as comparing the ratio of sight words and phonetically decoded words in the word reading test or comparing the Decoding and Spelling test scores. There are age-level norms for some of these comparisons, and there are criterion-referenced interpretations associated with particular performance levels (such as students who score at the 10th percentile or less are considered to be at "high risk for learning difficulties" [manual, p. 65] and might require further testing).

DEVELOPMENT. The original version of the DSPT was published in 1982, and was renamed to better reflect the test content. Many of the original words were retained, though some were adjusted to better match contemporary usage. A pilot study was conducted with 88 students (ages 7–14) to determine the appropriateness of the item difficulties and formats, and this study was followed by a re-norming study to standardize the test. An item analysis was conducted with the norming data to adjust the order of the items, ensuring that the easiest items come first.

TECHNICAL. The DSPT-R was administered to 1,409 children and young adults (ages 6–6 to 20+). Standardization testing took place across 16 states. The characteristics of the norming sample are compared to U.S. demographics in terms of gender, race/ethnicity, and region.

Coefficient alpha was used to estimate internal consistency for both forms of each section and for each age-level sample. These coefficients ranged from .75 to .99, with most values above .90. Not surprisingly, the alpha coefficients for the performance tests (Word Reading and Spelling) were higher than for the multiple-choice tests, which permitted guessing. When alphas were averaged across age levels for each form of each test, none was lower than .94.

Test-retest reliabilities were calculated with an average interval between testing sessions of 20 days using a sample of 79 examinees. Coefficients ranged from .65 to .66 for the multiple-choice tests and from .82 to .86 for the performance items that require students to read and spell words. There was also a study of 42 examinees to consider alternate forms equivalence. The correlation coefficients between the two forms of each test ranged from .71 to .97. Alternate form equivalence is the most conservative test of reliability, and these coefficients indicate that these tests could be used as pre- and post-measures. Standard errors of measurement (*SEM*) are provided for each of the forms of the four tests for each age-level group. Some of these are fairly small, such as for the Word Reading test (Form A, average *SEM* = 3.03), which would permit useful comparisons even at the 95% confidence interval, whereas others were large, such as for the Auditory-Visual Recognition test (Form A, average *SEM* = 5.21).

Validity evidence for the DSPT-R test scores was shown through an examination of the relationship of performance to age level, with older students outperforming younger ones. The biggest difference in this pattern was for the younger students, as expected, because these are the years in which normally developing word reading and spelling skills are most rapid. The DSPT-R was also found to be moderately related to measures of cognitive ability, and exceptional groups, including samples of learning-disabled students, underperformed the normative group. Finally, factor analysis confirmed that the tests appear to be similar and related, but with no single overarching construct. No concurrent validity studies were conducted with other decoding or spelling measures.

COMMENTARY. The structure of the DSPT-R addresses four related aspects of word knowledge: Students are asked to read words aloud, to distinguish appropriately spelled words from phonetically plausible yet incorrect spellings, to do so again with the words pronounced for them, and, finally, to spell words based on dictation. It is clear that the oral word reading or decoding measures provide useful information about student performance (we do care whether students can read or spell words), but it is less clear what the other two tests provide. Although the idea of testing whether students can recognize correct spellings is appealing, it is not clear that meaningful differences in performance are revealed by having the examiner read these words aloud. Performance differences between these two measures do not suggest one to be harder than the other, and given the relatively large *SEM*s for these tests, most comparisons would not be expected to tell much about student abilities; the factor analysis is not persuasive in this regard either. Given this limitation, and that the four tests are separate, the visual-auditory recognition test might be a candidate for exclusion.

The spiral-bound test manual combines administration information with technical information about the psychometrics of the instrument. This format is somewhat confusing. The directions for each test include scripted directions that the examiner is to say, along with various asides and directions to the examiner, all printed in bold and embedded within a larger narrative related to administration, making it hard to find the appropriate information at the right time. Some of the directions were unclear, such as the guidance for how to take students through the word reading test in a way that would allow sight word and decoding performance to be distinguished, and some of the preparation information would have been useful to have when administering the test.

Finally, it is not clear how one would use the individual test scores. If students score low in decoding or spelling, the test manual suggests teaching these skills, which seems self-evident. The guidance for use of the other tests seem more questionable, such as the suggestion that students who perform better on the Visual Recognition test than on the Auditory-Visual Recognition test may have a learning disability. Such interpretations are provided without any justifying evidence.

SUMMARY. The DSPT-R was designed to identify word reading and spelling abilities for students from first grade through early adulthood. Data suggest that older students do better than younger students on these tests and that individuals with learning disabilities perform less well than the normative average; nevertheless, there are no criterion validity studies comparing test scores with other measures of the same constructs. The Word Reading and Spelling tests have high reliabilities and would presumably compare well with other similar measures; the Visual and Visual-Auditory Recognition tests are not as reliable and the interpretations of the results of these measures seem questionable.

Review of the Decoding and Spelling Proficiency Test–Revised by KAY B. STEVENS, Associate Professor, Texas Christian University, Fort Worth, TX:

DESCRIPTION. The Decoding and Spelling Proficiency Test–Revised (DSPT-R) is a revision of the Diagnostic Spelling Potential Test (1982). The stated purpose is to give parents and professionals a "reliable and valid measure of a learner's ability to decode words, recognize correctly spelled words, and encode words correctly" (manual, p. 10) as a basis for remedial measures if necessary. The DSPT-R is norm-referenced and consists of four independent 90-item parts. The test includes no subtests but rather parts that stand alone. The norming population included 1,409 individuals ages 6-6 to 25 years. Two parallel forms are provided. Administration time is 30–45 minutes. The four parts include: (1) Decoding–orally read words of increasing difficulty from a list; (2) Visual Recognition–identify the correctly spelled word from four different phonetically plausible spellings of the word; (3) Auditory-Visual Recognition–same as Part 2 except an oral prompt is given to the examinee; and (4) Spelling–write individually dictated words of increasing difficulty.

Recommended starting points and basal-ceiling rules are provided for Parts 1, 3, and 4. For Part 2, students complete as many items as possible in 15 minutes. Instructions are clearly written; however, instructions to examinees are embedded in other narrative and difficult to find. Scoring for Parts 2, 3, and 4 is straightforward; the sum of correct responses equals the raw scores. Part 1 scoring is less direct. The examiner records "S" when the word is read correctly within 2 seconds;

"P" if read correctly within 2 to 10 seconds, when examinee self-corrects, or reads the word correctly with inaccurate syllable emphasis; "I" if the word is not read correctly within 10 seconds. Both S and P responses are counted as equally correct when calculating raw scores. Raw scores are converted to standard scores, percentiles, and age equivalents.

DEVELOPMENT. The DSPT-R assesses two areas of academic content: decoding and spelling. Changes made in the revision include addition of contemporary instructional practices (not described), a new name, reordering of parts to reflect a more natural sequence of literacy learning, streamlined procedures (not described), and updated norms.

"Many" of the words (item content) were retained from the original DSPT, but "some" were changed. The basis for item retention and/or change is not addressed beyond mentioning that changes were made to reflect contemporary usage. According to reviews written by Blachman (1983) and Reynolds (1983), a substantial weakness of the original DSPT was out-of-date item content from sources over 30 years old. Because many words were retained, the problem of words from old references remains, and because no information regarding the selection of new words is provided, content analysis is absent.

A pilot study consisting of 88 students, ages 7 to 14 years, was conducted. The study's single purpose was to determine the appropriateness of item difficulty for all ages. Based on raw score means, data representing three groups (a) all ages, (b) ages 7-10, and (c) ages 11-14 document that item difficulty is appropriate. However, the data are poorly described, and the data table includes an ill-defined "age" column. In addition, ages of study participants do not match the normative sample. What is known about examinees above the age of 14 related to upper-item difficulty? Based on these data the test author stated, "further item development was deemed unnecessary and the norming study could proceed" (manual, p. 66). However, a pilot study designed to determine overall item difficulty that includes limited age sampling and no description of content selection does not meet standards for test development (AERA, APA, & NCME, 1999).

Minimal information is provided regarding the norming study. Data from the normative group were analyzed using the Classical Test Theory (CTT) with no clear description of procedures.

Final item selection consisted of ordering the items from easiest to most difficult. Correlations between item position and item difficulty by age are strong. Based on these analyses, "all of the items utilized in the norming study were retained in the final published edition" (manual, p. 68).

TECHNICAL. Demographic data from the normative group, including gender, ethnicity, parent education, regions, and metro (urban/suburban vs. rural), are compared to figures from the 2000 U.S. Census. Gender, parent education, four of six ethnicities, and two of four regions are well represented. Overrepresented are African Americans (28.5% vs. 11.1%), southern states (47.6% vs. 35.6%), and rural areas (53.7% vs. 21.1%). Underrepresented are Caucasians (48.6% vs. 72.1%), northeast states (4.3% vs. 19.1%), and urban/suburban areas (46.3% vs. 78.9%).

The test author states that for optimal performance, administration should be conducted individually, and instructions to examinees are clearly written for individualized testing. However, the normative data were collected from group administrations for Parts 2, 3, and 4, a clear departure from recommended standardization procedures (Anastasi & Urbina, 1997). If individual administration yields optimal performance, it would follow that the students in the normative group were not given the opportunity for optimal performance. Included in an appendix of the test manual are detailed procedures for group administration of the DSPT-R. These procedures differ from those described for individual testing in many ways, which begs the question, were the group administration procedures included in the test manual the same procedures under which the test was normed? If so, a more serious standardization problem exists. Anastasi and Urbina (1997) clearly state, "Follow standardized procedures to the most minute detail" (p. 15) during test administration.

Reliability estimates measures include internal consistency, test-retest, and alternate forms. Coefficient alpha and split-half reliability were computed on all members of the standardization group. Coefficients for test-retest reliability administered an average of 20 days apart resulted in high internal consistency for Decoding and Spelling, .82 and .86, respectively, and moderate consistency for the two spelling recognition parts, .66 and .65 for Visual and Auditory-Visual, respectively. Ranges for all four parts are .65 to .86. The test manual is inconsistent regarding the number of test-retest examinees. The

narrative reports 37 examinees, the data table 79, and the demographic table 21. Alternate form reliability coefficients ranged from .71 to .97. Standard errors of measurement and confidence intervals are presented in an easy-to-read table. Interrater reliability was not evaluated; however, based on the cumbersome scoring procedures on Part 1, it should have been.

The test manual states that validity evidence is presented in the form of content validity and construct validity. However, no data are presented in the validity section related to content validity or whether the test items adequately represent the spelling and decoding domains. The user is referred to the development section for "information relevant to content validity" (manual, p. 79); however, this section consists only of the aforementioned "pilot study" data and the correlations between item position and difficulty. Because content evidence begins with item selection to ensure that items represent the domain the test claims to measure, without detailed information regarding item selection, other reported validity studies are less meaningful.

The description of construct evidence is more complete, consisting of: (a) moderate correlations between chronological age and DSPT-R raw scores demonstrating that spelling proficiency improves with age; (b) factor analysis data revealing no single underlying construct for the DSPT-R, which constitutes evidence of the lack of construct evidence for a "spelling factor"; (c) significantly lower DSPT-R scores for LD and ADHD students than for typical students providing support for exceptional group differences; and (d) moderate correlations between WISC-IV FSIQ scores and DSPT-R standard scores, which is expected and consistent with those found in other studies of the relationship between academic achievement and intelligence. However, the test authors' explanation regarding the relationship between cognitive tests and tests that assess specific skills taught in the classroom is somewhat inexplicable. Also, data on the relationship between the DSPT-R scores and the WISC-IV Index scores should have been presented. The validity data provide only weak evidence of construct validity. What is most evident in the validity section of the DSPT-R manual is what is *not* presented. For example, the manual does not include adequate description of the content selection process or of content validity. Concurrent evidence in the form of correlations with existing spelling tests are absent.

COMMENTARY. The most impressive revision in the DSPT-R is a larger and more representative standardization sample; increased validity measures in the revision; the design of a well-organized, user-friendly test manual that is easy to understand; and attractive materials. A progress-monitoring section was added in an appendix describing how to design graphs and plot raw test data if using the DSPT-R content for instructional purposes. The DSPT-R seems most useful as a criterion-referenced test for professionals who find the content appropriate for their use.

Major technical problems including the absence of information regarding content selection and analysis, contradictory standardization procedures (Parts 2, 3, and 4 were normed with groups only but may be administered individually), and limited validity negate the meaningfulness of norm-referenced scores. The test author is encouraged to follow the guidelines from the *Standards for Educational and Psychological Testing* (AERA, APA, & NCME, 1999) if the DSPT-R is revised in the future.

Other technically sound norm-referenced tests assess decoding and written spelling using the same procedures as the DSPT-R (e.g., Wide Range Achievement Test-4, 18:157; Test of Written Spelling-4, 15:266). Consumers should select tests that provide detailed descriptions of all aspects of test development.

Parts 2 and 3 assess what amounts to proof reading skills using a multiple-choice format, which is rather artificial because detecting misspelled words is most often required in continuous text. Further, multiple-choice format is potentially confusing because all distractors are phonetically plausible, which is not the case in actual proof reading.

SUMMARY. The DSPT-R was designed to compare students' performance in decoding and spelling to that of a norm group for a better understanding of relative standing with peers and to provide diagnostic information regarding skill strengths and weaknesses in order to help pinpoint remedial procedures. Due to its technical inadequacies, the DSPT-R leaves much to be desired as a norm-referenced index. Other technically sound, well-established norm-referenced tests are available to assess decoding and written spelling.

REVIEWER'S REFERENCES
American Educational Research Association, American Psychological Association, & National Council on Measurement in Education. (1999). *Standards for educational and psychological testing.* Washington, DC: American Educational Research Association.
Anastasi, A., & Urbina, S. (1997). *Psychological testing* (7th ed.). Upper Saddle River, NJ: Prentice-Hall.

Blachman, B. A. (1983). Test review: Diagnostic Spelling Potential Test (DSPT). *Journal of Reading, 22,* 134-138.
Reynolds, C. R. (1983). Some new and some unusual psychological and educational measures: Description and evaluation. *School Psychology Review, 12,* 481-488.

[49]
Decoding-Encoding Screener for Dyslexia.

Purpose: Designed to "quickly assess a student's specific reading difficulties."
Population: Grades 1-8.
Publication Date: 2006.
Acronym: DESD.
Scores, 5: DESD Grade Level, Reading Raw Score, Reading Standard Score, Sight-Word Spelling Raw Score, Phonetic Spelling Raw Score.
Administration: Individual.
Price Data, 2013: $121 per kit including stimulus booklet, 100 spelling response forms, 100 record sheets, and manual (63 pages); $29 per stimulus booklet; $10.50 per 100 spelling response forms; $47.50 per 100 record sheets; $58 per manual.
Time: (5-10) minutes.
Authors: John R. Griffin, Howard N. Walton, and Garth N. Christenson.
Publisher: Western Psychological Services.

Review of the Decoding-Encoding Screener for Dyslexia by MILDRED MURRAY-WARD, Professor of Education, Retired, California State University, Stanislaus, Turlock, CA:

DESCRIPTION. According to the authors, the Decoding-Encoding Screener for Dyslexia (DESD) was developed by Griffin, Walton, and Christenson as a quick-screening version of the more comprehensive Dyslexia Determination Test 3rd Edition (2003). The DESD's purposes are to act as a quick screening device for decoding and encoding, to provide a norm-referenced measure of sight-word recognition and qualitative indicators of sight-word retrieval and phonetic processing, to evaluate students' tendencies to reverse letters, and to characterize specific skills a child brings to the act of reading (manual, p. 3). The DESD provides a tool to assist in addressing the needs of learning disabled students, specifically those with dyslexia (*Diagnostic and Statistical Manual of Mental Disorders, Fourth Edition* [DSM-IV], American Psychiatric Association, 1994). Designed for use with students in Grades 1 through 8, the DESD helps clinicians and other professionals who work with children who may have reading problems. The DESD also can be used in schools or clinics as a quick screening tool with gifted students who are not reading at expected levels. The test authors also state some limitations of the test: The DESD cannot provide a definitive diagnosis of dyslexia or identify neurological factors that may be associated with dyslexia and poor reading performance.

The DESD consists of three different types of tasks: Letter Writing (Letter Writing Test), Decoding (Reading Test), and Encoding (Sight-Word Spelling Test and Phonetic Spelling Test). Test scores include a Reading Standard Score based on a mean of 100 and standard deviation of 15. Additional scores involve a DESD Grade Level and qualitative measures of Word Skill Classification–Sight Word-Analysis and Phonetic Analysis. The theoretical foundations of the DESD are well documented in the test manual and are based on previous research on the DDT, the DSM-IV, and additional research studies about reading development.

The test kit contains a manual with administration, recording, and scoring procedures, score interpretation, clinical uses, theoretical framework, development, standardization, and validity and reliability studies. Testing involves use of the DESD stimulus booklet, spelling response form, and record sheet.

The DESD takes 5 to 10 minutes to administer individually. As stated above, it is appropriate for students in Grades 1 through 8. In addition, the test authors stipulate that the DESD is only appropriate for use with students who speak English as a second language if they are fluent in English and have had at least 2 years of formal schooling in reading and writing English.

DESD administration is straightforward, with guidelines provided for establishing starting points, basal levels, and reversal and discontinuation rules. In addition, administration guidance includes creating the test environment, seating, establishing rapport, and taking consideration of respondents' cultural and regional language differences. Examiners record raw scores on the spelling response form and on the record sheet.

Scoring involves several steps. For the Letter Writing Test (used in Grades 1 through 4 only), students write the letters of the alphabet on the back of the spelling form. The Reading Test requires students to read from a list of 55 phonetically irregular words. The words are organized into groups of five and labeled on the record sheet with DESD Grade Levels. The test manual provides detailed instructions on establishing basal and maximum score levels, calculating the Reading Raw Score, and converting the raw score to a standard score. In the Encoding Test, students complete the Sight-Word

Spelling Test and the Phonetic Spelling Test. In the Sight-Word test, the student is asked to spell the 5 most difficult words passed in the Reading Test. In addition, in the Phonetic Spelling Test, students are asked to phonetically spell 5 words above their highest reading Grade Level. Again, the test manual provides detailed instructions on administering the test, recording student responses, scoring, and interpretation. All of the scores collected above are recorded on the interpretative summary. Using the form, the examiner is then able to calculate the interpretative range (from markedly below normal to above normal) for the Reading Standard Score and the two spelling tests. To aid in the interpretation process, the test authors provided four case studies.

DEVELOPMENT. For the DESD, the test authors examined the research and clinical practice literature regarding the history and neuroanatomy of dyslexia and reading. The DESD (an earlier version was The Dyslexia Screener [TDS]) was created as a shortened version of the DDT for a longitudinal study in which it was not possible to use the longer DDT. However, the 55 words used on the DESD were not part of the original DDT. The origins and rationale for the nature of the three sections of the DESD and the resulting DESD are well described in the test development section; however, the rationale and criteria for the selection of the words used in the DESD were not provided. The selection, order, and grouping of the words were determined using clinical judgment, and the word order was later validated with scaling analysis studies.

TECHNICAL.

Standardization. The standardization sample consisted of 678 children in regular classrooms in elementary and middle schools, most in Southern California. The gender and race/ethnicity of the sample were compared to 2001 U.S. Census figures. Although the sample matched well with the Census figures for gender, the same was not true for ethnicity with oversampling of Asian, African American, and Hispanic/Latino students and undersampling of white students. The possible effect of sampling on the reading scores was explored using effect sizes and revealed that these effect sizes were quite small. Although the sample effects were small ones, an interpretation issue remains, in that no students with dyslexia or screened for dyslexia or other reading difficulties were identified in the standardization sample.

The development of the Reading Standard Score norms involved a regression-based smoothing procedure to establish predicted mean raw scores and standard deviations for each grade level. These means and standard deviations were used to create the norms.

Reliability. The test authors examined internal consistency and test-retest stability for the DESD. To explore the DESD's internal consistency, the authors used coefficient alpha by grade. The resulting coefficients were at .88 or higher for Grades 1 through 6, and at .69 and .66 for Grades 7 and 8. Standard errors of measurement ranged from 2.12 for Grade 1 to 1.44 for Grade 8. The lower alpha coefficients observed in Grades 7 and 8 may have been influenced by the smaller sample sizes and restricted score ranges (some students had nearly perfect scores). However, the test authors do not address how interpretation of scores for higher grade students should be handled in view of these resulting coefficients.

Test-retest reliability for the Reading Standard Score was examined using two studies, each with a 1-week interval. The resulting correlation coefficient was .76 for Grades 2–8 and .78 for Grades 3–4. The word analysis skills Spearman coefficients, with a 1-week interval, were .80 and .91 for the sight-word and phonetic classifications, respectively. Again, suggestions for interpretation in view of these coefficients were not provided.

Validity. The test authors examined validity through several construct and concurrent validity studies with other measures of reading. However, no studies involving predictions for referral for dyslexia were offered. In the first study, the test authors explored the evidence supporting the placement of words in the grade level lists using Rasch mean logits for the groups of five words in each level. The results indicated that the words were of a wide range of difficulties and ordered with ascending mean difficulties. In another set of studies, the Rasch difficulties were correlated with the *EDL Core Vocabularies* word grade level assignments, thus establishing the increasing difficulties of words on the lists.

In addition to the study above, the test authors explored the stability of score classifications (markedly below normal to above normal) by comparing the proportion of students in the DESD standardization sample classified as mildly below normal to markedly below normal with that of the general population. Comparison revealed comparable pro-

portions in the standardization sample. However, it is important to note that no students with identified reading difficulties, especially dyslexia, were present or identified in the standardization sample.

Finally, the test authors examined concurrent validity evidence using the Norris Educational Achievement Test (NEAT), the Iowa Test of Basic Skills (ITBS) Vocabulary and Comprehension sections, and relevant subtests of the Woodcock-Johnson III Diagnostic Reading Battery. The NEAT Word Recognition scores and the DESD resulted in moderate correlation coefficients, suggesting that the NEAT and DESD measure similar constructs. The ITBS scores and the DESD Reading Raw Scores were strongly correlated. Correlations between an earlier version of the DESD (TDS) and the WJ Letter/Word Identification test, Word Attach test, and Passage Comprehension test yielded coefficients in the moderate range (-.68, -.58, and -.56, respectively). The test authors explain these moderate outcomes by describing the differences in the test structures, contents, and scores.

One additional study examined the predictive strength of the TDS in correctly identifying children diagnosed by the DDT as below normal in reading performances. The TDS correctly identified a strong proportion of these students. However, the value of the study is limited in light of the fact that the actual DESD was not involved in the study. Interestingly, the concurrent study mentioned in the development section of the test manual was not discussed as part of the validity evidence.

COMMENTARY. The DESD is a simplified version of the DDT and is a clinical instrument used to detect reading issues related to reading learning problems, specifically dyslexia. The instrument has a strong research base and a well-described set of tests. The DESD provides a Reading Raw Score and a Reading Standard Score as well as Sight-Word Spelling and Phonetic Spelling Raw Scores and skill levels. The development, administration, and interpretation of the test are clearly described. However, the standardization sample did not include students identified as having reading difficulties.

A number of studies explored the technical qualities of the DESD. The DESD displays strong reliability for the indices (.88 and above) for lower grade levels. However, the test authors did not provide suggestions for interpretation of scores for those students in the upper grades where lower reliability estimates were observed. Validity studies were extensive and explored test quality and uses.

Construct validity of the word lists was confirmed through a Rasch analysis. Concurrent validity was estimated by examining correlations of the DESD scores with several tests. Most correlation coefficients were in the moderate range. A major omission was the lack of predictive validity studies establishing the ability of the DESD to identify those students with reading difficulties, including dyslexia.

SUMMARY. Overall, the DESD is a quick-scoring version of the DDT. The test is easy to administer and score and could be appropriately used by teachers and other educational and clinical professionals. Test development is clearly described in the test manual. The DESD exhibits good technical qualities with strong to moderate internal reliability coefficients for the tests, ranging from .95 to .66. The test authors validated the test's scores with other tests, but not its accuracy of use in identifying children with reading difficulties.

Several cautions regarding use of the DESD should be noted. First, the standardization sample did not include students with reading difficulties, making identification of those students problematic. In addition, care should be exercised with using the DESD for identifying those "at risk" because no predictive validity studies to identify students with reading difficulties have been completed. Finally, as with all clinical decisions, determining whether children are in need of further screening for reading difficulties should involve use of multiple instruments and data sources.

REVIEWER'S REFERENCE

American Psychiatric Association (APA). (1994). *Diagnostic and statistical manual of mental disorders (4ᵗʰ ed.)*. Washington, DC: Author.

Review of the Decoding-Encoding Screener for Dyslexia by MONICA GORDON PERSHEY, Associate Professor, Speech and Hearing Program, School of Health Sciences, Cleveland State University, Cleveland, OH:

DESCRIPTION. The Decoding-Encoding Screener for Dyslexia (DESD) is an individually administered screening test of reading decoding and written language encoding for students in Grades 1 through 8. The DESD provides a norm-referenced measure of decoding as evidenced by sight-word recognition. The test provides a qualitative indicator of whether a student's encoding skills (i.e., written spelling) evidence the use of sight-word retrieval and/or phonetic processing strategies. A second qualitative indicator identifies whether a student's letter reversals (e.g., substituting *b* for *d*) are within normal limits for grade level.

The test includes three sections: Letter Writing, Decoding, and Encoding. The test kit includes an examiner's manual, word lists, a Word Viewer tool (a page cover that exposes one word at a time through a window), two student response forms (a record sheet for Letter Writing and Decoding and a spelling response form for Encoding), and an interpretive summary form.

The optional Letter Writing section qualitatively assesses a child's printing of the lowercase alphabet. The examiner may observe psychomotor considerations, for example, pencil grip, eye-hand coordination, erasures, and so on. Scoring reports the number of letters attempted and the number of reversals. Results are interpreted for children who have attempted to write at least 22 letters. The test manual notes the expected frequency of reversals for Grades 1-4. An appendix provides an informal procedure for allowing students who score poorly on Letter Writing to name and sound out single letters.

The Decoding section has one component, the Reading Test, which entails timed reading of a list of 55 single words of ascending difficulty that have phonetically irregular spellings. The examiner exposes a word through the Word Viewer window. The student must correctly pronounce each word within its 2-second time limit to demonstrate automatic sight-word recognition. Phonetically irregular words and time restrictions help ensure that a student does not phonetically analyze the words. The list presents 5 words for each of 11 grade ranges from kindergarten to college. Directions for obtaining a basal and ceiling are provided. The Reading Test yields a raw score (total number of correct words), which is converted to a norm-referenced Reading Standard Score (mean 100, standard deviation 15) and percentile rank, which fall into interpretive ranges of very high, above average, average, below average, and very low. A Grade Level comparison score represents the level at which the student correctly reads at least 3 words.

The Encoding section consists of two components: the Sight-Word Spelling Test and the Phonetic Spelling Test. For Sight-Word Spelling, the student writes the five most difficult words from the Reading Test that he or she read correctly, dictated singly by the examiner. The Reading Test and Sight-Word Spelling indicate whether the student brings visual word-recognition skills to bear during decoding and encoding. Phonetic Spelling, also presented by dictation, requires the student to write five words that he or she read in error on the Reading Test. The words are selected in sequence of difficulty, beginning at one grade level above the student's Reading Test Grade Level score. It is assumed that the student does not have a visual representation of each word that was misread. The examiner directs the student to attempt a phonetic spelling; a correct spelling is not necessary. The test manual provides scoring instructions regarding acceptable phonetically equivalent spellings, such as *kampane* for *campaign* (manual, pp. 4, 14, 53; see Commentary, below). The two Encoding measures are independently scored for percentage correct.

An interpretive summary is based upon all of the above scores. Regarding Decoding, any discrepancy between the Grade Level score and the child's actual grade level is calculated. Regarding Encoding, the interpretive summary estimates word analysis skills by using two measures. First, the grade level discrepancy (D = -3, -2, -1, 0, +1, +2, +3) is compared to the percentage correct on Sight-Word Spelling and assigned a qualitative descriptor of above normal to normal, borderline, mildly below, moderately below, or markedly below. In this way, a combined assessment of sight-word skills in decoding and encoding is obtained. Next, D is compared to the percentage correct on Phonetic Spelling. The same qualitative descriptors apply to performance when sight-word decoding is measured in conjunction with phonetic encoding. The test manual shows how scores suggest three forms of dyslexia: phonetic, sight-word, and sight-word–phonetic.

The DESD is intended for use with students who are fluent in English. Students who speak English as a second language should have English fluency and at least 2 years of formal schooling that includes reading and writing in English. Students are not to be penalized for word pronunciation that is affected by dialect or accent.

DEVELOPMENT. The test manual quotes the International Dyslexia Association definition of dyslexia and the DSM-IV criteria for diagnosis. The test is designed to disabuse the notion that letter reversals are indicative of dyslexia. The DESD is the screening version of the test authors' more comprehensive diagnostic measure, the Dyslexia Determination Test (DDT).

TECHNICAL. The Reading Test was standardized on a sample of 678 regular education students in Grades 1 through 8 in California and Wisconsin. Males and females were fairly equally

represented. Ethnicity data showed oversampling of minorities. Whereas the 2001 U.S. Census figures indicated that the population was about 29% minority, the standardization sample was about 70% minority. Effect size comparison of the means for each gender and ethnicity with the grand mean found no meaningful differences. Smaller effect sizes (range .03 to .33) were obtained (considering .20 as small and .50 as medium).

Derivation of Reading Standard Scores involved computing mean scores for grade levels. Each child's score was compared to grade level peers. A curvilinear regression model predicted mean scores for each grade, and a linear regression model predicted the standard deviations. The sample's obtained means and standard deviations followed the predicted trends very closely.

One subtest was tested for internal consistency. The Reading Test's reliability coefficients (alpha) across grades ranged from .66 to .95. The standard error of measurement confidence intervals for raw scores ranged from 1.44 for Grade 8 to 2.12 for Grade 1. Variability in performance decreased with age and may have contributed to the lesser margin around raw scores. Two test-retest reliability studies of 32 and 23 students across a 1-week interval yielded moderate Reading Standard Score correlation coefficients of .76 and .78, respectively.

The DESD's construct validity depends on the word list's increasing difficulty. The test authors selected words from grade level lists. Item response theory (i.e., the Rasch one-parameter model) was used to estimate item difficulty. Results attest to a linear increase in difficulty between the five-item sets. The amount of increase is fairly consistent between adjacent sets.

Validity of the Encoding Test as a dyslexia screener was demonstrated by comparing of the number of students in the standardization sample who scored at mildly below normal (or worse) to estimates of dyslexia in the general population. The approximate population rate for dyslexia is 5% to 17%. On Sight-Word Spelling, 10% of the standardization sample scored mildly below normal or worse. On Phonetic Spelling, 13% attained this level of performance. The proportion of students likely to be referred for further testing is comparable to the estimated prevalence of dyslexia.

COMMENTARY. The DESD's utility as a sight-word screener is evident. However, encoding testing is hampered by conceptual and procedural problems. First, the list of irregularly spelled words includes words that are not irregularly spelled, and to which phonetic rules and regularities apply. The test authors do not provide a rationale for designating these words as irregular. Second, the scoring guide for Phonetic Spelling consists of the test authors' list of 289 acceptable phonetic spellings for the 50 target words with no explanation of how this list was constructed. Reliability is reduced by some erratic scoring procedures: (1) Within the list of 289 phonetic spellings, 33 are designated unacceptable, but no explanation is provided for why these spellings were excluded. (2) For 31 of the 50 words, a correct spelling must be marked as incorrect. The test authors' rationale is that a correct spelling means that the student knows the word on sight, so the need to spell phonetically is obviated. That premise is not universally true. Further, it confounds diagnosis to penalize a student who has spelling strategies. It also is unclear why this penalty is in place for only about half of the words. (3) The test manual instructs examiners to use their own judgment if an examinee produces a spelling that is not listed as an acceptable variant.

SUMMARY. The DESD allows for rapid identification of sight-word recognition skills and provides a qualitative indicator of whether written spelling evidences the use of sight-word retrieval and/or phonetic processing strategies. Testing is designed to expose whether decoding difficulties are related to sight-word analysis skills, phonetic analysis skills, or both.

[50]

Dementia Rating Scale-2 Alternate Form.

Purpose: Designed as an alternate form of the Dementia Rating Scale-2, a measure of cognitive status, to reduce "the practice effects that occur with serial administrations of the DRS-2."

Population: Ages 56–105.

Publication Dates: 1973-2004.

Acronym: DRS-2: AF.

Scores, 6: Attention, Initiation/Perseverance, Construction, Conceptualization, Memory, Total.

Administration: Individual.

Price Data, 2013: $268 per introductory kit, including 50 scoring booklets, 50 profile forms, 1 set of stimulus cards, and professional manual supplement (2004, 29 pages); $144 per 50 scoring booklets; $48 per 50 profile forms; $46 per set of stimulus cards; $62 per professional manual supplement.

Time: [15-30] minutes.

Comments: As noted in the Dementia Rating Scale-2 Alternate Form professional manual supplement, "The

Professional Manual Supplement contains information on the development, reliability, and validity of the DRS-2: AF, as well as instructions for administration and scoring. However, this Professional Manual Supplement should be considered an adjunct to the DRS-2 Professional Manual," which must be purchased separately.

Authors: Kara S. Schmidt and Steven Mattis.

Publisher: Psychological Assessment Resources, Inc.

Cross References: For reviews by Iris Phillips and Pamilla Ramsden of the Dementia Rating Scale-2, see 15:75; see also T5:776 (63 references); for a review by R. A. Bornstein of the original Dementia Rating Scale, see 11:107 (2 references).

Review of Dementia Rating Scale-2 Alternate Form by MATTHEW E. LAMBERT, Texas Tech University Health Sciences Center, Department of Neuropsychiatry, Lubbock, TX:

DESCRIPTION. The Dementia Rating Scale-2 Alternate Form (DRS-2: AF) was developed to address potential practice effects that may occur with repeated administration of the Dementia Rating Scale-2 (DRS-2; Jurica, Leitten, & Mattis, 2001; 15: 75). As indicated in the DRS-2: AF manual, repeated DRS-2 administration has resulted in positive practice effects within cognitively impaired populations.

The DRS-2 is a 36-task evaluative tool to assess and track cognitive abilities in individuals, ages 56–105 years, with impaired cognitive functions. It assesses cognitive abilities arranged in five areas or subscales: Attention, Initiation/Perseveration, Construction, Conceptualization, and Memory. The test was designed to minimize floor effects for clinically impaired populations versus ceiling effects for normal high-functioning populations. As such, the DRS-2 has limited utility for assessing individuals functioning at average or higher intellectual levels. Those interested in reviews of the DRS-2 and its construction should consult *The Fifteenth Mental Measurements Yearbook* (Plake, Impara, & Spies, 2003).

The DRS-2: AF maintains an identical number of items arranged in the same five subscales. As with the DRS-2, administration utilizes a scoring booklet, 32 spiral-bound stimulus cards, pencils, and a stopwatch. Instructions are read verbatim from the scoring booklet and responses are recorded therein. Scoring instructions also are included in the scoring booklet with subscale tallies recorded on the booklet's front page. Detailed scoring instructions are included in the test manual to alleviate confusion over how to score particular item responses. Raw scores are converted to scaled scores and percentile ranges using the age-corrected Mayo's Older Americans Normative Studies (MOANS) tables included in the DRS-2 manual. Individual subscale scaled scores of 8 or below indicate impairment as does an overall test score of 123 or below. Percentile ranges are used to qualify the level of impairment associated with various scores. Total administration time is approximately 30 minutes.

DEVELOPMENT. Development of the DRS-2: AF was designed to mirror the DRS-2 such that it would include the same number of items contained within the same subscales. Although new items were created, there was also a determination of which DRS-2 items demonstrated practice effects. Previous DRS-2 research was reviewed to identify previously determined practice effects for specific items. Additionally, the DRS-2 was administered to five adults over age 60 years on two occasions, 2 weeks apart, to assess item practice effects. Practice effects were identified for items contained within the Initiation/Perseveration, Conceptualization, and Memory subscales, which ultimately impacted the Total Score. Eight DRS-2 items did not demonstrate practice effects, and these items were retained in the DRS2: AF while new items were written for the other 28 items. New verbal recall and verbal recognition items were written to match word frequency and syllable length of the commensurate DRS-2 items. As well, Construction items and figures were developed to match the number of straight and curved lines for the replaced DRS-2 items. New items were administered to five adults over 60 years of age to assess consistency of item difficulty. The final set of DRS-2: AF items was believed to reflect the original DRS-2 items.

TECHNICAL. Reliability of DRS-2: AF scores was assessed with 52 adults ranging in age from 60 to 91 years, 34 females and 18 males. Participants were drawn from a larger group screened to exclude those with neuropsychiatric disorders, substance abuse, or medications causing cognitive deficits. As such, participants in the reliability study were viewed as cognitively intact. Initially, the participants were administered several brief neuropsychological measures along with the DRS-2 and DRS-2: AF in a counterbalanced design. A second test session, conducted 2 to 4 weeks later, involved administration of additional neuropsychological measures and a second administration of the DRS-2: AF. All but four participants completed the entire testing, yielding 48 complete protocols.

Subscale test-retest reliability coefficients between the DRS-2 and DRS-2: AF ranged from .68 for the Initiation/Perseveration subscale to .90 for the Memory subscale. The coefficient for the Total Score test-retest reliability was .93, and all coefficients were significant at a $p < .001$ level. Comparison of DRS-2 and DRS-2: AF subscale and Total Score means indicated that order of administration had no significant effect.

Paired t tests comparing the two DRS-2 forms' subscale and Total Score means also did not reveal significant differences. However, the test manual notes a trend for mean scores to differ for the Conceptualization subscale. Correlation of the two forms' Total Score produced a coefficient of .82, whereas the subscale correlation coefficients ranged from .66 to .80 for all but the construction subscale as its distribution did not lend itself to analysis. As well, subscale generalizability coefficients (G) for the DRS-2 forms ranged from .63 for the Construction subscale to .90 for the Memory subscale. The Total Score generalizability coefficient was .92. Equipercentile equating of DRS-2 and DRS-2: AF scores further demonstrated the two forms' psychometric equivalence.

Construct validity was assessed by comparing the DRS-2: AF Total Score to Boston Naming Test scores for 49 nonimpaired individuals; a correlation coefficient of .61 ($p < .001$) was reported. As well, 94% of 35 nonimpaired individuals and 30 individuals diagnosed with dementia were accurately classified when an age-corrected MOANS scaled score of 7 was used. Similarly, the relationships between DRS-2: AF subscale scores, excluding Construction, and various cognitive measures were examined for 49 nonimpaired individuals. From this, convergent and divergent validity evidence similar to previous DRS-2 studies was reported. In the impaired sample of 30 individuals, DRS-2: AF scores were compared to Mini Mental State Examination scores and found to correlate significantly ($r = .64$; $p < .001$).

The data presented in the test manual indicate the DRS-2: AF has good evidence of reliability with and equivalence to the DRS-2. Acceptable levels of construct and convergent and discriminant validity are also indicated by the studies presented in the test manual. Yet, these studies are based on small sample sizes, and there are questions as to whether larger samples would yield the same results.

COMMENTARY. The DRS-2: AF provides a reasonable alternative form for users conducting serial administrations of the DRS-2 in clinical populations. There is no difference in administration or scoring procedures between the forms, and there should be no additional training required to use the DRS-2: AF other than ensuring familiarity. Alternate form reliability, as presented in the test manual, is adequate to demonstrate equivalence between the DRS-2 and DRS-2: AF in item content and scores. Validity evidence, also presented in the test manual, supports construct, convergent, and discriminant validity at levels that justify DRS-2: AF use for the purposes for which it is intended.

Yet, the reliability and validity data presented are based on small and restricted populations such that there is a need to ensure the DRS-2: AF's psychometric properties with larger and more diverse populations. This is especially so as the initial premise for the DRS-2: AF's development was to provide an alternate form for serial DRS-2 administrations. Do the DRS-2: AF reliability and validity data persist across populations when there are numerous administrations? How do repeated alternations between the DRS-2 and DRS-2: AF impact reliability and validity data? What are the practice effects of repeated DRS-2: AF administrations? These questions and others need to be addressed, and data related to the answers need to be included in the test manual. Because the DRS-2 is used in research protocols tracking the course of neurological diseases or responses to pharmacological interventions, these data are essential to drawing valid research conclusions.

SUMMARY. The DRS-2: AF provides great potential as an alternative form to address practice effects from repeated DRS-2 administrations. In clinical practice it can be a useful and valuable tool. With research applications, however, additional information regarding its psychometric properties is needed to ensure its reliability and validity as an outcome measure. Either the test manual needs to be revised to include these data or a supplement should be provided.

REVIEWER'S REFERENCES

Jurica, P. J., Leitten, C. L., & Mattis, S. (2001). *Dementia Rating Scale-2 professional manual.* Lutz, FL: Psychological Assessment Resources, Inc.
Plake, B. S., Impara, J. C., & Spies, R. A. (Eds.). (2003). *The fifteenth mental measurements yearbook.* Lincoln, NE: Buros Institute of Mental Measurements.

[51]

Developmental Indicators for the Assessment of Learning–Fourth Edition.

Purpose: Designed to "identify children ages 2:6 through 5:11 who are in need of intervention or diag-

nostic assessment in the following areas: motor, concepts, language, self-help, and social-emotional skills."
Population: Ages 2:6-5:11.
Publication Dates: 1983–2011.
Acronym: DIAL-4.
Scores: 9 regular form: Motor, Concepts, Language, DIAL-4 Total, Behavioral Observations, Parent Self-Help Development, Parent Social-Emotional Development, Teacher Self-Help Development, Teacher Social-Emotional Development; Speed DIAL-4: Total Score only.
Administration: Individual.
Forms, 2: Regular Form, Short Form.
Price Data, 2011: $625 per complete kit including manual (2011, 131 pages), 50 record forms (English), 1 record form (Spanish), 50 cutting cards, 25 Teacher Questionnaires (English), manipulatives, dials, Operator's Handbooks in English and Spanish for Motor, Concepts, and Language Areas plus the Speed DIAL and Training Packet; $45 per 50 Speed DIAL record forms; $275 per Speed DIAL kit in English/Spanish.
Foreign Language Edition: Available in Spanish.
Time: (30-45) minutes, regular form; (20) minutes, short form.
Authors: Carol Mardell and Dorothea S. Goldenberg.
Publisher: Pearson.
Cross References: For reviews by Gregory J. Cizek and Doreen Ward Fairbank of the Third Edition, see 14:116; see also T5:809 (2 references); for reviews by Darrell L. Sabers and Scott Spreat of an earlier edition, see 12:110 (1 reference); see also T4:762 (6 references); for reviews by David W. Barnett and G. Michael Poteat of an earlier version, see 10:89 (6 references); see also 9:326 (1 reference) and T3:696 (2 references); for reviews by J. Jeffrey Grill and James J. McCarthy of an earlier edition, see 8:428 (3 references).

Review of the Developmental Indicators for the Assessment of Learning–Fourth Edition by SHERRY K. BAIN, Associate Professor, Department of Educational Psychology and Counseling, and MICHELLE P. BLACK, Doctoral Student in School Psychology, Department of Educational Psychology and Counseling, The University of Tennessee, Knoxville, TN:

DESCRIPTION AND DEVELOPMENT. The Developmental Indicators for the Assessment of Learning–Fourth Edition (DIAL-4) is the most recent version of several iterations of the developmental screener. This latest version incorporates new norms, a new age range, new items, and a newly introduced Teacher Questionnaire.

The DIAL-4 is an individually administered developmental screener designed to identify children, 2–6 years to 5–11 years, who might need further assessment. The skill areas assessed include Motor, Concepts, Language, Self-Help, and Social-

Emotional. The current revision represents a shift downward in age focus from the DIAL-3 (Mardell-Czudnowski & Goldenberg, 1998).

The Self-Help and Social-Emotional areas are assessed by both the Parent Questionnaire (PQ) and the Teacher Questionnaire (TQ). A trained examiner administers Motor, Concepts, and Language area subscales (referred to as performance areas) directly to the child. Besides area scores, a DIAL-4 Total Score can be calculated. A short-form, the Speed DIAL-4, is also available, with one Total Score that is calculated. The full assessment takes about 30 to 45 minutes. A Spanish version is also included.

As with previous versions, the DIAL-4 provides detailed instructional material for training examiners, referred to as operators by the test authors, as well as detailed suggestions for preparing and managing testing stations. For easy administration of the Motor, Concepts, and Language areas, examiner's instructions are printed in red in the operator's handbook. The DIAL-4 kit also includes cover letters and blank score reports that can be photocopied as well as handouts for parents on developmentally appropriate activities. Items necessary for each performance area (Motor, Concepts, and Language) are stored in separate, easily identified tote bags.

When administrating the performance areas, the test authors suggest using a testing stations approach, with one coordinator and three station operators. Each operator is assigned to one performance area. The coordinator should be a professional in early-childhood education or a related field; the operators may be professionals or para-professionals trained to administer the DIAL-4. Behavioral checklists for each area are provided for noting observed behaviors, such as crying, whining, or separation anxiety. The PQ can be sent home before the testing day or filled out during administration of the performance areas. The TQ assesses these same areas in a classroom setting.

For the performance areas, item responses are converted from raw scores into weighted scores via tables in the record form, then entered on the cover page. The PQ and TQ are scored using a transparent overlay to obtain total scores for Self-Help and Social-Emotional areas; no conversions to weighted scores are necessary. Percentile ranks and standard scores with means of 100 and standard deviations of 15 can be obtained from tables in the user's manual.

The test authors designate score classifications as "OK" or "Potential Delay," depending upon several chosen cutoff points, ranging from 1 standard deviation to 2 standard deviations below the mean (p. 24). They caution that this designation should be used to prompt a referral for follow-up interventions and/or diagnostic testing, not for educational placement purposes, and that additional variables (e.g., cultural background, primary language) should be considered when making referrals.

TECHNICAL.

Standardization. For the performance areas, the standardization sample included 1,400 children ages 2-6 through 5-11 across 39 states. The sample was stratified to approximately match the 2008 U.S. Census data for race/ethnicity, gender, and geographic region. The test authors also collected information on mothers' education levels to control for ability and achievement. Additionally, the sample included children across educational settings, including daycare, school setting, or no program. Spanish-speaking children accounted for about 13% of the normative sample and were recruited from 14 states plus Puerto Rico.

Samples of 700 children provided data for the Self-Help and Social-Emotional areas, via their respective parents (guardians) or teachers filling out the PQ or TQ. About 30% of children who contributed to normative data for the performance areas also contributed data from these questionnaires.

Reliability. The test authors provide evidence and summaries for internal consistency, test-retest reliability, and the standard error of measurement (*SEM*). Internal consistency studies, based on the standardization sample, produced strong correlations across age groups according to Cohen's classifications (1988), with split-half coefficients ranging from .72 to .97 across the English and Spanish versions.

For test-retest reliability, 93 and 81 children were tested using the English and Spanish versions, respectively. Corrected coefficients across all domain areas, the DIAL-4 Total, and the Speed DIAL-4 were strong across both versions. The test authors discussed gain scores, but these reviewers could not locate information in the test manual about the length of the test-retest interval, causing difficulty in interpreting the impact of gain scores.

The *SEM*s for domain and total scores ranged from 0.9 to 3.1 across the two language versions. *SEM*s were based upon two types of scoring across domains, item weighted or raw score units, accounting for some of the difference in range.

Validity. The test authors provide tables and extensive discussion of validity results for the DIAL-4. Addressing content validity, the test authors report carrying out a comprehensive review of the literature and obtaining experts (including early childhood educators and behavioral experts) to review item content and evaluate new material added to the DIAL-4. Construct evidence of validity was provided via correlations among DIAL-4 subtests and total scores, as well as correlations with the measure's predecessor, the DIAL-3 (Mardell-Czudnowski & Goldenberg, 1998). For the English version, the correlation between the DIAL-4 Total and the Speed DIAL-4 was .94; the correlation coefficient for the Spanish version was .95. Domains that are expected to correlate at higher levels tended to produce higher correlations. For example, PQ Self-Help and Social-Emotional Development correlated at .52. Across the PQ and TQ, Self-Help and Social-Emotional correlated at moderate but probably acceptable levels—.33 and .34, respectively. Comparisons of DIAL-4 scores with those of the DIAL-3 produced strong correlations for the five domain areas across the board.

Between 60 and 70 children participated in concurrent validity studies, comparing the DIAL-4 with additional developmental screeners, a cognitive test, and a behavioral inventory. A comparison with the Early Screening Profiles (ESP; Harrison et al., 1990; 12:24) produced strong adjusted correlations between DIAL-4 Language and Concepts areas and the ESP Language subscale and Cognitive/Language Profile. Respective motor and self-help comparisons produced correlation coefficients in the moderate ranges, .30s and .40s.

Adjusted correlations between the DIAL-4 and the Battelle Developmental Inventory, Second Edition (BDI-2; Newborg, 2005; 17:15) fell at strong levels between the BDI-2 Communication domain and DIAL-4 Language area (.63) but less rationally between the BDI-2 Cognitive domain and DIAL-4 Motor area (.65). Comparing the DIAL-4 with the Differential Ability Scales, Second Edition (DAS-II; Elliott, 2007; 18:45), related domains correlated in a fairly rational pattern. Moderate to strong correlations occurred between the DIAL-4 Concepts area and DAS-II verbal and concept-based subtests ranging from .48 to .69. The DIAL-4 Language area produced correlations only slightly lower, compared to the same DAS-II subtests. The DIAL-4 Motor area correlated with the DAS-II visual-spatial and nonverbal reasoning subtests in the .50s.

The test authors compared the DIAL-4 results with the Parent/Caregiver Rating Form (PRF) and the Teacher Rating Form (TRF) of the Vineland-II Adaptive Behavior Scales (Sparrow, Cicchetti, & Balla, 2005, 2006; 18:150). Notably, the DIAL-4 Self-Help area produced adjusted correlations ranging from the .40s to the .60s (with one exception at .34) compared to the PRF and TRF Daily Living Skills subscales. Interestingly, the DIAL-4 Concepts area and the PRF and TRF Socialization subscales produced correlations in the .40s, a moderate strength (again with one exception at .28). Evidence of discriminant validity is offered in the test manual for samples of children with diagnoses of physical impairment, developmental delay, speech and language impairment, or autism, compared to a nonclinical sample matched on relevant demographic variables. Notably, none of the children from the clinical groups were severely impaired, and some were receiving therapy. Classification results are presented in the test manual based upon two cutoff levels, standard scores falling below 85, and below 90. The higher, less stringent cutoff score rendered sensitivity levels (correctly identifying children in respective clinical groups) of .76, .73, .67, and .82 for the four clinical groups, respectively. The lower cutoff level rendered higher sensitivity levels, as expected.

COMMENTARY. These reviewers found the DIAL-4 to be easy to administer and score, thanks to the clarity of directions and scoring procedures. The inclusion of model letters to parents and teachers is a welcome convenience, as are the separate, brightly colored bags for performance area items.

The reliability data seem adequate, and validity studies appear to generally support the separate subscales. However, the test authors do not provide a discussion or evidence of factor analytic results, based upon earlier versions or the current version of the instrument.

SUMMARY. The DIAL-4 is a screening instrument for identifying preschool and kindergarten children who might need further assessment for developmental delays. Areas examined include Motor, Concepts, Language, Self-Help, and Social-Emotional. These reviewers recommend use of this instrument as a broad-based screener in early educational settings. The DIAL-4 seems particularly useful in identifying children who may not have salient disorders but may display delays in developmental areas that might be ameliorated at an early age.

REVIEWERS' REFERENCES

Achenbach, T. M., McConaughy, S. H., & Howell, C. T. (1987). Child/adolescent behavioural and emotional problems: Implications of cross-informant correlations for situational specificity. *Psychological Bulletin, 101*, 213–232.

Cohen, J. (1988). *Statistical power analysis for the behavioral sciences* (2nd ed.). Hillsdale, NJ: Erlbaum.

Elliott, C. D. (2007). Differential Ability Scales, Second Edition (DAS-II). San Antonio, TX: Harcourt Assessment.

Harrison, P. L., Kaufman, A. S., Kaufman, N. L., Bruininks, R. H., Rynders, J., Ilmer, S., … Cicchetti, D. V. (1990). Early Screening Profiles (ESP). Circle Pines, MN: American Guidance Service.

Mardell-Czudnowski, C., & Goldenberg, D. S. (1998). Developmental Indicators for the Assessment of Learning, Third Edition (DIAL-3). Circle Pines, MN: American Guidance Service.

Newborg, J. (2005). Battelle Developmental Inventory, Second Edition (BDI-2). Itasca, IL: Riverside.

Sparrow, S. S., Cicchetti, D. V., & Balla, D. A. (2005). Vineland Adaptive Behavior Scales: Parent/Caregiver Rating Form (2nd ed.). Minneapolis, MN: NCS Pearson.

Sparrow, S. S., Cicchetti, D. V., & Balla, D. A. (2006). Vineland Adaptive Behavior Scales: Teacher Rating Form (2nd ed.). Minneapolis, MN: NCS Pearson.

Review of the Developmental Indicators for the Assessment of Learning–Fourth Edition by CLAUDIA R. WRIGHT, Professor Emerita, California State University, Long Beach, CA:

DESCRIPTION. The Developmental Indicators for the Assessment of Learning–Fourth Edition (DIAL-4), representing a revision of the DIAL-3 (see 14:116), is designed to identify children (ages 2-6 to 5-11), who may be at risk for academic underperformance and who exhibit behaviors consistent with developmental delays. As with the DIAL-3, DIAL-4 builds upon three core performance areas reflecting skills in Motor (gross and fine motor movements), Concepts (self-awareness, counting, sorting), and Language (articulation, naming objects/uses, and problem solving); data also are collected regarding Self-Help behaviors and Social-Emotional development. English and Spanish versions are available for both the DIAL-4 and the Speed DIAL-4, a short form of this edition of DIAL.

Test administrators are screened for appropriate backgrounds in early childhood and special education and undergo extensive, supervised training. Fluency is required in both English and Spanish for those who administer the Spanish version. The DIAL-4 is administered individually, with each performance area taking from 10 to 15 minutes to complete. More than one child can be tested at the same time using multiple administrators, with each responsible for a single performance area. Detailed set-up instructions are provided for the testing environment to minimize distractions for examinees. The attractiveness of testing materials has been maximized for young children with colorful, well-designed, research-supported manipulatives for the Motor, Concepts, and Language areas. Easy-to-follow bilingual instruction booklets for each area detail set-up for testing stations, use of materials, explicit directions to guide the testing process, appropriate response options, prompts for non-responders, and scoring.

The performance areas comprise several task categories with each category divided into multiple activities that are weighted using 2- to 5-point response scales; each area yields a maximum total score of 35. Motor includes such behaviors as copying a simple shape and is scored 0–2; Concepts, rapidly naming 25 objects, is scored 0–5 based on the number of objects correctly named. Language, naming objects or an object's use, is scored 0–1 (incorrect or correct). For each performance area, test administrators report an examinee's level of engagement (e.g., attention, persistence) using nine item-statements each scored 0–2, yielding a total possible score of 18. The Speed DIAL-4, reserved for special circumstances to assess whether further evaluation is needed, is made up of 10 core items and their related tasks. The 50-item Parent Questionnaire includes two parts that are scored. The first part consists of 22 item-statements regarding the occurrence in the home of self-help behaviors (e.g., dressing, hygiene) each scored 0–2. Part 2 has 28 items dealing with social-emotional behaviors (e.g., problem solving with others, cooperation), also scored 0–2. Part 3 (not scored) provides an opportunity for parents to convey concerns they may have regarding overall development. The 44-item Teacher Questionnaire focuses on 10 self-help and 34 social-emotional behaviors that occur in school settings.

DEVELOPMENT. Construction of the DIAL-4 included integration of current research and recent guidelines from professional, state, and federal agencies that informed and supported detailed rationales for selected constructs and alignment of item content. Expert feedback on the DIAL-3 guided decisions to lower the administration age to 2-6, to maximize the number of items predictive of school success, to simplify test administration and scoring, and to ensure consistency between the two language versions. To provide data for item performance and item/task bias analyses, a large DIAL-4 study was conducted with 224 administrators who tested 1,574 children (ages 2-6 to 5-11; 51% female; 59% Hispanic, 23% White, 15% Black, and 2% Other); 924 and 650 children completed the English and Spanish versions, respectively.

TECHNICAL.

Norms. The standardization sample was made up of 1,400 children between the ages of 2-6 and 5-11, selected from 385 sites across 38 states in four geographic regions (Northeast [15.7%], Midwest [22.9%], South [40%, including Puerto Rico], and West [21.4%]). The equating sample of 502 Spanish-speaking children was selected from 82 sites in 14 states across the four geographic regions (36% of sites were located in Puerto Rico). Demographic targets for gender, ethnicity, region, and mother's education level (SES) were guided by the U.S. Census Bureau (2008). Other factors included current school setting (no program, day-care, school), clinical diagnosis (< 7% of sample), premature birth (< 12%), low birth weight (< 8%), and drug/alcohol abuse during mother's pregnancy (< 5%). Excluded were children with conditions that would impair performance as were those with a primary language other than English or Spanish.

Data were subjected to Rasch-model analyses for developing scoring rules to differentiate among low, medium, and high scorers. This iterative process was used for generating weighted scores considering alignment with content and age, discrimination across performance levels, and differentiation between examinees with and without clinical diagnoses. IRT methods were employed to equate English and Spanish DIAL-4 performance areas yielding a single set of classification scores and norm groups. The technical manual includes a series of tables displaying percentile rank scores obtained for performance areas stratified by age grouping. Five cutoff-score classifications were selected based on distributions of scores from the standardization sample: 16%, 10%, 7%, 5%, and 2%.

Reliability. Satisfactory reliability evidence was obtained for both English and Spanish DIAL-4 versions including internal-consistency estimates, test-retest, and interscorer agreement. The sample of 1,400 examinees was divided equally across seven age groups (2-6 to 2-11, 3-0 to 3-5, 3-6 to 3-11, 4-0 to 4-5, 4-6 to 4-11, 5-0 to 5-5, 5-6 to 5-11; all $n = 200$). Internal-consistency estimates of reliability employed split-half (odd-even) weighted subscores, corrected for test length using the Spearman-Brown formula, for each of the DIAL-4 performance areas, DIAL-4 Total, and Speed DIAL-4. Based on raw scores, reliability estimates were generated for parent (PQ) and teacher (TQ) questionnaires. Obtained coefficients ranged from moderately high to high across age groups (means, using Fischer's z transformations, are provided parenthetically): Motor, .74 to .88 (.84); Concepts, .82 to .94 (.92); Language, .90 to .95 (.93); DIAL-4 Total, .90 to

.96 (.95); Speed DIAL-4, .84 to .94 (.91); PQ Self-Help, .80 to .86 (.83); PQ Social-Emotional, .79 to .90 (.85); TQ Self-Help, .72 to .90 (.83), and TQ Social-Emotional, .88 to .95 (.93). For the Spanish-speaking sample ($N = 502$), examinees were divided into four age groups: 2-6 to 2-11 ($n = 66$), 3-0 to 3-11 ($n = 140$), 4-0 to 4-11 ($n = 148$), 5-0 to 5-11 ($n = 148$). Reliability estimates (with means, using Fischer's z transformations, provided parenthetically) ranged as follows: Motor, .71 to .89 (.86); Concepts, .90 to .95, (.93); Language, .95 to .97 (.96); DIAL-4 Total, .94 to .97 (.96); Speed DIAL-4, .93 to .96 (.95); PQ Self-Help, .78 to .85 (.81); PQ Social-Emotional, .70 to .86 (.79); TQ Self-Help, .80 to .94 (.87), and TQ Social-Emotional, .86 to .92 (.90).

Estimates of test-retest reliability were obtained for scores on the English and Spanish versions. For 93 English-speaking examinees, coefficients were reported for nine areas for two age groupings (2-6 to 3-11, sample sizes ranged from 46 to 59; and 4-0 to 5-11, sample sizes ranged from 43 to 71). For the younger and older group, respectively, adjusted coefficients were for Motor, .70 and .73; Concepts, .78 and .77; Language, .79 and .90; DIAL-4 Total, .83 and .88; Speed DIAL-4, .78 and .84; PQ Self-Help, .68 and .65; PQ Social-Emotional, .78 and .72; TQ Self-Help, .87 and 72; and TQ Social-Emotional, .86 and .80. For both age groups, a comparison of means revealed increases in performance for each of the nine areas; however, no statistically significant differences were observed for younger examinees, suggesting relatively stable responses over time. For the older group, seven of the nine mean comparisons yielded statistically significant differences, with the largest found for Language (101.8 compared to 105.6, standard error of the difference = .33, $t = -3.99$, $p < .001$) and for DIAL-4 Total (103.4 compared to 108.3, standard error of the difference = .41, $t = -4.25$, $p < .001$). These findings are consistent with the idea that the testing interval was sufficiently long for schooling to support new learning.

For 81 Spanish-speaking examinees, test-retest coefficients for two age groupings (2-6 to 3-11, $n = 40$; and 4-0 to 5-11, $n = 41$) yielded for Motor, .83 and .80; Concepts, .84 and .86; Language, .87 and .92; DIAL-4 Total, .91 and .92; Speed DIAL-4, .89 and .89; PQ Self-Help, .74 and .73; and PQ Social-Emotional, .74 and .77. For a sample of 35 adult respondents who completed the teacher questionnaire, coefficients were .89 for TQ

Self-Help and .93 for TQ Social-Emotional. For the younger group, a comparison of means revealed small statistically significant gains for the performance areas with the greatest comparison observed for Motor scores (100.6 compared to 106.1, standard error of the difference = .35, t = -4.04, p < .001). For the older group, small statistically significant gains were observed for Concepts, Speed DIAL-4, and PQ Social-Emotional with the greatest gain for Language scores (93.2 compared to 97.1, standard error of the difference = .20, t = -3.81, p < .001). Overall, these observations are consistent with age-appropriate developmental patterns (e.g., strides in motor development for younger examinees and language development gains for older examinees).

Examination of interscorer agreement, provided by two independent scorers, was applied across age groups to tasks that involved subjective scoring (e.g., problem solving and copying). Intraclass correlation coefficients revealed high levels of agreement: Motor tasks ranged from .89 (writing name) to .98 (cutting); Language (English) was .97 for both expressive objects/actions and problem solving; and Language (Spanish) was .94 for expressive objects and actions and .90 for problem solving.

Validity. Modest to strong support was demonstrated for construct validity. DIAL-4 scores were correlated with scores from several other instruments designed to screen for developmental-related behaviors including DIAL-3 (14:116); Early Screening Profiles (ESP; 12:24), ages 2-0 to 6-11, assessing cognitive/language, motor, and self-help/social areas; Battelle Developmental Inventory, Second Edition (BDI-2; 17:15), ages birth to 7-11, focusing on adaptive, personal-social, communication, motor, and cognition; Differential Ability Scales, Second Edition (DAS-II; 18:45), including ages 2-6 to 3-5 and 3-6 to 6-11, emphasizing verbal ability, nonverbal reasoning, conceptual ability, and memory areas; and the Vineland-II Adaptive Behavior Scales—Parent/Caregiver Rating Form (PRF) and Teacher Rating Form (TRF; 18:150).

Sixty to 70 examinees provided responses for each analysis, with half completing the DIAL-4 first; the number of days between testing ranged from 1 to 25 (mean interval was 7 days). Examination of several multitrait-multimethod matrices based on standard scores revealed moderate to moderately high adjusted correlations between DIAL-4 and DIAL-3 scores: Motor, .58; Concepts, .84; Language, .75; PQ Self-Help, .66; PQ Social-Emotional, .66; and Speed versions, .83. Modest

to moderate adjusted correlations were found between ESP and DIAL-4 scores: EPS Cognitive/Language Profile and DIAL-4 Concepts, .59; and Language, .61; EPS Motor Profile and DIAL-4 Motor, .35; EPS Self-Help/Profile and DIAL-4 PQ Self-Help, .40; and PQ Social Emotional, .36. Low to moderate adjusted coefficients were observed among BDI-2 and DIAL-4 scores, with the highest obtained for total scores on each instrument, .61; for BDI-2 Communication Domain with DIAL-4 Motor, Concepts, and Language, .52, .54, and .63, respectively; BDI-2 Cognitive with the three DIAL-4 performance areas, .65, .47, and .49, respectively; BDI-2 Motor and DIAL-4 Motor, .49. Correlations between DAS-II and DIAL-4 scores yielded moderately high adjusted coefficients between DAS-II General Conceptual Ability and DIAL-4 Total, .73; and Speed DIAL-4, .67. Low to moderate correlations were observed between DIAL-4 Total and Vineland-II scores: PRF Daily Living Skills Domain, .43; Community, a subdomain of Daily Living Skills, measuring conceptual skills such as time, money, and rules, .58; and Socialization Domain, .37. Moderate to moderately strong adjusted correlations were obtained between DIAL-4 Concepts and TRF Daily Living Skills, .56; and TRF Socialization, .43; between DIAL-4 TQ Self-Help and TRF Daily Living Skills, .56; and TRF Socialization, .69; and between DIAL-4 TQ Social-Emotional and TRF Socialization, .54.

The referral efficiency of DIAL-4 scores was examined comparing matched samples (by age, gender, race, and SES) with no clinical diagnoses or with clinical diagnoses involving one of four conditions: physical impairment (mild fine motor to problematic gross motor movements), developmental delay, speech and language impairment (predominantly articulation disorders), or autism. Sample sizes for each condition ranged from 49 to 63. For each condition, estimates were obtained for sensitivity (proportion with clinical diagnoses identified as delayed), specificity (proportion correctly identified as okay), and agreement (proportion correctly identified as delayed and okay). Examinees were classified into one of two groups based on cutoffs for standard scores corresponding with the 16% cutoff level (< 85 or > 85) and the 10% cutoff level (< 90 or > 90). Examinees with physical impairments scored statistically significantly lower than did the comparison group on eight of nine DIAL-4 measures. The greatest difference in the means was observed for Motor (79.3 compared to 103.3, standard error of the difference = -1.88, $t[48]$ = -9.30, p < .001); for scores < 85, sensitivity, specificity, and agreement values were .67, .94, and .81 respectively; for scores < 90, agreement values were .76, .86, and .81, respectively. Examinees with developmental delays scored significantly lower on all nine DIAL-4 measures (all p < .001) than comparison examinees, with the greatest difference in means observed for DIAL-4 Total scores (82.1 compared to 102.9, standard error of the difference = -1.54, $t[62]$ = -8.65, p < .001). Sensitivity, specificity, and agreement values for scores < 85 were .57, .89, and .73, respectively; for scores < 90, agreement values were .73, .83, and .78, respectively. For examinees with speech and language impairments, five of nine DIAL-4 comparisons were statistically significant at the .01 level or lower for the comparison group, with Language scores representing the greatest difference in means (85.0 compared to 100.5, standard error of the difference = -1.17, $t[48]$ = -5.79, p < .001); sensitivity, specificity, and agreement values for scores < 85 were .49, .84, and .66, respectively; for scores < 90, agreement values were .67, .73, and .70, respectively. For examinees diagnosed with autism, statistically significant comparisons were observed on all nine DIAL-4 measures (all p < .001), with PQ decision statistics reported. For PQ Self-Help (75.8 compared to 102.4, standard error of the difference = -2.06, $t[49]$ = -10.28, p <.001), sensitivity, specificity, and agreement values for scores < 85 were .74, .90, and .82, respectively; for scores < 90, agreement values were .82, .82, and .82, respectively. For PQ Social-Emotional (78.1 compared to 100.1, standard error of the difference = -1.45, $t[49]$ = -7.24, p <.001), sensitivity, specificity, and agreement values for scores < 85 were .74, .82, and .78, respectively; for scores < 90, agreement values were .82, .76, and .79, respectively. Finally, for a group of 78 examinees from the standardization sample, classification comparisons were made between decisions based on the DIAL-4 Total score and the DAS-II General Conceptual Ability score. Sensitivity, specificity, and agreement values for scores < 85 were .33, .95, and .92, respectively; for scores < 90, agreement values were .78, .91, .90, respectively. In general, the test authors concluded that the DIAL-4 can adequately distinguish between groups with or without the conditions listed and would be useful as one indicator for identifying examinees for whom further testing would be appropriate.

COMMENTARY AND SUMMARY. The Developmental Indicators for the Assessment of Learning–Fourth Edition (DIAL-4) is a well-constructed and psychometrically sound developmental screening instrument. Sufficient evidence is provided for the reliability of scores and the construct validity of DIAL-4 performance scores using scores from other measures such as ESP, BDI-2, and DAS-II. The test developers clearly differentiate the DIAL-4 from tests of readiness, diagnostics (e.g., for learning disabilities), and intelligence–any use of the DIAL-4 for such purposes is strongly opposed and is considered ill-advised. Exceptional test development procedures, training and supervisory guidelines, resolution of articulation difficulties between the English and Spanish versions, and the inclusion of referral efficiency studies have contributed to an improvement of the DIAL-4 over the DIAL-3.

REVIEWER'S REFERENCE

U.S. Census Bureau. (2008). *Current Population Survey, March 2008* [Machine-readable data file]. Washington, DC: Author.

[52]

Developmental Teaching Objectives and Rating Form-Revised, 5th Edition.

Purpose: Designed "for assessing social and emotional development of children and youth."
Population: Ages 0-16.
Publication Dates: 1992–2012.
Acronym: DTORF-R.
Scores, 4: Behavior (Doing), Communication (Saying), Socialization (Relating), Cognition (Thinking).
Administration: Individual.
Levels, 5: Stage I, Stage II, Stage III, Stage IV, Stage V.
Forms, 3: Early Childhood, Elementary, Secondary.
Price Data, 2013: $200 annual fee per site and $5 per student for secure data entry, record management, group summaries, analysis, and reports (www.dtorf.com); $91 per textbook; $12 per user's manual.
Time: [30] minutes per individual student.
Comments: Textbook (2007, 346 pages) and CD distributed by PRO-ED, Inc.; User's manual (2012, 32 pages) distributed by Developmental Therapy Institute, Inc.; rating form filled out by people familiar with the child, following observations; older children (and their parents) participate in their own team ratings.
Authors: Mary M. Wood, Constance A. Quirk, and Faye L. Swindle.
Publisher: Developmental Therapy Institute, Inc.
Cross References: For a review by Sharon H. deFur of an earlier edition, see 14:118.

Review of the Developmental Teaching Objectives and Rating Form–Revised, 5th Edition by AN-

DREW A. COX, Professor, Counseling and Psychology, Troy University, Phenix City, AL:

DESCRIPTION. The Developmental Teaching Objectives and Rating Form–Revised, 5ᵗʰ Edition (DTORF-R 5ᵗʰ ed.) is an online version of the 171-item Developmental Teaching Objectives and Rating Form–Revised rating scale used by professional educators and others to assess the social and emotional development of children and youth from birth to age 16. The instrument can be used with children with or without special needs. Child functioning in the four developmental domains of Behavior, Communication, Socialization, and Cognition is assessed. Children's attainment of skills in these areas can be assessed to identify delayed competencies. There are three forms for use with children depending upon their age, ranging from early childhood, elementary level, and middle school–high school forms as well as a brief profile form to facilitate initial data gathering for a student. The DTORF-R (5ᵗʰ edition) does not represent an instrumentation change from the earlier DTORF-R.

All forms and materials to use the DTORF-R (5ᵗʰ edition) are available online through Letter-Press Software, Inc. (2013) and in print through the Developmental Therapy Institute. Within the online version, instrument users can assess students and youth and save student data across multiple assessments. Other available materials include behavioral intervention plans and individualized educational plan forms.

The test authors recommend at least three raters complete the instrument for a particular child or youth. Raters could include professionals, paraprofessionals, and parents who have in-depth knowledge of a particular child's functional level. Ratings are completed across the four developmental domains identifying specific developmental skills attained or not attained by the child or youth within home, neighborhood, and school settings. The ratings allow professional educators and other professionals to develop instructional goals to assist a child or youth in mastering unmet skills or in gaining needed prerequisite skills in order to master a particular developmental area as well as identifying skill strengths. Developmental age scores, proportional change ratios, goal attainment scaling, and visual descriptions of data can be obtained to estimate and describe assessed developmental functioning. Wood, Quirk, and Swindle (2007) provide examples to illustrate the rating procedure as well

as means to accommodate rating children or youth with special needs or specialized circumstances. The test authors also provide examples of how results can be used to document student progress and meet short- and long-term educational and instructional goals.

DEVELOPMENT. The test authors suggest that the DTORF-R/DTORF-R (5ᵗʰ edition) is a research-based functional behavioral system that meets assessment guidelines inherent within recent federal educational legislation. These guidelines are related to standards enumerated within the reauthorized Individuals with Disabilities Education Act and No Child Left Behind Act. The instrument is considered a criterion-referenced assessment with the Developmental Therapy–Developmental Teaching model as a theoretical backdrop. The instrument evolved from a Developmental Therapy-Developmental Teaching field project for children with social, emotional, and behavioral disabilities as summarized in deFur (2001). Additional "formative and summative evaluations of students' assessed needs and effective instructional practices" have been conducted over several decades (Wood et al., 2007, p. 238). This research has been completed with elementary children of various ages, teenagers, children with various disabling conditions, children at risk due to developmental or environmental factors, and children with adjustment problems but no developmental delays. A preponderance of research used in the instrument's development appears to have sampled children and youth experiencing developmental delays, as well as those with social, emotional, or behavioral deficits.

The DTORF-R (5ᵗʰ edition) builds upon the development of the DTORF-R that has taken place through three comprehensive validation studies and a study for a university preservice training program for university interns. These studies have evaluated the sustained effects of children's skill gains upon completion of an educational remediation program and after the passage of time. In 2001 (Wood et al., 2007), the DTORF-R was used in a study with a representative sample of 279 students ranging in age from 8 months to 20 years that evaluated an in-service program to train professional educators in the use of the instrument and the Developmental Therapy-Developmental Teaching program in different regions of the United States. The study examined a variety of special education placement options and assessed skill gains made by children by disability, severity of developmental delay, age, ethnic characteristics (African American and White), and gender. Though differential gains were made in relation to selected disability areas and grade level, the study suggests that the DTORF-R can assess individual gains in key developmental areas.

The use of the DTORF-R in international settings is also described by the test authors. Applications in Germany, Norway, and Italy are briefly described. The test authors describe evidence of the effectiveness of the DTORF-R and Developmental Therapy–Developmental Teaching in eight European, Asian, and Latin American countries, Canada, and the Virgin Islands. However, details and supporting data analyses regarding these studies or applications in multicultural settings are not described.

TECHNICAL. DeFur (2001) describes the basis for selection of the 171 items within the DTORF-R. Construct and content validation are described for the instrument. Construct validation evidence was derived from review of theoretical data and research on the constructs of social, emotional, and behavioral competence. However, details regarding reviewed theorists or research are not described within the test manual. Content validation evidence is based upon the original instrument's field testing as used for a 5-year time period. At a later time instrument changes were made to reflect research findings for children with autistic-like behavior or pervasive developmental delay, as well as research on moral development, interpersonal perspective taking, and adolescent development. Once again, limited information is provided regarding the nature or characteristics of this research. Content validity was expanded through item comparison with a number of well-respected developmental and childhood inventories and assessment scales. Item difficulty statistics are reported that appear to be adequate for the most part, although a lowered difficulty index is noted for the Cognitive domain.

Reliability estimates consist primarily of interrater reliability estimates among trained raters using the DTORF-R. Internal consistency and use of the standard error of measurement as reliability estimates are also reported. As noted in DeFur (2001), estimates are based upon a limited number of raters and with small research samples. Accordingly, additional studies of reliability may be needed.

COMMENTARY. The DTORF-R and DTORF-R (5th Edition) appear to be based upon several decades of educational research. Though summarized briefly in Wood et al. (2007) more de-

tails regarding this research would be helpful within test materials that are available to potential instrument users. Overall, the instrument appears to have merit in assessing the developmental characteristics of children from birth to age 16. It appears to assess key developmental skills required of children in school and community settings. Of particular value is the identification of attained and nonattained skills allowing child development practitioners and educators to develop training and instructional strategies to enhance attainment of needed child and youth developmental competencies.

The DTORF-R (5th Edition) is the assessment arm of the Developmental Therapy-Developmental Teaching instructional model with technical studies relating to this model presented as technical support for this instrument. An area of potential research would be to evaluate the utility of this instrument in other instructional or developmental intervention models or processes.

User materials appear to be adequate for the valid and effective use of the instrument. However, formal training in the use of the instrument would most likely be required for users with limited experience with the instrument in order to obtain valid and reliable developmental ratings. Much of the research related to reliability involves the use of trained raters. Scores obtained via ratings and developmental age scores would be useful to educational and child developmental practitioners in describing child and youth developmental strengths and weaknesses. Such scores would also be useful for consumers of score data such as parents and similar potential test consumers with limited knowledge of statistical concepts. Additional research is needed on the utility of the measure with children and youth from other cultural settings as research appears to have focused upon use with children from African American and Caucasian racial backgrounds. The test authors describe international applications of the DTORF-R and its associated educational model. However, very sparse detail regarding these applications or associated data are described in the test materials. Such detail of empirical studies and possible additional research would be required to ascertain the instruments utility in cross-cultural settings.

SUMMARY. The Developmental Teaching Objectives and Rating Form–Revised, 5th Edition appears to be a useful instrument for assessing and identifying the developmental competencies of children and youth from birth to age 16. The instrument would be useful in developing learning, instructional, and behavioral goals associated with individualized educational plans and similar developmental service documents. It would be of particular use in educational and child development programs using concepts associated with the Developmental Therapy–Developmental Teaching model. Additional research is needed to determine the instrument's utility within intervention programs using other child development concepts or strategies. At this time, the DTORF-R (5ᵗʰ Edition) would not be viewed as a replacement for other well-known developmental assessment measures such as the Vineland Adaptive Behavior Scales-II (18:150) or Battelle Developmental Inventory-2 (17:15).

It has been noted within this review that more detail regarding research depicting the technical characteristics and usage of the instrument in selected settings is needed. An updated technical report consolidating recent research compiled for the DTORF-R and DTORF-R (5ᵗʰ Edition) would be helpful. All described research is for the DTORF-R. No references are made to the DTORF-R (5ᵗʰ Edition) within the test manual or online materials leading to confusion among test users as to the version of the instrument being used. [Editor's Note: The publisher has provided the Buros Center with a user's manual that was not available at the time this review was written. One intent of the user's manual is to address these issues.] Sections within the test manual addressing research and effectiveness studies for the various editions of the DTORF-R/DTORF-R (5ᵗʰ Edition) would be helpful.

REVIEWER'S REFERENCES

deFur, S. H. (2001). [Review of the Developmental Teaching Objectives and Rating Form–Revised]. In B. S. Plake & J. C. Impara (Eds.), *The fourteenth mental measurements yearbook* (pp. 403-405). Lincoln, NE: Buros Institute of Mental Measurements.
LetterPress Software, Inc. (2013, January). Retrieved from http://www.dtorf.com
Wood, M. M., Quirk, C. A., & Swindle, F. L. (2007). *Teaching responsible behavior: Developmental therapy–developmental teaching for troubled children and adolescents* (4ᵗʰ ed.). Austin, TX: PRO-ED.

Review of the Developmental Teaching Objectives and Rating Form–Revised, 5ᵗʰ Edition by REBECCA GOKIERT, *Assistant Professor and Assistant Director, Faculty of Extension, and* REBECCA GEORGIS, *Ph.D. Candidate, Department of Educational Psychology, University of Alberta, Edmonton, Alberta, Canada:*

DESCRIPTION. The Developmental Teaching Objectives Rating Form–Revised, 5ᵗʰ Edition (DTORF-R 5ᵗʰ ed.) is a criterion-referenced assessment of social and emotional development for children from birth to 16 years. The 5ᵗʰ edi-

tion is an online adaptation of the DTORF-R (4ᵗʰ ed.), which is used within the Developmental Therapy–Developmental Teaching for Troubled Children and Adolescents system (Wood, Quirk, & Swindle, 2007). This review is based on the new online features of the DTORF-R (5ᵗʰ ed.) that can be accessed at www.dtorf.com, but it also draws heavily from the 4ᵗʰ edition manual and accompanying CD.

The tool consists of 171 hierarchically ordered items that measure social and emotional development of children across the following four domains: Behavior (doing), Communication (saying), Socialization (relating), and Cognition (thinking). Three forms are available (early childhood, birth–age 5; elementary school, ages 6–11; and middle/high school, ages 12–16), which are organized into five stages of social, emotional, and behavioral development. The forms can be accessed and completed online, or they may be printed for parents/guardians or students to complete. It is recommended that at least three people complete the form for a given child (e.g., parent or caregiver, primary teacher, and relevant clinical staff member working with the child). When appropriate, children are encouraged to participate as well. The DTORF-R can be used for many purposes: (a) to identify a child's strengths and needs, (b) to identify objectives that can form the basis for a student's individual education or intervention plan and instruction, (c) to monitor individual or groups of students' progress over time, and (d) to evaluate program effectiveness.

The online system provides detailed instructions about all aspects of setting up individual records, selecting appropriate forms, reporting at the individual or group level, and activating/deactivating student records that are saved in the database. A support email and phone number are provided if the user needs technical assistance. Raters are provided with the appropriate form based on the child's age, and each item on the form is stated as a learning objective that can be expanded by hovering the mouse over the item. Each item is rated as mastered, not mastered, or not ready for instruction. The skills that are rated as not mastered can become the focus of instruction and program planning for the student. There is a feature on the online program that will check for errors and requires the rater to confirm the results, as it will not accept missing items. It is important to confirm and save the evaluation for it to be added to the database; however, once this step has been completed, the rater cannot go back and modify the rating.

In addition to a student-generated report, the online system can automatically generate a Behavioral Intervention Plan (BIP) with identified intervention strategies for the student's stage and/or a summary of objectives for each of the four domains to complement a student's Individualized Education Plan (IEP). Furthermore, an estimate of severity of developmental delay (ranging from mild to severe in relation to same-aged peers) is computed by the online system by comparing the DTORF-R (5th ed.) scores to developmental age scores (DAS). Individual DTORF-R (5th ed.) ratings can be combined online to produce group or classroom level learning objectives. The tool can also be used as a repeated measure throughout the school year to monitor improvements and to enhance instruction that reflects current learning needs. These reporting features align nicely with the No Child Left Behind Act (NCLB; U.S. Department of Education, 2002) and the Individuals with Disabilities Education Act (IDEA; U.S. Department of Education, 1997, 2005), legislation that requires annual progress reports on student achievements of stated goals. In fact, both the BIP and IEP are required according to federal guidelines, and the ability of the DTORF-R (5th ed.) to automatically generate them for teachers and administrators is a strength of the tool.

DEVELOPMENT. In creating the DTORF, the authors wanted a tool that was scientifically based and possessed acceptable standards for validity and reliability as well as utility for classroom-based instruction. The DTORF-R (5th ed.) is the most recent version that was developed in 2004. The online version is exclusively in English; however, the tool has been translated into several languages (e.g., German and Norwegian) and there is a section in the textbook that describes the international applicability, which is of particular importance with significant changes in school-based demographics due to immigration. The tool that was previously reviewed (see deFur, 2001) has not changed in content when adapting the tool for online use. The technical information presented in the section to follow is based on the DTORF-R (4th ed.) materials unless otherwise stated. The test authors do not provide any comparison information about the online and paper-based versions, which would be useful for users and should be examined in the future.

TECHNICAL. The DTORF-R (5th ed.) is a criterion-referenced measure and, therefore, was not created to be administered through a standardized process whereby scores can be compared to a normative sample of children and adolescents. It has strength as a practical classroom-based assessment where objectives for instruction and intervention can be utilized in program planning and monitored over time for both individuals and groups of students. There is no reference to a sample that was used for piloting the original DTORF-R; however, all subsequent validation of effectiveness studies that have been conducted over the past 30 years have consisted of varying samples of children ages birth to 16 years, programs, and educators.

Reliability. Kuder-Richardson type reliability estimates of internal consistency yielded internal consistencies >.99 within each domain. A study examining the interrater reliability of two trained individuals evaluating 21 students resulted in agreement greater than or equal to 81%. This result led to the development of a rater training program that was tested with two individuals who independently rated 20 children. Their agreement posttraining was greater than or equal to 93% across all domains. In order to have consistent ratings on the forms, it is recommended that at least one rater have prior training in the rating procedures and an established reliability score. Interrater agreement of at least 80% is recommended.

Validity. The developers describe evidence of construct and content validity primarily in terms of the literature that guided the selection of constructs, development of items, and content review by educators, mental health professionals, and parents. More traditional statistical methods such as factor or item analysis would strengthen the construct validity evidence for the DTORF-R (5th ed.). Three distinct validation of effectiveness studies, with different foci in terms of target sample, are described in the 2007 manual. These studies have resulted in revisions to the rating system over time. The first study focused on measuring student gains over time and found that children made gains in more than 50% of the age-appropriate skills. The second comprehensive study examined teacher performance after receiving in-service training, which resulted in the recommendation that 30 hours of in-service training was needed to establish competence in applying the Developmental Therapy–Developmental Teaching model and, by extension, for effective use of the measure. The most recent pre-post intervention effectiveness study conducted in 2001 documented the progress of 279 students across six states who were monitored by experienced educators in training to become trainers. Students were selected if they had at least one recorded disability (e.g., emotional or behavioral disability, autism, pervasive developmental delay) and had two completed DTORF-R assessments from 2 months to <11 months apart. Findings indicate that collectively the 279 students made gains across all four DTORF-R domains even when considering gender and delay at time of entry (i.e., mild, moderate, or severe delay). Detailed information about the results of the effectiveness study by race, gender, and age level are provided in the test manual, as well as a complete reference list of studies conducted over the past 30 years.

SUMMARY. The DTORF-R (5th ed.) is a comprehensive criterion-referenced measure that assesses the social, emotional, and behavioral competence of children from birth to 16 years of age. It has significant strength as a classroom-based instructional and intervention tool as well as a tool for monitoring students' gains over time. The new web-based version makes generating Behavior Intervention Plans (BIP) that can contribute to Individual Education Plans (IEP) seamless. Reports also can be generated with descriptive and inferential statistics when pooling groups of students over time, to support ongoing group monitoring, to identify students who may require additional support, for information sharing with parents and staff, and for school or district level reporting requirements such as IDEA. Although there are no item or content changes from the previous version of the DTORF-R, the addition of an online platform for completing, storing, and monitoring progress over time contributes to the strength and comprehensive nature of the measure. Interested users can get a 30-day trial membership to access the online system; however, such access is challenging for users outside the U.S. without calling to set up a free account. The online system provides comprehensive instructions that guide raters in its use; however, it is recommended that users refer to the 4th edition materials for information about the theory, development, and psychometric properties of the test, as such information is not available online.

REVIEWERS' REFERENCES

deFur, S. (2001). [Review of the Developmental Teaching Objectives and Rating Form–Revised]. In B. S. Plake & J. C. Impara (Eds.), *The fourteenth mental measurements yearbook* (pp. 403-405). Lincoln, NE: Buros Institute of Mental Measurements.
Wood, M. M., Quirk, C. A., & Swindle, F. A. (2007). *Teaching responsible behavior: Developmental therapy–developmental teaching for troubled children and adolescents* (4th ed.). Austin, TX: PRO-ED.

[53]

Dimensional Assessment of Personality Pathology–Basic Questionnaire.

Purpose: Designed to "provide a comprehensive assessment of the basic dimensions of personality disorder and clinically relevant personality traits."
Population: Ages 18 and over.
Publication Date: 2009.
Acronym: DAPP–BQ.
Scores, 18: Affective Lability, Anxiousness, Callousness, Compulsivity, Conduct Problems, Cognitive Dysregulation, Identity Problems, Insecure Attachment, Intimacy Problems, Low Affiliation, Narcissism, Oppositionality, Rejection, Restricted Expression, Self-Harm, Stimulus Seeking, Submissiveness, Suspiciousness.
Administration: Group.
Price Data, 2012: $280 per hand-scoring examination kit including manual (149 pages), 10 test booklets, 25 answer sheets, 25 scoring sheets, 25 profile sheets, and 5 online administrations; $185 per Fax-In examination kit including manual, 5 test booklets, and 10 fax-in answer sheets; $37 per test manual.
Time: (35-50) minutes.
Authors: W. John Livesley and Douglas N. Jackson.
Publisher: SIGMA Assessment Systems, Inc.

Review of the Dimensional Assessment of Personality Pathology–Basic Questionnaire by NICHOLAS F. BENSON, Assistant Professor of School Psychology, The University of South Dakota, Vermillion, SD:

DESCRIPTION. The Dimensional Assessment of Personality Pathology–Basic Questionnaire (DAPP-BQ) is a self-report questionnaire designed to assess basic dimensions of personality disorder in clinical populations. As noted in the test manual, the DAPP-BQ consists of 290 items written at the 5th grade reading level and rated on a 5-point scale ranging from *strongly disagree* to *strongly agree*. Although the DAPP-BQ was designed primarily for use with clinical populations, the test authors note that test users may find its dimensional approach useful when assessing the full continuum of personality variation across clinical and nonclinical populations. The DAPP-BQ is designed for use with individuals aged 18 years and older and can be completed in approximately 35–50 minutes.

DEVELOPMENT. The test authors report that items were developed based on reviews of the clinical literature and subsequent evaluation by a panel of expert clinicians. The goal was to identify descriptive features of personality disorder and organize these features into trait descriptions essential for understanding, describing, and treating individuals with personality disorders. Items were selected to reflect these trait descriptions. Items were eliminated if they lacked internal consistency, yielded skewed patterns of endorsement, or correlated highly with measures of social desirability and general psychopathology. The remaining items were examined using principal component analysis and appear to represent 15 empirically derived factors in clinical, general population, and combined samples. However, rather than 15 scales the test authors developed 18 scales due to (a) a belief that separate anxiousness and identity problem scales were warranted based on theoretical and clinical relevance, despite empirical evidence indicating that these scales are primary measures of general distress or neuroticism; (b) a belief that a suspiciousness scale was clinically relevant, although suspiciousness was not a robust measure of any of the 15 empirically derived factors; and (c) inclusion of a Self-Harm scale not intended to measure a personality trait but developed for the express purpose of assessing suicidal ideation and self-harm. Empirical analyses suggest that the 18 DAPP-BQ scales can be organized into 4 higher order factors (i.e., Emotional Dysregulation, Dissocial Behavior, Social Avoidance, and Compulsiveness) and thus interpreted at a more general level. Finally, 8 items that correlated highly with measures of social desirability were retained in order to form a validity scale reflecting social desirability and impression management.

TECHNICAL. General population norms (n = 2726) and clinical norms (n = 656) are available for test users. The existing general population norms are composed of three separate samples including a sample from a mail-out study, a sample collected over time beginning in the early 1990s, and a sample of twins recruited from Canada for a research study. The clinical norms include patients with a primary diagnosis of personality disorder recruited from inpatient and outpatient settings. Information regarding representation of various ethnicities, education levels, and geographical areas is lacking.

Reliability studies reported in the test manual suggest that scores obtained from the DAPP-BQ demonstrate adequate reliability across the samples examined. Internal consistency reliability estimates ranged from .81 for Conduct Problems among female twins to .95 for Anxiousness in the clinical sample. Thus, respondents appeared to provide consistent answers within each of the 18 scales and each scale appears to be distinct and informative.

Test-retest reliability estimates following a 3-week delay ranged from .84 to .93, providing some preliminary evidence that the scores are temporally consistent and thus likely to represent traits rather than states.

A notable strength of the DAPP-BQ is that it has been utilized in research dating back more than 20 years. Thus, there is an impressive body of theoretical literature and empirical evidence to support score interpretation when attempting to understand and describe personality disorders. Research supports the dimensional approach underlying the DAPP-BQ and suggests genetic continuity between normal personality and disordered personality (for review, see Widiger, Clark, & Livesley, 2009). Research cited in the test manual suggests that the four-factor structure of the DAPP-BQ is consistent across samples obtained from several nations. Additionally, research cited in the test manual demonstrates convergence of DAPP-BQ self-report ratings with interview and rating scale formats designed to measure the same traits. Moreover, a joint factor analysis with the DAPP-BQ and the only other measure designed expressly for assessing personality disorder traits (i.e., the Schedule for Nonadaptive and Adaptive Personality; T8:2359) showed high convergence of content across the two measures (Clark, Livesley, Schroeder, & Irish, 1996). Thus, theory-consistent patterns of convergent and divergent relations have emerged from comparisons of DAPP-BQ scores with scores obtained from other measures of normal and disordered personality.

COMMENTARY. The DAPP-BQ assesses unique constructs and is well-aligned with current theory and research pertaining to the development of personality disorder. As a dimensional tool it may be used for assessing normal adaptive personality traits in addition to maladaptive personality traits. This dimensional approach seemingly facilitates understanding, description, diagnosis, and treatment of personality disorder.

The DAPP-BQ can be administered to individuals or groups using online, software, fax, or paper-and-pencil formats. There are a variety of options for scoring including an online platform and scoring software. If the paper-and-pencil format is preferred there are hand-scoring, fax-in, and mail-in options.

The DAPP-BQ norms are questionable given that information regarding representation of various ethnicities, education levels, and geographical areas is lacking. The test authors indicate that the current norms should be considered interim and that they intend to gather new normative samples. Meanwhile, norm-referenced score interpretations should be made cautiously.

There is fairly robust evidence to support the validity of DAPP-BQ score interpretations. However, empirical evidence supporting treatment utility is lacking. Although the test is touted on the publisher's website as a valuable tool for selecting interventions, there is little evidence to support this claim. The test manual provides seemingly useful treatment implications related to score interpretations, but evidence indicating that these interpretations contribute to beneficial treatment outcomes is lacking. Future research examining the treatment utility of DAPP-BQ scores is needed.

SUMMARY. The DAPP-BQ is a measure designed primarily to assess basic dimensions of personality disorder in clinical populations, although the test authors note that test users may find its dimensional approach useful when assessing the full continuum of personality variation across clinical and nonclinical populations. Reliability studies suggest that scores derived from the DAPP-BQ represent distinct traits that are temporally consistent. There is fairly robust evidence to support the validity of score interpretations. The DAPP-BQ has a long history as a research tool and is a promising clinical tool. The measure is likely to prove useful for researchers and clinicians alike who endeavor to assess personality disorders. However, users should proceed with caution when utilizing DAPP-BQ scores as part of the clinical decision process due to its questionable normative samples.

REVIEWER'S REFERENCES

Clark, L. A., Livesley, W. J., Schroeder, M. L., & Irish, S. L. (1996). Convergence of two systems for assessing specific trait disorders. *Psychological Assessment, 8,* 294-303.
Widiger, T. A., Clark, L. A., & Livesley, W. J. (2009). An integrative dimensional classification of personality disorder. *Psychological Assessment, 21,* 243-255.

Review of the Dimensional Assessment of Personality Pathology–Basic Questionnaire by PETER ZACHAR, Professor of Psychology, Auburn University Montgomery, Montgomery, AL:

DESCRIPTION. The Dimensional Assessment of Personality Pathology–Basic Questionnaire (DAPP-BQ) represents a cutting edge approach to assessing personality disorder. Rather than measuring the conventional categories of personality disorder encoded in official diagnostic manuals since the 1950s, the DAPP-BQ measures 18 clinically relevant dimensions of personality such as affective lability, low affiliation, and oppositionality. These dimensions cut across the conventional categories of personality disorder (e.g., Borderline and Histrionic) and also encompass the catch-all category of "Personality Disorder Not Otherwise Specified."

In addition to being relevant for assessing personality-related problems, the DAPP-BQ is potentially useful for better understanding psychiatric disorders in general. Personality pathology is a vulnerability factor for the development of psychiatric disorders such as mood, anxiety, and substance-use disorders (Oldham, Skodol, Kellman, & Hyler, 1995) and in some cases personality pathology lies on spectra that include other mental disorders such as Cognitive Dysregulation for the Schizophrenic spectrum (Lenzenweger, 2006). The DAPP-BQ's 18 dimensions can potentially illuminate these relationships.

DEVELOPMENT. The DAPP-BQ was developed using a modified version of the construct-oriented approach to test construction that is closely associated with Douglas Jackson. Jackson was one of the most influential developers of psychological tests in the latter half of the 20th century and is a co-author of the DAPP-BQ. The construct-oriented approach begins with a systematic analysis of the domain to be measured. The personality disorders listed in the *Diagnostic and Statistical Manual of Mental Disorders-III* (DSM-III) constituted the original framework for delimiting the domain. Each disorder was defined by over 50 traits as descriptors. Based on a survey of clinicians, this set of descriptors was reduced to only the most prototypical features for each disorder. Combining overlapping prototypical descriptors resulted in a list of 79 traits.

Items measuring the traits were written and subjected to a series of tests that led to the elimination of those items that correlated with social desirability and with a general measure of psychopathology. Items that were not appropriately correlated with their own scale were also eliminated, thus increasing internal consistency. Items to which most people responded toward the middle of the 5-point scale (*neutral*) and to which few people responded at the extremes (*strongly disagree* or *strongly agree*) were also eliminated, thereby increasing variance. The first item analysis indicated that the internal consistency of several trait scales was still not satisfactory and it was decided that they could be divided into two. Additional constructs were added to address changes made to the personality pathology domain in the *DSM-III-R* in 1987. The end result was an instrument measuring

100 trait scales. Another round of item analysis cross-validated the original findings and refined the scales further to maximize internal consistency while minimizing the number of items.

Normally, a Jackson-developed instrument would be nearly complete at this point. For the DAPP-BQ, the final version was determined by administering the instrument to a community sample and submitting all the scales to a principal components analysis. The best result was a solution of 15 correlated components. A similar result was found with a sample composed of patients diagnosed with personality disorder. The combination of statistical data and practical judgment that led to choosing the 15-scale solution was also used to add three more scales to the final version of the DAPP-BQ. One addition involved splitting an overly broad general distress factor into two scales. Two clinically relevant constructs (suspiciousness and self-harm) that were not represented in the 15-factor solution were also added.

The 290-item test has both hand-scoring and computerized-scoring options. Lists of items by scale and scoring criteria are provided for use in research. The computerized scoring options include faxing answer sheets to Sigma Assessment Systems, online administration, and loading the program onto a PC. The hand-scoring option is laborious relative to other tests from this same company and is not appropriate for regular clinical use. For example, the order of the scales on the profile form and T score and percentile rank tables are not aligned to expedite the plotting of profiles. [Editor's Note: The publisher advises us they have revised the order of the scales in the rank tables to alleviate this issue.]

TECHNICAL. The reliabilities of the 18 scales are very good. In four different samples, the internal consistencies hover around .90. Quite notable is the high internal consistency for the Suspiciousness scale. Traditionally, scales that measure paranoid features have lower reliability. The other DAPP-BQ scale measuring paranoid features, Rejection, is also good. This suggests that there are psychometric advantages to decomposing complex categories such as Paranoid Personality Disorder into unidimensional components.

The 3-week temporal stability of the scales assessed using both classical reliability theory (test-retest) and generalizability theory is also good, with coefficients being in the .80s and .90s. For statistical reasons alone, one can expect that unidimensional traits are more stable than DSM personality dis-

order diagnoses. If this pattern also holds for the DAPP-BQ scales, it should be demonstrated. In the future it would be helpful to assess stability of these dimensions over a longer period.

Norms are available for both a general population sample and a clinical sample of people with personality disorder diagnoses. The clinical sample excluded patients with certain comorbid psychiatric disorders. This may have made the sample less representative of the population of persons with personality disorder, but practically speaking the excluded groups are not appropriate candidates for psychological testing (e.g., those with psychotic disorders). Both T scores and percentile ranks are provided on the profile sheet, but the percentile ranks are more interpretively useful than the T scores (because the percentile rank of the mean score for some scales is not the 50th percentile due to skewed distributions). The possibility of misinterpretation by untrained persons certainly justifies limiting sale of the test to those with doctoral degrees in psychology.

Validity is a more complex issue. It is worth noting that the DAPP-BQ is not a measure of personality disorder per se. The scales of the DAPP-BQ are useful for conceptualizing particular cases of personality disorder once a diagnosis has been made. The general criteria for diagnosing personality disorder are not included in the DAPP-BQ, although scales such as Anxiousness, Identity Problems, Affective Lability, Low Affiliation, and Narcissism (that were all negatively skewed in the clinical sample) might be informative in this respect.

Because of the way the instrument was developed, it has very good factorial validity. The test manual also indicates that the factor loadings were similar in the general population and clinical samples. Furthermore, a second-order principal components analysis of the 18 dimensions yielded a four-factor structure composed of Emotional Dysregulation, Dissocial Behavior, Social Avoidance, and Compulsiveness. The loadings of the scales onto the second-order factors (or factor congruence) were also similar across several different samples. These second-order factors have been replicated across cultures and appear to have meaningful genetic components, although the test authors' claim that the DAPP-BQ scales represent "the underlying genetic architecture of personality" (technical manual, p. 78) appears overly enthusiastic.

The 18 scales have good criterion-related validity as assessed by correlations with tests measuring related constructs. The correlations with related personality tests are meaningful and in the expected directions. The same is true for joint factor analyses of the DAPP-BQ with each test. The manual explicates which dimensions might be expected to be prominent for the conventional DSM categories of personality disorder and which aspects of particular DSM diagnoses are not included in the DAPP-BQ item set. Explicit correlations between the dimensions with measures of DSM personality disorder constructs or with other measures of Axis I psychopathology such as mood and anxiety disorders are not presented.

The DAPP-BQ was correlated with a brief version of itself and with a structured clinical interview version of itself. The correlations were generally good, although some scales such as Narcissism and Compulsivity had a disappointing degree of overlap with their counterparts in the structured interview version (with just a little over 30% of the variance shared). Future work might explore how significant others rate patients on these dimensions. Paying more attention to what constitutes "clinically significant" is also important because the instrument includes some scales that are difficult to interpret. For example, if a person were to say "disagree" to all the items on the Callousness scale, he or she would still score at the 64th percentile on Callousness even after reporting being "not callous" at every opportunity. The Conduct Problems and Suspiciousness scales are also problematic in this same way.

Based on normal standards for assessing validity evidence, the DAPP-BQ is very adequate, but has some way to go before it can be said to be better than adequate–and the DAPP-BQ has significant potential to be better than adequate. Advocates for the dimensional model of personality pathology, of which the DAPP-BQ is a primary exemplar, make strong claims about the superiority of the dimensional model relative to the traditional categorical model, especially for treatment planning. Unfortunately, these claims of improved clinical validity are not demonstrated in the test manual, and probably not yet available. One would not expect to see this information in most test manuals, but when the developers of the instrument make claims about superior comparative validity relative to competing models, one might hope that such claims can be supported with evidence. Particularly useful would be information on which dimensions are more and less amenable to change.

One notable problem with using the DAPP-BQ in a clinical setting is its minimalist approach to assessing profile validity–which is primarily based on one short, positive impression scale. A broad menu of validity scales is itself a selling point for many tests, and determination of profile validity should be attended to carefully in clinical tests such as the DAPP-BQ. There are also very few reverse-scored items, which potentially sets up a response bias problem. After flipping through the test manual over a period of several weeks many of the pages are falling out–a quality control issue that should be remedied.

COMMENTARY. In the manual, the test authors claim that the DAPP-BQ was constructed using the assumptions of the lexical hypothesis in personality scale development. According to the lexical hypothesis all the relevant distinctions that can be made with respect to a domain such as personality have been encoded in natural languages. Alfred North Whitehead has referred to this kind of assumption as the fallacy of the perfect dictionary (Whitehead, 1926). Such an assumption also calls to mind Lord Kelvin's purported claim at the end of the 19th century that there is nothing new in physics to be discovered. The history of science has consistently shown that such "Whiggish" enthusiasm is misguided.

This lexical hypothesis motivates the test authors' claim that the DAPP-BQ represents a comprehensive assessment of personality pathology. Even if one went so far as to grant the plausibility of the lexical hypothesis, it is not clear that the DSM-III and the clinical literature of the late 20th century can be considered to represent all distinctions relevant to personality and adaptation. The test manual itself astutely highlights which aspects of the various DSM personality disorders are not measured by the DAPP-BQ. One could also find aspects of the 10 personality disorders originally described by Kurt Schneider (Schneider, 1923/1950) that are not measured by the DAPP-BQ. Therefore, the test authors' claim of comprehensiveness–or content validity–should be taken with a grain of salt.

A related issue is how to interpret the comparisons between the DAPP-BQ and other dimensional models of personality. In the past 20 years it has been advantageous for the advocates of dimensional models to form a tightly knit community, and this has created a proclivity to emphasize the similarities between the different models and downplay the divergences. For example, there are important, nontrivial differences between the DAPP-BQ and the Five Factor Model of personality (Krueger, et al., 2011). Construing them as competing models would be as scientifically helpful as asserting that they are "very loosely" measuring the same thing. Once a dimensional model is incorporated into the official diagnostic systems, one hopes this strategic consensus can be put aside.

SUMMARY. The Dimensional Assessment of Personality Pathology–Basic Questionnaire represents one of the most important advances in psychiatric conceptualization since the publication of the DSM-III in 1980. It provides information about personality pathology that is not available with most other clinical instruments. The test was developed using a rigorous methodology. The 18 dimensions of the DAPP-BQ were selected by a combination of clinical theory and empirical evaluation, and as a result offer a menu of more homogeneous constructs than the heterogeneous categories of personality disorder of the current diagnostic systems. Although the competitive advantages and disadvantages of the dimensional and the categorical models have not yet been tested in practice, it seems highly probable that the more scientifically adequate constructs of the dimensional model (including those of the DAPP-BQ) offer great potential for making advances in the treatment of personality disorder.

REVIEWER'S REFERENCES

Krueger, R. F., Eaton, N. R., Clark, L. A., Watson, D., Markon, K. E., Derringer, J., Skodol, A., & Livesley, W. J. (2011). Deriving an empirical structure of personality pathology for DSM-5. *Journal of Personality Disorders, 25*, 170-191.

Lenzenweger, M. F. (2006). Schizotaxia, schizotypy, and schizophrenia: Paul E. Meehl's blueprint for the experimental psychopathology and genetics of schizophrenia. *Journal of Abnormal Psychology, 115*, 195-200.

Oldham, J. M., Skodol, A. E., Kellman, H. D., & Hyler, S. E. (1995). Comorbidity of Axis I and Axis II disorders. *The American Journal of Psychiatry, 152*, 571-578.

Schneider, K. (1923/1950). *Psychopathic personalities* (M. W. Hamilton, Trans.). London: Cassell.

Whitehead, A. N. (1926). *Science and the modern world.* London: Cambridge University Press.

[54]

Early Language & Literacy Classroom Observation Tool, K-3, Research Edition.

Purpose: Designed to assess "the quality of both the classroom environment and teachers' practices" for language and literacy instruction.

Population: Kindergarten through third-grade classrooms.

Publication Date: 2008.

Acronym: ELLCO K-3.

Scores, 7: General Classroom Environment (Classroom Structure, Curriculum, Total), Language and Literacy (The Language Environment, Books and Reading, Print and Writing, Total).

Administration: Individual.

Price Data, 2010: $30 per user's guide (100 pages); $30 per 5 observation tools.

Time: (210) minutes.

Authors: Miriam W. Smith, Joanne P. Brady, and Nancy Clark-Chiarelli.

Publisher: Paul H. Brookes Publishing Co., Inc.

Review of the Early Language & Literacy Classroom Observation Tool, K-3, Research Edition by AMANDA NOLEN, Associate Professor, Educational Foundations/Teacher Education, College of Education, University of Arkansas at Little Rock, Little Rock, AR:

DESCRIPTION. The Early Language & Literacy Classroom Observation Tool, K-3, Research Edition (ELLCO K-3) is designed to assess the quality of language and literacy instruction in kindergarten through third-grade classrooms. It was originally published in 2002 as the Early Language and Literacy Classroom Observation (ELLCO) Toolkit, Research Edition, that was used for both prekindergarten and primary grades (Smith & Dickinson, 2002). The authors included "Research Edition" in the title of the ELLCO K-3 because, although it was based on the ELLCO it does differ substantially, and reliability and validity studies are still being conducted.

"The ELLCO K-3 consists of an observation instrument and a teacher interview designed to supplement the observation" (user's guide, p. 5). The observation tool includes an observation record where the observer can record information about the context of the observation (e.g., start time, date, number of male students, number of female students, number of students with disabilities, number of English language learners, etc.). The tool also contains five sections: Classroom Structure, Curriculum, Language Environment, Books and Reading, and Print and Writing. Each section is composed of items totaling 18 different observation points. An item contains an anchor statement, a description of artifacts and behaviors to look for, and a rating scale from 1 (Deficient) to 5 (Exemplary). Additionally, each item is accompanied by a holistic rubric to aid in focusing the attention of the observer and to distinguish among the criteria for levels of quality. Finally, the observation record provides space for the observer to record evidence he or she used to determine the score for each item.

Inspection of the rubrics used to determine scoring of the General Classroom Environment subscale yielded some concerns with their lack of clarity. The difference between a rating of "5"

(Exemplary) and a "4" (Strong) is described as the existence of "compelling" evidence in an exemplary case and "sufficient" evidence in a strong case. Consistently, in the opinion of this reviewer, the instructions on how to distinguish between compelling and strong evidence are confusing and seem subjective. For example, the Classroom Management item includes descriptions of "compelling" evidence that include notions that students understand and follow classroom rules, teachers and students are respectful of each other, and engage in meaningful behavior throughout the day. This same descriptor is provided for "sufficient" evidence but with an added clause that suggests that the teacher is more involved in classroom management. An argument can be made that this is an irrelevant difference and also that it requires subjectivity on the part of the observer. Also, this distinction has the potential to provide a confusing message to the teacher receiving the feedback.

The Teacher Interview section includes seven scripted questions and suggestions for probes. The observer is instructed to ask the questions after the classroom observation and advised that the information from the interviews is to be used to supplement the observation, not as evidence to determine scoring. The questions are designed to have the teacher describe typical processes in the classroom including curriculum, instruction, and assessment.

The primary objective of the ELLCO K-3 is to provide a somewhat standardized tool with which to assess accurately the language and literacy environment of the K-3 classroom as well as the literacy practices of the teacher. These uses could extend to curriculum developers, professional development facilitators and designers, teacher educators, and K-3 teachers.

The user's guide does specify qualifications of the observer as having a background in primary grade education, early language and literacy practices, and prior experience conducting classroom observations. It is suggested that the observer allot 3.5 hours at a minimum observing as much of the typical classroom day as possible. The observer is instructed to attempt to observe the teacher working with students in various settings in the classroom while remaining neutral, unobtrusive, and with minimal interaction with the teacher and students. Instructions for how to administer the assessment are clearly presented in the user's guide, and the observation tool is streamlined to allow the observer

to focus the appropriate attention on the activity of the classroom rather than on the tool itself.

DEVELOPMENT. Attempting to establish the theoretical foundation for the ELLCO K-3, the user's guide provides a general discussion of the increased accountability and standards around literacy at the national level. This section of the manual is followed with brief literature overviews of early reading and early writing. The authors conducted a critical literature review of these areas and adeptly connected the research and practices supported by the empirical literature to the underlying assumptions of the instrument itself.

The authors used the feedback they received from the users of the original ELLCO Toolkit in an effort to make the instrument easier to use as well as more robust. According to the description of the development of the ELLCO K-3, a significant modification included more reliance on indicators of how materials were used in the classroom when rating the literacy environment rather than a reliance on the number of materials. Although this distinction is an important and seemingly substantive improvement over the original ELLCO Toolkit, there is no further discussion or description of how the items or groups of items were developed. The reader is directed to a section of the user's guide to read the technical report of the original ELLCO Toolkit, Research Edition and how that instrument was revised to create two separate instruments: ELLCO Pre-K and the ELLCO K-3.

TECHNICAL. The authors describe the ELLCO K-3 as a "Research Edition," and the reader infers that the instrument is still in the development stages. Studies testing the reliability and validity of the instrument are planned, but as of this review, no findings have been reported. The authors do include substantial information about the technical merits of the original ELLCO Toolkit, with very respectable reliability measures. Studies were conducted across 147 pre-K through third grade classrooms from 1997 through 2002; and an additional 259 classrooms from 2002 through 2007. However, given that the ELLCO K-3 is substantially changed from the original version, these measures provide little support for the newer assessment instrument. A revised user's guide that includes findings from reliability and validity studies using the ELLCO K-3 would strengthen this instrument substantially.

COMMENTARY. The general description of the ELLCO K-3 provided by the authors in the user's guide states that this assessment "offers practitioners a vision for evidence-based practices that support students' language and literacy development in the primary grades" (p. 47). The usefulness of the ELLCO K-3 scores to estimate the language and literacy environment of primary grade classrooms is limited by the lack of supporting evidence. However, this instrument does appear to be a useful tool for researchers as well as practitioners. It is easily administered and scored, but requires considerable time on the part of the observer. Given the provenance of the tool from the original ELLCO Toolkit, the ELLCO K-3 has the potential for solid reliability and validity, but evidence has yet to be provided and is greatly needed.

SUMMARY. The Early Language & Literacy Classroom Observation Tool K-3, Research Edition (ELLCO K-3) consists of a classroom observation rubric designed to identify evidence of best practices in early language and literacy curriculum and classroom instruction in the primary grades. The current lack of validity and reliability data limits how this instrument can be used to evaluate teaching and classroom environments. However, the instrument is well-organized, clear, and easy to use, ensuring that the observer can provide constructive and evidence-laden feedback to practitioners and curriculum designers.

REVIEWER'S REFERENCE

Smith, M. W., & Dickinson, D. K. (with Sangeorge, A., & Anastasopoulos, L.) (2002). Early Language and Literacy Classroom Observation (ELLCO) Toolkit (Research ed.). Baltimore, MD: Paul H. Brookes Publishing Co.

Review of the Early Language & Literacy Classroom Observation Tool, K-3, Research Edition, by GRETCHEN OWENS, Professor of Child Study, St. Joseph's College, Patchogue, NY:

DESCRIPTION. The Early Language & Literacy Classroom Observation Tool, K-3, Research Edition (ELLCO K-3) is an observational measure designed to systematically evaluate the quality of the literacy and language experiences provided in kindergarten and early elementary classrooms. This is done by having an observer—whether a supervisor, literacy coach, curriculum coordinator, mentor, or researcher—appraise classroom activities during an extended period (recommended time is 3.5 hours). The rater considers both the general classroom environment (how the classroom is organized and the curriculum structured for learning) and what goes on while the teacher and children engage in their typical routines, particularly those related to language, reading, and writing.

Materials include a 41-page booklet for taking notes and scoring the observation, and a user's guide that, along with covering descriptive and psychometric information about the instrument, also reviews the literature on early reading and writing, provides a case study with vignettes to illustrate effective elements of early literacy instruction, and lays out detailed suggestions for how to incorporate the ELLCO K-3 into professional development programs and research. Recommendations for conducting observations and multiple examples of recording and scoring procedures are also provided.

To conduct an observation, the rater is instructed to take extensive notes in the "Evidence" pages of the form and to use those notes in subsequently assigning a level from 1 (Deficient) to 5 (Exemplary) for each of 18 topics. The authors provide a qualitative rubric for each item, consisting of anchor statements and descriptive indicators at each level. The anchor statements contain both the practice being addressed (e.g., "instructional efforts to expand students' spoken vocabulary") and the quality of the evidence that the outcome is being achieved ("compelling," "sufficient," "some," "limited," or "minimal" evidence). The anchor statements for each item are followed by "descriptive indicators," which represent examples of what might be seen or heard during the observation that would point toward a particular rubric score.

Scores for three to five related items are later combined to produce subtotals and mean scores (needed for intercomposite comparisons) for each of five composites: Classroom Structure, Curriculum, The Language Environment, Books and Reading, and Print and Writing. These in turn are grouped into two overall subscales: (a) General Classroom Environment and (b) Language and Literacy.

A teacher interview section is also included in the record booklet with suggested questions to determine whether the sample of activities observed was typical and to provide context for or to supplement what has been observed. The authors caution that the teacher responses are not to be used as evidence when scoring.

The authors suggest that the tool can be used effectively in both research and professional development efforts, whether structured around a literacy coach or employed in a study-group approach. The mean scores for each of the five sections can help identify areas of relative strength and weakness for individual teachers, allow for more effective targeting of professional development efforts, and identify areas of progress over time.

DEVELOPMENT. The ELLCO K-3 came out of research conducted in conjunction with the Center for Children & Families at Education Development Center, Inc., an international nonprofit organization based in Massachusetts. The authors devised the original and current versions based upon their review of the research literature on key components of early reading and writing instruction. After approximately 5 years of development that included pilot testing during several government-funded research studies (all designed to improve literacy practices in preschools and learning centers—mostly Head Start—that serve low-income communities in the Northeast), the authors published the ELLCO Toolkit, Research Edition (2002). Continued use of the published instrument and receipt of feedback from teachers and other users "across the country" (user's guide, p. xi) led to the authors' decision to modify the original research version according to age group. For the ELLCO K-3, they developed additional items appropriate to kindergarten and primary grade classrooms, in which reading and writing instruction are strongly emphasized. A separate tool, the ELLCO Pre-K, is available for 3- to 5-year-olds.

TECHNICAL. The authors note that this version "differs substantially" (user's guide, p. 1) from the previous one, and psychometric studies employing it have not yet been completed, so it is still being published as a research edition. They list their projected psychometric analyses and note that they plan to report them "as the tool is used in current and planned research" (user's guide, p. 61), but they give no indication how one could get access to those results. They do append to the present user's guide a technical report for the earlier version, but this report provides less than optimal evidence for the validity or reliability of the previous tool, and even less for the current one in light of the multiple changes that reportedly have been made.

Standardization. This instrument is not designed to be standardized, so normative data are not available. The authors present extensive descriptions of some of the samples from research studies employing the earlier version of the ELLCO, but these are notably limited in terms of socioeconomic level and geographic area. Absent claims that the measure is standardized, in the opinion of this reviewer it seems inappropriate to judge the re-search samples against accepted criteria for proper standardization practices.

Reliability and validity. The authors argue for the reliability and validity of the measure by again citing data from the variety of literacy instruction intervention studies they conducted in preschool classrooms in low-income communities, all of which used only the earlier edition of the Toolkit. When psychometric data eventually are provided for this edition, the authors may want to reconsider their decision to count a single classroom providing both pre- and postintervention scores as two classes in the classroom total, or to argue for "instructional sensitivity" (user's guide, p. 70) based on improved posttest scores from raters who presumably were not blind to the purpose of the grant-funded study (which was to demonstrate gains from a literacy intervention). In future psychometric studies, it also might be helpful to know what the rate of exact interrater agreement was (rather than reporting that 88%–90% of scorers' ratings were within 1 point on a 5-point scale). Finally, because some items are easier to score objectively (e.g., classroom materials are organized, appealing, and accessible) than others (e.g., instruction promotes students' breadth and depth of word knowledge), a breakdown of reliability by subscale also would be helpful.

COMMENTARY. One set of practical challenges has to do with the recording of observational data. The great majority of the items reflect ongoing, real-time activities and conversations that follow no predictable order, so the rater must flip pages frequently to locate the relevant item and record the evidence. Further, the amount of detail in some of the sample evidence pages presented in the user's guide suggests that such comprehensive observation should not be undertaken without use of electronic recording equipment. However, introducing audio or video equipment into a classroom for a one-day observation is likely to make it even more difficult to overcome the classic Hawthorne effect that results from the presence of an observer.

A second potential problem is that although the authors note in the user's guide that the specific indicators provided under each item are not a checklist but are simply examples that in some cases are quite specific to a given grade level, this caution is not mentioned anywhere in the 41-page record form. The resulting potential for confusion among casual users can be avoided only (a) if raters are willing to study the user's guide chapters covering how to use the indicators for assigning ratings thoroughly, and (b) if raters also have sufficient background expertise to adapt the examples to different grade levels.

In an era of increasing calls for performance-based assessments of teacher performance, administrators eager for an objective assessment tool might be tempted on first glance to consider adopting this instrument for teacher evaluations. However, practical issues argue against such a use at this time. First, few administrators are willing to spend 3.5 hours in each classroom, and even that amount of time may not allow them to see all the activities included in the ELLCO K-3 (e.g., "recognizing diversity" or "focused writing instruction"). Second, initial training is essential, and periodic retraining is strongly recommended. Without extensive training, rubric scores are likely to be insufficiently reliable for important personnel decisions.

The ELLCO K-3 should not be considered in any way a standardized test. Psychometric data from the earlier edition that are presented in the user's guide are not up to accepted standards for traditional psychoeducational measures (and would not be pertinent anyway because the ELLCO K-3 has been revised substantially and looks at a different age group than did the earlier version). As the authors conduct their planned psychometric analyses, it is hoped that they will obtain a broader, more representative standardization group and reconsider their approach to calculating sample sizes. However, because the ELLCO K-3 is not at this time being presented as a norm-referenced instrument, it should be judged on its own merits as a research and professional development tool, and it shows considerable promise for these purposes.

In terms of research applications, the user's guide specifically addresses some aspects of its implementation in educational research studies. Chapter 7 of the user's guide, though short, contains detailed recommendations on how to reduce measurement error in observations. These include suggestions for initial training of data collectors, directions for how to determine interrater agreement, and information about calibrating ratings and recalibrating them in the field.

Although the authors originally designed the ELLCO Toolkit for research purposes (i.e., to document improvements in teachers' literacy practices as a result of research interventions), its more beneficial and widespread applications are likely to be in the realm of professional development. For such uses, it is a plus that the ELLCO was developed by educators for educators. The rubrics could be used constructively by teachers, both new and experienced, as a practical guide to setting up their classrooms, self-evaluating their instructional practices, and making changes to improve their students' literacy skills. For districts offering professional development or mentoring, as well as for graduate and undergraduate teacher education programs, Chapter 6 of the user's guide provides a valuable primer for supervisors and literacy coaches on how to structure professional development activities. Included are practical hints about effective and respectful ways to create a positive climate, share results, create goals, encourage reflection, and support teachers as they make changes to improve their literacy practices. It is easy to imagine college instructors using the materials to advantage with their student teachers (e.g., guiding field observations, helping students structure their reflections, and illustrating best practices in literacy instruction).

SUMMARY. The ELLCO K-3 is an intriguing tool that provides a structured way to observe and record classroom structure and literacy environment systematically by using a series of rubrics built around best practices in literacy instruction. Few such instruments currently exist, so it could fill an important niche as schools move toward providing increased professional development activities and concurrently seek ways to track teachers' progress as they work to improve their practices and meet increasingly higher performance standards. Users must develop their own benchmarks, however, as the current tool is not a standardized instrument.

Though the ELLCO K-3 has many commendable features, it remains to be seen whether an instrument that requires 3.5 hours of a supervisor's or literacy coach's time for each observation, followed by additional feedback session(s), will find widespread use other than in research or for professional development in districts with unusually generous funding. Nonetheless, it has commendable features that make it potentially valuable even for those who have more limited resources. Such users could select specific components of the ELLCO K-3 to employ in more limited projects, including activities within informal learning communities or study groups, or as part of teacher education programs.

[55]

Early Language & Literacy Classroom Observation Tool, Pre-K.

Purpose: Designed as a way for educators and researchers "to examine the literacy-related features of classrooms."
Population: Center-based classrooms for 3- to 5-year-old children.
Publication Dates: 2008-2012.
Acronym: ELLCO Pre-K.
Scores, 7: General Classroom Environment (Classroom Structure, Curriculum, Total), Language and Literacy (The Language Environment, Books and Book Reading, Print and Early Writing, Total).
Administration: Individual.
Price Data, 2011: $50 per user's guide (101 pages) and 5 observation tools; $30 per 5 observation tools; $30 per user's guide.
Time: (210) minutes.
Authors: Miriam W. Smith, Joanne P. Brady, and Louisa Anastasopoulos.
Publisher: Paul H. Brookes Publishing Co., Inc.

Review of the Early Language & Literacy Classroom Observation Tool, Pre-K, by S. KATHLEEN KRACH, Associate Professor, Troy University, Montgomery, AL:

[Editor's Note: This reviewer had access to the 2008 User's Guide and the 2012 Addendum to the Technical Appendix.]

DESCRIPTION. The purpose of the Early Language & Literacy Classroom Observation Tool, Pre-K (ELLCO Pre-K) is to evaluate teachers' practices and the classroom environment in order to improve literacy and language skills for young children. The ELLCO Pre-K is part of a suite of tools to measure literacy and language issues and is specifically designed to be used to evaluate center-based classrooms for children ages 3 to 5 years (Smith, Brady, & Anastasopoulos, 2008). Researchers in the field, supervisors evaluating early literacy, in-service specialists attempting to evaluate needs in the school, and teachers desiring information for self-reflection can use data from the ELLCO Pre-K to improve literacy and language skills in young children. Other tools within the suite are designed for older children (e.g., ELLCO K-3 Research Edition; 19:54) and for home-based learning environments.

The ELLCO Pre-K is divided into two sections: classroom observations and a teacher interview. These two sections are expected to take at least 3.5 hours to complete. The authors of the ELLCO Pre-K do not provide information on how long each portion of the observation should take. One study by Wayne, DiCarlo, Burts, and Benedict (2007) used 5-minute observation periods. A different set of researchers (Grace et al., 2008) asserted that the observation tools should take "10 minutes maximum" (p. 75). The test authors are clear on the need for establishing a relationship prior to starting the assessment as well as choosing the observation periods in a planful manner. In addition, the authors emphasize the need for an unbiased and educated observer. They are less clear on how to ensure a lack of bias or to determine if an observer is qualified. In a separate study, researchers using the ELLCO asserted that the raters needed a minimum of 9 hours of training (Grace et al., 2008).

The classroom observation section has five subareas for evaluating the structure of the classroom, the curriculum and instruction used, the language environment, the books and book reading options, and the print and early writing opportunities within the classroom. Each of these subareas is broken down into specific items for observation (19 in all). The examiner is asked to evaluate each item on a 5-point rating scale, with 5 representing an exemplary level of organization and 1 representing a deficient level. Rubrics are provided to clearly define these ratings. These ratings are compiled as quantitative data at the end of the scoring form. In addition, examiners are asked to describe qualitative evidence supporting their ratings within the scoring form.

The teacher interview consists of seven questions, some of which address reasons why observation data may or may not represent a typical experience for the child. Other questions have to do with the curriculum, materials, class organization, available books, and literacy teaching methods. This qualitative data, along with the qualitative observation data, can be organized in a descriptive report to accompany the data represented from the observation ratings.

DEVELOPMENT. The ELLCO Pre-K was developed as part of the ELLCO Toolkit, Research Edition, published originally in 2002. Observation items and interview questions were based upon research defining positive classroom and teacher variables common in high-quality language and literacy instruction. Although several research studies were indicated, no single theory was put forth as guiding the development of the instrument. In addition, no specific information as to item development, selection, and analysis was provided.

TECHNICAL. The authors of the ELLCO Pre-K (Smith et al., 2008) provided technical information in a 2012 Addendum to the Technical Appendix as well as in the original manual accompanying the test kit. Data were obtained from at least six research projects funded by national organizations (e.g., the U.S. Department of Health and Human Services and the U.S. Department of Education); more than 250 classrooms were examined using the ELLCO system of tools.

Because the ELLCO Pre-K is not a normative-based instrument, true norms are not available. The authors provide some idea of "normal" by offering mean and standard deviation data for various portions of the instrument from the different projects presented in the manual. The problems with using the mean and standard deviation data as a comparison for use by consumers are described within the manual. Specifically, because many of these studies were funded to work with children from at-risk environments or lower-income homes, the data were not drawn from a representative group. Thus, these means and standard deviations can be used only as general information rather than for comparative purposes.

For reliability, the authors describe 74% interrater agreement. Internal consistency data (alpha coefficients) are provided for the five sections as well as the two composite scores. Coefficients for the General Classroom Environment composite (.86) and the Language, Literacy, and Curriculum composite (.92) show solid internal consistency. The coefficients for the Classroom Structure (.79), Curriculum (.72), Language Environment (.79), Books and Book Reading (.87), and Print and Early Writing (.89) scales fall within the range this reviewer considers acceptable.

Concurrent validity data were collected against the Classroom Profile (Abbott-Shim & Sibley, 1998). The authors of the ELLCO Toolkit felt that the Classroom Profile measured some aspects similarly to the ELLCO such as the Learning Environment subscale ($r = .31–.44$), thus providing modest support for convergent validity. Other areas, such as the Scheduling subscale, were predicted to provide divergent data, which was substantiated with the correlations provided ($r = .07–.12$). A study by Dickinson et al. (2000) provided some predictive validity data. According to the ELLCO Pre-K authors, the study found that data from the "Classroom Observation accounted for 80% of the between-classroom variance in vocabulary and 67% of the between-classroom variance in early literacy" (user's guide, p. 69).

COMMENTARY. Through legal requirements set forth in No Child Left Behind (NCLB, 2008) and the Individuals with Disabilities Education Act (IDEA, 2004), showing accountability data has become a necessity for most schools. Both IDEA and NCLB provide mandates for learning opportunities in language and literacy for children at the preschool level. The ELLCO Pre-K was designed to provide data needed for program planning and accountability for this age group. The ELLCO Pre-K appears to be a useful tool for gathering the data needed, with one caveat: It cannot be used as the only method. Information about the learning environment can be helpful when predicting learning outcomes, but direct assessment of the children should be conducted to obtain actual outcome data.

In addition to helping evaluate how well programs for young children meet optimal literacy and language needs, the ELLCO Pre-K can also be useful in other situations. Research by Grace et al. (2008) used a version of the ELLCO to monitor the effects of in-service training on language and literacy activities within the classroom. Researchers were able to use a portion of the ELLCO Toolkit to collect data for their research. Thus, in one study the researchers were able to see the benefits of the Toolkit for monitoring in-service needs and collecting research data.

Please note that although this reviewer is recommending the ELLCO Pre-K as a data collection tool, the instrument has some issues that should be considered by anyone using it. Although reliability data indicate a sound assessment tool, the validity data need more support. The predictive validity and concurrent validity data presented do seem positive. However, very little item development information is provided; thus, content validity cannot be assured. Also, there is no construct validity evidence presented. On its face, the ELLCO Pre-K seems like a valid instrument; however, more data in this area would be helpful.

SUMMARY. The ELLCO Pre-K was designed as part of a suite of tools called the ELLCO Toolkit, Research Edition. It was specifically designed to examine language and literacy issues within classroom environments for children 3 to 5 years of age. The items used in the instrument were selected based on research findings from several studies, but they lack a single, centralized theory to support their selection. Psychometric data from the instrument are promising. However, a personal evaluation of the instrument finds it to be a good tool to use solely for the purposes listed in the manual. Specifically, it should be considered for program planning, research, supervision, and self-assessment. The reviewer believes it would be inappropriate for any use outside of those listed.

REVIEWER'S REFERENCES

Abbott-Shim, M., & Sibley, A. (1998). *Assessment Profile for Early Childhood Programs*. Atlanta, GA: Quality Assist.

Dickinson, D. K., Sprague, K., Sayer, A., Miller, C., Clark, N., & Wolf, A. (2000). Classroom factors that foster literacy and social development of children from different language backgrounds. In M. Hopman (Chair), *Dimensions of program quality that foster child development: Reports from 5 years of the Head Start Quality Research Centers*. Poster session presented at the biannual National Head Start Research Conference, Washington, DC.

Grace, C., Bordelon, D., Cooper, P., Kazelskis, R., Reeves, C., & Thames, D. G. (2008). Impact of professional development on the literacy environments of preschool classrooms. *Journal of Research in Childhood Education, 23*, 52-81

Individuals with Disabilities Education Improvement Act, 20 U.S.C., § 1400 (2004).

No Child Left Behind Act of 2001, 20 U.S.C. § 6319 (2008).

Smith, M. W., Brady, J. P., & Anastasopoulos, L. (2008). *Users guide to the Early Language & Literacy Classroom Observation PRE-K Tool* (ELLCO Pre-K). Baltimore, MD: Paul H. Brookes Publishing Company.

Wayne, A., DiCarlo, C. F., Burts, D. C., & Benedict, J. (2007). Increasing the literacy behaviors of preschool children through environmental modification and teacher mediation. *Journal of Research in Childhood Education, 22*, 5–16.

Review of the Early Language & Literacy Classroom Observation Tool, Pre-K by JEFFREY K. SMITH, Professor of Education, University of Otago College of Education, Dunedin, New Zealand:

[Editor's Note: This review was prepared prior to receipt of the 2012 Addendum to the Technical Appendix and so reflects information in the 2008 User's Guide.]

DESCRIPTION. The Early Language & Literacy Classroom Observation Tool, Pre-K (ELLCO Pre-K) is designed to assess the quality of the literacy environment in prekindergarten classrooms (for children ages 3–5 years). It is not a measure of literacy abilities of children, but rather a measure of the quality of the literacy environment in which the children attend preschool. The ELLCO Pre-K is a revision and expansion of an earlier version of ELLCO. There is now a prekindergarten version (reviewed here) and a kindergarten through third grade version also reviewed in this volume (ELLCO K-3 Research Edition; 19:54).

The ELLCO Pre-K consists of conducting observations of the classroom being assessed and a supplemental interview with the teacher(s) in the classroom. It is divided into five main sections: Classroom Structure, Curriculum, The Language Environment, Books and Book Reading, and Print and Early Writing. The first two sections are then summed to form the General Classroom Environment subscale, and the last three sections are summed to form the Language and Literacy

subscale. Each of the main sections has three to five items pertaining to the classroom that are rated on a 1–5 scale from *deficient* to *exemplary*. Some items ask the observer to judge the quality and preparedness of literary instruction, for example. An item labeled "Discourse Climate" is one of the items in the section on The Language Environment, which gets summed into the Language and Literacy subscale. The rater would decide whether there is "compelling" evidence that this exists (yielding a rating of 5), "sufficient" (4), "some" (3), limited (2), or minimal (1).

The authors of the measure suggested that a rater should spend at least 3.5 hours in the classroom and observe a variety of classroom activities during this time. The teacher interview component of the measure is designed to assure the rater that the day was a typical one for the class, and results may be used for professional teacher development.

DEVELOPMENT. The original ELLCO was developed from roughly 1997 to 2002, and the current ELLCO Pre-K is based on that work and a second series of studies from 2002 to 2007. It is grounded on a set of explicit assumptions about what should happen with regard to literacy development in Pre-K classrooms. These assumptions primarily revolve around providing opportunities for language development, reading books, encouraging writing activities, and having materials in the classroom that foster the development of literacy skills.

There is neither much information provided as to how the 19 items were generated, nor about the development of the five main categories or the two major subscales. Whether the ELLCO Pre-K approach is appropriate for any given prekindergarten classroom would have to be determined by those considering using the instrument.

TECHNICAL. The technical material provided in the user's guide does not relate specifically to the ELLCO Pre-K, but rather to an earlier version of the measure (called the ELLCO Toolkit, Research Edition), which was revised to produce the ELLCO Pre-K. Thus, although the two versions are very similar in many respects, the technical information provided is not about the ELLCO Pre-K itself. It is clear from the user's manual that the ELLCO approach has undergone a substantial research and development process. Although it is not possible to speak to the technical qualities of the instrument being presented, and that is unfortunate, the authors are to be lauded for their sincere efforts to produce a measure that has been subjected to rigorous field testing.

Standardization. There are no standardization studies as such presented in the technical manual, although means and standard deviations from some studies are presented that would provide users with an indication of the kinds of scores that are obtained.

Reliability. The authors present information about both coefficient alpha internal consistency reliability on the two major subscales and interrater reliability on individual items (again, based on the ELLCO Toolkit, Research Edition). Coefficient alpha levels were reported on subcales at .83 and .86, and interrater reliability on observers trained and supervised in studies the authors were involved in are reported at 90%. It is not completely clear what "90%" means, but it appears that is 90% on agreement of categories within one scale point. It would be good to see what the reliability is when people are using the measure on their own as opposed to receiving formal training on its use.

Validity. There is some validity evidence presented from the Research Edition of the Toolkit that speaks to convergent, discriminant, and predictive validity of the measure. It is reasonable to conclude from these studies that the ELLCO Pre-K is probably providing a valid indicator of the degree to which classrooms observed are providing a literacy-rich environment for children, but direct evidence would be preferable.

COMMENTARY. There is much to like in the ELLCO Pre-K, particularly if the assumptions that the authors lay out concerning the quality of literacy environments in Pre-K classrooms are consonant with the perspectives of the potential users. It is not possible to give the measure an unqualified endorsement as the technical materials provided were not conducted on the measure itself, but on a precursor of the measure. It does not require a major inferential leap, however, to conclude from the data that are provided, that the newer instrument is of high quality.

SUMMARY. The ELLCO Pre-K appears to be a well-conceived, easy-to-use measure of the degree to which Pre-K classrooms are providing learning environments that would foster literacy development. It is usable by professionals without specific training in the instrument through careful attention to directions. The technical information, although sufficient for the Research Edition, clearly needs to be updated to reflect the qualities of the measure under consideration.

[56]

Earning Capacity Assessment Form-2nd Edition.

Purpose: Designed to "facilitate the systematic analysis and appraisal of loss of earning capacity."
Population: Ages 0 to 99.
Publication Date: 2010.
Acronym: ECAF-2.
Scores: 1 rating: Impairment to Earning Capacity.
Administration: Individual.
Price Data, 2012: $90 per complete kit, including manual (46 pages) and 25 rating forms; $35 per 25 rating forms; $60 per manual.
Time: [5-10] minutes.
Author: Michael Shahnasarian.
Publisher: Psychological Assessment Resources.

Review of the Earning Capacity Assessment Form-2nd Edition by MARTIN W. ANDERSON, Deputy Commissioner, Connecticut Department of Administrative Services, Hartford, CT:

DESCRIPTION. The Earning Capacity Assessment Form-2nd Edition (ECAF-2) is a rating scale consisting of 14 items with consumable record forms. Use of the assessment form is supported by a 40-page professional manual. The form is meant to be completed by an evaluator. The rating scales and form are appropriately used when completed for individuals who (a) possess an earning capacity, (b) contend their earning capacity has eroded due to an event that may prompt or is prompting litigation, and (c) are pursuing a claim of loss of earning capacity. The test author describes the ECAF-2 as being most effectively used in conjunction with a clinical interview, record review, and other vocational rehabilitation assessment methodologies. "The key determinant of the appropriateness of administering the ECAF-2 is whether the subject of a loss of earning capacity claim possessed an earning capacity" (professional manual, p. 5). The test author asserts that the ECAF-2 standardizes and objectifies the assessment of loss of earning capacity claims that are often at the center of litigation. The completion of the items translates to an overall rating ranging from "No Loss" to "Catastrophic" loss of earning capacity on the scale of mild, moderate, severe, and extremely severe, which translate roughly to percentages of impairment. Each of the 14 items are rated from 0 to 3 with anchored statements. The evaluator is able to note on the form that there is an "insufficient basis to assess" or that a scale item is "not pertinent" when rating scale items. The manual supplies recommendations for how these notations figure into an overall assessment. The professional manual includes two case analyses that include background information on the case, the analysis that was made, and how that translated to an impairment to earning capacity rating on the ECAF-2.

DEVELOPMENT. The test author reports that the scale items were variously derived from professional expertise, review of existing literature, lawyer scrutiny, and professional peer contributions. Shahnasarian and Leitten (2008) developed 9 postulates that form the underpinnings of the ECAF-2 and its constituent items with a 10th postulate added during the development of the instrument. Appointees to a state vocational rehabilitation agency and career counselors performed expert reviews in which they examined item content and utility. As a result of these reviews, some items and response choices were modified. The second edition of the ECAF differs from the first principally in the organization of items into inhibitor and driver categories. No additional details on the development of the scale are provided in the test manual. There are case studies in the manual that relate item ratings to presented cases, and the items are given thorough descriptions and meaning.

Inhibitor items relate to factors that can hinder a claimant's ability to realize his or her earning capacity that may or may not arise from that which gave rise to the loss claim. In contrast to inhibitor items, driver items relate to factors that can assist a claimant in realizing his or her optimal earning capacity. Although the number of inhibitor and driver items is not equal, each is given the same unit weight of importance. The explication and importance of each of the items are given good attention in the test manual as are the interpretive guidelines for ratings of inhibitor and driver items as well as their interaction.

TECHNICAL. Internal consistency in the form of coefficient alpha was reported as .82 across the 14 items for a group of 23 raters who had an average of 27 years of unspecified experience. Interrater agreement was reported as percentage agreement for ratings of a case study made by 23 raters using the ECAF, which ranged from 57% to 100% with agreement on 10 items at or above 70%. Temporal stability was assessed using 25 graduate students who rated case study vignettes over a 2-week interval. The inhibitor items demonstrated test-retest reliabilities ranging from .74 to .96. Coefficients for driver items ranged from .70 to .80.

The Impairment to Earning Capacity Rating Scale ratings had reliabilities ranging from .85 to .90.

The validity research was said to include assessments of internal structure and construct validity. The internal structure was assessed using correlations of ratings from experienced vocational raters who assessed 70 independent claims with the ECAF-2. The test author purports that the results lent support to the differentiation of the inhibitor and driver items collectively but not necessarily for items taken individually. The test author offered evidence to support construct validity through expert review of the items given that the "ECAF-2 is the only measure of its kind" (professional manual, p. 36). The vocational rehabilitation experts who rated the 70 independent claims agreed that the measure facilitated analysis of loss of earning capacity assessments in 52 of the 70 cases (74.3%).

COMMENTARY. The ECAF-2 was clearly meant to provide an objective means to assess the claim of loss of earning capacity, which is frequently at the center of legal damage arising from personal injury, medical malpractice, and work-related injuries and to quantify those claims. The test author convincingly offers that there are important person- and situation-specific contributors that cause or mitigate future earning capacity along with complex economic forces that will influence the ability of someone to regain or never regain full measure of his or her earning capacity. Some of the disappointments in the technical information reported in the manual included the fact that the lowest level of agreement among the raters (57% agreement) occurred for an item that assesses how the anticipated course of the claimant's impairment might affect any future vocational functioning, an issue that is at the center of most any claim. Going to the overall purpose of the ECAF scale, this is confusing and a little troubling even with strong agreement across other items, notably the driver items for which agreement among raters was nearly 100%. Additionally, it would be very helpful to potential consumers to have more explorations of the validity of the ECAF and its constituent item types, which should at least show useful and anticipated relationships with relevant real world indicators such as past earning histories, attained levels of education, job performance ratings, work attendance, measures of work history and advancement, and similar quantifiable data. In promotional materials found on the test publisher's website the test author suggests the ECAF has been well-validated through a number of published reliability and validity studies, but these are not reported in any detail in the professional manual. Still, there is little question that the ECAF can supply a structured and consistent way of approaching the assessment of persons who (a) possess an earning capacity, (b) contend their earning capacity has eroded due to an event that may prompt or is prompting litigation, and (c) are pursuing a claim of loss of earning capacity–as described in the manual. What is not fully borne out in the manual is how much consistency in ratings can really be expected for a case from evaluator to evaluator and what relationship these ratings have to real outcomes realized by individuals who were the center of litigation. In addition, it might be important to know more about the influence that the quality or sufficiency of information about a case has on the measurement qualities of the ECAF.

SUMMARY. The Earning Capacity Assessment Form-2nd Edition is a rating scale consisting of 14 items with consumable record forms. The form is meant to be completed by an evaluator. The test author recommends that "advanced training and years of clinical experience in many areas–including medical and psychosocial aspects of rehabilitation, vocational rehabilitation, career development, standardized testing, and the forensic process–are essential to the responsible and valid application of the ECAF-2" (professional manual, p.5). A limited number of studies and data are presented supporting the reliability and validity of the ECAF-2. The test author convincingly offers that there are important person–and situation-specific contributors that cause or mitigate future earning capacity along with complex economic forces that will influence the ability of someone to regain full measure of his or her earning capacity. The ECAF-2 seems to advance the ability of qualified users to consistently and systematically evaluate such earning capacity.

REVIEWER'S REFERENCE

Shahnasarian, M., & Leitten, C. L. (2008). The Earning Capacity Assessment Form: A study of its reliability. *The Rehabilitation Professional, 16*, 71-82.

Review of the Earning Capacity Assessment Form—2nd Edition by GARY J. DEAN, Professor and Chairperson, Department of Adult and Community Education, Indiana University of Pennsylvania, Indiana, PA:

DESCRIPTION. The Earning Capacity Assessment Form, 2nd Edition (ECAF-2), is designed to be used by rehabilitation professionals to assess the loss of earning capacity of individuals. The instrument consists of an overall Impairment

to Earning Capacity Rating Scale, rated on a percentage from 0% (no loss) to 100% (catastrophic). There are nine inhibitor items and five driver items that require the rehabilitation specialist to assess the person's capacity to continue with his or her current career or begin a new one. Each inhibitor and driver item is rated on a scale from 0 to 3 with 0 representing the most positive assessment and 3 representing the least positive assessment. Each item also contains two other possible responses: "Insufficient basis to assess" and "Not pertinent." Interpretation may be facilitated by plotting the rating assigned to each item. The professional manual contains a general overview of the instrument, instructions for administration and scoring, a review of the development, and technical data on the instrument.

DEVELOPMENT. The ECAF-2 consists of the same 14 items that were in the original edition first published in 2001. There are three primary differences between the two editions. First, in the second edition, the items have been grouped into two categories: inhibitor items and driver items. Second, "Insufficient basis to assess" and "Not pertinent" have been added as rating options for each item. Third, the second edition includes a professional manual.

The items were developed through professional expertise, the professional literature, and contributions from other professionals. There were 12 gubernatorial appointees to a state vocational rehabilitation agency and 35 career counselors who were consulted during item refinement.

TECHNICAL.

Reliability. Reliability was established in three ways: internal consistency, interrater agreement, and test-retest reliability. The internal consistency study was based on a sample of 23 expert raters with an average of 27 years of experience. Coefficient alpha, computed for the study, was .82.

Two studies were used to establish interrater reliability. In one study, 23 raters reviewed a vignette, and the ratings of the 14 items were compared among the raters. It was found that the percent of agreement among the raters ranged from a low of 57% to a high of 100%. In a second interrater reliability study ($N = 78$), a group of vocational rehabilitation counselors used the ECAF-2 to estimate impairment of earning capacity from case studies. Their ratings were compared to counselors who did not use the ECAF-2 to rate the same case studies. Estimates of impairment of earning capacity from the group using the ECAF were reported to have a significantly reduced variance compared to the estimates from the group not using it. No actual numbers were reported for this study.

The third method of establishing reliability was test-retest, in which 25 graduate students rated vignettes over a 2-week period. Test-retest correlation coefficients ranged from .74 to .96 for inhibitor items, .70 to .80 for driver items, and .85 to .90 for the overall Impairment to Earning Capacity Rating Scale.

Validity. Validity was assessed in two ways based on a single study in which five experienced vocational rehabilitators evaluated 70 independent claims using the ECAF-2. Construct evidence was based on the finding that the vocational rehabilitation experts agreed or strongly agreed that the ECAF-2 facilitated the assessment of loss of earning capacity in 52 of the 70 cases (74.3%).

The same study was used to calculate correlation coefficients among the 14 items of the ECAF-2. The findings generally supported the anticipated outcome that there would be positive correlations among all items, with stronger associations between items of the same type (inhibitor or driver). A number of exceptions to this general pattern occurred, however. The correlations among inhibitor items ranged from -.03 to .86, with 21 of the 36 comparisons being statistically significant. The coefficients for two items were low and did not show statistically significant findings with any of the other inhibitor items. Correlations among the driver items ranged from -.12 to .84 with 6 of the 10 coefficients being statistically significant. One item was not statistically significantly related to any of the other driver items. The comparison between inhibitor and driver items produced correlation coefficients that ranged from -.33 to +.64 with only one of the negative correlations being statistically significant, whereas 10 of the positive correlations were statistically significant.

COMMENTARY. The ECAF-2 and the professional manual appear to have been carefully developed for use by practitioners to assess loss of earning capacity. The instrument and the administration, scoring, and interpretation of it are clear and easy to understand and use. The professional manual is particularly strong for describing how to administer, score, and interpret the items. The examples provided in the manual are especially helpful.

The process of item development described in the professional manual for the ECAF-2 appears to have been very thorough, but more detail could have been reported on the actual development of item content. In addition, the reliability and validity studies reported indicate general support for the instrument. There are several areas of concern, however. First, there is scant information provided on the studies used to establish reliability and validity, making it difficult to judge the value of the research underlying the instrument. Second, the sample sizes employed in the studies were small. Third, the utility of dividing the ECAF-2 items into inhibitor and driver items has not been established.

SUMMARY. The ECAF-2 is designed to be used by vocational rehabilitation professionals to evaluate the loss of earning capacity for individuals. The instrument is well designed and appears straightforward in use and application. Its purpose is to reduce variance and increase standardization of claims assessments. The professional manual appears to be very helpful to practitioners in this regard. The research reported in general substantiates the development, reliability, and validity of the instrument; however, more details of the research need to be reported. In addition, evidence regarding the appropriateness and utility of dividing the instrument's items into the two categories of inhibitor and driver items is not compelling.

[57]

ElecTest (Form AR-C & Form B).

Purpose: For selecting electrical repair and maintenance candidates.

Population: Applicants and incumbents for jobs requiring practical electrical knowledge and skills.

Publication Dates: 1997-2010.

Scores, 10: Motors, Digital & Analog, Electronics, Schematics & Print Reading and Control Circuits, Basic AC/DC Theory and Electrical Maintenance, Computers & PLC and Test Instruments, Power Supplies, Power Distribution and Construction & Installation, Mechanical and Hand & Power Tools, Total.

Administration: Group.

Forms, 2: AR-C, B.

Price Data, 2011: $22 per consumable self-scoring test booklet or online test administration (minimum order of 20); $24.95 per manual (2008, 27 pages).

Foreign Language Edition: Available in Spanish.

Time: (60-70) minutes.

Comments: Self-scoring instrument; online version available; Form B is an alternate equivalent of Form A.

Author: Roland T. Ramsay.

Publisher: Ramsay Corporation.

Cross References: For a review by Eugene P. Sheehan of an earlier edition, see 18:47.

Review of the ElecTest (Form AR-C & Form B) by JOHN K. HAWLEY, Engineering Psychologist, U.S. Army Research Laboratory, Ft. Bliss Field Element, Ft. Bliss, TX:

DESCRIPTION. The various forms of the Ramsay Corporation's ElecTest are designed to provide measures of job knowledge and skill for those in the electrical trades. According to the test manual, the test is "intended for use with applicants and incumbents for jobs where practical electrical knowledge and skill are necessary parts of maintenance job activities" (p. 1). There are several forms of this test: Form AR-C, Form A-C, and Form B, although this reviewer only saw version AR-C. Each of the test forms samples from a range of electrical knowledge domains. These include Motors; Digital and Analog Electronics; Schematics, Print Reading and Control Circuits; Basic AC/DC Theory and Electrical Maintenance; Computers/PLC and Test Instruments; Power Supplies; Power Distribution and Construction/Installation; and Mechanical and Hand/Power Tools. Job analysis of the work performed by electricians and electrical maintenance personnel provided the general background for the knowledge and skill areas assessed. The knowledge and skill domains assessed in the test are routinely reviewed and edited to reflect job and underlying technology (e.g., analog vs. digital) changes over time.

Test versions AR-C and B are straightforward to administer and score. They are reported to be parallel test forms, although no supporting data are provided. Each test is composed of 60 multiple-choice items reflecting the specified electrical knowledge and skill domains. Directions are clear, and there are two introductory sample questions. Both versions contain traditional word items and also items referring to schematics or other diagrams. In both versions, items are organized by knowledge and skill domain. Form AR-C comes in a self-contained question and answer booklet in which answer alternatives align with corresponding spaces on a carbon answering sheet. Respondents' answers transfer via pencil pressure to a sealed answer sheet. The answer sheet can be torn open when the test is completed so that the scorer can easily determine which responses are correct. Form AR-C is also available in an online version. Test Form B has a separate answer sheet and is scored using a separate scoring overlay. The test manual indicates that the test is untimed but should take no longer than 60 minutes to complete.

DEVELOPMENT. The test manual indicates that the ElecTest was developed in consultation with five electrical trades subject-matter experts (SMEs). The job experts were incumbent electrical craft workers or supervisors of craft workers. These SMEs edited a list of potential knowledge and skill areas and ranked each in terms of importance. Rankings were averaged across raters, and each rater independently estimated the percentage of items that should be included in each knowledge and skill area. SMEs working in pairs then selected from a larger test bank items to be included in the test. Items were selected to reflect appropriate job content and difficulty. The test manual does not indicate the original source of the items in the larger test bank. The experts were instructed to ensure that each test area included a safety item, where applicable.

TECHNICAL. Final item selection for the ElecTest came after several hundred individuals had taken an early version of the test. Item selection was based on item point-biserial discrimination indices and item difficulty. This same approach has been used to refine and update the test over time.

Normative data expressed as test scores by percentile ranks are provided for both Form AR-C and Form B. Percentile ranks for Form AR-C are based on a sample of 34 maintenance employees in various industries. Similar ranks for Form B are based on a sample of 23 maintenance employees. The specific industries involved are not noted. The test manual also provides item difficulty indices and point-biserial correlations of items with test section scores for both Forms AR-C and B.

Reliability indices for the ElecTest are expressed in terms of KR-20 measures of internal consistency. Internal consistency reliability coefficients for the two versions of the test reviewed (AR-C and B) are generally high, .84 and .89, respectively. The reported reliability of Form AR-C is for the online version only. Odd-Even reliability for Form B is reported as .91.

Three types of validity evidence are discussed in the test manual: content-related, criterion-related, and construct. The evidence supporting content validity of the test is based on the fact that test items reflect the judgments of electrical trades SMEs drawn from a range of relevant industrial settings. The test manual asserts that the various forms of the ElecTest represent paper-and-pencil forms of a work sample.

To assess criterion-related validity, the scores of 95 employed maintenance workers were correlated with ratings provided by managers on several job dimensions. ElecTest scores correlated .50 with managers' ratings of technical skills, .23 with ratings of problem solving, and .32 with total performance. All of these correlations are statistically significant. The supervisor rating terms are not defined in the test manual. Although not stated, it appears that criterion-related validity results are pooled across various versions of the ElecTest series.

The ElecTest is a domain-referenced knowledge and skill test. In that sense, the construct measured is knowledge and skill in electrical maintenance. The test manual asserts that the test is useful in situations where electrical knowledge and skill is required. Suggested applications include diagnosing a person's knowledge and skill level prior to development of an individual training plan, hiring the most knowledgeable job candidate from a pool of applicants, and certifying electricians with respect to knowledge and skill in an electrical context.

COMMENTARY. The various forms of the ElecTest are easy to administer and score. Moreover, interpretation of test results is relatively straightforward. The test was developed in accord with generally accepted practices within the field of industrial-organizational psychology for the development of domain-referenced knowledge and skill tests. Test reliability assessed in terms of internal consistency is in the acceptable range. Criterion-referenced validity indices indicate that test scores are correlated with independent manager/supervisor ratings of on-the-job proficiency in the electrical trades.

The ElecTest is purported to measure both knowledge and skill in the electrical trades. However, it is not clear from a review of the items in Form AR-C that the test measures knowledge and skill equally. A distinction that is widely drawn in the learning sciences literature is between declarative and procedural knowledge (Anderson, 2000). Declarative knowledge is often characterized as "knowing about," whereas procedural knowledge (or skill) is described as "knowing how to do." The items in ElecTest Form AR-C appear mostly to reflect the former–knowing about. The extent to which the test measures skill, or the ability to perform competently on the job, is not clear. Criterion-related validity results suggest that test results are correlated with on-the-job performance, but those correlations are not high. In that sense, one can question whether the ElecTest actually could be called a work sample test. It might better be described as a knowledge test and used as such. Use as a job knowledge test is not inconsistent with the applications suggested in the test manual and cited in the previous section.

Potential ElecTest users are also advised to compare the job knowledge domains assessed with the requirements of their own work situation. Doing this might require users to perform a cursory job analysis of their own situation to determine the match between the domains assessed by the ElecTest and the job content of their own situation. Job domain mismatches are a potential source of invalidity in the way test results are used.

SUMMARY. The ElecTest assesses specialized knowledge for electricians and electrical technicians. The test is easily administered and scored, and the various forms of the test have acceptable psychometric properties. Results from the ElecTest can reasonably be used for the purposes suggested in the construct validity section of the test manual. Users should be cautioned, however, that the ElecTest is more properly categorized as a test of job-related knowledge than of job-related skill.

REVIEWER'S REFERENCE

Anderson, J. R. (2000). *Learning and memory: An integrated approach* (2nd ed.). New York, NY: Wiley.

[58]

Electrical Maintenance Trainee–Form UKE-1RC.

Purpose: Designed for selecting or evaluating electrical trainees with one year of training or experience.

Population: Applicants for jobs requiring electrical knowledge and skills.

Publication Dates: 1991-2010.

Scores, 12: Motors, Digital and Analog Electronics, Schematics and Electrical Print Reading, Control, Power Supplies, Basic AC/DC Theory, Construction Installation and Distribution, Test Instruments, Mechanical/Equipment Operation/Hand and Power Tools, Computers and PLC, Electrical Maintenance, Total.

Administration: Group.

Price Data, 2014: $23 per consumable self-scoring test booklet; $25 per online administration, scoring, and reports (20 minimum); $24.95 per manual (2008, 24 pages).

Time: (60-70) minutes.

Comments: Self-scoring instrument; available for online test administration.

Author: Roland T. Ramsay.

Publisher: Ramsay Corporation.

Cross References: For a review by David C. Roberts of an earlier edition, see 13:114.

Review of the Electrical Maintenance Trainee Test Form UKE–1RC by ELEANOR E. SANFORD-MOORE, Senior Vice-President of Research and Development, MetaMetrics, Inc., Durham, NC:

[Editor's Note: This review reflects information contained in the 2008 manual. The publisher advises that a new manual was released in 2013 after this review was written.]

DESCRIPTION. The Electrical Maintenance Trainee Test was developed by the Ramsay Corporation in 1990. The test is designed to measure an individual's knowledge and skills in training programs where electrical training and experience of up to 2 years of duration are required for entry. The test covers the following knowledge areas: motors, digital electronics, analog electronics, schematics and electrical print reading, control, power supplies, basic AC/DC theory, power distribution, test instruments, mechanical, computer and PLC, hand and power tools, electrical maintenance, construction and installation, equipment operation, and transducers.

The test can be administered via paper-and-pencil or online. Examinees are told that although there is no time limit, they should not need more than 60 minutes to complete the test. Test administrators are told to mark the time each examinee takes to complete the test on the test booklet, but no direction is provided in the test manual as to how this information should be used.

The Electrical Maintenance Trainee Test can be scored by the examiner (Form UKE–1RC), scored by the administrator using an overlay key (Form UKE–2C), or scored by computer (UKE–1RC online). The items are scored right-wrong, and the raw score is the test score.

DEVELOPMENT. The instrument was developed initially by having job experts rate the knowledge and skills previously identified as necessary based on the *Dictionary of Occupational Titles* and *O*NET* descriptions of the position. In addition to rating each topic in terms of importance to the job, raters also estimated the percentage of items in each topic that should be included on the test. Job experts then selected 119 relevant items (and safety items) from the existing item bank owned by the Ramsay Corporation.

Based on the pilot administration of the set of items, 60 items were retained on the final form of the test (UKE–1C). Items were selected for inclusion based on item point-biserial discrimination index (.32 to .75) and item difficulty (.17 to .90). Information is not provided on the range of item

point-biserial correlations and item difficulties for all items on the pilot test.

Currently, there are two forms of the Electrical Maintenance Trainee Test, UKE–1 and UKE–2, but no item-level information is provided to show that the forms are equivalent in content or difficulty. Item-level information is provided for Form UKE–1 and Form UKE–1C from two samples ($N = 88$ and $N = 28$). Although it is evident from the mean scores that the two samples are not equivalent in ability, item difficulties from the two samples are not consistent (the correlation between the item difficulties from the two samples is .69).

TECHNICAL.

Reliability. Reliability was calculated using the *KR20* formula and the associated standard error of measurement. Reliability coefficients ranged from .82 to .91 across five studies (*N*s ranged from 28 to 121). The standard errors for the samples ranged from 3.09 to 3.46 (based on 60 items). No information related to test-retest reliability is presented.

Validity. The validity information presented in the manual consists of two studies. The first study examined content evidence of validity and consisted of six raters evaluating each of the 60 items on the UKE–1C as to the extent of job-relatedness. The average job-relatedness rating across the items was 4.3 out of 5 (no scores below 2.5), and rater agreement was .72.

A second study examining criterion-related evidence of validity is also presented in the manual. For a small sample of examinees ($N = 32$), Electrical Maintenance Trainee Test scores were correlated with three criterion measures of job performance in electrical maintenance. The correlations of .41, .45, and .53 were described as significant.

Norms. Norms are provided using data from three populations. The first sample consisted of 88 applicants for electrical maintenance jobs at an integrated steel company. The second sample involved 33 students in secondary schools. As expected, the examinees in the first study scored higher ($M = 34.1$, $SD = 10.2$) than examinees in the second study ($M = 22.2$, $SD = 8.7$). The third set of normative data is based on 28 applicants for electrical trainee positions at a metals manufacturer. Contrary to expectation, these norms are lower ($M = 27.3$, $SD = 9.4$) than those in the original study even though the examinees in the two studies were comparable in experience and training.

COMMENTARY AND SUMMARY. The Electrical Maintenance Trainee Test is easy to administer and score. Interpreting the resulting scores is difficult, however. Although norms are provided in the test manual, the normative sample employed was very small, and the results are inconsistent with the results of other studies described in the manual.

Although revisions and additions have been made on the test (multiple forms, online administration), no additional studies beyond the initial development have been conducted to examine the reliability and validity of the test, to describe the equivalence of the forms, and to ensure that the knowledge and skills identified and initially assessed in 1990 are still applicable 20 years later for electrical maintenance trainees.

Review of the Electrical Maintenance Trainee Test—Form UKE-1RC by EUGENE P. SHEEHAN, Dean, College of Education and Behavioral Sciences, University of Northern Colorado, Greeley, CO:

[Editor's Note: This review reflects information contained in the 2008 manual. The publisher advises that a new manual was released in 2013 after this review was written.]

DESCRIPTION. The Electrical Maintenance Trainee Test, initially developed by the Ramsay Corporation in 1990, is designed as a test of knowledge for individuals with some training or experience in electrical maintenance. The Ramsay Corporation produced revisions and updates to the instrument in 1998 and in 2008. The test is very similar to the Ramsay Corporation's Elec-Test (Ramsay, 2001; 18:47), which this reviewer evaluated for *The Eighteenth Mental Measurements Yearbook* (Sheehan, 2010). Consequently, this review is similar in format and content to the earlier one.

As with the ElecTest, the Electrical Maintenance Trainee Test measures job knowledge and skill for those in the electrical trades, specifically electricians and electrical technicians, where practical electrical knowledge is critical to job functioning. The manual points to a distinction between trainees, toward whom this instrument is directed, and apprentices. Trainees enter the electrician field with higher skills than apprentices and complete about 2 years of training, whereas apprentices require 3 to 4 years of training. The Electrical Maintenance Trainee Test is designed to assess the knowledge and skills of applicants to a trainee program for which 2 years of training and experience are required for program entry. In essence, the test is an entry point into a training program to become an electrician. The

various job duties of electricians are detailed in the test manual.

According to the manual, the test draws from a range of knowledge and skill areas, including motors, digital and analog electronics, schematics and print reading, transducers, and hand and power tools. All the knowledge areas are clearly relevant to the field of electrical work. Job analyses of the work done by electricians and maintenance electricians provided the general background for the identification of the knowledge and skill areas. This reviewer does not have the job knowledge to ascertain whether any critical areas were omitted.

Test administration is straightforward. There are 60 multiple-choice items in the test, which comes in a self-contained booklet wherein answer alternatives align with corresponding spaces on a carbon-answering sheet. In the world of high technology testing today, this format might appear dated. However, its datedness is outweighed by its simplicity. The answers of the respondents transfer via pen pressure onto a sealed answer sheet. The answer sheet can be torn open when the test is completed so that the scorer can easily discern which responses are correct. An Online version also is available.

Both versions contain traditional word items as well as items referring to schematics or other diagrams. Items are organized by knowledge area: Basic AC/DC Theory; Schematics and Electrical Print Reading; Motors; Digital and Analog Electronics, Control; Power Supplies; Construction and Installation and Distribution; Test Instruments; Mechanical, Equipment Operation, and Hand and Power Tools; Computer and PLC; and Electrical Maintenance. All questions except one have four answer alternatives; the remaining question has five answer alternatives.

Directions are clear, and there are two sample questions. The test manual contains detailed instructions for administration, including suggestions to guide the behavior of the invigilator. There is no time limit.

DEVELOPMENT. The knowledge areas indicated above were derived from a longer list of knowledge areas that was reviewed and ranked by nine maintenance supervisors. The job experts also provided information on the percentage of items from each area of import that they thought should be in the test. These experts, working in pairs, then selected from a test bank those items they deemed suitable for the assessment. The manual does not indicate from whence the original items came. The experts also developed one extra item for each test area to address worker safety concerns.

Final item selection came after 121 individuals had taken an early version of the test. Two industrial psychologists selected the final 60 items. Item selection was based on item point-biserial discrimination indices and on item difficulty. Item point-biserial discrimination indices and item difficulty have been used to revise the instrument over time.

TECHNICAL. As mentioned, the Electrical Maintenance Trainee Test was initially developed using job experts to prioritize broad categories of work in electrical maintenance.

The psychometric data behind the instrument are generally solid. The manual contains information on reliability coefficients, standard errors of measurement, item analysis, validity (content, criterion-related, and construct), and normative data. The internal consistency reliability coefficients *(KR20)* are high, ranging from .82 to .91, across five different populations. Correlations between the various subsections of the test are also high and statistically significant. The manual also provides difficulty indices and point biserial correlations for each item.

Content validity evidence was obtained through the use of job experts during instrument development. Their job experience and knowledge ensures the test measures critical elements of work in electrical maintenance. The use of job experts in test development also aids with construct validity. Inter-rater reliability pertaining to the content validity of items averaged .72.

In a small sample (N = 32) study, conveyed via personal communication to the Ramsay Corporation, performance on the test correlated significantly (.41, .45, and .53) with three measures of job performance. Although a larger study with more details regarding the test takers would lend greater credence to the criterion-related validity evidence presented in the test manual, the reported study suffices as a good start for data regarding criterion-related validity.

Although no formal study was conducted to demonstrate evidence of construct validity, the authors draw conclusions about construct validity from the procedures used in test development. The logic here is akin to the logic used to demonstrate content evidence of validity. If the authors are going to mention construct evidence of validity, they need more evidence to demonstrate

this validity and to distinguish it from content evidence of validity.

Normative data are provided to facilitate the understanding of individual scores and the establishment of cutoff scores as well as to allow a comparison between groups.

COMMENTARY. The Electrical Maintenance Trainee Test certainly looks like a measure of knowledge of the electronics field. With job areas prioritized by job experts, the test has face, content, and construct evidence of validity. Criterion-related evidence of validity shows the instrument has some predictive powers, although more research needs to be done in this area. Reliability coefficients are also relatively high. The test is easy to administer, score, and interpret.

SUMMARY. The Electrical Maintenance Trainee Test measures specialized knowledge and skills needed for jobs in electronics. Easily administered and easily scored, the different forms of this instrument have reasonably good psychometric properties. Measures of internal reliability and of validity indicate the test has internal consistency and measures what it sets out to measure. Given the specificity of the instrument, the Electrical Maintenance Trainee Test should only be used to assess knowledge and skill in electrical work.

REVIEWER'S REFERENCES
Ramsay, R. T. (2001). *ElecTest*. Pittsburgh, PA.
Sheehan, E. P. (2010). [Review of ElecTest]. In R. A. Spies, J. F. Carlson, & K. F. Geisinger (Eds.), *The eighteenth mental measurements yearbook* (pp. 208–210). Lincoln, NE: Buros Institute of Mental Measurements.

[59]

ElectronTest (Form HR-C).

Purpose: Designed for selecting or evaluating candidates for industrial electronics jobs.

Population: Electronic technicians and applicants for electronics jobs.

Publication Dates: 1987-2010.

Scores, 7: Digital & Analog Electronics, AC/DC Theory & Schematics, Motors/Regulators/Electronic Equipment/Power Distribution, Power Supplies, Test Instruments, Computers and PLC, Total.

Administration: Group.

Price Data, 2011: $22 per consumable self-scoring test booklet or online test administration (20 minimum order); $24.95 per manual (2010, 17 pages).

Time: (60-70) minutes.

Comments: Self-scoring instrument; available for online test administration.

Author: Roland T. Ramsay.

Publisher: Ramsay Corporation.

Cross References: For reviews by K. Hattrup and Eugene (Geno) Pichette of an earlier edition, see 13:116.

Review of the ElectronTest (Form HR-C) by PHILLIP L. ACKERMAN, Professor of Psychology, Georgia Institute of Technology, Atlanta, GA:

DESCRIPTION. The ElectronTest (Form HR-C) is a 60-item multiple-choice test of electronics content. The test may be administered in paper-and-pencil format with a self-scoring test booklet, or it can be completed on a computer. The test is untimed, but the manual reports that "most examinees should not require more than 1 hour" (manual, p. 6) to complete the test. The instructions to the examiner regarding administration are clear and well-articulated. The directions to be read to the examinee are also clear. The test items in the booklet are clear and easy to read. The manual describes the test as one of achievement or skill assessment. The test is made up of six separate scales (e.g., Computers and PLC, Test Instruments, Power Supplies). A Total Score is the sum of correct answers on the test. There are no penalties for guessing on the test.

DEVELOPMENT. The ElectronTest (Form HR-C) is an evolution of several previous tests called the Electronics Test and the ElectronTest Form H-C. The current version of the test has a reduced set of items from the original Electronics Test, some of which have been updated since the collection of standardization, reliability, and validity information.

TECHNICAL.

Standardization. There is a common manual for Form H-C and Form HR-C of the ElectronTest. However, there are no explicit standardization data for the ElectronTest (Form HR-C). The manual instead reports percentile ranks from two samples that took earlier versions of the test (Form H [1996] and Form H-C [1998]). The respective standardization samples consist of 206 applicants and a mixed group of 65 applicants and job incumbents. It is not clear what information a test user can take from this standardization, given several factors: (a) the standardization data are 14 to 16 years old; (b) several of the actual items on the HR-C form are different from those of the earlier measures; and (c) it is unclear how to interpret scores from a "mixed" group of applicants and job incumbents, given that the median performance score of the applicant sample was higher than the median of the sample that was mixed with applicants and incumbents.

Reliability. Reliability data consist of Kuder-Richardson and odd-even forms of internal consistency reliability, but only for earlier versions of the test (Form H [1996] and Form H-C [1998]). One sample consisted of 209 applicants for electronics jobs, and the other sample consisted of 65 "various applicants and incumbents." (Note the differences in sample size for one group versus the standardization group–which presumably are the same individuals. No explanation is provided for these differences.) The KR-20 reliabilities were high (.92 in both samples). Item difficulties and correlations between items and the test section are reported, but again, these pertain to the earlier versions of the test–and use data that were collected in 2001. The manual reports that "There is [*sic*] no data available" for the current form of the test, "however, updated items reflect similar difficulty" (manual, p. 10). No internal consistency statistics were reported for the current form, and no test-retest reliability data were reported for any form of the test. Also, no information is provided about the psychometric properties of the individual scales, except for a list of the number of items in each scale.

Validity. The manual reports that the ElectronTest (Form HR-C) is an "achievement or skill test," and that as such, the "appropriate model for validity is content validity" (manual, p. 13). As such, the test has not been subjected to either criterion-related validation nor construct validation. However, the manual notes that based on work by Hunter and Hunter, it is suggested that a test with content validity will usually have "excellent criterion-related correlation coefficients" (p. 13). Content validity data are reported for earlier versions of the test (Form H-C and Forms F and G), with samples of three to seven raters. The items rated ranged from a count of 51 to 125 (the current version of the test has 60 items). The interrater agreements varied from .56 to .86, which appear to be relatively modest for the content makeup of the test. Ratings of "job relatedness" were also modest–ranging from an average of 3.0 to 3.7 across three of the four sets of raters. No direct contrasts are provided that compare job incumbents with nonincumbents, and no correlations are provided between the current test and other tests of similar content. No specific content validity data are provided for the current form of the test. There is no information in the manual to indicate how scores from the test should be interpreted (e.g., a "passing score"). Given that the test aims to be an achievement or skill test, it is unclear how one can interpret any score, except with reference to the underidentified standardization samples.

COMMENTARY. Although the test items appear well-constructed and content-validated, no information in the manual indicates that scores from the test can be interpreted in any practical fashion, mainly because the standardization samples have no clear reference to scores of individuals who are determined to be competent in the domain assessed by the test. Having only incomplete data on a small sample ($N = 65$) that is identified as a mixture of applicants and job incumbents, the manual does not provide sufficient information for test users to determine whether an examinee has achieved relative mastery of the test content. Absent comparative data from the standardization sample, there is no information that provides interpretation information about the percent correct on the test in comparison to a set of standards. Criterion-related evidence of validity would be helpful, but such data are not provided for any version of the test. Earlier reviews (e.g., Hattrup, 1998; Pichette, 1998) indicated these shortcomings with previous versions of this test, and the shortcomings persist in the current version.

SUMMARY. The ElectronTest (Form HR-C) is an achievement or skill test that appears to be well-constructed from a content perspective. However, the lack of information in the manual pertaining to the uses of the test (e.g., certification, selection), restrict the potential utility of the test. The test and manual appear to be a good starting point, but use of the test would require extensive development of norms, standards, reliability, and validity data.

REVIEWER'S REFERENCES
Hattrup, K. (1998). [Review of the Electronics Test–Form G2]. In J. C. Impara & B. S. Plake (Eds.), *The thirteenth mental measurements yearbook* (pp. 411–413). Lincoln, NE: Buros Institute of Mental Measurements.
Pichette, E. (1998). [Review of the Electronics Test–Form G2]. In J. C. Impara & B. S. Plake (Eds.), *The thirteenth mental measurements yearbook* (p. 413). Lincoln, NE: Buros Institute of Mental Measurements.

Review of the ElectronTest (Form HR-C) by PAUL MUCHINSKY, Joseph M. Bryan Distinguished Professor, University of North Carolina at Greensboro, Greensboro, NC:

DESCRIPTION. This test is one of many developed by the Ramsay Corporation designed to assess aptitude in the technical trades. This particular test is directed toward assessing aptitude in the field of electrical and electronic repair. The test is a revision of a previous version published in 1998, and then revised in 2004. This second revision was published in 2010. It is stated that the revision was made in response to changing technology in the field. The ElectronTest (Form HR-C) is in paper-and-pencil format, consists of 60 items, and is self-scored. The manual states the test is also available online. The test is untimed, but it is reported that most examinees complete the test in one hour.

DEVELOPMENT. The test is accompanied by a 17-page manual. The manual is well written and fully describes how the test was developed. The test was designed for the selection of applicants for the job of Electronics Mechanic. The relevant O*NET job code and job description are presented. Based on the job-analytic information, 13 specific knowledge areas (e.g., motors, digital electronics, power distribution) were identified. The manual states that the test was created by developing items covering the 13 knowledge areas aggregated into six major sections of the test. However, the six major sections were based on items covering only 11 of the 13 knowledge areas. For reasons that are not clear, two knowledge areas (radio control and mechanical) were omitted from the test plan. The manual states that seven job experts ranked the importance of the knowledge areas. The ranks were averaged across experts and became the basis for developing a test with knowledge area coverage proportional to its ranked importance. A total of 125 items were originally developed, and resulted in the test Electronics–Form G2. Those 125 items were reduced to 60 items on the basis of item analysis data (point-biserial coefficients and item difficulty), and these analyses resulted in the present test. The number of items comprising each section of the test ranges from 6 to 14. Perhaps items measuring radio control and mechanical were dropped in the revision process. Radio control is a rather small portion of the Electronics Mechanic job, but the mechanical area seems endemic to all maintenance jobs.

TECHNICAL. The manual provides a thorough description of the procedure the examiner should follow in administering the test. The manual covers such administrative concerns as room conditions conducive for testing and provides a script for the examiner to read when giving the test as well as directions for having the candidates review two practice items. This portion of the manual is well crafted.

The answer sheet is contained within the test booklet on a perforated page. Upon completion, the page is removed, and the reverse side of the page reveals the correct answers to the questions. The correct answers are tabulated to produce scores for each of the six subscales and the Total Score. A KR-20 reliability coefficient of .92 was computed for each of two administrations with sample sizes of 65 and 209. An item analysis is provided based on the sample of 209 examinees. Both the item difficulty and point-biserial coefficients are clearly in the theoretically desired range, a finding not surprising because these two indices guided the reduction of the original 125 items down to the current 60 items.

A section in the manual describes content, criterion-related, and construct types of evidence of validity. Based on four independent samples, job experts at each administration rated every item for overall job relatedness. The number of raters ranged from three to seven, and the degree of rater agreement (no specific statistical index was cited) ranged from .56 to .86. Although the average job relatedness was acceptable (ranging from 3.0 to 3.7 on a 5-point scale), the data are seemingly at odds with the structure of the current test. In none of the four administrations of the test was the number of items equal to the 60 items comprising the current test. This reviewer infers the discrepancy as being due to reporting items from previous versions of this test that were also included in this revision, plus the newly added items in this revision that were not previously included. The manual states that, as a skill test, the appropriate model for validation is content, not criterion-related, as per the Uniform Guidelines. Although this reviewer understands the difficulties of obtaining relevant criterion measures in such jobs, given that prior versions of the test have been in existence for more than a decade, having some minimal criterion data (such as shorter downtime for malfunctioning equipment, less turnover, or greater management satisfaction) does not seem unreasonable. Although the manual states that no formal studies of construct validity have been conducted, it describes professionally sound approaches to doing so. The publisher is to be lauded for even attempting to address an issue that could be easily and artfully avoided. The manual concludes with normative data consisting of percentile ranks for this version of the test and an earlier version. Based on these data, the test is difficult, even for examinees in an industrial context who were interested in such a job. The median score is 26 (out of 60).

COMMENTARY. The Ramsay Corporation has a long tradition of publishing tests designed for selection into jobs in the mechanical/electrical trades. In my opinion no other test publisher offers products with a similar purpose. Through a careful examination of the manual, the reader can infer the publisher is experienced and proficient in test construction. Although this reviewer is in general an admirer of the publisher's tests, they are not without some concerns.

First, the publisher carefully documents how the items are related to the knowledge domain to be assessed. But the content relevance of the questions was established in the very industrial facilities where the tests were subsequently used for making personnel decisions. As such, the questions, though job-related for those particular organizations, do not necessarily generalize to other types of manufacturing operations. Of the 13 knowledge areas originally identified, some, such as AC/DC theory, assess concepts and principles universally relevant in maintenance. Other knowledge areas, such as Test Instruments, represent a mixture of some items probably relevant for all manufacturing organizations and others that may be more organization-specific. Finally, one knowledge area, Schematics & Print Reading, is very organization-specific. Simply put, across the full spectrum of organizations that use schematics and prints, there are many varieties of each. This reviewer, in working as a consultant, had one client organization dismiss an entire Ramsay test on the grounds that the "print questions aren't like any prints we use in our business." Although this reviewer is highly sympathetic to the problems encountered in developing job knowledge tests, when such a test is designed primarily for one organization but is marketed to an entire industry, the apparent content relevance of the items is spuriously enhanced through what is called "fold-back" validation (Blum & Naylor, 1968).

A second concern is a common one with tests that report subscale scores. The normative data are based on the Total Score. Assume the organization agrees on a passing score for the test. The manual provides no advice on interpreting how that Total Score might be achieved. It could be reached by getting some questions correct in each subscale, or by getting all the questions correct in some subscales and none correct in others. The issue of minimal cut scores per subscale is not addressed. Presumably an organization is left to decide for itself how it will regard examinees with extremely skewed responses across the six subscales.

Finally, if nothing else, this writer is curious as to what happened to the radio control and mechanical knowledge areas. The reader is owed an explanation of their fate. The manual provided none.

SUMMARY. As a consultant, this reviewer has used Ramsay tests in the past and has been generally pleased with the results. As stated previously, to this writer's knowledge, no other test publisher is solely focused on meeting the needs of this particular market. The negative consequences for organizations making bad hiring decisions in this job can be enormous. This test will help organizations make fewer bad hiring decisions. Such was the purpose of its creation.

REVIEWER'S REFERENCE
Blum, M. L., & Naylor, J. C. (1968). *Industrial psychology: Its theoretical and social foundations.* New York, NY: Harper & Row.

[60]
Emotional Disturbance Decision Tree-Parent Form.

Purpose: Designed to help identify "children who qualify for the federal Special Education category of Emotional Disturbance."
Population: Ages 5-18.
Publication Date: 2010.
Acronym: EDDT-PF.
Scores, 11: Inability to Build or Maintain Relationships Scale, Inappropriate Behaviors or Feelings Scale, Pervasive Mood/Depression Scale, Physical Symptoms or Fears Scale, Emotional Disturbance Characteristic Scale Total Score, Resilience Scale, Attention-Deficit Hyperactivity Disorder Cluster, Possible Psychosis Cluster, Social Maladjustment Cluster, Severity Cluster, Motivation Cluster.
Administration: Group or individual.
Price Data, 2012: $155 per complete kit including 25 response booklets, 25 reusable item booklets, 25 score summary booklets, case, and manual (151 pages); $57 per 25 response booklets; $31 per 25 reusable item booklets; $21 per 25 score summary booklets; $57 per manual.
Foreign Language Edition: Spanish version available.
Time: (15-20) minutes.
Comments: Ratings by parents/guardians; modeled after the EDDT-TF (18:48; called EDDT in its own listing).
Author: Bryan L. Euler.
Publisher: Psychological Assessment Resources, Inc.

Review of the Emotional Disturbance Decision Tree–Parent Form by JEFFREY A. ATLAS, Director, Mental Health Services, SCO Family of Services, Queens, NY:

DESCRIPTION. The Emotional Disturbance Decision Tree–Parent Form (EDDT-PF) is a 185-item parent/caregiver questionnaire designed to supplement an earlier teacher version in contributing to school special education designations of students 5–18 years of age as "Emotionally Disturbed." The scale provides anchors of *Never, Sometimes, Frequently,* and *Almost Always,* with some behavioral and mood items reverse-scored, superimposed upon a carbonless scoring sheet. Four of the item classifications comprise operationalizations of federally described characteristics of emotional disturbance: impaired interpersonal relationships, inappropriate behavior or feelings, pervasive mood disorder, and physical symptoms/fears. Supplementary clusters provide evidence of Possible Psychosis, Attention-Deficit Hyperactivity Disorder, Level of Severity, and comorbid or differentiable Social Maladjustment. The test author provides a theoretical basis for the EDDT-PF by describing learning as entailing sociality, explicitly in the psychosocial stage theory of Erikson and implicitly in the cognitive-developmental stage theory of Piaget. In addition, the test author draws from the ego mastery and competence model of R. W. White. Although test items are not explicitly connected to these various influences, the nexus of theories provides a rationale for item development and face validity.

An Inconsistency score is provided to shore up the acceptability of the particular rating, and a Resilience Scale and Motivation Cluster are provided for possible indicators of intervention strategies.

DEVELOPMENT. The EDDT-PF was developed from the teacher form by eliminating items assuming educator expertise while utilizing the earlier measure's item-scale assignments. Item development and analysis followed goals of keeping the number of items to a reasonable amount, enhancing items' specificity, and eliminating items with low correlations to the total scale number. A final version was subject to standardization procedures outlined in the EDDT-PF manual.

TECHNICAL.
Standardization. The EDDT-PF was standardized on a normative sample of 889 children and 430 emotionally disturbed children meeting federal criteria.

The normative sample shows very good nationwide representation by male-female age stratification as well as ethnicity (Caucasian, African American, Hispanic, Other). There appears to be underrepresentation of Northeastern (13.2%) and Southern (25.6%) populations. The clinical sample shows dramatic underrepresentation of the South (8.1%) and overrepresentation of the Northeast (39.8%).

Although regression analyses yielded few age and gender effects on the scale scores, separate norms tables were developed for males and females to accommodate expectable cultural variations. Age groupings of 5–8, 9–11, 12–14, and 15–18 were established, in keeping with developmental literature and what one may view as common educational groupings.

The raw score distributions were converted to T-score distributions (mean of 50, standard deviation of 10) to establish norms tables, with provided descriptors of Normal (T-score 0–54), Mild At Risk (T-score 55–59), Moderate Clinical (T-score 60–69), High Clinical (T-score 70–79), and Very High Clinical (T-score equal or greater than 80).

Percentile ranges were developed (less than 1%, 2%–24%, 25%–74%, and above 75%) with attached qualitative labels of "Normal," "Mild at Risk," "Moderate Clinical," and "High Clinical" from the Emotional Disturbance Sample to provide for differentiation of cluster category scores. Groupings from the Emotional Disturbance Sample of ADHD ($N = 45$), Possible Psychosis ($N = 21$), and Socially Maladjusted ($N = 57$) students suggested expectable percentile contrasts to the normative ($N = 889$) group. The 430 students from the Emotional Disturbance sample similarly demonstrated expectable patterns of percentile contrasts for the Severity Cluster (e.g., 60% showing "Not Severe" and 2.1% showing "High Severity").

Reliability. The EDDT-PF demonstrated excellent internal consistency as indexed by alpha coefficients, which ranged from a median of .88 for cluster scores of the Emotional Disturbance sample to .91 for the normative sample on this measure and .90 for the normative sample scale score.

The reported test-retest (stability) data are harder to gauge, given a range of 1 to 54 days (8-day average) and a subsample of 117 with overrepresentation of Caucasian individuals (85.5%), but the median reliability coefficient of .96 is impressive.

Parent-parent interrater reliability coefficients ranged from a low of .57 for the Motivation cluster to a high of .88 on numerous scales and clusters, for a subsample of 165 individuals.

Scales and clusters common to the parent and teacher forms of the EDDT were compared for a representative sample of 112 individuals. The moderately high correlations, .65 to .72 for the scales and .60 to .76 for the clusters, highlight the need for multiple rater vantage points in assessments, as teacher ratings were reported as consistently higher across scales and clusters.

Validity. Intercorrelations between the normative EDDT-PF scales ranged from .62 to .93, with the cluster intercorrelations ranging from a low of -.01 between Motivation and Inability to Build or Maintain Relationships to .87 between ADHD and Inappropriate Behaviors or Feelings. Similar intercorrelations were found for the Emotional Disturbance reference group (.24 to .91 for the scales, -.05 to .82 for the clusters), suggesting satisfactory validity of most of the test scores in delineating different dimensional facets of emotional health and disturbance.

The EDDT-PF scores demonstrated convergent evidence of validity with select subscales of the Behavior Assessment System for Children, Second Edition Parent Rating Scales (BASC-2 PRS; Reynolds & Kamphaus, 2004) in normative ($N = 59$) and emotionally disturbed ($N = 99$) subsamples of children. Moderate to high correlations were demonstrated between the EDDT-PF and the BASC-2 PRS, respectively, in Social Maladjustment and Conduct Problems, Externalizing Problems Composite, and Aggression; in Pervasive Mood/Depression and the BASC-2 Depression scale; in ADHD and Externalizing Problems composite and Attention Problems; in Possible Psychosis/Schizophrenia and Atypicality; in Resilience and Adaptive Skills; and in the EDDT-PF Total Score and the BASC-2 Behavioral Symptoms Index.

Group differences between the Normative and Emotional Disturbance groups were calculated across all scales and clusters. Mean score comparisons showing greater disturbance in the clinical sample were all significant at a level below .001, offering evidence to support discriminant validity of the EDDT-PF's test scores.

COMMENTARY. The EDDT-PF shows evident utility as a potential component of Special Education deliberations concerning the designation of Emotional Disturbance.

The Motivation cluster is admittedly a weak link in the measure given weak specificity in many of the comparisons. Inspection of the norms tables in an appendix indicate percentile ranks ranging from about a fifth of raw scores over the 99th percentile to well over half, the low ceiling calling into question the degree of specifity of the scale as a whole and the need for its length, likely to take beyond the recommended 15–20 minutes when completed carefully.

A full 23 pages of the 151-page manual is taken up with illustrative fictional case studies. As with other instruments or case study discussions, the current reviewer finds such presentations less than compelling inasmuch as fictionalized data from real cases may engage our interest more fully even if they do not fit as snugly the features the test author is attempting to highlight. Of more concern, in this case, in an effort to be culturally sensitive the test author presents vignettes that entail cultural stereotypy (e.g., of an Asian boy excelling in Mathematics but showing social and emotional constriction; of an African American girl born addicted to cocaine, showing disruptive behaviors and depressive moods; of a Native American boy living in a shelter, born to an alcoholic father, himself seeking refuge in marijuana–attending powwows is one of the recommendations; and finally of an Hispanic teenage immigrant girl sexually abused by her uncle). These characters, or caricatures, are painful to read about as they hew closely to historical presuppositions that have led to overrepresentation of minority youth in Special Education (Atlas, 1992). A scale such as the EDDT-PF, contrariwise, can actually serve as an empirical corrective, given its generally sound psychometric properties, instead of perpetuating stereotypes.

The present reviewer piloted the EDDT-PF in a case of an 18-year-old male newly admitted to a Hard-to-Place group home after being AWOL from a previous placement. As this individual as well had resisted recent psychiatric and educational referrals, the EDDT-PF was given to his regular caseworker to aid in determining strengths and problem areas. The young man scored highest (above the 99th percentile) in the Inappropriate Behaviors subscale and was at the High Clinical level in ADHD, with Severity in the High Severity range. Inspection of his mental health chart indicated earlier Special Education placement for Emotional Disturbance, as well as an earlier ADHD diagnosis with a rule-out of Bipolar Disorder. Whether or not we are able to get this young man to remain in a stable environment and receive necessary services, the EDDT-PF provided some convergent validity, or confidence, that the earlier mental health diagnosis fits the spectrum of his disabilities and may become a focus of intervention pending confirmatory data.

SUMMARY. The EDDT-PF is a comprehensive, multidimensional instrument that may find a niche in psychologists' contributions to Special Education determinations. It compares favorably to the BASC-2 in mapping onto current federal guidelines defining Emotional Disturbance, but does not offer the age ranges of the BASC-2. Future work with one or both instruments may lead diagnosticians and clinicians to choose one or the other as augmentative measures in assessing students for Special Education.

REVIEWER'S REFERENCES
Atlas, J. A. (1992). Ideology in special education. *New Ideas in Psychology, 10,* 103–104.
Reynolds, C. R., & Kamphaus, R. W. (2004). BASC-2: Behavior Assessment System for Children (second ed.). Circle Pines, MN: AGS Publishing.

Review of the Emotional Disturbance Decision Tree–Parent Form by TONY C. WU, Faculty, College of Social and Behavioral Sciences, Walden University, Minneapolis, MN:

DESCRIPTION. The Emotional Disturbance Decision Tree–Parent Form (EDDT-PF) is a standardized, norm-referenced questionnaire that is used to identify children who might qualify for the Federal special education category of Emotional Disturbance (ED). The EDDT-PF is an individually administered paper-and-pencil scale to be completed by a child's parent or a caregiver who knows the child well. The test author indicates that this scale will be advantageous to school psychologists, clinical psychologists, counseling psychologists, educational diagnosticians, and allied health professionals interested in utilizing a uniform methodology to meet the Federal criteria for ED's five indicators, as differentiating constructs of ED is complex and highly subjective. The EDDT-PF is intended for use with the parents or caregivers of children and adolescents ages 5 through 18 years.

The EDDT-PF materials include a professional manual, an item booklet, a response booklet, and a score summary booklet. The scale can be completed and hand-scored with ease. The EDDT-PF generates scores for Inability to Build or Maintain Relationships (REL) Scale, Inappropriate Behaviors or Feelings (IBF) Scale, Pervasive Mood/Depression (PM/DEP) Scale, Physical Symptoms or Fears (FEARS) Scale, EDDT-PF Total Score (TOTAL), and Resilience (RES) Scale. It also produces cluster scores such as Attention-Deficit Hyperactivity Disorder (ADHD) Cluster, Possible Psychosis/Schizophrenia (POSSIBLE PSYCHOSIS) Cluster, Social Maladjustment (SM) Cluster, Level of Severity (SEVERITY) Cluster, and Motivation (MOT) Cluster.

The administration instructions are easy to follow; the test author claims that it can be completed by a parent/caretaker within a single session in a quiet and comfortable environment. The EDDT-PF is also available in Spanish. The EDDT-PF: Spanish Version (EDDT-PF:SV) contains a Spanish item booklet and Spanish response booklet. In terms of scoring options, it appears that only the hand-scoring method is currently available. Overall, the scoring, computing, and recording of the scale and cluster scores are straightforward. For hand-scoring, a calculator might be needed, but generally is not necessary, as scoring only involves addition of items. Once the raw scores are computed for each scale, the scoring sheet and score summary booklet are used to determine T scores and percentile ranks, which are separated by age and gender. In terms of interpretation, the test author claims that the ED Characteristic Scales, Resilience Scale, and Cluster scores will help to improve identification of children and youth who qualify for the special education category of ED. Finally, the test author recommends the analysis of items for inconsistency in order to allow the examiner to evaluate the validity of scores, response patterns, and reliabilities among different raters.

DEVELOPMENT. In the development of the EDDT-PF, the test author desired a test that would be beneficial to both school-based clinicians and researchers interested in ED evaluation. The purpose of this instrument is to offer school and other educational professionals a standardized way to obtain parent information about children's functioning as they relate to the federal ED definition. In addition to addressing the ED criteria, the scale investigates syndromes related to social maladjustment, severity, attention-deficit hyperactivity disorder (ADHD), psychosis, and strength, which are very useful for diagnostic purposes and treatment planning. The standardization sample of the EDDT-PF included 889 children ages 5 through 18 years. The test author notes that the demographic characteristics of ethnicity and race for this sample were well represented, compared to the national percentages for students with ED.

The EDDT-Parent Form: Spanish Version (EDDT-PF:SV) includes the same items as the English questionnaire. The test author notes that the first translation was created by a company that specializes in translating psychological tests. Later, an independent translation was also conducted. During the process, the two versions were compared and discrepancies were corrected. The test author claims that several iterations of back-translation and comparison took place before production of the final form. The validation sample included 67 parents who rated their children; the test author states that the Spanish and English forms were comparable.

TECHNICAL. Overall, meaningful estimates of reliability and validity are provided by the test author. Available data provide adequate evidence to support inferences made from the EDDT-PF test scores. The following discussion describes selected validity and reliability indicators for the questionnaire. Specific to reliabilities, internal consistency coefficients ranged from .88 to .96. With regard to test-retest reliabilities, coefficients ranged from .94 to .98. For the cluster scores, the test-retest coefficients were very high, ranging from .92 to .98. Interrater reliability coefficients between two parents were reported to range from .78 to .88 for the scales, and from .57 to .88 for the clusters. Likewise, validity evidence is provided by the test author to support conclusions drawn from the EDDT-PF. The test manual reveals that the intercorrelations between the EDDT-PF scales ranged from .62 to .93. It was also established that the correlation coefficient between the EDDT-PF Social Maladjustment cluster and the BASC-2 Conduct Problem scale was .76, and for the Aggression scale the coefficient was .77.

COMMENTARY. The EDDT-PF is a succinct and straightforward parent-completed questionnaire that has clinical and educational utility in the identification of children with ED under the Federal special education criteria. It features test items that specifically tap into the various constructs of different presentations of ED in a standardized and easy to understand fashion. Moreover, directions for recording, scoring, and interpretation are concise and easy to follow. The norms and comparison are based on both nonclinical and clinical individuals. Strong validity and reliability evidences are provided to support the inferences drawn from the results. The scale also includes a Spanish version, which provides an alternative for parents who might have difficulties in English. In future revisions of the EDDT-PF, the test author might consider computer scoring that includes test interpretation and treatment and education recommendations. The test author might also want to add a self-report measure as children oftentimes can provide unique and accurate perspectives on their own feelings and behaviors.

SUMMARY. The Emotional Disturbance Decision Tree–Parent Form (EDDT-PF) is a norm-referenced and standardized tool that can facilitate the identification of children and adolescents who qualify for special education under the ED category. The key feature of the EDDT-PF is its standardized approach to the loosely defined Federal ED criteria. This scale specifically taps into multidimensionality of ED symptoms and children's functioning. The test administration and psychometric properties are well founded and supported by the evidence provided in the test manual. Consequently, the EDDT-PF is recommended for educational and clinical use in school settings as one of the many tools for assessing ED in a comprehensive psycho-educational evaluation.

[61]

Emotional Eating Behavior Assessment.

Purpose: "Designed to assess a person's tendency to eat for reasons other than hunger and evaluate the underlying reasons for overeating."

Population: Under 17 through adult.

Publication Date: 2011.

Acronym: EMEBA.

Scores, 37: Health Locus of Control, Self-Discipline, Reward Dependence, Sense of Self-Efficacy, Depression, Anxiety, Resilience, Anger Control, Tolerance for Frustration, Eating Trigger (Deal with Emotional Pain, Avoid Confrontation, Loneliness, Boredom, Satisfy Need for Intimacy, Early Childhood Deprivation, Rebellion, Avoid New Challenges, Avoid Intimacy Due to Child Abuse, Feel Carefree, Fear of Other's Expectations, Self-Sabotaging Beliefs, Shame), Problem Solving, Information Seeking, Negotiation, Support Seeking, Positive Cognitive Restructuring, Emotional Regulation, Distraction, Rumination, Avoidance, Helplessness, Opposition, Social Withdrawal, Triggers, Coping Skills, Overall Score.

Administration: Individual.

Price Data: Available from publisher.

Time: (40) minutes.

Comments: Self-administered online assessment. The test publisher advises that the test manual is being updated to include more information about methodology and theoretical background used in the development of the test. The test publisher also advises that this information is available to clients, as are benchmarks for relevant industries and racial/ethnic group comparison data. However, this information was not provided to Buros or the reviewers.

Author: PsychTests AIM, Inc.

Publisher: PsychTests AIM, Inc. [Canada].

Review of the Emotional Eating Behavioral Assessment by TONY CELLUCCI, Professor and Director of the ECU Psychological Assessment and Spe-cialty Services (PASS) Clinic, and LESLEY LUTES, Clinical Health Psychology Faculty, East Carolina University, Greenville, NC:

DESCRIPTION. The Emotional Eating Behavioral Assessment (EMEBA) is a 149-item, online self-administered measure of emotional eating behavior and associated psychological constructs (see Psychtests at http://corporate.psychtests.com/). It is described as particularly applicable to patients in weight loss and eating disorder treatment programs and for related evaluations (e.g., pre-bariatric surgery). The estimated completion time is 40 minutes. The test is composed of an overall tendency toward emotional eating score, two subfactor scores (i.e., Coping Skills and Triggers) and nine associated personality subscales. The Coping Skills subfactor is further divided into 12 specific skills and the Triggers subfactor into 13 specific triggers. The nine associated subscales are: Health Locus of Control, Self-Discipline, Reward Dependence, Sense of Self-Efficacy, Depression, Anxiety, Resilience, Anger Control, and Tolerance for Frustration. All reported scores are standardized to fall on an interpretive scale of 0 to 100, with benchmarks for different groups available to professional users. A computerized report is provided to the test-taker that provides feedback on the various scales as well as strengths, areas of potential concern, and suggestions regarding triggers and use of coping skills. The test developer provides a technical manual that includes statistical information, but there is no narrative test or interpretative manual for the EMEBA.

DEVELOPMENT. There is limited information available on the development of the EMEBA. The test developer shared that she researched the related scientific literature and consulted subject matter experts to operationally define constructs (Dr. I. Jerabek, personal communication, 2012). The items themselves cover a broad range of content including abuse history and alcohol use. One administration concern is the scale anchors for the items change without warning between sections and on selected screens all items are worded negatively as opposed to balancing positive and negatively worded items. Descriptive statistical analyses of the various scales have been conducted and results are provided in the technical manual. According to the Test Development Procedures, the EMEBA would appear to be at Phase II involving preliminary statistical analyses with no information as yet on item modifications.

TECHNICAL.

Standardization. The test was standardized on a large (N = 5,743) self-selected sample, although the majority of respondents (79%) were women with only 10% men, and another 11% of test-takers not providing their gender. All participants took the assessment on Queendom.com and agreed to become a part of the validation study. The standardization sample is also divided into six age categories: below 17 years (22%), 18–24 (26%), 25–29 (10%), 30–39 (15%), 40–49 (10%), and 50+ years (8%), with 9% not reporting their age. These demographic variables are not currently used in scoring although the technical manual summarizes a large number of gender and age effects on the various scales. Specifically, there were 26 significant t-score differences out of 28 comparisons by gender and 33 of 38 significant one-way ANOVAs by age differences. The test developers also report significant education effects (i.e., high school or lower, junior college/technical school, Associates degree or higher) on 29 of the scales.

Reliability. The technical manual reports the alpha coefficients for each of the scale scores along with the associated number of items per scale. These appear to be acceptably high for the four composite score measures: Overall Tendency Toward Emotional Eating (.96), Personality Traits Related to Emotional Eating (.97), Emotional Eating Triggers (.92), and Coping Skills (.84). However, internal consistency varies considerably among subscale scores for Personality Constructs (.51 for Reward Dependence to .93 for Depression), Coping Scales (.58 for Negotiation to .90 for Helplessness), and especially Eating Triggers (.40 for Rebellion to .89 for Need for Intimacy). The latter individual trigger subscales are limited in that several consist of only 1–3 items with the Loneliness Trigger being 1 item.

Validity. Without more information than just taking the assessment, it is difficult to comment on the content validity of the items and their placement on particular scales. The personality-related scales do appear to cover important constructs in this area. More information is also needed as to the intercorrelations between the various scales that are not provided. A preliminary exploratory factor analysis (Dr. I. Jerabek, personal communication, 2012) is said to have identified eight factors: Depression/Poor Mental Health, Proactivity/Healthy Coping, Goal Orientation/Discipline, Emotional Management, Denial/Helplessness, Triggers/

Unhealthy Coping, Social Support, and Satisfaction with Life/Relationships. Further evidence is needed to support construct validity and the scale structure of the test.

The current evidence for the validity of test score usage rests primarily on two sets of analyses examining the scales' relationship to both weight and self-reported tendency toward emotional eating. In the first analysis, 1,000 respondents defined as overweight were compared to 979 test-takers with no weight problems. There were many expected differences; for example, the overweight group reported more anxiety and depression and greater reward dependence, whereas those without weight problems expressed more self-discipline, self-efficacy, tolerance of frustration, and resilience. Those without weight difficulties also generally had more positive coping skills and fewer triggers for emotional eating as well as a lower overall score (M = 41.6 versus 50.5, t = 12.78, p < .001). The second analysis involved a single criterion question, "Would you consider yourself to be an emotional eater?" coded as *Yes* (n = 1,200), *Somewhat* (n = 1,401), or *No* (n = 1,148). There were 33 significant differences between the criterion groups. Emotional eaters obtained higher overall scores (M = 53.6 versus 45.9 for the *Somewhat* group versus 38.7 for the *No* group) with F = 308.75, p < .001. They also reported more personality traits related to emotional eating, more emotional eating triggers, and fewer coping skills. In fact, the only scales that did not distinguish the groups were the emotional triggers of rebellion, avoid intimacy due to childhood abuse, and feeling carefree, as well as the coping skill of information seeking. As yet, the EMEBA scales have not been compared or correlated with other measures of similar constructs, nor is test information provided on clinical samples.

COMMENTARY. The EMEBA appears to be a promising instrument that needs further development. Published research in peer-related journals supporting both its psychometric structure and further evidence of scale construct validity is necessary prior to recommending clinical use. Factor analytic work and item analysis can help refine the scales. The strength of the test is the ambitious effort to measure a range of important constructs related to success in weight management. One possible omission may be assessing readiness to change eating patterns or stage of change. There is also a need for further basic research on the nature and predictive value of self-reported emotional eating as it relates to weight management and health (Adriaanse, de Ridder, & Evers, 2011).

There is no single competitive measure that is comparable to the EMEBA, but the test scales should be correlated with various validated measures of overlapping constructs, such as the Patient Health Questionnaire (PHQ-9/GAD-7; Spitzer, Kroenke, & Williams, 1999), the COPE Inventory (COPE; Carver, Scheier, & Weintraub, 1989), the Emotional Eating Scale (EES; Arnow, Kenardy, & Agras, 1995), the Eating Disorder Inventory-3 (EDI-3; Garner, 2004), and weight self-efficacy. It is also important to compare EMEBA scores for normal weight, overweight, and obese groups as defined clinically by the Body Mass Index, and to provide norms for patients with binge-eating disorder who constitute a significant percentage (about 25%) of overweight individuals (Ricca et al., 2009).

In addition, it seems important to consider whether the EMEBA should be considered a self-assessment or a clinical instrument. The feedback report is written for the respondent but one might argue that many individuals would require help to understand and effectively use the scale information provided. The advice listed may oversimplify the complexity of making difficult clinical and lifestyle changes. It is unclear whether certain scores precipitate a recommendation to seek help from a licensed professional, but this would seem to be an important ethical consideration.

SUMMARY. The EMEBA is a broad self-report measure of emotional eating and related constructs that warrants further research and development. Research-based guidelines for interpretation and recommendations for appropriate use with clinical populations are needed.

REVIEWERS' REFERENCES

Adriaanse, M. A., de Ridder, D., & Evers, C. (2011). Emotional eating: Eating when emotional or emotional about eating. *Psychology and Health, 26*, 23-39.

Arnow, B., Kenardy, J., & Agras, W. S. (1995). The Emotional Eating Scale: The development of a measure to assess coping with negative affect by eating. *International Journal of Eating Disorders, 18*, 79-90.

Carver, C. S., Scheier, M. F., & Weintraub, J. K. (1989). Assessing coping strategies: A theoretically based approach. *Journal of Personality and Social Psychology, 56*, 267-283.

Garner, D. M. (2004). *Eating Disorder Inventory–3 Professional Manual*. Odessa, FL: Psychological Assessment Resources.

Ricca, V., Castellinia, G., Lo Sauroa, C., Ravaldia, C., Lapib, F., Mannuccic, E., Rotellad, C. M., & Faravellie, C. (2009). Correlations between binge eating and emotional eating in a sample of overweight subjects. *Appetite, 53*, 418-421.

Spitzer, R. L., Kroenke, K., & Williams, J. B. (1999). Validation and utility of a self-report version of PRIME-MD: The PHQ Primary Care Study. *Journal of the American Medical Association, 282*, 1737-1744.

Review of the Emotional Eating Behavior Assessment by ANDREW A. COX, Professor, Counseling and Psychology, Troy University, Phenix City, AL:

DESCRIPTION. The Emotional Eating Behavior Assessment (EMEBA) is a 149-item computer-administered test that assesses characteristics associated with emotional eating and circumstances and feelings that may be associated with emotional binge eating. The test authors report that the instrument's purpose is to assess tendencies to eat for reasons other than hunger and to evaluate the underlying reasons for overeating. The question format involves self and situational assessment using a Likert scale format. The test authors report that the scale requires about 40 minutes to complete.

The EMEBA yields an overall (total) score, Coping Skills, Emotional Triggers, and 21 subscale scores. Subscales include Health Locus of Control, Self-Discipline, Reward Dependence, Sense of Self-Efficacy, Depression, Anxiety, Resilience, Anger Control, Tolerance for Frustration, Problem Solving, Information Seeking, Negotiation, Support Seeking, Positive Cognitive Restructuring, Emotional Regulation, Distraction, Rumination, Avoidance, Helplessness, Opposition, and Social Withdrawal. The EMEBA also provides scores for 9 subscales reflecting personality traits related to emotional eating. As the nature of the obtained scores are not described, it cannot be determined if scale scores are raw, weighted, or some other type of derived score. There are no data within the test manual that indicate how subscales or factor scores were identified or how they are related to the emotional aspects of eating behavior.

Upon completing the computer-administered inventory, a computer-generated report provides the test-taker with assessment results relative to the total, factor, and subscale scores. The report includes a strengths and limitations section relative to the test-taker's results along with recommendations for dealing with emotional eating and stress coping mechanisms.

DEVELOPMENT. Limited information is detailed regarding development of the EMEBA. The inventory was administered through Queendom. com, a clearinghouse for various computer-administered measurements. Sample statistics and validation data were derived from test-takers who completed the EMEBA on this website. An uncontrolled sample was used with test-takers self-selecting to take the assessment. The sample consisted of test-takers who "opted in to participate in the validation study" (manual, p. 2) with all validation data gathered through self-report. There is no information reported within the test manual regarding how items were selected for inclusion within the inventory or field testing of the final inventory.

TECHNICAL. A nonrandomized sample of 5,743 test-takers was used for validation purposes. Seventy-nine percent (4,543) of the sample were female, 10% (589) males, and 11% (611) of unknown gender. Age characteristics of the sample are reported with most test-takers being within the below 17 (22%), and 18 to 24 years (26%) age ranges. The remaining sample was within the 25 to 50 years or unknown age range. The test manual provides descriptive statistical tables and graphs for the overall, factor, and subscale scores for sample gender, age, educational level, and tendency towards emotional eating characteristics. The characteristics of the sample relative to ethnicity are not described. Though not reported within the test manual's sample description, sample characteristics for educational level are described within tables and graphs in terms of those within the sample possessing high school or less, junior college/college/trade-technical school, and associate degree or higher educational levels. The reader can review the descriptive statistics for this factor to determine the number of test-takers with a certain educational level responding in terms of total, factor, and subscale. Reliability (alpha) coefficients for the total, factor, and subscale scores are reported. No reliability coefficients below .40 are noted. The overall (total) score has a coefficient of .96. Seventy-nine percent of the factor/subscale scores have a coefficient of .70 or above. Approximately 24% of the subscales have coefficients less than .70. Lowest internal consistency estimates are noted on Health Locus of Control (.54), Reward Dependence (.51), Eating Triggers-Rebellion (.40), and Eating Triggers-Avoid Intimacy Due to Childhood Abuse (.51). The scales represented by these lower coefficients are composed of few items.

Validation evidence derives from t-test comparisons and analyses of variance for gender, age, and education. Data are reported via description of statistical analyses and bar graphs. No narrative describing the implications or interpretation of test data in terms of test score validity or relationship to eating behavior characteristics is provided. The type of validation evidence deriving from these analyses is not noted within the manual.

Analysis of variance data and associated data graphs are reported for test-takers manifesting a tendency towards emotional eating as compared to those not manifesting such a tendency, and test-takers self-reporting weight problems as compared to those without weight problems. However, once again, data are presented in terms of statistical analyses and bar graphs with no narrative describing implications or interpretation of test data. Inspection of these data appears to lend support to the fact that those considered as emotional eaters and those with and without weight issues seem to differ on key criterion variables. Those test-takers within the sample with weight issues had a significantly higher overall score than those without weight problems. Support is provided that those with weight problems had significantly higher scores on all variables associated with emotional aspects of overeating, whereas test takers without weight problems had significantly higher scores on healthy indicators of eating and lifestyle choices (i.e., Problem Solving, Support Seeking, Positive Cognitive Restructuring, Emotional Regulation, Distraction, and Coping Skills). If described more fully within the test manual and related to eating behavior/eating disorders literature, these data would seem to provide evidence bearing on construct or criterion-related validation of test score use.

COMMENTARY. The majority of the EMEBA's manual consists of graphs/histograms with limited descriptive or narrative information. Such narration involves descriptions of t-test and ANOVA results and scoring patterns. To some test users, such data presentation could be overwhelming or of limited use. The test manual's presentation resembles a chapter from a test technical/user manual describing statistical analyses involving the instrument rather than a comprehensive user's manual. It would be helpful to potential test users to have other chapters or information available that describe the instrument's uses, the nature and correlates of emotional eating and overeating, or even eating disorders as a psychopathology.

The test manual contains no literature review or references. Such literature is necessary to describe the inventory's interface and diagnostic information relevant to eating behavior and eating disorders literature. This is a major limitation and detracts from the instrument's potential validation, presented validation data, and clinical utility.

There is no information reported within the test manual concerning the use of the instrument other than for "therapy and counseling" (manual, p. 1). More detailed information regarding how the instrument would be useful in examining the correlates of or use in the diagnosis of eating behavior deficits or disorders would be useful to practitioners.

As the instrument is computer-administered and interpreted only, such administration limits the scale's applicability within the counseling and therapy practice realm. Test-takers and test administrators lose the capability for item analyses and the ability to review the test-taker's responses to each item, an important diagnostic and treatment technique that provides insight into the client's insight and thinking processes. The computer-administered format requires care and attention in responding to the instrument's items. The Likert-type scale changes throughout the test's administration making test-taker errors in responding possible without such care.

On a positive note, the computer-generated score report and interpretation is user-friendly and easily interpreted. The scale appears to have adequate internal consistency. Though more work appears to be needed on scale validation, ANOVA results suggest at least some criterion-related validation, though work is needed to relate this information to the construct of dysfunctional eating behaviors. Items appear to have face validity relative to the correlates of disordered eating behaviors as a dysfunctional coping mechanism.

SUMMARY. At this time, the Emotional Eating Behavior Assessment appears to be primarily a research instrument. It may have promise in assessing a specific area of eating behavior and possible dysfunction. However, more work and research on test score use and validation is recommended. Further development of norms that could include separate gender, educational level, and age norms along with research using a stratified research sample are recommended. More research and data relative to ethnic characteristics for the measure are needed as such data are not reported for the EMEBA. The instrument could play a role in research regarding both functional and dysfunctional eating behavior. The EMEBA could be used in research together with other personality and eating disorder measures with such research assisting in further validating the instrument.

The test manual requires much work to make it more useable for test users. The manual should have more narrative and descriptive information regarding the instrument and less reliance on graphs and review of statistical analyses. Revision of the test manual should include a synthesis of literature that details the instrument's relationship and use within the eating disorders treatment domain.

[62]
Emotional Quotient Inventory 2.0.

Purpose: Designed to measure emotional intelligence.
Population: Ages 18 and older.
Publication Dates: 1997-2011.
Acronym: EQ-i 2.0.
Scores: 21 content scores: Composite Scale Scores (Total EI, Self-Perception, Self-Expression, Interpersonal, Decision Making, Stress Management), Self-Perception Subscale Scores (Self-Regard, Self-Actualized, Emotional Self-Awareness), Self-Expression Subscale Scores (Emotional Expression, Assertiveness, Independence), Interpersonal Subscale Scores (Interpersonal Relationships, Empathy, Social Responsibility), Decision Making Subscale Scores (Problem Solving, Reality Testing, Impulse Control), Stress Management Subscale Scores (Flexibility, Stress Tolerance, Optimism), plus 1 Well-Being Indicator (Happiness) and 2 Response Style Indicators (Positive/Negative Impression, Inconsistency Index).
Administration: Individual or group.
Price Data: Available from publisher.
Foreign Language Editions: Translations available in Simplified Chinese, German, Spanish (European), French (Canadian and European), and Arabic.
Time: (20-30) minutes.
Author: Multi-Health Systems, Inc.
Publisher: Multi-Health Systems, Inc.
Cross References: For reviews by Andrew A. Cox and Robert M. Guion of an earlier edition entitled the BarOn Emotional Quotient Inventory, see 14:32.

Review of the Emotional Quotient Inventory 2.0 by JAMES C. DiPERNA, Associate Professor, School Psychology Program, Pennsylvania State University, University Park, PA, and LIA E. SANDILOS, Postdoctoral Scholar, Temple University, Philadelphia, PA:

DESCRIPTION. The purpose of the Emotional Quotient Inventory 2.0 (EQ-i 2.0) is to assess emotional and social skills that facilitate successful functioning in a variety of environments, such as the workplace and higher education. In addition, the inventory is intended to be used to assist with intervention planning in clinical and medical settings. Target examinees for the EQ-i 2.0 are individuals who are 18 years of age or older residing in the U.S. and Canada. Translations of the EQ-i 2.0 are available in a variety of languages.

The EQ-i 2.0 is a self-report measure, can be completed online or in paper format, and requires 20–30 minutes to complete. The inventory includes 133 items, and each item has five response options (*never, occasionally, sometimes, often, always/almost always*). Composite standard scores (mean = 100, standard deviation = 15) are generated for the total, scale, and subscale scores. The online EQ-i 2.0 portal can be used to create a Workplace Report. A Group Report and a Leadership Report are under development. [Editor's Note: The publisher advises that the Leadership Report is available as of December 2012. The Group Report is still under development.] Both client and coach printouts are available for each report. The coach printout includes information about the consistency of the client's responses, as well as information about the client's tendency to respond positively or negatively. Reports are clearly written and interpretable. Users of the EQ-i 2.0, such as psychologists, counselors, or other mental health professionals, should be familiar with psychometrics. Training is available for users who would like to obtain certification in the administration of the EQ-i 2.0.

In addition, a revision to the multi-informant version (EQ 360 2.0) was developed concurrently with the EQ-i 2.0 and is available to users through the online portal as well.

DEVELOPMENT. Reuven Bar-On, a clinical psychologist who conducted research on emotional intelligence, developed the theoretical framework upon which the EQ-i 2.0 is based. The EQ-i 2.0 is described as reflecting a "theoretically eclectic" (manual, p. 19) approach to conceptualizing emotional intelligence. Specifically, emotional intelligence is defined in the user's manual as "a set of emotional and social skills that influence the way we perceive and express ourselves, develop and maintain social relationships, cope with challenges, and use emotional information in an effective and meaningful way" (p. 31). The EQ-i 2.0 reflects a multifactor model composed of five primary scales (Self-Perception, Self-Expression, Interpersonal, Decision Making, and Stress Management), each of which is further divided into three subscales. The EQ-i 2.0 also includes two indicator scales (Happiness and Response Style).

The primary objective for creating the EQ-i 2.0 was to incorporate theoretical and empirical advancements regarding the construct of emotional intelligence since publication of the original version of the measure (EQ-i; Bar-On, 1997; 14:32). In addition, the revision was intended to address limitations noted by users of the original EQ-i (e.g., mismatch between rating scale and wording of certain items, lack of overlap in item content between the EQ-i self-report and the EQ 360). The development phase for the EQ-i 2.0 was guided by eight specific goals (e.g., aligning items

and response options, increasing symmetry between EQ-i 2.0 and EQ 360 2.0). As a result, 221 items were piloted with a large sample (N = 1,346) of adults. Based on the pilot, 133 items were retained for the standardization phase.

TECHNICAL. Data for the EQ-i 2.0 normative sample were collected from 4,000 participants living in all 50 U.S. states (n = 3,600) and 10 Canadian provinces (n = 400). Census information from the U.S. and Canada was used to determine the stratification of the standardization sample by key demographic variables (e.g., participants' age, gender, race/ethnicity, and education level). Univariate and multivariate analyses of covariance revealed small but significant age and gender effects, so both specific age/gender norms and overall norms were developed. Although the test manual reports that this inventory may be used internationally with various translations available, no data are provided about normative procedures with participants outside of the U.S. and Canada, and there is no information in the test manual regarding the development of translated versions of the EQ-i 2.0. [Editor's Note: The publisher advises that international norms were in development at the time this review was written. Since that time, additional normative information has been released for countries outside North America. Norms supplements are available for registered users of the online manual.]

Overall, scores from the EQ-i 2.0 demonstrate acceptable levels of reliability for screening and intervention planning purposes. Across the total normative sample, internal consistency reliability coefficients ranged from .77 to .91 for subscale scores and from .88 to .97 for composite scores. Test-retest stability data were collected on a subsample of participants (n = 204; r = .78–.92) at 2- to 4-week retest intervals and at an 8-week retest interval (N = 106; r = .70–.84). Although scores still fell within an adequate range, stability correlations tended to decrease as the time interval between testing increased.

The EQ-i 2.0 user's guide includes a detailed description of validity analyses. Unique samples were used to conduct exploratory (EFA) and confirmatory (CFA) factor analyses. Separate EFAs were conducted for each of the five hypothesized scales, and although criteria are specified in the test manual for factor retention and item loadings, the actual data are not reported in the manual. Fit indices for CFAs at the scale level are reported in the test manual and generally demonstrated acceptable fit.

The RMSEA and AGFI for the overall model, however, are not consistent with current criteria (e.g., Kline, 2005), raising some questions regarding the fit between the EQ-i 2.0 and the overall model that it is hypothesized to reflect.

The EQ-i 2.0 demonstrated low to moderate correlation coefficients with conceptually related subscales of other measures (e.g., Social Skills Inventory [SSI], NEO Five-Factor Inventory [NEO-FFI]) providing evidence of convergent validity. Low correlation coefficients between the EQ-i 2.0 and other measures of emotional intelligence (EI) (e.g., Mayer-Salovey-Caruso Emotional Intelligence Test [MSCEIT], Watson-Glaser II) are reported in the user's guide. Interestingly, these coefficients are interpreted as providing evidence in support of the EQ-i 2.0 because this measure conceptualizes EI as a trait, whereas the others conceptualize EI as an ability.

A number of group differences (e.g., degree of academic success, depressed vs. nondepressed populations) were examined. Findings were consistent with expectations based on theory. Differences in scores between corporate leaders and the general normative sample produced the largest effect sizes. Differences also were consistently observed across scales and subscales between Black, Hispanic, and White subsamples. Although the effect sizes across these three groups were generally small, members of the White sample consistently demonstrated the lowest scores, with several falling .33 *SD* (or more) below the group with the highest mean score. It is unclear whether these findings reflect true differences between the groups or could perhaps be an artifact of other characteristics (e.g., age, occupational achievement) that differed across the subsamples; however, they should be studied further. In addition, research examining differences among scores of individuals with a variety of clinical disorders would lend stronger support for the use of the EQ-i 2.0 in psychoeducational assessments and psychiatric settings. Predictive validity studies examining the long-term effects of coaching feedback on changes in EQ-i 2.0 ratings, as well as on observed changes in socioemotional functioning, would strengthen support for the use of this inventory as a tool for feedback and personal development.

COMMENTARY. The EQ-i 2.0 user's guide is impressive in its coverage of conceptual, practical (administration, scoring, interpretation, application to intervention), and technical aspects of the EQ-i 2.0. Equally impressive are the development efforts, pilot and standardization samples, and aspects of the psychometric evidence (e.g., reliability, scale structure, convergent validity, and expected differences between groups). Some questions remain, however, regarding structural validity evidence for the overall model that guided the development of the scale. In addition, data from predictive validity studies linking scores and recommended interventions (e.g., coaching) to outcomes are needed to strengthen support for the use of this inventory as a professional and personal development tool. Finally, further research examining the psychometric strength of EQ-i 2.0 scores with clinically and culturally diverse samples would provide valuable information about its use internationally and for psychodiagnostic purposes. Independent examinations of the psychometric properties of EQ-i 2.0 scores also are needed.

The user's guide notes that the EQ-i 2.0 should be used in conjunction with other assessment measures and that decisions should not be based solely on an EQ-i 2.0 score. Based on our review of the measure and current psychometric evidence, such an approach to use of the EQ-i 2.0 appears to be justified.

REVIEWERS' REFERENCES
Bar-On, R. (1997). *EQ-i technical manual.* Toronto, Canada: Multi-Health Systems. Inc.
Gardner, H. (1983). *Frames of mind: The theory of multiple intelligences.* New York, NY: Basic Books.
Kline, R. B. (2005). *Principles and practice of structural equation modeling.* New York, NY: The Guilford Press.
Leeper, R. W. (1948). A motivational theory of emotion to replace 'emotion as disorganized response.' *Psychological Review, 55,* 5–21.
Wechsler, D. (1940). Nonintellective factors in general intelligence. *Psychological Bulletin, 37,* 444–445.

[63]

Employee Attitude and Personality Test.

Purpose: "Designed to evaluate whether a person has the traits and skills needed to be a productive and successful worker."

Population: Under age 19 through adult.

Publication Date: 2011.

Acronym: EAPT.

Scores, 45: Social Skills, Forcefulness, Industriousness/Assiduity, Openness to Improvement, Openness to Change, Conformity, Resilience, Level-Headedness, Need for Supervision, Compliance, Trainability, Steadiness, Conscientiousness, Integrity, Approval-Seeking, Adaptability, Coping Skills, Emotional Stability, Creativity, Open-Mindedness, Innovation, Drive/Success Orientation, Calculated Risk-Taking, Street Smarts, Initiative, Independence, Leadership Potential, Dominance, Authoritarianism, Extroversion, Soft Skills, Agreeableness, Dynamism, Fair-Mindedness, Abrasiveness, Tension/Nervous Energy, Accident Proneness, Hotheadedness, Generalist, Specialist, Technical Skill, Kinesthetic Skill, Visual/Spatial Skill, Linguistic Skill, Analytical Thinking.

Administration: Individual.
Price Data: Available from publisher.
Time: (20) minutes.
Comments: Self-administered online assessment. The test publisher advises that the test manual is being updated to include more information about methodology and theoretical background used in the development of the test. The test publisher also advises that this information is available to clients, as are benchmarks for relevant industries and racial/ethnic group comparison data. However, this information was not provided to Buros or the reviewer.
Author: PsychTests AIM, Inc.
Publisher: PsychTests AIM, Inc. [Canada].

Review of the Employee Attitude and Personality Test by STEPHEN B. JOHNSON, Senior Psychometrician, Castle Worldwide, Inc., Greensboro, NC:

DESCRIPTION. The Employee Attitude and Personality Test (EAPT) is an individually administered online pre-employment screening tool. According to a sample report from the test publisher's website, the EAPT assesses the "type of work traits a person possesses, his or her primary, secondary, and minor traits/skills, and offers some helpful work tips" ("Test Descriptions and Sample Reports," n.d.) The intent of the tool is to provide a pre-employment or placement assessment about a "candidate's personality, attitudes, values, motivators, pet peeves, strengths and challenges" ("Candidate Selection," n.d.) that can be combined with data from customized benchmarks to assess the fit between the potential employee and the organizational mission and vision. The assessment also is described as supporting the interview process by providing guided interview questions for an interviewer based on the candidate profile.

The EAPT was designed for administration and interpretation by nonpsychologists; it is the type of test that was described before 1974 as requiring Class A qualifications. Typical respondents would take 45 to 60 minutes to complete the assessment, which is designed for purchase by human resource groups.

The test is composed of 85 questions that focus on asking respondents to select a behavioral or emotional response that best describes them. The majority of items are 5-option Likert-type questions with one- or two-word descriptions that ask respondents to describe how much they are like the descriptive word (exactly like me, a lot, somewhat, a little, not at all). These items are presented in blocks of nine per page. Another set of items,

presented in groups of six, asks respondents to select the best response to complete the sentence "I am a ..." Finally, sets of two items are presented that ask respondents to select an option that best completes the sentence "I am ..."

Administration is clear and simple to follow, and reporting is fast. The basic EAPT report provides an assessment of an individual in 45 areas. Nine of them are described as factors: Social Skills ("Ability to interact harmoniously with people; to build a rapport with others"); Forcefulness ("Assesses whether a person possesses a more commanding and controlling disposition, or an accepting and acquiescent one"); Industriousness/Assiduity ("Assesses degree to which a person is hard-working and diligent"); Openness to Improvement ("Assesses willingness to continuously learn and grow"); Openness to Change ("Extent to which a person is comfortable with variability in his or her environment"); Conformity ("Refers to obedient, unquestioning, and responsible conduct"); Resilience ("Ability to bounce back from adversity"); Level-Headedness ("Ability to maintain poise and control during difficult situations"); and Need for Supervision ("Assesses whether an individual possesses certain traits or behaviors that would make a supervised environment more beneficial"). The remaining 36 scales contain such concepts as Agreeableness, Extroversion, Accident Proneness, and Analytical Thinking. For each of the 45 factors and scales, a scaled score of 0 to 100 is provided with a one-paragraph description of the test taker's profile. There is no information available in the manual about how these nine factors and 36 scales were developed, what distinguishes the nine factors from the 36 scales, or what psychological theory informed their development.

The online report provides a number of easy-to-navigate tabs. The first tab (Introduction) describes the intent of the assessment. A Graphs tab provides for each of the 45 factors and scales an indicator of the scaled scores associated with the respondent. The Details tab provides for each scale a paragraph description of the respondent, his or her score, and a short description of the scale. A Dominant & Minor Traits tab categorizes the scales into three groups: traits/skills that play a dominant role in the respondent's life, traits/skills that influence a respondent's life to some degree, and traits/skills a respondent possesses to a minor degree. Finally, an Advice & Tips tab provides some general work style tips.

With 45 scales, many items loaded on more than one factor or scale. Within the two broad groups (nine factors and 36 scales), items also loaded on more than one factor or scale. For example, the number of items used for the nine factors totaled 197, ranging from 9 items (Forcefulness) to 33 items (Industriousness/Assiduity). For the 36 scales the number of items ranged from 5 to 25, although the majority of scales included 5 to 10 items.

There was no published information about how the traits/skills were assigned to the three categories provided in the Dominant & Minor Traits tab. The results obtained from the responses of this reviewer when he completed the measure and the example on the website indicate some use of a general benchmark. For example, for the responses of this reviewer, scales scoring 80 and above were described as "dominant," scales with scores from 60 to 79 were categorized as influencing life "to some degree," and scales scoring less than 60 were categorized as "minor."

The information provided in the Advice & Tips tab does not appear to be person-specific. This reviewer had the opportunity to respond to the assessment as a different user and noted that the advice tab contained the same general comments about being in the workplace.

Users are able to purchase additional modules that provide a comparison of a respondent with members of benchmark groups, such as the general population or workers in a specific industry (e.g., sales, IT, marketing). Users may also create their own benchmarks using internal data. The reporting also enables comparisons between individuals, and the system can provide interview questions that are customized based on a test taker's scores. This reviewer was not able to assess the quality of these group and comparative reports. Administration costs are available from the publisher upon request.

DEVELOPMENT. There was no information within the variety of online materials or the provided technical report that provided any details about the development process of the EAPT. The online test description describes the EAPT as compliant with the *Standards for Educational and Psychological Testing* (American Educational Research Association [AERA], American Psychological Association [APA], & National Council on Measurement in Education [NCME], 1999) and *Uniform Guidelines for Employee Selection*.

The provided technical report summarized an analysis of 959 "self-selected respondents."

The document provided summary data (*N*, mean, standard deviation) for each of the 45 scales by six descriptive categories: gender, age group (below 19, 20–24, 25–29, 30–39, 40–49, 50 and over), education level, socioeconomic status (assessed by income level), position (entrepreneur, manager, employee, not employed), self-reported academic grades (straight As, pretty well, average/poor), and supervisor ratings (excellent, good, satisfactory/poor). The data used to provide the categories were self-reported by respondents who opted to participate in the validation study when taking the assessment at the websites Queendom.com and Psychtests.com.

TECHNICAL. A "validation sample" of 959 respondents, 540 females, 286 males, and 133 who did not provide their gender, is used to report normative results. The sample had similar proportions in the seven age-group categories (below 19: 15%; 20–24: 13%; 25–29: 12%; 30–39: 19%; 40–49: 12%; 50 and over: 10%; and unreported: 19%). Further normative data are available for the demographic descriptors described above. ANOVA analyses are also reported for scale differences for the demographic descriptors. In addition, normative data (*N*, mean, and standard deviation) are provided for three groups of respondents described as excellent, good, and satisfactory for interpersonal skills. There is no information about how these 146-person groups were so identified.

For the 36 scales, the reported alpha coefficients (Cronbach, 1951) for the 959 respondents ranged from .63 (Steadiness, 5 items) to .91 (Leadership Potential, 25 items), with the majority of the coefficients in the .70 to .80 range. The nine factors had reported alpha coefficients of .75 (Forcefulness, 9 items) to .93 (Industriousness/Assiduity, 33 items), with most in the .80 to .90 range. These results are consistent with expectations for a general psychological measurement in terms of reliability estimates for the number of items. No information was provided on the correlations between the 45 scales.

There is very little validity evidence presented to support inferences made from the EAPT. The normative data presented do not represent strong validity evidence, and the lack of information about the procedures used to develop the scales substantially undermines the test author's contention that the test is compliant with the *Standards for Educational and Psychological Testing* (AERA, APA, & NCME, 1999). For example, Standard 3.7

clearly articulates the need to describe procedures used to develop, review, try out, and select items, as well as to document the qualifications of the individuals involved.

COMMENTARY. The EAPT is a simple, easy-to-use online assessment. At times, the assessment's 5-option Likert-type items felt like a vocabulary test. For example, one word provided was *perseverant*, an unusual presentation of the concept of perseverance. Although the item represented an appropriate use of such an adjective and someone with a strong vocabulary would be able to parse the word, the use of unfamiliar vocabulary might inject some level of measurement error for some respondents. Cases of such wording, as well as the lack of information about the development process, suggest that the authors may not have had a clear picture of the variety of persons who may be confronted with the assessment.

Although the individual and group reporting seems well designed, this reviewer was left with the impression that there was more involved in the score reporting than this reviewer was made privy. The clear example of this vagueness is the lack of clarity about how the scales were categorized into the three dominant trait groups.

Information about item and scale development, including who developed and reviewed the items (even a reference to an external site), item selection criteria, and review processes, would be very much appreciated. There also was no information provided about who reviewed the entire instrument and whether any bias review was conducted.

Finally, as a test reviewer who has worked with many different psychological instruments over the years, the concept that information on 45 separate scales can be adequately provided by 85 items appears highly problematic. Without information from correlation matrices, factor loading tables, or measurement models, this reviewer was left to conclude that many of these scales are essentially repeating the same information with slightly different descriptions applied to them. This lack of statistical information, along with an associated lack of a psychological theory supporting the development of the scales, should make one cautious about using this instrument.

SUMMARY. The EAPT is designed as a self-administered online measure of 45 traits and skills. It provides a clear and simple delivery interface and a well designed reporting infrastructure. The lack of information about how the scales were developed

and their psychological underpinnings undermines the delivery and reporting infrastructure. The defensibility of interpretations from using this tool would be highly problematic. The assessment may be slightly more effective as a comparative tool, particularly using in-house benchmarks, but the virtually nonexistent validity evidence does not recommend it as an appropriate job assessment tool. In the opinion of this reviewer, the lack of documentation results in a failure to meet professional test development and the *Uniform Guidelines*.

REVIEWER'S REFERENCES

American Educational Research Association, American Psychological Association, & National Council on Measurement in Education. (1999). *Standards for educational and psychological testing.* Washington, D.C.: AERA.
Candidate selection. (n.d.). Retrieved from http://www.archprofile.com/corporate/tests/hiring
Cronbach, L. J. (1951). Coefficient alpha and the internal structure of tests. *Psychometrika, 16,* 297–334.
Test descriptions and sample reports. (n.d.). Retrieved from http://corporate.psychtests.com/samples
U.S. Equal Employment Opportunity Commission, Department of Labor, Department of Justice, U.S. Civil Service Commission. (1978). *Uniform Guidelines on Employee Selection Procedures.*

[64]

Endler Multidimensional Anxiety Scales and EMAS Social Anxiety Scales.

Purpose: Designed to provide "a multidimensional measure of anxiety, with four related scales assessing transitory anxiety response, situational anxiety, perception of immediate threat, and social anxiety."

Population: Adolescents and adults.

Administration: Group.

Price Data: Not available.

Time: (25) minutes.

Publisher: Western Psychological Services.

a) ENDLER MULTIDIMENSIONAL ANXIETY SCALES.

Publication Date: 1991.

Scores, 12: Cognitive-Worry, Autonomic-Emotional, Total, Trait Social Evaluation, Trait Physical Danger, Trait Ambiguous, Trait Daily Routines, Perception Social Evaluation, Perception Physical Danger, Perception Ambiguous, Perception Daily Routines, Perception Threat.

Acronym: EMAS.

Authors: Norman S. Endler, Jean M. Edwards, and Romeo Vitelli.

b) EMAS SOCIAL ANXIETY SCALES.

Acronym: EMAS-SAS.

Publication Date: 2002.

Scores, 8: Trait Separation, Trait Self-Disclosure to Family Members, Trait Self-Disclosure to Close Friends, Trait Social Evaluation, Perception Separation, Perception Self-Disclosure, Perception Social Evaluation, Perception Threat.

Authors: Norman S. Endler and Gordon L. Flett.

Cross References: See T5:950 (6 references); for reviews by Deborah L. Bandalos and Steven D. Spaner of the Endler Multidimensional Anxiety Scales, see 12:138 (2 references); see also T4:905 (7 references).

[Editor's Note: The publisher advised that this test is out of print as of July 2012.]

Review of the Endler Multidimensional Anxiety Scales and EMAS Social Anxiety Scales by RENÉE M. TOBIN, Professor of Psychology, and JENNIFER L. ENGELLAND, Doctoral Student, Illinois State University, Normal, IL:

DESCRIPTION. Based on the interaction model of anxiety, the Endler Multidimensional Anxiety Scales (EMAS) are self-report measures designed to assess state anxiety, trait anxiety, and perceptions of threat primarily in adults. The EMAS scales include assessment of state anxiety with the EMAS-State scale (EMAS-S), of trait anxiety in four situations with the EMAS-Trait scale (EMAS-T), and of respondents' perception of threat in five domains with the EMAS-Perception scale (EMAS-P). The EMAS can be used in conjunction with, or independent from, the EMAS Social Anxiety Scales (EMAS-SAS), which assess trait anxiety in terms of separation, self-disclosure to family and friends, and social evaluation with the EMAS-SAS-Trait scale (EMAS-SAS-T) and the perception of threat in four domains with the EMAS-SAS-Perception scale (EMAS-SAS-P).

The state anxiety measure (EMAS-S) contains 20 items yielding Cognitive-Worry, Autonomic-Emotional, and Total State Anxiety scores. The trait anxiety measure (EMAS-T) contains 60 items (15 items assessing each of four situations), yielding scores for trait anxiety in Social Evaluation, Ambiguous, Physical Danger, and Daily Routines. The EMAS-P scale includes five questions using Likert-type scales and three open-ended questions, resulting in four raw scores and three narrative responses that are not scored. The EMAS-SAS-T yields one score for each of the four subscales. The items on the social evaluation (SE) subscale of the EMAS-SAS-T are the same as the social evaluation subscale on the EMAS-T; similarly, the items on the social evaluation (SE) and threat (TH) subscales of the EMAS-SAS-P are identical to the corresponding subscales on the EMAS-P.

The EMAS and EMAS-SAS are pencil-and-paper self-report measures that can be administered individually or in groups. The order of administration should always be state (EMAS-S), followed by trait (EMAS-T), and finally perception (EMAS-P). The scales are intended for use in applied, clinical,

and research settings with respondents who read and comprehend English at an eighth-grade level. Testing time for all three measures of the EMAS is 25 minutes. Testing time for both the EMAS-S and EMAS-P is less than 10 minutes, whereas the EMAS-SAS takes approximately 15 minutes to complete. Although this information is not provided in the test manual, the state, trait, and perception forms are available in hand-scoring, prepaid mail-in computer scoring, CD, and FAX service formats. The EMAS-SAS can be hand scored using AutoScore forms, but cannot be computer scored. A manual extension is available for hand-scoring. The scales may be administered by a paraprofessional, but the interpretation and communication of results require an expert in psychological assessment. The EMAS is intended for use as a diagnostic tool and for treatment planning for some anxiety disorders as part of a comprehensive assessment.

DEVELOPMENT. The EMAS is based on Endler's multidimensional interaction model of anxiety, which has received support in the research literature. The interaction model of anxiety has been used as a theoretical framework for understanding anxiety as a product of the interaction between a person's general tendency to be anxious in certain situations and the person's state response to that anxiety-provoking situation. This model has been applied to anxiety associated with diverse situations including stuttering (Ezrati-Vinacour & Levin, 2004; Messenger, Onslow, Packman, & Menzies, 2004), using the computer (Gaudron & Vignoli, 2002), exercising (Blanchard, Rodgers, Bell, Wilson, & Gesell, 2002), surgery with children (Clewes & Endler, 1994), public speaking (Muller, Endler, & Parker, 1990), job stress (Greenglass, 1985), and academic tests (Phillips & Endler, 1982). In terms of the EMAS, the interaction model of anxiety differentiates state anxiety from trait anxiety while analyzing the situational context. The test authors noted that the interaction between stressful situations and corresponding trait anxiety produces state anxiety. Similarly, the EMAS-SAS is based on the interactional nature of anxiety and includes the situations of separation and self-disclosure.

In its 30 years of development and use, the EMAS has been through multiple revisions based on the results of factor and correlational analysis. For the EMAS-T, factor analysis led to the development of items measuring interpersonal, physically dangerous, and ambiguous situations. Additional studies led to the development of items about daily routines and interpersonal anxiety as measures of social evaluation anxiety. For state anxiety, the original measure was based on the S-R Inventory of Anxiousness, and through several revisions using item-remainder and factor analyses, the current version of the EMAS-S was developed. Flood and Endler's (1980) Perceptions of Competitive Events (PCE) and Perception of Situations Rating Form (PSRF) preceded the EMAS-P. The development of the EMAS-SAS began in 1997 with the goal of providing greater assessment of aspects of social anxiety. Similar to other subscales of the EMAS, revisions to EMAS-SAS were based on empirical findings.

In the U.S., the EMAS was standardized with only undergraduates and adults, whereas it was standardized with Canadian adolescents, undergraduates, adults, psychiatric outpatients, and military personnel. The EMAS-SAS was standardized with these populations, excluding Canadian adolescents and military personnel, and including postpartum mothers and fathers. As with all measures, attention should be given to norm groups prior to administering and interpreting the EMAS and EMAS-SAS.

Hand scoring takes only about 5 to 10 minutes per form. Thus, scoring of all scales is easy and efficient. Reports are detailed and helpful, containing results summaries, graphs, integrated score profiles, score interpretations, and recommendations; nevertheless, this information should not replace clinical judgment. Scores provide information regarding respondents' anxiety in multiple situations; thus, it can be useful for the identification of antecedents and in treatment planning.

TECHNICAL. The norm groups for the EMAS are best described as convenience samples obtained from adults and undergraduate students in Ohio and New York for the U.S. sample, and adults, undergraduates, adolescents, psychiatric outpatients, and military personnel in Toronto and Peterborough for the Canadian sample. Norm groups for the EMAS-SAS excluded Canadian military personnel and adolescents, but included Canadian postpartum mothers and fathers. No EMAS or EMAS-SAS norms are available for U.S. adolescents or psychiatric outpatients. Thus, the normative samples are not representative of individuals in the U.S. or in Canada. In addition to geographic limitations of the normative sample, the test manual also does not provide data regarding race, ethnicity, education level, and socioeconomic status, although it does provide gender norms. Sample sizes for the subgroups ranged from 203 to 595 individuals with fairly equal numbers of men and women, totaling more than 1,800 respondents across age and gender groups for both the EMAS and the EMAS-SAS.

In terms of reliability, internal consistency was high for the EMAS-S (.78–.94), EMAS-T (.82–.96), and the EMAS-SAS scales for separation (.83–.94), self-disclosure (.87–.96), and social evaluation (.83–.95). In contrast, test-retest for the EMAS-S (the state measure) was low for males (.35–.46) and for females (.14 to .48); however, this is to be expected because the scale measures respondents' anxiety at the time of testing so fluctuation is expected. Three studies were conducted to examine test-retest reliability of the EMAS-T, with a 2-week interval for the first study and 4-week intervals for the other studies. Low to moderate test-retest reliability was reported in these studies (coefficients ranged from .50 to .79); thus, scores for trait anxiety were somewhat stable over time. Low test-retest correlations were found for the EMAS-P scale after a 1-month period for males (coefficients ranged from .03 to .72) and for females (coefficients ranged from .22 to .47). Nevertheless, items are based on respondents' current situation; thus, low test-retest reliability coefficients are expected. For the EMAS-SAS, a sample of 113 females and 27 males were tested twice over a 1-week period; moderate test-retest coefficients (.69–.77) were observed.

In terms of validity, Endler and his colleagues have done an outstanding job of strengthening the construct validity of the test scores over the years since the measure was created. Through peer-reviewed publications, they systematically provide evidence of convergent and discriminant validity of each of the subscale scores in a diverse set of applications. That is, research studies demonstrate that the EMAS scales do more than simply distinguish between individuals with anxiety disorders and those without or with other disorders. The cumulative effect of these validity studies is that the user can have greater confidence in the distinctiveness of each scale and the usefulness of respective scores in differential diagnosis and prediction of clinically relevant outcomes.

COMMENTARY. Overall, the EMAS and EMAS-SAS are quick and easy to administer and score. The EMAS-T and EMAS-SAS-T comprehensively cover situations in which individuals may experience anxiety. Social anxiety is extensively assessed on the two measures. In addition, the measures are useful in the assessment of Generalized Anxiety Disorder and Social Phobia. There is considerable empirical support for the EMAS and EMAS-SAS scales. The measures can distinguish between clinical and nonclinical populations and can be useful with treatment planning and evaluation. The measures have a clear theoretical foundation that has been supported through empirical studies over the last 30 years.

Despite the strengths, the EMAS and EMAS-SAS do not exhaustively cover anxiety disorders, such as Obsessive Compulsive Disorder. Narrative items on the EMAS-P and EMAS-SAS-P only pertain to state anxiety as opposed to trait anxiety. Items on the EMAS-S may lead respondents to become overly aware of their physical and mental states and begin reporting feeling more anxious. Probably its greatest weakness is its normative sample. Standardization of the measures was limited in terms of its sample size, regions, and age ranges. Although the age of the norms is likely of less concern than it would be for other types of measures (e.g., cognitive assessments), it is worth noting that the norms are 20 years old. Finally, the EMAS and EMAS-SAS can only be administered to individuals who read and comprehend English at an eighth grade level.

SUMMARY. The EMAS is a collection of assessment instruments designed to measure different types of anxiety primarily in adults. They allow for the assessment of an individual's present state of anxiety, the individual's general predisposition to experience anxiety, and his or her perception of situational threat. In combination, the EMAS and EMAS-SAS comprehensively measure state anxiety, trait anxiety, and perception of threat. Subscales cover anxiety during social evaluation, physical danger, ambiguous situations, daily routines, separation, and self-disclosure. The measures have strong theoretical and empirical support. They may be beneficial when used in conjunction with additional assessment measures for the diagnosis and treatment of anxiety disorders.

REVIEWERS' REFERENCES

Blanchard, C. M., Rodgers, W. M., Bell, G., Wilson, P. M., & Gesell, J. (2002). An empirical test of the interaction model of anxiety in an acute exercise setting. *Personality and Individual Differences, 32,* 329-336.

Clewes, J. L., & Endler, N. S. (1994). State-trait anxiety and the experience of elective surgery in children. *Canadian Journal of Behavioural Science/Revue canadienne des sciences du comportement, 26,* 183-198.

Ezrati-Vinacour, R., & Levin, I. (2004). The relationship between anxiety and stuttering: A multidimensional approach. *Journal of Fluency Disorders, 29,* 135-148.

Flood, M., & Endler, N. S. (1980). The interaction model of anxiety: An empirical test in an athletic competition situation. *Journal of Research in Personality, 14,* 329-339.

Gaudron, J., & Vignoli, E. (2002). Assessing computer anxiety with the interaction model of anxiety: Development and validation of the computer anxiety trait subscale. *Computers in Human Behavior, 18,* 315-326.

Greenglass, E. R. (1985). An interactional perspective on job related stress in managerial women. *Southern Psychologist, 2,* 42-48.

Messenger, M., Onslow, M., Packman, A., & Menzies, R. (2004). Social anxiety in stuttering: Measuring negative social expectancies. *Journal of Fluency Disorders, 29, 201-212.*

Muller, R. T., Endler, N. S., & Parker, J. D. A. (1990). The interaction model of anxiety assessed in two public speaking situations. *Personality and Individual Differences, 11,* 371-377.

Phillips, J. B., & Endler, N. S. (1982). Academic examinations and anxiety: The interaction model empirically tested. *Journal of Research in Personality, 16,* 303-318.

Review of the Endler Multidimensional Anxiety Scales and EMAS Social Anxiety Scales by TONY C. WU, Faculty, College of Social and Behavioral Sciences, Walden University, Minneapolis, MN:

DESCRIPTION. The Endler Multidimensional Anxiety Scales (EMAS) and Social Anxiety Scales (EMAS-SAS) are individually or group-administered paper-and-pencil self-report questionnaires for adolescents and adults to complete, designed for aiding the diagnosis and treatment planning of different types of anxiety disorders. The test authors indicate it will be advantageous to mental health and allied health professionals as well as researchers interested in differentiating the constructs of anxiety state and trait from other similar psychological characteristics and emotional states. The EMAS and EMAS-SAS were intended for use with adolescents and adults with normative and clinical samples from Canada and the United States.

The EMAS materials include three separate scales: EMAS-State (EMAS-S), EMAS-Trait (EMAS-T), and EMAS-Perception (EMAS-P). "Each scale can be either hand scored, using the EMAS AutoScore™ Forms, or computer scored, using the EMAS mail-in computer-scannable Answer Sheets" (manual, p. 6). The EMAS questionnaires generate scores for State Anxiety (Cognitive Worry and Autonomic-Emotional), Trait Anxiety (Social Evaluation, Physical Danger, Ambiguous Situations, and Daily Routines), and Perception of Threat (Social Evaluation, Physical Danger, Ambiguous Situations, Daily Routines, and Threat). The companion EMAS-SAS questionnaires further assess specific traits and symptoms associated with social anxiety by generating additional scores for Trait Anxiety (Separation, Self-Disclosure to Family Members, Self-Disclosure to Close Friends, and Social Evaluation), as well as Perception of Threat (Separation, Self-Disclosure, Social Evaluation, and Threat).

The administration instructions are easy to follow; the test authors claim that it takes approximately 25 minutes to complete each form of the questionnaire. In terms of scoring options, the test authors note that unlike the EMAS, the EMAS-SAS is currently available only in the hand-scoring method. Overall, the scoring, computing, and recording of the scale scores are not complicated. In fact, it is straightforward. For hand-scoring, a calculator might be helpful, but it is not necessary, as scoring involves only addition. Once the raw scores are computed for each scale, the profile sheet is used to determine T scores and percentile ranks, which are provided separately by genders. In terms of interpretation, the test authors claim that the scale scores will help to distinguish between state and trait anxiety in both the clinical and nonclinical groups. Finally, the test authors recommend the analysis of items for response inconsistency in order to allow the examiner to weigh the validity of the scores and response patterns.

DEVELOPMENT. In the development of the EMAS and EMAS-SAS, the test authors desired a test that would be beneficial to both clinicians and researchers interested in anxiety evaluation. The theoretical model for the EMAS is based on the interaction model of personality that has been utilized in various research conditions and environments. In this framework, anxiety is evaluated in four dimensions of general situational contexts: social evaluation situations, physically dangerous situations, ambiguous situations, along with daily routine situations.

The standardization sample for the EMAS included over 1,800 respondents of various age ranges in both the United States and Canada. Data from different samples were combined to produce norms for five populations: U.S. adults, Canadian adults, U.S. undergraduates, Canadian undergraduates, and Canadian adolescents.

For the companion EMAS-SAS, additional research was completed to validate the two newly developed scales as well as Separation Anxiety and Self-Disclosure Anxiety in the United States and Canada. The sample included 328 adults (150 men, 178 women) visiting a large science museum in Canada, as well as 502 university undergraduate students.

TECHNICAL. Overall, meaningful estimates of reliability and validity are provided by the test authors. Available data provide evidence to support inferences made from scores obtained from the EMAS and EMAS-SAS.

Specific to reliabilities, internal consistency coefficients for the Cognitive-Worry and Autonomic-Emotional subscales ranged from .78 to .91.

Similarly, it was reported that internal consistency estimates for the Total State Anxiety score ranged from .88 to .94. With regard to test-retest stability, the coefficients ranged from .35 to .46 for men and from .14 to .48 for women. The test authors noted that test-retest reliability analyses cannot be expected to be stable for the EMAS-SAS over time because state anxiety varies with situational factors.

Validity evidence is provided by the test authors to support the test conclusion drawn from the EMAS. Item-remainder correlations for the EMAS-S revealed moderate to high coefficients for males and females for most of the items on the Cognitive-Worry and Autonomic-Emotional subscales, with values ranging from .20 to .84. It was also determined that the correlations between the three EMAS-S subscale scores and the Speilberger State-Trait Anxiety Inventory–State for a group of male and female undergraduates were statistically significant at the .001 level.

Alpha coefficients for the EMAS-SAS ranged from .83 to .94 for the Separation subscale, .87 to .96 for the Self-Disclosure subscale, and .83 to .95 for the Social Evaluation subscale. Test-retest reliability coefficients ranged from .69 to .77. The concurrent validity of the EMAS-SAS, as estimated by using the normative sample of adults, indicated that the Pathological Worry, as assessed by the Penn State Worry Questionnaire, was associated with Anxiety in women ($r = .37, p < .01$).

COMMENTARY. The EMAS and EMAS-SAS are succinct and straightforward tests that have clinical utility in the differential diagnosis of anxiety disorders. They feature test items that specifically tap into the construct of different types of anxiety states and traits. Moreover, the recording, scoring, and interpreting are concise and easy to follow. The norms are based on both nonclinical and clinical individuals. Adequate validity and reliability evidence is provided to support the inferences drawn from test results. Even so, the EMAS was published more than 20 years ago (1991) with mostly Canadian samples, which raises questions about reliability and validity when the questionnaire is used with the United States population. For example, there is no information on the racial and ethnic composition of the normative sample available in the testing manual. In future revisions of the EMAS, the test authors might consider using representative samples of ethnic groups in order to clarify the applicability of the constructs for specific cultural groups in the United States. Additionally, the test authors might want to think about adding specific age ranges in the test administration section of the manual. Currently, the test authors note that this scale is suitable for use with both clinical and nonclinical populations who are fluent in English with a minimum reading level of Grade 8. Finally, computer scoring for the EMAS-SAS should be added to the questionnaire.

SUMMARY. The Endler Multidimensional Anxiety Scales (EMAS) and Social Anxiety Scales (EMAS-SAS) are norm-referenced, standardized tools that can facilitate the diagnosis and treatment for adolescents and adults who have anxiety problems. The key feature of the EMAS and EMAS-SAS is to assist in the detection of anxiety disorders and subsequent treatment planning. The EMAS and EMAS-SAS were developed in an attempt to ascertain the multidimensional symptoms and/or syndromes of these highly complex disorders, specifically tapping into transitory anxiety response, situational anxiety, perception of immediate threat, and social anxiety. The psychometric properties are supported by the evidence provided in the test manual. However, the authors of the EMAS should consider a revision given it was published about 20 years ago and standardized using a mostly Canadian population. Unfortunately, the EMAS cannot be recommended for clinical use at this time with the U.S. population. On the other hand, the EMAS-SAS was published in 2002 and is based on updated validation samples; hence, it is appropriate to use within a comprehensive psychological evaluation to assess social anxiety.

[65]

Entrepreneurial Aptitude Profile.

Purpose: Designed to "assess whether a test-taker's skills and personality traits match those required" to work as an entrepreneur.
Population: Potential entrepreneurs.
Publication Date: 2011.
Acronym: EntAP.
Scores, 19: Drive to Succeed (Independence, Passion, Goal-Orientation, Conscientiousness), Social Network (Social Skills, Leadership, Mentoring/Support), Outlook on Success (Self-Efficaciousness, Optimism, Status-Seeking), Openness to New Ideas (Interest in Knowledge, Innovation, Adaptability, Risk-Taking), Overall Score.
Administration: Individual.
Price Data: Available from publisher.
Time: (30) minutes.
Comments: Self-administered online assessment. The test publisher advises that the test manual is being updated to include more information about methodology

and theoretical background used in the development of the test. The test publisher also advises that this information is available to clients, as are benchmarks for relevant industries and racial/ethnic group comparison data. However, this information was not provided to Buros or the reviewers.
Author: PsychTests AIM, Inc.
Publisher: PsychTests AIM, Inc. [Canada].

Review of the Entrepreneurial Aptitude Profile by STEVEN W. SCHMIDT, Associate Professor of Adult Education, East Carolina University, Greenville, NC:

DESCRIPTION. The Entrepreneurial Aptitude Profile (EntAP) was designed to assess whether a test taker's skills and personality traits match those needed to work as an entrepreneur.

Results of the assessment are presented in a report that includes the following: an introduction to entrepreneurship, "An overview of the skills and traits needed to work as an entrepreneur" (p. 1); an overall entrepreneurship score; four scale scores (Drive to Succeed, Social Network, Outlook on Success, Openness to New Ideas); 14 subscale scores; and an advice section.

The test manual defines Drive to Succeed as "the ability and willingness to do what it takes to succeed" (p. 1). Included in this construct are the following subconstructs: Independence, the desire to stand alone, apart from the crowd; Passion, drive and enthusiasm for one's work; Goal-Orientation, setting objectives and following through to achieve them; and Conscientiousness, being organized, dependable and efficient.

Social Network is defined as "the ability to form strong social relationships with people" (p. 1). This construct includes Social Skills, the ability to relate easily with other people; Leadership, the ability to take charge and lead others effectively; and Mentoring/Support, strength of social networks to which to turn in times of trouble.

Outlook on Success "refers to whether an individual believes he or she has the potential for success" (p. 1). Subconstructs include Self-Efficaciousness, confidence one has in his/her own abilities; Optimism, the ability to stay positive despite adversity; and Status-Seeking, the role that social status and money play in an individual's drive to succeed.

Openness to New Ideas, "the inclination and desire to try out new ideas" (p. 2) includes Interest in Knowledge, the willingness to learn new things; Innovation, the ability to think productively; Adaptability, the capacity and willingness to accommodate change; and Risk-Taking, the extent to which an individual engages in reckless behavior.

Instructions for completing the EntAP are clear and easy to follow. Participants log on to a website and work through a series of prompts to access the survey. For each question, participants are asked to determine the degree to which the corresponding statement is like them or not like them. A 5-point Likert scale is used in this assessment, with 1 corresponding to *not at all like me* and 5 corresponding to *very much like me*. Questions are displayed 10 at a time, and progress is tracked through a bar at the top of the page that is filled in to indicate how much of the survey has been completed (and how much is yet to be completed). A reminder of the total number of questions and average completion time is also noted at the top of each page. Respondents are asked to complete the survey in one sitting.

Managers can access participants' scores on the same system. Managers have access to final scores and subscores, as well as to the interpretation of results. They do not have access to individual question responses.

DEVELOPMENT. The authors of the instrument and its manual presented very little background on the development of this survey instrument. They did provide information on a pilot study that was conducted as part of efforts to validate the survey. A total of 1,222 respondents participated in the pilot. All took the EntAP on-line at one of two different websites. The sample was uncontrolled; the subjects self-selected to take the assessment and opted in to participate in the validation study. All validation data were gathered through self-report.

The only demographic characteristics presented on participants in the pilot study were gender and age distribution. Both were well distributed. Data on job position and education level were also collected, but not reported (those data were used in validity-related content in the technical manual).

TECHNICAL. As noted above, 1,222 respondents participated in the pilot for the EntAP. Coefficient alpha reliability for the entire instrument was .96. Similar reliability coefficients for the four major constructs were as follows: Drive to Succeed, .86; Social Network, .90; Outlook on Success, .81; Openness to New Ideas, .89.

Reliability for the subscales was also presented. For the four subconstructs that comprise

Drive to Succeed, subscale reliability coefficient alphas ranged from .60 to .77. For the three subconstructs that comprise Social Network, subscale internal consistency reliability coefficients ranged from .70 to .84. For the three subconstructs that comprise Outlook on Success, reliability coefficients ranged from .75 to .79. For the four subconstructs that comprise Openness to New Ideas reliability ranged from .64 to .83.

According to Wallen and Fraenkel (2001), "For research purposes, a rule of thumb is that reliability should be at least .70 and preferably higher" (p. 101). The reliability coefficients noted for the main constructs of the EntAP construct were all well above that figure, ranging from .81 to .96. This is a major strength of this survey instrument. Furthermore, reliability coefficients for 12 of the 14 subconstructs were at or above .70.

Wallen and Fraenkel (2001) also note that "validity is the most important idea to consider when preparing or selecting an instrument for use" (p. 88). In the EntAP technical manual, validity analysis was discussed from the standpoint of demographic categories. Significant differences in scores on the 14 subconstructs were presented based on the following demographic categories: gender, age, education, and position. No additional validity information was presented, which is problematic.

COMMENTARY. A summary report is presented to all who take the EntAP. The technical manual focused on the statistics regarding the four major constructs associated with the instrument (Drive to Succeed, Social Network, Outlook on Success, and Openness to New Ideas). Although the authors note that the test assesses whether the respondent's skills and personality traits match those required to be an entrepreneur, the focus of the technical manual is pilot study data on the reliability and validity of the four major constructs. The technical manual contained no information about the introduction piece or the advice piece of the report provided to test takers, and a summary report example was not presented.

The authors used a large sample size for the pilot study as part of the survey development process. This is a strength of this survey. The survey is fairly quick and easy to take, which is an advantage as well.

On a different note, there are questions about the use of this instrument. The authors note that this instrument was designed to be an assessment tool used by human resource departments as a tool to assess the degree to which a respondent is suited for work as an entrepreneur. However, an entrepreneur is defined as "one who organizes, manages, and assumes the risk of a business or enterprise" (Merriam-Webster, 2005). Based on this definition, it would seem that an entrepreneur is someone who works for him/herself, rather than as an employee of an organization. Would human resource departments in organizations have use for this type of instrument? It is possible that there are some jobs in organizations that call for the same types of skills needed by entrepreneurs, so in these cases, this instrument may be appropriate.

SUMMARY. The EntAP was designed to be a testing system for entrepreneurship. The data on reliability presented indicates that it is highly reliable. The only validity evidence, however, was presented in the form of comparisons of different demographic groups and specific subconstructs of the instrument. There was no evidence presented with regard to the validity of the survey instrument as a whole. In order to make proper recommendations about the use of this instrument, this information should be presented.

REVIEWER'S REFERENCES
entrepreneur. (2005). In *Merriam-Webster's Collegiate* Dictionary (11th ed.). Springfield, MA: Merriam-Webster, Inc.
Wallen, N. E., & Fraenkel, J. R. (2001). *Educational research: A guide to the process.* Mahwah, NJ: Lawrence Erlbaum Associates.

Review of the Entrepreneurial Aptitude Profile by CHOCKALINGAM VISWESVARAN, Professor of Psychology, Florida International University, Miami, FL:

DESCRIPTION. The Entrepreneurial Aptitude Profile (EntAP) is a self-report inventory designed to assess whether a test taker's skills and personality traits match those required to work in entrepreneurial fields. The test is designed to be used for selection and training and is composed of 131 items. The estimated time for completion is 30 minutes. The inventory results in an overall entrepreneurship aptitude score as well as scores on Drive to Succeed, Social Network, Outlook on Success, and Openness to New Ideas. Drive to Succeed refers to the ability and willingness to do what it takes to succeed and assesses Independence, Passion, Goal-Orientation, and Conscientiousness. Social Network refers to the ability to form strong social relationships and assesses Social Skills, Leadership, and Mentoring. Outlook on Success examines whether individuals believe in their potential to succeed and takes into account Self-Efficaciousness, Optimism, and Status-Seeking. Finally, Openness to New Ideas assesses the inclination and desire to

try new ideas and includes Interest in Knowledge, Innovation, Adaptability, and Risk-Taking.

DEVELOPMENT. The manual provides no information on how the items were developed and refined. Responses from 1,222 participants were used to calculate the provided psychometric information. The sample was uncontrolled (i.e., self-selected), and comparisons of scores by gender, age, education, and job category are provided.

TECHNICAL. Technical data are very sparse. Included in the manual is a table summarizing coefficient alpha for the different scales. For the Overall Score, the reliability estimate is reported to be .96. Drive to Succeed, assessed with 35 items, has an alpha of .86. Social Network (31 items), Outlook on Success (29 items), and Openness to New Ideas (42 items) have alpha coefficients of .90, .81, and .89, respectively. Alpha coefficients are also reported for the subscales and range from .60 to .84.

Of the 1,222 respondents, there were 494 women and 524 men (hence, 204 were of unknown gender). Gender comparisons showed that men outscored women on Goal Orientation, Leadership, Status-Seeking, Adaptability, Risk-Taking, and Outlook on Success. Women outscored men on Conscientiousness, Risk Management, and Social Skills. Similar group differences were examined for age, educational level, and job category. The 1,222 respondents were grouped by age as younger than 18 (282 participants), 18–29 (484), 30–39 (138), over 40 (151), and unknown (167). The test manual notes, however, that when groups were not balanced, a smaller, random sample was chosen from the larger groups "to level out the numbers and conduct the analyses effectively" (manual, p. 3). Thus, the age group comparisons consisted of 140 participants who were under 18, 140 who were 18–29, 138 who were 30–39, and 151 who were over 40. Educational level group comparisons included high school or lower (100 participants), junior college or technical-trade school (100), some college (103), and bachelor's degree or higher (100). Job categories were entrepreneurs, managers, non-managers, and not officially employed. Before these results can be interpreted, potential test users need evidence of construct validity of this new measure with other established measures of entrepreneurship and personality. Although the technical manual refers to these group comparisons as validity analyses, it is difficult to make any strong inferences of validity.

COMMENTARY. No factor-analytic data have been presented to support the hypothesized factor structure. No empirical data have been provided to assess the convergent and discriminant validity with other related personality variables. Reliability data should include not only alpha coefficients but also test-retest estimates. If the 1,222 self-reports are to be used for normative data, more information about the appropriateness of the sample to the population of interest needs to be provided.

Item level analyses should normally be reported. Information about item difficulty (or endorsement rates) and item-total correlations is needed. It is critical to obtain construct validity data as well as results of predictive validity analyses. Although the manual provides data regarding group differences, no assessments of predictive bias can be made.

The data presented are from self-selected respondents and as such do not reflect high-stakes assessments. Given the self-reported nature of these interests and skills, the potential for faking in selection contexts needs to be addressed.

SUMMARY. In short, the manual for the EntAP provides impressive graphs comparing demographic groups from the self-selected sample based on gender, age, education, and job category on the different scales. Without information on the construct validity of these scales, however, inferences are ambiguous. Without criterion data, the predictive validity is unknown.

[66]

Entrepreneurial Personality Assessment.

Purpose: Designed to "provide information about which aspects of a person's personality are well suited to owning a business, and which aspects could be problematic."
Population: Under age 17 through adult.
Publication Date: 2011.
Acronym: EPA.
Scores, 7: Self-Sufficiency, Conscientiousness, Drive Orientation, Social Skills, Optimism, Risk-Taking, Networking Ability.
Administration: Individual.
Price Data: Available from publisher.
Time: (15) minutes.
Comments: Self-administered online assessment. The test publisher advises that the test manual is being updated to include more information about methodology and theoretical background used in the development of the test. The test publisher also advises that this information is available to clients, as are benchmarks for relevant industries and racial/ethnic group comparison data. However, this information was not provided to Buros or the reviewers.
Author: PsychTests AIM, Inc.
Publisher: PsychTests AIM, Inc. [Canada].

Review of the Entrepreneurial Personality Assessment by ROBERT K. GABLE, Director, Center for Research and Evaluation, Johnson & Wales University, Alan Shawn Feinstein Graduate School, Providence, RI, and MEGHAN KILEY, Admissions Associate, The Wheeler School, Providence, RI:

DESCRIPTION. The Entrepreneurial Personality Assessment (EPA) is a self-assessment online questionnaire containing 60 items to assess "whether a person possesses the skills and traits needed to succeed in owning their own business" (manual, p. 1). The assessment includes the following seven dimensions (number of items in each dimension): Self-Sufficiency (9), Conscientiousness (9), Drive Orientation (8), Social Skills (10), Optimism (8), Risk-Taking (8), and Networking Ability (12). Test takers respond to the items using a 5-point Likert scale. The developers indicate that information is also provided to test takers regarding their entrepreneurial style based on the typology in Wagner's (2006) text, *The Entrepreneur Next Door.*

DEVELOPMENT. Incomplete information is presented in the technical manual regarding the process used to develop and refine the dimensions and items included.

TECHNICAL. The norm sample consisted of 12,227 respondents who self-selected to take the assessment and participate in the validation study. Descriptive statistics (i.e., means and standard deviations) are presented for the total norm group. Other than these descriptive statistics normative information such as percentiles is not presented. Following administration, respondents are provided with a comprehensive summary score report with graphic display of the score for each dimension and a well-developed custom interpretative description for the respondent's score on each dimension. Coefficient alpha reliabilities for the data obtained for the total set of 60 items is .87; scale-level reliabilities ranged from .61 (Social Skills) and .62 (Self-Sufficiency) to .78 (Networking Ability). Given the adequate number of items in each dimension, the reliabilities in the low .60s for two of the dimensions (with 9 and 10 items) do not lend strong support for data interpretations for these dimensions.

An important source of validity, evidence based on test content, is not adequately addressed by the developers. The technical manual contains no judgmental evidence based on a literature review or expert panel to support what has been previously labeled content validity. The single reference to the entrepreneurial style based on the typology in Wagner's text is appropriate, but by itself does not allow the reviewers or intended test users–human resource professionals–to evaluate comprehensively support for the EPA's underlying theoretical framework. Regarding validity evidence based on the internal structure of the test, no empirical analyses are included. Analyses such as exploratory or confirmatory factor analysis and Rasch model item response theory are not included in the technical manual.

The technical manual does include evidence of validity based on relations to other variables. Analyses based on gender, age, education level, grades (self-reported academic achievement in school), position (entrepreneur, managerial, non-management, not officially employed), and socio-economic status (based on four levels of income) are included. For all analyses, graphic displays are included. Although the test developers note that large sample sizes can result in differences that are statistically, but not practically, significant when the differences between or among means are small, they proceed to report several t-test and ANOVA findings for large comparison groups (e.g., gender: males, $n = 1,799$; females, $n = 1,983$; age: below 17, $n = 950$; 18–24, $n = 1,055$; 25–29, $n = 565$; 30–39, $n = 688$; 40 and older, $n = 647$). The test manual states that "where the number of subjects in the validation sample was not equally balanced … a smaller, random sample was selected from the large groups whenever possible" (p. 3). However, no evidence that this procedure was applied is provided. No effect size statistics are presented, and occasionally an inappropriate statement appears, such as, "The 25–29 year olds ($M = 73.2$) were marginally outscored ($p < .10$) by the 30–39 age group ($M = 75.2$)" (manual, p. 15). The large sample sizes in the analyses often lead to statistically significant findings ($p < .001$) that could have little practical significance. An uninformed HR professional could be severely misled by the numerous text and graphic displays of t-test and ANOVA findings.

COMMENTARY. The reviewers find the reported information in the EPA technical manual to be incomplete from a comprehensive theoretical framework base. The reviewers are also concerned with two dimensions associated with a sufficient number of items to produce reliable data, but reported reliabilities were only .61 and .62. Finally, the large sample sizes used in the "relations to other variables" analyses often result in statistically significant findings that are most likely driven by the large sample sizes employed. Although the large number of t-tests and ANOVAs appear at first to be impressive, they may well be misleading when "statistically significant" findings could be associated with little practical value.

SUMMARY. Based on the information included in the EPA technical manual, the reviewers are hesitant to provide a strong endorsement for the use of the EPA by human resource professionals.

Review of the Entrepreneurial Personality Assessment by FREDERICK T. L. LEONG, Professor of Psychology and Psychiatry, Michigan State University, East Lansing, MI, and DZENANA HUSREMOVIC, Assistant Professor of Psychology, University of Sarajevo, Bosnia and Hercegovina:

DESCRIPTION. Entrepreneurship is a phenomenon that has received a lot of attention in social sciences, especially in economics, psychology, and sociology. The term "entrepreneur" (Ray & Ramachandran, 1996) refers to an individual or group of individuals who conceive, initiate, and maintain for a sufficiently long period of time a social institution that produces economic goods, or who perceive a business opportunity and create an organization to pursue it. The entrepreneurship literature includes different aspects, such as processes that lead to entrepreneurial behaviors and the role of the environment; relevant for this test is which traits or behaviors are defined as distinctive between entrepreneurs and non-entrepreneurs. The literature on entrepreneurial personality (e.g. Krueger, 2002) emphasizes a lack of clear evidence regarding which traits are distinctive for entrepreneurial behavior and recommends a focus on other important aspects of becoming a successful entrepreneur such as knowledge, interests, values, demographic characteristics, and environmental variables. In other words, having some characteristic such as internal locus of control or need for achievement does not imply that a person would manifest successful entrepreneurial behavior.

The Entrepreneurial Personality Assessment is a self-administered online psychological assessment designed to measure whether the test taker is well suited for successful performance in running one's own business. The test may also be used in an organizational setting to evaluate whether an employee has the traits and skills required to lead others and to work successfully on tasks that require entrepreneurial skills.

The test contains 60 questions that are answered on a 5-point Likert-type scale (1 = *exactly like me*; 5 = *not at all like me*). Results are organized into seven subscales: Self-Sufficiency, the ability to work independently; Conscientiousness, the ability to be organized, responsible, and diligent; Drive Orientation, the tendency to be competitive, driven, and impatient; Social Skills, the tendency to be people-oriented, relaxed, and easy-going in interactions; Optimism, ability to have a positive view of life and the future; Risk-Taking, the readiness and ability to take risks; and Networking Ability, the ability to form and utilize social connections.

The assessment can be completed in about 15 minutes. Results are generated in a report for the test taker and the manager who ordered the testing. The format of information presented to the manager protects the privacy of the participant. The participant's report is comprehensive with detailed descriptions of each measured characteristic, strengths and limitations, and general recommendations for future development.

DEVELOPMENT. The test manual provided by the publisher for this review contains no information concerning the theory or previous empirical findings that could be used to describe the rationale for test development.

TECHNICAL. The psychometric properties reported in the technical manual are obtained from the results of 12,227 participants who completed the questionnaire on one of three Internet sites, Queendom.com, Psychtests.com, and Psychology-Today.com. Sixty-nine percent of the sample did not report their gender, and 68% did not report their age, which means that statistical differences were calculated using only approximately 32% of the total sample, which was self-selected.

Subscale scores range from 0 to 100, and it is apparent that the scores are weighted for the scale, but there is no information in the report as to how the weighting is calculated. Individual scores are apparently compared to criterion measures, and interpretations are given based on differences between individual scores and criterion scores. However, there is no information in the test materials regarding how criterion scores are calculated. The calculated means for the subscales range from 55.43 (Risk-Taking) to 74.24 (Conscientiousness) with a mean standard deviation of 16.36.

Internal consistency reliability was calculated using coefficient alpha. Coefficients ranged from .61 (Social Skills) to .78 (Networking Ability) with a median value of .70. The test manual contains no information about test-retest reliability.

The technical manual provided to reviewers did not contain any information on content, criterion, or construct evidence of validity. The report did contain statistical information regarding group differences in terms of a few variables such as gender, age, education, and occupation. These comparisons, which the test manual labels "validity analyses," were calculated on data from 1,500 to 4,000 participants who reported these characteristics. Women scored significantly higher than men ($p < .001$) on Social Skills, Optimism, and Conscientiousness; men's scores were significantly higher ($p < .001$) on Drive Orientation and Risk-Taking.

COMMENTARY. The Entrepreneurial Personality Assessment is an online measure aimed at helping employers meet their professional needs in terms of development of leadership and management skills among their employees, and it is supposed to help evaluate whether an employee has the necessary traits and skills required to lead others. However, the authors did not provide a theoretical or empirical rationale for test development, nor did they provide evidence of content, criterion, or construct validity. Keeping that in mind, prospective test users should be aware of potential limitations of interpretations and predictions made from test scores. The only evidence found in the test manual is on differences by certain selected demographic attributes, which are not sufficient for predicting performance outcomes.

The authors of the instrument and the manual did not provide a printed version and detailed description of the test for reviewers. In order to see the test one of the reviewers had to take the measure online, and there was no way to go back once she finished the instrument to write additional notes. A printed copy of the instrument would be beneficial.

SUMMARY. The Entrepreneurial Personality Assessment was developed to help employers identify their employees with leadership and entrepreneurial potential. However, because there is no information on the theory used to guide test development and no content and criterion evidence of validity (especially for performance outcomes), the reviewers would like to recommend further validation evidence be provided to assist prospective test users in making an informed choice.

REVIEWERS' REFERENCES

Ray, S., & Ramachandran, K. (1996). Towards a framework for a comprehensive theory of entrepreneurship. *Journal of Entrepreneurship, 5*(1), 1-22.
Krueger, N. F. (2002). *Entrepreneurship: Critical perspectives on business and management* (Vol. 1). New York, NY: Routledge.

[67]
Entrepreneurial Readiness Inventory.

Purpose: Designed to "help individuals assess whether they have the personality characteristics, behaviors, and resources to successfully start and maintain their own businesses."

Population: Participants in career and employment counseling programs or educational programs that explore career and/or entrepreneurial options.

Publication Date: 2009.

Acronym: ERI.

Scores, 6: Vision, Risk Tolerance, Perseverance, Motivation, Independence, Resources.

Administration: Group.

Price Data, 2011: $21.95 per 10 assessment booklets.

Time: (20-25) minutes.

Author: John J. Liptak.

Publisher: JIST Publishing, Inc.

Review of the Entrepreneurial Readiness Inventory by MICHAEL J. FURLONG, Professor Counseling/Clinical/School Psychology Department, University of California-Santa Barbara, Santa Barbara, CA:

DESCRIPTION. The Entrepreneurial Readiness Inventory (ERI) is a career counseling and exploration assessment that assists an individual interested in pursuing entrepreneurial interests. It helps a person to examine systematically if his or her personal attitudes and related characteristics are aligned with those associated with the pursuit of small business activities. The instrument consists of a booklet that directs a person through a process from self-administering the ERI, to scoring, interpretation, and considering follow-up planning and activities.

The instrument includes 60 items that ask an individual to consider qualities related to six personal characteristics that research has associated with propensity to engage successfully in entrepreneurial activities, particularly business ventures. The response scale is: 1 = *not like me*, 2 = *a little like me*, 3 = *somewhat like me*, and 4 = *a lot like me*. Each subscale score ranges from 10 to 40, with scores of 31 to 40 described as being high, 21 to 30 as being average, and 11 to 20 as being low.

The six ERI subscales assess the following characteristics associated with successful entrepreneurial activity:

1. *Vision*: an individual has clear ideas about his or her future business plans.

2. *Risk Tolerance*: willingness of an individual to assume risks associated with undertaking a business venture.

3. *Perseverance*: an individual's sense of her or his willingness to pursue business objectives despite obstacles.

4. *Motivation*: an individual's level of self-motivation and confidence to carry out his or her business vision.

5. *Independence*: the degree to which an individual values self-employment and prefers to pursue personal goals.

6. *Resources:* an individual's perceptions of her or his access to financial and social capital that may be needed in a business venture.

DEVELOPMENT. The ERI was created to address the career counseling needs and interests of the growing segment of the population that is interested in pursuing independent business opportunities. Although the rewards of starting a successful business can be substantial, it is also true that many small business ventures do not realize substantial success. Hence, as part of the career counseling process, it is important that counselors have access to an assessment resource with which to consider and examine an individual's propensity to engage in successful entrepreneurial activity.

Limited information about the development and selection of the ERI items is provided in the administrator's guide. An unspecified number of items were developed to form a larger item sample pool and they were administered to 48 college students who were part of a campus entrepreneurial club. Based on the responses of these students and a review to address potential item bias (e.g., sex or ethnicity), 10 items were chosen for each of the six subscales.

TECHNICAL. The reliability and validity information presented is limited. Using the sample of 48 adults, reliability coefficients (split-half correlations) are provided for the six subscales and they range from .67 (Perseverance) to .95 (Vision). A subgroup of this sample completed the ERI after an interval of 1 month, with stability coefficients ranging from .60 (Perseverance) to .93 (Independence). Validity information is provided in the form of interscale correlations, using a subsample of just 24 adults, with only the correlation between Risk Tolerance and Perseverance (.41) being significant. The only other validity information provided is that the author argues that differences in the mean scores obtained from a sample of 74 males and 80 females is evidence of a type of discriminant validity; however, no statistical tests are used to compare mean score differences.

Norms. The only norms presented in the manual are means and standard deviations derived from a sample of just 154 adults. In addition, the administration booklet includes a self-scoring chart that the test-taker uses to plot her or his ERI profile across the six subscales. As noted, score ranges are provided indicating low, average, and high categories. These score ranges are not derived from a normative comparative sample, but are merely descriptive of an individual's average responses to the 4-point response scale.

COMMENTARY. The ERI clearly has a place in the range of self-exploration instruments that are available in college and adult career counseling centers to help individuals rationally consider if a small business entrepreneurial venture is a reasonable career aspiration. However, the psychometric characteristics and technical adequacy of the ERI are limited. Most critically, there is little convincing information presented in the administrator's guide about the ERI's construct validity. No exploratory or confirmatory factor analyses were conducted to show that the 60 items load specifically onto their referent subscales or that the items do not overlap with other subscales. Construct validity information is needed prior to using the ERI for most research purposes. The adequacy of the norm sample with only 154 adults requires further research, especially given the limited information about this sample. Finally, evidence is needed to demonstrate that responses to the ERI are associated with later successful entrepreneurial involvement.

SUMMARY. The ERI has potential utility as a counseling resource tool that provides individuals and career counselors a structured procedure through which to encourage the rational exploration of entrepreneurial activities as a viable career option. However, given the limited research supporting the technical adequacy of the ERI, it would be important that it be used only within a more integrative and comprehensive career assessment process. Career counselors using the ERI will want to review more recent research that has examined the relations between personality characteristics and entrepreneurial involvement, such as a meta-analyses by Brandstätter (2011) and Zhao, Seibert, and Lumpkin (2010).

REVIEWER'S REFERENCES

Brandstätter, H. (2011). Personality aspects of entrepreneurship: A look at five meta-analyses. *Personality and Individual Differences, 51,* 222–230. doi:10.1016/j.paid.2010.07.007

Zhao, H., Seibert, S. E., & Lumpkin, G. T. (2010). The relationship of personality to entrepreneurial intentions and performance: A meta-analytic review. *Journal of Management, 36,* 381–404. doi:10.1177/0149206309335187

Review of the Entrepreneurial Readiness Inventory by GREGORY SCHRAW, Professor, Department of Educational Psychology, University of Nevada-Las Vegas, Las Vegas, NV:

DESCRIPTION. The Entrepreneurial Readiness Inventory (ERI) provides an assessment of whether an individual has the personality characteristics, behaviors, and resources to start and maintain his or her own business. The ERI includes 60 items that measure six dimensions of entrepreneurship. Each item is answered using a 4-point Likert scale that ranges from *a lot like me* with a score of 4 to *not like me* with as score of 1. The test takes 20–25 minutes to complete and is self-scored. The test booklet includes a self-completed score profile, summary, and interpretation guide for each of the six dimensions. The ERI is appropriate for anyone able to create a business and is written at a seventh grade readability level.

The six dimensions include Vision, Risk Tolerance, Perseverance, Motivation, Independence, and Resources. High scores on each dimension indicate that the examinee possesses goals and drive to create a business (Vision), the ability to take risks and face consequences (Risk Tolerance), the determination to pursue goals despite obstacles and periodic setbacks (Perseverance), commitment to success, confidence, and an appropriate level of competitiveness (Motivation), a preference to not take orders and to be self-regulated (Independence), and have a sufficient amount of financial and personal resources to network and grow a business (Resources).

The test is interpreted by the examinee or scorer using three interpretive bands described in the manual, including scores from 10–20 (low), 21–30 (average), and 31–40 (high). Low scores indicate that an examinee does not possess many of the characteristics assumed to be essential to be a successful entrepreneur. An average score suggests the examinee possesses some of the characteristics and resources but needs to develop more. A high score indicates that the examinee possesses many of the characteristics and resources needed and should consider entrepreneurship further. The ERI is intended to be used in career and employment guidance centers in high schools or colleges, or for individuals returning to the work force who are interested in entrepreneurial opportunities.

DEVELOPMENT. The ERI includes a 17-page administrator's guide that discusses characteristics of entrepreneurship and several definitions of the term. The guide provides a summary of the types of individuals who consider entrepreneurial business ventures, as well as four reasons why they do so. These include discontent with 8 to 5 schedule, low need for job security, growth opportunities with small business, and comfort with change. Although the guide discusses characteristics of entrepreneurs and the need for an instrument to measure these characteristics, there is only an extremely limited description of the specific rationale, theoretical framework, or procedures used to develop the ERI.

TECHNICAL. The 17-page administrator's guide is well written, but provides very little information regarding the theoretical or conceptual framework for the ERI. The guide also provides minimal information about administration and score interpretation. It includes a very short illustrative case that is helpful to first-time scorers.

The six dimensions on the ERI are based loosely on the work of Baum, Frese, and Baron (2007). A set of items was developed and revised based on the six dimensions. It is unclear how many items were developed or who constructed, reviewed, and revised these items. Items were normed on members from an entrepreneurial club at a mid-size university. Item intercorrelations were used to discard items, although the statistical methods (e.g., correlation, factor analysis) are not described in the manual, nor are the omission criteria stated for item deletion.

A pool of 10 items for each dimension was administered to an unspecified group of potential entrepreneurs, from which 10 items for each of the six dimensions were selected. Business experts reviewed these items for clarity and bias prior to final validation.

There is a minimal amount of information about reliability. A sample of 48 unspecified individuals completed the 60-item scale. Split-half reliability ranged from .67 to .95 for the six scales and generally was good. A subset of 24 individuals from this sample retook the ERI after 1 month. Test-retest coefficients for the six scales ranged from .60 to .93.

Validity information is largely absent. The guide discusses means and standard deviations for the six scales for a sample of 154 individuals, including 74 males and 80 females. There were no statistical tests of differences between scales or between males and females. Raw scores are similar, although slightly higher for males on the risk tolerance and resources scales.

The guide also presents a table of pairwise correlations for the six scales based on a sample of 24 unspecified individuals. This table reveals low correlations and only one statistically significant pairwise correlation between risk tolerance and perseverance ($r = .41$). At face value, this finding suggests that the six scales are reasonably independent of one another.

It is important to note that there is no systematic discussion of content validity (i.e., appropriateness of items for each scale), criterion validity (i.e., relationship between the six scales and other indicators of entrepreneurship either currently or at a future point in time), or construct validity (i.e., statistical information that supports the six-scale structure). Nevertheless, the zero-order correlations indicate that the six scales measure six generally uncorrelated dimensions; thus, the use of a single composite score to determine low, average, and high entrepreneurial readiness may be unjustified.

COMMENTARY. The main strength of the ERI is that it fills the niche of entrepreneurial readiness that previously has been unfilled. The six scales described above appear a reasonable point of departure for such an instrument. The theoretical framework requires greater explanation, both in terms of using this framework to plan and build the instrument, as well as validating the results.

The reliability and validity of the ERI requires further research and higher quality information. One concern is that there is virtually no information about the relationship of the ERI to proximal or distal indicators of entrepreneurial success (i.e., no evidence of criterion validity). Despite the apparent face validity of the six scales, there is no evidence whatsoever that the ERI is related to relevant entrepreneurial outcomes. A still bigger concern is the lack of construct validity evidence and its implications for score interpretation. Future research is needed to explore the factor structure of the 60 test items. Zero-order correlations suggest a six-factor structure, which may preclude a meaningful interpretation of the composite score, as recommended in the test booklet. Preliminary evidence suggests that individual's scales may be better predictors than the composite score due to scale independence.

Overall, much more validation research is needed. Samples must be larger and better specified than those in the current version of the administrator's guide. In this reviewer's opinion, there is insufficient evidence to claim that the ERI is a valid instrument for a broad sample of potential examinees. If used at all, it should be interpreted with great caution and considered suggestive at best with regard to an individual's entrepreneurial potential.

REVIEWER'S REFERENCE

Baum, J. R., Frese, M., & Baron, R. A. (2007). *The psychology of entrepreneurship.* Mahwah, NJ: Erlbaum.

[68]

Examination for the Certificate of Competency in English.

Purpose: Designed as a test of general language proficiency in a variety of contexts; it assesses linguistic, discoursal, sociolinguistic, and pragmatic elements of the English language.

Population: Nonnative speakers of English.

Publication Dates: 1995–2011.

Acronym: ECCE.

Scores, 5: Writing, Listening Comprehension, GVR (Grammar/Vocabulary/Reading), Speaking, Overall Score.

Administration: Group.

Forms, 4: A, B, C, D.

Price Data: Available from publisher.

Time: (30) minutes for Listening; (80) minutes for Grammar/Vocabulary/Reading; (30) minutes for Writing; (10-15) minutes for Speaking.

Comments: Designed for nonnative speakers of English who would like official documentary evidence of intermediate proficiency in the English language, particularly for academic and professional purposes.

Author: The University of Michigan.

Publisher: Cambridge-Michigan Language Assessments.

Review of the Examination for the Certificate of Competency in English by ANTONY JOHN KUN-NAN, Professor, California State University, Los Angeles, CA, and ELVIS WAGNER, Assistant Professor, Temple University, Philadelphia, PA:

DESCRIPTION. The Examination for the Certificate of Competency in English (ECCE) is a partially group-administered paper-and-pencil standardized assessment of general language proficiency at the high-intermediate level of English as a foreign language. Scores are used as evidence of high-intermediate competence in English for personal, public, education, and occupational purposes. The test is administered to tens of thousands of test takers around the world at Cambridge Michigan Language Assessment (CaMLA) centers; CaMLA is a not-for-profit collaboration between the University of Michigan and the University of Cambridge. The majority of test takers whose data are included

in the November-December 2006 test report were from Europe–mainly from Greece–with smaller numbers from South America, Latin America, and Asia. The ECCE has four sections: listening; grammar, vocabulary, and reading (GVR); writing; and speaking. In total, the ECCE takes 2 hours and 35 minutes, although because of the need to schedule individual speaking administrations, test takers usually are required to be at the examination site for longer.

The listening section has 50 multiple-choice questions with three response options each and lasts for 30 minutes. Test takers record their responses on a bubble sheet. There are two parts to the listening section. Part 1 contains 30 items that involve listening to short recorded conversations followed by questions. For Part 2 of the listening section, a recorded radio interview is played. The interview is broken into segments, and groups of questions follow each segment.

The GVR section has 100 multiple-choice items with four response options each and takes 80 minutes. Part 1 is the grammar component with 35 items in which an incomplete sentence is followed by a choice of words or phrases to complete it. Part 2 is the vocabulary component, again with 35 questions. Part 3 is reading, with 30 questions presented in three parts. Part 1 involves a short reading passage followed by six comprehension questions, Part 2 has short texts that are presented as advertisements and accompanied by 11 or 12 questions, and Part 3 has a longer reading passage with 12 or 13 questions.

The writing section of the ECCE takes 30 minutes during which test takers write one sample. Test takers are given a very short article to read, and they can then choose to write either a letter or an essay in response to the article. These written samples are scored using a rating scale with four categories: content and development, organization and connection of ideas, linguistic range and control, and communicative effect. The holistic rating scale uses 5 points: A (high pass), B (pass), C (low pass), D (borderline fail), and E (fail).

The speaking section of the ECCE takes approximately 15 minutes. The test taker meets individually with an examiner. There are six components to the speaking test: opening/warm-up, stage 1 (conveying non-sensitive personal information), stage 2 (asking questions to get information), stage 3 (expressing an opinion and supporting it), stage 4 (elaborating on the topic), and a conclusion. The examiner who is both the interlocutor and the rater, rates speaking in three categories: language control-grammar, language control-vocabulary, and delivery and intelligibility. The 5-point scale used is the same as for the writing section.

The listening, GVR, and writing score sheets are sent to CaMLA for scoring. The listening and GVR sections are machine-scored; the writing section is scored by CaMLA trained and certified raters.

DEVELOPMENT. The ECCE is designed as a criterion-referenced competence examination to assess whether test takers have achieved the high-intermediate English language ability in alignment with the Common European Framework of References for Languages (CEFR). The CEFR describes language ability on a 6-level scale: A1 (lower basic), A2 (upper basic), B1 (lower intermediate), B2 (upper intermediate), C1 (lower proficient), C2 (upper proficient). The ECCE assesses whether test takers meet the threshold of B2.

The ECCE was designed to assess test takers' communicative use of English. A new form of the ECCE is written for each test administration. Items are written according to predetermined format and difficulty levels and are piloted on samples representative of the intended ECCE population of test takers.

TECHNICAL.

Standardization. Because the ECCE scores are aligned with the CEFR, the test is criterion-referenced, and thus, a standardization/norm sample does not exist. The CEFR describes language ability in terms of what a language user at a particular level can do. Because the ECCE seeks to assess whether test takers meet the B2 level of the CEFR, the items are designed to assess the abilities described at the B2 level and must possess the desired psychometric properties (e.g., discrimination indices, target difficulty range, and interitem correlations). Linking items are inserted into new operational tests and are used to equate new forms with previously administered forms.

Reliability. The May 2010 ECCE Test Administration Report indicates that 64.1% of the test takers passed the May 2010 examination. For the May 2010 administration, the reliability and standard error of measurement (*SEM*) estimates for the listening section were .89 and .34, respectively, and the reliability and *SEM* estimates for the GVR section were .93 and .27. The May 2010 test report does not indicate how these reliability estimates were computed, but the November-December

2006 report stated that item response theory with a three-parameter logistic model was used to estimate the reliability coefficient.

For the writing section of the ECCE, each response is rated separately by two raters trained and certified by CaMLA. If the two raters do not reach exact agreement on the score using the 5-point holistic rating scale, the writing response is rated by a third rater. For the writing section, rater agreement figures and pass/fail agreement figures are presented in the May 2010 test report. For the May 2010 administration, the rater agreement was 75.9%, and the pass/fail agreement was 89.6%.

As described earlier, the speaking samples are scored by the test interlocutor. These raters are trained using the ECCE Oral Examiner Training Manual and an accompanying DVD with videos of test takers taking the speaking test and numerous calibration samples and benchmarks. However, the performance of speaking test examiners is monitored locally, rather than by CaMLA, and thus no reports of scoring reliability are given for the speaking section. The May 2010 test report states that recordings of speaking tests are sent to CaMLA for review of how the speaking tests are conducted by the local examiners and for the accuracy of the ratings, although there is no mention of how CaMLA reviews these recordings, nor is there information about what the standards for accuracy and reliability are. In addition, the fact that the rater is also acting as interlocutor presents possible threats to reliable scoring, as does the fact that the speaking samples are scored by just one rater.

Validity. Validity evidence has been provided to support inferences made from the ECCE. Validation studies include Liao (2007), who investigated the construct validity of the ECCE by investigating the extent to which performance on the GVR section predicts performance on the listening section. Another validation study conducted by Lu (2005) examined the differences in discourse used by nonnative and native speaker examiners. The results of this study influenced subsequent oral examiner training on the ECCE. The May 2006 test report describes a study supporting the internal structure of the test. Factor analyses were conducted on the listening and GVR sections, which presented evidence in support of the models used to operationalize test items.

Fairness. An additional area of investigation that complements reliability and validity is fairness:

whether the ECCE is fair to test takers from different groups such as gender, age, and disability. DIF analyses were conducted, and about 14% of the items were flagged for DIF, with roughly half of these items favoring males and half favoring females. However, because test takers from different age groups take this test, it would be necessary to know whether the test tasks are of comparable difficulty for the different age groups of test takers. Finally, as more test takers with disabilities are taking such tests, it would be necessary to know what accommodations are provided to test takers with various disabilities and whether any studies have been conducted to ensure the accommodations provided are not biased in favor of or against test takers with disabilities. These studies would enhance the value of the ECCE.

COMMENTARY. The ECCE is a test of general language proficiency at the high-intermediate level of English as a foreign language. However, there are a number of issues that need to be considered in evaluating the ECCE's overall usefulness. First, the ECCE is linked with the CEFR as it examines whether test takers meet the threshold of B2 in the CEFR. However, the ECCE documents provided for review do not offer a study that verifies that the test is really at the B2 level. Second, although a human interlocutor in the speaking test is valuable as it enhances the authenticity of the interaction in the test and the validity of the inferences made from such an interaction, there is a possible loss of reliability and standardization by having a human interlocutor. Therefore, a study that provides evidence that having a human interlocutor who is also the rater does not result in a loss of reliability and standardization is essential. Finally, the ECCE needs to consider accommodations for test takers with disabilities.

SUMMARY. The ECCE is a partially group-administered paper-and-pencil standardized assessment of general language proficiency at the high-intermediate level of English as a foreign language at the B2 level of the CEFR. The test is well designed and serves the purpose of assessing test takers' communicative language competence in English.

REVIEWERS' REFERENCES
Liao, Y. (2007). Investigating the construct validity of the grammar and vocabulary section and the listening Section of the ECCE: Lexico-grammatical ability as a predictor of L2 listening ability. *Spaan Fellow Working Papers in Second or Foreign Language Assessment, 5,* 37–78.
Lu, Y. (2005). A validation study of the ECCE NNS and NS examiners' conversational styles from a discourse analytic perspective. *Spaan Fellow Working Papers in Second or Foreign Language Assessment, 3,* 73–99.

Review of the Examination for the Certificate of Competency in English by JUDITH A. MONSAAS, Executive Director, Assessment and Evaluation, Office of Access and Success, Board of Regents of the University System of Georgia, Atlanta, GA:

DESCRIPTION. The Examination for the Certificate of Competency in English (ECCE) is a standardized English-as-a-foreign-language examination that is developed and scored by the University of Michigan (UM) and administered twice a year at test centers around the world. A new form is developed for each administration. The ECCE is aimed at the B2 level of the Common European Framework of Reference (Council of Europe, 2001) and is used as evidence of high-intermediate competency in English for personal, social, educational, and occupational purposes.

There are four component sections of the ECCE. The listening test includes 50 multiple-choice items and is delivered via audio recording. Examinees respond to short conversational items on everyday topics. The second component, Grammar/Vocabulary/Reading (GVR), has 100 multiple-choice items and an 80 minute time limit. For the 35 grammar items, the examinee is to choose the word or phrase that correctly completes a sentence. The 35 vocabulary items also are formatted so the examinee identifies the correct vocabulary word needed to complete a sentence. For the 30 multiple-choice reading items, the examinee responds to texts similar to those written for a general audience, including magazines, newspapers, and websites. The writing component includes one task that is typically a short excerpt from a newspaper, memo, or other printed material, and the examinee can choose to write either a letter or an essay response. The first three components are completed in one sitting of up to three hours and both the multiple-choice answer sheets and the essays are sent to the University of Michigan to be scored.

The speaking section of the test is a structured one-on-one interaction between a local examiner and the examinee. It contains three tasks and takes about 10–15 minutes. One task involves using a picture form to engage the examinee in role playing based on the situation in the picture. The speaking section is administered and scored at the test site, and the rating, along with explanatory comments, are submitted with the answer sheets and essays to UM.

An examiner's manual is provided with very clear descriptions of examination procedures. Also provided are an oral examiner training manual and DVDs with sample oral administrations for the speaking section that are to be used for examiner training and practice. Rubrics for the writing and speaking sections are included. Scores on the four sections of the test are categorized into five performance levels: high pass, pass, low pass, borderline fail, and fail. The speaking and writing rubrics are organized from A to E. Low pass (or C) is considered to meet the standard. Examinees that pass three sections with low pass (C) or higher and receive no less than a borderline fail (D) in one section are awarded a Certificate of Competency.

DEVELOPMENT. A new form of the ECCE is written for each administration. Test and item specifications are guided by the stated purpose of the test, according to the November-December 2006 test report. A general description, prompt attributes, key and distractor attributes, and response attributes are determined in advance as is the format of items, response patterns, and the type of scoring procedures for each section. According to the 2006 report, "Because the ECCE is a criterion-referenced test, the cut scores represent the level required to meet the set standard" (Testing and Certification Division, English Language Institute, University of Michigan, 2008, p. 1). That statement represents the entire description of the process used to cut scores.

Test items are edited, pilot tested, and reviewed for content validity, clarity, and bias. Psychometric properties (discrimination, difficulty, interitem correlations) are all considered in rendering the decision of which items to include on each form. Linking items are included on each test form to facilitate equating the new test forms to the 2006 November-December ECCE test.

TECHNICAL. The ECCE is a criterion-referenced test and thus no normative data are provided. After each administration, a report is created with a description of the test and scoring, and a report of the results. Several thousand examinees take the test each time it is administerd, and the number of test takers and the names of the countries in which the test was administered are provided. Summary tables of pass rates are reported by first language background and by section of the test. It would be helpful if these reports included pass rates by age and gender for each test administration. This information is reported in the November-December 2006 report, but not in the other test administration reports.

Test score reliability estimates were determined using the three-parameter logistic item response theory (IRT) model for the two multiple-choice tests, listening and GVR. Reliability estimates are computed for each administration of the test; coefficients are in the upper .80s for the listening section and the lower .90s for the GVR section. Rater agreement on the writing section is about 75%, but the test manual reports that if raters do not reach exact agreement on the score, the section is rated by a third person. Overall, the reliability coefficients for the listening, GVR, and writing sections are acceptable. The speaking section is administered and scored locally, so no rater reliability is reported. The test manual notes that examiners for the speaking test are highly proficient and trained speakers. The performance of speaking test examiners is monitored, and recordings of the speaking tests are submitted to the test publisher. It would seem that these recordings could be used to evaluate the reliability of the raters.

The validity of test score use is supported by the description of the purpose of the test, the item specifications, and the administration and scoring procedures. According to the test manual this information provides evidence of content validity. Additional validity information is offered in the form of statistical analyses of the dimensionality of the test using factor analytic methods. The factor loadings on the listening section support the unidimensionality of this section. Factor loadings for the GVR section showed that one factor supported most of the vocabulary items and another factor supported most of the reading items. A third factor included about half of the grammar items and a few of the vocabulary items. The test manual states that this is not dissimilar to earlier factor analysis results. Testlet factor analysis supported the four factors of listening, grammar, vocabulary, and reading. These data support the factor structure of the two multiple-choice sections of the test.

Differential item functioning (DIF) analyses were conducted on gender. Careful examination of the content and wording of the 18 items flagged by the DIF analyses was conducted. The items were almost equally balanced in favor of males and females, so no gender bias was apparent.

There was no validity evidence provided for the writing and speaking sections of the test beyond descriptions of the test development process. Rubrics were created for these sections. Additional validity information should have been provided to support the use of both of these sections of the test.

COMMENTARY. The ECCE is a straightforward, relatively easy-to-administer test of English-language proficiency. It is widely used internationally and has a strong reputation. The description of the test and the administration and interpretation instructions are clearly written. The oral examiner training manual is comprehensive with sufficient examples at each proficiency level for the examiner to practice scoring. The test manual includes a recommendation that two examiners be present for the speaking portion of the test so one can record and the other conduct the conversation that is part of the interview. This process would be especially important for new examiners. The test manual does report that most speaking tests were conducted and rated by a single examiner. Audio recording of the tests also is recommended, but only some of the tests were recorded. The number and percent of speaking tests with just one examiner and tests that are recorded should be reported in the test manual. A main concern regarding this test is the spottiness of the data reported. More detail on the demographics of the tested population and their test scores should have been provided. The evidence supporting the reliability and validity of the speaking test scores is almost non-existent. Although it is difficult to obtain evidence from tests that are administered and scored locally, there should be some rater reliability studies conducted, possibly using the audio recordings of the tests.

SUMMARY. The ECCE was designed to test English-language proficiency for non-native English speakers and targets individuals who have high-intermediate language ability. The UM English Language Institute has a strong reputation and expertise in language assessment, and the test is comprehensive and professional. Adequate support is provided for the listening and GVR portions of the test, but a better description of the theoretical underpinnings of the test and evidence to support the validity and reliability of the speaking test scores would greatly enhance this test.

REVIEWER'S REFERENCES

Council of Europe. (2001). *Common European framework of references for languages: Learning, teaching, assessment.* Cambridge, UK: Cambridge University Press.

Testing and Certification Division, English Language Institute, University of Michigan. (2008). *Examination for the Certificate of Competency in English: November-December 2006 report.* Ann Arbor, MI: Author.

[69]
Examination for the Certificate of Proficiency in English.

Purpose: Designed "as a test of general language proficiency in a variety of contexts; it assesses linguistic, discoursal, sociolinguistic, and pragmatic elements of the English language."

Population: English language learners.

Publication Dates: 1953–2011.

Acronym: ECPE.

Scores, 5: Writing, Listening Comprehension, Grammar/Cloze/Vocabulary/Reading, Speaking, Overall Score.

Administration: Group.

Forms: 2 forms per year.

Price Data: Available from publisher.

Time: (150) minutes.

Comments: Administered twice a year at approved test centers around the world; aimed at the C2 level of the Common European Framework of Reference; designed for English language learners who would like official documentary evidence of advanced proficiency in the English language, particularly for academic and professional purposes.

Author: The University of Michigan.

Publisher: Cambridge-Michigan Language Assessments.

Review of the Examination for the Certificate of Proficiency in English by JORGE E. GONZALEZ, Associate Professor, School Psychology Program, Texas A&M University, and BRENDA LAGUNAS, Doctoral Student in School Psychology, Texas A&M University, College Station, TX:

DESCRIPTION. The Examination for the Certificate of Proficiency in English (ECPE) is designed to assess language proficiency for advanced English as a second language speakers for academic and professional purposes. The standardized exam tests Listening, Reading, Writing, and Speaking skills through a series of tasks.

Beyond stating that examinees may take the test at a center "only in the country in which you are a resident" (ECPE 2011 Information Bulletin, p. 6), little information is provided on the administration procedures at these centers. No information is provided on appropriate age ranges other than that the test is developed for "all people who wish to take the exam" (May/June 2010 Test Administration Report, p. 1). The Information Bulletin describes an ECPE Preliminary Test that assesses Grammar, Cloze, Vocabulary, and Reading; however, no information is provided about the relationship between the preliminary test and the ECPE Final Test format that also assesses these domains.

From the information in the test materials it is unclear whether the exam is taken individually or in a group at a test center. Information on the Speaking section indicates that it is rated and assessed by two certified oral examiners. The Writing section is scored by University of Michigan trained and certified raters. Both the Speaking (30–35 minutes to complete a five-stage interaction with another examiner) and Writing (30 minutes to write one essay) sections are reported to consist of "1 task" (Test Administration Report, p. 1) and are scored holistically using criteria specified in the test manual. The Listening section consists of 50 items reportedly taking 35–40 minutes to complete; Grammar, Cloze, Vocabulary, and Reading consist of 40, 20, 40, and 20 items, respectively, and take about 75 minutes to complete. According to the website, the entire test takes approximately 3 hours to complete.

With the exception of the Speaking and Writing sections, all remaining sections of the test are scored by a computer at the English Language Institute at the University of Michigan. According to the Administration Report, each item of the Listening portion and the Grammar, Cloze, Vocabulary, and Reading (GCVR) sections carries equal weight with no penalty for incorrect answers. Scaled scores are calculated using item response theory (IRT). The Listening and GCVR portions are multiple-choice questions. All examinees receive a report that provides an overall total performance rating as Honors, Pass, or Fail. In addition, examinees are provided scores for each section of the exam. Listening and GCVR score ranges are as follows: Honors 840–1000, Pass 750–835, Low Pass 650–745, Borderline Fail 610–645, and Fail 0–605. For Writing and Speaking, scores range from A to E for Honors to Fail, respectively. To pass the exam, test takers must obtain three section scores of Low Pass or higher and no more than one Borderline Fail score. According to the Test Administration Report, a passing score certificate is "valid for the holder's lifetime" (p. 2).

DEVELOPMENT. According to the test developers, passing the ECPE reflects a C2 level of English proficiency based on the Common European Framework of Reference for languages (CEFR; Council of Europe, 2001). The Information Bulletin indicates that a C2 level is considered "Proficient User, Mastery" (p. 7). Other than indicating that scaled scores are derived via IRT, neither the Test Administration Report nor the

Information Bulletin provides any information on item development and construction, selection, piloting, or technical properties.

TECHNICAL. The ECPE is a criterion-referenced test that is standardized in terms of administration and scoring. In addition, the Test Administration Report provides demographic information about the "Test-Taking Population" (p. 3). The Test Administration Report indicates that 25,606 examinees from 17 countries took the exam in May/June 2010 with the majority being 13–16 years old and largely female (61%). Results from the May/June 2010 test-taking population indicated that 60% of examinees passed the exam.

Although it is unclear what reliability estimate was used, the Test Administration Report indicates reliabilities for the Listening and GCVR sections were .86 and .93 with standard errors of measurement of .38 and .27, respectively. It is similarly unclear what the reliability estimates were for the individual GCVR domains. For the Writing section, the developers report two estimates for interrater agreement, exact agreement and pass/fail agreement. The interrater agreement was 76.7%, and the pass/fail agreement was 84.7%. Interrater agreement for Speaking is reported at 88.9% with no indication of a pass/fail agreement estimate. In the included CD provided to reviewers labeled "Recent ECPE Research Studies," Saito (2003) found coefficient alpha reliabilities of .80, .74, .72, and .87 for Grammar, Vocabulary, Reading, and Total, respectively, for the GVR section and .70 for the original (not factor analyzed) Cloze section.

No information is provided on the validity of the ECPE for its intended purposes, the relevancy of test content, or the differential validity of test scores across gender, racial, ethnic, or cultural groups (including differential item functioning). Construct evidence of validity of the Cloze section was studied in Saito (2003). In the paper, the author attempted to determine how the Cloze section items relate to the various parts of the GVR section and whether the Cloze test merits being a separate section of the ECPE. Results indicated that the Cloze section factor analyses produced two primary factors, Grammar Forms and Meaning, that were somewhat distinct from proficiency. Römhild (2008) investigated the factor invariance of the ECPE among two proficiency groups and found that the factorial structure of the ECPE differed across the low and high proficiency groups. In fact, the measurement properties of a substantial number of items as well as the factor variances and factor correlations were noninvariant, suggesting that group differences exist in the underlying latent construct measured by the five ECPE subtests. The measurement invariance analysis revealed many items with unequal measurement properties (i.e., 46%) with differences primarily in the Listening, Grammar, and Vocabulary subtests but not in the Cloze.

COMMENTARY. The ECPE has been indexed in previous volumes of *Test in Print*, but heretofore lacked sufficient technical documentation for a thorough review. Although the present version provides some reliability and sample information, it remains unclear whether the test is useful for its intended purposes. There remains insufficient reliability, validity, test construction, or test administration information to make a well-informed judgment about the test's adequacy. Without an articulated theoretical or conceptual framework, it is difficult to determine whether the assumptions underlying the dimensions of the ECPE represent adequate or complete measures of proficiency.

SUMMARY. It is difficult to assess the validity of the ECPE for its intended purposes. Moreover, it is not clear what the difference is between taking the ECPE or the more psychometrically sophisticated and researched Test of English as a Foreign Language (TOEFL). The TOEFL does remain the standard to which other measures of English as a foreign language are compared.

REVIEWERS' REFERENCES

Council of Europe (2001). *The Common European Framework of Reference for Languages: Learning, teaching, assessment.* Cambridge, UK: Cambridge University Press.

Römhild, A. (2008). Investigating the invariance of the ECPE factor structure across different proficiency levels. *Spaan Fellow Working Papers in Second or Foreign Language Assessment, 6,* 29–55. Ann Arbor, MI: University of Michigan English Language Institute.

Saito, Y. (2003). Investigating the construct validity of the Cloze section in the Examination for the Certificate of Proficiency in English. *Spaan Fellow Working Papers in Second or Foreign Language Assessment, 1,* 39–82. Ann Arbor, MI: University of Michigan English Language Institute.

Review of the Examination for the Certificate of Proficiency in English by MARÍA DEL R. MEDINA-DÍAZ, Professor, Program of Educational Research and Evaluation, Department of Graduate Studies, Faculty of Education, University of Puerto Rico-Río Piedras, San Juan, PR:

DESCRIPTION. The Examination for the Certificate of Proficiency in English (ECPE) consists of a combination of 170 multiple-choice (MC) items and two tasks in four sections, representing the language skills of Speaking (one task with a pair of examinees, 30–35 minutes); Writing (choose one of two topics and write a short essay, 30 minutes); Listening (50 MC items related to audio-recorded conversations, questions and topic

segments, 35–40 minutes); and Reading (20 MC items associated with four short passages), as well as Grammar (40 MC items), Cloze (20 MC items), and Vocabulary (40 MC items). This final section lasts 75 minutes, for a total administration time of 170–180 minutes. Instructions are easy to follow. The May/June 2010 Test Administration Report and sample test materials on CD are useful for understanding section requirements. The ECPE, a criterion-referenced test targeted at the C2 level of the Common European Framework of Reference for Languages (Council of Europe, 2001), "is open to all people who wish to take the exam, regardless of the school they attend or their participation in formal language study" (ECPE Information Bulletin 2011, p. 3). Procedures for requesting rescoring and provisions for invalidating scores obtained by cheating or misrepresentation are provided.

The Speaking task has five stages (introduction, summarizing and recommending, agreement, presentation and convincing, and justification and defending) in order to give the opportunity to each examinee to speak individually and in interaction with his or her partner. Each test taker is scored by two oral examiners present during the administration. They use a scoring rubric with five levels of performance (A, Expert; B, Consistent; C, Effective; D, Dependent; E, Limited) and three content areas (Discourse and Interaction, Linguistic Resources, Delivery and Intelligibility). Similarly, the examinees' written essays are scored by at least two raters. The Writing rating scale consists of five letters (A/Honors, B, C, D, E) with four content criteria (Rhetoric, Grammar/Syntax, Vocabulary, Mechanics). In both tasks, there is no clear indication of how the raters may apply these analytic rubrics and make decisions on criteria. The MC items are dichotomously scored by a computer at the University of Michigan.

Overall examinee performance is reported as Honors, Pass, or Fail. Scores are also shown by sections with five scoring levels (Honors, Pass, Low Pass, Borderline Fail, Fail). A certificate is awarded to "examinees who pass three sections with a Low Pass (or higher) and receive no less than a Borderline Fail in one section" (ECPE Information Bulletin 2011, p. 5). The test authors report that the certificate is valid for the lifetime of the examinee and is recognized in several countries and universities as evidence of advanced proficiency of English. However, documentation related to these uses and to predictive validity is absent.

DEVELOPMENT. Apart from describing the sections and mentioning that "all parts of the examination are written following specific guidelines, and items are pretested to ensure that they function properly" (ECPE Information Bulletin 2012, p. 1), no additional information is provided about how the test was designed and developed. Some trace is found in Saito's (2003) and Zhang's (2008) research. Saito (2003) argues that Grammar, Vocabulary, and Reading sections (GVR) represent Purpura's (1999) theoretical definition of grammar (i.e., language ability composed of grammatical forms and meanings and pragmatic knowledge) and reading comprehension (i.e., asking for explicit and inferential information from a text). Zhang (2008) refers to Bachman and Palmer's (1996) two-tier hierarchical structure of language proficiency: organizational knowledge (divided into grammatical and textual knowledge) and pragmatic knowledge (which includes lexical, functional, and sociolinguistic competences). This structure conveys that a proficient examinee should demonstrate both structural knowledge and efficient use of this knowledge (Zhang, 2008). Thus, the theoretical framework for developing the test is not quite clear. Many items in the 2010 ECPE Sample Test reflect North American English-language usage related to academic and professional contexts (e.g., biology and engineering). There is no discussion about the topic selection or content sampling, examinees' cultural differences in text interpretation and speech elaboration, or whether a multicultural committee reviewed the test items or specifications.

TECHNICAL.

Standardization. The ECPE is administered in June and November at testing centers in different countries. According to the test authors, "the ECPE testing program works closely with test centers to ensure that its tests are administered in a way that is fair and accessible to examinees" (ECPE Information Bulletin 2011, p. 3). Also, testing arrangements are provided for examinees with special needs. When an examinee does not take a test section, a modified certificate is issued showing the sections attempted and passed. However, little documentation is provided regarding testing conditions and accommodations, as well as raters' behaviors on grading writing and speaking tasks in the centers around the world.

Demographic data for examinees (i.e., age and gender) are shown in test administration reports. For example, in May/June 2010, a total of 25,606 examinees from 17 countries completed the exam, and 58% were between 13 and 19 years old. Fewer examinees (15,341) took the November 2010 ECPE in 14 countries, and 61% were younger than 20. In both administrations, 60% of examinees were female. The percentage of pass and fail by groups of first language backgrounds is reported as well. However, the statistics can be misleading without data such as the sample's distribution by language background.

Reliability. Reliability estimates are available for the 2010 administrations, but the test materials do not specify the type of reliability being reported. Acceptable estimates of reliability and standard error of measurement were calculated in the Listening section (.86 and .38, respectively) and the Grammar, Cloze, Vocabulary, and Reading (GCVR) section (.93 and .27, respectively) with May/June 2010 data. Similar reliability estimates were found with November 2010 examinees' responses (.85 in the Listening section and .93 in GCVR). Also, interrater agreement percentages are reported for written essay scoring and pass/fail decisions for that section. The raters agreed on approximately 77% and 79% of their scores for the Writing section in May/June and November 2010, respectively. The test authors indicate that if the raters do not reach exact agreement, a third rater is employed. No data are reported regarding these cases.

In the Speaking section, the two examiners discuss their scores and reach a consensus on the final score. Their agreement percentage is also acceptable (89%) for the May/June and November 2010 administrations. The test authors suggest that "the ECPE testing program monitors rater agreement for training purposes" (ECPE Test Administration Report, November 2010, p. 5), but there is no additional information about the raters' selection, training, and monitoring. Research on the effect of pairing examinees of different characteristics (e.g., ethnic and academic background, gender, age, and achievement level) in the speaking task and about the application of the scoring criteria to each examinee could enhance validity and reliability of the results.

Validity. Validity refers to the extent to which the accumulated evidence and theory from several sources support the use and interpretation of test scores (American Educational Research Association, American Psychological Association, and National Council on Measurement in Education, 1999). ECPE's validity evidence is fragmented in various independent studies included on a CD labeled "Recent ECPE Research Studies" that was provided to reviewers (Li, 2008; Plough, McMillan, & O'Connell, 2011; Römhild, 2008; Saito, 2003; Song, 2009; Wang, 2006; Zhang, 2008). Saito (2003) and Wang (2006) shed some light on construct validity evidence. For example, Saito (2003) conducted an exploratory (using promax rotation) and confirmatory factor analysis (applying Structural Equation Modeling [SEM]) of 12,468 examinees' answers to GCVR sections. Many of the Grammar and Vocabulary items (40 items each, alpha coefficients of .84 and .74, respectively) loaded on two factors (lexico-grammatical ability) and all 20 Reading items (alpha coefficient of .72) loaded on one (reading ability). As expected, this suggests that Grammar, Vocabulary, and Reading items are measuring different constructs. SEM results also confirm this two-factor structure. A Cloze section was also factor-analyzed and accounted for two factors (form and meaning), rather than higher-order text processing skills (Saito, 2003). Cloze scores based on these two factors showed low to moderate correlations (coefficients from .07 to .45) with Grammar, Vocabulary, and Reading variables of form and meaning, suggesting content redundancy between the two sections. These findings may justify merging or excluding Cloze from the GCVR section. Wang (2006) found low to moderate correlations (coefficients ranged from .20 to .62) among the Speaking (one item), Listening (50 items), and GCVR (100 items) sections and reported that a one-factor model (accounting for almost 92% of the variance of the scores) fit well using data collected from 2,011 examinees in 2005.

Römhild (2008) analyzed responses from 34,599 examinees who took the ECPE in 2005–2006. She found differences in the factor structure across high- and low-proficient groups. The measurement properties of a substantial number of items (46%) as well as the factor variances and correlations were non-invariant. Group differences were mostly found in Listening, Grammar, and Vocabulary items, but not in the Cloze section and only in two Reading items. These findings suggest caution in the interpretation of the composite scores (i.e., sum of section scores) from both groups of examinees. Similar research is needed comparing other groups of examinees. Differential item functioning (DIF) analysis can be conducted to evaluate test items that may favor (i.e., that are relatively easier) one examinee group over another (e.g., gender groups

and different language background groups) as a result of construct irrelevant variance (Haladyna & Downing, 2004).

On the other hand, Li (2008) studied the stability of item response theory (IRT) parameters (difficulty and discrimination) of 30 common items in Listening, Grammar, and Vocabulary across three administrations with 72,277 examinees. Four models with varying dimensions were used to calibrate and link the data. Samples of examinee answers were compared with simulation data generated under a multidimensional model. In general, the item difficulty parameters exhibited a very high degree of invariance across samples for one-dimensional and multidimensional models. In contrast, the degree of invariance of item discrimination parameters increased as the dimensions of the model augmented. This finding suggests that the selection of models for item calibration and linking can affect DIF detection. This issue could be explored comparing other test items and groups of examinees with different characteristics.

Score interpretation. The ECPE Sample Test Guide 2010 (p. 6) and other materials indicate that IRT is used for scoring MC items and that a combined scaled score is calculated. The test authors also argue that there is a high correlation between the number of correct answers and IRT scores. The scaled scores for a total of 170 items in the Listening and GCVR sections range from 0–605 (Fail) to 840–1000 (Honors). Besides the Song (2009) study with these sections, there is no other information reported regarding the applied IRT model, the linkage with the score distribution, or other score transformations. In addition, cutoff scores are set for each test section and used for awarding the final certification (e.g., a Certificate of Proficiency with Honors is awarded to an examinee with honor scores on all four sections). Based on November 2010 results, 0.25% and 61.53% of examinees received Honors/Pass and Pass, respectively. Zhang (2008) investigated the accuracy of proficiency classifications by different models of measurement (e.g., IRT and classical test theory [CTT]) with Listening (48 items) and GCVR (99 items). Overall, these scores were reliable (coefficients of .76 and .86, respectively) and achieved a slightly higher proficiency classification accuracy (85.0% in Listening and 88.5% in GCVR) using a three-parameter logistic IRT model than using CTT. Unfortunately, there is no technical information about the method employed for setting the passing scores.

COMMENTARY. The ECPE represents a valuable effort for measuring English language proficiency as a combination of different language components: Speaking, Listening, Writing, Grammar, Vocabulary, Cloze, and Reading. Reports show acceptable reliability estimates (above .80) for the scores. Also, raters' percentages of agreement of 80% or above in the Speaking and Writing tasks are good.

Nonetheless, the test author's claims of (a) assessing language proficiency in a variety of contexts; (b) assessing linguistic, discourse, sociolinguistic, and pragmatic elements of the English language; and (c) targeting the C2 level of the Common European Framework of Reference for Languages (Council of Europe, 2001) are not sufficiently documented. Some studies have shown that a one- or two-factor model may represent well the whole test structure, as language proficiency has been conceived in these manners (Saito, 2003; Wang, 2006). Additional information and research are required to sustain these arguments. The lack of a technical manual for summarizing and integrating validity evidence obliges the potential user to look for and to analyze the research reports. This is an extra burden for people interested in ECPE. A technical manual explaining test development and use, validity evidence, scaling and normalization, procedures for setting passing scores, and their interpretation is highly recommended.

SUMMARY. ECPE attempts to measure English language proficiency are worthwhile. The sample test materials and instructions are well organized and easy to follow. Acceptable reliability estimates of scores are reported. A set of studies provides relevant but partial validity evidence of the ECPE results. Because validation is an ongoing process, the explicit theoretical background of language proficiency and recent empirical evidence are needed for supporting the validity of the use and interpretation of test scores. Thus, inferences and decisions derived from them should be made with prudence.

REVIEWER'S REFERENCES

American Educational Research Association, American Psychological Association and National Council of Measurement in Education. (1999). *Standards for educational and psychological testing.* Washington, DC: American Educational Research Association.

Bachman, L. F., & Palmer, A. S. (1996). *Language testing in practice: Designing and developing useful language tests.* Oxford, UK: Oxford University Press.

Cambridge Michigan Language Assessments. (2012). *ECPE information bulletin 2012.* Retrieved from Cambridge Michigan Language Assessments website: http://www.cambridgemichigan.org/sites/default/files/resources/ECPE_IB.pdf

Council of Europe. (2001). *The Common European Framework of Reference for languages: Learning, teaching, assessment.* Cambridge, UK: Cambridge University Press.

Haladyna, T. M., & Downing, S. M. (2004). Construct-irrelevant variance in high-stakes testing. *Educational Measurement: Issues and Practice, 23*(1), 17–27.

Li, X. (2008). An investigation of the item parameter drift in the Examination for the Certificate of Proficiency in English (ECPE). *Spaan Fellow Working Papers in Second or Foreign Language Assessment, 6,* 1–28.

Plough, I. C., MacMillan, F. M., & O'Connell, S. P. (2011). *Changing tasks…changing evidence: A comparative study of two speaking proficiency tests.* Cambridge-Michigan Language Assessments Research Reports 2010-11. Ann Arbor, MI: University of Michigan.

Purpura, J. E. (1999). *Learner strategy use and performance on language tests: A structural equation modeling approach.* Cambridge, UK: Cambridge University Press.

Römhild, A. (2008). Investigating the invariance of the ECPE factor structure across different proficiency levels. *Spaan Fellow Working Papers in Second or Foreign Language Assessment, 6,* 29–55.

Saito, Y. (2003). Investigating the construct validity of the Cloze section in the Examination for the Certificate of Proficiency in English. *Spaan Fellow Working Papers in Second or Foreign Language Assessment, 1,* 39–82.

Song, T. (2009). Investigating different item response models in equating the Examination for the Certificate of Proficiency in English (ECPE). *Spaan Fellow Working Papers in Second or Foreign Language Assessment, 7,* 85–98.

Wang, S. (2006). Validation and invariance of factor structure of the ECPE and MELAB across gender. *Spaan Fellow Working Papers in Second or Foreign Language Assessment, 4,* 41–56.

Zhang, B. (2008). Investigating proficiency classification for the Examination for the Certificate of Proficiency in English (ECPE). *Spaan Fellow Working Papers in Second or Foreign Language Assessment, 6,* 57–75.

[70]

Expressive One-Word Picture Vocabulary Test–4: Spanish-Bilingual Edition.

Purpose: Designed to assess "an individual's ability to name–in either Spanish or English–objects, actions, and concepts shown in color illustrations."

Population: Ages 2–70+.

Publication Dates: 2001–2013.

Acronym: EOWPVT-4: SBE

Score: Total score only.

Administration: Individual.

Price Data, 2013: $175 per kit, including manual (2013, 105 pages), test plates, and 25 Spanish-Bilingual record forms; $55 per manual; $40 per 25 record forms; $80 per test plates.

Time: (20) minutes.

Comments: Co-normed with the Receptive One-Word Picture Vocabulary Test–4: Spanish-Bilingual Edition (19:141).

Author: Nancy A. Martin.

Publisher: Academic Therapy Publications.

Cross References: For a review by Jill Ann Jenkins of an earlier edition, see 16:88.

Review of the Expressive One-Word Picture Vocabulary Test–4: Spanish-Bilingual Edition by MICHAEL S. MATTHEWS, Associate Professor of Gifted Education, Department of Special Education and Child Development, University of North Carolina at Charlotte, Charlotte, NC:

DESCRIPTION. The Expressive One-Word Picture Vocabulary Test-4: Spanish-Bilingual Edition (EOWPVT-4: SBE) addresses expressive vocabulary, or the ability to name actions, objects, and concepts. An associated measure, the Receptive One-Word Picture Vocabulary Test: Spanish-Bilingual Edition (ROWPVT-4: SBE; 19:141) measures receptive vocabulary, or the ability to match spoken words to their associated pictures. Both expressive and receptive vocabulary skills are strongly related to reading comprehension, and therefore to academic achievement.

The EOWPVT-4: SBE assesses the individual's ability to name pictured objects, actions, and concepts using a single word in either English or Spanish. The test consists of 180 illustrations presented in an easel format in order of increasing difficulty (essentially from more common to less commonly known items). The test is untimed, but use of basal and ceiling items means that only a subset of these items is used with any given individual; because of this, most administrations will require approximately 20 minutes to complete, plus 5 to 10 additional minutes to compute manually the examinee's score. The basal is established by eight consecutive correct answers; the ceiling is set at six consecutive incorrect responses or by reaching the final illustration. Users will find that the instructions are extremely clear, occasionally to the point of being redundant. Scoring and interpretation are straightforward. Raw scores are converted to standard scores, percentile ranks, and age-equivalent scores using the age calculated on the response form and the tables provided in the test manual.

DEVELOPMENT. Though based initially on the English-language Expressive One-Word Picture Vocabulary Test, the number and order of items in this current version differ from both the current English and the previous bilingual version; consequently, the easel provided with this measure is not interchangeable with other versions of the test. Due to the death of the author of the previous bilingual edition (Brownell), this revision was conducted under new authorship (Martin). The prior version of this measure, published in 2001, was designed for use with children ages 4 through 12. The current version has been extended to permit its use with ages 2 to 70+. Extension of the test norms to include adults raises the intriguing possibility of using the measure diagnostically, such as with older individuals who may be showing early signs of Alzheimer's disease, according to the test manual.

TECHNICAL.

Standardization. The final standardization sample of 1,260 individuals was drawn from 54 sites representing 13 U.S. states and Puerto Rico. A map depicts the geographical location of standardization efforts and lists the cities and states involved. A majority of the 56 examiners were speech-language pathologists. In the standardization, responses that did not meet inclusion criteria were not used; the test author rejected those that were missing co-norming data from the receptive version of the measure, as well as those that had incomplete responses, and (it appears, but is not clearly stated) those who did not contribute to the standardization sample's representativeness of the overall population of U.S. Hispanics. The test manual did not report how many responses were discarded due to each of these reasons; including this information would increase the reader's confidence in the inferences being drawn from the standardization.

Reliability. Internal consistency reliability is very high, with coefficient alpha values ranging from .90 to .98 and averaging .95. Scores from 28 very low-scoring examinees were excluded from the computation of internal consistency reliability coefficients. According to the test manual, most of these examinees were autistic, and the low scores are consistent with vocabulary deficits that typically are associated with this condition. Test-retest reliability also was high, with a correlation coefficient of .99 for raw scores and .97 for standard scores. These values were determined over a period of 2–4 weeks (average 19 days) among 69 examinees who were retested by the same examiner. It is not clear how many different examiners were involved in this aspect of the standardization process. The standard error of measurement (*SEM*) is relatively small for all ages, and is widest at age 2 (as would be expected), with a 95% confidence interval of 9.48 standard score points (approximately +/- 1 year in age-equivalent terms). The *SEM* for most other ages falls in the range of 5–7 standard score points, or approximately +/- 3 to 6 months in age-equivalent terms. No information is provided regarding interrater reliability.

Validity. Content validity is supported by evidence of a wide variety of item difficulty levels and by the measure's reliance on relatively simple components of language that can be named orally even in the absence of writing ability. Construct validity is supported by evidence of moderate to high correlations between the EOWPVT-4: SBE and other measures of vocabulary, including standard scores from the previous edition of the measure (*r* = .66, *n* = 22) and to the current co-normed receptive measure (*r* = .67, *n* = 100 for standard scores, whereas *r* = .90, *n* = 127 for raw scores because their range is not truncated as it is for standard scores). A convenience sample of an unknown number of examiners provided scores from these other measures, and correlations with vocabulary measures from other test publishers are not provided.

Criterion-related validity evidence appears to be strong. The test author's discussion of test bias is commendably clear and concise. Scores from the EOWPVT-4: SBE show a positive correlation with age of the examinee, as would be expected because vocabulary develops with increasing age. Comparisons with disability groups (i.e., individuals with attention-deficit/hyperactivity disorder, autism spectrum disorder, and learning disabilities) in all cases revealed significantly higher scores for the matched sample without diagnosed disabilities, though it is not clear why only raw scores are reported for the autism/pervasive developmental disorder sample, whereas standard scores are used for the other two disability-related comparisons. It would be appropriate to report additional detail about how the matching process was conducted.

COMMENTARY. In reviewing the previous edition of this measure, Jenkins (2002) disagreed with Brownell's assertion that the test could be used as a measure of cognitive ability. The current edition (2013) no longer makes this claim; rather, Martin states in the test manual that because vocabulary is acquired through both cognitive ability and opportunity to learn, primarily via access to written content, "vocabulary tests such as the EOWPVT-4: SBE, therefore, do not offer a direct index of cognitive ability" (p. 14).

Instructions state that "all acceptable responses are printed on the Record Form; all other responses should be considered incorrect unless you are certain they are dialectical or regional variants of the acceptable responses" (manual, p. 29). This reviewer notes that more words are accepted as correct responses in Spanish than in English; examining the response sheet, depending on how one counts differences, there are approximately 40 more words allowed for Spanish responses than for English ones. It seems that items could have been selected so as to have the same number of possible responses in each language. It may be the case that those administering the test in the context of U.S. schools are considered more likely to be aware of additional correct responses in English than they would be in Spanish, or this may be simply a result of being inclusive of a wide variety of Spanish dialects whereas only American English is used.

As a former science teacher, this reviewer notes that among pictures depicting living organisms a few items may engender response errors because depictions of details of the natural world are not precisely correct. Without divulging specific test content that might compromise the measure's security, this reviewer would suggest that attending more carefully to natural (rather than cartoon-like) coloration and anatomy (Plate 38) and to nuances of naming (Plate 56) would address these relatively minor concerns. Plate 139 may confuse some bilingual respondents because the Spanish name is also used in English, with the same pronunciation as in Spanish, but in English it refers to a different animal.

This reviewer would have preferred that test developers include a comparison of academically advanced learners along with the comparisons of disability groups and their matched samples. Such a comparison would strengthen the case for the measure's criterion-related validity. More importantly, there are ongoing concerns and even litigation surrounding the issue of equitable representation in gifted education programming, as well as continuing discussion regarding the selection of suitable measures for matching academically advanced English language learners with appropriate programming (e.g., Lohman, Korb, & Lakin, 2008; Matthews & Kirsch, 2011). Appropriate and easily administered measures of vocabulary and reading ability such as the EOWPVT-4: SBE provides would fill an important gap if demonstrated to be suitable for use with this student population.

SUMMARY. The EOWPVT-4: SBE represents a timely and well-written update of this classic measure. Test users will find it straightforward and relatively rapid to administer and score. Used in conjunction with the companion ROWPVT-4: SBE and other relevant measures, it will inform both diagnostic and student placement decisions. Although a greater use of random selection in the norming process would be appropriate, as would further detail about some of the procedures used in the norming process, this reviewer believes these limitations do not detract from a positive overall recommendation for this measure.

REVIEWER'S REFERENCES
Jenkins, J. A. (2002). [Review of the Expressive One-Word Picture Vocabulary Test: Spanish-Bilingual Edition]. In R. A. Spies & B. S. Plake (Eds.), The sixteenth mental measurements yearbook (pp. 373–376). Lincoln, NE: Buros Institute of Mental Measurements.
Lohman, D. F., Korb, K. A., & Lakin, J. M. (2008). Identifying academically gifted English-language learners using nonverbal tests: A comparison of the Raven, NNAT, and CogAT. Gifted Child Quarterly, 52, 275–296. doi: 10.1177/0016986208321808
Matthews, M. S., & Kirsch, L. (2011). Evaluating gifted identification practice: Aptitude testing and linguistically diverse learners. Journal of Applied School Psychology, 27, 155–180. doi: 10.1080/15377903.2011.565281

[71]

Expressive One-Word Picture Vocabulary Test, 4th Edition.

Purpose: Designed to measure an individual's English-speaking vocabulary.

Population: Ages 2 to 80 years and older.

Publication Dates: 1979-2011.

Acronym: EOWPVT-4.

Scores: Total score only.

Administration: Individual.

Price Data, 2012: $175 per kit, including manual (2011, 99 pages), 25 record forms, and test plates in vinyl portfolio; $80 per set of test plates; $40 per 25 record forms; $55 per manual.

Foreign Language Edition: Spanish-Bilingual version available.

Time: (20) minutes.

Authors: 1990 and earlier edition by Morrison F. Gardner; 2000 edition by Rick Brownell; 4th Edition by Nancy A. Martin and Rick Brownell.

Publisher: Academic Therapy Publications.

Cross References: For a review by Alfred Longo of the 2000 edition, see 15:95; see also T5:994 (53 references) and T4:946 (23 references); for reviews by Gregory J. Cizek and Larry B. Grantham of an earlier edition, see 12:147 (6 references); for reviews by Jack A. Cummings and Gilbert M. Spivack of the Lower Level, see 9:403 (2 references).

Review of the Expressive One-Word Picture Vocabulary Test, 4th Edition by SANDRA M. HARRIS, Assessment Coordinator, College of Social and Behavioral Sciences, Walden University, Minneapolis, MN:

DESCRIPTION. The Expressive One-Word Picture Vocabulary Test, 4th Edition (EOWPVT-4) is an individually administered norm-referenced instrument used to assess a person's ability to name objects, actions, and concepts. The instrument can be administered to individuals 2–80+ years of age. Results from the assessment yield a single, total score.

The test material for the EOWPVT-4 consists of 190 illustrations that are arranged in order of increasing difficulty. The manual presents age-based starting points, which the examiner uses to establish a basal starting point for each examinee. The manual provides detailed instructions on how to establish the basal. During testing, individuals are shown one colored illustration at a time and asked to name the object or event in the illustration. Testing continues until the examinee reaches a ceiling, which occurs when six consecutive errors are made. The test is not timed and can be administered in 15 to 20 minutes. The manual indicates that results

can be scored in 5 to 10 minutes. Raw scores can be converted into scaled scores, standard scores, percentile ranks, and age equivalents.

Examiners should be trained professionals such as therapists, counselors, learning specialists, rehabilitation specialists, speech-language pathologists, and psychologists. The manual further advises that the test must be interpreted by individuals who have the following credentials: (a) background in psychometrics, (b) knowledge of how scores are derived from the test, and (c) knowledge of the limitations of the test. The complete test kit consists of a comprehensive manual (which includes directions, technical specifications, conversion charts, etc.), a spiral-bound easel (which contains the 190 color illustrations), and 25 record forms.

DEVELOPMENT. The EOWPVT was originally published in 1979. The original test targeted children ages 2–12 years. The test was amended in 1983 to extend the age range through 15 years, 11 months. The EOWPVT was also revised in 1990 and again in 2000. The 2000 revision contained significant changes and improvements. The stimulus words were enhanced, the instructions were rewritten, the administration procedures were streamlined, and color illustrations were included in the test material. The EOWPVT-4 builds upon previous versions of the instrument in several ways. First, the manual contains national norms for individuals 80 years of age and older. Second, new words were added to extend the testing age range. Third, the manual emphasizes use of the instrument as an early screening tool. Finally, the EOWPVT-4 was conormed with a measure of receptive vocabulary, the Receptive One-Word Picture Vocabulary Test, 4th edition (ROWPVT-4; 19:142).

TECHNICAL.

Norming. The normative sample for the EOWPVT-4 consisted of 2,394 English-speaking individuals from 26 states in the United States. Participants ranged from 2 to 103 years of age. The manual states that results should be interpreted with caution when being used to assess individuals who do not meet the description of the normative sample. The reported demographic data for the participants include gender, ethnicity, residential region of the U.S., whether participants live in rural or urban/suburban areas, and level of education. A total of 106 examiners participated in the standardization of the EOWPVT-4. The test manual indicated that the normative sample closely approximated the demographic distribution of the U.S. population at the time the test was administered.

Reliability. Internal consistency and test-retest reliability estimates were presented for the EOW-PVT-4. Internal consistency was estimated using coefficient alpha. Measures of internal consistency were computed using the standardization sample of 2,394 participants across varying age groups. Coefficient alpha values ranged from .93 to .97. The manual further reported a test-retest reliability of .97 across a period of 2 weeks to 4 weeks. A sample of $N = 78$ was included in the test-retest study. A standard error of measurement (*SEM*) was also reported by age group. The manual recorded a mean *SEM* = 3.29 [5.43, 6.45].

Validity. Three types of validity evidence were reported in the test manual: content, construct, and criterion-related. Content validity was addressed by asserting that the EOWPVT-4 is a fairly discrete naming task that does not tap into other skills. The manual also asserts that an item analysis was used to assess the item difficulty. However, there was no supporting empirical evidence regarding the specific indices or values that were used to assess item difficulty.

Construct validity was assessed by correlating standard scores from the EOWPVT-4 with scores from the previous (2000) edition. Results from a sample of 229 examinees ages 5 to 15 years yielded a high positive correlation of .95, which was not surprising because of the overlap in content on the two versions of the test. Criterion-related evidence of validity was addressed by correlating scores from the instrument with scores obtained from other instruments that assess abilities thought to be related to vocabulary skills. Scores from the EOWPVT-4 were positively correlated ($r = .69$) with reading scores as obtained by the STAR Reading test for a small sample of 33 examinees. A small positive correlation of .43 was obtained when scores from the EOWPVT-4 were correlated with the Wechsler Intelligence Scale for Children, Fourth Edition (WISC-4) Verbal Comprehension scores. Additionally, scores from the EOWPVT-4 showed a small positive correlation ($r = .35$) with full scale intelligence as measured by the WISC-IV.

Bias. The test manual presented several statistical procedures that were used to determine which items to include in the test protocol. The manual indicates that classical test theory (CCT), item response theory (IRT), and differential item functioning (DIF) were used to guide the selection of items and to address issues of bias. The manual indicated that results from the statistical analyses did not show any evidence of bias.

COMMENTARY. The revised version of the EOWPVT-4 continues to present the instrument as a valid tool for "evaluating vocabulary abilities across a wide range of ages" (p. 61). The manual is paperbound with a fairly attractive cover. The directions are straightforward and easy to follow. Testing procedures are simple and easily performed. The manual presents detailed and comprehensive instructions for test administration and scoring. The manual includes a sample of a completed and scored test protocol.

The manual presents some evidence regarding the psychometric properties such as reliability, bias, and validity. The manual presents evidence regarding the reliability of the instrument and also indicates the EOWPVT-4 was shown to have high internal consistency estimates as measured by coefficient alpha. The instrument also has high test-retest reliability.

The manual further lauds the validity of the instrument, but does not give adequate details regarding the empirical data used to draw conclusions about the validity. A major shortcoming of the manual is the lack of details regarding the statistical parameters used to guide the development of the instrument. The manual should contain details regarding the empirical results and parameters of the statistical procedures such as item analysis, DIF, classical test theory (CCT), and item response theory (IRT) that were used to guide the retention of items on the instrument.

The manual presents potential uses for the EOWPVT-4 as an evaluative tool for the following: vocabulary development, reading skill, screening for language delay, word/concept retrieval in aphasics, indirect measures of cognitive skills, and effectiveness of intervention programs. However, the manual fails to provide guidelines or directions on how scores from the instrument could be used to evaluate skills in the aforementioned areas. No guidelines are presented for interpreting or categorizing the raw or transformed scores. The manual issues a disclaimer regarding the categorization of scores obtained from the EOWPVT-4 by specifically stating "categorical terms are NOT delineated for the EOWPVT-4" (p. 36).

The manual presents information regarding the general demographic data for the normative sample; however, there are discrepancies in the age ranges presented in several charts. For instance, the chart that presents the age distribution is missing data for ages 14, 16, 18, and 19 as well as data for individuals in the age ranges of 21–49, 51–69, and 71–79. However, information presented on the same page for smoothed median raw scores does include information for 14-, 16-, 18-, and 19-year-olds. The same page presents data for ages 30, 40, and 60. Further, data from the reliability coefficients are not consistent with the age groupings presented in the age distribution table or the smoothed median raw scores table. The manual does not provide any explanation or rationale as to why there are differences in the age categories presented in the various tables.

SUMMARY. The EOWPVT-4 may have some practical use as a test to measure vocabulary. However, the instrument should not be used as a stand-alone measure of a person's vocabulary abilities and knowledge. The manual specifically references "expressive and receptive vocabulary tests, when combined with tests of other aspects of language" (p. 13). In addition, although the manual provides several references to various indications of validity, it also indicates that the validity of the instrument, like that of all measures, must be continually evaluated. Consequently, the greatest utility of the EOWPVT-4 may lie in the use of the instrument as a screening tool.

Review of the Expressive One-Word Picture Vocabulary Test, 4th Edition by KATHLEEN M. JOHNSON, Psychologist, Lincoln Public Schools, Lincoln, NE:

DESCRIPTION. The Expressive One-Word Picture Vocabulary Test, 4th Edition (EOWPVT-4) is "an individually administered, norm-referenced assessment of an individual's ability to name objects, actions, and concepts when presented with color illustrations" (manual, p. 5). The EOWPVT-4 is a revision of the previous EOWPVT 2000 edition and extends the utility of the instrument upward through adult and geriatric age groups.

The stated purpose of the EOWPVT-4 is to provide a quick and reliable measure of English expressive vocabulary skill, using a picture-naming paradigm. It is normed for individuals between the ages of 2 years, zero months and 80+ years. Used in combination with the Receptive One-Word Picture Vocabulary Test, 4th Edition (ROWPVT-4; 19:142), with which this test was conormed, a comparative assessment of single-word vocabulary can be obtained. The authors, Martin and Brownell, remind

examiners that vocabulary is only one component of language development albeit a very important one. The EOWPVT-4 was developed for use by trained professionals in speech-language pathology, psychology, and education. Based on the relationship between vocabulary and other cognitive and language skills, the authors recommend various uses for the EOWPVT-4. These uses include documenting vocabulary development, supplementing reading assessments, screening for early language delay, examining word/concept retrieval in aphasics, obtaining an indirect indication of some cognitive skills, and evaluating intervention programs.

The EOWPVT-4 can be administered in about 20 minutes. The testing materials include the user's manual, record forms, and 190 color illustrations in a spiral-bound book with an easel. The test items are sequenced by difficulty, and age-related starting points are provided to minimize the time needed for a thorough yet efficient assessment. Four practice items are used with all examinees to introduce the test and ensure they understand what is expected. The EOWPVT-4 test plates (illustrations) are presented at a comfortable pace for each individual; the test is untimed. Examinees are instructed to tell one word that names each picture. A useful summary of the administration directions is provided inside the record form, along with notations for the age-related start points. The basal and ceiling rules, along with the standard cues and prompts, are also printed in the record form. Standard scores are derived from the raw scores, and percentile ranks and age equivalent scores are provided to aid the examiner in the interpretation process.

DEVELOPMENT. The development of this normative revision and extension of the EOWPVT-4 was based heavily upon the development of the EOWPVT 2000 edition. The 174 items from the previous edition and 28 new items (words/images) were used in the development process. Some new items were added to extend both the floor and the ceiling of the test to increase test accuracy for the wider range of examinees. Other items were placed in the sequence to allow a gradual increase in difficulty level across the age span. The vocabulary/words used were primarily nouns, with some gerunds, verbs, and modifiers. Color illustrations depicting each object, action, or concept were carried over from the previous edition, revised from the previous edition, or newly created. The new items selected for younger ages were incorporated into the testing with examinees under age 13, and the new items selected for older examinees were incorporated into the testing with those age 13 and over. This procedure was used to obtain more accurate item analyses for the new vocabulary words. Both classical test theory (CTT) and item response theory (IRT) analyses were conducted, and some of the items were eliminated based upon the results of these analyses. The final edition of the EOWPVT-4 consists of 190 items sequenced by difficulty. The same basal (eight consecutive correct) and ceiling (six consecutive incorrect) rules were adopted from the previous edition. No evidence of item difficulty or item discrimination bias was found based on the CTT analyses. The Rasch (IRT) analysis showed no evidence of an interaction between ability and subgroup membership. Finally, differential item functioning (DIF) analysis was conducted to compare item functioning between groups (male-female, urban/rural, black/white, etc.). No evidence of item bias was identified through these analyses.

TECHNICAL. The standardization sample included 2,394 individuals from 26 states in the U.S., who ranged in age from 2 years 0 months to 103 years. The sample approximated the 2000 U.S. Census demographics for the variables of region, race/ethnicity, gender, parental education level, and residence area. Standard scores, percentiles, and age equivalents were derived from the raw scores obtained in the standardization process. The manual contains appendices that provide raw score to standard score conversions for specific age intervals, standard score conversions to percentiles and other commonly used derived scores, and raw score conversions to age equivalents.

Reliability and validity evidence is summarized by the authors in the EOWPVT-4 manual. Internal consistency coefficients were computed for each of 17 age groups (each year from age 2 to 12 and ages 13–14, 15–16, 17–19, 20–49, 50–69, and 70+). The coefficient alpha values for the age groups ranged from .93–.97. The median coefficient value was .95 across all the age groups. These values indicate a high degree of homogeneity within the pool of test items. Test-retest reliability was also reported as high (.97–.98), with an average of 19 days between testing sessions. Validity evidence provided in the manual includes some content (in the development section), construct, and criterion-related data and information. The authors provide evidence that the EOWPVT-4 measures the same construct as the previous edition of the test,

based on a high correlation (.95) between the two tests for the subgroup of 229 individuals in the standardization sample. The mean score earned on this updated edition was lower (12.6 standard score points) than the mean score earned on the older version, as might be expected with the more current normative edition. A moderate positive correlation (.69) between the standard scores on the EOWPVT-4 and the ROWPVT-4 was also found for the same subgroup. A lower positive correlation (.43) was reported based on the scores from the EOWPVT-4 and the Wechsler Intelligence Scale for Children-Fourth Edition (WISC-IV) Verbal Comprehension Index for a subgroup of 23 examinees. Limited criterion-related validity evidence is discussed in the manual. For a subgroup of 33 individuals, a moderate correlation (.69) was obtained when scores from the EOWPVT-4 were compared with scores from the STAR Reading assessment. For a subgroup of 24 children, a comparison of Full Scale IQ scores on the WISC-IV and the EOWPVT-4 standard scores yielded a lower correlation (.35). The authors provided data comparing five groups of individuals with disabilities with matched sample groups (without disabilities). The results indicated that the groups with verified disabilities scored at significantly lower levels than did those in matched sample groups.

COMMENTARY. The Expressive One-Word Picture Vocabulary Test, 4ᵗʰ Edition, which is both a normative update and an upward extension of the previous edition, continues to be a useful tool for quickly assessing expressive vocabulary knowledge. However, as the authors note, single-word vocabulary measures can only partially represent the wide scope of language development. Extending the normative sample through adulthood and geriatrics is likely to broaden its usefulness, especially in clinical settings. Having the EOWPVT-4 co-normed with the ROWPVT-4 provides a specific comparative analysis of single-word vocabulary, at least at a screening level. The test development procedures and standardization data are adequate and are documented in the manual. Administration of the test and scoring procedures are straightforward and effectively detailed in the manual. The color test plates are well-illustrated. Reported measures of internal consistency and test-retest reliability are high. In contrast, the construct and criterion-related validity evidence contained in the manual is more limited. The high correlation between the EOW-PVT-4 and the previous edition from 2000 is not unexpected given the high degree of item overlap (88%–90% of the items were the same). More research needs to be conducted in this area, especially with regard to how the EOWPVT-4 correlates with other measures of language development.

SUMMARY. The Expressive One-Word Picture Vocabulary Test, 4th Edition (EOWPVT-4) is an individually administered, norm-referenced measure of English expressive vocabulary skill, using a picture-naming format. It is an updated revision of the EOWPVT 2000 Edition and an upward extension through adult age groups. The test is now normed for individuals 2 years, 0 months through 80+ years of age. Development and standardization procedures are well-documented in the manual, and test administration time is a reasonable 20 minutes or less. The items are arranged in order of difficulty, and critical-range testing makes testing time-efficient. The EOWPVT-4 was conormed with the ROWPVT-4, which together provide comparative measures of expressive and receptive vocabulary skill. The primary usefulness of this instrument is as a screening tool for vocabulary knowledge, as one component of language development. The reliability and validity studies lend support for using the EOWPVT-4 for this specific purpose.

[72]

Firestone Assessment of Violent Thoughts–Adolescent.

Purpose: To "assess the underlying thoughts that predispose violent behavior in adolescents."
Population: Ages 11-18.
Publication Dates: 1999-2008.
Acronym: FAVT-A.
Scores, 9: Paranoid/Suspicious, Persecuted Misfit, Self-Depreciating/Pseudo-Independent, Overtly Aggressive, Total, Instrumental/Proactive Violence, Hostile/Reactive Violence, Inconsistency, Negativity.
Administration: Individual.
Price Data, 2011: $120 per introductory kit including professional manual (2008, 167 pages), 25 rating forms, and 25 score summary/profile forms; $55 per professional manual; $55 per 25 rating forms; $20 per 25 score summary/profile forms.
Time: 15 minutes.
Authors: Robert W. Firestone and Lisa A. Firestone.
Publisher: Psychological Assessment Resources, Inc.

Review of the Firestone Assessment of Violent Thoughts–Adolescent by DAVID F. CIAMPI, Post Doctoral Intern, Valley Mental Health Associates, Inc., Springfield, MA:

DESCRIPTION. The Firestone Assessment of Violent Thoughts-Adolescent (FAVT-A) is a self-reporting assessment instrument useful in the screening for violence potential among adolescents between 11 and 18 years of age. The test authors indicate that appropriate populations include incarcerated violent and nonviolent offenders, violent and nonviolent individuals on probation, outpatients with internalizing or externalizing disorders, and adolescents from the general population. The FAVT-A can be either individually or group-administered and scored on a carbonless, paper-and-pencil rating form in conjunction with the FAVT-A professional manual and the FAVT-A score summary profile form. The administration of the rating form is estimated to take 10 minutes.

The front side of the rating form contains instructions for completing the form. The backside of the document includes an area for recording the test-taker's demographic data, as well as a 35-item, 3-point, Likert-type scale with a rating range from 1 to 3 (1 = *Rarely, Almost Never*; 2 = *Sometimes*; 3 = *Frequently, Almost Always*) for indicating the frequency with which the test-taker experiences specific thoughts.

The FAVT-A is composed of four levels, which refer to distinctive genres of cognitions and thought processes that predispose adolescents to violent behaviors. Level 1 = Paranoid/Suspicious (P/S), Level 2 = Persecuted Misfit (PM), Level 3 = Self-Depreciating/Pseudo-Independent (SD/P), and Level 4 = Overtly Aggressive (OA). There are also two theoretical subscales: Instrumental/Proactive Violence (I/P) and Hostile/Reactive Violence (H/R), which, according to the test authors, reflect both static and dynamic functions of violence risk. There is also a Total FAVT-A raw score, T score, and percentile.

The rating form can be separated from the answer sheet by removing the perforated strip from the top of the rating form once the client completes rating all 35 items. This procedure is necessary to obtain the scoring sheet, which is used to calculate the total level and subscale raw scores. The raw scores are transferred to the score summary table on the score summary profile form. T scores and percentiles for each level are easily calculated by referencing the appendices in the FAVT-A professional manual. Additionally, both negativity and inconsistency scale directions and scoring are located on the score summary and profile form.

DEVELOPMENT. The FAVT-A was developed based on the constructs of separation theory, which was originally conceptualized by one of the test authors (R. Firestone, 1997) and encompasses both existential and psychoanalytic schools of thought. This instrument focuses on internal negative thought processes (referred to as "voices"), which are hypothesized as internalizations of negative attitudes that caretakers may have towards both themselves and their children. The identification of these cognitions (i.e., "voices") provides insight into how clients see themselves and others. According to the professional manual, the test authors note that specific thought processes are essentially the predictors and drivers of overt, violent behavior. Hence, the voices provide insight into the core dynamics of violent behavior towards self and others.

TECHNICAL.

Standardization. According to the manual, the FAVT-A standardization sample of 641 respondents was representative of the U.S. adolescent population based on age, gender, race/ethnicity, and grade level. This assessment instrument was administered to 315 adolescents (aged 11 to 14) and 326 teenagers (aged 15 to 18). According to the manual, the authors are from California and, as a consequence, 48.8% of the standardization sample was collected in a single geographic region the Western United States. The publisher collected the remainder of the standardization sample in the following regions: southern U.S. = 25.4%, midwestern U.S. = 21.8%, northeastern U.S. = 3.9%. For adolescents aged 11 to 14, 51.1% were male and 48.9% female. The breakdown of the FAVT-A sample according to race and ethnicity indicated that 61.2% were White, 15.2% Black, 16.5% Hispanic, and 6.7% designated as "Other."

For respondents in the 15 to 18 age band, 51.8% were male and 48.2% female. The racial and ethnic classifications for this age range were 62.8% White, 14.7% Black, 15.7% Hispanic, and 6.7% denoted as Other. The FAVT-A standardization demographic sample data closely approximate the U.S. Bureau of the Census (2003) statistics as highlighted by the test developers in their professional manual.

The designers of the FAVT-A applied several limitations throughout the standardization process. For example, adolescents were prohibited from participation if they were currently incarcerated, registered as an inpatient in a medical or psychiatric facility, under medical care for schizophrenia or other psychotic disorder, had uncorrected vision or hearing loss, inability to comprehend English, or read English at the third grade level, or were unable to provide informed consent.

The developers also collected demographic and FAVT-A data on two reference groups (i.e., the Incarcerated Reference Group and the Probation Reference Group) during the standardization procedure, which occurred between 2001 and 2008, and 1995 to 2008, respectively. Survey characteristics of the Incarcerated Reference Group were obtained in a juvenile facility for violent offenders and camps for juvenile offenders and from juvenile hall settings. Within this grouping, 56.3% of the respondents reported instances of being violent towards family members, friends, or someone they cared about. Data collection activities with the Probation Reference Group took place in probation schools located in California where students were formerly arrested and currently on probation. Among the cohorts in this group, there was a 34.8% reported history of violence towards family members, friends, or someone about whom they cared.

The normative data for the standardization sample were examined by investigating associations between demographic variables and the FAVT-A levels, the theoretical subscales, and the Total FAVT-A. According to the test authors, all the demographic variables were statistically significant: age ($F = 4.13$), gender ($F = 1.17$), and race/ethnicity ($F = 1.19$), all at $p < .01$ levels.

Reliability. Internal consistency and test-retest reliability data are presented in the FAVT-A professional manual. Alpha reliability coefficients range from .92 to .95 for the total FAVT-A score. The alpha values for Level 1 (P/S) range from .61 to .82; the Level 2 (PM) alpha values vary from .79 to .89; Level 3 (SD/P) demonstrates alpha coefficients that extend from .82 to .90; Level 4 (OA) alpha scores range from .83 to .91. The two reference groups have alpha coefficients that range from .61 to .86 for Levels 1–4.

The test authors provided an additional estimate of internal consistency by calculating average item-total correlations for each FAVT-A level, each subscale, and the Total FAVT-A. Overall, the coefficients ranged from .51 to .78. The authors reported that these results are in the moderate to desirable range.

Validity. The test developers note that the nature of validity is multidimensional and that no single statistical value can accurately estimate the degree of test score validity. Thus, the test authors examined the data in relation to content validity, construct validity, and criterion validity. Content evidence of test score validity was demonstrated for each of the four levels in the FAVT-A professional manual. As for evidence of construct validity, the test authors analyzed patterns of intercorrelations between Validity Sample 1, Validity Sample 2 and FAVT-A levels, the Theoretical subscales, and the Total FAVT-A. All of the correlations were significant at $p < .01$ with ranges .59 to .94. As the test developers observed, Overtly Aggressive (Level 4) and the Total FAVT-A achieved the highest correlations with respect to the psychological domains of both the Psychosocial Evaluation and Threat Risk Assessment (PETRA; Schneller, 2005) and Resiliency Problems. High correlations were also obtained for both the Proactive Violence subscale and the Hostile/Reactive Violence subscale when statistically compared with the Psychological domain and the Resiliency Problems domain, and the Aggression cluster of the PETRA. A comprehensive listing of all intercorrelations has been provided in the professional manual.

Sensitivity and specificity of the FAVT-A measures were examined in order to establish criterion-related validity. Receiver operating characteristics (ROC) analyses were conducted on each of the FAVT-A levels, as well as the Theoretical subscales in order to predict (a) which adolescents were incarcerated, (b) those who were not incarcerated, (c) those who were on probation, (d) adolescents who were not on probation, (e) those who had a history of arrest, and (f) individuals who have been violent to their friends, a family member, or to others about whom they cared. According to the test authors, Level 4 (Overtly Aggressive Level OA) and the Instrumental/Proactive Violence subscale performed somewhat better than the Total FAVT-A in predicting connections with the Level 4 Incarcerated AUC (i.e., area under the curve) = .71, Probation AUC = .75. The Theoretical subscale, Instrumental/Proactive Violence, obtained the following results: Incarcerated AUC = .71 and Probation AUC = .77.

The test authors noted that the accurate prediction of violent behavior is not an easy task due to difficulties with ROC and the associated AUC. As a consequence, the test developers utilized a subsample of the validity sample ($n = 476$) to establish the degree to which the FAVT-A could significantly improve the prediction of violence and arrest in

adolescent cohorts. The results of stepwise logistic regression analyses revealed that only age ($x^2 [3, n = 476] = 6.35, p < .05$), and Total FAVT-A ($x^2 [1, n = 476] = 11.74, p < .01$) reliably predicted violence toward a loved one within the final model. The test authors concluded that the FAVT-A significantly contributes to the prediction of violence and arrest when compared to demographic variables.

COMMENTARY AND SUMMARY. The FAVT-A is an important self-report measure of underlying thoughts that prompt violent behavior among adolescents. This instrument is easy and relatively fast to administer during the clinical intake process and appropriate when a clinician needs to ascertain the potential for violence. It is possible to assess the genre and intensity of violent thoughts that an adolescent experiences within approximately 10 to 15 minutes. Overall, meaningful estimates of reliability and validity are provided by the test developers.

The theoretical conceptualization of the FAVT-A is based on the recognized affinity between Separation Theory/Voice Therapy and cognitive processes (e.g., negative thoughts) that are drivers of violent behaviors. This instrument also has utility in integrating the FAVT-A scores into different treatment modalities, such as Rational Emotive Behavior Therapy and Dialectical Behavior Therapy. In summation, the FAVT-A appears to be an excellent, well-designed screening instrument for assessing violence potential among adolescents in the United States.

REVIEWER'S REFERENCES

Firestone, R. W. (1997). *Combating destructive thought processes: Voice therapy and separation theory.* Thousand Oaks, CA: Sage Publications.
Schneller, J. (2005). *Psychosocial Evaluation and Threat Risk Assessment (PETRA) professional manual.* Lutz, FL: Psychological Assessment Resources.
U.S. Bureau of the Census. (2003). *Current population survey, March 2003.* Washington, DC: U.S. Department of Commerce.

Review of the Firestone Assessment of Violent Thoughts–Adolescent by JEREMY R. SULLIVAN, Associate Professor of Educational Psychology, University of Texas at San Antonio, San Antonio, TX:

DESCRIPTION. The Firestone Assessment of Violent Thoughts–Adolescent (FAVT-A) was designed to assess violence potential among children and adolescents aged 11 to 18. According to the manual, "appropriate populations include incarcerated violent and nonviolent offenders, violent and nonviolent individuals on probation, outpatients with internalizing or externalizing disorders, and individuals from the general population" (manual, p. 17). The FAVT-A is based on the Separation Theory/Voice Therapy approach to conceptualizing and treating violent behavior, in which "voice" is defined as "a systematic pattern of negative thoughts antithetical to the self and hostile and suspicious toward others" (manual, p. 10). According to the theory, these negative thoughts are more likely to occur among children who have experienced environmental risk factors such as trauma or abuse (i.e., the child incorporates hostile or neglectful characteristics demonstrated by caretakers during childhood), and these thoughts lead to misperceptions of others' behaviors as threatening, thereby driving violent behaviors towards others. The FAVT-A is meant to assess the type and intensity of these thoughts as a way to screen for violence potential, assess the danger of specific threats, identify triggers of violent behavior, determine level of services or incarceration, provide direction for intervention, and monitor progress of identified youth.

The FAVT-A may be used individually or in a group setting. Test materials include the manual, rating form, and score summary/profile form. The test manual begins with an extensive literature review on violence among youth, thereby providing a rationale for the constructs included on the scale. The chapter on interpretation includes a model for conducting comprehensive risk assessments based on FAVT-A data in addition to other sources of information. Indeed, this section reads like a step-by-step guide for conducting risk assessments and as such will likely serve as a useful guide for professionals. The manual also provides a separate chapter on integrating the FAVT-A with various treatment modalities.

The self-report rating form includes 35 items, each of which represents a destructive thought or "inner voice." Examinees respond using a 3-point scale (1 = *rarely or almost never experience the thought*, 2 = *sometimes experience the thought*, 3 = *frequently or almost always experience the thought*). Thus, the items assess thoughts that predispose violent behaviors rather than behaviors themselves, with the premise that behaviors are heavily influenced by thoughts. The score summary/profile form is used to convert raw scores into *T*-scores and percentiles. Normative groups include younger (11–14 years) and older (15–18 years) males and females, in addition to two reference groups (incarcerated group and probation group) for optional comparison purposes.

Items are categorized into four levels. These levels are similar to subscales, and there is no item overlap among the levels. Level 1 (6 items) is Paranoid/Suspicious and includes thoughts of

mistrust of other people and the need to protect the self from harm. Level 2 (7 items) is Persecuted Misfit and includes thoughts of being misperceived, victimized, and humiliated by others. Level 3 (13 items) is Self-Depreciating/Pseudo-Independent, which assesses the tendency to be overly self-critical and to feel isolated or rejected by others. Level 4 (9 items) is Overtly Aggressive, which assesses open endorsement of violent behaviors, including lack of remorse for violent behaviors and acceptance of violence as an appropriate response to circumstances. Two Theoretical subscales are included to differentiate Hostile/Reactive Violence from Instrumental/Proactive Violence, with the understanding that these different types or functions of violent behaviors will require different treatment approaches. These two subscales are composed of items from the four levels. The Instrumental/Proactive Violence subscale (9 items) purports to identify instrumental (i.e., in order to gain something or achieve a certain outcome) or planned violence characterized by mistrust of others, feeling justified in using violent behaviors, lack of remorse or emotion, and a pattern of repeated violent behaviors. The Hostile/Reactive Violence subscale (9 items), on the other hand, purports to assess a propensity for violence that is based on emotional reactions to perceived threats. Thus, violent behaviors under this category are more spontaneous or impulsive rather than planned or deliberate. There also is a Total FAVT-A score, which is based on all 35 items and is interpreted as a broad index of the extent to which the examinee is experiencing a wide range of violent thoughts that are predictive of violent behaviors. Validity scales include Negativity (designed to assess extreme endorsement of violent thoughts) and Inconsistency (designed to identify inconsistent responses to pairs of items with similar content).

DEVELOPMENT. Separation Theory and Voice Therapy guided the development of items that capture the negative thoughts ("voices") that predict violent behaviors. Development also was informed by the process of establishing the Firestone Assessment of Violent Thoughts (FAVT; Firestone & Firestone, 2008; 18:52), which is the adult version of the FAVT-A, and the Firestone Assessment of Self-Destructive Thoughts (FAST; Firestone & Firestone, 2006; 14:149). For example, the FAVT-A includes a subset of items from the FAVT, and FAVT items were based on thoughts reported by individuals before and during committing acts of violence. The Rasch model was used to determine which items from the FAVT should be included on the FAVT-A, based on item-fit statistics and item redundancy. Exploratory factor analysis was used to assess the underlying structure of the FAVT-A items and to determine which items were removed from the final version based on low factor loadings. Unfortunately, detailed results of factor analyses are not presented for the four levels, so potential users are unable to evaluate the appropriateness of these processes.

The Instrumental/Proactive and Hostile/ Reactive Theoretical subscales were based on the adult versions of these scales (which were derived using expert review and categorization of the items) followed by interitem correlation analyses, item-total correlation analyses, internal consistency analyses, and exploratory factor analyses. Items are written at a second-grade reading level based on the Flesch-Kincaid system, which required some of the FAVT items to be reworded in order to be appropriate for the FAVT-A. Differential item functioning analyses were conducted using gender and race/ethnicity variables.

TECHNICAL.

Standardization. Standardization data collection occurred from 1995 to 2008. Stratified sampling procedures were used to obtain a representative sample in terms of age, gender, race/ ethnicity, and grade level according to the 2003 U.S. census data. The standardization sample included 641 adolescents who met certain inclusion criteria (e.g., not currently incarcerated or residing in an inpatient psychiatric facility), and who thus may represent a relatively "normal" sample. With regard to geographic representation, 48.8% of the sample came from the Western region of the U.S., which is larger than the proportions from other regions (Southern = 25.4%, Midwestern = 21.8%, Northeastern = 3.9%). Numerous statistically significant differences in FAVT-A scores were found for gender, race/ethnicity, and age, but separate norms for derivation of standard scores are provided only for age/gender (i.e., four groups: younger males, younger females, older males, older females). Demographic data also are provided for the two reference groups, which unfortunately are limited by small sample sizes (N for Incarcerated group = 87; N for Probation group = 137). It also is worth noting that many adolescents in the reference groups did not report a history of violent behaviors.

Reliability. Score reliability was assessed with internal consistency and test-retest reliability analyses. With regard to internal consistency, alpha coefficients are provided for all of the scales for the various age/gender and reference groups. Out of 42 reported alpha coefficients, 3 were in the .60s (all for Paranoid/Suspicious), 6 were in the .70s, 23 were in the .80s, and 10 were in the .90s. Notably, alpha coefficients for Total FAVT-A scores were in the .90s for all groups. Unfortunately, alpha coefficients were not compared across ethnic groups. The test authors also provide the mean item-total correlations for each scale; however, it would be more informative to see item-total correlations for each individual item so that potential users could identify any items that did not fit as well as the others.

Test-retest analyses were conducted with 28 participants from the standardization sample. The test-retest interval ranged from 7 to 42 days (mean interval = 19.93 days, SD = 8.97). All coefficients were statistically significant at $p < .01$, ranging from .88 to .99, suggesting a high degree of score stability over time.

Validity. The test manual provides an abundance of information related to validity; this description will be selective due to limited space. Evidence related to content validity is drawn from a review of research indicating that the content (i.e., the collection of items) of the four FAVT-A levels is related to violence potential. Additional evidence is provided by the development procedures described above.

Construct validity evidence derives from two sources. First, convergent and discriminant analyses were used to determine whether scores on the FAVT-A correlated with scores on similar and dissimilar measures in theoretically expected ways. Two different samples were used in these analyses (Sample 1 N = 150, Sample 2 N = 477). Some of the validity analyses used subsamples of these groups, thus the results are not based on the entire samples. In general, scores on the FAVT-A scales correlated with scores on other measures in predicted directions, with a few exceptions (e.g., this reviewer expected that Paranoid/Suspicious and Persecuted Misfit would correlate positively with the Alienation scale of the Psychosocial Evaluation and Threat Risk Assessment [Schneller, 2005], but the coefficients were .00 and -.04, respectively). Although there may be some concern about scores being too highly correlated with measures of more general psychopathology (e.g., anxiety, depression, suicidal ideation), the test authors justify these findings by noting the impact of emotional distress on violent ideation and behavior. Still, this raises the question of whether high scores on the FAVT-A truly can be interpreted as a high level of violence potential, or rather should be interpreted as psychopathology more generally.

Second, the factor analytic procedures described in the Development section were used as evidence of construct validity. This evidence is still limited, however, by insufficient detail of the factor analytic procedures.

Criterion-related evidence was assessed by examining FAVT-A scores for different groups. Comparison groups included normal adolescents (n = 347), adolescents who were incarcerated (n = 87), adolescents on probation (n = 137), adolescents receiving outpatient psychiatric services for internalizing disorders (n = 37), and adolescents living in group homes (n = 19). Across all of the levels, subscales, and the Total score, adolescents in the incarcerated, probation, and group home samples scored significantly higher than those in the normal and internalizing groups. Sensitivity and specificity analyses indicate that FAVT-A Total scores were moderately successful at identifying adolescents who were incarcerated or on probation, and adolescents in these groups showed a tendency to score higher on the various scales when compared to adolescents in the normal group. Regression analyses suggest that Total scores were predictive of violent behaviors and arrest among a subset of the validity sample. Although these results offer evidence that supports criterion-related validity, not all of the adolescents in the incarcerated or probation groups were violent offenders. Similarly, those adolescents living in group homes were placed due to experiencing abuse or teen pregnancy rather than for violent behaviors. Thus, the composition of these groups makes it less clear how to hypothesize why group members should be scoring in certain directions on the FAVT-A scales.

COMMENTARY. Strengths of the FAVT-A include the use of theory and research to guide the development of the test, the abundance and types of evidence offered to support the use of test scores in the proposed manner, and the thorough consideration of interpretation and intervention issues provided in the test manual. The items and scores may be helpful in identifying negative thoughts and distorted beliefs that could be addressed with cognitive-behavioral approaches.

Perhaps the most serious limitation of the FAVT-A is a lack of sufficient detail in the test manual to allow potential users to make informed conclusions or interpretations regarding psychometric properties. For example, more detailed information is needed on the construction of the various scales and item selection (e.g., number of people interviewed during the item generation process, item-total correlations for each item, factor loadings for each item on each level). Looking at the content of the four levels, Level 3 (Self-Depreciating/Pseudo-Independent) seems to be assessing the least unitary construct, as some of the items seem to be related to other thought patterns such as grandiosity, mistrust, and rationalization of violence. Users need to see factor analytic results that support the test authors' construction and interpretation of the levels. In the absence of this information, our knowledge of the factor structure is severely (and unnecessarily) limited.

In addition, more interpretation of convergent and discriminant correlation analyses would be helpful, as potential users are sometimes left to make their own interpretations of the data. This is especially important given that some of these results do not convince the potential user that FAVT-A scores can discriminate true violence potential from more general psychopathology or emotional distress. Finally, although the theoretical basis of the FAVT-A seems like a strength, it is unknown whether clinicians who do not use the Separation Theory/Voice Therapy approach will find the test applicable within their practices.

SUMMARY. The FAVT-A purports to assess violence potential among children and adolescents in order to help clinicians reach decisions regarding level of danger, placement, and intervention. Several other threat assessment instruments for use with adolescents have recently been developed, and each has its own limitations. The FAVT-A offers a unique approach by focusing on the thoughts that predict violent behaviors, rather than looking at more emotional or behavioral risk factors. Although much of the psychometric evidence provided in the test manual is promising, some of the statements made in the manual are speculative and await further empirical evaluation to show that FAVT-A scores are able to predict violence and inform placement and treatment decisions. It will be especially important to examine how the FAVT-A can be used with other threat assessment measures to improve the accuracy of these decisions. Until this information is available, the FAVT-A should be used with caution when making clinical decisions, perhaps by using the FAVT-A as a supplement to other methods in order to determine whether it provides valid information above and beyond that provided by other threat assessment methods.

REVIEWER'S REFERENCES

Firestone, R.W., & Firestone, L.A. (2006). *Firestone Assessment of Self-Destructive Thoughts/Firestone Assessment of Suicidal Intent professional manual.* Lutz, FL: Psychological Assessment Resources.

Firestone, R.W., & Firestone, L.A. (2008). *Firestone Assessment of Violent Thoughts professional manual.* Lutz, FL: Psychological Assessment Resources.

Schneller, J. (2005). *Psychosocial Evaluation and Threat Risk Assessment (PETRA): Professional manual.* Lutz, FL: Psychological Assessment Resources.

[73]

Franchisee Personality Profile Abridged–general version.

Purpose: Designed to assess "how well a person's personality and attitude fit the ideal franchisee profile."

Population: Potential franchise owners.

Publication Date: 2011.

Acronym: FPP-Ab.

Scores, 14: Leadership, Comfort with Sharing Cost and Profit, Self-Efficacy, Management Skills, Rule-Abiding, Community/Family Values, Go-Getter, Diligence, Innovation, Determination, Approachability, Self-Confidence, Positive Mindset, Entrepreneurial Spirit, Overall Score.

Administration: Individual.

Price Data: Available from publisher.

Time: (15) minutes.

Comments: Self-administered online assessment. The test publisher advises that the test manual is being updated to include more information about methodology and theoretical background used in the development of the test. The test publisher also advises that this information is available to clients, as are benchmarks for relevant industries and racial/ethnic group comparison data. However, this information was not provided to Buros or the reviewers.

Author: PsychTests AIM, Inc.

Publisher: PsychTests AIM, Inc. [Canada].

Review of the Franchisee Personality Profile Abridged–general version by FRANK M. BERNT, Professor, Education Department, Saint Joseph's University, Philadelphia, PA:

DESCRIPTION. The Franchisee Personality Profile Abridged–general version (FPP-Ab) is a 110-item, computer-administered, self-assessment instrument that aims to evaluate "how well a person's personality and attitude fit the ideal franchisee profile" (technical manual, p. 1). Suggested applications include screening and training of prospective franchisee owners within human resources contexts. The manual states that the FPP-Ab includes 11

subscales, clustered under two subfactors; it is not clear from the text what the subclusters are, nor is any evidence provided to support the subclusters. Thirteen scales are named: Leadership, Comfort with Sharing Cost and Profit, Self-Efficacy, Management Skills, Rule-Abiding, Community/Family Values, Go-Getter, Diligence, Innovation, Determination, Approachability, Self-Confidence, and Positive Mindset.

Items are anchored using a variety of 5-point rating scales, including *strongly agree* to *strongly disagree*, *exactly like me* to *not at all like me*, *no impact* to *major impact*, and *always* to *never*. The final 20 items use a variety of response options; there does not appear to be any evidence to support treating responses to these items as ordinal or interval data.

Completion of the FPP-Ab online is straightforward and can be completed in 15–20 minutes. The report produced online includes a summary, graphs, detailed results, strengths and limitations, and advice for the respondent. Each of these areas is, at first blush, very user-friendly, if not terribly precise or informative in its descriptions and analyses. There is liberal use of such modifiers as somewhat, reasonably, moderately, fairly–whereas indicators of relative position are absent from both test reports and from the technical manual.

DEVELOPMENT. Unfortunately, there is no discussion regarding how items were selected or developed, nor is there any presentation or analysis of individual items in the psychometric report. The title of the FPP-Ab suggests that it has been abridged; however, there is no record in the psychometric literature of any parent test from which it was abridged, nor is there any evidence of pilot testing (see discussion of norming sample, below). Given the aim to evaluate the respondent's "personality fit" to some ideal profile, reference either to some theoretical framework or to an empirical literature would help efforts to link the construction and structure of these scales to the larger field of personality assessment and business success.

TECHNICAL. The authors describe the norming sample as "uncontrolled": 855 subjects opted to participate in the validation study by taking the FPP-Ab on one of two websites. Description of the norming sample appears to be limited to age and gender variables; no indication of other demographic variables (race, income level, region, etc.) is provided.

Frequency distributions are reported for each subscale using a 100-point metric. Although not explicitly addressed in the technical manual, one might suppose that the average for all items on any given 5-point scale was simply multiplied by 20 to provide a common 100-point scale. If this is so, then scores provided on the individual test reports produced by PsychTests are decidedly not norm-referenced. If they are, in fact, norm-referenced, the technical manual provides no comment or data to explain, for example, exactly what a score of 70 means for a particular subscale. In addition, the 100-point range of most scales suggests a 6-point scale (ranging from 0 to 5) rather than the 5-point scale. Confusion regarding scoring and score interpretation needs to be clarified.

Number of items for each subscale range from 4 (Rule-abiding) to 33 (Leadership). Reported coefficient alphas are generally satisfactory; not surprisingly, three of the five subscales with 6 items or less (Comfort with Sharing Cost and Profit; Rule-Abiding; Community/Family Values) have alphas of .61 to .64; all others are .73 or above. There is no presentation of intercorrelations among subscales. There is also no indication of which items from which subscales comprise the Overall Score (only 92 items are included). In addition, the total number of items listed in the reliability analysis table exceeds the total number of items on the FPP-Ab, suggesting that many items are included on multiple subscales (which, in turn, suggests that subscales would be intercorrelated based upon shared items as well as similarity of the constructs themselves). There is no mention of estimates of temporal stability.

In the validation section of the psychometric report, the authors compare gender and age groups for each of the subscales and obtain statistically significant differences for several of the scales. The purpose and aim, as well as the implication of such comparisons, is not readily apparent. The absence of reported effect sizes (given the large sample) makes the practical significance of obtained statistically significant differences questionable. Graphic depictions of group differences throughout the report are scaled in such a way as to exaggerate differences. In the case of the comparison of franchise aspirants to nonaspirants for Management Skills, the bar chart ranges from a minimum of 72.6 (on a 100-point scale) to 74.0–a range of 1.4 points on a 100-point scale.

In addition to gender and age comparisons, results are presented for separate analyses comparing respondents with business experience to those without such experience, and those aspiring to own a franchise to those without such aspirations. Group differences for many of the subscales are in the direction that one might expect–for example, business owners scored higher than nonbusiness owners for Overall Score, Leadership, Comfort with Sharing Cost and Profit, Self-Efficacy, Diligence, Innovation, Determination, Approachability–and one or two other scales. In contrast, nonbusiness owners scored higher than business owners for Management Skills and Rule-Abiding subscales. Neither explanations nor hypotheses are offered for these findings to either support or contradict subscale validity; the report contains only statistics, with no comment or explanation. No data were presented concerning the correlation of FPP-Ab scores to external, objective measures of effectiveness as a franchise owner. No description of either exploratory or confirmatory factor analyses was provided to support the construct validity of the FPP-Ab.

SUMMARY. At present, there is simply not sufficient information available to support the widespread use of the FPP-Ab as a tool for screening or training. Interpretation and use of scores from the FPP-Ab should be viewed with caution and care until such time as a more detailed description of the test's development and norming procedures is made available, and until such time as more extensive studies are reported addressing criterion and construct validity issues. The FPP-Ab may hold promise as a means of identifying and training franchisees; however, at this time, that promise is largely unrealized. Several reviews of the literature reveal that very little has been done in the area of the personality profiles of franchisees (see Weaven, Grace, & Manning, 2009, for an example of empirical work being done in this area). Exploring ways to connect test development in this specific area to the more general question of personality and success in the business world seems to be a fruitful direction to consider.

REVIEWER'S REFERENCE

Weaven, S., Grace, D., & Manning, M. (2009). Franchisee personality: An examination in the context of franchise unit density and service classification. *European Journal of Marketing, 43*, 90–109.

Review of the Franchisee Personality Profile Abridged–general version by EUGENE P. SHEEHAN, Dean, College of Education and Behavioral Sciences, University of Northern Colorado, Greeley, CO:

DESCRIPTION. Franchises are ubiquitous. There is hardly a corner in any large American city that does not have some type of franchise. The variety is almost endless, including coffee shops, different types of restaurants, sandwich shops, small convenience stores, tire stores, gymnasiums, spas, tanning salons, storage units, and hotel chains. Franchises are among the most well-recognized corporations in the United States. These franchises offer the prospect of owning a business, while adopting a proven business model and benefitting from corporate name recognition and regional and national advertising. Assumed personality characteristics of those wishing to own a franchise are that they seek autonomy and independence and that they can tolerate financial risk. Given the financial commitment invested in a franchise it would be beneficial to know whether one had the requisite personality and the risk tolerance prior to opening a franchise. It is these characteristics that the Franchisee Personality Profile Abridged–general version seeks to measure. The manual asserts that the test assesses whether an individual's personality and attitudes fit the profile of an ideal franchise owner.

Taken online, the Franchisee Personality Profile Abridged–general version is an individually administered 110-item questionnaire that attempts to predict whether one has the potential to be a successful franchise owner. Franchise corporations could use the instrument to select individuals applying for a franchise, and individuals seeking to open a franchise could use the instrument to assess their compatibility with franchise ownership. The assessment takes roughly 30 minutes to complete, although this reviewer completed the questionnaire in 20 minutes. Administration instructions are remarkably clear and easy. A bar at the top of the screen allows a test-taker to monitor progress through the test. Test items cover dimensions of personality pertinent to being a franchise owner, along with specific situations one would likely encounter as a franchise owner.

Upon completion of the test, respondents immediately receive a report that begins with an overall summary of their potential to own a franchise. This potential is shown graphically on a 100-point scale and is followed by a short reminder of the pros and cons of franchise ownership. This summary includes the notice that only between 30% and 50% of small businesses survive the first 5 years. The next section in the report is a graphical representation, again on a 100-point line, of scores on the various scales. A narrative section describes the meaning of each score. These meanings are summarized in a section titled "Strengths & Limitations." The last section in the report contains advice for becoming a successful franchise owner. For example, this advice includes

making sure one's customers feel appreciated and choosing the business and location carefully.

DEVELOPMENT. The Franchisee Personality Profile Abridged–general version was developed by Arch Profile/Psychtests. The organization's brochure claims that their instruments undergo rigorous development procedures, including meeting educational and psychological testing standards advocated by the American Educational Research Association, American Psychological Association, and the National Council on Measurement in Education (AERA, APA, & NCME, 1999). Although many of the items have a face validity aligned with franchise ownership, the manual provides little detail about test development. There is no conceptual framework provided regarding why the personality dimensions on the test were used. The manual indicates two subfactors and 11 subscales: a total of 13. However, this reviewer notes the following: Overall Score, Leadership, Go-Getter, Diligence, Innovation, Determination, Approachability, Comfort with Sharing Cost and Profits, Self-Efficacy, Self-Confidence, Positive Mindset, Management Skills, Rule–Abiding, Community/Family Values, and Entrepreneurial Spirit. That list tallies to 15 scales. It is also not readily discernable as to which are the subfactors and which are the subscales.

TECHNICAL. The standardization sample comprised 855 individuals. The manual contains information about their gender and age distribution, along with the caveat that the sample was self-selected and that validation data were based on self-report. Normative data are provided by gender and by age group. The manual is not clear regarding how the standardization sample was used to develop scores on the various scales.

There are no data about the item writing or item selection process in the manual. Nor do we know which items load on which scales.

Coefficient alpha reliability ranges from a high of .94 on the Overall Score and Leadership scales to a low of .62 on the Rule-Abiding scale and .61 on the Community/Family Values scale. Therefore, the instrument generally has robust, if somewhat variable, internal-consistency reliability. No other reliability data are available.

The Franchisee Personality Profile Abridged–general version has face validity in that the items could easily be construed as measuring a personality profile that is congruent with franchise ownership and running one's own business. The hypothetical situation items are especially high on face validity.

Quantitative validity data in support of the ability of the instrument to differentiate between groups and to predict successful franchise ownership are not strong. Validity information relies on two comparison data sets. The first is a comparison between business owners and nonbusiness owners. There were about 130 in each group. Unfortunately, no demographic or descriptive information about these groups was provided in the manual. Operationally, business ownership could include a wide range, from individuals who sell products that are offshoots of a hobby to individuals who own multiple franchises and yet others who have been successful in business without any franchise involvement. Additionally, we know nothing of the success of these business owners–critical to determining the predictive validity of this instrument. *T*-test comparisons between the groups revealed statistically significant differences, in the expected direction, between the groups on five of the scales. Interestingly, there were no significant differences between the groups on the Overall score.

The second validity data set is a comparison between those who answered affirmatively that they would like to own their own franchise and those who indicated they would not. There were about 75 in each group. Again, there are no demographic data about these groups. We do not know about their leadership or business experience, for example. Nonetheless, as with the business owners, there are statistically significant differences, all in the expected direction, between the two groups on 11 scales.

COMMENTARY. The Franchisee Personality Profile Abridged–general version contains a set of 110 questions that any potential franchise owner should reflect on prior to investing in a franchise. Some of the items are very specific, dealing with incidents a franchise owner might encounter. Other items deal with broader personality constructs. The instrument is relatively short and very easy to administer, take, and score–all online. Scoring is immediate and results in a report that should provide potential franchise owners with information to consider prior to going down a statistically risky investment path. Psychometric data, on the other hand, are relatively weak. Although reliability appears robust, as measured by coefficient alpha, data on the validity of the instrument do not lead to the conclusion that the instrument can accurately identify a successful franchise owner. Because the items have face validity, rather than direct use

as a diagnostic tool, the Franchisee Personality Profile perhaps could be used as a device to provoke thoughtful conversation and reflection about franchise ownership.

SUMMARY. The Franchisee Personality Profile is designed to assess the personality dimensions deemed necessary for successful ownership of a franchise. Developed by PsychTests, taken and scored online, the 110-item instrument provides scores and a report on a range of relevant dimensions: Overall Score, Leadership, Go-Getter, Diligence, Innovation, Determination, Approachability, Comfort with Sharing Cost and Profits, Self-Efficacy, Self-Confidence, Positive Mindset, Management Skills, Rule-Abiding, Community/Family Values, and Entrepreneurial Spirit. The psychometric data supporting the instrument do not provoke confidence in its validity. Although coefficient alpha is reasonably strong, other reliability data are lacking. Further, the standardization sample is not described in sufficient detail to allow for meaningful comparisons to be drawn, and hard validity data are not comprehensive. Perhaps the best use of the instrument is its potential to raise questions for those considering an entrepreneurial career as a franchise owner.

REVIEWER'S REFERENCE
American Educational Research Association, American Psychological Association, & National Council on Measurement in Education. (1999). *Standards for educational and psychological testing.* Washington, DC: American Educational Research Association.

[74]

Garos Sexual Behavior Inventory.

Purpose: "Designed to assist forensic specialists and mental health professionals in making assessments and treatment decisions about individuals with problems related to sexuality and sexual behavior."

Population: Ages 18 and over.

Publication Date: 2008.

Acronym: GSBI.

Scores, 8: Discordance, Sexual Obsession, Permissiveness, Sexual Stimulation, Sexual Control Difficulties, Sexual Excitability, Sexual Insecurity, Inconsistent Responding.

Administration: Individual or group.

Price Data, 2010: $99.50 per complete kit including 25 AutoScore forms, 5 reusable administration cards, and manual (63 pages); $42.50 per 25 AutoScore forms; $27.50 per 5 reusable administration cards; $55 per manual.

Time: (20-30) minutes.

Comments: Administration card is entitled Sexual Attitudes Inventory.

Author: Sheila Garos.

Publisher: Western Psychological Services.

Review of the Garos Sexual Behavior Inventory by NORMAN A. CONSTANTINE, Research Program Director, Public Health Institute, Oakland, CA, and Clinical Professor of Community Health and Human Development, University of California, Berkeley, and NANCY BERGLAS, Research Scientist, UC Public Health Institute, Berkeley, CA:

DESCRIPTION. The Garos Sexual Behavior Inventory (GSBI) is a self-report measure of sexual attitudes and behavior developed to assist forensic and mental health specialists in making assessment and treatment decisions. Its purpose is to assist clinicians in identifying disorders of sexual frequency and control, and to assess dimensions of overall sexual adjustment. It is designed to be used in combination with available clinical data. Unlike many measures of sexual dysfunction, it has been norm-referenced to the general population. The GSBI is intended to be used with adult clients with varying degrees of sexual dysfunction or psychopathology, including sex offenders, substance abusers, survivors of sexual abuse, and clients with eating disorders.

The GSBI consists of 70 items that describe varied sexual attitudes, feelings, values, and preferences; each is measured on a 5-point Likert scale from *strongly disagree* to *strongly agree*. The examinee is given a reusable "Sexual Attitudes Inventory" Administration Card with the 70 items and a personal AutoScore Form to record his or her responses by circling the appropriate number (1–5). This process helps protect the confidentiality of responses and facilitates scoring by the administrator. The instructions for both the administrator and examinee are straightforward, and items are written at a sixth-grade level. It is estimated to take 20–30 minutes to complete.

The GSBI provides four Main scales, three Masking scales, and an Inconsistent Response Index score. The Main scales use 35 items to address the atypical sexual behaviors of Discordance, Sexual Obsession, Permissiveness, and Sexual Stimulation. The 25 items comprising the Masking scales are included to make the atypical behaviors of the main scales less obvious to the respondent, reducing the likelihood of socially desirable responses. The Masking scales measure common difficulties in sexual relationships, including Sexual Control Difficulties, Sexual Excitability, and Sexual Insecurity. Sixteen pairs of items are used for the Inconsistent Responding Index to detect unusual response combinations that may indicate poor attention to item content.

The test manual provides instructions for scoring the responses, and the AutoScore Form assists in this process. The form uses carbon tissue to transfer the examinee's responses to a scoring worksheet. Scoring instructions and simple visuals direct the administrator to calculate the Inconsistent Responding Index, assign item scores to the appropriate scales, and determine a total raw score for each of seven scales. The administrator transfers these scores to the GSBI Profile Sheet, where they are transformed into normalized *T*-scores and percentile ranks. High scores are shaded in gray for easy identification. The administrator is instructed to circle the values and connect them across scales to produce a graphical representation of results, although it is not specified how this plot is to be used. The test author notes that the GSBI can be administered by a paraprofessional, but scores should be interpreted by a trained clinician. Three case studies are included to illustrate interpretation and use of results.

DEVELOPMENT. The GSBI was developed to fill the need for a psychometrically sound measure to help clinicians in the identification of sexual disorders of frequency and control. According to the test author, previous instruments did not meet standards of reliability, validity, and clinical utility; were designed for use only with sex offenders; and were unnecessarily intrusive, expensive, and subject to response bias. Because no specific criteria for uncontrolled sexual behavior exist in the DSM-IV, the GSBI is based on a conceptual model derived from a combination of sources, including DSM-IV criteria for substance dependence, interviews with sex addicts, expertise from psychotherapists, existing instruments, and a review of the literature. After developing a definition for disorders of sexual frequency and control, the test author generated more than 300 items across 15 constructs. Items were tested using a panel of individuals with diagnosed sexual disorders, reviewed by expert panels, and piloted with a diverse sample drawn from inpatient treatment centers, recovery groups, and the general community (*n* = 495). Internal consistency estimates and principal components factor analysis were conducted, and 70 items were retained and tested with a second sample of individuals (*n* = 496) for scale refinement. The final GSBI was standardized with a nonclinical population. Detailed information about the sample populations, procedures, and analyses are presented in the test manual.

TECHNICAL. The GSBI was normed using a standardization sample of 1,029 adults drawn from nonclinical community settings. This sample was demographically diverse across age, gender, sexual orientation, and marital status. Ethnic minorities, most notably Hispanic respondents, were underrepresented relative to the U.S. population; information about social class is not provided. Based on this sample, normalized T-scores were developed (mean = 50, sd = 10) and are used for comparison across the seven scales. The test manual presents mean T-scores for each demographic subgroup. Although some statistically significant differences were found, the test author argues that these are most likely due to the large sample size and do not appear to be clinically meaningful.

The test manual presents reliability evidence based on internal consistency and stability. Alpha coefficients varied across the seven scales from .57 to .82, suggesting moderate to strong homogeneity of items within scales. Test-retest reliability estimates were computed using a 1-week interval from a subsample of 85 respondents in the standardization sample (range .70 to .93) and at 19 days from an independent sample of 54 college students (range .62 to .84). Both samples indicated adequate or better temporal stability of the scales.

Validity of GSBI test scores was addressed through content, construct, and discriminant evidence presented in the test manual and published literature (Garos & Stock, 1998a, 1998b). Content evidence was provided through the item development and assessment process, including item review by expert panels.

Construct evidence is presented through factor analysis conducted for the development of the seven distinct scales and correlational analyses. The four Main scales derived through factor analysis showed similar patterns of within-scale item loadings for both males and females. But factor loadings are provided only between items and the scale in which they were placed, constraining the user's ability to fully evaluate the instrument's factorial validity. Item-to-scale correlations presented in the reliability section can help address this issue. Among the 35 Main scale items, 28 had higher correlations with their assigned scale than the other scales, whereas 7 were equally well-correlated with another scale. The interscale correlations for the Main scales are low to moderate in magnitude (range -.11 to .39) and moderate for the Masking scales (.48 to .58). Additionally, the Main scales were correlated with six related instruments–including the Sexual Opinion Survey, Sexuality Scale, and Beck Depression Inventory–during development (N = 369). These correlations generally provide support for the construct validity of the scales, with a few exceptions (e.g., the low correlations between the Sexual Addiction Screening Test [SAST] and the GSBI sexual obsession scale, as compared to the much higher correlations between the SAST and the GSBI discordance scale).

Discriminant evidence of test score validity was assessed through analyses of the standardization sample by demographic subgroup, yielding results consistent with prior research. Additionally, responses of the nonclinical standardization sample were compared to those of several other groups, most importantly a sample of self-identified sex addicts. This analysis correctly predicted nonaddiction for more than 99% of the nonaddict standardization sample. Among the sex addicts sample, however, only 26.5% were correctly identified, yielding an exceptionally high false negative percentage of 73.5%. The test author reports in a prominent table an overall correct classification percentage of 92.7%; however, this is misleading and due to the much larger size of the nonaddict sample (338 versus 34). The test author briefly addresses this issue and suggests that it is probably a methodological artifact. We agree with this explanation; nevertheless, the fact remains that the GSBI was able to correctly identify only 9 of the 34 self-identified sex addicts.

COMMENTARY. The GSBI is described as a brief and easily administered measure of excessive or uncontrolled sexual behavior for adult clients. Its content is well founded in prior research, and its underlying theoretical model is clearly articulated. A key strength of the GSBI is its standardization with nonclinical populations allowing for its use in varied settings. Its primary weakness involves issues of construct validity. Although promoted as a measure of behavior, a large preponderance of items ask about attitudes, feelings, values, or preferences. The descriptions of the individual scales also are not behavior focused. This confusion is illustrated by the administration form's title of "Sexual Attitudes Inventory." This issue is further reinforced by the absence of essential construct validity evidence of the GSBI's ability to correctly classify self-identified sex addicts. The test author acknowledges the need for additional studies in this regard. In the meantime, we recommend cautious utilization of the GSBI for its intended use as a supplement to available clinical data in assessing disorders of sexual frequency and control.

SUMMARY. The GSBI was developed to meet the need for a brief, self-administered measure of disordered sexual behaviors that can be used by mental health professionals and forensic specialists to assess adult clients. It is straightforward to administer and score, and is estimated to take 20 to 30 minutes to complete. Evidence presented provides some support for its primary intended use, yet further evidence is needed before it can be used with full confidence.

REVIEWERS' REFERENCES

Garos, S., & Stock, W. A. (1998a). Investigating the discriminant validity and differentiating capability of the Garos Sexual Behavior Index. *Sexual Addiction & Compulsivity, 5,* 251–267.

Garos, S., & Stock, W. A. (1998b). Measuring disorders of sexual frequency and control: The Garos Sexual Behavior Index. *Sexual Addiction & Compulsivity, 5,* 159–177.

Review of the Garos Sexual Behavior Inventory by M. MEGHAN DAVIDSON, Assistant Professor of Counseling Psychology, University of Nebraska-Lincoln, Lincoln, NE:

DESCRIPTION. The Garos Sexual Behavior Inventory (GSBI) is a self-report measure intended to assess problems related to sexuality and sexual behavior. The GSBI is not intended to be a diagnostic measure of sexual disorders or sexual dysfunction, but is designed to be utilized to develop hypotheses about potentially problematic sexual behavior and to identify general issues regarding sexuality. The test author states the GSBI is appropriate for adults 18 years of age and older, and may be used with a wide range of individuals including clinical (i.e., inpatient and outpatient clients) and nonclinical (i.e., people from the general population) samples, as well as incarcerated and/or correctional populations (e.g., sex offenders, substance abusers, and sexual addicts). In conjunction with other clinical data, the GSBI can be utilized as a screening measure for treatment and an inventory to monitor client progress and change. As well, the GSBI may be used with sexual assault and/or trauma survivors and clients with eating disorders to ascertain overall sexual adjustment. A total of 20–30 minutes is required to complete the GSBI.

The GSBI is composed of 70 items that describe a variety of sexual behaviors and attitudes. Each item is answered with a 5-point response scale ranging from 1 (*strongly disagree*) to 5 (*strongly agree*). These 70 items are scored by summing the item scores that correspond to four Main scales and three Masking scales. These 7 raw scale scores are then converted to *T*-scores. The Main scales are

Discordance, Sexual Obsession, Permissiveness, and Sexual Stimulation, whereas the Masking scales are Sexual Control Difficulties, Sexual Excitability, and Sexual Insecurity. The Discordance scale measures the degree to which the respondent feels conflict, shame, or fear regarding sexual behavior, whereas the Sexual Obsession scale assesses the extent of preoccupation a person has with sex and/or sexually stimulating material. The Permissiveness scale measures the person's sexual values in terms of liberality, and the Sexual Stimulation scale assesses the respondent's degree of comfort with feelings of sexual stimulation and arousal. Regarding the Masking scales, the Sexual Control Difficulties scale measures the sense of control over sexual urges, the Sexual Excitability scale assesses reactivity to sexually stimulating common experiences, and the Sexual Insecurity scale is an indicator of insecurity in sexually intimate relationships. Additionally, an Inconsistent Responding Index is computed by examining 16 item pairs and summing the number of pairs for which the response values differ by 2 or more points. A total score is not computed. The GSBI AutoScore Form is a perforated booklet composed of an answer sheet for responding to items, a Scoring Worksheet, and a Profile Sheet; the AutoScore Form is used in conjunction with the GSBI Administration Card that comprises the 70 items.

DEVELOPMENT. The GSBI is not rooted in any one theory. A conceptual model to understand disorders of sexual frequency and control was first developed using *DSM-IV* criteria for Substance Dependence, interviews with self-labeled sex addicts, information from therapists working in this area, and a review of the extant literature. Next, a set of 300 rationally derived items focused on constructs consistent with excessive or problematic sexual behavior was generated. These items were then reviewed by a panel of people diagnosed with some sexual disorder related to frequency and/or control, resulting in both item elimination and generation to yield a total of 338 items. This compilation of items was then presented to four subsets of expert panels who engaged in "rationally derived item elimination procedures" (manual, p. 32), yielding 80 items.

This 80-item version of the GSBI was analyzed using data from a sample of 495 individuals recruited from three inpatient treatment facilities ($n = 56$), sexual addiction programs ($n = 68$), 12-step groups ($n = 58$), and the general community (*n* = 310). This sample was predominantly White (87%), female (61%), and heterosexual (86%); the mean age was 31.4 years (*SD* = 12.2) for females and 34.5 years (*SD* = 14.1) for men. Internal consistency estimates (i.e., coefficient alphas) were first examined and ranged from .52 to .82. Additionally, a principal components analysis was performed yielding six factors with 70 items; however, two of these factors were deemed too heterogeneous. The remaining four scales demonstrated alpha coefficients ranging from .76 to .89.

These 70 items were then administered to a second sample composed of individuals recruited from college classes, conferences, neighborhoods, and employment settings. This sample was similar to the first development sample in sex, age, race, and sexual orientation, and their data were combined and analyzed using a maximum likelihood factor analysis. Data were explored separately by males (*n* = 396) and females (*n* = 595), and then by the total sample (*N* = 991). A four-factor model with 35 items was observed for males, females, and the total sample, thus it was deemed appropriate to create the GSBI Main scales of Discordance, Sexual Obsession, Permissiveness, and Sexual Stimulation. The remaining items were retained as they demonstrated a reliable structure of their own; these items are used as the Masking scales and the Inconsistent Responding Index. The Masking scales of Sexual Control Difficulties, Sexual Excitability, and Sexual Insecurity are used in an effort to decrease defensiveness in respondents.

TECHNICAL. A standardization sample of 1,029 individuals was obtained to evaluate the GSBI, and was composed of some nonclinical respondents from the original development sample as well as additional individuals recruited from a range of nonclinical settings. This sample was predominantly White (81%) although attempts at greater racial diversity were made. Additionally, the sample was almost evenly divided across sex (52% female), had a mean age of 38.3 years (*SD* = 16.9), and was mostly heterosexual (87%). Estimates of internal consistency (alpha coefficients) for the Main scales of the GSBI based on this standardization sample were as follows: .80 for Discordance, .79 for Sexual Obsession, .68 for Permissiveness, and .57 for Sexual Stimulation. Regarding the Masking scales, alpha values were .82 for Sexual Control Difficulties, .81 for Sexual Excitability, and .72 for Sexual Insecurity. One-week test-retest reliability estimates were reported, based on a sample

of 85 respondents. Coefficents ranged from .70 to .84 for the Main scales and .71 to .93 for the Masking scales. Additionally, this standardization sample was used to obtain average raw scores to create normalized *T*-scores for each of the scales comprising the GSBI. Finally, pairs of items that demonstrated correlation coefficents of .40 or higher in this sample were selected to create the Inconsistent Responding index.

Regarding construct evidence of test score validity, the test author first discusses the internal structure of the measure, citing the GSBI interscale correlations as evidence supporting interpretability of the scales as distinct constructs. Other indices of construct validity have been demonstrated via correlations with scores on the Sexual Opinion Survey (Fisher, Byrne, White, & Kelley, 1988), the Sexuality Scale (Snell & Papini, 1989), the Zuckerman-Kuhlman Personality Questionnaire (Zuckerman, Kuhlman, Joireman, Teta, & Kraft, 1993), the Beck Depression Inventory (Beck & Steer, 1993), the Sexual Addiction Screening Test (Carnes, 1989), and the Rosenberg Self-Esteem Scale (Rosenberg, 1962) for a sample of 389 individuals from the development samples (218 female, 171 male). Finally, evidence for the ability of the GSBI scores to distinguish people with known sexual behavior or attitudinal problems from individuals without such problems is provided as indicators of discriminant validity. Criterion-related evidence and predictive evidence are not provided.

COMMENTARY. The GSBI is a brief and easy-to-administer measure that has the potential to further our knowledge and intervention in the area of sexual behavior. The primary strength of the GSBI is in its careful development and construction, utilizing a number of large-scale samples. Another strength is the use of the Masking scales to decrease discomfort in responding to the measure, as well as the use of the Inconsistent Responding index to assess for random response sets. Despite these strengths, the psychometric evidence for the GSBI needs further empirical support, specifically with more racially diverse populations as well as with individuals who identify as lesbian, gay, bisexual, transgender, queer, and questioning as the representativeness of the standardization sample is limited. Finally, the GSBI is lacking a theoretical foundation; thus, future research could advance the measure's utility by testing various theoretical models.

SUMMARY. The Garos Sexual Behavior Inventory (GSBI) is a self-report measure of problems related to sexuality and sexual behavior. The assessment can be useful in identifying general concerns regarding sexuality as well as in hypothesizing about potentially problematic sexual behavior. The GSBI has demonstrated adequate empirical evidence supporting its psychometric properties and is likely to be useful in a variety of clinical settings. Professionals seeking ways to assess sexual behavior and attitudes for clinical intervention and treatment would likely find the GSBI a useful measure. Further investigation regarding theoretical models and psychometric evidence including more diverse samples with regard to race, ethnicity, and sexual orientation would greatly enhance the validity of the GSBI.

REVIEWER'S REFERENCES

Beck, A. T., & Steer, R. A. (1993). *Beck Depression Inventory: Manual* (2nd ed.). San Antonio, TX: Psychological Corporation.

Carnes, P. (1989). *Contrary to love*. Minneapolis, MN: CompCare.

Fisher, W. A., Byrne, D., White, L. A., & Kelley, K. (1988). Erotophobia-erotophilia as a dimension of personality. *Journal of Sex Research, 25*, 123-151.

Rosenberg, M. (1962). The Rosenberg Self-Esteem Scale. Department of Sociology, University of Maryland, College Park.

Snell, W., & Papini, D. (1989). The Sexuality Scale: An instrument to measure sexual esteem, sexual depression and sexual preoccupation. *Journal of Sex Research, 26*, 756-763.

Zuckerman, M., Kuhlman, M., Joireman, J., Teta, P., & Kraft, M. (1993). A comparison of three structural models for personality: The big three, the big five, and the alternative five. *Journal of Personality and Social Psychology, 65*, 757-768.

[75]

Gesell Developmental Observation–Revised.

Purpose: Designed as a comprehensive developmental screening that measures social/emotional/adaptive skills, physical/neurological growth, language skills, and cognitive behaviors such as thinking, memory, perception, attention to task, ability to follow directions, short term visual and auditory memory, cognitive-perceptual thinking, organizational skills, logical mathematical thinking skills, and application of what is learned.

Population: Ages 2.5 through 9 years.

Publication Dates: 1964-2012.

Acronym: GDO-R.

Scores: 26 tasks: Cubes, Interview, Name and Numbers, Copy Forms, Incomplete Man, Right and Left, Visual I, Visual II, Naming Animals, Interests, Prepositions, Digit Repetition, Comprehension Questions, Color Forms, Three-Hole Form Board, Action Agents, Identifying Letters and Numbers, Numeracy, Counting, One-to-One Correspondence, Conservation, Calculations, Fine Motor, Gross Motor, Overt Behavior, Social/Emotional/Adaptive.

Administration: Individual.

Levels, 2: Ages 2.5 to 6.5; ages 7 to 9.

Price Data, 2013: $97.80 per Questionnaire bundle including 30 GDO-R forms, 30 Parent/Guardian Questionnaires, and 30 Teacher Questionnaires; $59.95 per 30 student record forms; $23.65 per 30 Teacher Questionnaires; $23.65 per 30 Parent/Guardian Questionnaires; $30.85 per 30 Spanish language Parent/Guardian Ques-

tionnaires for 30 families; $184.40 per examiner's manual (2011, 230 pages); $92.65 per examiner's script; price information for technical manual available from publisher.

Foreign Language Edition: Parent/Guardian Questionnaires are available in Spanish.

Time: Untimed; (20-45) minutes.

Comments: 5 strands: A (Developmental Tasks), B (Letters/Numbers), C (Language/Comprehension), D (Visual/Spatial Discrimination), E (Social/Emotional/Adaptive); original version of the test was called The Gesell School Readiness Test.

Author: The Gesell Institute of Child Development.

Publisher: Gesell Institute of Child Development.

Cross References: See T5:1085 (4 references) and T4:1035 (13 references); for reviews by Robert H. Bradley and Everett Waters of an earlier version, see 9:438; see also T3:953 (6 references) and T2:1703 (4 references); for excerpted reviews by L. J. Borstelmann and Edith Meyer Taylor, see 7:750 (5 references).

Review of the Gesell Developmental Observation–Revised by THERESA GRAHAM LAUGHLIN, Adjunct Faculty, Nebraska Methodist College of Nursing, Omaha, NE:

DESCRIPTION. The Gesell Developmental Observation–Revised (herein referred to as GDO-R) is a "standardized, performance-based, criterion-referenced instrument" (technical report, p. 12) intended to assess five components of development among children ages 2.5 to 9 years. The five components or "strands" include Developmental, Letters/Numbers, Language/Comprehension, Visual/Spatial Discrimination, and Social Behavior, Emotional Development and Adaptive Skills. Each strand consists of different tasks. For example, Development includes 5 tasks: Cubes, Incomplete Man, Copy Forms, and Fine and Gross Motor. Other strands include more tasks. For example, Letters/Numbers consists of 9 tasks. Developmental, Letters/Numbers, Language/Comprehension, and Visual/Spatial Discrimination are assessed using the same 26 tasks included in the 2007 GDO. Emotional Development/Adaptive Skills is based on a newly created Parent/Guardian Questionnaire and Teacher Questionnaire. It is intended to evaluate children's developmental and academic performance on a "developmental continuum" (examiner's manual, p. 2). In addition, information is used to assist educators in their curriculum development and to identify children who may need academic or social intervention.

The GDO-R should be administered individually by a trained examiner and is estimated to take between 20 and 45 minutes, depending on the age of the child. Scoring is estimated to take between 15–20 minutes. It is recommended that examiners complete a 3-day workshop offered by the Gesell Institute to learn test administration and scoring protocols. Given the complexity of administration and scoring and reliance on examiner judgment, extensive training is necessary to ensure standard administration and interpretation. An Examiner's Script is provided to ensure standard administration. In addition, for each task, the examiner's manual provides information regarding the rationale, the materials needed, administration guidelines with decision trees, protocol for recording child behavior, and tips for scoring, including detailed scoring rubrics. The examiner's manual provides guidelines regarding starting points. Decision Trees are utilized to determine end points. Three forms are included in the GDO-R: the Child Recording Form, the Parent/Guardian Questionnaire, and the Teacher Questionnaire.

The Child Recording Form is a comprehensive recording instrument that provides space for recording and coding child behavior. Because the GDO-R relies on examiner observation, the Child Recording Form includes space for process and qualitative information. In addition, the Child Recording Form contains the Summary Profile, which is used to score each strand and to record Developmental Age and Overall Performance Level. For each task, rubrics are provided to determine the child's Developmental Age. Strand scores, based on the subset of tasks within each strand, are calculated using the Strand Scoring Worksheet provided in the examiner's manual. Scores are converted to Performance Level Ranges using cut scores. For each strand, children's performance is summarized in terms of the following three categories: Age Appropriate, Emerging, and Concern. Finally, Overall Performance Level is determined by the examiner's "collective impression of the child" (examiner's manual, p. 57) and should be consistent with the Performance Level Definitions provided in the examiner's manual. Overall Performance Level can be categorized as Age Appropriate, Emerging, and Concern. Although performance is dependent on child performance on task, significance weight is also placed on verbal and nonverbal behavior observed by the examiner.

The Parent/Guardian Questionnaire and the Teacher Questionnaire should be completed within 2 weeks of administration of the GDO-R and are intended to offer insight into different character-istics of the child, including social engagement and temperament. Three components are assessed in the questionnaires: social behavior, emotional development, and adaptive skills. The recording chart for the two questionnaires is included in the Child Recording Form. Guidelines for scoring are provided in the examiner's manual. Cut scores are used to interpret the questionnaires and are categorized as Age Appropriate, Emerging, or Concern.

DEVELOPMENT. The GDO-R is based on a number of developmental principles, most notably the ideas of Arnold Gesell and his maturational developmental theory. *The Mental Growth of the Pre-School Child* (Gesell, 1925) outlined developmental milestones in motor, adaptive, language, and personal social behavior that were used to develop the tasks used in the GDO-R. The examiner's manual summarizes Gesell's work, outlines typical behavior of children across the age groups included in the GDO-R, and provides age-related implications for administering the GDO-R. Although it is clear that the GDO-R is based on developmental principles, no information is provided regarding specific item development. In part, this is due to the fact that the items used in the GDO-R are the same as those that were developed for earlier versions of the test.

The Parent/Guardian and the Teacher Questionnaire are based on analysis of other unnamed questionnaires. According to the examiner's manual, the questionnaires reflect "current thinking on child behavior continuums, best practice in early childhood classrooms, and current cultural influences" (p. 57). However, no specific information is given regarding item development or analysis.

TECHNICAL. Scant technical information is found in the examiner's manual although there is a chapter titled "Standardization, Reliability, and Validity." A separate technical report on the GDO-R provides more in-depth information regarding the standardization study completed. Prior to the standardization study, an online survey was conducted to gather information from customers using the GDO. In general, respondents ($N = 153$) indicated that the GDO was time-consuming and not culturally sensitive. Feedback on the Child Recording Form led the test authors to make adjustments in the form prior to the GDO study. Respondents' comments on the scoring and rubrics led the test authors to establish strand scoring and update rubrics in the GDO-R. Finally, a review of the GDO by five experts in the early childhood field prompted changes in two items on the Interview task and the addition of the Teacher and Parent/Guardian Questionnaire.

The GDO study included 1,287 children ages 3–6 years, recruited from 53 schools (62% private; 38% public) in 23 U.S. states. Of the total participants, 45% were from private schools, and 55% were from public schools. No standardization information or data were gathered for children under age 3 or for children ages 7–9 years. The sample was divided into seven age bands, in 6-month increments. The actual number of children within each age band differed widely, ranging from 53 for 3-year-olds to 278 for 5-year-olds. Information regarding ethnicity and gender distribution across the age groups tested is provided. Ethnic distribution differed significantly across the age groups. For example, over 40% of the sample of 3-, 3.5-, and 4-year-olds were African American, whereas less than 6% of the sample of 5.5- and 6-year-olds were African American. No information regarding participant socioeconomic status is provided. Discrepant information regarding the training of the examiners who administered the GDO study is provided in the examiner's manual and the technical report. The examiner's manual indicates that test administrators either completed a 3-day GDO workshop or viewed a training DVD. The technical report makes no mention of the training video. Scoring of the GDO-R was completed by Gesell Institute National Lecture Staff. This discrepancy is important given the reliance on examiner judgment.

Reliability. Reliability was based on internal consistency coefficients for each task within the strands for each age band. Internal consistency coefficients are generally higher for tasks with more items and, for the most part, are within an acceptable range. Internal consistency coefficients for the strands were lower than the values reported for the tasks. For example, the internal consistency coefficients for the Visual/Spatial Discrimination Strand ranged from .01 for 6-year-olds to .54 for 5.5-year-olds. The internal consistency coefficients for the three components included in the Teacher Questionnaire were high. However, no data were provided for the Parent/Guardian Questionnaire.

Descriptive information regarding child performance and p-values across the various tasks was provided. Child performance increased, as expected, across the various age bands. Older children were more successful on tasks than younger children. Two tasks that are usually administered to children older than 6 years were not included in the study.

No test-retest evaluation was performed. However, interrater reliability was assessed on subsamples of 122 and 132 children for two tasks: The Incomplete Man and the Copy Forms items, respectively. Four individuals with experience administering the GDO produced high interrater reliability for assigning Developmental Age on these two tasks. No interrater reliability was provided for any of the other items.

Validity. Evidence of content-related validity was based on a comprehensive review of child development, discussions with experts in the field, and online surveys of past users of the GDO-R. Construct validity evidence was based on intercorrelations performed between tasks by age band. Moderate to small to no correlation was found between tasks. Moreover, it was clear that items within a strand were often unrelated. The test authors stated that the strands were based, then, on a theoretical framework rather than on correlations between tasks. No other indicators of validity were provided. Moreover, the GDO-R was not compared with other preschool assessments nor tied to any prediction of future behavior.

COMMENTARY AND SUMMARY. The GDO-R is intended to measure a wide array of significant cognitive, language, motor, and social-emotional components of development in children ages 2.5 to 9 years of age. The assessment relies on examiner observation of children performing a variety of tasks and from parent/guardian and teacher questionnaires. The cornerstone of this measure is its history in the tradition of Arnold Gesell and his followers.

Unfortunately, the utility of the current version of the GDO-R is compromised by a number of factors raised in the standardization study conducted. First, the study only includes children between the ages of 3–6 years of age. Without data for children ages 7–9 years of age, it is difficult to confirm reliability and validation for this age group. Moreover, clearly there is a relationship between socioeconomic status and the achievement of many of the milestones measured in the GDO-R. Without any specific data on SES and oversampling of children enrolled in Head Start, it is possible that some of the data gathered might be skewed, which in turn may adversely affect the cut scores generated and interpretation of data.

In addition, one of the new components to the GDO-R is the inclusion of the Teacher and Parent/Guardian questionnaires. Although descriptive data are presented from the Teacher Questionnaire, no data are presented from the Parent/Guardian questionnaire. Although the test authors provide a variety of explanations for the lack of data, they offer no suggestions on how to improve return rates for future users of the GDO-R.

Finally, although many of the tasks included in the GDO-R are very useful in providing a picture of preschool development, it requires a well-skilled examiner to administer and score the test. It is unlikely that many teachers have the resources or time to devote 3 days for intensive training: a significant investment of time and energy to provide teachers information to inform their curriculum and classroom instruction. It is unlikely that the measure is useful at the classroom level. In sum, the current standardization study does not provide enough information to assess the validity and reliability and utility of the GDO-R for the entire age group for which this measure is intended.

REVIEWER'S REFERENCE

Gesell, A. (1925). *The mental growth of the pre-school child: A psychological outline of normal development from birth to the sixth year, including a system of developmental diagnosis.* New York, NY: Macmillan.

Review of the Gesell Developmental Observation–Revised by TIMOTHY R. KONOLD, Professor of Research, Statistics, and Evaluation, and KATHAN SHUKLA, Doctoral Student in Research, Statistics, and Evaluation, University of Virginia, Charlottesville, VA:

DESCRIPTION. The Gesell Developmental Observation–Revised (GDO-R) assessment system is designed to provide an assessment of children's developmental progress for purposes of guiding instruction. This revised version of the GDO incorporates word revisions to some tasks, newly developed observation forms, and a technical manual.

The GDO-R consists of an individually administered direct assessment as well as informant-based parent and teacher observation forms. The direct assessment measures both developmental and academic (i.e., Letters/Numbers, Language/Comprehension, and Visual/Spatial Discrimination) domains through the measurement of 26 tasks, and the parent-teacher observation forms assess home and classroom Social/Emotional/Adaptive experiences of the child. Child level score reports are available in the form of summary profiles that reveal patterns of strengths and weaknesses across tasks, as well as an overall performance level rating.

The direct assessment is designed to be individually administered to children between 2 years 6 months to 9 years of age. Users of the GDO-R are required to complete a 3-day workshop on the assessment system that covers developmental theory, an overview of the GDO-R, and administration and scoring instructions. Administration is said to take approximately 20–45 minutes for trained examiners, and those with experience with the instrument can expect to complete the scoring profile form within 15–20 minutes. GDO-R materials include separate teacher and parent/guardian questionnaires, a child recording form, an examiner's manual, an examiner's script (i.e., standardized instructions for administration), manipulatives, and a technical report (available upon request) that describes the psychometric characteristics of the GDO-R.

DEVELOPMENT. Arnold Gesell's maturational-developmental theory served as the primary framework for development of the GDO-R. Gesell's early childhood theory outlines general stages of development, and provides the framework for reasonable growth expectations. Following Gesell's work, general developmental characteristics that are typical of children in the areas of motor behavior, language behavior, personal-social behavior, and learning behavior are described in the examiner's manual for 6-month periods that span the ages of 2 years 6 months to 9 years. These characteristics provide foundation for the test blueprint that guided the GDO-R item development.

TECHNICAL.

Standardization. The GDO-R was administered to a sample of 1,287 children (55% from public schools) between 3 and 6 years of age by 101 examiners within 53 schools (38% public) that were located within 23 different states across the U.S. Although the GDO-R is advertised for use with children between 2 years 6 months through 9 years of age, the standardization sample did not include children between 7 and 9 years of age, or between 2 years 6 months to 3 years of age. The tested sample is described as being composed of typically developing children from schools that normally administer the GDO. Ethnic diversity was present in the total sample of tested children. However, some racial groups appear to be underrepresented across age groups. At the same time, there were approximately equal numbers of boys and girls across the included age bands. All examiners had either participated in the required 3-day workshop necessary to become trained in the administration and scoring of the GDO-R, or were presented with a training DVD within 5 years of testing.

The standardization sample was employed to provide users with various descriptive statistics across the GDO-R tasks and strands. Separate tables are provided for 6-month increments ranging from 3 to 6 years of age. Summary tabled descriptive statistics include the number of items in each task or strand, the number of tested children, maximum number of obtainable points, means and standard deviations, and estimates of internal consistency and difficulty values. No data are provided for children 2–2.5 years of age or 7–9 years of age.

Reliability. Several investigations into the reliability of scores are presented in the form of internal consistency measures at both task level and strand level. A review of the technical report reveals that there is wide variability in these estimates across both tasks and strands. In many instances, internal consistency estimates are within reasonable expectations (i.e., > .80). At the same time, a number of age-level strand and task estimates are well below expectations (i.e., < .50), which the test authors attribute to fewer numbers of items. Users should be mindful of how these errors of measurement might impact interpretation of these measures.

Interrater reliability evidence is presented using correlation coefficients between developmental ages assigned by the pairs of raters on a subsample (approximately 10%) of children for two tasks (i.e., Incomplete Man and Copy Forms). Results suggest high interrater agreement (coefficients of .92 and .91, respectively) between developmental ages assigned by two raters. No information on interrater reliability is provided for other tasks on the GDO-R. In addition, estimates of test-retest reliability are not provided.

Validity. It is widely recognized that validity refers to the accumulation of evidence to support the interpretation of test scores in the context of their purpose. The primary form of validity evidence provided for the GDO-R is in the form of content validity, which was appropriately based on review of child development theory and consultations with educational experts for determining contemporary educational goals, and knowledge and skills highlighted in early childhood curricula.

Overall, the intercorrelations between tasks of different strands is higher than within strand tasks. There are some moderate to high correlations (.30–.77), but many extremely low correlations are also found. For example, correlations between the Fine Motor task and all other tasks in its strand is less than .22 for all ages, with one exception (age 4 with Gross Motor, $r = .33$). Correlational estimates between tasks within strands are smaller

in general at younger ages. For example, at age 3, the correlation between Visual 1 and Color Forms is .01, and between Visual 1 and 3-Hole Form Board is .16. The test authors attribute this outcome "to the relatively larger measurement error that typically occurs in data from very young children" (technical report, p. 50). However, even at age 6, correlations between Comprehension and all other tasks of its strand are less than .22.

COMMENTARY. Development of the GDO-R appears to be based on a strong theoretical foundation that served as a blueprint for its development. Further, much work appears to have gone into establishing a system of scoring that would be useful to the end user. At the same time, several psychometric characteristics of the instrument are less than desirable or unknown from the information provided in the GDO-R's user's manual and technical manual. Beyond a strong basis to support the content validity of the instrument, there is little evidence provided to support the GDO-R's associations with external measures of current or future academic skills (i.e., concurrent and predictive validity), and no empirical evidence is provided to link the tasks with the strands that they purportedly measure. Users would benefit from factor analytic work to provide additional support for the construct validity of this instrument. For example, it is unclear why letter identification and writing are in the same strand with numbers but separated from language/comprehension. There are limited data for some age groups for which the GDO-R is intended (e.g., 3 years and 7–9 years of age). The need to complete a 3-day workshop prior to administering and interpreting the instrument may be considered a limitation to some users and may place the GDO-R at a disadvantage to other similar instruments that are more easily accessible to educators.

Given the technical and other limitations, this instrument at best may serve as supporting evidence for a child's development, and more psychometric evidence is needed to support its use as a sole source for use in high stakes decision making.

SUMMARY. The GDO-R is a multidimensional assessment tool that allows for the measurement of children's developmental, academic, and social-emotional-adaptive skills. It appears to be a carefully constructed, individually administered assessment tool that aligns with a respected theory of children's development. This revision incorporates some word changes to tasks, informant-based reports, and an optional technical report. It is designed to provide insight into strengths and weaknesses that may be useful for guiding future instruction, and to serve as a communication tool for teachers and parents. Users would benefit from additional psychometric studies that evaluate additional forms of reliability (e.g., test-retest) and validity (e.g., concurrent, predictive, dimensionality) to provide users with greater confidence that the scores resulting from use of this assessment with children are indeed related to their intended uses.

[76]

Gesell Early Screener.

Purpose: Designed as a brief developmental screening instrument to "identify children who may have a learning problem or condition that could affect his or her potential to learn."
Population: Ages 3-6.
Publication Dates: 2011-2012.
Acronym: GES.
Scores: 14 scores in 4 strands: Cognitive Strand (Cubes, Copy Forms, Prepositions, One-to-One Correspondence, Conservation, Identifying Numbers), Language Strand (Interview), Motor Strand (Tiptoe, Balance on One Foot, Hop on One Foot Forward, Skip, Catch, Throw), Social/Emotional/Adaptive.
Administration: Individual.
Price Data, 2013: $247.15 per English version complete kit including 30 child recording forms, 30 parent/guardian questionnaires, 30 teacher questionnaires, Copy Form cards, Numbers cards, 10 hardwood cubes, beanbag, tote bag, examiner's manual (2011, 78 pages); $252.30 per Spanish version complete kit; $36 per 30 child recording forms; $82.35 per examiner's manual; price data for technical report (2012, 104 pages) available from publisher.
Foreign Language Edition: Spanish edition includes Spanish instead of English parent/guardian questionnaires (all other materials are in English).
Time: (15-20) minutes.
Author: Gesell Institute of Child Development.
Publisher: Gesell Institute of Child Development.

Review of the Gesell Early Screener by JEAN N. CLARK, Associate Professor of Educational Psychology, University of South Alabama, Mobile, AL:

DESCRIPTION. The Gesell Early Screener (GES) is individually administered to children ages 3–6, for the purpose of screening for signs of potential difficulties in learning. Using eight measures from the longer and more comprehensive Gesell Developmental Observation–Revised (GDO-R; 19:75), the screening tool is composed of tasks and interview items administered in about 15 minutes, along with Teacher and Parent/Guardian Questionnaires. The assessment has eight tasks, which are subsumed into four categories or "strands": Cognitive, Language, Motor, and Social/Emotional/Adaptive.

There is a recording form that includes examiner observation of reported ethnicity, weight, distinguishing physical features, and expressive language indicators including speech patterns, native language, and English fluency. This section is followed by an interview protocol used to assess language abilities, with two questions asking the child about self, and three questions about home. Subsequent sections contain tasks in the four strands: Cognitive tasks include building with cubes, copying forms, demonstrating prepositions, one-to-one correspondence in counting pennies, and number identification; Language assessment includes observations of speech patterns and fluency during the five-item interview; Gross Motor assessment includes walking on tiptoe, standing on one foot, hopping, skipping, and throwing/catching a beanbag; and Fine Motor development is assessed by a categorical observation checklist including handedness and pencil grasp.

The 45-item teacher rating scale consists of a 5-point Likert-type scale, plus one open-ended probe; sections include Social/Emotional Development, Classroom Activities, and Self-Expression, Adaptive Abilities. An 80-item parent/guardian checklist elicits information about Family Background, Medical/Educational History, Home Environment, Adaptive and Academic Skills, and Social/Emotional Development. There is a summary profile for recording observation and feedback data, where scores are translated into Performance Level Rating categories of Age Appropriate, Emerging, or Concern.

DEVELOPMENT. The parent instrument of the GES is the Gesell Developmental Observation (GDO), with technical data dating back to 1979. This instrument was most recently revised based on data collected from 2008–2010, and the revised instrument (GDO-R; 19:75) was published in 2011 and is also reviewed in this *Yearbook*. The data were collected by teachers in public (55%) and private (45%) schools, who had a mean of 12 years of teaching experience and a mean of 7 years experience in using the GDO. In addition, there was a required refresher training with intensity and length based on recency of prior training. Based on the perceived need of a short screening tool to meet federal mandates of Headstart, No Child Left Behind (NCLB), and the Individuals with Disabilities Education Act (IDEA, 1990, 1997), six performance tasks and an interview from the original GDO were modified to fit the screening time of 20 minutes. Questionnaires for teacher (TQ) and parent/guardian (PQ) were added to both the GDO-R and the GES. Both questionnaires elicit feedback in rating social, emotional, and adaptive levels. The PQ elicits demographic and personal history, and the TQ provides observation of language development. One item ("seems shy") was eliminated from the original TQ because there was no clear determination of whether this was a positive or negative attribute. Standing Long Jump and Jump in Place tasks were eliminated because of measurement and validity issues. Six performance tasks from the GDO were retained in the GSE. In summary, the GES includes four domains or strands: Cognitive, Language, Motor, and Emotional/Social/Adaptive. The cognitive domain is assessed by six performance tasks (building with cubes, copying forms, demonstrating prepositions, identifying numbers, one-to-one correspondence, and conservation using pennies); gross motor level is assessed by six activities (walking on tiptoe, standing on one foot, hopping on one foot, skipping, beanbag throw, and beanbag catch); Emotional/Social/Adaptive level is assessed in the TQ and PQ, and Language is assessed by recording observations during a 5-item interview. Based on scoring rubrics and developmental definitions from experts, outcomes are reported by Performance Level Ratings in each strand. Development of cut scores for the performance categories of Age Appropriate, Emerging, Concern, or blended (e.g., Emerging/Concern), consisted of GDO data, expert opinion, and current developmental theory literature.

TECHNICAL. The age range of the standardization sample was 2 years 9 months to 6 years 3 months, given that the instrument is used to assess children ages 3–6. Using the same sample of 1,287 children from the GDO study, the current instrument (GES) was developed. The sample included participants in 23 states, and encompassed all regions of the contiguous United States. Eligibility for free or reduced lunch (28.2%) was used as a proxy for low socioeconomic status (SES). The ethnicity of the total sample approximated the U.S. Census: 14.8% African American, 60.7% Caucasian, 15.3% Hispanic, 4.5% Asian American, 2.9% American Indian, and 1.8% other. Data were

analyzed in 6-month age bands (e.g., age "3" = 2 years, 9 months to 3 years, 2 months, 29 days). The test authors purport that content validity evidence for the instrument was established by reviewing child development theory, and that the test authors "met with education experts" (Technical Report, p. 18). However, no record of the process was described. To assess reliability, a subsample of 10 children per age strand from the GDO sample were examined, and Pearson product moment correlations were used for two raters in assessing six tasks in the Cognitive strand of the GES. One rater was a graduate intern at the Gesell Institute who "independently scored selected GES items from the original GDO Child Recording Form completed by the GDO examiner" (Technical Report, p. 78). Coefficients ranged from .89 (one-to-one correspondence using pennies) to 1.00 (copying circles, using the prepositions "on," "under," and "beside," and number identification). These coefficients are reported on the total set of sample scores (n = 60), but are not broken down by age strands. Using alpha coefficients, the internal consistency of four tasks in the Cognitive strand were estimated and ranged from .39 to .71 with p-values (item difficulty) ranging from .25 to .42. Finally, for the Cognitive strand, descriptive data were used to report what percent of children in each age band were assessed at each performance (Age Appropriate = 50–55% over the 7 age bands; Emerging = 24.3–29.6%; Concern = 15.7–23.1%). The cutoff scores for these performance levels were set independently by two researchers and then reviewed by the team. No statistical analyses of these ratings, or their review process, were presented. No analyses of the PQ or the TQ were presented.

COMMENTARY. The examiner's manual has clear and concise training tips and literature review, a sample letter to notify parents/guardians about the assessment, and careful summaries of the components of the assessment kit. One potential concern is that the manual directs administrators to record children's interview responses verbatim, to record patterns of fluency, sentence construction, grammatical errors, and other language indicators; however, the manual also states that many children may speak too quickly for such literal transposition and there is no alternative (such as audio recording) suggested. Although the manual describes the importance of the Teacher Questionnaire (TQ) in assessing language development, there were no reported analyses, such as interrater reliability, to demonstrate strength of the tool in the assessment paradigm. Likewise, the Parent/Guardian Questionnaire (PQ) provides demographic information that is critical in conducting instrument validation analyses; however, many parents/guardians did not complete the form. In balance, the absence of many PQs was explained and addressed, with focus on student well-being over data collection. However, because both of these instruments were added to the GDO-R and the GES as new components, some type of analysis or feedback would be important in considering its generalizability, use, and application. A second general area of concern is that, although there are several descriptive sets of data related to facets of the GDO, analyses of the screening instrument at hand consisted of the three data sets described earlier. Additionally, the interrater reliability described one rater who scored items completed by another rater, rather than two raters actually completing same-sample observations. Thus, the reliability assessment was not based on two independent observations, but on two people independently scoring one set of observations. A final concern relates to the sample diversity. Although the overall sample ethnicity distribution paralleled that of the U.S. Census, this approximation did not hold with all age bands. Thus, the application may be less generalizable and those assessing some minority groups are advised to consult the Technical Report to see if certain children are fairly represented.

SUMMARY. As a screening tool, administration of the GES is quick and easy, requiring no special training for completion. Scoring and interpretation guidelines are available in the examiner's manual, to be used by persons with varying degrees of expertise. The instrument meets early childhood assessment standards for both the Individuals with Disabilities Education Act (IDEA, 1990, 1997) and Head Start. Used as intended, the instrument gleans enough information about the comparative developmental level of the child to substantiate the performance level indicators (Age Appropriate, Emerging, Concern). As the examiner's manual points out, the more extended version (GDO-R) is an alternative for cases in which there are areas of concern or questions that merit closer evaluation.

Review of the Gesell Early Screener by JO-SEPH C. KUSH, Associate Professor and Director of the Doctoral Program in Instructional Technology and Educational Leadership, Duquesne University, Pittsburgh, PA:

DESCRIPTION. Arnold Gesell, Ph.D., M.D. studied child development throughout his career. He helped establish the clinic now known as the Yale Child Study Center as well as the Gesell Institute of Child Development, and he developed the Gesell Schedules and the Gesell Developmental Observation (GDO). Originally published in 1925, the GDO has been widely used to assess infant and child development, and was updated in 1940, 1965, and 1979. The most recent update occurred in 2011 with the publication of the Gesell Developmental Observation–Revised (GDO-R; 19:75), an instrument suitable for children between the ages of 2.5 and 9 years. Using questions from the GDO-R, and adding Parent/Guardian and Teacher Questionnaires, the Gesell Early Screener (GES) was created as a screening device, designed to assess quickly the developmental levels of children between 3 and 6 years of age. The instrument evaluates four domains of a child's development: Cognitive, Language, Motor, and Social/Emotional/Adaptive Skills. The measure can be administered by professionals and paraprofessionals and consists of an examiner's manual, a Child Recording Form (CRF-S) that includes a standardized script and Summary Profile form, a set of manipulative objects, Teacher and Parent/Guardian Questionnaires, and an autocalculating version of the GES Scoring Worksheet. As a brief screening device, the GES can be completed in approximately 15 minutes with an additional 5 minutes to complete the Summary Profile Form.

The Gesell Early Screener (GES) complete kit includes all the necessary materials for administering the GES to children ages 3 to 6. An alternative Spanish version contains a Spanish-language Parent/Guardian Questionnaire.

DEVELOPMENT. The GES serves as a screening device designed to quickly measure the developmental level of a child and identify children who are at risk for developmental delays. The GES was published in 2011 and uses selected developmental tasks derived from the GDO-R. The GDO-R is a more detailed instrument that also evaluates child development and is used to determine a Developmental Age and assist with the development of classroom curricula.

The GES was developed by selecting specific tasks from the GDO-R with the goal of identifying a child's three-level Performance Level Rating (Age Appropriate, Emerging, or Concern) in each of the four domains (Cognitive, Language, Motor, and Social/Emotional/Adaptive) in 15 minutes or less. Tasks were selected such that the GES would be easy to administer, objective to score, reliable and valid when administered by individuals with varying levels of experience and ability, and meet all federal mandates for screening young children.

The GES is used to quickly record direct observations of behaviors in four domains of development, and scores are compared with rubrics of expected performance levels of typically developing age-matched peers. Identified children may then be referred for more in-depth psychoeducational evaluations.

The Gesell Early Screener measures cognitive capacities such as short-term memory, numeracy, planning, and organization of thoughts; language abilities such as expressing thoughts and needs, understanding conversational exchanges, and understanding the use of words in their appropriate context; motor planning for small and large muscle groups including gait, balance, and coordination; and social, emotional, and adaptive functioning with adults and peers, as reported by parents and teachers. Qualitative rubrics are provided for each of the four strands and allow the examiner to choose one of three summary conclusions for each strand: Age Appropriate, Emerging, or Concern.

The four GES strands include: The Cognitive strand measures visual-motor perception and coordination, and short-term visual memory. It also assesses a child's exposure to and proficiency with numbers via one-to-one correspondence. The Language/Comprehension strand evaluates a child's attention span, articulation, and expressive and receptive language. The Motor strand evaluates a child's fine and gross motor skills. The Social/Emotional/Adaptive strands (Teacher and Parent/Guardian Questionnaires) provide information to evaluate the quality of a child's interactions with peers and adults, emotional regulation behaviors, and self-help skills both at home and at school.

The complete GES kit includes six components: (a) The GES Child Recording Form (CRF-S) contains the information necessary for the examiner to record the child's responses to all screening tasks. (b) The GES Summary Profile Form provides a summary of a child's scores and is designed to facilitate communication between parents and teachers. (c) The GES Strand Scoring Worksheet (GES-SSW) assists with strand or summary scoring. (d) The Teacher Questionnaire (TQ) allows the teacher to record social,

emotional, and adaptive behavior observed in the classroom. (e) The Parent/Guardian Questionnaire (PQ) is similar to the TQ and records parent descriptions of early health history, and social, emotional, and adaptive behaviors that are exhibited in the home. (f) The GES examiner's manual contains information about the rationale, purpose, and development of the GES and provides specific information about the administration, scoring, and interpretation of all GES tasks. GES manipulative materials include 10 one-inch red cubes, a beanbag, a small jar with pellets, task cards, and a number card.

A number of specific tasks are measured by the GES. The set of tasks comprising Cubes provides information about horizontal and visual perception, fine motor coordination, attention span, premathematical skills, short-term and visual memory, and spatial judgment. The Interview questions assess a child's speech and language skills, as well as the ability to recall everyday experiences. Responses provide an overview of the child's cognitive organizational skills, ability to stay on task, and ability to follow directions. The set of tasks comprising Copy Forms examines a child's competence in integrating visual information with motor abilities, visual tracking skills, and discrimination abilities. Specifically assessed skills include handwriting, reading comprehension, and ability to recognize and recall letters and numbers. The Prepositions task assesses the child's understanding of spatial position of an object and his or her ability to apply that knowledge to a corresponding object. The Identifying Numbers task requires the child to identify random numerals 1–12 by name. The Numeracy task consists of two measures: One-to-One Correspondence and Conservation. The child is asked to count a set of four items, using one-to-one correspondence, and then to tell how many there are in the set altogether. Fine and Gross Motor Skills are observed through the Cubes and Copy Forms task as well as pencil grasp (Fine Motor) and by items related to large motor skills, such as balance, gait, and coordination as the child walks on tiptoe; balances on one foot, hops, skips, throws, and catches (Gross Motor). Social Behavior, Emotional Development, and Adaptive Skills assess a child's interactions with peers and adults, ability to self-regulate, and self-help skills.

TECHNICAL. Norms for the GDO-R were developed as part of a nationwide study in 2008–2010 that collected technical data for children 3–6 years of age on all 20 GDO-R tasks, as well as Overt Behavior and Social/Emotional/Adaptive measures. Data were collected from 53 schools across 23 states and included a total of 1,287 children between the ages of 3 and 6 years. Attempts were made to include children representative of diverse ethnic, geographic, and SES backgrounds. Data were collected by 101 trained examiners with a mean of 12 years of teaching experience. Public schools provided 55% of the normative data with the remaining 45% coming from private schools.

With regard to reliability, the GES technical manual provides correlation coefficients for each of the tasks within a strand as well as the correlation of tasks between strands. As would be expected for diverse cognitive tasks given to young children, the correlations are relatively low, yet still adequate for a scale of this type. For example, for the young 3-year-old group, the fine-motor task of stacking cubes shows a modest correlation (.37) with the verbal Prepositions task that assesses language comprehension. Correlation coefficients between the individual tasks and the corresponding strand totals are, as expected, much higher, and again quite adequate. Additionally, interrater reliability coefficients are reported, evidencing extremely high values; however, the number of cases reported in the technical manual was very small and the results should be seen as preliminary. The complete GDO-R Technical Report and the complete GES Technical Report are both available online on the publisher's website (http://www.gesellinstitute.org/technical-reports).

COMMENTARY. The GES is a well-crafted instrument, designed to assist in the screening and early identification of developmental delays. Because its sole purpose is that of a screening instrument, it cannot be used for diagnostic purposes, a characteristic clearly pointed out in the examiner's manual.

The GES examiner's manual includes a well-written section describing the methods for administering and scoring the instrument as well as information on preparing for the administration of the instrument including suggestions for establishing rapport with the child, and preparing to interview the parents and teachers and complete the corresponding questionnaires. Additional training is also available from the publisher.

As with any criterion-referenced measure of early childhood development, the content may or may not match the behaviors deemed important by the school or agency, and a careful examination of the four strands should be undertaken before administration. There may be instances where an "in-house" compilation of desired behaviors is deemed a better alternative, for example, in a case where a school district is attempting to identify young children for early admission to a kindergarten program. In this instance the district could identify specific behaviors deemed necessary for their unique curriculum (e.g., can the child use scissors, is the child fully toilet-trained, does the child know all his or her primary colors, can the child count to 35?), and could subsequently develop a cutscore; for example, the child could be admitted early if they demonstrated 20 of the 25 identified behaviors.

Program placement, however, is not one of the intended uses of the GES and should not be seen as a limitation. Rather, as stated in the technical manual, "The GES is designed to be used with large numbers of children to identify any child who may benefit from further in-depth evaluation. It provides an estimate of a child's performance in four domains, but does not provide a developmental age or inform instruction" (p. 69).

The GES examiner's manual explicitly states that the instrument (as well as all screening instruments) is not a readiness test or an IQ test and should not be used to diagnose or label a child. Additionally, the test manual states that the GES should never be used as the sole determinant of a child's placement in school, and that multiple assessments, including parent observations, teacher observations, medical history, and a portfolio of a child's work should always be utilized. Similarly, and as indicated in the examiner's manual, the GES must be combined with other sources of psychoeducational assessment data when making diagnostic decisions. However, Developmental Ratings of "Concern" on any of the strands of the GES may signal an area to monitor for periodic rescreening or for referral for specialized evaluation.

SUMMARY. The four domains/strands assessed by the GES have great intuitive appeal (face validity), and the individual tasks provide raw scores and summary statistics across 6-month intervals for each of the 3 years covered by the scale. Again, because of the screening nature of the instrument, no developmental ages are provided. However, users can compare individual scores to the average scores reported in the technical manual and also can easily determine the three-level summary conclusion:

Age Appropriate, Emerging, or Concern. When these data are combined with additional information provided by the child's teacher and parents, the GES provides a solid alternative to the more detailed, but time-intensive Gesell Developmental Observation–Revised (GDO-R; 19:75).

[77]

Green's Emotional Perception Test.

Purpose: Designed to measure "the ability to judge emotion expressed in another person's tone of voice."
Population: Ages 6 to 90.
Publication Dates: 1986-2008.
Acronym: EPT.
Scores: Total score only.
Administration: Individual.
Price Data, 2010: $200 per 20 test uses and manual (2008, 44 pages); $4 per individual use.
Foreign Language & Other Special Editions: Nonsense version available for non-English speakers.
Time: (6) minutes.
Comments: Test is administered using Microsoft Windows.
Authors: Paul Green, Lloyd Flaro, and Roger Gervais.
Publisher: Green's Publishing Inc. [Canada].

Review of the Green's Emotional Perception Test by GEORGE ENGELHARD, JR., Professor of Educational Measurement and Policy, and AMINAH PERKINS, PhD candidate, Educational Studies, Emory University, Atlanta, GA:

DESCRIPTION. Green's Emotional Perception Test (EPT) is designed to provide a measure of a person's ability to judge emotions from tone of voice. The EPT is a computer-administered assessment. It uses the recorded voice of a professional actress reading several sentences in different ways in order to convey various emotions that are then identified by the test-taker. The specific five emotions included in the EPT (ordered from hard to easy to detect emotion) are (1) Happy, (2) Angry, (3) Frightened, (4) Neutral, and (5) Sad. The test-taker listens to 45 items (a combination of three sentences read to reflect the five different emotions). Test-takers must identify the correct emotion based on listening to the voice of the actress. The test score is based on a count of the total errors made by the test-taker in identifying the emotional tone represented by the 45 items. The computerized version of the EPT takes approximately 6 minutes to administer. A target population for this assessment is not specified in the user's manual. Rather, the test appears to be intended for use with "general"

audiences and several potential applications are suggested. Directions for opening and using the EPT program are provided in the test manual along with directions for administering the assessment.

DEVELOPMENT. Early versions of the EPT were used to determine whether or not abnormal differences existed between left ear, right ear, and binaural scores on immediate story recall for healthy adults and psychiatric inpatients in clinical settings. Differences in emotional perception were noticed in these early studies, which prompted the recommended use of the EPT for the measurement of emotional perception. Pilot testing of the EPT was conducted with a sample that included 41 nonpsychiatric patient volunteers who worked in a psychiatric hospital and 34 psychiatric inpatients.

TECHNICAL. Evidence in support of the reliability of EPT scores is based on the correlations between scores obtained from 3 item subsets (based on 15 item subsets). These correlation coefficients range from .80 to .84, and provide support for the internal consistency of the EPT scores. The test authors do not report other traditional indices of score reliability, such as coefficient alpha and test-retest reliability coefficients. Descriptive statistics such as items p-values and item discrimination are not provided. The test manual includes short descriptions of several studies in support of the technical adequacy and use of EPT scores. The test authors suggest several uses for scores obtained on the EPT including career counseling, selection of candidates for employment, and use as evidence in court testimonies. Limited information is provided regarding the validity of test scores on the EPT for these recommended uses.

COMMENTARY. The concept of affective prosody or the ability to perceive emotions based on tone of voice is very complex (Kiss & Ennis, 2001). The EPT is designed to measure these complex emotional perceptions, and it has the potential to provide useful scores within clinical contexts. Unfortunately, there currently is insufficient validity evidence provided in the user's manual to support the proposed uses of the EPT scores. The current work lacks a clear statement of the underlying theory used to guide the development of the EPT.

One of the weaknesses of the EPT is the use of error counts as scores. The items used to measure emotional perception vary in difficulty, and therefore, a score made on the basis of simple counts does not have a clear interpretation. For example, 10 errors on a set of easy items does not imply the same ability to judge emotions as 10 errors on a set of hard items. A second weakness regarding score interpretation is that the assessment is timed, and if a test-taker does not answer the items promptly, then the computer proceeds to the next item resulting in an error score. Speededness in a 6-minute test may confound the meaning of the EPT scores. A third potential weakness is that no information is provided regarding the meaning of EPT scores for individuals from various social and cultural backgrounds. No evidence is reported regarding differential item functioning across subgroups of test-takers. A final complicating factor in interpreting the EPT scores is the frequent use of the Word Memory Test (WMT; Green, 2003) to measure "effort." According to the test authors, "the test scores shown are those remaining after those failing effort testing have been dropped from the analysis" (user's manual, p. 16). Additional information is needed in order to understand how the measurement of effort mediates the interpretation and use of scores on the EPT.

SUMMARY. Caution should be exercised in using the EPT to measure emotional perceptions. Insufficient information is provided in the user's manual to support the reliability and validity of the scores from the EPT for the recommended uses. In the user's manual (2008), the test authors conclude that the "EPT seems to be a reliable and valid measure of judgment of emotion expressed in tone of voice" (p. 39). Our review of the EPT indicates that additional research is needed to support this conclusion.

REVIEWERS' REFERENCES

Green, P. (2003). *Manual for the Word Memory Test for Windows*. Edmonton, Canada: Green's Publishing Inc.

Kiss, I., & Ennis, T. (2001). Age-related decline in perception of prosodic affect. *Applied Neuropsychology, 8*, 251-254.

Review of the Green's Emotional Perception Test by TRACEY WYATT, Academic Dean and Associate Professor of Psychology at York College, York, NE:

DESCRIPTION. Green's Emotional Perception Test (EPT) is an individually administered assessment of one's ability to perceive the emotional intonation of another. The test authors claim the assessment will measure the ability to judge emotion expressed in another person's tone of voice, a fundamental human ability underlying effective communication. The value of such an assessment would be to provide practitioners and employers with a tool to quantify a test-taker's judgment of emotional cues potentially crucial to employment situations or social settings. Earlier research suggests

impaired perception may be the result of damage, as detected through an MRI, to the right temporal/parietal lobe as exhibited by brain lesions.

The EPT is a simple, convenient, and fully automated, computer-based assessment using point and click instructions. The EPT was developed for people ages 6 to 90 years of age. It contains a series of three sentences in the form of questions, each tied to a set of five separate emotional cues: Happy, Angry, Frightened, Neutral, and Sad. Respondents listen through computer speakers or headphones to each of the 15 questions and score their response. The EPT takes approximately 6 minutes to complete. The scoring is automatic.

DEVELOPMENT. Originally piloted in 1986 as a means to assess the emotional perception of psychiatric patients, the test authors conducted a pilot study selecting 41 healthy volunteers, mostly staff from Alberta Psychiatric Hospital Edmonton and 34 psychiatric patients of mixed diagnoses, primarily depression, schizophrenia, or schizoaffective disorder, to determine if their psychiatric impairment impacted their ability to judge emotional intonation in communication. The EPT builds upon a body of clinical knowledge suggesting that right temporal/parietal lobe lesions are associated with impaired perception of emotion in tone of voice. The test authors developed the EPT as a clinical means to assess this condition. The study suggested that emotional perception impairment is a correlate of certain psychiatric disorders. Later research suggests that the EPT is a valid assessment for persons who have experienced traumatic brain injury (TBI).

TECHNICAL. In the original study group, errors of perception were found to be significant between the 41 hospital staff members and the 34 psychiatric patients. The differences averaged 11.1 errors in perception (SD = 4.8) for healthy adults and 19.5 errors (SD = 8.5) for the psychiatric patients. Significant differences were not found to exist within each group when tested for three listening conditions, left ear, right ear, and binaural. Both groups demonstrated internal consistency on the EPT despite listening conditions. Using the original study group, the test authors divided the 45 questions into 3 subsets of 15 and reported internal reliability coefficients of r = .80, r = .80, and r = .84 between the first, second, and third set of scores, respectively, and the overall total score. The test authors report that the scores on the first 30 items correlate at r = .60 with scores on the last 15 items.

Since the development of the EPT in 1986, additional studies have been conducted to expand understanding of scoring and interpreting the results relative to the variables of age, gender, and intelligence level. The EPT has no static norm group, and no single cutoff score can be applied to all people due to significant differences in the aforementioned variables. Central to a proper administration of the EPT is connecting the results with the appropriate norm group. The test authors report that a significant confounding variable to the outcome of the assessment was the amount of effort or "weakness of effort" on the part of the test-taker. Unless controlled in the norm group, there is a misleading sense of impairment to assess emotional perception. The test authors report that in all normative groups, effort testing was conducted to control "weakness of effort," thus retaining only the variables of age, gender, and intelligence level. The authors provide a detailed examination of these variables. Age was found to be the most significant variable subject to impact the scoring. In assessing a sample of 98 school-age children, the test authors report estimates of reliability for the 3-sentence combination using the test-retest method of assessing reliability of $r = .78$ ($n = 34$, ages 6–8, mean 6.9), ($n = 32$, ages 9–11, mean 10), ($n = 32$, ages 13–15, mean 14). In groups, across all age ranges, in one administration, women who passed effort testing, there was a significant difference among age groups ($F = 3.2$; df 5, 343; $p = .007$, $n = 349$). Gender, as a variable affecting emotional perception, was likewise found to be significantly different between men and women. Women scored fewer errors than men and girls less than boys. The test authors report a high, positive effect of gender on performance outcome for test-takers ($F = 28$; df 1, 846; $p < .0001$; $n = 848$). In consideration of gender and age, there were gender differences in healthy children aged 6–15. The gender differences begin to manifest at about the age of puberty and accelerate thereafter. Girls begin to outpace boys in the recognition of voice intonation despite homogeneity of group in the variable of IQ and age. People with severe mental or psychiatric impairment experience a greater negative impact on emotional perception–severe more than mild impairment ($F = 17$; df 1, 339; $p < .0001$).

COMMENTARY. Test scores from the EPT appear to offer a reliable and valid means by which to judge emotions for adults and children by groups of age, gender, and intelligence level. The measure works well with people who have suffered right hemispheric insult to the brain and who may be entering into social or employment settings where the accurate perception of emotion is crucial to success. However, the necessity of matching the score of the test-taker with the appropriate norm reference group should give pause relative to the administration of the assessment outside of the hands of a trained professional. For example, employers using this test could inadvertently deny employment to an otherwise qualified individual based on an assumed impairment.

SUMMARY. As we age, our ability to perceive emotions in others declines. Although perception of emotion changes over time for both males and females, males decline at a faster rate than females regardless of control for intelligence and overall mental health stability. In scoring the EPT, individuals must be matched with a similar norm group for age, gender, and intelligence level–otherwise the results will be invalid. Although the test authors suggest EPT use in employment settings where accurate emotional perception is crucial to job performance, it would be important for any administration and scoring to be supervised by a qualified professional to ensure proper interpretation in view of the necessity of matching test-taker with appropriate norm group.

[78]

Green's Medical Symptom Validity Test.

Purpose: Designed as a computerized "verbal memory screening test with built-in effort testing."
Population: Ages 6 to 68.
Publication Dates: 2003-2004.
Acronym: MSVT.
Scores, 5: Primary Effort (Immediate Recognition, Delayed Recognition, Consistency), Memory (Paired Associates, Free Recall).
Administration: Individual.
Price Data, 2013: $340 per manual (2004, 102 pages), program on CD for use with Microsoft Windows, and 30 test uses; $6 per individual use.
Foreign Language Editions: Available in Danish, Dutch, French, German, Norwegian, Portuguese, Spanish, and Swedish.
Time: [5-15] minutes.
Author: Paul Green.
Publisher: Green's Publishing Inc. [Canada].

Review of Green's Medical Symptom Validity Test by MARK A. ALBANESE, Professor Emeritus of Population Health Sciences, University of Wisconsin School of Medicine and Public Health, Madison, WI:

DESCRIPTION. Green's Medical Symptom Validity Test (MSVT) is a brief computerized verbal memory-screening test that assesses the examinee's memory as well as whether the effort put into taking the memory test was sufficient for the resulting scores to be valid. Effort is especially important to assess in memory testing when incentives exist for the examinee to show impaired memory (e.g., an accident victim suing for memory loss resulting from head injury). The MSVT is proprietary, and the test author argues forcefully that divulging either the nature of the test or the theory underlying it will invalidate its use. Because of this constraint, the description of the instrument is vague. What can be understood from the description is that the operational part of the memory test contains a series of 10 paired words shown at the rate of one word pair every six seconds. Each pair of words together represents a common object (e.g., French-fries, ballpoint-pen), and all words are no higher than the third grade reading level. The set of 10 word pairs is repeated, after which three subtests assessing examinee effort are administered.

The Immediate Recognition (IR) subtest requires the examinee to choose the target word from the original list in each of 20 new word pairs (e.g., choose ballpoint from the word pair ballpoint-iron). After 10 minutes of distracter activities, the Delayed Recognition (DR) subtest begins. This subtest is basically an alternate form of the IR subtest in which different incorrect words are used (e.g., ballpoint-ballpark). Besides separate scores from the IR and DR subtests, differences in the responses to the two subtests are used to create what is described as a Consistency score (CNS). Following completion of the DR subtest, the examinee is asked to sit away from the computer so he or she cannot see the screen. The test administrator then administers two measures of memory ability. The first is the Paired Associates (PA) test in which the first word from each word pair is given by the test administrator and the examinee is asked to provide the second word. The second measure is Free Recall (FR) in which the examinee is asked to recall as many words as possible from the list.

The test manual also describes a "stealth version of the MSVT" (manual, p. 11), which looks and feels just like the actual MSVT, but is much more difficult. The stealth version is a sham exam included as one of various defenses built into the program to frustrate attempts to "game" the MSVT. The effort exams are computer-administered with the test administrator simply making certain that all is going well before leaving the room. Scores are expressed as percentage correct. A minimum criterion for the three effort scores is set at >85% based upon more than 10 studies in which this performance level was shown to be easily reached by children and adults except for the most cognitively impaired individuals. If any one or more of the three effort scores is 85% or less, insufficient effort is concluded.

DEVELOPMENT. The development of the MSVT is not directly described in the test manual. The test author makes a substantial point that effort testing has much in common with other forms of assessment that are proprietary and that the underlying conceptual development of the instrument provides information that could compromise the validity of the instrument. The MSVT is a direct descendant of the Word Memory Test (WMT; T8:1178) developed by the test author in 1994–5. From comparison tables included in the test manual, the WMT uses the same five scores as the MSVT. The difference between the MSVT and the WMT is that the MSVT is half as long with only 10 word pairs as compared to 20 pairs in the WMT. The MSVT word pairs are also less complex, differing along a single dimension, whereas the WMT words vary along two dimensions. Empirical data from dual use show the five MSVT scores tend to be higher than those obtained from the WMT.

The basic conceptual progression in the four MSVT subtests is: 1. stimulated immediate recognition, 2. stimulated delayed recognition, 3. stimulated recall, and 4. free recall. These tasks sequentially place greater demands on memory, so one would expect the scores to progressively decline. The Consistency score is based on the number of answers in agreement (right or wrong) on the IR and DR scales. One would generally expect the Consistency score to be equivalent to or lower than the IR and DR scores, so the expectation is for scores to be flat or to decline as one progresses in the sequence.

The passing standard of >85% for the effort tests' scores was based upon a large number of studies in which examinees of all types were found to exceed 85% with little difficulty. Interpreting scores on the PA and FR tests is more complicated, and users are advised to select results from various patient populations in their database for making an interpretation. Reports can be requested from the database by users. Passing scores of 80% for the PA and 50% for the FR are implied.

TECHNICAL.

Scoring. Computer administration of the MSVT provides automatic scoring and reporting of results. Scoring the MSVT involves recording whether the examinee 1. chose the correct option in the recognition subtests, 2. recalled correctly the word paired with the stimulus word in the PA subtest, 3. recalled correctly any of the 20 words on the original list in the FR subtest. The score is the percentage correct on the particular task. Effort test failure occurs if any IR, DR, or CNS score is 85% or below. The PA and FR scores require clinical determinations, and reports from various patient populations can be generated to assist in interpreting results.

Standardization. There is no single standardization sample, but there is a relatively large amount of data reported in the test manual. The populations included are quite variable with some being nonclinical adults and children whereas others have dementia, mental retardation, learning disabilities, and so on. Some data are provided from examinees who were instructed to simulate memory impairment. Because the use of the instrument is primarily clinical, users need to identify the types of examinee data in the database that will be appropriate for interpreting results from a given examinee.

Reliability. The closest data that might be considered reliability evidence comes from examinees who were administered both the MSVT and the WMT. Because the MSVT is primarily a shorter version of the WMT, the consistency of scores on the two instruments might be considered an estimate of alternate form reliability. Data from 248 adults found mean effort scores on the MSVT and the WMT yielded a correlation coefficient of .80. MSVT scores plotted against WMT scores showed a linear trend, but with compression from ceiling effects. Scores are much more variable below 85%. A study of 145 patients receiving a neuropsychological assessment found 81% agreement between the MSVT and WMT effort scores. This reviewer corrected the values for chance agreement, yielding a kappa coefficient of .55. Comparable data from another 256 patients found percentage agreement and kappa to be 81% and .58, respectively. Considering the complexity of the quality being assessed, these values reflect relatively good agreement.

Validity. Cross-validation data were reported using four types of groups: (a) examinees who were given the MSVT and one or more other effort or memory assessments (WMT, Amsterdam Short

Term Memory Test [ASTM; 17:6], Test of Memory Malingering [TOMM; 14:392], Computerized Assessment of Response Bias [CARB], Rey-15 item test, and California Verbal Learning Test [CVLT]); (b) various clinical and nonclinical populations (e.g., adult outpatients, children, children with diagnosable conditions [mental retardation, ADHD, fetal alcohol syndrome], dementia patients); (c) examinees who were instructed to simulate poor memory; and (d) examinees who were tested in a language unknown to them. The descriptions of the validation studies were at varying levels of detail, which makes it hard to judge the quality of the studies. Taking the studies at face value, the MSVT showed extremely good consistency with the WMT, TOMM, CARB, and ASTM. Examinees who failed the effort test on these instruments were very likely to fail the effort test on the MSVT. However, the MSVT failed more examinees. Of 24 cases that failed the TOMM, 22 also failed the MSVT, but 50 failed the MSVT. In a separate study involving 188 participants, 13% failed the TOMM and 27% failed the MSVT. In a third study involving 195 participants, 10.3% failed the TOMM compared to 24.6% who failed the MSVT. There was a consistent ratio of approximately 2 to 1 failures on the MSVT versus the TOMM over the three studies.

Relative to the expected patterns of performance from the various populations who took the MSVT, with few exceptions, performance on the effort section of the test exceeded the fail cut score (85%).

For individuals who were instructed to simulate memory loss, five studies in three different countries showed almost 100% sensitivity of the WMT to poor effort. The test author argues that because of the relationship of the WMT and MSVT, the results should generalize to the MSVT.

Three studies examined the impact of giving the MSVT in a language not spoken by the examinee. They all showed effort-test performance that met the passing standard, but low performance on the PA and FR scores.

COMMENTARY. Measuring a psychological process that a person is trying to fake is a very challenging task, particularly if the stakes are high. Many situations in which the MSVT would be used are high stakes, such as the determination of damage awards following a car accident. Thus, thwarting people from faking memory loss is an important task that the MSVT has been designed to achieve.

The MSVT has a number of strengths, chief of which is its derivation from the WMT, an effort and memory assessment that has a relatively long history of use and a fairly large base of studies supporting its validity. The fact that the MSVT is a derivative of the WMT, but seems to be an improvement in some respects, is also a strength. The sensitivity of the effort test of the MSVT appears to have been improved by making the content simpler than the effort test on the WMT. The computer version of the MSVT is preferable to the oral version, because it is more sensitive to poor effort. The MSVT is also a relatively short and simple examination. Although no specific time estimate is given in the test manual, one can estimate that it probably takes less than 20 minutes for most examinees. It also provides numerous databases so normative data can be tailored to the specific characteristics of the examinee. The computer version also produces different graphs that illustrate the examinee's performance profile relative to different groups and to the passing criterion. If one considers the association of scores between the MSVT and the WMT as alternate form reliability, the reliability coefficient is about .80. The argument and data provided make a strong case that the MSVT effort score is not confounded by the difficulty of the verbal content used in its assessment. Relationships to other instruments purporting to measure effort, such as the TOMM, show it is most likely more sensitive to poor effort.

However, the MSVT also has some weaknesses. The test manual is relatively painful to read. Acronyms are used throughout, some of which are never defined (e.g., TOMM, CARB, Rey-15). This omission makes interpreting the results difficult unless one is already familiar with these comparison instruments. Because the underlying theory and some elements of the computer administration are considered proprietary, one must trust that the theory is valid and that the components added to mask the intent of the exam do not add construct irrelevant variance to the scores. There is no direct attempt to address the reliability of the scores. None of the studies reported results from multiple attempts to take the test, and correlations between the five MSVT scores are not reported. Thus, it is unclear how stable MSVT scores are across multiple test administrations. It is likely that the correlations among the three effort scores are disconcertingly low because of ceiling effects; however, this possibility should be addressed in the test manual.

The greatest general weakness of the studies reported in the user's manual stems from the inconsistency with which they are reported. In some cases, many details are provided; in others, only a synopsis of results is provided with no mention of sample sizes or study populations. Some of the graphs and figures are mislabeled, which produces some confusion. The unevenness of the data presentation makes a critical assessment of the MSVT difficult and also leaves one wondering whether negative information is selectively omitted. The greatest clinical weakness is the lack of recommendations for how to use the MSVT in relation to the WMT, TOMM, and other instruments mentioned in the test manual. Guidance about when to use the stealth version of the MSVT would be a welcome addition. It also would be very helpful to clarify whether the MSVT is a new and improved version of the WMT, or a shorter, more focused version that still leaves the WMT as the "gold standard." It is clear in some of the cases that professionals use a battery of examinations, not just a single test, to assess memory deficits as well as effort being applied. Guidance about how the MSVT fits into the larger panoply of instruments and the conditions under which it and its stealth version should be used would be very helpful.

SUMMARY. Green's Medical Symptom Validity Test (MSVT) is a brief computerized verbal memory-screening test that assesses the examinee's memory as well as whether the effort put into taking the memory test was sufficient for scores to be considered valid. The MSVT is proprietary, and the test author argues forcefully that divulging either the nature of the test or its underlying theory will invalidate its use. Three scores combine to be an effort score with values less than or equal to 85% correct on any one constituting a failure. The memory test portion produces two scores based upon stimulated recall and free recall of 10 word pairs. A "stealth version of the MSVT" (manual, p. 11) exists and is similar to the MSVT, but is much more difficult. In essence, the stealth version serves as a sham exam to frustrate attempts to "game" the MSVT.

The MSVT is a direct descendent of the Word Memory Test (WMT) reporting the same five scores, but the MSVT is half as long and less complex. Users can select from various databases that which will be appropriate for a given examinee. No classical reliability estimates are reported, but mean effort scores on the MSVT and WMT correlate at about the .80 level, and percentage agreement in passing scores is approximately 80% (55–58% when corrected for chance).

Cross-validation studies showed reasonably good consistency with other measures of examinee effort, although the MSVT failed more examinees. A number of studies in which the MSVT was administered to a wide range of examinees–from children and adults with cognitive impairments to normal individuals who were intentionally trying to fake their results–suggest that the MSVT operated effectively in identifying poor effort. In general, the test author makes a strong argument for the validity of the MSVT.

The weaknesses of the MSVT include no direct estimate of the reliability of the scores; it is unclear how stable MSVT scores are based upon multiple administrations. The inconsistency with which the validity data are presented limits the ability to make a critical assessment of the MSVT. Recommendations for how to use the MSVT in relation to the stealth version and to other like instruments (WMT, TOMM, etc.) would be helpful.

Measuring a psychological process such as memory loss that a person may be trying to fake is a very challenging task, particularly if the stakes are high. The MSVT is a very carefully designed assessment of examinee effort embedded in a verbal memory test that has a good pedigree with substantial use in the field. It should be used by a credentialed examiner who can select companion tests to use as well as to determine which of the many databases are appropriate for performance comparisons.

[79]

Green's Non-Verbal Medical Symptom Validity Test.

Purpose: Designed as a "computerized nonverbal memory-screening test, which allows the person's effort on testing to be measured."
Population: Children and adults.
Publication Dates: 2006-2008.
Acronym: NV-MSVT.
Scores, 7: Primary Effort (Immediate Recognition, Delayed Recognition, Consistency, Delayed Recognition-Variations, Delayed Recognition-Archetypes), Memory (Paired Associates, Free Recall).
Administration: Individual.
Price Data, 2010: $300 per manual (2008, 116 pages), program on CD for use with Microsoft Windows, and 30 test uses; $6 per individual use.
Time: [5-15] minutes.

Author: Paul Green.
Publisher: Green's Publishing, Inc.

Review of the Green's Non-Verbal Medical Symptom Validity Test by MATTHEW E. LAMBERT, Texas Tech University Health Sciences Center, Department of Neuropsychiatry, Lubbock, TX:

DESCRIPTION. The Green's Non-Verbal Medical Symptom Validity Test (NV-MSVT) is a brief, nonverbal, computer-administered, memory test to assess effort in individuals being evaluated for medical or cognitive complaints. As well, the NV-MSVT assesses dementia or severe cognitive impairment in order to exclude their confounding effects on effort determination. No limitations are presented for usage based on age, gender, ethnicity, medical/psychological conditions, or patient/claimant types. As such, it appears the NV-MSVT is viewed as appropriate for use with all persons or groups in which effort should be assessed.

The NV-MSVT is installed on one computer by using either an installation CD or via internet download through the publisher's web address. The program allows unlimited NV-MSVT administrations during the first year of usage. From the second year forward, administrations are purchased in lots of 30. The remaining administrations number is presented in the computer screen's lower right hand corner. Computer system requirements are basic to all Windows 98 SE-based or later computers.

Test instructions are printed on a Quick Guide or Large-Print Testers Guide, which are found as appendices in the test manual. A "degraded foils sheet" is also required for presentation between the second and third subtests. Administration begins with general encouragement followed by the examiner reading the test instructions. Examiners must remain with the examinee for task orientation, to ensure accurate item naming during the first two trials, provide instructions and distraction between the second and third subtests, and administer the fourth and fifth subtests. Otherwise, the examinee self-administers the test using the computer mouse.

NV-MSVT administration consists of six trials. List Presentation involves presenting 10 image pairs for 4 seconds per pair with the examinee verbalizing each image's name. The pairs list is presented twice. Immediate Recognition follows with presentation of 10 new image pairs with one image having been seen previously. The examinee again verbalizes the image names then clicks the cursor on the previously seen image. The degraded foils sheet is subsequently presented for 60 seconds followed by 9 minutes of alternative, nonmemory activity. The Delayed Recognition trial then presents a previously learned image paired with a degraded image foil and the examinee again clicks the image previously seen. Following this step, the examinee sits to the side for the Paired Associates subtest, but within view of the computer screen. As an image is shown the examinee names the image originally paired with it as the examiner enters the response. Finally, for the Free Recall subtest the examinee is asked to recall all images seen during the List Presentation trial. Total time for NV-MSVT administration is about 15 to 20 minutes (including the 9-minute interval that precedes the Delayed Recognition trial).

Once test administration is completed, access to scores is through the program's "Reporting" menu. Four effort and two memory scores are calculated: Immediate Recognition (IR), Delayed Recognition (DR), Delayed Recognition-Variations (DRV), Delayed Recognition-Archetypes (DRA), Paired Associates (PA), and Free Recall (FR). In addition, consistency of responses between immediate and delayed recognition is used to form the Consistency Score (CNS). For each effort measure, the computer generates a categorical interpretation of "Pass," "Low," or "Very low"; with Low being below the fifth percentile of a comparison group and Very low being below any of the comparison group scores. The program also determines good effort "Pass" or "Fail" judgments based on a stepwise progression of decision rules.

DEVELOPMENT. The goal in developing the NV-MSVT was to create an effort test that was sensitive to both effort and severe cognitive impairment or dementia. This would allow for discrimination of individuals failing simple tests due to poor effort from those who fail because of dementia or severe cognitive impairment.

Although verbally based symptom validity tests have typically been more sensitive to effort than visual-spatial tests, this factor was not believed to preclude development of a visual-spatial test that could effectively assess effort. As such, characteristics of paired associate learning and multiple brief subtests with differing objective levels of difficulty were used to guide test development. Alternatives to typical target-foil discrimination were also developed to assess effort. Such strategies have been used in verbally based effort tests such as the Word Memory Test [WMT] (Green, 2003a) or Medical

Symptom Validity Test [MSVT] (Green, 2003b). As such, the NV-MSVT was developed to utilize colorful paired images instead of words.

There is no description in the test manual, however, of how specific images were selected, paired, or used as foils other than using Jungian psychology for the foils in the DRA subtest. Nor is there any information about the statistical relationships, difficulty level, or distractibility indices for the learned images or foils.

Data are presented to support the NV-MSVT's nonverbal nature as children demonstrated equivalent correlations between FR scores and verbal and performance IQs (i.e., .24 and .23, respectively). This relationship was also reported for a group of adults seeking compensation and giving good effort on a verbal symptom validity test and the NV-MSVT. As well, two temporal lobectomy patients with intact verbal memory demonstrated impaired NV-MSVT Free Recall scores. Difficulty levels for the various subtests were determined by administration to 15 children with Fetal Alcohol Spectrum Disorder (FASD) and low cognitive functioning. All but one child scored 90% correct or better on the easy NV-MSVT subtests. From this result, theoretical development of four criteria emanated to determine if a score profile indicated good effort, poor effort, or severe cognitive impairment.

Criterion A assesses whether the mean of the IR, DR, CNS, DRV, DRA, and PA scores is less than or equal to 90% correct; or if the mean of the DR, CNS, DRV, and DRA scores is less than or equal to 88% correct. Meeting Criterion A implies good effort is questionable. Criterion B1 assesses whether the PA score is not at least 11 points below the mean of the previous four scores. Meeting Criterion B1 is seen as the "Pinocchio principle" in which performance on a more difficult subtest is better than for the easy subtests. Criterion B2 determines if the mean of the IR, DR, and CNS scores is not at least 20 points higher than the mean of the PA and FR subtests; whereas Criterion B3 determines whether the standard deviation of IR, DR, CNS, DRA, and DRV is 12 or greater. The latter criteria are used to assess whether meeting Criterion A is due to the presence of poor effort or severe cognitive impairment. Passing the NV-MSVT implies good effort was given.

These criteria were applied to a larger group of children with FASD, children with multiple diagnoses referred for clinical assessment, end stage renal disease (ESRD) patients, and adult volunteers asked to give their best effort. All but two children with FASD passed the NV-MSVT and 94% of the child clinical group, 90% of the ESRD group, and all of the adult good effort group passed. All of a group of parents seeking returned custody of their children also passed the NV-MSVT. The last group was believed to have external motivation to give good effort. Several dementia groups were also reported to show a pattern of 80% to 90% correct across the easy subtests followed by decreased performance on the PA and FR subtests. A group of 39 simulators was then compared to the dementia patients with the simulators showing the Pinocchio profile characteristic of poor effort.

Unfortunately, information underlying NV-MSVT development is not well-organized in the test manual, which makes understanding its development difficult. This is particularly notable for the Consistency Index used in the "Pass-Fail" decision rules.

TECHNICAL. No focused standardization or reliability studies are presented in the manual. There are no studies presented that assess variations in NV-MSVT profiles based on sex, race, or cultural factors. Validity data appear to come from the test author and 16 researchers in four other countries who administered the NV-MSVT as part of clinical evaluations or other studies.

NV-MSVT profiles were compared to good effort individuals who had passed the Test of Memory Malingering [TOMM] (Tombaugh, 1996), WMT, and MSVT. As predicted, the IR through PA subtests were found to be very easy whereas the FR subtest was found to be difficult. Yet, NV-MSVT profiles were also examined for individuals who had passed the TOMM, or passed the TOMM and failed the WMT. Those examinations indicated a high number of TOMM good effort false positives, as numerous NV-MSVT and WMT performances showed poor effort profiles.

Additionally, mild traumatic brain-injured patients indicated greater effort failure profiles for the NV-MSVT and other symptom validity tests than moderate and severely injured patients. This finding occurred despite greater cognitive impairment being expected for the moderate and severely brain-injured groups. NV-MSVT and other symptom validity test failures were shown to have a negative relationship to California Verbal Learning Test performances and greater suppression of neuropsychological test performances. Suppression was most notable for memory tests.

Age and intellectual level also are not noted to be factors in NV-MSVT profiles after 8 years of age. Moreover, using the NV-MSVT, WMT, and MSVT allowed for nearly all cases of dementia or cognitive impairment being correctly discriminated from simulators of cognitive impairment. And in another study using the NV-MSVT alone, it was noted that only 1 of 61 simulator cases demonstrated a poor effort profile.

COMMENTARY. The NV-MSVT presents a novel nonverbal approach to understanding effort when evaluating individuals with medical or cognitive complaints. It adheres to its theoretical model and is consistent with the theoretical underpinnings of current symptom validity tests. Evidence also supports the use of test scores to determine "adequate" effort in medical and cognitive examinations. Little in the NV-MSVT can be used to characterize effort as anything other than poor or adequate. No current symptom validity tests allow effort to be measured on an ordinal scale.

Significant information is missing from the test manual, which is poorly organized and difficult to read. A complete description of the NV-MSVT's developmental process is not presented. As well, there is no indication of how scores change as a function of effort feedback or multiple testings. Although inconsistent with the theoretical basis, there is a need to present how NV-MSVT profiles are affected or not by gender, race, cultural background, and various legal statuses.

Practical issues also need to be addressed, including when the NV-MSVT should be administered in an evaluation battery. Will effort vary when the NV-MSVT is administered early or late in the battery? And, is there a need to use more than one symptom validity test to accurately assess effort? These issues need to be addressed in a well-organized and readable test manual as they comprise potential discovery questions in compensation evaluations or litigation.

SUMMARY. The NV-MSVT is an innovative and potentially valuable tool to assess effort in cognitive and medical assessments. At this point it appears to demonstrate good validity evidence, but there are still questions about its psychometric properties in relation to various examinee variables. Those questions are not addressed in the test manual, which is difficult to read and needs improvement. Addressing those issues will allow the NV-MSVT to have great utility in a wide array of psycholegal and medicolegal contexts.

REVIEWER'S REFERENCES

Green, P. (2003a). *Green's Word Memory Test for Windows: User's manual.* Edmonton, Canada: Green's Publishing.

Green, P. (2003b). *Medical Symptom Validity Test for Windows: User's manual.* Edmonton, Canada: Green's Publishing.

Tombaugh, T. N. (1996). Test of Memory Malingering. Toronto, Canada: Multi-Health Systems.

Review of Green's Non-Verbal Medical Symptom Validity Test by JANET S. REED, Board Certified in Clinical Neuropsychology, Division of Neuropsychology, Henry Ford Behavioral Health Services, Detroit, MI:

DESCRIPTION. The Non-Verbal Medical Symptom Validity Test (NV-MSVT) is a nonverbal test for use in clinical and forensic cognitive evaluation to assess test-taking bias, effort, and/or malingering of memory disorder for children and adults. The measure is a briefly administered (5 minutes plus about 10 minutes of nonmemory activity), computer-administered and scored instrument that yields several indices, normative data, a profile, and specific criteria for examining test-taking effort.

The NV-MSVT comprises six subtests. To set up the memory tasks, the patient is presented (4 seconds each) with 10 pairs of pictures on the monitor, each presented twice, and is instructed to name aloud each item. The first subtest (Immediate Recognition; IR) consists of pairs of items, one that was presented previously and one that was not ("foil image"). The examinee is instructed to name each item and select with the mouse the item that was included in the List Presentation task. The examinee is next presented (for 60 seconds) with a sheet of drawings that is degraded in quality ("degraded foil sheet"). The second subtest is administered after a 9-minute delay. Pairs of items are presented on the computer. The examinee is required to identify the item in the pair that was previously presented on the monitor (Delayed Recognition; DR). A consistency score (CNS) is computed by comparing IR and DR values. Within the DR subtest, there are two embedded tasks that comprise the third and fourth subtests using foils that are similar to the target in subtle ways (Delayed Recognition–Variations; DRV) and others that are images considered to be of high salience (Delayed Recognition–Archetypes; DRA). The fifth subtest consists of presentation of one item of the originally presented pair and requires the examinee to name the other item in the pair (Paired Associates; PA). On this subtest, the examiner controls the mouse, and subtle feedback regarding accuracy is provided via the examiner checking a check box or cross to indicate whether the response was correct or incorrect, respectively. The sixth subtest requires the examinee to name all items that were presented from the original list of 10 pairs (Free Recall; FR).

The test yields several indices, a graphical profile, and several algorithms for determining a pass or fail. Seven scores (IR, DR, CNS, DRA, DRV, PA, FR) are produced and can be compared to a number of simulation and diagnostic groups used in the validation studies. Interpretation involves comparing the performance of a single examinee to that of the similar diagnostic groups.

Several criteria for determining whether the examinee "passes" or "fails" were developed and evaluated for sensitivity and specificity against samples of diagnostic and simulator groups. Cutoff scores and profile patterns for differentiating those simulating or demonstrating poor effort from those with genuine deficits are provided.

A number of features were incorporated into the program to minimize the impact of coaching on dissimulation. The examiner is able to obtain item-level reports, profile patterns, algorithms, and other indices from the automated scoring program.

DEVELOPMENT. The NV-MSVT paradigm is based on the method used in the Word Memory Test (WMT), developed by the same author. It was designed to address the identified problem of high rate of false positives on other measures of symptom validity for those with dementia (genuine impairment). One desirable characteristic of symptom validity measures is high specificity to differentiate those with a poor score due to effort (or feigned impairment) from those with genuine cognitive deficits. Another desirable characteristic of symptom validity tests is insensitivity of test performance to age and intellectual level, such that the very young and those with intellectual disabilities perform similarly to typical adults without intellectual disabilities. The NV-MSVT was developed and validated for these characteristics.

TECHNICAL. The NV-MSVT has demonstrated insensitivity to age (as young as 9 years) and intellectual level. Low but significant correlations between verbal, nonverbal, and full scale intellectual scores and the NV-MSVT were found. There was little difference between correlations with verbal and nonverbal indices, indicating that the NV-MSVT may function similarly in both domains. The NV-MSVT was shown to be sensitive to lateralized dysfunction. In two cases with nondominant temporal lobectomy, FR performance was impaired, whereas verbal learning and memory were spared, indicating sensitivity for visual memory.

Predictive validity evidence was provided as the NV-MSVT demonstrated sensitivity to effort across groups. A group of adults with mean intellectual functioning in the low average range who were motivated to appear positively (those seeking custody of children removed from their care) passed criteria for adequate effort. In another study comparing the performance of those with dementia and simulators, one subtest demonstrated specificity in being able to distinguish between groups. Moreover, specific patterns of performance across subtests were able to discriminate groups with genuine and simulated memory impairment. In a cross-validation study using patients with probable dementia or mild cognitive impairment ($N = 19$), 14 patients failed the NV-MSVT; only 1 met all four criteria for failing.

Performance of the NV-MSVT was directly compared to four other well-established measures of symptom validity in several clinical groups. Those with traumatic brain injury, neurological disorders, fetal alcohol syndrome, and psychiatric diagnoses passed the NV-MSVT and all three other measures of effort. The NV-MSVT identified more simulators and those judged to be malingering than the Test of Memory and Malingering, representing greater sensitivity. A direct linear relationship was found between performance on the NV-MSVT and performance on memory measures with the number of memory complaints significantly greater in those who failed than those who passed the NV-MSVT.

COMMENTARY. The NV-MSVT was developed and evaluated based on state of the art practice in symptom validity assessment. Validation and cross-validation studies show that the test is relatively insensitive to intellectual level and developmental factors while retaining sensitivity to detect suboptimal effort and improving specificity in differentiating those with genuine memory impairment. The NV-MSVT requires little language or reading proficiency and is a valuable addition to the neuropsychologist's armamentarium of effort tests.

The test manual could be improved by the presentation of demographic characteristics of examinees (e.g., age, race, gender), and more in-depth examination of these characteristics. Given the task demands of naming, the measure would benefit from validation on individuals with anomia or aphasia as it is not entirely a nonverbal measure.

SUMMARY. The NV-MSVT is one in a series of measures developed by the same author for the purpose of symptom validity assessment in cognitive evaluations used in clinical and forensic neuropsychological evaluation. The NV-MSVT is designed to be used along with these measures, is similar in its sound conceptual model, and offers novel characteristics in the form of profile analysis to improve specificity when identifying poor effort and interpreting underlying factors. It is brief and easy to administer, score, and interpret, but must be used by appropriately trained professionals.

[80]

Green's Word Memory Test.

Purpose: Designed to "measure verbal and nonverbal memory."
Population: Ages 7 and over.
Publication Dates: 1995-2005.
Acronym: WMT.
Scores, 6: Immediate Recognition, Delayed Recognition, Multiple Choice, Paired Associates, Free Recall, Long Delayed Free Recall.
Administration: Individual.
Price Data, 2010: $300 per Green's WMT for Windows first year (unlimited use).
Foreign Language Editions: Oral, Spanish, French, German, Dutch, Portuguese, Turkish, Russian, Danish, and Hebrew translations available.
Time: Administration time not reported.
Comments: For use with Microsoft Windows; two scores are designed to be sensitive to "poor effort or exaggeration of cognitive difficulties, yet they are insensitive to … cognitive impairment."
Author: Paul Green.
Publisher: Green's Publishing Inc. [Canada].
Cross References: For reviews by M. Allan Cooperstein and Michael P. Gamache of an earlier version, see 14:424.

Review of Green's Word Memory Test by SANDRA D. HAYNES, Dean, School of Professional Studies, Metropolitan State University of Denver, Denver, CO:

DESCRIPTION. Green's Word Memory Test (WMT) is designed to measure verbal memory, specifically, the ability to learn a list of 20 word pairs. Additionally, the WMT measures the test taker's effort to ascertain validity of responses and indicate possible malingering. The WMT is individually and partly self-administered via computer. The test author asserts that the WMT can be used for a wide range of conditions that could lead to cognitive impairment, although he also acknowledges that further research on highly litigating populations (e.g., fibromyalgia) is warranted. An appropriate age range for testing is not identified except to mention that the "very young or the elderly" (manual, p. 8) may need more monitoring during testing. The WMT has been translated into nine languages with all translations available on the test CD.

The test is divided into six subtests of increasing difficulty. No information is provided by the examiner prior to starting the test except an explanation of which keyboard keys should be used during testing; the test taker is to alert the examiner when a screen requesting a password appears. After starting the test program, brief instructions are provided to the examinee including an admonishment to pay attention, and an explanation that 20 sets of word pairs will appear on the screen, one pair at a time, at 6 seconds per pair. The word-pair list repeats instantly followed by the Immediate Recognition (IR) subtest. There is a 30-minute delay between IR and the second subtest, Delayed Recognition (DR), during which the patient should be involved in an activity other than verbal memory testing. DR is introduced by the tester and is immediately followed by another subtest, Multiple Choice (MC). All three subtests require the examinee to select words that form the original word pairs.

To avoid intervention by the examiner, the test author advises that the test administrator leave the testing room while the examinee is taking the first three subtests except when a password is needed to continue or when clarification is requested from the examinee. The examiner's presence is necessary for the last three subtests starting with Paired Associates (PA). During PA, the examiner presents the first word of each original word pair and records the examinee's response when he or she tries to complete the pair. The next subtest is Free Recall (FR) in which the patient is asked to recall as many words from the list in any order, paired or not. Long Delayed Free Recall (LDFR), the last subtest, is administered 20 minutes after the end of the FR subtest. LDFR is conducted in the same way as FR.

Scoring is automatic, and subtest scores are immediately calculated upon completion. Scores are reported as the percentage of correct responses. The test author recommends a three-step process for interpretation. In the first step, primary effort measures are analyzed and scores are accompanied by "pass," "fail," or "caution" notation. The primary effort scores are derived from IR and DR as well as a Consistency score, which is a measure of the consistency of responses between the IR and the DR subtests. "Pass" indicates that any one of these

scores is above 90%, and "fail" indicates any one of these scores is at or below 82.5%. "Caution" is given if any one of these scores is between 83% and 90%. "Fail" indicates that individuals are not making a full effort to do well or are trying to do poorly, not only on the WMT but also on other tests if a battery is used.

Step 2 involves interpretation of the MC and PA subtest scores. The test author suggests examining the number of standard deviation units associated with the test taker's scores in relation to the individual's comparison group. The word "warning" is associated with scores below a level that would indicate suspicious effort, severe dementia, or amnesia.

In Step 3, the Free Recall scores are interpreted only if the primary effort scores are passed. If this threshold is not met, the Free Recall scores are considered invalid. If effort score validity is established, the process from Step 2 is followed for interpreting the Free Recall scores.

More detailed reports may be generated to assist with interpretation. For all steps, the program can generate graphs with all subtest scores, comparison group norms, and what might be considered the area that defines abnormal performance. If desired, interpretation can be accomplished with numerical rather than graphical reports. No information is given on the interpretation of verbal memory as it is expected that all but the most severely impaired patient will pass the subtests; the focus is on effort.

DEVELOPMENT. Scant attention is given to test development in the test manual. No information is provided on item selection or steps undertaken in the selection of the final set of items for the test. Additionally, no information is provided regarding evaluation of the appropriateness of these items for measuring constructs of interest. [Editor's Note: A detailed description of test development processes employed for the earlier version of this test is provided by Cooperstein; see 14:424.]

TECHNICAL. Although evidence for validity is reported, little attention is paid to theory or the underlying assumptions. Many studies have been conducted with various populations and sample sizes to approximate convergent test validity, and the test has face validity based on memory assessment theory. Experiments are not consolidated for an overview of test validity and in general are not peer-reviewed. The only mention of reliability estimates is in test-retest measures where a coefficient of .97 emerged using a retest interval of 1–7 days.

COMMENTARY. The test author's emphasis throughout the manual on the test's ability to assess effort seems to indicate that detection of exaggeration of cognitive difficulties is the primary function of the test. As such, the WMT appears to be a useful instrument. It is less clear how useful the test is as a test of word memory. In both areas, the WMT is likely a good addition to a battery of tests to support other word memory tests, but particularly as a test of effort and detection of possible malingering.

SUMMARY. Malingering remains an issue in psychological evaluation especially in cases in which secondary gain is at stake. It is crucial to assess the response bias of a test in any test battery. Green's WMT can provide a useful addition in that regard. The test author is encouraged to rewrite the test manual for ease of use and to ensure that all standards of good test design including normative data, validity, and reliability are contained in the revised manual.

Review of Green's Word Memory Test by ANITA M. HUBLEY, Professor of Measurement, Evaluation, and Research Methodology, University of British Columbia, Vancouver, British Columbia, Canada:

DESCRIPTION. Green's Word Memory Test (WMT) is a verbal memory test designed to assess effort or symptom validity in children or adults with a Grade 3 reading level or higher and is of particular use in cases where an examinee may gain personally or financially from impaired performance. Green (2005) argues that effort has a larger effect on memory and other cognitive performance measures than severe brain injury and that the inclusion of participants showing poor effort in research can mask other effects or produce spurious results.

The WMT begins with examinees twice being shown a list of 20 word pairs on a computer screen at a rate of one pair every 6 seconds. Six subtests are administered that increase in difficulty level: two learning and primary effort tests (i.e., Immediate Recognition [IR], 30-minute Delayed Recognition [DR]) and four memory tests (i.e., Multiple Choice [MC], Paired Associates [PA], Free Recall [FR], 20-minute Long Delayed Free Recall [LDFR]). The first three subtests typically are completed by the examinee at the computer; the last three subtests are administered by the examiner. Administration of the WMT is straightforward, and detailed instructions are provided in the test manual.

Scores, including a CNS score that represents the consistency of responses between IR and DR, are produced at the end of each subtest and displayed as a percentage of the maximum possible score.

Cutoff scores are applied to the primary effort measures and to MC and PA to determine whether poor effort is indicated. MC and PA scores are then compared to the primary effort and FR and LDFR scores to determine whether the score profile suggests inconsistent effort. The Report Builder in the WMT Windows program provides three different graphing options: a bar chart and a line chart–both of which show the percent correct–and a line chart showing z-scores. According to the WMT website (www.wordmemorytest.com), the Windows program has incorporated more than 80 comparison groups (e.g., normal adult controls, simulators of cognitive impairment, patients with brain injuries). Mean scores from up to five different comparison groups can be added to a graph at any given time using either standard set, best fit, or custom fit options. These graphs may be saved, printed, or copied to other documents. The test manual presents examples of the different graphs to demonstrate different patterns of performance. FR and LDFR are only interpreted if good and consistent effort is shown. According to the WMT website, an Advanced Interpretation (AI) program is available that automatically extracts all data from the WMT and uses a simple flow chart to show and apply the steps in interpreting results.

DEVELOPMENT. An oral WMT was first developed by Green in 1994 (Green & Astner, 1995) and a computerized version using DOS appeared in 1996 (Green, Allen, & Astner, 1996). In 2003, the WMT was produced in a Windows format. According to the test manual (Green, 2005) and website, the oral and computerized versions of the test have the same structure and word content; the test is given orally now only in limited circumstances. Although the manual is available only in English, the WMT has been translated into more than 10 languages, and each version is included in the program. Few details have been provided about the translation/adaptation processes used for each language version.

Little information is provided about the development of the WMT besides the idea that the subtests were to be very sensitive to poor effort but insensitive to all but the most severe cognitive impairment. [Editor's Note: A detailed description of test development processes employed for the earlier version of this test is provided by Cooperstein; see 14:424.] The test manual indicates that all subtests should be administered (i.e., not just the effort measures) because (a) it is the relative complexity and speed of the WMT that help make it resistant to an examinee creating a credible false impression of impairment even if coached, (b) actual memory impairment is more convincing when all of the effort scores are well above cutoff scores and the memory tests show a pattern of performance consistent with known memory impairment, and (c) inconsistency across measures of equal difficulty may be an indicator of insufficient effort. This partly explains the number of subtests. In another place in the test manual, the selection of the cutoff score for the primary effort measures is explained. No information is provided about the choice of word pairs and subtests for the WMT or the rationale for the number of word pairs, presentation rate, or length of delay intervals. Although it may be understandable that test development information is not provided in the test manual in an effort to "protect the integrity of the program and to deter coaching" (manual, p. 2), the lack of such information also makes it difficult to appreciate and evaluate the test development process.

TECHNICAL. The most notable aspect of the WMT is the impressive number and range of comparison groups that have been incorporated into the Windows program. At present, there are more than 80 comparison groups representing more than 3,000 cases. Fifty of these groups are described in the test manual and include, for example, normal adult controls, children with clinical conditions (e.g., conduct disorder, learning disabilities), adults simulating cognitive impairment, and adults with clinical conditions (e.g., severe brain injury, major depression, chronic pain). Some groups are identified based on whether they passed the WMT and whether they have disability/financial claims. The size of the groups varies widely, from two cases to 883 cases. Mean level performance is provided, but there do not appear to be norms for the primary effort measures. The AI program provides T-scores by age, gender, and education for the FR and LDFR scores although the website does not describe the group used to produce the normative data.

Much, but not all, of the available data on the WMT involve English and computerized versions of the test. Although it is typically possible to identify when a non-English version was used, it is not at all clear when the oral version was used.

Notably, Hoskins, Binder, Chaytor, Williamson, and Drane (2010) found that mean effort scores were generally equivalent for the oral and computerized English WMT in a mixed clinical and forensic outpatient sample, but there was some nonequivalency in the inpatient epilepsy sample. No significant differences were found for either group in the rate of failure on the WMT. These findings need to be replicated, however, as the samples used in this study were small.

Although reliability of scores is important, it is not clear how well it can be estimated with memory and effort tests such as the WMT. In terms of internal consistency, split-half reliability was reported to be "very high" (manual, p. 35) but no details were provided that describe the sample, the subtests examined, the type of split-half reliability, the rationale for this approach, or the values obtained. Test-retest reliability was examined over a 1-day to 1-week interval in a sample that combined two groups: (a) good effort (n = 12; 9 adults and 3 children), and (b) simulators (n = 8; all adults). Test-retest reliability coefficients ranged from .92 to .99. Combining good effort and simulator groups increased variability (and thus the size of correlations) but does not make sense given the invalid scores in the latter group. Given the extensive exposure of examinees to the test stimuli over multiple subtests, test-retest reliability is not a good indicator of the reliability of memory or effort scores.

The *Standards for Educational and Psychological Testing* (AERA, APA, & NCME, 1999) describe five sources of validation evidence: test content, response processes, internal structure, relations to other variables, and consequences of testing. Current validation evidence for the WMT appears to focus exclusively on relations to other variables, which includes known-groups, convergent and discriminant, and criterion-related validation.

The bulk of the validation evidence for the WMT in the test manual focuses on group differences. There is good evidence that the primary effort measures are relatively insensitive to brain damage in that similar scores are obtained by healthy volunteers and individuals with a variety of neurological diseases, moderate to severe brain injury, or cognitive impairment; this evidence has been reported for the English, German, and Spanish versions of the WMT. There is also very good evidence from several studies that the WMT is able to successfully differentiate individuals instructed to put forth good effort from those asked to simulate memory impairment: In each case, 100% or close to it are identified correctly; this evidence has been reported with English, German, and Turkish versions of the WMT.

Several studies cited in the test manual have examined effort failure rates on the WMT compared to other tests of effort given to the same sample. It is often argued that inconsistency of results across different effort tests provides evidence of suboptimal effort, further suggesting that effort tests passed by a person with inconsistent results were not sensitive to low effort. Although there might be something to be said for this argument, using one measure of effort as a criterion against which one judges the WMT (or any other measure of effort) is not appropriate (e.g., Green, Flaro, & Courtney, 2009). More convincing is the research presented in the test manual that shows individuals passing an effort test but showing cognitive performance results that are implausible (e.g., far below groups with severe brain injury or dementia).

Some research in the test manual provides interesting information about the WMT effort and memory measures but does not qualify as strong validation evidence because what is missing is presentation of either a strong theoretical rationale (e.g., a known lack of age, education, or verbal IQ effects on effort measures in the extant literature) or a strong criterion of malingering (e.g., when unexpected correlations were found between effort and severity of brain injury or abnormal [vs. normal] brain scan results in samples with compensation claims, it was suggested that individuals with mild brain injuries or normal scans are more likely to put forth less effort so they may look more impaired).

COMMENTARY. Overall, the WMT is a well-conceptualized test that uses cutoffs and profiling of multiple subtests to assess effort. The WMT Windows program is straightforward to load and use and permits automated administration, scoring, profiling, and data storage. Additional strengths of the WMT include that it can be used with children or adults, the availability of the test in multiple languages within the Windows program, the inclusion of an exceptionally large number of diverse groups that can be used for comparison purposes, and, in particular, the ability of the program to identify groups of best fit for comparison based on performance.

Considerable research has been generated that attests to the usefulness of the WMT as a measure of effort, but there is also emerging evi-

dence that raises questions about high false positive rates and whether effort is the sole construct being measured by WMT effort indicators. Research by Batt, Shores, and Chekaluk (2008) raises questions about high false positive rates on the WMT in full effort and distraction groups and suggests that the primary effort measures require cognitive capacity in addition to effort. This suggestion is supported by Allen, Bigler, Larsen, Goodrich-Hunsaker, and Hopkins (2007) and Larsen, Allen, Bigler, Goodrich-Hunsaker, and Hopkins (2010), who reported brain activation in areas associated with task difficulty, memory load, and cognitive effort during DR performance. [Editor's Note: The test author advises that some research published in peer-reviewed journals demonstrates low false positive rates on the WMT.]

The most frustrating aspects of the WMT are the poorly organized test manual and website, which make it difficult to find and assess the quality of the psychometric evidence that is presented. The test manual should be completely revised with better organized chapters; evidence more clearly presented by administration version (i.e., oral, computerized), language version, and age (i.e., child, adult); information from the appendices integrated into the chapters; page references added to tables and graphs so they can be located more easily; and the addition of an index.

Because the exchangeability of the different language versions of the WMT has not been clearly established, these groups should not be combined or compared to one another without evidence of measurement invariance. The finding of equivalent scores, even with matched samples, is not enough to establish invariance (e.g., Rienstra, Spaan, & Schmand, 2009). Thus, further evidence is needed that examines the measurement invariance of the different administration and language versions. Additional psychometric evidence is needed to address issues related to reliability, test content validation, convergent and discriminant validation, response processes, and consequences of testing (see Hubley & Zumbo, 2013). The development of alternate forms of the WMT and inclusion of alternate forms reliability would be beneficial, particularly given the possibility that an examinee may be evaluated more than once.

A great deal of research has been published examining the utility of the WMT as a test of effort, but this information has not been presented in a systematic and organized manner, which is a great disservice to this test. The test manual is quite disorganized and out of date in this regard and despite Green's attempts to provide updates and current information on his website, the information is scattered across different webpages and links, which makes it difficult to locate and evaluate. Regarding documentation of the earlier version of the test, Hartman observed (2002, p. 712), "If this was an intentional attempt to befog attorneys attempting to decode the test, well, it has the same effect on neuropsychologists." This statement applies equally well to test documentation in the current manual and website.

SUMMARY. Overall, the WMT is recommended for use as part of an assessment to determine whether an examinee is exerting sufficient effort that scores on other measures of memory, cognitive ability, and neuropsychological functioning should not be deemed invalid or of questionable utility. The computerized WMT is a well-conceptualized test available in multiple languages, using multiple indicators of effort, and allowing for comparison with a multitude of comparison groups. The test manual needs to be much better organized with a clearer presentation of the available psychometric evidence. There is considerable evidence that supports the usefulness of the WMT as a measure of effort, but there is also some emerging evidence that raises questions about high false positive rates on the WMT and whether effort is the sole construct being measured by its effort indicators. Particularly strong competitors to the WMT include the Test of Memory Malingering (TOMM; Tombaugh, 1996; 14:392) and the Medical Symptom Validity Test (MSVT) for Windows, which is a short-form version of the WMT (Green, 2003/2005).

REVIEWER'S REFERENCES

Allen, M. D., Bigler, E. D., Larsen, J., Goodrich-Hunsaker, N. J., & Hopkins, R. O. (2007). Functional neuroimaging evidence for high cognitive effort on the Word Memory Test in the absence of external incentives. *Brain Injury, 21*, 1425–1428.

American Educational Research Association, American Psychological Association, & National Council on Measurement in Education. (1999). *Standards for educational and psychological testing*. Washington, DC: American Educational Research Association.

Batt, K., Shores, E. A., & Chekaluk, E. (2008). The effect of distraction on the Word Memory Test and Test of Memory Malingering performance in patients with a severe brain injury. *Journal of The International Neuropsychological Society, 14*, 1074–1080. doi:10.1017/S135561770808137X

Green, P. (2003, revised 2005). *Medical Symptom Validity Test for Windows: User's manual and program*. Edmonton, Alberta, Canada: Green's Publishing.

Green, P. (2005). *Green's Word Memory Test for Microsoft Windows user's manual*. Edmonton, Alberta, Canada: Green's Publishing.

Green, P., Allen, L., & Astner, K. (1996). *Manual for the Computerised Word Memory Test*. Durham, NC: CogniSyst.

Green, P., & Astner, K. (1995). *Manual for the Oral Word Memory Test*. Edmonton, Alberta, Canada: Neurobehavioural Associates.

Green, P., Flaro, L., & Courtney, J. (2009). Examining false positives on the Word Memory Test in adults with mild traumatic brain injury. *Brain Injury, 23*, 741–750.

Hartman, D. E. (2002). The unexamined lie is a lie worth fibbing: Neuropsychological malingering and the Word Memory Test. *Archives of Clinical Neuropsychology, 17*, 709–714. doi:10.1016/S0887-6177(01)00172-X

Hoskins, L. L., Binder, L. M., Chaytor, N. S., Williamson, D. J., & Drane, D. L. (2010). Comparison of oral and computerized versions of the Word Memory Test. *Archives of Clinical Neuropsychology, 25*, 591–600.

Hubley, A. M., & Zumbo, B. D. (2013). Psychometric characteristics of assessment procedures: An overview. In K. F. Geisinger (Ed.), *APA handbook of testing and assessment in psychology*. Washington, DC: American Psychological Association.

Larsen, J. D., Allen, M. D., Bigler, E. D., Goodrich-Hunsaker, N. J., & Hopkins, R. O. (2010). Different patterns of cerebral activation in genuine and malingered cognitive effort during performance on the Word Memory Test. *Brain Injury, 24*, 89–99.

Rienstra, A., Spaan, P. E. J., & Schmand, B. (2009). Reference data for the Word Memory Test. *Archives of Clinical Neuropsychology, 24*, 255–262.

Tombaugh, T. N. (1996). *Test of Memory Malingering*. Toronto, Canada: Multi-Health Systems.

[81]

Hairstylist Aptitude Personality & Attitude Profile.

Purpose: Designed to "assess whether a test-taker's skills and personality traits match those required to work in the hairdressing industry."

Population: Hairstylists and prospective employees in hairdressing industry.

Publication Date: 2011.

Acronym: HAPAP.

Scores, 18: Competitiveness, Willingness to Learn New Skills, Integrity, Passion, Time Management, Neatness, Physical Hardiness, Stress Management, Self-Efficacy, Social Skills, Self-Control, Reliability, Creative Problem-Solving, Self-Motivation, Networking, Common Sense, Entrepreneurial Spirit, Overall Score.

Administration: Individual.

Price Data: Available from publisher.

Time: (30) minutes.

Comments: Self-administered online assessment. The test publisher advises that the test manual is being updated to include more information about methodology and theoretical background used in the development of the test. The test publisher also advises that this information is available to clients, as are benchmarks for relevant industries and racial/ethnic group comparison data. However, this information was not provided to Buros or the reviewer.

Author: PsychTests AIM, Inc.

Publisher: PsychTests AIM, Inc. [Canada].

Review of the Hairstylist Aptitude Personality & Attitude Profile by JOHN S. GEISLER, Professor Emeritus, Western Michigan University, Kalamazoo, MI:

DESCRIPTION. The Hairstylist Aptitude Personality & Attitude Profile (HAPAP) is a 79-item self-report measure of the personal attitudes, beliefs, and values of adults who are interested in the possibility of entering the hairstyling occupation. The test is administered online and can be completed in 30 minutes. The HAPAP is scored using a 5-point Likert scale format (range 1–5) on 17 scales: Competitiveness, Willingness to Learn New Skills, Integrity, Passion, Time Management, Neatness, Physical Hardiness, Stress Management, Self-Efficacy, Social Skills, Self-Control, Reliability, Creative Problem-Solving, Self-Motivation,

Networking, Common Sense, and Entrepreneurial Spirit. All scales consist of 5 items, except Common Sense (8) and Entrepreneurial Spirit (6). In addition, an Overall (total) Score is reported. It appears that raw scale scores (range 1–5) are converted (raw score x 20) to a scoring system with a range from 20 to 100. However, a table in the test manual lists score ranges of 0–100, 20–100, and 12–97 for different scales. This information must be considered problematic because it is inconsistent and unclear. The test authors also report that 1,943 participants were in the normative sample.

DEVELOPMENT. Scant development information is provided. No information is provided in the test manual regarding the background, theoretical foundations, psychological constructs, or rationale for item choices. No information is provided as how to interpret the scores. No preliminary field testing research studies were reported in the test manual.

TECHNICAL. The only reliability data that are reported in the manual are alpha internal consistency coefficients ranging from .38 to .80 for individual scales, with an Overall Score coefficient of .93. The number of participants who provided data for the reliability analysis was not provided.

No concurrent, predictive, construct, or content validity data were provided. Mean scale scores, standard deviations, analyses of variances (ANOVA) and associated *t*-test data were reported across all scales on the following variables: gender (*n* = 276); age (*n* = 1,797–five levels); education (*n* = 876–three levels); experience (*n* = 352) or no experience (*n* = 350) as a hairstylist, and success as a hairstylist (*n* = 402–four levels).

COMMENTARY AND SUMMARY. The title of the instrument is misleading. The HAPAP does not appear to assess or measure aptitude or personality traits relative to the occupation of hairdressing. It does not assess the skills of hairstylists despite this statement in the manual: "This … assessment will evaluate whether a person has the skills and traits to be successful in this field." The best that can be said is that it does measure self-reported attitudes, beliefs, and values relative to hairstyling as a potential career choice. However, the instrument cannot be said to do so in a rigorous, well-developed, thorough, validated, and scientific manner. The reliability data are questionable because of the lack of information provided, and the validity data are either nonexistent or inadequate. In addition, more information should

have been provided about the normative sample (e.g., How many of the normative sample are experienced hairstylists?). The one table that does report persons having hairstyling experience lists only 352 people. Thus, it would appear that a majority of the normative sample participants are not hairstylists. The descriptive statistics table reports minimum and maximum scores (i.e., ranges) for each of the scales. The minimum scores vary from 12 to 20, and 16 of the minimum scores are 0. This information seems highly questionable. The range of the Overall Score is 12 to 97. This score range is implausible, and the utility of such a score is seemingly questionable. No information is provided as to how the scale scores were converted into a secondary scoring system. Also, no information is given as to how to interpret the Overall Score or any of the 17 scale scores.

The overlay of quasinormal curves on the descriptive statistics graphical displays has no meaning because the distributions generally do not approximate normal distributions. The 46 pages of bar graphs provided in the test manual are not necessary because these data also are reported in the text and accompanied with thorough analyses of significant mean differences. Whether the statistically significant mean differences have pragmatic value is debatable, and the authors should be commended for making this point in the manual. The sample sizes also raise questions. The total sample size is reported to be 1,943, but gender analyses are conducted on much smaller samples (e.g., gender *n* = 276).

Unless and until more rigorous, thorough, and complete validity data are provided; sound theoretical and psychological foundations established; predictive and follow-up data collected and analyzed; material relative to interpretation provided; and improved scoring, test item content and procedures established, the HAPAP cannot be recommended.

[82]

Halpern Critical Thinking Assessment.

Purpose: Designed to assess "critical thinking skills."

Population: Ages 15 and over.

Publication Date: 2010.

Acronym: HCTA.

Scores: 3 scores for each dimension of critical thinking (Verbal Reasoning, Argument Analysis, Thinking as Hypothesis Testing, Likelihood and Uncertainty, Decision Making and Problem Solving): Total Critical Thinking Score, Critical Thinking Score-Constructed Responses, Critical Thinking Score-Forced Choice Responses.

Administration: Individual.
Forms, 2: Form S1, Form S2.
Price Data: Available from publisher.
Foreign Language Editions: The management software is available in 13 languages; translations of the HCTA are available in 10 languages including Chinese, Spanish, Dutch, and Turkish.
Time: (20) minutes for short-form recognition items; (60-80) minutes constructed response and recognition items.
Comments: Computer administered and scored using the Vienna Test System.
Author: Diane F. Halpern.
Publisher: Schuhfried GmbH [Austria].

Review of the Halpern Critical Thinking Assessment by JULIA Y. PORTER, Professor of Counselor Education, Mississippi State University-Meridian, Meridian, MS:

DESCRIPTION. The Halpern Critical Thinking Assessment (HCTA) uses 25 scenarios from everyday life to assess five critical thinking skills: (a) Verbal Reasoning, (b) Argument Analysis, (c) Thinking as Hypothesis Testing, (d) Likelihood and Uncertainty, and (e) Decision Making and Problem Solving. The two forms (Form S1/Standard and Form S2/Screening) of the HCTA are administered and scored using a computer. The HCTA may be administered individually or in groups and is recommended for clients who are 18 years of age and older. Because there are two forms of the HCTA (Version A and Version B), clients may take the HCTA twice without concerns for test-retest effects.

Although both forms use the same 25 scenarios, Form S1 includes forced-choice and constructed-answer questions and takes 45–80 minutes to complete. The test administrator interprets the responses to constructed-answer items following a set of computerized interpretation questions. Form S2, which includes only the forced-choice questions, takes 15-25 minutes to complete and is scored by the computerized testing program. There is no time limit for either of the forms.

Five scenarios taken from events that occur frequently in everyday life are presented for each of the critical thinking skills being assessed. Scores for each of the five scales are weighted based on their significance to the overall critical thinking process using the following weights: (a) Verbal Reasoning = 12%, (b) Argument Analysis = 21%, (c) Thinking as Hypothesis Testing = 24%, (d) Likelihood and Uncertainty = 12%, and (e) Decision Making and

Problem Solving = 31%. Reported scores for Form S1 of the HCTA include a Total Critical Thinking Score as well as scores for the forced-choice section and the constructed-answer section. For Form S2, an overall score is generated based on the forced-choice items. Both forms also report scores for each of the five critical thinking skills being evaluated. Results are reported as percentile ranks that fall into the following three categories: (a) <16 below average, (b) 16–84 average, and (c) >84 above average.

Suggested uses for the HCTA include assessing common constructs of critical thinking skills, improving educational assessment by measuring whether educational institutions are increasing the critical thinking skills of students, and improving the selection and promotion of employees in business and industry.

DEVELOPMENT. The HCTA is based on critical thinking skills, which were identified through an examination of expert definitions for critical thinking. During the past two decades, the HCTA has been refined and improved based on analysis of the results from administrations of the instrument. The current forms include 25 scenarios that are representative of situations encountered in the lives of many individuals. The scenarios are written in commonly used language at a reading level that would be used in newspaper or magazine articles. Forced-choice questions and constructed-response questions about the scenarios were developed to measure the cognitive processes of free recall and recognition. The forced-choice responses include multiple-choice, ranking, and rating of alternatives. The constructed-response questions ask for analytical responses to information presented in the scenarios. Research on the HCTA in ongoing, and current studies include testing the HCTA in multiple languages in several countries.

TECHNICAL. The HCTA was normed with 450 adults from the United States whose ages ranged from 18 to 72 (mean age = 29). Normative data are reported as percentile ranks and T scores. The norm sample included 62% females (280), 27% males (120), and 11% whose gender was unreported (50). Statistically significant differences were not found between the scores of males and females.

The interrater reliability coefficient for the Critical Thinking–Constructed Responses score was .83 for a group of 200 respondents from the standardization sample. Alpha coefficients were used to examine the internal consistency of the measure. Results for Form S1 were .79, .84, and .88 for Critical Thinking–Forced Choice Responses, Critical Thinking–Constructed Responses, and Total Critical Thinking, respectively. The coefficient for Total Critical Thinking for Form S2 was .79. Values generally support the internal consistency of both forms.

Validity studies were conducted to collect evidence related to content, construct, and criterion sources of validity information. Content evidence of validity was determined by matching items on the HCTA with constructs commonly used in definitions of critical thinking. Four studies conducted to assess construct and criterion evidence of validity of the HCTA used sample sizes ranging from 50 to 355. Computed correlations between constructed-response and forced-choice scores ranged from .39 to .51. The test developer also conducted two factorial structure studies that indicated the constructed-response format and multiple-choice format measured different critical thinking skills. The HCTA manual includes additional detailed information about each of the validity studies.

COMMENTARY. The HCTA provides an objective method for evaluating critical thinking skills that have been identified as necessary for success in the 21st Century (American Management Association, 2010; Riggio & Halpern, 2006). One form of the assessment (Form S1) uses both constructed-response items and forced-choice items. Constructed-answer questions generally require higher-level thinking than multiple-choice questions to respond correctly. A limitation is that respondents with poor writing skills may score lower on the constructed-answer section of the HCTA because of a deficit in their language skills, rather than in their higher-order thinking skills.

Test administrators may need technical assistance to install the HCTA, which is part of the Vienna Test System. Advantages of being part of this system are that other test results may be entered into the system to compare with HCTA results, and the HCTA may be included as part of a test battery for a client. Test administrators new to the system may need practice before administering the HCTA. Advanced capabilities of the system such as changing test items require additional training time. Modifications to the computer used to run the test such as turning off protection programs may also be required for the test system to operate correctly. Test administrators should check compatibility and capability of their computer system to run the Vienna Test System to administer the HCTA.

An electronic tutorial manual provided as part of the test system can be downloaded or printed. The manual is easy to read and provides detailed instructions for using the Vienna Test System as well as the HCTA.

SUMMARY. A computerized assessment instrument, the HCTA measures critical thinking skills on five dimensions (Verbal Reasoning, Argument Analysis, Thinking as Hypothesis Testing, Likelihood and Uncertainty, and Decision Making and Problem Solving). A long form (Form S1) and short form (Form S2) are available depending on the ability of the client being tested and the purpose of the assessment. Some administrator training typically is required before use. Assessment results provide information about the current critical thinking skills of an individual. These data may be helpful in planning educational training for individuals and groups, in selecting individuals for jobs that require higher-order thinking skills, and in evaluating worker performance on critical thinking tasks.

REVIEWER'S REFERENCES

American Management Association. (2010). AMA 2010 Critical Skills Survey. Executive Summary. http://www.p21.org/storage/documents/Critical%20Skills%20Survey%20Executive%20Summary.pdf
Riggio, H. R., & Halpern, D. F. (2006). Understanding human thought: Educating students as critical thinkers. In W. Buskist & S. F. Davis (Eds.), *Handbook of the Teaching of Psychology* (pp. 78-84). Malden, MA: Blackwell Publishing.

Review of the Halpern Critical Thinking Assessment by GERALD TINDAL, Castle-McIntosh-Knight Professor of Education, College of Education, University of Oregon, Eugene, OR:

DESCRIPTION. The Halpern Critical Thinking Assessment (HCTA, version 22) is depicted as a test of critical thinking to be used in educational psychology and personnel selection; it is designed for respondents who are 18 years and older. The test is computer-based in administration, scoring, and reporting and is bundled with four different booklets (Manual, Help File Manual, Vienna Test System, and Vienna Test System Installation), a CD, and a USB port dongle (for loading software to a PC). The Help File is 105 pages and contains information for test administrators on the basics of computerized psychological diagnostics, as well as a description of the Vienna Test System and the Test Generator. Most of the information about development and technical adequacy are reported in a 44-page manual.

The author of the test manual describes the theoretical background of the test with an informal review of the term "critical thinking," referencing synonyms such as "skeptical" and including terms such as reasoning, judgment, reflection, questioning, metacognition, and mental processes. In the end, critical thinking is defined as a multidimensional construct composed of five categories: (a) Verbal Reasoning, defined as "skills that are needed to comprehend and defend against the persuasive techniques that are embedded in everyday language" (manual, p. 7); (b) Argument Analysis, defined as "identifying conclusions, rating the quality of reasons, and determining the overall strength of an argument" (manual, p. 7); (c) Thinking as Hypothesis Testing, reflecting the use of the scientific method in attempting to explain, predict, and control events in life; (d) Using Likelihood and Uncertainty, implying the correct use of probability and likelihood concepts, along with recognition of base rates; and (e) Decision Making and Problem Solving skills, which involve using multiple statements to define problems, identify possible goals and alternatives, and judge among them.

"Taken together, these five categories define an organizational rubric for a skills approach to critical thinking...focusing on skills that are teachable, testable, and generalizable" (manual, p. 8). Two forms of the test are available: S1 includes both forced-choice and constructed-response options and requires 45–80 minutes; S2 includes only multiple-choice options and requires only 20 minutes on average. The author of the test manual asserts that these two response types take advantage of different cognitive processes, with the constructed response items requiring higher-level processing (critical thinking–free recall) and the forced-choice responses requiring lower-level cognitive skills (critical thinking–recognition). The test manual also acknowledges shortcomings of both response types, noting that constructed response items may result in an underestimation of skills for respondents who are mediocre writers and that forced-choice items are "less ecologically valid" (manual, p. 11). In the words of the test author, the HCTA "offers an easy way to assess learning outcomes for programs that aim to enhance critical thinking and as a means of assessing levels of critical thinking for ages 18 through adulthood" (manual, p. 41).

DEVELOPMENT. The author notes that this test has been in development for more than two decades with numerous refinements and improvements. It consists of 25 everyday scenarios that are presented in common language. Each scenario describes a situation requiring the respondent to answer an open-ended question followed by a multiple-choice question. The scenarios are described as reflecting issues depicted in multiple disciplines such as medical research, social policy, and "numerous other disciplines" that might be found in "newspapers and in everyday conversations" (manual, p. 10). The test manual notes that there are five scenarios for each critical thinking category, but that "some categories were worth more total points than other categories in their contribution to the total critical thinking score" (manual, p. 9). Decision Making and Problem Solving contributes 31% to the total, Verbal Reasoning contributes 24%, Thinking as Hypothesis Testing contributes 24%, Argument Analysis contributes 21%, and Likelihood and Uncertainty contributes 12%. The main variables include critical thinking as both a free recall score and a recognition score; the two are added to obtain the Total Critical Thinking Score. Differentiated (component) variables include each of the five dimensions of critical thinking with total scores as well as separate free recall and recognition scores for each dimension.

TECHNICAL.

Standardization. The norm sample reported in the manual is based on data gathered between 2009 and 2012. To construct the 2012 norm sample, 450 respondents ages 18-72 (mean of 29 years, median of 24, and standard deviation of 13) were used. The sample was predominately female (280 representing 62%) with 120 males (27%) and 50 people whose gender was not reported (12%). Various counts and percentages are presented on school attendance and graduation in two states (California and Texas). A norms table in the test manual presents values for three main variables: critical thinking–total, critical thinking–recall, and critical thinking–recognition. Each of the five domain norms is then presented in a similar manner as a total score and differentiated by recall and recognition.

Reliability. Interrater reliability coefficients are reported for a sample of 200 respondents ages 18–72 from different community colleges, state and private universities, and the community. Reliability coefficients for the free recall portions ranged from .53 (Decision Making and Problem Solving) to .82 (Likelihood and Uncertainty). For the critical thinking–recall score, the coefficient was .83, with a total critical thinking score coefficient of .93. Internal consistency (coefficient alpha) was calculated using data from the normative sample. Alpha coefficients were .79 and .84 for critical thinking–recognition and critical thinking–recall, respectively, and .88 for the total critical thinking score.

Validity. Research is reported in the test manual for three "facets of validity" (p. 16): content validity, construct validity, and criterion validity.

Content validity is addressed by simply stating that it "can be assumed due to the item design process" (manual, p. 17) even though the process focused on matching constructs to commonly listed definitions of critical thinking with no references cited. No steps are described for constructing either the scenarios or the choices (for the recognition format).

Construct and criterion validity are addressed by describing several studies that focus on internal structures. A major tenet in this research is to document the difference between the two item formats (free recall and recognition) that are used to measure different dimensions of critical thinking across five domains. Constructed response reflects utilization, and multiple-choice references recognition.

Four small-scale studies are described in the test development process that evaluate the correlation between free recall and forced choice critical thinking.

Study 1 was conducted with 98 students at "a selective Catholic University in Southern California" (manual, p. 17). Study 2 used a Spanish "translation of the HCTA with a community sample of 355 working adults in Spain" (p. 17). Study 3 used a Dutch language translation that "was administered to all first year university students majoring in education in Belgium" (p. 17). In Study 4, 50 students were tested at a U.S. community college that had open admission. The correlation coefficients between free recall and forced choice scores in these studies were .39, .49, .42, and .51, respectively.

A confirmatory factor analysis was conducted using the data set from the "U.S. norm sample" (manual, p. 18) that compared three models: (a) the two response formats were related but separable, (b) both formats were indistinguishable, and (c) the two formats were unique. Using several criteria for goodness of fit, the first model was considered the most plausible; furthermore, factor loadings from each dimension onto its latent trait (format type) were medium to high. Another study using undergraduate students from a nonselective U.S. university ($n = 153$) and a highly selective Hong Kong university ($n = 142$) tested for cultural invariance. Four models were compared: (a) correlated

dimensions and formats, (b) two latent factors reflecting the formats, (c) correlated domains within formats, and (d) correlated domains within correlated formats. The last model fit best indicating 10 separable first-order factors for the five domains in each format and two correlated higher-order factors (for the two domains). The authors of the manual noted that scores from the two formats (free recall and recognition) can therefore be used to calculate a global critical thinking score. Finally, the factor structure of the 10 subdomains was investigated. Configural invariance (same general factor structure in both samples) was compared to (a) a weak measurement invariance model (all domain scales contribute equally to the formats), (b) a weak measurement invariance and weak structural invariance model (correlated formats), and (c) a structural uniqueness model (equal unique variances across both samples). Results supported the configural invariance model as fitting the data well "indicating that the factor structure of the test is identical in America and China … however, they also indicate the need to provide culture-specific norms and to evaluate the psychometric characteristics of adaptations of HCTA in another culture" (manual, p. 21).

Convergent and discriminant validity is reported through a series of studies. In the first study, "80 high school juniors and seniors in California were compared with 80 college students at a nonselective state university" (manual, p. 22). All students also took the Arlin Test of Formal Reasoning. College students scored higher than high school students on both tests; the correlation coefficient for scores on the two tests was .32 for the combined sample. The authors of the test manual reported no differences by gender or college major. With 177 students (both graduate and undergraduate) from a nonselective state university, a number of measures (grade point average, SAT and GRE scores, and scores on the Need for Cognition Scale and the Conscientious Scale) were correlated and compared. Graduate students scored higher than undergraduates on the HCTA, and correlations were moderate with GPA, SAT and GRE scores, and scores on the Need for Cognition Scale, but not with scores on the Conscientiousness Scale. In a study with a Chinese and U.S. sample of students, low to moderate correlation coefficients were documented between the HCTA and several other scales. Finally, two studies provide quasiexperimental evidence of construct validity. Students from "low performing" high schools in California took the HCTA as a pre-post test with a "critical thinking intervention" (manual, p. 24) provided to an experimental group with students randomly assigned (and paid in the first study). A number of findings are presented on pre-post test differences and correlations with other measures (e.g. GPA, California Standards Test, California High School Exit Exams). Finally, HCTA scores were compared with Decision Outcome Inventory scores using respondents from three "qualitatively different populations" (manual, p. 25): community college students ($n = 35$), state university students ($n = 46$), and community adults ($n = 50$). Low to moderate (negative) correlations were found, although they increased with each sample, respectively. On the basis of a hierarchical regression analysis to document difference across the samples, the authors concluded, "The results indicated that neither uniform, nor nonuniform predictive bias existed ... the relation between critical thinking and quality of everyday life decision turned out to be invariant across the three subsamples" (manual, p. 26).

COMMENTARY AND SUMMARY. The HCTA is a computer-based test designed to assess the very complex construct of critical thinking using constructed-response items and forced-choice. Although test takers complete the assessment on a computer, scoring is not automatic, as the test giver must respond to prompts from the computer and render specific qualitative judgments about the free recall responses before scores can be generated. In the opinion of this reviewer, the technical support for the instrument is insufficient. Although some sample scenarios are provided in the test manual, it is not clear how the scenarios used in the assessment were developed. Moreover, the test manual does not describe how the content aligns with the constructs of interest. Limited information is given regarding the data collection procedures, student recruitment strategies, and the participation rates of those recruited versus those who participated in the studies. Gender information is sometimes provided for the student samples used in various studies, but little additional demographic information (e.g., age, race, language) is included. Because studies involving undergraduates and graduate students were often described in the same paragraph, this reviewer found the presentation of the correlations with GPA (where collected) somewhat confusing. Age and maturation are confounded with comparisons across groups of students, and most of the statistical analyses take advantage of a wide age span that may

spuriously inflate results. More detailed descriptions of the norm sample would be welcome. Participants' gender and education level are presented, but only two specific geographic locations are identified. The sample was drawn from selective and nonselective colleges/universities in Texas and California and included a range of educational levels, as well as "adults living in the community (from various parts of the United States)" (manual, p. 28).

Ironically, as a test of critical reasoning, the HCTA manual reflects anything but critical reasoning. The presentation of research is inadequate, the evidence is of mixed quality, and the conclusions appear overstated. The research reported in the HCTA manual does not yet appear to be up to professional standards and, as a consequence, this test should not be used in high stakes applications until a more complete description of technical adequacy is provided and reviewed.

[83]

Harris Infant Neuromotor Test.

Purpose: Developed as a "family-focused screening tool" for use "in clinical and research settings for the early identification of developmental disorders in infants."
Population: 2.5 months to 12.5 months.
Publication Dates: 2009-2010.
Acronym: HINT.
Scores: Total score only.
Administration: Individual.
Price Data, 2010: $36 per manual (2010, 39 pages); $60 per 50 test forms.
Time: (15-25) minutes.
Comments: Additional materials required for administration, but not included: brightly colored ring with string attached, black and white contrasting pictures or designs, disposable paper tape measures for measuring head circumference; after getting a total raw score, it is possible to obtain standard scores based on age norms.
Authors: Susan R. Harris, Antoinette M. Megans, and Linda E. Daniels.
Publisher: Infant Motor Performance Scales, LLC.

Review of the Harris Infant Neuromotor Test by LESLIE R. HAWLEY, Postdoctoral Trainee, Nebraska Center for Research on Children, Youth, Families and Schools, University of Nebraska-Lincoln, Lincoln, NE:

DESCRIPTION. The Harris Infant Neuromotor Test (HINT) consists of 21 items distributed across seven sections. The HINT is administered to infants ranging from 2.5 months to 12.5 months. It is designed to differentiate between infants who are at increased risk for developmental delay and those who are developing normally. The test is not intended for those who have been previously identified as having a disorder. Items evaluate infant motor behavior, locomotion, transition skills, posture, movements, behavior, and head circumference. Additional materials needed to conduct the assessment include a brightly colored ring with attached string, black and white contrasting pictures, tape measure, and head circumference-for-age charts. These materials must be supplied by test administrators. Intended users of the test include health professionals and early childhood educators. Test users are encouraged to attend a 2-day training workshop to learn proper administration and scoring.

Prior to administration, examiners are encouraged to collect background information about the infant and complete the Questions to Parent/Primary Caregiver form. HINT items are scored based on the frequency of behaviors observed by the test examiner throughout a testing session. Administration time is expected to vary based on the age of the infant. After observing or administering all items and prior to calculating a Total score, examiners are instructed to provide an overall clinical impression of the infant's neuromotor performance. Total scores range from 0 to 76, with a higher score corresponding to less mature development. Instructions are provided for calculating appropriate chronological and corrected ages. Examiners use the infant's actual or corrected age along with the HINT scoring decisions (based on normative data) to make recommendations about the need for repeat screening, further assessment, or early intervention services.

DEVELOPMENT. Preliminary content was based on research from the Movement Assessment of Infants (MAI), a review of the literature on early identification of neurodevelopmental impairments and the first test author's own clinical experience. The early research version of the HINT was further developed through a content validity study. A panel of 26 experts in physical therapy, occupational therapy, psychology, pediatrics, and early childhood special education provided item feedback on aspects such as the appropriateness of administration, content coverage, and ability to screen for developmental delay. The comments and revisions suggested by the expert panel informed the current version of the HINT (Clinical Edition of the HINT Version 1.0).

Scoring is based on a normative sample of Canadian infants. Means and standard deviations are provided for 10 intervals ranging from ages 3 to 12 months. Age ranges extend 2 weeks on either side of the age category, so norms apply to infants as young as 2.5 months and as old as 12.5 months. Scores are interpreted within each age interval, and Total scores more than 1 standard deviation above the mean indicate increased risk of less mature development.

TECHNICAL. The standardization sample consisted of 412 Canadian infants ranging in age from 3 to 12 months. At least 40 infants were included in each of the 10 age intervals, and each interval had a minimum of 20 boys and 20 girls. The distribution of education levels for primary caregivers was disproportionately high for university graduates compared to Canadian normative data, but additional research failed to find a significant association between maternal education and infant development as measured by the HINT. The distribution of ethnicity in the norming sample was similar to Canadian population demographics, except for infants of Hispanic ethnicity because Statistics Canada does not include a Hispanic ethnic group category. The test manual notes that additional research found no difference between HINT scores for groups of infants from the United States and Canada as well as Canadian infants with Asian and European origins.

Information is reported on intrarater, interrater, and test-retest reliability of HINT Total scores and item-level scores using a convenience sample of 54 high-risk infants between 3 and 12 months old. Reported intra-class correlation coefficient (ICC) values for intrareliability ranged from .98 to .99 for Total HINT scores. Reported interrater reliability estimates for HINT Total scores also were high (ICCs ranged from .98 to .99). Of the 21 individual items, the test manual reports that 18 (85.7%) had ICCs greater than .70, but 2 items had very low ICCs (-.059 and .124 for eye muscle control and stereotypical behaviors, respectively). Test-retest reliability was evaluated using a sample of 30 infants who were retested between 2 and 9 days after initial testing. The ICC from HINT Total scores was high (.98), and the majority of items (14; 66.7%) had values greater than .70. Two items had noticeably lower ICC values for test-retest reliability (.00 and .38 for eye muscle control and stereotypical behaviors, respectively). Additional research should evaluate these 2 items, so examiner training can be adapted and standardized accordingly.

The test manual reports evidence to support concurrent and predictive validity of test score use.

In terms of concurrent validity evidence, Total HINT scores demonstrated moderately strong to strong relationships with the Mental and Motor scales of the Bayley Scales of Infant Development, Second Edition (BSID-II; 13:29; rs = -.73 and -.89, respectively), the Alberta Infant Motor Scale (AIMS; rs = -.83 and -.85, respectively) and the Ages and Stages Questionnaire (ASQ; rs = -.82–.84). Predictive validity estimates were not as strong and varied across domain scales. Correlations between the HINT raw scores during infants' first year of life and raw scores from the Mental and Motor scales of the BSID-II obtained during infants' second year of life were modest to poor (rs = -.11 and -.49 for the Mental and Motor scales, respectively). Similar analyses were conducted with HINT scores from two time points in the infants' first year, scores on the BSID-II Motor scale during infants' second year, and Gross Motor and Fine Motor subscales of the Bayley Scales of Infant and Toddler Development-Third Edition (Bayley-III; 17:17) at 3 years old. Correlations between HINT scores from younger and older infants in their first year of life and the BSID-II Motor outcomes at year 2 ranged from low to moderate (rs = -.36 and -.55 for younger and older, respectively) but improved with the Bayley-III Gross Motor outcomes at year 3 (rs = -.45 and -.55 for younger and older, respectively). Correlation coefficients were negative because high scores on the HINT indicate less mature development, whereas high scores on the BSID-II/Bayley-III scales, AIMS, and ASQ reflect more mature development (less risk).

Total scores for a sample of known groups of high- and low-risk infants (n = 466) provide additional validity evidence. In age groupings with sufficient numbers of high-risk infants (n = greater than or equal to 6) to test for significant differences, mean HINT scores from high- and low-risk infants were shown to be significantly different in 4 out of 10 possible age groupings. The test manual provides information about the low sensitivity of first-year HINT scores to detect later motor delays on the Bayley-III (accuracy less than 25%) and high specificity of the HINT scores to identify typically developing infants (greater than 98%) in later years. Additionally, the test manual reports that positive predictive values for the 2 SD cutoff were greater than 80% for both time points in year 1, and the negative predictive values for the 2 SD cutoff were moderate (61.9% and 63.2%) across both time points.

COMMENTARY. The HINT is a brief and easy assessment to administer and score. Strengths are the extensive test development process used to create the items and the degree of research conducted on the item-level and Total scores. The majority of the items and the Total score demonstrate acceptable psychometric properties. There are some questions as to the predictive validity of the test scores to domains other than motor behaviors, the sensitivity of the test, and the negative predictive value.

There is a noticeable weakness with regard to the HINT's norming sample. To their credit, the test authors made specific efforts to include infants from several racial/ethnic groups, but the majority of the infants (> 70%) were Caucasian. The norms should be strengthened using a more diverse sample, especially if this assessment is to be used with infants outside of Canada. An additional weakness is the lack of guidance provided for test users regarding the integration of information from the parent questionnaire, the administrator's clinical impression, and HINT Total scores. Without standardized procedures, it is not possible to determine how test users are to integrate these sources of evidence into their decisions. The psychometric information provided in the test manual may not be relevant if test users are basing clinical decisions on their own summative judgments or a combination of factors.

SUMMARY. The Harris Infant Neuromotor Test (HINT) is a brief screening tool for the early identification of infants who are at increased risk for developmental delay. HINT item-level and Total scores demonstrate acceptable psychometric properties. Users should be cautioned that the normative sample has some limitations that may hinder the applicability of the assessment to all environmental contexts and that the test manual lacks specific guidance for the integration of additional information (clinical impression, parent questionnaire) collected during the assessment.

Review of the Harris Infant Neuromotor Test by MARY J. McLELLAN, Department of Educational Psychology, Northern Arizona University, Flagstaff, AZ:

DESCRIPTION. The Harris Infant Neuromotor Test (HINT) is presented as "a family-focused screening tool" for use "in clinical and research settings for the early identification of developmental disorders in infants" (manual, p. 1). In effect this test has been in development via research and earlier versions since 1984. The publisher, Infant Motor Performance Scales, LLC, also publishes the Test of Infant Motor Performance (TIMP; 19:169), which is also reviewed in this volume.

The HINT is administered to children between the ages of 2.5 months and 12.5 months and is specifically intended to identify children with developmental disorders. One of the test authors is a physical therapist, and strong emphasis is placed on the neuromotor functioning of the child. The test manual specifies that this test is to be used as a screening tool and not a diagnostic instrument. Professionals who have experience with infant assessment are authorized to utilize the test; a 2-day training workshop is recommended for test users.

The protocol of the HINT provides specific information about the items administered; the test manual is not used during test administration. The protocol has seven sections with a total of 21 items. The examiner follows specific instructions to score the infant's performance based on descriptions provided on the protocol. Lower scores reflect higher skill level and therefore lower risk. Conversely, higher scores reflect lower levels of ability and higher risk. Items 1–18 are specific to motor skill development, Items 19 and 20 are related to behavior and emotional regulation, and Item 21 reflects the child's head circumference, which is then compared to normative charts from established reference sites to determine relative standing. A Total score is calculated and compared with norms established in Canada that are grouped by monthly intervals. The final section of the test is devoted to overall impressions. The examiner rates the child as being qualitatively normal, qualitatively suspect, or qualitatively abnormal prior to calculating the infant's Total score, which is compared with the normative data and categorized developmentally appropriate, immature or slightly delayed, or significantly delayed. The normative sample's mean, standard deviation, and variation from the mean are provided on the protocol for quick calculation.

DEVELOPMENT. The HINT was developed through apparent years of experience and research by the primary author, who has an extensive history of publications in the field of physical therapy and working with children at risk developmentally. Items were selected to address issues with reliability and validity that were identified through research on the Movement Assessment of Infants (MAI), a measure that was developed in the early 1980s. About one-quarter of the items on the HINT were written and added to those selected from the MAI to form the HINT. The test author received a grant to establish content validity for the first research edition of the HINT from the British Columbia Health Research Foundation. The development team used content experts who rated the test well in the areas of neuromotor and developmental delay identification, but average to poor in the area of cognitive delay identification. A revised research edition was established based on recommended changes in 1993, and the current edition is the same as the revised research edition.

TECHNICAL. The standardization sample for the HINT consisted of 412 children with at least 40 children at each of the 10 age intervals. The sample was stratified by age and gender with attempts to make the sample mimic the 1998 data on population statistics from Canada. Infants that were full term, of typical birth weight, and with no risk indicators were recruited for the study. The majority of the sample was Caucasian, and data were gathered in British Columbia between 2000 and 2003.

Reliability. Interrater, test-retest, and intrarater reliability coefficients were calculated using the second research edition of the HINT and a convenience sample of 54 high-risk infants between the ages of 3 and 12 months. All coefficients were found to be quite high and within acceptable ranges, suggesting the reliability of this measure is acceptable.

Specifically, interrater reliability estimates were based on evaluations of 28 infants by two independent raters (from a panel of five therapists). Coefficients ranged from .06 to .99 for the 21 items, with all but 3 items yielding coefficients of .70 or higher. The coefficient for the Total HINT score was reported as .99. Test-retest reliability was assessed by using the same examiner–who did not have access to the first set of scores–to retest a sample of 30 infants over a 2- to 9-day interval. Coefficients ranged from 0 to 1.0 across the 21 items comprising the HINT, with all but 7 items yielding coefficients greater than .70. The coefficient for the Total score was reported as .98. Intrarater reliability estimates were determined by videotaping 20 administrations of the HINT and asking the original evaluators to re-score the measure, without referring to their original scores. The resulting coefficients for the Total score were all above .97.

Validity. Scores from the Bayley Scales of Infant Development, Second Edition (BSID-II; 13:29) were used for comparison to provide evidence of concurrent and predictive validity. Concurrent validity evidence appeared strong, as demonstrated by correlation coefficients of .73 for the Bayley Mental scale and .89 for the Bayley Motor scale. The HINT scores also appear to correlate strongly with scores from the Ages and Stages Questionnaire, where correlation coefficients ranging from .82 to .84 were observed. The test manual also reports results from a longitudinal study that used a sample of 121 typically developing infants for whom the HINT and the Alberta Infant Motor Scales (AIMS) were completed on two occasions. Correlation coefficients of .83 and .85 were produced at the time the infants were 4–6.5 months old and 10–12.5 months old, respectively. In this reviewer's opinion, predictive validity evidence was not as compelling when infants' scores were examined across time, as they mature. However, users of the HINT need to keep in mind that predictive powers of measures administered at very young ages are often limited. It is not too surprising, then, that low (.11) to moderate (.49) correlation coefficients emerged when the HINT was used to predict scores on the BSID-II that were obtained some 3 to 12 months later.

COMMENTARY. The HINT is a relatively short screening measure that is targeted to identify risk for infants ages 2.5 months to 12.5 months. This test is affordable and relatively self-explanatory. Proper use of the instrument requires a solid foundation of infant development with emphasis on motor development. The test authors recommend training to learn proper administration. The test publisher's website (http://thetimp.com) lists upcoming training sessions. The protocol is self-contained with the instructions, scoring criteria, and normative data all included. The protocol also offers a section for the examiner that identifies possible actions to take, depending on the outcome. The test authors are very clear that an outcome of suspect or atypical warrants, at a minimum, follow-up screening or referral for a comprehensive standardized assessment.

SUMMARY. The HINT provides a low-cost screening measure for children who may be at risk for developmental delay. The age range is restricted to 2.5 to 12.5 months, and the most appropriate use may be in a pediatric clinic setting where a multidisciplinary team evaluates children who may be at risk. The instrument requires training to be administered properly, but the protocol is self-contained and very few materials are needed. Head circumference statistics need to be accessed from another source to complete one of the items. The HINT has limited utility, but is very adequate for use with infants ages 2.5–12.5 months as a screening tool for neuromotor or developmental delays.

REVIEWER'S REFERENCES

Harris, S. R., & Daniels, L. E. (1996). Content validity of the Harris Infant Neuromotor Test. *Physical Therapy, 76*, 727–737.
Harris, S. R., & Daniels, L. E. (2001). Reliability and validity of the Harris Infant Neuromotor Test. *The Journal of Pediatrics, 139*, 249–253.
McCoy, S. W., Bowman, A., Smith-Blockley, J., Sanders, K., Megens, A. M., & Harris, S. R. (2009). Harris Infant Neuromotor Test: Comparison of US and Canadian normative data and examination of concurrent validity with the Ages and Stages Questionnaire. *Physical Therapy, 89*, 173–180.

[84]

Hogan Development Survey [Revised].

Purpose: Designed to "assess eleven common dysfunctional dispositions."
Population: Ages 16 and over.
Publication Dates: 1995-2009.
Acronym: HDS.
Scores, 11: Excitable, Skeptical, Cautious, Reserved, Leisurely, Bold, Mischievous, Colorful, Imaginative, Diligent, Dutiful.
Administration: Group.
Price Data: Available from publisher.
Foreign Language Editions: Available in 42 languages: Czech, French Canadian, French Parisian, German, Slovak, Spanish, Castilian Spanish, Brazilian Portuguese, Danish, Turkish, UK English, US English, Italian, Swedish, Dutch, Norwegian, Indian, Greek, South African, Kenya, Bahasa Malaysian, Bahasa Indonesian, Japanese, Korean, Icelandic, New Zealand English, Simplified Chinese, Traditional Chinese, Polish, Russian, Finnish, Romanian, Bulgarian, Thai, Australian, Greek English, Arabic, Estonian, Hungarian, Macedonian, Serbian, Vietnamese.
Time: (15–20) minutes.
Comments: Available for online administration.
Authors: Robert Hogan and Joyce Hogan.
Publisher: Hogan Assessment Systems, Inc.
Cross References: For reviews by Glen Fox and E. Scott Huebner of an earlier edition, see 14:168.

Review of the Hogan Development Survey [Revised] by STEPHEN AXFORD, Executive Officer for Special Services, Falcon School District 49, Colorado Springs, CO, and Adjunct Professor, University of Colorado at Colorado Springs, Colorado Springs, CO:

DESCRIPTION. The Hogan Development Survey (HDS), based on Socioanalytic Theory, is a multifactor, group-administered measure of "interpersonal competencies" (manual, p. 2) or, conversely, "dysfunctional dispositions" (manual, p. 6) essentially corresponding to DSM-IV-TR personality disorders. Specifically and respectively, the 11 HDS Scales paralleling dysfunctional DSM Behavioral Traits include: Excitable (Borderline Behavioral Traits), Skeptical (Paranoid), Cautious (Avoidant), Reserved (Schizoid), Leisurely (Passive-Aggressive; retained in the revised HDS but acknowledged by the test authors as being removed from the DSM), Bold (Narcissistic), Mischievous (Antisocial), Colorful (Histrionic), Imaginative (Schizotypal), Diligent (Obsessive-Compulsive), and Dutiful (Dependent). However, the test authors provide the following qualification regarding clinical application: "the HDS is not designed to measure personality disorders–the personality disorders are manifestations of mental disorder, and we are assessing self-defeating expressions of normal personality" (manual, pp. 6-7). The test authors go on to further clarify that "behavioral traits" are transient and contextually dependent; whereas "personality disorders" are "enduring and "pervasive." Nevertheless, as the HDS is designed to be used for hiring and promotion decisions (particularly for leadership positions), and thus constitutes a high stakes measure, users are cautioned to heed the authors' cautionary statements regarding avoiding diagnostic or clinical application of the HDS, although human resource application of the HDS includes prescriptive professional development information referred to as "Developmental Recommendations" (Leadership Forecast Challenge Report). These recommendations and applied interpretations of test results are in the form of helpful advice for improving interpersonal relationships and collaboration within the work environment.

The test booklet and manual administration instructions for the 168-item, dichotomously scored (i.e., true/false) HDS are clear and easy to follow. A Flesch-Kincaid reading analysis for the HDS indicated it is written at a Grade 6.9 level. The manual includes administration instructions for accommodating individuals with disabilities, using the Online Internet System, using language translations of the HDS, and informed consent. The test items are easy to comprehend, and a bubble format answer sheet is utilized, scored by the test publisher, with follow-up interpretive reports provided. However, online administration is also available. The test requires 15 to 20 minutes to administer and is available in 42 languages, including English. Although ages are not specified, the manual states that the HDS is intended for use with "normal" adults, and not children, adolescents, or clinical/psychiatric

populations. Test results reports are provided for the test administrator and test-taker, providing percentile ranks for the 11 scales and interpretive information available for making personnel selection decisions and for career advisement. The Hogan Development Survey Manual is well-written and organized, and includes information pertaining to theoretical foundation, test development, reliability, validity, interpretation, utilization, administration, and norms.

DEVELOPMENT. The test authors provide considerable information regarding the development of the HDS, starting with a comprehensive review of the relevant literature relating interpersonal competencies with leadership and organizational dynamics. This is viewed from the standpoint of "performance risks" resulting from dysfunctional dispositions arising out of the individual's social development. From this perspective, all individuals manifest these risks, but to different degrees. From an organizational perspective, this may be conceptualized as managerial competence.

The central construct of the HDS is interpersonal competency theoretically affecting organizational health. Eleven normatively distributed factors representing dimensions of interpersonal competency are identified. The 11 factors essentially correspond to DSM personality disorders, although the test authors emphasize that the HDS is not intended to be a measure of pathology. Rather, the HDS normative scales collectively indicate "good interpersonal skills, to flawed skills, to non-existent skills" (manual, p. 8). Thus, a few people are "highly effective" based on the scales; a few on the other end of the spectrum are consistently incompetent; and most individuals are somewhere in the middle. However, an individual may score high or low on any particular dimension or scale. The test authors cite several personality taxonomies–including Horney's "neurotic needs," Wiggins's "interpersonal circumplex," and Bentz's "overriding personality defects"–as being the theoretical foundation of the HDS.

TECHNICAL. The test manual provides considerable technical information, with numerous tables summarizing data addressing the development, validation, and renorming of the HDS. Several studies validating the HDS are reviewed in detail, including meta-analysis results for scales aligned with competency domains. The final norming sample consisted of 109,103 participants, which included 46,135 managers/executives; and reflected demographics matching the U.S. Census Bureau's

American Fact Finder program (2006)–corresponding distribution tables are provided for age, gender, and ethnicity.

Reliability. Alpha coefficients ranged from .43 (Leisurely Scale) to .68 (Cautious and Colorful Scales). Test-retest reliability was conducted using retest intervals of less than 3 months and 9–12 months. Pearson correlation coefficients, considered acceptable, ranged from .64 to .75 for the former and .52 to .75 for the latter, with regard to the 11 scales. Normalized Euclidean Similarities coefficients respectively ranged from .76 to .85 and .75 to .85.

Validity. Several studies are reported investigating validity evidence in support of HDS score use. In consideration of construct validity evidence, HDS correlation coefficients were examined for various personality, interests, abilities, and preferences measures, including: the Hogan Personality Inventory (HPI), the California Psychological Inventory (CPI), the NEO PI-R, the International Personality Item Pool, the Sixteen Personality Factor Questionnaire (16PF), the Motives, Values, Preferences Inventory (MVPI), the Campbell Interest and Skill Survey, the Jackson Personality Inventory, the Hogan Business Reasoning Inventory, and the Watson-Glaser Critical Thinking Appraisal subtests. In general, the resulting coefficients were in the directions predicted. Validity was further assessed through correlation of others' descriptions, including ratings from observers, co-workers, spouses, and coaches–satisfactory levels of concordance were observed. Finally, meta-analysis was used to examine the validity of test score interpretation for the HDS, using 26 independent samples (*N* = 3,059) from various professional publications between 1997 and 2008. The meta-analysis specifically examined the relationship between personality and job performance competence. The results of the study were consistent with predicted outcomes.

COMMENTARY AND SUMMARY. The test authors provide a compelling review of the literature supporting the importance of interpersonal competencies as to their impact on organizations, particularly as this relates to individuals in leadership positions. Indeed, for anyone who has worked in a complex organizational setting, the truth of this seems obvious–all too often painfully obvious. Thus, the importance of the work invested by Robert Hogan and Joyce Hogan in developing the HDS and in conceptually framing leader effectiveness as it relates to personality is monumental. Fortunately,

the care that went into developing the HDS as a psychometrically adequate and user-friendly tool for aiding personnel selection and professional growth lives up to the need. The HDS manual is well-written and organized, as are the HDS Survey (test booklet), and spiral-bound reports (Select, Development, Lead). Human resource managers and selection committees should find the HDS to be a very useful tool in objectively considering personality factors that potentially impact job performance. Typically, this evaluation is more often done haphazardly through the interview process. The HDS, perhaps in combination with performance measures and authentic assessments, holds the promise of a more objective method of considering how personality factors impact interpersonal job performance.

This reviewer recommends the HDS as a tool to be used in combination with other sources of information for screening candidates seeking leadership positions. The HDS also promises utility as a staff development tool in targeting specific skill areas for enhancing interpersonal competence. The HDS meets accepted psychometric standards, and the test authors have done an excellent job of addressing technical features in the respective published HDS test materials.

Review of the Hogan Development Survey [Revised] by THEODORE L. HAYES, Personnel Research Psychologist, U.S. Office of Personnel Management, Washington, DC:

DESCRIPTION. The Hogan Development Survey (HDS) is a paper- or web-administered 168-item self-report measure of 11 "dysfunctional dispositions ... flawed interpersonal characteristics ... themes that enhance and inhibit effective performance" (manual, pp. 6, 9, & 11). The target respondent audience includes working-age adults. Suggested applications include personnel selection, professional development or coaching, counseling, and research. The test authors state repeatedly that the HDS is not meant to diagnose psychological disorders and should only be used in nonclinical situations. The HDS and test reports are available in 42 languages including English. Items, which are on average 9.8 words long and are pitched at a Grade 6.9 (13-year old) reading level, are administered using an Agree/Disagree response format. The 11 scales each contain 14 items. The scales, which bear resemblance to personality disorders in the *Diagnostic and Statistical Manual of Mental*

Disorders, Fourth Edition, Text Revision (American Psychiatric Association, 2000), are labeled Excitable, Skeptical, Cautious, Reserved, Leisurely, Bold, Mischievous, Colorful, Imaginative, Diligent, and Dutiful. Graphical and interpretive reports are provided for the 11 scale scores. There are no overall or otherwise aggregated scores.

DEVELOPMENT. The HDS is the result of work begun during the late 1980s to develop a test of dysfunctional dispositions that related empirically to nontest outcomes. The time was marked in behavioral science by the resurgence of interest in developing measures of normal personality attributes known as the "Big Five" (Goldberg, 1992; Hogan, 1991). Empirical research established that Big Five personality measures are taxonomically consistent and linked to consequential work outcomes (e.g., Barrick & Mount, 1991). The HDS broadened the realm of psychometric personality assessment to include subclinical dysfunctional dispositions while also capitalizing on the groundswell of acceptance of personality measurement within organizations. Outside of the HDS, some research has attempted to align Big Five measures with counterproductive criterion behavior (e.g., Salgado, 2002) or to create "syndrome scales" as part of omnibus personality test development (Schmit, Kihm, & Robie, 2000). Other competency- (van Velsor & Leslie, 1995) or personality-based (Brandon & Seldman, 2004) approaches exist that are more modest and atheoretical. Overall, the HDS is probably the only assessment of its kind.

TECHNICAL.

Standardization. Scale score standardization and normative value setting for this edition of the HDS are executed exceptionally well. Over 109,000 complete cases were used to develop percentile ranks and expected values for major demographic groups, typically interactions of groups (e.g., Table 6.14, "Norming sample scale means and standard deviations for ethnic groups by females under 40," manual, p. 170). Single demographic tables are provided for ethnicity, not age and gender. No score tables are presented by occupational category. No scale score mean difference analyses, such as *t*-tests, are provided. Visual inspection indicates that most scale scores are consistent across demographic categories. A test user should have confidence that these normative values are current and applicable, especially for professional development or counseling purposes.

Reliability. The test publisher has chosen both test stability and internal consistency for the HDS

reliability model. The test manual indicates that its test development approach considers external behavior more important than internal consistency. As a consequence, the alpha coefficients for the 11 scales range from .43 to .68 (median = .61), which are notably low. Additionally, alpha coefficients are higher for 10 of the 11 scales when data were gathered for professional development compared to data gathered for selection purposes. A planned HDS revision incorporating homogeneous item composites (manual, p. 12) will remedy the internal reliability issue. Stability estimates are presented for retesting within 3 months (average = .70) and between 9 to 12 months (average = .64). These values are within the range expected for the Minnesota Multiphasic Personality Inventory (MMPI; Parker, Hanson, & Hunsley, 1988) and somewhat higher than found for Big Five personality attributes (Roberts & Del Vecchio, 2000).

Validity. Content-oriented validity evidence for use of HDS test scores is highly sophisticated. Items were written to reflect dysfunctional criterion behaviors while also maintaining subtlety. Most items are written to reflect behavior in a work setting. There is no item overlap between scales.

Conceptual or construct-level validity evidence supporting HDS test score use is the strongest suit. The underlying theories are rich and cannot be adequately described here. In brief, HDS scales reflect Horney's (1950) tripartite model of flawed social interaction strategies. Young people develop interpersonal skills and affective tendencies as results of beliefs and expectations regarding how others will treat them, leading to adaptation of interpersonal schemas. Interpersonal deficiencies are based on flawed strategies used to manage schema-based interaction expectations. These flawed strategies include moving away from people (Excitable, Skeptical, Cautious, Reserved, Leisurely), moving against them (Bold, Mischievous, Colorful, Imaginative), or moving toward them (Diligent, Dutiful). Higher HDS scale scores reflect flawed strategies that lead to workplace dysfunction. The test manual notes in passing that exceptionally low scores also reflect flawed strategies as if by dint of an extraordinary deficiency of any strategy. The test manual provides developmental feedback ideas for each scale to correct flawed schemas.

Criterion-oriented validity evidence is more diffuse. The test authors are leaders in aligning criteria with predictors using job analyses (e.g., Hogan & Holland, 2003). A large appendix in the test manual shows meta-analyzed correlations using this approach combined with adjectival ratings, and other tables show similar adjectival ratings criteria arising from implementation of the HDS in a community survey. These data indicate that self-reports from the HDS align with adjectival ratings made by others. Separately, the HDS seems to correlate with workplace multicourse ratings in theoretically consistent ways (Kaiser & Hogan, 2007; Kaiser, Le Breton, & Hogan, in press). At the same time, there is no body of correlational data linking the HDS and discrete organizational outcomes such as failure to promote, early termination, and so forth; even more so than with at-work theft, it may be exceptionally difficult to capture these criteria. It seems that criterion validity evidence for the HDS is more explanatory than predictive.

COMMENTARY. The HDS test manual is among the best this reviewer has ever reviewed for the *Mental Measurements Yearbook*, and is clearly superior to its predecessors and competition. The undergirding theoretical basis for the HDS is much stronger than for the Big Five.

The test publisher has positioned the HDS as being useful for multiple purposes, including pre-employment testing. Because the great majority of test-takers are likely to have some elevated score–and again, low scores also are problematic–and because there is no apparent way to set a cutscore, it would seem the HDS is better suited for professional development than selection. A selection application might be appropriate in situations where the applicants' test materials were first reviewed by trained consultants who then could present the portfolio of strengths and limitations, "bright side" and "dark side," for all candidates so that a hiring manager or selection committee could be aware of the potential new hire's developmental challenges.

The approach taken in the HDS is that dysfunctional dispositions can derail individuals or teams at any level. Other approaches focus on derailment of high-potential leaders (e.g., Civil Service College of Singapore, 2010; McCall & Lombardo, 1983). The focus on identified leaders is more operational and may allow for easier criterion capture. Derailment seems to be a special case of dysfunction, though, and not all dysfunction is at the manager/leader level.

Although HDS scores have satisfactory empirical stability, an open question, and one not addressed in the HDS manual, is: how much *behavioral* improvement, not *scale score* change, would

be expected for an individual with dysfunctional tendencies in a professional development engagement? Optimistic approaches to this question are offered by Davies (2009) and Gentry and Chappelow (2009), though compelling empirical evidence is lacking. Smither, London, Flautt, Vargas, and Kucine (2003) found that managers working with executive coaches after multisource feedback engaged in positive developmental activities, such as developing goals, and seemed to get improved ratings relative to managers not working with coaches. The answer to the question of whether and how much improvement occurs may depend on the skill of the coach, motivation of the recipient, type of dysfunction, and type of change sought. Given this framework, change in criterion dysfunctional behavior should be associated with changes in HDS/criterion correlations even if the HDS scores themselves do not change over time.

Finally, the HDS materials and the feedback it provides are entirely adequate, especially when integrated with the suite of tests offered by the test publisher. However, the score bar graph reports are both static-looking and oriented at single-scale feedback, compared to configural scale clusters based on the Horney classifications. Enhanced Web 2.0 reporting features might explore higher quality graphics, configural feedback, and possibly even interactive reporting that would allow clients to build personalized reports or goal-setting plans.

SUMMARY. The HDS is alone in its test space and it has been developed with exceptional psychological and psychometric care. Its proper place in an assessment battery may not yet be apparent. Unlike most tests, one does not review HDS feedback with a sense of personal esteem, mastery, or interpersonal competence. Maybe that is the point.

REVIEWER'S REFERENCES

American Psychiatric Association. (2000). *Diagnostic and statistical manual of mental disorders* (4th ed., text rev.). Washington, DC: Author.

Barrick, M. R., & Mount, M. K. (1991). The Big-Five personality dimensions and job performance: A meta-analysis. *Personnel Psychology, 44,* 1-26.

Brandon, R., & Seldman, M. (2004). *Survival of the savvy: High-integrity political tactics for career and company success.* New York, NY: Free Press.

Civil Service College of Singapore. (2010). *Research study: Understanding management derailment* (technical report). Singapore: Centre for Leadership Development.

Davies, M. R. (2009). Unlocking the value of exceptional personalities. In R. B. Kaiser (Ed.), *The perils of accentuating the positive* (pp. 137-156). Tulsa, OK: Hogan Press.

Gentry, W. A., & Chappelow, C. T. (2009). Managerial derailment: Weaknesses that can be fixed. In R. B. Kaiser (Ed.), *The perils of accentuating the positive* (pp. 99-113). Tulsa, OK: Hogan Press.

Goldberg, L. R. (1992). The development of markers for the Big Five factor structure. *Psychological Assessment, 4,* 26-42.

Hogan, J., & Holland, B. (2003). Using theory to evaluate personality and job-performance relations: A socioanalytic perspective. *Journal of Applied Psychology, 88,* 100-112.

Hogan, R. (1991). Personality and personality measurement. In M. D. Dunnette & L. M. Hough (Eds.), *Handbook of industrial and organizational psychology* (vol. 2, 2nd ed., pp. 327-396). Palo Alto, CA: Consulting Psychologists Press.

Horney, K. (1950). *Neurosis and human growth.* New York, NY: Norton.

Kaiser, R. B., & Hogan, R. (2007). The dark side of discretion: Leader personality and organizational decline. In R. Hooijberg, J. Hunt, J. Antonakis, & K. Boal (Eds.), *Being there even when you are not: Leading through strategy, systems, and structures. Monographs in Leadership and Management, vol. 4* (pp. 177-197). London, England: Elsevier Science.

Kaiser, R. B., LeBreton, J. M., & Hogan, J. (in press). The dark side of personality and ineffective leadership. *Applied Psychology: An International Review.*

McCall, M. W., & Lombardo, M. M. (1983). *Off the track: Why and how successful executives get derailed.* Greensboro, NC: Centre for Creative Leadership.

Parker, K. H., Hanson, R. K., & Hunsley, J. (1988). MMPI, Rorschach, and WAIS: A meta-analytic comparison of reliability, stability, and validity. *Psychological Bulletin, 103,* 367-373.

Roberts, B. W., & Del Vecchio, W. F. (2000). The rank-order consistency of personality traits from childhood to old age: A quantitative review of longitudinal studies. *Psychological Bulletin, 126,* 3-25.

Salgado, J. F. (2002). The Big Five personality dimensions and counterproductive behaviors. *International Journal of Selection and Assessment, 10,* 117-125.

Schmit, M. J., Kihm, J. A., & Robie, C. (2000). Development of a global measure of personality. *Personnel Psychology, 53,* 153-193.

Smither, J. W., London, M., Flautt, R., Vargas, Y., & Kucine, I. (2003). Can working with an executive coach improve multisource feedback ratings over time? A quasi-experimental field study. *Personnel Psychology, 56,* 23-44.

Van Velsor, E., & Leslie, J. B. (1995). Why executives derail: Perspectives across time and cultures. *Academy of Management Executive, 9,* 62-72.

[85]

How I Think about Drugs and Alcohol Questionnaire.

Purpose: Designed to "measure adolescents' behaviors and attitudes related to drug use."

Population: Grades 9-12.

Publication Date: 2008.

Acronym: HIT-D&A.

Scores, 16: Behavior Scale (Soft Drug Use, Hard Drug Use, Drug Abuse, Drug Dependence), Attitude Scale [3 Cognitive Distortion Referent subscales (Self-Centered, Blaming Others and Assuming the Worst, Minimizing and Mislabeling) or 4 Drug Referent subscales (Alcohol, Nicotine, Marijuana, Hard Drugs)], Validity Screener, Drug Use Screener, Drug of Choice Ranking.

Administration: Group.

Price Data, 2011: $25.95 per manual (65 pages) and 20 questionnaires, $23.95 per 20 questionnaires.

Time: (5-10) minutes.

Authors: Alvaro Q. Barriga (test and manual), John C. Gibbs, Granville Bud Potter, M. Konopisos, and K. T. Barriga.

Publisher: Research Press.

Review of the How I Think about Drugs and Alcohol Questionnaire by COLLIE W. CONOLEY, Professor of Counseling, Clinical and School Psychology, and ELISA VASQUEZ, Doctoral Student, University of California, Santa Barbara, Santa Barbara, CA:

DESCRIPTION. The How I Think about Drugs and Alcohol (HIT-D&A) Questionnaire is a 52-item paper-and-pencil self-report measure composed of both drug-related Behavior and Attitude scales and intended for use with the adolescent population. An adult proctor is to be used to administer and hand-score the questionnaire. The measure is intended to take between 5 and 10 minutes to complete and consists of declarative sentences to which the participant responds based on a 6-point Likert scale ranging from *agree strongly* to *disagree strongly*. The questionnaire manual includes normative information for community adolescent populations. Reported ages of participants in the normative sample ranged from 14 to 19 years.

The measure is scored using computation forms that are provided within the questionnaire manual. Scores can then be compared to summary scale profiles, indicating the severity of drug problems and attitudes based on a normative sample. Additional forms are available within the manual that can be used by the administrator for scoring and interpretation purposes.

DEVELOPMENT. The development of the HIT-D&A stemmed from the original How I Think Questionnaire (HIT; Gibbs, Barriga, & Potter, 2001), which was derived from the theoretical model of self-serving cognitive distortions (Gibbs, Potter, & Goldstein, 1995). The four types of self-serving distortions (self-centered, blaming others, minimizing and mislabeling, and assuming the worst) provided the basis for the development of the items used in the questionnaire. After a confirmatory factor analysis, the four distortion types were reduced to three factors that comprise the Attitude scale: Self-Centered, Blaming Others and Assuming the Worst, and Minimizing and Mislabeling.

The bulk of the items concerning attitudes were adapted to focus on drug and alcohol use from original HIT questions that exhibited strong evidence of validity and reliability. However, the criteria for determining which statements were chosen from the original measure were not explicated. Additional items were included to serve as a social desirability validity check through analyzing rarely rejected responses. The Validity Screener, as the test authors termed the scale, was equated to amount of denial or poor reading comprehension, which could cause the HIT-D&A results to be invalid. The Behavioral scale included items that represent drug abuse and dependence symptoms found in the *DSM-IV-TR* (American Psychiatric Association, 2000).

The preliminary survey (62 items) was administered to the normative group, 925 adolescents ranging in age from 14 to 19 years who were students at one public high school in Pennsylvania. The term preliminary was used because in the commercial assessment (52 items) several items have been removed but the existing items are as used in the initial survey.

TECHNICAL.

Standardization. The normative sample data were gathered from the data obtained from the preliminary HIT-D&A survey. As stated previously, the sample consisted of 925 adolescents from a single high school in Pennsylvania. Ages ranged from 14 to 19 years, with an average age of 16.2 and a standard deviation of 1.16. The test author found that there was a small effect size for age and suggests that this is expected, as older adolescents will likely have had more opportunities for exposure to drugs and alcohol. There is no age adjustment for interpretation. Of the participants, 52% were males and 48% were females. The test author reported that males tended to have higher scores on the scales and subscales than did females. There is no sex of subject adjustment for interpretation. The sample was 92% Caucasian, with the remaining individuals indicating various ethnic identities. The test author reported negligible differences in questionnaire scores based on ethnic identification. Socioeconomic status was also assessed with the significant correlation coefficients (3 out of 13) not of concern to the test author.

A clinical sample was recruited consisting of 69 adolescents who had been referred to an outpatient clinic for drug and alcohol evaluation and/or treatment. The sample was 81% male and 19% female with ages ranging from 13 to 19 years (average age 16.1, standard deviation 1.55). No differences were found for gender, and consistent with the normative sample, age was positively correlated with scale/subscale scores. Ethnic/racial data indicated 56% African Americans, 32% Caucasians, 9% with mixed ethnicities, 2% Latinos, and 2% Native Americans.

Reliability. Test-retest reliability coefficients over a one-week period were computed from a convenience sample of 33 undergraduate college students, whose demographic information was not presented in the test manual. The older age of the college test-retest sample presents a concern because the sample is older than the recommended and normed high school HIT-D&A group. The older ages of the test-retest sample may overestimate the reliability coefficients. The resulting Pearson correlation coefficients for the Attitude and Behavior scales were .90 and .95, respectively. The subscales of the Behavior scale yielded coefficients that were all above .91. The subscales of the Attitude scale yielded coefficients that ranged from a low of .69 for Blaming Others and Assuming the Worst to a high of .89 for Minimizing and Mislabeling.

The normative sample was used to determine internal consistency, which allows more confidence in these data because the sample better reflects the population recommended for the test. Alpha coefficients of .92 for the Behavior scale and .93 for the Attitude scale were observed.

The subscales within the Behavior scale were reported as having the following alpha coefficients: Soft Drug Use (.76), Hard Drug Use (.88), Drug Abuse (.77), and Drug Dependence (.83). The subscales within the Attitude scale were reported as having the following alpha coefficients: Self-Centered (.84), Blaming Others and Assuming the Worst (.76), Minimizing and Mislabeling (.84), Alcohol (.84), Nicotine (.75), Marijuana (.87), and Hard Drugs (.61). The lower coefficients (.61 to .77) raise concern about the internal consistency of the subscales.

Validity. A confirmatory factor analysis was conducted to evaluate the structure of the measure and inclusion of items. Results indicated support for the division of the Attitude scale into three cognitive distortion referent subscales as well as for the division of the Attitude Scale into four drug referent subscales. Also, the division of the Behavior scale into Drug Abuse, Drug Dependence, Hard Drug Use and Soft Drug Use subscales was supported by further analysis.

Criterion group validity was examined by comparing normative and clinical samples. Results showed that the clinical sample scored significantly higher than the normative sample on all subscales except the Alcohol referent subscale. In another criterion group validity study, the normative sample was divided based on participation in school-sponsored sports and school-sponsored activities other than sports. As expected, involvement in sports indicated lower scores on all but two scales/subscales, and involvement in an activity other than sports indicated lower scores on all scales/subscales.

Convergent validity was examined using external criteria including the Youth Behavior Rating Scale (YBRS; Barriga, 2006) and the school variables of GPA, detentions, and suspensions. Results indicated significant correlations (at the p <.001 level) between all HIT-D&A subscales and problem behavior symptoms of the YBRS. Additionally, GPA negatively correlated with scale/subscale scores, and detentions and suspensions positively correlated with HIT-D&A scores.

Divergent validity was determined by examining age and socioeconomic status. The correlation between scores and these demographic variables was weak, but significant, for age on 8 of 13 subscales (positive correlations) and SES on 3 of 13 subscales (negative correlations). The test author concluded that there was little evidence for bias based on age or SES. These reviewers disagree with the test author's conclusions regarding the influence of age. The two superordinate scales were significantly correlated with age; the Behavior scale had a correlation coefficient of .11, and the Attitude scale had a correlation coefficient of .07.

COMMENTARY. The purpose of the HIT-D&A is to assess the drug- and alcohol-related attitudes and behaviors of adolescents. The inclusion of both attitudes and behaviors, along with the short administration time of the instrument, are significant strengths. Also, the use of a validity scale helps to determine whether adolescents are being forthright in their responses, information that can aid in the prevention of misinterpretation. Additionally, the measure was tested on both clinical and nonclinical samples, suggesting that it can be used for discriminating levels of drug and alcohol use, dependence, and abuse for adolescents who will accurately self-report.

The test author provides helpful information in the manual regarding confirmatory factor analysis of scales, subscales, and items. Additionally, the test manual includes suggestions for interpretation and further interview guidelines and forms to use with adolescents who may endorse specific problematic behavior. Unfortunately, the interview guidelines are complex and not well explicated. A knowledgeable alcohol and drug counselor could probably use them.

Some concerns exist. First, the assessment manual clearly states that only administrators knowledgeable about the American Psychological Association ethical codes regarding assessment who have at least a master's degree in psychology or a related field, as well as having taken a course in assessment should use the HIT-D&A. However, the HIT-D&A is for sale through Internet bookstores with no verification of expertise. A concerned parent could easily buy the assessment for a family investigation and misinterpret the results.

Additionally, directions to the test taker on the HIT-D&A Questionnaire state, "Your answers will be kept private." The statement appears misleading, as the test author cannot know with certainty how the test results will be used by individuals who administer the measure.

The normative sample consists of 925 high school students from a town in western Pennsylvania. The town has a population of less than 10,000 and is high in majority culture population (more than 92%) compared to other U.S. cities. Using one area for gathering normative data that is suburban, small in size, and culturally different from most U.S. cities is of concern.

Finally, there is a validity concern regarding using the HIT-D&A with African American and perhaps Latino/a, Native American, and mixed racial/ethnic groups. The test authors interpreted absence of significant differences in means between Caucasians and minorities as good because there are no "demographic biases" (manual, p. 33). However, the clinical sample contained 56% African Americans whereas the normative sample was 2% African American. No attempt was made to explain the vast difference in representation that appeared in the clinical as compared to the school sample. No attempt was made to explain how the vast difference in representation in the clinical sample may prompt concern for the accuracy of the HIT-D&A survey discriminating risk in the high school sample. Also, the mixed ethnicity category increased from 3% in the normative sample to 9% in the clinical sample, and the Latino/a and Native American groups increased from 1% to 2%. A consistent bias appears but is not identified in the measure or explained by the test author.

SUMMARY. The HIT-D&A consists of a scale measuring self-reported drug use behavior, an attitude scale measuring cognitive distortions associated with drug use, and a screener measuring validity of responses. The measure seems to be valid for measuring differing levels of drug and alcohol attitudes and experiences of Caucasian adolescents. Construct validity was established using confirmatory factor analysis. The measure's normative group is limited in that the group is from one high school in a town that is not reflective of most U.S. cities. The normative sample was predominately Caucasian. As a result, the validity of using test scores obtained from non-Caucasian respondents is questionable. The test manual provides additional forms that may be useful for both clinicians and researchers interested in drug and alcohol attitudes and behaviors in adolescents.

REVIEWERS' REFERENCES

American Psychiatric Association (2000). *Diagnostic and statistical manual of mental disorders* (4th ed., text rev.). Washington, DC: Author.

Barriga, A. Q. (2006). The Youth Behavior Rating Scale (YBRS). Unpublished questionnaire. Greensburg, PA: Seton Hill University, Psychology Department.

Gibbs, J. C., Barriga, A. Q., & Potter, G. B. (2001). The How I Think (HIT) Questionnaire. Champaign, IL: Research Press.

Gibbs, J. C., Potter, G. B., & Goldstein, A. P. (1995). *The EQUIP program: Teaching youth to think and act responsibly through a peer-helping approach.* Champaign, IL: Research Press.

Review of the How I Think about Drugs and Alcohol Questionnaire by ROBERT K. GABLE, Director, Center for Research and Evaluation, Johnson & Wales University, Alan Shawn Feinstein Graduate School, Providence, RI, and MEGHAN KILEY, Admissions Associate, The Wheeler School, Providence, RI:

DESCRIPTION. The How I Think about Drugs and Alcohol (HIT-D&A) Questionnaire developed by Barriga, Gibbs, Potter, Konopisos, and Barriga (2008) contains 52 items rated using a 6-point Likert scale (*agree strongly* to *disagree strongly*). It includes three scales and 11 subscales: a Validity Screener; a Behavior scale, including Soft Drug Use subscale, Hard Drug Use subscale, Drug Abuse subscale, and Drug Dependence subscale; and an Attitude scale, which includes a Self-Centered subscale, a Blaming Others and Assuming the Worst subscale, and a Minimizing and Mislabeling subscale, or four drug referent subscales (Alcohol, Nicotine, Marijuana, and Hard Drugs). Administration takes 5 to 10 minutes and can occur individually or in small groups. In clinical assessment situations, the HIT-D&A can be scored quickly to allow for an immediate follow-up interview. The HIT-D&A is primarily intended for use with adolescents 14 to 19 years of age. The questionnaire provides for the normative assessment of the use of 10 common drugs. The classes of drugs have been divided into "soft" and "hard" drug use subscales, in addition to separate subscales for assessing abuse and dependency symptoms. The interpretive guidelines are based on a normative sample consisting of 925 adolescents from a suburban high school and a clinical sample of 69 adolescents referred to a drug and alcohol outpatient clinic.

DEVELOPMENT. Prior to describing the development of the HIT-D&A, the test author presents a comprehensive literature review regarding the problem of adolescent drug use and the challenge of assessment in this area. Included are descriptions of other assessment instruments and how the HIT-D&A provides a more direct focus on the drug-related behaviors and attitudes that underlie such behaviors. The theoretical framework was based on adapting Gibbs, Potter, and Goldstein's (1995) four category typology of self-serving cognitive distortions (i.e., Self-Centered,

Blaming Others, Minimizing and Mislabeling, and Assuming the Worst) to adolescent drug use. For the Behavior scale the list of drugs generated from the Substance-Related Disorders chapter of the *DSM-IV-TR* was reviewed by six drug and alcohol counselors. The Attitude items were based on the test author's previous work in which four categories of self-serving cognitive distortion were crossed with four categories of commonly used drugs. A Validity Screener containing items commonly agreed with was included to identify any students with "naysayer" response sets.

A well-designed hand-scoring matrix is included for the Behavior and Attitude scales and subscales. A Drug Use Screener provides percentile ranks linked to reported use (heavy, medium, light, and none) and includes a Drug of Choice ranking. A particularly notable feature is the display of Behavior and attitude scale percentile ranks matched with problem severity descriptors (severe, significant, moderate, mild, and not a problem). The initial 62 item instrument was reduced to 52 items using judgment and empirical analyses (i.e., exploratory and confirmatory factor analyses). Item complexity and readability were examined; a grade level of 4.6 on the Flesch-Kincaid readability index resulted.

TECHNICAL. Two samples of students were analyzed: normative and clinical. The normative sample consisted of 925 adolescents from one suburban high school in western Pennsylvania. Of this group 92% were Caucasian and 8% were minorities. Average socioeconomic status was found to be middle class. The clinical sample consisted of 69 adolescents who had been referred to an outpatient clinic for drug and alcohol evaluation and/or treatment.

The generalizability of the normative sample data to other populations can be considered a limitation. Although the ethnicity of the clinical sample (32% Caucasian) differed from the normative sample, the test author presents a defendable argument that the differences do not rule out comparisons of the two groups.

Normative sample (*N* = 917) alpha coefficient reliabilities for the Behavior scale (.92) and subscales (.76–.88) and the Attitude scale (.93) and subscales (.61–.87) are presented in the test manual. The Attitude subscale Hard Drugs was associated with the lowest alpha reliability estimate; the reliability data for the remaining Attitude subscales are acceptable. For a convenience sample of 33 college students, the one-week retest correlation coefficients were

.95 for the Behavior scale and .90 for the Attitude scale; subscale correlation coefficients ranged from .91 to .96 for the Behavior scale and .69 to .89 for the Attitude scale.

Using different terminology than that used in the *Standards for Educational and Psychological Testing* (AERA, APA, & NCME, 1999), the test author carefully covered the relevant types of validity evidence. As noted earlier, evidence based on test content was carefully addressed through previous research conducted by the test developer and colleagues and through a content review by six drug and alcohol counselors. Regarding evidence based on internal structure of the test, several confirmatory factor analyses were used to generate the final structure of the instrument. It would have added to the structure and data interpretation issue if the developer had included Rasch model item response theory analyses to examine the spread of students and items across each targeted scale. Successful application could lead to finer interpretations of high and low scoring students.

Regarding convergent and discriminant validity evidence based on relations to other variables, the developer presents several supportive analyses. Correlation coefficients consistent with theoretically predicted relationships are present for the HIT-D&A Behavior and Attitude scales and subscales and the problem behavior syndromes (mood problems, attention deficits, aggressive behavior, and conduct problems) assessed by the Youth Behavior Rating Scale (Barriga, 2006) as well as with the following school variables: GPA (-.27 to -.39), detentions (.22 to .34), and suspensions (.19 to .28). Discriminant validity correlation coefficients with age (.03 to .14) and socioeconomic status (-.01 to -.13) were low and in the predicted direction to support the claim that construct invariance was present for these demographic variables. Of particular importance was the finding that mean scores on the Behavior and Attitude scales were higher for the clinical (i.e., referred for drug and alcohol treatment) group than for the normative sample. As predicted, lower HIT-D&A Behavior and Attitude scale means were observed for students involved in school sports and other co-curricular activities than for those not involved. Finally, the tendency for males to score higher than females was present with a small effect size, and no differences were found between ethnic groups (821 Caucasians, 57 minorities).

COMMENTARY. The HIT-D&A is an efficient instrument to gather important data that can be calculated with a hand-scoring matrix. The user's manual contains comprehensive validity evidence based on test content, internal structure, and relations to other variables. Score interpretation with normative percentile ranks and guidelines for a semistructured follow-up interview are included. The data from the clinical sample in comparison to the normative sample are supportive of test validity. For all the analyses concerning convergent and discriminant validity, it would be helpful to include and discuss effect sizes along with the usual statistical significance levels (e.g., $p < .001$) that the test developers report. It is well known that large samples such as the 917 used from the normative group can lead to statistical significance; effect sizes would assist readers in considering the practical significance of the findings. This suggestion is not to indicate that the reported correlations or t-test values are misleading; they are consistently in predicted directions and magnitudes. A primary concern of these reviewers is the extent to which the normative sample demographics allow for meaningful comparisons and generalizations to other groups. Further differential item functioning/ construct invariance analyses using Rasch modeling should be considered by the test developer.

SUMMARY. Based on the underlying theoretical base, literature review, evidence of sources of validity, data reliability, scoring method, and interpretation guidelines, How I Think about Drugs and Alcohol (HIT-D&A) Questionnaire is recommended for use.

REVIEWERS' REFERENCES

American Educational Research Association, American Psychological Association, & National Council on Measurement in Education. (1999). *Standards for educational and psychological testing*. Washington, DC: American Educational Research Association.

Barriga, A. Q. (2006). The Youth Behavior Rating Scale (YBRS). Unpublished questionnaire. Greensburg, PA: Seton Hill University, Psychology Department.

Gibbs, J. C., Potter, G. B., & Goldstein, A. P. (1995). *The EQUIP program: Teaching youth to think and act responsibly through a peer-helping approach*. Champaign, IL: Research Press.

[86]

i-Ready Diagnostic and Instruction.

Purpose: Designed to identify "student strengths and weaknesses in reading and math" through computer adaptive testing and to provide differentiated online instruction.

Population: Grades K-8 (Diagnostic) and K-6 (Instruction).

Publication Date: 2011.

Scores, 14: Reading (Overall Scale Score, Overall Placement, Phonological Awareness, Phonics, High-Frequency Words, Vocabulary, Comprehension—Literature, Comprehension—Informational Text); Mathematics (Overall Scale Score, Overall Placement, Number and Operations, Algebra and Algebraic Thinking, Measurement and Data, Geometry).

Administration: Group.

Price Data, 2012: $27 per one-year Diagnostic and Instruction subscription (reading or math); $6 per one-year Diagnostic subscription (reading or math); 20 license minimum per subject for new customers; multi-year pricing available.

Time: (45) minutes per diagnostic (reading or math).

Comments: Diagnostic test may be purchased with or without instruction component. [Editor's Note: The publisher advises that an updated and expanded version, i-Ready K-12 Diagnostic and K-8 Instruction, was made available in 2013. It will be reviewed in the next edition of the *Mental Measurements Yearbook*.]

Author: Curriculum Associates.

Publisher: Curriculum Associates, LLC.

Review of the i-Ready Diagnostic and Instruction by RIC BROWN, Adjunct Faculty of Statistics, Department of Education Psychology, College of Education, Northern Arizona University, Flagstaff, AZ:

DESCRIPTION. The i-Ready Diagnostic and Instruction is an online approach to reading and math that diagnoses individual student needs, reports such information to the district teachers and administration to aid in instructional decision-making, has an instructional component tailored to the diagnosis, and monitors progress as instruction and assessment occur.

The comprehensive information provided about the i-Ready indicates that the diagnostic component (K-8) draws from an item bank with thousands of test items and selects from among those items based on student ability level. Each successive item is based on the previous response to ensure an exact performance level to report to the teacher (scale score and grade level). Based on the diagnostic information, downloadable instructional materials matched to student performance are available. The i-Ready Diagnostic may be purchased with or without the instructional component.

The i-Ready Instruction (K-6) provides reading and math topics by domain (for example, Phonological Awareness for reading, and Number and Operations for math). As noted previously, the instruction is tied to the diagnostic assessment.

A wide variety of online reports are available. For example, the individual student profile report for reading provides a scale score for the diagnostic test and a grade placement level for each test taken

and each content domain. Steps for improvement and tools for instruction are suggested along with a guide to the instructional component. There are also class profiles and a report for which Common Core standards are involved. District-level reports also can be generated.

A 42-page user's guide for teachers is provided containing an overview of both the diagnostic and instructional components. There is also a step-by-step guide for using each product and a list of additional resources. The 43-page user's guide for administrators also provides an overview of both the diagnostic and instructional components. This guide also covers managing the teacher component and getting district-level reports.

DEVELOPMENT. The i-Ready Diagnostic was developed along guidelines set by the Testing Standards of the American Educational Research Association, the American Psychological Association, and the National Council on Measurement in Education. The technical manual identifies test and item design, which employed item response theory and Rasch modeling. Items were based on state standards as well as the Common Core State Standards. The items were field tested with more than 17,000 students across 18 different states. More than 33,000 assessments were administered for reading and math. Demographic data for the diversity of the students tested in terms of ethnicity, poverty level, special education status, and English language learner status are reported. After taking the i-Ready Diagnostic, instruction in the area assessed is individualized and based on the content areas covered. The web-based i-Ready Instruction is asynchronous and delivered to students at their specific performance levels.

TECHNICAL. The reliability of the i-Ready Diagnostic is presented in terms of test design (IRT) and Computer-Adaptive Testing modeling. The i-Ready Diagnostic utilizes an item bank approach, and the manual points to continuing item analysis for item revisions or deletion. The comprehensive technical manual outlines the construct maps that were developed and how the maps were followed. For both reading and math, the development of scale scores, standard errors of measurement, and the progression of scale scores across the grade levels are meticulously presented. As well, reliability estimates are detailed.

Validity evidence for the diagnostic tool is presented in terms of expert knowledge used in item development, review by a panel of expert advisors (members are listed in the manual), and use of best practices in online test development.

For the instructional component, four examples representing different groups of students (at risk, Title I, special education, and lowest quartile) are presented showing positive results. A complete curricular map is presented by domain and topic across the K-6 spectrum.

COMMENTARY. In addition to the printed test materials this reviewer examined online examples provided by the test publisher. Two student screens, a teacher screen, and an administrator screen were reviewed for Grade 4. As noted in the user's guide, the administrator screen provided opportunities to review different reports, as well as monitoring of student and teacher information. The teacher screen provided overall class data and individual student profiles. Both landing pages were clear, and the various tabs were easy to navigate.

The student diagnostic was visually appealing, involving animated characters and choice of background setting. Questions on the test were presented with a four-choice (multiple-choice) answer format. After a series of questions, a short video game appeared to break up the test.

As with any software (online or not), the success will ultimately depend on the ability of teachers to use the system and their willingness to follow through with it. This statement is not to say that the system is difficult to use (it does not seem so), but it will require a commitment beyond the regular classroom operation or substitute for something currently in place.

The user's guide for teachers appeared relatively clear and complete. However, a "help desk" website or phone number was not apparent. If teachers are to refer questions to a district-level employee, that person will need to be technically proficient and have the personal skills necessary to deal with what might seem mundane questions (Brown, 2011). Mass teacher professional development may be a start, but adult learning theory suggests some teachers will need what they need, when they need it (Papa & Papa, 2011).

The i-Ready Diagnostic technical manual is comprehensive and provides enough information for a district-level measurement expert to use for decision-making. However, the four case studies used to document the evidence for the i-Ready Instruction component are less specific. To be useful for decision-making, they need to be more detailed.

SUMMARY. The i-Ready Diagnostic and Instruction is a well-developed diagnostic tool with a matching (optional) instructional component. The reading and math areas covered represent acceptable topics in K-6 curriculum and are aligned with the Common Core State Standards. Technically, the diagnostic meets all standards for reliability and validity, and the instructional component follows state-of-the-art curricular models. A district with the resources (curriculum budget and hardware to meet student and system needs) would find the i-Ready Diagnostic and Instruction welcome tools in the K-6 teaching and learning arena.

REVIEWER'S REFERENCES

Brown, R. (2011). Administration of technology: Teaching, learning, and resource management. In R. Papa (Ed.), *Technology leadership for school improvement* (pp. 45–60). Thousand Oaks, CA: Sage.
Papa, R., & Papa, J. (2011). Leading adult learners: Preparing future leaders and professional development of those they lead. In R. Papa (Ed.), *Technology leadership for school improvement* (pp. 91-108). Thousand Oaks, CA: Sage.

Review of the i-Ready Diagnostic and Instruction by JENNIFER N. MAHDAVI, Associate Professor of Special Education, Sonoma State University, Rohnert Park, CA:

DESCRIPTION. A computer-based adaptive diagnostic assessment of mathematics and reading skills for students in grades kindergarten through 8, the i-Ready Diagnostic and Instruction can be taken independently by students, with each successive item delivered based on performance on the previous item. A full testing session in mathematics or in reading takes approximately 45 minutes. Test developers recommend the assessment be administered no more frequently than every 13 weeks, which means a student may take it as many as three times each year.

The i-Ready Diagnostic test items and achievement indicators are based on, but not statistically correlated with, the Common Core State Standards (CCSS), so it is possible to use the assessment to evaluate indirectly whether a student is meeting those standards. The reports generated indicate whether all or part of many individual standards were met. Teachers are able to look at reports of individual student growth and progress, as well as class-wide indicators of which students are at, above, or below grade level. The program then generates diagnostic analyses of student performance that the teacher may use to select appropriate lessons to address student needs. If the instructional component was purchased, the system will automatically select individualized lessons for students to work through on the computer.

This assessment yields scale scores, ranging from 100–800, with 400 as the central value. The scale scores on the i-Ready Diagnostic are specific to the grade level of the student who took the assessment and indicate the proper placement of the student for instruction. For example, a first grader achieving a scale score of 500 on the diagnostic will be placed in level one (or first grade) math lessons; however, a sixth grader achieving the same scale score will be placed in level five (or fifth grade) lessons. As such, the i-Ready Diagnostic scale scores are not useful in tracking progress for an individual student over time. The program also generates a level for each student's achievement, which is similar to a grade level.

DEVELOPMENT. Research in reading led to the development of the following construct strands for assessment and instruction: High-Frequency Words, Phonics, Phonological Awareness, Comprehension, and Vocabulary. The mathematics strands, following the recommendations of the National Council of Teachers of Mathematics and research in the field are: Algebra, Geometry, Measurement, and Number and Operations. Within each strand, multiple-choice items were developed to assess critical skills; these items were later reviewed and critiqued by a panel of content specialists including experienced teachers, reading specialists, curriculum specialists, and college professors. Once the content of items had been reviewed twice, presentation aspects were created, including technical, visual, and audio content so that the assessment may be presented online. According to the technical manual, more than 2,700 items were developed for use in the i-Ready Diagnostic.

Item response theory (IRT), specifically the Rasch model, was used to scale the diagnostic assessment. Test developers state that this model "provides sample-free item difficulty estimates and item-free person ability estimates ... [and] a mechanism to generate an interval level scale..." (technical manual, p. 6).

As a computer-adaptive test, the i-Ready Diagnostic is able to present items to a student according to his or her success on the previous item. Testing for each student begins with items that are considered below that student's grade level, unless the assessment has been taken before, in which case previous ability determines the current start point. After each item is completed, the computer program evaluates the student's estimated ability to deliver the next item that is appropriate. A maximum of 72 reading items or 48 math items are presented to a student during a testing period.

TECHNICAL.

Standardization. A convenience sample of 58 school sites using Curriculum Associates products was drawn from 18 states. These schools were nearly all in the eastern and southern regions of the United States, with only one school site in Nevada representing the western third of the country. From these sites, 17,000 students in grades K-8 participated in the item pilot and reliability tests. Although children living in poverty, those eligible for free or reduced lunch, children with special needs, and English language learners were sampled in percentages that closely reflect population estimates, ethnic demographics were not as representative. African American children were sampled at more than twice their national percentage, and Hispanic students were slightly undersampled. Caucasian children made up about half the group, but represent nearly three-quarters of the U.S. population. The male-female ratio was not reported.

Although the number of students participating in the development of the test is impressive, the lack of random or strategic sampling, as well as the absence of reports regarding differential performance of students according to demographic categories is a concern.

Reliability. The i-Ready technical manual provides two types of reliability evidence, standard errors of measurement (*SEM*), and separation indices. These results are preliminary and apparently will be updated as the measures are used by more students and more data for analysis become available.

Separation indices give an indication of how much score variance is related to person or item differences. With values of 2.0 indicating that less than 20% of variance is due to error, the i-Ready reports a person separation of 2.89 in reading and 1.81 in math, and an item separation of 12.93 in reading and 9.74 in math. Although impressive, these statistics are not disaggregated by any student demographic characteristics, nor by domain within reading or mathematics. There is no way of knowing whether the assessment is more reliable for some students, or grades, or within certain domains.

Person and item reliability, similar to *KR20* reliability coefficients, are also reported. Within-person reliability measures are strong, .89 for reading and .77 for math. Item reliability is extremely consistent in both areas, reported as .99. Again, reliability coefficients are not disaggregated by student characteristics, by grade, or by academic domain.

SEM, which describes the standard deviation of errors within a test, is reported by grade and by subject. Lower *SEM* values indicate a more reliable assessment. *SEM* values on i-Ready mathematics are fairly consistent, with a low of 14.84 in Grade 6 and a high of 15.79 in kindergarten (where the standard deviation of 2.9 indicates relatively more variability in scores). There is somewhat more spread in the reading *SEM*s, from a low of 12.42 in kindergarten to a high of 14.51 in Grade 8. These statistics are within acceptable limits for reliability of a test with scale scores that range from 100–800, as the scores on the i-Ready do.

Validity. The authors of the i-Ready Diagnostic do not offer the types of validity evidence one expects to see in a technically adequate measure. Rather than provide predictive or concurrent evidence of validity, the authors address construct evidence of validity and mention the face validity of the measure. Because the i-Ready was constructed to align with the Common Core State Standards, which have been adopted by most of the states in the U.S., there is implied validity from a construct perspective; the assessment measures skills deemed important by many American educators. Sample items provided in the manual are shown alongside the CCSS strand and grade level that the item addresses. In addition to building on the CCSS, test developers used documents provided by important professional groups, such as the National Council of Teachers of Mathematics. A review of reading research is provided, with extensive references to important studies conducted by well-known reading instruction researchers. No similar report is provided for mathematics.

Test authors indicate that they have plans to perform differential item functioning (DIF) analyses as well as to collect additional concurrent evidence of validity with state tests; these results were not available at press time.

COMMENTARY. The automation of the i-Ready gives classroom teachers and school administrators a great deal of information at a glance. Errors students make are analyzed by the computer program, and teachers are given a report about skills each student has and areas that need improvement. The program can create groups of students who need similar skills and can indicate percentages of students who are achieving at, below, or above grade level. However, there is no possibil-ity of seeing specific items that students answered or of doing additional analyses of error patterns. Teachers must not be lulled into a sense of security based upon these results; they must review reports with a professional and critical eye to ensure that the results of this diagnostic assessment fit with other assessments and observations. This process is particularly important if the instructional modules are used because in such a case, the teacher may have little interaction with the student when new lessons are assigned.

Given the scope of the skills assessed and the number of students involved in piloting the measure, the lack of technical adequacy information provided in the manual is disturbing. Claims made in the manual of the utility of the measure may be overstated.

SUMMARY. As a 21st Century, computer-based measure, the i-Ready Diagnostic and Instruction may save teachers time, as well as provide efficient suggestions about how to help students advance in basic reading and mathematics skills. Its explicit references to the CCSS may also be valuable to school administrators and teachers. At the same time, until additional information about reliability and validity are provided, this measure should be used with caution and in conjunction with other reading and mathematics assessments.

[87]

Independent School Entrance Exam, 3rd Edition.

Purpose: Designed to "assess verbal reasoning, quantitative reasoning, reading comprehension, and mathematics achievement for use in admissions into independent schools."

Population: Grades 4-11, or candidates for Grades 5–12.

Publication Dates: 1989–2010.

Acronym: ISEE.

Scores, 4: Verbal Reasoning, Quantitative Reasoning, Reading Comprehension, Mathematics Achievement.

Administration: Group.

Levels, 3: Lower, Middle, Upper.

Price Data: Available from publisher.

Time: (140) minutes.

Comments: Test booklet title is ISEE.

Author: Educational Records Bureau.

Publisher: Educational Records Bureau.

Cross References: For reviews by Mary Anne Bunda and Joyce R. McLarty of an earlier edition, see 11:174.

Review of the Independent School Entrance Exam, 3rd Edition by C. DALE CARPENTER,

Interim Dean and Professor of Special Education, College of Education and Allied Professions, Western Carolina University, Cullowhee, NC:

DESCRIPTION. The purpose of the Independent School Entrance Exam (ISEE) is to assist independent schools in making admission decisions for students seeking admission to Grades 5–12. It is a group-administered instrument.

The ISEE 3rd Edition is a revision of the ISEE 2nd Edition published in 1999. The Technical Report 2009–2010 details the changes from the original edition in 1989; however, it is not as clearly specific about the changes from the second to the third edition. That may be because the report refers to earlier reviews of the original edition that appeared in *The Eleventh Mental Measurements Yearbook* (Bunda, 1992; McLarty, 1992).

The current ISEE is composed of five sections, four of which are scored: Verbal Reasoning, Quantitative Reasoning, Reading Comprehension, Mathematics Achievement, and an essay. The essay, which is not scored, is written in response to a provided prompt and sent to schools selected by the student.

Verbal Reasoning consists of vocabulary items in which a word and possible synonyms are presented in a multiple-choice format and modified cloze format items in which a sentence is presented and students choose a word or phrase that best completes a missing element of the sentence.

Quantitative Reasoning consists of word problems and quantitative comparisons (e.g., greater than, less than).

Reading Comprehension uses a traditional format in which 300- to 700-word passages are presented followed by items measuring main idea, inference, supporting idea, vocabulary, organization/logic, and tone/style/figurative language.

Mathematics Achievement is made up of traditional test items requiring calculation.

Depending on whether the Lower Level (Grades 5–6), Middle Level (Grades 7–8), or Upper Level (Grades 9–12) tests are used, sections or subtests allow 20 to 40 minutes for completion and have between 25 items (Lower Level Reading Comprehension) and 47 items (Middle and Upper Level Mathematics Achievement). Combined testing time, not including directions and the essay (30 minutes) is 110 minutes for the Lower Level and 130 minutes for the Middle and Upper Levels.

DEVELOPMENT. The technical report states that the ISEE is "not strictly an achievement test or an aptitude test" (p. 4), but that verbal and quantitative reasoning are more in the aptitude category, and reading comprehension and mathematics achievement are more traditionally achievement measures. The report includes a brief literature review of the cognitive ability research relating to the test and discusses how the sections of the instrument are aligned with the standards of the National Council of Teachers of Mathematics, the International Reading Association, and the National Council of Teachers of English.

The report also details the item-writing and field testing processes as well as the norming process. More than 13,000 test-takers from 79 schools participated in the field testing.

TECHNICAL.

Standardization. The ISEE 3rd Edition was administered for the first time in the 2009–2010 school year to more than 41,000 students. Norms for the scaled scores and percentile ranks as well as stanines are based on the most recent 3 years of test-takers. Demographic information about test-takers for even the first year are not provided in the manual so it is not possible to see how many students completed each form at each level or to know other typical information such as gender, age, SES data, and geographical representation.

Reliability. Internal consistency coefficients using coefficient alpha are reported based on the 2009–2010 administration. Only 5 of 36 reported coefficients for three forms of the four scored sections at three levels were below .80, and all were above .75 showing what this reviewer considers acceptable internal reliability estimates. No other kinds of reliability information are provided.

Validity. Content evidence of validity data are provided in the discussion of the item-writing and field-testing information as well as in the brief review of literature in the manual. Construct evidence of validity is provided through intercorrelation coefficients for each of the sections with each other. The information and coefficients are consistent with what was included in the previous reviews based on the original ISEE. That is, Verbal Reasoning (VR) and Reading Comprehension (RC) scores correlate well (i.e., .70 and above), as do Quantitative Reasoning (QR) and Mathematics Achievement (MA), whereas VR and RC do not correlate well with QR and MA (i.e., .61 and below). Finally, criterion-related evidence of validity is provided in the form of correlations between ISEE 3rd Edition and the Comprehensive Testing

Program, 4th Edition (CTP4), an achievement test used by some schools. Correlation coefficients are provided from the administration of the ISEE 3rd Edition used as an admissions tool and the CTP4 subtests that are closely related and used as an achievement test for students already admitted to independent schools. Verbal subtests on the ISEE 3rd Edition correlate well (i.e., .40 and above) with the same kinds of subtests on the CTP4 and the same is true for quantitative tests from each instrument.

COMMENTARY. Criticisms in earlier reviews concerning the original ISEE have been addressed in part although not always satisfactorily. There is more information about items and how field-testing occurred. There is ample information about the properties of each item. Unfortunately, there are also unanswered questions.

If the purpose of the instrument is to predict success in the schools using the data, predictive (criterion-related) evidence of validity showing the correlation of ISEE 3rd Edition scores with measures of success in independent schools is a primary need. That information is not available. Correlation data of the ISEE 3rd Edition with the CTP4 is helpful but not conclusive.

The fact that the two verbal measures on the ISEE 3rd Edition correlate with each other and the two quantitative measures correlate with each other begs the question of whether two scores rather than four scores are most meaningful and useful given the intended use of the instrument. Other technical concerns are the lack of detailed norm sample information, the lack of alternate-form reliability given the use of three or four forms for each level, and a need for a cogent theoretical model for the test.

One of the advantages of the ISEE 3rd Edition is that it is administered to a select group–those students who seek admission to independent schools–and the scores are normed for that group. Therefore, schools can compare scores of applicants to others seeking admission. If schools consider the constructs measured helpful, ranking applicants along those constructs may be a needed service. However, it is possible other instruments with more information about the psychometric properties of the test, including norm samples, may also serve the purpose as well.

SUMMARY. The Independent School Entrance Exam, 3rd Edition is a revised edition of an instrument intended to be used as an admissions tool for independent schools for Grades 5 through 12. The domains and items are generally accepted areas

on such tests. Field-testing, internal reliability, and some validity data are provided and meet general guidelines for acceptability. However, there remains a lack of critical information that test users should expect when choosing an instrument. Most critical among that information is evidence that results of the instrument adequately predict success in the independent schools using the ISEE 3rd Edition.

REVIEWER'S REFERENCES

Bunda, M. A. (1992). [Review of Independent Schools Entrance Examination]. In J. J. Kramer & J. C. Conoley (Eds.), *The eleventh mental measurements yearbook* (pp. 400–401). Lincoln, NE: Buros Institute of Mental Measurements.
McLarty, J. R. (1992). [Review of Independent Schools Entrance Examination]. In J. J. Kramer & J. C. Conoley (Eds.), *The eleventh mental measurements yearbook* (pp. 402–403). Lincoln, NE: Buros Institute of Mental Measurements.

Review of the Independent School Entrance Exam, 3rd Edition by THANOS PATELIS, Vice President of Research and Analysis, Research and Development Department, The College Board, and Research Scholar, Graduate School of Education, Fordham University, New York, NY:

DESCRIPTION. The Independent School Entrance Exam, 3rd Edition (ISEE 3rd Edition) is designed to be used in the admission process for students applying to independent schools entering 5th through 12th grades. The ISEE 3rd Edition is composed of five sections and offered in three levels. These three levels are the Lower Level for students in Grades 4 and 5 who are applying for admission to Grades 5 and 6; the Middle Level for students in Grades 6 and 7 who are applying for admission to Grades 7 and 8; and Upper Level for students in Grades 8 through 11 applying for admission to Grades 9 through 12. The five sections of Verbal Reasoning, Quantitative Reasoning, Reading Comprehension, Mathematics Achievement, and an essay are administered to all three levels with the Lower Level taking 110 minutes and the Middle and Upper Levels taking 130 minutes. The essay, which takes 30 additional minutes, is not scored, but copies are provided to schools designated by the test taker. The other four sections are composed entirely of multiple-choice items and are right-only scored (i.e., without any adjustment for incorrect answers). For each of these four sections, raw score, scaled score, percentile rank, and stanine are provided. The scaled scores for each of the four sections range from 760 to 940. Fees for registration and scoring/reporting services are indicated online at www.erblearn.org. Online versions of the ISEE are offered for students seeking admission to Grade 4 and in the fall of 2011 Grades 2–3. No information about these tests was made available, and they are not considered as part of this review.

DEVELOPMENT. The 3rd edition represents a revision of the previous edition with a focus on two cognitive areas of reasoning in verbal and quantitative areas and achievement in reading comprehension and mathematics. A literature review is provided in one of the appendices of the 2010 technical report supporting the conceptual basis of the reasoning and achievement sections of the test referring to the literature of cognitive functions for the reasoning components and anchoring the basis of the achievement components to standards from the National Council of Teachers of Mathematics (NCTM) and National Council of Teachers of English (NCTE). With these aspects forming the basis, the publishers utilized a committee of representatives from the schools to review and revise the test specifications from the previous version. Additionally, teachers and administrators from more than 100 Educational Records Bureau (ERB) schools were trained by the publisher to produce and select the items, reading passages, and writing prompts according to the test specifications. The items and passages comprised 10 forms per section per level and were field tested on a sample of more than 13,000 students from 79 schools that were members of ERB. In order to ensure the comparability of the 3rd Edition with the 2nd Edition, a set of common items were used (i.e., common item equating design) with a Rasch one-parameter item response model (IRT) using the field trial data. Classical item statistics, Rasch IRT statistics, and differential item functioning (DIF) analyses for gender and ethnic groups were calculated using the field trial data. These statistics were reviewed by a committee of experienced and trained ERB member school educators. Three base forms at the Lower Levels and four base forms at the Middle and Upper Levels with embedded field test items were developed along with additional field test forms.

TECHNICAL. In the 2009–2010 school year, more than 41,000 students across the three levels represented the first operational administration of the 3rd Edition of the ISEE. Using a common item equating design with Rasch one-parameter IRT, scores from the multiple base forms were equated including the conversion of the 3rd Edition scores to the 2nd Edition scores using regression parameters (i.e., slope [A] and y-intercept [B] parameters). Norms are developed each year by including 3 years of administration data. The 3rd Edition included old 2nd Edition data for normative data. Speededness or completion rates are provided for each section at each level based on the percentage of items completed and the ratio of the variance of the number of items not reached to the total score variance. Coefficient alpha reliability is reported for each level, section, and form. The reliability estimates ranged from .76 to .95. Validity evidence is provided by (a) examining the degree to which the test forms align to the test specifications, (b) examining the extent to which the sections of the test show positive correlation coefficients, and (c) examining the relationship of performance on the ISEE 3rd Edition and an achievement test, the Comprehensive Testing Program, 4th Edition (CTP4).

COMMENTARY. The revision of the ISEE was carefully undertaken by the publisher, ERB (Educational Records Bureau), and its contractor, Measurement, Inc. (MI). However, there are some aspects that should be added to the technical report. The test development was thoroughly undertaken utilizing the literature, professional content standards, and subject matter experts involving educators in the schools that utilize the ISEE in their admissions process. The test development process was carefully designed and undertaken in a thorough manner. The technical report, however, fails to report the characteristics of the field test and operational test samples to permit effective evaluation of psychometric information provided. Because interpretation of the test scores is normative, a more detailed description of the sample comprising the norms is quite important. There was some variability by form within level for various psychometric indicators (e.g., section completion rates, variance index, and coefficient alpha). Additional information about the conditional standard error of measurement should be provided. The sample score reports indicate the range of performance by section, but their values were not provided in the technical report or described in the score report. Finally, the validity evidence provides some evidence in support of the development of the ISEE 3rd Edition and evidence that the scores are related to achievement test scores (i.e., Comprehensive Testing Program, 4th Edition, CTP4). Sample information from the validity study examining student performance on the ISEE 3rd Edition and the CTP4 was not provided, making it difficult to understand the statistical conclusion and external validity of this study. Additional validity evidence is needed with criteria that are more aligned to performance or even success in the independent schools. Such criteria could include indicators such as grades, cumulative grade point average, persistence through middle and high school, or high school graduation. Furthermore, unless the admission process for each school is the same, school-specific validity studies should become a part of the ongoing assessment program. These predictive validity studies should use as many predictors as can be used and representative of the admission process at the school. Such studies may only be possible, however, in larger schools with sufficiently large numbers of students.

SUMMARY. The ISEE 3rd Edition has been improved from earlier versions with a thorough test development process, large field test sample, and strong psychometrics that include Rasch IRT scaling and equating. The reliability based on coefficient alpha is at acceptable levels, even though there were subtests with values less than .8, but no less than .76. Additional information representing the conditional standard error of measurement would be helpful. Although large samples were used to establish norms, more information describing the normative sample would be helpful to the test users. There is validity evidence to support the strength of the alignment of the test to the test specifications and the positive relationship between ISEE 3rd Edition scores and an achievement test. However, predictive validity evidence is needed using criteria closer to representing success in the independent schools such as course grades, cumulative grade point average, persistence through grades, and high school graduation. Additionally, these predictive validity studies should include as many predictors as possible that are representative of the admissions process at typical schools.

[88]
Inventory of Legal Knowledge.

Purpose: "Designed to assist the forensic examiner in assessing response styles of defendants undergoing evaluations of adjudicative competence" and to measure "a defendant's approach to inquiries about his or her legal knowledge."
Population: Ages 12 and over.
Publication Date: 2010.
Acronym: ILK.
Scores: Total score only.
Administration: Individual.
Price Data, 2010: $129 per complete kit including 10 reusable item booklets, 25 response sheets, and manual (56 pages); $40 per 10 reusable item booklets; $55 per 25 response sheets; $45 per manual.

Time: (15) minutes.
Comments: "The ILK is not a test of adjudicative competence....The ILK is solely a measure of response style; more specifically, it is a measure of a defendant's approach to inquiries about his or her legal knowledge."
Authors: Randy K. Otto and Jeffrey E. Musick; Christina B. Sherrod (manual only).
Publisher: Psychological Assessment Resources, Inc.

Review of the Inventory of Legal Knowledge by ROSEMARY FLANAGAN, *Associate Professor, Touro College, Graduate School of Psychology, New York, NY:*

DESCRIPTION. The Inventory of Legal Knowledge (ILK) was designed to help forensic examiners assess a defendant's response style when undergoing evaluation of adjudicative competence. The 61-item ILK is composed of simply written true-or-false items about the legal process. Based on the *Dusky* (1960) standard, this information is needed to determine whether a defendant is capable of consulting with his or her attorney with a reasonable degree of rational understanding, and whether the individual has a factual and rational understanding of the proceedings against him or her, both distinct from adjudicative competence. The *Dusky* standard requires that examiners consider that adjudicative competence is a "present" state issue concerned with ability. It must be determined whether a defendant's ignorance is based on deficient cognitive ability or adequate ability obscured by knowledge deficits that may be feigned or remediable. The standard is flexible and contextual (Otto, 2006) because it is a matter of degree, as capacity must be sufficient and suggestive of a reasonable degree of rational understanding. Although identifying mental disorders (and in the case of adolescents, developmental immaturity) is important, their relevance is the potential negative impact on a competence-related ability.

Mental health professionals must consider whether the examinee's approach to responding to questions is honest, defensive, feigning, malingering, or irrelevant. More than one response style in a given interview is possible. The threshold for determining whether defendants are feigning symptoms or impairments should be high.

The ILK is designed for English-speaking persons ages 12 and older. Examinees must be able to listen to, as well as understand and process items that are written at a fifth-grade level, so they may provide responses to true-false questions. Because the items focus on the American legal system, examinees should have some knowledge of it; thus, the ILK may not be an appropriate instrument for some individuals who are foreign-born.

Test materials include a manual, a reusable item booklet, and a two-page carbonized answer sheet that is attached with a perforated tear strip. The first page is for recording identifying information and responses; the second page is the scoring sheet. The reusable item booklet contains administration instructions and 61 items, which are scored "0" or "1." The examiner completes the response sheet and records the responses. The items do not appear on the scoring sheet; thus, if the answer sheet is required by the court, test security is maintained.

Administration procedures for the ILK are standardized; instructions and individual items are read verbatim to the examinee. The examiner records the response and tells the examinee whether the response is correct. It is important that the examiner obtains a response for each item before proceeding to the next. Scoring is accomplished by separating the sheets and by summing the number of correct responses for each of the two columns. Correct responses appear in shaded grid boxes.

Interpretation of the ILK is based on the total score, which is the number of correct responses; the possible range of scores is 0 to 61. The detection strategies are to be used sequentially. The examinee's score is first compared to tabled values for below-chance performance, followed by comparison of the examinee's score to the tabled cutoff for the combined adult or juvenile reference groups. It may also be useful to compare the examinee's score to the tabled data for particular comparison group(s).

DEVELOPMENT. The item pool was developed based on the test authors' experience conducting evaluations for adjudicative competence as well as their knowledge of criminal law. The initial item pool was more than 100 items; following several revisions and preliminary studies, 61 items were retained. Revisions to items included review of language to ensure meaning was clear and the items were comprehensible. It was also important to have a similar number of items for which the correct responses would be true or false. Items were subsequently reviewed by a varied panel of experts; no biases related to gender, race, ethnicity, and so forth, were found. Pilot studies were subsequently conducted to determine (a) whether items should be discarded, (b) how well the ILK total score differentiated feigning from honest response styles, (c) whether the terms "attorney" and "lawyer" as well as "prosecution" and "prosecutor" would be interpreted by respondents as having equivalent meaning, (d) whether the word "prosecutor" should be replaced by equivalent terms used in localities, such as "state attorney."

TECHNICAL.

Standardization. The community control group comprises adults, college students, and juveniles (N = 615). The clinical/forensic reference sample (N = 515) includes psychiatric inpatients, adults adjudicated incompetent to proceed to trial, those acquitted by reason of insanity, adult competency examinees, juvenile competency examinees, and juveniles adjudicated incompetent to proceed to trial; individuals from these groups constitute the typical population for which the ILK was designed. Scores within a 90% confidence interval of chance responding (30 items; range 24–36) fall below the mean score of 51.86 (8th percentile) for control group respondents. Classification utility statistics were computed using a college student control sample (N = 207) and a combined psychiatric sample (N = 199). Sensitivity, specificity, and base rates for feigning are reported for cutoff scores ranging from 36–53. A cutoff score of 47 is recommended because: (a) at the p ≤.05 level, the base rate for feigning is .86, (b) specificity (absence of feigning in one who is not feigning) is .99, and (c) sensitivity (the presence of feigning in one who is feigning) is .84. These values are acceptable.

Means, standard deviations, and ranges are available for all reference samples and subsamples. The mean score for the Adult Community Control is significantly higher than the mean score for Community Psychiatric Inpatients who were told to respond honestly (55.93 vs. 53.04; p = .009). This minimal raw score difference between groups underscores the need for a multistep detection procedure as the test authors have outlined. The differences between group means for the Juvenile Community Control and Juvenile Adjudicated Incompetent to Proceed, also significant, are more pronounced (48.96 vs. 43.69)

Reliability. Using the data from the Adult Community Control sample (N = 211), the mean item-total correlation was .32 (range = .10–.53). Coefficient alpha, however, indicates ample internal consistency (.88). Using a subset of individuals from the College Student Control (n = 61) who were administered the ILK twice within an interval of 5–11 days (M = 7.1), test-retest reliability was .76. This result suggests a slight practice effect. This may not be surprising as the administration procedures call for the examinee to receive feedback as to the correctness of each response.

Validity. Using the College Student Control (CSC; *n* = 207), the Community Psychiatric Inpatients (CPI; *n* = 100), and those Not Guilty by Reason of Insanity (NGRI; *n* = 99) groups, individuals were divided into subgroups and were administered the ILK under standard conditions (respond honestly) or under conditions in which they were told to fake bad. Data indicate means that are substantially different; Cohen's *d* ranged from 1.31–2.45. To quantify the classification utility, the Receiver Operating Characteristic (ROC) curve was used. The area under the curve for the CSC, CPI, and NGRI groups was .97, .90, and .86, respectively. These values are considered "excellent" to "good." For scores ≤ 47, which is the cutoff score, sensitivity, specificity, positive predictive power, and negative predictive power were computed. For the CSC sample, these values were: .84, .99, .98, and .93, respectively. For the CPI sample, these values were .76, .82, .81, and .77, respectively. For the NGRI group, these values were .77, .77, .72, and .81, respectively. These data suggest that the ILK is likely to perform well, correctly identifying and predicting those who are feigning, as well as those who are not. Evidence of convergent validity (Otto, Musick, & Sherrod, 2011) is based on a study of diverse defendants ages 9–68 years, who were administered the ILK and at least one of three other measures of response style that are sensitive to feigning rsponses and malingering.

COMMENTARY. The ILK is a promising measure that was developed with the requirements of the legal system in mind. The rationale for its development is clear, and psychometric properties are acceptable. More studies are needed to establish its validity and utility with certainty.

SUMMARY. The ILK was developed to provide an assessment of a defendant's response style during evaluation of his or her adjudicative competence. Administration and scoring is straightforward, with interpretation being objective, using a cutoff score that is supported by adequate sensitivity, specificity, positive predictive power, and negative predictive power. There is ample internal consistency reliability; the evidence of construct and convergent validity is encouraging.

REVIEWER'S REFERENCES

Dusky v. United States, 362 U.S. 402 (1960).
Otto, R. K. (2006). Competency to stand trial. *Applied Psychology in Criminal Justice, 2,* 82-113.
Otto, R. K., Musick, J. E., & Sherrod, C. B. (2011). Convergent validity of a screening measure designed to identify defendants feigning knowledge deficits related to competence to stand trial. *Assessment, 18,* 60-62.

Review of the Inventory of Legal Knowledge by JEFFREY A. JENKINS, *Professor of Justice Studies, Roger Williams University, Bristol, RI:*

DESCRIPTION. The legal standards for the adjudicative competence (also known as competency to stand trial) of a criminal defendant are clear: the defendant must be able, with a "reasonable degree of rational understanding" (professional manual, p. 1), to understand the nature of the criminal proceedings and to assist in his or her defense (*Godinez v. Moran,* 509 U.S. 389, 1993; *Dusky v. United States,* 362 U.S. 402, 1960). This includes the ability to consult with or waive the right to an attorney, as well as the capacity to plead guilty (*Drope v. Missouri,* 420 U.S. 162, 1975). Thus, a person's ability to participate in a proceeding in which criminal charges are asserted depends upon an assessment of his or her mental capacity in general but, more specifically, his or her understanding of the criminal proceedings. To complete this assessment, forensic examiners rely on a variety of assessment tools and methods. The Inventory of Legal Knowledge (ILK) is intended to measure a limited, but important, aspect of evaluating adjudicative competence: response style. Specifically, the ILK seeks to help examiners determine whether a respondent is likely to be malingering (feigning a mental illness or cognitive deficit), most often for the purpose of avoiding trial altogether or gaining some other perceived benefit as a result of feigned adjudicative incompetence. The ILK employs two methods to accomplish this. First, it compares a respondent's score on the instrument to answers that would be expected by chance. To the extent that the respondent scores significantly below a chance level, it is considered to be indicative of feigning. Second, a respondent's score is compared to that of various reference groups, such as criminal defendants acquitted by reason of insanity or adults hospitalized with serious mental illness (see "Development" below for further discussion of normative reference groups). If a respondent scores significantly below scores obtained by these norm groups, the respondent is likely to have given feigned responses.

The ILK consists of an item booklet and a perforated response sheet with a scoring sheet beneath, as well as a professional manual that guides administration, scoring, and score interpretation. The item booklet includes 61 true-false items that are read verbatim to the examinee. The items include basic statements relating to the criminal justice system. Responses are recorded by the examiner on the response sheet by circling "T" or "F." When each response is recorded, the examiner tells the respondent whether the answer given was correct or incorrect before proceeding to the next item. Scoring is accomplished by separating the response sheet from the scoring sheet, upon which the circled responses are transferred and shown as ones and zeros, indicating correct and incorrect responses, respectively. Examiners need only sum the correct scores to produce a total ILK score. This score is compared to reference values reported in the appendices of the professional manual to assist the examiner in reaching a conclusion about whether the respondent has feigned a deficit in legal knowledge.

DEVELOPMENT. The ILK was developed for use with English-speaking respondents 12 years of age and older. It presumes the respondent has the ability to understand language at a fifth-grade reading level and has a basic familiarity with the American legal system. The test authors chose the administration format of providing respondents with feedback on the correctness of their responses in order to (a) allow those who respond honestly but simply lack understanding of aspects of the criminal justice system to learn and potentially improve their performance on subsequent items and (b) encourage those who feign to downgrade their performance if they believe they are giving too many correct answers.

More than 100 items were initially created to reflect a broad range of factual information relating to the criminal justice system in areas such as pleas, evidence, rights, and courtroom procedures. Duplicates and flawed items were eliminated, resulting in the final 61 items. Items were revised for clarity and reading level. Items were phrased so that there were approximately equal numbers of correct and incorrect items and reviewed by a panel consisting of five psychologists, one psychiatrist, two attorneys, and a clergy member. The ILK then underwent a series of pilot tests that involved examining the performance of the items with adult psychiatric inpatients, adults adjudicated incompetent, adults and adolescents being evaluated for adjudicative competence, and adults living in the community. The items on the ILK survived this process with only minor variations in word choice.

TECHNICAL. The normative groups for the ILK are reference samples obtained from nine different populations/settings. These include three control groups: adults living in the community, college students (some of whom were asked to feign), and juveniles living in the community. The remaining six samples were obtained in clinical or forensic settings: adult psychiatric inpatients, adults adjudicated incompetent to proceed, inpatients found not guilty by reason of insanity, adult defendants evaluated for adjudicative competence, juvenile defendants evaluated for adjudicative competence, and juveniles adjudicated incompetent to proceed. Mean ILK total scores and cutoff scores as well as cumulative percentile scores for comparison are provided.

The technical characteristics of the ILK are discussed in the professional manual. Reliability is reported in terms of internal consistency and test-retest reliability. Estimates were derived from the adult community control group ($N = 211$) or a subset ($N = 61$) of the college student sample. Coefficient alpha was reported to be .88 for the ILK total score, which is adequate for a knowledge-based measure. Test-retest reliability with an average 7-day retest interval resulted in a reliability coefficient of .76. Both of these reliability estimates should be interpreted with caution for two reasons. First, as the test authors themselves point out, the purpose of the ILK is to assess response style, not legal system knowledge. Because the reliability estimates are based on the ILK total score, they estimate the reliability of the ILK as a measure of knowledge about the legal system. Second, reliability estimates that were based on a sample of adults living in the community used a sample that was chosen by oversampling on characteristics of criminal defendants such as males, racial minorities, and lower socioeconomic status, which is a reasonable sampling approach. However, it seems that the likelihood of feigning by this group would be low. Although it may be valuable to include this group for reference purposes, estimates derived from this group do not necessarily apply to the group of respondents for which the ILK was intended: actual criminal defendants whose adjudicative competence is in doubt and who are more likely to engage in feigning their responses.

The professional manual also provides various sources of evidence of validity for the ILK. First, the discriminant validity of the ILK was assessed by comparing the means of the reference samples. No significant differences were found among the community-based control groups, which would be expected given their selection as controls. With only one exception, no significant differences were found among the forensic/clinical groups, which also would be expected given the similarity among these groups as reference samples. However, the community control groups were found to have scored significantly higher than the forensic/clinical groups, demonstrating that the ILK does produce different results in populations with presumed differences in their propensity to feign about their legal knowledge. Of particular importance for an instrument such as the ILK (which seeks to distinguish feigning response styles) is its ability to classify. The test authors report several studies comparing respondents who were given the standard ILK instructions and those who were given "fake bad" instructions; that is, instructed to feign their knowledge of the legal system. Those in the "fake bad" group reported significantly lower ILK scores than those in the standard group, a difference in the expected direction. Finally, convergent validity evidence was provided, based on a process that compared scores with scores from three other measures of feigning/malingering. These comparisons yielded validity coefficients of approximately .60, well within an acceptable range for such estimates.

COMMENTARY. As a measure of response style, the ILK has much to recommend it. It is easy to administer and score in nearly any setting and provides a quick evaluation of feigning behavior in the assessment of adjudicative competence. Its rationale is sound and the development of items and support for the technical characteristics of the instrument is commendable. With the single caution regarding interpretation of the reliability coefficients noted above, the ILK can be relied upon as a quick measure of potential feigning to be used as part of a thorough evaluation of adjudicative competence.

SUMMARY. The ILK is a measure of response style relating to the evaluation of adjudicative competence that seeks to distinguish honest and feigned responses to items involving the legal system. The development of the ILK is research-based and generally reflects a sound approach to instrument development. Although no one instrument should be used alone to assess feigned responses, the ILK may be used with confidence to help evaluate this aspect of response style for those who require an assessment of adjudicative competence.

REVIEWER'S REFERENCES

Drope v. Missouri, 420 U.S. 162 (1975).
Dusky v. United States, 362 U.S. 402 (1960).
Godinez v. Moran, 509 U.S. 389 (1993).

[89]
IT Aptitude Personality & Attitude Profile.

Purpose: "Designed to assess certain aspects of a person's work habits, work attitudes, and analytical skills that pertain to success in a career in the IT industry."
Population: Under age 17 through adult.
Publication Date: 2011.
Acronym: ITAPAP.
Scores, 21: Meticulousness, Concentration, Prioritization, Attitude Towards Team Work, Team vs. Individual Preference, Adaptability, Pattern Recognition, Classification, Analogies, Logic, Creative Problem-Solving, Patience, Time Management, Reaction to Stress, Attitude Towards Dishonesty, Impression Management, Acquiescence, Work Habits, Work Attitudes, Analytical Skills, Overall Score.
Administration: Individual.
Price Data: Available from publisher.
Time: (30) minutes.
Comments: Self-administered online assessment. The test publisher advises that the test manual is being updated to include more information about methodology and theoretical background used in the development of the test. The test publisher also advises that this information is available to clients, as are benchmarks for relevant industries and racial/ethnic group comparison data. However, this information was not provided to Buros or the reviewers.
Author: PsychTests AIM, Inc.
Publisher: PsychTests AIM, Inc. [Canada].

Review of the IT Aptitude Personality & Attitude Profile by LAURA L. B. BARNES, Associate Professor of Research and Evaluation, Oklahoma State University, Tulsa, OK:

DESCRIPTION. The IT Aptitude Personality & Attitude Profile is "designed to assess certain aspects of a person's Work Habits, Work Attitudes, and Analytical Skills that pertain to success in a career in the IT industry" (manual, p. 1). Beyond this proposed purpose, there is no description provided in the manual. The test is administered online and contains "133 plus" (manual, p. 1) questions. The online version provided by the publisher for this review contained 137 questions. Fifteen subscales are said to contribute to the subfactors of Work Habits, Work Attitudes, and Analytical Skills, plus there are two validity subscales. A total score is also generated based on all content subscales except Team vs. Individual Preference. Although the test manual (p. 4) records the number of items for the total score as 128, the sum of the items listed for 15 subscales is 144. Therefore, the actual composition of the subscores and the total score is not clear. The test items are described as "situational and self-assessment and images" (manual, p. 1). The Work Attitudes Scale is said to measure "an employee's attitude in the workplace in terms of how they fit in with the existing team and how they will handle new situations as they arise" (manual, p. 1). Work Habits is said to assess "the ability to work efficiently and productively" (manual, p. 1), and Analytical Skills to assess "analytical reasoning skills and the ability to understand complex abstract concepts in order to find the appropriate solution to a problem" (manual, p. 1). The subscale descriptions are not provided in the manual but are part of the report provided to examinees upon completion of the online test.

The test is taken in an online environment and is administered via the ArchProfile testing portal. The test should maintain examinees' interest with varied item formats and content. Upon completion, a report is generated that describes examinee performance for each subscale. A narrative summary of examinee strengths, potentials, and limitations is also provided. Other features of the online report are brief descriptions of what is tested in each area as well as a list of suggestions for improving skills in the tested areas.

DEVELOPMENT. No information about the development of the test is provided in the manual nor was it available from the publisher's website. There is no information about its theoretical foundation, or about how the items were constructed or analyzed.

TECHNICAL.

Standardization. The standardization sample consisted of 1,045 self-selected volunteers who took the test on Queendom.com, Psychtests.com, or PsychologyToday.com over an unspecified period of time. The sample was evenly balanced by gender and ranged in age from "below 17" (14%) to "50+" (4%). Unknown gender constituted 9% and unknown age constituted 7% of the sample. The national origin of the sample is not provided. The test manual does not provide information regarding how volunteers were recruited to take the test. The normative sample was not scientifically obtained: "The sample was uncontrolled," according to the test manual (p. 3). Such haphazard data collection is not likely to result in norms that are representative of the intended population (AERA, APA, & NCME, 1999, p. 55). Descriptive statistics computed on this sample are provided for all subscales and subfactors and for the Overall Score. Separate means and standard deviations are provided for males and females and for age levels; however, they are neither presented as subgroup norms nor should they be interpreted as such. Rather, these comparisons are reported as part of the test's "validity analysis" (manual, p. 17). The online score report generates scores on a 0–100 scale for the subscales, subfactors, and the total score. No information was available regarding the method of score transformations from raw scores to scale scores. Presumably, these are scores derived from comparison to a standardization sample. However, because the standardization sample was not scientifically obtained, but consisted of self-selected volunteers who took the test at various websites, the validity of the derived scores is questionable.

Reliability. Alpha coefficients of internal consistency were computed on an unspecified sample and are reported for subscales, subfactors, and the total score. Although internal consistency coefficients for the subfactors and the overall score are adequate, reliability for half of the subscales is well below even minimally acceptable standards. Subscale coefficients range from .47 for Classification to .84 for Meticulousness. Three subscales have coefficients below .50; the median alpha coefficient is .71. Subfactor coefficients are .82, .88, and .91, and the internal consistency of the Overall Score is reported as .92. No information regarding the stability of the scores over time (test-retest reliability) is provided.

Validity. A systematic approach to presenting validity evidence is absent. The publisher provides no information about the theoretical foundation of the instrument, no description of item content, no factor-analytic studies supporting the construction of the subscale or their relationships to the subfactors, and no construct validity evidence of any kind. Numerous tables and charts are presented showing the results of significance testing for various group comparisons on each subscale as noted above. The standardization sample provided the data for these comparisons. In addition to the inflated Type I error rate associated with this type of unrestrained analysis, the value of these comparisons is dubious because we are given no basis for interpreting the meaning or even the direction of the subscale scores. For instance, how does one interpret the finding that college graduates had a higher score than all other groups on Team vs. Individual Preference (manual, p. 43)? Two of the comparison variables, (a) experience in the IT field and (b) supervisor's ratings, provide some indication of a relationship of the scores to job performance. Those with IT experience significantly ($p < .05$) outscored those without IT experience on each of the subfactors and subscales except Patience. Higher scores on the tests also were associated with better self-reported performance reviews. However, no information was given regarding how IT experience was defined, and the validity of self-reported performance reviews is questionable. Most troubling is the lack of evidence that test performance bears any empirical relationship to actual job performance other than that which was self-reported. No information regarding performance in specific IT jobs is provided.

COMMENTARY. The publisher's website shows that this measure is one of many tests developed and marketed by PsychTests (PsychTests AIM Inc., 2013). According to the website's catalog information (PsychTests AIM Inc., 2012), the ITAPAP complies with APA and EEOC standards. Further, the catalog advertises that coefficient alpha values for the ITAPAP range from .82 to .92. In fact, only six of the 21 scores reported in the manual made available for review have alpha coefficients in this range. The test publisher has failed to meet the requirements of the *Standards for Educational and Psychological Testing* (AERA, APA, & NCME, 1999) in a number of ways beginning with a lack of an integrated validation strategy regarding the use and interpretation of test results (AERA, APA, & NCME, 1999, p. 9), failure to present a sound scientific basis for test development and interpretation (e.g., Standards 3.1, 3.2, 3.4, 3.7, 3.9), use of nonscientific sampling methods for collecting normative data (Standards 4.5, 4.6), and providing inadequate documentation in general (AERA, APA, & NCME, 1999, pp. 67–70).

SUMMARY. The ITAPAP has a very attractive online delivery system. In addition to scores and interpretations presented in both graphic and narrative formats, the score report provides information regarding examinees' strengths, potentials, and limitations for employment in an IT environment. Feedback is provided to examinees to help them understand their scores and to give recommendations for improving their work habits and skills. The test has a number of technical inadequacies, however, including the poorly defined standardization sample, the lack of any systematic approach to assessing the validity of the test scores, and the relatively poor reliability of a number of subscales. Information regarding test development is absent, as is any reference to how the test is scored. The

following quote is from the publisher's website: "Each test is well researched and designed according to the APA (American Psychological Association) standards for educational and psychological testing" (PsychTests AIM Inc., 2013). Based on documentation provided for this review, those claims would not appear to include the ITAPAP. Given its substantial limitations, this reviewer does not recommend the use of this test at this time.

REVIEWER'S REFERENCES

American Educational Research Association, American Psychological Association, & National Council on Measurement in Education. (1999). *Standards for educational and psychological testing.* Washington, DC: American Educational Research Association.
PsychTests AIM Inc. (2013). PsychTests. Retrieved from http://corporate. psychtests.com/tests/?sec=tests
PsychTests AIM Inc. (2012). ITAPAP Personality and Attitude Profile. Retrieved from http://corporate.psychtests.com/pdf/catalog_arch_profile.pdf

Review of IT Aptitude Personality and Attitude Profile by TRACY KANTROWITZ, Director of Research & Development, SHL, Atlanta, GA:

DESCRIPTION. The IT Aptitude Personality & Attitude Profile (ITAPAP) is an assessment of work habits, work attitudes, and analytical skills for use in selecting and training information technology (IT) professionals. The test uses "133 plus" (manual, p. 1) situational and multiple-choice items to assess 15 markers of success in the IT field. The test is available in a web-based format with clear instructions. The test is untimed, but the authors indicate that approximately 30 minutes should be allotted to complete the test.

DEVELOPMENT. The authors sought to develop a test of characteristics that pertain to success in the IT industry. The authors chose to report results in terms of 15 dimensions of IT success that are organized into 3 subfactors: Work Attitudes, Work Habits, and Analytical Skills. However, no information is provided about the development of the ITAPAP that would help evaluate the rigor with which the assessment was developed. There is no reference to job analytic or classification work to identify the specific types of jobs targeted by the test, even though resources exist for gathering information about knowledge, skills, experience, and characteristics needed for IT roles (see O*NET, for example). In addition, no information is provided in the test manual about the theoretical or empirical support for the 15 subscales and three subfactors, literature on characteristics related to IT success, information on the item writers and their qualifications, the item writing process, how scoring was determined, how items were piloted, and how the final set of items was selected.

TECHNICAL. The standardization sample for the ITAPAP consisted of 1,045 examinees who completed the assessment via one of three websites where the test was made available. No information is provided in the test manual about how examinees were recruited to participate or whether the examinees were employed in the IT industry. Such information would assist in determining how relevant and generalizable the norms would be for the target use of the test. Normative data are presented for the overall sample, but are not readily interpretable because information about scaling is not provided. Norms could be in the form of percentages or percentile ranks, but there is no explanation about the data provided in the tables. Norms also are reported in terms of gender and age. The sample was fairly equally composed of men and women, and various age groups were sufficiently represented.

Reliability evidence is presented in the form of internal consistency estimates. Reliability estimates were calculated using a sample of 1,045 (presumably the same group of examinees used to generate the normative data noted above). The internal consistency of the Overall Score is quite high (alpha = .92), as were the estimates of the three subfactors (.91 for Work Habits, .88 for Work Attitudes, and .82 for Analytical Skills). Reliability estimates for the 15 subscales ranged from .47 to .84, with 13 of the 15 lower than .80. This is likely due to the brevity of the scales. According to published texts (e.g., Gatewood & Feild, 2000), tests used for pre-employment selection should reach a reliability threshold of .85. Authors should indicate to users how decisions should be made on the basis of the Overall Score and/or the subfactor scores.

The authors report subgroup difference information for gender and age. (Note: the test authors label this information as "validity analysis," which is probably inappropriate because it does not express information in terms of traditional types of evidence of validity–content, construct, or criterion-related). Results are presented in terms of mean differences at the individual scale level and indicate few significant differences for gender. A variety of significant differences were found for age, with those younger than 20 generally scoring lower than other age groups. Perhaps most importantly, significant differences between age groups were found for the Overall Score, indicating that younger examinees may generally score lower than older examinees.

Validity evidence is presented in the form of criterion-related validation with self-reported grades, self-reported experience in the IT field, and self-reported supervisor ratings. Little information is included about the nature of the criteria measures or the sample used to collect this information. Again, such information is critical to judge the relevance of this information in light of the intended uses of the test. Academic achievement, for example, is an insufficient criterion to validate the test scores if the intended application is selection and training of IT professionals. In terms of the academic achievement criterion, mean differences were calculated via analysis of variance (ANOVA) to determine whether there were significant differences between: (a) those with "straight A's" (n = 132), (b) those with "good grades" (n = 132), and (c) those with "average/below average" grades (n = 132). Several significant differences were found, and post-hoc analyses generally showed that those who reported earning straight A's scored higher on the ITAPAP. ANOVA results show some evidence of validity, but correlational analysis would be more appropriate to judge the strength of the relationship between test scores and this criterion.

The validity of the ITAPAP was also examined in the context of performance reviews. On its face, this set of analyses appears to be a more accurate criterion to validate a test designed for employment uses. However, no information was provided that details how performance was measured, the nature of the sample, or the characteristics of managers who provided ratings. Mean differences were calculated via analysis of variance (ANOVA) to determine significant differences between: (a) those with "excellent" performance (n = 138), (b) those with "above average" performance (n = 138), and (c) those with "average/poor" performance (n = 137). Several significant differences were found, and post-hoc analyses generally showed that those with "excellent" evaluations received higher test scores. Again, correlational analysis would be appropriate to include to judge the strength of the relationship between test scores and this criterion.

No construct validation evidence is provided to establish convergent or discriminant validity for the test. Such information would inform whether characteristics measured in this test are highly correlated with similar characteristics measured in more established tests.

COMMENTARY. The ITAPAP is intended to be used for selection and training of IT professionals, a set of jobs known to be in demand in a workforce increasingly characterized by knowledge and technical jobs. The normative data are based on a large group of individuals but need to be updated to reflect job applicants applying for target jobs for which the test is designed to be used. Reliability estimates are based on a large group of individuals, and the test's Overall Score exhibits a high degree of internal consistency. Most critically, however, validity evidence is very limited, and the theoretical basis supporting the assessment and details regarding the test development process are unknown. In future documentation and development, the authors should document better the rationale and development of their assessment and conduct additional research to provide criterion-related and construct evidence of validity to provide more information to consumers about the usefulness of the test.

The use of the phrase "133 plus" test questions is peculiar and is confusing to the examinee. This reviewer is unsure whether the instrument is computer adaptive, whether there are 133 scored items and an unspecified number of variable/experimental/unscored items, or what else might explain the additional questions in the test. The web interface also indicates that the test requires 30 minutes, but there is not a time limit. This statement could also be potentially confusing to examinees. Furthermore, the test does not include practice questions so examinees can get a feel for what to expect in the test. Addressing such items would enhance test taker reactions and perceptions of fairness in the test.

SUMMARY. The ITAPAP test was designed to measure characteristics important for success in IT roles. The test shows evidence of reliability and has some norms to facilitate comparisons across examinees, but the test manual severely lacks technical information needed to support the inferences made about the ITAPAP. More information is needed for critical evaluation.

REVIEWER'S REFERENCES

Gatewood, R., & Feild, H. S. (2000). *Human resource selection.* South-Western College Publishers.
O*NET. (2012). *Find occupations.* Retrieved from http://www.onetonline.org

[90]

Jordan Left-Right Reversal Test, 3rd Edition.

Purpose: Designed "to identify children who may have difficulty recognizing the correct orientation of letters and numbers, or who may reverse words or other letter sequences."
Population: Ages 5-0 through 18-11.
Publication Dates: 1973-2011.

Acronym: Jordan-3.
Scores, 2: Accuracy, Error.
Administration: Group.
Levels, 2: Ages 5 through 8, Ages 9 through 18.
Price Data, 2012: $110 per test kit, including manual (2011, 88 pages), 25 record forms, 25 Remedial Checklists (optional), and 25 Laterality Checklists (optional); $30 per 25 record forms; $20 per 25 Remedial Checklists; $20 per 25 Laterality Checklists; $40 per manual.
Time: (20-30) minutes.
Author: Brian T. Jordan.
Publisher: Academic Therapy Publications.
Cross References: For reviews by Christine W. Burns and Jeffrey H. Snow of the 1990 Edition, see 12:203 (1 reference); see also T4:1326 (4 references); for reviews by Mary S. Poplin and Joseph Torgesen of the Second Revised Edition, see 9:557; see also T3:1224 (2 references); for reviews by Barbara K. Keogh and Richard J. Reisboard, and excerpted reviews by Alex Bannatyne and Alan Krichev, see 8:434 (5 references).

Review of the Jordan Left-Right Reversal Test, 3rd Edition by DARRELL L. SABERS, Professor Emeritus of Educational Psychology, and AMY M. OLSON, Doctoral Student, University of Arizona, Tucson, AZ:

DESCRIPTION. The Jordan Left-Right Reversal Test, 3rd Edition (Jordan-3) assesses the ability to recognize picture, letter, number, sequence, and word reversals. It comprises five subtests (two given to children ages 5 to 8 and all five given to students ages 9 to 18). Two subtests new to this edition include reversals in line drawings and reversals in nonword letter sequences.

The Jordan-3 can be administered individually or to small groups and requires 20 to 30 minutes for testing and about 10 minutes for scoring. The directions for administration are clear and easy to follow. Scores are interpreted from percentile ranks: Scores in the 25th to 99th percentile range are considered Average, those in the 11th to 24th percentile range are Borderline, and scores in the 1st to 10th percentile range are Atypical. Age equivalent scores are also provided, but not recommended for general use by the test author.

DEVELOPMENT. The Jordan-3 is the latest revision of the test (previously published in 1974 and 1990) intended to "identify children who may have difficulty recognizing the correct orientation of letters and numbers, or who may reverse words or letter sequences" (manual, p. 8). Improvements in the current edition include providing additional information about the national representation of the standardization sample and providing separate scores for Accuracy and Errors. The new items in the Jordan-3 include both easier and more difficult items to increase the range of the test.

TECHNICAL. Norms were based on 1,334 examinees from 43 sites in 22 states across the United States, who were tested individually. The sample characteristics compare reasonably well with the 2000 U.S. Census Bureau data with respect to gender, ethnicity, and parent education. There are separate norms tables for boys and for girls. The sample includes 185 students identified with some type of disability.

Internal consistency reliability estimates were calculated for the Accuracy scores on two subsamples, ages 5 to 8 and ages 9 to 18. The resulting alpha coefficients for Part 1 (the first two subtests) were .89 and .81, respectively. For Part 2 (three subtests administered to those ages 9 to 18), the alpha coefficient was .91. Stability estimates over an average interval of 20 days are reported for a group of 68 test takers whose ages were not reported. Coefficients were .68 and .66 for Accuracy and Error scores, respectively. In that the test is used to identify cut scores based on percentile ranks, it is important to have good norms and good cut scores. Prospective test users would benefit from a presentation of conditional standard errors near the cut scores for the intended purpose of the test.

Validity information is presented as three types of validity evidence: content, criterion-related, and construct. The stated content domain includes reversals, inversions, and transpositions. The test author explains that letter reversals (d vs. b), inversions (b vs. p), transpositions of adjoining letters (post vs. pots), and reversals of letter sequences (was vs. saw) can change the meaning of words, but that "objects can be perceived without regard to position in space or directional orientation" (manual, p. 8). However, as a concession to the youngest test takers who may not be familiar with letters and numbers, the first subtest assesses an individual's ability to detect incorrect object orientation. The Jordan-3 does not assess letter inversions on any of the subtests and only assesses transpositions in nonword sequences of letters. Thus, the content relevance of the subtests appears acceptable (i.e., has evidence of face validity), but the content representativeness is potentially problematic.

Criterion-related validity information shows moderate correlations between Accuracy and Error scores on the Jordan-3 and scores on subtests of the Wechsler Intelligence Scale for Children–Fourth Edition (WISC-IV; 16:262) and the Woodcock–Johnson III (WJ III; 15:281). Correlation coefficients with WISC-IV Perceptual Reasoning Index (PRI) and WJ III Achievement (Broad Reading) ranged from .36 (Jordan-3 Error score with WISC-IV PRI) to .44 (Jordan-3 Accuracy score with WISC-IV PRI). In the reviewers' opinion, neither test represents a good criterion measure for the purpose of the Jordan-3, and thus higher coefficients would not really be expected or desirable.

Construct validity evidence is viewed as the most important validity consideration for the Jordan-3 and receives the most discussion in the test manual. Developmental changes, correlations with other measures, and group differences are all discussed and supported by data.

COMMENTARY. The collection of two types of mistakes (omissions and errors) is an improvement over previous versions of the Jordan that focused only on one type of error, particularly if these errors should lead to different decisions about test takers. With more development, these scores may become useful as separate measures in future versions of this test (as initially suggested by Keogh, 1978). Similarly, future development could focus on scoring patterns (e.g., recommendations for students who score in the average range on Accuracy and in the atypical range on Error or vice versa).

The scoring example in Figure 3.1 (manual, p. 23) contains a mistake. Although this mistake is not replicated in the key in the back of the manual, it may cause confusion in learning to score the instrument. [Editor's Note: The publisher advises that this error was corrected in the second printing of the manual.] Additionally, in scoring the new subtest on reversals in nonword letter sequences, a correct score is given when the entire sequence is underlined. For example, when the sequence "S T R" is reversed to "R T S," all three letters are to be underlined. A potential inconsistency in scoring may occur if students misunderstand and only underline the "S" and the "T." The instructions are not clear as to whether the scorer should count this as one sequence (and not mistakenly as two) or give no credit.

In some places, the test author makes suggestions without providing adequate instructions. For example, the test can be used in conjunction with diagnostic test batteries for specific learning disability, but there are no explanations for how the Jordan-3 complements the larger batteries. In the section on score interpretation, the test author cautions that underlying attention processes must be taken into account when interpreting scores, but how this is to be done is unclear. The test also comes with two checklists (laterality and remedial) that are not described in the test manual. Instructions for their use and evidence for their effectiveness would improve the test [see Poplin (1985) and Heydorn (1984, 1985) for criticisms of remediation].

Users may want to consider issues of standardizing administration. For example, for 5-year-olds who have not entered school, the examiner writes each prompt of the letter and number reversal subtest on another sheet of paper or on a blackboard, and students compare what the examiner wrote to what is on their paper. Similarly, in a subtest for students ages 9 to 18, the examiner writes a practice prompt on the board while demonstrating the directions. Whenever possible, users should consider standardizing prompts so that individual differences in handwriting, use of capital versus lower case letters, and so forth, do not affect performance.

In general, these observations also point to the largest problem with the test: It is unclear what construct the test is intended to measure. If the results help detect potential problems with reading, the number reversals contained in one of the subtests seem inappropriate. However, if results should be linked to mathematics, the concurrent validity studies might include a measure of mathematics achievement. The examiner might want to know whether a child's performance on the Jordan-3 relates to a general problem or to a more specific problem in either mathematics or reading. Boone (1986) found that reversals as measured by the Jordan-2 were equally related to mathematics, language, and reading.

SUMMARY. Although the Jordan-3 does seem to measure reversals, more evidence is needed to demonstrate that the construct being measured impacts student outcomes and that the suggested remediation improves student achievement. Test users who find the previous versions useful can be assured of the Jordan-3's improvement, but critics of previous versions (Poplin, 1985; Torgeson, 1985) are not likely to be satisfied with the continuing issues regarding the validity of the construct addressed by the test.

REVIEWERS' REFERENCES

Boone, H. C. (1986). Relationships of left-right reversals to academic achievement. *Perceptual and Motor Skills, 62*, 27-33.

Heydorn, B. L. (1984). Treatment versus non-treatment in reduction of symbol reversals by first-grade children. *Perceptual and Motor Skills, 59*, 36-38.

Heydorn, B. L. (1985). Effect of practice of correct symbol reversals on reading achievement by first-grade children. *Perceptual and Motor Skills, 60*, 509-510.

Keogh, B. K. (1978). [Review of the Jordan Left-Right Reversal Test, Revised Edition.] In O. K. Buros (Ed.), *The eighth mental measurements yearbook* (pp. 588-589). Highland Park, NJ: Gryphon Press.

Poplin, M. S. (1985). [Review of the Jordan Left-Right Reversal Test, Second Revised Edition.] In J. V. Mitchell, Jr. (Ed.), *The ninth mental measurements yearbook* (pp. 761-763). Lincoln, NE: Buros Institute of Mental Measurements.

Torgesen, J. (1985). [Review of the Jordan Left-Right Reversal Test, Second Revised Edition.] In J. V. Mitchell, Jr. (Ed.), *The ninth mental measurements yearbook* (pp. 763-764). Lincoln, NE: Buros Institute of Mental Measurements.

Review of the Jordan Left-Right Reversal Test, 3rd Edition by JAMES P. VAN HANEGHAN, Professor and Director of Assessment and Evaluation, College of Education, University of South Alabama, Mobile, AL:

DESCRIPTION. The Jordan Left-Right Reversal Test 3rd Edition (Jordan-3) is designed to detect letter, word, and number reversal problems in children and adolescents ages 5 years to 18 years, 11 months. The test consists of two parts, with each part having subtests. Subtest 1-A involves identifying the reversed figure in a row of line drawings. It is new to this edition, although no rationale for its inclusion is described in the test manual. Subtest 1-B involves identifying reversals from rows of uppercase letters, lowercase letters, and numbers. Only these two subtests are given to children 5 years through 8 years, 11 months. Children 9 years and older receive these subtests and Part 2, which contains three subtests. Subtest 2-A involves finding reversals among rows of words. Subtest 2-B involves finding word reversals in sentences. Subtest 2-C is new and involves looking at two columns of letter sequences. The child is to identify which letters are out of sequence in the second column. Other than a mention in the preface of the test manual of an interest in adding complexity, there is no clear rationale for the addition of this new subtest. Typically, the test takes 20–30 minutes to administer. It may be administered individually or in a group. The test author cautions users to remove stimuli in the test environment that might cue students (e.g., letters and words on bulletin boards). There are two types of raw scores generated from the test: an Accuracy score that indicates the number of reversals found and an Error score comprising the sum of reversals missed and correctly oriented items identified as reversed. These scores are used to determine percentile ranks for different age groups developed from a national sample of 1,300 children. These percentiles ranks are the scores that the test author focuses on for test interpretation. The lower the Accuracy score and the higher the Error score, the lower the percentile rank for a child. Tables are included in the appendices to transform scores to age equivalents and standard scores of different sorts. Generally speaking, in normally developing children the scores tend toward ceiling from around age 9 years and older.

DEVELOPMENT. There is little information presented in the test manual about the development of the items on the Jordan-3. There is no discussion or examination of pilot testing for the new subtests. All that is presented in this section of the test manual are mean raw scores on the subtests at each age level and a note that percentile rank cutoffs were determined by the test author by looking at the score distributions. In the opinion of this reviewer, with the addition of two new subtests, it would be important to learn in detail why those subtests were added, how they might add to the predictive power of the test, and how scores on the new edition correlate with scores on the older editions. Further, more history of the development of the test in its earlier forms seems warranted.

TECHNICAL. The standardization sample included 1,334 individuals from 22 states. The test author claims that the sample demographics approximate the 2000 U.S. Census data. However, the sample appears more educated, rural, Hispanic, and from the West than the general population. The sample was derived from a network of professionals including a list of previous customers for the test. The examiners were told to randomly choose students and were encouraged to find individuals "… representing a wide range of disability status" (manual, p. 38). Hence, although the plan encouraged the drawing of a representative sample, the sampling plan was not a formal one.

Two forms of reliability evidence are presented: internal consistency reliability and test-retest reliability (over an interval that averaged 20 days). The internal consistency reliability coefficients concerning Accuracy scores are in the .80s. As the test author notes, they are adequate, but not as high as desired for making clinical decisions. The test-retest correlation coefficients are reported for raw Accuracy and Error scores. The test-retest coefficient for Accuracy scores is .68, and the coefficient for Error scores is .66. These values indicate some stability, although depending upon the age makeup of the sample and the variation in the interval between tests, the results could be attenuated due to variation in retest interval and restriction of range.

The test author refers the reader to the development section for evidence of content validity. In that section, there are brief descriptions of subtests, an analysis showing that the test scores reach ceiling around 9 or 10 years, and a description of Accuracy and Error scores. Criterion- and construct-related evidence presented comes in the form of moderate correlations of Accuracy and Error scores with the Perceptual Reasoning Index of the Wechsler Intelligence Scale for Children–Fourth Edition (WISC-IV; 16:262) and the Broad Reading score from the Woodcock–Johnson III (WJ III; 15:281). Further criterion-related evidence that students with attention-deficit disorder, learning disability, and reading disability, score lower than matched samples of normally developing children is also presented. No evidence of convergent and discriminant validity is presented, nor is there evidence presented concerning consequential validity.

COMMENTARY. As noted by several authors (e.g., Brooks, Berninger, & Abbott, 2011) reversals are complex phenomena that have several different possible mechanisms and are not even a common part of dyslexia. Although this does not rule out their significance, it makes it incumbent upon the test author to make a strong case for why it is useful and necessary to include a test for reversals in a test battery.

Based on the test manual, one can conclude that the Jordan-3 appears to reliably diagnose reversals. The test is in its third edition, so it has a long history as an assessment of letter reversals. However, modern validity theory (e.g., Kane, 2006) demands more evidence be presented by the test author to clarify the meaning of the letter reversal construct. For example, the test author suggests using the test as a screener for reading problems, but provides no evidence of sensitivity and specificity at different age levels. The test author does demonstrate that children with learning disabilities and attention-deficit disorder achieve lower scores, but the author does not conduct any kind of classification analysis. Further, the test author does not present any predictive validity evidence to show that test scores are predictive of future reading problems. The test author includes a series of exercises for improving laterality, but presents no published evidence that the exercises actually improve scores on the test. A further concern is that the test author presents little evidence that the test adds anything functional to a clinical battery. The three sample case studies presented say little specifically about reversals or their remediation. Although the test author correctly points out that the test cannot be used as a stand-alone measure, the inclusion of the test in a battery suggests that it adds some unique information that can be included in clinical recommendations. Reviews of prior editions by Burns (1995), Snow (1995), Poplin (1985), Torgesen (1985), and Keogh (1978) all reported that there was very little evidence presented to support use of the test. It would be expected that the validity issues raised by previous reviewers would have been addressed more completely by now. Standards for psychological testing dictate that test authors provide evidence that supports the various uses of test scores and explain the cognitive processes that underlie the measure (e.g., American Educational Research Association, American Psychological Association, & National Council on Measurement in Education, 1999). The test manual is lacking in specifics when it comes to showing that the test is useful as part of a battery of tests for students with suspected learning disabilities. Without providing better justifications for its use and a more detailed description of what performance means for whom, it is hard to recommend its use for clinical purposes.

SUMMARY. On a basic level, the Jordan-3 appears to yield consistent (reliable) reversal identification performance in children. However, the new edition of the test adds little to an already muddied picture of the validity of the Jordan Left-Right Reversal Test for the purposes outlined by the test author. Given that this is the third edition of a test with a long history, validity evidence for the test should be better documented. Without those data, it is hard to justify the time and expense of using the test diagnostically.

REVIEWER'S REFERENCES

American Educational Research Association, American Psychological Association, & National Council on Measurement in Education. (1999). *Standards for educational and psychological testing.* Washington, DC: American Educational Research Association.
Brooks, A. D., Berninger, V., & Abbott, R. D. (2011). Letter naming and letter writing reversals in children with dyslexia: Momentary inefficiency in the phonological and orthographic loops of working memory. *Developmental Neuropsychology, 36,* 847-868. doi:10.1080/87565641.2011.606401
Burns, C. W. (1995). [Review of the Jordan Left-Right Reversal Test (1990 Edition)]. In J. C. Conoley & J. C. Impara (Eds.), *The twelfth mental measurements yearbook* (pp. 525-526). Lincoln, NE: Buros Institute of Mental Measurements.
Kane, M. T. (2006). Validation. In R. L. Brennan (Ed.), *Educational measurement* (4th Ed., pp. 17-64). Westport, CT: American Council on Education and Pra250 eger Publishers.
Keogh, B. K. (1978). [Review of the Jordan Left-Right Reversal Test, Revised Edition]. In O. K. Buros (Ed.), *The eighth mental measurements yearbook* (pp. 433-434). Highland Park, N.J.: Gryphon Press.
Poplin, M. S. (1985). [Review of the Jordan Left-Right Reversal Test, Second Revised Edition]. In J. V. Mitchell, Jr. (Ed.), *The ninth mental measurements yearbook* (pp. 761-763). Lincoln, NE: Buros Institute of Mental Measurements.
Snow, J. H. (1995). [Review of the Jordan Left-Right Reversal Test (1990 Edition)]. In J. C. Conoley & J. C. Impara (Eds.), *The twelfth mental measurements yearbook* (pp. 526-527). Lincoln, NE: Buros Institute of Mental Measurements.
Torgesen, J. (1985). [Review of the Jordan Left-Right Reversal Test, Second Revised Edition]. In J. V. Mitchell, Jr. (Ed.), *The ninth mental measurements yearbook* (pp. 763-764). Lincoln, NE: Buros Institute of Mental Measurements.

[91]

Leadership Potential Assessment.

Purpose: Designed "to measure whether one has the right attitudes, behaviors, and skills to be an effective leader."

Population: Under 17 through adult.
Publication Date: 2011.
Acronym: LEAP.
Scores, 20: Transactional Leadership, Transformational Leadership, Leadership Potential, Delegating, Giving Feedback, Goal Setting, Rewarding Performance, Motivating, Coaching, Problem Solving, Vision, Collaboration, Setting an Example, Agreeableness, Conscientiousness, Open-Mindedness, Extroversion, Emotional Stability, Impression Management, Overall Score.
Administration: Individual.
Price Data: Available from publisher.
Time: (30) minutes.
Comments: Self-administered online assessment. The test publisher advises that the test manual is being updated to include more information about methodology and theoretical background used in the development of the test. The test publisher also advises that this information is available to clients, as are benchmarks for relevant industries and racial/ethnic group comparison data. However, this information was not provided to Buros or the reviewers.
Author: PsychTests AIM, Inc.
Publisher: PsychTests AIM, Inc. [Canada].

Review of the Leadership Potential Assessment by JOHN K. HAWLEY, Engineering Psychologist, U.S. Army Research Laboratory, Ft. Bliss Field Element, Ft. Bliss, TX:

DESCRIPTION. The Leadership Potential Assessment (LEAP) developed by PsychTests AIM, Inc. is intended to measure whether a test taker has the right attitudes, behaviors, and skills to be an effective leader. Leadership is defined in the test report summary as "getting other people to follow you towards a common goal, bringing out the best in people around you, and helping people find a greater meaning in the everyday tasks they are asked to perform." Assessment results are presented in terms of an overall leadership aptitude score and three subfactor scores. The leadership subfactors are Transactional Leadership, Transformational Leadership, and Leadership Potential. Transactional Leadership is defined as the ability to set clear guidelines for behavior, reward good performance and punish poor performance, provide feedback, and take a management role in assigning tasks to others. Separate subscores for the Transactional subfactor are provided for Delegating, Goal Setting, Giving Feedback, and Rewarding Performance. Transformational Leadership is defined in terms of motivating and coaching employees, sharing a vision for the company or organization, problem-solving, decision-making, and setting an excellent example.

Separate subscores are provided for each of the Transformational subfactors. Leadership Potential is defined as the level of suitability for a leadership role. Leadership Potential subscores are Agreeableness, Conscientiousness, Open-Mindedness, Extroversion, and Emotional Stability. All scores are presented on a 0–100 scale. The assessment report also provides an Impression Management score, which assesses the test taker's tendency to respond to the test items in a socially desirable manner. The Impression Management score is analogous to the lie scale included with other psychological tests. The LEAP report provides the test taker with a summary of test results stated in terms of leadership-related strengths, potential strengths, and limitations. Tips on how to help members of an organization reach their highest potential also are provided.

The LEAP comprises 100 Likert-type and situational items. Likert-type items ask respondents to rate themselves on specific traits and personal characteristics. With situational items, test subjects are asked to indicate how they might view or relate to a particular organizational situation. Test takers are given 30 minutes to complete the assessment. The LEAP is available online only, and the printable assessment report is available immediately. Only one version of the assessment is available.

DEVELOPMENT. The LEAP is a trait-based leadership assessment tool. As described above, the assessment is based on the notion that aptitude for leadership reflects a combination of transactional and transformational skills, traits, and attitudes. Transactional and transformational leadership are operationally defined in terms of the subfactors listed in the previous section. LEAP documentation reflects this view and further asserts that the assessment's conceptual structure is based on extensive research. However, no research citations to support the claim are provided. The 100 items comprising the measure are mapped across the three leadership subfactors and their associated subscales. The number of items per subscale ranges from 6 to 12. No information is provided as to the source of the items, and no information is provided concerning how individual item responses are combined to form subscale scores. Similarly, no information is provided concerning how subscale scores are combined to form subfactor scores, or how subfactor scores are combined to form the Overall Score.

TECHNICAL. Per the assessment manual (2011), the LEAP has been administered to 37,869

participants. This calibration sample was uncontrolled, and participants self-selected to take the assessment and also to participate in a follow-on "validation study" (manual, p. 2). Summary statistics for these participants (minimum score, maximum score, mean, and standard deviation) are provided for the Overall Score, the three leadership subfactors, and each of the subscales comprising the assessment. Normative data for assessment participants are provided separately by gender, age, educational level, school grades, job position, socioeconomic status, satisfaction with job field, and performance in job field. All of these background data items are self-reported. The assessment manual also presents ANOVA results comparing the various assessment scores across the above categories. Most of these comparisons are statistically significant. However, given the large sample sizes, any score differences across groups, no matter how small, will be significant. The practical significance of most of these reported differences across calibration sample subgroups is thus questionable. Differences across subgroups are not discussed in the manual.

Reliability indices for the LEAP are expressed in terms of coefficient alpha measures of internal consistency. Internal consistency reliability indices for the overall leadership aptitude score and for the three leadership subfactors are generally high, ranging from .81 to .95. These high numbers possibly reflect the large calibration sample and a large number of assessment items. Reliability indices for the subscores are generally lower (reflecting a smaller number of component items) and range from .34 to .82. The internal consistency reliability index for the Impression Management score (lie scale) is .77.

None of the traditional types of validity evidence are addressed in the LEAP manual. The assessment's content and construct evidence of validity are based on the fact that items are included to address the subscales defining each of the three subfactors characterizing overall leadership aptitude. Essentially, assessment scores reflect a relatively simple roll-up from trait/skill subscale to leadership subfactor to overall leadership aptitude. No criterion-related evidence of validity is provided relating assessment results to independent measures of leadership performance in small groups or larger organizational situations. Also, there is no discussion of how the various scores have been shown to relate to actual leadership performance, merely a blanket claim that they are related. In terms of how assessment results are to be used, the manual merely states that the results are useful for "pre-employment testing" (p. 1).

COMMENTARY. The LEAP is easily taken online, and results are immediately available. All of the various scores have a rather simple intuitive meaning, much like the results provided by other popular psychological and personality tests and measures. The construct underlying the assessment is consistent with trait-based perspectives on leadership (see Zaccaro, 2007, for a recent review of this field). However, users must bear in mind that "Leadership represents complex patterns of behavior, likely explained, in part, by multiple leader attributes, and trait approaches to leadership need to reflect this reality" (Zaccaro, 2007, p. 6). Bennis (2007, p. 2) also cautions that research on the subject of leadership is "vast, amorphous, and slippery." These comments suggest caution when interpreting results from an assessment instrument like the LEAP.

That said, this reviewer believes the LEAP has some potential uses in pre-employment screening. The construct underlying the LEAP is consistent with a relatively simplistic view of leadership that is perhaps best applied to participation in and leadership of small groups. The assessment might reasonably be used to identify personnel who could function smoothly in or possibly lead small groups or teams. The subfactors included in the assessment generally reflect traits, attributes, and attitudes that would facilitate or detract from smooth team functioning or the ability to effectively lead a small group. Also, given that the reported distribution of LEAP scores from the calibration sample is generally negatively skewed and truncated on the top end of the distribution (possibly reflecting how the scores are scaled), the results might be more useful to identify personnel who should not be assigned to participate in or lead a small group. Scores on the lower end of the distribution reflect traits, attributes, and attitudes that would not be conducive to smooth team functioning or effective team leadership.

SUMMARY. The LEAP is easily administered online, and results are immediately available. Results are stated in nontechnical terms and are intuitively appealing. The assessment has acceptable internal consistency reliability indices. However, little validity-related information is provided, and validity-related discussions are cursory and unsupported by research citations. The assessment can reasonably be used for the purpose suggested in the assessment manual: pre-employment screening, and possibly in other ways. Users should be cautioned, however, that the LEAP is a rather simple trait-based leadership assessment tool that is perhaps best applied at the small group or team level to identify who should or should not participate in or be assigned to lead such a group.

REVIEWER'S REFERENCES
Bennis, W. (2007). The challenges of leadership in the modern world: Introduction to the special issue. *American Psychologist, 62*(1), 2-5.
Zaccaro, S. J. (2007). Trait-based perspectives of leadership. *American Psychologist, 62*(1), 6-16.

Review of the Leadership Potential Assessment by KARL N. KELLEY, Professor of Psychology, North Central College, Naperville, IL:

DESCRIPTION. The Leadership Potential Assessment (LEAP) is an online test designed to measure personality traits that characterize good leaders and to provide feedback on how to utilize these traits if given a leadership position. This 50- to 65-minute "A" level test is designed for individuals 18 or older. The 100 situational self-report items yield an overall leadership score, three primary factor scores, and 15 scale scores that are commonly associated with effective leadership behaviors and an Impression Management Score.

DEVELOPMENT. The LEAP measures three factors and 15 scales that are theoretically consistent with predictors of effective leadership. This test is marketed by PsychTests, a subsidiary of Plumeus, Inc. Plumeus is responsible for research and development of a wide variety of assessments, and PsychTests has served as the online delivery system of those tests (http://corporate.psychtests.com/) since 1977. The target audiences for these psychological assessment products and services include human resource personnel, therapists, academics, and researchers. The LEAP serves primarily as a leader development tool and is not marketed as a selection test. However, the manual for the LEAP reports that it is in compliance with both APA and EEOC standards (specifically regarding gender, disability, and ethnicity).

TECHNICAL. A 146-page technical manual is provided along with the test. It presents detailed descriptive psychometric data. A normative sample of 37,869 individuals from a variety of ages, education levels, academic performance (grades), and socioeconomic backgrounds participated in the development of this test. The representativeness of this large sample is not clear.

The test is administered only in an online version. Test takers respond to 100 situational self-report items that address interpersonal and leadership situations. The situational items are clearly written and provide multiple behavioral options. Results include an overall leadership score and three factor scores including Transactional Leadership (28 items), Transformational Leadership (48 items), and Leadership Potential (41 items). Each of the factors includes several specific scales. Transactional Leadership is defined the ability to effectively communicate with others and to assign appropriate tasks. The four scales for this transactional dimension include Delegation, Giving Feedback, Goal Setting, and Rewarding Performance. Transformational Leadership focuses on leader behaviors that are motivational and inspirational. The subscales for this dimension are Motivating, Coaching, Problem Solving, Vision, Collaboration, and Setting an Example. Leadership Potential measures personality dimensions consistent with the Big 5 scale of Agreeableness, Conscientiousness, Open-Mindedness, Extroversion, and Emotional Stability. The assumption is that high scores on each of these personality dimensions are related to effective leadership.

After taking this test, participants receive a 12- to 13-page evaluation that clearly explains the results in a narrative format interspersed with multiple graphs. Participants can easily understand the constructs being measured and their relative performance. Terms and scores are clearly defined, and examples are used to put the information in context. In addition, the report provides a list of an individual's strengths and limitations followed by an advice section. Links to additional online information and sources also are provided.

The overall test mean score was 74.68 with a standard deviation of 10.70. The test, factors, and scales generally yielded strong internal reliability scores with alpha coefficients ranging from .52 to .95. A much lower alpha coefficient for the six-item reward performance scale was .34.

The trends in the descriptive data were theoretically consistent with factors such as age and education. Scores on factors and scales increased with age and with increased education. In addition, managers typically performed better than non-managers and those who were unemployed.

Some indirect criterion-related evidence of validity was presented. Individuals with higher job satisfaction scored higher on most dimensions than those with lower job satisfaction. When job performance data were available, those with good job performance scored significantly higher on most factors and scales than those with average performance.

COMMENTARY. Overall the Leadership Potential Assessment (LEAP) appears to represent an adequate test of this construct. The measure has strong intuitive appeal and excellent face validity. This instrument can be used as a good starting place for employee development and training. Without any criterion-related evidence of validity presented, screening job applicants or making final hiring decisions is not suggested.

The basic reliability and psychometrics are good and the trends are logically consistent with the test constructs, but more information would be very helpful. More data regarding content, construct, and criterion evidence of validity are needed. The criterion-related evidence presented for validity is especially limited. In addition, information on test-retest reliability would be helpful.

As an employee development tool, this test identifies theoretically important constructs in developing effective leaders. Because the test is self-report, employees can easily provide the best answer rather than the most personally accurate answer. It would be helpful to provide a multi-trait multi-method matrix to see whether these self-reports are consistent with the views of others.

[92]

Listening Skills Inventory.

Purpose: Designed "to evaluate one's listening abilities."
Population: Under age 18 through adult.
Publication Date: 2011.
Acronym: LiSI.
Scores, 10: Physical Attentiveness (External Distractions, Conversation Flow, Speaker to Listener Transition, Body Language), Mental Attentiveness (Internal Distractions, Attention Span, Hearing a Person Out), Overall Score.
Administration: Individual.
Price Data: Available from publisher.
Time: (15) minutes.
Comments: Self-administered online assessment. The test publisher advises that the test manual is being updated to include more information about methodology and theoretical background used in the development of the test. The test publisher also advises that this information is available to clients, as are benchmarks for relevant industries and racial/ethnic group comparison data. However, this information was not provided to Buros or the reviewers.
Author: PsychTests AIM, Inc.
Publisher: PsychTests AIM, Inc. [Canada].

Review of the Listening Skills Inventory by
VICTORIA A. COMERCHERO, Assistant Professor
of School Psychology, Touro College, New York, NY:

DESCRIPTION. The Listening Skills Inventory (LiSI) is a computer-based self-assessment instrument. The purpose of the test is to evaluate an individual's listening abilities to be applied to pre-employment testing. According to the test manual, the LiSI "measures how attentive you are to a speaker, and whether you're an active participant in the listening process." The total score is composed of 2 subfactors and 7 subscales. The report, which is computer-generated, includes an introduction that gives an overview of the topic of listening skills and a general score that equates to the overall listening score. Results and interpretations, with scores ranging from 0–100, are provided in two major areas, Physical Attentiveness and Mental Attentiveness, as well as seven subscales that comprise the broader abilities. The Physical Attentiveness factor includes the following subscales: External Distractions, Conversation Flow, Speaker to Listener Transition, and Body Language. Mental Attentiveness includes subscales measuring Internal Distractions, Attention Span, and Hearing a Person Out. At the end of the generated report an advice section gives the examinee tips to enhance his or her individual listening skills based on the test taker's individual strengths and weaknesses. The target population is "below 18 through 40+" (manual, p. 2). However, the test manual does not specify the minimum and maximum ages for the testing population, making it a bit unclear as to who is eligible to take this test. Additionally, no specific administration instructions are provided in the test manual, perhaps because it is a computer-administered test (directions likely are given once the examinee begins the test).

DEVELOPMENT. The test manual does not provide information with respect to the theory or assumptions that guided the development of the various items, subfactors, and subscales. Additionally, no information appears that addresses the process of item development (e.g., item analysis).

TECHNICAL. The standardization sample consisted of 23,220 participants with 49% of the sample specified as women, 31% specified as men, and 20% specified as "unknown gender" (manual, p. 2). Given that one fifth of the sample was unknown in gender and given the relatively larger number of reported females taking the test than males, it is difficult to draw conclusions about the role of gender despite the very large sample size. However, the test authors noted that smaller, random samples were selected from the larger groups whenever possible, in order to "level out the numbers and conduct the analyses effectively" (manual, p. 2).

Another drawback with respect to the sample was the method in which it was drawn. Specifically, the test authors reported that the sample was not controlled and that the participants self-selected to take the assessment and voluntarily opted to participate in the validation study. With respect to age, the distribution of age groups is also hard to validate because (a) the age range for the category "below 18" is not known, and (b) 16% of participants' ages were unknown. Finally, no evidence is presented in the test manual that indicates the test developers explored cultural, linguistic, or ethnic variables within the validation sample.

Normative data (means, minimums, maximums, and standard deviations) are presented for each of the two subfactors, Physical Attentiveness and Mental Attentiveness, and for the 7 subscales (External Distractions, Conversation Flow, Speaker to Listener Transition, Body Language, Internal Distractions, Attention Span, and Hearing a Person Out). Descriptive statistics for all of the scores are neatly presented in histograms that provide the reader with an effective visual interpretation of the data.

Based on the normed sample ($N = 23,220$), strong reliability evidence was documented. Internal consistency using coefficient alpha yielded moderate to high reliability estimates with the majority of subtests demonstrating coefficients above .80 and ranging from .69 to .89. The alpha coefficient for the entire test was reported as .91. However, no evidence of temporal stability or test-retest reliability was documented. Additional reliability data would be helpful for the examiner to better assess the overall psychometric properties of the test.

Validity evidence is presented in a highly structured and systematic manner with validity analyses conducted using various comparison variables including gender, age, grades in school, and performance in current field. The type of validity evidence that the test authors tried to establish is not clear; however, the authors do provide organized visual graphs and highly descriptive, though sometimes overly technical, summaries of the results. Based on the stated purpose of the test–to evaluate listening abilities for pre-employment screening–the final comparison variable, "performance in current field," might be analyzed to infer construct validity. The results of the various ANOVAs that were implemented seem to indicate that those who performed at the good or satisfactory levels in their current fields significantly outscored those who performed poorly on most scales.

COMMENTARY. The LiSI (Listening Skills Inventory) seems to be a good screening tool for its intended purpose. The large sample size (N = 23,220) and the large range of ages assessed (under 18 to over 40) were impressive. However, significant detail is lacking, specifically with respect to the theory and assumptions that guided the development of the items used for the various subscales.

SUMMARY. The LiSI, a computerized self-assessment created for the purposes of evaluating one's listening abilities and for pre-employment screening, should be used with caution in making formal interpretations because there is no theory presented guiding the development of the test. Additionally, the test manual offers no information about how the items were developed and refined. In conclusion, the test manual needs to include additional details that will provide the examiner with the necessary information used to determine the appropriateness of the test for its intended purposes.

Review of the Listening Skills Inventory by RAY FENTON, President, FentonResearch, Tucson, AZ:

DESCRIPTION, The Listening Skills Inventory (LiSI) is a computer-delivered self-assessment of listening skills. It is available through Queendom.com. The publisher indicates that the purpose of the LiSI is to assess "how attentive a person is to a speaker, and whether he or she is an active participant in the listening process." The emphasis is on listening etiquette and the self-reported interest in actively attending to others. The test is presented as being useful in pre-employment screening, as a training tool, and for professional skills development. Examinees are presented with 54 questions including scales and multiple-choice items keyed to specific situations and demographic questions such as age, gender, education level, success in school, and success in employment.

Test items are clearly stated and transparent. Estimated time for completion of the computerized assessment is 20 to 30 minutes. Reports are available immediately and include a summary report, a brief introduction to good listening behaviors, a narrative interpretation of scores, indicators of individual strengths and limitations, and advice on how to improve listening skills. Recommended age level for the online inventory is 18 and older.

Marketing materials indicate that performance benchmarks are available for the general population and 33 industries.

DEVELOPMENT. No detailed information is provided about the development of the instrument, although the items present commonly understood elements of good listening behavior and relate to behaviors emphasized in most listening training programs. Listening skill items (42) are grouped under two major factors: Physical Attentiveness (23) and Mental Attentiveness (21). Physical Attentiveness consists of subscales including External Distractions (12), Conversational Flow (9), Speaker to Listener Transition (9), and Body Language (15). Mental Attentiveness consists of subscales including Internal Distractions (9), Attention Span (22), and Hearing a Person Out (20). No information is provided about how individual items are credited toward each of the 100-point scales. No information is provided about how or why individual items and the scales or scale scores were developed. No information is provided about scoring.

TECHNICAL. Information is provided about a large sample of participants who have taken the Listening Skills Inventory on Queendom.com. The sample is self-selected, and validation information was collected through self-reporting. The time over which data from the 23,220-participant sample were accumulated is not reported. The group is described as comprising 7,154 men (31%), 11,491 women (49%), and 4,575 participants (20%) who did not report gender. Age distribution is below 18 (23%), 18-24 (31%), 25-29 (8%), 30-39 (10%), 40+ (12%) and unknown age (16%). Means, standard deviations, and alpha coefficients are provided based on the 23,220 cases for Overall Score (64.57, 14.52, .91); Physical Attentiveness (67.40, 14.18, .85), and Mental Attentiveness (61.73, 16.04, .87). Physical Attentiveness consists of subscales including External Distractions (36.77, 17.01, .81), Conversational Flow (69.62, 18.12, .73), Speaker to Listener Transition (65.55, 18.44, .69), and Body Language (69.83, 16.95, .87). Mental Attentiveness consists of subscales including Internal Distractions (38.17, 18.30, .83), Attention Span (60.48, 17.64, .89) and Hearing a Person Out (62.97, 15.86, .86).

Validity analyses used ANOVAs and *t*-tests to compare the scores of various groups on Overall Score and subscores. Significant differences are reported in scale scores of men, women, and the various age groups, self-reported grades in school, and performance in current field. Results showed higher listening scores for females, older age groups, those reporting higher grades, and those reporting a higher level of performance in their current field. No external indicators of validity are provided. No information is provided about the benchmark scores or the 33 industries mentioned in promotional materials. Overall, information provided about reliability and validity is limited and incomplete.

COMMENTARY. The LiSI is a quick and easy inventory of self-reported listening skills. The strength of the inventory is the face validity of the items and the association between items and behaviors emphasized in programs for improving listening skills. Information is lacking on scale construction, and validity evidence is extremely limited. It would be helpful for the test authors to provide more detail about test construction, the validity of narrative interpretation of scores, strengths and limitations, and advice that is provided based on scale scores. External validity evidence is also needed.

SUMMARY. The Listening Skills Inventory (LiSI) is a computer-delivered self-assessment of listening skills. The publisher indicates that the purpose of the LiSI is to assess "how attentive a person is to a speaker, and whether he or she is an active participant in the listening process." It may be useful as part of a pre-employment screening or a self-assessment of listening skills. Unfortunately, very limited validity evidence is provided.

[93]

MacArthur-Bates Communicative Development Inventories, Second Edition.

Purpose: Designed as parent-completed assessments "of key language milestones" yielding "information on the course of language development."

Publication Dates: 1993-2007.

Acronym: CDI.

Administration: Individual.

Price Data, 2011: $121.95 per complete kit, including 20 Words and Gestures forms, 20 Words and Sentences forms, CDI III, and user's guide (2007, 207 pages); $99.95 per kit including 20 Words and Gestures forms, 20 Words and Sentences forms, and user's guide; $25 per 20 Words and Gestures forms; $25 per 20 Words and Sentences forms; $20 per 25 CDI-III forms; $59.95 per manual.

Foreign Language Edition: Spanish edition available.

Time: (20-40) minutes.

Comments: Previous version known as MacArthur Communicative Development Inventories.

Authors: Larry Fenson, Virginia A. Marchman, Donna J. Thal, Philip S. Dale, J. Steven Reznick, and Elizabeth Bates.

Publisher: Paul H. Brookes Publishing Co., Inc.
a) WORDS AND GESTURES.
Population: Ages 8-18 months.
Scores, 7: Early Words (First Signs of Understanding, Phrases Understood, Starting to Talk, Vocabulary Checklist), Actions and Gestures (Early Gestures, Later Gestures, Total Gestures).
b) WORDS AND SENTENCES.
Population: Ages 16-30 months.
Scores, 7: Words Children Use (Vocabulary Checklist, How Children Use Words), Sentences and Grammar (Word Endings/Part 1, Word Forms, Word Endings/Part 2), Combining Words (Examples of the Child's Three Longest Sentences, Complexity).
c) CDI-III.
Population: Ages 30-37 months.
Scores, 3: Vocabulary Checklist, Sentences, Using Language.
Cross References: See T5:1528 (8 references); for a review by Carol Westby of the MacArthur Communicative Development Inventories, see 13:188 (14 references).

Review of the MacArthur-Bates Communicative Development Inventories, Second Edition by TIFFANY L. HUTCHINS, Assistant Professor, University of Vermont, Burlington, VT:

DESCRIPTION. The MacArthur-Bates Communicative Development Inventories (CDIs) are a set of parent-informant measures designed to evaluate the communicative skills of young children from their "early signs of comprehension, to their first nonverbal gestural signals, to the expansion of early vocabulary and the beginnings of grammar" (technical manual, p. 7). The test authors state that the CDIs can be used to screen for language delay, identify older children with language impairment, evaluate the effects of treatment, and to screen or match children on the basis of language skills in the context of research.

The CDIs are composed of two major forms: the CDI: Words and Gestures and the CDI: Words and Sentences. According to the technical manual, each form takes between 20–40 minutes to complete depending on the extent of the child's communicative skills. The CDI: Words and Gestures is designed for typically developing children ages 8–18 months as a measure of emerging receptive and expressive vocabulary and the use of communicative or symbolic gestures. It has two major parts. Part I, Early Words, is divided into four sections. Section A, First Signs of Understanding, includes three yes-no items intended to determine whether the child has started to respond to language. Section B,

Phrases, is a 28-item checklist designed to tap the understanding of everyday language in the context of interactional routines. Section C, Starting to Talk, consists of two items to assess the frequency (i.e., *never, sometimes, often*) with which a child imitates words and labels objects. Section D, the largest section, is called the Vocabulary Checklist. It is a 396-item checklist organized into 19 semantic categories. Ten of these reflect different noun classes but a variety of other categories are also represented (e.g., verbs, adjectives, pronouns, quantifiers). For each item, the respondent indicates whether the child "understands" or "understands and says."

Part II, Actions and Gestures, is divided into five sections. Section A, First Communicative Gestures, includes 12 items to assess the frequency (i.e., *never, sometimes, often*) of nonverbal communicative acts (e.g., reaching, pointing, nodding). Section B, Games and Routines, is composed of six yes-no items (e.g., playing a particular game). Section C, Actions with Objects, uses 17 yes-no items (e.g., using eating utensils). Section D, Pretending to be a Parent, includes 13 yes-no items where respondents indicate the kinds of actions a child engages in during pretend play with a stuffed animal or doll (e.g., showing affection). Section E, Imitating Other Adult Actions, includes 15 yes-no items intended to assess the child's attempts to simulate the actions of adults using real or toy implements.

Unlike the CDI: Words and Gestures form, which is designed to evaluate receptive and expressive language, the CDI Words and Sentences form is intended to assess expressive language only. It is designed for typically developing children ages 16–30 months as a measure of developing expressive vocabulary and a number of aspects of early grammar development. Part I, Words Children Use, is divided in two sections. Section A, Vocabulary Checklist, is a 680-item checklist organized into 22 semantic categories similar to those used in the CDI: Words and Gestures form. For each item, respondents simply indicate those items the child "says." Section B, How Children Use Words, includes five items to assess the frequency (i.e., *never, sometimes, often*) with which a child talks about things and people that are not in the here-and-now. Part II, Sentences and Grammar, is divided into five sections. Section A, Word Endings/Part 1, uses four items to assess the frequency (i.e., *not yet, sometimes, often*) with which the child produces early-emerging morphemes that appear at the end of words (e.g., plural –s, regular past tense –ed). Section B, Word Forms, is a checklist

of 25 items intended to tap production of irregular nouns and verbs. Section C, Word Endings/Part 2, is a 45-item checklist of overregularized nouns and verbs that occur naturally in children's speech. A single question (Combining) then asks whether the child has begun to combine words (*not yet, sometimes, often*). Section D, Examples, is intended to provide a basis for estimating mean length of utterance (MLU). Here, the respondent is asked to write three examples of the longest sentences that the child has said recently. Section E, Complexity, is a 37-item checklist designed to assess syntactic complexity. Each of the 37 items is composed of a pair of sentences that contrast in complexity. Using a forced-choice format, respondents are asked to judge which sentence in each pair sounds most like the way their child talks.

The CDIs also include a third form called the MacArthur-Bates Communicative Development Inventory-III. This form is a brief measure representing an upward extension of the CDI: Words and Sentences form. It is intended for use with 3-year-olds. The test authors describe this form as being at a "relatively early stage of development" (technical manual, p. 161).

Detailed administration and scoring procedures (with examples) are provided in the technical manual and comprehensive descriptive data are presented for all CDI sections. Percentile ranks for the sexes combined and separate percentile rank data for boys and girls using 1-month intervals are provided for all sections except two sections of the CDI: Words and Gestures form (i.e., First Signs of Understanding, Starting to Talk) and two sections of the CDI: Words and Sentences (i.e., How Children Use Words, Word Endings/ Part 1). When percentile ranks are not provided, the percentage of affirmative answers is calculated for comparison with the percentages given in the manual. When percentile ranks are provided, they can be unstable. Specifically, restriction in the range of scores sometimes occurred for ages at which the skills in question were just emerging. When this happens, small differences in raw scores can have dramatic effects on the associated percentile ranks. "Because relatively few items can have such a large effect on the child's percentile scores in these instances, users should be very cautious in drawing strong conclusions based on these reported values" (technical manual, pp. 33-34). Because scores for each age group are frequently skewed, standard scores are not provided.

Original and expanded versions of a Basic Information Form are included in the CDI. The forms are designed to gather demographic information useful in interpretation of test scores. It should be noted that CDI short forms are also available (Fenson et al., 2000). As noted in the test manual, the short forms likely lack the precision of the full CDIs and must be administered and interpreted with caution. Members of the CDI advisory board have developed Mexican Spanish versions (including short forms) of the CDIs (Jackson-Maldonado et al., 2003). The measures have also been developed in a number of languages other than English by other researchers and many have supporting normative data. A comprehensive list of these versions is available on the CDI web site (http://www.sci. sdsu.edu/cdi/adaptations.htm). This web site also provides a link to a free automated scoring program. The program is easy to use, takes less time to score compared to the hand-scoring method, and will generate reports and letters describing the results of the CDIs.

DEVELOPMENT. As explained in the technical manual, "the first systematic attempts to use questionnaires to tap parents' knowledge about their children's language skills" (manual, p. 1) were conducted by Elizabeth Bates (a co-developer of the CDIs) and colleagues in the 1970s and 1980s (e.g., Bates, Camaioni, & Volterra, 1975). These inventories were later refined to tap parents' knowledge of their children's vocabulary and grammar and laid the foundation for the development of the first edition of the CDIs. The primary purposes of the second edition (2007) of the CDIs are to report data for an expanded normative sample and to expand upon the reliability and validity of the tool by incorporating new data.

As a parent-informant measure, the CDIs have several advantages over observation and direct testing methods. As discussed in the technical manual, parent-report can provide more representative data because parents have the opportunity to observe their child over time in a wide range of contexts. Moreover, parent-report measures are not vulnerable to child characteristics like temperament or personality or transitory states related to motivation and mood that can influence the results of laboratory-based measures. In addition, parent-report measures are generally inexpensive, quick, and easy to administer. Given these advantages, the CDIs are offered as parent-report measures that yield reliable and valid indices of several dimensions of children's early communicative skills. As cautioned by the developers, no measure (including the CDIs) should be used in isolation for the purpose of identification. For such purposes, the CDIs should be used as one tool in a broader assessment protocol.

TECHNICAL.

Standardization. The CDI: Words and Gestures is normed on a sample of 1,748, and the CDI: Words and Sentences is normed on a sample of 2,591 when the original and updated normative samples are combined. The normative sample reveals a relatively even distribution of girls and boys across the age ranges sampled. Although the 2007 expanded norms more closely approximate national demographic statistics than the original norms, the test developers note that the sample still underrepresents children and families with low educational and/or socioeconomic backgrounds. In addition, Caucasians are slightly overrepresented whereas Hispanics are underrepresented (a likely result of exclusion criteria requiring children to be from a home where English was the primary language).

Reliability. Two types of reliability evidence are offered in the technical manual. Data for internal consistency (i.e., the degree to which items on a test measure the same content domain) generally indicate homogeneity of content (coefficients above .70) with a few exceptions. Values lower than .70 are interpreted as statistical artifacts (i.e., low occurrence, ceiling effects) for some sections. For other sections, lower values are taken as evidence for the multidimensionality of the construct being tapped.

The test-retest reliability of the CDI: Words and Gestures utilized 137 pairs of forms from a site in New Haven, Connecticut, with an average test-retest interval of 1.35 months (range: .90–2.37 months). A series of Pearson correlations computed separately for each month revealed good temporal stability of the comprehension items with correlation coefficients in the upper .80s. One exception to this occurred for children age 12 months ($r = .61$), which was interpreted as reflecting a "general cognitive reorganization" (technical manual, p. 101) that may occur at this point of development. Test-retest reliability for the production items was also strong with the following exceptions: "Stability for production was low in the 8- to 10-month range, probably due to the restricted range (i.e., a floor effect), but stabilized in subsequent months, with correlations in the mid-.80s. Gesture scores were also in the .80 range for each monthly level ... except at 12 months, at which point a coefficient of .60 was obtained–parallel to the reduction in month-to-month stability for vocabulary comprehension" (technical manual, p. 101). Test-retest reliability of the CDI: Words and Sentences was based on 216 pairs of forms from the Connecticut site with an average interval of 1.38 months (range = .73–2.94). Correlation coefficients for all sections were above .90 for each age.

Validity. Several kinds of validity evidence are offered in the technical manual. First, the CDIs demonstrate excellent evidence related to content, or the degree to which the test covers the intended content domain. The content of the CDIs was developed in line with the language development literature, is supported by more than 30 years of child language research, and has been credited as adequately sampling early vocabulary and grammar development (e.g., Westby, 1998). Additional validity evidence (what the test authors term "convergent validity") is offered that recognizes the fact that various CDI sections "correspond closely to the developmental functions that have been reported for the same variables in observational studies" (technical manual, p. 103). Concurrent validity evidence is based on the relationship between CDI scores and various child performance measures and is particularly impressive. As reported in the test manual, moderate to high correlation coefficients have been reported across numerous studies on typically developing children as well as children with language impairment and developmental delays. For example, sections of the CDI are significantly correlated with standardized tests designed to assess expressive and receptive vocabulary as well as language sample measures like the Index of Productive Syntax (Scarborough, 1990) and Number of Different Words (NDW).

COMMENTARY. The CDIs offer several advantages as tools to assess early communicative skills. They are well-validated and are relatively quick, easy, and inexpensive to administer. As parent-report measures, they are not vulnerable to child characteristics (e.g., motivation, shyness) and situational factors (e.g., familiarity with an examiner) that can influence the results of direct assessments. As noted by the developers, parent-report may also yield a more representative sample of child skills. Moreover, the CDIs can be used appropriately for a range of clinical and research purposes, and they sample a broad range of communicative skills (e.g., verbal, nonverbal, lexical, syntactic domains) that are salient in early de-

velopment. Limitations of the CDIs include the fact that for some percentile ranks, restriction of range in the data can create unstable scores and so there is a potential for misinterpretation in such cases. In addition, the test authors present evidence suggesting that there is the potential for mothers with the most limited education to overestimate their young children's language comprehension. For these reasons, scores from items tapping word comprehension for children "younger than 1 year should be treated with caution, particularly with children whose parents have lower education levels" (technical manual, p. 88). In a related vein, the CDIs would benefit from an even more expanded normative sample to create a truly representative sample with regard to education and income level as well as race and ethnicity.

SUMMARY. The CDIs have endured the test of rigorous scientific scrutiny, and there is now tremendous evidence in support of their reliability and the validity of test score uses in the manner suggested by the test authors (Hutchins, 2011). For the reasons cited above, the CDIs have become well-respected measures. Their popularity lends support to the notion that parents are valuable, reliable, and accurate sources of information, and the CDIs have been particularly welcomed from a family-centered perspective (e.g., Westby, 1998). In short, when professionals adhere to the conventions and suggestions for use and are cautious in their interpretation of percentile ranks, the CDIs can be highly recommended as research and clinical tools.

REVIEWER'S REFERENCES

Bates, E., Camaioni, L., & Volterra, V. (1975). The acquisition of performatives prior to speech. *Merrill-Palmer Quarterly, 21*, 205-226.

Fenson, L., Pethick, S., Renda, C., Cox, J. L., Dale, P. S., & Reznick, J. S. (2000). Short-form versions of the MacArthur Communicative Development Inventories. *Applied Psycholinguistics, 21*, 95-116.

Hutchins, T. L. (2011). The MacArthur Communicative Development Inventories (CDIs). In F. Volkmar & R. Paul (Eds.), *Encyclopedia of autism spectrum disorders.* Available at http://referencelive.springer.com/login.php

Jackson-Maldonado, D., Thal, D. J., Fenson, L., Marchman, V. A., Newton, T., & Conboy, B. (2003). *MacArthur Inventarios del Desarrollo de Habilidades Communicatives users guide and technical manual.* Baltimore, MD: Paul H. Brookes Publishing Co.

Scarborough, H. S. (1990). Index of productive syntax. *Applied Psycholinguistics, 11*, 1–22.

Westby, C. (1998). [Review of the MacArthur Communicative Development Inventories]. In J. C. Impara & B. S. Plake (Eds.), *The thirteenth mental measurements yearbook* (pp. 631–632). Lincoln, NE: The Buros Institute of Mental Measurements.

Review of the MacArthur-Bates Communicative Development Inventories, Second Edition by HOI K. SUEN, Distinguished Professor of Educational Psychology, Pennsylvania State University, University Park, PA:

DESCRIPTION. The MacArthur-Bates Communicative Development Inventories (CDI), Second Edition is an assessment of English-language development for infants and toddlers from

8 months to 2.5 years of age. There are two major forms. The Words and Gestures form is designed for 8- to 18-month-olds; the Words and Sentences form is designed for 16- to 30-month-olds. Both are checklists of words, gestures, phrases, and/or sentences that infants and toddlers may understand, do, or say. The Words and Gestures form consists of a checklist of a few signs of understanding, 28 phrases, 396 vocabulary words, and 63 gestures. The Words and Sentences form consists of a vocabulary checklist of 680 words and 112 sentences and grammar items. The test authors report that it takes 20–40 minutes to complete one of these forms. A third form, the MacArthur-Bates Communicative Development Inventory-III, comprises an upward extension that may be used with 3-year-olds. Although the test authors describe the psychometric properties of this form as "encouraging," it is still considered to be in development.

The respective form is to be completed by a parent. For example, if the parent thinks that the child understands the word "frog," the parent would check that word as one that the child understands. Children using different baby-talk pronunciations of a given word are counted as having used the word. For instance, if the child has said "sketti" for "spaghetti," the child is considered to have used the word "spaghetti." Items are checked based on the parent's knowledge of the child and not on whether the child can repeat a particular word at the moment of assessment.

Parents completing the forms need to be literate. For an illiterate parent, it is acceptable to have someone read the items to the parent and mark down the responses from the parent. Parents may also ask others such as nannies, child care providers, and other family members to supplement their own knowledge and help fill out the form.

Each form produces a number of scores for different areas of language development. Specifically, the Words and Gestures form yields a fitted percentile score for each of the following areas: Phrases Understood, Words Understood, Words Produced, Total Gestures, Early Gestures, and Later Gestures. The Words and Sentences form yields a fitted percentile score for Words Produced, Complexity, Examples/M3L (mean length of child's three longest sentences), Word Forms, and Word Endings/Part 2. For a few other areas, the CDI does not produce percentile scores. Instead, it reports the percent of children reported to accomplish a specific task at a certain age, and the test authors

provide instructions for how to interpret the scores in these areas.

The test authors caution that it is not appropriate to use the CDI as a diagnostic tool. They also caution that the CDI should not be used alone for important clinical decisions. However, they suggest that the CDI can be used as a preliminary screening tool for language delay, to evaluate language delay of older children beyond 30 months of age, and to help formulate intervention strategies.

DEVELOPMENT. For a typical assessment tool, there are several phases of mutually related developmental activities. These can be divided into those related to contents of the tool; those related to scaling, norming, and equating of scores; and those related to quality control such as reliability, validity, and bias analyses. For the CDI, detailed information is provided about the scaling and norming processes as well as reliability and validity information. However, information about the development of the content is less clear.

It appears that the lists of words, phrases, gestures, and sentences have originated from research and development work in the 1970s and 1980s, primarily by the late Dr. Elizabeth Bates, as well as by some of the current authors of the CDI. It appears that these earlier efforts have led to a number of precursor inventories. The word lists in these early inventories were used as the basis to develop the two current CDI forms. The processes through which the word lists had been generated for these earlier precursor inventories are not described in the CDI technical manual. To form the current CDI, words on these earlier inventories that were found to be infrequently used (by less than 5% of the children) were removed. Some equivalent words listed together previously were separated as two different words. Some items were regrouped under new and different categories, such as "Actions and Gestures." Thirty-five new words were added to the Words and Sentences form. There is no information on how these 35 new words were chosen.

Detailed information is provided about the norming process. For the second edition of the CDI, an updated sample of 544 girls and 545 boys was used for the norming of Words and Gestures; an updated sample of 728 girls and 733 boys was used for that of Words and Sentences. Care was taken to ensure there were sufficient cases within each age group to enable norming. The samples seem to be drawn primarily from eight towns or cities around the U.S. where major universities are located. In terms of geographic representation, the Midwest appears to be quite underrepresented. When compared against data in the 2000 U.S. Census, the sample overrepresents the white population while underrepresenting the Hispanic population substantially. When maternal education is used as a proxy measure of socioeconomic status, mothers with a college education are substantially overrepresented.

With slightly different scoring rules for various areas of language development, raw scores can be produced. Based on the distribution of raw scores in the norming sample, percentile scores were derived. These were smoothed through logistic functions to produce fitted percentile scores.

TECHNICAL. Comparisons between boys and girls were made for various scores. In most cases, differences in scores were found; but in almost all cases, the effect size was small. Children from low SES families were found to score lower in general than children from higher SES backgrounds.

Coefficient alpha values were high for most scales. For the Words Understood and Words Produced scales, the coefficients were as high as .95–.96. For a few other areas, alpha coefficients were found to be in the .60 range, with that for Question Words scores being as low as .56. These are most probably related to the differences in the number of items for each of these areas. Reliability estimates obtained via test-retest methods also show uniformly high values over about a 6-week interval, on average. No information on rater-related measurement error or reliability is reported.

Validity evidence derives primarily from correlations with scores on other existing measures of language skills. High correlations were found in almost all cases between CDI area scores and corresponding scores on the Bayley Language Scale, Peabody Picture Vocabulary Test, Reynell Developmental Language Scales, Preschool Language Scale–Revised, Language Sample NDW, and others.

Construct validity was mentioned as part of instrument development, but no information is provided to specifically support the correspondence between scores and the underlying theoretical constructs of language skills. The test authors report correlations found between two sets of scores obtained from two administrations of the CDI to the same group of children 6 months apart. They frame these correlations as "predictive validity" while also claiming that they can be regarded as a measure of reliability. These correlations were found to be in the range of .60. As evidence for "predictive validity," these values are quite high. However, as reliability estimates, they can be considered low. Because the CDI measures language development among children at an age when language is developing rapidly, the exact interpretation of these nonstandard "predictive validity" correlations is difficult to discern.

COMMENTARY. As with most assessment tools, the CDI is strong in some areas but less so in other areas. The norming process and the updated sample used for the purpose, in spite of the substantial underrepresentation of Hispanics, the underrepresentation of children from the Midwest, and the significant overrepresentation of upper-middle-class respondents, is generally quite good and large. The process of stratifying the sample by age has ensured an adequate number of cases within each age group to produce meaningful norms. A great deal of care was taken in ensuring the precision of percentile scores by the use of growth-curve, logistic functions to smooth the percentiles. Reliability estimates are generally high–ensured by the large number of vocabulary items. Evidence of validity based on correlations with other similar measures is very strong and compelling.

Unfortunately, its weaknesses are in the two most critical areas: content representation and relevance, and potential random and systematic rater errors. These two areas are central to the design and utility of the CDI. They are, in this case, the Achilles heels of validity for CDI test scores.

Content representation and relevance. The test authors have described the CDI as "a 'catalogue' of all the words that are used by many different children" (Words and Sentences form, p. 2). A child's level of "language development" is determined entirely on the basis of what percent of the child's age group understands or uses fewer of these particular words than the child does. There is a subtle but extremely important difference between a child's "language development" and the child's understanding of these particular words/phrases chosen by the test authors. For the interpretation of the score as indicative of relative language development, this "catalogue" of words and phrases needs either to be exhaustive or to form an unbiased representation of the elements in any young child's potential repertoire. This piece of evidence of content representation and relevance is perhaps the most critical piece of validity evidence in this particular case.

The words and phrases were largely taken from inventories developed in the 1970s and 1980s. There is no description of how these inventories were formed and what steps were taken to ensure that these words and phrases are representative of the potential language development of a child. The test authors also state that the words and phrases were "drawn from the developmental literature and from suggestions made by parents in response to earlier versions of the instrument" (technical manual, pp. 102-103) without describing how they were drawn.

Language evolves constantly. As the social environment changes over time, infants and toddlers necessarily acquire different vocabularies from their surroundings. The United States in the 1970s and 1980s was quite different from the U.S. today in terms of cultural and technological environment surrounding a young child. These changing environments present different opportunities to learn different words and phrases. Most if not all items in the CDI word lists appear to reflect a middle to upper-middle class, Caucasian home environment from a decade or two ago. Some of the items are likely to be in the process of disappearing from a typical child's environment today. Others may be too strongly related to geographic location and socioeconomic status of the family. Meanwhile, new words such as "video game" or "(computer) mouse" that did not exist 30 years ago are likely to be learned by a child today. The risk of having a word list that is not all-inclusive is that a child may be mistakenly assessed as having possible language delay based on CDI scores when in fact the child is quite advanced in an overlapping but different set of words and phrases. Another related issue is that the domain of "communicative skills" appears to be overly broadly defined. For instance, various actions or activities (such as using eating utensils) are counted as gestures. Perhaps the test authors need to conduct a formal systematic evaluation to ensure that the word lists are indeed a catalogue of all the words used by most children today.

Rater reliability. In an extensive discussion in the technical manual, the test authors acknowledge the limitation of using parents as raters. It is partly due to these limitations that the test authors caution against using the CDI in isolation for diagnostic purposes. Parent ratings may contain systematic biases and random judgmental errors. In the case of the CDI, these problems are further exacerbated by a lack of standardized administrative procedure. The checklist is considered self-explanatory to par-

ent raters. For illiterate parents, however, another person can read the word to the parent and record the parent's response. Parents may also consult nannies, caregivers, and/or other family members when completing the checklist. Furthermore, parents are instructed to consider baby talk pronunciations of a word as indications of using the word. The test authors also report that lower SES parents may overreport their children's language skills. All these variations and issues point to a high probability of substantial random judgment errors and systematic rater biases. Yet there has been no attempt to assess the magnitude of these potential errors. Perhaps the test authors should consider conducting small scale generalizability studies using samples of children with more than one parent/caregiver as independent raters to evaluate both score reliabilities and magnitude of error variances attributable to parent raters.

Other limitations. In addition to the two major concerns above, there are several relatively minor precautions in the use of the CDI. One such limitation is the exact purpose to which the CDI is put. The test authors recommended that the CDI can be used as a preliminary screening tool for language delay, to evaluate language delay of older children, and to help formulate intervention strategies. These suggestions need to be taken with some precautions. As a preliminary screening tool, the CDI is too lengthy and too narrow to be of practical value. Because older children were not in the norming sample, there is no information on how parents evaluate older children on these particular items. Extrapolating beyond the norms is risky. Finally, as a preliminary screening tool, the CDI may not be sufficiently precise to help formulate intervention strategies.

Although comparisons were made between boys and girls in terms of performances in the different language areas within the CDI, there is no means of discerning whether the observed difference is due to an inherent gender difference or an indication of test bias. Evaluation of possible gender bias will need to await results of more formal differential item functioning analyses.

Finally, due to a significant overrepresentation of children from upper-middle class and substantial underrepresentation of certain ethnic/cultural minority children, the CDI should be used with extreme caution when evaluating the language development of a child from a lower SES family or from a cultural minority family.

SUMMARY. Overall, the CDI is an easy-to-use, albeit lengthy, checklist that is based on considerable research. It produces percentile scores that appear most accurate for children from upper-middle class Caucasian families. The resulting scores correlate very well with many other early childhood language measures. However, caution should be taken when interpreting the meaning of the percentiles due to a number of limitations. The more important limitations include a lack of evidence that rater errors are minimized, a lack of evidence of content representation and relevance, and uncertainty about the measure's appropriateness for low income and cultural minorities.

[94]

Machinist Test–Form AR-C.

Purpose: Designed for selecting or evaluating applicants or incumbents for machine shop jobs.
Population: Machinist job applicants or incumbents.
Publication Dates: 1981-2007.
Scores, 10: Heat Treating, Layout/Cutting and Assembly, Print Reading, Steel/Metals and Materials, Rigging, Mechanical Principles and Repair, Machine Tools, Tools/Material and Equipment, Machine Shop Lubrication, Total.
Administration: Group.
Price Data, 2011: $22 per consumable self-scoring test booklet (20 minimum order); $24.95 per manual (2007, 19 pages).
Time: (60-70) minutes.
Comments: Self-scoring instrument; previously listed as Ramsay Corporation Job Skills-Machinist Test; available for online test administration.
Author: Roland T. Ramsay.
Publisher: Ramsay Corporation.
Cross References: For reviews by John Peter Hudson, Jr. and James W. Pinkney of an earlier edition, see 13:253.

Review of the Machinist Test–Form AR-C by SUSAN M. BROOKHART, Consultant, Brookhart Enterprises LLC, Helena, MT:

DESCRIPTION. The Machinist Test–Form AR-C is a test of machining job knowledge. It is an updated (in 2007) version of the Ramsay Corporation Job Skills Machinist Test Form AC, which was last revised in 2000. According to the *Manual for Administration & Scoring*, it is intended for use with "applicants and incumbents for jobs where machining knowledge and skill were necessary parts of job activities" (p. 1). This one sentence is the only information about test use that is provided. The test manual does not give any specifics for how the test should be used with applicants and incumbents.

Simply by saying "applicants," the manual implies that the test could be used as part of a job application process. There is no advice about how to employ the test in such a situation, so users might vary widely in their approaches, with some comparing applicants' scores to each other and some requiring a certain level of attainment. Neither of these approaches is supported with appropriate validity evidence provided in the manual, and users are also not cautioned to establish their own validity evidence for use. Similarly, simply by saying "incumbents," the manual implies that the test could be used as part of promotion or training processes. Again, there is no information in the manual about how to do that.

The test consists of 60 multiple-choice items organized into 9 subsections. Only the Total Score is intended to be interpreted. The test booklet is clearly printed and easy to read. Many of the items have diagrams associated with them, and the diagrams are clear. Many of the items require the respondent to apply knowledge to solve a problem, as opposed to merely recalling definitions or principles. The directions for administration and scoring are clear and complete. The test administrator should have no trouble following them and creating the standardized conditions as intended.

DEVELOPMENT. The Ramsay Corporation Job Skills Machinist Test Form A was developed in 1989 with 120 items. A shortened form (Form AC, 60 items) was developed in 1998 and revised in 2000 to include 28 new items on "geometric dimensions and tolerances, CNC machines, and new questions in tooling, assembly, and print reading" (manual, p. 1). Definitions for the job title Machinist are provided from two U.S. Department of Labor sources: the *Dictionary of Occupational Titles* and *O*NET OnLine*. The manual claims that job analysis activities determined these definitions applied to the content of the test, but no description of those job analysis activities is given, unless the publisher construes job expert ratings of a prepared activity list to constitute that job analysis.

The job expert ratings seem to have occurred for Form A (1989), but the time line is not clear because the results are presented in terms of the newer 60-item forms. Six job experts independently edited and ranked a prepared list of knowledge and skill areas. Ranks were averaged across raters and used to identify the proportion of items for each subsection of the test. Pairs of job experts then selected items from Ramsay Corporation's item bank. The 120 items on Form A were reduced to 60 in 1998 on the basis of item statistics, specifically point-biserial correlations and item difficulty indices, based on data from 245 examinees. For both the revision in 2000 and the current Form AR-C revision in 2007, the manual claims that "care was taken to make sure that [the] difficulty level of each of the categories remained consistent" (p. 6). Later in the manual, the 2007 update to Form AR-C is described as replacing 11 items and revising three items.

In summary, it appears that most of the test development work was done in 1989, with six job experts, and with test revisions since then based on mostly statistical concerns. However, the test manual does not present enough description about the development process to conclude this for certain.

TECHNICAL.

Standardization. Normative data, in the form of a table of percentile ranks, are presented for a sample of 82 applicants for machinist jobs at one refining plant who took Form AC of the test. The small sample size calls into question the stability of the ranks. The limited source of the sample calls into question how representative the sample is of machinist candidates and machinists in general. The fact that the norms are based on a previous form of the test calls into question how relevant they are for Form AR-C because almost a quarter of the items in Form AR-C are new or revised.

Reliability. Reliability data for the Total Score are presented for three separate samples ranging in size from 72 to 126. *KR20* values are .81, .83, and .87. Two of these values (.83 and .87) were reconstructed for Form AC by using data from 60 of the items in Form A (1989). The lowest value (.81) was based on Form AC (2000). None of the values are based on Form AR-C (2007) and thus do not reflect the presence of the 14 new or revised items. One can conclude that the reliability of Form AC is probably adequate, but there is no solid information about the reliability of Form AR-C.

Validity. The test manual gives information about the validity of interpretation of the Total Score as indicative of level of machining job knowledge. Although in several places the manual reads "knowledge and skill," this reviewer believes that is just an editorial issue. It seems clear that the test is intended to measure knowledge, not skills.

Evidence that the test samples the body of knowledge judged by experts to be required for the job of machinist comes from the job expert reviews during the test development phase, described above. Additional evidence that the test samples the body of knowledge judged by experts to be required for the job of machinist comes from two studies, one in the metals manufacturing industry and one in the ceramics industry. In each case, five raters were asked to rate the job relatedness of each item. Average job relatedness values, on a scale of 0 through 5, were 4.2 for metals manufacturing and 4.0 for ceramics. This evidence supports the validity of the content selection, but again for the previous Form AC, not for the new Form AR-C.

COMMENTARY. The Machinist Test–Form AR-C is a test of machining job knowledge. It is an updated (2007) version of the Ramsay Corporation Job Skills Machinist Test Form AC, which was last revised in 2000. Evidence for test development and reliability and normative data for Form AC is provided. The evidence is based on small samples; therefore, although the evidence presented is supportive of the validity of the test, it is not conclusive. Two major issues are as follows: (a) the evidence presented is for a previous form of the test; and (b) although the manual implies the test could be used for job-related appraisals, there is no validity evidence about the relationship between examinee knowledge as measured by the test and examinee knowledge on the job.

Given the intended use of the Machinist Test–Form AR-C with applicants and incumbents for machinist jobs, this reviewer makes a strong recommendation that studies be designed and implemented to show that scores on the Machinist Test are related to knowledge used in actual job performance in some way. The manual ends with a request of users that they furnish "normative data, test results, or validation information" (p. 19) to the Ramsay Corporation to enable them to update the manual, which suggests that the publisher is aware that instrument quality evidence is thin.

SUMMARY. The Machinist Test–Form AR-C is a test of machining job knowledge. The test items are clear and easy to read. Administration and scoring descriptions are clear. The test manual provides preliminary, and promising, instrument quality evidence; however, the evidence presented in the manual is inadequate to support the use of Form AR-C (2007). Most of the information is more pertinent to supporting the use of Form AC (1998, 2000), and 23% of the items have been replaced or revised in Form AR-C.

Review of the Machinist Test–Form AR-C by CAROLYN H. SUPPA, Licensed Psychologist, Coordinator of Human Services Education, Office of Career and Technical Instruction, West Virginia Department of Education, Charleston, WV:

DESCRIPTION. The Ramsay Corporation Job Skills Machinist Test was developed as part of a series of skills tests. Its intended use was with "applicants and incumbents for jobs where machining knowledge and skill were necessary parts of job activities" (manual, p. 1). The test was shortened to 60 items and reformatted as Machinist Form AC in 1998. In 2000 Form AC underwent a content revision resulting in 28 items being added and three items being revised. In 2007 the updated Form AR-C was published with 11 questions being replaced and three being revised. No further history regarding the test's development, purposes, or use is provided in the limited manual.

The administration and scoring instructions are clear and easy to follow. Testing is available in both pencil-and-paper and online formats. The paper-and-pencil format is a self-scoring booklet in which respondents mark their answers on a carbonless form that transfers to a keyed box on a scoring grid attached to the scoring sheet. The scorer must remove a perforated seal to reveal the scoring grid. Subsection scores are summed for a total test score. The manual states that "there is no time limit" to complete the 60 exercises but that respondents "should not need more than 1 hour" (p. 10). Directions to administrators add that everyone should be allowed to finish.

DEVELOPMENT. The manual introduction provides definitions of Machinist from both the *Dictionary of Occupational Titles* (DOT; U.S. Department of Labor, 1991) and *O*NET OnLine* (U.S. Department of Labor, 2006) and references "job analysis activities conducted during development of this test" (manual, p. 1) as having relevance to these two definitions. No details regarding these activities were specified. There is a two-sentence section on item analysis in the manual (p. 12) that states only that Form AC test data for 82 machinist job applicants were analyzed and that a table showing item difficulties and point-biserial discrimination indexes is provided. However, there is no item analysis provided for the new version.

The manual presents the knowledge and skill areas sampled by all forms with no reference to the origin of these areas. They are: Heat-Treating; Layout, Cutting, and Assembly; Print Reading; Steel, Metals, and Materials; Rigging; Mechanical Principles and Repair; Machine Tools (operation, maintenance, and use); Tools, Material, and Equipment; and Machine Shop Lubrication. Safety was reported as a skill pervasive throughout all of these knowledge areas.

The manual's three-paragraph description of the development of the measure describes a process for selecting the number of items for each knowledge area. Six unidentified job experts were given a list of the selected knowledge areas and asked to edit and independently rank their importance. These rankings were applied to the number of planned items for the test. Pairs of unidentified job experts then selected "relevant test items" (manual, p. 6) with appropriate content and difficulty from Ramsay Corporation's item bank and assigned them to each category. A safety item was included for each test section where applicable. The job experts provided correct answers for items, which were submitted to an unidentified destination for verification.

Pilot testing involved the administration of Form A (1989) to 245 individuals (although no demographic details were provided). Then two unidentified "industrial psychologists selected the best 60 items according to criteria of item point biserial discrimination indexes and item difficulty" (manual, p. 6). These 60 items made up Form AC (1998). No technical details were provided for the methods of revising Form AC in 2000 or for developing Form AR-C other than a statement saying "care was taken to make sure that [the] difficulty level of each of the categories remained consistent" (manual, p .6).

TECHNICAL. Normative data for a sample of 82 applicants for machinist jobs at a refining plant who took Form AC were presented in a table with percentile ranks. No demographic data for these applicants and no other information regarding the norming process were provided; no normative data for Form AR-C were described.

Results of two content validation studies performed for Ramsay Corporation clients in 2000 and 2001 using a 45-item short form of the test (Form AC-SF) were provided. There is no further discussion of the process. Results of these two studies report rater agreement for the five raters to be .75 for a client in the metals manufacturing industry and .70 for a client in the ceramics industry. Average job relatedness of the shortened form was reported from 0 to 5. Metals manufacturing reported a 4.2, and ceramics reported a 4.0. However, there is no content validity evidence reported for the current 60-question form.

The manual reports that there have been no criterion-related or construct validity studies conducted for this test. Although the authors assert that the construct of machining knowledge or skill could be applied to the development of a training plan, assessment of knowledge prior to hire, and certification of machinists, there is no evidence in the manual to support the use of this test for these purposes.

COMMENTARY. Although the U.S. Department of Labor's O*NET skills sets have gained popularity in technical education, this test does not provide evidence to support the use of these skill sets in its development. Although it is possible that there is an underlying theoretical model to support test development, it is not described in this manual. In fact, the manual consists of only 19 pages, some of which display only a few sentences or a table. No current research is described or suggested.

Although the scoring sheet is not difficult to use and online testing is available, all psychometric aspects of this test must be strengthened before use is recommended. When additional information is available, the manual needs to be significantly enhanced. Empirical evidence to support the assertion that the knowledge and skills tested are indicators of machinist job requirements as well as to relate these requirements to various industries is a critical need.

SUMMARY. Although the RCJS Machinist Test–Form AR-C purports to assess machinist job knowledge and skills, very little evidence is provided to support this claim. Therefore, other measures of machinist job knowledge and skills as related in DOT and O*NET definitions, including performance assessments, should be used instead.

REVIWER'S REFERENCE

U.S. Department of Labor. (1999). *Dictionary of occupational titles* (4th ed., rev.). Washington, D.C.: U.S. Government Printing Office

[95]
Maintenance Electrician A Test (Form BTA-RC).

Purpose: Designed for selecting manufacturing or processing maintenance candidates.
Population: Applicants and incumbents for jobs requiring electrical knowledge and skills at the highest level.
Publication Dates: 2000-2009.
Scores, 8: Motors, Digital Electronics and Analog Electronics, Schematics & Print Reading and Control Circuits, Power Supplies/Power Distribution and Construction & Installation, Basic AC/DC Theory and Electrical Maintenance & Troubleshooting, Test Instruments and Computers & PLC, Mechanical Maintenance, Total.
Administration: Group.
Price Data, 2011: $22 per consumable self-scoring test booklet or online test administration (minimum order of 20); $24.95 per manual (2009, 18 pages).
Time: (60-70) minutes.
Comments: Self-scoring instrument; available for online test administration.
Author: Roland T. Ramsay.
Publisher: Ramsay Corporation.
Cross References: For a review by Kevin R. Kelly of an earlier edition, see 17:112.

Review of the Maintenance Electrician A Test (Form BTA-RC) by EMILY BULLOCK-YOWELL, Associate Professor of Psychology, University of Southern Mississippi, Hattiesburg, MS:

DESCRIPTION. The manual for the Maintenance Electrician A Test Form BTA-RC states that the test was "intended for use with applicants and incumbents for jobs where electrical knowledge and skill are necessary parts of job activities" (p. 1). Additionally, the test was created for the highest level of electrical skills and was developed as a part of several skills tests offered by the publisher, Ramsay Corporation. The BTA-RC is a 60-item, multiple-choice test that can be administered via paper and pencil or taken online. An overall score, ranging from 0–60, can be calculated through the self-scoring mechanism included in the test booklet. The manual notes that the knowledge areas included are Motors; Digital Electronics and Analog Electronics; Schematics & Print Reading and Control Circuits; Power Supplies, Power Distribution, and Construction & Installation; Basic AC/DC Theory, and Electrical Maintenance & Troubleshooting; Test Instruments and Computers & PLC; and Mechanical Maintenance. Additionally, safety is represented across all domains.

The testing materials are attractive and easy to read. The manual provides detailed and appropriate administration and scoring information for test users. The manual states that the test is untimed but that one hour should be sufficient testing time for most applicants. The scoring grid is a bit difficult to understand initially, but it is likely mastered with practice.

According to the test manual, the original version of the test was created in 1991 as the RCJS Maintenance Electrician A Test Form BTA. Version BTA-C was developed in 2000, with the main revision being the incorporation of self-scoring.

In 2005, Form BTA-C was revised by replacing two items and rewording one. The current 2008 BTA-RC version was released after 26 items were revised or replaced. At that time, the publisher also offered an online version available at www. ramsaycorp.com. All development and standardization information provided in this review is based on the paper-and-pencil version of the test as no relevant information for the online version was provided in the test manual.

To develop the RCJS Maintenance Electrician A Test Form BTA (1991), 10 job experts were asked to choose the most relevant maintenance electricians' knowledge and skills areas from a list the author developed after a review of the relevant Dictionary of Occupational Titles and O*NET descriptions. Experts also were asked their opinion on the percent of items appropriate for each area. This information was averaged across raters, and the percentage of questions suggested was used to determine the number of planned items for each area. The author created items and used job experts to rate which items were most relevant and to choose a safety item for each area.

Following administration of the test to 50 individuals, the author employed two industrial psychologists to select the best 60 items based on item difficulty and point-biserial correlation coefficient discrimination indexes. According to the test manual, the test was kept fairly consistent from the BTA version to the BTA-C version. The current BTA-RC version being reviewed underwent some substantial changes, in that 26 questions were replaced or revised. The test manual does not provide information about how these new items were selected or evaluated, but it does state that the new items were similar in difficulty to the items they replaced.

TECHNICAL.

Standardization. For the BTA-C version, means of 26.22 and 25.74 and standard deviations of 6.79 and 6.89 were reported for a group of 49 applicants at a Midwest automotive plant and 68 applicants and incumbents in various industries, respectively. Percentile ranks for administration of the BTA-C to 68 test takers were provided in the manual. For instance, a score of 40 and above was equated to a 99.3 percentile rank, and a score of 13 and below was 0.7 percentile rank. The group's demographics were not described. Standardization information for the BTA-RC version was not provided in the manual.

Reliability. The test manual provides information regarding the internal consistency of the test when the BTA and BTA-C versions were administered. Using a sample of 167 test takers, internal consistency ($KR20$) ranged from .74 to .87, depending on the sample and test version. Reliability data for the BTA-RC 2008 version were not provided in the manual. It should be noted that the reliability coefficients for the more recent Form BTA-C were lower than the coefficient reported for the older BTA version.

Validity. Content evidence of validity for the BTA version is well supported, based on the test development process described above. Rater agreement among the experts was reported to range from .74 to .82. However, the test manual made no mention of any expert review of the new or revised items that were added to create Form BTA-RC. Criterion-related evidence of validity seems to be particularly important for a test of this nature. A common use of the test would likely be to make hiring decisions. Therefore, it would be important to know whether test scores actually predict job performance and differentiate between entry and upper-level employees, as claimed by the authors. The test manual acknowledges no formal criterion-related validity studies have been conducted. The authors of the test manual identify the construct being assessed by the test as "knowledge and skill in electrical maintenance" (manual, p. 15). Yet, no formal studies to establish construct evidence of validity have been conducted. A factor analysis to determine the items chosen for the designated content areas actually adhere to that area would be an appropriate beginning to provide some initial construct evidence of validity. Additionally, discriminant validity studies among the electrician oriented tests offered by the publisher could be used to determine whether the different tests actually differ in the intended skill-level manner.

COMMENTARY. It is likely that the RCJS Maintenance Electrician A Test Form BTA-RC fills a unique niche for assessing high-level electrical skills and knowledge in an easy-to-use and readily available format. However, because the manual reports little information about the development or standardization of this current form, little confidence can be placed in either the content or the results of the test. A thorough description of the revision process, data on the equivalency across versions, assessment of this form's internal consistency, investigation of construct evidence of validity, and some formal criterion-related evidence of validity studies are suggested to increase confidence in the use of Form BTA-RC.

SUMMARY. The RCJS Maintenance Electrician A Test Form BTA-RC is published with a series of other skills tests by the Ramsay Corporation. It has undergone two main revisions since 1991. Inadequate description of the test's development and validation data are provided for the current version, reducing confidence in the content or results of the test.

[96]

Management and Leadership Questionnaire.

Purpose: Designed to "provide information about an individual's management and leadership competencies and skills."
Population: Ages 18-64.
Publication Date: 2011.
Acronym: MLQ30.
Scores, 36: Strategic and Creative Thinking, Thinking and Managing Globally, Developing Strategy and Acting Strategically, Managing Knowledge and Information, Creating and Innovating, Managing costs and Financial Performance, Leading and Deciding, Attracting and Managing Talent, Motivating People and Inspiring Them to Excel, Coaching and Developing People, Managing Culture and Diversity, Making Sound Decisions, Developing and Changing, Displaying Initiative and Drive, Showing courage and Strength, Learning and Developing Continuously, Managing and Implementing Change, Adapting and Coping with Pressure, Implementing and Improving, Executing Strategies and Plans, Improving Processes and Systems, Managing Customer Relationships and Services, Analyzing Issues and Problems, Managing Plans and Projects, Communicating and Presenting, Facilitating and Improving Communication, Influencing and Persuading People, Managing Feelings and Emotions, Speaking with Confidence and Presenting to Groups, Writing and Reporting, Relating and Supporting, Relating and Networking, Listening and Showing Understanding, Building Trust and Modeling Integrity, Identifying and Resolving Conflict, Cultivating Teamwork and Collaboration.
Administration: Group.
Forms, 2: Normative and Ipsative.
Price Data, 2011: $14.95 per test.
Time: (30) minutes.
Comments: Assessment, scoring, and feedback conducted online.
Author: MySkillsProfile.com.
Publisher: MySkillsProfile.com Limited [England].

Review of the Management and Leadership Questionnaire by PATRICIA A. BACHELOR, Professor Emeritus, California State University, Long Beach, Long Beach, CA:

DESCRIPTION. The theoretical basis of the Management and Leadership Questionnaire (MLQ30) is a 30-dimension competency model of leadership and management skills and abilities across transformational or transactional aspects covering six key areas. Specifically, leadership competencies consist of three transformational aspects: Strategic and Creative Thinking, Leading and Deciding, and Developing and Changing. The management competencies are assumed to be three transactional aspects: Implementing and Improving, Communicating and Presenting, and Relating and Supporting. Each of the resultant six key areas are assessed by five scales, thereby producing the 30 dimensions/scales of the MLQ30. Each dimension is measured by a 6-item scale, resulting in a 192-item instrument including 12 items relating to deception. The test developers prepared an ipsative version and a normative version, MLQ30i and MLQ30n, respectively. The MLQ30i presents examinees with 100 sets of three competency statements, and test takers are asked to rate themselves on levels of competency from *best* to *least*. The ipsative version, as the name suggests, is used as a self-improvement/enhancement instrument. The MLQ30n can offer self-insight; it is most likely used to compare an examinee's performance with others in an effort to identify areas of strengths and/or weaknesses on the 30 dimensions/scales. The normative version asks examinees to rate their current performance on 30 scales/dimensions of management and leadership competencies using a 5-point Likert scale (1 = *emerging*, 2 = *developing*, 3 = *competent*, 4 = *superior*, and 5 = *elite*). In an effort to ensure test takers are not being deceptive in their answers, an additional (seventh) factor, self-impression, was developed to consist of two 6-item scales–self-deception and impression management. Each version takes no more than 30 minutes to complete. Both versions of the MLQ30 are only available online.

DEVELOPMENT. There is no description in the test manual of the theoretical basis upon which the MLQ30 was modeled or constructed. No evidence was provided as to how items were generated and revised. It is expected that the next user's manual would incorporate the practical nature of the MLQ30 dimensions and subsequent scales and items that would enable an understanding of the practical aspects of item development and revisions, scale development, and factor structure.

Further discussion of the assumptions underlying factor analysis would better serve as evidence of criterion-related evidence of validity.

TECHNICAL.

Standardization samples. Three samples were used to assess the psychometric qualities of the MLQ30: the standardization sample (n = 878), the trial questionnaire sample (n = 163), and the ipsative sample (n = 481). The standardization sample consisted of "incidental" examinees who completed the test online as part of a corporate assessment or as an individual customer (manual, p. 59). The sample had roughly equal numbers of males (n = 436) and females (n = 442). Seventeen percent were from the United Kingdom (n = 150) and 37% were from the United States (n = 322), with the remaining 46% (n = 406) from the rest of the world. Participants' ages were distributed in categories ranging from 18 to 64. Specifically, 18- to 24-year-olds (n = 122) made up 14% of the sample; 25- to 34-year-olds (n = 231), 26%; 35- to 44-year-olds (n = 279), 32%; 45- to 54-year-olds (n = 177), 20%; and 55- to 64-year-olds (n = 69), 8%. The average age was reported to be 37. Managerial levels of employees were categorized as junior (n = 358), 41%; middle (n = 254), 29%; senior (n = 91), 10%; and no managerial responsibilities (n = 175), 20%. The ipsative sample consisted of 481 "incidental" members who completed the questionnaire on the Internet. Approximately equal numbers of males (n = 252) and females (n = 229) took the MLQ30i. Twelve percent were from the United Kingdom (n = 60), 31% were from the United States and Canada (n = 149), and the remaining 57% (n = 272) were from the rest of the world. Ages were distributed in categories ranging from "up to 24" years to 65 years or older. Specifically, up to 24 years old (n = 80) made up 17% of the sample; 25 to 34 years (n = 150), 31%; 35 to 44 years (n = 139), 29%; 45 to 54 years (n = 86), 18%; 55 to 64 years (n = 24), 5%, and 65 years or older (n = 2), 0.4%. The average age was 36. Managerial levels were categorized as junior (n = 190), 39%; middle (n = 145), 30%; senior (n = 42), 9%; and no managerial responsibilities (n = 104), 22%. The trial questionnaire sample consisted of 163 employees who were administered the MLQ30n and also recalled their prior work performance review on a 4-point scale (*excellent, good, satisfactory*, and *unsatisfactory*). Their scores were correlated to assess whether the MLQ30n and the prior review measured the same skill set. The trial questionnaire sample was also used to calculate internal consistency estimates of reliability, (i.e., coefficient alpha for the MLQ30n). Ignoring a small sample, no other demographic or normative information is available about these employees. Additionally, even though a category on the 4-point performance review is unsatisfactory, no distribution of the scores on the prior reviews is presented; hence, there is a strong possibility that the category is seldom, if ever, used because such employees are dismissed. Without distributions for the MLQ30n scores and scales scores and without the prior reviews' distribution, there is little empirical evidence available to accept the resultant correlations as meaningful to establish the construct evidence of validity of the MLQ30. Without knowledge of the range of scores on the 4-point scale for job performance or the distribution of the scores on the MLQ30n, there is a possibility of a restricted range, hence depressing the correlation between the scores.

Reliability. Internal consistency reliability estimates for the 32 scales of the MLQ30 were calculated using coefficient alpha. Alpha is often the most appropriate measure of internal consistency of measures that consist of items scored on a Likert-type scale. Data were used from the 192 items of the MLQ30n given to the 878 members of the standardization sample. Alpha values for each of the 32 scales ranged from .78 to .92, indicating adequate internal consistency. Similarly, data were used from the 186 items comprising 31 scales of the MLQ30n (without the 6-item self-deception scale) given to the 163 members of the trial questionnaire sample. Alpha values for each of the 31 scales ranged from .84 to .95. Hence, despite a significantly lower sample size for the trial questionnaire sample, the internal consistency estimates of alpha were substantial.

Validity. A factor analysis was performed with an oblique two-factor rotated structure, and scale intercorrelations were provided. No discussion of test construction and revision was offered. Principal factor extraction was used, and an oblique two-factor rotated structure was presented. Results indicated that the first factor was considered a social interaction/people management factor based on the scales that attained the highest factor loadings. The second factor could be considered managing strategically various resources, finances, and information with a global view due to the highest factor loadings on task and conceptual activities associated with strategy management and managing tasks and resources with global vision. The factor loadings were of sufficient size to conclude that only one factor could be supported by the data. The items assessing leadership and management included people and task skills as well as communicating and directing people. Hence, the skills that are measured on the MLQ30n do not appear to be assessing six factors or 30 dimensions but rather aspects of the one factor of a complex outstanding leader who has global vision and interpersonal skills combined with management of tasks inherent in top performance in a global corporation. Given no theoretical basis for the leadership/transformational and management/ transaction key areas and the resultant 30 scales, one must step back from number-driven solutions to reasonable assumptions about leadership and management skills. This reviewer interprets these analyses to indicate a one-factor solution due to high factor intercorrelations.

Criterion-related evidence of validity could be assessed using the high number of statistically significant correlations between the performance of current employees and their performance on the MLQ30n. However, there may be other effects in existence. It would be helpful to examine the scores of those who took the MLQ30n and their scores on their prior review to rule out any distributional anomalies in the data.

COMMENTARY. The MLQ30 is an captivating tool to identify leadership and management talent, yet the psychometric properties are yet to be verified. It must be considered a research tool at this point. If the data were provided, perhaps the reservations about this questionnaire could be resolved favorably. Demographic information to enable meaningful comparisons based upon the trial questionnaire sample would have been preferred to the lengthy presentations about scale interpretation. No discussion of the theoretical model upon which the MLQ30 was based, item development and revision, scale construction, or item analysis was offered. Distributions of job performance and the scores on the MLQ30n are needed for understanding the correlations in the discussion of criterion-related validity. This reviewer believes that factor analysis revealed a one-factor solution due to high factor loadings and statistically significant scale intercorrelations.

SUMMARY. The MLQ30n is a 30-dimension competency model of leadership and management skills covering transactional and transformational aspects. Test-taking strategies were evaluated by two additional scales–impression management and deception. Despite contradictory statements about utilizing coefficient alpha to assess internal consistency, estimates of alphas were calculated with values adequate to support the claim that the 32 scales of the MLQ30n are each internally consistent. Preliminary evidence suggests there is emerging evidence to support criterion-related evidence of validity; however, the distribution of the job performance and the distribution of scores on the MLQ30n need to be examined before a definitive conclusion can be reached. Item review, scale descriptions, and factor analysis results led this reviewer to conclude that a one-factor model best fit the data, especially based on the factor loadings and scale intercorrelations.

Review of the Management and Leadership Questionnaire by JANET HOUSER, Academic Dean of the Rueckert-Hartman College for Health Professions (RHCHP), and LYNN WIMETT, Professor, RHCHP, Regis University, Denver, CO:

DESCRIPTION. The Management and Leadership Questionnaire (MLQ30) is an online 192-item self-assessment tool designed to identify perceived competency areas, provide feedback for personal leadership development, and possibly serve as a guide for supervisor-manager evaluation. The MLQ30 consists of 30 scales (6 items per scale) based on a concept model that includes key leadership skills (manual, p. 4).

There are two forms of the MLQ30, a normative version and an ipsative version. This review is of the normative version. The normative questionnaire requires test takers to rate their performance on the competencies using a 5-point Likert scale from *emerging* to *elite*. The ipsative version includes 100 blocks of three items that represent a competency. On the ipsative version, test takers rate the item they do best and least well. The average time for completion is less than 30 minutes for both versions of the questionnaire.

The stated purpose of the questionnaire is "to provide information about an individual's management and leadership competencies and skills" (manual, p. 4). On the instrument's web page (MySkillsProfile.com), the authors suggest that the test could be used for self-reflection, understanding differing managerial styles, and to benchmark leadership performance. An interpretive summary report is provided for test takers that includes suggestions for improving leadership style and competency. The user's manual also suggests that the assessment may help in the selection of candidates by offering a framework for normative comparison, a starting point for a competency-based interview, and a way to discuss potential candidate strengths and weaknesses. The MLQ30 is also described as useful for staff development, team building, coaching, and counseling.

The intended population includes existing and potential leaders and managers. Currently, the test is available only online at MLQ30.com or MySkillsProfile.com. The website is attractive and easy to navigate. It provides clear directions, a link to the user's manual, and a direct pay option.

DEVELOPMENT. The test manual contains little information about the development of the test items. A theoretical framework is provided that represents six key areas of management and leadership competence. The test items were based on this model that, in the authors' words, "cover the transformational and transactional aspects of managerial and leadership activity" (manual, p. 4). Three of the concepts are specific for leadership and include Strategic and Creative Thinking, Leading and Deciding, and Developing and Changing. The remaining concepts relate to management and include Implementing and Improving, Communicating and Presenting, and Relating and Supporting. These concepts are further subdivided into 30 dimensions of management and leadership. The model appears as a figure in the manual, without literature reference, and has no reporting of analysis supporting its validity or application.

There is no information in the manual regarding specific steps in the development, testing, and refining of individual items. There is no description of the process taken to identify the competency areas from the original 192 items. If a factor analysis was used to discern the six subscales, it is not reported in the manual.

TECHNICAL. Normative data were provided by a convenience sample of 878 Internet-based respondents. The test authors report that the group included individuals who were assessed as part of a corporate effort and individuals who accessed the test directly and voluntarily. Gender, age, and nationality of the respondents were described. Of key interest was the managerial level of respondents, which was described as junior, middle, senior, or no managerial responsibilities. The distribution of managerial personnel levels appears to approximate reasonably the overall population distribution of managers, with the majority at the junior level.

Standardized scores are reported as ranges by item. The tables are somewhat difficult to interpret, as categories (e.g. "1", "2", "3"…"10") are reported for each range of scores by item, but the categories are not defined. After re-reading the "interpretation" section of the test manual, it appears that the categories are sten scores, with a competency level defined in a table. However, the linkage between scoring, interpretation, and standard scores is neither explicit nor clear.

Internal consistency reliability estimates based on coefficient alpha and raw and sten score *SEM*s for the normative version are provided by the authors in the user's manual. The stated alpha range is .84 to .95 with a median reliability of .89 for the trial questionnaire and .78 to .92 with a median of .86 for the standardization sample. Intercorrelations and reliability are also reported in table format in the user's manual, with a reported median percentage of reliable variance for the MLQ30 scale pairs of 72. According to the test manual, "about one quarter of the scale pairs in the normative questionnaire share less than 60 percent common variance" (p. 48). The standard error of difference importance is briefly explained and documented as ranging from 0.82 to 1.1 with a median of 1 for the normative questionnaire.

There is limited evidence of validity considerations and the section of the manual devoted to reliability and validity of the instrument focused more on reliability. It does appear that construct validity was possible–given the provision of subscales–but there is no description of the process from item to scales.

COMMENTARY. The MLQ30 is an online self-assessment tool that can be used by managers and others in leadership roles to identify their competency areas as they perceive them. This may well be a helpful exercise in establishing a personal leadership development plan or as a guide for supervisor-manager evaluation. A key strength is the instrument's accessibility and ease of administration; it is also quick to administer and has low respondent burden.

The instrument appears to be reliable internally, and item analysis was used to refine a few items. However, little information is provided about the development of items and determination of scales. It is impossible to discern how scales were formed. Future testing of the instrument could include additional factor-analytic research to determine whether these concepts are, indeed, captured by these scales, as they appear to be in the initial analyses presented in the manual.

An assessment of the validity of the instrument is mostly absent. This instrument would not be a good choice for an inferential research study without stronger confidence that it actually represents transformational and transactional aspects of managerial and leadership activity. Particularly troubling is the lack of any tests for criterion-related and predictive evidence of validity; without them, this instrument would not be appropriate for pre-employment testing or as a basis for employment decisions, as the authors suggest.

SUMMARY. The MLQ30 is a self-assessment tool developed for managers as a basis for a personal development plan or as a starting point for a manager/supervisor conversation about performance. The instrument is easy to access and use, and it provides helpful summary reports that include both personalized feedback and suggestions for improvement. Its psychometric properties have not been well tested, and as a result, this instrument would not be appropriate for pre-employment testing or employee counseling. It would probably not be a valuable test of the constructs it intends to measure to use in a research study. However, it could be used reliably to determine an individual's perceptions of his or her basic leadership competence.

[97]

Management Skills and Styles Assessment.

Purpose: Designed to assess "basic managerial functions" to "determine an individual's overall management skills and style."

Population: Under 17 through adult.

Publication Date: 2011.

Acronym: MANSSA.

Scores, 40: Intrapersonal Skills (Comfort with Authority, Concentration, Coping Skills, Decision-Making, Locus of Control, Optimism, Perfectionism [Self-Directed], Self-Confidence, Integrity), Interpersonal Skills (Communication Skills, Flexibility, Soft Skills, Perfectionism [Other-Directed], Self-Monitoring, Sensitivity to Social Cues), Executive Skills (Creativity, Drive, Goal-Setting, Time Management, Vision, Risk-Taking, Organizational Skills, Cognitive Ability), Transactional Leadership (Delegating, Giving Feedback, Rewarding Performance), Transformational Leadership (Coaching, Motivating, Problem-Solving, Communicating Vision, Collaboration), Leadership Ability, Impression Management, Setting an Example, Overall Score.

Administration: Individual.

Price Data: Available from publisher.

Time: (45) minutes.

Comments: Self-administered online assessment. The test publisher advises that the test manual is being updated to include more information about methodology and theoretical background used in the development of the test. The test publisher also advises that this information is available to clients, as are benchmarks for relevant industries and racial/ethnic group comparison data. However, this information was not provided to Buros or the reviewers.

Author: PsychTests AIM, Inc.

Publisher: PsychTests AIM, Inc. [Canada].

Review of the Management Skills and Styles Assessment by FREDERICK L. OSWALD, Professor of Psychology, Rice University, Houston, TX:

DESCRIPTION. The Management Skills and Styles Assessment (MANSSA) consists of 196 multiple-choice items that cover eight broad areas of managerial skill that presumably distinguish between effective and ineffective managers. Scores on the MANSSA scales could be used for the purposes of identifying promising managers; selecting, promoting or transferring employees into management positions; and training and developing existing managers. The test is administered online, with subsets of items presented on the screen, radio buttons to allow for responding to each item on a 1–5 Likert scale (*agree* to *disagree* for each statement), and a progress bar to indicate the extent of test completion.

DEVELOPMENT. The MANSSA scales span a range of skills that reflect interpersonal interactions, intrapersonal strengths, and leadership functions. There is also a social desirability scale, reflecting the extent that the examinee scores high on presenting oneself in a favorable light.

TECHNICAL. The MANSSA Psychometric Report provides results based on a large sample of 4,988 test takers that are diverse along various demographic categories: gender (49% female); age (note that 10% of the sample was below 17 and likely lacked managerial experience; 15% was 18–24, 12% 25–29, 22% 30–39, 19% 40–49, 10% 50 and older, and 12% unknown); education (a fairly even distribution across high school, technical/trade school, and post-secondary degrees); socioeconomic status (ranging from less than $20,000 to $100,000 or more); and position (a fairly even distribution between entrepreneur, managerial, employed, and not officially employed). Demographics on race/ethnicity are not provided. Additional information was collected on whether test takers were currently in a management position (56% were). The test developers caution that although the sample is large, it is also "uncontrolled"; test takers opted to complete the assessment through one of three websites (queendom.com, psychtests.com, and psychologytoday.com).

The MANSSA Psychometric Report provides descriptive statistics (means, standard deviations) at the level of the scales (not the items). The number of items per scale is 29–88 at the level of the scales, and 3–12 at the level of the subscales. Coefficient alpha was .97 for the Overall Score and .86–.94 across the scales. Alpha coefficients were more variable across the subscales (.53–.89), as might be expected given that there are fewer items. Correlations between scales and subscales are not reported, although the labels of the scales suggest that correlations between some of the scales may be high (e.g., Vision and Communicating Vision). Histograms for each scale are helpfully reported; they indicate that many of the scales are negatively skewed, meaning that many people report being on the higher end of the skills assessed, more so for some skills (e.g., Motivation, Goal-Setting) than others (Perfectionism [Self-Directed and Other-Directed]).

The MANSSA Psychometric Report also provides more refined descriptive statistics (means, standard deviations) and analyses (t-tests and ANOVAs) within levels of the various subgroups previously described: gender, age, education, socioeconomic status, and managerial position.

COMMENTARY. The MANSSA contains measures for a very wide range of management skills. Although the conceptual distinctions between many of the scales and subscales are clear (e.g., Time Management vs. Giving Feedback), more empirical evidence from future psychometric and validation work would greatly help to support these distinctions, especially given that the measure is entirely self-report (vs. peer ratings and/or prediction of managerial outcomes). Correlation matrices between scales, confirmatory factor analyses, and the prediction of managerial outcomes would together strengthen inferences to be made with regard to the reliability, validity, and other correlates and group differences associated with the MANSSA. This work might be conducted on more focused samples of employees who are candidates for management positions or who are already in those positions and are eligible for managerial training or promotion.

The authors of the MANSSA Psychometric Report make the point that statistically significant mean differences between groups may not be practically significant. Their graphs of mean differences help to reinforce this important point (e.g., a statistically significant difference may be a very small difference in the number of points on the scale given the large sample size). The information provided also allows one to compute standardized mean differences (d-values) between subgroups as a quantitative index of practical significance. Keeping the nature of the sample in mind, those computations indicate that some statistically significant results are practically significant whereas others are not.

SUMMARY. The Management Skills and Styles Assessment (MANSSA) measures a wide range of skills across interpersonal, intrapersonal, and leadership domains. The test is administered online in a user-friendly format (simple 1–5 scale responses across items, with a bar to indicate progress visually). Psychometric information is based on a large web-based sample, but that sample potentially includes people less relevant to managerial positions (e.g., young, unemployed). MANSSA scales are generally found to be reliable at the scale level (high alpha coefficients), but reliability varies across subscales. Future psychometric information that would be highly informative might include correlational and factor analyses (to determine how empirically distinct the scales are), as well as evidence of validity for predicting organizational outcomes (e.g., managerial performance and training success). Clients making use of this test might consider the potential benefits of the large sample but relatively limited results provided in the MANSSA Psychometric Report along with the feasibility and value of collecting reliability and validity results for their own test takers.

Review of the Management Skills and Styles Assessment by RICHARD REILLY, Professor Emeritus, Stevens Institute of Technology, Hoboken, NJ:

DESCRIPTION. The Management Skills and Styles Assessment (MANSSA) is an individually administered online measure. The estimated time for the test is 45 minutes. The manual states that the purpose of the test is to "determine an individual's overall management skills and style. It assesses basic managerial functions" (p. 1). The manual states that the application of MANSSA is for HR testing (screening and training). According to the authors the MANSSA includes 196 items. The total number of items for the version reviewed was 186 items.

Respondents are advised that they should be in a quiet place and have enough time to complete the test in one sitting. Respondents are told that the purpose of the MANSSA is to "evaluate certain personality characteristics and/or specific skill sets. This information will be used to provide insight about what is important to you and/or in which settings you would most likely thrive." Respondents are advised to select "answer choices that reflect how you usually feel or act–those that most accurately describe your general feelings or behaviors." Respondents also are told: "There may be some questions describing situations that do not apply to you. In these cases, select the answer that you would most likely choose if you ever found yourself in such a situation." Respondents are warned that "there are measures in place that are intended to pick up attempts at self-misrepresentation. If there is an indication that you are not being truthful or taking the test carelessly, the results might be considered invalid."

The test instructions are clear and easy to follow. A progress indicator that shows the percentage of the test completed is displayed at the top of each page. Respondents must complete all items in order to advance to the next screen. Throughout the test, respondents are presented with a variety of different item types. These include personality items, attitudinal items, and scenario-based items. The test includes a variety of item-response scales, most of which are 5-point scales that assess attitudes or frequency of behavior. The exceptions are the scenario-based questions, which present work-related scenarios and ask respondents to choose one of several alternatives. A radio button format is used for all responses. Upon completion of the test the respondent is informed that his or her scores have been saved.

A computer-generated score report can be accessed immediately after finishing the assessment. The report begins by describing the "personality type" of the respondent with a paragraph relating this personality type to potential success as a manager. The remainder of the report is organized around four main aspects necessary to excel in management. These are Intrapersonal Skills, Interpersonal Skills, Executive Skills, and Leadership Ability. The report also includes an overall "suitability for management" score. This score, like all other scores on the MANSSA, is reported on a 0 to 100 scale, where higher scores reflect better suitability for a management career. Summary scores for Intraper-

sonal Skills, Interpersonal Skills, Executive Skills, and Leadership Ability, as well as their subscores, are reported. The summary score for Interpersonal Skills is based on the subscores Comfort with Authority, Concentration, Coping Skills, Decision-Making, Locus of Control, Optimism, Perfectionism (Self-Directed), Self-Confidence, and Integrity. The summary score for Interpersonal Skills is based on the subscores Communication Skills, Flexibility, Soft Skills, Perfectionism (Other-Directed), Self-Monitoring, and Sensitivity to Social Cues. The summary score for Executive Skills is based on subscores for Creativity, Drive, Goal-Setting, Time Management, Vision, Risk-Taking, and Organizational Skills. In addition to an overall Leadership Ability score, the report includes a Transactional Leadership score, which is based on subscores for Delegating, Giving Feedback, and Rewarding Performance and a Transformational Leadership score, which is based on subscores for Coaching, Motivating, Problem-Solving, Communicating Vision, and Collaboration. A score for Impression Management is also included in the report.

DEVELOPMENT. The test manual presents very little information about the development of the items or scores included in the MANSSA. No theory or rationale for the selection of items, subscales, or summary scores is presented. No information is given to support content validity, nor how items were developed or selected, whether item analysis was used to remove items, or whether items were reviewed by content experts.

TECHNICAL. The test manual indicates that the Overall Score is based on 196 items with an alpha coefficient of .97. Alpha coefficients are reported for 40 different scores including scores for Setting an Example (based on 36 items, alpha = .88) and Cognitive Ability (based on 10 items, alpha = .53), neither of which are included in the report. The manual does not explain why the number of items making up the various subscores is much larger than the 196 items reported for the Overall Score. Although the range of the scores appears to be 0–100, the manual does not explain how the scores were scaled, or how any of the scores were derived. The manual reports a sample size of 4,988 participants (2,472 women, 1,935 men, and 591 of unknown gender) and notes that all took the MANSSA online at one of three websites. The test manual further notes that the sample was uncontrolled and self-selected and that all "validation items were gathered through self-report" (p.

3). The manual reports sample sizes, minimum and maximum scores, and means and standard deviations for all scores listed above as well as scores for Setting an Example and Cognitive Ability. The manual reports the age distribution for the sample, and it should be noted that the 10% of those reporting age were below 17 years old, which would seem to be outside the range for viable candidates for management jobs. The manual also includes a series of frequency charts for the various scores. The distribution of most of the scales appears to be fairly normal although no statistics are given to support normality.

The section labeled Validity Analysis presents a series of comparative analyses. First, a series of *t*-tests with accompanying bar charts are reported for males vs. females on all of the scores with results varying depending upon the scale. It should be noted that the degrees of freedom for the *t*-tests vary considerably, but these differences are not explained. For the Overall Score, graphic results appear to show a higher score for women, although this Overall Score is not included in the list of *t*-test results. The next section includes a series of analyses of variance (ANOVA) using age as an independent variable and each of the MANSSA scores as dependent variables. Age is divided into six categories ranging from below 17 to 50 and older. Sample sizes are 513 for the below 17 group, 583 for the 25 to 29 group, and 496 for the 50 and older group. The remaining three groups have sample sizes of 500, but the test manual does not explain how these samples were selected or if they were selected. ANOVAs and post-hoc analyses generally showed that the 17 and under age group scored lower than other age groups. This section also includes a series of bar charts showing the distribution of each construct by age. The next section reports a series of ANOVAs with education as the independent variable and the various MANSSA scores as dependent variables. The total sample was divided into nine categories based on education level attained ranging from some high school to Ph.D. The within-group sample sizes for seven of the groups was 130, but for technical/trade school the sample size was 148 and for Ph.D.s the sample size was 102. The test manual does not explain how or why the subsamples were selected. A variety of significant results are reported with consistently lower scores for those with some high school. The analysis for the Overall Score showed a significantly higher mean for those with master's degrees vs. those with

some high school and those with college degrees. (It should be noted that education would logically be confounded with age, given the distribution of age reported.) A later section reports a series of ANOVAs with socioeconomic status (SES) as the independent variable and MANSSA scores as the dependent variables. SES was divided into six categories based on income ranging from $100,000 or more to $20,000 or less based on the question, "How would you classify your socioeconomic status?" Within-group sample sizes were 200 except for the $20,000 to $25,000 category, which had a sample size of 177. No explanation is given for why or how these subsamples were selected. The general trend of these analyses showed lower MANSSA scores for the lowest SES categories. Results for the Overall Score showed significantly higher scores for the highest SES groups compared with the lowest SES groups. These results may be confounded with other variables including age and education. The next section includes a series of comparisons between those who responded "yes" and those who responded "no" to the question, "Are you currently working in a managerment position?" The sample sizes for these analyses were 2,227 (yes) and 1,719 (no). The manual does not state how these samples were selected. The results showed consistent significant differences between the two groups with higher scores for those currently employed as managers. The remainder of the manual includes a series of tables with means and standard deviations for the various score-subsample combinations. In sum, there is limited evidence provided for the validity of the MANSSA and the various subscales on which feedback is provided. There is no discussion of item analyses, correlations between subscores, or factor analytic results that might support the constructs included in the test. It is not clear how summary scores are arrived at from the manual, and there is scant evidence of validity. The primary evidence for validity of the MANSSA is the series of comparisons showing differences for responses to the question "Are you currently working in a management position." However, the credibility of this evidence is mitigated by the uncontrolled nature of the sample, the self-report nature of the items, and potential response bias. In addition, the results for the "currently working as a manager" question are subject to a number of potential confounds (age, gender, SES, education), which are not controlled and which, as the manual reports, have significant relationships with the MANSSA scores.

COMMENTARY. The MANSSA includes a mix of personality, attitudinal, and situational items that could potentially predict performance in management. Unfortunately, little evidence is provided to support the validity of the MANSSA for this purpose. In addition, the extensive detailed report that provides feedback to candidates on a variety of summary scores and subscores requires that these scores have some evidence of construct validity. The manual provides no evidence for the validity of these constructs either with respect to the content of the various measures or with respect to empirical evidence that these constructs are distinct. The manual would benefit from a narrative that explains how the MANSSA was developed with a complete description of how the items and scales were selected or developed. Most critically, the manual should include credible evidence of criterion-related validity for performance in managerial jobs.

SUMMARY. The MANSSA is designed to assess an individual's overall management skills and style. It provides an overall recommendation for potential as a manager and detailed feedback on a variety of subscores. The manual provides little evidence for the validity of the various scores reported. All data were collected from an uncontrolled sample, and the limited validity evidence provided is of dubious quality. The use of the MANSSA for selection or development cannot be recommended as the evidence does not meet the minimum scientific/professional requirements for validity.

[98]
MATRICS Consensus Cognitive Battery.

Purpose: "A self-contained battery that includes copyrighted materials from various sources" that is designed "to provide a relatively brief evaluation of key cognitive domains that are relevant to schizophrenia and related disorders."

Population: Adults with schizophrenia and related disorders.

Publication Date: 2006.

Acronym: MCCB.

Scores, 18: Speed of Processing [Brief Assessment of Cognition in Schizophrenia: Symbol Coding, Category Fluency: Animal Naming (Fluency), Trail Making Test: Part A], Attention/Vigilance [Continuous Performance Test—Identical Pairs], Working Memory [Wechsler Memory Scale—Third Edition: Spatial Span, Letter-Number Span], Verbal Learning [Hopkins Verbal Learning Test—Revised], Visual Learning [Brief Visuospatial Memory Test—Revised], Reasoning and Problem Solving [Neuropsychological Assessment Battery: Mazes], Social Cognition [Mayer-Salovey-Caruso Emotional Intelligence Test: Managing Emotions], Overall Composite Score.

Administration: Individual.

Price Data, 2012: $1,275 per complete kit, including manual (2006, 163 pages), 25 MCCB administrator's forms, 25 MCCB respondent's booklets, 2 software discs in plastic sleeves [one with the CPT-IP and the second with the MSCEIT™ and MCCB scoring programs], 1 Scoring Template for the BACS Symbol Coding Task, 1 WMS-III™ Spatial Span board, 25 HVLT-R test booklets–Form 1, 1 BVMT-R Recall Stimulus booklet, 25 Executive Functions Module response booklets–Form 1, and 25 NAB Mazes Test record forms–Form 1, in an MCCB box; $510 per Retest Packet, including 25 MCCB administrator's forms, 25 MCCB respondent's booklets, 25 NAB Executive Functions Module response booklets, 25 NAB Mazes Test record forms, and 25 HVLT-R test booklets.

Foreign Language Editions: Simplified Chinese, German, Hebrew, Hindi, Italian, Japanese, Kannada, Marathi, Romanian, Russian, Spanish (Central and South American), Spanish (Spain), Tamil, and Telugu versions available.

Time: (90) minutes.

Comments: Distributed by Psychological Assessment Resources, Inc., 16204 N. Florida Ave., Lutz, FL 33549-8119; Multi-Health Systems, Inc., P. O. Box 950, North Tonawanda, NY 14120-0950; Pearson Assessments, Inc., P. O. Box 599700, San Antonio, TX 78259.

Authors: Keith H. Nuechterlein and Michael F. Green.

Publisher: MATRICS Assessment, Inc.

Cross References: For review of Brief Visuospatial Memory Test—Revised by Anita M. Hubley and Terry A. Stinnett, see 15:40; see also T8:367. For review of Hopkins Verbal Learning Test—Revised by Timothy Z. Keith and Wendy J. Steinberg, see 16:108; see also T8:1264. For reviews of Mayer-Salovey-Caruso Emotional Intelligence Test by S. Alvin Leung and by Catherine Cook-Cottone and Scott T. Meier, see 16:143; see also T8:1634. For reviews of Wechsler Memory Scale—Third Edition by Ric Carl D'Amato and Cecil R. Reynolds, see 14:416; see also T6:2695.

Review of the MATRICS Consensus Cognitive Battery by THOMAS P. HOGAN, Professor of Psychology, University of Scranton, Scranton, PA:

DESCRIPTION. The MATRICS Consensus Cognitive Battery (MCCB) is not a test in the traditional sense of that term. Rather, it is a collection of 10 existing tests (or parts of tests) assembled for a particular purpose. The tests and the parts included in the MCCB are Category Fluency: Animal Naming; Trail Making Test–Part A; Brief Assessment of Cognition in Schizophrenia: Symbol

Coding; Continuous Performance Test–Identical Pairs; Letter–Number Span; Wechsler Memory Scale–Third Edition: Spatial Span; Hopkins Verbal Learning Test–Revised: Immediate Recall; Brief Visuospatial Memory Test–Revised: Immediate Recall; Neuropsychological Assessment Battery: Mazes; and Mayer–Salovey–Caruso Emotional Intelligence Test: Managing Emotions. All 10 of the tests have well-established identities in their own right; some are the subject of separate Buros *Mental Measurements Yearbook* (MMY) reviews. MCCB organizes the tests into seven domains, with three tests in one domain (Speed of Processing), two in another domain (Working Memory), and one each in five domains (Attention/Vigilance, Verbal Learning, Visual Learning, Reasoning and Problem Solving, and Social Cognition). Thus, MCCB yields 18 scores: one for each of the original 10 tests, seven domain scores (domain scores are equivalent to test scores for the five domains that have one test), and one Overall Composite Score.

According to the MCCB manual, the MCCB is designed to serve "as an outcome measure for clinical trials of cognition-enhancing drugs for schizophrenia, as an outcome measure for studies of cognitive remediation, as a sensitive measure of cognitive change …, as a cognitive reference point for non-intervention studies …" (p. 2). The emphasis is on use of the battery as a change measure. The manual specifically disavows use for formal clinical evaluation to support a diagnosis of schizophrenia.

MCCB materials consist, for the most part, of the 10 existing tests. However, the MCCB has its own administrator's form and a respondent's booklet, each containing directions for administering and spaces for responding, respectively, to all or parts of the existing tests. Some of the existing tests simply stand alone in their original forms. The total administration time for all 10 tests is given as 60–90 minutes. There is also an MCCB computer scoring program used to input raw scores for conversion to normed scores; the scoring program was not supplied for this review.

The MCCB has a single manual covering description of purpose and development, technical matters, administration and scoring procedures, and tables of norms. Supplied to this reviewer with the manual were four journal articles devoted exclusively to the MCCB: Green et al. (2008), Kern et al. (2008), Kern et al. (2011), and Nuechterlein et al. (2008). Some of the information connected with the articles is available only as online supplements. Considerable overlap exists in the information provided by the articles and the manual, although each also has some unique information.

DEVELOPMENT. Development of the MCCB was motivated by a perceived need of the U.S. National Institute of Mental Health (NIMH) for a measure sensitive to change in cognitive functioning in schizophrenia, specifically to evaluate the effectiveness of new drugs. That is, for NIMH to fund drug studies, it wanted to ensure availability of a useful outcome measure. Nuechterlein et al. (2008) described the process for selecting MCCB's 10 tests. Relying primarily on a compilation of judgments and formal ratings by a variety of expert panels in a sort of Delphi procedure, the process began with identification of approximately 90 tests, the list was cut to 36 tests, and then further reduced to 20 tests comprising a beta battery. This battery was administered to 176 participants diagnosed with schizophrenia (the patient sample), and re-administered four weeks later to 167 of these participants. Based on data in this tryout, as well as data already available for these tests, panel members rated the 20 tests on five criteria: test-retest reliability, utility as a repeated measure, relationship to functional status, potential for showing change, and practicality and tolerability (to the examinees). The article provided median panel ratings on these criteria and described the rationale for selection of the final 10 tests based on these ratings. The entire developmental process was managed by the NIMH-funded project Measurement and Treatment Research to Improve Cognition in Schizophrenia (MATRICS).

TECHNICAL.

Norms. The authors correctly noted the need for norming the MCCB tests on a single group to facilitate profile analysis. Each of the constituent tests has its own norms, but they derive from varying samples, administrative procedures, and time periods. MCCB norms are based on what the manual refers to as the "community sample" of 300 cases drawn from five sites and selected to be reasonably representative of the United States adult population in the age range 20–59. Norms are presented in the form of *T*-scores and percentiles based on the community sample. The scoring program allows for use of three options for converting raw scores to normed scores: no demographic correction; age and gender correction (recommended for most uses); and age, gender, and education correction.

Reliability. The test manual, as well as Nuechterlein et al. (2008), reported test-retest reliability over a 4-week interval based on 167 members from the 176-member patient sample. Coefficients, given as both Pearson product-moment correlations and intraclass correlation coefficients (with inconsequential differences between the two indices), for the 10 MCCB tests ranged from .68 to .85, with a median of .75. This single study, based on one sample, is the only reliability information provided. Reliability data for domain scores and the composite score are not provided.

Validity. The MCCB manual included one study viewed as a form of validity. This one study provides correlations between the 10 MCCB tests and principal components (labeled work, social, independent living, and a total score) derived from the Social Functioning Scale and the Social Adjustment Scale. Median correlations of the 10 MCCB tests with the total score and with the work dimension were approximately .20, whereas median correlations with the social and independent living dimensions were approximately .05. Correlations for domain scores and the composite score were not provided. Green et al. (2008) reported a study of correlations between MCCB tests and what are referred to as "co-primary measures ... intended to serve as face valid indicators of the consequences of underlying changes in cognition" (p. 223) based on the patient sample. (The MCCB manual does not include results from this study.) The co-primary measures included three scores from the Maryland Assessment of Social Competence, two scores from the UCSD Performance-Based Skills Assessment, three scores from the Schizophrenia Cognition Rating Scale, and four scores from the Clinical Global Impression of Cognition in Schizophrenia test, for a total of 12 scores. Many of these measures had limited reliability: about half had test-retest reliability coefficients under .70. The quality of the co-primary measures is not at issue in this review. They are important as possible indices of criterion-related validity for MCCB. The main article provided only the correlations of the MCCB Overall Composite score with the 12 co-primary measures. The median correlation with the 12 co-primary measures was .31. The online supplement to the article gave correlation coefficients for the co-primary measures with the 10 separate MCCB tests, but not with MCCB domain scores. Correlations of individual MCCB tests with the various co-primary measures ranged widely, but averaged around .20. Kern et al.

(2011) compared performances of the 300-member community sample with the 176-member patient sample on each of the MCCB tests. Not surprisingly, the groups differed, primarily on Speed of Processing measures.

COMMENTARY. The norming process was a reasonable one and should provide a meaningful basis for comparing results of the 10 MCCB tests. As often happens, particularly with individually administered tests, the effect of self-selection bias (i.e., participation by those "who were interested in participating" [Kern et al., 2008, p. 215]), is unknown. Kern et al. (but not the MCCB manual) also noted certain additional limitations to the community sample, (e.g., its modest size, overrepresentation of urban areas, and lack of stratification by ethnicity). It would have been useful to compare data from the MCCB community sample norms with norms from the original sources, particularly for some of the tests acknowledged to have excellent norming procedures, such as the Wechsler Memory Scale–Third Edition.

The normative tables in the manual have two odd features. First, both the MCCB manual and Kern et al. (2008) consistently describe the age groups in the community sample according to three categories: 20–39, 40–49, and 50–59 (three tables in the manual evidently mislabel the youngest group as 29–39). But the manual presents age-based norms not on these three groups but in eight 5-year intervals (from 20–24 to 55–59). Second, in the tails of the distributions, percentile norms proceed in increments of .1% rather than using the normal end points of 1% and 99%. Could there really be clinical utility in distinguishing between percentiles of, say, .2 and .3 or 99.7 and 99.8? These minute differences consume nearly one-third of the normative tables.

According to the test manual and Nuechterlein et al. (2008), the authors considered a test-retest reliability of .70 as acceptable. That is a rather low standard. Five of the tests have reported reliabilities below .75. High reliability is particularly important for change measures. Oddly, although MCCB normative tables and computer reports provide scores for domains and an Overall Composite score (as well as for the 10 individual tests), no reliability information is presented for the domain or composite scores. The *Standards for Educational and Psychological Testing* (American Educational Research Association, American Psychological Association, & National Council on Measurement in Education,

1999) clearly call for reporting reliability for all scores. These reliabilities would almost certainly be higher, and the composite score reliability is likely much higher than that of even the most reliable individual tests. This reliability information could easily be developed from existing data (i.e., based on data from the patient sample).

Validity data in the form of correlations with several other measures and the contrast between the patient and community samples are useful. However, evidence related to the measurement of change—MCCB's main purpose—is lacking. The internal structure of the battery also warrants attention. Although the authors reported principal components analysis of some of the other measures, they did not report such analysis for the MCCB itself, nor even provide a simple matrix of correlations among the 10 subtests.

MCCB would profit from a revised manual that integrates information currently scattered throughout the manual and several articles. A revision should consistently report information (e.g., reliability and correlations with other measures) for the composite and domain scores, as well as for the 10 subtest scores.

SUMMARY. MCCB is intended as a measure sensitive to cognitive changes in schizophrenia in response to intervention, especially to drug therapy. It consists of 10 extant tests. Selection of the tests depended primarily on expert judgment. Norms provide a useful common metric for interpretation. Individual tests in the battery, on average, have modest reliability evidence. Some validity information in the form of correlations with other measures and group contrasts is available. Validity information specifically related to sensitivity of change is currently lacking. MCCB appears to be a promising start to providing a measure sensitive to change, but data related to that purpose have yet to be obtained and evaluated.

REVIEWER'S REFERENCES

American Educational Research Association, American Psychological Association, & National Council on Measurement in Education. (1999). *Standards for educational and psychological testing*. Washington, DC: American Educational Research Association.
Green, M. F., Nuechterlein, K. H., Kern, R. S., Baade, L. E., Fenton, W. S., Gold, J. M., ... Marder, S. R. (2008). Functional co-primary measures for clinical trials in schizophrenia: Results from the MATRICS psychometric and standardization study. *American Journal of Psychiatry, 165*(2), 221–228.
Kern, R. S., Nuechterlein, K. H., Green, M. F., Baade, L. E., Fenton, W. S., Gold, J. M., ... Marder, S. R. (2008). The MATRICS Consensus Cognitive Battery, part 2: Co-norming and standardization. *American Journal of Psychiatry, 165*(2), 214–220.
Kern, R. S., Gold, J. M., Dickinson, D., Green, M. F., Nuechterlein, K. H., Baade, L. E., ... Marder, S. R. (2011). The MCCB impairment profile for schizophrenia outpatients: Results from the MATRICS psychometric and standardization study. *Schizophrenia Research, 126*, 124–131.
Nuechterlein, K. H., Green, M. F., Kern, R. S., Baade, L. E., Barch, D. M., Cohen, J. D., ... Marder, S. R. (2008). The MATRICS Consensus Cognitive Battery, part 1: Test selection, reliability, and validity. *American Journal of Psychiatry, 165*(2), 203–213.

Review of the MATRICS Consensus Cognitive Battery by OREN MEYERS, Psychologist, Case Western University, Department of Psychiatry, and SOLUTIONS (private practice), Beechwood, OH:

DESCRIPTION. The MATRICS Consensus Cognitive Battery (MCCB) is a compilation of 10 tests used to measure seven domains of cognitive function: Speed of Processing (Brief Assessment of Cognition in Schizophrenia: Symbol Coding, Category Fluency: Animal Naming, Trail Making Test: Part A); Attention/Vigilance (Continuous Performance Test–Identical Pairs); Working Memory (Wechsler Memory Scale–Third Edition: Spatial Span, Letter–Number Span); Verbal Learning (Hopkins Verbal Learning Test–Revised); Visual Learning (Brief Visuospatial Memory Test–Revised); Reasoning and Problem Solving (Neuropsychological Assessment Battery: Mazes); and Social Cognition (Mayer–Salovey–Caruso Emotional Intelligence Test: Managing Emotions). Because many of the component tests of the MCCB have been previously reviewed (and were developed and normed separately), the scope of the present review is on the battery as a whole. The MCCB was developed as a brief evaluation of cognitive deficits to be used in schizophrenia research. The battery is administered individually by trained personnel. Scoring is straightforward, with the exception of the figure-drawing task, which requires more intensive training.

DEVELOPMENT. The effort to develop the MCCB was funded by the National Institute of Mental Health with the recognition that a standardized, broad-based battery of cognitive abilities was critical to evaluating the efficacy of medications being developed for schizophrenia with the potential for enhancing cognitive functioning. The committee first developed a list of cognitive domains to be assessed and a set of criteria for candidate measures of these domains. The essential elements were geared toward the eventual use of the battery in a clinical trials context and emphasized test-retest reliability, utility for repeated measurement, relationship to functional outcome, and tolerability and practicality. A committee rated each of the candidate measures on these criteria in order to narrow the list to a beta battery. This battery of measures was tested in a field standardization study (Kern et al., 2008), resulting in the final list of 10 tests, which cover seven cognitive domains.

TECHNICAL. Various psychometric properties of the instruments making up the MCCB were evaluated during the course of the standardization study. Despite the fact that the component tests had been developed independently and can stand on their own from a measurement properties perspective, the MATRICS committee appropriately recognized the need to reassess the psychometrics of each test as used in the battery and as applied to the defined patient group (patients with schizophrenia identified by the Structured Clinical Interview for *DSM-IV*). In terms of test-retest reliability (in this case over a 4-week span), the reliability coefficients (*r*) range from a low of .71 for the Brief Visuospatial Memory Test–Revised to a high of .85 for the Brief Assessment of Cognition in Schizophrenia: Symbol Coding. Intraclass correlation coefficients (ICCs) for these tests were also .71 and .85, respectively, and represent the top and bottom of the range. The test developers demonstrated that practice effects are small for the included tests, thus making the battery suitable for the repeated measures that are necessary to show efficacy in a clinical trial. The test authors performed analyses aimed at demonstrating the relationship between the MCCB components and independent measures of functional outcome across the domains of work, social functioning, and independent living, as well as global functioning. Although limited in some respects by the design of the study, especially in terms of restriction of range at some of the clinical sites and wide variation in mean levels of functioning across sites, the results demonstrate a modest relationship to these functional outcomes.

COMMENTARY. The seven cognitive domains chosen for inclusion in the MCCB were carefully selected and vetted in a scientific process but are ultimately the result of a committee process. The recommendation that a cognitive summary be based on equal weighting of the seven domains assumes that they are equally important and relevant as outcomes to physicians, patients, and their families and that they equally influence functional outcomes. These assumptions are reasonable but require testing and supporting data. The developers of the battery clearly did thorough and comprehensive work in developing the MCCB. They make the claim that the MCCB "is now recommended as the standard instrument for all clinical trials of cognition-enhancing agents in schizophrenia" (manual, p. 15). No reference is provided for this claim. However, there is some evidence that there has been uptake by the pharmaceutical industry, insofar as the MCCB is being used in a number

of industry-sponsored clinical trials (see www.clinicaltrials.gov). However, the real testament to the success of the MATRICS effort will be achieved when evidence collected via the MCCB in pivotal Phase 3 clinical trials becomes the basis for an efficacy claim for one or more new medications with an indication for cognitive impairment associated with schizophrenia.

REVIEWER'S REFERENCE

Kern, R. S., Neuchterlein, K. H., Green, M. F., Baade, L. E., Fenton, W. S., Gold, J. M., ... Marder, S. R. (2008). The MATRICS Consensus Cognitive Battery, part 2: Co-norming and standardization. *American Journal of Psychiatry, 165*(2), 214–220.

[99]

Mechanic Evaluation Test–Forms A1R-C, B1-C, C1-C, C1R-C.

Purpose: Designed for selecting or evaluating industrial mechanics.

Population: Mechanic job applicants or incumbents.

Publication Dates: 1992-2013.

Administration: Group.

Levels, 3: C Mechanic, B Mechanic, A Mechanic.

Price Data, 2011: $22 per consumable self-scoring booklet or online test administration (20 minimum order); $24.95 per manual (18 pages).

Foreign Language Edition: Available in Spanish.

Time: (60-70) minutes.

Comments: Self-scoring instrument; available for online test administration.

Author: Roland T. Ramsay.

Publisher: Ramsay Corporation.

a) A MECHANIC.

Scores: 6 areas: Welding & HVAC, Pneumatics and Lubrication, Print Reading and Shop, Electrical, Mechanical & Miscellaneous, Total.

b) B MECHANIC.

Scores: 5 areas: Welding/ Plumbing & HVAC, Pneumatics and Lubrication, Print Reading/ Mechanical & Shop, Electrical, Total.

c) C MECHANIC.

Scores: 6 areas: Welding/ Plumbing & HVAC, Pneumatics and Lubrication, Mechanical & Print Reading, Electrical, Shop/ Tools & Machines, Rigging & Miscellaneous, Total.

Cross References: For reviews by David O. Anderson and Alan C. Bugbee of an earlier edition, see 13:254.

Review of the Mechanic Evaluation Test, Forms A1R-C, B1-C, C1-C by STEPHEN B. JOHNSON, Senior Psychometrician, Castle Worldwide, Inc., Greensboro, NC:

DESCRIPTION. The Mechanic Evaluation Test is intended for the assessment of applicants and incumbents in positions requiring mechanical knowledge and skills. It is designed to be aligned with the occupational outline for general maintenance and repair workers promulgated by the U.S. Department of Labor. These are positions that focus on installing, maintaining, and repairing commercial or industrial machinery.

The Mechanic Evaluation Test consists of three progressively harder versions, from C Mechanic (Beginning Journey-Level) to A Mechanic (Advanced Journey-Level). Each version consists of an untimed 60-item test available as paper-and-pencil or online versions in English and Spanish. All items are four-option multiple-choice questions. There are no qualifications required for test administration. The tests can be self-administered, but are designed and priced to be administered in a group format, typically in groups of 20 per test administrator. The test is designed to take no more than 60 minutes to complete.

Each version of the Mechanic Evaluation Test assesses 10 areas of knowledge (Print Reading, Lubrication, Welding, Mechanical, Pneumatics, Machine Shop, Electrical, Rigging, Heating/Ventilation/Air Conditioning [HVAC], and Plumbing). C Mechanic items are grouped into five areas: Welding/Plumbing & HVAC, Electrical, Pneumatics and Lubrication, Shop/Tools & Machines/Rigging & Miscellaneous Mechanical, and Mechanical and Print Reading. B Mechanic items are grouped into four areas: Welding/Plumbing & HVAC, Print Reading/Mechanical & Shop, Pneumatics and Lubrication, and Electrical. The A Mechanic items are grouped into five areas: Welding & HVAC, Pneumatics and Lubrication, Print Reading & Shop, Mechanical and Miscellaneous, and Electrical. Each version has different numbers of items for each knowledge area. For example, the Electrical section includes 11 items for A Mechanic, 14 for B, and 10 for C.

The Mechanic Evaluation Test can be scored by hand on the test-consumable booklet. A total score for each of the item groupings is calculated and charted on the score profile section.

Alternative forms of the tests are available. A separate *Manual for Administration & Scoring* is available for each version. The guides provide details about the intent and development of each version of the test as well as basic measurement statistics. The manuals also provide normative data for samples of test takers.

DEVELOPMENT. The forms of the Mechanic Evaluation Test are based on an analysis of the mechanical knowledge and skills necessary to meet the requirements of two positions defined

by the U.S. Department of Labor: Maintenance Repairer, Industrial (U.S. Department of Labor, 1991); and Maintenance and Repair Workers, General (U.S. Department of Labor, 2006). The definitions and associated tasks are provided in the administrative guides. From this foundation, the authors identified the 10 knowledge areas, each of which consists of two to 15 subareas. The knowledge and skill areas were provided to two maintenance supervisors who independently ranked them for importance. The supervisors also provided the percent of time a person of each level spent in each of the item groupings identified above. The two job experts then reviewed an existing item bank to identify all potential items appropriate at each level that would meet the content outline. A total of 116, 117, and 125 items were identified for C, B, and A, respectively.

Following identification of the items, they were administered to samples of candidates. The items were analyzed by two industrial psychologists who selected the 60 best items based on item point-biserial correlations and item difficulty criteria. Alternative forms were also developed by two industrial psychologists.

TECHNICAL. The *KR20* reliability coefficients vary by form and sample. The A Mechanic ranged from .63 (N = 47, Form A1-C) to .93 (N = 15, Form A-1 & A1-C combined). For the B Mechanic the range was .78 (N = 61, Form B-2) to .86 (N = 122, Form H-2 & B1-C combined). The C Mechanic ranged from .82 (N = 40, Form C1-C) to .90 (N = 70, Form H-1 and C-1 combined). Standard errors of measurement (*SEM*) also are provided. The *SEM*s differ by level, form, and sample, but range from 2.42 to 3.48 across the three levels. The C Mechanic is the most stable.

The presented validity evidence consists of construct-related validity as outlined in the development of the material, and content-related validity specified by the item rater agreement by the judges of the knowledge areas for each of A, B, and C Mechanic. No other validity information is available. Normative data for one or two samples of candidates are available to enable comparisons of test-taker performance.

COMMENTARY. As someone who works in the adult certification world, this reviewer has personal experience working with organizations interested in assessing mechanical and technical capabilities similar to those assessed through the Mechanic Evaluation Test. This reviewer is well aware of the challenges faced in the development and administration of assessment tools for industrial situations. The paper-and-pencil consumable version provided evidence that the developers had deep experience working with a candidate population whose notion of time well spent may not include testing. The brevity of the instrument, use of appropriate language in the items, clear layout, integration of schematics, ease of use, and scoring, all provided ample evidence that the developers had a strong notion of the target audience for this tool.

Although the design of the test booklet provides evidence of clear experience with the target audience, the associated administration manuals were somewhat less valuable. The material for such manuals requires addressing the needs of both the test administrators and those assessing the validity and technical aspects of the instrument for their needs. These goals were not achieved.

The information in the manual on test administration and scoring was clear, concise, and obviously written with a nontechnical audience in mind. However, the material was undermined by the design of the manual as a whole and the gaps in information required to meet the needs of a technical reviewer (or one determining whether to use the test based on psychometric information).

The developmental history of the instruments provided limited information on the appropriateness of the job experts selected. It was not possible to assess whether the same job experts were used across studies, or what their experiences were. The job importance rating procedure would not be possible to replicate based on the limited information provided. For example, did the raters rate the 10 knowledge areas, all of the subareas, or the groupings of knowledge areas? What were the results? Overall, the information on how the knowledge areas were rated and weighted was not consistent with the intent of Standards 3.1 and 3.5 (p. 43) of the *Standards for Educational and Psychological Testing* (American Educational Research Association, American Psychological Association, & National Council on Measurement in Education, 1999).

Information on item development, such as who developed and reviewed the initial bank of items (or even a reference to an external site) would have been appreciated. There was also no information provided on who reviewed the entire instrument, and whether any bias review was conducted.

The item selection criteria employed by the psychologists who reviewed item analysis data were not enumerated, and the data provided were restricted to the 60 "best" items chosen. It also was not clear whether the final 60 items were reviewed by content experts before the instrument was finalized.

The administration manuals indicated multiple forms of the tests exist. However, it was unclear from the manuals and the Ramsay Corporation website whether all the forms are available, whether some had been retired from use, or if more than one was available, what the equating studies concluded.

The administration manuals also were unclear about the target audience and appropriate use of the results. For example, the use of U.S. measurements in the items, with no translations into metric units, implied usage by only a U.S. only workforce. Although a reader of the manual may infer that the use of U.S. Labor occupational definitions necessitates that U.S. personnel are the only potential test takers, from personal experience this reviewer believes that other countries use the U.S. Department of Labor's well-designed sources for their labor force definitions. This reviewer also is aware of how many individuals in the instrumentation, mechanical, and related fields are required to work in both unit systems.

Finally, information on how to use the scores was limited. The scoring section provided clear, simple-to-follow instructions on how to score, but apart from the normative table for the total score did not provide any additional information as to appropriate or inappropriate uses of the results, or information on the sample group's performance on the item groupings. Although such data may be unreliable it is potential information, with appropriate provisos to be provided by the developers.

SUMMARY. In summary, the Mechanic Evaluation Test is a tool that provides sufficient evidence to be usable for the purposes of assessing some core knowledge areas defined by the U.S. Department of Labor for U.S.-based mechanics. The clarity of language and ease of use for the test taker are clear signs that the developers understand their test audience.

The lack of metric conversions, and even what type of measurements are being used for some items, does not support the use of the Mechanic Evaluation Test outside of the U.S. As the mechanic/instrumentation world often and increasingly involves multinational companies and tools, and equipment designed under both systems, this adaptation would be an appropriate and simple fix.

The administration manuals could be improved. The clarity of the target audience evidenced in the test booklet fails to be replicated in the manuals. The administration manuals are required for two essential audiences, the test administrator and the individual(s) assessing the appropriateness of the instruments. For example, a clear separation of the test administration and scoring section (e.g., target audience statement, purposes of the instrument, administration and scoring, normative data) from the item and test development materials (e.g., development process, reliability, item analysis, validity data) would enhance the credibility of the instrument.

The gaps in information about item and test development are, in the opinion of this reviewer, substantial enough to warrant concern that the Mechanic Evaluation Test would struggle to meet existing test development standards. This lack could be problematic for organizations that intend to use this instrument for placement decisions. In the opinion of this reviewer, the needed changes are simple documentation fixes as the information that is provided suggests that more details should be available.

REVIEWER'S REFERENCES

American Educational Research Association, American Psychological Association, & National Council on Measurement in Education. (1999). *Standards for educational and psychological testing*. Washington, DC: American Educational Research Association.
National O*NET Consortium for the U.S. Department of Labor. (2006). *O*NET Online* [Online]. Available: online.onetcenter.org.
U.S. Department of Labor. (1991). *Dictionary of occupational titles* (4th ed., rev.). Washington, DC: U.S. Government Printing Office.

Review of the Mechanic Evaluation Test, Forms A1R-C, B1-C, C1R-C by CHARLES A. SCHERBAUM, Associate Professor of Psychology, Baruch College, City University of New York, New York, NY:

DESCRIPTION. The Ramsay Corporation Mechanic Evaluation Test is designed to assess mechanical knowledge of A, B, and C level mechanics. The test was developed to be used for selection and promotion in jobs requiring mechanical knowledge and skills including mechanical repairer, industrial (*Dictionary of Occupational Titles* No. 899.261–014) and maintenance and repair worker, general (O*NET No. 49–9071.00). Forms A1R-C, B1-C, and C1R-C each contain 60 items that assess mechanical knowledge of welding, plumbing, HVAC, pneumatics and lubrication, mechanical and print reading, electrical, shop tools and machines, rigging, and safety. These knowledge areas are divided into four to five subsections of the test with each section containing between 10 and 19 items. The administration instructions are clear and provide sufficient detail. A single administrator can administer the test to up to 20 test takers at one time. The test is untimed, but the technical manual states that it should take less than an hour to complete. The test booklet is self-scoring and the test manual includes appropriate detail about how to record scores. Scores can be computed for each section of the test and for the entire test. There is no discussion in the manual of how the test scores should be used to make employee selection and promotion decisions. The testing forms and test administration instructions ask examinees to report their Social Security numbers, a request that may create a negative reaction and concern among test takers.

DEVELOPMENT. The Mechanic Evaluation Test series was developed in 1987 and has undergone several revisions and name changes since that time. The current technical manual provides little information about the development and revision processes that have been used over the past 26 years. The original forms and subsequent forms were developed on the basis of the opinions of a small number of job experts regarding the importance of various knowledge and skills for the job of a mechanic. No information is provided about the item development, review, revision, and pilot testing processes that have been employed throughout the test construction and revision process. Subsequent revisions have been based on reviews by industrial and organizational psychologists of item-level characteristics derived from a small sample of test takers. Little information is provided about the criteria used in these reviews to determine which items remained on the test, which items were revised, or which items were removed. On the forms reviewed here, several items were revised or removed from the previous versions, but it is unclear which content areas these items came from or which aspects of the item analyses led to these items being identified for revision or removal. The test items appear well written and rely on traditional multiple-choice style knowledge items as well as items that use graphical stimuli. None of the items require an actual demonstration of mechanic skills.

TECHNICAL. Very little information is presented about the norm samples, and little normative data are available for these tests. The normative data reported in the manuals for forms B1-C and C1R-C come from earlier versions and forms of these tests. Given the lack of more current information, the use of the reported norms is not recommended.

For each form of the test, estimates of the internal consistency of the scores are reported. Based on the information in the technical manual, it appears that the majority of the estimates reported come from different forms and versions of this test. The reliability estimates emerge from different, seemingly non-equivalent, versions or forms and should not therefore be used as a substitute or proxy for the reliability of the scores on these forms. The technical manual reports an internal consistency estimate for Form A1R-C, the only instance in which it is clear that a reliability estimate was computed independently on one of the forms included in this review. The reliability evidence presented for Form A1R-C ($KR20$ = .81) is within the range of what would be considered professionally acceptable on a high stakes test. The interpretation of the reliability evidence in the manual uses terms such as "excellent" or "very good," whereas the numerical values of the reliability coefficients are appropriately interpreted as adequate, but toward the lower end of the acceptable range. No test-retest reliability estimates are reported. Based on the information available at this point, there is very little evidence on the reliability estimates for Forms A1R-C, B1-C, and C1R-C.

The test manual includes results from classical item analyses that included indices of item difficulty (item means) and item discrimination (point-biserial correlations). It is important to note that the point-biserial correlations are based on the items' correlations with the test section and not the total test. Also, it is not noted whether the corrected or uncorrected point biserial correlations are reported. (Corrected correlations adjust the correlation of the impact of the item on the total test score and are preferred.) Therefore, the values for the item discrimination may be inflated. The item analyses reported in the manual for Forms B1-C and C1R-C appear to come from different, seemingly non-equivalent forms and versions of the test. The item analysis reported for Form A1R-C indicates that the test is difficult with low item discrimination overall. Overall, the item analyses should be interpreted very cautiously. No evidence is reported for the factor structure of the test.

No studies demonstrating criterion-related evidence of validity are reported, and the manual appears to suggest that criterion-related evidence of validity is not appropriate for a job knowledge test. No correlations with other tests of mechanical knowledge, skill, or ability are reported. Although all three forms mention content validity evidence, little to no such information is provided about the content validity studies. The representativeness of the job experts or adequacy of the procedures used to gather the content validity data are unknown. It appears that the majority of the content validity evidence comes from a single industry or organization; therefore, the generalizability to other industries and organizations is unknown. Based on the information presented in the manuals, there is no content-related evidence of validity directly presented for Forms B1-C and C1R-C. For Form A1R-C, a single content validity study is reported, but due to the lack of information about the content validity study it is not possible to evaluate adequately the evidence presented. Based on the information available at this point, there is very little validity evidence for Forms A1R-C, B1-C, and C1R-C.

No analyses are reported on differential item functioning or group differences in test scores.

COMMENTARY. The format and content of the tests have many positive aspects, including an intuitive design and thorough administrative instructions. The serious limitation is that given the limited information and evidence available at this point in time, this test does not meet a number of the professional and legal standards for tests used in high stakes decisions including the *Uniform Guidelines for Employee Selection Procedures* (1978) and the *Principles for the Validation and Use of Personnel Selection Procedures* (SIOP, 2003). Much more additional data and information are needed to support the use of these tests in any employment contexts.

SUMMARY. Based on the available evidence, the Mechanic Evaluation test cannot be recommended for its stated use in high stakes decision-making. There is little evidence to support the reliability or validity of scores on these tests. Most professional and legal standards would not be met at this point. Future research and additional evidence may eventually support the use of the test for selection and promotion decisions, but until that evidence is available, the test is not recommended for use in making personnel decisions.

REVIEWER'S REFERENCES

Equal Employment Opportunity Commission, Department of Labor, Department of Justice, & U.S. Civil Service Commission. (1978). *Uniform Guidelines on Employee Selection Procedures. Federal Register, 43*, 1607.1–1607.18.
Society for Industrial and Organizational Psychology, Inc. (2003). *Principles for the validation and use of personnel selection procedures* (4th Edition). Bowling Green, OH: Author.

[100]

Mechanical Aptitude Test (Form MAT-3-C).

Purpose: Designed for evaluating mechanical aptitude.
Population: Applicants for jobs that require the ability to learn mechanical skills.
Publication Dates: 2002-2010.
Scores: Total score only covering 4 areas: Household Objects, Work-Production and Maintenance, School-Science and Physics, Hand and Power Tools.
Administration: Group.
Price Data, 2011: $22 per consumable self-scoring test booklet or online test administration (minimum order of 20); $24.95 per manual (2010, 21 pages).
Foreign Language Edition: Available in Spanish.
Time: 20(30) minutes.
Comments: Self-scoring instrument; available for online test administration.
Author: Roland T. Ramsay.
Publisher: Ramsay Corporation.
Cross References: For a review by M. David Miller of an earlier edition, see 17:116.

Review of the Mechanical Aptitude Test (Form MAT-3-C) by JAMES T. AUSTIN, Senior Research Specialist, Center on Education and Training for Employment, The Ohio State University, Columbus, OH:

DESCRIPTION. This 36-item multiple-choice measure is one in a long line of tests of mechanical ability and aptitude. As such it is subordinate to a higher-order factor proposed by Vernon in 1961 and supported in Carroll's 1993 reanalysis-synthesis (specifically, k:m represents a mechanical-practical factor as opposed to v:ed, which represents verbal-educational). The test purpose is defined on the developer-publisher's website as the "ability to learn production and maintenance job activities" within an organization. This statement implies that the construct assessed would be used primarily to select apprentice-level applicants into job training programs and validated by either content or criterion strategies. Test administration is offered through paper-and-pencil (self-scoring) or online modes. This review is based on a copy of the test and its manual (2010) as well as a review of the test publisher's website. Although the manual also describes the alternate equivalent Form MAT-B, that test is not a focus of this review.

DEVELOPMENT. The manual details the history of the test dating to the MAT-A in 2002. The job analysis is not described in detail, but reference is made to apprentices performing general tasks of maintenance or production jobs using the U.S. Department of Labor's Dictionary of Occupational

Titles and the online Occupational Information Network (O*NET). The manual further states that test items were written by industrial-organizational psychologists to revise the earlier test. An outline of content categories was derived from unspecified textbooks, tests, and training manuals. The categories (and the numbers of items) are household objects (11), maintenance-production work (9), school science (6), and tools (10). Subscores, however, are not provided for the content categories.

TECHNICAL. Three types of technical information are presented in the manual. First, reliability evidence is provided for seven groups ranging in size from 109 to 1,867 and consisting of postsecondary students, applicants, and incumbents. For the six groups that took the MAT-3-C, the range for KR-20 estimates is .61 to .80, and the standard error of measurement ranged from 1.85 to 2.73. Only internal consistency estimates of reliability are provided. Second, item analysis results are provided for the combined pool of applicants and incumbents (n = 1,867). The range of item difficulty values is .39 to .97, and the point-biserial correlation coefficients range from .12 to .50. Third, validation evidence is described using pre-1999 categories of validity. The evidence was developed using content (13 studies) and criterion-related (2 studies) strategies, as well as a study that employed a construct (convergent) strategy: correlating MAT-3-C scores with those from two other mechanical tests. The content validation studies were conducted across a range of organizations. The results indicate intraclass correlations (presumably an estimate of reliability) for the 3 to 15 individuals who rated item job relatedness. Average job relatedness and the number of items with job relatedness ratings below 2.5 are also reported (although no details for the rating scale are provided, the context seems to indicate a 5-point scale). Unfortunately, only two of the validation studies used the MAT-3 test series. Two criterion-related studies (one with an incomplete reference to Development Dimensions International) were reported, but neither specifically used the MAT-3-C. Construct-related evidence of validity is claimed from the results of several undated studies that examined relationships of MAT-3-C scores with the Wiesen Test of Mechanical Aptitude (r = .72) and with the Bennett Test of Mechanical Aptitude (r = .78, r = .75). The manual provides percentile rankings for the combined sample of 1,867 applicants and incumbents. The manual also asserts that test scores show less adverse impact regarding gender than other available measures (.5 *SD* vs. 1.2 *SD*), but it is unclear how this comparison was made.

COMMENTARY. The MAT-3-C items are current and sample broadly from work, school, and home contexts. The manual reports moderate internal consistency reliability, but as Miller (17:116) pointed out in an earlier review, it may be difficult to justify selection decisions solely on the basis of this test. Additional types of reliability evidence might add support. The validity evidence could be presented more clearly in the manual. Clarification of item overlap among the test forms dating to 2002 would be helpful. A larger item bank also would be useful. Comparison of paper-and-pencil and computer administration might also be useful. Test security is given adequate attention in the administration instructions.

SUMMARY. This test is a solid and inexpensive tool, but it should not be used alone in apprentice selection. Continuation of the technical research within the new categories of validity evidence provided by the revision of the *Standards for Educational and Psychological Testing* (AERA, APA, & NCME, 1999) will support continued use of the MAT-3-C.

REVIEWER'S REFERENCES

American Educational Research Association, American Psychological Association, & National Council on Measurement in Education. (1999). *Standards for educational and psychological testing.* Washington, DC: American Educational Research Association.

Carroll, J. B. (1993). *Human cognitive abilities.* Cambridge, UK: Cambridge University Press.

Vernon, P. E. (1961). *The structure of human abilities.* London, UK: Methuen.

Review of the Mechanical Aptitude Test (Form MAT-3-C) by KARL N. KELLEY, Professor of Psychology, North Central College, Naperville, IL:

DESCRIPTION. The Mechanical Aptitude Test (Form MAT-3-C) is a short (20 minute), self-scoring measure of mechanical aptitude designed to be used in employee selection. Mechanical aptitude refers to an individual's ability to learn and perform production and maintenance job activities. The assumption is that individuals who can assess accurately the function and use of common objects and elements can perform related job tasks. They will also possess basic mechanical knowledge that will allow them to be trained on similar tasks. The measure is well suited for identifying the potential for success in an apprenticeship or trainee program focusing on maintenance mechanics and production jobs, including machine operators and tool setters. The MAT-3-C is free of references to city/rural or gender-based content.

DEVELOPMENT. Ramsay Corporation developed the original version of the Mechanical Aptitude Test (Form MAT-A) in 2002 and revised it in 2004 (MAT-AR2-C) as a self-scoring form. The current version (MAT-3-C) is a minor modification of the earlier version, replacing one question completely and making minor changes to four other items. In addition, the Ramsay Corporation publishes online (Form MAT-3-C [Online]), Spanish (Form MAT-3-SP), and alternate equivalent (Form MAT-B) versions. The current version of the test was developed to coincide with and be applicable to data found on the U.S. Department of Labor's O*NET Online database, specifically jobs related to industrial machinery mechanics. Job titles for this general heading include maintenance mechanic, maintenance technician, mechanic, engineering technician, master mechanic, industrial machinery mechanic, machine adjuster, overhauler, industrial electrician, and industrial mechanic. In addition, 38 recognized apprenticeable specialties are directly related to these job skills.

TECHNICAL. The test includes 36 image-based items with multiple-choice response options. The items are drawn from four knowledge areas: Household Objects (11 items), Work–Production and Maintenance (9 items), School–Science and Physics (6 items), and Hand and Power Tools (10 items). The test is designed to be completed in 20 minutes.

A 21-page manual provided with the test presents relevant psychometric data, references, a brief introduction to the test, and protocols for administration and scaling.

A normative sample of 1,867 from a variety of food production, entry-level manufacturing, and manufacturing apprenticeship programs yielded a mean score of 26.5 and a standard deviation of 5.24. Internal consistency reliability of this test was adequate, with KR-20 coefficients ranging from .61 to .80 for various studies. Item analysis using the point-biserial index (correct/incorrect item response correlated with total test score) ranged from .12 to .53. An item difficulty index was also presented, but not well explained.

Test items were developed after reviewing recent books and training materials for mechanical jobs. These items were then presented to a sample of subject matter experts from various industries. It appears that items were evaluated for job relatedness on a 5-point scale (1 = *not related* to 5 = *highly related*). Average job relatedness (for all 36 items) ranged from 3.4 to 4.7. Lawshe's (1975) content validity index was not presented. Some evidence for criterion-related validity was presented. Among a sample of post-secondary school students, scores on a form of this test were significantly correlated with a test of mechanical job knowledge (r = .48; p < .01), and technical school GPA (r = .40; p < .01). No source was presented for this research. A second study by Winter, Lin, Jones, and Schultz (2005, as cited in test manual) reported that MAT scores were significantly correlated with supervisor ratings indicating "ability to troubleshoot equipment" (r = .27, p < .05).

Construct-related evidence of validity was assessed by comparing MAT scores to scores on two other mechanical aptitude tests. MAT scores correlated significantly with scores on the Wiesen Test of Mechanical Aptitude (r = .72; p < .01) and the Bennett Test of Mechanical Aptitude (r = .78; no p-value reported).

COMMENTARY. Overall, the Mechanical Aptitude Test (Form MAT-3-C) represents an adequate test of this construct. Although it can be a useful tool for screening job applicants, it is recommended that employers seek additional information before making final hiring decisions.

The basic psychometrics are good, but more information would be very helpful. The internal consistency reliability of this test is adequate, and appropriate analyses were used (KR-20). The sections on content validity could be strengthened by using Lawshe's (1975) content validity ratio with modifications suggested by Wilson, Pan, and Schumsky (2012). More details about the computation of the item difficulty index and job-relatedness evaluations would be particularly helpful.

The evidence presented for criterion-related evidence of validity is limited, and it is strongly advised that locally produced correlation and regression-analyses be used until sufficient evidence exists to support widespread use of this test in employment decisions.

The conclusion of the technical manual calls for further peer-reviewed research to be conducted on this test. The Ramsay Corporation requests to be kept informed of any of these projects.

REVIEWER'S REFERENCES

Lawshe, C. H. (1975). A quantitative approach to content validity. *Personnel Psychology, 28,* 563-575. doi:10.1111/j.1744-6570.1975.tb01393.

Wilson, F., Pan, W., & Schumsky, D. A. (2012). Recalculation of the critical values for Lawshe's content validity ratio. *Measurement & Evaluation in Counseling & Development, 45,* 197-210. doi:10.1177/0748175612440286

[101]

Mechanical Maintenance Trainee (Form UKM-1C).

Purpose: Designed for selecting mechanical maintenance trainees.
Population: Applicants with mechanical training and experience necessary for entry into a training program.
Publication Dates: 1998-2010.
Scores, 13: Hydraulics, Pneumatics, Print Reading, Welding, Power Transmission, Lubrication, Pumps, Piping, Rigging, Maintenance, Shop Machines, Tools/Material & Equipment, Total.
Administration: Group.
Price Data, 2011: $22 per consumable self-scoring test booklet or online test administration (minimum order of 20); $24.95 per manual (2008, 22 pages).
Time: (60-70) minutes.
Comments: Self-scoring instrument; available for online test administration.
Author: Roland T. Ramsay.
Publisher: Ramsay Corporation.
Cross References: For a review by Kevin J. McCarthy of an earlier edition, see 17:117.

Review of the Mechanical Maintenance Trainee (Form UKM-1C) by PATRICIA A. BACHELOR, Professor Emeritus, California State University, Long Beach, CA:

DESCRIPTION. The Mechanical Maintenance Trainee test (Form UKM-1C) was developed in 1998 as a series of tests for selection of maintenance trainees in a Midwestern steel plant. Trainees differ from apprentices in that they have a minimum of 2 years of training; an apprentice usually begins at a basic level and generally requires 3 or 4 years on the job. The Mechanical Maintenance Trainee test (Form UKM-1C) has a self-scoring format, and was shortened from the original 120 items to 60 items, then reviewed in 2005 and reviewed again in 2007 to ensure that items reflect relevant and current technology. An alternate version of the test (Form B) was prepared in 2005. The Mechanical Maintenance Trainee test (Form UKM-1C) was made available for online testing in 2007. It is administered to those with proper identification, in groups of no more than 20, with no interactive electronic devices allowed. Number 2 pencils are required for use on the separate self-scored answer sheet included with the test booklet. An hour is usually sufficient to complete the test, although the test is not timed.

The Department of Labor's definition of *Maintenance and Repair workers, General,* was used to initiate test construction, using the characteristics of the tasks involved, work duties, and various job titles of a maintenance trainee. Tasks were specified using action verbs, which established clear skills and knowledge expected of a trainee. These enabled a successful assessment of an individual for selection into a training program of up to 2 years duration. The final version (2007) of the Mechanical Maintenance Trainee (Form UKM-1C) is composed of 60 items designed to cover 12 subareas. These subareas and the number of items used to assess those areas were Hydraulics (6 items); Pneumatics (5 items); Print Reading (5 items); Welding (4 items); Power Transmission (6 items); Lubrication (5 items); Pumps (3 items); Piping (3 items); Rigging (3 items); Maintenance (9 items); Shop Machines (4 items); and Tools, Material, and Equipment (7 items). All items required practical, specific knowledge and/or applications such as computation skills based on a given diagram with measurements or knowledge of specific dimensions/calibrations.

DEVELOPMENT. Items were designed to assess an examinee's knowledge and skill of tasks one would likely be faced with on the job. In that effort, eight "job experts" (maintenance supervisors) independently rated tasks on the Maintenance Activity List using a 3-point scale (2 = *important* or 1 = *done but not one of the most important parts of the job* or 0 = *not done by a person on the job.*). Each rater also estimated the percent of time an incumbent might spend on each task. The same job experts also independently ranked the importance and percent of items that should be generated for each of the knowledge and skill areas. These rankings ultimately generated the number of items for the test. Two industrial psychologists employed techniques of item analyses to reduce items on the 1998 version of the Mechanical Maintenance Trainee (Form UKM-1C) from 120 items to 60 items. Using item difficulty (ideal range from .40 to .60) and point-biserial discrimination indices (correlations between item score and scale score, subarea, in the present case) they were able to eliminate 60 items. Of the 60 items on the version currently in use and developed in 1998, the Mechanical Maintenance Trainee (Form UKM-1C), 40 items have item difficulties ranging from .34 to .65; 12 items have item difficulties between .19 and .31; and 8 items range in difficulty from .71 to .81. These are obviously near the desired ideal ranges, as one would expect. Point-biserial discrimination indices ranged from .36 to .68. Twenty-eight indices were in the .50s;

17 in the .40s; and 14 in the .60s. Again, these are the items on the final version of the test; hence, items remaining on the test had met criteria for inclusion. Point-biserial discrimination indices are usually performed using the total test score and the item's score with the item's score eliminated from the total or else risks overestimating the value of the correlations. It is particularly important to note that 10 subareas were of 3 to 6 items, hence item to subarea correlations are mathematically inflated, especially in point-biserial correlations, with a right/wrong score (0 or 1) correlated with a subarea score, which could be as low as 3 and at maximum 9.

TECHNICAL.

Reliability. Estimates of internal consistency are generally calculated using KR20 when the items on a test are scored correct or incorrect. Items on the Mechanical Maintenance Trainee (Form UKM-1C) were scored "1" for correct answers, whereas missing, duplicate, or wrong answers were scored "0" as specified in the test manual. The KR20 estimates attained for each of the five standardization samples ranged from .82 to .89. Hence, there is support of the claim of internal consistency for the Mechanical Maintenance Trainee (Form UKM-1C).

Standardization samples. Data from five standardization samples were used to estimate internal consistency via KR20 of the Mechanical Maintenance Trainee (Form UKM-1C). The first four samples were administered the 60-item version; the last sample was administered the 120-item version. A study including 91 applicants for maintenance training jobs at various manufacturing plants in the Midwest comprised Sample 1 and attained a KR20 value of .82. The second sample consisted of 29 applicants for maintenance jobs in a Mid-Atlantic electrical plant; a KR20 of .89 was found. Sample 3 consisted of 93 applicants for mechanical trainee positions. The KR20 value was .82. Sample 4 was made up of 127 candidates for various skilled and unskilled craft jobs and a KR20 of .88 was found. Sample 5 consisted of 1,071 applicants for production and maintenance jobs in a Midwest metals industry. This sample was administered the 120-item version of the Mechanical Maintenance Trainee (Form UKM-1C). The KR20 estimate of internal consistency was found to be .87. Mathematically, the value of KR20 would have been expected to be increased due to the increased number of items (120 rather than 60 items) administered to the four prior samples. As noted above, all samples' KR20 values fell within the range of .82 to .89.

Validity. Content evidence of validity is appropriate due to the purpose of the Mechanical Maintenance Trainee (Form UKM-1C). Knowledge and skills to perform tasks associated with being a mechanical maintenance trainee were demonstrated by incorporating the assessment of eight job experts (mechanical maintenance supervisors) who independently rated tasks, independently ranked importance of skill and knowledge, and independently estimated the percent of items on the test based on relevance of the task knowledge and/or skill area. These same job experts were asked to rate the importance of items independently for each of 12 skill areas in an effort to establish the number of items per each subarea. The interrater agreement of .72 is indicative of adequate agreement among job experts in terms of tasks performed by a mechanical maintenance trainee. Clearly, data collected from the eight independent job experts demonstrated adequate support for the claim of content evidence of validity of the Mechanical Maintenance Trainee (Form UKM-1C).

COMMENTARY. The test manual provided detailed information about the specific knowledge and skill areas needed by a mechanical maintenance trainee. Eight job experts (maintenance supervisors) independently ranked the skills and knowledge each area of competency's importance (on a 3-point scale) and the percentage of time a candidate would be expected to spend on the task under review. Additionally, these same job experts independently ranked the importance of skills and knowledge of the tasks used on the job to estimate the number of items on the test. Two industrial psychologists performed item analyses to select the 60 items to constitute the final version of the Mechanical Maintenance Trainee (Form UKM-1C). The standardization samples were described only as applicants for mechanical, maintenance, or craft positions in various Midwest and Mid-Atlantic industries who were administered the Mechanical Maintenance Trainee (Form UKM-1C). Normative comparisons and statements regarding performance to others is limited, hence the Mechanical Maintenance Trainee (Form UKM-1C) must be viewed currently as a research tool. The data employed in the item analysis are based upon the 60 items from the 1998 version, yet that version had 120 items and is now 14 years old. There is no explanation of how the current versions (2005 and 2007) were reviewed or revised. Item difficulty or point-biserial index values were presented on 60 items from the original 1998 version; these items were obviously well within ideal ranges. The current versions (2005 and 2007) were said to have been reviewed for currency of technology, yet data from the original version were presented as documenting the psychometric quality of the 60 items on the current version. Clarification is anticipated along with an overdue revision.

SUMMARY. The Mechanical Maintenance Trainee (Form UKM-1C) was designed to assess skills and knowledge of individuals who applied for a mechanical maintenance trainee program. The current version consisted of a total of 60 items designed to assess skill and knowledge of 12 subareas. Estimates of internal consistency were analyzed using five samples including applicants for mechanical or maintenance type positions from the Midwest or Mid-Atlantic. No additional demographic information is provided; hence, normative comparisons are not credible at this time. Estimates of KR-20 of five samples ranged from .82 to .89 indicating support for adequate internal consistency for the 60-item version of the Mechanical Maintenance Trainee (Form UKM-1C). The largest sample who took the 120-item version had an internal consistency estimate of .87 lending additional evidence for the value of the results of item analyses. Content evidence of validity was supported by eight job experts who independently rated and ranked test content based on required skill and knowledge needed on the job. However, their work was performed on the 1998 version of the Mechanical Maintenance Trainee (Form UKM-1C), which had 120 items, yet the data presented were for 60 items, presumably those continuing as this latter form of the test.

Review of the Mechanical Maintenance Trainee (Form UKM-1C) by KATE HATTRUP, Professor, Department of Psychology, San Diego State University, San Diego, CA:

DESCRIPTION. The Mechanical Maintenance Trainee Test (Form UKM-1C) is a job knowledge test for mechanical maintenance workers at the trainee level. As the manual for the test points out, trainee level workers begin at a more advanced level than do apprentices, who generally start at a more basic level of training. Thus, the stated purpose of the test is for the selection of applicants for training programs in mechanical maintenance, where sufficient knowledge and skills are required for entry into an advanced training program lasting about 2 years.

The test is composed of 60 multiple-choice items, each having four response options. The items were written to reflect job-specific knowledge in each of 12 areas: Hydraulics (6 items), Pneumatics (5 items), Print Reading (5 items), Welding (4 items), Power Transmission (6 items), Lubrication (5 items), Pumps (3 items), Piping (3 items), Rigging (3 items), Maintenance (9 items), Shop Machines (4 items), and Tools, Materials, and Equipment (7 items).

The test is administered in a proctored group setting in a paper-and-pencil format or online. The manual provides very detailed instructions about the group administration, including important testing conditions, required materials, suggestions for conducting the test administration, and a detailed script to read to examinees. Although there is no time limit for the test, examinees are instructed that they should be able to complete the test within 1 hour. The test booklet itself is very user-friendly and easy to understand, and provides two practice items. Various diagrams are provided throughout the test for reference in answering certain test items. The physical layout of the test allows for very easy self-scoring, and instructions for scoring the test are provided in the manual and at the end of the test booklet itself.

DEVELOPMENT. The Mechanical Maintenance Trainee test (Form UKM-1) was developed initially by the Ramsay Corporation in 1990 as part of series of skill tests for maintenance trainees in a Midwestern U.S. steel plant. Form UKM-1C is a shorter 60-item version of this original test, and was developed as a self-scoring instrument in 1998 and then reviewed for currency in 2005 and 2007. An equivalent Form B of the test is also available.

A job analysis of the position of mechanical maintenance trainee was conducted to serve as the basis for defining the target construct domain and writing test items. This included a review of the *Dictionary of Occupational Titles* (U.S. Department of Labor, 1991) and O*NET for the positions of Maintenance Repairer (any industry) and Repair Workers-General, respectively. These sources provided a comprehensive list of tasks that might be performed in the target job. In addition, eight subject matter experts, all maintenance supervisors, rated a series of job tasks in terms of their relevance to the job using a 3-point scale (2 = *important*, 1 = *done, but not one of the most important parts of the job*, 0 = *not done by a person on the job*). They then ranked a set of knowledge and skills areas for the

job, and indicated what percentage of test items should be written for each knowledge and skill area. Subject-matter experts then selected relevant items for the test from Ramsay Corporation's item bank. Finally, using data collected from a sample of 1,071 applicants at the Midwestern U.S. steel plant, two industrial psychologists selected the best 60 items based on item difficulty and item discrimination (point-biserial correlations). These item analysis statistics are provided in the manual for the final set of 60 items.

TECHNICAL. The manual provides internal consistency reliability coefficients (KR-20) and standard errors of measurement for total test scores for five samples of examinees, with sample sizes ranging from 29 to 1,071 examinees. Reliabilities range from .82 to .89 in these samples, which is on the lower end of what might be considered acceptable for a test used in high stakes decision making (where this reviewer believes that reliabilities should normally exceed .90). Separate reliabilities are not provided for the 12 subscales of the measure. Item difficulties (p-values) range from .19 to .81, and point-biserial correlations range from .41 to .68, in the initial sample of 1,071 respondents.

Very little additional information is available to support inferences regarding the content, construct, or criterion-related validity of the test. The manual explains that content evidence of validity is supported by the test development procedures, which involved having subject-matter experts evaluate the job-relevance of the skills and knowledge measured by the test. Although the manual claims that the test is a "paper-and-pencil form of a work sample" (p. 17), it is a sample only of job knowledge and not of job behaviors. The manual reports intraclass correlation coefficients for ratings of job relevance, but it is not clear whether these are for individual raters or for the sets of raters.

Additional validity evidence is needed to support inferences regarding the underlying constructs measured by the Mechanical Maintenance Trainee test, and its usefulness as a predictor measure. Correlations might be computed between the test and measures of other cognitive constructs, such a general mental ability (GMA), and medium size results should probably be expected. Correlations with some unrelated noncognitive constructs could also be evaluated, and here, low correlations would support the discriminant validity of the test. Pre-training scores can be compared to posttraining scores; a significant improvement in scores would support inferences about the constructs measured by this test. Mean differences across groups that differ in experience could also be examined. In this regard, it is noteworthy that mean test scores differed quite substantially across the five samples used in evaluating reliability, as reported in the manual, with mean differences reaching as much as 2 standard deviations between some groups. This is probably due to differences in the experience and skill levels of these groups; it is unfortunate that the manual reports these differences without commenting on their meaning or implications for interpreting test scores.

Differences between these groups also show up in the norm tables, and again, there is no guidance provided in the manual about how these norms can be used in practice and compared to scores obtained in the user's sample. Separate norms for male and female examinees, and for different ethnic groups, would be a useful addition to the manual.

COMMENTARY. The Mechanical Maintenance Trainee test (Form UKM-1C) is a very focused measure of job knowledge for mechanical maintenance trainees. It does not assess knowledge of electrical component repair or of building maintenance, such as carpentry or plumbing. It is therefore especially relevant for use as a pre- or posttraining assessment for the specific job of mechanical maintenance trainee. Because of the limited evidence supporting the reliability and validity of the test, it is probably less appropriate for use in making high stakes decisions, such as in personnel selection. Moreover, users must consider carefully whether a focused job knowledge test for a fairly narrow set of jobs is needed, or whether a test of a more general cognitive construct, such as GMA would be appropriate. Tests of narrow constructs will predict specific criteria, such as performance in mechanical maintenance training in the present case, whereas tests of broader constructs may predict a wider range of outcomes, such as performance in a variety of training programs including mechanical maintenance training. The present test seems potentially useful for identifying applicants who possess sufficient knowledge to benefit from mechanical maintenance training. But until additional evidence is provided that supports the reliability and validity of the test, users are urged to exercise caution in interpreting and using observed scores when making selection decisions with this test.

SUMMARY. The Mechanical Maintenance Trainee test is a measure of a very narrow construct,

namely knowledge of mechanical maintenance at the trainee level. It therefore has a limited range of uses compared to tests of more general cognitive constructs such as GMA. But, in those contexts where assessment of specific knowledge relevant to mechanical maintenance at the trainee level is needed, the Mechanical Maintenance Trainee test (Form UKM-1C) does an adequate job. However, given the limited evidence of the test's reliability and validity, its use is probably most appropriately restricted to those contexts where psychometric considerations are secondary.

REVIEWER'S REFERENCE

U.S. Department of Labor. (1991). *Dictionary of occupational titles* (4th ed., rev.). Washington, DC: U.S. Government Printing Office.

[102]

Mechanical Technician A (Forms AR-XC and MTA-YC).

Purpose: Designed for selecting or evaluating above journey level maintenance technicians for jobs in the metals or manufacturing industry.

Population: Applicants and incumbents for jobs requiring mechanical maintenance knowledge and skills at the highest level.

Publication Dates: 2003-2009.

Scores, 6: Hydraulics & Pneumatics, Print Reading, Power Transmission & Lubrication, Pumps & Piping, Mechanical Maintenance Principles, Total.

Administration: Group.

Forms, 2: AR-XC, MTA-YC.

Price Data, 2011: $22 per consumable self-scoring test booklet or online test administration (minimum order of 20); $24.95 per manual (2009, 24 pages).

Time: (60-70) minutes.

Comments: Self-scoring instrument; available for online test administration; Form MTA-YC is an alternate equivalent of Form AR-XC.

Author: Roland T. Ramsay.

Publisher: Ramsay Corporation.

Cross References: For reviews by Michael D. Biderman and Bart L. Weathington and by Mary L. Garner of an earlier edition, see 17:118.

Review of the Mechanical Technician A (Forms AR-XC and MTA-YC) by ALLEN I. HUFFCUTT, Caterpillar Professor of Psychology, Bradley University, Peoria, IL:

DESCRIPTION. This test is designed for selection of maintenance technicians above the journey level in metal or manufacturing industries, in particular technicians at the highest levels. It has 60 items and is available both online (minimum of 20) and as a self-scoring booklet. The price ($22 per test; $24.95 for the manual) seems reasonable, as does the administration time (generally 60–70 minutes). There are two versions, Form AR-XC (2009) and MTA-YC (2003). This review is focused on Form AR-XC, although comparative reference is made to Form MTA-YC.

The test itself is very professional and attractive. The items are clearly presented, the drawings are crisp and sharp, and the use of a blue color for the items and drawings adds a degree of professionalism and even warmth that contributes to an overall favorable impression of this test. Job candidates taking the AR-XC should feel that their skills were assessed in a very competent, fair, and professional manner.

One note of curiosity is the designations for the two forms, currently AR-XC and MTA-YC. The AR-XC previously was the MTA-XC, the latter being descriptive (MTA = mechanical technician A). It is unclear where "AR" comes from or what it represents. Having MTA for one form and AR for the other is confusing, but overall is a minor point.

A major distinction between the two forms is that the AR-XC is a self-scoring booklet whereas the MTA-YC uses a separate answer sheet and is scored with an overlay (see page 8 in the manual). Unfortunately, the manual does not provide any information on the relative advantage of each scoring format, leaving potential users either to contact the test publisher or to guess. The test publisher is encouraged to provide more information on the rationale for having two different scoring formats in the next version of their manual. A further distinction is that the AR-XC is available online, an issue addressed later in this review.

DEVELOPMENT. The test publisher used both the *Dictionary of Occupational Titles (DOT)* and *O*NET* to identify the job groupings, titles, and duties for which this test is applicable. Such a practice is commendable, and prevents ambiguity regarding when this test is applicable. However, the manual still lists number and definitions from the *DOT*. Given that *O*NET* has largely replaced the *DOT*, it is recommended that the test publisher pulls all of their information from *O*NET* in the next version of their manual.

Regarding the selection of test items, the interrater agreement of .90 among 18 maintenance supervisors rating the importance of knowledge and skill areas is exceptional. However, the test publisher should clarify whether .90 is the average interrater reliability or whether it represents an intraclass correlation. Further, the manual refers to

a "Maintenance Activity List" that the supervisors used to rate importance, but there is no description of what that instrument was.

These 18 job experts then picked 80 test items from the developer's database, although it is not clear whether they picked these items based on the importance of the knowledge and skill areas or on the time spent in them (another evaluation the maintenance supervisors made). This should also be clarified. These 80 items were then reduced to 60 using biserial and item difficulty methodology, which is a sound and widely accepted practice. In a February 2009 revision, 6 items were replaced and 7 were revised. Although such revisions are common and a normal part of test development, the test publisher is encouraged to provide a little more information about the nature of these changes and the reasons for making them.

TECHNICAL. The directions provided for administration and scoring of the booklet version are excellent and should result in controlled, standardized testing. Because such control cannot be ensured with online testing, organizations using this test might consider using the booklet form if logistics permit.

The KR20 reliability estimates provided in the manual (p. 15) are excellent for the first two samples (.91 and .94, respectively), but much less so for the third sample (.72). It is unclear whether the difference between the third and first two samples is the result of normal sampling error or some specific feature of the third sample (e.g., type of job, experience of the candidates). It would be helpful if the test publisher provided some insight into these differences. The test publisher is further encouraged to increase the sample size, as a total of 177 (across the three samples) is not particularly large.

The item analysis results for Form AR-XC look reasonable, although they are based on a sample of only 44. Psychometrically, this is a problem because there are more test items than test takers, which adds a high degree of uncertainty to the results. The test publisher is once again encouraged to perform the analyses on a larger sample.

The test publisher provides information on content evidence of validity but not on criterion evidence of validity. Although content validity certainly is appropriate for this type of test, the test publisher is strongly encouraged to add criterion-related information in the future. Corrections will need to be made for range restriction and performance ratings unreliability in such an analysis, but such corrections are relatively straightforward to make.

COMMENTARY. Form AR-XC is a very well-constructed test. The items appear to be an excellent representation of the key knowledge areas for a high-level maintenance technician. The test booklet itself is very professional, and the self-scoring format is easy to use. The directions for test administration are very precise and should ensure uniform testing. The limitations noted in preceding sections pertain either to clarifications of information already in the test manual (e.g., whether the test items were selected based on importance or on time spent) or to the need for further psychometric analysis of test properties (e.g., criterion-related validity, larger samples).

SUMMARY. There is much to commend about Form AR-XC of the Mechanical Technician A test, and organizations evaluating candidates for the job groupings described in the manual would be well-advised to consider this test.

Review of the Mechanical Technician A (Forms AR-XC and MTA-YC) by YUANZHONG ZHANG, Faculty, Miami-Dade College, Miami, FL:

DESCRIPTION. The Mechanical Technician A is a standardized test developed by the Ramsay Corporation to evaluate knowledge and skills required of maintenance technicians at the advanced journey-level as part of the inventory of assessment of mechanical abilities. The version of the test focused in the review is the self-scoring format of Form AR-XC updated in 2009. An alternate version equivalent to the current one is Form MTA-YC. The main audience of the test includes prospective and in-service technical employees in the occupations of mechanical maintenance and repairs across industries as detailed in the Manual for Administration and Scoring (2009). The Mechanical Technician A is available in both paper-and-pencil and online format. The time allowed for examinees to complete the test is not specified but it should take about an hour to complete. It is recommended that the examiners pay close attention to the work of the examinees during the test.

DEVELOPMENT. The Form AR-XC of Mechanical Technician A consists of 60 multiple-choice items related to multiple content areas including Hydraulics and Pneumatics, Print Reading, Power Transmission & Lubrication, Pumps & Piping, and Mechanical Maintenance Principles. The number of test items organized respectively

into each content area is as follows: 18 items in the section of Hydraulics and Pneumatics, 5 in Print Reading, 15 in Power Transmission & Lubrication, 11 in Pumps & Piping, and 11 in Mechanical Maintenance Principles.

The test instrument is developed and refined through collaborative efforts between job experts outside the test developing group who assume supervisory roles in maintenance and industrial psychologists who are versed in testing development. The job experts provide input about essential knowledge and skills for maintenance technicians. An interrater agreement at .90 was obtained among the 18 job experts involved in ranking the importance level of competency areas. The industrial psychologists were responsible for selecting representative test items in accordance with the indexes of item difficulty and item point biserial correlations after the initial administration of the test. The previous two forms of the test–Forms MTA-X and MTA-Y were refined and redesignated as Forms AR-XC and MTA-YC.

As a self-scoring test, the Form AR-XC enables test takers to score their answers by themselves upon completion of the test. The keys are included in the test booklet (Mechanical Technician A Form AR-XC), and the scoring instructions are provided. The correct response for each individual question is marked in a boxed area.

TECHNICAL.

Standardization. Administered by a uniform procedure, standardized tests are developed by a disciplined approach including the proposal of the idea, evaluation of the proposal, item tryouts, revision, and publishing. Standardized tests make assumptions about the representativeness of the samples who took the test. Information about percentile ranking of raw scores obtained from the test is provided to reflect the position of a certain score in the tested population.

Mechanical Technician A is apparently built with common features of standardized tests to demonstrate its objectivity. According to the Manual for Administration and Scoring (2009), the knowledge areas identified in the test are divided into eight cluster groups, and listed under each cluster group are several concepts or skills. The items in the test are arranged in accordance with corresponding knowledge areas. The directions for administration and scoring, and the conversion of table for score reporting are provided. Although historical background of the test development is not described in detail, it is evident that the test grows out of a longitudinal trajectory of development first introduced in 1995.

Reliability. The reliability is reflected particularly in the balanced choice of items of varying difficulty level. The range of difficulty level of items is from .14 to .89. As the most difficult items in the test (#6, #19, and #20), only 14% of the responses are correct. As the least difficult items in the test (#9 and #16), 89% of the responses are correct. Chi-square analysis shows that there are no significant differences in the test items in the overall distribution of difficulty level (chi-square = 2.40, $p > .05$). All individual sections of the test reflect a similar balanced pattern of item difficulty, with the exception of Pumping and Piping (chi-square = 5.89, $p < .05$). The results of the chi-square test for all other sections are as follows: chi-square = .22, $p > .05$ for Hydraulics & Pneumatics; chi-square = .20, $p > .05$ for Print Reading; chi-square = 1.66, $p > .05$ for Power Transmission & Lubrication; and chi-square = .82, $p > .05$ for Mechanical Maintenance and Principles.

The reliability data were derived from three groups who were administered three different forms of the test: AR-XC, MTA-XC, and MTA-YC. The results of reliability coefficient (KR_{20}) and odd-even reliability of the test items are above .90 for Form AR-XC and MTA-XC, and extend in range from .72 to .84 for Form MTA-YC. Although the test items achieve high levels of reliability, the *F* test calculated based on the data of Mean and Standard Deviation provided in Table 3 of the test manual reveals that the differences among the test scores of the three groups are statistically significant ($F_{(2, 174)} = 9.15$, $p < 0.05$). The differences in test-retest scores can be attributed to a host of factors including the method of administration and the normative samples taking the test. It is needed for the test maker to investigate the possible causes of variation and the interaction between the difficulty of items and the outcomes of the test.

Validity. Observations about the status of validity are made in the reviews of the previous versions of the test (Biderman & Weathington, 2007; Garner, 2007). The updated version of the test addresses validity under three headings: content-related, criterion-related, and construct validity. The content-related validity is reflected in the high degree of congruence among the panel of job experts who rate the areas of knowledge and skills in the preparation phase of test development. The criterion-related validity is based on the assumption of predictability in that knowledge and skills measured by the test share the essential traits as those required of job performance. Given the high correlation coefficients with positive job performance evaluations by supervisors in other similar vocational tests developed by the Ramsay Corporation, it is argued that the criterion-related validity of the test in question can be concurrently established by analogy. The construct validity is discussed on the grounds of subjective judgment of experts, whereas empirical/objective evidence through formal studies is needed to generate more data and documentation about the relationships between the set of traits measured by the test and the qualifications expected in the workplace.

COMMENTARY. The Mechanical Technician A adheres to sound models of testing development. The content of the test is aligned with the descriptions of related job titles presented in the *Dictionary of Occupational Titles* (U.S. Department of Labor, 1991). The blueprint of the knowledge and skills of maintenance mechanics charted in the test is helpful for employers to establish professional expectations of advanced-level mechanics technicians. The test manual gives in-depth information on the procedures of administration and scoring, whereas the technical aspects of testing are addressed by varying lengths and extents. It is desirable for the test designer to include more data and information related to reliability and validity from subsequent trials of test administration. It is also advisable to customize the general definition of reliability and validity to fit into the specific purpose of the current test instrument.

SUMMARY. Mechanical work is essentially a hands-on, field-based career. Developing a psychometric instrument to measure such hands-on knowledge represents an innovative effort to validate the expertise of technicians by turning the practices into professional and technical terms and phrases (Biderman & Weathington, 2007). The test provides an example of applying the discrete-point written test to calibrate hands-on skills. The items in the Mechanical Technician A can be viewed as encompassing such classifiable knowledge and skills as declarative (factual), procedural, and conditional knowledge (Paris, Lipson, & Wixson, 1994). As pointed out in the Manual for Administration and Scoring, future research is anticipated to address the existing issues with reliability and validity and suggest ways to interpret the test scores.

REVIEWER'S REFERENCES

Biderman, M. D., & Weathington, B. L. (2007). [Review of the Mechanical Technician A]. In K. F. Geisinger, R. A. Spies, J. F. Carlson, & B. S. Plake (Eds.), *The seventeenth mental measurements yearbook* (pp. 515–517). Lincoln, NE: Buros Institute of Mental Measurements.

Garner, M. L. (2007). [Review of the Mechanical Technician A]. In K. F. Geisinger, R. A. Spies, J. F. Carlson, & B. S. Plake (Eds.), *The seventeenth mental measurements yearbook* (pp. 517–518). Lincoln, NE: Buros Institute of Mental Measurements.

Paris, S., Lipson, M., & Wixon, K. (1994). Becoming a strategic reader. In R. Ruddell & H. Singer (Eds.), *Theoretical models and processes of reading* (4th ed.) (pp. 788–810). Newark, DE: International Reading Association.

U.S. Department of Labor. (1991). *Dictionary of occupational titles* (4th ed.). Washington, DC: U.S. Government Printing Office.

[103]

Mechanical Technician C (Forms CR-XC and MTC-YC).

Purpose: For selecting or evaluating entry-journey level maintenance technicians for jobs in the metals or manufacturing industry.

Population: Applicants and incumbents for jobs requiring mechanical knowledge and skills.

Publication Dates: 2003-2008.

Scores, 8: Hydraulics & Pneumatics, Print Reading, Burning/Fabricating/Welding & Rigging, Power Transmission & Lubrication, Pumps & Piping, Mechanical Maintenance Principles, Shop Equipment & Tools, Total.

Administration: Group.

Forms, 2: MTC-YC, MTC-XC.

Price Data, 2011: $22 per consumable self-scoring test booklet or online test administration (minimum order of 20); $24.95 per manual (2008, 25 pages).

Time: (60-70) minutes.

Comments: Self-scoring instrument; available for online test administration; Form MTC-YC is an alternate equivalent of Form CR-XC.

Author: Roland T. Ramsay.

Publisher: Ramsay Corporation.

Cross References: For a review by Russell W. Smith of an earlier edition, see 17:120.

Review of the Mechanical Technician C (Forms CR-XC and MTC-YC) by JAMES A. ATHANASOU, Adjunct Professor, Faculty of Arts & Social Sciences, University of Technology, Sydney, Australia:

DESCRIPTION. The Mechanical Technician Form C is not for the naïve test user as it requires extensive technical and engineering experience. A sample item (not one of the actual test questions) from the website for the test is: "The capacity of a piston metering pump can be changed by varying the: (A) vane spacing, (B) connecting rod stroke, (C) impeller size, (D) drive motor speed."

The Mechanical Technician Form C was first developed in 1995 and the latest form is a shortened 60-item version. This measure was updated in 2007 and the revision involved replacing 5 questions and revising 1 item.

This test covers 72 discrete areas of knowledge. The 60 items were selected by 18 content experts on the basis of importance for the work. Items were selected from a database and the resultant items for the seven content categories are: Shop Equipment & Tools (7 items), Mechanical Maintenance Principles (12), Pumps & Piping (7), Power Transmission & Lubrication (11), Burning/Fabricating/Welding & Rigging (10), Print Reading (4), and Hydraulics & Pneumatics (9). The intended use of this measure is in selecting metals or manufacturing candidates for positions such as maintenance repairer, maintenance mechanic, or millwright. Details of the relevant job descriptions from the *Dictionary of Occupational Titles* and the *O*NET* are provided.

The test is administered as a self-contained booklet that contains the questions, the answer sheet, and a sealed carbon imprint marking sheet. The instructions are clear and the marking is straightforward. The manual provides explicit advice and the overall presentation is professional. It is user-friendly and better than many comparable paper-and-pencil tests.

Each item has only one correct response. The scoring is simple. One counts the number of correct responses for a total in each of the seven subsections.

DEVELOPMENT. The standardization sample is only 63 applicants for mechanical maintenance jobs and comes from an earlier version of the measure. The manual states that "No data is [sic] presently available for the newly revised version of the test ... however, the five new questions are of similar difficulty to those that they replaced. It is expected that the updated test will yield similar data" (p. 16). Strictly speaking, this use of earlier data is not acceptable and in any event the sample size is terribly small. In the opinion of this reviewer, at the very least one might expect a sample that is 5–10 times the number of questions.

Fortunately, this standardization sample matches the intended population but its use as a selection measure means that the normative data (Table 6, p. 23) are hardly relevant. Cutoff points for competence would have been more useful for selection. In any event, it is not clear how normative data from job applicants could ever be used to "facilitate the comparisons of persons scoring at a given level with a reference group, e.g., employed workers, skilled craft workers, etc." (manual, p. 22).

The 50th percentile for Form XC was a score of 46 out of 60 and for Form YC it was 48 out of 60. Inspection of the item difficulty values and point-biserial discrimination indices for the 60 items shows that the majority of items were well above .5 in difficulty and that some point-biserial correlations were well below the .2 cutoff. This finding probably reflects the selective nature of the standardization sample.

The evidence for score consistency is based on Kuder-Richardson (KR-20) estimates of .75 for a sample of $N = 63$ and .71 for a sample of 42 job applicants. These estimates are well below the criterion of around .9 many consider desirable for high stakes decisions. Also there are no reports of the internal consistency reliability of the seven subsection scores and these are likely to be lower when there are as few as 4 items for the Print Reading section. In any event, internal consistency is only a partial indicator of the likely stability of test scores over time.

There are no formal studies of the criterion or construct validity of the assessment. The major argument for the validity of the results is that of content validity. This is important for an achievement test and it is likely to offer concurrent and predictive validity but the outcome is not certain. Both the validity and reliability coefficients would in all likelihood be substantially higher within a general sample of the population compared to the restriction of range in this selective cohort.

COMMENTARY. The overall strength of this test is that it has stood the test of time and found ready application in industry. It has the face validity that would make it attractive to commercial users and it is relatively easy to use. The results are directly interpretable when selecting candidates for a job.

There is a caveat, however, in this conclusion. There is the nagging concern that there are limitations in the evidence that supports the test results in terms of standardization, reliability, or validity, especially the newer evidence that some consider consequential validity evidence. Additional advice on the use of the test as a competency assessment with cutoff points for performance is required.

SUMMARY. Among the major publishers of mechanical reasoning tests, there is probably no equivalent to this measure in this reviewer's knowledge. It is a specific measure with considerable content validity. There is much to commend the Mechanical Technician C (Forms CR-XC and MTC-YC) as an achievement test of mechanical knowledge in selection contexts. Its use as a measure of aptitude, however, requires additional support that has not been forthcoming in the latest revision and manual (March 2008). One suspects that this assessment has quality and substance but the evidence basis for it is not forthcoming at this time.

Review of the Mechanical Technician C (Forms CR-XC and MTC-YC) by CHRISTA E. WASH-INGTON, Associate Professor of Psychology, Saint Augustine's University, Raleigh, NC:

DESCRIPTION. The Mechanical Technician C (Form CR-XC and MTC-YC) is a test that measures knowledge and skills from mechanical technicians. This test is intended to be used with new applicants and incumbents. There are three hierarchical levels of the test. The original RCJS Mechanical Technician C represents the beginning levels of knowledge and skills. There is an alternate version in the RCJS Mechanical Technician C Form MTC-Y (1995). An abridged version of each form consists of 60 items. The individual is given 60 multiple-choice questions and is asked to select the correct answer for each question. The following areas are tested: (1) Hydraulics & Pneumatics, (2) Print Reading, (3) Burning/Fabricating/Welding & Rigging, (4) Power Transmission & Lubrication, (5) Pumps & Piping, (6) Mechanical Maintenance Principles, and (7) Shop Equipment & Tools. Also, in each category there is an item on safety. Safety is not a stand-alone category.

The test instructions are clear and easy to follow. There is no time limit, but the test should not take longer than 1 hour to complete. The test is scored by counting the number of correct responses. The number of correct responses is also counted for each subsection and these sums are added together for the total test score. Scores are used to compare the individual's knowledge with the skills required to perform the job duties.

The score is a raw score and based on that number the individual is compared to norms data to be assigned a percentile. There was no specific information given to differentiate the percentiles.

DEVELOPMENT. The test was developed by 18 job experts (maintenance supervisors). The applicable job titles are as follows: maintenance repairer, industrial, maintenance mechanic, and millwright. A total of 80 items were selected from the Ramsay Corporation's database. The test was designed to measure knowledge and skills for the following areas: (1) Hydraulics & Pneumatics, (2)

Print Reading, (3) Burning/Fabricating/Welding & Rigging, (4) Power Transmission & Lubrication, (5) Pumps & Piping, (6) Mechanical Maintenance Principles, and (7) Shop Equipment & Tools. A number of individuals were tested with the RCJS Maintenance Technician C Form MTC-X and RCJS Maintenance Technician C Form MTC-Y and both forms consisted of 80 items. From these tests, two industrial psychologists decided to select 60 of the 80 items to create the RCJS Mechanical Technician C (Form MTC-XC) and the RCJS Maintenance Technician C (Form MTC-YC). In December 2007, the test was renamed the RCJS Mechanical Technician C (Form MTC-XC) (manual, p. 8). Five of the test items were replaced. These items were not specified. Also, one item was revised and no detailed information was provided on the revision. There was very little information provided on the item selection and analysis procedures. The RCJS Mechanical Technician C (Form MTC-X) and the RCJS Mechanical Technician C (Form MTC-Y) were evaluated and compared using the Ramsay Corporation items analysis. Overall, there was only limited information on item selection and analysis.

TECHNICAL. There are no current data available for the RCJS Mechanical Technician C (Form CR-XC). As a result, there is no information on the participant demographics. Also, there were no normative data for the RCJS Mechanical Technician C (Form CR-XC). Without any information on the test norms, it is difficult to assess the overall standardization, reliability, or validity. However, the earlier version of this test, the RCJS Mechanical Technician C (Form MTC-XC) (2003, 2005), evidenced very good reliability and the RCJS Mechanical Technician C (Form MTC-YC) (2003) was also considered to have good reliability. With the new test questions (5 items), the test is expected to yield similar results.

COMMENTARY. The RCJS Mechanical Technician C (Form CR-XC) appears to be a reasonable measure. When the experts reduced the items from 80 to 60, this shorter measure seems more feasible. The administration of the test is simple and should not present problems. The scoring method is simple addition of each section. Far too little information relative to the norms is available in the manual. Without any new data for this revised version of the test, it is difficult to offer evaluative comments regarding the strengths and weaknesses of the test.

The previous tests were lacking in validity and it would be best if this test has greater validity analyses and support.

SUMMARY. The Mechanical Technician C (Form CR-XC) is a test designed to measure the knowledge and skills required for mechanical technicians. The test meets the partial goals of assessing mechanical skills such as Hydraulics, Pneumatics, Print Reading, Burning, Fabrication & Welding, Power Transmission, Lubrication, Pumps, Piping, Rigging, Mechanical Maintenance Principles, Shop Equipment & Tools, and Safety. There were no data regarding the validity and reliability to support the test meeting the goals of testing mechanical knowledge in a professional manner.

[104]

MecTest (Forms AU-C and BV-R).

Purpose: Designed for selecting or evaluating journey-level maintenance mechanics.

Population: Applicants and incumbents for maintenance jobs.

Publication Dates: 1991–2012.

Scores, 9: Hydraulics and Pneumatics, Print Reading, Welding and Rigging, Power Transmission, Lubrication, Pumps and Piping, Mechanical Maintenance, Shop Machines/Tools/Equipment, Total.

Administration: Group.

Forms, 2: AU-C, BV-R.

Price Data, 2013: $23 per consumable self-scoring test booklet (20 minimum order); $25 per online administration; $24.95 per manual (2012, 28 pages).

Foreign Language Edition: Available in Spanish.

Time: (60-70) minutes.

Comments: Self-scoring instrument; available for online test administration; Form BV-R is an alternate equivalent of Form AU-C.

Author: Roland T. Ramsay.

Publisher: Ramsay Corporation.

Cross References: For a review by Robert J. Drummond of an earlier edition, see 13:197.

Review of the MecTest (Forms AU-C and BV-R) by NANCY T. TIPPINS, Senior Vice President and Managing Principal, CEB, Greenville, SC:

DESCRIPTION. The MecTest (Form AU-C) is a measure of the knowledge and skills necessary to perform the duties of maintenance mechanic jobs. The test is intended to be used for employee selection and can be administered individually or in group settings via paper and pencil or computer. There are two forms of the test, AU-C and BV-R, consisting of 60 items currently in use, which produce nine scores, a total score and eight subscores.

The items in the test represent eight areas related to mechanical maintenance: Hydraulics and Pneumatics, Print Reading, Welding and Rigging, Power Transmission, Lubrication, Pumps and Piping, Mechanical Maintenance, and Shop Machines, Tools and Equipment. Each knowledge area includes subcomponents. For example, "pumps" includes seven subcomponents: horizontal, vertical, seals, alignment, thrust, positive displacement, and centrifugal.

The 60 items are multiple-choice and ask the test taker to demonstrate his or her knowledge or skill by indicating the correct response. Some items require knowledge recall; others require the test taker to study diagrams and answer questions about them. The instructions for test administration and scoring are clearly written and easy to follow. Administration of the test items is untimed; however, the administration instructions indicate that most test takers will require no more than one hour. The amount of time required for scoring is not stated in the administration instructions, but scoring appears to be a simple task composed of inspecting the answer sheets for items with multiple answers and counting the correct responses.

DEVELOPMENT. The 60 items in the MecTest were written to evaluate knowledge in the eight areas of mechanical maintenance described above and the subcomponents of these areas. These topics are aligned with the *Dictionary of Occupational Titles* definition for maintenance mechanic and the O*NET definition for industrial machinery mechanics. The rationale for the number of items included for each knowledge area in the first version of the test, Form A, is based on the expert judgment of five job experts, who ranked the importance of each knowledge area. The test manual does not explain how the depth of knowledge in a particular area was taken into account. For example, "steam" is a subcomponent of piping, but it is not clear if the maintenance mechanic should know simply that steam is a gaseous form of water or to understand more complex topics such as the enthalpy of vaporization.

After these subject matter experts' rankings were averaged, the subject matter experts were asked to estimate the percent of items to be developed for each area. The average percentage was multiplied by the total number of items contemplated for the first version of the test to derive the number of items for each knowledge area. To develop the first form of this test (A), job experts in groups of two chose relevant items for each knowledge area from Ramsay Corporation's item bank. The job experts chose one safety item for each knowledge area where applicable. The number of job experts used is not specified nor is the total number of items used in the first form. The extent to which each item represents one or more subcomponents of the eight areas is also not clear. Thus, a test user who is not an expert in mechanics cannot tell if a subcomponent is adequately represented. For example, there are nine subcomponents of pneumatics, but only five questions were assigned to the knowledge area. Whether or not one item covers multiple subcomponents cannot be easily determined by the test user who lacks skills in this area.

In 1987, an industrial psychologist chose the best 60 items based on data from several hundred testings using criteria of item point-biserial discrimination indexes and item difficulties. Exactly how these criteria were applied is not clear. For example, one can assume that items with extreme item difficulties (i.e., too easy, too hard) were not chosen, but the decision rules used are not specified. The "best" 60 items constitute Form AU (1991) and Form AU-C (1998, 2000, 2006). Again, it is assumed that the same 60 items were used in both forms. The test manual does state that the proportions of items in each content area were the same across Forms A, AU, and AU-C. The 2000 version of the MecTest changed fractions to decimals in four questions. The 2006 version contained minor changes to the wording of 6 items.

Form BV of the MecTest was developed in 1998 by two industrial psychologists who selected the best 60 items from Form B (1994). Although it is assumed that Form B of the MecTest was developed in the same manner as Form A, the test manual provides no information about its history.

In January 2007, the RCJS MecTest (1998, 2000, 2006) was made available in an online version through Ramsay Corporation's website, www.ramsaycorp.com.

No data are presented on the equivalency of the two forms currently in use, although the proportion of items in both Form AU-C and Form BV-R, reflects the importance of each knowledge area as determined by the original set of job experts.

TECHNICAL. The test manual provides descriptive statistics for five groups of test takers that include both job applicants and incumbents, ranging in sample size from 31 to 2,048. The means and standard deviations potentially allow a test user to establish an expected level of test performance based on the data from other organizations' experiences; however, the test user should be cautious about the data from some groups. For example, the two largest groups are defined as "applicants and incumbents nationwide" (n = 2,048). Most test users using the MecTest for employee selection of maintenance mechanics would not find the data collected from applicants to unrelated jobs or incumbents in unrelated jobs useful. These descriptive statistics report both *KR20* and odd-even reliability for each group. *KR20* reliabilities range from .74 to .89. Odd-even reliabilities range from .69 to .88.

For a sample of data from Form AU-C (n = 2,048) and a sample of data from Form BV-R (n = 31), item difficulties and point-biserial correlation coefficients (item to total in a test section) are presented. The item difficulties on Form AU-C, ranging from .34 to .91, indicate that the extremely difficult or hard items were identified and eliminated. The item difficulties on the smaller sample of Form BV-R data reflect a wider range of item difficulties (.10 to .97), consistent with a small sample. The point-biserial correlations suggest moderate levels of consistency in the construct being measured with correlations ranging from .28 to .75 on Form AU-C data and more variable levels of consistency among the data from the smaller sample of BV-R data (-.10 to .81).

Percentile rankings are presented for each score using data from two samples (AU-C, n = 2,048; BV-R, n = 31). Note that both of these samples are labeled as "applicants and incumbents" with no job designated.

A content-oriented approach to establishing evidence of validity for the intended use is typically used with job knowledge tests. Items for Forms AU-C and BV-R were derived from sets of items selected to represent areas of knowledge determined appropriate by five subject matter experts for a mechanical technician job that was a combination of three jobs: millwright, pipefitter, and welder. In addition, the test manual summarizes nine content validation studies of Forms AU-CGR, AU-C, AU-CLG, and AU-CG. (There is no other information on Forms AI-CLG and AU-CG nor is there validation information on Form B and its derivatives.) The details of the studies in terms of what judgments subject matter experts were asked to make and what anchors were used are not provided; however, the average job relatedness, which is assumed to be an average of the ratings of job relatedness across all items and all raters, ranges from 3.6 to 4.7 on a 5.0 scale. No test had any items of job relatedness below 2.5, which must indicate a point on the scale below which an item would not be considered job related. Intraclass correlations used to assess rater agreement range from .60 to .89.

One criterion-related validity study is reported in the appendix to the test manual (n = 95). Scores on the MecTest were correlated significantly with supervisors' ratings of technical skills (.496, p < .001), problem solving (.236, p < .05), and performance total (.313, p < .01).

No studies were documented in the test manual using a construct approach to validity.

COMMENTARY. The MecTest is an excellent source of items measuring mechanical craft skills; however, the test is only useful if the items reflect the requirements of the job for which it is being used. Maintenance jobs vary considerably from company to company and even from plant to plant within a company depending on organizational structure, bargaining unit, product being made, etc. Thus, it is unlikely that one set of test items representing mechanical knowledge is applicable to all jobs. It is incumbent upon the user to establish the job relevancy of the items for his or her job. This process could be facilitated if the publisher provided more detailed definitions of the knowledge areas that included information about the level of knowledge required. The usability of the test could be further strengthened with more descriptive information based on test scores from samples that include only incumbent maintenance mechanics. Data regarding the equivalency of the various forms would also be useful when users must give retests.

SUMMARY. The MecTest was developed to measure job knowledge required in mechanical maintenance jobs and to inform employee selection decisions. Because employee selection procedures that are lawful and meet best business practices must be job relevant, the publisher should acknowledge the wide variation in mechanical knowledge requirements commonly found and encourage each test user to establish validity using a content-oriented strategy and should not imply that validity derived from content approaches generalizes to all mechanical maintenance positions.

Review of the MecTest (Forms AU-C and BV-R) by SHELDON ZEDECK, Professor of the Graduate School, University of California at Berkeley, Berkeley, CA:

DESCRIPTION. This review covers the Ramsay Corporation Job Skills MecTest (Form AU-C), as described in the test's accompanying *Manual for Administration and Scoring* and covers the latest version from 2012. The test purports to measure the practical knowledge and skills necessary for maintenance jobs, particularly Maintenance Mechanic and Industrial Machinery Mechanics as these jobs are described in the *Dictionary of Occupational Titles* (U.S. Department of Labor, 1991) and the *O*NET Online* (U.S. Department of Labor, 2006), respectively. The original version, titled RCJS MecTest Form AU, was developed in 1991, changed in scoring format in 1993, and reprinted as RCJS MecTest Form AU-C in 1998, 2000, 2006, and 2008. Another form, RCJS MecTest BV, was developed in 1998, but it is not the focus of the current review.

The MecTest (Form AU-C) is a 60-item, self-scoring, multiple-choice test that purports to measure eight knowledge areas covering Hydraulics and Pneumatics, Print Reading, Welding and Rigging, Power Transmission, Lubrication, Pumps and Piping, Mechanical Maintenance, and Shop Machines, Tools, and Equipment. The number of items for each of these areas varies from 4 through 15. The test is available for online administration; it is untimed, but the expectation is that it can be completed in not more than one hour.

DEVELOPMENT. The purported use of the test, as planned in 1991, was to select applicants for jobs that involved practical mechanical knowledge and skills that are part of maintenance job activities. The test was developed by having five job experts who were incumbent craft workers or supervisors of craft workers review a list of knowledge and skill areas (see list in the above "Description") purportedly needed for "Technician Mechanical" and to (a) rank each for importance and (b) estimate the percent of items that should be developed for each area. No information is presented on the "expertness" of the five raters, nor is any information presented on their backgrounds (e.g., age, experience, gender, ethnicity, nature of their work, and the like).

Job experts (here, again, no information is provided on the number of such experts, much less background on them) then selected relevant items from Ramsay Corporation's item bank to represent each of the eight knowledge areas. The result of their efforts was RCJS Technical Mechanical Form A (1987). After testing "several hundred individuals" on this form, "an industrial psychologist

selected the best 60 items according to criteria of item point biserial discrimination indexes and item difficulty" (manual, p. 6), which in turn resulted in the current form. The individual item statistics are presented in Table 4 of the manual, and in general, represent reasonable values that one would desire in such a test.

Overall, little information is provided about how the knowledge areas were reduced to a set of eight, what instructions were given to the raters, and what definitions were provided for the knowledge areas; no information is provided on the backgrounds of the raters, nor the cutoff criteria used for final selection of items. In addition, for the item analysis, there is little information on the sample on which the data were generated and analyzed (see below, Technical section).

TECHNICAL. The reliabilities reported for the test are ones of internal consistency (Kuder-Richardson 20), and that range across 5 "samples" from .74 to .89. These are reasonable values, but the ability to judge their "appropriateness" is hampered by a lack of information about the studies on which they are based. The manual simply reports 5 samples that are described as (a) maintenance employees in processing plants throughout the USA, (b) applicants for a mechanical job in the energy industry, (c) incumbents at a Mid-Atlantic electrical power utility, (d) applicants and incumbents nationwide, and (e) combined applicants and employed workers (manual, p. 13). The five samples are also combined into a total group. Unfortunately, there are no descriptions of the jobs being applied for by the applicants or performed by the incumbents, nor are there descriptions of the companies at which the data were collected. Most glaringly missing, however, are background and demographic characteristics of the samples on which the reliability data were collected.

Three strategies for validity evidence are presented. One, "content validity," is presented as established for the test because the "behaviors required on the test are also required on the job. It is a paper-and-pencil form of a work sample" (manual, p. 19). The manual states that the "appropriate model for validity is content validity" (p. 20). Yet, no detailed information is presented as to how content validity evidence was obtained or established, or how the test items and their content were linked to job content. The manual merely states that the RCJS MecTest Form AU-C is a shortened version of a test for the job of Mechanical Technician and that the "resulting number of questions were determined by a group of 5 job experts at a metal processing plant in the Midwest" (p. 19). (See comments above about lack of information regarding the five experts.) Further evidence for presumed content validity is presented in the form of a table (Table 6, p. 20) that summarizes data from nine "content validation studies." These data are in the form of intraclass correlations and average job relatedness–but no detail is presented on how the data were collected, who exactly provided the data, or why the analytical output (the correlations) represent evidence for content validity.

A second strategy presented pertains to "criterion-related validity" (manual, p. 20). The bases for this evidence are correlations between test scores and "supervisor's performance ratings for 95 maintenance workers" (manual, p. 20) with various performance competencies such as Technical Skill, Problem Solving, and Performance Total. Again, this description and level of detail is deficient. Who were the raters? Who were the ratees? What were their backgrounds? What were the definitions and ratings scales for the three "competencies" rated?

The third strategy presented is "construct validity." The description of the strategy is confusing. The manual states that "The construct measured by RCJS MecTest is knowledge and skill in mechanical maintenance" (p. 21). The next sentence states, however, that "No formal studies of construct validity have been conducted, but construct validity may be enhanced by the procedures of development" (manual, p. 21). I fail to see, based on these sentences, how construct validity can be argued for the test.

Normative data are presented in the manual (Table 7), which shows percentile rankings for the raw scores on the test. However, there is no discussion of how these data and results were obtained nor is there any discussion of how the results for specific test takers are to be interpreted and used for selection or hiring. In addition, there are no descriptions on how different demographic groups might perform on the test (e.g., males vs. females, Caucasian vs. African American and other potentially underrepresented ethnic groups, college-educated vs. less than college education, and the like).

One final table (Table 8, p. 25) shows the intercorrelations among the eight knowledge areas; the results range from approximately .37 through .69, which reflects both some independence and some overlap among the areas. However, the meaningfulness of the intercorrelations among the eight areas is unknown because there is no discussion of whether the decisions made based on the test are provided by the total score or area scores, or both.

Finally, with respect to directions for test administration, there is some confusion in the instructions. The manual states that "The time limits specified must be observed precisely as specified for each test" (p. 9). Yet the manual further states that there are no time limits, and it is unknown what is meant by "each test," because to the best of this reviewer's knowledge, the test is administered as a total and not as an "area by area" test. Furthermore, the administrator is asked to observe examinees at work and note any behavior that might indicate that the test results may not represent accurate measurements of ability. Again, this reviewer is at a loss to understand what is meant or being requested of the administrator. The suggestion that the administrator might fulfill the request by determining that the "examinee has less than six years of education and reads with difficulty" (manual, p. 9) is not one that can be met by *observing* the examinee. Related to test administration, no information is provided to the examinee as to whether he or she should guess and whether there will be a correction for guessing.

COMMENTARY AND SUMMARY. From a "face validity" perspective, the 60 items appear to be measuring aspects of mechanical knowledge. Yet the manual is quite deficient in presenting information that would allow the user to determine whether inferences can be made about the ability of applicants to perform mechanical maintenance. This lack of information is surprising because the test has been available since the early 1990s, and the presumption is that considerable use has been made of the test that should have generated sufficient information that is necessary to be part of any test manual–information that would allow the user to make sound judgments about the nature and quality of the test, the resulting scores, and the interpretations based on the test scores. Also, contributing to the surprise is that a number of the concerns addressed above were presented in a previous review, by Drummond (1998).

REVIEWER'S REFERENCES

Drummond, R. J. (1998). [Review of the MecTest (A Test for Maintenance Mechanics)]. In J. C. Impara & B. S. Plake (Eds.), *The thirteenth mental measurements yearbook* (pp. 653-654). Lincoln, NE: Buros Institute of Mental Measurements.
U.S. Department of Labor. National O*NET Consortium. (2006). O*NET Online. Available: online.onetcenter.org
U.S. Department of Labor. (1991). *Dictionary of occupational titles* (4th ed., rev.). Washington, DC: U.S. Government Printing Office.

[105]

Memory for Intentions Test.

Purpose: Designed to measure "everyday aspects" of prospective memory performance.

Population: Ages 18 to 95.

Publication Date: 2010.

Acronym: MIST.

Scores, 8: 2-Minute Time Delay, 15-Minute Time Delay, Time Cue, Event Cue, Verbal Response, Action Response, Prospective Memory Total, Retrospective Recognition Total; 1 optional score: Delayed Prospective Memory Task.

Administration: Individual.

Forms, 2: A, B.

Price Data, 2010: $240 per complete kit including 25 Form A record forms, 25 Form B record forms, 25 Form A word search sheets, 25 Form B word search sheets, 25 score summary sheets, 25 request for records forms, digital clock, carrying case, and manual (62 pages); $180 per introductory kit including 25 Form A record forms, 25 Form A word search sheets, 25 score summary sheets, 25 request for records forms, digital clock, carrying case, and manual; $40 per 25 record forms (Form A or Form B); $25 per 25 word search sheets (Form A or Form B); $30 per 25 score summary sheets; $25 per 25 request for records forms; $15 per digital clock; $65 per manual.

Time: (30) minutes.

Comments: Additional materials required for administration, but not included in test materials: red pen, postcard, envelope, tape recorder, pencil.

Authors: Sarah Raskin, Carol Buckheit, and Christina Sherrod (manual).

Publisher: Psychological Assessment Resources, Inc.

Review of the Memory for Intentions Test by JEANETTE W. FARMER, Professor of Special Education, Marshall University Graduate College, South Charleston, WV:

DESCRIPTION. The Memory for Intentions Test (MIST) is an individually administered assessment of "prospective memory," which refers to the ability to recall and perform tasks necessary at a future time. The life skill can be related to remembering to take medication on a schedule, remembering doctor appointments, remembering to take cooked food from the oven, and so forth. Prospective memory (PM) is reported to be the most common form of memory problems.

Forms A and B are available to counter practice effects for examinees who will be administered the test on separate occasions. The test kit comes in a black canvas case, and includes a battery-powered digital clock (battery included), professional manual, a package of 25 record forms, pad of 25 score summary sheets, pad of 25 word search puzzles,

and a pad of 25 request for record forms. Other materials to be supplied by the examiner are a red pen, postcard, envelope, tape recorder, and pencil.

A brief script is provided for the examiner on the record form. Prospective memory is assessed by presenting eight tasks that require a verbal or motor response. Retrospective recognition tasks (RRT) are assessed with eight multiple-choice questions related to examiner requests made during the earlier PM series. Responses are scored either 0, 1, or 2. The test manual includes tables for converting raw scores into percentiles by age and educational levels. A table is provided to interpret the percentiles into five rankings: very superior, high average, average, below average, or impaired.

DEVELOPMENT. Earlier prototypes include the Prospective Memory Screening Test (PROMS) by Sohlberg and Mateer in 1989 and the Assessment of Intentional Memory (AIM) by Raskin and Buckheit in 1998. The MIST has added different aspects of prospective memory, and has shortened administration time from 1 hour to 30 minutes.

Over 700 participants were included in the norm group. Men and women, ages 18 to 94 years, represented the educational levels, ethnicity, and geographic regions of the United States Census of 2007. Tables are included in the professional manual to present this specific information. Reviews investigated differences of skill levels by age, gender, and education.

TECHNICAL. Mean scores and standard deviations are provided for each examinee's prospective memory response (verbal and action), following a 2-minute delay, a 15-minute delay, with a time cue, and with an event cue. The test authors report data for internal consistency (.93 coefficient alpha from the six subscales, with the Spearman-Brown split-half reliability coefficient at .97). Interrater reliability is reported, as well as test-retest reliability. Content and convergent evidence for test score validity is supported with much research assessing various populations, including individuals with Alzheimer's disease, with brain injury, Parkinson's disease, Human Immunodeficiency Virus (HIV), multiple sclerosis, schizophrenia, older adults, those with mild cognitive impairments, and survivors of "intimate partner violence." Information on each of these populations related to PM is presented in the MIST manual.

COMMENTARY. Overall, the MIST is recommended to aid an examiner in assessing prospective memory functioning of individuals. Once a ranking (very superior, high average, average, below average, or impaired) is established, a program of remediation may need to be established, if appropriate. The strengths of the MIST are in the relative ease in administrating and interpreting the results, and in presenting information regarding prospective memory research among a variety of populations. The MIST is for diagnosis and does not indicate steps for restoration.

SUMMARY. The test authors note that there is evidence of examinees improving their prospective memory through "restorative approaches," yet no examples of such approaches were included. This assessment measure takes a relatively short time to administer, score, and interpret. Strong validity and reliability information is provided.

Review of the Memory for Intentions Test by MICHAEL J. FURLONG, Professor, and VICTORIA M. GONZALEZ, Doctoral Student, Counseling/Clinical/School Psychology Department, University of California-Santa Barbara, Santa Barbara, CA:

DESCRIPTION. The Memory for Intentions Test (MIST) measures prospective memory functioning in adults. Prospective memory (PM) facilitates a person's ability to recall and to perform a future task, or "remembering to remember" (professional manual, p.1), which is an important clinical consideration for individuals with neurological conditions that require time- and event-based treatment management. PM is a complex cognitive task in that it involves multiple memory functions including intention formation, storage, and "timely" retrieval. The target population of this assessment is adults ages 18–95, undergoing evaluations for neuropsychological impairments. The intended use of this instrument is to assess a person's ability to perform a future task, which requires a person to remember his or her intentions of performing a task and then carrying out the task, such as remembering the timing and dosage of medications. Event-based tasks are prompted by external cues (e.g., hearing a phone ring, and remembering to call and make a medical appointment); whereas specific times or dates (e.g., seeing the clock, and remembering to make a phone call at a specific time) prompt time-based tasks.

There are two versions of MIST (Form A and Form B). Administration takes approximately 30 minutes, with one optional follow-up item that is assessed 24 hours after the initial administration. A nonfocal stimulus is used to distract the examinee from the prospective memory tasks. The distractor is a word search puzzle that the examinee is instructed to use throughout the assessment.

Instructions are read aloud, and the test begins once the examiner is confident that the examinee fully understands the instructions. After the first item is administered, the examiner starts a timer and keeps track of and records the time that each item is administered, and when a response is given. Tracking time is necessary in order for the examiner to know when to administer a prompt, and when the examinee should provide a response. The examinee is also instructed to attend to the timer in order to provide responses at specific times. During the test, the examinee is also instructed to continue to complete the word puzzle. There are eight instructions (trials) given to the examinee, and examinees are directed to provide responses at different times. For example, the first item directs the examinee to ask for a break after 15 minutes. Before the 15 minutes are over, the examinee is given seven other instructions.

The MIST is divided into the following three variables: time delay, cue type, and response type. Two subscales measure each variable, which produces six subscale totals, each having a score ranging from 0–8. The *time delay* variable is composed of measures of shorter time delay assessment (2 minute and 15 minute) and another for a longer time delay (24 hours). *Cue type* has two subscales measuring time-based cues and event-based cues. *Response type* is divided into two subscales measuring verbal responses and action responses. Additionally, two composite scores are reported: *prospective memory* total (PMT) and *retrospective recognition* total (RRT). The PMT score ranges from 0–48, and is the sum of all six subscales. The RRT score is obtained by posing to the examinee questions about each trial, which includes the total of correct responses given for eight questions corresponding to the eight trials on the exam.

The instrument measures five types of errors, which might cause individuals to fail the prospective memory tasks. The five types of errors include: prospective memory failure, task substitution, loss of content, loss of time, and random errors. The error codes provide clinical qualitative information about which types of errors are occurring and when they occurred. Percentile rank conversions of raw scores are provided by age and education level for PMT total score, RRT total score, and six subscale scores (time delay, cue delay, and response type). The test manual provides percentile rank conversions from raw scores for the RRT and MIST subscales by age and education level.

DEVELOPMENT. The MIST was developed to serve as an ecologically relevant assessment of prospective memory independent of other memory or executive functioning assessments. The test authors comment that the MIST was designed as a brief measurement of intended memory, which could be used in conjunction with a battery of neuropsychological and rehabilitation assessments. The rationale for the development of the MIST was based on a study that examined individuals with brain injuries and found that their most prominent difficulties were with prospective memory in carrying out daily activities. Subsequently, the Prospective Memory Screening Test (PROMS) was developed to evaluate (a) individuals who required treatment of PM, and (b) the efficacy of PM treatment. Because this assessment did not measure different aspects of PM, the Assessment of Intentional Memory (AIM) was developed to measure these different aspects. However, due to the length of time needed for the AIM assessment, the MIST was then developed with the same content coverage as AIM, but with only half of the administration time. The initial version of the MIST was called the Memory for Intentions Screening Test.

TECHNICAL. The standardization sample for the MIST consisted of 736 adults ages 18–94 years; 50.3% of the sample was male. Overall, the standardized sample provides a fairly good representation of ethnic and cultural groups as compared to the U.S. Census. The White participants made up 65.8% of the MIST sample along with 14.5% African Americans. Hispanics comprised 16.0% of the total sample. Normative data are provided by age group (18–29, 30–59, 60–69, 70–79, and 80+) and by years of education (<12, 12, 13–15, and $\geq$16). The test authors commented that they excluded individuals from their sample who reported a history of neurologic disorders, severe brain injuries, hearing or visual impairment, significant polysubstance abuse, or of psychiatric hospitalizations. Form A and Form B scores were compared for 99 participants and the results suggested nonsignificant differences.

Coefficient alpha based on the six subscales that make up the PMT score was .93 (Spearman-Brown split-half reliability was .97). Coefficient alpha for the six individual subscales ranged from

.54 to .64. Correlations between each trial score and each total score indicated significant correlations at the $p < .01$ level. To establish interrater reliability, two trained examiners scored 50 MIST protocols. Two-way, single measure intraclass correlation coefficients (ICC) for each trial code and error code ranged from .81 to .96, and perfect agreement was achieved for the Trial 7 score and error codes. Form A was administered to 30 adults (ages 19–82 years) with a 15-day gap and the stability coefficient of the PMT score was satisfactory at .78.

Convergent validity evidence was compiled by comparing the MIST with two items from the Rivermead Behavioral Memory Test (RBMT), because the test authors note that no other instrument measures PMT alone. The correlation between the MIST and the RBMT's two items was favorable (.80). The MIST was compared to the Mini-Mental State Examination, Second Edition with no significant correlations reported. The test authors used this comparison to support the validity of the MIST as a measure of memory with an intentional component, which differentiated it from instruments measuring general cognitive impairments. Construct validity evidence was supported by reporting studies conducted with clinical samples: Alzheimer's Disease, Acquired Brain Injury, Parkinson's Disease, Human Immunodeficiency Virus, Multiple Sclerosis, Schizophrenia, and Mild Cognitive Impairment. The test manual provides a few paragraphs for each clinical sample explaining how these individuals scored on the MIST as compared to nonclinical samples.

COMMENTARY. The MIST assessment provides an opportunity for clinicians to better understand an individual's prospective memory functioning. This instrument might be helpful in assessing treatment needs and evaluation of interventions used to improve PM. The MIST manual is comprehensive, and after thorough review, a trained clinician should be able to accurately administer the assessment. However, there are many details that require careful attention when administering and scoring this assessment. In particular, tracking errors and recording error code instructions are complicated. Further, the scoring procedures appear to be somewhat convoluted, with little empirical evidence to support the rationale for scoring methods. It will be helpful in future studies to show how the MIST predicts or relates to real-world applications of the assessment results. Existing clinical PM assessments offer a unique glimpse of how specific aspects of memory affect one's daily living functioning, and the MIST offers the first brief version of assessing these aspects.

SUMMARY. The MIST gives clinicians working with elder clients and others affected by memory impairment an efficient way to assess PM and thereby better understand what aspects of memory to attend to and how to plan treatment. The direct assessment approach of the MIST is supported by research as being superior to client self-report, but family or caregiver self-reports also provide a viable assessment option. Raskin (2009) provides an overview of MIST research in a special issue of the journal *Brain Impairment* (volume 10[1]) that examines the topic of prospective memory.

REVIEWERS' REFERENCE
Raskin, S. A. (2009). Memory for Intentions Screening Test: Psychometric properties and clinical evidence. *Brain Impairment, 10*, 23–33. doi:10.1375/brim.10.1.23

[106]

Michigan English Test.

Purpose: Designed to assess "general English language proficiency" by measuring "listening, reading, grammar, and vocabulary skills in personal, public, occupational, and educational contexts."
Population: Adolescents and adults at or above a secondary level of education.
Publication Dates: 2009-2011.
Acronym: MET.
Scores, 3: Section I: Listening, Section II: Reading and Grammar, Final Score.
Administration: Group.
Forms: 11 forms per year, one per month excluding December.
Price Data: Available from publisher.
Time: (135) minutes.
Comments: A paper-and-pencil test that is administered monthly, except December, only at authorized test centers.
Author: The University of Michigan.
Publisher: Cambridge-Michigan Language Assessments.

Review of the Michigan English Test by SANDRA T. ACOSTA, Assistant Professor of Bilingual Education, Educational Psychology, Texas A&M University, College Station, TX:

DESCRIPTION. The Michigan English Test (MET) was developed by Cambridge Michigan Language Assessments (CMLA) and is published by the University of Michigan English Language Institute (ELI-UM). The MET is a multilevel, international English proficiency assessment for nonnative English speakers. Although some proficiency assessments measure test takers' preparedness for

functioning linguistically in a particular setting (e.g., Test of English as a Foreign Language [TOEFL]), other assessments such as the MET assess test takers' global proficiency level (Madsen, 1983). In the case of the MET, English learners' (EL) test scores are mapped to the Common European Framework of Reference for Languages (CEFR) standards for English. The MET's target population is ELs, ranging in age from early secondary adolescents to post-secondary adults, with upper beginner to lower advanced English proficiency.

Using authentic American-English content drawn from educational, social, and business contexts, the MET consists of 135 items presented in a multiple-choice format with four answer options. The MET measures basic language skills–listening, reading, grammar, and vocabulary. The test comprises two sections: (a) Listening, and (b) Grammar and Reading Comprehension. Vocabulary is tested in both the Listening and Reading sections. The prerecorded listening section has three parts (60 items) and takes approximately 45 minutes to administer. Test takers hear short conversations between two people, followed by somewhat longer conversations, and finally four lectures or talks. The Grammar and Reading Comprehension section (90-minute administration time) consists of 25 questions and 50 questions, respectively. Reading Comprehension tasks feature four thematic units with three texts from real-life scenarios per unit. Texts are written in a variety of formats from flyers to research notes. Additionally, items in both listening and reading sections assess understanding at three levels: locally (i.e., at the sentence level; e.g., vocabulary knowledge), globally (e.g., main idea), and inferentially (e.g., inferring supporting details). The MET is paper-based and computer scored. All test items have the same scoring weight with no penalty for wrong answers. Test takers receive a score report from the University of Michigan (UM) that includes scaled scores (maximum of 80 points) for each section—Listening and Grammar/Reading Comprehension—and a total score for the two sections. Although score reports provide a CEFR proficiency level for each section, they do not provide corresponding CEFR proficiency levels for total scores. Score reports are valid for 2 years from the test administration date (MET Testing Program, 2011).

DEVELOPMENT. The MET is a test of receptive language skills that uses the CEFR, a reference document of proficiency standards for language learning and teaching established by the Council of Europe, to describe EL's language ability. The Council was founded in 1949 and is headquartered in Strasbourg, France.

The process of the MET's development and standardization occurred in two phases. The first phase, item development, followed the item and test guidelines published by CMLA (B. Dobson, personal communication, January 3, 2012). Additionally, Barbara Dobson, the assistant director of CMLA, provided a copy of the CMLA guidelines, a 1-page description of the item and test development process from item writing to trialing of assessment products. Although the MET item development process was not explicitly described in the CMLA guidelines, The Michigan English Test: 2012 Information Pack addressed fairness and topic bias in item content.

The second phase, standardization, included pilot testing, item analysis, and standard-setting (i.e., establishing the cut scores for the CEFR standards). The sample group (n = 3,279) took the MET in July 2008 at nine test centers in Colombia (Dobson, personal communication, January 3, 2012). Item response theory (IRT), a mathematical model applied to testing data, was used to analyze MET scores. IRT modeling of scores allows a more precise measurement of item difficulty and its relation to ability, in this case language proficiency (Bachman, 2004). The next step was mapping MET scores to the CEFR standards (i.e., proficiency levels).

In December 2008, a panel of experts or judges, representing the nine Colombian testing centers, met over a 3-day period in Cali, Colombia, to recommend cut scores from the pilot data. The expert panel comprised center personnel employed as English teachers, teacher trainers, academic directors, and academic advisors. To evaluate the scores, each judge received instruction in the CEFR proficiency standards (i.e., levels) and statistical information about the data (e.g., means, reliability indices). According to procedures outlined by the Council of Europe for CEFR standard setting, the expert panel's standards meeting was subsequently evaluated according to three categories of validation: procedural validation consisting of the meeting organization and instructions to the judges; internal validation consisting of the accuracy of the results (i.e., the cut scores for the CEFR proficiency standards); and external validation consisting of confirmation by an external source of the standard setting meeting outcomes, that

is, MET score ranges for each CEFR proficiency level. External validation of cut scores followed one of the alternatives accepted by the Council of Europe—comparing ratings of student proficiency levels by the academic director of one of the testing centers to the students' MET scores.

TECHNICAL.

Standardization. Reports differed on the pilot testing sample size. Although the CMLA reported 3,279 test takers, the ELI-UM reported that 660 test takers took the pilot test, MET Form A (Papageorgiou, 2010). Additionally, no descriptions of the sample's characteristics were reported (e.g., age, gender).

Reliability. Two types of reliability indices were reported in various MET technical reports published by ELI-UM. The first were reliability indices of judges' discrimination of CEFR standards descriptors; the second were IRT-based reliability indices of MET scores. The reliability evidence was generally high. For example, ELI-UM provided indices to support evidence of agreement among judges (coefficient alpha) and judges' consistency in cut score selection for each of the three CEFR proficiency levels (intraclass correlation [ICC] and Kendall's W). Indices ranged from good (W .79–.84) to high (ICC .98; alpha .98) in listening, grammar, reading, and vocabulary skills. Likewise, the intrajudge reliability evidence, reported as Spearman correlations, was reasonable and ranged from a low correlation of .62 to a high of .97 for all four basic language skills. In addition, ELI-UM reported monthly IRT-based reliability indices for MET scores for the period 2009–2010. These indices ranged from .90 to .93 and demonstrated high score reliability and consistency over the 2-year period.

Validity. There were gaps in the validity evidence. Procedural, internal, and external validation procedures supported the standard setting process and appeared adequate. However, descriptions of the MET item specification and development process were absent. In addition, MET technical reports published online did not incorporate a theoretical explication of the constructs.

COMMENTARY. The MET has two principal strengths. These are its alignment to the CEFR, which permits test score interpretation recognized worldwide, and the use of IRT as the analytical approach for modeling test scores. Conversely, the MET also has weaknesses related to the absence of a theoretical framework and information about item development and testing.

Theoretical framework. In the MET technical reports, there is no clearly articulated theoretical framework explicating the constructs measured by the MET and how those constructs are related and operationalized. Furthermore, there are inferences to receptive task performance as a predictor of productive skills. For example, in describing grammar cloze multiple-choice tasks as a type of recall cue, there is the following statement: "Each MET grammar item should elicit a 'tip-of-the-tongue' effect" (MET Testing Program, n.d., p. 6). Yet, no supporting empirical evidence is proffered for this claim. In a second example from the same document, the CEFR descriptors listed in the grammar subsection are descriptors for grammar accuracy (Council of Europe, 2001, p. 114, as cited in MET Testing Program, n.d.). Descriptors such as "uses some simple structures correctly" and "communicates with reasonable accuracy in familiar contexts" infer that receptive grammar performance predicts productive language skills (e.g., speaking). As a self-described high-stakes test (Papageorgiou, 2010), a possible consequence of this assumption could be the misuse of the MET resulting from misinterpretation of test results (e.g., over- or underestimating test takers' productive English language skills).

Item development and testing. As mentioned earlier, the CMLA does not explicitly describe the process of MET item development and testing. This omission represents a gap in the validity evidence. Another issue is the absence of information about IRT model fit. Although IRT analytical approaches offer advantages such as increased measurement precision, Bachman (2004) states that IRT models must be evaluated empirically by describing how well the model fits the data.

SUMMARY. The MET, a foreign language examination of American-English, measures and categorizes ELs' performance on receptive language tasks according to the CEFR proficiency standards. Test forms are generated monthly from test item banks, published, and sent to testing centers. I recommend the MET with reservations. Major concerns are gaps in specific validity evidence related to item development and testing and the lack of a theoretical framework. As a high-stakes test, implications for possible misuse of the MET include interpreting ELs' language ability too globally by inferring productive skills not evaluated by the MET.

REVIEWER'S REFERENCES

Bachman, L. F. (2004). *Statistical analyses for language assessment.* Cambridge, UK: Cambridge University Press.
Madsen, H. S. (1983). *Techniques in testing.* New York, NY: Oxford University Press.
MET Testing Program. (2011). *Michigan English Test (MET): 2012 Test administration report.* Ann Arbor, MI: Author.
MET Testing Program. (n.d.). *Michigan English Test: 2012 information pack.* Ann Arbor, MI: Author.
Papageorgiou, S. (2010). *Setting cut scores on the Common European Framework of Reference for the Michigan English Test.* Ann Arbor, MI: English Language Institute-University of Michigan.

Review of the Michigan English Test by MILDRED MURRAY-WARD, Professor of Education, Retired, California State University, Stanislaus, Turlock, CA:

DESCRIPTION. The Michigan English Test (MET) was developed by the University of Michigan in 2009. It is an assessment of English-language proficiency needed in a variety of North American English linguistic environments, including social, educational, and workplace contexts. The MET can be used as a final test after completion of English language courses and for evaluation for employment purposes, such as applying for a position or a promotion (Michigan English Test–MET Information Bulletin, 2011, page 3). In addition, the MET can be used as a "bridge" to a higher English proficiency level exam, but the Information Bulletin does not explain the authors' definition of a "bridge." The publisher also indicates a limitation of the test: The MET should not be used as a college admissions test in the United States, Canada, or the United Kingdom.

The MET is a 135-item multiple-choice test consisting of two sections: Listening (understanding social, educational, and workplace conversations) and Reading and Grammar (grammar; understanding social, educational, and workplace contexts in written materials). Vocabulary is assessed within the Listening and Reading and Grammar sections. The two sections result in scaled scores from 0 to 80 based on IRT ability estimates on all test items. The scores are linked to proficiency levels contained in the Common European Framework of Reference (CEFR). Although the general content of the test is described in the MET Information Bulletin, no information is provided on the theory of language development underlying selection of tasks nor is a blueprint or detailed origins of content for topics covered by items provided by the test developers.

Total examination time is 2 hours and 15 minutes. Responses to the multiple-choice items are recorded on MET answer sheets, with no penalty for guessing. The MET is offered every month except December at authorized test centers in several countries and is scored by the University of Michigan. Scores are available 4 weeks after test administration, and are valid for 2 years. The scores for the two test sections are used to place the examinee on a continuum of language proficiency tied to the CEFR. In addition, a final score consists of the sum of the two scores; however, no CEFR interpretations are offered for the total score. The CEFR contains six levels ranging from A1 to A2 (Basic User), B1 to B2 (Independent User), and C1 to C2 (Proficient User). The MET items fall within A1 to C2, with best discrimination between B1 and B2. The MET Testing Program offers recommendations for using the MET for decision making. These include consideration of changes in proficiency levels due to frequency of use of English and knowledge of a professional field and general intellect. However, no guidance as to how to judge the impact of these factors on score use or interpretation is offered.

The MET publishes an Information Bulletin, describing the test and scoring procedures. It can also be explored by visiting the MET website: www. lsa.umich.edu/eli/testing/met. The website contains general information, test background, sample items, the technical description of standard setting for the CEFR levels, and a complete 135-item sample test.

DEVELOPMENT. The MET uses an item bank that results in new test forms at every administration. The multiple-choice items use four options and the sample items found in the Michigan English Test–MET: Sample Test Form A follow accepted rules for quality multiple-choice item construction. The Michigan English Test–MET: Test Administration Report 2010 indicates that the test items are written to specific guidelines, and are pretested to assure that items work properly. However, no information as to the guidelines and standards used to judge proper item functioning or descriptions of the content base or blueprint are offered in the MET materials. The Michigan English Test–MET: Setting Cut Scores on the Common European Framework of Reference for the Michigan English Test technical report provides a detailed description of the process of setting cut scores for the CEFR levels and is discussed in detail below.

The 0-to-80-point scaled score uses a mathematical model based on Item Response Theory. However, the document on setting cut scores states that the scores are based on a scaled score range from 0 to 100 reported to examinees. No information on how this 0 to 100 scaled score has been transformed to the 0 to 80 scaled scores reported to students is provided.

TECHNICAL. Because the MET is an item bank, no standardization of a specific set of score forms was completed. However, information on item quality is available through the Michigan English Test–MET: Test Administration Report 2010 and the Michigan English Test–MET: Setting Cut Scores on the Common European Framework of Reference for the Michigan English Test technical report.

Information on validity of interpretation of test scores against the CEFR criteria is available in the MET document on setting cut scores, and information on the sample of examinees assessed in a 2010 IRT reliability study of items used in that year are found in the MET Test Administration Report for 2010. In the 2010 reliability study, a total of 6,767 examinees completed the MET at test centers in Colombia, Brazil, and Chile. Of that group, approximately 46% were male and 53% were female. The examinees' ages ranged from 12-years-or-younger, to 40-or-more-years, with the vast majority in the ranges of 17–19, 20–22, 23–25, and 26–29 years. Most of these persons attained scores at the B1 or B2 levels (Intermediate CEFR levels) on both the Listening and the Reading and Grammar Sections. No statements of significance, interpretation, or discussion of these data were offered.

Because the scores of the MET are interpreted against the CEFR criteria, a major validity activity of the test creators was construction of cut scores for the CEFR proficiency levels. The process of setting cut scores attended to procedural validity (examining procedures used), internal validity (accuracy and consistency of the standard setting results), and external validity (evidence from independent sources to support the standard setting results). The standard setting followed a three part process following the methods proposed by Angoff (1971) and others. In the first part of this process, the 13 judges or panelists from the nine Bi-national Centers in Colombia where the MET is administered, led by a facilitator from the University of Michigan English Language Institute, were asked to think of 100 borderline examinees for each of three CEFR levels associated with the center-most levels of performance (i.e., those near the borders of A2 and B1, B1 and B2, and B2 and C1). In preparation for this task, the judges were trained in the CEFR system by classifying a number of reading, vocabulary, and grammar sentence level descriptors from the CEFR. The judges were asked to sort the statements into CEFR levels and then estimate the numbers of borderline examinees who could answer the items correctly. Using this process, the judges then classified the reading, grammar, vocabulary, and listening items that had been assigned a correct CEFR level. When the median level assignments did not agree with the assigned level or the range of judgments was three or more levels, the group discussed the chosen levels.

The judges used a two-step process for practice with CEFR level scores. In Step 1, the judges took the MET and then estimated the percentage of examinees who would pass the item at each of three transition points in the CEFR scale–A2/B1, B1/B2, and B2/C1. The judges calculated an overall proportion passing for the level. In the second step, the judges were presented with statistics for each of the items they had just examined. These statistics included number of examinees, number of items, mean score, standard deviation, maximum and minimum score, coefficient alpha, facility and point-biserial correlations of each item, and histograms of score distributions. The judges were then asked to re-examine their estimates in light of the data and were allowed to retain or to change those estimates. The overall results indicated that the judges were able to place items in the correct order, with all but one Spearman correlation coefficient for individual judges' estimates and actual ratings in the .69 to .97 range. Interrater agreement among the judges was examined through the intraclass correlation coefficient and Kendall's W, yielding values of .98 and .79 to .84 for the four test areas.

Actual cut scores were set using the Step 2 cut scores, resulting in Level B1, B2, and C1 cuts for both sections of the MET. These scores were then examined for method and decision consistency. Method consistency was explored using the standard error of judgment; the error estimate was found to be too high due to extreme ratings. Removal of extreme ratings adjusted the cut scores by small amounts. Decision consistency was explored through an agreement coefficient, and Kappa values showed good agreement. Reasonableness of the cut scores was explored using external criteria: the correlation of the judges' estimates with estimates from a test center's independent classification of 302 examinees. The MET developers stated that the percentages of correct classification were acceptable; however, Pearson correlations for Sections I and II of the MET were moderate for exact classifications and at 96% for Section I and 87% for Section II for those

exact or one level difference. The test authors did not explore the issue of false positives or negatives in this high-stakes test in which course passage or employment decisions could be affected by an examinee's classification. Interestingly, after the process of setting the cut scores, the test authors indicated that additional IRT analyses of 2009 live administrations resulted in a change in cut scores to present levels. No explanation or rationale for these changes was offered by the test authors. Furthermore, the entire process involved a scaled score ranging from 0–100. The final scaled scores were reported on a scale of 0–80. No explanations for the change or the process of converting scores to this new scale were provided by the test publisher.

Reliability. Reliability of the MET was explored through reliability estimates of results of IRT-based reliability coefficients and standard errors of measurement (*SEM*s) for monthly administrations of the MET in 2010. The reliability coefficients for the 11 test administrations ranged from .91 to .93 for Section I: Listening. *SEM*s for this section ranged from .24 to .35. For Section II: Reading and Grammar, the reliability coefficients varied from .91 to .93, with *SEM*s of .18 to .31. In this reviewer's opinion, these reliability estimates are at highly acceptable levels for individual test interpretations.

In addition to item reliability, estimates of inter- and intrajudge reliability during the cut score setting activities revealed acceptable to strong reliabilities. The interjudge reliability was explored using decision consistency, with agreement coefficients for each CEFR level ranging from .88 to .97 for Section I and .86 to .95 for Section II. Intrajudge reliability was explored with correlations between the mean judge ratings and estimates of empirical difficulty. The correlations were calculated at the first and second round of cut score setting. The resulting Spearman rho coefficients for Section I were .42 for Round 1 and .83 for Round 2. The rho coefficients for Section II were .73 and .92, respectively. These Round 2 coefficients were quite strong.

COMMENTARY. The MET is a multiple-choice test for English-language development used in various contexts. The test can be used to determine levels of English-language proficiency and as a tool for employment selection. The instrument uses CEFR proficiency levels, a clear and well-documented system of language development. The MET provides scaled scores for both Section I: Listening and Section II: Reading and Grammar. The scaled scores are based on a scale from 0 to 80 and report the examinee's placement on the CEFR continuum of English-language proficiency. In addition, the examinees receive a total score from the two sections. Interestingly, the cut scores described in the MET cut score setting document were established and changed once during the process and a final time after the process was completed. However, the rationale for the final change in cut scores was not discussed. Furthermore, the initial scaled score ranged from 0–100 and was changed to a range of 0–80. No explanation for this change was provided by the test authors. The development, administration, and interpretation of the test scores were clearly described. However, the overall description of and rationale for item content in the two test sections were not provided. The overall data reported for the 2010 administrations covered three countries and include statistics on gender and ages of the groups. Information about the examinees' education levels and English-language experiences, which could be factors in valid examinee classifications, was not provided.

A number of studies were conducted to explore the technical qualities of the MET. The MET cut score setting process was complex and well-documented. The MET also displayed strong reliability for the indices for the two sections' items, as well as strong inter- and intrajudge reliabilities. Validity studies of the cut scores were extensive and involved comparison of classifications with those of an independent judge at the MET test center. However, item development data and content validity studies were not discussed.

SUMMARY. Overall, the MET is a test of English-language proficiency for adults from non-English-speaking countries. The test is used for determination of examinee success in English courses and as a tool to determine English proficiency for the North American work environment. The test is administered at authorized MET test centers and scored at the University of Michigan. The test's development was described in the publisher's materials. The MET exhibits good technical qualities with strong to moderate reliabilities for the test forms administered over 1 year. The test authors completed a detailed and well-described cut score setting process but did not clarify the rationale for or sources of item content. More importantly, the test developer changed the cut scores for each CEFR level and the scaled score ranges from 0–100 during development to 0–80 in the final form. There were no explanations for these changes.

Several cautions in using the MET should be noted. First, two major problems with the score interpretation should be noted: (a) the change in the scaled score range and the lack of discussion about possible impacts using the CEFR score continuum, and (b) the lack of specific item content descriptions. Second, as with all life decisions such as completion of English programs and eligibility for employment decisions, use of the MET should be accompanied by multiple indicators and data sources.

[107]

The MLR Visual Diagnostic Skills Test.

Purpose: Designed to "provide an objective measure of one's ability to identify common technical-physical performance problems and to prescribe appropriate remedies."
Population: Undergraduate through graduate school.
Publication Dates: 1983–2008.
Scores: Total score only.
Subtests, 2: Woodwind, Brass.
Administration: Group.
Price Data, 2010: $50 per Visual Diagnostic Skills Test CD-ROM, including composite test, brass subtest, woodwind subtest, test manual, and answer sheets.
Time: (45) minutes.
Comments: This test can be used as a pre-test/post-test companion to the Visual Diagnostic Skills Program; the two additional subtests (Woodwind, Brass) are provided to accommodate pretest/posttest visual diagnostic skills assessment but no studies have been undertaken to determine the subtests' reliability, content validity, and construct validity.
Authors: James O. Froseth and John R. Woods.
Publisher: GIA Publications, Inc.

Review of the MLR Visual Diagnostic Skills Test by MARY L. GARNER, Professor of Mathematics, Kennesaw State University, Kennesaw, GA:

DESCRIPTION. The MLR Visual Diagnostic Skills Test is designed to measure prospective music teachers' ability to identify common problems in beginning instrument students' techniques in playing brass and woodwind instruments, specifically the trumpet, trombone, flute, clarinet, saxophone, and horn. The test consists of 32 slides; each slide shows a series of images of a student playing an instrument and demonstrating one particular problem in technique. Each slide is associated with two multiple-choice questions, one in which the respondent identifies the problem and another in which the respondent chooses an appropriate remedy for the problem. As illustrated in the practice test on the administration CD, there are usually five problem choices, which vary slightly according to the instrument, and five possible remedies after the problem is identified. Remedies also vary slightly according to the problem and instrument.

No special skills are required for test administration. Answer sheets, test manual, and test are provided on a CD-ROM. The test is delivered by running the slide show on a computer. The slide show begins with an explanation of the purpose of the test; two practice items are then presented with solutions explained. Each student image (sometimes with multiple perspectives) is shown for 12 seconds; the possible problems and remedies are shown for 20 seconds. The respondent records the letter indicating the problem and the number indicating the remedy on an answer sheet. There are 16 woodwind items, including 9 clarinet, 2 flute, and 5 saxophone. There are 16 brass items, including 4 trumpet, 7 trombone, and 5 horn. Each item is scored 0 if the incorrect problem is chosen, 1 if the correct problem is chosen but an incorrect remedy is chosen, and 2 if the correct problem and correct remedy are chosen. The total possible score is 64. The slide show requires approximately 35 minutes. The CD also includes two 16-item subtests, one for woodwind items only and one for brass items only.

DEVELOPMENT. There is a rich history of scholarship associated with the test. Research began in the 1970s at the University of Michigan with observations of novice instrumental music education students assigned to teach elementary students in Ann Arbor. These observations led to the development of "Visual Diagnostic Skills (Training) Programs" for selected wind instruments, violin, and percussion. James O. Froseth published *Introducing the Instruments* in 1976 and the *MLR Teacher Education Series: Visual Diagnostic Skills Program for Flute, Clarinet, Alto Saxophone, Trumpet, Horn, and Trombone* in 1978. The program was revised in 2007 with the publication of *Visual Diagnostic Skills Program, Woodwind and Visual Diagnostic Skills Program, Brass* by James O. Froseth and Michael T. Hopkins in 2007. In 1975 and 1976, initial versions of the test, based on the Visual Diagnostic Skills Programs, were administered to graduate and undergraduate students at the University of Michigan, the Ohio State University, and Bowling Green State University. Various revisions were made to the test as a result of these studies.

Three experts in the field of elementary education (public school teachers) were asked to judge each problem by estimating how many typical beginning instrumental students would be likely to demonstrate the problem according to the following scale: (1) Few students, (2) Less than half, (3) About half, (4) Many, and (5) All. Items with a score of 2.65 or less were eliminated. There is no rationale provided for the cutoff score. The problems on the current, final version of the test had a mean rating of 3.92 with a range of 3.00 to 5.00.

The test was also presented to a panel of three university music education faculty who were asked to score the problem according to the following scale: (1) An inadequate visual representation, (2) an adequate visual representation, or (3) an excellent visual representation. All items with a rating of less than 2.00 were eliminated. The items on the current, final version of the test had a mean rating of 2.79 with a range of 2.00 to 3.00. Twenty items received a mean score of 3.00.

Items were also reviewed by two faculty members of the Performance Department at the Ohio State University, one a woodwind specialist and the other a brass specialist. Each faculty member rated the remedies for the problems as (1) Unacceptable remedy, (2) Acceptable remedy, or (3) Excellent remedy. Items with a mean rating less than 2.00 were eliminated. The items on the current, final version of the test had a mean rating of 2.79 with a range of 2.00 to 3.00. Twenty-one remedies were rated excellent (3.00) by both faculty members.

TECHNICAL. The test was administered initially to 60 undergraduate students at the Ohio State University during the Spring quarter of 1977. The authors provide an item difficulty index (percentage answering incorrectly) and item discrimination index (difference between upper quartile and lower quartile answering correctly) for all 64 multiple-choice questions based on this administration of the test. The item difficulty ranges from .02 to .86 and item discrimination ranges from .07 to .66.

Norms in the form of percentile ranks for scores 1 to 64 are provided for four populations: a population of 237 undergraduate students before training with the MLR Visual Diagnostic Skills Programs; a population of 203 undergraduate students after training; a population of 334 graduate students before training; and a population of 201 graduate students after training. The undergraduates were students from the University of Michigan, the Ohio State University, and the Eastman School of Music, during the period from 1977 to 1982. The graduate students were workshop participants or students enrolled in graduate courses at colleges in Ohio, Michigan, Pennsylvania, Wisconsin, Kentucky, Texas, Illinois, Maryland, and New York during the period from 1977 to 1982. The authors warn that the populations do not represent a scientific sampling. The test appears to perform as expected, with a highest score of 47 representing the 99th percentile before training and a highest score of 54 representing the 99th percentile after training among undergraduates. The highest score of 52 represents the 99th percentile before training and a highest score of 62 represents 99th percentile after training among graduate students.

As evidence for reliability of the test, the authors present a study in which the test was administered to 77 undergraduate students at the Ohio State University and again after 1 week. The correlation between test and retest scores was .80; the mean pretest score was 31.13 and mean posttest score was 36.85. No other evidence of reliability is provided.

The test is designed to "provide an objective measure of one's ability to identify common technical-physical performance problems and to prescribe appropriate remedies" (manual, p. 6). Evidence for the content validity of the test is provided by the evaluations of three public school teachers, several music education faculty members, and two performance faculty members as described above in "Development." The major assumption underlying use of the test is that teachers who score well on the test would be more able to identify and remedy technical-physical performance problems in their students. Evidence for the validity of this use of the test is provided through a study, conducted in 1977, in which 20 elementary instrumental music teachers' scores on the test were compared with ratings of their students' performance behaviors. A significant correlation of .64 was found between teacher scores and student scores.

Evidence for the validity of the test is also provided in a study showing that practice and training using the Visual Diagnostic Skills Program improved test scores significantly. In this study in 1977, pretest scores were compared with posttest scores of a group of 18 instrumental music teachers attending a workshop at the University of Michigan. The pretest mean was 30.50 and the posttest mean was 43.27.

Norms in the form of percentile ranks for the 16-item woodwind subtest and the 16-item brass subtest are also provided, but no further analysis of the subtests is provided.

COMMENTARY. The development and testing of the MLR Visual Diagnostic Skills Test involved an impressive collaboration between a variety of schools involved in educating music teachers. Furthermore, the test has a solid foundation in a research-based pedagogical methodology—the Visual Diagnostic Skills Program. It is clear, however, that any music education program could use the test even if the Visual Diagnostic Skills Program is not part of the curriculum. The test is very easy to administer and requires only printing answer sheets and showing a slide show; the slide show provides an introduction to the test and very clear instructions.

The authors have a variety of studies showing the validity of the test including a study of the relationship between actual student instrumental performance and teachers' scores on the test; this study, conducted in the 1970s, would serve as a model today in the much bigger debate about using student performance to judge teacher quality. The norms provided, although not based on a random sampling of the population, are mostly appropriate. It would have been useful to see the distribution of scores on the various administrations of the test. In addition, recall that each item (or image of a student playing an instrument) had two associated questions, one about the problem and one about the remedy. The score on the remedy is not independent of the score on the problem; hence, it would have been useful to report item difficulties (percentage incorrect) and item discrimination conditional on getting the problem correct.

Analysis of the test is lacking in certain areas. The domain from which the items are taken is not clearly delineated in the test manual. In other words, the authors do not answer the question: What does the domain of all technical-physical performance problems look like and how are the problems chosen for this test representative of that domain? In addition, analysis of the test should take into account the structure of the test and should analyze the test as 32 rather than 64 items, each with a rating scale of 0 to 2. No analysis is provided regarding variability of performance on the test according to instrument type. No analysis of differential item functioning is provided across gender or cultural group. The populations of students who were administered the tests are not adequately described; it is implied but not stated that all are music education students.

SUMMARY. The MLR Visual Diagnostic Skills Test has been used since the 1970s to measure the ability of undergraduate and graduate music education students to identify problems and remedies for common technical-physical performance problems in playing woodwind and brass instruments. Everything needed for the test is provided on a CD-ROM and the test is very easy to administer and score. Although the test is based on the Visual Diagnostic Skills Program (Froseth, 1978; Froseth & Hopkins, 2007a & 2007b), it appears to be valid for any program teaching skills necessary for instrumental instruction. The test manual is well-written and easy to understand, with percentile norms provided for undergraduate and graduate students. Some convincing evidence is provided for reliability and validity of the test. Analysis of the test would be enhanced by more thorough descriptions of the domain, the populations who were administered the test, the performance of the rating scale, and differential item functioning.

REVIEWER'S REFERENCES

Froseth, J. O. (1978). *MLR teaching education series: Visual diagnostic skills program for flute, clarinet, alto saxophone, trumpet, horn, and trombone.* Chicago, IL: G.I.A. Publications, Inc.

Froseth, J. O. & Hopkins, M. T. (2007a). *Visual diagnostic skills program, woodwind.* Chicago, IL: G.I.A. Publications, Inc.

Froseth, J. O., & Hopkins, M. T. (2007b). *Visual diagnostic skills program, brass.* Chicago, IL: G.I.A. Publications, Inc.

Review of the MLR Visual Diagnostic Skills Test by CHRISTOPHER JOHNSON, Professor of Music Education and Music Therapy and Director, Music Research Institute, The University of Kansas, Lawrence, KS:

DESCRIPTION. The MLR Visual Diagnostic Skills Test is a 32-item test administered by playing a movie file on a compact disc and completing an answer sheet. As the manual describes: "Test items include common performance problems on flute, clarinet, saxophone, trumpet, trombone, and horn. Performance problems are limited to technical-physical behaviors including posture, instrument position, hand position, embouchure, and mouthpiece placement" (p. 6). All the test items are presented visually on 35mm slides and all the test items contain two parts. "First, a slide demonstrating a specific performance problem is projected for twelve seconds. Then, a second slide presents an answer format which requires two responses: 1) identification of the problem, and 2) selection of the appropriate remedy. The respondent is given twenty seconds to record responses on an answer sheet" (manual, p. 6).

All testing materials (manual, answer keys, and answer sheets) come in PDF files on the same CD-ROM. It is presumed that if one purchases the test, one is free to print all materials contained on the disc. The tests themselves are separate files and the movies are in QuickTime Movie format. There are three versions of the test. There is a woodwind subtest, a brass subtest, and a full test that sequences the two subtests.

The CD-ROM is a disc with the 10 necessary files. It does not have any files built to install the test or any aspects of the test to one's computer. Purchasers simply put the disc in the computer and access the necessary files; there is no installation needed. Further, the files use standard technologies, so that all the test items can be played on almost any modern computer.

There is no training required to administer the product. It is feasible that any interested person could administer and grade the test. The test is a paper-and-pencil format and the answer sheets must be hand graded. The instructions for test administration and grading are in the manual. Instructions for the test takers are imbedded in the movies. Each of the subtests is 19 minutes long and contains 16 test items. The full test is 33 minutes and 10 seconds long and contains all 32 items.

It should be noted that the CD-ROM case references a companion Visual Diagnostic Skills Program for brass and woodwind instruments; that program was not provided to this reviewer. However, this test covers rather common materials to instrumental music education, and can easily be utilized without the aforementioned program.

DEVELOPMENT. The development of this test began in the 1970s with slides of six elementary school children modeling common mistakes found with people playing flute, clarinet, saxophone, trumpet, trombone, and horn. Original versions of the test used slides accompanied by a cassette tape in the presentation.

The first pilot test utilized the services of 16 graduate students. This administration occurred in the summer of 1975. Testing times and material edits occurred as a result of this pilot. The second pilot test occurred later that summer at a neighboring university. This time, 10 graduate students completed the test. It was determined that the quickened timing of the pictures was too quick, and verbiage on the answer slides was again shortened.

A third pilot was conducted. This time the test was administered three times. The first was in the summer of 1975 at another neighboring Big Ten institution. A total of 24 graduate students participated in this administration. Two more administrations took place at the original two schools, but with undergraduate students and during the regular school year. These administrations resulted in another answer sheet format change, as well as the elimination of nondiscriminating test slides.

The final pilot study occurred in the spring of 1976 with 22 music majors. Results of this administration created the test as it has existed in its analog format ever since.

TECHNICAL. Reliability of the MLR Visual Diagnostic Skills Test was established via 77 undergraduate students at the Ohio State University using a test-retest paradigm. The manual describes how testing occurred under matched conditions and environments separated by one week's time. The reliability coefficient of the two administrations was .80.

Content validity was established in three phases. The first phase used experts in the field of elementary instrumental education. They reviewed the pictures and offered assessments on how typical the problems illustrated were among beginning instrumental students. Only problems estimated to be representative of "about half" of the typical students or more were kept. In the second phase, a panel of music education faculty reviewed the slides to assess the adequacy of the visual representation. Only slides that were deemed to be adequate representations were retained. In the third phase, performance faculty determined the remedy for each test item as being pedagogically acceptable or not. Only items deemed acceptable or better were retained. The final aspect pertaining to content validity was an item analysis. Results of the item difficulty analysis are given in the manual. Further, no inversely discriminating or nondiscriminating items were retained.

Construct validity was determined in two ways. The first was that experienced teachers took the MLR Visual Diagnostic Skills Test. Ten randomly selected students from each of the 10 teachers' classes were then auditioned. Performance scores from each of those students were compared to their respective teacher's test scores, and a correlational score of .64 was obtained. The second method of establishing construct validity was that students were given the MLR Visual Diagnostic Skills Test as a pretest, given instruction in visual identification of beginning instrumentalist errors, and then took the posttest. Significant gains were noted.

COMMENTARY. The MLR Visual Diagnostic Skills Test is the only test of its kind to the best of this reviewer's knowledge. The CD-ROM is easy to use. The files are clean and self-explanatory. The instructions for administering the test are clear and easy to follow. The answer sheets are likewise very easy to understand. The authors also make it very clear what this test does and does not do—it measures visual skills in identifying common instrument performance problems.

The test itself is rather dated. The pictures of the students look very much like the time period in which they were created—the 1970s. Also, the graphics of the testing movie are photos of the pieces of paper still in what appears to be the original testing booklet. There was no effort made to update the testing materials, even with modern graphics or slides. That having been said, for the purpose of what this test serves, there is probably little benefit to do any updating. How to teach a beginning player to hold the clarinet has not changed in the past 100 years, much less the past 30–40. And though the pages of text could be made snazzier, it would not be of much functional help.

In the manual, the authors do offer a snapshot of norms for the test. However, it should also be noted that the authors normed this test using a very specific, convenience sample, and that these scores should be taken as less than completely scientific, but more so as general reference.

SUMMARY. The MLR Visual Diagnostic Skills Test is the only test this reviewer knows of that examines the visual diagnostic aspects of instrumental music instruction. The pictures are dated, but still relevant. The manual is very good and extremely informative, as are the other included materials. The test administration instructions are clear. The CD-ROM presentation makes this test infinitely usable in any number of venues. This test has a very narrow, specific purpose, but all evidence indicates that it measures those aspects effectively.

[108]

Modified Wisconsin Card Sorting Test.

Purpose: Designed "to assess problem solving and the ability to shift cognitive strategies in response to changing environmental contingencies."

Population: Ages 18–92.

Publication Date: 2010.

Acronym: M-WCST.

Scores, 5: Number of Categories Correct, Number of Perseverative Errors, Number of Total Errors, Percent of Perseverative Errors, Executive Function Composite.

Administration: Individual.

Price Data, 2013: $240 per introductory kit including professional manual (102 pages), 50 record forms, and one card deck; $48 per 25 record forms; $68 per card deck; $90 per professional manual.

Time: (10-15) minutes.

Comments: A modification of the original Wisconsin Card Sorting Test that eliminates all 80 cards from the original 128-card deck that share more than one attribute with a stimulus card.

Author: David J. Schretlen.

Publisher: Psychological Assessment Resources, Inc.

Review of the Modified Wisconsin Card Sorting Test by ANITA M. HUBLEY, Professor of Measurement, Evaluation, and Research Methodology, University of British Columbia, Vancouver, British Columbia, Canada:

DESCRIPTION. The Modified Wisconsin Card Sorting Test (M-WCST) is one of several modifications of the Wisconsin Card Sorting Test (WCST; Heaton, Chelune, Talley, Kay, & Curtiss, 1993; 14:420). As a measure of executive function, it "provides information about an examinee's abstract reasoning ability and ability to shift cognitive strategies" (manual, p. 11).

Examinees are presented with a deck of 48 response cards with symbols varying in form (triangles, stars, circles, crosses), color (red, blue, yellow, green), and number (from 1 to 4) that they must sort under one of four key cards (four blue circles, three yellow crosses, two green stars, or one red triangle) according to rules they must figure out. Response cards are presented in a specific order. Examinees are told whether each response is correct or incorrect. Whichever rule/category (i.e., color, form, number) an examinee uses first is treated as correct; the second category used is also treated as correct as long as it differs from the first category, and the third category must be the remaining one. The subsequent three categories must follow the same order as the first three categories. The examiner records this order and the category used for each response. Consecutive correct responses within each category are numbered; after each set of six consecutive correct responses, the examinee is told that the rule has changed. The test is completed when either (a) all six sorting categories have been completed correctly, or (b) the entire deck of cards has been sorted. Administration time is 10–15 minutes.

Four primary scores are computed: Number of Categories Correct (i.e., number of sequences of six consecutive correct responses), Number of Total

Errors, Number of Perseverative Errors, and Percent of Perseverative Errors. Perseverative errors occur when the examinee incorrectly uses the same category as the immediately preceding response. Raw scores can be converted to T-scores and percentile ranks based on sex, age (14 groups), and education (four levels) using tables in the test manual. If the Calibrated Neuropsychological Normative System Software Portfolio (CNNS-SP; 19:25) is used to obtain norms, one can choose from among eight prediction models based on various combinations of sex, age, education, race, and Hopkins Adult Reading Test score. An Executive Function Composite score, which is the sum of the T-scores for the Number of Categories Correct and the Number of Perseverative Errors can be computed and presented as a standard score and a percentile rank. Qualitative labels also are available for all scores. Scoring is estimated to take 2–3 minutes. The test manual contains examples of recording procedures and scoring. Two case examples also are provided.

DEVELOPMENT. Nelson (1976) modified the WCST to remove ambiguity in scoring perseveration, simplify the test (particularly for older examinees), and reduce examinees' frustration and noncompliance. Specifically, she removed any response card that shared more than one rule with a key card, altered the requirement that sorting occur in order from color to shape to number, explicitly informed the respondent when a rule changed, and reduced the criterion from 10 to six consecutive correct responses before changing rules. As a result, the number of response cards was reduced from 128 to 48 (i.e., two identical decks of 24 cards), the test administration time is shortened, respondent frustration and fatigue are reduced, and both administration and scoring of the test are simplified.

TECHNICAL. The normative sample consists of 323 adults (56.3% women); the age range is unclear but appears to be 18 to 92 years. It is impressive that this sample underwent brain magnetic resonance imaging (MRI scans), blood tests, physical and neurological examinations, psychiatric interviews, and cognitive testing. The normative sample is small, predominantly White, relatively highly educated, and geographically limited. Norms are presented in 112 tables in combinations of 14 age groups and four educational levels by sex, which suggests, on average, fewer than three individuals form the basis of each table. The exact number, age, and years of education of individuals per normative grouping is not provided. No rationale is provided for the demographic variables used in presenting the norms; previous research suggests that M-WCST scores are affected by age, education, and intelligence, but not sex (e.g., de Zubicaray, Smith, Chalk, & Semple, 1998, Lineweaver, Bondi, Thomas, & Salmon, 1999; Obonsawin et al., 1999).

Test-retest estimates of reliability ranged from .26 to .49 across seven M-WCST scores in older adults after a minimum 6-month (M = 7.47 months) period, despite MRI and neurological retesting to confirm their healthy status at retest (de Zubicaray et al., 1998). Lineweaver et al. (1999) reported stability coefficients ranging from .46 to .64 for number of categories correct and numbers of perseverative and nonperseverative errors in middle-aged and older adults after a 2-year period, despite neurological retesting to confirm their healthy status at retest. Reliable change indices indicated that, in order for significant change to occur across two assessments, the number of categories completed, number of perseverative errors, and number of nonperseverative errors must differ by more than 2, 6, and 10, respectively. Only nonperseverative errors appeared to be sensitive to practice effects (Lineweaver et al., 1999). Bird, Papadopoulou, Ricciardelli, Rossor, and Cipolotti (2004) found that stability coefficients ranged from .16 to .38 for number of categories correct and numbers of perseverative and total errors in healthy middle-aged and older adults after a 1-month period. Finally, the M-WCST manual reports an Executive Function Composite test-retest reliability estimate of .50 over 5.5 years in a standardization subsample. Test-retest intervals in these reliability studies are generally too long. Intervals should be long enough that recall of responses or practice effects are minimized but short enough that real changes in the underlying construct(s) have not occurred. Current reliability estimates for M-WCST scores are inadequate; test users must be aware of the notable error that is apparent across testing sessions and consider this when determining whether real change has occurred over time. Reliability information is also poorly presented in the test manual. Data from only two studies are presented with no information provided about the samples on which this evidence is based. Further, a reliability estimate is provided for the Executive Function Composite score but not for any other available scores.

Three main forms of validation evidence are provided in the test manual: comparisons of the sensitivity of the M-WCST to that of the WCST, correlations with measures of cognitive ability, and comparisons of M-WCST performance among various clinical groups or with a control group. The test manual is somewhat selective in its reporting, but generally the results are mixed in terms of the sensitivity of the M-WCST relative to that of the WCST and depend on the sample being studied and the scores used.

Using the standardization sample as well as a pooled sample that also included "324 adults with significant medical conditions or psychiatric disorders" (manual, p. 21), both the Number of Categories Correct and Number of Perseverative Errors correlated moderately and most strongly with Trail Making Test Part B scores, followed by Brief Test of Attention (15:39) total scores. Weaker correlations were found with mental status, working memory and attention, verbal fluency, facial discrimination, visuo-constructional ability, and explicit memory scores. Although these correlations might provide some convergent and discriminant evidence, they would have been more convincing if a strong theoretical rationale had been presented in advance hypothesizing expected relationships (e.g., nomological network) and reliability estimates had been reported for all measures.

Finally, numerous studies are presented in the test manual to show one or more M-WCST scores distinguish either healthy controls from clinical samples or between individuals with and without different clinical conditions. It is important to distinguish between (a) validation research, and (b) clinical research conducted to determine whether groups differ on a supposed measure of executive functioning. In known-groups validation studies, for example, a measure is evaluated by determining whether it is able to distinguish between groups that are already well known to differ on the construct of interest. A single study cannot serve both purposes. Most, if not all, of the studies cited in the test manual address the purpose of clinical, rather than validation, research. There has long been evidence suggesting that card sorting tests do not discriminate well between patients with frontal and nonfrontal lesions (e.g., Reitan & Wolfson, 1994; van den Broek, Bradshaw, & Szabadi, 1993); this evidence needs to be appropriately addressed in the test manual.

COMMENTARY. The key strength of the M-WCST is that it improves administration and scoring issues identified by Nelson (1976) with the WCST. The key weaknesses are the normative sample, test manual, and psychometric evidence. The normative sample of 323 is small given the 112 (sex by age by education) groups for which norms are provided and is not representative of the U.S. population in terms of geography, educational level, and race. Test users should also consider normative data provided by Lineweaver et al. (1999), Obonsawin et al. (1999), and Caffarra et al. (2004), although these studies also have their faults in terms of sample size, sample composition, or consideration of demographic factors.

The test manual appears to have been compiled quickly with more attention paid to presenting norms and getting the test on the market than assisting the test user in understanding the benefits of the M-WCST over other available card sorting tests, providing a rationale for decisions made in the test, clarifying the test instructions, and providing a thorough, well-considered, and clearly presented review of reliability and validity evidence to support inferences made from the test. For example, the response cards for the M-WCST are presented in a particular order, but the test manual does not make clear why this order differs from that presented in de Zubicaray et al.'s (1998) standardization and does not follow the WCST rule of no two consecutive response cards having the same color, form, or number. No explanation is given for why four scores were selected over others (see Cianchetti, Corona, Foscoliano, Contu, & Sannio-Fancello, 2007; van den Broek et al., 1993). An Executive Function Composite score is introduced, but neither its meaning nor the rationale behind combining T-scores for the Number of Categories Correct and the Number of Perseverative Errors to produce it is presented. M-WCST instructions, taken from Nelson (1976), do not make it clear to the new examiner that response cards are matched one at a time to one of the stimulus cards (as opposed to each of the four stimulus cards at once) and assume knowledge of WCST procedures. Also, the instructions suggest to the examinee that a different rule must be found each time, which can be a problem when examinees reach the fourth category and rules must be repeated. The standardized instructions provided by de Zubicaray et al. (1998) are much clearer.

Overall, reliability estimates for M-WCST scores are inadequate and do not support the use of the test, particularly over time. However, additional test-retest reliability studies are needed with adults of different ages and education levels

using shorter intervals (e.g., 2 weeks to 3 months). The *Standards for Educational and Psychological Testing* (AERA, APA, & NCME, 1999) describe five sources of validation evidence: test content, response processes, internal structure, relations to other variables, and consequences of testing. Validation evidence presented in the test manual relies exclusively on relations to other variables. If the M-WCST is expected to measure elements of executive functioning, such as abstract reasoning ability and ability to shift cognitive strategies, but perhaps also working memory, planning, set switching, attentional flexibility, and response inhibition, then further evidence of this is needed through the use of correlational or factor analytic studies with carefully selected convergent and discriminant measures, examination of internal structure, and studies of response processes using techniques such as think-aloud protocols, observation, and eye tracking. Finally, attention needs to be paid to the appropriateness of various M-WCST scores for different groups (e.g., age, culture/ethnicity/race, educational level, intelligence, socioeconomic status, language).

SUMMARY. The M-WCST was designed to be an improved, shorter version of the WCST. Unfortunately, available reliability estimates of the M-WCST scores are inadequate and little strong validity evidence exists to support inferences made from the test scores as a measure of executive functioning and, in particular, abstract reasoning ability and ability to shift cognitive strategies. The test manual needs to be much better organized with a more thorough and clear presentation of the available psychometric evidence. Although the M-WCST cannot be recommended for clinical use at this time, it is not clear that other card sorting tests do not suffer from similar psychometric issues.

REVIEWER'S REFERENCES

American Educational Research Association, American Psychological Association, & National Council on Measurement in Education. (1999). *Standards for educational and psychological testing.* Washington, DC: American Educational Research Association.

Bird, C. M., Papadopoulou, K., Ricciardelli, P., Rossor, M. N., & Cipolotti, L. (2004). Monitoring cognitive changes: Psychometric properties of six cognitive tests. *British Journal of Clinical Psychology, 43,* 197–210.

Caffarra, P., Vessadini, G., Dieci, F., Zonato, F., & Venneri, A. (2004). Modified Card Sorting Test: Normative data. *Journal of Clinical and Experimental Neuropsychology, 26,* 246–250.

Cianchetti, C., Corona, S., Foscoliano, M., Contu, D., & Sannio-Fancello, G. (2007). Modified Wisconsin Card Sorting Test (MCST, MWCST): Normative data in children 4–13 years old, according to classical and new types of scoring. *The Clinical Neuropsychologist, 21,* 456–478.

de Zubicaray, G. I., Smith, G. A., Chalk, J. B., & Semple, J. (1998). The Modified Card Sorting Test: Test–retest stability and relationships with demographic variables in a healthy older adult sample. *British Journal of Clinical Psychology, 37,* 457–466.

Heaton, R. K., Chelune, G. J., Talley, J. L., Kay, G. G., & Curtiss, G. (1993). *Wisconsin Card Sorting Test manual, revised and expanded.* Lutz, FL: Psychological Assessment Resources.

Lineweaver, T. T., Bondi, M. W., Thomas, R. G., & Salmon, D. P. (1999). A normative study of Nelson's (1976) modified version of the Wisconsin Card Sorting Test in healthy older adults. *The Clinical Neuropsychologist, 13,* 328–347.

Nelson, H. E. (1976). A modified card sorting test sensitive to frontal lobe defects. *Cortex, 12*, 313–324.

Obonsawin, M. C., Crawford, J. R., Page, J., Chalmers, P., Low, G., & Marsh, P. (1999). Performance on the Modified Card Sorting Test by normal, healthy individuals: Relationship to general intellectual ability and demographic variables. *British Journal of Clinical Psychology, 38*, 27–41.

Reitan, R. M., & Wolfson, D. (1994). A selective and critical review of neuropsychological deficits and the frontal lobes. *Neuropsychology Review, 4* (3), 161–198.

van den Broek, M. D., Bradshaw, C. M., & Szabadi, E. (1993). Utility of the Modified Wisconsin Card Sorting Test in neuropsychological assessment. *British Journal of Clinical Psychology, 32*, 333–343.

Review of the Modified Wisconsin Card Sorting Test by DENISE E. MARICLE, Professor of School Psychology, Director of Clinical Training, Doctoral Program in School Psychology and AMANDA GRAY, Ph.D. Candidate in School Psychology, Texas Woman's University, Denton, TX:

DESCRIPTION. The Modified Wisconsin Card Sorting Test (M-WCST) is a variation of the Wisconsin Card Sorting Test (WCST; Heaton, Chelune, Talley, Kay, & Curtiss, 1993; 14:420) and the Wisconsin Card Sorting Test-64 Card Version (WCST-64; Kongs, Thompson, Iverson, & Heaton, 2000; 15:280).

The M-WCST kit consists of a professional manual, record forms, 48 response cards, and four key cards. According to the test author, the M-WCST was standardized for use with English-speaking adults between the ages of 18 and 92. Administration time is reportedly 10–15 minutes. Directions for administration and scoring will be familiar to users of the WCST or WCST-64. For those unfamiliar with the WCST, the directions for administration and scoring provided in the professional manual are clear and concise, and examples are given to enhance clarity.

The examinee is to place the cards one by one under the four key cards according to an unspecified sorting principle (form, number, or color). Whatever category the examinee chooses first is designated "correct" by the examiner who proceeds to acknowledge responses as "correct/incorrect" until a run of six correct responses has been achieved. At this point the examinee is told that the rule has changed and is instructed to "find another rule." Whichever category the examinee chooses next is designated correct as long as it differs from the first category. The third category is the one not previously selected. The order of the next three categories is the same as the first three categories. The test continues until all six consecutive categories of cards are sorted or the 48 cards are used up. In contrast, on the WCST the cards are sorted in a fixed order (color, form, number) with 10 consecutive sorts required for each category.

Four scores are calculated: Number of Categories Correct, Number of Perseverative Errors; Number of Total Errors, and Percent of Perseverative Errors. In addition to these four scores, it is possible to calculate an Executive Function Composite. Scores are first converted to scaled scores and then to age-, education-, or sex-calibrated *T*-scores. The user can obtain *T*-scores using the appendices in the test manual or can purchase a separate software program, the Calibrated Neuropsychological Normative System Software Portfolio (CNNS-SP; 19:25), available through the publisher. According to the test author, the CNNS-SP provides more precise conversions because it uses exact values for the demographic predictors and allows the user to select from eight prediction models that use various combinations of demographic variables (age, race, sex, and education). In addition to scaled scores and *T*-scores, percentile ranks can be obtained, and qualitative label classifications are provided.

DEVELOPMENT. The test author introduces the M-WCST as a simplified version of the WCST. The M-WCST is said to improve upon the WCST by simplifying the task for the individual being tested, thus avoiding frustration or noncompliance, and by removing the ambiguity in interpreting perseverative responses. The M-WCST, WCST, and WCST-64 are all based on card sorting tasks introduced into the literature by Berg (1948), Grant and Berg (1948), and Nelson (1976). The M-WCST is based primarily on Nelson's work. The M-WCST eliminated from the WCST all cards that shared more than one attribute with a stimulus card. As with the WCST and the WCST-64, the M-WCST is considered a measure of executive function, as it evaluates abstract reasoning ability and the ability to switch cognitive set when given feedback. Additionally, it is intended to evaluate perseveration, working memory, planning, attentional flexibility, and novel problem-solving.

TECHNICAL. A professional manual accompanies the M-WCST material. The information provided in the manual is clear and easy to read, albeit limited. Users familiar with the WCST will have little or no difficulty following the administration, scoring, and interpretive guidelines for the M-WCST.

The standardization sample appears to have consisted of 323 cognitively intact adults recruited from Baltimore, MD, and Hartford, CT. The professional manual notes some participants were excluded from the final standardization group based on a number of exclusionary criteria, only some of which were specified in the professional manual. It remains unclear whether the final standardization sample included any participants with neurological impairment or a disability of any sort. There were more females (56.3%) than males (43.7%), and the standardization group was primarily Caucasian (79.9%) with a representative sample of African American individuals (18.3%). Although means and standard deviations for age and education level of the entire sample were provided, no other information about the standardization sample was given. It is unclear how many men and women were obtained in each age decade. The professional manual indicates the test is appropriate for individuals ages 18–92; age-based norms extend from 18 to 86 and older. Information from two normative studies (Lineweaver, Bondi, Thomas, & Salmon, 1999; Obonsawin et al., 1999) that is not specifically reported in the professional manual shows the performance of cognitively intact individuals is affected by both age and education. Including this information would have been important.

The professional manual provides minimal reliability and validity evidence in support of the M-WCST. Reliability and validity information appears to be focused on the commonly reported indices of Number of Perseverative Errors and Number of Categories Correct. The professional manual reports test-retest reliability based on prior research by Lineweaver and colleagues (1999) and on a small research study conducted on a subsample of the standardization group ($n = 103$). Lineweaver et al. (1999) report adequate reliability (coefficients of .64 and .65, respectively) for two of the four scores (Number of Perseverative Errors and Number of Categories Correct) over a 2-year period, whereas the Executive Function Composite demonstrated a 5.5-year test-retest correlation coefficient of .50 for the subsample of the standardization group.

The test author presents evidence of convergent and discriminant validity based on the correlations of Number of Categories Correct and Number of Perseverative Errors with a variety of subtests that measure similar constructs. The correlation coefficients all appear to fall in the poor to adequate range (.20–.55 for Number of Categories Correct and .16–.51 for Number of Perseverative Errors). The test author also claims that a growing collection of scientific research supports the use of the M-WCST as a clinical measure and cites external studies supporting the validity of the M-

WCST for clinical populations such as those with Parkinson's disease, amyotrophic lateral sclerosis (ALS), Huntington's disease, Korsakoff's syndrome, and subcortical vascular dementia, among others. Additionally, the professional manual reports a clinical sample consisting of individuals diagnosed with schizophrenia, bipolar disorder, possible dementia, and mixed clinical presentations was examined to evaluate the validity of the Executive Function Composite. Means and standard deviations for each group were reported, with individuals diagnosed with schizophrenia and individuals with possible dementia demonstrating below normative performance.

No factor analytic studies of the M-WCST were reported in the professional manual. Repeated factor analytic studies (see Greve, Stickle, Love, Bianchini, & Stanford, 2005) have demonstrated that the WCST does not evaluate a unitary domain of executive functioning, but generally assesses three factors (concept formation/perseveration, nonperseverative errors, and failure to maintain set). Because the M-WCST is so reliant on the WCST interpretively, the lack of factor analytic data is problematic.

COMMENTARY. The test author lists several advantages of the M-WCST including that (a) it takes less time to administer than the WCST, (b) perseverative responses are unambiguous errors in contrast to the WCST where a response might be coded as correct and perseverative, and (c) its shorter administration time results in less frustration for impaired examinees. Although it would appear that the M-WCST has the advantage of reducing fatigue, as well as eliminating distress a test taker might experience when the category shifts unexpectedly, it would seem that alerting the individual to the shift in sorting category changes the nature of the task significantly. Thus, the test author's implication that the M-WCST is the same as the WCST and can be interpreted comparably is called into question. Indeed, it has already been called into question by de Zubicaray and Ashton (1996), who noted that the M-WCST is a different test than the standard version of the WCST. Only one study could be found that examined the comparability of the M-WCST and the WCST (van Gorp et al., 1997). The results were mixed, with younger cognitively intact individuals performing comparably on the two forms of the test, but with the clinical sample of older adults with dementia showing differential performance. Van Gorp et al. (1997) concluded that the M-WCST and the WCST are not clinically comparable in a population with central nervous system dysfunction.

A greater concern centers on the psychometric properties of the M-WCST. The small standardization sample raises concerns about the statistical power of the analyses used to derive the standardized scores, as well as the representativeness and generalizability of the standardization sample to a variety of examinees. Norms need to be strengthened using a larger and more ethnically and geographically diverse sample. Additionally, the conversion of raw scores to scaled scores and then T-scores is impacted by the raw score distribution, which is highly skewed rather than normally distributed. The means and standard deviations of such highly skewed distributions are difficult to understand and interpretively misleading. Reliability evidence is lacking, and what is reported is merely adequate (.50–.60). For diagnostic purposes it would be critical to have reliability coefficients in the .80–.90 range. Validity evidence is also scant and again, what is reported would indicate only poor to adequate validity. In contrast to the WCST, there are few reports that describe the performance of cognitively intact individuals and clinical populations using the M-WCST or that describe the relationship between M-WCST performance and demographic variables, general intellectual ability, general neurological functioning, or specific executive functions.

SUMMARY. The M-WCST was designed to be an individually administered measure of executive function, specifically abstract reasoning and cognitive set-shifting abilities. The M-WCST is purported to be a simplified variant of the WCST. As such, the M-WCST appears to derive much of its reliability and validity support on the literature base and clinical reputation of the WCST. Unfortunately for the M-WCST, there is insufficient normative data to support its use, and the modifications may have resulted in an instrument not directly comparable to previous versions (WCST, WCST-64). Additionally, the reported reliability statistics, while adequate, are diagnostically insufficient, and although there appears to be some diagnostic sensitivity within clinical populations, the validity of the M-WCST is far from established. Given these concerns, the M-WCST cannot be recommended for clinical use at this time.

REVIEWERS' REFERENCES

Berg, E. A. (1948). A simple objective test for measuring flexibility in thinking. *Journal of General Psychology, 39*, 15–22.
de Zubicaray, G. I., & Ashton, R. S. (1996). Nelson's (1976) Modified Card Sorting Test: A review. *The Clinical Neuropsychologist, 10*, 245–254.

Grant, D. A., & Berg, E. A. (1948). A behavioral analysis of degree of reinforcement and case shifting to new responses in a Weigl-type card-sorting problem. *Journal of Experimental Psychology, 38*, 404–411.
Greve, K. W., Stickle, T. R., Love, J. M., Bianchini, K. J., & Stanford, M. S. (2005). Latent structure of the Wisconsin Card Sorting Test: A confirmatory factor analytic study. *Archives of Clinical Neuropsychology, 20*, 355–364.
Heaton, R. K., Chelune, G. J., Talley, J. L., Kay, G. G., & Curtiss, G. (1994). *Wisconsin Card Sorting Test manual: Revised and expanded.* Lutz, FL: Psychological Assessment Resources.
Kongs, S. K., Thompson, L. L., Iverson, G. L., & Heaton, R. K. (2000). *Wisconsin Card Sorting Test-64 Card Version.* Lutz, FL: Psychological Assessment Resources.
Lineweaver, T. T., Bondi, M. W., Thomas, R. G., & Salmon, D. P. (1999). A normative study of Nelson's (1976) modified version of the Wisconsin Card Sorting Test in healthy older adults. *The Clinical Neuropsychologist, 13*, 328–347.
Nelson, H. E. (1976). A modified card sorting test sensitive to frontal lobe defects. *Cortex, 12*, 313–324.
Obonsawin, M. C., Crawford, J. R., Page, J., Chalmers, P., Low, G., & Marsh, P. (1999). Performance on the Modified Card Sorting Test by normal, healthy individuals: Relationship to general intellectual ability and demographic variables. *British Journal of Clinical Psychology, 38*, 27–41.
van Gorp, W. G., Kalechstein, A. D., Moore, L. H., Hinkin, C. H., Mahler, M. E., Foti, D., & Mendez, M. (1997). A clinical comparison of two forms of the Card Sorting Test. *The Clinical Neuropsychologist, 11*, 155–160.

[109]

Multi-CrafTest (Forms MC-C and B).

Purpose: Designed for selecting or evaluating maintenance employees.

Population: Applicants and incumbents for jobs requiring mechanical and electrical knowledge and skills.

Publication Dates: 2000-2009.

Scores, 8: Hydraulics & Pneumatics, Welding & Rigging, Power Transmission/Lubrication/Mechanical Maintenance & Shop Machines/Tools and Equipment, Pumps/Piping & Combustion, Motors/Control Circuits & Schematics and Print Reading, Digital Electronics/Power Supplies/Computers & PLC and Test Instruments, Basic AC & DC Theory/Power Distribution and Electrical Maintenance, Total.

Administration: Group.

Forms, 2: MC-C, B.

Price Data, 2011: $22 per consumable self-scoring test booklet or online test administration (minimum order of 20); $24.95 per manual (2009, 23 pages).

Foreign Language Edition: Available in Spanish.

Time: (60-70) minutes.

Comments: Self-scoring instrument; Form B is an alternate equivalent of Form MC-C; available for online test administration.

Author: Roland T. Ramsay.

Publisher: Ramsay Corporation.

Cross References: For a review by Vicki S. Packman of an earlier edition, see 17:128.

Review of the Multi-CrafTest (Forms MC-C and B) by BRUCE BISKIN, Senior Associate, Delaware Valley Career Solutions, Newtown, PA, and Adjunct Assistant Professor of Graduate Education, Leadership, and Counseling, Rider University, Lawrenceville, NJ:

DESCRIPTION. The Ramsay Corporation Job Skills Multi-CrafTest (the Multi-CrafTest) is described as "a diagnostic test of maintenance skills" on the cover of the manual. The manual discusses the development of the test, includes instructions for administration and scoring of two forms (MC-C and B), and provides technical information such as normative data, item statistics, score reliability, and validity evidence. Each form comprises 60 multiple-choice items that generate seven section scores: Basic AC & DC Theory, Power Distribution, and Electrical Maintenance (8 items); Digital Electronics, Power Supplies, Computers & PLC, and Test Instruments (8 items); Motors, Control Circuits & Schematics, and Print Reading (9 items); Pumps, Piping, & Combustion (9 items); Power Transmission, Lubrication, Mechanical Maintenance, & Shop Machines, Tools and Equipment (12 items); Welding & Rigging (7 items); and Hydraulics & Pneumatics (7 items). The section scores are summed to get the total score. Form MC-C, originally developed in 2000, was revised slightly in 2006 and 2008.

Forms MC-C and B are both available in a paper-and-pencil form. However, Form B has separate booklets and answer sheets (template scoring), whereas the answer sheet and scoring key for the paper-based Form MC-C are both integrated into the test booklet, and hand scoring requires no template. Form MC-C is also available for online administration through the publisher's website. In the online format, the Multi-CrafTest is scored automatically. Although the Multi-CrafTest is not timed, instructions to examinees suggest that they should complete work within an hour. Most qualified examinees should complete the 60 items in far less time.

DEVELOPMENT. The operational items for Form MC-C were initially taken from the publisher's 153-item Maintest (Form NL-1), though a small percentage have subsequently been revised or replaced in minor revisions. (Form B was created as an "alternate equivalent" test to Form MC-C; however, the manual provides no information about how it was developed.) Content coverage for the Maintest was based on a job analysis, though the details of the job analysis were not included in the Multi-CrafTest manual. The job analysis resulted in detailed content specifications comprising 21 knowledge areas and 128 specific topics that pertain to the work of journey-level maintenance workers. The Multi-CrafTest covers the same 21 knowledge areas but combines them into seven sections. The Multi-CrafTest manual does not explain whether the topics included in the 21 knowledge areas were clustered into seven through empirical evaluation

of subscore relationships, subject matter expert judgments, or some other method. Each of the final seven content clusters corresponds to one of the seven section scores computed.

TECHNICAL. Although the Multi-CrafTest manual covers the administration and scoring for paper-based versions of both Form MC-C and Form B, technical information related to norms, reliability estimates, and validity evidence is presented only for Form MC-C. No explanation for failure to include technical information for Form B is offered. The manual includes some data from online administration of Form MC-C, but it does not describe factors inherent in automated test administration that could affect scores (e.g., method of item presentation, how graphics are displayed, item review options). As a result, this section does not include evaluations of the online version of the Multi-CrafTest (Form MC-C).

Administration and scoring. The manual provides detailed instructions for administering both paper-and-pencil forms (MC-C and B) of the Multi-CrafTest. These instructions are important because of the substantial differences in the structure of the booklets and answer sheets for the two forms. Instructions to examinees are intended to be read aloud, whether the Multi-CrafTest is administered to a single individual or to a group of examinees. The manual emphasizes to the test administrator, "The directions for the test must be followed exactly. … [T]he examiner should read them verbatim" (p. 9). This is particularly important with the paper version of Form MC-C because the answer format may be unfamiliar to many examinees.

The self-contained answer format for Form MC-C eliminates the need for separate scoring templates. However, the Form MC-C scoring sheet is crowded and printed in light blue-gray. Arrows link answers by section to facilitate section scoring. It is difficult to follow all the arrows because of the coloring and crowding. If practicable, this reviewer would encourage the publisher to consider printing the scoring sheet with a higher contrast ink or printing the arrows in a contrasting color to reduce the risk of scoring errors. Form B, which comes with reusable booklets and separate answer sheets, is hand-scored more conventionally using templates.

Online administration is available through the publisher's proprietary Online Testing System. Administration instructions for the online version of Form MC-C are not included in the Multi-CrafTest manual. Online scoring is done automatically at the end of the administration. The online version of Form MC-C was not evaluated.

Time limits. The Multi-CrafTest does not have a formal time limit. The directions to the examinee state, "There is no time limit, but you should not need more than 1 hour." Most qualified examinees will finish in much less than an hour, although the manual does not provide a range or distribution of examinee completion times. If the publisher has such information for each form and administration format of the Multi-CrafTest, it should be included in the next revision of the manual.

Norms. A table of total scores and corresponding percentile ranks is included in the manual for "3,484 applicants and employed multicraft workers in various industries" (p. 21) who took Form MC-C. Because the table does not report applicants and employees separately, and because the relative proportion of each group is unknown, the table has limited value. In addition to reporting norms for the two groups separately, the publisher should consider describing the normative sample in more detail by including potentially relevant demographic variables such as education, training, experience, age, sex, and ethnicity. If the normative data cannot be specified in a more usable way, the publisher should consider eliminating them from the manual.

Reliability. The Multi-CrafTest manual reports internal consistency reliability estimates for total score and section scores for Form MC-C only; no reliability estimates are reported in the manual for Form B. For total scores on the Multi-CrafTest, internal consistency reliability estimates are provided for three groups comprising both applicants and employed workers from: (a) one large delivery company (N = 2,854–mechanics), (b) various industries throughout the U.S. (N = 427–multicraft workers), and (c) online administration in various industries throughout the U.S. (N = 203–multicraft). The manual reports KR-20 estimates of .87 to .89, and split-half (odd-even) reliability estimates of .88 to .90, for the three groups. These estimates suggest Form MC-C is internally consistent across sections. This level of internal consistency is often found for well-designed achievement tests of about the same length that assess a broad but unified domain of knowledge.

With respect to section scores, KR-20 estimates only were reported for the combined group of 3,484 applicants and workers. These estimates range from .46 for both Hydraulics & Pneumat-

ics and Welding & Rigging, to .67 for Motors, Control Circuits & Schematics and Print Reading (median KR-20 = .57). The section score reliability estimates are substantially lower than those for the total score, and are too low to recommend to use individually for making high-stakes decisions. However, reliability estimates are greatly affected by the number of items on which they are based, so the fact that section scores are less reliable than total scores is understandable.

Another method of estimating score reliability is to correlate scores from two forms of the same test. Considering two forms of the Multi-CrafTest are available–Forms MC-C and B–it was surprising that no evidence of alternate-form reliability was included in the manual. As a result, inferences about the comparability of scores across the two forms of the Multi-CrafTest cannot be made.

Validity. Validity refers to the accuracy of inferences, interpretations, and decisions made using test scores. Therefore, the degree to which test scores are valid depends on how they are used, and the uses of test scores should be consistent with the stated purpose of the test. Surprisingly, the manual does not clearly state the purpose of the Multi-CrafTest, nor does it offer specific guidance about how scores might be used. The introduction includes a statement that the test is intended "for use with applicants and incumbents for jobs where practical mechanical and electrical knowledge and skill are necessary parts of maintenance job activities" (p. 1). The only other suggestion of purpose is in the instructions to examinees, stating that the Multi-CrafTest is a "series of exercises to be used in *employee selection*...so that we can compare your skills with those *required to learn and perform the job*" (p. 10, emphasis added). Taken together, this evidence suggests that Multi-CrafTest scores may be intended for use in making employment decisions for maintenance workers. A clearer statement appears on the publisher's website: "Ramsay Corporation's Multi-CrafTest is for use in selecting maintenance employees [at the journey level] who have knowledge in seven different craft areas" ("MultiCrafTest-Form MC-RC," n.d.). It might be useful for the publisher to add a statement similar to this one at the beginning of the manual and to focus employee selection in the remainder of the material in the manual.

Content-related validity evidence reported in the Multi-CrafTest manual is a table that summarizes six different content validation studies, three using Form MC-C and three using other undocumented forms. The table does not provide enough information to evaluate how well the studies support the validity of the Multi-CrafTest. For example, although raters in all studies found virtually all items to be "job related," it is unclear whether the entire pool of items was rated for representativeness in assessing journey-level maintenance workers. The manual also reports the results of two criterion-related studies as evidence of validity, both involving correlations of Multi-CrafTest scores with supervisor ratings. Again, there is insufficient information about the studies to evaluate the evidence they contribute. In one study, scores from 201 maintenance workers were correlated with supervisor ratings of "know-how," technical knowledge, supervisory skills, problem solving, interpersonal skills, and total performance, and five of the six correlations were statistically significant, ranging from .22 (supervisory skills) to .57 (technical knowledge). The second study was much smaller in scope, including 24 equipment service associates whose scores on Form MC-C correlated .42 with "supervisory performance ratings." Neither study described the methodology (including rating scales) in enough detail to evaluate critically. One might question whether supervisors knew the workers' Multi-CrafTest scores at the time the ratings were made. The manual did not mention any application of validation study results to setting cut scores for employee selection. The publisher should include more information in the manual about the validation studies in the next revision so that the validity evidence can be critically evaluated by test users.

The manual also included a short section on construct-related evidence for validity. Without a clearly articulated purpose for the Multi-CrafTest, however, this section seemed forced and unconvincing. The result is a small set of questionable statements that detract from the case being made for the validity of Multi-CrafTest scores.

COMMENTARY. Although the Multi-CrafTest manual covers both Form MC-C and Form B, information for Form B relates almost exclusively to administration and scoring. The lack of technical information for Form B was surprising, particularly because it was identified as being developed as an alternate to Form MC-C. This weakness was noted in an earlier review of the Multi-CrafTest (Packman, 2007). Without convincing evidence to support its use as an alternative to Form MC-C, Form B should be avoided except for research purposes. Instructions to administrators and examinees

for the online version of the Multi-CrafTest and other information reflecting differences with the paper version should be included in the manual.

The Multi-CrafTest (Form MC-C) seems to be a reasonable choice to consider for a quick assessment of knowledge required for maintenance workers in a wide range of work settings. Although it may have value as an employment screening tool for journey-level maintenance workers, the validity evidence in the Multi-CrafTest manual is meager for that or any other specific purpose. The manual also should include a general discussion about how to use test scores for high-stakes decisions such as employee selection. Although test publishers should not be expected to validate test score use for all possible contingencies, they should anticipate likely uses and identify issues related to these uses in the manual. Indeed, the publisher already addresses test validation issues in selection generally in a document on its website (Ramsay Corporation, 2010), parts of which could be used to frame the validity section in the Multi-CrafTest manual.

SUMMARY. The Multi-CrafTest Form MC-C is a reliable measure of knowledge required by maintenance workers. The publisher has tweaked Form MC-C several times since it was introduced in 2000 and has continued to update and improve it. However, the evidence included in the Multi-CrafTest manual fails to make a case for using Form MC-C in employee selection of journey-level maintenance workers. No technical information about Form B was included in the manual and so it could not be evaluated.

[Note: A new form, Form MC-CR, was released shortly before this review was completed (Ramsay, 2011). Except for three replacement items, Form MC-CR appears to be identical to Form MC-C.]

REVIEWER'S REFERENCES

MultiCrafTest–Form MC-RC. (n.d.). Retrieved December 27, 2011 from the Ramsay Corporation website, http://www.ramsaycorp.com/catalog/view/?productid=749
Packman, V. S (2007). [Review of the Multi-CrafTest]. In K. F. Geisinger, R. A. Spies, J. F. Carlson, & B. S. Plake (Eds.), *The seventeenth mental measurements yearbook*. Retrieved from the Buros Institute's *Test Reviews Online* website: http://www.unl.edu/buros.
Ramsay, R. T. (2011). *Manual for administration & scoring: Multi-CrafTest Form MC-RC (2000, 2006, 2008, 2011), Form B (2007)*. Pittsburgh, PA: Ramsay Corp.
Ramsay Corporation. (2010). Test validation brochure. Retrieved from http://www.ramsaycorp.com/docs/info/validation-services.pdf.

Review of the Multi-CrafTest (Forms MC-C and B) by M. DAVID MILLER, Professor, Research and Evaluation Methods, University of Florida, Gainesville, FL:

DESCRIPTION. The Ramsay Corporation Job Skills (RCJS) Maintest Form NL-1 was developed in 1991 for use with workers having or applying for jobs that require practical mechanical and electrical knowledge and skills. The RCJS Multi-CrafTest Form MC-C was developed in 2000 and revised in 2006 and 2008 as a shortened version of RCJS Maintest Form NL-1. RCJS Multi-CrafTest Form B was developed in 2007 as an alternative equivalent version of RCJS Multi-CrafTest Form MC-C.

The RCJS Multi-CrafTest Forms MC-C and B were developed to measure the knowledge and skills of multicraft mechanics. Job analysis showed that the Maintest Form NL-1 was applicable to the job titles of Maintenance Repairer, Industrial and Maintenance and Repair Workers, General as defined by the U.S. Department of Labor.

The Multi-CrafTest Forms MC-C and B are available with two methods of administration: paper-and-pencil and online. Clear standardized directions for test administration and scoring are available. Each form consists of 60 multiple-choice items. Scoring provides a total score as well as scores for the following subtests: (a) Hydraulics & Pneumatics, (b) Welding & Rigging, (c) Power Transmission, Lubrication, Mechanical Maintenance, & Shop Machines, Tools and Equipment, (d) Pumps, Piping, & Combustion, (e) Motors, Control Circuits & Schematics and Print Reading, (f) Digital Electronics, Power Supplies, Computers & PLC, and Test Instruments, and (g) Basic AC & DC Theory, Power Distribution, and Electrical Maintenance. Each subtest contains 7 to 12 items.

DEVELOPMENT. The Multi-CrafTest Form MC-C is a shortened form of the RCJS Maintest Form NL-1. Two industrial-organizational psychologists selected 60 items from the pool of 153 items based on item statistics and content specifications. Two revisions of the form have led to changes in 11 and 7 items, mostly based on minor wording changes. In 2007, the RCJS Multi-CrafTest Form B was developed as an alternate equivalent version of Form MC-C. Minimal information is reported for the development of the alternate form. In addition, all reliability, validity, and item analyses are reported only for Form MC-C. No evidence of the alternate form being parallel to Form MC-C is provided in terms of the content specifications.

Item analyses for Form MC-C show that the items behave well statistically. The item difficulties range from .16 to .81. Item discriminations or point-biserial correlation coefficients with the subtest scores range from .19 to .63. Item discriminations

with the total score are not reported. Finally, the content of the items matches the test specifications.

TECHNICAL. Validity and reliability data are presented for the Multi-CrafTest Form MC-C. No data are provided for the Multi-CrafTest Form B. The data for the reliability and validity studies include data from 3,484 applicants and employed multicraft workers in various industries. Sampling is not described for the data on which the reliability and validity studies are based. The data combine paper-and-pencil and online administrations.

Reliability. The Multi-CrafTest Form MC-C reports the standard error of measurement and two types of reliability for the total score: internal consistency (KR20) and split half (Odd-Even). In addition, the reliability estimates are reported for subsets of the sample: mechanics at a large delivery company, multicraft workers at industries in the U.S., and online test administrations for multicraft workers at industries in the U.S. Some of these data may be from applicants rather than job incumbents. In all cases the reliability estimates are high, ranging from .87 to .90. However, the total score reliabilities are only reported for Form MC-C. Form B has no reported reliabilities including no alternate form reliabilities to show consistency with Form MC-C.

Internal consistency estimates (KR20) and standard errors of measurement are also reported for the seven subtests of Form MC-C. The reliability estimates range from .46 to .67 with a median of .57.

Validity. Two types of validity evidence are provided. First, evidence is provided to show that the body of knowledge measured by the assessment is related to specific jobs. Second, evidence is provided that the assessment correlates with job performance ratings.

To assess the match between the behaviors required on the job and the content of the test, six clients (i.e., sites) were identified to study. The six clients included five job titles (e.g., maintenance mechanic, shift utility mechanic) in five industries (e.g., food production, chemical company). For each job, raters (4–10 per site) rated the job relatedness of the items from Multi-CrafTest Form MC-C or other forms of the measure on a 6-point scale (i.e., 0–5). The results showed that the average ratings of items across the six sites ranged from 3.2 to 3.9 with fewer than 1% of the items having ratings below the midpoint of the scale. Thus, the Multi-CrafTest Form MC-C showed good evidence of job relatedness for the selected job titles/industries. No description was given of how the specific industries or job titles were selected; however, the job titles provided a reasonable sample for the study.

To assess the criterion-related evidence of validity of the assessment, job performance ratings were correlated with scores on the items making up the Multi-CrafTest Form MC-C. The correlations with ratings of technical knowledge, supervisory skills, problem solving, and total job performance were .57, .22, .27, and .36, respectively. Based on the 95–97 maintenance employees from the Fortune 500 company, the correlations were significant, showing reasonable criterion-related validity.

Norms. Norms are presented for the Multi-CrafTest Form MC-C. The norms are based on the 3,484 applicants and employed multicraft workers in various industries that were used to report the item analyses and reliabilities. Again, there was no description of the population or the sampling methods.

COMMENTARY AND SUMMARY. The Multi-CrafTest Form MC-C and Form B are short forms of the RCJS Maintest Form NL-1. The assessments can be administered using paper and pencil or online. The assessments are intended to be used for job applicants and workers where practical mechanical and electrical knowledge and skills are necessary parts of maintenance job activities. The multiple-choice items are clearly based on knowledge about specific skills, but not skilled performance.

Although two forms of the test are available, the data on reliability, validity, item analyses, and norms are based solely on Form MC-C. Even the development process for the second form is not well described. The basic information about alternate-form reliability and content is not available to assess the quality of Form B. Consequently, the discussion of the quality of the assessment below applies only to Form MC-C, and I would not recommend using Form B without additional information being provided.

The Multi-CrafTest Form MC-C provides sufficient evidence to use as an achievement test measuring the knowledge needed for multicraft applicants and employees. The total score has a high level of reliability and reasonably strong validity evidence including content development, job relatedness, and relationship with job performance.

However, several cautions need to be exercised in using the Multi-CrafTest Form MC-C. First, subtests do not have reliability coefficients that would lead to their effective use. Second, use of the norms must be done cautiously with the lack of a description of the population upon which the norms are based. Finally, any use of the assessment that involves decisions will need careful consideration of what are "acceptable" levels of achievement. No studies of specific cutoffs have been reported, and companies will need to establish reasonable cutoffs for any specific decisions based on the assessment.

[110]

Multi-dimensional Emotional Intelligence Quotient, 7ᵗʰ Revision.

Purpose: Designed to assess "the ability to recognize and understand emotions, understand sentiments in oneself and to handle one's feelings in a productive manner, as well as the ability to understand what it takes to motivate oneself."

Population: Below 18 through adult.

Publication Date: 2011.

Acronym: MEIQ-R7.

Scores, 36: Emotional Identification/ Perception/ and Expression, Emotional Facilitation of Thought, Emotional Understanding, Emotional Management, Moderating Emotional Intelligence Factors, Emotional Self-Awareness, Awareness of Strengths and Limitations, Impulse Control, Self-Control, Resilience/Hardiness, Rumination, Comfort with Emotions, Assertiveness, Coping Skills, Problem Solving, Self-Esteem, Contentment, Values Integrity, Positive Mindset, Independence, Self-Motivation, Goal Setting, Striving, Emotional Selectivity, Social Responsibility, Flexibility, Empathy, Adaptable Social Skills, Conflict Management Behavior, Social Insight, Recognition of Other's Emotions, Emotional Integration, Conflict Management Knowledge, Emotional Reflection, Impression Management.

Administration: Individual.

Price Data: Available from publisher.

Time: (60) minutes.

Comments: Self-administered online assessment. The test publisher advises that the test manual is being updated to include more information about methodology and theoretical background used in the development of the test. The test publisher also advises that this information is available to clients, as are benchmarks for relevant industries and racial/ethnic group comparison data. However, this information was not provided to Buros or the reviewers.

Author: PsychTests AIM, Inc.

Publisher: PsychTests AIM, Inc. [Canada].

Review of the Multi-dimensional Emotional Intelligence Quotient, 7ᵗʰ Revision by NINA W. BROWN, Professor and Eminent Scholar of Counseling, Old Dominion University, Norfolk, VA:

DESCRIPTION. The Multi-dimensional Emotional Intelligence Quotient, 7ᵗʰ Revision

(MEIQ-R7) was published in 2011 and is the seventh revision for the test first published in 1998. The test publishers offer both a long and an abbreviated version. The abbreviated version was not reviewed, only the 234-item long version that has 4 scales, 1 moderating factor, and 29 subscales. The test authors recommend its use as a supplement for pre-employment screening for sales positions, customer service training, and for personal, leadership, and team development. The target population is adults, although the standardization sample included participants who were younger than age 18. The administration is individual, takes about 60 minutes on the computer, and is scored immediately.

Items on the test are scenario, image-based, and self-reports of behavior and attitudes using multiple-choice and a 5-point Likert scale format. The original scoring was revised in 2007 from standardized (with scores between 0–100) to IQ Scale, in which scores ranged from 55 to 155 with 100 as the average. The rules for scoring and interpretation were developed by subject matter experts and are computer generated by system experts and algorithms.

Test-takers and recruiters/administrators are provided with an overall Emotional Quotient IQ and percentile rank, scores for each of the four core abilities, and scores for each of the moderating emotional intelligence factors. The report does not provide separate scores for self-report and ability as is indicated by the test authors as what the test is intended to measure, and on the profile provided to test takers. The report includes 18 pages of scores and personal interpretations; a summary of strengths, potential strengths, and limitations; and advice for the four scales that appears to be general and not related to the individual test-taker's scores.

DEVELOPMENT. The test was initially developed to assess two broad factors: Emotional Knowledge and Emotional Behavior. Beginning with the 6ᵗʰ Revision, the test was constructed to use the mixed model of emotional intelligence that incorporates both self-report of behavior and self-assessment of abilities. Four core abilities are assessed in the 7th Revision: Emotional Identification, Perception, and Expression with 4 subscales and 60 items; Emotional Facilitation of Thought with 5 subscales and 33 items; Emotional Understanding with 4 subscales and 64 items; and Emotional Management with 9 subscales and 70 items. An additional 42 items assess the moderating emotional intelligence factors. The instrument also evaluates seven factors that are related to how emotions are perceived, understood, expressed, and managed, in addition to the extent of social desirability in answering the items.

Test development procedures for the first six versions had three phases: test design and initial launch, preliminary statistical analysis, and large scale statistical analysis. Phase III followed common statistical analysis procedures by establishing reliability using coefficient alpha, and providing evidence related to content, criterion-related, internal consistency-convergent, and discriminant-validity, and used a principal component factor analysis with Varimax rotation. It was not clear how the 7th Revision differs from previous versions, or how criterion and construct validity evidence was gathered.

TECHNICAL.

Standardization. The sample for the MEIQ-R7 consisted of 821 participants who self-selected to participate in the validation study of which 62.5% were female and 29.5% were male, with 8% not indicating gender. Ages were distributed from below 18 (lowest limit not specified) to 40+ (highest age not specified) with 12.2% not specifying age. For the purpose of comparison, it would be helpful to have other information such as the sample's racial/ethnic composition and educational levels, but this information was not provided. It is not clear that the instrument can be used cross-culturally.

Reliability. Alpha coefficients provided for the four scales range from .86–.95 indicating good to excellent internal consistency. The 42 items measuring the moderating emotional intelligence factors have alpha coefficients ranging from .56 for Emotional Reflection to .82 for Empathy, with 11 subscales having coefficients in the .60–.70 range, and 15 with coefficients in the .70–.80 range. Numerous scales and subscales share or have items in common indicating some overlap.

Validity. The test authors assert that the test demonstrates evidence of content validity, as items for the previous versions were approved by experts, and many of the items have been subjected to psychometric and statistical analyses since 1998. Content validity for the R7 version was not described or specified in the test materials provided fro the purpose of this review.

The process of obtaining other types of validity evidence for the R7 version relied on self-reports of self-selected test-takers. Differential validity for age and gender study used matched sample sizes to equalize the comparison groups, post hoc analyses were conducted by age, gender (N = 242 each group), and groupings for self-report on academic achievement (3 groups, N = 118 each), socioeconomic status (4 groups, N = 117–138 each), self-assessment of performance reviews (3 groups, N = 49 each), popularity (3 groups, N = 73 each), and relationship satisfaction (4 groups, N = 58 each). Some sample sizes may be too small to provide stable estimates, a problem that may be compounded by limited fluctuation due to sampling error. Evidence for the R7 is lacking other forms of validity such as criterion, predictive, and construct validity.

COMMENTARY.

Strengths. The use of the mixed model that assesses emotional intelligence for both self-ratings and ability underscores the assumption that emotional intelligence is not unidimensional. This can be seen as a strength. The operational definitions for the four scales are useful.

Weaknesses. There are several areas that need strengthening: descriptions for the standardization sample such as inclusion of participants' racial/ethnic identity and educational levels, assessing two dimensions but only reporting results in one score, description of the development for the R7 version, establishment of validity, and information that presents and explains contradictory results.

Lack of information about some important demographics of the standardization sample suggests that it may not be cross-culturally appropriate, and may not be useful for test-takers from cultures other than those of the normative group.

Although the test results note that there are two parts (self-report and ability), two scores are not reported. The lack of some important information about the norm group makes it difficult to determine how individual scores compare to the norm group, and/or describe the person taking the test.

A description of the process of development for the R7 would be helpful, especially to understand how it differs from previous versions. Validity information for the separate 29 subscales is inadequate, and any reliance on subscale scores for the stated purposes of HR screening and counseling can be problematic, and may even prove misleading for some test-takers.

The test authors provide a disclaimer on the profile of test results that notes that there can be contradictory results for the self-report and ability components. However, because the profile does not report the separate scores for self-report and ability,

the test-taker cannot know if there is a discrepancy or contradiction.

SUMMARY. The Multi-dimensional Emotional Intelligence Quotient, 7th Revision does not appear to be appropriate for the intended use of counseling pending further study and analyses to establish construct validity. This is especially true for the 29 subscales that do not have sufficient evidence to support test score use. The stated use for HR pre-employment screening for sales positions and customer service training does not have adequate predictive validity evidence to support this use. It may be advisable to use caution when interpreting the results to be used for personal, leadership, and team development, especially when the subscale scores are a part of this process.

Review of the Multi-dimensional Emotional Intelligence Quotient, 7th Revision by JAMES C. DiPERNA, Associate Professor, and CHRISTOPHER ANTHONY, Doctoral Candidate, School Psychology Program, Pennsylvania State University, University Park, PA:

DESCRIPTION. The Multi-dimensional Emotional Intelligence Quotient, 7th Revision (MEIQ-R7) is a 234-item questionnaire designed to measure Emotional Intelligence (EI), which reflects an individual's ability to self-motivate, form close relationships, and manage the feelings of themselves and others. The MEIQ-R7 is intended for screening and training purposes in human resource and counseling settings. The measure can be administered individually or in groups, and approximate time for completion is 60 minutes. (The test manual indicates that shorter forms are available, however.)

The MEIQ-R7 is completed online, and scores are generated automatically upon completion. Specifically, the measure yields an overall Emotional Intelligence score as well as scores reflecting four core ability scales: (a) Emotional Identification, Perception, and Expression, (b) Emotional Facilitation of Thought, (c) Emotional Understanding, and (d) Emotional Management. The MEIQ-R7 also includes a Moderating Emotional Intelligence Factors scale that assesses personal factors (e.g., assertiveness, self-esteem) hypothesized to influence the four core EI abilities. Across these five scales, there are a total of 29 subscales. In addition, the MEIQ-R7 includes a brief Impression Management (social desirability) scale. The online score report generates a profile of individual strengths, limitations, and suggestions for improving relatively weak areas of EI.

DEVELOPMENT. Although no information is provided in the MEIQ-R7 technical manual regarding development of the measure, some insights can be gleaned from the introduction in the score report. Specifically, the report indicates that the measure is based on Mayer, Caruso, and Salovey's (1999) definition of EI: "the ability to recognize the meanings of emotions and their relationships, and to reason and problem-solve on the basis of them... [including] the capacity to perceive emotions, assimilate emotion-related feelings, understand the information of those emotions, and manage them" (p. 267).

In addition, the report notes that questions on the MEIQ-R7 reflect a "mixed-model" that includes both direct-assessment questions (e.g., identifying emotions expressed by individuals in a photograph) and self-report questions (e.g., indicating how one is likely to respond in a certain situation). The former type of questions reflect an ability model suggesting that EI is an internal and stable individual characteristic, analogous to cognitive intelligence. In contrast, the latter type of questions allow for the assessment of related factors such as motivation and interpersonal relationships.

Based on a review of the items, many appear to be consistent with the working definition/model of EI; however, some appear to be less relevant. Also, a number of items were quite lengthy and required repeated readings to understand clearly. In addition, some of the pictures featured in the direct assessment items appeared to have valid alternative interpretations. Unfortunately, no additional information or data are provided in the technical manual regarding item development, pilot testing, or final item selection, so it is difficult to determine the adequacy of the items retained in the final version of the MEIQ-R7.

TECHNICAL.

Standardization. The MEIQ-R7 standardization sample included 821 participants who completed the measure online via the test publisher's website. Approximately 63% of the standardization participants were women, and 55% of the sample fell between the ages of 18–39. No other demographic data were reported for the standardization sample in the technical manual.

Reliability. Internal consistency (alpha) coefficients based on data from the standardization sample are high for the overall score (.95) and five scale scores (.86–.92). Subscale coefficients are lower and range from .56 (Emotional Reflection) to .82 (Empathy). Neither short- nor long-term stability coefficients are reported in the technical manual.

Validity. The primary forms of validity evidence reported in the MEIQ-R7 technical manual are comparisons based on demographic variables (age, gender, socioeconomic status), personal accomplishments (academic achievement, work performance reviews), and interpersonal relationships (popularity, satisfaction). It is important to note that all of these data were self-reported, and the responses for each variable often were recoded into a smaller number of categories for comparison purposes. Also separate analyses were conducted for each scale, subscale, and grouping variable. Observed patterns generally are consistent with expectations based on the construct (e.g., women tended to score higher than men). Aside from reliability coefficients, no other evidence of internal structure is reported in the technical manual. Similarly, no evidence is reported regarding the relationships between the MEIQ-R7 scores and scores from other measures of the EI construct.

COMMENTARY. The MEIQ-R7 has been developed based upon prominent theories of EI and features item formats often used to assess the construct. In addition, the online administration, real-time scoring, and comprehensive report make the measure convenient to use. The measure, however, does require a significant amount of reading and approximately 60 minutes to complete. The standardization sample is relatively small and minimal demographic data are reported in the technical manual. As such, it is impossible to determine if the sample is representative of the target population for the MEIQ-R7. In addition, no information is provided regarding item development, testing, and selection for the current version of the measure. Internal consistency coefficients are generally appropriate for screening purposes, and observed group differences are consistent with expectations based on theory and extant research. No other forms of reliability and validity evidence are reported in the technical manual.

SUMMARY. Although the MEIQ-R7 has some positives, the limited information regarding its development, standardization sample, and psychometric properties preclude recommendation of its use at this time. Specifically, studies regarding stability of scores, structural validity, and relationships with other measures of EI (as well as related constructs) are necessary to provide evidence that scores from the MEIQ-R7 are consistent with its intended purpose. In addition, the standardization sample must be representative of the target population to ensure appropriate normative interpretation of scores from the MEIQ-R7.

REVIEWERS' REFERENCE

Mayer, J. D., Caruso, D. R., & Salovey, P. (1999). Emotional intelligence meets traditional standards for an intelligence. *Intelligence, 27*, 267–298.

[111]

Multi-Dimensional Intelligence Test.

Purpose: Designed to measure "several factors of intelligence, including logical reasoning, math skills, language abilities, spatial relations skills, knowledge retained and the ability to solve novel problems."
Population: Below 17 through older adult.
Publication Date: 2011.
Acronym: MIT.
Scores, 15: Overall Score, Fluid Intelligence, Crystallized Intelligence, Vocabulary, Analogies, Arithmetic, Graphs & Charts, Matrices, 2D/3D Images, Arguments, Puzzles, Verbal, Numeric, Spatial, Logical.
Administration: Individual.
Price Data: Available from publisher.
Time: (40) minutes.
Comments: Self-administered online assessment. The test publisher advises that the test manual is being updated to include more information about methodology and theoretical background used in the development of the test. The test publisher also advises that this information is available to clients, as are benchmarks for relevant industries and racial/ethnic group comparison data. However, this information was not provided to Buros or the reviewers.
Author: PsychTests AIM, Inc.
Publisher: PsychTests AIM, Inc. [Canada].

Review of the Multi-Dimensional Intelligence Test by JASON C. IMMEKUS, Assistant Professor, California State University, Fresno, Fresno, CA:

DESCRIPTION. The Multi-Dimensional Intelligence Test (MIT) is an individually completed, online measure of specific factors of intelligence, including: logical reasoning, math skills, language abilities, spatial relations skills, knowledge retained, and novel problem-solving. It is vaguely reported that it is applicable to human resource (HR) testing to screen and train employees and for "educational purposes" (manual, p. 1). It is designed for individuals below age 17 through older adults, but no information is available regarding the youngest and oldest ages for whom the instrument would yield psychometrically sound scores. Test administration requires the examinee to log in to the publisher's website to complete the instrument that has presumably been assigned by a manager or HR representative. There is one version of the test and it is administered via a pop-up window that begins with general instructions for completing the 109 multiple-choice and true-false items. It is reported that the instrument takes 40 minutes to complete, but there is no built-in feature in the online testing environment that reports how much time has been spent completing individual items or the overall test.

The administration instructions are generally clear. However, no information is available regarding standardized administration of the instrument or computer capabilities beyond Internet access. Items are administered in item sets with shared content and require examinees to record their responses by selecting their answer. Examinees progress through the test by clicking on the "next" button at the bottom of each page. Examinees are allowed to use a calculator to solve math problems, but are not allowed to use additional resources. Items are clearly written and how to proceed to the next set of items is self-explanatory. Responses are electronically scored and results are available immediately upon completion of the instrument. Test performance is reported according to 15 scores, including 3 total scores and 12 subscale scores. Total scores include: Overall IQ, Fluid Intelligence (54 items), and Crystallized Intelligence (55 items). The 6 Fluid subscales include: Spatial, Matrices, 2D-3D Images, Logical, Arguments, and Puzzles. The 6 Crystallized subscales include: Verbal, Vocabulary, Analogies, Numerical, Arithmetic, and Graphs & Charts. The number of items comprising each subscale ranges from 10 (Graphs & Charts) to 30 (Logical, Verbal). No information is available on the extent to which test accommodations or modifications should be provided for individuals with disabilities.

DEVELOPMENT. One of several major limitations of the MIT is that there is no information available on its development. This absence includes information on its theoretical framework, selection and development of subscales, justification for the number of items in each subscale, why a 40-minute time limit was suggested, how to interpret the subscales, and rationale for composite scores. For example, based on the reporting of Fluid and Crystallized composite scores, it can only be presumed that the instrument is based on Horn and Cattell's (1966) two-factor model of intelligence. However, no information is provided regarding the theoretical dimensions of intelligence (e.g., General Visualization, General Fluency) the subscales are designed to measure. It is also unclear why composite scores are reported by IQ scale scores ($M = 100$, $SD = 15$) and percentile ranks, whereas subscale performance is restricted to IQ scale scores. Based on the *Standards for Educational and Psychological Testing* (*Standards*; American Educational Research Association [AERA], American Psychological Association [APA], & National Council on Measurement in Education [NCME], 1999), information is needed on purposes of testing, standardization sample, analyses used to pilot test and select items, and recruitment of sample.

TECHNICAL. The standardization sample was based on 1,544 individuals who completed the Classical IQ Test on Queendom.com, Psychology Today, or Psychtests.com, and self-selected to complete the MIT and participate in the validation study. The publishers report that validation items were based on self-report. It is unclear what is meant by validation items, except that perhaps it refers to the standardization sample's demographics. The sample consisted of 42% each of men and women, with 16% reported "Unknown." The majority of the sample was below the age of 17 ($n = 572$), with the lowest sample for the 25–29-year-old age group ($n = 138$). No information is provided by race/ethnicity, disability, geographic region, or socioeconomic status. No attempt was made to obtain a sample representative of the larger population.

Normative data are reported separately with respect to the sample's demographics. This breakdown includes: gender, age group, education, grades, position, socioeconomic status, satisfaction with field, and performance in field. Frequency distributions and descriptive statistics are used to report the score distributions for the entire sample across subscales and composite scales. Statistical comparisons were used to conduct mean score differences across demographic groups. Specifically, 14 *t*-tests were used to compare the performance of men and women across all scale scores. One-way ANOVAs were used to examine the statistical score differences across other demographic groups (e.g., age group, education). However, these analyses raise a number of concerns, including the low sample sizes for certain subgroups limiting statistical power, conducting a large number of statistical comparisons without controlling for Type I error, and no reporting of effect sizes.

Coefficient alpha (internal consistency) is the only reliability evidence reported for the scale scores. The reliability of composite scores exceeded .89, whereas those for subscale scores ranged from .69 (Arguments) to .87 (Logical). Additional information on the reliability of scores is clearly needed, such as test-retest to examine stability of scores over time.

Another major limitation of the MIT is that no information is reported on test score validity. Validity evidence is clearly needed in terms of the evidence supporting the content validity, predictive validity, and concurrent validity, of the instrument, among others. Specifically, if the MIT is designed for the screening and training of employees in a corporate setting, predictive validity evidence is needed to determine the extent to which scores predict job performance indicators. Furthermore, factor-analytic results are needed to examine the dimensionality of the item- and test-level data to provide empirical data on the internal structure of subscale and composite scores.

COMMENTARY. The MIT represents a general measure of intelligence that can be efficiently administered and scored online. The primary strength of the instrument is that subscale and composite scores report accepted levels of internal consistency reliability, with the exception of Matrices, 2D-3D Images, and Arguments, which are less than .70. Otherwise, the publishers need to report considerably more documentation on the development of the instrument (e.g., theoretical structure), fairness in testing, and testing application, as per the *Standards* (AERA et al., 1999). For example, if the instrument is to serve as a credible measure across employment and educational settings, the norms need to be improved by including a larger, representative sample that represents the diversity of the target population. Such a sampling is particularly important given the limited amount of information on the characteristics of the standardization sample. With the addition of documentation on the development and psychometric properties of the instrument, test users will have available the information needed to judge the extent to which the instrument can be used for informed decision making.

SUMMARY. The MIT was designed to measure specific factors of intelligence for HR testing and screening, and for educational purposes. Unfortunately, the limited amount of information on the development of the instrument and its psychometric properties for the entire sample, and such information across subgroups raises concerns regarding the extent to which the instrument can be used to measure intelligence as designed. The absence of validity evidence is particularly troubling given the time that employers and examinees may dedicate to administering and using the MIT in applied settings. Furthermore, the publishers need to specify the instances in HR testing and screening in which the instrument could be expected to be used for decision-making purposes. This enumeration of uses also includes identifying what is meant for using the MIT for "educational purposes," such as: program placement, diagnosis, and screening. For any designated purpose of testing, validity evidence would be needed to substantiate score use. Consequently, the lack of information on the MIT results in the recommendation that the instrument not be used as a credible measure of specific factors of intelligence.

REVIEWER'S REFERENCES

American Educational Research Association, American Psychological Association, & National Council on Measurement in Education. (1999). *Standards for educational and psychological testing.* Washington, DC: American Educational Research Association.
Horn, J. L., & Cattell, R. B. (1966). Refinement and test of the theory of fluid and crystallized general intelligences. *Journal of Educational Psychology, 57*(5), 253–270.

Review of the Multi-Dimensional Intelligence Test by WILLIAM SCHAFER, Affiliated Professor (Emeritus), University of Maryland College Park, College Park, MD:

DESCRIPTION. The Multi-Dimensional Intelligence Test (MIT) is one of numerous assessments available at the web site of the publisher: www.archprofile.com. The MIT is intended for adults, 18 years of age and older. It is primarily marketed to organizations for dealing with personnel matters such as screening and training as well as educational uses, but more specific applications are not suggested.

The MIT consists of 109 items administered by computer. All items are multiple-choice or very short answer (e.g., a number or a letter). In-house testing is recommended but the assessment could be completed at home. The test is not timed, but it is suggested that users will be able to complete it in about 40 minutes. That estimate appears to be less than half of what a more realistic time for the test should be in this reviewer's opinion; the publisher does not provide a basis for their 40-minute estimate.

The test results are incorporated into a lengthy computer-generated presentation beginning with an informative history of intelligence testing that places the assessment in context. It continues with a graphical display of the individual's Overall score and percentile rank, followed by the individual's Fluid and Crystallized Intelligence scores and percentile ranks. Each of the latter is supported by subscores that are also graphed; for Fluid Intelligence, these are Spatial, Matrices, 2D-3D Images, Logical, Arguments, and Puzzles; and for Crystallized, there are Verbal, Vocabulary, Analogies, Numerical, Arithmetic, and Graphs & Charts. The next section of the report interprets the scores of the test taker on each of these scales and subscales verbally. The personalized section ends with a one-page summary of the strengths, potential strengths, and weaknesses of the test taker. A final section gives general advice on the topics of: taking intelligence tests; taking tests in general; dealing with test anxiety; improving memory; improving ability to learn, process information, and solve problems; answering logic problems; and improving mathematical ability.

DEVELOPMENT. The domain of the test, although seemingly reflective of the literature on intelligence, is only informally developed and validated.

The materials provided by the publisher indicate that items may be weighted, but which items and how they are weighted is deemed proprietary and is not shared. Scoring is not described in subsequent materials, either. The materials provided by the publisher indicate that Rasch analyses are used to score the test. Interpretive procedures are described as proprietary and are not made available.

The examinee is not told how item responses are combined into scores. For example, the impacts of an "I don't know" versus a wrong answer are not compared.

TECHNICAL. The publisher has written a standard-by-standard discussion of compliance with the current *Standards for Educational and Psychological Testing* (American Educational Research Association, American Psychological Association, & National Council on Measurement in Education, 1999). See http://corporate.psychtests.com/pdf/APA_Standards_Plumeus.pdf.

The test report claims that the test is in its third revision and that the total sample size for validation studies numbers over one million. But there is no discussion of how these data were used and what they indicate about the quality of the current revision except an indication that the alpha reliability for the entire test is .94.

Analyses were carried out on a sample of users from various sources who self-reported their demographic data. The 1,544 participants were a self-selected, convenience sample. Sixteen percent were of unknown gender and the rest were equally split between men and women. Ten percent were of unknown age; of the remainder, 37% were below the age of 17 years. The conditions under which the participants were recruited and what they were told about how their data would be used were not presented; the predominance of adolescents (and perhaps even younger individuals) in the sample suggests concern to this reviewer about how seriously they approached the task. Given that information, it is thus impossible to evaluate the adequacy of the sample for the purpose of supporting the assessment.

The publisher provided a table that documents the means and standard deviations of IQ-scale scores of the sample on the overall assessment, on the Fluid and Crystallized subscales, and on the 12 component scales; a second table presents the alpha reliabilities (except that the Vocabulary subscale is omitted; probably an oversight). The numbers of items on the Fluid scale (54) and the Crystallized scale (55) sum to the number of items on the overall scale (109), but the number of items on the 11 reported subscales sum to 203 (even without Vocabulary), suggesting that at least some items are scored on multiple subscales, probably compromising their distinctiveness. Documentation of scaling is particularly weak; were the 1,544 participants in the psychometric sample also those on whom the scaling was performed and how are IQ-scale scores computed from the raw item scores?

The alpha reliabilities of the Overall, Fluid, and Crystallized scores are adequate for individual interpretation (at .94, .89, and .90, respectively, based on the 1,544 participants). The reliabilities of some of the shorter subscales (ranging between 10 and 30 items) do not in general appear supportive for individual use; they range from a low of .56 (Matrices) to a high of .87 (Logical) with a median of .75. Perhaps there are too many subscales for the total number of items.

It is difficult to judge the adequacy of support for interpreting scores without either the method of score development or the procedures used for interpretation. Conditional standard errors of measurement are not presented, even though Rasch analyses should make them very easy to estimate, depending on how scoring is done. Such a presentation would be particularly helpful to both individuals and organizations in their own interpretations of the results. The publisher does not recommend any specific uses for which they feel empirical support is needed.

Supportive analyses, such as internal factor analyses and scale correlations as well as correlations with other assessments would be helpful as documentation of success of the program. The materials claim that analyses such as these are performed but are not reported because they are proprietary. However, these are standard analytic methods and the publisher cannot reasonably claim that they are specific to these assessments. One must question why the publisher is so guarded about sharing the results of common evaluation methods.

The publisher provided several histograms that describe the distributions of the sample on each of the subscales. Inconsistencies in how the results were presented were unexplained. For example, the Matrices subscale and the 2D/3D Images subscale each has 12 items, yet the histogram for Matrices groups the participant results into eight score categories whereas the histogram for 2D/3D Images groups them into only five.

Several analyses comparing the scores of demographic groups (gender, age, education, grades, position, socioeconomic status, satisfaction with field, and performance in field) appear in the technical materials. The analyses are limited to statistical significance tests among the groupings; effect sizes would have been helpful for follow-up interpretations.

The publisher has indicated that a manual is being prepared. In lieu of a manual, the material provided for this review was quite sparse.

COMMENTARY. Uses of the assessment are not very specific. Documentation of what decisions may be based on the scores and of the validity of the scores for those interpretations are absent. This is a major barrier to confident use of the assessment. A priority for research should be aimed at technical documentation.

Additional work is also needed to document the psychometric properties of the assessment. Data from a representative sample should be collected and a complete technical analysis, including a modern item response theory scaling with reported conditional standard errors of estimate should be included in the documentation. Reports of the exploratory and confirmatory factor analyses the publisher claims were carried out should be shared with potential users. Without these resources, an informed evaluation of the MIT is not possible and therefore its use can only be recommended for research purposes, which falls far short of the uses suggested by the publisher.

SUMMARY. The MIT is easy to administer and can be completed in a variety of settings. Although it is likely that it could be supportable technically, those analyses, assuming they have been performed, have not been reported. In the absence of supportive documentation from the publisher, it is suggested that organizations planning to use the MIT gather their own documentation to evaluate its utility in their local settings before considering ways it can support their particular goals.

REVIEWER'S REFERENCE

American Educational Research Association (AERA), American Psychological Association (APA), & National Council on Measurement in Education (NCME). (1999). *Standards for educational and psychological testing.* Washington, DC: American Educational Research Association.

[112]

MultiCraft Trainee Test.

Purpose: For selecting MultiCraft (mechanical and electrical) trainees.

Population: Applicants for jobs where some knowledge and skill in mechanical and electrical areas is needed.

Publication Dates: 2004-2009.

Scores, 8: Hydraulics & Pneumatics, Welding/Cutting & Rigging, Power Transmission/Lubrication/Mechanical Maintenance & Shop Machines and Tools & Equipment, Pumps/Piping & Combustion, Motors/Control Circuits and Schematics & Print Reading, Digital & Analog Electronics/Power Supplies/Computers & PLC and Test Instruments, Basic AC/DC Theory/Power Distribution and Electrical Maintenance, Total.

Administration: Group.

Price Data, 2011: $22 per consumable self-scoring test booklet or online administration (minimum order of 20); $24.95 per manual (2009, 19 pages).

Foreign Language Edition: Available in Spanish.

Time: 60-70 minutes.

Comments: Reusable test with separate answer sheets and key; available for online administration.

Author: Roland T. Ramsay.

Publisher: Ramsay Corporation.

Review of the MultiCraft Trainee Test by NANCY L. CRUMPTON, Adjunct Professor, Walden University, School of Counseling and Social Service, Mental Health Counseling Program and Troy University, College of Education, Counseling Department, Montgomery, AL:

DESCRIPTION. The Ramsay Corporation Job Skills (RCJS), MultiCraft Trainee Test, Form A, is a group or individually administered paper-and-pencil test with an online administration option (www.ramsaycorp.com). The purpose of the assessment is to select applicants for a 2-year MultiCraft Training Program in the areas of Electrical and Mechanical Maintenance. There are seven categories tested with specific questions included to measure knowledge and skills required for each. Categories include: (a) Hydraulics & Pneumatics, (b) Welding & Rigging, (c) Power Transmission, Lubrication, Mechanical Maintenance & Shop Machines, and Tools & Equipment, (d) Pumps, Piping & Combustion, (e) Motors, Control Circuits & Schematics and Print Reading, (f) Digital Electronics, Power Supplies, Computers & PLC and Test Instruments, and (g) Basic AC & DC Theory, Power Distribution, and Electrical Maintenance. The test is composed of 60 multiple-choice items that measure the individual's knowledge of electrical and mechanical processes, maintenance, and repair. The test is not timed; however, the time required for completion is noted on the answer sheet. Typical time for completion is less than one hour. Test instructions are to be read verbatim and there are two practice questions prior to starting the test. An overlay key is used to hand score the test. The number of correct answers is entered on the answer sheet and converted to a percentile score using the Percentile Rank Table provided in the test manual. Applicants are selected for the MultiCraft Training Program based in part on their score.

DEVELOPMENT. The MultiCraft Trainee Test, Form A, was developed by the Ramsay Corporation in 2004 to provide a method of selecting applicants with mechanical and electrical experience to participate in a training program. Job analysis was completed for the MultiCraft training program using the *Dictionary of Occupational Titles* (DOT) and the O*NET to identify occupational descriptions of the requirements for the MultiCraft position. Sixty questions from the pool of questions included in the Ramsay Corporation Job Skills (RCJS) Electrical Maintenance Trainee Test (Form UKE-1C) and Ramsay Corporation Job Skills (RCJS) Mechanical Maintenance Trainee Test (Form UKM-1C) were selected to be included in the (RCJS) MultiCraft Trainee Test, Form A, based upon item statistics for applicability to the MultiCraft position. Two industrial/organizational psychologists were responsible for selecting the items and a technical review resulted in 10 items being edited to update and clarify the original questions.

Normative data for the test were determined by test administration to 59 "various test-takers, ranging from applicants at a Midwestern manufacturing facility to job experts at a chemical manufacturer in March, 2009" (manual, p. 13).

TECHNICAL.

Standardization. Specific information about the normative population noting ages, gender, ethnicity, years of experience, level of training, etc., of the 59 participants was not described. It appeared that the results of testing by this group were primarily used to determine the level of difficulty of the 60 questions on the test. An item analysis representing difficulty of the questions based on the seven categories of test items was included in the manual. Details of the selection decisions of items for the assessment were limited.

Reliability. The discussion of reliability noted a KR20 reliability coefficient of .90; however, specific details of the study in which this coefficient was determined were not presented. The only description of the group of 59 participating in the norming data was "Employees and applicants in several industries" (manual, p. 12). Only one administration of the test was noted. How the results on the MultiCraft Trainee Test, Form A, as represented by characteristics of this group, indicated dependability or consistency was not available to provide evidence of reliability.

Validity. In this section, as in the other technical areas, statements regarding supportive analyses are not in evidence due to the minimal information available. Based on using the content of DOT and O*NET job descriptions to define the knowledge and skill areas to be evaluated by the questions on the test, it may be expected that performance on the test would have useful inferences to success in training. Neither the meaningfulness of the test results nor how the rater agreement was determined were described. It was noted that there were six "raters" of the 60 items on the test, but the test form studied was noted as EUM, not Form A. To support content evidence of validity, qualifications of the raters and how they determined that the items on the test were representative of the content domain would be required. That the manual described the one job title of Utility Mechanic within the chemical industry was also confusing in terms of how this information would be supportive of using the MultiCraft Test to predict success in training.

Criterion evidence of validity would be most critical in support of using this assessment, in that the purpose of the test is to predict success in training. Having criterion-related evidence of validity

rather than the statement (in a 1984 article) that content validity reflects criterion validity is needed.

COMMENTARY. Although the MultiCraft Trainee Test, Form A, has potential to be a useful, standardized screening tool for individuals participating in the MultiCraft Training, detailed information regarding the process of developing the test, increasing the numbers of the norming population, and providing details of the individuals in that group are needed. The limited information available regarding test development does not provide psychometric evidence of standardization. The limited validity and reliability information does not support the use of the assessment as presented. The general directions for the test examiner as well as specific instructions for administering the test are clearly presented to provide consistency in administration. Having the online option for taking the test is a benefit for applicants. Scoring is easily completed.

SUMMARY. The Ramsay Corporation Job Skills (RCJS), MultiCraft Trainee Test, Form A, is a group or individually administered paper-and-pencil test with an online administration option (www. ramsaycorp.com). The purpose of the assessment is to select applicants for a 2-year MultiCraft Training Program in the areas of Electrical and Mechanical Maintenance. Although there is a lack of evidence at this time of standardization of the test and other psychometric information, this measure has potential to be a useful assessment in screening for participation in multicraft training.

Review of the MultiCraft Trainee Test by FREDERICK L. OSWALD, Professor of Psychology, Rice University, Houston, TX:

DESCRIPTION. The MultiCraft Trainee Test consists of 60 multiple-choice items that cover seven broad areas of mechanical and electrical knowledge. The test is intended for applications to multicraft traineeships where applicants already have some multicraft experience; thus, the knowledge requirements are higher and the training time is less than that for apprenticeships. Only a pencil is required for the paper version of the test; there is also an online version of the test (see www.ramsaycorp. com). The test is scored simply by subtracting the number of incorrect and missing answers from the number of correct answers, and thus a maximum score of 60 is possible.

The MultiCraft Trainee Test may be individually or group administered to applicant trainees, with the test manual recommending there should be one examiner per 20 examinees. The test manual contains informative guidelines for administering the test successfully, as well as a script containing clear and specific directions for test-taking that are to be read aloud to the examinees. Examinees are told that although there is no time limit to the test, the test should not take more than an hour.

DEVELOPMENT. The MultiCraft Trainee Test development was based on selecting items from two other tests produced by the Ramsay Corporation: The Electrical Maintenance Trainee Test (Form UKE-1C) and the Mechanical Maintenance Trainee Test (Form UKM-1C). Test content areas are typical of other tests of mechanical and electrical knowledge: (a) Hydraulics and Pneumatics (7 items); (b) Welding and Rigging (7 items); (c) Power Transmission Lubrication, Mechanical Maintenance, and Ship Machines, Tools and Equipment (12 items); (d) Pumps, Piping, and Combustion (9 items); (e) Motors, Control Circuits, and Schematics and Print Reading (9 items); (f) Digital Electronics, Power Supplies, Computers and PLC, and Test Instruments (8 items); and (g) Basic AC/DC Theory, Power Distribution, and Electrical Maintenance (8 items).

TECHNICAL. The MultiCraft Trainee Test examiner's manual indicates that the content of the MultiCraft Trainee Test was judged by six raters in the chemical industry to be highly job-related (the items receiving an average rating of 4.1 on a 5-point scale). Although this is a limited set of raters, these results are promising. Additionally, scientific research and meta-analyses support the general idea that domain-specific job knowledge tests are predictive of training performance and job performance in organizations.

Based on an item analysis of the MultiCraft Trainee Test, the examiner's manual makes the claim of "excellent reliability" and provides a table of cutoff test scores; however, these reliability and cutoff-score results are based on a single sample comprising "59 various test-takers ranging from applicants at a Midwestern manufacturing facility to job experts at a chemical manufacturer" (manual, p. 13). (A KR-20 reliability of 90 was found with this diverse sample of 59 individuals.) Psychometric results in the examiner's manual should, therefore, be viewed as tentative at best. For example, 4 of the 60 test items were reported to have less than 25% endorsement, the percent that would be guessed correctly from random guessing. Therefore, instead of relying on the psychometric results in the test manual, a client using the MultiCraft Trainee Test might prefer psychometric information derived from client data or on the basis of data that closely resemble the client's industry and employees (e.g., internal consistency reliability, convergent and discriminant validity, group differences, and other psychometric information). To that end, the Ramsay Corporation offers validation services to its clients.

COMMENTARY. Although the psychometric information in the test manual is based on very limited samples, the content of the MultiCraft Trainee Test appears to be based on sound and representative sampling of electrical and mechanical knowledge domains. A broad test of this nature has the benefit of sampling across these domains that are relevant for multicraft positions, but it also has the drawback that a least some specific information within electrical and mechanical areas and subareas must be sacrificed as a result. Perhaps a company wanting to test both domains in greater depth could use the two aforementioned tests by Ramsay Corporation that were used to develop the MultiCraft Trainee Test.

It also should be directly noted that despite the test manual identifying "knowledge and skill areas," the MultiCraft Trainee Test is a test of knowledge, not of skills. Knowing something often implies the ability to do it, but that does not mean that knowledge and skills are the same thing. Therefore, in some cases, companies that use this test might seek further confirmation that the knowledge expressed by the test-taker can, in fact, be expressed in terms of a skill. For instance, MultiCraft Trainee Test scores could confirm the prior job experience found in a resumé, where skills in the past can be inferred; the test could also serve as an initial screen to select test-takers to perform hands-on skills tests, assuming the client believes that skills tests are needed in order to support the assumption that a test-taker's specialized knowledge can be applied.

As mentioned previously, despite the test manual's support for representative content of electrical and mechanical knowledge in the MultiCraft Trainee Test, and despite the provision of a small-sample item analysis and table of cutoff scores, much more psychometric evidence is needed for a client to make solid inferences about the reliability, validity, and other correlates and group differences associated with the test.

SUMMARY. The MultiCraft Trainee Test merges item content from the electrical and mechanical knowledge tests already developed by the company. Thus, a bit of depth within each domain is sacrificed in the service of measuring greater breadth across domains. The administration guidelines and test instructions are clear, relevant, and can be easily implemented. The test manual reports psychometric results based on quite a limited set of sample data (one rater sample and one job sample, each with small sample sizes); however, these results demonstrate at least tentative support for the content relevance and overall reliability of the test. Because of these limited data, however, the cutoff scores reported in the manual should be used with great caution. Furthermore, data pertaining to criterion-related evidence of validity and subgroup differences related to protected classes (e.g., gender and race) are not reported. A client making use of this test should request large-sample psychometric results and/or ask that those results be computed for their own test-takers.

[113]

Multidimensional Anxiety Scale for Children 2nd Edition.

Purpose: Designed as "a comprehensive, multi-rater assessment of anxiety dimensions in children and adolescents...to [aid] in the early identification, diagnosis, treatment planning and monitoring of anxiety-prone youth."
Population: Ages 8–19.
Publication Dates: 1997–2013.
Acronym: MASC 2.
Scores, 13: Separation Anxiety/Phobias, Generalized Anxiety Disorder (GAD) Index, Social Anxiety: Total (Humiliation/Rejection Subscale, Performance Fears Subscale, Total), Obsessions & Compulsions, Physical Symptoms: Total (Panic Subscale, Tense/Restless Subscale, Total), Harm Avoidance, Anxiety Probability Score, Inconsistency Index (response style), Total Score.
Administration: Individual or group.
Forms, 2: Self-Report, Parent.
Price Data, 2013: $189 per complete hand-scored kit (including manual, 25 each of self-report and parent QuikScore™ forms); $88 per manual (2013, 136 pages); $219 per complete online kit (including manual, 25 self-report and parent online forms); $329 per complete scoring software kit (including manual, scoring software [USB key], 25 each of self-report and parent response forms).
Time: (15) minutes.
Comments: Revision includes addition of parent form, new norms, and some new scales. Online and paper/pencil versions available.
Author: John S. March.

Publisher: Multi-Health Systems, Inc.
Cross References: For reviews by John C. Caruso and Robert Christopher of an earlier edition, see 14:246.

Review of the Multidimensional Anxiety Scale for Children 2nd Edition by JERRELL C. CASSADY, Professor of Psychology, Department of Educational Psychology, and Director, Academic Anxiety Resource Center, Ball State University, Muncie, IN:

DESCRIPTION. According to the test authors, the Multidimensional Anxiety Scale for Children 2nd Edition (MASC 2) is a comprehensive assessment system to identify domains of elevated anxiety for children ages 8 to 19 years. It is proposed to serve as an early identification assessment as well as a tool for evaluating the efficacy of intervention efforts to alleviate anxiety symptoms or in basic research.

The MASC 2 is a revision of the popular Multidimensional Anxiety Scale for Children (MASC), with several ambitious updates that enhance the validity of its scores and the diversity of anxiety symptoms that can be identified. The updates include the creation of a parent form (MASC 2-P) that allows multiple parents or guardians to provide reports of anxiety symptoms in children. The data collected with the parent form not only provide additional points of information for review, but the scoring protocol also provides guidance for identifying when two parents' reports differ significantly from one another, or when they differ from what the child self-report (MASC 2-SR) offers. In addition to this new form, the MASC 2 has added new dimensions of anxiety for diagnostic support, including a Generalized Anxiety Disorder Index, the Obsessions & Compulsions scale, and an overall Anxiety Probability Score (which provides a likelihood indicator for the child having at least one anxiety disorder).

The MASC 2-SR and the MASC 2-P can be completed as a paper-pencil version or through the Multi-Health Systems Online Assessment Center. The MASC 2 is reported to have a reading level of 2.0; children without sufficient literacy skills can have the measure read aloud by a trained administrator. The MASC 2-P has an estimated reading level of 2.2. The test manual suggests an administration time of 15 minutes or less, which was verified during this review.

Reports from either form of data collection can be generated that provide a simple review of the individual assessment (Assessment Report), changes in scores over time by individual students (Progress Report), or comparative analyses of scores gathered from different raters (Comparative Report).

Scores are generated on the following scales and subscales: Separation Anxiety/Phobias, Generalized Anxiety Disorder Index, Social Anxiety: Total (composed of Humiliation/Rejection subscale and Performance Fears subscale), Obsessions and Compulsions, Physical Symptoms: Total (composed of Panic subscale Tense/Restless subscale), and Harm Avoidance. In addition, a Total score; an Anxiety Probability score; and an Inconsistency Index, designed to measure response patterns, are generated.

DEVELOPMENT. The test manual outlines the history of the revisions for the MASC 2, again building on the MASC's long history of success. The impetus for developing the MASC and MASC 2 was the high rate of anxiety disorders in the population (estimates range up to nearly 30%) as well as the finding that early onset of anxiety is common. The advantages of the MASC 2 are the presence of quality norming samples and the addition of the parent form for obtaining external ratings of anxiety symptoms.

Psychometrically, the MASC 2 built upon the previously validated MASC. To identify the final items for the MASC 2, all original items from the MASC along with an additional 18 items addressing obsessions and compulsions and two items focusing on generalized anxiety were used in the data collection effort. Analyses of the item characteristics led to the removal of one original MASC item. In addition, data from the 18 obsessions and compulsions items led to the selection of 10 items for the final scale. Validation of the factor structure using this new collection of items was conducted through confirmatory factor analysis, with acceptable fit indices produced. The analyses of the intercorrelations supported the conclusion that MASC 2 provides a multidimensional and nested representation of anxiety symptoms.

The new normative sample included 1,800 children ages 8 to 19 for the MASC 2-SR and 1,600 parent raters for the MASC 2-P. Review of the demographic characteristics for this sample collected from the United States ($n = 1,355$ for MASC 2-SR; $n = 1,126$ for the MASC 2-P) and Canada ($n = 445$ for MASC 2-SR; $n = 474$ for MASC 2-P) indicated reasonable representation of targeted categories, including race/ethnicity, gender, parental education level, and age of children. The sampling process for developing the normative data

for the MASC 2-SR and the MASC 2-P drew from an overall data collection effort exceeding 5,000 respondents.

In addition to the normative sample, data were collected from a clinical sample including more than 1,000 children with a diagnosed clinical disorder (including generalized anxiety disorder, panic disorder, social phobia, major depressive disorder, social anxiety disorder, obsessive compulsive disorder, and attention-deficit/hyperactivity disorder). The data from these children were used to identify the utility of the MASC 2 for identifying differences between the clinical and normative samples.

The revisions for the MASC 2 also involved developing an Anxiety Probability Score, which purportedly estimates the probability that a child has a clinical anxiety disorder. This probability is defined by elevated responses on one or more of three anxiety scales that assess the constructs of separation anxiety disorder, generalized anxiety disorder, and social anxiety disorder. The utility of the Anxiety Probability Score was assessed by identifying the likelihood that a respondent who had elevated levels on one or more of these anxiety scales would be a member of the clinical sample. The results of this analysis demonstrated that as the number of elevated anxiety scale scores increased, the probability of being a member of the clinical sample also increased.

The Inconsistency Index was created by isolating eight pairs of items on the MASC 2-SR and the MASC 2-P that were found to have the highest correlations. When differences in student or parent responses on those item pairs are detected, the absolute value of the difference is identified. The sum of those absolute values is then compared to established cut scores that indicate inconsistent responses and suggest that the reported levels of anxiety may be suspect. In the normative sample, fewer than 5% of respondents were found to demonstrate inconsistency.

TECHNICAL. The technical manual is very detailed in outlining the psychometric qualities of the MASC 2-SR and the MASC 2-P. The test authors provide detailed explanations of the procedures used to establish the T-score values for each age range in the normative sample. Careful review of the normative sample confirmed that separate norms were required based on age and gender. The scoring protocol provides simple identification for males and females separately across three age ranges (8–11, 12–15, 16–19).

Scale reliability estimates for internal consistency, test-retest reliability, and stability were offered. Internal consistency estimates were sufficient for all reported subscales, with Total score alpha coefficients of .92 for the MASC 2-SR and .89 for the MASC 2-P.

Test-retest reliability was examined with a small subset (n = 98 children; n = 95 parents) of participants. The average times between the test and retest administrations were 19.8 and 18.9 days, respectively. The correlation coefficients for the test and retest values for the various subscales ranged from .80 to .94 for the MASC 2-SR and .80 to .93 for the MASC 2-P. Although these analyses used a limited sample, the data support the conclusion that test-retest reliability is strong. Stability estimates were also calculated with this subsample by examining whether a respondent's value on the MASC 2 subscales differed from one administration to the next by less than 1 standard deviation. These analyses confirmed that respondent scores were stable over time.

Validation evidence for the MASC 2 is strong. Discriminant validity was established using the aforementioned clinical sample. Effect size comparisons for the clinical subsamples (disaggregated by type of diagnosis) are offered and repeatedly confirm expectations for identifying differences from the general population as well as among the clinical samples.

Convergent validity evidence is also offered in the test manual based on a study examining consistency of responses for the MASC 2 with the Beck Anxiety Inventory for Youth (15:31) and the Conners Comprehensive Behavior Rating Scales (18:33). Moderate correlation coefficients were noted for both external measures of anxiety through the self-report scales. Similar evidence emerged in an examination of the parent form for the Conners scale and the MASC 2-P.

Finally, interrater consistency in identifying anxiety symptoms was examined as construct evidence of validity. Comparisons between parent and child ratings on the MASC 2-SR and the MASC 2-P provided quality evidence of interrater consistency, with moderate correlation coefficients noted (range .43–.68).

COMMENTARY. The MASC 2 is a well-constructed assessment tool for examining a diverse range of anxiety symptoms in children ages 8–19. The clinical utility of the scale was validated through the comparison of data from a large normative sample and clinical samples, demonstrating expected divergence of scores for the groups. The scale has been exhaustively reviewed psychometrically, demonstrating strong reliability and validity evidence. The creation of T scores for each subscale using the substantial normative sample is useful for making comparisons across groups or within individuals across the multiple dimensions of anxiety measured.

The administration and scoring of the protocols is well supported by the test manual and can be learned with minimal review and training. In addition, the inclusion of the Inconsistency Index and established guidelines for detecting inconsistencies in reports from multiple raters provide confidence in scores obtained.

SUMMARY. Clinicians and researchers alike will find the MASC 2 to be a valuable tool for identifying students with elevated levels of anxiety symptoms as compared to a normative sample. The durability of the scale also supports the test authors' suggestion that efficacy of treatment programs for reducing anxiety symptoms can be effectively documented by repeated testing over time, aided by the careful attention to standard age differences noted in response patterns.

Review of the Multidimensional Anxiety Scale for Children 2nd Edition by MERILEE McCURDY, Associate Professor, and JILL HOLTZ, Doctoral Student, Department of Educational Psychology, University of Nebraska-Lincoln, Lincoln, NE:

DESCRIPTION. The Multidimensional Anxiety Scale for Children 2nd Edition (MASC 2) is a measure of anxiety symptoms in children and adolescents ages 8–19 years intended for use as a component of a comprehensive clinical evaluation. While retaining features of the original MASC (1997), the MASC 2 includes a parent form with items parallel to those on the self-report form, new demographically representative norms, and new scales (i.e., General Anxiety Disorder [GAD] Index, Obsessions & Compulsions scale, Anxiety Probability Score).

The MASC 2 contains two forms: a self-report form (MASC 2-SR) for youths to report their own anxiety symptoms and a parent form (MASC 2-P) for parents to report the anxiety symptoms of a youth. Items follow a 4-point, Likert-type format. The MASC 2 can be administered via paper-and-pencil and scored by hand or with software; online administration and scoring also are available. Procedures for administering the MASC

2 using either method are clearly described in the test manual. Administering the MASC 2-SR or the MASC 2-P to an individual or group takes approximately 15 minutes.

The test manual includes instructions for calculating raw scores, converting raw scores to *T*-scores, and calculating the Anxiety Probability Score. The MASC 2 yields 13 scores: the Total Score (sum of 50 items), scale scores (i.e., Separation Anxiety/Phobias, GAD Index, Social Anxiety: Total, Obsessions & Compulsions, Physical Symptoms: Total, and Harm Avoidance), subscales (i.e., Social Anxiety subscales: Humiliation/Rejection, Performance Fears; Physical Symptoms subscales: Panic, Tense/Restless), Anxiety Probability Score, and Inconsistency Index. Guidelines for interpreting scores are adequately described. The test manual provides a case study to assist assessors in examining item-level responses and integrating results from multiple sources.

DEVELOPMENT. In the test manual, the author describes how the original MASC's scales were constructed to conceptualize childhood anxiety broadly, including using an empirical, bottom-up approach that involved categorizing a pool of items into symptom domains and then performing a series of exploratory factor analyses to arrive at a solution consisting of four factors (Physical Symptoms, Social Anxiety, Separation/Panic, and Harm Avoidance) and six subscales (Tense/Restless, Somatic/Autonomic, Perfectionism, Anxious Coping, Humiliation/Rejection, and Performance Fears). The MASC was designed to assess a spectrum of anxiety symptoms rather than a specific DSM anxiety construct. It has found application in areas of anxiety research including treatment outcome studies (March & Parker, 2004), etiological studies (e.g., McLaughlin & Hatzenbuehler, 2009), and studies defining the spectrum of anxiety (e.g., Saavedra & Silvermann, 2002). Development of the MASC 2 was guided by objectives to collect new normative data to enhance interpretability of scores, to assist in conducting more comprehensive evaluations by including both parent and youth reports about anxiety symptoms, and to increase the utility of the test through the development of scales measuring additional anxiety dimensions (i.e., generalized anxiety, obsessive-compulsive disorders).

New normative and clinical data were collected for the MASC 2, including a normative sample of 3,400 ratings from an equal number of males and females ages 8 to 19 and a clinical sample of more than 1,000 ratings of youths diagnosed with clinical disorders. Data collection forms included all items from the original MASC, 18 new items assessing obsessions and compulsions, and two new items measuring symptoms of generalized anxiety.

To strengthen the measure's psychometric properties, changes were made to its factor structure, including removing the Harm Avoidance subscales (Anxious Coping and Perfectionism) and creating an eight-item Harm Avoidance scale that encompassed both. To validate the fit of the revised factor structure, confirmatory factor analyses (CFAs) were completed using data from both normative and clinical samples. Separate CFAs were conducted for the MASC 2-SR and the MASC 2-P.

Although most scales from the MASC were retained in the MASC 2, changes were made. The Somatic/Autonomic subscale was renamed the Panic subscale, and the Separation/Panic scale was renamed the Separation Anxiety/Phobias scale. The GAD Index (10 items that differentiate GAD cases from normative ones), the Obsessions & Compulsions scale (10 items measuring aspects of OCD), and the Anxiety Probability Score (a score estimating a youth's chances of having an anxiety disorder) were developed.

TECHNICAL.

Standardization. Data collected from normative samples (i.e., 1,800 self-report ratings from youths ages 8 to 19 for the MASC 2-SR and 1,600 parent ratings for the MASC 2-P) were weighted to match U.S. and Canadian census data with respect to race/ethnicity, education level, and geographic region. Data provided on the demographic characteristics of both the MASC 2-SR and MASC 2-P normative samples indicate that normative samples are similar to the census results (all within 3.5%) in terms of race/ethnicity, geographic region, and parental education level.

Norming procedures examined gender and age trends in the data. A series of ANCOVAs and MANCOVAs was performed to assess the effects of age, gender, and their interaction on raw scale scores. Age was found to significantly affect scale scores; thus, norms are separated into three age groups: 8–11 years, 12–15 years, and 16–19 years. Gender was found to significantly affect all scales on the MASC 2-SR and some scales on the MASC 2-P, so gender-specific norms also were developed. Separate norms were not developed for racial or ethnic groups.

Reliability. Overall, the MASC 2 exhibits strong internal consistency. Coefficient alpha for the

Total score is .92 for the MASC 2-SR normative sample (median alpha value for scales and subscales is .79) and .89 for the MASC 2-P normative sample (median alpha value for scales and subscales is .78). For the anxiety disorder sample (a subset of the clinical sample), coefficient alpha is .95 for the MASC 2-SR (median alpha for scales and subscales is .86) and .95 for the MASC 2-P (median alpha for scales and subscales is .84). Alpha values for the GAD Index (.72 for the MASC 2-SR and .66 for the MASC 2-P) are lower than alpha values for other domains.

The MASC 2 demonstrates good temporal stability. To assess test-retest reliability, 98 youths and 95 parents completed the test a second time after a 1- to 4-week interval. Corrected retest values for the MASC 2-SR ranged from .80 to .94 and from .80 to .93 for the MASC 2-P.

Validity. To demonstrate evidence of discriminative validity, diagnostic information from youths was obtained. ANCOVA and MANCOVA were conducted to investigate whether scores on the MASC 2 could distinguish between the general population and clinical groups. Results indicated that the MASC 2 scale scores differentiated between youths diagnosed with an anxiety disorder and the general population of youths. Also, the MASC 2 anxiety scale scores (i.e., Separation Anxiety/ Phobias, GAD Index, Social Anxiety: Total) differentiated among groups of youth with different anxiety disorders.

The MASC 2 also demonstrates evidence of convergent validity. Beck Anxiety Inventory for Youth (BAI-4; 15:31) and MASC 2-SR Total scores were found to be moderately correlated (corrected r = .73). Of the scales available on both the MASC 2 and the Conners Comprehensive Behavior Rating Scales (CBRS; 18:33), moderate correlations were found between scale scores that were conceptually related on the MASC 2-SR and the CBRS self-report (corrected r = .42 to .64). Moderate correlations were found between scale scores that were conceptually related on the MASC 2-P and the CBRS parent form (corrected r = .28 to .64).

Analyses were conducted to determine whether similar scores are obtained across race/ ethnic group samples from the normative samples. Results revealed that on both the MASC 2-SR and the MASC 2-P, White youths scored significantly higher than Hispanic/Latino and Black youths on the Total score and on subscales; however, overall, effect sizes were trivial for the MASC 2-P and for

the majority of the MASC 2-SR scales. The test author claims that the lack of meaningful differences between racial and ethnic groups supports the validity of the use of the MASC 2 test scores with various ethnic groups.

COMMENTARY. Overall, the MASC 2 is a well-standardized, psychometrically sound measure of anxiety dimensions in youth. The addition of new norms and the MASC 2-P as well as the GAD Index, Obsessions & Compulsions scale, and the Anxiety Probability Score allow for a more comprehensive assessment of anxiety symptoms than did the original MASC. Generalized anxiety and obsessive-compulsive disorders were dimensions of anxiety not previously assessed by the MASC, and development of these scales allows assessors to more effectively measure these constructs. However, the MASC 2, by itself, should not be regarded as a comprehensive measure of anxiety and should not be used alone in making a clinical diagnosis. Additionally, caution should be used in interpreting scores with respect to racial/ethnic groups, despite some empirical findings that support its use across racial and ethnic groups.

SUMMARY. The MASC 2 is a useful tool for assessing anxiety symptoms in youths as part of a comprehensive clinical evaluation. Like the MASC, it can be used as a screener or a tool to monitor treatment effects in a variety of settings (e.g., schools, clinics, research facilities) where repeated measures are needed. The test manual is well written and organized. Administration and scoring procedures are clearly explained, and guidelines for interpretation are provided. The MASC 2 is intended for use by psychologists, school psychologists, clinical social workers, counselors, physicians, psychiatric workers, and pediatric/psychiatric nurses.

REVIEWERS' REFERENCES

March, J. S. (1997). *Manual for the Multidimensional Anxiety Scale for Children (MASC).* Toronto, Canada: Multi-Health Systems, Inc.

March, J. S., & Parker, J. D. A. (2004). The Multidimensional Anxiety Scale for Children (MASC). In M. E. Maruish (Ed.), *The use of psychological testing for treatment planning and outcomes assessments: Instruments for children and adolescents.* Hillsdale, NJ: Lawrence Erlbaum Associates.

McLaughlin, K. A., & Hatzenbuehler, M. L. (2009). Stressful life events, anxiety sensitivity, and internalizing symptoms in adolescents. *Journal of Abnormal Psychology, 118,* 659–669.

Saavedra, L. M., & Silvermann, W. K. (2002). Classification of anxiety disorders in children: What a difference two decades make. *International Review of Psychiatry, 14,* 87–101.

[114]

Multidimensional Verbal Intelligence Test.

Purpose: Designed "to evaluate a person's verbal ability."
Population: Under age 17 through adult.
Publication Date: 2011.
Acronym: MVIT.

Scores, 7: Definitions, Antonyms, Sentence Completions, Analogies, Reading Comprehension, Vocabulary, Overall Score.
Administration: Individual.
Price Data: Available from publisher.
Time: (30) minutes.
Comments: Self-administered online assessment. The test publisher advises that the test manual is being updated to include more information about methodology and theoretical background used in the development of the test. The test publisher also advises that this information is available to clients, as are benchmarks for relevant industries and racial/ethnic group comparison data. However, this information was not provided to Buros or the reviewers.
Author: PsychTests AIM, Inc.
Publisher: PsychTests AIM, Inc. [Canada].

Review of the Multidimensional Verbal Intelligence Test by THANOS PATELIS, Vice President of Research and Analysis, Research and Development Department, The College Board, and Research Scholar, Graduate School of Education, Fordham University, New York, NY:

DESCRIPTION. The Multidimensional Verbal Intelligence Test (MVIT) is designed to evaluate verbal ability through a self-administered online assessment. The manual indicates that the application of the results from the MVIT could be used for pre-employment testing. The initial directions were clear, the online display of the questions was easily visible, and the response formats were clear. On small screens, as found on laptops, respondents need to scroll down the page and cannot access the directions without scrolling back. Additionally, once the respondent moves to the next page, the respondent cannot move backward. Scoring is instantaneous, and score reports are provided immediately with suggestions for increasing subsequent performance. An overall score is provided, as well as scores on six scales representing (a) Vocabulary, (b) Definitions, (c) Antonyms, (d) Sentence Completions, (e) Analogies, and (f) Reading Comprehension. Each scale has a maximum of 155 with the minimum ranging from 55 to 63 depending on the scale. Multiple-choice responses included an "I don't know" option, but information about how this option was scored was not provided. The sample used for norms represented a large sample ($n = 8,600$) of convenience. Gender and age distributions were provided.

DEVELOPMENT. The manual represented a series of tables and figures with some narrative indicating and interpreting a number of the analyses. Although the statistical analysis for each of the tables and figures was provided, the conceptual basis of the construct being represented, the basis for the design of the instrument, information and results about pilot testing including sensitivity review, and the logic of the sample used for the analyses were not provided.

TECHNICAL.

Standardization. The sample used for norms represented a large sample ($n = 8,600$) of convenience. Gender and age distributions were provided. However, information about geographic and racial/ethnic representation was not provided. The distributions of the scales seemed normally distributed, but for some of the scales including the overall score, the distributions appeared negatively skewed. The scoring rules were not provided.

Reliability. Reliability in the form of coefficient alpha was provided for each scale and for the overall score. The overall score comprised 58 items and had the highest coefficient alpha at .93, representing a high level. For the other six scales, alpha coefficients ranged from .75 to .89. No other reliability information was provided including the standard errors of measurement. The correlation coefficients between scales were not provided.

Validity. Validity was assessed primarily by comparing performance on each scale across a number of self-reported responses to the following variables: gender, age, education levels, grades in school, current position, socioeconomic status, satisfaction with current field, and performance in current field. Mean differences across each level for each scale were examined. Statistically significant differences were found in many relevant areas. The effect sizes of these differences were not reported.

COMMENTARY. The ease of administration and immediacy of the score report are two of the most positive features of this instrument. Although the test questions appear to be consistent with questions represented on other verbal ability tests, the lack of a substantive basis for the scales, the absence of a description of the test development process including piloting and revision, and the failure to mention a sensitivity review and differential item functioning results raise concerns over the appropriateness of the test questions used. More information is needed in the manual to describe the development process and scoring rules. Although the overall internal consistency for the sample mentioned was sufficiently large at .93, internal consistency of the individual scales was smaller than .90. Additionally, although the mean scores show statistically significant differences at different levels of selected variables in patterns that one would expect to see, the effect sizes were not reported, making it difficult to understand whether the scales offered meaningfully relevant information at each level. Next, if the goal is to use this measure in pre-employment testing, such an important application requires more direct evidence to support its use in personnel selection situations. Finally, in the score reports provided, there is a need to include the standard error of measurement in the communication of the results and to provide validity evidence to support the advice provided.

SUMMARY. The MVIT is an online instrument that is easily administered and scored with immediate score reporting. In addition to the overall score, six scale scores are provided (i.e., Vocabulary, Definitions, Antonyms, Sentence Completions, Analogies, and Reading Comprehension). A large sample is used for the norms, but the representativeness of the sample is difficult to judge. The internal consistency of the overall score is high (i.e., .93), but the internal consistency values of the individual scales are all less than .90. Some validity evidence suggests that the scores on each scale are statistically significantly different at different levels of some relevant variables (e.g., grades, education levels, current position, etc.), but how meaningful the differences are is difficult to assess. Additionally, for the intended application of pre-employment testing, more direct evidence to support these inferences is needed. Finally, although the score reports are descriptive, offering interpretation of scores and advice to improve performance, validity evidence to support these claims is needed.

Review of the Multidimensional Verbal Intelligence Test by KATHLEEN QUINN, Professor of Education, Director, Fall and Spring Reading Clinic, Holy Family University, Philadelphia, PA:

DESCRIPTION. The Multidimensional Verbal Intelligence Test (MVIT) is a computer-administered measure of verbal intelligence designed for use with persons ages 17 and above. The authors believe it can provide a quick estimate of verbal cognitive ability for pre-employment testing. The test includes 60 multiple-choice items to be completed in 30 minutes. Results are reported on the following scales: Vocabulary, Definitions, Antonyms, Sentence Completions, Analogies, and

Reading Comprehension. Because the measure is computer administered, the examinee cannot go back to a previous screen to review or change an answer, which is a distinct disadvantage to a more traditional paper-and-pencil test. Most items are composed of phrases or sentences. However, the Reading Comprehension items contain two separate articles, scientific in nature, taken from two professional sources. Because no readability statistics were provided, this reviewer calculated these to be between 15.2 and 16.6 on the Flesch-Kincaid scale. This value would be considered at least college and/or graduate level material. This level is certainly above the expected reading level of even most proficient 17- to 18-year-old high school graduates. As a result, these passages could certainly have a negative impact on an individual's overall score and on their Reading Comprehension scale score in particular for the population for which this test is intended.

The test is self-administered and though the guidelines state it requires approximately 30 minutes the reviewer was able to take longer than that to complete it. In addition, unless the administration is monitored in some way, it would be fairly easy for someone to use various resources as aids in answering many of the questions.

The test is scored automatically and quickly upon completion. A full report is provided to the examinee giving her or him the overall results reported as a Verbal IQ score along with the percentile rank, a diagram of where the examinee places on the normal curve, a narrative explanation of what the test measures, the examinee's performance strengths and needs, and similar information for the scales. The report also gives brief advice such as "The best way to develop word skills and to increase your verbal intelligence is to practice, practice, practice! Besides that, here are some specific tips to help you improve" (p. 6 of report). "Increasing Vocabulary: Pay attention. Make an effort to be more mindful of the words you read and try to look up those that you don't know instead of skipping to the next sentence" (p. 6 of report). Although of some limited value, the advice/tips often sound canned and generic.

DEVELOPMENT. In developing the MVIT, the authors wanted to design a brief measure of general verbal ability for a wide age range that could be used for pre-employment purposes. The authors provide no information as to how the items and scales were developed. There is no mention of a pilot and process of revision for items nor is there a factor analysis or item analysis provided to support the labeling of the scales. Upon examination of the test itself, the reviewer does concur that the items are similar in nature to other verbal ability tests; however, no concurrent validity data are provided. In addition, there is no discussion of why this test would be valuable for pre-employment testing nor is there any indication of how one would use it for this purpose or in what fields. As a result, it is difficult to evaluate this process.

TECHNICAL. The standardization sample for the MVIT included 8,600 adults (ages 17–50+) who self-selected to take the test online at Queendom.com, Psychtests.com, or Psychologytoday.com. There was no attempt to have a fairly representative group based on U.S. or Canadian population data or any other demographic. The manual does provide descriptive statistics for all subjects in the sample with a breakdown by the following subcategories: Gender, Age, Education, Grades in School, Employment Position, Socio-Economic Status (income based), Satisfaction Level in Current Field of Employment, and Performance in Current Field of Employment. There is no mention of a category specific to ethnicity, language proficiency, geographic regions, nationality, or groups with special needs.

Reliability is reported for internal consistency using coefficient alpha for both the overall score and the individual scales. Values range from .75 to .93 and are all within the acceptable range in the opinion of this reviewer. Standard deviations are rather high, ranging from 20.39 to 34.68. In the psychometric report, a series of t-tests and ANOVAs is presented in both graphic (normal curves and bar graphs) and narrative form indicating significant differences observed on each scale and on the overall score for each subcategory. The results indicate that men significantly outscored women on the overall score and on all scales except Antonyms ($p < .05$).

The standardization sample subcategory of age was divided into six ranges: below 17, 18–24, 25–29, 30–39, 40–49, and 50 and above. Those in the below 17 age group scored significantly below all other age groups on the Sentence Completions, Analogies, and Reading Comprehension scales and on the overall score ($p < .05$). There were 10 categories for the education variable with the number of participants in each category ranging from 142 to 221. Those with any form of postsecondary education generally outperformed

those who did not. All postsecondary preparation categories scored higher than those who had high school or lower. When comparing reported grades in school, those who reported top or good grades significantly outperformed those who reported average or below average grades, except on the Antonyms scale. In the category of position, those who reported being entrepreneurs, managers, or nonmanagers significantly outperformed those who reported that they were unemployed ($p < .05$) in the vast majority of scale comparisions. For the four categories of SES, those reporting incomes of \$25,000 to \$49,000, \$50,000 to \$74,000, and \$75,000 and above significantly outperformed those who reported incomes below \$25,000 ($p < .05$). For the three subcategories of satisfaction with current field, those who were very satisfied significantly outperformed those who reported being somewhat satisfied and unsatisfied in all scores except Reading Comprehension and Analogies ($p < .01$). For Reading Comprehension, those who reported being very satisfied outperformed those who reported being unsatisfied ($p < .05$). Those who reported good performance in their jobs outperformed those who reported satisfactory performance in their jobs on all scales. Aside from these statistical results of comparisons for subcategories of the sample, no other evidence of validity is reported. A request was made for further information as indicated on the publisher's website (http://corporate.psychtests.com/tests/science_validity) on September 4, 2012, but no reply was received.

As a result, based on limited information, it is not possible to fully evaluate the construct, content, concurrent, or predictive validity of this test. There is no information regarding the theoretical or philosophical base for this test in the manual. There is a brief summary of the publisher's definition of intelligence in the score report. There is no information about item development, item analysis, or factor analysis, although the publisher's website (cited above) states that developers conducted "factor analysis (both exploratory and confirmatory) to evaluate the structure of the assessment, and compare groups of subjects on a number of variables… In addition, our intelligence tests are subjected to Rasch analysis. Results of these analyses are reported in statistical reports available to our clients." There is no information about the difficulty level of the items or the readability level of the items or passages used. Further, there are no data to support the predictive nature of this test as a pre-employment screening measure nor is there any explanation as to how, when, and why one should use the measure for this purpose.

No test-retest reliability was reported. No standard error of measurement (*SEM*) was reported. There was no indication that test bias was examined.

COMMENTARY. Although the measure is similar to many other measures of verbal cognitive ability, the authors do not provide thorough or complete psychometric information in the manual that accompanied the MVIT to warrant its use. The MVIT also lacks data to support its content, construct, predictive, and concurrent validity along with limited information regarding reliability and item difficulty and development. Although ease of administration and automatic interpretation may seem like advantages, they may not be in this case. The computer administration could lead to a variety of deceptive responses and does not allow examinees the opportunity to review and revise their responses. Without a professional evaluation of responses, the scores are autogenerated with a canned report that also provides prescriptive and sometimes euphemistic advice. Until further exposition of all of the technical and theoretical issues addressed in this review, the MVIT should not be used.

SUMMARY. The MVIT is a computer-administered, scored, and interpreted test of verbal cognitive ability designed for use as a pre-employment screening for those ages 17 and older. There is not enough technical or theoretical information to support its use at this time in the opinion of this reviewer.

REVIEWER'S REFERENCE

PsychTests AIM, Inc. (2011). MVIT (Multidimensional Verbal Intelligence Test). Montreal, QC: Pt/psychtests. http://corporate.psychtests.com/tests/science_validity (downloaded on 9/4/2012).

[115]

Negotiation Aptitude Profile.

Purpose: Designed to assess "ability to negotiate effectively in a business environment."

Population: Under 17 through adult.

Publication Date: 2011.

Acronym: NAP.

Scores, 35: Memory for Faces, Memory for Names, Stress Management, Patience, Anger Control, Perspective, Self-Monitoring, Communication Skills, Listening Skills, Social Skills, Persuasiveness, Conflict-Resolution Skills, Assertiveness, Networking Skills, Social Insight, Empathy, Flexibility, Willingness to Withhold Judgment, Integrity, Use of "Dirty" Tactics, Mental Speed, Problem-Solving Skills, Knowledge of Negotiation Tactics, Knowledge of Negotiation Principles/Terminology, Preparation and

Planning, Clarification and Justification, Bargaining and Problem-Solving, Closure and Implementation, Memory Skills, Self-Control, People Skills, Agreeableness, Cognitive Acuity, Knowledge of the Negotiation Process, Overall Scores.

Administration: Individual.

Price Data: Available from publisher.

Time: (30) minutes.

Comments: Self-administered online assessment. The test publisher advises that the test manual is being updated to include more information about methodology and theoretical background used in the development of the test. The test publisher also advises that this information is available to clients, as are benchmarks for relevant industries and racial/ethnic group comparison data. However, this information was not provided to Buros or the reviewers.

Author: PsychTests AIM, Inc.

Publisher: PsychTests AIM, Inc. [Canada].

Review by the Negotiation Aptitude Profile by NORA P. REILLY, Professor of Psychology, Radford University, Radford, VA:

DESCRIPTION. The Negotiation Aptitude Profile is designed to assess the ability to negotiate effectively in a business environment. Its application is pre-employment testing for adults ages 17 and older. It is a self-administered, online assessment that uses 186 items that ostensibly compose 28 subscales: Memory for Faces, Memory for Names, Stress Management, Patience, Anger Control, Perspective, Self-Monitoring, Communication Skills, Listening Skills, Social Skills, Persuasiveness, Conflict-Resolution Skills, Assertiveness, Networking Skills, Social Insight, Empathy, Flexibility, Willingness to Withhold Judgment, Integrity, Use of "Dirty" Tactics, Mental Speed, Problem-Solving Skills, Knowledge of Negotiation Tactics, Knowledge of Negotiation Principles/Terminology, Preparation and Planning, Clarification and Justification, Bargaining and Problem-Solving, and Closure and Implementation. These subscales compose six factors: Memory Skills, Self-Control, People Skills, Agreeableness, Cognitive Acuity, and Knowledge of the Negotiation Process, all of which are used to provide an Overall Score. The examinee is presented with brief and simple instructions and is expected to complete the assessment in a single session lasting approximately 30 minutes.

The factors are briefly defined in the manual (p. 1). Memory Skills refers to the "ability to memorize and recall important information." Self-control refers to the "ability to monitor and regulate emotions and behavior." People Skills describes the "ability to relate to and deal with others." Agreeableness "refers to overall good-naturedness and likeability." Cognitive Acuity describes the "ability to learn quickly and apply knowledge effectively." Finally, Knowledge of the Negotiation Process "assesses one's understanding of the steps in the negotiation process." A rationale for each factor's contribution to negotiation aptitude is not provided even though this field is well-researched. Although the factors have face validity, as do most of the 28 subscales, an overall justification for how these factors constitute the content domain of the test's purpose is missing as are references in support of the presumed factor structure. Scoring information is not provided, nor are the items identified that contribute to each subscale. The number of items per subscale and factor are provided. The manual states that "advice and information regarding the different negotiating styles covered on the test" is provided in the test report, but the negotiating styles themselves are not identified in the manual. A sample test report was not included in the manual.

DEVELOPMENT. No information regarding the development of the test was provided in the test manual. It would be helpful to know the literature on which the factors were based as well as to know how the factors are useful for pre-employment screening. At minimum, subject matter experts should have been used to verify the categorization of items into subscales and subscales into factors. It is unusual but not unacceptable to have a varied number of response options to different items in the same subscale, but because of the lack of information about the scoring process, one cannot tell whether various responses are weighted or whether only one option is scored as correct. In sum, the description of the process involved in the test's development is lacking.

TECHNICAL. Standardization of the Negotiation Aptitude Profile seems to have been based on a convenience sample (the test manual refers to it as "uncontrolled") of 3,195 respondents. The demographics described in the manual included gender, age, education, grades, position (employment status), socioeconomic status, and the extent to which negotiating plays a role in a respondent's career. The sample sizes associated with each of the demographic analyses vary dramatically, with the latter group comprising 257 respondents. The manual refers to the demographic analyses as "validity analyses." However, although means and standard deviations are provided for each subscale,

these data are purely descriptive and constitute the characteristics of the normative sample. Although the data provide useful information about the representativeness of the sample, they do not provide evidence of validity beyond that of the generalizability of average scores. Analyses of variance were conducted within each level of the demographic variables. Given the sample size, traditional statistical significance is largely irrelevant. Effect sizes within a demographic should have been reported. For the most part, these would have been small.

Reliability analyses were reported. All such analyses are reported as alpha coefficients. The number of items associated with estimating subscale reliabilities ranges from 2 to 40. At least eight of the subscales did not approach acceptable levels of reliability. Further, coefficient alpha is inappropriate for use on a speeded test (e.g., the Mental Speed subscale). The aggregation of items into the factor reliabilities improved the reported alphas, although one factor (Cognitive Acuity) remained unacceptable (alpha = .32); there is more error variance than true score variance associated with the 47 items in that factor. Finally, if there is supposed to be some independence among the factors, an overall reliability is not typically calculated. If one is, it is subject to the same inflation as coefficient alpha due to an increase in the number of items, although the homogeneity may still be reduced.

COMMENTARY AND SUMMARY. In addition to the data that are provided in the test manual, it would have been extremely useful to have intercorrelations among items as well as among subscales and factor scores. Either a confirmatory or principal components factor analysis–if not a structural equation model–should have been used to determine the factor structure, especially in the absence of establishing content validity via subject matter experts. Once factors were established, it would have been useful to provide correlations with relevant external criteria to demonstrate that the Negotiation Aptitude Profile is, in fact, related to behaviors or observer ratings of negotiating skills and their relative success. Without such information, in the opinion of this reviewer, this profile would not stand up to legal scrutiny if used for employment screening or for any legitimate feedback regarding negotiating skills and abilities. These analyses are essential in order for this test to fulfill its stated purpose.

Furthermore, the manual needs considerable revision for it to be useful. While the author(s) clearly invested considerable effort into generating the test, collecting data, and creating the manual, the Negotiation Aptitude Profile falls short of a psychometrically sound instrument at this point. The statistical evidence for drawing valid inferences about negotiation skills and abilities does not yet exist in its current form.

Review of the Negotiation Aptitude Profile by F. STASKON, Adjunct Faculty, Saint Xavier University, Chicago, IL:

DESCRIPTION. The Negotiation Aptitude Profile (NAP) is an online, individually administered measure that assesses one's negotiation skills. From the publisher's document on operational definitions the NAP assesses one's "Overall ability to negotiate ... possess the traits and skills that are conducive to productive and effective negotiating." The NAP was developed to assess someone at least 18 years of age, working in a business setting where negotiation is practiced. The PsychTests AIM website catalogue has the NAP as part of a number of tests available for pre-employment applications, training tools, or skill development applications. Based on six domains of competencies, scores are obtained from 186 items and interpreted with the following segmentations: (a) Scores from 0–20 indicate a major deficiency, where improvement is essential. (b) Scores from 20–40 suggest some basic skill, but improvement is highly recommended. (c) Scores from 40–60 indicate the person has at least basic skill and the potential for growth. Improvement is still recommended. (d) Scores from 60–80 indicate a fair amount of skill, knowledge, and potential in the person, with improvement suggested. (e) Scores 80 and above indicate the respondent possesses a great deal of skill, knowledge, and potential.

The test publisher's documentation did not provide scoring procedures given that this measure is a web-based assessment for which a brief test report is immediately generated. In addition, test documentation provided no information on the scoring algorithm used to generate 35 scores from the 186 items. In the example report for a female on the test publisher's website, scores are presented for the following domains: Memory for Faces, Memory for Names, Stress Management, Patience, Anger Control, Perspective, Self-Monitoring, Communication Skills, Listening Skills, Social Skills, Persuasiveness, Conflict-Resolution Skills, Assertiveness, Networking Skills, Social Insight, Empathy, Flexibility, Willingness to Withhold Judgment,

Integrity, Use of "Dirty" Tactics, Mental Speed, Problem-Solving Skills, Knowledge of Negotiation Tactics, Knowledge of Negotiation Principles/Terminology, Preparation and Planning, Clarification and Justification, Bargaining and Problem-Solving, Closure and Implementation, Memory Skills, Self-Control, People Skills, Agreeableness, Cognitive Acuity, Knowledge of the Negotiation Process, as well as Overall Scores.

DEVELOPMENT. There is no documentation providing detail on methodology for item selection. In a document provided by the publisher titled "Negotiation Skills Test–Theoretical Background," there is a statement that subject matter experts provided information on negotiating that served as a basis for a qualitative analysis that identified characteristics and skills relevant to effective negotiating. A research document containing response distributions and information about differential validity states that all respondents self-selected to participate and completed the NAP on either Queendom.com or Psychtests.com. Validation items were gathered at the same time as questionnaire items.

NAP items are from a variety of constructs that the test developers believe are associated with effective negotiators. These could be viewed as six factors divided into 28 scales: (a) Memory Skills (18 items: Memory for Faces and Memory for Names); (b) Self-Control (35 items: Stress Management, Patience, Anger Control, Perspective, and Self-Monitoring); (c) People Skills (53 items: Communication Skills, Listening Skills, Social Skills, Persuasiveness, Conflict-Resolution Skills, Assertiveness, Networking Skills, Social Insight, and Empathy); (d) Agreeableness (26 items: Flexibility, Willingness to Withhold Judgment, Integrity, and Use of "Dirty" Tactics); (e) Cognitive Acuity (47 items: Mental Speed and Problem-Solving Skills); and (f) Knowledge of the Negotiation Process (19 items: Knowledge of Negotiation Tactics, Knowledge of Negotiation Principles/Terminology, Preparation and Planning, Clarification and Justification, Bargaining and Problem-Solving, and Closure and Implementation). The content of these items indicates a large share of the test is based on social skills or interpersonal communication styles, followed by self-regulation characteristics, and finally cognitive attributes of problem solving, recall memory and speed of decision making. The latter construct appears to be measured with response times for related items rather than with item content.

TECHNICAL. The NAP is not a standardized assessment tool, but one based on a rather large development sample of 3,195 participants, self-selected through the two websites mentioned above. As noted previously, scoring algorithms are not presented, and the cut points for score interpretation have no established reference or benchmark.

Reliability is presented as internal consistency alpha coefficients, where the total score coefficient is .94, based on 186 items. The six factors have reported reliability coefficients ranging from .32 for Cognitive Acuity to .90 for People Skills. Other coefficients are .66 for Memory Skills, .88 for Self-Control, .86 for Agreeableness, and .67 for Knowledge of the Negotiation Process.

The validity analysis in the publisher's documentation addresses mean differences within the nonrandom sample of 3,195 using the demographic variables gender, age, education, grades, employment position, and socioeconomic status. The descriptive statistics and statistical comparisons (using ANOVA and t-test results) report mean scores across levels of each background characteristic and p-values resulting from comparisons across levels.

COMMENTARY. The NAP claims to assess one's aptitude for effective negotiating skills in a typical business setting. Ironically, the research in social psychology and decision-making often finds the social context a primary influence upon negotiation outcomes, overriding individual differences. But, assuming individuals do differ in being competent in negotiation, a test like the NAP can facilitate assessments of current skills that an individual uses in typical transactional business negotiations. For this test to measure individual differences in relation to a type of social behavior, the assumption is that the latter is a rather static context. However, each negotiation has a propensity toward uniqueness, making assumptions about prototypical processes questionable. A wiser choice might be to use simulations or assessment center techniques addressing the relevant business context within which the individual will be required to exhibit negotiation skills.

Coefficient alpha is a common reliability coefficient for scales measuring social behaviors/style, but not the best approach for reliability estimates for a test with a variety of content domains. Also, when response formats result in skewed distributions, as the publisher's documentation indicates for memory and cognitive acuity factors, this distribution may reduce the reliability coefficient.

Rating scales vary across most factors. For memory, exercises consist of pairings of word/image, simple equations, or number sequences, and respondents are asked to indicate whether a pair matches as fast as they can. For knowledge of negotiation, multiple-choice test items are used. However, many factors are measured with rating scales using four labels with check boxes, where labels vary by factor (i.e. *exactly like me* vs. *not at all like me*; *most of the time* vs. *almost never*; *completely true* vs. *completely false*; *strongly agree* vs. *strongly disagree*; and *almost always* vs. *almost never*). The latter sets of scales have higher reliability coefficients than those for Cognitive Acuity. It is assumed by this reviewer that this difference results from the use of the rating scales compared to bivariate choices for Cognitive Acuity. The rating scales' distributions appear not as skewed as with the Cognitive Acuity factor.

Again, the publisher's documentation provides no information on scoring algorithms, norms, or benchmarks. However, the publisher's catalog indicates that benchmarks are available in the general population and 51 industries. Finally, the catalog states the NAP complies both with APA standards and EEOC standards for disability, but again, the supporting materials provided would not be enough to establish these claims.

SUMMARY. From the supporting documentation provided by the publisher, it is difficult to evaluate the validity and utility of the NAP for its intended purposes. Likely, as an assessment aid for training or skill development, the NAP has face validity and predictive validity perhaps would be feasible given decent reliability estimates. However, as a selection instrument, the documentation does not warrant an endorsement. As stated above, negotiation has been researched and explained more as a social behavior where individual differences have been discounted. The associated literature on negotiations has not established consistent individual difference influences that impact outcomes across the variations in negotiation settings, so comparison with other similar assessment tools is rather subjective.

[116]
NEO Personality Inventory-3.

Purpose: Designed to measure "the five major dimensions, or domains, of personality and the most important traits or facets that define each domain."
Population: Ages 12 and older.
Publication Dates: 1978-2010.

Administration: Group.

Price Data, 2013: $330 per complete NEO-FFI-3 Adult Form S Kit including NEO Inventories professional manual (2010, 145 pages), 10 reusable NEO-FFI-3 Form S Adult item booklets, 10 reusable Form R item booklets (5 male and 5 female), 25 handscorable answer sheets, 25 Form S Adult profile forms, 25 Form R Adult profile forms, 25 Adult Combined-Gender profile forms (Form S/Form R), and 25 Your NEO Summary feedback sheets in a soft-sided attaché case; $330 per complete NEO-FFI-3 Adolescent Comprehensive Kit including NEO Inventories professional manual, 10 reusable Form S item booklets, 10 reusable Form R item booklets (5 male and 5 female), 25 handscorable answer sheets, 25 Form S Adolescent profile forms, 25 Form R Adolescent profile forms, 25 Adolescent Combined-Gender profile forms (Form S/Form 4), and 25 Your NEO Summary feedback sheets in a soft-sided attaché case; $65 per NEO Inventories professional manual: NEO-PI-3, NEO-FFI-3, NEO PI-R.

Comments: A major innovation of this edition is the modification of the NEO PI-R in which 37 items were replaced; the NEO-PI-3 is now "suitable for assessing personality in middle school-aged children and adolescents, as well as adults"; clinicians may continue using the NEO PI-R; "The NEO-FFI-3 is a revision of the NEO-FFI in which 15 … items have been replaced to improve readability and psychometric properties."

Authors: Robert R. McCrae and Paul T. Costa, Jr.

Publisher: Psychological Assessment Resources, Inc.

a) NEO PERSONALITY INVENTORY-3.

Acronym: NEO-PI-3.

Scores, 35: 30 facets in 5 domains: Neuroticism (Anxiety, Angry Hostility, Depression, Self-Consciousness, Impulsiveness, Vulnerability), Extraversion (Warmth, Gregariousness, Assertiveness, Activity, Excitement-Seeking, Positive Emotions), Openness (Fantasy, Aesthetics, Feelings, Actions, Ideas, Values), Agreeableness (Trust, Straightforwardness, Altruism, Compliance, Modesty, Tender-Mindedness), Conscientiousness (Competence, Order, Dutifulness, Achievement Striving, Self-Discipline, Deliberation).

Forms, 2: Form S (self-report), Form R (observer ratings).

Time: (30-40) minutes.

b) REVISED NEO PERSONALITY INVENTORY.

Acronym: NEO PI-R.

Scores, 35: 30 facets in 5 domains: Neuroticism (Anxiety, Angry Hostility, Depression, Self-Consciousness, Impulsiveness, Vulnerability), Extraversion (Warmth, Gregariousness, Assertiveness, Activity, Excitement-Seeking, Positive Emotions), Openness (Fantasy, Aesthetics, Feelings, Actions, Ideas, Values), Agreeableness (Trust, Straightforwardness, Altruism, Compliance, Modesty, Tender-Mindedness), Conscientiousness (Competence,

Order, Dutifulness, Achievement Striving, Self-Discipline, Deliberation).

Forms, 2: Form S (self-report), Form R (observer ratings).

Time: (30-40) minutes.

c) NEO FIVE-FACTOR INVENTORY-3.

Acronym: NEO-FFI-3.

Scores, 5: Neuroticism, Extraversion, Openness, Agreeableness, Conscientiousness.

Forms, 4: Form S (self-report), Form R (observer ratings), Adolescent, Adult.

Time: (5-10) minutes.

Cross References: See T5:2218 (135 references); for reviews by Michael D. Botwin and Samuel Juni of the Revised Edition, see 12:330 (50 references); see also T4:2263 (49 references); for reviews by Allen K. Hess and Thomas A. Widiger of an earlier edition, see 11:258 (5 references); for a review by Robert Hogan of an earlier edition of a, see 10:214 (6 references).

Review of the NEO Personality Inventory-3 by NICHOLAS F. BENSON, Assistant Professor of School Psychology, The University of South Dakota, Vermillion, SD:

DESCRIPTION. The NEO Personality Inventory-3 (NEO-PI-3) was designed to measure five factor-analytically derived domains of personality. The NEO-PI-3 consists of 240 items, 37 of which are new to this revision. The new items serve as replacements for deleted items and are believed to be more appropriate for middle-school-aged children and adolescents because they are easier to read and have better psychometric properties. Items are rated on a 5-point scale ranging from *strongly disagree* to *strongly agree*. The NEO-PI-3 is designed for use with individuals aged 12 years and older, includes both self-report and observer rating options, and can be completed in approximately 30 to 40 minutes. The instrument also includes the previous version (i.e., the Revised NEO Personality Inventory; NEO-PI-R) and an abridged version (i.e., the NEO Five-Factor Inventory-3; NEO-FFI-3). The NEO-PI-R is included primarily for researchers and clinicians who elect to continue using the previous version and norms. As the NEO-PI-R previously was reviewed by Botwin (1995) and Juni (1995), this review will focus on the NEO-PI-3 and NEO-FFI-3. The NEO-FFI-3 is a revision of the NEO Five-Factor Inventory in which 15 of 60 items were replaced.

DEVELOPMENT. The NEO-PI-3 is the latest revision of the original inventory, which was designed to measure three domains represented by the acronym NEO (i.e., Neuroticism, Extraversion, and Openness to Experience). The test authors added the Agreeableness and Conscientiousness domains in subsequent revisions. The five-factor structure originated from the lexical hypothesis, which posits that natural languages develop to include words that societies can use to identify and describe salient differences between people (Allport & Odbert, 1936). In accordance with this hypothesis, several researchers developed personality items from words viewed as describing personality traits and subjected these items to factor analyses (Goldberg, 1993). Debate ensued regarding the uniqueness, precision, and objectivity of the resulting solutions. McCrae and Costa favored the five-factor solution and thus developed a set of items to measure five domains of personality. As noted in the test manual, McCrae and Costa selected items for inclusion in their questionnaire based on factor loadings as well as the balance of positively and negatively keyed items. Positively and negatively keyed items were balanced in an attempt to control for response acquiescence.

Like the NEO-PI-R, the NEO-PI-3 and NEO-FFI-3 have a hierarchical structure. In addition to five domains, the NEO-PI-3 measures 30 facets of personality. Each domain is composed of 6 facets, and each facet is intended to represent a meaningful division within its respective domain. Scores for these facets were included in an effort to increase predictive utility. In contrast, although 28 of 30 facets are represented on the NEO-FFI-3, only scores representing the five domains can be derived from this abridged version.

TECHNICAL. Adult and adolescent norms for the NEO-PI-3 self-report (n = 635 and 500, respectively) and observer rating (n = 649 and 465, respectively) scales are available. Separate male and female norms are provided. The NEO-PI-3 adult and adolescent norms also are utilized when scoring the NEO-FFI-3. Supplementary norms for the NEO-PI-3 are available, including norms for adults ages 21 to 30 (n = 218), norms for adults 31 and older (n = 417), and international norms based on observer ratings for adolescents ages 12 to 17. Separate male and female norms also are provided for the supplementary norms. Information regarding representation of various ethnicities, education levels, and geographical areas in the normative samples is lacking. The test authors do note that the adolescent sample was recruited from 26 states and that the majority of respondents were high academic achievers. The test authors also note that

the adult sample was recruited from 29 states, most respondents had obtained more than a high school education, and 92.6% of the sample was White.

Internal consistency estimates for adults who completed the self-report NEO-PI-3 ranged from .89 to .93 for domains and from .54 to .83 for facets. Internal consistency estimates for observer ratings were slightly higher. Internal consistency estimates for adolescents are not provided. The evidence reported suggests that each domain appears to be distinct and informative, whereas unreliability precludes the interpretability of at least some facet scores.

Test-retest reliability estimates for the NEO-PI-3 and NEO-FFI-3 are not available. Therefore, estimates obtained from NEO-PI-R data are included in the test manual as substitutes. These estimates suggest adequate temporal stability across the samples examined, although the generalizability of estimates obtained from NEO-PI-R data to scores obtained from the most recent revisions is unknown. Notably, a reliability generalization study of the NEO-PI-R by Caruso (2000) found that Agreeableness scores obtained from self-reports had modest reliability. Test-retest reliability for self-report Agreeableness scores was found to be particularly problematic (mean of .58 across 4 samples), as was the internal consistency of Agreeableness within clinical samples (mean of .62 across 7 studies). Moreover, use of the abridged form was found to result in problematic reliability for self-report ratings of Agreeableness (mean of .67 across 20 samples) and Openness to Experience (mean of .65 across 20 samples). In sum, reliability evidence for the latest revision is lacking. However, existing evidence suggests that domain scores, with the exception of scores representing Agreeableness, tend to display adequate reliability.

Goldberg (1993) noted that extensive external validity research examining relationships between the NEO Inventories and a wide variety of personality questionnaires did much to increase acceptance of the five-factor model. This tradition has continued and the five-factor structure is now considered integral to dimensional models of assessment and classification that overcome some important limitations of categorical systems by focusing on normal adaptive personality traits in addition to maladaptive personality traits (Widiger, Clark, & Livesley, 2009). As described in the test manual, research suggests that personality domains measured by the NEO Inventories play an important role in a variety of psychological phenomena, including but not limited to psychological well-being, coping, defense mechanisms, motivation, acculturative stress, and prejudice. Moreover, research suggests that personality domains are important influences on both academic and job performance (Kanfer, Wolf, Kantrowitz, & Ackerman, 2010) and that Conscientiousness plays a role in academic performance that is largely independent of intelligence (Poropat, 2009).

COMMENTARY. The NEO-PI-3 and NEO-FFI-3 can be administered to individuals or groups using a paper-and-pencil format or an optional software format. Answer sheets are available for hand-scoring and scanning. The scannable answer sheet can be sent to the publisher for scoring or scanned by the user if optional on-site scanning software is purchased.

The appropriateness and representativeness of the normative samples is questionable. Norm-referenced score interpretations should be made carefully given that the samples do not appear to approximate U.S. Census projections with regard to variables such as geographical region, race/ethnicity, linguistic status, and education level. The inclusion of separate norms for males and females is beneficial given that recent research suggests females tend to score higher than males and that these differences are reasonably robust even when some assumptions of measurement invariance are violated (Marsh et al., 2010).

Although five domains of personality traits have been identified consistently using exploratory factor analysis, the five factor structure has shown poor fit when evaluated using other methods such as confirmatory factor analysis (CFA). Thus, the structural fidelity (Loevinger, 1957) of the NEO Inventories (i.e., correspondence between inter-item structure and the five-factor structure) is debatable. As some attribute this lack of correspondence, at least in part, to overly restrictive assumptions of CFA, the use of a new technique known as exploratory structural equation modeling (ESEM) has been proposed (Marsh et al., 2010). Although ESEM suggests better correspondence with the five-factor structure than does CFA, the adequacy of this correspondence is still relatively modest. Notably, CFA and ESEM studies examining the factor structure of the NEO-PI-3 and NEO-FFI-3 are not available at this time.

Juni (1995) commented extensively on concerns regarding the format of NEO-PI-R items.

These concerns relate to features shared by some items that likely produce construct-irrelevant variance and contribute to poorly fitting CFA and ESEM models. Some of these concerns were addressed in the revision process. As a number of items have been revised in an effort to improve readability and psychometric properties, it would not be surprising if future CFA and ESEM studies of the NEO-PI-3 and NEO-FFI-3 indicate improved model fit relative to studies involving the NEO-PI-R and NEO-FFI.

There is a large body of theoretical literature and empirical studies to support score interpretation when attempting to understand and describe personality using the NEO Inventories. In fact, a bibliography of more than 2,500 publications pertaining to the NEO Inventories is available at the publisher's website. Notably, external validity evidence for NEO-PI-3 and NEO-FFI-3 scores is lacking and must be extrapolated from studies involving earlier versions. Also notably absent is evidence that covariance among the self-report and observer rating scales is caused by personality domains rather than method artifacts. The proportion of construct-related variance in the observed variance of self-report and rater versions (Cronbach & Meehl, 1955) could be studied by developing confirmatory factor analytic models and analyzing data from participants for whom both self-report and observer rating scales have been completed.

SUMMARY. The NEO-PI-3 is the latest revision of the NEO Inventory and is designed to measure five domains of personality. The NEO-FFI-3 is an abridged version of the NEO-PI-3. The NEO Inventories have a long history and there is a large body of theoretical literature and psychometric studies to support the validity of score interpretations. However, most of this reliability and validity evidence must be extrapolated to the NEO-PI-3 and NEO-FFI-3 from studies pertaining to earlier versions. Additional research pertaining to test-retest reliability, internal structure, and external validity is needed to determine the extent to which existing reliability and validity evidence generalizes to scores derived from the NEO-PI-3 and NEO-FFI-3.

REVIEWER'S REFERENCES

Allport, G. W., & Odbert, H. S. (1936). Trait names: A psycho-lexical study. *Psychological Monographs, 47*(1, Whole No. 211).

Botwin, M. D.(1995). [Review of the Revised NEO Personality Inventory]. In J. C. Conoley & J. C. Impara (Eds.), *The twelfth mental measurements yearbook* (pp. 862-863). Lincoln, NE: Buros Institute of Mental Measurements.

Caruso, J. C. (2000). Reliability generalization of the NEO personality scales. *Educational and Psychological Measurement, 60*, 236-254.

Cronbach, L. J., & Meehl, P. E. (1955). Construct validity in psychological tests. *Psychological Bulletin, 52*, 281-302.

Goldberg, L. R. (1993). The structure of phenotypic personality traits. *American Psychologist, 48,* 26–34.

Juni, S. (1995). [Review of the Revised NEO Personality Inventory]. In J. C. Conoley & J. C. Impara, (Eds.), *The twelfth mental measurements yearbook* (pp. 863–868). Lincoln, NE: Buros Institute of Mental Measurements.

Kanfer, R., Wolf, M., Kantrowitz, T. M., & Ackerman, P. L. (2010). Ability and trait complex predictors of academic and job performance: A person-situation approach. *Applied Psychology: An International Review, 59*(1), 40–69.

Loevinger, J. (1957). Objective tests as instruments of psychological theory. *Psychological Reports, 3,* 635–694.

Marsh, H. W., Lüdtke, O., Muthén, B., Asparouhov, T., Morin, A. J. S., Trautwein, U., & Nagengast, B. (2010). A new look at the Big Five factor structure through exploratory structural equation modeling. *Psychological Assessment, 22,* 471–491.

Poropat, A. E. (2009). A meta-analysis of the five-factor model of personality and academic performance. *Psychological Bulletin, 135,* 322–338.

Widiger, T. A., Clark, L. A., & Livesley, W. J. (2009). An integrative dimensional classification of personality disorder. *Psychological Assessment, 21,* 243–255.

Review of the NEO Personality Inventory-3 by ANNETTE S. KLUCK, Associate Professor, Auburn University, Auburn, AL:

[Note: This review addresses the following forms: NEO-PI-3 Form S; NEO-PI-3 Form R; NEO-FFI-3 Form S; NEO-FFI-3 Form R.]

DESCRIPTION. The NEO Personality Inventory–3 (NEO-PI-3) and NEO Five-Factor Inventory–3 (NEO-FFI-3; collectively NEOs-3) represent the most recent revision to the NEO inventories, maintaining the approach and structure of the NEO Personality Inventory–Revised (NEO-PI-R). The NEOs-3 are appropriate for use with adolescents (ages 12 to 20) and adults (ages 21 and older) to measure individual differences in normal personality traits. The administration allows for individual or group assessment, and offers parallel self-report (Form S) and informant (Form R) options, as well as a short form (the NEO-FFI-3). The NEO inventories are available in over 50 languages. The manual that accompanies the NEOs-3 contains information regarding the NEO-PI-R development, and research on the NEO-PI-R is often offered as evidence for the validity and reliability of the NEO-PI-3. Although valid criticisms remain regarding the empirical support for the NEO-PI-R, previous reviewers (Botwin, 1995; Hess, 1992; Juni, 1995) have examined these concerns. This review is limited to the development and evaluation of data specific to the NEOs-3.

The NEOs-3 administration is simple; the test manual and item booklet directions are clear. Evaluators give respondents the appropriate item booklet and response form, based upon the rater, age (adolescent or adult), length, and preferred scoring. The administration typically takes 30 to 40 minutes (5 to 10 minutes for the NEO-FFI-3), but will be longer for individuals with weak reading skills (the NEO-PI-3 has a fifth grade reading level). New to the test manual is a table with easy-to-understand definitions for 28 less familiar words, which can be provided to respondents (manual, p. 8).

Hand scoring for the NEO-PI-3 requires the use of the hand-scorable answer sheet, which contains information needed to compute the raw scores. Scannable answer sheets should be used for computer/scanned scoring available through the publisher's Professional Report Service. NEO-FFI-3 is only available for hand scoring and the combined item-response booklets contain all scoring information. Scoring requires approximately 5 minutes. The test manual provides scoring procedures for both NEOs (identical to NEO-PI-R procedures), computation of factor analytic domain scores, as well as checking for invalidity due to item omission, acquiescence, nay-saying, and random responding. The NEO-PI-3 yields 35 scores, with six facet scales comprising each of the following five domains: Neuroticism, Extroversion, Openness, Agreeableness, and Conscientiousness. The NEO-FFI-3 yields only the five domain scores. Both versions contain three face-valid validity questions.

DEVELOPMENT. Primary goals for the development of the NEO-PI-3 were to (a) make the test appropriate for use with adolescents, (b) update the norms, and (c) retain strengths of the NEO-PI-R (McCrae, Costa, & Martin, 2005). The literature on factor analytic approaches to personality assessment is extensive and provides ample empirical support for the Five-Factor Model (FFM). The FFM is derived from a trait approach to understanding personality through empirical methods rather than classic developmental theories (McCrae & Costa, 2003). NEOs-3 authors argue that "personality assessment should begin at the top and work down" (manual, p. 59), maintaining the focus on domains and their specific traits.

The revision of the NEO-PI-R involved obtaining current norms and replacing hard-to-read and psychometrically weak items. Based on omitted items and low item-facet correlations ($rs < .30$), 48 items were deemed problematic. Alternative questions for each of these items were piloted with the NEO-PI-R on adolescent ($N = 500$; ages 14–20) and adult ($N = 635$; ages 21–91) mixed gender samples, primarily recruited from acquaintances of undergraduate research assistants (McCrae, Costa et al., 2005; McCrae, Martin, & Costa, 2005). Older (18–20) adolescents tended to be in college and were overrepresented in the adolescent sample. Pilot participants completed Forms S and R, the latter for another participant or unknown target

(McCrae, Costa et al., 2005; McCrae, Martin et al., 2005). In the adolescent sample, 84.6% were White and 7.6% were Asian/Pacific Islander, and 92.6% of the adult sample was White such that Hispanic and African American individuals were substantially underrepresented compared to current U.S. Census data (Humes, Jones, & Ramirez, 2011). Three-quarters of adults had more than a high-school education and over one-quarter had at least a bachelor's degree (McCrae, Martin et al., 2005). Based on omission frequencies and correlations with respective facets and nonparent domains in the adolescent sample, 37 items were replaced. Similar findings were obtained for the 37 new items on the adult sample. To evaluate item performance and readability in younger individuals a third sample of 424 middle-school students (ages 12–13, primarily Grades 6–8) completed only the NEO-PI-3. The NEO-PI-3 contains the same number of items and facets as the NEO-PI-R and 11 facets remained unchanged (McCrae, Costa et al., 2005).

In the revision of the NEO-FFI, 9 items with low factor loadings in previous research and 5 hard-to-read items were identified. The 180 items not originally considered for inclusion in the short form were considered to replace the 14 problematic items. Fifteen items were replaced based on item-factor correlations and facet scale representation.

TECHNICAL. The previously described adolescent and adult samples were used for computing NEO-PI-3 norms. The adolescent norms were derived from responses from 242 males and 258 females for Form S and 211 males and 254 females (ages 14–20) for Form R. The adult norms are based on 279 men and 356 women for Form S and 301 men and 348 women for Form R. The adolescent and adult respondents were from 26 and 29 states, respectively, with the majority from Pennsylvania (McCrae, Costa et al., 2005; McCrae, Martin et al., 2005). Adolescent and adult norms are available by gender and combined. Norms for the NEO-FFI-3 were derived from the NEO-PI-3 responses of the norming samples.

Studies on the reliability of the NEOs-3 provide support for their use. NEO-PI-3 internal consistencies across adolescents and adults are good for domains (.87–.93 and .88–.95) and ranged from unacceptable to good on the facet scales (.48–.83 and .56–.86 for Forms S and R, respectively), with slightly lower internal consistency values obtained for the adolescent sample (McCrae, Costa et al., 2005; McCrae, Martin et al., 2005). NEO-FFI-3

internal consistency values for the domains are lower (ranging from .66 to .88 for the norming samples). There are no test-retest reliability studies on the NEOs-3. NEO-PI-3 reliabilities across self- and other-report (interrater reliability across the parallel-worded Form S and Form R) were similar to those obtained for the same samples using NEO-PI-R items and scoring (McCrae, Costa et al., 2005; McCrae, Martin et al., 2005), with reliabilities being lower for adolescents (.38 to .60 for domains, .21 to .59 for facets) than adults (.52 to .65 for domains, .39 to .68 for facets) (manual, p. 79). NEO-FFI-3 correlations between parallel-form reliabilities were similar to those obtained for the NEO-PI-3 domains.

Criterion-related validity of the NEO-PI-3 is supported by strong correlations with the NEO-PI-R for adolescents (rs = .98–.99 for domains, .83–.98 for altered facets) and adults (rs = .98–.99 for domains, .86–.99 on facets) in the norming sample. The weakest correlations between the previous and current edition were found for A6: Tender-Mindedness, a facet on which half of the items were replaced. Correlations between the NEO-FFI-3 and NEO-PI-3 ranged from .34 to .60, and were often lower in the adolescent sample.

Examination of the factor structure of the NEO-PI-3 offers construct evidence of validity. In the adult norming sample, all facets loaded onto their assigned domain. Similar to the NEO-PI-2 factor structure and research findings, a few facets had moderate to high loadings (in one case, E3: Assertiveness, equal) on second factors. Consistent gender (similar to the NEO-PI-R) and age effects were found, supporting the use of gendered and aged norms (McCrae, Martin et al., 2005).

COMMENTARY. The NEOs-3 appear to retain the strengths of their predecessors as easily administered measures of individual differences in nonpathological domains of personality. The NEO-PI-3 norming sample is more geographically, and likely educationally, representative than the NEO-PI-R, and norms are now available for adolescents. The NEO-PI-3 is psychometrically similar to the NEO-PI-R, with improved psychometrics when used with adolescent individuals. Finally, the availability of parallel forms continues to be a strength of the NEO inventories.

Many criticisms of the NEO-PI-R remain true of the NEO-PI-3. Face-valid items are used to assess validity. Although attempts to correct for socially desirable responding have been unsuccessful, the authors' dismissal of the concern is problematic. In clinical work, providers administering tests with validity scales sometimes obtain results that are invalid *unexpectedly*. One does not always know when a person is motivated (consciously or otherwise) toward biased responding. Because one of the purported uses of the NEO-PI-3 is in clinical settings, concerns regarding assessment of valid responding limit the confidence clinicians can place in the results. Although the NEO-PI-3 can likely be used for establishing rapport and increasing self-understanding, clinical decisions should be grounded in measures with adequate validity checks. A new limitation of the NEO-PI-3 is the ethnic/racial composition of the norming sample. Although some research has found the factor structure to replicate across cultures, this is unlikely to convince individuals concerned about the appropriateness of using the NEO-PI-3 with non-White clients. Finally, test-retest reliability evidence, even with much of the measure remaining the same, needs to be strengthened.

SUMMARY. The NEOs-3 are updated scales of the NEO series and can be used as valid measures to assess individual differences in personality for adolescents and adults. Psychometrically, the NEO-PI-3 is similar enough to the NEO-PI-R that previous research findings and clinical familiarity and cautions should generalize to the new version.

REVIEWER'S REFERENCES

Botwin, M. D. (1995). [Review of the Revised NEO Personality Inventory.] In J. C. Conoley & J. C. Impara (Eds.), *The twelfth mental measurements yearbook*. Retrieved from EBSCO*host*.

Hess, A. K. (1992). [Review of the NEO Personality Inventory.] In J. J. Kramer & J. C. Conoley (Eds.), *The eleventh mental measurements yearbook*. Retrieved from EBSCO*host*.

Humes, K. R., Jones, N. A., & Ramirez, R. R. (2011, March). Overview of race and Hispanic origin: 2010 Census briefs (United States Census Bureau Publication No. C2010BR-02). Retrieved from http://www.census.gov/prod/cen2010/briefs/c2010br-02.pdf

Juni, S. (1995). [Review of the Revised NEO Personality Inventory.] In J. C. Conoley & J. C. Impara (Eds.), *The twelfth mental measurements yearbook*. Retrieved from EBSCO*host*.

McCrae, R. R., & Costa, P. T., Jr. (2003). *Personality in adulthood: A five-factor theory perspective* (2nd ed.). New York, NY: Guilford Press.

McCrae, R. R., Costa, P. T., Jr., & Martin, T. A. (2005). The NEO-PI-3: A more readable revised NEO Personality Inventory. *Journal of Personality Assessment, 84*, 261-270. doi: 10.1207/s15327752jpa8403_05

McCrae, R. R., Martin, T. A., & Costa, P. T., Jr. (2005). Age trends and age norms for the NEO Personality Inventory-3 in adolescents and adults. *Assessment, 12*, 363-373. doi:10.1177/1073191105279724

[117]

New York Longitudinal Scales Adult Temperament Questionnaire, Second Edition.

Purpose: Designed to measure the nine NYLS dimensions of temperament in adulthood.
Population: Ages 13-89.
Publication Dates: 1995-2008.
Acronym: ATQ2.

Scores, 9: Activity Level, Rhythmicity, Adaptability, Approach, Intensity, Mood, Persistence, Distractibility, Threshold.
Administration: Group.
Price Data, 2011: $69.95 per complete kit including test manual (2008, 34 pages), user's guide, and 25 questionnaires with scoring and profile sheets; $49.95 per 25 questionnaires with scoring and profile sheets; volume discounts available.
Time: (10-15) minutes.
Comments: Self-report ratings; Internet scoring available using ATQ2 iReport Writer software.
Authors: Stella Chess and Alexander Thomas.
Publisher: Behavioral-Developmental Initiatives.
Cross References: For reviews by James A. Athanasou and Stephen N. Axford of the original edition, see 16:166.

Review of The New York Longitudinal Scales Adult Temperament Questionnaire, Second Edition by GYPSY M. DENZINE, Assistant Vice Provost and Professor of Educational Psychology, Northern Arizona University, Flagstaff, AZ:

DESCRIPTION. The New York Longitudinal Scales Adult Temperament Questionnaire, Second Edition (ATQ2) provides updated and expanded norms for use in measuring the nine temperaments in adults derived from the New York Longitudinal Study (NYLS) of Thomas, Chess, and colleagues that began in the late 1950s (Thomas, Chess, Birch, Hertzig, & Korn, 1963). The NYLS began with 135 infants, who have been assessed across their lifespan for the existence and significance of behavioral style (originally referred to as "primary reaction patterns"). The ATQ has been useful in identifying relatively stable aspects of behavior that influence how people interact with the environment. Distinct from personality, temperament in adulthood is useful in understanding functionally how people adapt to the events in their lives (Thomas, Chess, Lerner, & Lerner, 1989). The authors designed the ATQ as a tool for clinicians and researchers to understand better the role of temperament in adult adjustment. The ATQ2 test manual and user's guide were developed to provide new information about the online testing and scoring procedures and to contain the updated and expanded normative data for age and gender groups.

The ATQ2 contains 54 items, plus nine additional questions. The items comprise both situational and self-assessment types. In addition to the 54 frequency items assessing the nine temperament traits, the ATQ2 contains a question for each of the nine temperaments asking respondents to rate general impressions of their temperament in comparison with other adults they know using a 6-point Likert scale. The measure can be completed via paper and pencil and scored by hand or by using iReport Writer software. It can also be administered online, and a computer-scored report summary may be generated. The test authors indicate that in addition to being administered and scored by clinicians and researchers, the ATQ2 can be self-administered, self-scored, and self-interpreted.

This reviewer found the process of reading the instructions and completing the items in the online test to be a very straightforward task taking approximately 15 minutes. The iReport Writer software allows the input of data from a completed paper-and-pencil assessment. This reviewer's experience logging onto the iReport Writer system, completing the ATQ2, and obtaining the results from the iReport Writer was a positive one. Reports consist of a three-page document that contains the temperament profile, interpretations of temperament categories, and validity checks on the client's ratings. The temperament profile is a graphical representation of the respondent's temperament. The authors of the test manual note that counselors may give the temperament profile directly to the client or choose to interpret the results for the client. The profile also contains text descriptors of high and low values for each of the nine temperaments. According to the authors of the manual, temperament scores are considered average when they fall between +.90 and -.90 standard deviations from the mean. The validity checks report contains information about missing data, ratings/perceptions discrepancies, temperament scores, and raw scores for each ATQ2 item, including the impressions of temperament questions. If a responder does not complete at least 80% of the questions, a warning about being cautious in interpreting the results is printed at the bottom of the profile.

DEVELOPMENT. Grounded in person-environment interaction theory (Chess & Thomas, 1984), Chess and Thomas began working on the ATQ in 1995. The final 54-item ATQ was developed from an original pool of 140 items. Samples of college students, as well as the 135-person NYLS sample, were used in the ATQ item and scale development processes. Using a 7-point Likert-type scale, the ATQ is a brief self-report measure based on frequency data obtained on nine temperament traits: Activity Level, Rythmicity, Adaptability, Approach, Intensity, Mood, Persistence, Distractability, and Threshold.

Although the manual contains a reference that indicates the original ATQ was developed from clinical observations, the manual for the ATQ2 does not address the theoretical and/or empirical foundation of the ATQ/ATQ2.

TECHNICAL. Evidence for the reliability of the ATQ is presented in the ATQ2 test manual; however, no new studies are presented for the ATQ2. Internal consistency for the ATQ ($N = 135$) produced scale alpha reliability coefficients ranging from .69 to .83. Test-retest reliability data for the ATQ ($N = 25$) were gathered from a sample of college students from Winona State University and yielded coefficients of .89 for the total scale, with scale coefficients ranging from .64 to .90. The authors of the test manual do not report how they handled issues of missing data, nor do they address the extent to which the items met assumptions related to normality, homogeneity of variance, and so forth.

Perhaps the greatest concern is the lack of evidence in support of construct and predictive validity. The ATQ was initially derived from a pool of 140 items contained in a young adult version for measuring temperament in the NYLS sample. Using the 140 items, Thomas et al. (1982) investigated the concurrent validity of the scale by correlating ATQ scores with interview ratings. In the ATQ2 test manual, the manual authors suggest the need for investigating the NYLS temperament model with other temperament frameworks (i.e., Myers-Briggs, Keirsey, and the Guilford-Zimmerman); however, no empirical work is either presented or referenced.

The ATQ2 test manual contains updated and expanded norms for ages from 13 to 89 arranged by age groups and gender. The updated ATQ2 sample is composed of the original NYLS sample and the new sample of 3,284 participants (2,275 female and 1,009 male) who completed the online version of the ATQ between 2003 and 2007. The test developers compared the means and standard deviations for the ATQ2 scales based on the original NYLS sample and the new online sample. In general, the new online sample rated themselves slightly more difficult in temperament compared to the NYLS sample. The greatest difference was in the Adaptability category, with the new sample scoring more than half a point (.58) higher than the NYLS sample. The new and larger sample allowed for cross-sectional analysis on the nine temperaments across gender and the lifespan. The authors of the measure note that significant gender differences were found in adult temperament; however, no interpretations of the results are presented. Nor are any references cited in the test manual that may help explain gender differences in adult temperament. Similarly, the authors of the manual report that adults become more regular and less active over time (as indicated by the Activity Level and Rhythmicity scales), whereas emotional Intensity and initial Approach appear to decrease with age. Based on cross-sectional analyses, it appears that Distractibility and Persistence show relative stability from the teens to the 60s.

Beyond the statistical results presented in the test manual for the original sample used for test development, this reviewer found no recently published articles about the psychometric properties of the ATQ/ATQ2.

COMMENTARY AND SUMMARY. Given the research to date on item and scale development, the ATQ2 can be recommended for use with nonclinical populations of adults and for research purposes. The authors of the manual provided evidence that the ATQ/ATQ2 meets the bare minimum standards for educational and psychological testing (AERA, APA, & NCME, 1999). The manual authors claim the ATQ2 can be used to help clients through vocational choice decisions. However, without more research in the area of career development, this reviewer is reluctant to recommend the ATQ2 for use in career decision-making. The major limitation of the ATQ was the limited standardization sample, both in terms of number of participants and the demographic representation. Thus, the ATQ2 is an improvement because of the expanded norms.

Persons hoping for an in-depth treatment of temperament theory applied to adult adjustment and/or career development will be disappointed in the test manual and in the measure itself. Although the reporting of new norms is useful, the test manual falls short by not reporting new reliability analyses or validity information such as an updated principal components analysis of the data obtained from the online standardization sample.

In conclusion, the ATQ2 is fairly straightforward in its administration, scoring, interpretation, and suggestions for use. However, the test manual provides insufficient evidence that the scale is a psychometrically sound measure of the nine temperaments in adulthood. The ATQ2 may be appropriate for self-awareness or in clinical settings for discussing adjustment issues or personal

growth, but it may not be an appropriate tool for high-stakes assessment. The best use of the ATQ2 may be research, as this reviewer cannot recommend it as a diagnostic tool at this time.

REVIEWER'S REFERENCES

American Educational Research Association, American Psychological Association, & National Council on Measurement in Education. (1999). *Standards for educational and psychological testing.* Washington, DC: American Educational Research Association.

Chess, S., & Thomas, A. (1984). *Origins and evolution of behavior disorders from infancy to early adult life.* New York, NY: Brunner-Mazel.

Thomas, A., Chess, S., Birch, H. G., Hertzig, M., & Korn, S. (1963). *Behavioral individuality in early childhood.* New York, NY: NYU Press.

Thomas, A., Chess, S., Lerner, R., & Lerner, J. (1989). *Behavioral individuality in adult life. Final report for NIMH research grant.* Unpublished.

Thomas, A., Mittleman, M., Chess, S., Korn, S., & Cohen, J. (1982). A temperament questionnaire for early adult life. *Educational & Psychological Measurement, 42,* 593-600.

Review of The New York Longitudinal Scales Adult Temperament Questionnaire, Second Edition by GREGORY A. LOBB, Clinical Director and Licensed Psychologist, Family Psychological Associates, Kittanning, PA:

DESCRIPTION. The New York Longitudinal Scales Adult Temperament Questionnaire, Second Edition (ATQ2) is an updated version of the ATQ published in 2003. The purpose of the ATQ2 remains the same as the original version: The measure is a self-report instrument used to assess the primary reaction patterns or temperament traits of an individual. The authors of the measure provide several reasons for updating the instrument. The first reason was described as the need to extend the reach of the instrument by extending the norm group to provide more information about adult temperament across the life span. Second, the development of online testing has enabled test developers to gather more extensive data from participants across a wider geographic area, thus allowing for a larger norm group. Finally, the usefulness of the ATQ has increased the need for a more up-to-date instrument that assists researchers and clinicians in understanding temperament in adulthood.

The ATQ's 54 items—plus nine items asking respondents to rate their general impressions of their temperament as compared with others they know—have not been changed for the ATQ2. Results are reported for nine temperament traits: Activity Level, Rhythmicity, Adaptability, Approach, Intensity, Mood, Persistence, Distractibility, and Threshold. Changes from the previous version include updating the norms to include participants ages 13–89 years, refining the interpretations of the nine temperament traits from three levels to five, and adding the computerized scoring process to the user's guide.

The technical manual provides detailed descriptions for each of the nine temperament traits, including five descriptions of potential results for each trait. A user's manual provides a brief overview of the ATQ2, instructions for administration and scoring, use of the web-based software, use of the iReport Writer for online scoring, and interpretation of the temperament profile.

The detailed administration and scoring procedures provided in the ATQ2 manual are easy to follow. However, the test manual contains some inconsistent information regarding online administration. It does not appear that an individual can complete the ATQ2 online, but instead must complete the questionnaire in paper-and-pencil format before responses can be transferred to the web portal for scoring and interpretation. Alternatively, hand scoring can be performed by tabulating results by hand and transferring them to the profile sheet for interpretation. Directions for hand scoring are slightly tedious and require attention to detail to prevent error, but they are adequate for any professional trained in the use of psychological testing instruments. Computer scoring requires a login and a password. The online software allows the examiner to select a desired norm group prior to scoring. The user selects one of the newly developed norm groups or the original (now referred to as "classic") norm group. The software generates a Temperament Report that contains a bar graph profile, a written interpretation of the temperament profile, validity checks, raw scores, z scores, and individual item responses. Users must purchase blocks of uses (3, 10, 25, 50, or 100) from the test publisher.

The test publisher indicates that ATQ software on a CD has been "contracted for development but is not available at this writing" (user's guide, p. 3).

DEVELOPMENT. The original ATQ emerged from a notable behavioral study in the 20th century—the New York Longitudinal Study (NYLS), which began in the late 1950s and extended nearly to the end of the century. This pioneering study followed a group of participants from infancy, resulting in nine classifications of temperament that were then studied from childhood through adulthood. Despite the name of the measure, the normative data for the ATQ2 are cross-sectional, not longitudinal, a fact that the test developers acknowledge in the user's manual. The authors of the measure also acknowledge a potential limitation of the instrument is the possibility that sampling differences may account for some or all of the statistical changes observed over time.

The items have not changed from the original ATQ, but the development of the ATQ2 appears to address the previous version's major criticism—that of a limited standardization sample—as the normative sample increased from 135 for the original instrument to more than 3,000 for the ATQ2.

TECHNICAL. The measure's authors have made significant improvements in broadening the normative sample for the ATQ2. Of the new participants, 2,275 were female, and 1,009 were male, demonstrating a significantly disproportionate number of female participants. Data from the new sample were combined with the original data for a total standardization sample of 3,418 for the ATQ2. The increase in the standardization sample seems to address adequately the limitations of the previous version related to issues with demographic representation and generalization. The ages of participants range from 13 to 89 years, which is greatly expanded from the original version. Analysis of the ages and genders of the participants resulted in a determination that normative groups could be developed for each decade (teens, 20s, 30s, 40s, 50s, and 60s and older) and for specific school-aged groups (high school and college age). This grouping does create some partial overlap in the age ranges of the norm groups. There are a total of eight norm groups, each of which was additionally subdivided into male and female groups. Sample sizes per group range from 76 in the 60 years and older group to 694 in the teen group.

No new reliability or validity data are reported for the ATQ2, which contains the same items as the ATQ. Internal consistency coefficients ranging from .69 to .83 are reported for the nine temperament traits, each of which is composed of six items.

COMMENTARY. Overall the test developers have done an excellent job of expanding the standardization sample. This expanded standardization group has greatly increased the number of participants and broadened the demographic representation allowing for a more expansive generalization of results.

The user's manual is well written, concise, and descriptive for any professional planning to use the instrument. However, there continue to be some questions regarding the value of the nine general impressions of temperament items as an indicator of self-awareness. Although there has been research to support the distinction between ratings and perception in infants and children, additional research is necessary for this relationship to be confirmed in adulthood.

The technical manual indicates that the authors of the ATQ2 "believe that adults should be able to complete temperament instruments themselves and score and interpret their own results without the involvement of professionals" (p. 12). The authors of the measure acknowledge the need for additional research to determine the effects of self-administration vs. use with professional assistance. This comparison is somewhat contradictory to the user's manual, which lists specific user qualifications, requiring users to be individuals licensed or certified to provide behavioral health services. Upon review of the publisher's website, it does not appear that the publisher requires a purchaser or user to complete a standard qualification form, which many publishers of psychological testing instruments do, nor that the publisher scrutinizes or verifies any educational or licensure requirements. There is a brief statement in the user's manual that instructs any individual who is not qualified to administer, score, or interpret the measure to return the materials for a refund.

SUMMARY. With the addition of the expanded standardization sample, it appears that the utility of the ATQ2 has also expanded. The previous version was likely best suited primarily as a research tool, but now it appears that it has some additional clinical utility. Although it still does not seem to be an instrument to be used as the primary source for making high-stakes decisions with clients, in a clinical setting, the ATQ2 could be helpful in assisting clients in their personal exploration of temperamental dimensions of personality and in increasing self-awareness and understanding of the impact of temperament on an individual's functioning. In a clinical setting it would be wise to use the ATQ2 in conjunction with other more well-established personality instruments. The relationship between temperament and other better known personality characteristics is still in need of further research.

REVIEWER'S REFERENCES
Athanasou, J. A. (2005). [Review of The New York Longitudinal Scales Adult Temperament Questionnaire]. In R. A. Spies & B. S. Plake (Eds.), *The sixteenth mental measurements yearbook* (pp. 696–697). Lincoln, NE: Buros Institute of Mental Measurements.
Axford, S. N. (2005). [Review of The New York Longitudinal Scales Adult Temperament Questionnaire]. In R. A. Spies & B. S. Plake (Eds.), *The sixteenth mental measurements yearbook* (pp. 697–699). Lincoln, NE: Buros Institute of Mental Measurements.

[118]
NICU Network Neurobehavioral Scale.

Purpose: Designed to examine "the neurobehavioral organization, neurologic reflexes, motor development, and active and passive tone as well as signs of stress and withdrawal of the at-risk or drug-exposed infant."

Population: Infants between 30 to 48 weeks corrected or conceptional age.
Publication Date: 2005.
Acronym: NNNS.
Scores, 13: Habituation, Attention, Handling, Quality of Movement, Regulation, Nonoptimal Reflexes, Asymmetry, Stress/Abstinence, Arousal, Hypertonicity, Hypotonicity, Excitability, Lethargy.
Administration: Individual.
Restricted Distribution: Examiners must obtain training and certification to administer the test.
Price Data, 2010: $349 per complete test kit including manual, scoring sheets, and tool kit (includes ball, bell rattle, flashlight, foot probe, and head supports); $50 per manual (242 pages); $30 per 20 scoring sheets; $325 per tool kit.
Time: (20) minutes.
Comments: Examiners are instructed to gather observations and then complete the scoring sheet; scores should not be completed while conducting the examination. The standardized administration procedures are designed to accommodate the current state of arousal and age of the infant being assessed. The authors state that the scale is "not appropriate for infants who are younger than 30 weeks gestational age."
Authors: Barry M. Lester and Edward Z. Tronick.
Publisher: Paul H. Brookes Publishing Co., Inc. [Editor's Note: Paul H. Brookes Publishing Co., Inc., advises that it is no longer publishing this scale as of 2012 and that publication rights are reverting to the scale's authors.]

Review of the NICU Network Neurobehavioral Scale by JANET S. REED, Board Certified in Clinical Neuropsychology, Division of Neuropsychology, Henry Ford Behavioral Health Services, Detroit, MI:

DESCRIPTION. The NICU Network Neurobehavioral Scale (NNNS) is a structured observational tool for quantifying and characterizing behavior of drug-exposed and high-risk (pre-term) infants 30 weeks gestational age to 48 weeks corrected or conceptual age. It was developed for clinical and research use as part of the NIH Maternal Lifestyle Study (MLS), a large prospective longitudinal study of prenatal cocaine exposure in infants. It consists of a Tool Kit containing all the materials necessary for conducting the examination, an 8-page recording form for recording scores, and a manual that includes several reproducible forms (the NNNS Clinical Classification, Parts I and II; the NNNS Consultation Sheet; and the NNNS Feedback Sheet). Examination by an experienced examiner is reported to take 20–30 minutes.

The NNNS exam assesses 115 items in three categories: (a) neurological items that assess active and passive muscle tone, primitive reflexes, and central nervous system integrity; (b) behavioral state, sensory, and interactive responses; and (c) stress/abstinence items. Of the 115 items rated from the clinical examination, 45 items require direct manipulation of the infant. Once the clinical examination is complete and recorded on the NNNS Scoring Sheet, scores are transferred to Parts I and II of the Clinical Classification Sheet. This results in ratings of Typical, Suspect, or Atypical on 13 Summary scores representing infant states and neurological status: Habituation, Attention, Handling, Arousal, Regulation, Quality of Movement, Reflexes, Active Tone, Passive Tone, Asymmetrical Responses, Hypertonicity, Hypotonicity, and Stress/Abstinence Signs.

The examination is conducted on infants during specific states of arousal, and procedures for scoring each of the 115 items are provided in detail. Scoring and transfer of the items into Summary Scores is detailed in the test manual. Administration of the NNNS requires training and supervision, but minimum educational requirements or experience are not described. Video training, reliability training, and certification are available. It is reported that those trained on the Neonatal Behavior Assessment Scale (NBAS) can achieve training sufficient for certification in 2 days. For those without experience handling infants, practice with 20–30 infants is recommended.

DEVELOPMENT. The NNNS was developed due to the need to document infant status for infants prenatally exposed to cocaine and opioids, for use in the MLS. The NNNS was tested at four sites (Brown University, University of Miami, Wayne State University, and the University of Tennessee at Memphis) with 1,388 infants 1-month of age who were at high risk for, or with confirmed prenatal drug exposure. The conceptual model for the NNNS is based on normal neonatal development and clinical symptoms of prenatal drug exposure and withdrawal. The test authors state that the NNNS can be used for clinical and research purposes. Clinical applications include management in the intensive care nursery, discharge planning, serial assessment, and working with protective services.

TECHNICAL.

Standardization. The samples on which the scale was developed and for which descriptive statistics were reported include 1-month-old infants prenatally exposed to cocaine and opioids, by maternal admission or meconium testing (Exposed

Group n = 658); and a Comparison Group (n = 730) of infants whose mothers denied use of opioids and cocaine during pregnancy, but who may have used alcohol, marijuana, or tobacco. Participants were recruited from the four sites. All infants were examined between 42 and 44 weeks postgestational age. Examiners were blind to infant exposure status. Descriptive statistics (mean, standard deviation, range, and percentile ranks) by conceptual age, gender, race, and study site for 1-month-old infants are reported for each group (Exposed and Comparison) and summary score. Relevant studies reporting dose-response relationships between exposed and matched control groups are cited.

Similar descriptive statistics for a sample of newborns selected for optimal health status are reported. Newborns were recruited at the well-child nursery at one hospital. Inclusion criteria included at least 38 weeks gestational age, second (5-minute) APGAR score greater than or equal to 7, and discharge from the hospital within 3 days of delivery (4 days for infants delivered by C-section).

Reliability. Procedures for training and establishing reliability between examiners are described for research assistants in the sample of healthy newborns, but no measures or indices of interrater reliability are presented. Test-retest reliability is reported, with correlations of .30 to .44 across two studies and three test sessions that occurred over 4- and 6-week intervals. Internal consistency in the form of coefficient alphas of items comprising each Summary score is reported, with a range from .37 to .84 across Summary scores.

Validity. Face validity is established, with the conceptual model related to the assessment of the infant within its environment, consistent with the model developed by Brazelton (Neonatal Behavioral Assessment Scale) for the neurobehavioral assessment of the typical infant; and with added scales to assess abstinence symptoms. Divergent validity is reported, with citations of differences between exposed and nonexposed groups. Construct validity is reported via citations of studies indicating sensitivity to treatment effects and varying levels of exposure.

COMMENTARY.

Strengths. The NNNS represents a highly structured process of examination and scoring of behavior of the drug-exposed infant during specific states of arousal and alertness. It provides for detailed evaluation of infant behavior for high-risk infants who may have experienced prenatal exposure and display abstinence symptoms. The test manual provides for objective criteria, examples, and illustrations to facilitate scoring of observations and manipulation of the infant. It appears to have utility for high-risk infants and repeated testing to assess neurobehavioral status for clinical purposes during the early postnatal period. The NNNS shows promise for use in research on long-term outcomes with the additional documentation of training, interrater reliability (item-by-item, with kappa coefficient statistics), establishment of internal consistency, test-retest reliability, and predictive and convergent validity.

Weaknesses. Although the NNNS may be useful clinically to document recovery and neuro-developmental growth of an individual infant after prenatal exposure to substances, the normative data do not permit interpretation regarding severity of abnormal findings relative to a well-defined or representative sample. Descriptive statistics are available only for 1-month-old high-risk comparison and exposed groups and for healthy newborns. Both groups were recruited at one or more of the four study sites, and there is no information reported on the representativeness of the population, thus limiting generalizability of the findings. The test authors claim that the tool may be applied similarly as the Bayley Scales of Infant Development (BSID; Bayley, 1993). However, the NNNS does *not* possess adequate psychometric characteristics (e.g., representative samples of the population, normal distribution of scores, interrater reliability at the item or summary score level) to be applied to evaluation of infants in a manner similar to the BSID. Consequent to the poor psychometric qualities of the instrument, the application of the NNNS to research studies is limited. Demonstration of reliability and validity would be improved by presenting data from studies conducted with the measure; and evaluating the representativeness of drug-exposed infants who participated in the study relative to those who did not participate.

The administration of the NNNS is reported to take 20–30 minutes, but the scoring and completion of summary forms is cumbersome, time-consuming, and somewhat redundant. The Scoring Sheet would benefit from inclusion of abbreviated scoring criteria.

Adequacy of model. The conceptual model for the development of the NNNS is based on research conducted on prenatally exposed infants enrolled in a multisite longitudinal study. As such,

the measure incorporates concepts associated with neurodevelopmental functioning as well as stress/abstinence symptoms.

SUMMARY. The NNNS was designed specifically for the purpose of documenting and relating prenatal drug exposure to behavior and neurobehavioral functioning of the neonate. The conceptual model on which the instrument was developed corresponds well with neurobehavioral findings in drug-exposed and high-risk infants. However, reliability and validity data are limited and normative data are available for 1-month-olds only, restricting its utility for infants of varying ages and for assessment of change over time. The NNNS appears to have its greatest application in the training and supervision of clinical observation of infants at high risk for prenatal drug exposure, but it would not be appropriate for legal or research purposes. Norm-referenced measures such as the Bayley Scales of Infant Development (Bayley, 1993) with nationally representative norms to compare infant development and change would be more appropriate for such purposes.

REVIEWER'S REFERENCE

Bayley, N. (1993). Bayley Scales of Infant Development. San Antonio, TX: Pearson.

Review of the NICU Network Neurobehavioral Scale by CATHERINE RUTH SOLOMON SCHERZER, Associate Professor, Department de Psychologie, Université de Montreal, Montreal, Quebec, Canada:

DESCRIPTION. The NICU Network Neurobehavioral Scale (NNNS) was designed for the neurobehavioral assessment of drug-exposed and other high-risk infants, especially preterm infants (Lester, 1998). The age range for which it is suited is from approximately 30 weeks gestational age to 48 weeks adjusted age (gestational age plus age since birth). It was developed for the National Institute of Health (NIH) for the longitudinal, multisite Maternal Lifestyle Study of prenatal drug exposure and child outcome in preterm and full-term infants. Because prenatal drug exposure often occurs in the context of multiple risk factors, both biological and social, the scale was developed to broadly assess the infant at risk. According to the test authors it evaluates neurobehavioral organization, neurologic reflexes, motor development, active and passive tone, and signs of stress and withdrawal from drugs. It can also be used to evaluate a variety of non-drug-exposed high-risk infants, because it evaluates classical reflexes, tone, posture, and social and self-regulatory competences. As stated in the test manual, the comprehensive NNNS assessment includes three parts: (a) classical neurologic items that assess active and passive tone and primitive reflexes as well as items that reflect central nervous system (CNS) integrity; (b) behavioral items including state, sensory, and interactive responses; and (c) stress abstinence items appropriate for high-risk infants.

The scale was designed for both research and clinical work. Research applications involve the study of the effects of various factors occurring during pregnancy such as illegal drug use, environmental toxins, abuse of prescription medications, use of tobacco, poor nutrition, inadequate prenatal care, and other social-related factors on the neurobehavior of the infant. Clinical applications include developing a profile of the infant to write a managerial plan while in the hospital, evaluating the infant close to discharge as part of the discharge plan, and evaluating the infant during the transition to home that involves the caregivers in the examination in order to inform them of the infant's capacities and limitations. Post-discharge it can be used to determine whether the infant qualifies for early intervention services. In order to use the NNNS one must be trained and certified in the administration and scoring of the test. Training requires the trainee to have considerable experience with all types of infants, full-term, preterm, low birth weight, drug-exposed, and other high-risk infants. In the test manual the authors have taken care to describe the various infant states and to emphasize the importance of infant state and the effects of examiner-infant interaction for the administration of the NNNS. The test manual also presents very detailed scoring instructions for each infant ability to be evaluated, and instructions for how to proceed and how often to present the various stimuli and how long to wait between presentations. Each concept is fully explained. Scoring examples and case studies are provided. The test authors present the limits of the test and suggest other tests for use when the NNNS is not appropriate. For instance, it is not designed for use with full-term healthy infants or for measuring particular neurological syndromes.

The NNNS Scoring Sheet consists of 115 items divided in three parts: Part I, 45 examination items that involve direct manipulation of the infant, is followed by 70 items divided into Parts II and III. Part II Examiner Ratings provide for the recording of observations taken during the course of the examination. Part III Stress/Abstinence records the presence or absence of signs of drug dependency or environmentally related stress as observed over the entire examination. The examination takes about 30 minutes.

The items on the Scoring Sheet are broken down into 11 packages that are administered beginning with a change in position of the infant or of focus of the examination. The packages produce a standard sequence with which to challenge the infant, and are designed to reduce unnecessary manipulation and state changes. The order of administration of the packages and items is meant to be relatively invariant, although it can be modified to accommodate to the state of the infant being examined for clinical purposes. The state in which the infant must be for each item is clearly specified and to be noted on the scoring sheet. As in the test manual, directions are provided about how to proceed, how often to present the various stimuli, and how long to wait between presentations. The attribution of scores is also clearly specified and optimal responses are printed in bold. The Scoring Sheet provides several summary scores for different domains such as Autonomic subtotal, CNS subtotal, Skin subtotal, Visual subtotal, Gastrointestinal subtotal, and State subtotal, providing a detailed picture of the infant's functioning in several areas. Tables are provided that permit comparisons of these totals with those of an at-risk sample of prenatally drug-exposed infants and with a sample of normal healthy infants. The test authors describe several other ways for the examiner to summarize the NNNS results for clinical purposes. A second way is to interpret the construct measured by the summary scores as well as the individual items that comprise the summary score. A third way offered is to write a clinical summary using the constructs of the summary scores but without actually scoring the individual items. A fourth way is to use an abbreviated chart format, the NNNS clinical classification, which also includes a profile sheet for recording results of multiple examinations. The NNNS clinical classification allows the examiner to quickly scan the summary score descriptions and check the ones that most closely resemble the infant's pattern of response.

DEVELOPMENT. As stated above, the NNNS was developed for the National Institutes of Health for the longitudinal, multisite Maternal Lifestyle Study of prenatal drug exposure and child outcome in preterm and full-term infants. The sample included 1,335 infants at four National Institute of Child Health and Human Development Neonatal Research Network sites. They were examined between 42- and 44-weeks post-conceptual age. The study was conducted in two phases: acute outcome and longitudinal outcome. For the longitudinal study, infants were part of the exposed (to cocaine) group (N = 658) or the comparison group (N = 730), and were matched on race, sex, and gestational age. The NNNS is closely related to several other published tests. It draws on the Neonatal Behavioral Assessment Scale (NBAS; Brazelton, 1973), the Neurological Examination of the Full-Term Newborn Infant (Prechtl, 1977), the Neurological Evaluation of the Maternity of Newborn Infants (Amiel-Tison, 1968), the Neurobiological Assessment of the Preterm Infant (Korner & Thoman, 1990), the Assessment of Preterm Infants' Behavior (Als, Lester, Tronick, & Brazelton, 1982), and on the Neonatal Abstinence Score (Finnegan, 1986). In order to develop the NNNS, the scoring of items on the NBAS was expanded to include the behavior of at-risk infants, and new items were added. In contrast to the NBAS, the NNNS places more emphasis on the responses of the infant to the test items and less emphasis on the responses of the infant to the examiner.

TECHNICAL. The test manual states that test-retest reliability was established in two ongoing studies. In both studies the infants were tested at 34, 40, and 44 weeks' gestational age. The test authors report the correlation coefficients between the test sessions as summary scores ranging as from .30 to .44 across the three tests.

Validity evidence is reported to have been documented in a study of full-term newborns in 1996. Infants with cocaine and alcohol exposure were compared with infants with alcohol exposure alone and those without prenatal drug exposure. Differences were found between these groups and an unexposed group. There are no data reported on longer term predictive validity in the manual.

COMMENTARY. The NNNS appears to have excellent face validity. It is based on several well-known and highly regarded tests. The test manual presents and details every aspect of every concept required to administer and score the test. The scoring sheet is equally well-presented and detailed. Aspects of test reliability and validity are not as clearly presented. Predictive validity is not addressed.

SUMMARY. The NNNS appears to be an excellent test of the neurobehavioral organization of at-risk or drug-exposed infants. It would be useful to have more information about the technical features of the test.

REVIEWER'S REFERENCES
Als, H., Lester, B. M., Tronick, F. C., & Brazelton, T. B. (1982). Towards a research instrument for the assessment of preterm infants' behavior (A.P.I.B.). In H. E. Fitzgerald, B. M. Lester, & M. W. Yogman (Eds.), *Theory and research in behavioral pediatrics, Vol. 1* (pp. 85–132). New York, NY: Plenum.
Amiel-Tison, C. (1968). Neurological evaluation of the maturity of newborn infants. *Archives of Disease in Childhood, 43*, 89–93.
Brazelton, T. B. (1973). Neonatal Behavioral Assessment Scale. In *Clinics in Developmental Medicine, No. 50*. Philadelphia, PA: J. B. Lippincott.
Finnegan, L. P. (1986). Neonatal abstinence syndrome: Assessment and pharmacotherapy. In F. F. Rubatelli and B. Granati (Eds.), *Neonatal therapy and update*. New York, NY: Experta Medica.
Korner, A. F., & Thoman, V. A. (1990). *Neurobehavioral assessment of the preterm infant*. New York, NY: The Psychological Corporation.
Lester, B. M. (1998). The Maternal Lifestyle Study. *Annals of New York Academy of Science, 846*, 296–306.
Prechtl, H. (1977). *The neurological examination of the newborn infant: Clinics in developmental medicine, No. 63*. Philadelphia, PA: J. B. Lippincott.

[119]

Non-verbal IQ Test.

Purpose: "Designed to test intelligence while minimizing cultural or educational background unfairness."
Population: Below age 17 through adult.
Publication Date: 2011.
Acronym: NVIQT.
Scores: Overall Score only.
Administration: Individual.
Price Data: Available from publisher.
Time: (30) minutes.
Comments: Self-administered online assessment. The test publisher advises that the test manual is being updated to include more information about methodology and theoretical background used in the development of the test. The test publisher also advises that this information is available to clients, as are benchmarks for relevant industries and racial/ethnic group comparison data. However, this information was not provided to Buros or the reviewers.
Author: PsychTests AIM, Inc.
Publisher: PsychTests AIM, Inc. [Canada].

Review of the Non-verbal IQ Test by STEPHAN DILCHERT, Assistant Professor, Department of Management, Baruch College, City University of New York, New York, NY:

DESCRIPTION. The Non-verbal IQ Test (NVIQT) is a nonverbal measure of cognitive ability, developed to assess spatial ability and pattern recognition. The stated purpose of the test is to serve as a measure of intelligence that minimizes irrelevant cultural or educational influences on test scores. The technical manual accompanying the test does not further delineate the nature of the construct that the test is intended to assess. Limited information is provided on the intended target population or intended uses of the test. It can be used as a pre-employment test, according to the manual.

The NVIQT presents 20 figural reasoning items of the "matrix" type, where patterns in a 3-by-3 matrix need to be recognized and completed by correctly identifying the missing cell among five response options. The test is administered online and takes an estimated 30 minutes to complete. The technical information and the test-taker instructions do not indicate whether the test is timed, or how missing items are handled once test-takers exceed the 30-minute time-frame. Upon completion, test reports include a brief introduction on "cross-cultural IQ tests," followed by the total test score and brief narrative interpretation.

DEVELOPMENT. The accompanying technical manual provides only scant information about the development of the test. First, it is not clear whether the test was developed based on a set of test specifications that defined the content of the test, item format, or desired psychometric properties. Second, no information is provided on item development, including how items were written, pretested, or selected for inclusion on the final version of the test. It is unclear whether the set of 20 items was selected from a larger pool of items based on appropriate psychometric characteristics, or if they were the only items developed for this purpose.

The technical manual presents normative information for the test based on one large sample. This sample is not characterized as a development sample, and the normative and validity information provided suggests that the sample was rather used for standardization purposes. Thus, this reviewer assumes that the publisher either omitted results from any potential development sample from the technical manual or that the development sample also served as the normative sample.

TECHNICAL.

Standardization. The test was completed by 9,954 individuals who self-selected to complete the test on three publicly accessible websites. Gender information was available for less than half of the sample (approximately balanced between groups). Age information was available for 78% of individuals. The age distribution was highly skewed, with an overrepresentation of teenagers and young adults (42% of participants for whom age information was available were 17 years of age or younger; 16% were 18–24). No information is provided on race

and ethnic group representation. Because the test materials do not specify an intended target population, the appropriateness of the standardization sample cannot be evaluated. However, at least with regard to age, the present sample is not representative of the general or working populations of most industrialized countries.

With regard to the scoring of test performance, it is unclear whether the test is scaled on a traditional IQ metric. The descriptive statistics on the total test score provided for the standardization sample (M = 105.6, SD = 19.6, range 55–155) suggest that this might have been the intention of the test developers. In the standardization sample, test scores displayed roughly normal distributional properties, as judged by a visual inspection of the cumulative frequency distribution (information on skew and kurtosis were not provided).

Reliability. A single reliability estimate is provided for NVIQT scores, presumably obtained on the standardization sample discussed above–however, no associated sample size is provided. Coefficient alpha (20 items) is reported as .77. Although internal consistency reliability estimates above .70 are often regarded as adequate (Nunnally, 1978), such a value is on the low end of reliability estimates typically obtained for cognitive ability test scores (Jensen, 1980). Regarding the suitability of this type of reliability estimate, it is a reasonable assumption that items on the latter half of the test on average receive fewer numbers of correct responses. An examination of item content by this reviewer revealed that items on the second half of the test indeed display higher difficulty than those on the first half (item difficulty is not discussed in the technical manual). Hence, instead of internal consistency estimates, this reviewer believes that alternate measures of reliability (e.g., test-retest reliability) would have been more appropriate. Such estimates are not reported by the test publisher.

Validity. The technical manual presents results of analyses that relate test scores to demographic and background variables. The findings discussed here might be regarded as initial evidence of the test's construct validity, but do not address criterion-related validity.

The developers report a statistically significant sex difference on total test scores. A Cohen's *d* value computed by this reviewer based on the group mean scores reveals that sex differences were moderate in absolute magnitude (.45 standard deviation units), and thus higher than those on most other types of cognitive ability measures (see Hyde, 2005).

Analyses on age group differences are presented only in the form of ANOVA results. Computations by this reviewer based on group descriptives reveal that largest differences were found between the ages 25–29 and the youngest and oldest age groups (Cohen's d = .40 and .39, respectively; 25–29-year-olds scoring higher). It should be noted that the age-based subsamples for which data were provided were small (Ns = 609–718) and selected by the test developers in order to present age groups of roughly equal sizes.

Educational background (highest degree obtained) is positively related to total scores on the NVIQT. In the standardization sample, there was a near perfect gradation showing that individuals with postgraduate degrees on average outscored college graduates, who outscored high school graduates, who outscored individuals without high school degrees.

Finally, the technical manual reports means and standard deviations for groups based on educational achievement (measured as self-reported grades in four categories: below average, average, good, and top grades). The observed differences are mostly in the expected direction, but modest in magnitude (average d value between adjacent groups = .13, as computed by this reviewer). Individuals with self-reported top grades outscored all other groups, and those with good grades outscored lower groups as well. There was a small difference between those with average and below average grades, albeit in the opposite direction. The largest difference between any two groups was between individuals with top grades and those with average grades (d = .48).

The stated purpose of the NVIQT is to provide a measure of cognitive ability that minimizes educational influences on test scores. On first inspection, the results discussed above might suggest that the developers have succeeded in this regard, compared to other, more traditional cognitive ability measures. However, several factors limit the interpretability of these findings. First, information on educational background and grades was self-reported by participants. These data likely suffer from overreporting and an artificial reduction in variance, reducing the observed relationship with cognitive test scores. Second, the categorical measure of grades artificially polytomizes the scale, resulting in observed effects that are further attenuated compared to their true magnitudes. Third, the grade category

labels are ambiguous, and most likely contribute to measurement unreliability on the criterion measure, even further attenuating observed effects. Although it is likely that the nonverbal character of the test reduces the influence of extraneous factors (such as literacy or native language skills, for example), NVIQT scores do relate to educational background, as would be expected of any test measuring general mental ability or a lower order primary ability.

As stated above, beyond educational achievement, the technical manual does not provide evidence of the test's criterion-related validity. Judgments of appropriateness for any potential uses would thus have to be based solely on content validity. Furthermore, the lack of validity information precludes analyses of differential validity for various legally protected groups, which is important before the test can be used in most applied settings, especially in employment settings.

COMMENTARY. The NVIQT can draw on a long tradition of cognitive ability tests that measure basic reasoning ability with nonverbal, figural item content (see, e.g., Cattell, 1940). In fact, it is clear that the development of the NVIQT must have been inspired by, or even purposefully mimicked, one of the most popular and well-supported examples of this type of assessment–the Raven's Advanced Progressive Matrices (T8: 2233). This similarity is a positive indicator of the test's validity. However, beyond this basic evidence, important information on the test's development, psychometric characteristics, fairness, and criterion-related evidence of validity is lacking. The information and evidence presented by the test publisher does not satisfy important national and international testing standards and guidelines (e.g., *Standards for Educational and Psychological Testing* [American Educational Research Association, American Psychological Association, & National Council on Measurement in Education, 1999] or the *International Guidelines for Test Use* [International Test Commission, 2000]). Although some information might simply have been omitted from the technical manual, it is also clear that during the development of the test, many important decisions were based on considerations of convenience. The lack of control over testing conditions and the extreme imbalance in age distribution of the standardization sample suggest that the test in its current form cannot be supported for most practical applications.

SUMMARY. In principle, the NVIQT might show promise as a measure of figural reasoning.

However, several important principles of test design have been disregarded during its development (e.g., using multiple, appropriate samples; documenting item characteristics and selection decisions; assessing criterion-related evidence of validity). Statements about the psychometric quality of the test currently cannot be substantiated based on evidence provided by the test publisher. Hence, use of the test should be discouraged, especially in environments where important outcomes are associated with test scores (e.g., work settings, admissions decisions) or in populations poorly represented during test development (e.g., race- and ethnic-minority groups, older adults) until more results from research studies have accumulated. Users interested in similar, empirically well-supported measures might alternatively consider tests such as the Raven's Advanced Progressive Matrices (T8: 2233) or the Naglieri Nonverbal Ability Test (14: 252), both of which have been reviewed in previous volumes of the *Mental Measurements Yearbook*.

REVIEWER'S REFERENCES

American Educational Research Association, American Psychological Association, & National Council on Measurement in Education. (1999). *Standards for educational and psychological testing.* Washington, DC: American Educational Research Association.
Cattell, R. B. (1940). A culture-free intelligence test. *Journal of Educational Psychology, 31,* 161-179.
Hyde, J. S. (2005). The gender similarities hypothesis. *American Psychologist, 60,* 581-592.
International Test Commission. (2000). *International guidelines for test use.* Retrieved from http://intestcom.org
Jensen, A. R. (1980). *Bias in mental testing.* New York, NY: Free Press.
Nunnally, J. C. (1978). *Psychometric theory* (2nd ed.). New York, NY: McGraw-Hill.

Review of the Non-Verbal IQ Test by STEFAN C. DOMBROWSKI, Professor and Director, School Psychology Program, Rider University, Lawrenceville, NJ:

DESCRIPTION. The Non-Verbal IQ Test (NVIQT) claims to be a measure of a fluid/nonverbal intelligence and was developed with the intent of minimizing the influence of language, education, reading ability, culture, and social context. The test presents a 20-item battery that evaluates spatial aptitude, inductive reasoning, and perceptual accuracy. It appears to be modeled after J. C. Raven's (1965) Progressive Matrices. The NVIQT reports higher correlations with nonverbal (fluid) aspects of IQ than with verbal (crystallized) IQ, although the actual correlations are not furnished in the manual. The test manual indicates that this measure is useful for pre-employment testing. It requires a computerized testing session with an estimated completion time of 30 minutes. However, there does not appear to be a test time limit so more persistent examinees can linger in taking the test for as long as they wish. Scoring of the NVIQT occurs online with a resulting feedback report that produces a standard score and percentile rank in accord with the commonly used metric for IQ tests (mean = 100; standard deviation = 15). The report feedback also offers examinees advice on how to improve one's intelligence test scores. This advice includes test-taking tips, tips to improve verbal IQ, and a guide to improving nonverbal IQ. Additional descriptive information regarding the NVIQT in the manual or report feedback is unavailable.

DEVELOPMENT. The normative sample was uncontrolled and participants self-selected to take the assessment and participate in the validation study on Queendom.com, Psychtests.com, or Psychologytoday.com. The sample included 9,954 participants with a breakdown as follows: 22% female, 24% male, and 54% unknown. The age of participants was predominantly below age 17 (42%) with the remaining ages stratified as follows: 18 to 24 (16%), 25 to 29 (7%), 30 to 39 (7%), 40 plus (6%), and unknown (22%). The normative sample had a score range of 55 to 155 with a mean of 105.64 and a standard deviation of 19.63. A graph in the manual for the instrument depicts a score distribution that looks approximately normal. However, statistical validation of this visual approximation was not furnished. Performance on the NVIQT by age, gender, education (Grade School/Some High School, High School, Some College, and Post-Graduate Work/Degree), and Grades (Top, Good, Average, Below Average) were included. The Post-Graduate Work/Degree group (M = 112.1) outscored the Grade School/Some High School group (M = 104.2). The Top Grades category (M = 113.4) outscored the Average (M = 104.0) and the Below Average (M = 105.7) groups. Analyses of variance with follow-up post-hoc procedures were used to determine differences among groups. No further descriptive information was furnished in the manual.

TECHNICAL. The NVIQT was normed online by individuals who self-selected to take the instrument through Queendom.com, Psychtests. com, or PsychologyToday.com. The sample was uncontrolled and all demographic information was gathered through self-report. The manual reports a reliability analysis for the 20 items (coefficient alpha = .77) but no further reliability information is available. The manual reports "validity analysis" by comparing examinees' performance by self-reported gender, age, education, and grades using analysis of variance and post-hoc procedures. No further technical information regarding the structure of the instrument or the normative sample was furnished.

COMMENTARY AND SUMMARY. Created as a measure of pre-employment testing, the NVIQT assesses individuals' nonverbal/fluid reasoning and claims to be free from cultural, educational, reading, and language bias. The item content is reminiscent of J. C. Raven's Progressive Matrices (1965). Whether the content is free from cultural or language bias has yet to be determined psychometrically or even through expert consensus. The instrument's instructions are offered in English in a half page of online text. And one of the response choices for each item is also offered in English (e.g., "I don't know"). This questions whether the instrument is truly a language-free measure. The NVIQT lacks even nominal analyses of its underlying psychometrics including validity, reliability (other than the internal consistency reliability provided), item analysis, and representativeness of sample. The normative sampling is problematic because it is based on self-selection and may not be representative of the population who may be administered the instrument. Nearly 42% of those who self-selected were under the age of 17. This lack of balance in the sample raises questions about the instrument's suitability for ages older than 17. The score report feedback offers a "guide" to improving IQ test performance including verbal IQ. However, this reviewer considers the report feedback guide inaccurate because no extant evidence suggests that IQ test performance can be improved. Online administration and scoring facilitates the scoring and administration of the instrument, but also may pose test security problems. Severe psychometric limitations including an unrepresentative normative sample and nonexistent validity and limited reliability evidence makes drawing definitive, quantitative conclusions from the NVIQT ill-advised.

REVIEWER'S REFERENCE

Raven, J. C. (1965). *Advanced Progressive Matrices: Sets I and II: Plan and use of the scale with a report of experimental work carried out by G. A. Foulds and A. R. Forbes.* London, England: H. K. Lewis.

[120]

Number Sense Screener, K-1, Research Edition.

Purpose: Designed "for screening early numerical competencies in kindergarten and early first grade."
Population: Students in kindergarten and first grade.
Publication Date: 2012.
Acronym: NSS.
Scores, 7: Counting Skills, Number Recognition, Number Comparisons, Nonverbal Calculation, Story Problems, Number Combinations, Total Score.

Administration: Individual.
Price Data, 2012: $89.95 per kit including user's guide (66 pages), stimulus book, quick script for administrators, and 25 record sheets; $25 per 25 record sheets.
Time: (15-20) minutes.
Authors: Nancy C. Jordan, Joseph J. Glutting, and Nancy Dyson.
Publisher: Paul H. Brookes Publishing Co.

Review of the Number Sense Screener K-1, Research Edition by ARTURO OLIVÁREZ, JR., Professor, Teacher Education Department, University of Texas at El Paso, and NORMA MARTINEZ, Graduate Research Assistant, Teacher Education Department, University of Texas at El Paso, El Paso, TX:

DESCRIPTION. The Number Sense Screener (NSS) is a 29-item test for screening early numerical competencies in kindergarten and early first grade. It is an individual measure that may take between 15 to 20 minutes to administer. The instrument itself is composed of six different, but interrelated subareas linked to number sense computational topics: Counting Skills (3 items), Number Recognition (4 items), Number Comparisons (7 items), Nonverbal Calculation (4 items), Story Problems (5 items), and Number Combinations (6 items). The Counting Skills subtest assesses knowledge of a count sequence to at least 10, principles of one-to-one correspondence, cardinality, and order; the Number Recognition subtest assesses the ability to name written symbols for numbers; the Number Comparisons subtest assesses number order, magnitude, and distance between stimuli for each item; the Nonverbal Calculation subtest assesses addition and subtraction calculations with the use of tokens to perform the given number sense tasks with little to no verbal cues; the Story Problems subtest assesses three addition and two subtraction problems by providing specific verbal format using pennies in the instruction for each operation allowing for the use by the examinee of a variety of counting strategies; and the Number Combination subtest assesses four addition and two subtraction problems that are orally phrased as "How much is m and n?" Each item is scored 0 (incorrect) or 1 (correct) with a total raw score of 29. The administration of the NSS is straightforward and the examiner can calculate the subarea raw score totals, the entire exam raw score total, and the conversion of these raw scores into standard scores and percentile ranks using norm sample tables in the appendix section of the user's guide.

DEVELOPMENT. The NSS is a research-based tool for the screening and identification of early numerical competencies in young children. These numerical competencies are used to predict student achievement and developmental growth in kindergarten and first grade level mathematics. The developers followed the Common Core State Standards for kindergarten mathematics (National Governors Association Center for Best Practices & Council of Chief State School Officers, 2010). The test authors' main rationale for its development is derived from the extant research literature that informs practice as to the likelihood for higher rates of failure by students in the middle school that tend to increase dramatically due to the underachievement in mathematics in the early school years (National Mathematics Advisory Panel, 2008). Similarly, Gersten, Jordan, and Flojo (2005) have concluded that early detection of students with math difficulties can be traced back to the problem of identifying students who have exhibited deficiencies with number sense. Furthermore, Geary, Hamson, and Hoard (2000) have found that young children with weak math number sense skills result in series of poorly developed counting procedures, slow fact recall and retrieval, and inaccurate computation skills. On the other hand, when research studies have been conducted to determine the importance that number sense plays in a student's ability to do well in school tasks, the results indicate that even high-risk students exhibit significant gains on math outcomes (Griffin, Case, & Siegler, 1994). Several research studies indicate that there is high predictability on math achievement up to third grade due to demonstrated proficiency with number sense skills by kindergarten and first-grade students (Jordan, Glutting, & Ramineni, 2009; Jordan, Kaplan, Ramineni, & Locuniak, 2009; Locuniak & Jordan, 2008).

TECHNICAL. The standardization norms for the NSS used a longitudinal sampling approach where a cohort of children was evaluated on three occasions: Kindergarten Fall 2003, Kindergarten Fall 2004, and First Grade Fall 2004. The normative sample accounted for participants' age, gender, race, and region of residence. There were closely balanced proportions in terms of the participants' age, gender, and–to a lesser extent–SES variables. A less balanced representation from the variables of race and classification status was obtained for these variables. All participants were from the state of Delaware. The NSS's raw scores were converted to standard scores using a mean of 100 and a standard deviation of 15. To allow for sample scores interpretation and comparison purposes, the NSS provides both standard scores and percentile ranks. The normative analyses were derived from students who participated in the item tryout phase ($N = 425$) of the NSS's development, thus all psychometric information is derived from this sample.

The test developers included scale reliability information by using person- and item-separation indices by the application of modern test-score theory. The results yielded acceptable levels on person-reliability (.84) and highly satisfactory item-reliabilities (.99) providing evidence of validity (item index) and reliability (person index) for the NSS scale. Classical true-score theory approaches were also presented by the test developers. High internal consistency and test-retest stability indices of reliability were observed for the total sample and, in the case of internal consistency, for males and females. All coefficient alpha reliabilities were in the high range (equal to or greater than .82). The test-retest correlation coefficients ranged from a low of .61 to a high of .86 (using an interval of 2 to 17 months) with lower reliabilities observed only when the testing period exceeded one year.

Evidence of construct, predictive, discriminant, and content validity studies were performed on the NSS by using various children samples in which the researchers independently determined the different types of validity evidence. In support of the most important type of validity evidence for this type of measuring tool, the test authors examined the NSS construct validity by using the Calculation and Applied Problems portions of the Woodcock-Johnson III (W-J III) as a convergence criterion and the Dynamic Indicators of Basic Early Literacy Skills–Sixth Edition (DIBELS) as a divergent criterion. The results obtained provided evidence of this type of validity for both first-grade and third-grade samples. The NSS exhibited high levels of association ($r = .62$) with the mathematics criterion (W-J III subtest) and lower levels of association ($r = .37$) with the reading criterion (DIBELS). Finally, the test authors provided evidence of treatment validity, focusing on the idea that the NSS scale can be sensitive to effective interventions that may allow for the "boosting" of children's skills in number sense. The results of this study provided ample evidence that the students in the treatment condition exhibited higher levels of number sense performance than the control group, as measured by the NSS scale. The rest of the validity evidence work is found in the *NSS Research Edition User's Guide K-1*.

COMMENTARY. Overall, the NSS scale provides the user with a measuring tool that uniquely targets a student population who can benefit greatly with the early identification and diagnosis of intrinsic mathematical deficiencies typically gone undetected by parents and elementary school personnel. The NSS offers an affordable, easy, and straightforward measurement tool that has been developed by a highly experienced and respected team of researchers who have examined the issue and the damaging impact that inherent weaknesses in young children's number sense skills may have in future mathematics performance. The psychometric studies conducted for this scale provide clear evidence of its construct and treatment validity. Thus, the common user as well as a seasoned researcher will have the opportunity to gather student data and trust the data will lead them to appropriate decision making in early intervention efforts and adjustment of individualized educational plans of students identified with weak number sense skills. The test developers have aligned the scale to well-established state and national standards of mathematics learning. On the other hand, the test developers need to conduct additional research studies where other populations of elementary students can be examined because the majority of their research employed students from a single region in the country. This version of the NSS is labeled as the "Research Edition" and, as such, it may indicate that the scale is still under development. The test authors may increase its utility by adding different geographical regions to enhance the generalizability properties of the scale. Additionally, there may be a need for a Form B of the NSS because several items are repeated and these items may produce misleading results of actual student performance in a particular subarea. Rather than repeating an item in different subareas, it would be better to introduce parallel or equivalent items so that students solve them and the solution is not influenced by the test taker's practice effects or "carry-over effects" innate to the test-taking task.

SUMMARY. All in all, the Number Sense Screener, K-1, Research Edition is an ideal tool that can assist parents and teachers to support their children in detecting mathematics problems due to weaknesses in the child's proficiency with number sense before it is too late. Early identification can lead to simple interventions and adjustment in the teacher's mathematics instruction at the elementary school level. The unidimensionality of the NSS speaks loudly about the simplicity and usefulness of detecting this pivotal mathematical single skill, which can assist in preventing serious educational and vocational consequences to students. As it currently stands, the NSS is a psychometrically sound instrument to be used with confidence by any school personnel to make timely interventions for students identified as lacking this important mathematical skill.

REVIEWERS' REFERENCES

Geary, D. C., Hamson, C. O., & Hoard, M. K. (2000). Numerical and arithmetical cognition: A longitudinal study of process and concept deficits in children with learning disability. *Journal of Experimental Child Psychology, 77*(3), 236–263.

Gersten, R., Jordan, N. C., & Flojo, J. R. (2005). Early identification and interventions for students with mathematical difficulties. *Journal of Learning Difficulties 38*(4), 293–304.

Griffin, S., Case, R., & Siegler, R. (1994). Rightstart: Providing the central conceptual prerequisites for first formal learning of arithmetic to students at risk for school failure. In K. McGilly (Ed.), *Classroom lessons: Integrating cognitive theory and classroom practice* (pp. 24–49). Cambridge, MA: MIT Press.

Jordan, N. C., Glutting, J., & Ramineni, C. (2010). The importance of number sense to mathematics achievement for first and third grades. *Learning and Individual Differences, 20*(2), 82–88.

Jordan, N. C., Kaplan, D., Ramineni, C., & Locuniak, M. N. (2009). Early math matters: Kindergarten number competence and later mathematics outcomes. *Developmental Psychology, 45*, 850–867.

Locuniak, M. N., & Jordan, N. C. (2008). Using kindergarten number sense to predict calculation fluency in second grade. *Journal of Learning Difficulties 41*, 451–459.

National Governors Association Center for Best Practices & Council of State School Officers. (2010). *Common core state standards for mathematics.* Retrieved November 15, 2010, from http://www.corestandards.org/CCSSI_Math%20Standards.pdf

National Mathematics Advisory Panel. (2008). *Foundations for success: The final report of the National Mathematics Advisory Panel.* Washington, DC: U.S. Department of Education.

Review of the Number Sense Screener, K-1, Research Edition by G. MICHAEL POTEAT, Associate Professor, Department of Psychology, East Carolina University, Greenville, NC:

DESCRIPTION. The Number Sense Screener, K–1, Research Edition (NSS) is a "research based tool for screening early numerical competencies in kindergarten and early first grade" (user's guide, p. 1). The NSS was developed in response to the mathematical underperformance of students in the U.S. The NSS assesses areas of competency aligned with the Common Core State Standards for kindergarten mathematics developed by the National Governors Association. The instrument is designed to both assess and provide remediation strategies for deficits in mathematical fluency. The NSS measures (a) Counting Skills, (b) Number Recognition, (c) Number Comparisons, (d) Nonverbal Calculation, (e) the ability to solve Story Problems, and (f) the ability to perform Number Combinations. In addition to the test manual (the user's guide), the NSS materials include a quick script card to aid in administration, a stimulus booklet, and record sheets. Black dots or tokens must be purchased separately, and a box with an opening must be constructed by the user for the Nonverbal Calculation task. The NSS consists of only 29 items and is designed for a specific purpose. It combines traditional test development with the more recent focus on curriculum-based assessment.

DEVELOPMENT. The development of the NSS was supported by grants from the *Eunice Kennedy Shriver* National Institute of Child Health and Human Development and represents an attempt to develop an instrument to identify specific problems with early mathematics referred to as number sense. Number sense is defined for young children (basically 3 to 6 years of age) as involving the ability to count, to recognize that the final count represents the number of items in the set, to discriminate between small quantities, to compare small quantities, and to transform sets (e.g., addition and subtraction). The NSS is also designed to aid in the identification of children with learning problems and in the assessment of progress as part of the response to intervention model.

TECHNICAL. The norms for the NSS were developed using longitudinal sampling conducted over three stages (fall and spring of kindergarten and fall of first grade). The norms are based on 300 children (135 girls and 165 boys) who participated in all three stages. The results were normalized to provide standard scores with a mean of 100 and a standard deviation of 15. The norms are based on a sample that has a higher number of children identified as African American or Hispanic than the national population. Children from low SES groups were also overrepresented in the norms. Separate norms are presented for children at each of the three stages.

The NSS requires individual administration using a standardized administration procedure. The instructions for administration are adequate but could be more concise. The NSS quick script is designed to assist the administrator; eight pages of the test manual are devoted to administration and scoring. The stimulus booklet is spiral-bound and does not include instructions for administration. Although the NSS can be used by psychologists or other specialists, it is primarily a screening instrument and will probably be used most frequently by classroom teachers. The test manual states that the instrument takes approximately 15 to 20 minutes to administer.

The psychometric properties of the NSS are excellent in most aspects. Item statistics are based on Rasch analysis of 26 items used in the development of the NSS and demonstrate that the ordering of the items is appropriate. Only one item demonstrated item-bias analysis between boys and girls, with girls outperforming boys on this item. Average internal consistency ($N = 425$) based on coefficient alpha was .85. The NSS was developed using a longitudinal approach and a number of test-retest correlation coefficients are provided. The NSS provides stable data ($rs > .80$) for as long as 4 months and the test-retest stability was .61 for children tested in September in kindergarten and again in February of first grade.

Validity of test score use was evaluated using a number of procedures. Content validity is evident in that the basis for selecting material corresponds with the common core standards. A repeated measures analysis of variance using NSS scores as the criterion variable compared children who did or *did not* demonstrate proficiency on the Delaware Student Testing Program (DSTP) in Mathematics, administered in the third grade as the predictor variable. The results showed that performance on the NSS is related to mathematics proficiency later in school. The results are complex, but the difference in fall kindergarten NSS scores between proficient and nonproficient third-grade students was approximately 18 points (more than a standard deviation). Considerable evidence is also presented demonstrating the predictive validity of the NSS compared to a number of other measures (e.g., matrix reasoning, vocabulary) using measures of mathematical achievement on the Woodcock-Johnson III (WJ-III) as the criterion variable. Two subtests on the WJ-III (Math Calculation and Math Applications) were used as criterion variables. The scores on the two subtests were also combined and labeled overall math achievement. The analysis used a block entry regression model and the regression coefficients for the NSS were significant for all comparisons. The effect size (Cohen's f) of the NSS as a predictor of overall math achievement in the first grade was .29 and overall math achievement in third grade was .21. These effect sizes would be classified as between moderate and large using Cohen's criteria. The effect sizes with math calculation as the criterion variable were smaller (.10) for first grade and larger for the third grade (.26). The largest effects were based on the math applications. The respective effect sizes were large (.44 and .45) for the first grade and the third grade math application scores. Other evidence is also presented for convergent and divergent validity and for treatment validity. The latter study used the NSS as an outcome variable to evaluate an intervention to improve numeracy in a sample of kindergarten children from low-income households.

COMMENTARY. The NSS is not a typical standardized instrument designed to offer scores that are useful for identification and classification. It is also not just a criterion-referenced measure based on judgments of what children should know at certain ages. Instead, it represents an approach that combines tasks based on a recently developed set of national core standards for curriculum combined with evidence of reliability and validity. The norms are obviously not representative of the U.S. population but this form of instrument should be normed at a state or local level. The NSS also produces information useful for educational remediation. It provides a score for each of the six areas assessed, but norms are provided only for the total score.

This reviewer's primary suggestion is that the test authors provide a concise synopsis of the research on reliability and validity. The instructions for administration need to be combined with the stimulus booklet to make administration easier. Now the instructions for administration are intermingled with the rationale for the items. Even psychologists and educators trained in psychometrics will find the technical specifications difficult to interpret.

SUMMARY. The NSS is an instrument designed to assess a specific area of academics that is of national concern. It appears to be carefully developed, and the evidence of reliability and validity is impressive. The norms provided should be used with caution. Local norms should be constructed. This version of the NSS is labeled as a research edition, and it could be used as a screening instrument or as a criterion variable for programs focusing on mathematical performance in kindergarten and first grade. It is an instrument designed with laudable goals and represents a new approach to standardized assessment. Overall, the NSS is an excellent instrument for its stated purpose and should be useful in research and application.

[121]

Offender Reintegration Scale.

Purpose: "A self-report assessment designed to measure the concerns and potential barriers faced by offenders and ex-offenders" regarding reentry into society.

Population: Offenders in various statuses, including incarceration, work release, probation, or parole.

Publication Date: 2008.
Acronym: ORS.
Scores: 5 scales: Basic Needs, Job Search, Family Concerns, Life Skills, Career Development.
Administration: Group.
Price Data, 2011: $41.95 per 25 assessments; free downloadable Administrator's Guide (2008, 8 pages).
Time: (20) minutes.
Author: John J. Liptak.
Publisher: JIST Publishing, Inc.

Review of the Offender Reintegration Scale by MICHAEL G. KAVAN, Professor of Family Medicine and Professor of Psychiatry, Associate Dean for Student Affairs, Creighton University School of Medicine, Omaha, NE:

DESCRIPTION. The Offender Reintegration Scale (ORS) is a 60-item self-report instrument designed to assess concerns of and potential barriers to offenders and ex-offenders as they are released from prison and attempt to reenter society. The ORS covers concerns related to basic needs, searching for a job, general life skills, family, and career development. The test author suggests the ORS may be administered to offenders during the intake process, in work release programs, on probation or parole, or in post-release situations. It is meant to assist offenders in developing an individualized plan that will enhance their success in reentering society.

The ORS is meant to be used by correctional treatment specialists, counselors, officers, and other staff associated with the correctional team and requires no special training to administer or interpret. The ORS may be administered to individuals or to groups and takes approximately 20 minutes to complete. It is a self-administered inventory in which examinees are asked to complete basic demographic information and then to read the directions along with the test administrator to ensure a clear understanding of the instructions. Examinees are then asked to respond to the items by circling a number from 1 (*no concern*) to 4 (*great concern*) and then totaling their scores for each of five sections. Scores for each scale may range from 12 to 48. These scores are then plotted on a profile and used to steer the examinee toward areas most likely to pose barriers to reentry. Suggestions for overcoming barriers are provided within the test booklet along with space to develop an action plan for successful reentry. No alternative language versions of the ORS are available from the test publisher.

DEVELOPMENT. The ORS was developed to be a "quick, reliable instrument to help offenders and ex-offenders identify their concerns about being released from prison and reintegrating into society" (Administrator's Guide, p. 5). The test author indicates that the ORS should meet the following guidelines: (a) measure a wide range of concerns; (b) be easy to use; (c) be easy to administer, score, and interpret; and (d) contain items that are applicable to offenders and ex-offenders of all ages.

To accomplish these objectives, the test author conducted a review of the literature related to the reentry of offenders into society. In addition, "academic and professional" sources were used to identify the five scales for the ORS: Basic Needs, Job Search, Family Concerns, Life Skills, and Career Development. An item pool representing the five scales was developed, reviewed, and edited for clarity, style, and appropriateness, and then screened to eliminate reference to gender, race, culture, and ethnic origin. Adult prisoners completed draft versions of the ORS and, based on data collected, a pool of 12 concerns was chosen that best represented each of the five scales.

TECHNICAL. Normative data consisting of means and standard deviations for the five scales are provided for offenders currently in prison ($n = 78$), currently enrolled in work release programs ($n = 50$), recently released from prison ($n = 43$), and for all offenders and ex-offenders ($N = 171$) who took the ORS. No additional demographic data are provided on these groups.

Internal consistency estimates (split-half correlations) are presented to justify the selection of items best representing each scale. Estimates from a sample of 48 adults are provided for the five scales and show coefficients between .87 (Basic Needs) and .94 (Job Search). Interscale correlations ranged from .06 (Life Skills and Career Development) to .56 (Job Search and Career Development). The test author notes that most correlations are small and, thus, support the independence of each scale. No test-retest data are provided within the Administrator's Guide.

With regard to content validity, the test author reviewed the literature on offenders, along with their reentry, reintegration, and barriers to success, and identified the five ORS scales as being areas of concern to offenders attempting to reenter society. Items were then developed based on these scales. The test author also reports that evidence for the validity of the ORS comes from the means and standard deviations for three different offender types: those currently incarcerated, those in work release programs, and those recently released from prison. Currently incarcerated offenders demonstrated a high level of concern across all five scales with their greatest concerns in the areas of Family Concerns (mean = 43.28), Life Skills (mean = 40.92), and Basic Needs (mean = 40.29). The test author suggests that this group of offenders is naturally less concerned with Job Search (mean = 39.26) and Career Development (mean = 39.94) issues, which supports the validity of these scales with this population of prisoners. Offenders who are in work release programs were reported to have similar concerns as those currently incarcerated, but tended to be more concerned with Career Development (mean = 45.36), Life Skills (mean = 43.46), and Family Concerns (mean = 42.58). It is suggested that because these participants are currently in job release programs, Job Search issues are less of a concern than Career Development issues. Finally, compared to the other two groups, those offenders recently released from prison showed the least concern across the five areas with their highest area of concern being Job Search (mean = 37.81). Means and standard deviations are also provided for the total sample ($N = 171$). All five scale concerns were in the "high" range with mean scores ranging from 37.85 for Job Search to 40.69 for Family Concerns. The Administrator's Guide includes an illustrative case study using the ORS with one 41-year-old male finishing a 5-year state prison sentence. No data are provided to support the classification of the "content-referenced" scores into the low, average, and high categories. No other validity data are provided within the Administrator's Guide.

COMMENTARY. As of December 31, 2010, state and federal correctional authorities had jurisdiction over 1,612,395 prisoners with 708,677 prison releases in 2010 alone (Guerino, Harrison, & Sabol, 2010). Therefore, the need for a reliable and valid instrument to assist in offender reintegration into society is great. The ORS was developed as an instrument to assist offenders and ex-offenders in identifying concerns and potential barriers about being released from prison and reentering society. The test author suggests that the ORS should measure a wide range of concerns, be easy to use, be easy to administer, score, and interpret, and be applicable to offenders and ex-offenders of all ages.

In terms of breadth, the ORS covers an appropriately diverse set of potential concerns of offenders (Brown, 2011; Griffiths, Dandurand, & Murdoch, 2007). The ORS does provide correctional treatment specialists, counselors, officers, and other staff associated with the correctional team with an easy to use and relatively quick method of determining offender concerns about reentry into society. Although it requires no special training for administration, special training in corrections, psychological and career counseling, and possibly social services would likely facilitate more useful interpretation, discussion, and planning beyond that provided within the test booklet, especially because many of the issues confronting offenders and ex-offenders are quite complicated and may require a more concentrated and thorough interdisciplinary collaboration to planning and follow-up (Griffiths et al., 2007). The test author suggests that the ORS should be applicable to offenders and ex-offenders of all ages with the Administrator's Guide indicating that the ORS is appropriate for "all juvenile and adult offenders" (p. 3) in or recently released from prison. However, normative data are limited to 171 offenders who are assumed to be adults only. In addition, the ORS is limited to English language speakers only, and no data are provided within the Administrator's Guide as to the reading level required for the instrument. Interpretation of the ORS is hampered by limited normative data and a lack of criterion and predictive validity evidence. In regards to the latter, does the ORS truly impact the successful reentry of offenders into society? Intuitively, one would believe that an instrument such as the ORS could be beneficial in examining issues relevant to reentry. However, no data are provided within the Administrator's Guide to support its relevancy in successfully reintegrating offenders into society. Further research is necessary to assess the utility of the scale scores and the impact of using the ORS in assisting with offender reentry.

SUMMARY. The ORS is a 60-item self-report instrument designed to assess offenders' and ex-offenders' concerns and potential barriers as they attempt to reenter society. Based on the large number of Americans incarcerated, there is certainly a need for a reliable and valid instrument of this type. The ORS is a reliable instrument that allows offenders and those working with them to consider potential concerns and barriers to their successful reintegration. However, because of limited validity data, it is uncertain whether using the ORS truly impacts the successful reentry of offenders into society.

REVIEWER'S REFERENCES
Brown, C. (2011). Vocational psychology and ex-offenders' reintegration: A call for action. *Journal of Career Assessment, 19*, 333-342.
Griffiths, C. T., Dandurand, Y., & Murdoch, D. (2007). The social reintegration of offenders and crime prevention. The International Centre for Criminal Law Reform and Criminal Justice Policy. Retrieved from Public Safety Canada http://www.publicsafety.gc.ca/res/cp/res/soc-reint-eng.aspx.
Guerino, P., Harrison, P. M., & Sabol, W. J. (2012). Prisoners in 2010 (Revised). Bureau of Justice Statistics, Office of Justice Programs. Retrieved from http://bjs.gov/content/pub/pdf/p10.pdf.

Review of the Offender Reintegration Scale by ROMEO VITELLI, private practice, Hamilton, Ontario, Canada:

DESCRIPTION. The Offender Reintegration Scale (ORS) was developed by John J. Liptak, Ed.D. as a brief assessment instrument to help offenders and ex-offenders identify needs, barriers, and essential skills that offenders must have to be reintegrated into society. As Associate Director of the Experiential Learning and Career Development office at Virginia's Radford University, Dr. Liptak has created a number of career and job search measures and is well-respected for his work with federal and state offenders.

Developed to be easy to use, score, and interpret, each ORS booklet contains 60 statements representing concerns about prison release, reentering society, and returning to the workforce. The ORS items are scored along the following five scales:

Basic Needs. This scale assesses the extent to which the offender needs assistance in meeting basic needs such as shelter, medical care, finances, or getting in contact with the necessary government agencies.

Job Search. This scale evaluates whether the test taker needs help searching for a job, such as organizing an effective job search campaign, networking, and learning effective interview strategies and how to talk about prison experiences.

Family Concerns. This scale assesses concerns about the offender's relationship with friends and family members. Items loading on this scale examine the test taker's ability to resolve conflicts, communicate effectively, and strengthen emotional ties.

Life Skills. High scores on this scale reflect concerns about ability to function effectively in society, overcome barriers such as substance abuse problems, and maintain a positive attitude despite having been in prison.

Career Development. This scale assesses the extent to which the test taker has developed a strong career plan with a realistic appraisal of potential problems. Deficits on this scale can indicate a need for vocational testing and/or counseling.

The ORS is a pencil-and-paper instrument that can be completed in approximately 20 minutes. The first page provides detailed instructions for test takers to endorse the 60 test items on a response scale ranging from 1 (*no concern*) to 4 (*great concern*). After completing the assessment, test takers are given instructions on how to score and interpret the results, including understanding specific barriers to reintegration identified by the test. All scoring instructions are provided in the test booklet. After the 60 items are completed and scored, the raw scores are transferred to the test profile. Scale scores range from 12 to 48 with scores between 37 and 48 being ranked as "high" and indicating problem areas to be addressed during feedback sessions.

As part of the profile feedback, test takers are provided with suggested activities to overcome those barriers and helped to develop an action plan to follow upon release. Counselors and test administrators meet with test takers to discuss the action plan and to help form specific strategies to implement the plan.

The ORS manual provides an illustrative case in which the test is used to help a male completing a state prison sentence develop an action plan with specific problem areas being identified and addressed. The test manual includes recommendations for the optimum time for the ORS to be administered (ideally as part of the prison intake process). The ORS also can be used for offenders on probation and parole to monitor progress in the community.

DEVELOPMENT. Helping offenders reintegrate into society remains the most difficult aspect of offender rehabilitation. Although almost all prisoners return to society eventually, successful reentry involves a tradeoff between considerations for public safety and providing adequate community support to prevent recidivism. Although it is widely recognized that hundreds of thousands of individuals are released from state and federal prisons across the United States each year, the need for successful community placement is often neglected. Considering that prisoners are spending longer periods of incarceration with fewer rehabilitation programs being made available in prison, the problems that prisoners face after release can lead to as many as two-thirds of prisoners being rearrested within 3 years of their release.

With a growing recognition of the need for better resources geared toward helping released prisoners make a successful transition to society, the U.S. Department of Justice has developed a new reentry court system to facilitate offender rehabilitation. Under the new system, offenders are encouraged to develop a reentry plan that draws upon personal support networks and community-based resources to address issues they might face upon release. That includes education, job training and job search, and treatment of clinical issues such as substance abuse.

Developing reentry plans does not eliminate the very real barriers that prisoners can face on release, however. Along with life-skill deficits, family issues, educational and career planning needs, and other barriers that every prisoner faces upon release, the careful evaluation of those barriers remains a critical element of the reentry plan. The ORS was developed to correspond to the five areas of offender concern identified by Don Andrews and James Bonta (Andrews & Bonta, 2010) and other sources. These areas include community resources, employability, family issues, life skills, and career planning.

TECHNICAL. As part of the ORS item selection process, a large pool of potential items was standardized using adult prison populations with gender and racial bias being carefully addressed. Standardization of potential items involved administering early ORS drafts to members of adult prison populations with correctional experts weeding out items that were too similar.

The ORS manual includes reliability information including separate normative data for incarcerated and community-based offenders. Split-half correlation coefficients for the five ORS scales range from .87 to .94 while interscale correlations yield modest correlations among the five scales. Means and standard deviations are also provided for three different offender groups: currently incarcerated prisoners, offenders in work release programs, and recently released offenders. Comparisons between the different groups reflect the concerns most characteristic of the problems being faced while incarcerated or in the community.

COMMENTARY. The Offender Reintegration Scale fills a long underserved niche and provides vocational counselors as well as offenders with a valuable tool to assist in generating effective plans for returning to society. Although validity data remain limited, the ORS is an easy-to-use instrument to assist offenders in state and federal prisons in recognizing barriers that might prevent successful community reintegration. Although tailored to general offender populations, more specialized versions may be needed for offenders facing additional problems that might prevent successful reintegration (e.g., registered sex offenders or offenders dealing with high-profile offenses) by creating additional barriers to rehabilitation.

SUMMARY. Although further research is needed to evaluate how useful the ORS can be in helping offenders in the community and offenders facing release, the value of an instrument of this nature cannot be underestimated. Although it is designed as a stand-alone instrument that can be self-scored and interpreted, the ORS should be used only in consultation with social workers or other professionals assisting offenders with reentry into the community. As the problem of offender reintegration continues to escalate and more offenders return to society, the ORS and similar instruments will become increasingly needed.

REVIEWER'S REFERENCE

Andrews, D. A., & Bonta, J. (2010). *The psychology of criminal conduct* (5th ed.). New Providence, NJ: Matthew Bender & Co.

[122]

OPQ32.

Purpose: A "personality questionnaire ... designed to give information on individual styles or preferences at work."

Population: Employees and job applicants.

Publication Dates: 1984-2011.

Scores: 32 Personality Characteristics in 3 Domains, plus Consistency Scale: Relationships with People (Persuasive, Controlling, Outspoken, Independent Minded, Outgoing, Affiliative, Socially Confident, Modest, Democratic, Caring), Thinking Style (Data Rational, Evaluative, Behavioral, Conventional, Conceptual, Innovative, Variety Seeking, Adaptable, Forward Thinking, Detail Conscious, Conscientious, Rule Following), Feelings and Emotions (Relaxed, Worrying, Tough Minded, Optimistic, Trusting, Emotionally Controlled, Vigorous, Competitive, Achieving, Decisive).

Administration: Group.

Forms, 3: OPQ32r, OPQ32n, OPQ32i.

Price Data: Available from publisher.

Foreign Language Editions: Available in more than 30 languages; contact publisher for information.

Time: (30) minutes.

Comments: Administrators must be trained through SHL OPQ training course; a previous edition was titled Occupational Personality Questionnaire.

Author: SHL Group Ltd.

Publisher: SHL [United Kingdom].

Cross References: See T5:1822 (7 references); for a review by Thomas M. Haladyna of an earlier edition, see 11:267.

Review of the OPQ32 by S. ALVIN LEUNG, Department of Educational Psychology, The Chinese University of Hong Kong:

DESCRIPTION. The Occupational Personality Questionnaire (OPQ) is a personality measure developed to measure personality characteristics or behavioral preferences that are essential in work-related contexts (e.g., personnel selection, team development, needs analysis, research, career counseling). The 32 scales of the OPQ32 are organized into three domains: Relationships with People (Persuasive, Controlling, Outspoken, Independent Minded, Outgoing, Affiliative, Socially Confident, Modest, Democratic, Caring), Thinking Style (Data Rational, Evaluative, Behavioral, Conventional, Conceptual, Innovative, Variety Seeking, Adaptable, Forward Thinking, Detail Conscious, Conscientious, Rule Following), and Feelings and Emotions (Relaxed, Worrying, Tough Minded, Optimistic, Trusting, Emotionally Controlled, Vigorous, Competitive, Achieving, Decisive). The OPQ32 is available in a normative format (OPQ32n), a forced-choice (ipsative) format (OPQ32i), and—most recently—an IRT-scored, forced choice normative form (OPQ32r). In the normative format, respondents respond to 230 items (an average of 7 items per scale) using a 5-point Likert scale (1 = *strongly disagree*, 5 = *strongly agree*; average completion time is 35 minutes). In the ipsative format, respondents complete 104 blocks of 4 items, yielding a total of 416 statements (average completion time is 45 minutes). The OPQ32r requires responses to 104 blocks of 3 items, effectively comprising a subset of the OPQ32i (average completion time is 30 minutes). A social-desirability scale is included in all versions to reflect a "fake good" tendency in responding. Due to item content difficulty and the structure of the OPQ32, the instrument is most appropriate for college graduates with managerial-related aspirations. Individuals with lower levels of education and/or backgrounds in manual positions might find the content to be less relevant.

The users of the OPQ32 are managerial, personnel and human resource specialists, and psychologists who have received training on the use of the instrument. The OPQ32 is administered via three channels: online, PC-based expert system, and paper and pencil. A number of computer-generated reports are available to users (e.g., leadership, team impact, person-job match).

DEVELOPMENT. The OPQ32 did not originate from a comprehensive theory of personality. Rather, the underlying framework was formulated through the synthesis of existing personality models and measures relevant to job performance in occupational fields, which resulted in an initial model of personality typology consisting of 40 bipolar scales. The first phase of the project (1981–1984) continued with the development and use of an adjective checklist to examine the relevance and unique content of the scales, and the total number of scales was narrowed to 32. Items were then generated to measure the 32 scales (including Likert ratings, multiple-choice, ranking, and forced-choice items) and field tested on more than 700 participants. Psychometric analyses were performed to examine item-scale relationships and the internal consistency of scales, and the number of scales was further reduced to 30. Studies were conducted to examine and refine the factor structures of the scales as well as to establish normative data. The process resulted in a number of initial OPQ versions encompassing the concept and factor models using different item formats (Likert, forced-choice, multiple-choice).

The second period (1984–1994) of development of the OPQ involved refinement of the original items, concept, and factor models; research endeavors to standardize interpretation (e.g., to establish a U.K. general population norm), survey ethnic minority groups to examine cross-cultural differences, and map scale items with the five-factor model of personality; and the development of applied models targeting specific occupational groups (e.g., using OPQ scales to construct the Customer Service Questionnaire, Sales Personality Questionnaire).

The OPQ32 was launched in the third phase (1994–1999) of the project. This phase involved developing the application and relevance of the OPQ concept model across cultural and occupational groups, refining scale reliabilities and scale differentiations, and optimizing the length of the instrument. Quantitative and qualitative data were collected among selected cultures and regions, and new items were developed aiming to capture the meaning of scales in ways that could be understood across cultures. The finalized OPQ32 consisted of a normative version (OPQ32n) and an ipsative version (OPQ32i). The third version, the OPQ32r, was developed later and essentially replaces the OPQ32i, according to information provided by the test publisher that was not included in the test materials. [Editor's Note: The OPQ32n remains in use primarily for research purposes and in limited use in the U.S. and the U.K., according to the test publisher.] The OPQ32 was standardized in the U.K. and a number of other countries. OPQ32 items were translated into different languages, and normative information and evidence on cross-cultural validity is provided in the technical manual. The OPQ32 is now available for use in more than 30 countries.

TECHNICAL.

Standardization. An impressive number of norms are available to assist in the interpretation of the OPQ32. There are 86 norm groups for the OPQ32n and OPQ32i versions, including norms for different translations of the instrument (e.g., German, French, Japanese, Complex Chinese), general population norms, and norms for specific users (e.g., managerial and professional, financial services). The OPQ32r technical manual notes that in addition to the new norms (developed via application of IRT scoring to OPQ32i responses), "all previously available OPQ32i population, user, and local norms can be used with the OPQ32r" (p. 19). The size of the normative groups is also impressive. The mean sample size of the OPQ32n version was 1,475 and the mean for the OPQ32i version was 2,054. Sten scales (range from 1 to 10) were used in reporting OPQ32 scores with the mean set at 5.5 and the standard deviation at 2.

Reliability. Internal consistency reliabilities were computed for the various general population, language translations, and specific user groups. Alpha coefficients computed on a majority of OPQ32 scales were above .70 for most of the population samples. For the OPQ32n version, the median alpha coefficients for the U.K. trial sample ($N = 1,228$) and general sample ($N = 2,028$) were .84 (range from .70 to .90) and .79 (range from .65 to .87), respectively. Reliability coefficients were similar for the U.S. general occupational sample ($N = 1,053$; $Mdn = .83$, range from .72 to .90) and South African data sets (two samples with ethnicity not reported, $N = 322$ each; $Mdn = .81$, range from .69 to .91). For the OPQ32i version, the median alpha coefficient of the U.K. standardization sample ($N = 807$) was .81 (range from .67 to .88). In two South African data sets, the median alpha coefficient of white South Africans ($N = 2,894$) was .80 (range from .67 to .88), but for black South Africans ($N = 3,159$), the median coefficient was substantially lower at .69 (range from .57 to .87). The alpha coefficients found for a Japanese sample ($N = 601$; $Mdn = .75$, range from .60 to .89) and a European composite data set (N = 40,922, Mdn = .77, range from .66 to .86) were also slightly lower than the U.K. standardization sample. For the OPQ32r, empirical reliability estimates were based on IRT information functions for the calibration sample (n = 518). Estimates for the measured traits ranged from .68 (Conventional) to .91 (Controlling), with a median value of .84. Test-retest reliability information was limited and less satisfactory. Coefficients (Mdn = .79, range from .64 to .91) were reported for the OPQ32n version for only one group of U.K. undergraduate students (N = 107) who took the test twice within a period that averaged one month. The OPQ32r technical manual reports test-retest reliability estimates for a sample of 168 (mostly female, young, white) volunteers from the U.S., U.K., and West Indies, using a 2-week test-retest interval. Coefficients ranged from .69 (Tough Minded, Variety Seeking, and Evaluative) to .84 (Outgoing), with a median value of .78.

Construct validity. First, OPQ32 scales were found to correlate with scales measuring similar personality constructs (e.g., scales from 16PF, Myers-Briggs Type Indicator [MBTI], Hogan Personality Inventory [HPI]). Second, factor analysis procedures were conducted on the OPQ32 items to map them with the five-factor model of personality (FFM). Exploratory factor analysis on data sets from several countries identified personality factors similar to factors in the FFM. Subsequent confirmatory factor analysis showed a good degree of fit between the data and the FFM factors. Meanwhile, the OPQ32 scales correlated with FFM instruments in the expected direction, and the average convergent correlations were found to range from .32 to .55.

Criterion-related validity. Evidence on criterion-related validity is important to the OPQ32 because the instrument was designed to measure personality characteristics in work-related contexts. The technical manual summarized findings from research studies, including findings from meta-analysis on the criterion-related validity of earlier versions of the OPQ and the OPQ32. Overall, findings showed that OPQ32 composite scales were related to hypothesized competency measures/ratings of professionals (e.g., managers, technology consultants, sales managers and representatives). The test publisher's Universal Competency Framework was used to conceptualize work competencies into dimensions. The correlation between the predictor composite scales and competency ratings of hypothesized competency dimensions (by supervi-

sors, peer, and/or self) were found to range mostly from .20 to .25, with some reaching as high as .45. These findings provided empirical support on the connection between personality factors and their behavioral manifestation (e.g., competency ratings) in work-related settings.

COMMENTARY AND SUMMARY. The OPQ32 is a personality measure that is systematically developed with close attention to meeting measurement and psychometric standards. The long test development process that began in the 1980s reflected this commitment: Items were developed in reference to existing personality theories and measures, multiple test formats (e.g., normative, ipsative, and IRT-based versions) were used to capture the constructs fully, diverse norms were established, and research studies were carried out as ongoing efforts to ensure that the OPQ32 met and exceeded technical standards in terms of reliability, validity, and relevance. Most importantly, the OPQ32 aspired to be an international personality measure, a measure that could be used across cultural, geographic, and language boundaries. In many ways, the OPQ32 has achieved this aspiration through the development of different language translations and regional norms. Evidence on reliability and measurement equivalence suggests that the OPQ32 could be used across cultures even though further criterion-related and predictive evidence of validity are still needed. Meanwhile, both the technical manuals and the user manuals of the different OPQ versions are well written, and they provide comprehensive, technical, and practical information including case examples to assist users in understanding and using the instrument.

The relationship between the normative and ipsative versions of OPQ32 is somewhat unclear. The test authors suggested that the two versions "measure constructs that are close but not exactly the same" (technical manual, p .61). Profile analyses further suggested that test takers whose preferences on the OPQ scales were not differentiated were more likely to receive dissimilar profiles from the two versions than test takers whose preferences were differentiated. With the arrival of the OPQ32r version, however, it would appear that understanding the distinctiveness and the unique functions of the two original versions has become less urgent.

Small- to medium-size gender differences (typically smaller than one sten score or half a standard deviation) in the OPQ32 scale scores were consistently found across countries. The consistent gender differences did not result in a recommendation to use gender-specific norms in profiling and scale interpretation. The justification for not using gender-specific norms, however, is not clearly articulated in the OPQ32 technical manual.

The OPQ32 is a well-developed personality measure for users in diverse cultural and language settings. The instrument could be used to enhance understanding and development, especially to address work- and career-related concerns. If the OPQ32 were to be used in high-stakes situations such as personnel selection or career advancement, it should be used along with a battery of measures so that a comprehensive set of information could be obtained to assist in making decisions.

Review of the OPQ32 by SAMEANO F. PORCHEA, Test Development Manager, American Nurses Association/American Nurses Credentialing Center, Silver Spring, MD:

DESCRIPTION. The Occupational Personality Questionnaire (OPQ32r) is a multitrait personality questionnaire. It is administered via the Internet and has been designed primarily as a workforce tool. The OPQ32r assesses three primary domains of personality (composed of 32 scales): Relationships with People (Persuasive, Controlling, Outspoken, Independent Minded, Outgoing, Affiliative, Socially Confident, Modest, Democratic, and Caring); Thinking Style (Data Rational, Evaluative, Behavioral, Conventional, Conceptual, Innovative, Variety Seeking, Adaptable, Forward Thinking, Detail Conscious, Conscientious, and Rule Following); and Feelings and Emotions (Relaxed, Worrying, Tough Minded, Optimistic, Trusting, Emotionally Controlled, Vigorous, Competitive, Achieving, and Decisive). Additionally, a secondary domain, Dynamism (Vigorous, Achieving, and Competitive) is interwoven across the three primary domains, and a measure of examinee response consistency is included. There are 104 blocks that consist of three statements each for examinees to consider. Examinees are required (forced-choice) to select one of the three statements as "most like me" and one as "least like me"; test takers do not endorse the third statement. The questionnaire is designed to be administered internationally and has been translated into more than 30 languages. The measure is not timed, but takes approximately 30 minutes if uninterrupted. Professionals in human resources and industrial organization are best suited to administer the questionnaire and interpret the results.

Such individuals must be trained through the test publisher's OPQ training course. The questionnaire is scored automatically upon completion. Results are provided to a preselected designee through the Internet in a set of standard reports (currently 17) with the option of obtaining additional reports. Reports include standardized scores for each scale based on an appropriately selected norm group. Reports also include visual comparisons by scale within domain and explanations regarding their interpretation.

DEVELOPMENT. The OPQ32r is the latest version in the family of Occupational Personality Questionnaires (OPQ). Prior to the development of this questionnaire, two forms were available: OPQ32n (normative) and OPQ32i (ipsative), which were both scored using classical test theory (CTT). The OPQ32n was used as a basis for developing the OPQ32i. Although the OPQ32n and OPQ32i were widely used and documented as well developed, due to the nature of CTT the normal variation absolute profile locations were distorted and caused a distortion of comparisons between profiles. Materials furnished by the test developer (including the 2006 technical manual, OPQ32 Big Five technical supplement, OPQ32 Great Eight technical supplement, OPQ32; international norm technical supplement, OPQ32n U.S. supplement to the 2006 technical manual, OPQ32r technical manual, OPQ32r U.S. norm supplement, OPQ32r user manual, references, and sample reports) were thorough and provided an in-depth history of the questionnaire development. The definitions provided for each scale and each domain were brief but sufficiently descriptive allowing for delineation across related topics. Although the constructs underlying several scales appear to overlap, due to the nature of personality the concept model was designed such that less than 50% of the reliable variance is shared across any two scales. The developer provided detailed information regarding the factor analysis used to determine like concepts and to develop each of the scales. Additionally, the developer provided adequate references to support claims.

TECHNICAL. To develop the three-statement item form found in the OPQ32r, the OPQ32i four-statement items were recoded as pairwise comparisons. Applying IRT scoring resulted in fully equivalent scores between the two forms. The OPQ32r produces normative scale scores in the form of theta values. The Thurstonian IRT model is used to measure the latent trait and ranges from -3 to +3 as described by Brown and Maydeu-Olivares, 2011. The developers included information regarding both overall and subgroup (gender, industry, ethnicity, and age) norms obtained from a group administered the U.S. English version. The overall norms were based on a total of 2,473 examinees. Norms for gender, industry, ethnicity, and age were based on 2,473; 2,027; 1,060; and 169 examinees, respectively. In some instances categories within subgroups had sample sizes that were inadequate to make conjectures (i.e. 20 or younger $n = 0$, recruitment industry $n = 1$, Native Hawaiian $n = 5$). In these instances groups were combined for analysis. Ethnicity was reported in two categories, Minority and White; age was reported as 40 and under and 41 plus.

Reliability estimates were calculated for each of the 32 scales based on the entire sample and each of the combined subgroups. Estimates for the overall sample across the 32 scales ranged from .68 ($SE = 0.27$) to .92 ($SE = 0.56$) with a mean reliability coefficient of .84 ($SE = 0.39$), which was approximately equal to the median. Mean estimates for men, women, minority, and white examinees were all .84. The mean standard error only varied by -.01 for the minority and white subgroups. The effect sizes for gender were all small to medium indicating little to no effect, and the effect sizes for ethnic groups were all small (Cohen, 1988). Effect sizes for age (40 and under and 41 plus) were small to medium. The overall and subgroup effect sizes indicated no practical significance. These results were consistent with those from the OPQ32n.

With regard to construct validity, the developers' methodology included intercorrelations across scales within the OPQ32r and a comparison to the same intercorrelations on the OPQ32n. Additionally, the developers presented data indicating that scale scores on the OPQ32r had a strong positive correlation with those on both the OPQ32n ($Mdn = .70$) and the OPQ32i ($Mdn = .71$). Due to the nature of the IRT scores, the developers were also able to conduct factor analyses. Three separate exploratory factor analyses were conducted further confirming the generalizability of the OPQ32r data. The developers addressed criterion-related evidence of validity using the test publisher's Inventory of Management Competencies and Universal Competency Framework, which is utilized in the OPQ32r. The two instruments were mapped, and median correlations between performance ratings

for each rater category and composite personality predictor were calculated. None of the results were statistically significant.

COMMENTARY. A major difference between the OPQ32i and the OPQ32r is that the latter questionnaire has blocks of three statements instead of four, drastically reducing the number of decisions an individual has to make. The OPQ32r is therefore less challenging cognitively, and the completion time is reduced by 50%. Too, the scores on the OPQ32r are no longer ipsative. The OPQ32r is scored using an IRT model that provides a better estimate of trait standings. Combined, these features drastically improve the examinee's experience while maintaining the validity of the inferences made from the results of the questionnaire. Additionally, the developers have equated the OPQ32r to its predecessor, the OPQ32i, and provided conversion tables so examinees can easily convert their scores from one version to the other. It is notable that the median reliability estimate of the shorter OPQ32r exceeded that of the longer OPQ32i version of the questionnaire.

The number of examinees who participated in the normative sample and were associated with consulting as their industry was drastically out of proportion. Therefore there is a lack of industrial data. This deficiency may indicate that consulting firms predominantly use the questionnaire and that results may be less relevant to those in other industries. In sum the developers have done an admirable job paying close attention to the detail of the questionnaire's previous designs and comparing them to the new IRT-based design. Additionally, they have provided more than adequate detail in their technical and administration manuals. The developers have been very diligent about including both the proper and improper uses of the questionnaire results in addition to specifically providing the limitations related to the self-report instruments.

SUMMARY. The developers of the OPQ32r have successfully produced a questionnaire that results in very valuable information regarding workplace personality traits. The instrument is easily accessible, and the only barrier to administration is the required training. The reports produced upon completion are thorough and easy to read. The test authors have provided case studies to assist with interpretation and continue to develop additional reporting tools. They have considered differences in results based on examinee background characteristics such as reading ability, ethnicity, gender, age, and locality. Additionally, they have sufficiently addressed the topic of varying uses and multiple interpretations of similar results. Evidence in the way of qualitative reviews, multiple tests of reliability, cross validation studies, case studies, and piloting is provided in detail and indicates that the developers have put forth great effort in assuring the questionnaire provides psychometrically sound results and is therefore an asset to the user.

REVIEWER'S REFERENCES

Brown, A., & Maydeu-Olivares, A. (2011). Item response modeling of forced-choice questionnaires. *Educational and Psychological Measurement, 71*, 460–502.

Cohen, J. (1988). *Statistical power analysis for the behavioral sciences* (2nd ed.). Hillsdale, NJ: Erlbaum.

[123]

Oral and Written Language Scales, Second Edition: Listening Comprehension and Oral Expression.

Purpose: Designed to measure oral language "across receptive and expressive processes."

Publication Dates: 1995-2011.

Acronym: OWLS-II LC; OWLS-II OE.

Scores, 5: Listening Comprehension, Oral Expression, Oral Language Composite, [Receptive Language Composite, Expressive Language Composite (when used with OWLS-II Listening Comprehension and Oral Expression Scales)].

Administration: Individual.

Price Data, 2013: $499 per software kit including 10 LC/OE record forms, LC easel, OE easel, unlimited-use computer-scoring CD, Foundations of Language Assessment handbook, LC/OE manual (2011, 282 pages), and carrying case; $399 per hand-scored kit (includes everything except computer-scoring CD); $52.50 per 25 LC/OE record forms; $136.50 per easel (LC or OE); $68.50 per Foundations of Language Assessment handbook; $68.50 per LC/OE manual.

Time: [10-30] minutes per scale.

Comments: May be used alone or in combination with OWLS-II Reading Comprehension and Written Expression (19:124).

Author: Elizabeth Carrow-Woolfolk.

Publisher: Western Psychological Services.

a) FORM A.

Population: Ages 3-21.

b) FORM B.

Purpose: Designed as a parallel form for retesting.

Population: Ages 5-21.

Price Data, 2013: $236.50 per Form B pack, including 10 LC/OE record forms-Form B, LC easel-Form B, OE easel-Form B; $52.50 per 25 LC/OE record forms-Form B; $136.50 per Form B easel (LC or OE).

Cross References: For reviews by Steve Graham and Koressa Kutsick Malcolm of an earlier edition, see 14:266.

Review of the Oral and Written Language Scales, Second Edition: Listening Comprehension and Oral Expression by BETHANY BRUNSMAN, Assessment/Evaluation Specialist, Lincoln Public Schools, Lincoln, NE:

DESCRIPTION. The Oral and Written Language Scales, Second Edition: Listening Comprehension and Oral Expression (OWLS-II, LC/OE) consists of 130 Listening Comprehension (LC) items and 106 Oral Expression (OE) items. Companion Reading Comprehension (RC) and Written Expression (WE) tests are also available and may be used with the LC and OE tests. Two parallel forms of the tests (A and B) are available. LC measures oral language reception or listening to and comprehending spoken language. OE measures speaking. The tests are designed to cover several categories of linguistic structures: lexical/semantic (vocabulary), syntactic (grammatical morphemes–function words, inflections, sentence structure), supralinguistic (nonliteral language), and pragmatic (functional and social characteristics of language), but do not yield separate subscores for these structures. LC and OE can be combined to create an Oral Language Composite score. LC and OE can also be combined with RC and WE to generate additional composite scores if those tests are also given.

OWLS-II was developed to identify language delays and disabilities and to inform the design of appropriate interventions to teach language. It is meant to help guide decisions about eligibility for Special Education services and interventions. The test author recommends the use of the LC and OE scales with Reading Comprehension (RC) and Written Expressions (WE). Form B was developed to measure progress as a result of intervention and is appropriate for ages 5–21. It is not clear why the RC and WE instruments are packaged separately, given that all four instruments are intended to be used together.

The tests are individually administered to examinees ages 3 to 21. LC items are multiple-choice with four responses each. OE items are open-ended. For both tests, the examiner reads the item aloud and the respondent references a picture or pictures before responding. The pictures are full-color drawings. For the listening component, respondents point to a response from the pictures/words on the easel. For the speaking component, respondents respond orally. To score the OE items, the examiner compares the oral responses to the scoring criteria, which contain exemplars.

The test manual specifies that the tests are intended for examinees whose primary language is English. The tests would also have limited use for people with visual disabilities because the test author does not recommend using the norms if the text is enlarged.

Both tests include recommended starting points based on age and basal and ceiling rules. When scoring, any items the respondent does not answer at the beginning of the test are counted correct and any items after the ceiling rule are counted as incorrect. The basal and ceiling rules should be relatively easy to apply because they are consistent across the instruments. The test manual suggests that test administrators need experience and training administering assessments to children. The test author recommends professional training and experience in speech and language, child development, psychology, or education or supervision by a professional in one of these areas to interpret and apply results. Given the judgment involved with applying the OE scoring criteria and with decisions about identification and services for children and youth with disabilities, these recommendations seem reasonable.

A paper/pencil answer document along with the norms manual or computer software can be used to generate scores. The test author recommends using scores in conjunction with other assessment results and observations to plan interventions for children. Raw scores, scale scores, age- and grade-based percentile ranks, and age and grade equivalents are available. More frequent norming windows are provided for younger examinees (e.g., ages 3–5) for the age norms than for older examinees (e.g., ages 16–21). Grade norms are available for spring and fall of each year, beginning with the spring of Kindergarten. The directions for administration and scoring are very specific and clear and include several examples with score interpretation. The scoring software runs on Windows 7/XP/Vista. It requires a USB key be in the USB port anytime the software is running. Detailed reports, including error analysis, are available using the scoring software. The reports include a narrative analysis discussing examinee strengths and weaknesses.

The test manual provides recommendations for interpreting scores and patterns of results, including several detailed examples. For the OE scale, analysis of acceptable/preferred responses may provide additional information for intervention design. A worksheet is provided in the back of the test booklet to show the pattern of results by linguistic structure. Test administrators are encouraged to use this information to help interpret the results. The examples are detailed and concrete and should be helpful to examiners.

DEVELOPMENT. The OWLS II LC/OE is an update of the Oral and Written Language Scale: Listening Comprehension and Oral Expression, published in 1995. It contains additional and revised items, including a second form and new artwork, new norms, and alternative scoring criteria for individuals who speak African American English or a similar dialect. One of the strengths of the revisions is the new pictures, which are in full color and represent diverse people.

The theoretical basis for the instruments is detailed in *Foundations of Language Assessment*, a companion manual to the test manual. As part of the revision process, the test author conducted a user survey for the OWLS. She conducted two pilot studies and evaluated items using a one-parameter Rasch model. Pairs of items (one for each form) were selected based on similar difficulty and content, balancing the categories of linguistic structures and the types of pictures in the items. The test manual states that the items were reviewed by "language professionals" and that "practicing speech pathologists" were consulted regarding the development of the scoring criteria for OE, but no specific information about how many reviewers were involved, the qualifications of these people, exactly what reviews occurred, or how that information was used is included in the materials.

TECHNICAL. Norm data were collected from 2,123 respondents over 14 months beginning in 2010. The scoring rules and exemplars for the OE scale are based on data collected in the pilot and norm studies. Both the pilot groups and the norm group were relatively diverse with respect to gender and ethnicity. The norm group also included representation from each of four geographic regions in the United States and four parental educational levels similar to the 2009 U.S. Census numbers.

The two forms of the OWLS II were evaluated for equivalence. A small group of examinees (n = 319) took both forms and this information was used to compare scale scores and composites across both forms. It is not clear if this subsample was representative of the norm sample or how they were selected. The resulting coefficients ranged from .67 to .96, with a median value of .78.

To provide further evidence of reliability of scores, the test author conducted analyses using split-half and test-retest methods. The reliability coefficients for the norm group were .92 and higher for split-half and ranged from .73 to .94 for LC, OE, RC, and WE scores from Forms A and B (n = 62 and n = 55, respectively) using a test-retest method with a 2-week delay. Interrater reliability estimates for OE scores for a random sample of 25 participants in the norm group with two trained raters were above .90 (coefficients of .96 and .93 for Forms A and B, respectively).

Collectively, these data suggest acceptable levels of reliability for scores for the norm group. A little more information, however, about the training of the raters for the OE interrater study would be helpful to determine if we can expect those levels of consistency for scorers given only the instructions and examples provided in the test manual.

Results from several studies are presented to provide construct-related validity evidence for the proposed uses of the scores. The test author used confirmatory factor analysis to verify the relationships among the scales for both forms A and B. The WE and RC scales (not included in this review but reviewed in a separate listing in this volume) were also included in these analyses. Goodness of fit indices supported a two-factor model, with OE and WE loading on an expressive language factor and LC and RC loading on a receptive (comprehension) language factor. Correlations among the subscales and with other similar measures (the original OWLS and the Clinical Evaluation of Language Fundamentals, 4th Edition; CELF-4; Semel, Wiig, & Secord, 2003; 16:53) yielded moderate to strong correlation coefficients. Comparisons of scores obtained by a group of 241 respondents with speech and language disorders with scores of a control sample matched on gender and age revealed differences in the expected direction with effect sizes ranging from .58 to .90 for LC and OE. Additional analyses suggested that scores of respondents with articulation disorders were less different from the control group scores than from those with expressive or receptive language impairments or those with reading disorders. In a separate study, scores of students who spent a significant portion of the school day receiving special education services outside the regular classroom were significantly lower than those of students in a matched control group. The test author did not propose different interpretations of scores based on

gender, ethnicity, race, or culture groups other than those related to African American dialects. No data related to bias were provided, although bias analyses were mentioned as part of the development process.

COMMENTARY. The theoretical basis for the OWLS II LC/OE scales is clearly detailed in the testing materials along with practical information about how to calculate and apply the scores to make determinations about student needs and design interventions. The examples of several students' scores and resulting decisions should be helpful to practitioners. The development process for the instruments as described by the test author is reasonable and the data included in the manual support the use of the instruments for the purposes described. The comparisons of scores for students with language-related disabilities with those in a control sample support the use of the instruments to identify individuals with disabilities.

Some critical information about scale development was not available in the test manual, however. What were the qualifications of specific reviewers and what were their specific roles in the instrument development process? Who were the consultants who assisted with the development of the alternative scoring criteria for speakers of African American dialects and what were their qualifications? Were the items reviewed for bias? What criteria were used to evaluate empirical evidence of lack of bias and why were those data not included in the test manual? Can we assume that scores can be interpreted the same way for individuals who differ in gender and ethnicity/race?

No empirical support for the use of the alternative scoring criteria for respondents who speak African American dialects was provided and there is very limited guidance in the materials about how to interpret or use those scores. Do examiners need specific expertise to determine if the alternative scoring criteria are appropriate, to apply them, or to interpret scores based on them? Can these scores be used interchangeably with the scores calculated using the regular scoring criteria?

Additionally, the value of Form B scores for progress monitoring for interventions is questionable. Teachers, speech therapists, and other professionals need timely, specific data to monitor the progress of children and youths when they are providing language interventions. The test author provides evidence that Form B scores are similar to those produced by Form A, can distinguish children and youth with language disabilities from those without, and are related to scores on other language measures. What is missing are data to suggest that scores from this type of measure would be sensitive to language development intervention and would provide the type of feedback students and practitioners need.

SUMMARY. The OWLS II LC/OE, in conjunction with other measures and data, may be used to identify students with listening and speaking language impairments and develop interventions to support their needs. The materials provide a clear theoretical basis for the instruments and practical examples to support their use. Some additional content- and construct-related evidence to support the proposed uses of scores, particularly confirmation that experts agree that item content is appropriate and free from bias would strengthen the measures. Users should be particularly cautious about using the alternative scoring criteria for respondents who speak African American dialects because no empirical evidence to support the use of these scores was provided.

REVIEWER'S REFERENCE

Semel, L., Wigg, E., & Secord, W. A. (2003). Clinical Evaluation of Language Fundamentals, Fourth Edition. San Antonio, TX: Pearson.

Review of the Oral and Written Language Scales, Second Edition: Listening Comprehension and Oral Expression by CAROLYN MITCHELL-PERSON, Associate Professor in the Speech–Language Pathology Department at Southern University and A&M College, Baton Rouge, LA:

DESCRIPTION. The Oral and Written Language Scales, Second Edition is a set of four interrelated scales (Listening Comprehension, Oral Expression, Reading Comprehension, and Written Expression) that provide a global assessment of language to aid in the evaluation and identification of children with significant language disorders in the areas tested. The OWLS-II enables assessment of oral language skills for ages 3 to 21 and written language skills for ages 5 to 21. The OWLS-II is designed to identify strengths and weaknesses in language including problems related to autism, mental retardation, and hearing impairment; specific language difficulty or bilingual language; or a generalized lag in language related to environmental factors.

Use of the scales and application of results presumes experience and training in administration and interpretation of individual assessments of children and is appropriate for use in schools, clinics, hospitals, private practice, and intervention programs.

Of the four interrelated scales, this review is of the Listening Comprehension Scale (LC) as well as the Oral Expression Scale (OE). The Listening Comprehension (LC) Scale, which measures the understanding of spoken language, consists of 130 items arranged in order of increasing difficulty. The three LC components are the Lexical/Semantic items that measure the range of linguistic structures, the Syntactic items that require comprehension of noun and verb modulators, and Supralinguistic items that comprise tasks requiring language analysis on a level higher than decoding literal lexical or syntactic structures. The Oral Expression (OE) Scale, which measures the use of spoken language, has 106 items that are also arranged in increasing order of difficulty. The OE Scale contains four categories of items. The examinee must use nouns, verbs, modifiers, idioms, words with double meanings, and concepts of direction, quantity, and spatial relationships (Lexical/Syntactic items). The OE Syntactic items require the use of noun and verb modulators as well as syntactic constructions. The OE Pragmatic items require appropriate responses in specific situations. Supralinguistic items require language analysis on a nonliteral level. Both the LC and OE Scales require the use of test easels (LC Easel A and OE Easel A, respectively) that contain instructions, pictures, items, prompts, and information about skill measured by each item. During testing the examiner provides verbal stimuli to elicit nonverbal or verbal responses from the examinee while he or she looks at one or more colored pictures.

The administration and scoring instructions for the LC and OE Scales are clear and easy to follow. Specific instructions are provided for recording responses on the Listening Comprehension/Oral Expression Record Form A (the primary form designed for use in single assessments and on the first occasion of a repeat testing protocol). The Parallel Form B (LC/OE Form B) is available for each scale if an examiner wishes to retest individuals aged 5 to 21 after a short time interval. All scales administered for the same assessment must be from either Form A or Form B and cannot be mixed. Instructions for how to start and end each test as well as how to determine raw scores and convert them to standard scores are also provided. The OWLS-II scales can be administered and used separately. The instructions for the general administration of the OWLS-II state that it is designed so that one, two, three, or four of the scales may be administered. For this reason, there is no set order of scale administration, and scales can be administered in random order. Additionally, each item on each scale is labeled by the linguistic structures it measures to aid in concrete identification of strengths and weaknesses.

DEVELOPMENT. The OWLS-II is a revision of the original OWLS (Oral and Written Language Scales: Listening Comprehension and Oral Expression). The goal of the original OWLS was to create a comprehensive measure of language based on the Integrative Language Theory. The test author's goal in developing the OWLS-II was to preserve the strongest features of the OWLS in addition to developing a new test of reading comprehension, new nationally representative norms, updated artwork, and revised scoring software.

The underlying assumptions of the OWLS-II are built upon a carefully constructed theory of language measurement (Integrative Language Theory) put forth by its author in previous publications (Carrow-Woolfolk, 1988, 1994; and Carrow-Woolfolk & Lynch, 1982) and supported by contributions of current and prominent theories of language as symbolic behavior, theories of form and meaning in language, theories of language performance, knowledge, and use, theories of language acquisition, as well as theories of language disorders. Integrative Language Theory divides language into separate elements that represent processes required to use language effectively as well as categories of linguistic structures. A full and clear discussion of the theoretical framework, its relation to the separate elements (processes and linguistic structures) that help provide a better understanding of language knowledge and performance, as well as the OWLS-II theoretical model are provided in the *Foundations of Language Assessment* (Carrow-Woolfolk, 2011) included with the test materials.

Each item of the LC and OE Scales underwent a tryout process involving two trials to ascertain fitness for inclusion in the scales before the standardization process. Items selected for each scale were evaluated and paired with a similar item with one being assigned to Form A and the other to Form B.

The test author provides detail about how the suggestions from the reviewers and users of the original OWLS guided the revision process for the OWLS-II. Some of those suggestions addressed sociolinguistic variation by calling for alternative scoring rules for speakers of nonstandard English dialects. In response to those suggestions, each item was reviewed for unfairness, bias, or stereotyping during scale development. The OWLS-II author acknowledges that children and young adults may respond with the dialectal variation of English they use in communicating in their everyday social, cultural, and regional settings. To account for such differences, the OE Scale provides the examiner with alternative acceptable responses.

TECHNICAL. A total of 2,123 individuals who were proficient in English were selected for the standardization sample. The characteristics of the sample as shown in the LC/OE manual indicate that the sample is representative of the U.S. population in terms of ethnicity, gender, and parental education level. At face value, such a sample does not appear to reflect cultural bias, gender bias, language disability discrimination, or any other possibilities for unfair testing or negative bias.

Reliability has to do with the consistency or reproducibility of the examinee's performance on the LC and OE Scales that was estimated with four different methods: internal reliability, test-retest reliability, interrater reliability, and alternative forms reliability. In the first method, both scales were split into two halves of equal length using an odd-even strategy to assess the consistency of results across items within the OWLS-II (internal reliability). Split-half reliability represents the reliability of a test only half as long as the actual test; therefore, the Spearman-Brown formula was used to correlate and adjust raw scores of both halves. The reliability coefficients were greater than or equal to .92 and consistent across both forms. In the second method, the OWLS-II was re-administered to 117 students from the standardization group to assess the degree to which the tests scores were consistent from one test administration to the next (test-retest reliability). This group was balanced for gender, age in years, ethnicity, and parents' educational level. Correlation coefficients for Form A and Form B of the LC and OE Scales ranged from .73 to .91 and are satisfactory for tests of developing abilities. In the third method, the degree of agreement among the different raters who scored the OE Scales (interrater reliability) was studied because raters with identical training and coding instructions were required to make subjective judgments about the quality of oral responses to OE Scale items. Intraclass correlation coefficients were used to determine how strongly the raters' judgments resembled each other. Responses from 25 participants were randomly selected from the standardization study. For OE Form A, the intraclass correlation was .96 and it was .93 for OE Form B, indicating a high level of agreement between different raters who used the same written instructions to score the OE Scales. In the fourth method, responses from 319 students from the standardization sample who took both the LC/OE Form A and LC/OE Form B were compared. The correlation coefficient between the two forms (alternative forms reliability) ranged from .67 to .96, providing support for the equivalence of Form A and Form B.

Validity of the OWLS-II is the degree to which it is appropriate to use its scores in the manner proposed by the test author or developer. Three methods were used to provide evidence of validity: construct validity, convergent validity, and discriminative validity. As previously mentioned, the underlying assumptions of the OWLS-II are built upon the Integrative Language Theory of language measurement. Construct validity refers to the degree to which the OWLS-II actually measures and supports those theoretical constructs. Analysis results indicate that the factor structure of the OWLS-II supports the underlying constructs of the Integrative Language Theory as well as the independent and separate scoring and interpretation of the OWLS-II scale scores. Convergent validity refers to the relationship of the OWLS-II to existing measures of similar constructs. As previously mentioned, the test author's goal in developing the OWLS-II was to preserve the strongest features of the OWLS; therefore, links were established to the convergent validity studies of the original OWLS. The OWLS-II measures were found to significantly correlate with their counterparts in the original OWLS with strong associations for the oral language scales and composite. These results support that the original OWLS convergent validity evidence demonstrates validity of the OWLS-II. Discriminative validity refers to the capacity of the OWLS-II test scores to distinguish between groups of participants who are expected to differ in the ability measures. As previously mentioned, the OWLS-II is designed to identify strengths and weaknesses in speech and language related to special populations or a generalized lag in language related to environmental factors. Validity analysis indicated that the OWLS-II scores distinguish typically developing individuals from those with speech and language disorders, as well as those with behavioral and developmental disorders.

COMMENTARY. The LC and OE Scales have well-crafted technical properties and offer evidence-based measures of oral expression as well as listening comprehension. As measures of language founded on sociolinguistic variations, these two scales represent an assessment of receptive and expressive language for children and young adults. The tests provide professionals with information needed to identify and assess communication problems as well as to design intervention and help that individuals aged 3–21 need to build critical language and literacy skills. The test author warns that neither tool should be used for final diagnostic and treatment decisions. As designed, the OWLS-II will also possibly identify the root cause of reading and writing problems through an individual's difficulty with language.

This reviewer applauds the inclusion of case examples illustrating scoring and interpretation of scores as well as the use of test results. Additionally, the discussion of intervention principles with case examples is excellent. The test author and contributors demonstrate how assessment provides the structure for intervention.

SUMMARY. The LC and OE Scales of the OWLS-II were designed to measure oral language "across receptive and expressive processes" based on the Integrative Language Theory of language measurement. The test meets its goals of assessing oral language reception (listening to and comprehending spoken language) and oral language expression (speaking). The OWLS-II scores were found to distinguish typically developing individuals from those with speech and language problems related to autism, mental retardation, and hearing impairment; specific language difficulty or bilingual language; or a generalized lag in language related to environmental factors.

REVIEWER'S REFERENCES

Carrow-Woolfolk, E. (1988). *Theory, assessment and intervention in language disorders: An integrative approach.* Philadelphia, PA: Grune & Stratton.
Carrow-Woolfolk, E. (1994). *Learning to read: An oral language perspective of beginning reading.* San Antonio, TX: Psychological Corporation.
Carrow-Woolfolk, E. (2011). *Foundations of language assessment.* Torrance, CA: Western Psychological Services.
Carrow-Woolfolk, E., & Lynch, J. (1982). *An integrative approach to language disorders in children.* New York, NY: Grune & Stratton.

[124]

Oral and Written Language Scales, Second Edition: Reading Comprehension and Written Expression.

Purpose: Designed to measure "written language across receptive and expressive processes."
Population: Ages 5-21.

Publication Dates: 1996-2011.

Acronym: OWLS-II RC; OWLS-II WE.

Scores, 5: Reading Comprehension, Written Expression, Written Language Composite, [Receptive Language Composite, Expressive Language Composite (when used with OWLS-II Listening Comprehension and Oral Expression Scales)].

Administration: Individual.

Price Data, 2013: $499 per software kit including 10 RC/WE record forms, 10 WE response booklets, RC easel, WE easel, unlimited-use computer-scoring CD, Foundations of Language Assessment handbook, RC/WE manual, and carrying case; $399 per hand-scored kit (includes everything except computer-scoring CD); $52.50 per 25 RC/WE record forms; $26.50 per 25 WE response booklets; $136.50 per easel (RC or WE); $68.50 per Foundations of Language Assessment handbook; $68.50 per RC/WE manual.

Time: [10-30] minutes per scale.

Comments: May be used alone or in combination with OWLS-II Listening Comprehension and Oral Expression (19:123).

Authors: Elizabeth Carrow-Woolfolk (test and manual) and Kathleen T. Williams (Written Expression scale and manual).

Publisher: Western Psychological Services.

   a) FORM B.

   Purpose: Designed as a parallel form for retesting.

   Price Data: $236.50 per Form B pack, including 10 RC/WE record forms-Form B, 10 WE response booklets-Form B, RC easel-Form B, WE easel-Form B; $52.50 per 25 RC/WE record forms-Form B; $26.50 per 25 WE response booklets-Form B; $136.50 per Form B easel (RC or WE).

Cross References: For reviews by C. Dale Carpenter and Koressa Kutsick Malcolm of an earlier edition, see 14:267.

Review of Oral and Written Language Scales, Second Edition: Reading Comprehension and Written Expression by SHARON HALL deFUR, Professor of Special Education, Curriculum and Instruction, The College of William and Mary, Williamsburg, VA:

DESCRIPTION. The Oral and Written Language Scales, Second Edition (OWLS-II) is a revision of the original OWLS (Carrow-Woolfolk, 1995, 1996; 14:26). OWLS-II maintained the same purpose as OWLS: to provide an individual comprehensive measurement of oral and written language skills, both receptive and expressive, for children and youth. OWLS-II includes four individually administered norm-referenced scales that generate composite scores as well as skill-specific scores. This review focuses on Form A from two scales, the Reading Comprehension (RC, Carrow-

Woolfolk & Williams, new with OWLS-II) and the revised Written Expression (WE, Carrow-Woolfolk), both of which use an easel format for administration. The author of the test manual asserts that all scales were developed based on Integrated Language Theory and provide diagnostic data on linguistic structures. Such data can be used to inform eligibility for clinical services (e.g., speech-language, special education) and yield data that can help determine the presence of language delays or disabilities; an item analysis procedure facilitates intervention decisions.

According to the RC/WE manual, there are parallel forms for both RC and WE (Forms A and B), thus facilitating retesting options. The RC identifies language factors that may be interfering with or promoting reading comprehension. Similarly, the WE assesses various linguistic aspects of writing. When used together, a composite score for Written Language can be generated. Although these scales are considered comprehensive, the test author cautions that OWLS-II should not be used as the only measure to determine eligibility or intervention decisions. The RC and WE are age and grade normed for English-speaking children and youth ages 5–21. OWLS-II is not valid for use with examinees not fluent in English or for examinees who require test adaptations.

The OWLS-II, although not a restricted assessment, does require examiners with experience in the use of psycho-educational assessments with children. Furthermore, interpretation of the results of both the RC and WE requires a depth of knowledge of language structure and professional training in speech and language, child development, or education. The comprehensive RC/WE manual provides the theoretical background for the scales as well as practical case examples and scoring guidelines for both scales. The examiner easels include a guide for test administration instructions as well as a summary of skills measured by each item.

The OWLS-II RC and WE can be used independently, administered at different times, and have no set order of administration if both are given. When both scales are given, a Composite Written Language Score can be generated. These scales can also be used with the OWLS-II Oral Expression and Listening Comprehension Scales to generate additional Composite Scores. Guides for item analysis for both scales provide additional diagnostic information as to whether errors represent a consistent linguistic delay in one or more specific language components. These analyses could benefit intervention foci. The test manual devotes a chapter to the interpretation of the OWLS-II RC and WE results and provides a procedure to determine the significance of differences in scores between RC and WE.

The RC includes 140 multiple-choice items of increasing difficulty; items require the examinee to read a prompt and choose one of four response options. The RC begins with simple word reading and progresses to items requiring complex comprehension skills. The RC has items that measure understanding of syntax, lexical/semantics, supralinguistic understanding (e.g., inference, humor, logic), and pragmatics. Examinee age determines the starting item. For the RC, a basal is achieved with seven consecutive accurate responses and a ceiling is achieved when the examinee has four successive errors. Raw scores convert to standard scores for analyses; confidence intervals, percentile ranks, age, and grade scores can be generated for comparison with other norm-referenced tests. Administration of the RC takes 10–30 minutes depending on the skills and engagement of the examinee.

The WE has 50 prompts that are divided into age-based sets with the expectation that the examinee will complete one age-based set (14–18 items) taking 15–30 minutes. An easel format provides visual prompts, but primarily the examinee writes in a response booklet. Responses to prompts are not timed, but the test manual suggests moving forward if the examinee has not responded within 30 seconds. Each WE item has a gateway written expectation that must be passed to obtain any credit for that item. Written responses are scored based on a range of language components including semantics, syntax, conventions, pragmatics, and text structure. The test manual provides scoring examples (100 manual pages) of correct and incorrect responses to the WE.

Scoring tables are provided in the manual for both the RC and WE. Reportedly there is also computerized scoring software that can be used with these scales. The record form offers a summary of scores on both scales as well as a profile graph and score comparison. Forms are provided in the response record form to facilitate item analyses for both scales.

DEVELOPMENT. Reviews of the original OWLS, expert reviewers, and feedback from users of the original OWLS contributed to the revision goals for OWLS-II. These revision goals included maintaining the strongest features of OWLS, adding an RC Scale, developing new national norms, improving the scoring software, and developing up-to-date artwork. In addition, the test authors sought to develop parallel OWLS-II forms to allow for repeated assessment. The original OWLS was developed using Integrated Language Theory as its framework.

The test developers added RC to include a measure of reading comprehension as part of the OWLS-II assessment that reflected the theoretical language framework. RC items reflect one of four categories of language: (a) Lexical/Semantic, (b) Syntactic, (c) Supralinguistic, and (d) Pragmatics. The test authors used an item pool of 294 items in a tryout study with 781 individuals; all items were maintained and divided to create two parallel RC scales for the standardization protocol. Using data from the tryout study, RC items were ordered by difficulty and parallel forms were developed.

In revising the WE scale, the test author (Carrow-Woolfolk) consulted multiple state curricula standards for Writing. Influenced by these standards, the author developed additional WE items that would enable the creation of a parallel form of the WE scale. The author revised the scoring system and identified a gateway WE item to increase the ease of scoring. The author conducted an initial tryout with 501 children and youth, followed by a second tryout with 5,118 individuals. The final item selection used the tryout items that reflected multiple linguistic structures, thus enabling measurement of more written expression skills with fewer items. Sixty-one item pairs were selected for the WE standardization.

TECHNICAL. The OWLS-II RC and WE were standardized based on data from a sample of 2,123 English-speaking children and youth, ages 5–21. The sample was drawn from 31 states that included all four major U.S. Census regions and included national representation based on gender, ethnicity, parent education, and geographic region. Standard scores were developed for each of the scales as well as Composite scores.

Split-half reliabilities were calculated for the RC (Form A and B), which yielded reliability coefficients above .96 for all age levels. Using a Rasch analysis, the WE (Form A and B) generated reliability coefficients ranging from .93 to .99. These scores imply strong internal reliability for these measures. Test-retest reliability estimates for the RC and WE along with effect sizes are reported in the test manual. The RC (both Form A and B) had low test-retest effect sizes suggesting that retesting produced a minimal learning effect. The same was true for the WE, Form A. Test-retest using Form B of the WE generated an effect size of .22, suggesting a small, yet measurable impact of retesting.

Factor analysis revealed strong factor loadings for RC correlation with OWLS-II Listening Comprehension Scale, forming a factor for Receptive Language. Similarly, the WE factored with the OWLS-II Oral Expression Scale formed a factor for Expressive Language. These factors support the language processing model hypothesized by the Integrated Language Theory.

The test authors present convergent validity evidence for both the WE and RC. Moderate to strong correlations are reported between OWLS-II and the original OWLS. The OWLS-II RC showed a strong correlation with the Woodcock Johnson–III Normative Update (WJ-III NU) Broad Reading Composite ($r = .86$). The WE also strongly correlated with the WJ–III NU Broad Writing Composite ($r = .78$). The test author examined possible dialectical differences for the WE. Small, but observable, differences were found. Responses were then coded to allow for an alternative correct response for nonstandard-English speakers. Using the alternative coding protocol to accommodate dialectical differences reduces the penalty for students who speak nonstandard English.

Using a randomized matched control group drawn from the standardization sample, the test author examined differential performance on the OWLS-II for students identified with speech and language impairments (SLI) ($n = 241$) and for students described as a clinic-referred sample ($n = 114$). A MANOVA found that students with SLI scored significantly lower than those from the control group. A comparison of means of the SLI and control group found a moderate effect size for both RC (.66) and WE (.65) (Form A). Comparing means resulted in even more substantive effect sizes for the clinic-referred students. For RC, the difference between the means of clinic-referred and control group participants resulted in effect sizes of 1.82 and 1.79 for Forms A and B, respectively. For WE, the effect sizes were 1.68 and 1.91, respectively. The strong effect sizes support the claim that OWLS-II can be used to help differentially identify students with SLI, reading comprehension, written expression, and written language delays.

COMMENTARY. The OWLS-II RC and WE are comprehensive norm-referenced measures of receptive and expressive written language that provide in-depth diagnostic information for both eligibility purposes as well as intervention decisions for children and youth experiencing difficulties in one or more components of language. The OWLS-II offers a tool to explore differences specific to receptive language, expressive language, and reading disorders. The technical measures applied to the development of the OWLS-II RC and WE and scoring were comprehensive and rigorous demonstrating that these norm-referenced tests can achieve the intended purposes of providing a comprehensive measure of written language that can be used diagnostically to identify language disorders and that can be used as tools to help guide language-based interventions.

Although the OWLS-II RC and WE are not restricted-use norm-referenced tests, interpretation of the results of these scales independently or as a composite require a depth of clinical understanding of language beyond what might typically be expected from introductory courses in language, reading, or writing. The case examples provided in the test manual offer resources for studying how the OWLS-II test results can be applied and interpreted in a report format. Use of OWLS-II RC or WE for diagnostic or eligibility purposes without deep content knowledge of language development may result in inappropriate interpretations.

The RC, new with OWLS-II, is easily administered in a familiar easel/multiple-choice format. Scoring appears relatively straightforward. Translating raw scores using the tables requires careful attention to detail. The RC assesses multiple linguistic components, and as the test authors claim includes items that measure lexical/semantic skills such as word-to-picture matching, fill in the blank with the best word, and so on. There are items that assess syntactical understanding such as recognizing when to use an irregular verb or sentence structure. The test authors use the term supralinguistic to describe comprehension demands that require inference, world knowledge, figurative language, and so forth. There are also items to assess comprehension of text that demonstrate an understanding of social norms or pragmatics and items that require understanding of text structure such as summarizing or recognizing point of view.

The WE also assesses multiple linguistic components including conventions, lexical/semantic skills, syntactic skills, pragmatic skills, as well as text structure. Although this scale uses an easel format, most responses are written in a response booklet. The prompt is sometimes on the easel, but not always, potentially making the administration somewhat awkward without practice. Use of a gateway item as a signal for correct response facilitates administration of the WE informing the examiner when basal and ceilings are reached. Somewhat confusing is the use of an age-based item set that limits the demonstration of exceptional writing skills, although, with further study, it is understandable that this minimizes the time and writing demands during a single test administration.

Although the WE was revised to update pictures and prompts, with the fast paced change of technology and knowledge dissemination of this era, some prompts quickly become outdated.

The test authors should be commended for including norms that allow for adjustment for nonstandard English enabling diagnosticians to more appropriately identify true language delays or disorders for individuals who speak nonstandard English. It is disappointing that validity evidence does not support the use of the test with students who require test adaptations such as enlarged print, read-aloud, or technology-enhanced responses such as word-processing. However, use of the RC and WE will enhance diagnosis and intervention for students with learning and other developmental disabilities.

SUMMARY. The OWLS-II, RC and WE are individually administered measures of reading comprehension and written expression that specifically address the components of written language providing comprehensive diagnostic data regarding written language for children and youth ages 5–21. Test development and technical adequacy meet or exceed standards for norm-referenced tests. Results from these assessments can be used reliably as one tool in identifying children and youth as eligible for clinical or educational services as well as providing diagnostic data for intervention planning. Interpretation of test results requires content expertise in language development and analysis.

Review of The Oral and Written Language Scales, Second Edition: Reading Comprehension and Written Expression by SANDRA WARD, Professor of Education, The College of William & Mary, Williamsburg, VA:

DESCRIPTION. The Oral and Written Language Scales, Second Edition (OWLS-II) is a norm-referenced instrument developed to identify strengths and weaknesses in language through the administration of four interrelated scales. The Reading Comprehension (RC) and Written Expression (WE) scales assess the receptive process of written language and the expressive process of written language, respectively, in students between the ages of 5 and 21 years. The two scales combine to produce a Written Language (WL) Composite. The OWLS-II: RC and WE includes two equivalent forms. Form A is to be used for single assessment or for the first assessment if repeated testing is planned.

Although the RC and WE scales are intended for individual administration, the WE scale can be administered to a small group if the examinees take the same item set. The RC scale includes 140 multiple-choice items that assess the four linguistic structures: Lexical/Semantic, Syntactic, Supralinguistic, and Pragmatic. Additional items measure all four categories under the heading of Text Structure. The WE scale includes 50 items in overlapping item sets that are sequenced by age level and measure the same four linguistic structures as the RC scale. Additionally, the WE scale assesses Conventions (Spelling, Capitalization, Punctuation, and Letter Form) and Text structure (Text Organization, Use of Details, and Cohesion). The RC and WE items are presented in an easel format that includes straightforward administration directions on the examiner's side. For the RC items, the examinee reads a prompt and selects one of four response choices by responding verbally (stating the corresponding number of their choice) or nonverbally (pointing to their selection). On the WE scale, the examinee writes responses in the response booklet. Scoring for the RC scale is simple, and the test authors (Carrow-Woolfolk & Williams) provide clear descriptions and helpful examples of the basal and ceiling rules. The test author (Carrow-Woolfolk) includes specific instructions and practical examples for the use of the item set approach for the WE scale. An entire chapter of the test manual is devoted to the scoring of the WE items. In addition to general guidelines, the authors provide detailed scoring examples for each item. The scoring guidelines are thorough, but require precise knowledge of written language conventions. This reviewer would recommend that first-time users of the WE scale obtain supervision of the item scoring by an experienced examiner.

Raw scores for the RC scale are easily converted to standard scores (mean of 100, standard deviation of 15), with corresponding percentile ranks, confidence intervals, and grade and age equivalents. Due to the item set approach on the WE scale, raw scores must first be converted to Rasch ability scores that are then converted to standard scores. Standard scores can be based on age or grade norms, but the test authors recommend the use of age norms unless the examiner is administering the OWLS-II for curriculum planning. The RC and WE standard scores combine to produce a WL composite score, percentile rank, and confidence interval. Qualitative descriptive categories are provided in the test manual. The front of the record form provides useful space to statistically compare the RC and WE standard scores and analyze the difference for significance (at the .05 level) and frequency in the standardization sample. The item analysis worksheets represent another functional component of the OWLS-II scoring that allow the examiner to qualitatively evaluate strengths and weaknesses across language structures.

DEVELOPMENT. The OWLS-II represents a revision of the original OWLS. Major revisions include the addition of the RC scale and a parallel form. The OWLS II-RC and WE scales were developed based on the integrative language theory (Carrow-Woolfolk, 1988), which distinguishes between the skills required to process language (expressive and receptive) as well as the components of language (oral and written ability). This theory is reviewed in a separate manual. For the WE scale, new items were created to assess additional aspects of written language, establish a higher ceiling for assessing high ability students, and develop a parallel form. Based on qualitative analyses of initial tryout data, new items were developed. Data from a second tryout study with 194 items were used to determine item bias, difficulty level, similarity within item pairs, response variability, and linguistic structures measured. Based on this review, 61 item pairs were included in the standardization form. Scoring criteria for WE were developed based on collaborative input from the test author, speech-language pathologists, and testing experts. Final selection of WE items was based on data collected during standardization and estimates of item difficulty based on the Rasch measurement model. These data were considered in light of variability in item type, coverage of linguistic structures, and similarity between item pairs. The test author

is commended for her approach to developing the WE item sets. The final WE scale included 50 items in five overlapping sets.

The RC scale was added to provide a measure of reading comprehension that is consistent with the integrated language theory. The scope and format of the RC scale is intended to correspond with the other scales. The test authors developed a blueprint of 139 item pairs that measured one of the four linguistic structures. After a review by the publisher, the item pool increased to 147 pairs. Based on a tryout study with 781 individuals between the ages of 5–21 years, minor edits were made to items, and 147 item pairs were included in the standardization form. The final selection of RC items was based on data collected during standardization. Item responses from both forms were analyzed together to estimate difficulty and fit to the Rasch measurement model. Items were ordered by difficulty so that test takers of any age get a diverse set of linguistic structures.

TECHNICAL. The data for the standardization of the OWLS-II was collected from 2,123 individuals from 31 states who were proficient in English. The test authors admit that the norms are not appropriate for examinees who do not have strong English ability. Individuals with disabilities were included in the sample, if they spent most of the school day in the regular classroom. The standardization sample closely matched the 2009 U.S. Census data for gender and ethnicity except for a slight overrepresentation of Black/African Americans. Socioeconomic status was indicated by parent education level. The standardization sample underrepresented parents with some college and overrepresented parents with 4 years of college or more. These differences in parents' education level can represent a problem for a test of language skills related to education level. With respect to geographic regions, the western region was slightly underrepresented, and the eastern region was slightly overrepresented. The standardization sample appropriately included proportionally more students in the 5–11 age range to account for more rapid language development and the need for narrower normative age groups at these younger levels. Norms for ages 3–7 are in 3-month intervals, and norms for ages 8–12 are presented in 6-month intervals. Although the test authors point to small mean score differences to support the equivalence of forms, they ignore the large standard deviations that suggest variability in performance across forms.

The internal consistency reliability coefficients reported in the test manual are sufficient for the intended purpose of the OWLS-II RC and WE. Split-half reliability coefficients for RC exceeded .95 across age levels for both forms. Rasch analysis was used to compute internal consistency of the WE scale due to the item set organization. Reliability coefficients exceeded .92 across age levels for both forms. The reliability coefficients for the WL composite exceeded .97 across age levels for both forms. Test-retest reliability was estimated using 117 cases with a 2-week test-retest interval. The correlations for Form A were .94, .89, and .94 for the RC, WE, and WL, respectively. The correlations for Form B were .84, .75, and .85 for the RC, WE, and WL, respectively. The lower test-retest coefficients suggest more variability in performance across time on Form B.

Interrater reliability coefficients based on 24 WE record forms randomly selected from the standardization sample averaged .96 for Form A and .94 for Form B across pairs of raters. A subset of 319 individuals from the standardization sample took both forms of the OWLS-II to compute alternate form reliability. These reliability coefficients ranged from .80–.91 for RC, .83–.95 for WE, and .89–.96 for WL. Some of the lower reliabilities suggest that the two forms may not be completely parallel, depending on the age range.

The test authors provide modest support of the construct validity of the OWLS-II. Although a confirmatory factor analysis appears to support the two-factor model of language processing (expressive and receptive), the analysis was completed on all ages combined, so the factor structure by age is unknown. Furthermore, the receptive and expressive language factors correlated at .99, which may suggest a single factor model. The test authors did not test any alternative models. The confirmatory factor analysis only marginally supports the two-factor language component model (oral and written) for ages 5–6. This two-factor model is not supported for the older age groups.

Evidence for convergent validity was adequate. Although correlations between the OWLS-II with the original OWLS, Clinical Evaluation of Language Fundamentals, 4th Edition (CELF-R), and Woodcock-Johnson II Normative Update Tests of Achievement (WJ-III NU) were sufficient, they were computed on only clinical samples of small sizes. The test authors provide strong support for the discriminative validity of the OWLS-II. These studies used data collected from a group of 241 students who were receiving speech and language services and compared their scores with those of randomized matched control groups from the standardization sample. The results indicated that the RC, WE, and WL mean scores were significantly lower, with strong effect sizes, for the speech- and language-impaired group. Additional analyses were completed with subgroups of the larger speech- and language-impaired sample, including receptive language, expressive language, reading disorder, and articulation disorder. The RC, WE, and WL mean scores were significantly lower, with moderate to strong effect sizes, for all subgroups except the articulation disorder group where mean scores were significantly lower, but effect sizes were too small for clinical significance. The OWLS-II was not designed to measure articulation disorders. Although the test authors report findings from a study of children with autism, the comparisons are made with the original OWLS, and are not pertinent to the discriminative validity of the OWLS-II.

COMMENTARY. The OWLS-II RC and WE is a brief instrument that is easy to administer in order to assess the receptive and expressive processes of written language in individuals 5–21 years of age. Scoring is straightforward, but users are encouraged to obtain supervision in scoring the WE items on initial administrations. The test authors used a sound theoretical model and applied accepted standards in the instrument's development. The OWLS-II RC and WE is well-standardized and the authors appropriately use narrower normative age groups at the younger levels for computation of standard scores.

Reliability data support the use of the instrument as part of an assessment battery to determine language strengths and weaknesses. Test-retest reliability was sufficient for Form A, but the lower coefficients for Form B indicate more variability in performance. Alternate form reliability coefficients were lower and provide further evidence that the forms may not be parallel. Evidence for convergent validity is adequate, and the test authors did an excellent job in establishing discriminative validity. However, data to support the construct validity of the OWLS-II RC and WE is inadequate. The test authors only tested the two-factor theoretical models of the integrative language theory and combined data across all ages. With respect to language process, the high correlation between receptive and expressive processes suggests a single-factor model.

Additionally, within the language component the two-factor model was not supported above age 7, which suggests a single-factor model as well. An exploratory factor analysis of the standardization data would provide some evidence of the strength of the underlying structure. Without this analysis or a test of alternative models, interpretation of the Overall Language Composite may be the most appropriate.

SUMMARY. The OWLS-II RC and WE is a user-friendly instrument that can be used as one part of a comprehensive battery to identify language difficulties. The technical adequacy of the instrument, including standardization and reliability, is robust. However, data suggest that performance on Form B is more variable. Convergent and discriminative validity evidence for test score use is adequate. Confirmatory factor analysis does not completely support the two-factor model. Consequently, users should interpret individual RC and WE scale scores with caution and place more emphasis on the WL composite.

REVIEWER'S REFERENCE

Carrow-Woolfolk, E. (1988). *Theory, assessment and intervention in language disorders: An integrative approach.* Philadelphia, PA: Grune & Stratton.

[125]

Parent Adolescent Relationship Questionnaire.

Purpose: Designed to "examine and understand the parent-adolescent relationship."

Population: Parents of adolescents ages 11-18 and adolescents ages 11-18.

Publication Date: 2009.

Acronym: PARQ.

Scores, 31: Conventionalization, Global Distress, Communication, Problem Solving, School Conflict, Sibling Conflict, Eating Conflict, Malicious Intent, Perfectionism, Ruination, Cohesion, Coalitions, Mother-Father Coalition, Spouse-Adolescent Coalition, Parent-Adolescent Coalition, Triangulation, Adolescent in Middle, Parent in Middle, Spouse in Middle (Parent Form), Mother Communication, Father Communication, Mother Problem Solving, Father Problem Solving, Mother School Conflict, Father School Conflict, Autonomy, Unfairness, Father-Adolescent Coalition, Mother-Adolescent Coalition, Father in the Middle, Mother in the Middle (Adolescent Form).

Administration: Group.

Forms, 2: Parent Profile Form, Adolescent Profile Form.

Price Data, 2013: $265 per introductory kit including professional manual (171 pages), 10 parent reusable item booklets, 25 parent response booklets, 25 parent profile forms, 10 adolescent reusable item booklets, 25 adolescent response booklets, 25 adolescent profile forms;

$70 per professional manual; scoring software is available from publisher.

Time: (15-20) minutes, Parent Form; (15-20) minutes, Adolescent Form.

Authors: Arthur L. Robin, Thomas Koepke, Ann W. Moye, and Rebecca Gerhardstein.

Publisher: Psychological Assessment Resources, Inc.

Review of the Parent Adolescent Relationship Questionnaire by MICHAEL J. SCHEEL, Associate Professor, Department of Psychology, University of Nebraska-Lincoln, Lincoln, NE:

DESCRIPTION.

Purposes. The Parent Adolescent Relationship Questionnaire (PARQ) is intended for use in clinical settings to assess the nature of relationships between adolescents with a psychiatric diagnosis (e.g., Attention-Deficit/Hyperactivity Disorder [ADHD], Oppositional/Defiant Disorder [ODD], anxiety disorders, mood disorders, eating disorders) and their parents. A multidimensional profile is obtained regarding the parent-adolescent relationship across three broad dimensions: overt conflict/skill deficit, extreme beliefs, and family structure. The profile is designed for use in planning family therapy interventions. The test authors also endorse the PARQ for adolescent individual therapy, in schools to augment Individualized Educational Programs, and in pediatric medical settings for adolescents with chronic diseases or problems with adherence to medication regimen. Finally, the test authors recommend the PARQ for research, citing several studies in which PARQ scales are used as outcome measures.

Scales and scoring. The PARQ is a self-report measure consisting of an adolescent form of 168 true/false items and a parent form with 152 true/false items. Both parents complete the parent version when possible. The number of items for which responses are required depends on whether one or both parents live in the home and whether adolescents have siblings living with them. Both versions include validity scales (i.e., Inconsistency, Conventionalization), six Overt Conflict/Skill Deficit scales (i.e., Global Distress, Communication, Problem Solving, School Conflict, Sibling Conflict, and Eating Conflict), and three Family Structure scales (i.e., Cohesion, Coalitions, and Triangulation). Each version includes three Beliefs scales (i.e., Ruination, Malicious Intent, and Perfectionism completed by each parent and Ruination, Anatomy, and Unfairness completed by the adolescent). The Adolescent form also includes separate ratings of mothers and fathers on Communication, Problem Solving, and School Conflict.

The PARQ is either hand- or computer-scored, and a computer-generated interpretive report is available. Scores are reported as *T*-scores and percentile ranks with *T*-scores graphed to form profiles. The instrument is appropriate for adolescents between ages 11 and 18 and their parents. A replacement procedure is included for missing items as well as a method of computing a Reliable Change Score. The summary profile is used in place of a total scale score, allowing for a holistic, visual interpretation of multiple dimensions.

TEST DEVELOPMENT.

Underlying assumptions and theories. PARQ development was based on extensive clinical experience leading to a comprehensive instrument containing multiple dimensions of the parent-adolescent relationship. Robin and Foster's (1989) Behavioral Family Systems Therapy (BFST) model forms the basis of test development. The approach consists of (a) problem-solving training, (b) communication training, (c) cognitive restructuring, and (d) structural interventions. The parent-adolescent relationship is defined by conflict, extreme individual beliefs about parent and adolescent roles and expectations, and family structure (i.e., cohesion, coalition, triangulation).

Item development. Item development began in 1982 through a rational-deductive method producing 18 scales. Experts judged the original bank of 1,000 items for clinical utility, clarity, and importance. Only items rated high on the three criteria were retained. This process resulted in parallel forms of 409 and 395 items, respectively, for parents and adolescents. The initial pilot study included 577 middle class families residing in Eastern Michigan and grouped as externalizing behavior disorders, ADHD, eating disorders, nonclinical, and nondistressed. The PARQ discriminated between the externalizing behavior disorders and the nondistressed groups. Items that correlated highly with their own scale and not with other scales were retained, resulting in a reduced total scale of 250 parent and 284 adolescent items. The scaled down instrument demonstrated moderately high alpha coefficients (i.e., .70 or better) for Family Structure and Overt Conflict/Skill Deficits but lower values for Beliefs. Principal components analysis produced a three-factor solution explaining 61% of the variance for mothers and fathers and 59% for adolescents.

The PARQ was refined between 2006 and 2008 using a standardization sample of 742. Using specific criteria for choosing to keep only the highest performing items, scales were reduced to the 8 to 10 best performing items. The PARQ Adolescent form went from 315 items to 168, and the Parent form went from 280 to 152 with several scales being eliminated. The refined versions maintained sufficient internal consistency reliability and *t*-test comparisons significantly (*p* < .05 or better) differentiated between clinical and nonclinical groups.

Generally higher correlations were found between scales within the same domain (Overt Conflict/Skill Deficits, Beliefs, Family Structure) in comparison with scales of other domains. Principal components analyses of the adolescent, mother, and father samples were similar to pilot study results from two decades earlier by strongly supporting a three-factor solution and accounting for more than 60% of the variance in each analysis.

The Inconsistency Scale was developed to test the validity of responses using pairs of items that strongly correlate. Consistency levels are designated as acceptable, elevated, or highly elevated on a scale of 0 to 8.

TECHNICAL.

Standardization. The standardization sample consisted of 602 adolescents, 332 mothers, and 292 fathers. Stratified sampling achieved demographics representative of the U.S. with respect to several factors. Individuals residing in a medical or psychiatric facility or receiving medical treatment for a psychiatric disorder were excluded. African American and Hispanic adolescents were adequately represented, but other ethnic groups (e.g., American Indian; Asian American) were not. A significant change index was calculated and is available by level of statistical significance.

Reliability. Internal consistency reliability estimates were reported for PARQ scales, with 70% to 80% of alpha coefficients greater than .70. Test-retest reliability was strong (*p* < .01) for time intervals of approximately 2 weeks to 1 month. In the adolescent sample, correlation coefficients ranged from .78 to .96 on the Overt Conflict/Skill Deficit scales, .62 to .76 on the Beliefs scales, and .68 to .89 on the Family Structure scales. In the parent sample (mothers and fathers combined), coefficients ranged from .83 to .94 on the Overt Conflict/Skill Deficit scales, .76 to .90 on the Beliefs scales, and .83 to .96 on the Family Structure scales. Interrater consistency was calculated by pairing adolescents with their mothers, adolescents with their fathers, and mothers with fathers. Resulting correlation coefficients ranged from .25 to .83 across all scales.

Validity. Content validity evidence was gained by anchoring the PARQ to the BFST approach and writing items to fit the broad functional domains of Overt Conflict/Skill Deficit, Cognitive Distortions (Beliefs), and Family Structure. Clinicians also reviewed the original bank of items.

Construct validity. The construct measured is the adolescent-parent relationship. It is defined as multidimensional with parameters identified through BFST. Factor analysis confirmed a factor structure similar to the BFST approach through the three factor solution of (a) Overt Conflict/ Skill Deficits (i.e., Cohesion, Problem Solving, Communication, Global Distress, Sibling Conflict, and Eating Conflict), (b) Beliefs (Ruination, Unfairness, Autonomy, Conventionalization, and School Conflict), and (c) Family Structure (Triangulation and Coalition). The Mother PARQ and the Father PARQ factor analyses also produced three factor solutions varying only slightly from the results of the PARQ Adolescent factor analysis.

In a convergent validity study, Koepke (1986) found that observer ratings organized by the PARQ domains of interactions and interviews of families of a clinical sample (N = 51) demonstrated concordance with the appropriate PARQ scale scores. Interestingly, the mothers' PARQ ratings were the most highly correlated with observer ratings of the family. Support for the Beliefs scale comes from a study by Koepke, Hull, and Robin (1990) in which the Family Beliefs Inventory (FBI; Vincent-Roehling & Robin, 1986) and the PARQ Belief scores were significantly correlated ($p < .01$) for most PARQ scales. Correlation coefficients between PARQ and FBI scores were .51 to .72 for mothers, .20 to .70 for fathers, and .53 to .60 for adolescents. Webb (1988) found support for the Family Structure scales of the PARQ through comparisons with the Direct Question Checklist (DQC) Cohesion scale, the McMaster Family Assessment Device for fathers, and the Structured Interview Rating Scale (SIRS) Cohesion scale.

A large convergent and discriminant validity study organized by the PARQ authors compared the PARQ to corresponding scales of the Family Environment Scales (FES), the Personality Assessment Inventory-Adolescent (PAI-A), the Conners-Wells Adolescent Self-Report Scales: Short Form of the Conners' Rating Scales-Revised (CASS:S),

the Revised Children's Manifest Anxiety Scale (RCMAS), and the Children's Depression Inventory (CDI). Overall, the scales that were predicted to correlate with one another did so.

Criterion-related validity. The PARQ Adolescent standardization sample (normal group) was compared to a clinical sample. Generally, the Conflict and Beliefs scales of the PARQ differentiated between the nonclinical groups and the clinical groups, but the Family Structure scales did not. The test authors suggest that Family Structure does not necessarily vary as a function of diagnostic categories in the way that extreme beliefs or family conflict would. Webb (1988) reported a study comparing blended families with families having two biological parents in which stepfathers reported more triangulation.

COMMENTARY. The Behavioral Family Systems Therapy (BFST) model proved to be an accommodating three-factor structure upon which to base the PARQ. The factor structure was confirmed repeatedly across refinements of the instrument in both the adolescent and parent versions. Strengths of the PARQ include its practical utility. Test results translate nicely into practice because the PARQ structure is derived from and mirrored in the BFST therapeutic approach. The instrument has accumulated a wealth of evidence over 30 years to support the validity of test score use in the prescribed manner. It discriminates well between nonclinical and clinical samples that include a wide range of diagnoses. The PARQ is unique in that the systemic and dynamic nature of the parent-adolescent relationship can be depicted through comparisons of parent and adolescent profiles. Consequently, interventions can be targeted to address family conflict, faulty beliefs, and dysfunctional family structures. The few weaknesses of the instrument may lie in limitations of ethnicity, race, and family culture in the normative sample.

SUMMARY. The PARQ has undergone several iterations of development and is strongly anchored within a theoretical structure. The test authors were successful in designing an instrument that aids the treatment of clinically diagnosed adolescents and their families. It compares very favorably to established instruments in the field and is easily administered, scored, and interpreted. The multidimensional nature of the PARQ provides a wealth of avenues to pursue in treatment conceptualization to facilitate systemic as well as behavioral change. Research supporting the development of the PARQ is impressive in providing strong evidence of construct, criterion-related, and discriminate validity.

REVIEWER'S REFERENCES

Koepke, T. (1986). *Construct validity of the Parent Adolescent Relationship Inventory: A multidimensional measure of parent-adolescent interactions* (Unpublished doctoral dissertation). Wayne State University, Detroit, MI.

Koepke, T., Hull, B., & Robin, A. L. (1990). *Construct validity of the Family Beliefs Inventory and the PARQ Beliefs scales.* Unpublished manuscript, Wayne State University, Detroit, MI.

Robin, A. L., & Foster, S. L. (1989). *Negotiating parent-adolescent conflict: A behavioral-family systems approach.* New York, NY: Guilford Press.

Roehling, P. V., & Robin, A. L. (1986). Development and validation of the Family Beliefs Inventory: A measure of unrealistic beliefs among parents and adolescents. *Journal of Consulting and Clinical Psychology, 54,* 693-697.

Snyder, D. K. (1997). *Marital Satisfaction Inventory, Revised manual.* Los Angeles, CA: Western Psychological Services.

Webb, D. B. (1988). *Discriminant and concurrent validity of the structural scales of the Parent Adolescent Relationship Questionnaire: A multidimensional measure of parent adolescent interactions* (Unpublished doctoral dissertation). University of South Carolina, Columbia, SC.

Review of the Parent Adolescent Relationship Questionnaire by CHRISTOPHER A. SINK, Professor and Chair, School Counseling and Psychology, and LAUREN D. MOORE, Doctoral Student, Counselor Education, Seattle Pacific University, Seattle, WA:

DESCRIPTION. The Parent Adolescent Relationship Questionnaire (PARQ) was designed with clinicians (e.g., mental health therapists, school counselors, pediatricians) in mind, particularly as they attempt to (a) "identify and assess the nature and extent of relationship problems between parents and an adolescent" (manual, p. 5) and (b) detect incongruities between parent and adolescent perceptions of family dynamics. Based on Robin and Foster's (1989) Behavioral Family Systems Therapy (BFST), these multidimensional self-report surveys quantitatively estimate critical dimensions of parent-adolescent relationships. Although the test manual describes the numerous scales and subscales associated with both the parent and adolescent versions, potential test administrators will need to refer to the parent and adolescent profile forms to obtain an overall perspective on the measure's underlying dimensionality and scale composition. These forms identify the three broad parent-adolescent relationship dimensions (Overt Conflict/Skill Deficits, Beliefs, and Family Structure) and which scales and subscales are associated with each dimension. Although the parent (152 true/false items) and adolescent (168 true/false items) versions have most scales in common, the overall number of scale and subscale scores differs (19 parent; 25 adolescent). There are other noteworthy differences between PARQ versions as well. For example, within the Beliefs domain, the adolescent version includes Ruination, Autonomy, and Unfairness, whereas the parent form includes Ruination, Malicious Intent,

and Perfectionism. Furthermore, related to the Overt Conflict/Skill Deficits domain, adolescent respondents must complete both "mother" and "father" subscales.

The test manual provides ample test administration, scoring, interpretation, background, and technical information about the parent and adolescent versions of the PARQ. The test authors suggest that knowledgeable examiners can use the PARQ to assist with planning family therapy interventions, to investigate family dynamics more thoroughly, to monitor the effectiveness of counseling interventions, to provide information for special education evaluations, and to help increase compliance with a medical regimen.

Items comprising the parent/caregiver form are written at a sixth-grade reading level. The adolescent instrument is appropriate for children and youth between the ages of 11 and 18 years and requires a fifth-grade reading level. Both forms require about 15 to 20 minutes to administer. The PARQ test kit includes two-ply perforated, carbonless response booklets for both parents and adolescents, allowing for relatively straightforward determination of scale and subscale raw and transformed scores. Alternatively, the PARQ may be computer scored using the Parent Adolescent Relationship Questionnaire Scoring Program (PARQ-SP) available from the test publisher. Instructions for calculating raw scores, *T*-scores, and percentiles for each scale and subscale are presented in a largely understandable and step-by-step manner. Respondent score patterns are displayed using uncomplicated profile forms.

DEVELOPMENT. The scale development and standardization processes are logically and well described in the test manual. Beginning in the early 1980s, the conceptual and research groundwork for the instrument was initiated (Robin & Foster, 1989). Over the next 25 or so years, the PARQ progressed through several phases of revision and refinement. Three theoretical strands were influential in shaping scale and item content: social learning/behavioral psychology, family systems theory, and cognitive therapy. Item and scale construction took into consideration vital characteristics of adolescent development as well as the stages of family development. The theoretical foundation and pertinent supportive research for individual scales are adequately summarized in the test manual. In short, fundamental concepts and constructs are carefully explained, and an overview of each scale is provided with its essential nature/attributes, purpose, and applications.

The sample size for the exploratory phase of scale development was acceptable ($N = 577$ families, including mothers, fathers, and adolescents), although the sample was not representative of the U.S. population. Early psychometric analyses conducted on the sample data provided some evidence for the internal consistency and factorial validity of the major scales. From 2006 to 2008, the PARQ scales were further refined, and standardization samples were collected. The test manual details the norming process including the samples tested, as well as the extensive item, reliability, and factor analytic analyses (principal components with appropriate rotations) conducted on the scales. If confirmatory factor analyses were conducted on the derived scales, they are not reported in the test manual.

TECHNICAL. The standardization procedures reported in the test manual appear to follow conventional psychometric research practices, including substantial attention to maintaining statistical rigor. The PARQ standardization samples were largely composed of more traditional parent-adolescent/caregiver-adolescent relationships (i.e., biological parents, stepparents, adoptive parents). Given the difficulty of soliciting large numbers of families to participate in the norming process, these reviewers consider the adolescent and parent sample sizes (respondents were not all related) to be marginally adequate ($n = 602$ adolescents; $n = 332$ mothers; $n = 292$ fathers). The test authors attempted to stratify respondents according to U.S. Census data on key demographic variables, including adolescent age, gender, and ethnicity. Certain groups of potential respondents were intentionally omitted from the standardization sample (e.g., prison inmates, individuals with weak English language skills, individuals on probation, and those in inpatient hospital treatment). The predominant non-White ethnicities represented in the standardization sample were African American and Hispanic. Hence, the applicability of the PARQ to Asian American families and other minorities appears to be equivocal. Scale score interpretations derived from respondents in these groups are probably suspect.

Reliability evidence for both versions of the PARQ is extensively reviewed in the test manual and in several germane studies (e.g., Robin, Koepke, & Moye, 1990; Sizane & van Rensburg, 2011; Wysocki, 1993). Internal consistency (alpha), stability (Pearson r), and interrater reliability (Pearson r) coefficients are reported. In an attempt to summarize the internal consistency results over several PARQ-related publications, the reviewers aggregated alpha coefficients from individual scales within each of the three dimensions. With some exceptions, the overall magnitude of the alpha coefficients reported in these sources was largely satisfactory for the adolescent and parent versions, with the majority of values ranging from .65 to .85.

Test-retest stability coefficients were estimated from small groups of respondents ($N = 31, 32\%$ for adolescents and parents, respectively) following a span of 14 to 38 days after the initial testing. Across the three PARQ dimensions, the correlation coefficients ranged from moderately strong to strong for both versions: Skill Deficits/Overt Conflict, adolescent .78 to .96, parent .68 to .94; Beliefs, adolescent .62 to .76, parent .76 to .90; Family Structure, adolescent .68 to .89, parent .83 to .96.

Interrater reliability estimates were given as correlations among three groups of paired respondents (adolescent-mother pairing, $N = 442$; adolescent-father pairing, $N = 246$; and mother-father pairing, $N = 104$). Overall results indicate modest interrater reliability across the PARQ's three dimensions, with the Skill Deficits/Overt Conflict area generating the highest correlations among respondent group pairings (adolescent-mother correlations ranged from .40 to .66; adolescent-father, .38 to .68; mother-father, .48 to .83). The range of interrater reliability coefficients for the other two dimensions (Beliefs and Family Structure) were generally lower for the three groups of paired respondents.

The test manual reports in some detail three forms of validity evidence for the two versions of the PARQ. First, content validity evidence appears to be demonstrated by: (a) carefully devising the PARQ scales and subscales based on an established theoretical model (BFST), (b) reviewing other comparable questionnaires and closely inspecting individual items to determine how investigators assessed similar constructs, (c) having scale definitions and the initial pool of items reviewed by a panel of 16 family therapists, and (d) establishing moderate to strong internal consistency estimates indicating homogeneity of content.

Criterion-related validity was assessed in Robin, Koepke, and Moye (1990) by contrasting score patterns across three adolescent samples:

distressed (*n* = 174), nondistressed (*n* = 69), and normative (*n* = 314). According to these researchers, significantly higher scores on the scales comprising the Skill Deficits/Overt Conflict and Beliefs dimensions for the behavior-disordered group compared to the normative group supports criterion-related validity. Further, those families who were screened for "positive adjustment" performed better on scales from the above dimensions than the unscreened normative group, again supporting criterion-related validity (Robin et al., 1990). The validity for the Family Structure scale was less consistent, most likely due to the respondents' score patterns on the Triangulation and Coalition subscales. Robin et al. (1990) provided various plausible explanations for the differences found among the three comparison groups, suggesting, for example, that acting out behavior disorders are not associated with the item content of the Triangulation and Coalition subscales and the inability of respondents to accurately self-report issues related to these subscales.

The test manual provides further evidence for the criterion-related validity of the PARQ across multiple respondent groups with differing diagnoses (e.g., attention-deficit/hyperactivity disorder, anxiety, depression, eating disorder, myelomeningocele or spina bifida). Similar to the findings reported in Robin et al. (1990), the PARQ Skill Deficits/Overt Conflict and Beliefs subscales appear to satisfactorily distinguish individuals in relation to defined criteria; however, few group differences were found for the Family Structure scales.

Finally, evidence for construct validity is exhaustively documented in the test manual and essentially demonstrated in four ways: (a) PARQ scores were compared to interview-based ratings of the same constructs; (b) direct observations of family interactions were coded and analyzed; (c) convergent and discriminate correlational analyses comparing PARQ scores to five differing instruments were conducted; and (d) exploratory factor analyses were computed to show PARQ's factorial validity. Although it is clear that the researchers meticulously addressed construct validity, due to the sheer volume of information reported, it would be beneficial if this section of the test manual were more cogently organized and summarized. In short, the empirical documentation marshaled in support of the instrument's construct validity was more than passable for self-report noncognitive inventories (see Nunnally & Bernstein, 1994).

COMMENTARY. The test manual documents the value of the adolescent and parent responses to the PARQ in providing an accurate estimate of respondents' perceptions of the family dynamics that may be used in subsequent planning of family counseling interventions by trained practitioners. In general, the two versions appear to yield test scores that are reliable and valid for use in a variety of therapeutic clinical settings (e.g., mental health clinics) as screening and perhaps as diagnostic tools. The standardization sample is marginally adequate, requiring some caution when interpreting derived scores, particularly when clinicians use either measure for diagnosis and treatment planning with non-White clients. Additional evidence is needed to show that PARQ scores can lead to effective interventions for adolescent-family problems. Moreover, because the school-based evidence for the PARQ's reliability and validity is scant, in these reviewers' opinion, neither version should be employed in school settings as a diagnostic or treatment planning measure.

SUMMARY. The adolescent and parent versions of the PARQ are relatively user-friendly, reliable, and efficient instruments for appraising respondents' perceptions of family dynamics. They can be administered and scored by a variety of assessment competent clinicians. The case studies provided in the test manual offer a very helpful guide for practitioners to follow in their assessment of family dynamics and counseling work with adolescents and their parents. Given the PARQ's sophisticated theoretical underpinnings and large number of scales and subscales, score interpretation should be left to well-trained and licensed professionals. Clinically based validity evidence for the measures is well within the accepted professional testing standards for attitudinal-like screening/diagnostic questionnaires. Additionally, even though both versions of the PARQ require further validation research using confirmatory factor analysis procedures, their scores can be prudently applied to evaluate the outcomes of family counseling interventions.

The test manual is less than clear in some sections (e.g., validity evidence). Extensive background in psychometrics is needed to decipher the presented outcome data. If school-based mental health professionals decide to use the measure, they must take into account the PARQ's clinical/family systems foci and norms as they cautiously interpret and apply respondents' scores. At present, the PARQ should not be used with limited English speakers or in school settings.

REVIEWERS' REFERENCES

Nunnally, J. C., & Bernstein, I. H. (1994). *Psychometric theory.* New York, NY: McGraw-Hill.

Robin, A. L., & Foster, S. L. (1989). *Negotiating parent-adolescent conflict: A behavioral-family systems approach.* New York, NY: Guilford Press.

Robin, A. L., Koepke, T., & Moye, A. (1990). Multidimensional assessment of parent-adolescent relations. *Psychological Assessment: A Journal of Consulting and Clinical Psychology, 2*(4), 451-459. doi:10.1037/1040-3590.2.4.451

Sizane, N. F., & Van Rensburg, E. (2011). Night shift working mothers: Mutual perceptions with adolescent children. *Journal of Psychology in Africa, 21*(1), 71-78.

Wysocki, T. (1993). Associations among teen-parent relationships, metabolic control, and adjustment to diabetes in adolescents. *Journal of Pediatric Psychology, 18*(4), 441-452. doi:10.1093/jpepsy/18.4.441

[126]

Parent Success Indicator [Revised Edition].

Purpose: Designed to "identify favorable qualities of parents and aspects of their behavior where education seems warranted."

Population: Ages 10-14 and parents of ages 10-14.

Publication Dates: 1984-2009.

Acronym: PSI.

Scores, 6: Communication, Use of Time, Teaching, Frustration, Satisfaction, Information.

Administration: Group.

Forms, 2: Parent, Adolescent.

Price Data, 2010: $73.90 per starter set including manual (2009, 31 pages), 20 Parent Inventory booklets, 20 Child Inventory booklets, and 20 profiles; $15.80 per manual.

Foreign Language Editions: Spanish, Japanese, and Mandarin versions available.

Time: (15-20) minutes.

Comments: Parents provide self-assessments, adolescents provide observations of their parents.

Authors: Robert D. Strom and Paris S. Strom.

Publisher: Paris & Robert Strom (the authors).

Cross References: For reviews by C. Ruth Solomon Scherzer and Suzanne Young of an earlier edition, see 16:179.

Review of the Parent Success Indicator [Revised Edition] by ROSEMARY FLANAGAN, Associate Professor, Touro College, Graduate School of Psychology, New York, NY:

DESCRIPTION. The Parent Success Indicator [Revised Edition] (PSI) focuses on parents with a child aged 10-14 years in order to identify favorable parental qualities as well as aspects of their behavior for which education seems indicated. Uses for the PSI include to: (a) determine how adolescents perceive the strengths and shortcomings of their parents, (b) learn how parents perceive their own strengths and shortcomings, (c) compare adolescent and parent impressions of parent performance, (d) provide feedback about attitudes and behaviors, (e) design curriculum for particular groups with shared characteristics, and (f) detect how parent interaction changes in response to an intervention to consider changing. These data can be used to stimulate the growth and development of parenting curricula.

There are two parallel versions of the PSI, one for parents, one for adolescents; the order of the items is the same on both forms, the only difference is that sentence stems on the parent questionnaire begin with "I…" and on the adolescent form, the sentence stems begin with "My parents…." Using the PSI questionnaires, both parents provide data about their functioning as parents; adolescents share observations of their parents. The PSI comprises 60 Likert-type items that are divided into six subscales: Communication (skills of advising children and learning from them), Use of Time (making decisions about the ways in which time is used), Teaching (the scope of guidance and instruction expected of parents), Frustration (attitudes and behaviors of children that bother parents), Satisfaction (aspects of the parent role that bring satisfaction), and Information Needs (things parents need to know about their child).

The forms are straightforward questionnaires that are readily completed. Parent participation can be via mail; adolescents should complete the forms at home or in school. An invitational letter to be sent to the parents is in the appendix of the test manual and should be mailed to the parents along with an informed consent form/permission for child participation (also in the appendix). It is important to make certain that all items are answered. Phone follow-up is indicated for parents who do not fully complete the questionnaires and teachers should review the forms filled in by adolescents for completeness. Adolescents complete forms for the parent(s) with whom they reside on a regular basis; the forms should be completed in 15–20 minutes. A profile form is available for reporting comparison information together, facilitating pre- and post-intervention data comparison.

The items are scored on a 4-point scale with 1 = *never*, and 4 = *always*. Raw scores for the items are summed for each scale. Higher scores indicate a more positive view of parenting, as item scores of 1 are considered highly unfavorable, and item scores of 4 are considered highly favorable. The scoring procedure is the same for both the parent and adolescent forms.

DEVELOPMENT. The PSI was developed by using an open-ended survey based on theory. A random sample of 2,893 individuals from a Phoenix, AZ suburb, including 1,286 parents, 700 teachers, and 907 children completed an open-ended survey. Corresponding items appeared on each form, with items about parent competence being ranked in importance. The preliminary measure was called the Parental Strength and Needs Inventory (PSNI), which addressed six aspects of parenting. Internal consistency reliability, based on data from a sample of 900 adults and children ranged from .88 to .96 for the overall instrument, and from .67 to .93 for the subscales.

Factor analysis was employed to obtain a preliminary estimate of validity. Data obtained from 612 parents and children were analyzed. This resulted in some revision to individual items and content of scales. Following these modifications, the scale was renamed the Parent Success Indicator (PSI).

TECHNICAL.

Reliability. Additional studies were conducted to determine the psychometric properties of the PSI. Data obtained from 1,634 parents and children indicate ample internal consistency. Coefficient alpha for the full scale ranged from .92–.95 for samples of Black, White, and Hispanic mothers and children. Coefficient alpha for the subscales ranged from .75–.95.

Validity. Principal components analysis was used to determine whether the 60-item PSI did indeed support the hypothesized six-factor structure. A principal components analysis, using a varimax rotation, produced eigenvalues ranging from 13.600 to 1.514, which accounted for over 48% of the variance. Of the 60 items, 58 produced loadings of at least .40 on six factors. These 58 items loaded cleanly on one factor. The data are available in the test manual for inspection.

Preliminary evidence of cross-cultural validity (Beckert, Strom, Strom, Yang, & Singh, 2007) comes from an investigation of the responses of Chinese parents (n = 429) and their adolescent children (n = 411), whose data were compared to those of 1,618 American parents (n = 794) and their children (n = 824). The scale was translated to Mandarin and back-translated to English to ensure that the meaning of the items would be equivalent. Mothers and fathers were included in both samples. The six-factor solution accounted for 46–54% of the variance. Alpha coefficients for the total scale were greater than .90 for each subsample. These data suggest that the PSI holds promise for

multicultural applications, as the aggregated data obtained from the Chinese parents are similar to those obtained from American parents.

An additional validity study based on responses to the PSI given by a diverse (Black, White, Hispanic) sample of 806 adolescents and 739 mothers generally indicated favorable ratings of parenting, although there were differences in the rated perceptions of parenting success. This is believed to provide a basis for developing a national parenting reference standard (Strom, Strom, Strom, Shen, & Beckert, 2007). Comparisons at the item level reveal significant differences between mothers and adolescent children on most items. The sampling procedure for this investigation did not reflect census tract data, and the test authors weighted some samples in order to compensate for uneven sampling. Using this same sample, the predictive power of independent variables on PSI scores was examined. An important finding that emerged from the study data is that the amount of time that a mother spent with an adolescent each week was the only studied variable that significantly impacted all six PSI subscales. Ethnicity, a parent home after school, the child's grades, and mother's level of education impacted some PSI scales. Additional substantiation of the importance of time spent with an adolescent each week comes from a later investigation (Beckert, Strom, Strom, Derre, & Weed, 2008).

Although some validity studies are encouraging, other recent data suggest that more data are needed to establish the utility of the PSI. Beckert, Strom, and Strom (2006) studied Black and White American fathers (n = 228) and 10-to 14-year-old adolescents (n = 289) to investigate the (parenting) curriculum needs of fathers. Data indicate significant main effects for both generations of respondents and ethnicity on four of the six scales. Significant main effects for child gender were reported in two subscales. Of note and in contrast to much of the literature on the PSI as well as the normative data, this validity study provided information about fathers.

COMMENTARY. A number of studies have been conducted by the test authors and their collaborators and have been commented upon in reviews of an earlier edition of the PSI. It is important to note that the earlier studies examined data from mothers, but not fathers. Happily, there has been some change and now some data from fathers are available (e.g., Beckert, Strom, &

Strom, 2006), which is an encouraging start. Also encouraging is that the PSI has been studied with varied populations (Japanese, Taiwanese, Chinese, Vietnamese, Central Americans, Black Americans, and gifted youth) and appears helpful in identifying barriers to parental success; these studies are summarized in the test manual. A continued concern with the PSI is that data obtained from mothers have been used to develop norms that provide a basis for comparisons. The use of this instrument by practitioners will be limited by the absence of representative norms.

SUMMARY. The PSI was developed to assist with the identification of favorable parenting qualities as well as to identify areas of parenting that might benefit from education. Administration and scoring are straightforward. Development is based on a factorial model. Internal consistency reliability is ample, and there is evidence of construct validity, as well as potential utility for parents and children from diverse cultures. Much of the available data were obtained from samples of mothers; some data are now available from fathers, which may broaden the utility of the instrument. More research is needed to establish the utility of the measure prior to it being used widely to assess needs of groups. Nevertheless, it appears to be a useful tool for researchers, and should prove useful to determine needs on an individual basis.

REVIEWER'S REFERENCES
Beckert, T. E., Strom, R. D., & Strom, P. S. (2006). Black and White fathers of early adolescents: A cross-cultural approach to curriculum development for Parent Education. *North American Journal of Psychology, 8*, 455-470.
Beckert, T. E., Strom, R. D., Strom, P. S., Derre, K., & Weed, A. (2008). Single mothers of early adolescents: Perceptions of competence. *Adolescence, 43*, 275-290.
Beckert, T. E., Strom, R. D., Strom, P. S., Yang, C., & Singh, A. (2007). Parent Success Indicator: Cross-cultural development and factorial validation. *Educational and Psychological Measurement, 67*, 311-327. DOI: 10.1177/0013164406292039.
Strom, R. D., Strom, P. S., Strom, S. K., Shen, Y., & Beckert, T. E. (2007). Black, Hispanic, and White American mothers of adolescents: Construction of a national standard. *Family Therapy, 34*, 191-208.

Review of the Parent Success Indicator [Revised Edition] by GEOFFREY L. THORPE, Professor of Psychology, University of Maine, Orono, ME:

DESCRIPTION. The Parent Success Indicator (PSI) was published in 2009 as a revision of the previous edition of 1998, although the name of the test has not been altered. According to the test manual, the PSI "identifies favorable qualities of parents and aspects of their behavior where education seems warranted" (manual, p. 2). In addition to the manual it consists of three test booklets: the PSI for Parent (of Child Ages 10 to 14), the PSI for Child (Ages 10 to 14), and the PSI Profile. Recommended uses of the PSI include assessing parents' perceptions of their strengths and weaknesses,

assessing children's perceptions of their parents' strengths and weaknesses, comparing parents' and children's assessments, providing feedback concerning possible areas for change, designing curricula for remediation, and evaluating changes following interventions. In a typical administration, a mother and a father each complete a Parent test booklet and a child completes the Child test booklet. Six subscales assess basic aspects of parenting: Communication, Use of Time, Teaching, Frustration, Satisfaction, and Information Needs.

The PSI for Parent test booklet contains a Parent Identification Form with 12 questions; the test proper, with 60 questions each answered on a 4-point scale (*Always, Often, Seldom, Never*); and an additional open-ended question asking if the parent wishes to add anything. The Parent Identification Form items assess demographics, relationship to child (parent, stepparent, or grandparent), and a couple of general questions such as how much time is spent with the child each week. The 60 test items are presented in successive blocks of 10, each representing one of the subscales; each item within a subscale begins with the same stem (e.g., "I am good at ..." for Communication items). Responses are classified as *Highly Favorable, Slightly Favorable, Slightly Unfavorable,* or *Highly Unfavorable.* The 1–4 scale used to code responses is reversed for half of the subscales so that "4" always reflects the *Highly Favorable* rating. The Profile indicates the scoring and classification of a parent's own responses.

The PSI for Child booklet parallels the Parent booklet and presents the same questions, rephrased as appropriate (e.g., "My parent is good at ...").

The Identification Forms for parents and children and the Profile are available from the publisher in Spanish. The test authors may be contacted for Japanese and Mandarin versions of the PSI.

DEVELOPMENT. The test authors' rationale for developing the PSI was that changes in society and technology have left parents ill-equipped to guide their adolescent children confidently, with a consequent need for theory-based assessment to select parents who might benefit from suitable educational programs.

The PSI originated from an open-ended survey administered to 2,893 people (1,286 parents, 907 children, and 700 teachers) who had been randomly selected from a chiefly upper-middle class suburb of Phoenix, Arizona. Initial published reports date from 1985 and 1987. An example of a survey question was: "What things does your child do that you consider frustrating?" Responses that raised concerns about parenting competence were identified, and for each grade level a hierarchy of such responses was established. The interrater reliability of the assignment of responses to coded categories was 96%. The highest ranked topics were selected to form a questionnaire, initially named the Parental Strengths and Needs Inventory, with Likert-scale response options for each item. High values for internal consistency were observed in the original six subscales and for the test as a whole in a sample of 900 parents and children; and a factor analysis identified six factors, the most prominent of which measured communication and use of time. The PSI was formed following further modifications that revised or deleted items with multiple or unclear factor loadings.

A significant recent event in the development of the PSI has been its cross-cultural validation in samples of Chinese (n = 840) and American (n = 1,618) parents and their adolescent children, reported in 2007. For the Chinese (Taiwanese) sample the PSI was translated into Mandarin, with appropriate methodology including the adoption of suitably idiomatic language and back-translation. The original six-factor structure of the PSI was replicated in the four respondent groups, and item-to-factor correlations showed goodness of fit for 51 to 56 of the 60 items.

TECHNICAL. The internal consistency of the PSI and its six subscales was assessed in samples of Black, White, and Hispanic mothers and their children (data reported in 1998). The sample sizes ranged from 133 (Hispanic mothers) to 391 (White mothers), and coefficient alpha values ranged from .75 to .95 for the subscales. In the Chinese and American samples reported in 2007, the alpha values for subscales ranged from .74 to .94. Data on test-retest reliability are not reported.

As presented in the test manual, information on the validity of the PSI derives from factor analyses with principal components extraction. Item intercorrelation matrices from the responses of an ethnically diverse sample of 612 low- and middle-income parents and children produced eigenvalues greater than 1 on all of the specified six factors. All but 4 items loaded .40 or greater on at least one of the factors. Similar results were obtained in a confirmatory analysis with a larger sample. Correlations of the PSI and its subscales with other tests or scales purporting to measure similar constructs are not reported.

The test manual refers to several studies of various parent and child samples who have responded to the PSI in addition to those previously noted. These often large samples include White fathers, fathers and mothers in Taiwan, Japanese mothers, Black mothers, parents of gifted adolescents, Asian and South American immigrants, parents of mentally handicapped adolescents, and deaf parents of hearing adolescents. Although a substantial recent research literature is cited in the test manual, there is no reference to standard scores, percentiles, or the properties of distributions of scores. Hence, information on test standardization is not provided.

One of the appendices tabulates mean scores and standard deviations for 1,097 mothers and 1,104 children on the six subscales, with the results of independent t-tests comparing the means for the two generations. The means are significantly different for five of the six subscales, not always in the same direction. For example, in the Frustration subscale the mean score for mothers (3.03) is significantly higher than the mean for children (2.98).

COMMENTARY. The PSI test item and Profile booklets appear to be well-designed and convenient to use. The test authors have provided detailed information on the psychometric properties of the test, chiefly in the form of factor analytic work on the data from large samples of respondents with different racial and ethnic identifications and in different countries. The six component subscales of the PSI have been well-established by this work, and it is clear that they map onto the pertinent constructs identified in the test authors' extensive review of the theoretical background on parenting. The availability of the PSI in Mandarin and Japanese obviously extends its range of applicability widely.

The internal consistency of the PSI and its subscales has been documented, but their test-retest reliability has not. Validity has been assessed only with respect to the test's multidimensional subscale structure and the strong correlations of items with factors. Normative data have not been presented specifically, consistent with the developers' goals of providing idiographic feedback to particular parents and children, of acquiring research data, and of setting the scene for the design of remedial programs. Also consonant with the research and program development goals is the provision in the test manual of sample letters and permission forms from schools to parents, and consent forms for children (Young, 2005). Test users are, of course, free to compare the scores of their respondents with those of over 1,000 mothers and over 1,000 children whose data are tabulated in an appendix, and to derive standard scores and percentiles as desired.

Some might question the inclusion of the Frustration items as reflecting aspects of parent behavior in need of remediation. Having the items for a given subscale listed together in a block could lead to a response set that would inflate internal consistency values (Scherzer, 2005). Comparing the mean subscale scores of mothers and children could be of interest, but in the table presented in the manual (Appendix H), the large sample size produced statistically significant values for *t* even when the actual difference between the means was as low as .05.

It was not immediately clear how the PSI of 2009 differs from the PSI of 1998, but the prefatory review of research on family relationships in the 2009 manual (with sections on parent education, generation as culture, and perceptions of youth), and the rationale for the subscales under Instrument Description, are notably up-to-date (all citations are from 2002 to 2008, with one exception). A highlight of the test authors' recent research on the PSI as featured in the test manual is its validation with Taiwanese and American respondents and the confirmatory evidence of its factor structure.

SUMMARY. The PSI is a multidimensional self-report inventory of parenting strengths and weaknesses with separate forms for parents and children. Its six subscales have been established by factor analytic work, and the test has shown its applicability with samples from groups varying in socioeconomic status, racial and ethnic identification, and nationality and language. The PSI is not offered as a clinical instrument with standardization and normative data. Instead, it is used to provide feedback on parenting strengths as perceived by parents and their children, and for use in research and program development.

REVIEWER'S REFERENCES

Scherzer, C. R. S. (2005). [Review of the Parent Success Indicator.] In R. A. Spies & B. S. Plake (Eds.), *The sixteenth mental measurements yearbook (pp. 748-750).* Lincoln, NE: Buros Institute of Mental Measurements.
Young, S. (2005). [Review of the Parent Success Indicator.] In R. A. Spies & B. S. Plake (Eds.), *The sixteenth mental measurements yearbook (pp. 750-751).* Lincoln, NE: Buros Institute of Mental Measurements.

[127]

Parenting Stress Index, Fourth Edition.

Purpose: "Designed to evaluate the magnitude of stress in the parent-child system."

Population: Parents of children ages 1 month to 12 years.

Publication Dates: 1983-2012.

Administration: Group.

Forms, 2: Full Length, Short Form.

Foreign Language Editions: Validation studies done for Chinese, Portuguese, French Canadian, Finnish, and Dutch populations.

Author: Richard R. Abidin.

Publisher: Psychological Assessment Resources, Inc.

a) FULL LENGTH.

Acronym: PSI-4.

Scores, 18: Total Stress (Child Domain [Distractibility/Hyperactivity, Adaptability, Reinforces Parent, Demandingness, Mood, Acceptability, Total], Parent Domain [Competence, Isolation, Attachment, Health, Role Restriction, Depression, Spouse/Parenting Partner Relationship, Total], Total), Life Stress, Defensive Responding.

Price Data, 2013: $210 per introductory kit, including professional manual (2012, 174 pages), 10 reusable item booklets, 25 answer sheets, and 25 profile forms; $70 per professional manual; $65 per 10 reusable item booklets; $72 per 25 answer sheets; $25 per 25 profile forms.

Time: (20) minutes.

b) SHORT FORM.

Acronym: PSI-4-SF.

Scores, 5: Total Stress (Parental Distress, Parent-Child Dysfunctional Interaction, Difficult Child, Total), Defensive Responding.

Price Data, 2013: $135 per short form kit, including professional manual (2012, 174 pages) and 25 short forms; $80 per 25 short forms.

Time: (10) minutes.

Cross References: See T5:1889 (20 references); for reviews by Julie A. Allison and by Laura L. B. Barnes and Judy J. Oehler-Stinnett of the Third Edition, see 13:221 (51 references); see also T4:1933 (22 references); for reviews by Frank M. Gresham and Richard A. Wantz of an earlier edition, see 10:271 (2 references).

Review of the Parenting Stress Index, Fourth Edition by MARY M. CLARE, Professor of Counseling Psychology, Lewis & Clark College, Portland OR:

DESCRIPTION. The fourth edition of the Parenting Stress Index (PSI-4) is a tool for supporting early identification of parent/child systems experiencing stress known to have harmful effects on children's emotional development. As such, the PSI-4 is specifically intended as an enhancement for clinical service delivery. The PSI-4 consists of a 101-item inventory that uses a 5-point response scale (*strongly agree* to *strongly disagree*) and is composed of a Child Domain and a Parent Domain that together render a Total Stress scale.

Six subscales within the Child Domain provide measures associated with these titles: Distractibility/Hyperactivity, Adaptability, Demandingness, Mood, Acceptability (child fulfills parental expectations), and Parent Reinforcement. The first four subscales represent relatively stable child temperament characteristics and were identified over time when parents seeking clinical support consistently presented one of these four as their primary concern. The last two subscales represent interactive circumstances based in the parent's affective sense of acceptance of and relational gratification with their child.

The seven subscales within the Parent Domain provide measures that carry these titles: Competence, Depression, Attachment (sense of closeness), Health, Isolation, Role Restriction (due to parent role), and Spouse/Parenting Partner Relationship. The first three subscales reflect the parents' functional personality assessing the respondents' sense of competence, level of depression and sense of attachment to and investment in the child. The next four scales reflect situational circumstances related to health, and social connections.

The 101 items of the PSI-4 are followed by an optional 19-item Yes/No questionnaire composing the Life Stress Scale. This scale extends understanding of the parent-child relationship by offering a measure of the family's social context based on global situational factors such as family debt, parent drug use, marital and employment circumstances, and recent family deaths.

With regard to administration and scoring, the PSI-4 can be considered "user-friendly." The forms completed by parents and those provided in support of scoring and interpretation are clear and minimally cluttered. Rich case illustrations arising from the considerable history of PSI application provide context to support clinical interpretation of scaled scores in each domain.

An abbreviated version of the PSI, the Parenting Stress Index–Short Form (PSI-SF) includes 36 items comprising three domains: Parental Distress, Parent-Child Dysfunctional Interaction, and Difficult Child, all combining to provide a short-form Total Stress scale. This brief form captures the primary components of the parent-child system by assessing parent factors, child factors, and the nature of parent-child interaction. The PSI-SF thus meets the needs of practitioners who have limited time with patients and require a screening index that could be completed in 10 minutes or less.

DEVELOPMENT. The PSI originated from the test author's desire to support the earli-

est possible identification of stressors to parent/child systems so that preventive programming can be made available for enhancing attachment and thus the young child's developing emotional health. Originally published in 1983, the PSI is based on the four assumptions of grounding in current empirical knowledge, integration of that knowledge with clinical practice to support healthy parent/child systems, and the two understandings that stress is additive in nature and that each stressor is multidimensional. These foundational insights arose chronologically from the test author's own experience and observations as a parent, his therapeutic support of parent/child client systems and his consultation with pediatric physicians who revealed a general need for strategies to apply in gaining clinical insights into the families they served. The primary observation underlying the four assumptions emerged over time. In the test author's words,

> I recognized that there was no set pattern of parenting skills or attributes that was best for facilitating the development of children. ... [E]very parent experiences stresses that, depending upon their number, their intensity, and available coping resources, determine whether dysfunctional parenting occurs. The natural consequence of dysfunctional parenting is that children often develop behavioral and emotional problems. (manual, p. iv)

Each subsequent revision of the PSI has focused on updating empirical bases and improving psychometrics. The revision effort leading to the fourth edition of the PSI had as its goals: (a) Strengthening items revealed to be weaker in studies accomplished since the publication of the third edition in 1995, (b) updating while retaining psychometric and clinical integrity, and (c) updating the norm sample to reflect current U.S. demographics.

TECHNICAL. The scale structure and content of the PSI have well-established reliability (internal consistency and test-retest) and content validity. The extent of the relevance (practically) and validity (psychometrically) is powerfully illustrated in the stability of the PSI's measured factor structure, validity, and reliability across the 40 languages into which it has been translated. In addition, country-specific norms and psychometric data have been generated in eight countries in addition to the U.S.-based publication that is the focus of this review (Canada [French], China, Germany, Italy, Japan, Korea, Netherlands, and Portugal). Extending the psychometric basis of the U.S. index are explicit investigations of Hispanic (n = 223) and Lesbian/Gay (n = 27) parent samples, each indicating no significant variation from the larger norm sample.

Related to investigations of specific parent samples is the emphasis in this revision on enhancing sample consistency with education level and ethnicity in current U.S. demographics. The current sample includes 1,056 adults (534 mothers, 522 fathers) from 17 states in all four regions of the U.S., matching distributions of ethnicity and education levels reflected in current census data, and in equal proportion across child gender and age bands. Scoring adjustments were made to reflect the small variations evident in this revised sample (e.g., fathers' scores were slightly higher on Child Domain responses).

Based on these norm sample adjustments, the current revision emphasized two interrelated goals of strengthening the psychometric strength of individual items and updating language to more accurately draw responses reflecting behavioral patterns associated with target constructs (see scale descriptions above). As one particular example, "spouse" references were shifted to read "spouse/parenting partner."

Worth noting are the more than 250 reference citations in the current test manual that represent only the most recent and immediately relevant publications related to this measure. Finally, the correlation between the PSI-3 and PSI-4 indicate the continued psychometric strength of this index in its latest iteration.

COMMENTARY. The PSI-4 has the distinction of being grounded in psychometric and clinical rigor that has been systematically enhanced over the 30 years of its existence. Due in large part to the test author's foundational commitment to treatment validity–that is, immediate relevance to parents, children and the service providers supporting them–the PSI-4 represents an instrument of practical power and empirical legitimacy. In spite of this validation, the test author offers, early in the narrative of the test manual for the PSI-4, what reads as either an apology or justification. Reaching into the abstracted realms of personality research, the test author explains that research has not upheld theoretical (i.e., clinically observed) connections between temperament early in life and later behavioral tendencies. He then indicates that the Child Domain Scale of the PSI-4 is based in these predictive temperaments, nonetheless.

Perhaps this is simply the obfuscation that arises when scholars raised on strict empiricism write about otherwise strong and helpful clinical psychometrics. As continues to be the case in many practically focused measurement tools, distraction into defending clinical authority floats subtly throughout the PSI-4 manual. This is likely because there are still gatekeepers for whom a clinically focused measure is suspect regardless of its empirically demonstrated practical superiority and psychometric integrity. This reviewer mentions this dynamic in the hope that stating it here in the *Mental Measurements Yearbook* can encourage testing professionals to persist in moving past the necessity for apologetics that unnecessarily detract from the clear description of an immediately relevant tool. Certainly test authors (as contrasted with those who apply these tools) must keep in mind the fraction of their audience who are the gatekeepers determining which innovations may enter the knowledge base. If those gatekeepers remain the few most privileged by the system, the obfuscation will continue.

SUMMARY. The Parenting Stress Index, Fourth Edition is by the test author's description a measure of the "goodness of fit" in a parent-child system. Based on parents' responses to a 101-item paper-and-pencil inventory, the PSI-4 provides scaled scores reflecting children's behavior and temperament tendencies alongside scores indicative of parent skills, personality traits and socio-emotional circumstances. Thirty years of rigorous psychometric and clinical refinement support the strength and utility of the PSI-4 for its stated purpose. The descriptive data from these scales indicate points of strength and weakness in parent-child relationships that may guide clinical interventions for enhancing the security of attachment and reliability of nurture most supportive of healthy child development and related prevention of future behavior and emotional problems.

Review of Parenting Stress Index, Fourth Edition by SUZANNE YOUNG, Professor of Educational Research, University of Wyoming, Laramie, WY:

DESCRIPTION. The Parenting Stress Index (PSI) was first published in 1983 and the current revision, the Fourth Edition, was published in 2012. The primary goals of the fourth revision were to address changes in population demographics and to revise items to account for current research in the use of the PSI. The PSI has been used in clinical settings to screen parents for parent-child relationships that may lead to subsequent behavioral and emotional difficulties for either parents or children. Additionally, the PSI has been used in research studies that examine stressors in parents, children, and the parent-child system. The target population for the PSI is parents of children ages 1 month to 12 years.

The index includes both a full inventory (PSI-4) and a short form (PSI-4-SF). The PSI-4 contains two scales (101 items) plus an optional Life Stress scale (19 items); the two scales, Child Domain (47 items) and Parent Domain (54 items), combine to form a measure of Total Stress. In addition, the Child Domain scale consists of six subscales that tap into parent perceptions of child temperament characteristics that may impact parent stress. The Parent Domain is made up of seven subscales that assess parents' perceptions of the adequacy of their parenting.

The PSI-4-SF consists of 36 items and includes the following three scales: Parental Distress, Parent-Child Dysfunctional Interaction, and Difficult Child. Scores from the three scales combine to form the Total Stress scale. Items on the three scales are taken from the full inventory. The intention of the short form is to provide clinicians and researchers a way to quickly assess parent stress in situations where time is an issue.

Administration, scoring, and interpretation of the PSI should be conducted by professionals who have expertise in areas such as clinical psychology, educational psychology, or other fields with a specific emphasis on the use and interpretation of tests and measurement. Individuals without such training may administer and score the PSI. The PSI can be administered in an individual or a group setting. There is no time limit for the inventory but typically respondents will be able to complete the full inventory within 20 minutes and the short form within 10 minutes. Parents should be able to read and understand at a fifth grade level but administrators can provide some clarification. Both forms of the PSI may be administered by paper-and-pencil, using an eight-page booklet with an answer sheet, or by computer software.

The PSI can be hand-scored or scored by the available software portfolio program. If hand-scored, responses are placed on an answer sheet and automatically transferred to a connected scoring sheet. The scorer must calculate raw total scores for each scale and subscale. The scorer then enters the subscale and scale scores on the Profile Form and determines percentile ranks and T-scores using the appropriate age tables provided in the test manual. If using the computer software, percentile ranks and T-scores are automatically generated. Scorers may also enter item responses or scale totals from a hand-administered inventory into the software program for a report and interpretation.

DEVELOPMENT. The test author, as a parent and a clinical psychologist, was motivated to develop the PSI because of a need in the clinical setting to assess parent stress related to psychological and/or behavioral issues. In response to this need, the test author examined research and developed an initial set of dimensions and test items to use in piloting the instrument. Professionals in the field of parent-child relationships also examined and rated the items. The first version of the PSI was revised three more times, leading to the fourth edition. For its standardization, an expanded sample was used to represent the current population in education level and ethnicity. Items in the PSI-4 were reviewed and revised based on current literature, feedback from experts, and data collection from the standardization sample. Finally, reliability and factor structure of the new items were used to identify any items not contributing to the scales and the overall inventory.

The PSI-4-SF was developed based on factor analytic studies conducted on full-length versions of the PSI. These studies indicated that a short form was psychometrically possible and that the inventory contained three factors, or scales, related to the parent-child system. The test author proposes that these three factors (Parental Distress, Parent-Child Dysfunctional Interaction, and Difficult Child) may be combined to influence parenting behaviors and child outcomes.

TECHNICAL. The standardization sample for the PSI-4 was much more diverse than the sample used for previous versions of the PSI. The sample included mothers and fathers of children ranging in age from less than 1 year to 12 years old and from varied regions of the U.S. Care was taken to ensure that the sample matched the education level and ethnicity of the U.S. population reported in the 2007 U.S. Census. Conversion tables for raw scores to percentile ranks and T-scores are presented based on child age. The test author did not include any information about the standardization sample for the short form.

The reliability of the PSI-4 is reported in the test manual. Coefficient alpha is shown for Versions 3 and 4, indicating increased reliability for the two scales and the total scale. Increases are also shown for most of the subscales within the two scales. The Child Domain scale demonstrates a high level of internal consistency overall, with an alpha coefficient of .96 and subscale coefficients ranging from .78 to .88. The Parent Domain scale also demonstrates a high level of internal consistency, with an alpha coefficient of .96 and subscale coefficients ranging from .75 to .87. The alpha coefficient for the Total Stress scale is .98. Test-retest reliability is reported for 3-week, 3-month, and 1-year intervals, indicating stability over time. For the Child Domain, correlation coefficients range from .55 to .82. Correlations for the Parent Domain range from .70 to .91. The Total Stress correlations range from .65 to .96. Reliability of the optional Life Stress scale was not reported.

The validity of the PSI-4 is supported by evidence related to its development based on the literature, content experts, and, to a lesser degree, by factor analysis. In addition, the construct and predictive validity is supported by evidence from numerous studies including those conducted in diverse locations and with diverse populations. General findings of selected studies are reported in the test manual; specific validity coefficients are not provided. Research studies indicate relationships between parenting stress and maternal anxiety, children living in at-risk situations, child attachment, childhood ADHD, child abuse, and others constructs. The test author refers the reader to the publisher's website for a more extensive bibliography. The author reports factor loadings for the Child Domain and Parent Domain subscales and items. Factor loadings do not reflect unique loadings for all items and subscales, and some loadings do not meet the criterion to exceed .30. Additionally, 91 of the items use a Likert response scale (*strongly disagree* to *strongly agree*); 10 of the items use varied response formats. Similar to reliability, validity of the Life Stress scale was not addressed in the test manual. Reliability and validity of the PSI-4-SF are reported for the three scales and the Total Stress scale. Internal consistency coefficients range from .88 (Difficult Child) to .95 (Total Stress). The test author also reports correlations between scales and subscales of the PSI-4 and scales of the PSI-4-SF. The Parental Distress scale of the short form correlates strongest with the Parent Domain of the full inventory (r = .94). The Difficult Child scale of the short form correlates most strongly with the Child Domain

scale of the full inventory (r = .95). The Parent-Child Dysfunctional Interaction scale on the short form correlates most strongly with both the Child Domain and Total Stress scales of the full inventory (r = .91). The Total Stress scales for the two forms demonstrate a very strong correlation (r = .98). Correlations with the Life Stress scale were provided as well, indicating moderate relationships (coefficients range from .41 to .48) with the short form. Given the strong correlations between the short form and the full inventory, with the exception of the Life Stress scale, and the fact that the short form was developed using items from the full inventory form, the test author suggests the short form is equally as valid as the full inventory. However, 3 of the 36 items use response formats that differ from the other 33 Likert items, yet they are combined to form additive measures of parenting stress.

COMMENTARY. The PSI-4 appears to be a strong measure of parental stress as it relates to the family system. The test author gave considerable attention to current literature when making revisions to the PSI, in addition to using a standardization sample that represents changing demographics of the U.S. population. The test author suggests that the PSI-4 is appropriate for use in research conducted in a number of countries but is silent on its usefulness in clinical settings in those countries. The optional Life Stress scale received little attention from the test author; reliability, validity, and scale development were not addressed. The test author indicates scores above the 90th percentile on the Life Stress scale should be cause for considering a recommendation of professional assistance. However, in light of the lack of development and technical information provided, this scale appears to be inappropriate for clinical use. Barnes and Oehler-Stinnett (1998) reviewed the third edition and also noted the lack of reliability provided for the Life Stress scale. In addition, as Barnes and Oehler-Stinnett (1998) also addressed, 10 of the items use response formats that differ from the other 91 items on the scale, yet they are included in summative measures of the scales and subscales. These 10 items should not be included in reliability measures or factor analysis, nor should they be combined with items using different response scales. Finally, reliability and validity of the paper-and-pencil and computerized versions were not discussed separately, indicating that each version is equally valid and reliable; that may not be the case.

The PSI-4-SF as a rapid measure of parental stress is supported in the test manual, even though the test author suggests it is in the early stages of development. Because it is aligned very well with the full version of the instrument and because factor analysis supports its structure, the validity evidence of the short form appears strong. However, similar to the full inventory, three items use different response formats from the others yet are added to form scale and Total Stress scores. Similar to the full inventory, these items should not be analyzed or combined with items that use different response scales. Internal consistency indicates that the PSI-4-SF is a reliable measure, even with the three mismatched items. The moderate correlations with the Life Stress scale of the full inventory is another indication that the Life Stress scale is not yet well-developed. Similar to the full inventory, reliability and validity of the paper-and-pencil versions are not presented and discussed separately.

SUMMARY. With the exception of the Life Stress scale, and even considering items that should be excluded from the scales because of their mismatched response formats, the PSI-4 and the PSI-4-SF appear to be strong measures of stress in the parent-child relationship. Both forms of the instrument seem to be especially useful in a clinical setting, although they can certainly be used for research purposes. This reviewer does not recommend the Life Stress scale be used or interpreted until it is more fully developed and analyzed.

REVIEWER'S REFERENCE

Barnes, L. L. B., & Oehler-Stinnett, J. J. (1998). [Review of Parenting Stress Index, Third Edition.] In J. C. Impara & B. S. Plake (Eds.), *The thirteenth mental measurements yearbook* (pp. 724-727). Lincoln, NE: Buros Institute of Mental Measurements.

[128]

PDD Behavior Inventory-Screening Version.

Purpose: Designed as "a screening tool to help clinicians quickly identify children at risk for" autism and other pervasive developmental disorders.
Population: Ages 1-6 to 12-5.
Publication Dates: 1999-2011.
Acronym: PDDBI-SV.
Scores, 3: Social Pragmatic Problems, Social Approach Behaviors, Social Deficits.
Administration: Group.
Price Data, 2013: $98 per introductory kit, including 50 rating forms and professional manual (2011, 41 pages); $58 per 50 rating forms; $54 per professional manual.
Time: (5-10) minutes.
Comments: Derived from the PDD Behavior Inventory (17:142).
Author: Ira L. Cohen.
Publisher: Psychological Assessment Resources, Inc.

Review of the PDD Behavior Inventory-Screening Version by LUCY BARNARD-BRAK, Associate Professor, Education EPL, and DAVID M. RICHMAN, Chair of the Burkhart Center, Texas Tech University, Lubbock, TX:

DESCRIPTION. The PDD Behavior Inventory-Screening Version (PDDBI-SV) is an abbreviated version of the PDD Behavior Inventory (PDDBI; Cohen & Sudhalter, 2005; 17:142) to screen for children who may be at risk for a pervasive developmental disorder such as an autism spectrum disorder. The primary advantage of the PDDBI-SV as presented by the author is that it covers a broader span of ages (18 months to 12 years, 5 months) than other similar screening tools. As a screening tool, the test author notes, and these reviewers would like to reiterate, that the PDDBI-SV should not be used to make diagnostic decisions but rather to inform clinicians whether to pursue diagnostic assessment. The PDDBI-SV consists of a one-page rating form of 18 items across two subscales, which can be completed in approximately 5 to 10 minutes. Each subscale, Social Pragmatic Problems (SOCPP-SV) and Social Approach Behaviors (SOCAPP-SV), consists of 9 items. All 18 items produce one composite score, the Social Deficits (SOCDEF) score. These items map onto criteria for the identification of pervasive developmental disorders from the *Diagnostic and Statistical Manual of Mental Disorders, Fourth Edition, Text Revision* (*DSM-IV-TR*; American Psychiatric Association [APA], 2000) or autism spectrum disorder per the *DSM-5* (APA, 2013). Formal training or a graduate degree is not required to administer or score the PDDBI-SV, but administration and interpretation should occur under the supervision of a qualified professional.

DEVELOPMENT. The PDDBI-SV was developed from the PDDBI items and its standardization sample (Cohen & Sudhalter, 2005). From the PDDBI, the items that best predicted the difference between the SOCAPP and SOCPP *T* scores (referred to as the SOCDSC score) were considered most appropriate for inclusion in the PDDBI-SV because the SOCDSC score performed best in reliably predicting autism spectrum disorders. For the SOCDSC score, higher scores indicate less severity of symptoms; the SOCDEF score for the PDDBI-SV presents the reverse of this presentation in which higher scores indicate greater severity of symptoms. The correlation between PDDBI SOCDSC score and the PDDBI-SV SOCDEF was excellent with a Pearson product-moment correlation coefficient (r) of -.97.

TECHNICAL. The standardization sample consisted of 369 parent ratings for children ages 18 months to 12 years, 5 months with an autism spectrum disorder. The test manual reports that most of the parents were mothers and Caucasian with more than two-thirds having pursued higher education. No further details are provided. Approximately 92% of the sample had a diagnosis of autism from either the Autism Diagnostic Interview-Revised (ADI-R) or the Autism Diagnosis Observation Scale (ADOS). In more than one place in the testing manual, the authors note that further details regarding the standardization sample can be found in the PDDBI manual. As a result, these reviewers requested and received the PDDBI manual and test materials from the publisher. The PDDBI manual provided more information about the age distribution of the standardization sample along with a variety of other detailed demographic information such as the children's gender and ethnicity, and parents' years of education (Cohen & Sudhalter, 2005). The PDDBI manual also provided information regarding the norming procedure that was used in the development of the PDDBI (Cohen & Sudhalter, 2005), which was subsequently relied upon in item selection for the PDDBI-SV. These reviewers consider referring to the PDDBI manual for this information to be an undue burden on the consumer and suggest that this information regarding the standardization sample be included in the PDDBI-SV manual as well.

In terms of internal consistency, the alpha coefficient for the data obtained was .87, which may be considered sufficient. For interrater reliability, the ratings of mothers and fathers were compared revealing a correlation coefficient of .62 after the removal of statistical outliers, which would not be considered strong evidence for interrater reliability. Further examination of interrater reliability should be conducted among parents and other caregivers who may be in contact with children before entering school given that the age of onset is considered to be prior to 3 years old (APA, 2000).

Sensitivity analyses were conducted on a limited sample (n = 100) by employing receiver operating characteristic (ROC) curve analyses, which revealed a high degree of sensitivity with an area under the curve (AUC) value of .96 (95% confidence interval was .92 to .99). From these ROC analyses, the test authors produced cutoff scores to determine the level of severity of symptoms across six levels ranging from unlikely to extreme. The determination of these cutoff scores would appear to be premature given the limited sample of 100 children with a mean age of 3.6 years (SD = 1.0). The PDDBI-SV purports to screen a broader range of ages (children ages 18 months to 12 years, 5 months) than data collected for ROC curve analyses represent. Because the determination of cutoff scores and severity levels were derived from this limited sample, these severity levels and associated cutoff scores should be viewed with caution.

In terms of evidence of criterion-related validity, the PDDBI-SV varies in its correlation with similar screening instruments with correlation coefficients ranging from .54 to .83. Evidence of criterion-related validity appears to be variable and warrants further examination.

COMMENTARY. The author of the PDDBI-SV indicates that item development was based on *DSM-IV-TR* criteria, and there have been changes with the *DSM-5* to the diagnostic criteria, which may affect the reliability and validity of this screener. This is of particular concern given that the taxonomy of *DSM-5* removes Pervasive Developmental Disorder-Not Otherwise Specified and Asperger's Disorder, and collapses all autism diagnoses under Autism Spectrum Disorder (ASD) with three symptom severity levels. Additionally, the new diagnostic criteria for ASD are designed to be more thorough with strict guidelines for determining the presence of ASD characteristics, which calls into question the reliability and validity of all autism-related screening and diagnostic instruments. With this possible limitation acknowledged, potential users of PDDBI-SV should also bear in mind that the 18 items exclusively assess the "social" domain of ASD symptomatology. As indicated by subscale names and total composite score name, all 18 items assess socialization, social communication, and adaptive social skills. There are no items covering the other two broad categories of autism symptomology: (1) restricted repetitive and stereotyped behavior, interests, or activities, and (2) impairments in communication. Close examination of individual questions suggests that some items are not relevant to children as young as 18 months (e.g., "has problems understanding the need to be polite"). Finally, a strength of the screener is the breadth of coverage of socialization difficulties frequently observed in children with ASD.

SUMMARY. Overall, the effort to create a screening instrument for pervasive developmental disorders for a broad age range of children is needed and appreciated. However, the PDDBI-SV requires further development based upon the limited psychometric/normative data presented. The limited standardization sample noted in a review of the PDDBI (Carey, 2007) was not expanded for the creation of this abbreviated, screening version. In conjunction with changes to diagnostic criteria with the publication of the *DSM-5* (APA, 2013), these reviewers cannot recommend the clinical use of the PDDBI-SV.

REVIEWERS' REFERENCES

American Psychiatric Association. (2013). *Diagnostic and statistical manual of mental disorders* (5th ed.). Washington, DC: Author.

American Psychiatric Association. (2000). *Diagnostic and statistical manual of mental disorders* (4th ed., text rev.). Washington, DC: Author.

Carey, K. (2007). Review of the PDD Behavior Inventory. In K. F. Geisinger, R. A. Spies, J. F. Carlson, & B. S. Plake (Eds.), *The seventeenth mental measurements yearbook* (pp. 614–616). Lincoln, NE: Buros Institute of Mental Measurements.

Cohen, I. L., & Sudhalter, V. (2005). *PDD Behavior Inventory professional manual.* Lutz, FL: Psychological Assessment Resources.

Review of the PDD Behavior Inventory— Screening Version by STEVEN R. SHAW, Associate Professor of Educational and Counselling Psychology, McGill University, Montreal, Quebec, Canada:

DESCRIPTION. The PDD Behavior Inventory-Screening Version (PDDBI-SV) is a screening instrument intended to identify children at risk for an autism spectrum disorder (ASD) as defined in the *DSM-IV-TR* or to assist in general screening for pervasive developmental disorders. There are several stated goals for the PDDBI-SV: to provide a rapid screening tool for caregivers or clinicians who have concerns about a possible ASD diagnosis, to be useful for a broad range of ages, to cover a wide range of adaptive and maladaptive behaviors, to provide a standardized score for an estimate of degree of severity as well as degree of confidence, and to create a screening tool that would be useful for multiple applications (Cohen, Schmidt-Lackner, Romanczyk, & Sudhalter, 2003).

The PDDBI-SV is an 18-item parent-completed screener based on the PDD Behavior Inventory (PDDBI; Cohen & Sudhalter, 2005; 17:142). The PDDSI-SV yields a composite score called the Social Deficits (SOCDEF) score. There is also a Social Pragmatic Problems scale based on 9 items related to social problems and a Social Approach Behaviors scale based on 9 items related to social skills and abilities. Scores are reported as *T* scores. There are also qualitative descriptions of severity that correspond to differences of 0.5 or 1 standard deviations. These six levels of severity

are Level 1, Unlikely; Level 2, Borderline; Level 3, Mild; Level 4, Moderate; Level 5, Severe; and Level 6, Extreme.

Formal training or graduate education is not required to administer or score the PDDBI-SV. However, a supervising professional with graduate training in psychology, psychiatry, pediatrics, or other allied health profession should ensure that the administrative, scoring, and interpretation guidelines are followed exactly. The PDDBI-SV requires 5 to 10 minutes to complete and should be completed by parents or caregivers. The PDDBI-SV can be hand scored from a carbonless form using instructions provided in the test manual or completed on screen and computer scored.

DEVELOPMENT. The PDDBI-SV was derived from the PDDBI, which is a detailed instrument to be used in the assessment of ASD. On the PDDBI, the best subtest for discriminating between young children with ASD and children matched on age and performance IQ without ASD was the SOCDEF scale. The 48 items originally composing the SOCDEF scale were reduced to 18 items for purposes of developing the screening version. Items were selected based on discriminative ability. Also considered were items that best fit the literature on social behaviors that best predict ASD in young children.

TECHNICAL.

Standardization. The standardization sample for the PDDBI-SV is the same sample used for the PDDBI. This sample includes 369 parent ratings for children who had been diagnosed with an ASD. The standardization sample included children ranging in age from 1 year, 6 months to 12 years, 5 months. The majority of the sample respondents were White and female. More than two-thirds of the respondents had a college education or above. Seventy percent of the standardization sample had an ASD diagnosis through the Autism Diagnostic Interview-Revised (ADI-R), 63% had an additional Autism Diagnostic Observation Schedule-Generic (ADOS-G) diagnosis, and 92% had an ASD diagnosis based on either one of these measures. The remaining 8% of the sample was diagnosed by an experienced diagnostician using the *DSM-IV-TR* criteria.

Reliability. Reliability is reported as internal consistency, stability, and interrater reliability. Internal consistency was calculated based on records from a sample of 100 children who were used to establish cutoff scores. Records from the standardization sample were selected according to specific criteria described in the test manual, involving the use of other measures as well as clinical judgment. The alpha coefficient for the composite SOCDEF score was .87. No alpha coefficients were reported for the Social Pragmatic Problems and Social Approach Behaviors scales. Stability was determined through a sample of 38 children who were assessed with a 12-month interval between testing sessions. Selection criteria for the 38 children were not described. The Pearson correlation coefficient, used to examine test-retest stability, was .74. Over the course of 12 months, the mean score decreased by approximately 2 points, which was not a statistically significant change. Evidence for interrater reliability was based on a doctoral dissertation from 2006. This study involved 126 mothers and fathers of children with an ASD. The intraclass correlation between mothers and fathers was .53. There was also a small, but significant, mean score difference between mothers and fathers. The mean score was 2 points higher for fathers than for mothers. Although more detail would be welcomed, there is sufficient evidence of reliability for this instrument.

Validity. Validity evidence is reported as supporting predictive or diagnostic validity, criterion validity, and clinical validity. Predictive and diagnostic validity evidence is reasonably strong for a screening instrument. At the cutoff point between Borderline and Unlikely classifications, there is a sensitivity of .98 and a specificity of .70. The very high sensitivity means that the probability of a positive ASD diagnosis given a Borderline classification is quite high. The moderate specificity means that the probability of no diagnosis given an Unlikely classification is modest. Therefore, there is likely to be a large number of false positives, but few false negatives, when using the PDDBI-SV. Given the value of early identification and intervention and the cost of a full diagnostic assessment for ASD, these are not unreasonable numbers. Criterion-related validity was reported based on correlations with the Modified Checklist for Autism in Toddlers (M-CHAT), Social Responsiveness Scale (SRS), and the Childhood Autism Rating Scale (CARS). Scores from the PDDBI-SV SOCDEF scale correlated with the M-CHAT critical items failed score at .67 and the total number of items failed at .73. The PDDBI-SV and the Social Responsiveness Scale demonstrated a correlation coefficient of .83. The Pearson correlation coefficient between the PDDBI-SV and the CARS was .54, which represents the lowest coefficient among the several comparisons. This result is likely due to the extent to which CARS emphasizes behavioral aspects of autism, as opposed to the emphasis on social deficits shown in the PDDBI-SV. Clinical validity was addressed by investigating the severity classifications on the PDDBI-SV to the full PDDBI, scores on the Vineland Adaptive Behavior Scales, classifications on the ADI-R, and functioning from a sample of children recovered from intraventricular hemorrhage. All of these relationships demonstrate that the severity classification is useful in discriminating among groups in the expected direction.

COMMENTARY. There is some lack of clarity concerning the appropriate age range for the PDDBI-SV. All children in ages from 1 year, 6 months to 12 years, 5 months are scored in the same manner. There is no consideration of the qualitative differences in ways children of different ages manifest symptoms of ASD. The PDDBI-SV focuses exclusively on social skills, whereas the definition of ASD includes language development and stereotyped, ritualistic, or restricted behaviors. In addition, the definition of ASD changed with the *DSM-5* in 2013. Therefore, there are limitations in some clinical applications of the PDDBI-SV. As with all screening instruments, a major factor in the effectiveness of the PDDBI-SV is the nature of the screening program. Given the high incidence of ASD, universal screening with the PDDBI-SV could be a reasonable option for a school district or outpatient clinic. The more information that professionals have, the less useful such a screening measure would be. For example, if a professional knows that a child is 3 years old without speech and does not make eye contact, then the PDDBI-SV is unlikely to add any information and may be unnecessary. However, when no information is known, as in the case of universal screening, the PDDBI-SV could be a useful instrument for improving early identification.

SUMMARY. The PDDBI-SV is a convenient and brief screening measure of social skills and behaviors that are predictive of autism spectrum disorders. The test manual reports modest psychometric data, yet the evidence is supportive. The PDDBI-SV could be an excellent screening tool for assisting in early identification of ASD in children from ages 1 year, 6 months to 12 years, 5 months.

REVIEWER'S REFERENCES

Cohen, I. L., Schmidt-Lackner, S., Romanczyk, R., & Sudhalter, V. (2003). The PDD Behavior Inventory: A rating scale for assessing response to intervention in children with pervasive developmental disorder. *Journal of Autism and Developmental Disorders, 33*, 31–45.

Cohen, I. L., & Sudhalter, V. (2005). *PDD Behavior Inventory: Professional manual.* Lutz, FL: Psychological Assessment Resources.

[129]

Pediatric Test of Brain Injury.

Purpose: Designed to "estimate a child's ability in applying neurocognitive-linguistic skills that are vulnerable to pediatric brain injury and relevant to functioning well in school" and track "recovery starting in the acute phase and continuing until…performance indicates functioning in the normal range."

Population: Ages 6-16 who have sustained traumatic brain injury or acquired brain injury.

Publication Date: 2010.

Acronym: PTBI.

Scores, 11: Orientation, Following Commands, Word Fluency, What Goes Together, Digit Span, Naming, Story Retelling-Immediate, Yes/No/Maybe, Picture Recall, Story Retelling-Delayed, Overall Performance Rating.

Administration: Individual.

Price Data, 2010: $349.95 per complete test kit including examiner's manual (127 pages), stimulus book, and test forms; $49.95 per 10 test forms.

Time: (30-35) minutes.

Comments: Specialists trained to assess children and adolescents with cognitive-communication impairments, including brain injury, are qualified to administer the PTBI. Results from each score are reported in a performance profile pattern and are combined to provide a level of overall performance.

Authors: Gillian Holtz, Nancy Helm-Estabrooks, Nickola W. Nelson, and Elena Plante.

Publisher: Paul H. Brookes Publishing Co, Inc.

Review of the Pediatric Test of Brain Injury by ANDREW S. DAVIS, Associate Professor, and W. HOLMES FINCH, Assistant Professor, Department of Educational Psychology, Ball State University, Muncie, IN:

DESCRIPTION. The Pediatric Test of Brain Injury (PTBI) is a criterion-referenced measure designed to assess children ages 6–16 with acquired (ABI) or traumatic (TBI) brain injuries for the purpose of measuring current functional abilities as well as assessing skills that are essential to reintegration into school. The test questions were developed and evaluated using item response theory (IRT) methods and classical test theory. The test authors indicate speech-language pathologists, psychologists, and other specialists who work with children with brain injuries are qualified to use the PTBI; these individuals will be able to quickly learn how to administer and score the PTBI. The administration time is about 30 minutes, and the test authors suggest a methodology for breaking the administration

into two separate sections to be given on the same day, if necessary. Test materials include a stimulus book, examiner's manual, and test form (protocol). The examiner's manual provides a good overview of the test, including information about the background and rationale for the creation of the PTBI, directions for administration and scoring, technical analysis of the measure, and a case example. The test protocol is easy to follow and use and there is space on the front page to describe the child's medical history and demographic information. The test protocol also includes a behavioral observation checklist for each subtest.

Ability scores are obtained for each of the 10 subtests comprising the battery based on the number of correct items with each item carrying a different weight. The ability scores for each subtest can be compared to tabulated data presented in an appendix that is organized into 11 tables (one for each age from ages 6–16) and descriptions of performance: very low, low, moderate, and high. Standard errors of measurement (*SEM*) that allow for the calculation of confidence intervals are available for each subtest, broken down into 11 age groups. The test protocol also provides a space to summarize performance across subtests using guidelines provided in the test manual.

DEVELOPMENT. The test authors noted "the coauthors drew on their expertise in the areas of pediatric brain injury, child language development, and neuropsychology to develop a conceptual framework that would include cognitive and linguistic skills important to children who are developing typically as well as those skills most vulnerable to brain injury" (examiner's manual, p. 11). Test development began with a series of pilot studies involving 500 children, although these studies are not described in the examiner's manual. Development of the PTBI (Research Edition) is described in a separate journal article by Hotz, Helm-Estabrooks, and Nelson (2001). The test manual describes development of the PTBI, which proceeded in two phases. The first phase, conducted in 2007, included data from 32 children with TBI and 12 typically developing children ranging in age from 6–16. The second phase, conducted in 2008, used a "research version" (examiner's manual, p. 11) of the PTBI primarily in pediatric hospitals with children either in the acute or rehabilitative phase of TBI. The test authors indicate that feedback from the clinicians at the sites was considered in creating the final version of the test. The test authors note that the final version of the PTBI was administered to 134 children with TBI, 46 children with acquired brain injuries, and 77 children who did not have a brain injury. Ages of these children ranged from 6–16.

The test authors provide a conceptual framework and rationale for the creation of the overall test as well as the subtests. The 10 subtests in the final version of the PTBI assess "constrained skills" (skills that children obtain early in development and that remain relatively stable throughout the lifespan) and "unconstrained skills" (skills that continue to develop as children age; these are the types of skills that usually necessitate age-based norms). The three constrained subtests are Orientation, Following Commands, and Naming; the seven unconstrained subtests are Word Fluency, What Goes Together, Digit Span, Story Retelling-Immediate, Yes/No/Maybe, Picture Recall, and Story Retelling-Delayed. The test authors provide a factor analytically derived model to support the use of these measures.

TECHNICAL. The technical properties of the test are included in a chapter in the examiner's manual. The test authors indicate that the cutoff scores for the performance categories were calculated based upon the performance of 103 children who had not been diagnosed with a brain injury. The test authors note "The differences in the percentages of children classified into the different performance categories reflects naturally occurring differences in the range of performance that children in the general population show in these different skill areas" (examiner's manual, p. 43). One issue that is not addressed is how the cutoff scores were determined. There was no information regarding how the criteria were established or validated, making interpretation of these classifications somewhat difficult.

Discussion of the technical aspects of the instrument is somewhat uneven. For example, very little information is provided regarding the various samples used in the psychometric studies such as demographic information (e.g., age, gender, ethnicity) or how the individuals were sampled. On the other hand, the test authors did report fairly detailed demographic information for individuals included in these samples. A number of pieces of validity evidence are presented in the technical summary of the PTBI. For example, the test authors report on a study in which mean scores for the 10 subsets were used to compare the performance of typical children (ages 6–16 years) to that of children with TBI and acquired brain injuries. It is unclear why the

researchers elected to make these comparisons using t-tests rather than analysis of variance (ANOVA) with appropriate post hoc testing. In addition, there is no indication that any efforts were made to control the Type I error rate associated with conducting such repeated tests (30 in this case). Therefore, significant differences that were identified using an alpha of .05 must be interpreted with caution. It should be noted that the observed significant differences supported the construct validity of the PTBI. Mean scores obtained by the typical sample were significantly higher than those of both the TBI and ABI groups, with the exception of the TBI groups Following Commands subtest where the difference was not significant.

Convergent validity was investigated by calculating Pearson correlation coefficients between scores on the unconstrained skills of the PTBI and scores on the Glasgow Coma Scale and the Rancho Los Amigos Scale. The sample included 38 children between 7 and 16 years of age who had been diagnosed with TBI. Correlations ranged between -.05 and .58, with most lying between .40 and .58. The test authors conclude that these results provide convergent validity evidence, although it is also clear that the PTBI diverges to some extent from these other measures. The test authors also calculated the correlation between what they term the "calculated ability scores" with ability estimates obtained using the Rasch IRT model. The exact nature of these calculated ability scores was not made clear; however, they were highly correlated with the Rasch model based ability estimates, with all of the Pearson's r values lying between .75 and 1.00 and all but two correlations being .90 or greater. This analysis was conducted using the 257 children (ages between 6–16) from the initial standardization sample. This sample was also used to explore relationships among the unconstrained PTBI subscales using both Pearson r among subtest scores and exploratory factor analysis with Varimax rotation. The correlation coefficients among the subtest scores ranged from .29 to .79, with the majority falling between .45 and .60. The test authors conclude that the factor analysis revealed three factors among the unconstrained skill subtests. However, an examination of the factor loading matrix reveals that factors 2 and 3 each have only one observed subtest loading on them. Furthermore, two of the subtests (Word Fluency and What Goes Together) were cross loaded with multiple factors. Given these analytic problems, it was unclear how a practitioner might use the factor analysis results to gain insights into the construct validity of the PTBI. Finally, validity evidence was provided in terms of correlations between age and PTBI scores for typically developing children. The PTBI was administered to a sample of 77 children between ages 6 and 16, and Pearson's r was calculated between scores on the unconstrained skills subtests and age. The resulting values ranged from .39 to .70, indicating that performance on each of the subtests was better for older children.

As well as investigating various aspects of instrument validity, the test authors also report on two studies regarding the reliability of the PTBI. They report results for test-retest reliability from a sample of 40 children (ages 6 to 16) with no diagnosis of TBI or acquired brain injury. Participants were given the PTBI twice with sessions between 3 and 6 weeks apart (mean interval 32 days), and Pearson's r, adjusted for restriction of range, was calculated for scores from each subtest. These correlation coefficients ranged from .75 to 1.00. Interrater reliability was estimated using a sample of 41 children (ages 6 to 17), 15 of whom were diagnosed with TBI, 15 with acquired brain injury, and 11 with no brain injury. Each subtest was scored by a research assistant and one of 14 clinicians. Pearson's correlation coefficients were calculated between the clinician and research assistant scores. These values ranged from .98 to 1.00, indicating nearly exact agreement to exact agreement for each subtest.

In addition to evaluating the validity and reliability of the PTBI, the test authors report on research examining the possible presence of bias in the instrument. Of particular interest was the investigation of bias based upon some demographic factor (gender, ethnicity) in the assignment of diagnostic category for individual children. The distributions of diagnostic category for 70 white and 31 minority (24 African American, 4 Hispanic, 1 Asian, and 2 of "other" ethnicity) children were compared in terms of frequency counts. The test authors conclude that the groups fell into diagnostic groups at a "similar" rate; however, no formal hypothesis testing was conducted, nor were percents or proportions presented, making interpretation of the results somewhat difficult for the reader. Finally, the test authors conducted a Differential Item Functioning (DIF) analysis to identify specific items that might contain bias with respect to gender, ethnicity, or language status (mono- versus multilingual). They

report using an outdated approach known as the delta plot, and found some items exhibiting DIF, which were subsequently removed from the final scale. It was not clear why a more widely used method such as the Mantel-Haenszel test was not employed instead.

COMMENTARY. Although the PTBI is a somewhat brief measure, it still assesses multiple domains (e.g., memory, attention, executive functioning, language) that can be negatively impacted in children who sustain a TBI. The test authors note that they intended the test to be "brief enough to be usable in early acute phases but also broad enough to continue through later phases of rehabilitation, school reentry, and new learning" (examiner's manual, p. 15). Practitioners who are used to assessing children with brain injury will recognize some of the subtests as derivations of classic measures, a feature that assists with the validation of the PTBI. The examiner's manual provides a nice description of the theoretical constructs used in the creation of the measure, a good description of the sequelae of TBI in children, as well as an explanation of how the subtests assess these domains. The test is easy to administer and score, and the small number of test materials required to administer the test make it particularly useful for bedside evaluations (for which test materials are typically brought to a patient's room).

During the discussion of the case example, the test authors indicate the PTBI can be administered on a weekly basis; it would have been helpful for some comment regarding practice effects if this is done. The case example at the end of the examiner's manual is highly useful as it provides an example of how the subtests are scored, how the front page of the protocol is completed, how test results can be reported, and in which cases the PTBI would be useful.

In terms of the psychometric properties of the PTBI, there is much positive to say. There is a great deal in the way of validity evidence, and much of it points to the excellent coverage that the PTBI has of the constructs of interest. The PTBI was able to accurately differentiate among individuals with and without TBI, and scores on the PTBI were somewhat correlated with the Glasgow Coma Scale and Rancho Los Amigos Scale. In addition, investigations of item and instrument bias were conducted, results of which should prove particularly useful to practitioners interested in using the PTBI with a demographically varied population.

Although a notable strength of the psychometric evaluation of the PTBI is the number of validity and reliability studies that were reported, there are questions about how some of these studies were conducted. For example, as noted above, the comparison of means involved the use of 30 t-tests rather than ANOVA or MANOVA. The researchers also reported the supremacy of a 3-factor solution for their exploratory factor analysis despite the fact that 2 of the factors consisted of only a single subtest, and with no statistical evidence regarding the fit of this solution (e.g., proportion of variance explained, results of a parallel analysis). Also, the studies did not provide sufficient information regarding how the samples were selected. The test authors reported the demographic characteristics of each sample, but did not indicate whether they were randomly selected, purposefully selected, or convenience samples.

SUMMARY. The PTBI will be a useful addition to many practitioners who routinely evaluate children with brain injuries. It is particularly valuable in that a wide range of functional domains are able to be considered in a relatively short period of time; this is often helpful as fatigue and inattention are common features of children with TBI that can necessitate the use of shorter batteries. The PTBI uses cutoff scores and performance categories to describe performance, but some users may wish standard scores were available and for a more thorough description of how these cutoff scores were obtained. The test is easy to learn to administer and score, and interpretation is facilitated by following the extensive case example provided in the examiner's manual. The manual provides a large number of studies testifying to the psychometric qualities of the instruments though the questions raised above should be considered. In sum, the PTBI is a valuable tool that allows for the quantification of brain injury across multiple domains that are important for school reintegration following TBI, although some questions remain about the psychometric properties reported in the manual. As with any new test, future independent studies regarding the psychometric properties of the PTBI will be helpful.

REVIEWERS' REFERENCE

Hotz, G., Helm-Estabrooks, N., & Nelson, N. W. (2001). Development of the Pediatric Test of Brain Injury. *The Journal of Head Trauma Rehabilitation, 16*, 426-440.

Review of the Pediatric Test of Brain Injury by RAMA K. MISHRA, Neuropsychologist, Department of Psychiatry, Medicine Hat Regional Hospital, Medicine Hat, Alberta, Canada:

DESCRIPTION. The reported purpose of the Pediatric Test of Brain Injury (PTBI) is to estimate neurocognitive-linguistic skills of children between the ages of 6 and 16 years who have sustained brain injury. This test is also intended for tracking recovery from an acute phase to mild or normal range of functioning.

The battery consists of 10 subtests, 3 of which are described as constrained skills and the other 7 as unconstrained skills. The constrained skills include Orientation, Following Commands, and Naming; these skills develop early and remain consistent after that. Therefore, except for those with severe brain injury, children would be expected to obtain full scores on these tests. The tests that represent unconstrained skills include; Word Fuency, What Goes Together, Digit Span, Story Retelling-Immediate, Yes/No/Maybe, Picture Recall, and Story Retelling-Delayed. The test taker's responses can be recorded in the provided space. Clinicians can also record behavioral observations by checking off the given descriptions or writing additional observations in the space provided for each subtest. All items in each subtest are administered to all children except the Story Retelling subtest. In this subtest children are presented with one of three stories based on their grade level (Grades 1–3, 4–7, or 8–11). The estimated time to complete all 10 subtests is 30 minutes. With the exception of Word Fluency, each item of the subtests is represented by an ability score based on Item Response Theory (IRT). The Word Fluency score is the total number of words produced. The examiner is simply required to sum the scores of the correct responses for each subtest and compare the total to the tabulated values in an appendix to determine the level of performance (e.g., very low, low, moderate, and high) for the child's age group.

DEVELOPMENT. The test authors claim the PTBI uses a "conceptual framework of cognitive-linguistic abilities that are both developmentally appropriate for children and adolescents and particularly at risk following brain injury" (examiner's manual, p. 15). However, the test manual does not provide any description of how these abilities differentiate into higher level skills as the child develops from age 6 to age 16. Moreover, there was no description as to how the item contents in subtests were selected to reflect the developmental skills of the conceptual framework. Further, there were no descriptions of the impact of type and severity of head injury at different developmental stages.

The test authors report results of an exploratory factor analysis. They chose to report a 3-factor solution for the seven unconstrained subtests, where only one subtest, Digit Span, had a respectable loading of .97 on Factor 3. Factor 2 was a mixed bag with factors loadings of .57, .67, and .87 for Word Fluency, What Goes Together, and Picture Recall, respectively. Factor 1 had appreciable factor loadings from both Story Retelling subtests and the Yes/No/Maybe subtest.

This test is claimed to be a criterion-referenced test that provides threshold values for each subtest for each age for four severity classifications: very low, low, moderate, and high. There was no explanation as to how these classifications were determined.

Nevertheless, the test authors did accomplish their goal to keep the length of the test short enough to be usable during the acute phase of brain injury and broad enough to be useful through rehabilitation and return to school.

TECHNICAL. The final version of the test was administered to 134 children with Traumatic Brain Injury (TBI), 46 children with Acquired Brain Injury (ABI), and 77 children who were described as "typically developing" with a total sample of 257 children obtained from 14 hospital settings including two sites in Canada. There was no indication how the "typically developing" children were selected and the extent to which they were representative of the United States and Canadian population distributions with respect to age, gender, race, socioeconomic status, and so forth. Moreover, the test authors did not consider other possible comorbid conditions such as learning disability or developmental language disorder in their "typically developing" children; children with these comorbid conditions could have specific weaknesses on certain subtests.

The age and gender distributions of the total sample are presented in the test manual. There were more males in the TBI category (87 males compared to 47 females) and more females in the "typically developing" category (29 males compared to 48 females). Moreover, 32 cells (50%) had fewer than 3 subjects. The final determination of the performance category was based only on age, but not on gender, presumably due to minimal difference in IRT ability scores on subtest items for boys and girls. It would have been helpful to show the level of significance of the mean difference for boys and girls for all subtests including the Word Fluency

subtest where differential item functioning (DIF) could not be calculated.

Test-retest reliability coefficients for an average time lag of 32 days were reported and ranged from .75 to .99 for a group of 40 children without any history of TBI or ABI. The means and *SD*s for both Time 1 and Time 2 are presented in the examiner's manual. However, it has not been indicated if there was a significant difference between the two time scores for any subtest to explain possibilities of practice or fatigue effect.

Interrater reliability coefficients for a sample of 41 children consisting of 15 children with TBI, 15 children with ABI, and 11 without any brain injury were reported with values ranging from .98 to 1.00. The protocols of these 41 children were originally scored by 14 clinicians, presumably from the test sites, and then rescored by a research assistant using the recorded responses. It would have been useful to report whether these 41 children were randomly selected from the standardization sample of 257 children. Other reliability estimates, such as internal consistency, are not reported.

With respect to validity, the test authors claim that criterion-related validity and construct-identification validity have been demonstrated. Criterion-related validity correlation coefficients were reported using the Glasgow Coma Scale (GCS) and the Rancho Los Amigos Scale (RLAS). The correlation coefficients of the unconstrained subtests of the PTBI were reported to be between -.5 and .58 with GCS and between .03 and .56 with RLAS. The test authors also demonstrated that children with TBI and ABI scored significantly lower than children without brain injury on all unconstrained tests, indicating possible construct related validity. However, no cognitive or linguistic tests were used as criterion measures.

COMMENTARY. The goal of assessing current ability levels of children with brain injury on the subtests included in the PTBI has been achieved. However, it has not been shown how tracking changes over time can be accomplished. No parallel versions of the tests were developed to minimize practice or familiarity effects. The sensitivity and specificity of the test have not been reported for severity of brain injury or for recovery following brain injury. As a result, it is not clear if improvement following brain injury can be captured by this test. There are no guidelines to show how frequently the clinician should re-administer this test so that changes in cognitive and linguistic skills can be documented after taking the standard error of measurement (*SEM*) into account. In fact, some of the subtest *SEM*s are so large that it would be difficult to show improvement following rehabilitation.

The test authors have suggested that for an acute phase of brain injury the test can be divided into two sessions, with Subtests 1–5 in Session 1 and Subtests 6–10 in Session 2. The test authors note that both sessions must take place on the same day. Comparisons of test scores from a single session to a split session for matched samples have not been reported.

The major strengths of this test are that it is clinician friendly and takes only 30 minutes to complete. As a result it is quite likely that clinicians would be able to use the entire battery even for children in acute care settings.

The major drawbacks of this test lie in an inadequate conceptual framework, and incomplete descriptions of procedures used in item selection, sample selection, test development, and validity indicators. In this regard, it would have been helpful to report the results of a confirmatory factor analysis based on the conceptual model. In addition, the reported factors could be used to group the subtests into factors for reporting the performance of children.

It has not been clarified how the selected subtests capture important skills lost during brain injury. Important information such as localization of injury, severity, and time since injury, and their impact on the selected subtests has not been taken into account.

It is presumed that some items were dropped or modified for the final version of the test based on the item characteristics based on IRT model and other criteria during the pilot studies. It would have been useful to provide the Item Characteristic Curves (ICC) for the final items in each subtest so that the clinicians and researchers could see the distribution of difficulty indices and understand relative importance of that item for specific children in their clinical practice or research studies.

Many other important aspects of language such as reading, writing, organization of narratives, and so on have not been included in this test battery. The cognitive domain is extremely limited. It would be difficult to prepare a comprehensive intervention plan based on the skills assessed by this test.

No attempts were made to include criterion measures to validate the test with respect to its cognitive and linguistic domains. No achievement

tests were used to show how school performance can be predicted from this brief test, which is one of its stated purposes.

SUMMARY. The test authors' efforts to develop this test is commendable. Almost 10 years ago Hotz, Helm-Estabrooks, and Nelson (2001) articulated their vision for this test, which has finally become a reality. They had a very ambitious goal of assessing "full range of cognitive-linguistic impairments following brain injury" (Hotz, Helm-Estabrooks, & Nelson, 2001, p. 426) in as little as 30 minutes. They also wanted to track changes, make recommendations for treatment planning, and help children function well in school. The PTBI may have the potential to achieve some of these goals by focusing on a very specific objective, including tests based on a conceptual model as well as confirmatory factor analysis, adaptive testing procedures (progressive starting and discontinuing points), developing parallel forms for tracking progress, objective scoring criteria to increase internal consistency and interrater reliability, and using multiple criterion measures that are similar and dissimilar in characteristics. The sample selection could be improved by including Census-matched characteristics with respect to gender, age, ethnicity, geographical location, socioeconomic status, and family background for the non-brain-injured children. It would be quite risky for clinicians to use this test in its present form for this highly sensitive population not only from a clinical point of view, but also because of litigation and insurance settlement issues associated with TBI and some cases of ABI.

REVIEWER'S REFERENCE

Hotz, G., Helm-Estabrooks, N., & Nelson, N. W. (2001). Development of the pediatric test of brain injury. *Journal of Head Trauma Rehabilitation, 16*(5), 426-440.

[130]

Preschool Language Scales, Fifth Edition.

Purpose: Designed to "identify children who have a language delay or disorder."

Population: Ages birth to 7-11.

Publication Dates: 1969-2011.

Acronym: PLS-5.

Scores, 5: Auditory Comprehension, Expressive Communication, Total Language; 2 optional scores: Articulation, Mean Length of Utterance.

Administration: Individual.

Price Data, 2013: $349 per complete kit with manipulatives including examiner's manual (2011, 119 pages), administration and scoring nanual (2011, 191 pages), picture manual, 15 record forms, and 25 Home Communication Questionnaires; $288 per basic kit without manipulatives including examiner's manual, administration and scoring manual, picture manual, 15 record forms, and 25 Home Communication Questionnaires; $133 per set of manipulatives; $61 per 15 record forms; $10.30 per 25 Home Communication Questionnaires; $57.75 per examiner's manual; $167 per picture manual; $109 per administration and scoring manual.

Foreign Language Edition: Spanish edition available.

Time: (25-50) minutes.

Comments: Fifth edition includes some new items, scoring changes, and norms based on 2008 U.S. Census data.

Authors: Irla Lee Zimmerman, Violette G. Steiner, and Roberta Evatt Pond.

Publisher: Pearson.

a) ARTICULATION SCREENER.

Purpose: Designed to evaluate articulation in single words.

Population: Ages 2-6 to 7-11.

Scores: Total score only.

Comments: "Criterion-referenced" optional subtest.

b) LANGUAGE SAMPLE CHECKLIST.

Purpose: Designed to evaluate spontaneous speech.

Population: Ages 1 to 7-11.

Scores: Mean Length of Utterance.

Comments: Supplemental measure to help validate information obtained from the Expressive Communication scale.

c) HOME COMMUNICATION QUESTIONNAIRE.

Purpose: Designed to give "the caregiver's perspective of a child's communication behaviors" at home, preschool, or daycare.

Population: Ages birth to 2-11.

Scores: Not scored.

Time: (10-15) minutes.

Comments: Supplemental questionnaire.

Cross References: For reviews by Terri Flowerday and Hoi K. Suen of a previous edition, see 16:198; see also T5:2045 (6 references); for reviews by J. Jeffrey Grill and Janet A. Norris of a previous edition, see 13:241 (26 references); see also T4:2084 (24 references); for an excerpted review by Barton B. Proger of a previous edition, see 8:929 (3 references); see also T2:2024 (1 reference); for a review by Joel Stark and an excerpted review by C. H. Ammons, see 7:965.

Review of the Preschool Language Scales, Fifth Edition by THOMAS McKNIGHT, Psychologist, Private Practice, Spokane, WA:

DESCRIPTION. According to the test authors, the Fifth Edition of this instrument continues to have a number of uses for children, birth through 7 years 11 months, including measuring possible language delay, assessment of relative strength and weakness of language development, determining

eligibility for early intervention programs, and evaluating the efficacy of speech and language treatment programs. The test authors claim that the instrument can be used with children over the upper age limit "who function developmentally within this age range" (examiner's manual, p. 3). Supplemental measures include a Home Communication Questionnaire, Language Sample Checklist, and Articulation Screener. There is notation this instrument can be administered, scored, and interpreted by speech-language pathologists, early childhood specialists, psychologists, educational diagnosticians, and "other professionals" with training in individual assessment and experience working with children. "Paraprofessional staff can be trained" (manual, p. 8) to administer test items and record responses but scoring and interpretation "should only be done by a clinician who has training and experience in diagnostic assessment" (manual, p. 8).

DEVELOPMENT. The stated goal of this revision was to improve the instrument's psychometric properties, reflecting changes in the population of the United States based on the 2008 Census, needs of clinicians, best practices in speech-language assessment of young children, and current research. Changes were also made due to "current legislation" and recommendations, coming from 500 clinicians who used the Fourth Edition.

TECHNICAL. Standardization data for the PLS-5 were collected from 1,400 individuals during a 9-month period in 2010. The normative sample was stratified according to the 2008 Census data, reflecting the increasing diversity of the U.S. population. Inspection of reported data indicates this goal was generally achieved with information reported about geographic region, race/ethnicity, sex, child's learning environment, and age/educational level of the primary care provider.

Assessment results can be reported as standard scores, percentile ranks, and age equivalent scores for the Auditory Comprehension and Expressive Communication scales, and a Total Language score can be calculated. Standard scores range from 50 to 150. Norm based criterion scores are reported for the Articulation Screener, beginning at 2 years, 6 months.

The range of interrater reliability coefficients, reported by age groups, is .96 to .99. There were 25–28 participants in each of the 6 cells (birth to 3:11 and 4:0-7:11 for Auditory Comprehension, Expressive Communication, and Total Language). Interscorer agreement, for items that required scoring judgment, ranged from 91.9% to 100%. Split-half reliability for each of the 18 age groups across three scales varied from .80 to .98. Coefficients were higher for more narrow ability ranges (.96–.98 for children with a "language disorder" and .93–.97 for those identified as "language delayed"). Test-retest reliability coefficients (unadjusted) ranged from .78 to .94. Correcting for the variability of the sample resulted in adjusted coefficients of .86 to .95.

Concurrent validity evidence for the PLS-5 derived from comparisons with its Fourth Edition and the Clinical Evaluation of Language Fundamentals Preschool–Second Edition. These comparisons yielded coefficients that ranged from .64 to .84 (.66 to .85 adjusted), rather expected given the differences between instruments. Again, coefficients were inflated when "corrected for variability." Studies found the PLS-5 efficiently distinguished between language-delayed children and nonclinical, matched samples. Effect size was large, with standard differences above 1.5 and significant at the .01 level.

COMMENTARY. The PLS-5 face validity is good, rather expected given the feedback of speech/language pathologists, and others, who have used the four earlier editions. Drawings are colorful and expected to appeal to the children for whom the instrument was designed. The administration and scoring manual is detailed and clear, as is the record form. However, this is a complicated instrument and prospective users should not simply assume prior experience with other instruments qualifies them to administer and score the PLS-5. Inadequate preparation may result in administration and scoring mistakes that can produce significant interpretive errors that can, in turn, seriously impact a child's education. Qualified examiners who choose to train a paraprofessional must provide specific training, to include observation and rescoring of multiple practice administrations. Too, all notations and responses to items must be reviewed to assure clarity and accuracy before scoring.

The PLS-5 has added items to "reflect current research on language development…in gestural communication, theory of mind, and emergent literacy" (examiner's manual, p. 41); what this means, however, is not entirely clear. Of concern is the limited number of individuals comprising the normative sample, which leads to extremely low numbers in individual cells.

SUMMARY. Like previous editions of the Preschool Language Scale, the Fifth Edition will be a useful instrument in the assessment of language development/delay in young children. Speech/language pathologists, developmental or school psychologists, and early education specialists are expected to embrace this revision. Additional validity studies, using larger numbers of children and other instruments of similar kind, are needed.

Review of the Preschool Language Scales, Fifth Edition by KATHY L. SHAPLEY, Assistant Professor of Speech Pathology, University of Arkansas Little Rock/University of Arkansas for Medical Sciences, Little Rock, AR:

DESCRIPTION. The Preschool Language Scales, Fifth Edition (PLS-5) is an individually administered test for children ages birth to 7 years 11 months. The purpose of the PLS-5 is to identify children who have a language delay or disorder. The PLS-5 consists of an administration and scoring manual, examiner's manual, picture manual, record form, and home communication questionnaire. Manipulatives can be purchased with the kit, or clinicians can use their own items.

The PLS-5 can be used to identify both receptive and expressive language delays/disorders. The categories assessed in the Auditory Comprehension (AC) scale include attention, gesture, play, semantics, language structure, integrative language, and emergent literacy. The items on the AC scale require children to follow directions and point to items/pictures. The skills assessed in the Expressive Communication (EC) scale include vocal development, gesture, social communication, semantics, language structure, integrative language, and emergent literacy. Children are asked to name objects, express quantity, and use specific grammatical markers and sentence structures.

Administration time varies from 25–50 minutes depending on the age of the child. Colored adhesive tabs are provided to label the administration and scoring manual for easy access to each age group. Suggested starting points are included in 2-month intervals from birth to 11 months and in 6-month intervals from 1:0 to 7:11. For ages birth to 2:11, Caregiver report (CR), Observation (O), and Elicitation (E) can be used to assess skills. Scoring criteria and examples are provided for each item. All items, for all ages, are scored as 1 or 0. Basal and ceiling rules are the same for both the AC and EC scales. A basal is achieved when three consecutive numbered items are scored as 1. A ceiling is achieved when six consecutive numbered items are scored as 0.

The PLS-5 provides norm-referenced scores (standard scores, percentile ranks, and age equivalents) for the AC and EC scales. A norm-referenced Total Language score can also be calculated. Scores are available at 3-month intervals for birth through 11 months, and 6-month intervals for 1:0 to 7:11. Norm-based criterion scores are reported for the Articulation Screener for children 2:6 to 7:11. Growth scale values can be calculated to monitor progress over multiple test administrations for children ages birth through 7:11. The PLS-5 can also be used as a criterion-referenced measure for children who are older but who function developmentally within the birth to 7:11 age range.

The PLS-5 includes three supplemental measures: the Language Sample Checklist, the Articulation Screener, and the Home Communication Questionnaire. The Language Sample Checklist (LSC) can be used with children who speak in connected utterances. The LSC provides an overview of a child's spontaneous utterances and an estimate of the mean length of utterance (MLU). The Articulation Screener (AS) is used to determine whether a diagnostic evaluation of articulation is warranted. The LSC and the AS are included in the record form. The Home Communication Questionnaire is a separate form and provides the clinician with the caregiver's perspective of a child's communication skills.

DEVELOPMENT. The PLS-5 is the fourth revision of the Preschool Language Scale. Approximately 25% of the items remained unchanged from PLS-4, 50% of the PLS-4 items were modified either by reducing the number of subitems or changing the number of practice items. Twenty-five percent of the items are new. The development cycle included both a pilot phase and a tryout phase.

During the pilot phase, a bias review panel consisting of six experts reviewed the modified and new items to determine whether the items were appropriate and fair for children from different ethnic groups, socioeconomic status, and regions of the country. Panel members were selected based on their expertise in assessment, cultural/linguistic diversity, and/or regional issues. Two field tests were conducted: one with children ages birth to 7:11 (n = 42) and one with children ages 7:0–7:11 (n = 35). Items were eliminated and administration directions were modified based on these results.

During the tryout phase, data were collected from two samples: a nonclinical sample of children (n = 455) and a clinical sample (n = 169). The pilot

bias review panel members and four additional speech-language pathologists were asked to review the test prior to data collection. Reportedly, results from traditional Mantel-Haenszel bias analyses and Item Response Theory (IRT) bias analyses were used to analyze the data. At this stage items were either rewritten to correct the bias or dropped from the item set for the standardization. Scoring guidelines were also refined during this stage.

TECHNICAL. The standardization sample includes data from 1,400 children collected by 189 examiners in 42 states with additional samples for reliability and validity studies. From birth to 11 months the sample size was 50 per each 3-month age group. For ages 1:0–5:11 the sample size was 100 per each 6-month age group. For 6:0–7:11 the sample size was 50 per each 6-month age group. The sample is representative of the 2008 U.S. Census data for race/ethnicity, geographic region, and primary caregiver's level of education for children birth to 7:11. Males and females were equally represented. Children with various educational classifications and diagnoses were included in the normative sample, including those with speech-language disorders and developmental delays who comprised 3.9% and 1.1% of the total sample, respectively.

The following evidence of reliability was provided: A sample of 195 children from the normative sample was used to estimate test-retest reliability. The children ranged in age from birth to 7:11 and the demographic characteristics percentages of the test-retest sample were representative of the 2008 U.S. Census. The test interval was an appropriate range for the construct being assessed (i.e., 3 to 28 days with an average of 7.8 days). The average corrected coefficients range from .86–.95 for the different age ranges indicating good to excellent test stability. To assess how consistently the items measure the construct, internal consistency estimates were examined (AERA, APA, & NCME, 1999). Split-half reliability coefficients were reported for the normative sample: AC ranged from .80–.97 and EC ranged from .82–.97. Split-half reliability coefficients were also calculated for children with diagnosed language disorder (n = 229) and ranged from .96–.98, and for those with language delay (n = 23) ranged from .93–.97. Overall, the internal consistency of the test ranged from good (r > .80) to excellent (r > .90), indicating the items measure the same constructs (purportedly, receptive and expressive language). Interrater reliabilities ranged from .96–.99, and interscorer agreement for items that required scoring judgments ranged from 91.9%–100.0%. These results suggest that the scoring rules were clear and objective.

The following evidence of content validity was provided: Test items were developed based on literature review, user feedback, and expert review panels. Response process was assessed at each phase of development to ensure that items assessed intended skill and were age appropriate, and that confounding processes were minimized (e.g., picture supports were provided to minimize auditory memory). Evidence of construct validity was provided based on adjusted correlations between the PLS-5 and other language ability tests. One study examined scores on PLS-4 and PLS-5 for 134 children ages birth to 6:11. Correlation coefficients between scores on the two tests were .80 (AC and EC) and .85 (Total Language), indicating a high correlation between the two tests. Adjusted correlations between scores on the PLS-5 and Clinical Evaluation of Language Fundamentals Preschool–Second Edition (CELF-P2) for 97 children ages 3:0–6:11 ranged from .70 (PLS-5 AC/CELF-Preschool 2 Receptive Language) to .82 (PLS-5 EC/CELF-Preschool 2 Expressive Language and PLS-5 Total Language/CELF-Preschool 2 Expressive Language), indicating a moderate to high correlation between the two tests. Positive and negative predictive power (PPP and NPP) are included for five different base rates: screening at 20%; referral at 70%, 80%, and 90%; and 50% for a matched clinical sample. Results indicate the further below the mean a child's score lies, PPP is higher and NPP is lower; sensitivity and specificity are .83 and .80, respectively.

COMMENTARY. The PLS-5 is a comprehensive language assessment for children ages birth to 7:11. It is easy to administer and simple to score. The test manual includes clear and concise administration directions and scoring examples. The standardization sample is robust and reflects the current ethnic minority and socioeconomic status distributions in the United States. The inclusion of a limited set of items to assess play skills and emergent literacy strengthen the versatility and utility of the test. The test has been expanded to include children ages 7:0–7:11. The examiner's manual is easy to read and provides explanations of psychometric evidence in user-friendly terms.

Criticisms of the previous edition included the lack of positive and negative predictive power

and a factor analysis. The PLS-5 includes PPP and NPP for five base rates; however, a factor analysis was not conducted.

SUMMARY. The PLS-5 is a norm-referenced assessment of preschool and early language development. The test publisher provides multiple sources of evidence of reliability and validity that the test is appropriate for measuring a young child's language ability. Overall, the evidence of the psychometric properties of the PLS-5 is strong.

REVIEWER'S REFERENCE
American Educational Research Association, American Psychological Association, & National Council on Measurement in Education. (1999). *Standards for educational and psychological testing.* Washington, DC: American Educational Research Association.

[131]
Preschool Language Scales—Fifth Edition Screening Test.

Purpose: Designed "to assist in the identification of children who may need in-depth assessment of their speech and language abilities."

Population: Ages birth to 7-11.

Publication Date: 2012.

Acronym: PLS-5 Screening Test.

Administration: Individual.

Levels and Forms: 8 forms, 9 age-group levels.

Price Data, 2013: $153.50 per complete kit including stimulus book/test manual (255 pages) and 25 record forms for each age; $133 per stimulus book/test manual; $35.75 per 25 record forms (age birth to 11 months, age 1, age 2, age 3, age 4, age 5, age 6, or age 7).

Foreign Language Edition: Spanish edition available.

Time: (5-10) minutes.

Authors: Irla Lee Zimmerman, Violette G. Steiner, and Roberta Evatt Pond.

Publisher: Pearson.

  a) AGE BIRTH TO 0:11.

  Scores, 3: Language, Feeding, Social/Interpersonal.

  Comments: Form is subdivided into two age-group levels: ages 0-0 to 0-5 and 0-6 to 0-11.

  b) AGE 1.

  Scores, 3: Language, Feeding, Social/Interpersonal.

  c) AGE 2.

  Scores, 3: Language, Social/Interpersonal, Articulation (ages 2-6 to 2-11).

  d) AGE 3.

  Scores, 6: Language, Articulation, Connected Speech, Social/Interpersonal, Fluency, Voice.

  e) AGE 4.

  Scores, 6: Language, Articulation, Connected Speech, Social/Interpersonal, Fluency, Voice.

  f) AGE 5.

  Scores, 6: Language, Articulation, Connected Speech, Social/Interpersonal, Fluency, Voice.

g) AGE 6.
Scores, 6: Language, Articulation, Connected Speech, Social/Interpersonal, Fluency, Voice.
h) AGE 7.
Scores, 6: Language, Articulation, Connected Speech, Social/Interpersonal, Fluency, Voice.

Review of the Preschool Language Scales–Fifth Edition Screening Test by AIMÉE LANGLOIS, Professor Emerita, Department of Child Development, Humboldt State University, Arcata, CA:

DESCRIPTION. The Preschool Language Scales–Fifth Edition Screening Test (PLS-5 Screening Test) purports to identify in less than 10 minutes children between birth and 7 years and 11 months of age who may need to be referred for in-depth speech and/or language assessment. The test includes eight scoring forms, one for each of eight age levels with the earliest form subdivided into two ages: 0:0-0:5 and 0:6-0:11. For infants and toddlers, Language, Feeding, and Social/Interpersonal skills are screened; Feeding is not tested in older children whose Articulation, Connected Speech, Fluency, and Voice are checked. The test includes a stimulus book/test manual and 25 record forms for each age. In addition, testers who screen infants and toddlers under the age of 3 years must procure up to 15 manipulatives.

The test manual delineates users' responsibilities, explains test administration procedures, and provides psychometric data about the test. Examiners must become familiar with the materials, follow the instructions exactly, and ensure the children's comfort. Yet, the seating arrangement is awkward as the child faces the easel stimulus book while the examiner, seated at a right angle to the child (or at the left angle to the child if the examiner is left-handed), must read the instructions on the easel's opposite side, see pictures to which the child points, and point to pictures the child is to identify. Testers must therefore move back and forth between the side of the easel with pictures and the side with instructions. They must also simultaneously score the child's response and flip the stimulus book's pages, while maintaining rapport with the child.

The score sheets specify scoring procedures and passing scores for each area tested, yielding a screening summary that identifies areas for additional testing. At first glance, scoring appears straightforward. However, several factors complicate the process; one relates to the subjectivity required to score many items, which reduces reliability between examiners. Another refers to a lack of precision about

involving caregivers. The test authors provide general guidelines for doing so but the likelihood of variability among examiners as well as caregivers is high. Because testers must adhere to the instructions, lest reliability and validity are compromised, the scripts (or questions provided) for talking to caregivers and directives to follow when they do not comply need to be followed. The last factor involves scoring items for which dialectal variations exist. To decide what dialect children use requires examiners to have prior knowledge of their background, an endeavor that can add minutes to screening time in some environments. The test manual is unclear about this issue and the record form does not include a space in which to enter a child's dialect.

DEVELOPMENT. The test authors intended to meet "the need for a broad-based speech and language screener that is comprehensive and based on sound research, yet quick to administer" (manual, p. 1). As such, the PLS-5 Screening covers critical communication development areas and is reported to take less than 10 minutes to administer. Given that essential requirements of a speech and language screening test are comprehensiveness and rapidity of administration, the test appears sound. Although the PLS-5 Screening Test was revised from the PLS-4 Screening Test, the rationale for the revision and an explanation of how this new test differs from the prior version are not provided.

Item development. The test authors selected the items and tasks for the language and articulation sections of the test from those on the PLS-5 (a comprehensive language assessment tool) that had previously discriminated best between children with typical language skills and those with language disorders. No data are provided on this aspect of item development. The test authors provide a sound rationale for selecting items for the feeding, connected speech, social/interpersonal, voice, and fluency sections from the literature.

TECHNICAL.
Standardization. The 1,400 children from across the country who were part of the standardization process for the PLS-5 became the norming group for the PSL-5 Screening Test. They ranged in age from birth to 7:11 years with 100–200 children per age level, and included equal numbers of boys and girls. They also represented the U.S. population in terms of geographical area, race/ethnicity, and primary caregiver's education level. Given that age is the basis upon which PLS-5 Screening Test users select a form to administer, 100 or more children at

each age level is a number high enough to ensure that norms are stable. Yet, lacking from the group's description is information about the children who spoke different dialects of English. Because the test manual provides dialectal variations in order to score many grammatical items, data on these children is essential lest they be confused with those on ethnicity and race.

Criterion scores. The criterion scores for Language, Articulation, Social/Interpersonal skills in 3- to 8-year-olds, Voice, and Fluency reflect data gathered during the development of the PLS-5 and the PLS-5 Screening Test. Those for Feeding, Connected Speech, and Social/Interpersonal skills from birth to 3 are based on the literature. Although the test authors present numerous statistics and focus on the relevant literature, their reliance on scores from previous tests raises questions as to why this test was designed and how it differs from earlier versions.

Reliability. Test-retest reliability coefficients are only provided for the Language and Articulation scores gathered during the development of the PLS-5; these are high and suggest that results of testing in these areas are stable over time. However, there is neither evidence of test-retest reliability in the other areas screened nor of interrater reliability. Because subjectivity is inherent in scoring parts of the test, the absence of data about both types of reliability raises questions about the test's potential for false positive and false negative identifications.

Validity. Because the Language and Articulation items on the PLS-5 Screening Test were selected from the most discriminating items on the PLS-5, the section on content validity refers to that of the parent test and provides no data. Likewise, although the test authors state that "the tasks elicited intended responses" (manual, p. 31), information about response process validity research is not given.

Criterion validity was established only for the language scores by comparing those obtained on the PLS-5 Screening Test to those obtained on three other tests. The data collected reveal high correlation coefficients and percentage of agreements, thus indicating that the test accurately identifies children with typical language skills and those with delays and disorders. However, the data leave in doubt the predictive validity of the whole test because scores from the other areas screened were not similarly researched nor were the screening summaries. Absent this information, its usefulness

is compromised. The test authors also researched the sensitivity and specificity of the test by analyzing language scores only. They obtained probability levels of 80% and higher for both children with language delay and those with language disorders, indicating that the chances of correctly identifying children for whom additional information is needed in the language area are good. However, there is no information on specificity and sensitivity for the entire test and for children with typical speech and language skills, further eroding the predictive validity of the test.

Qualifications of examiner. Experienced professionals who work with children qualify as examiners as do teachers' aides and other ancillary personnel. Yet, because the test uses terms mostly familiar to speech-language pathologists (e.g., "sound combination," "pragmatic functions," "post-noun elaboration," "modifying noun phrase") other examiners may lack such knowledge and thus misunderstand the instructions. This varied group might also differ from those who administered the test for its standardization, whose professional background is unknown. In light of absent interrater reliability, this issue needs to be addressed.

COMMENTARY. The PLS-5 Screening Test is a quick and comprehensive instrument that leads to the identification of children who need further evaluation to determine whether a speech and/or language disorder exists. The strength of the test lies in the short amount of time it takes to administer and in its breadth. In addition, standardization is based on adequately large groups of children representative of the U.S. population, and the extensive review of the literature that guided item selection demonstrates good content validity.

However, several concerns about test administration discussed above and major concerns about the test's reliability and validity raise questions about its soundness. Specifically, there are no test-retest reliability data for the entire test and no interrater reliability information is offered. Likewise, there is no predictive validity evidence for the whole test nor for children with normally developing communication skills. Because standardized screening tests must be psychometrically sound in order to be adequate (Crais, 2011), the PLS-5 Screening Test falls short of adequacy.

SUMMARY. The PLS-5 Screening Test covers a wide age range, and is comprehensive and quick to administer. However, unless the issues raised above are addressed and appropriate psychometric studies conducted, its clinical value is uncertain. Unfortunately, a test that meets the above three criteria and is psychometrically sound does not exist.

REVIEWER'S REFERENCE

Crais, E. R. (2011). Testing and beyond: Strategies and tools for evaluating and assessing infants and toddlers. *Language Speech and Hearing Services in Schools, 42*, 351–364.

Review of the Preschool Language Scales–Fifth Edition Screening Test by SHAWN POWELL, Dean, Social and Behavioral Sciences, Casper College, and MARIA I. KUZNETSOVA, Assistant Lecturer of Psychology, University of Wyoming, Casper, WY:

DESCRIPTION. The Preschool Language Scales–Fifth Edition (PLS-5) Screening Test is an individually administered, norm-referenced speech and language screening measure. It is not designed as a diagnostic instrument to determine the presence of a speech or language disability, but rather as a screening tool that may indicate the need for further evaluation. The PLS-5 Screening Test is suitable for the brief assessment of speech and language abilities in children from birth to 7 years 11 months of age. The test is not timed. The test authors state administration should take 5 to 10 minutes, although the test manual specifies breaks are allowed to ensure valid testing results are obtained.

For infants under the age of 2 years, caregivers are asked questions about the child and are asked to follow standardized instructions to elicit certain target behaviors from the child that are rated by the evaluator (i.e., a caregiver may be asked to hold the child while others are talking in proximity to the child to determine the child's response to others' conversation). The test manual allows credit to be given on some test items when an infant's behavior is not directly observed by the evaluator based on the caregiver's report (i.e., if an infant is nonresponsive to a given situation and the caregiver reports the infant displays the behavior in other settings, then credit for the item is allowed). When using the PLS-5 Screening Test to assess children from birth up to and including ages 2 years 11 months, examiners must provide manipulatives (e.g., infant toys, spoon, keys) that are not included in the testing kit.

The test can be administered by professionals trained and experienced with standardized testing procedures. Paraprofessionals are allowed to administer the PLS-5 Screening Test after practicing administration and scoring several times under supervision.

The PLS-5 Screening Test has eight separate record forms for the following age groups: birth to 11 months, age 1, age 2, age 3, age 4, age 5, age 6, and age 7. Depending on the child's age, different domains are assessed including: Language, Feeding, Articulation, Connected Speech, Social/Interpersonal, Fluency, and Voice. The examiner uses a spiral-bound manual with an easel format to show individual stimulus pages to the child and administers items appropriate for the child's age. There are pass criterion scores provided for each domain and each age group.

DEVELOPMENT. The PLS-5 Screening Test is the latest version (copyright, 2012) of a test that has been in use for over 40 years (Zimmerman & Steiner, 1970). The original PLS was intended to measure language development in young children. This goal has continued to be the primary focus of the revisions of this language assessment scale since its inception. The PLS-5 Screening Test was based on the fifth edition of the Preschool Language Scales (PLS-5; Zimmerman, Steiner, & Pond, 2011). The test authors selected items from the PLS-5 that had the best psychometric properties in developing the shorter screening version of their speech and language assessment instrument. Items from the PLS-5 that were used in the PLS-5 Screening Test reportedly were ones that best differentiated children with language disorders from children with normal language development, assessed receptive and expressive language skills, and included developmentally appropriate speech sounds in regard to the "initial, medial, and final positions of words" (manual, p. 22).

The test authors cite recent literature addressing feeding development, speech and language development, language disorders, social and interpersonal development, and psycholinguistics, which they used in adapting and developing test items. The developers do not specify which theoretical approach they used to guide the selection of literature used for item construction.

TECHNICAL. The standardization sample for the PLS-5 consisted of 1,400 children ages birth to 7 years and 11 months. It should be noted there was not a separate standardization process for the PLS-5 Screening Test. The test authors claim that their sample was representative of U.S. Census demographics based on sex, race/ethnicity, caregiver's education level, and geographic region. The test manual does not include the specific geographical locations that were used when the normative sample was collected beyond four regions of the United States (e.g., Northeast, Midwest, South, and West).

Evidence of test-retest stability for language total scores was based on a study that used a sample of 189 children, where percentage of classification agreement ranged between 88.9% and 95.7% depending on the age group. Test-retest stability for articulation scores was determined based on a sample of 133 children, where percentage of classification agreement ranged between 91.7% and 100% across the age groups.

The test authors present an extensive section in which they offer evidence in support of the validity of test score use in the manual. The validity sources listed include literature reviews, users' feedback, expert review, comparisons with other measures, and indications of specificity and sensitivity for specific clinical populations. To support construct validity the developers compared the PLS-5 Screening Test to the Clinical Evaluation of Language Fundamentals Preschool–Second Edition (Wiig, Secord, & Semel, 2004). This comparison used a sample of 96 children. The classification accuracy for these two measures was reported as 99%. The developers also conducted a study comparing performance on the PLS-5 Screening Test in clinical samples (children with developmental delay and language disorder) with that of a non-clinical matched sample, and reported statistically significant differences in the language total scores between these groups.

Sensitivity and specificity of the measure were reported. For children with developmental language delays, the reported PLS-5 Screening Test sensitivity was .80 and specificity was .84. For children identified as having language disorders the reported sensitivity was .83, with .84 specificity. As a result, false positives, identified as children needing a more in-depth assessment when, in fact, these children did not have a language delay/disorder, accounted for 44%. Conversely, false negatives, identified as children who passed the test when, in fact, they should have been referred for further speech and language assessments, accounted for only 5%.

COMMENTARY. The PLS-5 Screening Test is the latest version of a well-established speech and language assessment. It appears to demonstrate strong evidence of good construct validity in making screening decisions regarding the need to refer or not to refer a child for additional evaluation compared to other language assessment instruments. The high false positive rate may be attributed to variations

that occur in language development among young children, especially as the test's age range was lowered in this version. Nonetheless, the high rate of false positives may result in excessive and unnecessary in-depth speech and language assessments.

The PLS-5 Screening Test was developed based on the normative sample for the PLS-5. Because the PLS-5 Screening Test was not separately administered to a standardization sample, it is difficult to draw direct conclusions regarding its own normative properties. The reliability and validity information presented is sufficient to support the use of the PLS-5 Screening Test in clinical and school-based settings. The adequacy of the theoretical underpinnings of the PLS-5 Screening Test is difficult to determine based on presented evidence. As this is a screening measure based on a more comprehensive assessment, namely the PLS-5, which is developmentally sequenced in its administration, the empirical basis for its use appears sound. Although having eight different record forms allows for flexibility in administration and ordering, the number of different protocols for this screening instrument is somewhat unwieldy.

SUMMARY. The PLS-5 Screening Test is the latest version of a popular language assessment screening instrument. It is designed to be given in an individual format and administered by trained professionals and/or supervised paraprofessionals. This test has expanded age groups compared to other language screening instruments. The PLS-5 Screening Test has adequate reported reliability and validity properties. The test authors appear to have updated this speech and language assessment measure on a regular basis by following recent research in the area of language development. It is a cost-effective measure that can be used in a variety of settings to assist in determining whether a child needs a more in-depth language evaluation.

REVIEWERS' REFERENCES

Wiig, E. H., Secord, W. A., & Semel, E. (2004). Clinical Evaluation of Language Fundamentals Preschool–Second Edition. San Antonio, TX: Harcourt Assessment.
Zimmerman, I. L., & Steiner, V. G. (1970, April). *Validity and evaluation of the preschool language scale.* Paper presented at the Western Psychological Association Convention, Los Angeles, CA.
Zimmerman, I. L., Steiner, V. G., & Pond, R. E. (2011). Preschool Language Scales–Fifth Edition. San Antonio, TX: Pearson.

[132]

Preschool Language Scales—Fifth Edition Spanish.

Purpose: A "dual-language assessment" designed "to identify a language delay or disorder in children who are monolingual Spanish speakers or bilingual Spanish-English speakers."

Population: Children from birth to age 7-11 whose primary language is Spanish.

Publication Date: 2012.

Acronym: PLS-5 Spanish.

Scores, 5: Auditory Comprehension, Expressive Communication, Total Language; 2 optional scores: Articulation, Mean Length of Utterance in Words.

Administration: Individual.

Price Data, 2013: $386 per complete kit with manipulatives including examiner's manual (135 pages), picture manual, administration and scoring manual (217 pages), 15 record forms, and 25 Home Communication Questionnaires; $335 per basic kit without manipulatives including examiner's manual, picture manual, administration/scoring manual, 15 record forms, and 25 Home Communication Questionnaires; $55 per Spanish manipulatives set; $10.45 per package of two Spanish children's books; $67 per 15 record forms; $10.30 per 25 Home Communication Questionnaires; $56.70 per examiner's manual; $167 per picture manual; $109 per administration and scoring manual.

Foreign Language Edition: English edition available.

Time: (30-65) minutes.

Comments: Administrators need "native or near-native proficiency in Spanish"; examiner's manual is written in English; administration and scoring manual is written in English and Spanish; normative data based on children whose primary language is Spanish, including the bilingual Spanish-English speakers in the sample; the English edition (PLS-5; 19:130) should be administered to children whose primary language is English.

Authors: Irla Lee Zimmerman, Violette G. Steiner, and Roberta Evatt Pond.

Publisher: Pearson.

a) ARTICULATION SCREENER.

Purpose: Designed to evaluate articulation in single words.

Population: Ages 2-6 to 7-11.

Scores: Total score only.

Comments: "Criterion-referenced" optional subtest included in the record form.

b) LANGUAGE SAMPLE CHECKLIST.

Purpose: Designed to evaluate spontaneous speech.

Scores: Mean Length of Utterance in Words.

Comments: Supplemental measure included in the record form to help validate information obtained from the Expressive Communication scale.

c) HOME COMMUNICATION QUESTIONNAIRE.

Purpose: Designed to give "the caregiver's perspective" of a child's communication behaviors at home, preschool, or daycare.

Population: Ages birth to 2-11.

Scores: Not scored.

Time: (10-15) minutes.

Comments: Supplemental questionnaire.

Review of the Preschool Language Scales-Fifth Edition Spanish by ARTURO OLIVÁREZ, JR., Professor, Teacher Education Department, and NORMA MARTINEZ, Graduate Research Assistant, Teacher Education Department, University of Texas at El Paso, El Paso, TX:

DESCRIPTION. The Preschool Language Scales–Fifth Edition Spanish (PLS-5 Spanish) is an individually administered test designed to identify language delay or disorder in children from birth through 7 years, 11 months of age who are Spanish speakers (monolingual or bilingual). The test provides parallel items in Spanish and English. Monolingual Spanish speakers are presented all the items in Spanish; bilingual speakers are presented all the items in Spanish first and in English for missed items only. The test consists of two standardized scales: Auditory Comprehension (AC; 67 items), which evaluates the extent of children's comprehension of language in concordance with their age, and Expressive Communication (EC; 60 items), which determines the level of communication between the child and others according to the participant's age. Supplemental measures include a Language Sample Checklist for gathering information about a child's spontaneous utterances, a criterion-scored Articulation Screener, and a Home Communication Questionnaire that can be completed by caregivers of children up to 2 years, 11 months of age. The primary objectives for revising the test were to update its normative information, improve on the test properties, and add the benefit of dual language assessment. The length of time required to administer the PLS-5 Spanish ranges from 30 to 65 minutes, depending on the child's age, cooperation levels during the test, and the child's degree of bilingualism. A fluent Spanish-speaking examiner is recommended for test administration to Spanish monolingual children. Results should be interpreted only by a clinician who is experienced, has received training in diagnostic assessment, and has content knowledge in language development.

DEVELOPMENT. The PLS-5 Spanish materials provide little explanation as to the theoretical underpinnings for the utilization of only the AC and EC language constructs apart from references to research that points to the utilization and application of these constructs in the English language. In revising and developing the PLS-5 Spanish, the authors sought to update the previous version (PLS-4 Spanish) by making changes to test content and scope that incorporated best practices in assessment when using an examinee's dual language skills. In addition, the new version was developed to conform to legislative changes on early intervention services for children with communication delays. Modifications include changes to some items, the addition of new items, modifications to administration procedures, and revisions to the scoring criteria. The test developers referenced current research studies that suggested the use of a conceptual scoring approach whereby bilingual children are given the opportunity to put to use all their global language skills, thus leveling the playing field and reducing referrals to special education intervention programs (Bedore, Peña, Garcia, & Cortez, 2005; Pearson, Fernández, & Oller, 1993; Peña, Bedore, & Zlatic-Giunta, 2002; Umbel, Pearson, Fernández, & Oller, 1992). A detailed set of criteria is provided concerning the development of the final pool of test items across age levels. About 35% of the items were modified from the earlier version, and about 25% of the items are new. Nonclinical (n = 341) and clinical (n = 69) samples were used in tryout testing that led to the development of the PLS-5 Spanish.

TECHNICAL. The PLS-5 Spanish examiner's manual describes the standardization process and provides evidence of the scale's psychometric soundness. The normative process involved a sample of 1,150 children stratified by age, gender, geographic region, and primary caregiver's education level with 50 to 75 children in each of the 18 age categories. Reliability analyses and results indicated that scales and the total test yielded high levels of stability with corrected test-retest correlation coefficients (with an interval between 3 and 15 days) ranging from .85 to .92 across three major age categories (N = 193). Evidence for internal consistency reliability using the split-half method yielded moderate to high coefficients for the normative sample (from .80 to .97) for the AC and EC scales and the Total Language scale. The measure also demonstrated high levels of internal consistency (coefficients were .98 or higher) with a clinical sample (N = 170). Normative sample data were used to calculate standard errors of measurement for the construction of confidence intervals across each age category to aid in the interpretation of scores.

The test manual provides evidence of validity based on test content as far as relevance and coverage of what is being assessed. Additional evidence is based on the internal structure of the separate scales and the total scale, on the measure's relationship to similar scales, and on comparisons between clinical and nonclinical groups of test takers. According to the test authors, content validity evidence is based on extant review of the literature, user feedback, and expert review. A second approach for evidence of validity is based on the internal structure of the test. These results indicated high levels of item homogeneity within and across the scales with a reported correlation coefficient between the AC and the EC scales over all ages of .69. Comparing scores from the PLS-5 Spanish with scores from the PLS-4 Spanish and scores from the Clinical Evaluation of Language Fundamentals Preschool–Second Edition-Spanish (CELF Preschool-2 Spanish; 17:49) yielded moderate to high correlation coefficients with both external measures. Finally, scores of children with a diagnosed language disorder (N = 170) were compared with scores from a matched sample of children without language disorders. Children with language disorders scored significantly (p < .01) lower than children from the matched sample on the AC, EC, and Total Language scores, with large effect sizes reported.

COMMENTARY. The developers of the PLS-5 Spanish should be commended for their efforts to make their scale a psychometrically sound instrument. These efforts will greatly support school personnel and parents in determining the correct diagnosis of any of the many communication disorders or delays that children may demonstrate. The use of ancillary measures such as the Articulation Screener, the Language Sample Checklist, and the Home Communication Questionnaire add to these efforts to minimize the misclassification of Spanish speakers into special education programs. Revisions reside on a well-established conceptual approach for assessing young children by the use of the child's own dual language fund of knowledge and abilities. The normative data also attest to this advantage given that dual language learners scored at least 3 to 4 points higher than students who are not completely bilingual in terms of overall performance. These few crucial points may define a child's academic future of success or failure. Additionally, the PLS-5 Spanish makes many other time-sensitive updates needed in this type of assessment because schools are inundated with students who are language challenged and who will require school personnel who are prepared to provide the most appropriate educational services to all learners.

Although there are a good number of favorable modifications in this version of the test, the PLS-5 Spanish continues to have several weaknesses. The materials provided little explanation as to the theoretical underpinnings for the utilization of the AC and EC language constructs except for providing some references to relevant research. Problems with the literal translation of test items and instructions continue to be observed in this version. For example, on two items, the examiner is given instructions to count one or more options as incorrect, even though the option could be considered correct. There also appears to be some level of inconsistency between the administration manual and the record form. Furthermore, instructions, item translation, age-appropriateness of vocabulary terms, incorrect selection of response options, and heavy reliance on memory may lead to errors in scoring and interpretation. Although the Home Communication Questionnaire is optional, the administrator should be able to corroborate the parent responses given that some parents may minimize their child's actual communication problems. Upon inspection of the translated content of some items, some of the Spanish options offered to examinees may lead to ambiguity and confusion, imperiling interpretation of the child's true language ability. Overall, the instrument appears to be difficult to administer because it requires examiners to pay close attention concurrently to three or more different test materials (i.e., manipulatives, picture manual, protocol, and so forth) and test administration tasks on top of keeping the test taker's attention and interest in the entire evaluation process. There is a need to streamline the entire test administration process to make the use of the scale more efficient. Finally, the developers continue to rely heavily on older measurement theories rather than implementing more modern assessment models (e.g., confirmatory factor analysis, item response theory, partial credit model) that would enhance the overall assessment as well as construct validity evidence as previously recommended by Restrepo and Silverman (2001) for an earlier edition of the scale.

SUMMARY. In conclusion, the PLS-5 Spanish is a tool developed to assist clinicians in identifying language delays or disorders in Spanish-speaking (monolingual or bilingual) children. The incorporation of the test taker's dual language abilities is a tremendous improvement, but it can lead to the introduction of other nonsystematic errors of assessment with this population. Because of the identified weaknesses, the test user is alerted to pay close attention to possible sources of error that could be introduced in administration and interpretation. The PLS-5 Spanish would benefit from additional objective explanations regarding construct validity beyond its heavy reliance on content validity as attested to by experts. It also needs to be streamlined to promote effective use of the test that may, in turn, help alleviate current problems with misclassification of students into special education programs.

REVIEWERS' REFERENCES

Bedore, L. M., Peña, E. D., Garcia, M., & Cortez, C. (2005). Conceptual versus monolingual scoring: When does it make a difference? *Language, Speech, and Hearing Services in Schools, 36*, 188-200.

Pearson, B. Z., Fernández, S. C., & Oller, D. K. (1993). Lexical development in bilingual infants and toddlers: Comparison to monolingual norms. *Language Learning, 43*, 93-120.

Peña, E. D., Bedore, L. M., & Zlatic-Giunta, R. (2002). Category-generation performance of young bilingual children: The influence of condition, category, and language. *Journal of Speech, Language, and Hearing Research, 41*, 938-947.

Restrepo, M. A., & Silverman, S. W. (2001). Validity of the Spanish Preschool Language Scale-3 for use with bilingual children. *American Journal of Speech-Language Pathology, 10*, 382-393.

Umbel, V. M., Pearson, B. Z., Fernández, M. C., & Oller, D. K. (1992). Measuring bilingual children's receptive vocabularies. *Child Development, 63*, 1012-1020.

[133]

Preschool Language Scales—Fifth Edition Spanish Screening Test.

Purpose: A "dual language assessment" designed to identify "monolingual Spanish or bilingual Spanish-English-speaking children who may need in-depth assessment of their speech and language abilities."

Population: Children from birth to age 7-11 whose primary language is Spanish.

Publication Date: 2012.

Acronym: PLS-5 Spanish Screening Test.

Administration: Individual.

Levels and Forms: 8 forms, 9 levels.

Price Data, 2013: $164 per kit including stimulus book/test manual (282 pages) and 25 record forms for each age; $133 per stimulus book/test manual; $36 per 25 record forms (age birth to 11 months, age 1, age 2, age 3, age 4, age 5, age 6, or age 7).

Foreign Language Edition: English edition available.

Time: (5-10) minutes.

Comments: Normative data based on children whose primary language is Spanish and who understand and converse fluently in Spanish or Spanish and English; publisher "highly recommends" examiners who administer the assessment to monolingual Spanish speakers be fluent or near-fluent Spanish speakers; examiners who administer the test to bilingual Spanish-English speakers should be bilingual themselves. If an examiner does not have fluent or near-fluent proficiency in Spanish, the test can be administered in collaboration with a trained and qualified interpreter.

Authors: Irla Lee Zimmerman, Violette G. Steiner, and Roberta Evatt Pond.

Publisher: Pearson.

a) AGE BIRTH TO 0:5 MONTHS.
Scores, 3: Language, Feeding, Social/Interpersonal.
b) AGE 0:6 TO 0:11 MONTHS.
Scores, 3: Language, Feeding, Social/Interpersonal.
c) AGE 1.
Scores, 3: Language, Feeding, Social/Interpersonal.
d) AGE 2.
Scores, 3: Language, Social/Interpersonal, Articulation (ages 2-6 to 2-11).
e) AGE 3.
Scores, 6: Language, Articulation, Connected Speech, Social/Interpersonal, Fluency, Voice.
f) AGE 4.
Scores, 6: Language, Articulation, Connected Speech, Social/Interpersonal, Fluency, Voice.
g) AGE 5.
Scores, 6: Language, Articulation, Connected Speech, Social/Interpersonal, Fluency, Voice.
h) AGE 6.
Scores, 6: Language, Articulation, Connected Speech, Social/Interpersonal, Fluency, Voice.
i) AGE 7.
Scores, 6: Language, Articulation, Connected Speech, Social/Interpersonal, Fluency, Voice.

Review of the Preschool Language Scales–Fifth Edition Spanish Screening Test by MARÍA DEL R. MEDINA-DÍAZ, Professor, Program of Educational Research and Evaluation, Department of Graduate Studies, Faculty of Education, University of Puerto Rico-Río Piedras, San Juan, PR:

DESCRIPTION. The Preschool Language Scales–Fifth Edition (PLS–5) Spanish Screening Test was designed to identify the need for in-depth assessment of speech and language abilities of monolingual Spanish or bilingual Spanish-English-speaking children from birth (0:0) to 7 years, 11 months (7:11) in six domains: Language (5 items for children of all ages), Articulation (7–10 sounds for children ages 2:6–7:11), Connected Speech (3 items for children ages 3:0–7:11), Social/Interpersonal (4 atypical behaviors for children birth to 11 months, 6 atypical behaviors for children 1:0 to 2:11 years; 6 typical behaviors for children 3:0–7:11 years), Fluency (3 typical and 5 atypical characteristics for children 3:0–7:11 years of age), and Voice (1 typical and 5 atypical characteristics for children 3:0–7:11 years). Feeding domain scores are included for ages birth-1:11 with six and seven atypical feeding and swallowing behaviors that influence speech and language development and may also have health implications.

The test kit includes a color-tag organized and easel-style manual with items, administration and scoring directions, and a set of color-coded protocol (Protocolo) sheets for recording and scoring the answers of each age group. Several objects or toys (not included) are needed for 0:0–3:11 age group administration: a squeaky toy, a ball, a teddy bear, a box with removable lid, keys on a key ring, a rattle, a spoon, a bowl, an infant toy, bubbles, a cup, cloth, sealable bag, personal toys, age-appropriate snack, and watch with second hand or stopwatch. The examiner's manual and protocol directions are clear and easy to follow. A qualified examiner fluent in Spanish or Spanish-English administers the test individually to the child (with her or his caregiver) in Spanish (for monolingual Spanish-speaking children) and in dual language (first in Spanish and then, in English), according to the child's first responses. First, the items are asked and scored in Spanish. If the answer is incorrect, the item can be formulated in English. The score includes both language answers. Because of this and other arrangements that can be implemented to suit the child's age, language comprehension, and attention (e.g., taking the test with a translator), and at the examiner's discretion, the test is not strictly "standardized." Also, testing flexibility is allowed in terms of altering the item sequence "to maximize the child's performance and attention when it seems appropriate" (manual, p. 12) using the floor or a low-table for conducting the test with 1- to 3-year-old children (manual, p. 10) and extending the administration time for a bilingual child (manual, p. 5).

Language items (in blue print) are in Spanish for caregivers of 0:0–2:11 age children. The test manual provides Feeding and Social/Interpersonal items in Spanish for caregivers of children birth-1:11. For ages 2:0-2:11, the test manual provides Social/Interpersonal items in Spanish. For children ages 3:0-7:11, the PLS-5 Spanish Screening Test provides Social/Interpersonal, Connected Speech, Fluency, and Voice items in Spanish for caregivers. For children ages 0:0-0:11, items in the test manual are presented in Spanish only so the caregivers can report an observed behavior. For children ages 1:0-1:11, the test manual includes two items (Items 1 and 2) that may require a dual-language administration. Items 3-5 include caregivers' questions in Spanish. The test manual and protocols include items and responses in both languages for children ages 2:0-7:11. Alternative words and responses in Spanish are provided. Others could be added (e.g., "mamadera," "vacía," "canasta," and "sapo" used in Puerto Rico). Also, some questions and time suggestions may be helpful for testing different word combinations in the playing sessions (ages 3:0–3:11, p. 77). Drawings for children ages 2:0–7:11 are colorful and include children from different races and gender. However, several show boys and girls engaged in activities that might be considered sexist or stereotypic. Sensitivity item review is recommended for addressing this issue and Spanish-language dialectical differences.

A passing criterion or score is included for each section in the protocol and in the test manual's technical information section. If a child does not meet the criterion, the examiner checks a box for obtaining additional information. Any of these marked in the protocol's Screening Summary is a signal for referral and requesting a diagnostic or in-depth assessment of the child's performance. The examiner also reports test session behaviors and administration conditions during the test.

The passing scores originate from different sources and procedures. The Language criterion scores for each group were based on the standardization research data of the PLS-5 Spanish with 1,084 typically developed and 96 language-disabled children, "applying Receiver Operating Characteristic curve analysis on the raw scores on the selected items" (manual, p. 34) of the PLS-5 Spanish Screening Test. The results of this procedure are not shown. Also, the Articulation criterion score (number of phonemes produced for 90% of the children in each age group) were determined from the PLS-5 Spanish standardization data at each age. The passing scores for Feeding and Connected Speech sections are grounded in brief cited research. The Social/Interpersonal, Fluency, and Voice sections criteria were based on data obtained during the development of the PLS-4 Screening Test, as well as the literature reviewed. This documentation for setting the passing scores is slim for supporting the screening decisions derived from PLS-5 Spanish Screening Test scores.

DEVELOPMENT. According to the test authors, the test "was developed by selecting a subset of items from PLS-5 Spanish for the Language and Articulation sections, and by compiling a list of descriptive statements for the other sections (e.g., Connected Speech, Social/Interpersonal, Fluency)" (manual, p. 25). The rationale for including each section is supported with literature and research.

PLS-5 Spanish back- and decentered-translation processes are discussed briefly, but without empirical evidence of the validity of the translated test scores. The procedure for selecting, tryout, and translating all the items for the PLS-5 Spanish Screening Test depends on the PLS-5 Spanish. Thus, one may ask: What is the difference between the two tests? No item analysis of the PLS-5 Spanish Screening Test for determining item selection and quality was provided in the test documentation.

TECHNICAL. Normative data are based on PLS-5 Spanish standardization, administered by 111 examiners in 18 states of the U.S.A. and Puerto Rico, from May 2010 through March 2011. The nonrandom stratified sample of 1,150 children was classified on the basis of age (65% between 1:0 and 5:11 years old); gender (50% boys and 50% girls), geographic region (47% U.S.A. South and 29% Puerto Rico), race/ethnicity (97% Hispanic), primary caregiver's country of origin (53% Mexican and 30% Puerto Rican), and primary caregiver's education level (36% with Grade 11 or less). This demographic profile shows a fair ratio of children whose primary language is Spanish. However, there is no information available about the distribution of children by geographic region and gender through age groups and of PLS-5 Spanish scores, as well as the procedure for selecting and excluding children. PLS-5 Spanish Screening Test scores were not used in the norming procedure described.

Test-retest reliability estimates are provided using percent agreement on passing the Language (190 children ages 0:0–7:11) and Articulation (123 children ages 2:6–7:11) sections from the PLS-5 Spanish test. "The testing interval ranged from 3 to 15 days, and both tests were administered by the same examiner" (manual, p. 36). The percentage of agreement ranged from 91% to 100% across age groups for both domains. Again, these estimates do not appear to have been obtained from the PLS-5 Spanish Screening Test.

The main concern of the PLS-5 Spanish Screening Test evidence of construct validity is its capacity to differentiate children who develop language skills normally versus children who need additional assessment for detecting language deficiencies. The test authors relied on the relation with other language tests and discrepancies in performance demonstrated between language-disordered and non-language-disordered children. As evidence, the test authors cite: (a) mean standard (Language) scores of PLS-5 Spanish Screening Test were higher than Clinical Evaluation Language Fundamentals Preschool–Second Edition Spanish Core Language scores, but the classification accuracy of 80 children 3:0–6:11 years old was high (94%) (manual, p. 44); (b) items chosen for PLS-4 and PLS-5 "demonstrated the greatest differences in performance between children with typically developing language skills and children identified as having a language disorder, [...] and were identified by logistic regressions as being the most predictive of a child's group membership" (manual, p. 39); (c) mean Language scores of PLS-5 Spanish Screening Test (Mean = 1.8) was lower for a group of 73 children (1:0–7:11 years of age) diagnosed with language disorder than of the typically developing children (Mean = 3.9), and effect size for the first group is above 1.0 (Cohen's d = 1.49 as standard difference of the two means) (manual, pp. 45–46). It is interesting to notice that in all these studies the Language total score (e.g., criterion score of 77 or less) is used, but the explanation of its derivation and the correlation coefficients between scores are omitted.

The accuracy of child classification is another critical issue for supporting the validity of the use of test scores. According to the test authors, "PLS-5 Spanish Screening Test [total Language score] correctly classified 79% of the [71] children who were identified on PLS-5 Spanish [total Language score of the standardization sample] with a language disorder and 95% [out of 1,105] who were identified as typically developing" (manual, p. 42). Diagnostic accuracy of PLS-5 Spanish Screening Test (Language scores) classification was also examined using the scores of the language disorder group (no number provided of children on ages 0:0–7:11). The results show high levels of sensitivity (.85) and specificity (.79), as well as 5% false negatives for screening populations in which the base rate of language disorders is estimated to be 20% (manual, pp. 48–49). However, these findings should be interpreted cautiously due to the small sample, the range of criterion scores less than 77, and the differences in the age groups. The test authors argue that there is no evidence of negative consequences of the PLS-5 Spanish and PLS-5 Spanish Screening Test (manual, p. 49).

COMMENTARY. The test authors state that the test is a reliable and valid tool that could be used in the first level of assessing a bilingual child's language abilities (dual language assessment). This claim is supported with references and PLS-5 Span-ish tryout research addressing bilingual children score differences. The PLS-5 Spanish Screening Test examiner considers children's responses in Spanish and English and combines them in the Language score. However, no results are provided regarding the differences in each age group item responses, order effects, and scores between bilingual and monolingual Spanish children answering the PLS-5 Spanish Screening Test sections. Also, no differential item functioning (DIF) analysis is reported comparing scores of different groups in some variables, such as gender, age, and primary language. Because the items can be administered either in Spanish or English, and scored in either language according to the child responses, more evidence is necessary for supporting the examiner's language selection and scoring decisions (meeting or not meeting the criteria). Without this evidence, the validity of test score use (especially, the claim of dual language assessment) and reliability across age groups are misleading.

The test authors indicate that because the Language and Articulation items of the PLS-5 Spanish Screening Test are a subset of the PLS-5 Spanish items, they relied on previous reliability estimates to support the stability of the classification. Specifically, the test authors state, "data collected from PLS-5 Spanish were sufficient for PLS-5 Spanish Screening Test data analysis. Additional data were not collected" (manual, p. 39). This is not sufficient evidence for establishing the score reliability of the PLS-5 Spanish Screening Test (American Educational Research Association, American Psychological Association, & National Council on Measurement in Education, 1999). Reliability estimates of inter- and intrarater agreement with two or more examinees, internal consistency, and standard error of measurement are required for the test and for each age group. Also, there is no explanation of the item selection process and item or test response analysis model (e.g., classical test theory or item response theory), as well as the PLS-5 Spanish Screening Test items psychometric features.

Test scores validity is sustained using documentation of content selection and response process evidence from previous tests. The test authors posit that responses and scores for the PLS-5 Spanish Screening Test would be similar to those of the Preschool Language Scale–Fourth Edition (PLS-4) and Preschool Screening Language–Fifth Edition (PLS-5) "because both tests used the same methodology in selecting items" (manual, p. 39).

Also, the "extensive examination" of the responses of PLS-5 Spanish tryout and standardization studies accounts for validity evidence on response processes. However, the Spanish and Spanish-English language variations in children's thinking and responses to PLS-5 Spanish Screening Test items are worth exploring.

The PLS-5 Spanish Screening Test is a short and promising instrument for screening some language domains and related behaviors of Spanish- and Spanish-English-speaking children. The manual and protocols are useful and organized with clear and easy-to-follow directions for administering and scoring the test. Notably, they include items and responses in Spanish and English. The test authors employed various sources of evidence for evaluating the validity of test scores. Nevertheless, the evidence is presented together with empirical results and score analyses derived from other tests, specifically of Language scores of the PLS-5 Spanish Test. This hardly sustains the validity of PLS-5 Spanish Screening Test score interpretations, according to the purpose and content of the whole test.

SUMMARY. The PLS-5 Spanish Screening Test is based on Language and Articulation items of the PLS-5 Spanish test. Therefore, its quality depends in large measure on the influence and research results of its source. This is demonstrated with the normative data and validity evidence provided by the test authors. The literature reviewed and related studies support each test domain, as well as content validity. However, a question remains about the selection and quality of PLS-5 Spanish Screening Test items and validity of the test scores for fulfilling their purpose. Additional data are needed regarding relevant psychometric features of the test, such as score reliability, item discrimination, DIF analyses for bilingual and monolingual Spanish-speaking children and for children of different ages and gender.

REVIEWER'S REFERENCE

American Educational Research Association, American Psychological Association, & National Council on Measurement in Education. (1999). *Standards for educational and psychological testing*. Washington, DC: American Educational Research Association.

Review of the Preschool Language Scales–Fifth Edition Spanish Screening Test by RICHARD RUTH, Associate Professor of Clinical Psychology, BENJAMIN MORSA, Graduate Student, and LAURA W. REID, Graduate Student, The George Washington University, Washington, DC:

DESCRIPTION. The Preschool Language Scales–Fifth Edition (PLS-5) Spanish Screening Test indicates whether more comprehensive or diagnostic assessment of speech/language abilities is needed in children, ages birth to 7–11, who are monolingual in Spanish or considered to be bilingual in Spanish/English. It is a clinical instrument, administered individually, scored, and interpreted by speech/language pathologists or other early childhood professionals with native or near-native fluency in both Spanish and English or, when this is not feasible, by professionals able to work with skilled interpreters. In children considered Spanish/English bilingual, the measure assesses whether benchmark speech/language competencies have been acquired in either language. The dual language conceptual scoring approach, considered a best practice approach, minimizes the likelihood that children in the process of second-language acquisition will be misidentified as having a speech/language disorder.

Depending on the child's age range and the competency being screened, items are scored based on caregiver report, examiner observation, or the child's response to a standardized stimulus or prompt, according to well-specified administration protocols that vary by age level. Administration is to take place in quiet, comfortable, distraction-minimized settings. As with many tests for use with young children, the caregiver's nonintrusive presence is allowed when considered clinically facilitative.

For children considered bilingual, items are "administered in Spanish and English simultaneously" (manual, p. 17) for the youngest children (those 1 year through 1 year, 11 months) and, for children age 2 and older, first in Spanish and then, if not passed in Spanish, in English. Some items use verbal prompts only; others use picture stimuli, or a list of items considered commonly found in the child's environment. Examiners should bear in mind that some of these items may not be commonly present in the homes of disadvantaged or relatively unacculturated children, especially those from rural or indigenous backgrounds.

Scoring is clearly described and user-friendly. For each competency area assessed (as outlined in the accompanying descriptive materials that vary by age range), component items are scored pass (1) or fail (0). For some items, scoring involves determining whether a threshold number of problem behaviors or demonstrated skills is evidenced. For other items, scoring involves determining whether a threshold number of subitems is passed. Item scores are then summed and, depending on the number of points required to meet a criterion level, the competency—Language, Feeding, Articulation,

Connected Speech, Social/Interpersonal, Fluency, Voice–is rated "pass" or "obtain more information" (i.e., refer for comprehensive/diagnostic assessment of the competency).

DEVELOPMENT. The PLS-5 Spanish Screening Test draws upon empirical findings and identified best practices in language development, language disorders, psycholinguistics, and foreign language and bilingual test development literatures. This information was used to identify key competencies to be screened and based on item development approaches found useful in crafting the PLS-4, the PLS-5, the PLS-5 Spanish, and the PLS-5 Screening Test, measures widely considered conceptually and technically sound.

PLS-5 Spanish Screening Test Language items were chosen from PLS-5 Spanish items that best discriminate between typically developing and language-disordered children in relevant domains of receptive and expressive language. Item selection was further refined using logistic regression to select items that best predicted classifications based on PLS-5 Spanish Total Language score. Items in other competency areas were chosen based on criteria for typical and atypical functioning identified in the empirical literature.

PLS-5 Spanish Screening Test items were translated from Spanish into English. Then, the English translations were translated back into Spanish and checked for linguistic equivalence, and additionally checked for accuracy resolution using a decentering method. Although this process is in accordance with recommended practices in foreign language/bilingual test development, several PLS-5 Spanish Screening Test items have English-into-Spanish errors of grammar, usage, and rhetoric that may be noticeable to monolingual speakers of Spanish and Spanish-primary bilingual children. Choices about use of the subjunctive in prompts and in examples of correct/incorrect responses may not parallel usage patterns in some regional populations. Although acceptable regional vocabulary variations are noted among response alternatives, these do not seem comprehensive, and some examiners may find the guidance they offer limited. Some of the picture stimuli may not be as familiar to monolingual Spanish speakers and relatively unacculturated children as they are to acculturated bilingual children. Clinical judgment would need to be used in case-specific determinations whether such factors affect a given child's performance on relevant items and competencies.

Criterion cutoff scores for Language were determined using receiver operating characteristic curve analysis to maximize true positive and minimize false positive findings. Conceptual criteria based on findings in the empirical literature establish cutoffs for other competency determinations. These reviewers believe the procedures are acceptable for a screening measure.

TECHNICAL. The PLS-5 Spanish Screening Test standardization sample was composed of 575 male and 575 female children. Either 100 or 150 children from each age cohort were included. Parent educational levels were diverse; family socioeconomic status in the sample was not assessed directly. The children predominantly lived in the South, the West, and Puerto Rico (998 out of 1,150). Place of birth was the U.S. for 681 children; 338 children lived in Puerto Rico; the remainder were immigrants with varying years of residence in the U.S. Of some concern, 614 children were of Mexican ethnicity and 351 were Puerto Rican; Latino children of other ethnic backgrounds were less well-represented. Similarly, 633 children were monolingual in Spanish; 160 had some English but were Spanish-primary; only 153 of the sample were reported equally conversant in English and Spanish. Thus, examiners in some U.S. regions and working with some clinical populations will find the children they assess less than well-represented among the standardization sample.

Reliability was assessed with test/retest comparisons (interval 3–15 days, mean approximately 6.7 days) of classification agreement (pass vs. obtain more information) on Language and Articulation scores, a reasonable approach to reliability determination given the test's purpose and composition. The reliability study sample was age-stratified and roughly congruent with the standardization sample for other demographic variables. Agreement was very good (90.8–93.2% for Language, 97.7–100% for Articulation). It would have been preferable had retests not been performed by the examiner who performed the initial assessments.

The PLS-5 Spanish Screening Test manual offers qualitative narratives supporting convergent validity of the measure's results and results of other tests in the PLS series and content validity deriving from use of the dual language conceptual approach and from strong relationships between test responses and clinically meaningful signs and symptoms. Further evidence of convergent validity was developed through comparisons between PLS-5

Spanish Screening Test results and results of the PLS-5 (94.8% agreement for nonclinical populations, 78.9% for language-disordered children) and results of the PLS-5 and the Clinical Evaluation of Language Fundamentals (CELF) Preschool-2 Spanish (93.8%). A diagnostic accuracy study of the PLS-5 Spanish Screening Test with language-disordered children found .85 sensitivity and .79 specificity. Although these are not ideal sources of evidence supporting validity of test score use, they are within an acceptable range for a screening test.

COMMENTARY. The PLS-5 Spanish Screening Test seeks to screen a broad diversity of children who understand and/or converse in Spanish in some ecological contexts. This poses inherent challenges; it assumes identifications of children as monolingual in Spanish or bilingual have been made correctly (in clinical practice in some settings, not always the case) and does not consider the possibility that some clinical populations may be bilingual in Spanish and some language other than English (for example, children from Bolivia bilingual in Spanish and Quechua or Aymara, and children from Mexico and Guatemala bilingual in Spanish and Mayan languages). Those using the test need to be mindful of such possibilities and their implications and use clinical acumen when selecting monolingual versus bilingual administration protocols and interpreting findings.

Instruments based on dual language conceptual scoring do not predict whether a bilingual child will perform to expectations in school settings using Spanish- or English-medium instruction. The PLS-5 Spanish Screening Test makes clear that its sole purpose is to predict whether further assessment of a given competency area is suggested and thus, used properly, is not vulnerable to this predictive validity problem.

With a conceptual framework and specific items largely derived from the widely used and well-regarded PLS-4 and PLS-5 diagnostic tests, the PLS-5 Spanish Screening Test has a generally sound technical and conceptual infrastructure and well-thought-out administration and scoring procedures. It was developed using conceptual and statistical methods that prioritize minimizing possibilities of false negative results; the test manual notes that, in doing so, there is a heightened risk of false positive findings. This is not an unreasonable choice in a screening test. Examiners are assumed to have substantial familiarity with patterns of bilingual language usage and development in young children and to be able to use professional discretion in selecting among possible regional variations in item and response wording. Examiners are also assumed to be able to score items based on clinical observations and subjective appraisals of target competencies and to accompany findings with salient qualitative observations.

Items are well-chosen to help the PLS-5 Spanish Screening Test provide careful, empirically supported, ecologically valid screenings, when the test is used properly, of key early speech/language competencies relevant to developmental, educational, psychological, neuropsychological, and health-related concerns. Although systematic translation and back-translation procedures consistent with best practice guidelines have been used, particularly for some regional populations there is a chance that some item wordings might produce artifactual results in some children. Although such occurrences are unlikely to affect pass/fail determinations, the chance exists, and examiners will need to use their best clinical and professional judgment to use the test effectively in such instances.

SUMMARY. The PLS-5 Spanish Screening Test is highly useful in screening whether young children, monolingual or bilingual in Spanish, need to be assessed for language disorders. It is less clearly useful in identifying whether children bilingual in Spanish and another language need to be assessed for such disorders. It is well-conceptualized and designed and readily usable for adequately trained professionals. Reliability and validity are acceptable for a screening test. Test users need to be aware that the test is not a diagnostic measure. Issues with the cultural content of some stimuli and the comprehensibility of some Spanish item translations may make findings questionable when used with members of some populations. As with most bilingual measures, examiners will need to use professional discretion in interpreting findings.

[134]

Preschool-Wide Evaluation Tool™ (Pre-SET™), Research Edition.

Purpose: Designed "to measure an early childhood program's implementation fidelity of program-wide positive behavior intervention and support."

Population: Evaluators and other observers of early childhood programs.

Publication Date: 2012.

Acronym: PreSET.

Scores, 9: Expectations Defined, Behavioral Expectations Taught, Responses to Appropriate and Challenging

Behavior, Organized and Predictable Environment, Monitoring and Decision Making, Family Involvement, Management, Program Support, Total Percent Implemented.
Administration: Individual programs.
Price Data, 2012: $99.95 per CD-ROM that includes all necessary printable forms; $50 per manual (125 pages).
Time: (60) minutes.
Comments: Administration time applies to programs with 1-2 classrooms; time will increase approximately 20 minutes for each additional classroom; intended for use with early childhood programs that implement the program-wide positive behavior intervention and support (PW-PBIS) model.
Authors: Elizabeth A. Steed, Tina M. Pomerleau, and Robert H. Horner (forms).
Publisher: Paul H. Brookes Publishing Co., Inc.

Review of the Preschool-Wide Evaluation Tool™ (PreSET™), Research Edition by MALINDA HENDRICKS GREEN, Professor of Educational Sciences, Foundations and Research, University of Central Oklahoma, Edmond, OK:

DESCRIPTION. The Preschool-Wide Evaluation Tool (PreSET), Research Edition is designed to measure an early childhood program's implementation of the program-wide positive behavior intervention and support (PW-PBIS) model. The PreSET manual and accompanying CD both are attractive and easy to navigate. The manual is readable with clearly labeled chapters and sections, including guidance for using the PreSET and an overview of the PW-PBIS system. Implementing the PW-PBIS system is recommended to take 2–3 years with professional development, including ongoing classroom coaching. The PreSET is administered once or twice a year to monitor the progress of the implementation. The PreSET assesses eight areas of the PW-PBIS system: Expectations Defined, Behavioral Expectations Taught, Responses to Appropriate and Challenging Behavior, Organized and Predictable Environment, Monitoring and Decision Making, Family Involvement, Management, and Program Support. Data collection for the 30-item PreSET requires completion of the Administrator Interview Form, the Classroom Interview and Observation Form, and the Classroom Summary Form. The Classroom Interview and Observation Form includes questions for the lead teacher, other teachers, and several children. All forms can be printed from the CD provided. The Administrator Interview Form includes a list of materials to be supplied by the site administrator and

questions regarding the eight areas to be assessed with 3-point scoring along a scale. The Classroom Interview and Observation Form includes space for three teachers' responses to two questions, three children's responses to two questions, eight questions for the lead teacher, and notes. The Classroom Summary Form provides a matrix for recording scores for 10 classrooms. Administration takes approximately 1 hour for small programs with 20 minutes for each additional classroom. Scores are calculated for the eight areas listed above as well as the Total Percent Implemented score for the PW-PBIS system as a whole.

DEVELOPMENT. The PW-PBIS was developed with the goal of improving young children's social and emotional development and decreasing unacceptable behavior in the school setting. The PW-PBIS is an adaption of the earlier school-wide positive behavior interventions and support (SW-PBIS) system utilized in elementary, middle, and high schools. Specifically focused, the PreSET's purpose is to monitor the adoption and long-term implementation of PW-PBIS practices. Hence, the PreSET is the early childhood version of an evaluation measure, the School-wide Evaluation Tool (SET), used to monitor a specific system of student management that a school, district, or state has adopted. The manual for the measure provides details about the behavior management system, its purpose, and implementation. Revisions were made to the SET's language, content, and subscales to provide applicability to the preschool setting. The modifications focused upon the unique nature of classroom routines and family involvement in early childhood settings. Particularly, the children's interview questions are asked by the teacher, rather than by the outside observer, using language targeted to the children. The PreSET technical data were collected from 138 early childhood classrooms located in the West, Northwest, and Southeast United States.

TECHNICAL. An appendix in the manual reports technical properties and evidence using data from early childhood classrooms. A logical case was presented for the structure of the PreSET, including revisions made allowing a better fit "with the more constructivist theoretical approach" (manual, p. 103) prevalent among early childhood programs. Data analyses were based upon 138 classrooms in various locations within the U.S. and various types of early childhood settings including Head Start, private child care, and public or nonprofit programs.

Data were drawn from single classrooms in 127 of the program settings and two or more classrooms in the remaining 11 settings.

Analyses included descriptive statistics, correlations among subscales, interrater reliability, and correlations with scores from another instrument developed to measure implementation of the PBIS system. Standard administration was to be achieved through training of the observer-data collectors using the PreSET and the staff implementing the PW-PBIS system. Evidence of reliability for the PreSET included item-subscale correlations (coefficients ranged from .16 to .90), item-total correlations (.12 to .75), and subscale-total correlations (.39 to .71). Internal consistency (coefficient alpha) values for the subscales ranged from .55 to .94. Interrater reliability was calculated using data from 22 classrooms in which two observers conducted independent assessments. Agreement on ratings for individual items ranged from 68% to 100%, with an average agreement of 95%.

Evidence of validity was presented as correlations with scores from another instrument (Teaching Pyramid Observation Tool) developed to measure implementation of the PBIS system. Differences in content, data collection, and scoring between the two measures was provided along with the expectations of the PreSET's authors as to the results of the analysis. Results were drawn from data collected in 31 classrooms by an external evaluator who collected data from both instruments in the same classroom. Correlation coefficients between subscales ranged from .19 to .58 with six of the eight achieving statistical significance. Additional evidence of validity was provided in the form of data collected pre- and post-implementation of the PW-PBIS system in 29 early childhood classrooms during the 2006–2007 academic year. The paired t-test results were statistically significant at the .001 level.

COMMENTARY. The PreSET materials are well prepared and clear for users seeking to assess implementation fidelity of the PW-PBIS system of behavior management in early childhood settings. The materials include information needed to ascertain the appropriateness of the instrument to a particular application. The measure's authors make no claims in the manual regarding the usefulness of the PreSET to settings not utilizing the PW-PBIS. Certainly the arena of early childhood education has a need for clear, concise, and efficient methods of assessing their programs. In fact, the

PreSET authors stress that success of the measure and hence the behavioral system includes administrator support, adequate materials and planning time, and professional development for teachers using the system. The PreSET CD includes feedback and PW-PBIS action plan forms that would appear useful for sharing results. However, no comprehensive study and data analysis of the entire PreSET was reported for a large-scale implementation of the PW-PBIS system. Such an analysis would provide stronger evidence supportive of the quality of the instrument. The PreSET does not purport to be a standardized test, but rather it is a measure of the fidelity of the implementation of a single behavioral system; hence, no information is provided in the manual for differing groups such as gender or ethnicity.

SUMMARY. The Preschool-Wide Evaluation Tool (PreSET), Research Edition is an excellent first step towards effective assessment of early childhood programs that adopt the PW-PBIS system of positive behavior intervention and support. Although the technical evidence is incomplete, the authors have certainly begun to accumulate statistical evidence supportive of the viability of the PreSET as a useful tool in early childhood education. The reporting forms included on the CD appear to be assets for simplifying the sharing of results. One weakness concerns limited statistical evidence of reliability and validity. Caution should be used when these measures are administered for summative evaluation and this reviewer hopes the PreSET's authors will continue efforts to build upon initial evidence of validity and reliability. Early childhood programs that implement the PW-PBIS system could find the PreSET helpful for monitoring their efforts to use this approach based upon behavior analysis, inclusion, and person-centered planning.

Review of the Preschool-Wide Evaluation Tool™ (PreSET™), Research Edition by GIULIANA LOSAPIO, Assistant Professor of School Psychology, Touro College, New York, NY:

DESCRIPTION. The Preschool-Wide Evaluation Tool (PreSET), Research Edition is an evaluation instrument designed to measure implementation fidelity of program-wide positive behavior intervention and support (PW-PBIS) in early childhood programs (Fox & Hemmeter, 2009). PW-PBIS is adapted from the school-wide positive behavior intervention and support (SW-PBIS) model used in elementary, middle, and high schools (Spaulding, Horner, May, & Vincent, 2008). The PreSET is based on the School-wide Evaluation Tool (SET; Sugai, Lewis-Palmer, Todd, & Horner, 2001), which reportedly has well established psychometric properties and is a widely used measure of school-wide positive behavior intervention and support (SW-PBIS) fidelity. As recommended, the PreSET is administered twice per year in the initial phases of implementation (for the first few years) then once annually if the center chooses to reduce the number of yearly administrations. The administration involves an interview with the program administrator that should take approximately 15–20 minutes, followed by observations and interviews with teachers, other staff, and a sample of children. The authors of the manual report administration takes approximately one hour in small settings with one to two classrooms, with an increase of about 20 minutes for each additional classroom. The authors recommend knowing each classroom's transition times to assist in scheduling observations because observing a transition from a less structured to a more structured activity is required.

The PreSET is presented as a 3-point Likert scale (0-*not yet implemented*, 1-*partially implemented*, 2-*fully implemented*) and includes 30 items that are divided into eight face-valid subscales that measure features of PW-PBIS. Each subscale is scored by converting Likert ratings to "percentage implemented" scores. A Total Percent Implemented score is derived by computing the mean percentage implemented score of all eight subscales. The PreSET provides a score that is an aggregate of multiple classrooms assessed in a preschool program.

Results from administration of the PreSET inform educators about what areas of PW-PBIS they are most successful in implementing, the areas that need improvement, and those they are not yet implementing. This feedback is useful for measuring progress from year to year and for indicating areas in need of professional development or revision. The PreSET assesses classroom and program-wide variables across eight categories (Expectations Defined, Behavioral Expectations Taught, Responses to Appropriate and Challenging Behavior, Organized and Predictable Environment, Monitoring and Decision Making, Family Involvement, Management, and Program Support).

DEVELOPMENT. In developing the Pre-SET, the authors sought to create a reliable measure to evaluate the impact of PW-PBIS in early child-

hood settings. The PreSET measures the program's implementation of key aspects of PW-PBIS. It also measures program-wide supports needed to promote long-term maintenance of PW-PBIS practices. The PreSET is based on the framework of the School-wide Evaluation Tool (SET; Sugai, Lewis-Palmer, Todd, & Horner, 2001). Items were modified by the authors to apply to early childhood settings, changes were made to language used to describe subscales, and content was changed to correlate better with language used in preschools. Organized and Predictable Environment and Family Involvement subscales were added, and the PreSET clarifies that rules and expectations need to be posted in word and other visual formats as the young children in such settings are emergent readers. The PreSET also includes items concerning the use of supports during transitions, when young children seem to exhibit more challenging behavior.

The SET, from which the PreSET was adapted, has strong psychometric properties (Horner, et al., 2001; Vincent, Spaulding & Tobin, 2010). The SET reportedly has strong test-retest reliability, interobserver agreement, and construct evidence of validity (Horner et al., 2001) as well as high internal consistency (Vincent et al., 2010). The PreSET authors report that preliminary data on reliability and validity demonstrate high internal consistency and item-total correlations across eight subscales. Construct evidence of validity has also been assessed as adequate as was the scale's sensitivity to change.

TECHNICAL. The technical information in the PreSET manual is based on data from 138 early childhood classrooms. The majority of these classrooms were in the Pacific Northwest (101) with many less (31) in the southeastern U.S. and only 6 in other western states in the U.S. Settings included 66 Head Start classrooms, 26 private child care classrooms, 16 state-funded preschool classrooms, 15 special education classrooms, 11 public/nonprofit settings, and 4 preschool classes in elementary schools. Most programs (127) provided data from a single classroom. Although the sample is somewhat representative of the intended population, there were no schools in the northeastern or central U.S. included in the sample. Furthermore, Head Start programs made up almost half of the schools included whereas all other schools made up the other (slightly more than) half. Overall, the sample could have been better distributed, but does represent a wide range of preschool settings.

The authors assessed interobserver reliability on a subset of data collected. Two trained data collectors independently collected PreSET data in the same 22 classrooms. The average percent of agreement on items was 95%, ranging from 68% to 100%. Interrater agreement was high across PreSET items and total scores in these settings. Item-subscale correlations were moderately strong with a mean of .56 and a median of .58. Item-total correlations ranged from .12 to .75. Subscale-total correlations were moderately strong, ranging from .39 to .71. The authors report having completed a series of principal component and exploratory factor analyses to determine whether the eight subscales conformed to a single score. Results supported the use of the total score for interpretation.

Validity was assessed from a construct perspective by correlating scores with the Teaching Pyramid Observation Tool (TPOT; Fox, Hemmeter, & Snyder, 2008 as cited in Steed & Pomerleau, 2012), which also measures implementation fidelity of PBIS in early childhood settings. Convergent evidence is provided for subscales for which the TPOT and PreSET measure similar constructs. Correlations were modest to moderate. Divergent evidence of validity in areas only measured by one of the tools was also assessed. As expected, there were no significant positive correlations between subscales that are not conceptually linked. Additionally, pre- and post-implementation data were collected at 29 sites to estimate the tool's sensitivity to change. All classrooms demonstrated an increase in their PreSET scores from fall to spring following instruction from behavior specialists, training in PBIS, and individualized coaching.

COMMENTARY. The PreSET is a convenient tool used to measure PW-PBIS implementation fidelity that shows good promise. The psychometric properties of the PreSET were examined using data from 138 preschool classrooms. The schools, however, were not representative of some regions in the U.S. Technical information could be strengthened by including data from a more geographically diverse and representative sample.

The PreSET seems easy to use, and the time commitment necessary seems appropriate for the amount of information gathered. Strengths of the PreSET include administration time, although based on this limited review, it seems that it might take slightly longer than specified to complete. Given that the classroom observation includes a mandatory observation of a transition, even if the observer plans his or her observation ahead of time, it seems likely that the evaluation would require more time. Other strengths are the convenient CD containing spreadsheets for data collection and ease of use. The recommended two administrations per year, although useful, might be difficult for some programs to provide. Overall, the PreSET seems to be a useful and much needed tool for preschools following the PW-PBIS protocol.

SUMMARY. The PreSET is an evaluation tool designed to measure implementation fidelity of PW-PBIS in early childhood programs. The measure is based on the SET, which was designed for schools implementing SW-PBIS. The PreSET would be of particular interest to administrators and directors of early childhood settings currently using PW-PBIS or considering implementation of the behavior intervention. As a measure for evaluating treatment fidelity, the PreSET would be valuable in many early intervention settings across the U.S.

REVIEWER'S REFERENCES

Fox, L., & Hemmeter, M. (2009). A programwide model for supporting social emotional development and addressing challenging behavior in early childhood settings. In W. Sailor, G. Dunlop, G. Sugai, & R. Horner (Eds.), *Handbook of positive behavior support* (pp. 177–202). New York, NY: Springer Publishing Co. doi:10.1007/978-0-387-09632-2_8

Horner, R. H., Todd, A. W., Lewis-Palmer, T., Irvin, L. K., Sugai, G., & Boland, J. B. (2004). The School-Wide Evaluation Tool (SET): A research instrument for assessing school-wide positive behavior support. *Journal of Positive Behavior Interventions*, 6, 3–12. doi:10.1177/10983007040060010201

Spaulding, S. A., Horner, R. H., May, S. L., & Vincent, C. G. (2008). *Implementation of school-wide PBIS across the United States* (OSEP Technical Briefs). Retrieved from http://www.pbis.org/evaluation/evaluation_briefs/nov_08_(2).aspx

Steed, E. A., & Pomerleau, T. M. (2012). *Preschool-Wide Evaluation Tool (PreSET), Research Edition manual.* Baltimore, MD: Paul H. Brookes Publishing Co.

Sugai, G., Lewis-Palmer, T., Todd, A., & Horner, R. H. (2001). School-wide evaluation tool. Eugene, OR: University of Oregon.

Vincent, C., Spaulding, S., & Tobin, T. J. (2010). A reexamination of the psychometric properties of the School-Wide Evaluation Tool (SET). *Journal of Positive Behavior Interventions*, 12, 161–179. doi:10.1177/1098300709332345

[135]

PrinTest (Forms A-C and BR-C).

Purpose: Designed for selecting or evaluating entry-level production or maintenance employees where the reading of prints and drawings is required.

Population: Applicants or incumbents for jobs requiring print reading abilities.

Publication Dates: 1990-2010.

Acronym: RCJS-PrinTest.

Scores: Total score only.

Administration: Group.

Price Data, 2011: $22 per consumable self-scoring test booklet or online test administration; $24.95 per manual (2010, 23 pages).

Time: 35(45) minutes.

Comments: Online administration available.

Author: Roland T. Ramsay.

Publisher: Ramsay Corporation.

Cross References: For reviews by James W. Pinkney and Nambury S. Raju of an earlier edition, see 13:258.

Review of the Ramsay Corporation Job Skills PrinTest (Forms A-C and BR-C) by JANET HOUSER, Academic Dean, Rueckert-Hartman College for Health Professions (RHCHP) and LORA CLAYWELL, Associate Professor, RHCHP, Regis University, Denver, CO:

DESCRIPTION. The Ramsay Corporation Job Skills (RCJS) PrinTest (Forms A-C and BR-C) were originally developed in 1988 and 1994, respectively, as 33-item, self-scoring tests intended to measure the ability to read mechanical prints and drawings. The two forms of the test, A-C and BR-C, are identical in content and diagrams; however, measurements in Form BR-C are expressed as decimals instead of fractions as in Form A-C. Both forms are available for online administration or in paper-and-pencil format. Form A-2, developed in 2008, is a parallel equivalent, and is not included in this review. All forms appear to be offered only in English.

The target audience for the tests includes both applicants and those currently employed in jobs where the reading of prints and drawings is a necessary part of the role. These include Maintenance Mechanics, Apprentices, and Drafters, as well as Industrial Machinery Mechanics and Mechanical Drafters. The test is intended to diagnose gaps in knowledge in order to determine a training plan, determine knowledge prior to hiring, and for certification of mastery of a body of knowledge or competency testing.

Specific instructions for the paper-and-pencil format have been provided and include rules for the testing environment as well as an examiner script. The instructions and script are clear and easy to follow. The website is provided for access to the instructions for the online versions. All PrinTest forms are readily accessed via www.ramsaycorp.com. Paper-and-pencil format tests are limited to 35 minutes in duration. The length of time allotted for online administration is not provided. Both the self-scoring paper-and-pencil version and the online tests are compatible with the Ramsay Corporation's exam scoring system. Specific examiner instructions for scoring paper-and-pencil tests are clear and reasonable.

DEVELOPMENT. The authors note that the RCJS Reading Prints and Drawings Form A was developed based on content areas suggested by job experts in maintenance and engineering. The content areas are listed in the manual as: Views and Surfaces, Simple Drawings: Dimensions, Intermediate Drawings: Dimensions, Complex Drawings: Dimensions, and Complex Drawings: Finishes. There is no information regarding how the authors developed the specific items based on the content areas, or how it was determined that the items reflected these specific content areas. The authors make note that the drawings used as reference in the instrument were developed by an engineering firm using standard drafting and CAD materials.

Each question presents a drawing and identifies a plane or line that must be calculated. Answers are presented in multiple-choice format. The drawings begin with simple measures and progress in the first dozen questions to complex calculations.

There is no information about the theoretical assumptions that form the detailed basis of actual test construction. There is no information provided about pilot testing of the instrument. Information about development of the instruments is wholly lacking from the test manual, and so the reader cannot evaluate the effectiveness of processes used to write, refine, and finalize the test items.

TECHNICAL. The test was administered to 199 technical institute students and 134 incumbents and applicants for technical jobs as a basis for the normative data reported in the manual, but there is no indication that any of these were used as pilot data to revise or refine the instrument. Additional reliability data were provided by a sample of 111 employees at a manufacturing plant. This sample represents the target population relatively well overall; there were no data presented describing the specific jobs or titles of the subjects, although the distribution of gender was reported. Although standardized scores were not developed, the authors do report a raw score-to-percentile table that can be used to determine an individual's score relative to those in the normative sample.

The manual accompanying RCJS Reading Prints & Drawings Form A, RCJS PrinTest (Form A-C and Form BR-C) includes information regarding reliability in the form of KR-20 Kuder-Richardson coefficients and descriptive statistics, including mean, standard deviation and standard error of measurement. The Kuder-Richardson approach to reliability is an appropriate test of reliability for a test composed of dichotomous answers (correct/incorrect) and an overall test score that is a sum of the correct answers. Two tables are provided for interpretation of the internal reliability data. The item analysis data demonstrate midlevel to high point-biserial correlations. Two test items were subsequently changed as a result of low point-biserial correlations.

In 2001, the reliability of scores on the RCJS PrinTest Form B-C (2001) was estimated with 130 people, though the classification of the participants is unknown (they were applicants and incumbents at an oil refinery). The point-biserial indices for items on these forms demonstrate low to midlevel correlations, resulting in the revision of 6 of the 33 questions.

There was no mention of a split-half reliability in the manual, which is appropriate as all forms of the test are timed. As there appears to be no interest in trending the results of this test over time, test-retest reliability is of little concern and no data are provided.

No specific validity analyses were described in the test manual. The authors note that test questions were devised by an engineering company, and define both content-related and criterion-related validity in the manual, but admit that no studies of either were conducted. Also, no evidence of construct validity is provided. The authors refer to U.S. Department of Labor findings from 1970 that similar tests were predictive of success in jobs, but report no studies of predictive validity. This is unfortunate, given the stated purpose of the test for pre-employment evaluation. There is no description of the fairness of the instrument, which is particularly important to assure the test does not discriminate on the basis of some characteristic other than the criterion of interest.

COMMENTARY. The RCJS PrinTest (Forms A-C and BR-C) are short, easily administered tests. This may be a good test to use as a basis for employee development or training. A key strength is its accessibility and ease of administration; it is quick to administer and has low respondent burden.

The instrument appears to possess mid- to high-level reliability. However, there is little evidence about the specific process used to develop individual items or how it was determined these items were the most important skills for these employee groups.

Validity analyses are absent. Particularly troubling is the lack of any tests for criterion-related and predictive validity, given the authors propose the test be used as a pre-employment screen. Without evidence that these items do, indeed, predict some level of job performance in a nondiscriminatory way, this instrument would not be appropriate for pre-employment testing or as a basis for employment decisions without local validity studies.

SUMMARY. The RCJS PrinTest (Forms A-C and BR-C) are 33-item self-scoring, timed, online or paper-and-pencil tests intended to measure the ability to read prints and drawings. The target audience, according to the manual, is composed of both applicants (requiring predictive test characteristics) and current employees as a diagnostic tool for knowledge gaps.

The manual that accompanies the tests includes examiner instructions and script sufficient for administering the paper-and-pencil form. The online version is accessed via www.ramsaycorp.com. According to the manual, the items are based on standards of practice related to drafting and CAD; however, few specific development details were provided.

Review of the PrinTest (Forms A-C and BR-C) by CHOCKALINGAM VISWESVARAN, Professor of Psychology, Florida International University, Miami, FL:

DESCRIPTION. The PrinTest (Forms A-C and BR-C) was developed to assess proficiency in reading prints and diagrams. It is designed for use with job applicants and incumbents in jobs such as Industrial Machinery Mechanics and Mechanical Drafters (as described in the O*NET database). The test comprises 33 items administered over 35 minutes and has five types of questions: Views and Surfaces (4 items), Simple Drawings: Dimensions (10), Intermediate Drawings: Dimensions (7), Complex Drawings: Dimensions (10), and Complex Drawings: Finishes (2). Compared to the previous versions of this test, the only change seems to be the splitting of the 12 items in the Complex Drawings Category into two groups. However, the test is designed to provide not five scores but one total score on the proficiency to read mechanical prints and drawings.

DEVELOPMENT. The test was initially developed in 1988 as Form A and revised in 1990 (when 2 items were changed). Both these earlier versions have been reviewed in the *Thirteenth Mental Measurements Yearbook* (*13th MMY*). Form B was designed in 1994 using the same diagrams but with measurements expressed in decimals instead of fractions. The Introduction to the test manual states that the PrinTest Form A-C was revised in 1998 and Form B-C was revised in 2001 and 2010. It is noted that a parallel form was developed in 2008 (Form A2). The descriptions of the different forms and their links are difficult to follow and no data are provided on the empirical equivalence of scores across the multiple forms.

The manual describes data from (a) a sample of 199 technical institute students, (b) a sample of 23 incumbents and applicants from a manufacturing plant, (c) a sample of 111 employed males and females from a southern manufacturing plant, and (d) a sample of 199 applicants and employees in a refinery in eastern U.S.A. (69 took Form A-C and 130 took Form B-C). The first three samples responded to Form A. Looking back at the reviews found in the *13th MMY*, it appears that only the third and fourth samples are an addition using the revised forms. The manual also provides detailed instructions to test examiners to ensure a standardized assessment across all examinees.

TECHNICAL. The technical data presented in the manual include item difficulty levels and item-total point-biserial correlations for the 33 items in Form A. These data are provided for the three samples ($N = 199, 23$, and 111) separately as well as for the combined sample. Normative data for Form A-C and Form B-C came from a sample of 199 applicants and incumbents at an eastern U.S. refinery. Most of the point-biserial correlations were positive and high (in the .50s and .60s) suggesting that the 33 items assess a relatively homogeneous construct.

The raw scores can be converted to percentiles for Form A either using one of the three samples or the combined sample of 333 respondents. However, a normative sample of 23 is probably not informative. The manual also provides a table to convert raw scores in Form A-C (1998) and Form B-C (2001) based on the responses of 199 respondents (Sample 4). It is not clear why data for these two forms were combined.

Internal consistency estimates (assessed as KR-20) are reported for the different forms. For Form A, based on a combined sample of 333, an alpha of .91 is estimated for the total score. For Forms A-C and B-C, the internal consistency estimates were .79 and .86, respectively. The standard deviation of the scores for those taking Form A was higher (7.34) compared to those taking other forms (5.54), and this difference in variability of scores is likely to account for the slight difference in the reliability estimates.

No criterion-related validity information is provided. The manual states that content validity of the test is assured when the behaviors required on the test are also required on the job. A table apparently summarizes two content validation stud-

ies. The first states that Form CMB was analyzed and is dated December 1996 (even before the first version of the test was available in 1998); it reports an interrater agreement of .83 across 10 raters and 21 items. The second study seems to focus on Form OMB and is dated April 1997 and reports an interrater agreement of .81 across 10 raters and 20 items. No further information on rater sampling, scales used, and how the 20 and 21 items were chosen from 33 items are available.

The manual reports that no formal studies of construct validity have been conducted. It is asserted that construct validity will be enhanced by the procedures of test development. The item difficulties reported for Form A, however, indicate that students found the items to be easier than employees and incumbents. As such, it is imperative that the correlation between the test scores and cognitive ability be investigated.

COMMENTARY. The technical manual is inadequate and needs to be revised. There should be clear descriptions of what samples are analyzed for reliability, item analysis, etc. If data from different forms are combined, empirical data demonstrating the equivalence of the different forms is needed. Reliability is assessed with KR-20 internal consistency coefficients but alternate forms reliability and test-retest coefficients are also needed. Criterion-related validity data should be gathered as well as analyses conducted for predictive bias across ethnic groups and gender. Group differences are not reported but should be available from the test publisher given the gender composition of the samples. These group differences need to be reported in the manual. Normative data should not be based on a combined sample of incumbents and applicants. Given motivational differences, norms for job applicant samples are likely to differ from those of incumbents.

SUMMARY. The manual is too cryptic and is missing important information. Some of this information (e.g., predictive validity, construct validity) awaits further data collection whereas others (equivalence across forms, demographic group differences, differential item functioning, etc.) should be incorporated into the manual. What is disheartening is that some of these limitations were pointed out in the earlier reviews in the *13th MMY* (1998) and have not yet been addressed. The positive aspect is the provision of clear and detailed directions to test examiners on how to obtain standardized scores across examinees.

[136]
Profile of Mood States, Second Edition.

Purpose: Designed for the "assessment of transient and fluctuating feelings, as well as relatively enduring affect states."

Publication Dates: 1971-2012.

Acronym: POMS2.

Scores, 8: Anger-Hostility, Confusion-Bewilderment, Depression-Dejection, Fatigue-Inertia, Tension-Anxiety, Vigor-Activity, Total Mood Disturbance, Friendliness.

Administration: Individual or group.

Forms, 4: Adult, Adult Short, Youth, Youth Short.

Price Data, 2013: $144 per complete online kit, including manual (2012, 128 pages), 10 online adult forms, 10 online adult short forms, 10 online youth forms, and 10 online youth short forms; $88 per manual; $2.50 per online form.

Authors: Juvia P. Heuchert and Douglas M. McNair.

Publisher: Multi-Health Systems, Inc.

> *a)* PROFILE OF MOOD STATES 2ND EDITION—ADULT.
> **Population:** Ages 18 and older.
> **Acronym:** POMS2—A.
> **Time:** (8-10) minutes.
> *b)* PROFILE OF MOOD STATES 2ND EDITION—ADULT SHORT.
> **Population:** Ages 18 and older.
> **Acronym:** POMS2—A Short.
> **Time:** (3-5) minutes.
> *c)* PROFILE OF MOOD STATES 2ND EDITION—YOUTH.
> **Population:** Ages 13 to 17.
> **Acronym:** POMS2—Y.
> **Time:** (8-10) minutes.
> *d)* PROFILE OF MOOD STATES 2ND EDITION—YOUTH SHORT.
> **Population:** Ages 13 to 17.
> **Acronym:** POMS2—Y Short.
> **Time:** (3-5) minutes.

Cross References: See T5:2076 (187 references) and T4:2122 (191 references), 9:998 (46 references), and T3:1904 (84 references); for reviews by William J. Eichman and Thaddeus E. Weckowicz of an earlier edition, see 8:651 (33 references); see also T2:1337 (17 references).

Review of the Profile of Mood States, Second Edition by IRA H. BERNSTEIN, Professor of Clinical Sciences, and HELEN MAYO, Research and Liaison Librarian, The University of Texas Southwestern Medical Center at Dallas, Dallas, TX:

DESCRIPTION. The Profile of Mood States, Second Edition (POMS 2, 2012) by Juvia P. Heuchert and the late Douglas M. McNair is a revision of a 1971 test that, in turn, dates back to work to the 1950s by McNair, Maurice Lorr, and Leo Droppleman. As noted in the test manual, it is intended to be applicable to clinical, medical, research, and athletic settings. The present form is a reworking of the original test. The authors of the test manual note five reasons for the revision: (1) improved psychometric information, (2) better defined positive mood states, (3) modernized item wording, (4) elimination of culturally specific items, and (5) extension of the range of the test downward in age to adolescents.

DEVELOPMENT. The general format of the items is to respond to questions of the general form "How do you presently feel?" for each of a series of mood descriptors using a 5-point scale ranging from 0 = *not at all* to 4 = *extremely*. Six scales collectively define a Total Mood Disturbance (TMD) score: Anger-Hostility (AH), Confusion-Bewilderment (CB), Depression-Dejection (DD), Fatigue-Inertia (FI), Tension-Anxiety (TA), and Vigor-Activity (VA). There is also a separate Friendliness (F) scale that is not part of the TMD score. There is a full-length adult version (POMS 2-A), a full-length youth version (POMS 2-Y), a short adult version (POMS 2-A Short), and a short youth version (POMS 2-Y Short). These respectively consist of 65, 60, 35, and 35 items. The adult versions are intended for individuals age 18 and above, and the youth versions are intended for individuals ages 13–17. The measure may be administered either online or in a paper version with results generated online only. Results are reported in a conventional *T*-score metric (mean of 50 and standard deviation of 10). The adult scores may be compared to overall or gender-specific norms, and the youth scores may be compared to overall or age- and gender-specific norms. Automated results are available from the administration in question or as a comparison of up to four prior administrations. The original version of the POMS was designed for psychiatric outpatients, but subsequent use has spanned a wide range of both nonclinical and clinical applications. One purpose among many is to evaluate and monitor therapeutic effects.

TECHNICAL.

Standardization. Considerable time and care went into the establishment of normative samples, which were stratified by geographical location in Canada and the United States, age, and gender. Additional information was obtained regarding ethnicity and educational level. Particular care went into obtaining a geriatric sample. The test manual describes a variety of analyses of these demographic variables among others.

Reliability. According to the test manual, the normative sample yielded alpha coefficients ranging from .82 to .93 for the individual scales and .96 for the composite (TMD) in the full 2-A version. Not surprisingly, the F scale, with only 5 items, had the lowest internal consistency. The full 2-Y values were nearly identical as were the values obtained from a clinical sample. The one exception was that the F scale was noticeably more internally consistent in the 2-Y clinical sample (alpha coefficient was .96). This might be due to a greater variance in this sample but such data were not presented, perhaps because it is generally redundant with regard to the values of coefficient alpha. By definition, the scales are not designed to be highly stable over time. The obtained adjusted test-retest correlation coefficients for individual scales ranged from .43 to .65 over a 1-week period, changing but slightly when disattenuated. This is not surprising in view of the high internal consistency observed for the individual scales. It is also not surprising that the values fell slightly to .30–.63 when a 30-day period was used. The 2-Y data were similar. Perhaps more surprisingly, the short form internal consistency and temporal stability data differed little from the longer versions.

Validity. The test authors present four lines of evidence for the validity of the POMS 2 scales: (a) appropriateness of the factor structure, (b) discriminative validity, (c) convergent validity, and (d) generalization across relevant racial/ethnic groups.

Most appropriately in the opinion of these reviewers, the test developers used a parcel approach to factor analysis by grouping correlated items, which minimizes the problems of factoring items. The primary factor model tested was hierarchical with all individual scales other than F proposed to load on a higher order factor. The fit was acceptable save for the RMSEA measure, which was .10 for both full scales and thus slightly high. The slight misfit seems to reflect the VA scale, for which the correlations with other scales were generally lower than the other measures.

The basic evidence presented for discriminative validity comes from a series of analyses of covariance, both univariate and multivariate. The relevant groups consisted of anxiety disorder, mood disorder, and nonclinical reference groups with age, ethnicity, gender, and education level used as covariates. In general, the mood-disordered groups obtained the highest (most pathological) scores except for the TA and VA scales where, as expected, the patients

with anxiety disorders were most elevated. Effect sizes were generally in the medium range, which reflects relatively small differences between the two impaired groups and a larger difference between these groups and the nonclinical reference group. Specifically, the effect sizes in terms of the partial eta squared values (correcting for the demographic variables) ranged from .06 to .14 for the POMS 2-A. Corresponding values for the POMS 2A-Short ranged from .04 to .13, which, in relation to the long form, is impressively large. In addition, comparable partial eta squared values for the POMS 2-Y and POMS 2-Y Short ranged from .02 to .40 and from .05 to .38, respectively.

The evidence provided for convergent validity consists of the correlations between the POMS 2-A and Watson and Clark's (1994) Positive and Negative Affect Schedule–Expanded Form (PANAS-X), which is a 60-item self-report measure of emotions. Report was limited to scales measuring similar content (e.g., the POMS 2-A TA scale with the PANAS-X Fear scale and the POMS 2-AH scale with the PANAS-X Hostility scale). Correlation coefficients between the five pairs of measures so chosen on a nonclinical sample ranged from .57 to .84 (all $ps < .001$, $df = 73$). This is certainly relevant evidence considering the methodological difference between the two scales (clinical evaluation vs. self-report) and the difficulty finding comparable scales in the literature. There were no comparable data for the POMS 2-Y nor for the two short forms. Recognizing the limited time between publication of the various versions of the POMS and the writing of this review, it is hoped that these blanks will be filled in shortly.

The final supporting evidence presented for the POMS 2-A is that it generalizes across ethnicities. This evidence derived from a comparison of African Americans, Whites, and Hispanic/Latinos controlling for age, gender, and education level (parents in the case of the POMS 2-Y). The test authors use a more conservative criterion ($p < .01$) to reduce the occurrence of Type I errors that may appear when multiple analyses are implemented. Only the AH scale differed at a level approaching significance among ethnicities ($p = .015$) when these other demographic variables were controlled. Its effect size (partial eta squared) was .009 with the remainder being .006 or less. The error df varied from 923 to 926. All ethnicity effects were significant beyond the .05 level for the POMS 2-Y, but the effect sizes only ranged from about

.01 to .07 based upon an error *df* of 442. Given the relatively large sample sizes, these effects do not seem extremely large.

The POMS 2 (2012) manual concludes with a series of useful appendices that provide a partial listing of representative research using the original version, standard error of measurement values by gender for both youth and adult versions and by age and gender for the adult version, data on change scores, and the 60+ norm group. The research listing contains a count by area of the roughly 3,000 published POMS studies and an annotated listing of a selected number of these studies indicating the breadth of research that has been conducted using the previous version of this measure.

COMMENTARY. At this time, there is basically no research published using the recently released POMS 2 that was not part of its initial validation. Given the success of the original POMS and the similarity of the POMS and POMS 2, a substantial degree of validity generalization should be expected. The underlying theoretical model seems eminently reasonable, and it reflects current views on mood states quite well.

SUMMARY. Quite simply, this is an updating of a successful test. The logic used in its development appears quite sound. More than sufficient effort has gone into its development. It seems quite suitable for its intended purposes of assessing mood states in a variety of contexts.

REVIEWERS' REFERENCE

Watson, D., & Clark, L. A. (1994). *Manual for the Positive and Negative Affect Schedule, Expanded Form.* Iowa City, IA: The University of Iowa.

Review of the Profile of Mood States, Second Edition by JOSEPH C. KUSH, Associate Professor and Director of the Doctoral Program in Instructional Technology and Educational Leadership, Duquesne University, Pittsburgh, PA:

DESCRIPTION. The Profile of Mood States, Second Edition (POMS 2) is a collection of four instruments designed to assess the mood states of individuals 13 years of age and older. Created as a revision of the Profile of Mood States (POMS), these self-report scales allow for the quick assessment of transient, fluctuating feelings and enduring, affective states. The POMS 2 is designed for use in clinical and research settings, for both assessment and treatment monitoring.

The POMS 2 includes separate scales to assess two age ranges: adults aged 18 years and older (POMS 2–A) and adolescents 13 to 17 years of age (POMS 2–Y). Both POMS 2 instruments are avail-able as full-length and shortened versions, and can be administered using online or paper-and-pencil formats. However, all scales are scored exclusively online using the MHS Online Assessment Center. All scales produce *T*-scores with a mean of 50 and a standard deviation of 10.

POMS 2 Full-Length Versions. The POMS 2–A consists of 65 items, whereas the POMS 2–Y is composed of 60 items. Both full-length versions yield multiple scale scores: Anger-Hostility, Confusion-Bewilderment, Depression-Dejection, Fatigue-Inertia, Tension-Anxiety, and Vigor-Activity. A Total Mood Disturbance score can also be calculated as a total of the six scale scores. A newly created Friendliness scale can be scored separately. The publisher indicates that the full-length versions of the POMS 2 are recommended when a thorough evaluation of mood is desired.

POMS 2 Short Versions. Two abbreviated versions of the POMS 2 are also contained within the package: one for adults and a second for adolescents. The shortened versions of these scales each contain a subset of 35 items taken from the full-length versions. The publisher indicates that the subset was derived from the five items on each of the POMS 2–A and POMS 2–Y scales that exhibited the highest item-total correlations and best predicted their respective scale scores. Shortened versions are designed to be used for screening purposes or when multiple administrations are required (e.g., when used to monitor or evaluate treatment programs).

DEVELOPMENT. The Profile of Mood States was first developed and released by Mc-Nair, Lorr, and Droppleman in 1971. The original POMS consisted of 65 self-report items that required participants to rate their current mood on a 5-point scale ranging from *Not at all* to *Extremely*. The POMS was designed to measure six factors including Tension-Anxiety, Depression-Dejection, Anger-Hostility, Fatigue-Inertia, Confusion-Bewilderment, and Vigor-Activity. The first five scales were scored negatively (higher scores reflected negative emotions) and the Vigor-Activity scale was scored positively, with a higher score reflecting more vigor. The original POMS was reviewed in the *Eighth Mental Measurements Yearbook* (Buros, 1978) and since its original publication, over 4,000 research studies have been published with both clinical and nonclinical populations. Although it was originally designed for use with adult outpatient clinical populations, the POMS has been researched in a variety of alternative settings with a wide variety of populations including studies with cancer patients, meditation, sports psychology, psychopharmacology, and neuropsychology. The POMS has also become popular outside of the United States and has been translated into over 40 languages other than English.

The Profile of Mood States, Second Edition (POMS 2) is a revision of the Profile of Mood States (POMS). All three of the original test authors are now deceased; however, their contributions to the long-term development of the scales are fittingly acknowledged in the POMS 2 manual. The test manual provides five factors that motivated the revision of the POMS: (a) To update the norms; (b) to focus on positive mood states, in particular Friendliness; (c) to modernize the language of the scale items; (d) to eliminate scale items considered to be culture-specific or difficult to translate into languages other than English; and (e) to create a version of the scale for adolescents.

Administration guidelines, both prior to and during the administration, are well-described in the test manual. All forms of the POMS 2 can be administered individually, in groups, or remotely. The test manual indicates that all POMS 2 components are designed to be administered by psychologists, clinical social workers, physicians, counselors, psychiatrists, and psychiatric nurses. All scale interpretation should be undertaken by individuals with MHS b-level qualifications. The full-length versions of the scales require approximately 10 minutes to complete whereas the shortened version can be completed in approximately 5 minutes. Questions are intended to be read by the examinee and require an eighth grade reading level. Alternative methods of administration, such as the administrator reading items aloud or entering the responses into the computer manually, can be undertaken. The typical response prompt is "How have you been feeling during the PAST WEEK, INCLUDING TODAY?" Additional ways of asking this question and other examiner directions to be considered after the administration are also provided.

Step-by-step directions for interpretation are well-described in the POMS 2 manual. Directions are given for converting raw scores to T-scores and percentile ranks and for computing and interpreting confidence intervals. The chapter describing scale interpretation concludes with a brief case study.

TECHNICAL. Data collection for the POMS 2-A occurred during 2004 to 2009 and data collection for the POMS 2-Y occurred during 2006 to 2009. Data were collected from 62 sites in the United States and Canada. Stratification variables included age, gender, race/ethnicity, level of educational attainment, and geographic region. For both the adult and adolescent version, the race/ethnicity and parent education level variables deviated from the 2000 U.S. Census and necessitated statistical weighting to correct for these deviations.

Normative data for the adult versions (POMS 2–A) for both standard and abbreviated formats were derived from 1,000 individuals. Adult norms are grouped for ages 18–29, 30–49, and 50 plus, in addition to an optional 60 plus group. Normative data for the adolescent versions (POMS 2–Y) were based on 500 individuals aged 13 to 17 years. Analyses reported in the test manual indicate an absence of gender differences on the POMS 2-A Total Mood Disturbance Scale. However, males were found to evidence greater Anger-Hostility, Depression-Dejection, whereas females displayed significantly more Friendliness. Significant age differences were also evidenced with younger adults displaying more negative emotions than older adults. For the adolescent sample, neither age or gender differences were evidenced on the POMS 2-Y.

The psychometric properties of the POMS 2 are also presented in the test manual. Strong internal consistency (coefficient alpha) was evidenced for both the POMS 2-A Total Mood Disturbance (alpha ranged from .94 to .97) and the POMS 2-Y Total Mood Disturbance (alpha ranged from .95 to .98) normative samples. Subscale correlations were slightly lower but still quite adequate for the POMS 2-A as well as the POMS 2-Y (alpha ranged from .76 to .95). The use of alpha coefficients is an improvement over the original POMS analyses that used *KR20* to report internal consistency. For the clinical sample, internal consistency estimates were comparable, with a slightly wider range (.76 to .96), as might be expected, that reflect strong coefficients.

Test-retest correlation coefficients are reported for the POMS 2-A after one week ($r = .48$ to .72) and after 30 days ($r = .34$ to .70), as well as for the POMS 2-Y after one week ($r = .45$ to .75) and after 30 days ($r = .02$ to .59). The test manual reports that because the POMS 2 assesses fluctuating mood states "these test-retest stability results align with expectations for a measure of mood states" (p. 37). Although moods (as contrasted to personality traits) certainly can be expected to vary over time, a 30-day test-retest correlation of .02 reflects an almost perfectly random relationship and calls into question the stability and ultimately the utility of what is purported to be assessed.

Regarding validity, the test manual reports that a confirmatory factor analysis was performed on data from both the normative and clinical samples. Although it appears that the analysis was performed properly (e.g., multiple criteria for model fit), the description of the analysis is inadequate and omits important information necessary for proper interpretation and replication. Similarly, a series of ANCOVAs and MANCOVAs comparing clinical and nonclinical groups are reported in an attempt to establish the discriminant validity of the scale. Again, these findings are not clearly described and are based on relatively small samples. Convergent validity is reported through correlations with the Positive and Negative Affect Schedule–Expanded Form. Resulting correlation coefficients were computed on a relatively modest sample of 74 individuals with values ranging from .57 to .84. Finally, in an attempt to support the use of the scales with diverse populations, the test manual reports analyses that compared race/ethnicity performance. The results are somewhat unexpected, with no differences on the POMS 2-A but multiple race/ethnicity differences occurring on the POMS 2-Y. Specifically, for the adolescent group, White adolescents scored significantly higher on many of the scales than the Hispanic/Latino and African American youth. In attempting to explain these findings, the test manual offers the statement "These results indicate that there are some small and consistent differences between the race/ethnic groups on the POMS 2-Y" (p. 48). However, the manual continues, "practitioners do not have to be concerned that the constructs measured by the POMS 2-Y are biased against minority groups" and "these results may indicate that African American and Hispanic youth may slightly under-report, or White youth may slightly over-report, their negative moods" (p. 48). It is unclear how the test authors arrived at these interpretations as no supportive data are offered and no previous research or theoretical explanations are provided to help explain these differences.

COMMENTARY. There is much to like about the revised POMS 2; however, it still contains limitations. When considering the field of mood scales or surveys, the POMS is by far the most popular instrument and the most well-researched. The questions contained on the scales have high face validity and the intention of the publisher to update the language of some of these questions is

admirable. The test manual is easy to read and the multiple administration formats will provide users with welcome alternatives. The POMS 2 now offers standard length and abbreviated forms for adults and adolescents.

Unfortunately, however, much of the revision is a bit disappointing. Only a small number of new items were created and added to the revised scales, and the process describing the revision is not described in sufficient detail. For example, it is not clear if the new questions were reviewed by a panel of experts or a single individual. Relatedly, the qualifications of these individuals are not described within the test manual.

Additionally, more extensive reliability and validity studies, with larger sample sizes conducted prior to the publication of the scale, could have greatly improved the integrity of the instrument. Additional research with clinical or exceptional populations also would have served to increase the generalizability of the POMS-2 scores. It also should be noted that the standardization sample only included three race/ethnicity groups: African American, Hispanic/Latino, and White. It does not appear that Native Americans, Asian Americans, or any "Other" classifications were included, and results obtained from these populations should be interpreted with great caution.

The scale possesses a number of psychometric shortcomings that significantly limit the usability of the instrument. Internal consistency is adequate for the overall scale but subscale reliabilities vary substantially. In the absence of strong test-retest data, potential users of the POMS-2 will be unable to determine whether changes in an examinee's score over time reflect normal fluctuation, possible abnormal developmental etiology, or simply items that are being measured inconsistently across time by the instrument.

Additionally, the test manual provides no evidence of incremental validity, or the extent to which information obtained from the scale will increase the accuracy in predictions derived from other sources of information. Finally, the test authors make no mention of the limitations associated with self-report instruments (e.g., responses may be distorted by social desirability).

SUMMARY. If this scale were a software product, it would be more appropriate to characterize it as a minor update (e.g., POMS 1.5) rather than a comprehensive revision as claimed by the publisher. Perhaps when used as a research instrument, the POMS 2 will stimulate a more rigorous validation process.

Ultimately, many of the limitations of the POMS 2 can be leveled against any scale purporting to measure moods. By definition, moods are fleeting and transitory and far less stable than personality traits. It is not uncommon for an individual to wake up in a grumpy mood only to have encounters with the world that change one's attitude and places that individual in a "good mood" within a few hours. Moods can change rapidly, that is the nature of the construct; hence, the Catch-22 for scales like the POMS 2. If the POMS 2 was given to this hypothetical individual, it would be expected that two very different scores would be produced, even following the brief time interval of a few hours. Assuming the scale accurately yielded a low mood score in the morning and then produced an elevated score after a good lunch with friends and a walk in some fresh air, we could conclude that the POMS 2 was producing "true" or valid scores, as the scale accurately measured changes in mood that occurred over this brief period of time. However, in the same situation the test-retest reliability of the scale would be low. Does validity trump reliability? This is the first step on the slippery slope. If we suspend the requirement of psychometric guidelines that govern other rating scales, how do we interpret an instrument that yields low reliability, even in the short term? More specifically, one of the purported uses of the POMS 2 is for treatment monitoring. How do we confidently conclude that the changes in mood that we hope to see following 30 days of therapy or pharmacological intervention are truly the result of the treatment and not just fluctuations in the scale? Although these questions cannot be sufficiently answered in the test manual of a rating scale such as the POMS 2, the context should have been discussed more completely in the test manual. This context, along with the associated cautions, would allow users to better understand and interpret the questionable psychometric properties associated with the scale. Additional discussion examining the diagnostic accuracy of the scale, including the rate of identified false positives and false negatives, also would have been of great value. Although the POMS 2 remains the most popular rating scale of moods, until such time as more extensive reliability and validity studies are completed, great caution should be exercised when using the scale, particularly with adolescents from diverse racial and ethnic backgrounds.

REVIEWER'S REFERENCE

Buros, O. K. (Ed.) (1978). *The eighth mental measurements yearbook.* Highland Park, NJ: The Gryphon Press.

[137]

Progressive Achievement Test of Mathematics, 2nd Edition.

Purpose: To assist classroom teachers in determining the mathematics skills of their students.

Population: Ages 8–14.

Publication Dates: 1974–2007.

Acronym: PAT Mathematics.

Scores: Total score only.

Administration: Group.

Levels, 7: Individual tests for 7 year levels.

Price Data, 2011: NZ$4 per test booklet; NZ$1.78 per 10 answer sheets; NZ$20 per teacher's manual (2007, 64 pages); NZ$2.40 per marking key; price data for specimen sets for split year levels available from publisher.

Time: (35–45) minutes.

Comments: Electronic marking service available to generate specific reports for each child/classroom/year level.

Authors: Charles Darr, Alex Neill, and Andrew Stephanou.

Publisher: New Zealand Council for Educational Research [New Zealand].

Cross References: For reviews by Linda E. Brody and Suzanne Lane of an earlier edition, see 12:313; see also T3:1911 (1 reference); for a review by Harold C. Trimble of an earlier edition, see 8:288; for reviews by James C. Impara and A. Harry Passow of an earlier Australian edition, see 11:309.

Review of the Progressive Achievement Test of Mathematics, 2nd Edition by MARY L. GARNER, Professor of Mathematics, Kennesaw State University, Kennesaw, GA:

DESCRIPTION. The Progressive Achievement Test of Mathematics, 2nd Edition (PAT: Mathematics) is a series of nine paper-and-pencil tests designed to measure and chart the growth of the mathematical proficiency of individual students in Years 3 through 10 in New Zealand schools. Items are based on the New Zealand curriculum and can be grouped into the following five content categories: Number Knowledge, Number Strategies, Geometry and Measurement, Algebra, and Statistics. Each test consists of 30 to 45 multiple-choice items, with the number of items increasing with the age of the student. A booklet is provided for each test, along with answer sheets that can be scored electronically or by hand. A conversion table for each test is provided so the total raw score can be converted to a scale score with a range of approximately 0 to 100. The scale score can be used to compare an individual's scores across years and to track growth in mathematical proficiency. For each test, stanines are provided at three adjacent year levels, showing how a student's scale score compares with those of a representative sample of students in the same year level. Specific instructions are provided for administering the test. Each test requires 55 minutes of class time, 10 for instructions and 45 for taking the test. Calculators, rulers, and protractors are not allowed.

Individual test results are reported in two ways. A template for a PAT: Mathematics student report is provided for each test, showing the student's level of proficiency, raw score, scale score, stanine, reference group, the relative difficulty of the items on the test, and exactly which items the student answered correctly. Also provided is a Scale Descriptor Report for each content category; as described in the test manual, the Descriptor Report shows "the types of mathematical knowledge and skills required to answer test items that are located at different parts of the scale" (manual, p. 16).

DEVELOPMENT. The first edition of PAT: Mathematics was published in 1974 and revised in 1993. The current edition represents the first time that the tests were analyzed and put on a common scale using Rasch measurement theory. The test authors state that specifications were established for designing the revised tests and that a panel of mathematics education experts reviewed new and revised items, but no further details are provided. A total of 280 items emerged from the revision; these items were divided into 13 forms and piloted nationally with 1,753 students from Years 4 to 10. The Rasch measurement model was used to analyze the national data using Quest software, but details of the analysis are not provided. The test manual states that the items had good Rasch measurement properties, but no specifics are provided about the statistics used to judge the quality of the items. The items were reviewed by a panel to identify possible bias.

TECHNICAL. The raw scores, which represent ordinal measurement, are converted into "patm" units. The scale for the patm units is set so that the mean location of all items is 50 patms, and the logits provided by the Rasch analysis (which usually range from approximately -3 to 3) are converted to patms by multiplying by 10 and adding 50.

Norms in terms of stanines are provided for each test for three adjacent years. For example, Test

4 has three sets of stanines for Years 6, 7, and 8. The norming study was conducted in two phases. Norms for Tests 1 through 7, Years 4 through 10, were established in March of 2005; norms for Tests 1A and 6A, and Year 3, were established in April and May of 2006. In both the 2005 and the 2006 studies, a stratified random sampling of schools based on school decile (socio-economic status) and school type was performed using information from the Ministry of Education. The test authors used a bootstrap procedure on the achieved sample to generate a sample with the intended national proportions of students and compared means and standard deviations of the generated sample with the achieved sample before norming. Approximately 1,500 students were sampled from each year, 4 through 10. For Year 3, 688 students were sampled. The norming studies are described in detail in the test manual.

Evidence for internal reliability of Tests 1 through 7 is provided through reliability coefficients (type not specified) generated by the Quest software. The "Quest coefficients" reported for each test ranged from .89 to .92. No coefficients are provided for Tests 1A and 6A. Scale score standard errors and item difficulty standard errors are also reported in a Rasch analysis and provide evidence for reliability of the test.

Evidence supporting the validity of test score use accrues in the clear progression of item difficulties and mean scores from the lower end of the scale with Year 3 students to the upper end of the scale with Year 10 students. Scores from the PAT: Mathematics were correlated with scores from an achievement test developed by the Australian Council for Educational Research (ACER) and "a direct and consistent relationship was established" (manual, p. 27) according to the test authors. In addition, the test authors argue for the validity of the test scores by stating that each test item "has been subjected to thorough scrutiny by practicing teachers and mathematics specialists and examined by others with expertise in test construction" (manual, p. 27).

COMMENTARY. PAT: Mathematics is an excellent example of how Rasch measurement theory can be used to create a reliable measurement instrument, a ruler along which items and persons can be positioned, to track development in knowledge and skills across many years. Furthermore, the test manual is well written and does an excellent job describing the scale and providing a means to effectively communicate test information to students and parents. The student report and Scale Descriptor Report are clear and effective displays of the detailed information about student performance that can be achieved through objective measurement. This sequence of tests is clearly a useful instrument to educators in New Zealand.

There are a few gaps in the analysis of the tests. Although the test authors state that items not fitting the Rasch measurement model were eliminated from the test, they do not indicate the specific criteria used to define misfit. Furthermore, on a test with five different categories of items, it could be argued that the possibility of multiple dimensions is strong; it is not clear that the fit criteria used would be adequate to ensure the unidimensionality of the tests.

SUMMARY. PAT: Mathematics is a series of nine tests designed to provide New Zealand educators with the ability to measure and chart the growth of the mathematical proficiency of individual students in Years 3 through 10 along a single continuous scale. A report can be generated for each student describing the student's level of proficiency, raw score, scale score, stanine, reference group, the relative difficulty of the items on the test, and exactly which items the student answered correctly. Furthermore, the student's location on the scale can be described in terms of the expected development of knowledge with regard to each of the content categories assessed: Number Knowledge, Number Strategies, Geometry and Measurement, Algebra, and Statistics. Although there are some gaps in the evidence provided regarding analyses, the tests appear to be reliable and to demonstrate validity of test score uses in the prescribed manner.

[138]

Progressive Achievement Tests of Reading [2008 Revision].

Purpose: Designed to "assist classroom teachers to determine the level of achievement attained by their students in reading comprehension and reading vocabulary."

Population: Years 4-10.

Publication Dates: 1969-2008.

Scores, 2: Reading Comprehension, Reading Vocabulary.

Administration: Group.

Levels, 7: 1, 2, 3, 4, 5, 6, 7.

Price Data: Available from publisher.

Comments: Scores on the tests are converted to scores on the Reading Comprehension and Reading Vocabulary measurement scales. This allows progress to be measured across tests.

Authors: Charles Darr, Sue McDowall, Hilary Ferral, Juliet Twist, and Verena Watson.

Publisher: New Zealand Council for Educational Research [New Zealand].

a) READING COMPREHENSION.

Acronym: PATC.

Time: (55) minutes.

b) READING VOCABULARY.

Acronym: PATV.

Time: (35) minutes.

Cross References: See T5:2094 (3 references); for a review by Herbert C. Rudman of an earlier edition, see 12:314 (3 references); see also T4:2141 (7 references) and T3:1912 (2 references); for a review by Douglas A. Pidgeon, see 8:738 (1 reference); see also T2:1579 (1 reference); for excerpted reviews by Milton L. Clark and J. Elkins, see 7:699.

Review of the Progressive Achievement Tests of Reading [2008 Revision] by LISA F. SMITH, Professor of Education and Dean, University of Otago College of Education, Dunedin, New Zealand:

DESCRIPTION. The Progressive Achievement Tests of Reading Comprehension and Reading Vocabulary (2nd Edition) are designed to evaluate New Zealand students in Years 4 to 10, analogous to Grades 3 to 9 in the United States. There are seven reading comprehension tests (PATC) and seven vocabulary tests (PATV) in multiple-choice format, administered in group settings. The tests can be administered at any time during the school year; however, when choosing which test level to administer, it should be noted that norming data were collected at the beginning of the 2007 school year.

The PATC uses narrative texts, poems, and various reports, explanations, procedural texts, and persuasive texts to assess students' ability to construct meaning. The multiple-choice questions comprise retrieval items, local inference items based on small sections of text, and global inference items from across larger sections of text.

The PATV assesses comprehension of key words embedded in text by asking the examinee to choose the best synonym from five options. The test authors state that the key words represent the 10,000 most frequently used word families in the English language, chosen from a New Zealand corpus and a British corpus; no mention of an external or expert review of the words is provided.

The tests are intended to be scored either by hand, using templates provided, or through automated marking available from the test publisher. Scores from the previous edition can be converted to the current scale scores to permit comparison of results over time across the old and new tests.

The teacher manual is among the best one could hope to have. It is clearly written, easy to follow for even novice teachers, presented in a logical fashion, and instructive for those who may not be familiar with technical concepts related to test development, administration, and interpretation. The test authors provide additional information that should be welcomed by teachers, such as instructions on how to construct a student report, how to use test results, how to avoid student stress while taking the tests, and how to communicate results to students and parents. Appropriate cautions regarding interpretation of scores are also provided.

DEVELOPMENT. The Progressive Achievement Tests of Reading Comprehension and Reading Vocabulary (2nd Edition) is the first revision of this test since 1991. The test authors credit New Zealand literacy professionals and psychometricians from the Australian Council for Educational Research with assisting with the test development. For the PATC, the teacher manual states that the test content and questions were almost completely changed and the number of questions per test was reduced. Although there is now only one test form for each year, the test questions are unique for each test and are organized in a series that increases in difficulty. The amount of revision that was done on the PATV is less clear; the test authors state that many vocabulary items from the previous edition were replaced, and sentences and response options were updated to accommodate current New Zealand usage and/or social context. As with the PATC, questions are unique for each test.

An advantage over the previous edition of The Progressive Achievement Tests of Reading Comprehension and Reading Vocabulary is that the Rasch measurement model was used to construct the scales for the 2nd edition. Test items are shown in figures grouped by test and by text for the PATC, and by test for the PATV. Figures of achievement by year level show that the mean scale score for the PATC increases at a fairly constant rate. For the PATV, achievement growth is greater on average between Years 4 and 6 as compared to after Year 6.

TECHNICAL.

Standardization. The norming study, begun in 2005, used robust methods. Thirteen trial tests for both reading comprehension and vocabulary were administered to a stratified random sample from across New Zealand, comprising 1,650 students in Years 4, 5–6, 7–8, and 9–10, and representing small, medium, and large schools across low, mid, and high socioeconomic areas. The number of schools and number of students were for the most part sufficient in each category and appear representative of the intended population. The trial tests yielded the following for the norming study, which included more than 1,200 students: seven tests designed for reading comprehension and vocabulary at the desired year levels, six tests to provide item links, and three tests with items from New Zealand and Australian versions of the tests. From these, the final test booklets were developed and subjected to a poststratification procedure that used 200 iterations of subsampling. Stanine scores were calculated by year level, using an assumption of a normal distribution of population scores and based on the means and standard deviations estimated in the poststratification procedure.

Reliability. Coefficients alpha are provided for each of the norming tests. The reported values range from .89 to .91 for the PATC and from .90 to .93 for the PATV.

Validity. The test authors state that practicing teachers, reading specialists, reading advisors, and curriculum developers were consulted and assisted in the construction of the tests. This provides some level of evidence in terms of test content; however, no detail is provided regarding these experts beyond referring to them generically. Similarly, the test authors state that a direct and consistent relationship was established between the PATC and the PATV with the Australian counterparts to these tests; however, data were not provided to permit an evaluation of this claim. Increased achievement over years is also provided as evidence of validity of test score use. Although this information speaks to the issue of validity, it is not particularly strong evidence. A DIF analysis for gender and group differences is described but no data are provided to substantiate the statement that only marginal differences were obtained that did not warrant the deletion of any items.

COMMENTARY. Although there could have been more data supplied for some of the technical aspects of the PATC and PATV, overall The Progressive Achievement Tests of Reading Comprehension and Reading Vocabulary (2nd Edition) offer a well thought out revision. The content of the tests reflects the current New Zealand context, is engaging, and fits well with the New Zealand curriculum. Beginning on page 78 of the teacher manual, scale descriptions of the PATC and PATV are provided to assist with interpretation of competencies at various levels. These qualitative explanations should be very helpful for teachers.

The tests are intended for use in New Zealand. New Zealand content will be problematic for other countries, as might the British spellings.

SUMMARY. The test authors clearly state that these tests should be used in conjunction with other tests or evaluations for complete evaluations, which is sound advice in general. Used as intended, The Progressive Achievement Tests of Reading Comprehension and Reading Vocabulary (2nd Edition) will provide solid, broad diagnostics for both individual students and groups of students.

The materials are user-friendly for teachers and attractive for students. The test authors are to be commended for providing a teacher manual that is also a primer for understanding sampling, and basic concepts in test theory. Overall, New Zealand teachers will find The Progressive Achievement Tests of Reading Comprehension and Reading Vocabulary (2nd Edition) a valuable tool for their teaching and their students' learning.

Review of the Progressive Achievement Tests of Reading [2008 Revision] by RAYNE A. SPER-LING, Associate Professor of Educational Psychology, The Pennsylvania State University, State College, PA:

DESCRIPTION. The Progressive Achievement Tests of Reading (PAT: Reading) is a standardized assessment that contains both reading comprehension (PATC) and vocabulary (PATV) assessments. The comprehension tests provide examinees texts to read and corresponding questions to answer. The vocabulary tests contain five-option multiple-choice items. There are seven booklets designated as Reading Tests 1–7, each of which include both a comprehension test and a vocabulary test. Reading Test 1 was developed for students in Year 4 in New Zealand schooling, which approximates age 8. Test 7 is appropriate for secondary students in Grades 9–10. These tests are progressive and scaled such that scores can be interpreted across tests over time.

The teacher manual states that the PAT: Reading tests were developed to help teachers to determine students' individual reading achievement in order to make appropriate instructional decisions (p. 7). The target population for the PAT Reading tests is school-aged learners in New Zealand. The intended use of the assessments is to determine an individual student's reading comprehension and vocabulary. The tests are designed such that an individual student's reading ability can be tracked over time across test booklets. The teacher manual also suggests that in addition to other diagnostic purposes, scores can be used to measure progress over time, group students for instruction, and identify students for additional support or enrichment.

The PAT: Reading tests can be administered to classes of students by the classroom teacher. Detailed administration directions are outlined in the teacher manual and in addition to a suggested 10 minutes for each test in administration time, the comprehension tests are administered in about 45 minutes and vocabulary tests are administered in about 25 minutes. The testing procedure is clear and should be familiar to even the youngest school students.

Scores are reported in raw scores, scale scores, and stanines for each test. Detailed directions for how to develop a student report are provided in the teacher manual. Descriptive interpretation of scores is available for an individual student's success at the item level and the teacher manual adequately supports such detailed reporting. Each booklet provides an easily used scoring key. For a small additional fee, tests may also be sent to the New Zealand Council for Educational Research (NZCER) for electronic scoring.

The well-prepared teacher manual effectively provides critical information regarding use, scoring, and interpretation of the tests. The accompanying website also serves as a significant resource for those who seek more information regarding the tests or who elect to use these assessments (http://www.nzcer.org.nz/).

DEVELOPMENT. Previous versions of the Progressive Achievement Tests as well as revisions to other subject area tests served as the foundation for this edition of the PAT: Reading. Of importance, Rasch modeling was used to develop this edition of the PAT Reading Tests, resulting in interval scale scores that support the ability to track and interpret student performance across tests. Information for interpretation across editions is found in the teacher manual.

The PAT: Comprehension test defines the construct of interest, comprehension, in a manner consistent with international, research-based perspectives. The comprehension test passages vary in form and include narrative, poetry, explanation, reports, recounts, and persuasive and include comprehension tasks such as following instructions. Some comprehension items, retrieval questions, require the reader to find an answer present in the text. Other items require the reader to make local or global inferences. Across the test booklets, well-established comprehension components are targeted, including skill in using abstract information, using information from distant parts of a text, bringing pieces of information together, using implied information, identifying and rejecting competing information, using vocabulary, and skill in complex grammatical structure.

Item development specifications were created for each of the tests. Expert panels worked to examine previous items and to consider inclusion, revision, and exclusion. New items were also constructed consistent with the specification framework. The Rasch modeling implementation is a significant enhancement found in this edition. As noted, comprehension items were developed to assess retrieval, local, and global inferences. These outcomes are consistent with expectations of reading assessments. The vocabulary measures were designed to target the most common word families and are representative of the New Zealand Component of the International Corpus of English and the British National Corpus.

Variance in passage selection is a strength of the PATC. Noun count readability was reported and employed as a strategy to assure appropriateness of passages and is reported for each passage. Although more commonly used in the Pacific, noun count readability formulas are an accepted measure of passage difficulty. This reviewer selected several passages and calculated Flesch Kincaid and Fry readability estimates and found the passages to approximate the same levels across these readability measures. Examination of the PAT: Reading, as well as this reviewer's own pilot testing, suggests that these tests measure the constructs of interest, namely reading comprehension and vocabulary, over time.

TECHNICAL. Items were piloted to an unreported small number of students prior to the national trial. The national trial assessed 1,650 students. Item-level data from the national trial were used to determine the materials for the norming study. Thus, 16 booklets were prepared for the norming study. The norming study included a stratified sample representative of the national population of students by grade level and school size. More than 12,000 students participated in the norming study.

The PAT: Reading test was normed for the beginning of the school year, and for interpretation of individual scores, the test might best be administered at the beginning of the school year. For individual diagnostic information, however, it is important to note that the leveled tests can be used at other times during the academic year and in adjacent grades as well.

The teacher manual provides reliability estimates for each of the tests. The Quest test reliability for the comprehension and vocabulary tests are reported around .90. Care in development lends some initial validity support for the assessments. The teacher manual reports that Differential Item Functioning (DIF) analyses were conducted on the items and no changes were deemed necessary. The teacher manual also reports that the PAT: Reading assessments were found to be correlated with other standardized reading measures. Although some information is provided, more data regarding construct validity studies for this assessment are warranted.

COMMENTARY. There are many strengths of the PAT: Reading Comprehension and Vocabulary tests. Both these sets of assessments are well-designed and prepared and appear to adequately capture the constructs of interest. Variance in types of passages and types of items to reflect increasingly challenging comprehension tasks is an important strength of the PATC. The PATC tests include many important characteristics of the reading comprehension construct. The care taken to ground the choices in word selection for the PATV is a significant strength of the measure. The supporting documentation for the tests is an important resource for practitioners.

Although the PATC and PATV are designed for students in New Zealand, the measures may be effective for use in other populations. In pilot administrations, this reviewer found the Test 1 measure appropriate for administration to average readers finishing U.S. second grade, despite English language use and spelling variations. In pilot administrations with older learners across the other tests, the passages were comprehended as expected, with some minor information provided (e.g., name replacements for animals).

SUMMARY. The PATC and PATV assessments represent a comprehensive set of tests to measure student reading achievement over time. Both the Comprehension and Vocabulary assessments were well-planned and care was taken to adequately capture the constructs of interest.

Although designed for students in New Zealand the test might also be used effectively as an additional source of data regarding student reading achievement in other populations. The test is well-designed and developed. The detailed teacher manual is well-prepared and provides adequate information for accurate scoring and interpretation. The tests may be used appropriately by researchers and practitioners alike.

[139]

Quick Neurological Screening Test, 3rd Edition.

Purpose: Designed to assess "the development of motor coordination and sensory integration."
Population: Ages 5 and older.
Publication Dates: 1974-2012.
Acronym: QNST-3.
Scores, 16: Hand Skill, Figure Recognition and Production, Palm Form Recognition, Eye Tracking, Sound Patterns, Finger to Nose, Thumb and Finger Circle, Double Simultaneous Stimulation of Hand and Cheek, Rapidly Reversing Repetitive Hand Movements, Arm and Leg Extensions, Tandem Walk, Standing on One Leg, Skipping, Left-Right Discrimination, Behavioral Irregularities, Total.
Administration: Individual.
Price Data, 2012: $120 per test kit, including manual (2012, 124 pages), 25 record forms, and 25 remedial guidelines (developmental activities) forms in vinyl folder; $35 per 25 record forms; $20 per 25 remedial guidelines forms; $65 per manual.
Time: (20-30) minutes.
Authors: Margaret C. Mutti, Nancy A. Martin, Norma V. Spalding, and Harold M. Sterling.
Publisher: Academic Therapy Publications.
Cross References: For a review by Edward E. Gotts of the 2nd Revised Edition, see 14:306; see also T5:2141 (1 reference) and T4:2183 (3 references); for a review by Russell L. Adams of an earlier edition, see 9:1027.

Review of the Quick Neurological Screening Test, 3rd Edition by BRADLEY MERKER, Neuropsychology Division Head, and BRENT A. FUNK, Postdoctoral Fellow, Henry Ford Health System, Detroit, MI:

DESCRIPTION. The Quick Neurological Screening Test, 3rd Edition (QNST-3) is an individually administered measure of 15 tasks purported to elicit neurological soft signs. The major update to this edition is an expanded normative sample that covers ages 4–80+ according to the appendix, though the introduction in the test manual states the measure is for ages 5 and older. Earlier editions of the measure argued its usefulness in detecting learn-

ing disabilities among children. The new revision argues for additional uses that include assessment related to symptoms associated with Attention-Deficit/Hyperactivity Disorder (ADHD), Autism Spectrum Disorders, traumatic brain injury (TBI), and certain neurological diseases.

Task administration instructions are clear and simple to follow. The test requires approximately 20 minutes to administer and 10 minutes to score. The first 13 tasks are based upon the examinee's performance and the last 2 upon observations. Multiple errors are described and can be scored for each task, with each error scoring either 1 or 3, with 3 designating more severe impairment and 0 indicating no problem or error. As with previous editions, and described by Gotts (2001), no justification is provided regarding the differentiation between 1 and 3 point errors. Additionally, several tasks have only 1-point errors that may be scored.

Scoring criteria for some of the tasks are unclear and may relate to neurological deficits, but also psychiatric, non-neurological motor difficulties, or other factors. Additionally, any tremor is penalized without accounting for non-neurologic causes of tremor (i.e., anxiety). Other tasks contain penalties for irregular hand positions and speech irregularities, even for tasks that do not measure expressive language difficulties. Additionally, behavioral or psychiatric concerns may contribute to scores on some items, such as a 3-point error for refusal of a particular task and 1-point errors on another task for defensiveness, anxiety, and social withdrawal. On some tasks, typical neurological signs are not scored, whereas other tasks deviate from the typical neurological examination without justification.

Cutoff scores are provided for "normal," "moderate," and "severe" levels of impairment across age groups for each task and the total score based upon percentile ranks. As Gotts (2001) reported in reviewing the 2nd edition, an examinee can score within normal or moderate ranges across individual tasks, yet their total score may fall in a severe range of impairment. Finally, relatively few errors can result in a severe range score, making the problems described above of concern as this may falsely identify neurologic impairment that may not reflect any actual neurological deficit

DEVELOPMENT. The 15 tasks used in this edition are the same as those used in the previously published editions. These tasks were not originally selected due to any underlying theory of neurological function, but rather selected as a representative sample of neurological soft signs that are commonly assessed during neurological examination.

The test manual provides a brief review of literature related to neurological soft signs among some clinical conditions of focus, with a lengthier literature review regarding learning disabilities taken from a chapter from the 2nd edition, contained in one of the appendices. As in previous editions, there is a lack of evidence indicating the full diagnostic value of each task and the overall score does not relate to specific clinical conditions. Of importance, the test authors caution that this is only a screening measure and more extensive evaluation will be necessary for diagnostic considerations.

One major concern related to the expansion of this measure to additional clinical conditions is the test authors' review of the literature regarding the relationship of soft signs to TBI, ADHD, ASD, and so on. Their review focuses largely on the symptoms of these disorders, and not on the underlying diagnostic classification system. Unfortunately, no indication of the duration following an injury during which the QNST-3 is useful for TBI is discussed, nor is the severity level of the neurodegenerative conditions. For example, one might expect greater neurologic deficits as an immediate sequalae of a mild TBI with a gradual reduction, and return to neurologic baseline after adequate recovery periods.

TECHNICAL. The QNST-3 standardization sample comprises 1,400 individuals between ages 4 and 97 years. Sampling was conducted at 43 separate sites across the United States. This expanded normative sample represents the greatest improvement of this edition over its predecessors. The test authors assert that the sample was representative of U.S. population demographics based upon U.S. Census data from 2000 and 2010. A review of the demographic characteristics of the sample provided in the test manual largely supports this claim. Within age groups, sample sizes ranged from as few as 10 (ages 90–99) to 102 (age 10), with most groups containing 40 or more. Normative comparisons are collapsed into age groups and the test manual does not provide a discussion of whether other demographic variables influenced performance. Given that the number of elderly individuals in the normative set is relatively small, the test manual contains a warning regarding the limits of meaningful interpretations for individuals in this age group. There is little information regarding how examiners were trained.

Reviews of previous editions of this measure cited reliability of the test as a major concern. Adams (1985) specifically called attention to the lack of interrater reliability, in view of the fact that scoring is based upon subjective interpretations of performance. Not only was this problem not addressed during the previous revision, but evidence of interrater agreement in scoring is not mentioned anywhere in the QNST-3 manual. Data provided in the test manual regarding reliability address only internal consistency and test-retest stability.

Due to the low variability of performance within each item, internal consistency was assessed using mean item difficulty indexes calculated for each individual task. Across age groups most tasks are passed by neurologically intact individuals and, therefore, each item is relatively easy. It remains curious given that item difficulty was assessed, that the test authors did not apply these to their recommended cutoff scores for classifying individuals as normal, moderate, or severely impaired within individual tasks across age groups. Test-retest coefficients (average time between testing was 20 days) were adequate ($r = .49$–$.96$) for most tasks and the overall scores. However, for those tasks that were not stable over time, no discussion is provided.

Given the weaknesses noted among the reported reliability studies, it is difficult to adequately assess the validity of this measure. In the validity section of the test manual, the test authors turn to validating the QNST-3 as a measure of motor and sensory functioning, with little mention of screening for specific clinical conditions. Content validity is supported by the fact that the tasks that make up the measure are typically components of a standard neurological examination.

Criterion-related validity evidence was assessed by comparing this measure to other motor tests, a behavior checklist, and a cognitive screening measure. The QNST-3 correlated very weakly ($r = -.34$ to $.21$) with all of the other measures. The test authors explicitly state that this was expected because the tasks comprising the QNST-3 are sufficiently different from those it was compared against, making this an unusual strategy to assist in establishing criterion-related validity. Furthermore, it is stated in the test manual that because the QNST-3 total score reflects higher numbers of errors and other measures' scores are higher based on intact or good performance levels, the correlation coefficient was expected to not only be negative but also low. Although, it is entirely understandable that negative correlations were expected, it remains unclear why low correlations were expected simply because an error-based score was correlated with those based upon intact performances.

Construct validity evidence is supported by the fact that groups of individuals that would be expected to display more neurologic soft signs (e.g. younger/older populations and clinical groups) tend to score higher on the QNST-3, indicating greater impairment. As examples, there is a significant jump in errors at age 80 and errors tend to decrease through age 15. One problem within the construct validity section is that divergent validity is argued via the weak correlations with other tasks that were used in an attempt to provide evidence of criterion-related validity. It is unclear to these reviewers how the findings can support both criterion-related validity arguments and divergent validity. Finally, a factor analysis was performed to explore the relationship among tasks and to provide further evidence of construct validity. Unsurprisingly, given that most individuals will perform these tasks without error, all tasks except "Hand Skill" loaded onto one factor, which was interpreted as supporting the idea that the total score represents the single construct of neurological soft signs.

A final issue within the validity data provided in the test manual is that an attempt was made to validate the use of the total score in differentiating clinical groups with ADHD, developmental delays, learning disabilities (LD), Autism, Alzheimer's, and Parkinson's from matched normal controls. Although all of the statistical analyses examining the differentiation of clinical groups from neurologically intact individuals were reported as significant, a number of problems exist with interpreting these data. First, no definition is provided regarding the clinical classifications, nor is severity of the disorder discussed. Second, the sample sizes in the Alzheimer's groups ($N = 9$ for clinical and matched controls) and Parkinson's groups ($N = 6$) are far too small to make any meaningful conclusions about these groups' performances on this measure. Next, it is unclear as to whether the clinical condition may be the underlying reason for performance on the QNST-3, or whether other factors may play a role (e.g., physical or psychiatric difficulties). Furthermore, no between-group comparisons were made across the clinical conditions studied. This means that poor performance on the QNST-3 may be indicative only of the existence of a condition of clinical concern, but not which condition may

be the underlying etiology. For example, the mean scores for the clinical Alzheimer's and Parkinson's groups are nearly identical, as are performances of the LD and ADHD groups. Further analyses of the profile of difficulties for each group (i.e., on which specific tasks errors were made) or the use of multivariate comparisons across relevant clinical groups rather than pairwise comparisons between clinical and matched control groups would perhaps be useful in making a differential diagnosis. Finally, some of the clinical and matched groups have significant demographic mismatches. Examples of mismatches include a disproportionate number of Caucasians (40) compared to African Americans (4); in the ADHD match group, 29 Caucasians contrasted with only 1 African American for the LD matched group, and only Caucasians in the Alzheimer's, Parkinson's, and their respective matched groups.

The test manual consistently cautions that this is a screening measure, and cannot be used in isolation for diagnosis of a clinical condition. An analysis of the receiver operating characteristics of the measure, its predictive value in identifying clinical conditions, or how it may guide a more comprehensive evaluation for any of the clinical conditions is absent. Such analyses would be useful in determining the incremental validity of adding this screening measure to an assessment, as opposed to simply proceeding with a full evaluation of the clinical condition in question. Finally, despite the numerous clinical groups discussed in the test manual, no case examples are provided, which may be helpful for clinical usage and interpretation.

COMMENTARY. The QNST-3 is a brief and easily administered screening test of neurological soft signs. The key strength of this edition is an expanded normative sample and study that is roughly representative of the U.S. population. Additionally, it has a simplified administration process as compared to the 2nd edition, as the examiner may now use the test manual directly for administration rather than cue cards for each of the different tasks. However, the data for its reliability, validity, and application to clinical samples remains suspect and it has not significantly improved upon these problems from previous editions. Prior reviewers (Adams, 1985; Gotts, 2001) described the primary strengths of the QNST as being able to identify those who would present abnormally on neurologic examination and the test manual providing a critical review of the literature relating soft signs to learning disabilities. Unfortunately, the manual for the current edition makes little mention of these strengths and relegates the previously lauded review of learning disabilities to an appendix without any update or adequate justification for the proposed expanded focus on other clinical conditions. One final improvement, as compared to the 2nd edition, is that the QNST-3 manual is a simpler read and does not contain nearly the number of editorial errors as the previous edition.

SUMMARY. The status of the QNST-3 is similar to prior editions reviewed by Adams (1985) and Gotts (2001). It remains a promising measure that would standardize and normatively compare performances on simple neurological tasks, though it continues to lack demonstrable evidence of reliability and has failed to establish validity, despite a significant update to normative studies. Notably lacking is empirical evidence of determinations for severity of impairment at the task level and for the overall score, as well as solid evidence of its ability to rapidly screen for the clinical conditions discussed. Additionally, the incremental validity of using a screening measure in addition to standard evaluation methods for the identified conditions is limited. Therefore, considerably more research on the instrument will be necessary before it can be recommended for regular clinical use.

REVIEWERS' REFERENCES

Adams, R. L. (1985). [Review of the Quick Neurological Screening Test, Revised Edition.] In J. V. Mitchell, Jr. (Ed.), *The ninth mental measurements yearbook* (pp. 1256–1258). Lincoln, NE: Buros Institute of Mental Measurements.
Gotts, E. E. (2001). [Review of the Quick Neurological Screening Test, 2nd Revised Edition.] In B. S. Plake & J. C. Impara (Eds.), *The fourteenth mental measurements yearbook* (pp. 979–981). Lincoln, NE: Buros Institute of Mental Measurements.

Review of the Quick Neurological Screening Test, 3rd Edition by SHAWN POWELL, Dean, Social and Behavioral Sciences, Casper College, Casper, WY:

DESCRIPTION. The Quick Neurological Screening Test, 3rd (QNST-3) is the third edition of an instrument initially published in 1974. It is an individually administered, norm-referenced assessment of motor coordination and sensory integration. The QNST-3 is a screening instrument intended to be used by a variety of professionals to assist in determining if an individual is manifesting neurological soft signs, defined as "poor motor coordination, sensory perceptual changes, and difficulty sequencing complex motor tasks" (Seidl, Thomann, & Schröder, 2009, p. 525). It can be administered to individuals from age 4 to 80 years and older.

The QNST-3 presents 15 tasks common to neurological and neuropsychological assessments to assess motor maturity and development, sensory processing, fine and gross motor muscle control, motor planning and sequences, sense of rate and rhythm, spatial organization, visual and auditory perception, balance and vestibular function, attention, and the ability to discriminate between left and right orientations. The test is untimed and administration takes 20 to 30 minutes.

The QNST-3 includes a manual and two record forms. The manual contains chapters on the test's description, general testing considerations, administration and scoring procedures, interpretation, development, standardization, reliability, validity, age norm tables, and implications of detecting neurological soft signs. The first record form is a protocol used to record and grade examinees' performance on the 15 tasks with an examinee's performance on each task placed into a category of either No discrepancy, Moderate discrepancy, or Severe discrepancy. The second record form provides prescriptive remedial guidelines that can be incorporated into treatment planning to improve deficit areas. The remedial guidelines form is intended for use with clients who display severe discrepancies on any of QNST-3 Tasks 1–13.

In administering the QNST-3, examiners use a spiral-bound manual that includes standardized instructions. The manual provides scoring criteria with examples for assigning point values to each of the tasks. Results are measured in the errors an examinee commits in completing the presented tasks. Thus, higher scores suggest greater levels of deficits.

DEVELOPMENT. The original QNST was developed to detect neurological soft signs in young children. In its current version the QNST-3 is based on a set of national norms that extended its use from childhood to geriatric populations. The test may be used to detect markers for brain injury, neurodegenerative diseases, and to track ability changes over time.

The test manual includes definitions of nine different types of neurological soft signs that may be detected during administration of the QNST-3 (e.g., overflow, involuntary movements, dysrhythmia, dysmetria, dysdiadochokinesia, dysgraphesthesia, intention tremor, astereognosis, and impaired fine-motor coordination). These neurological soft signs are intended to be detected to better understand an examinee's status in relation to neural pathway development that governs motor planning and motor execution. The QNST-3 manual provides comparative information for six clinical groups that include populations of individuals diagnosed with attention difficulties, learning disabilities, developmental delays, autism, Alzheimer's disease, and Parkinson's disease.

TECHNICAL. The national standardization sample for the QNST-3 included 1,289 individuals from the ages of 4 years to 97 years. The test manual reports the sample was representative of United States Census Bureau demographics based on gender, ethnicity, education level, geographic region, and metro status (i.e., urban compared to rural). In reviewing the demographic information, there are several reasons to question whether the sample was truly reflective of the United States population. There are marked differences in the QNST-3 national sample compared to the United States Census Bureau data in several demographic areas: the percentage of individuals in the sample of Hispanic origin, 21.5%, compared to the Census Bureau data, which showed a national percentage of 12.1%; the percentage of Caucasians in the sample, 61.6%, was less than the Census Bureau data indicating 72.1% of the United States population is Caucasian; in the sample 53.4% of participants live in urban or suburban areas, whereas data from the Census Bureau showed 79% of the population live in urban or suburban areas; and 46.6% of the sample live in rural areas whereas according to the Census Bureau data 21% of the population live in rural areas.

The normative sample was collected from four regions of the United States (e.g., North Central, North East, South, and West). The number of states involved in the data collection for the national sample was 22. In considering the regions of the United States in an east to west manner it is clear the vast majority of states involved in data collection for the QNST-3 national sample are from the eastern part of the country. Among the 22 states involved in the national sample, 6 states (about 27%) are west of the Mississippi River whereas 16 states (about 73%) are located east of the Mississippi River. Thus, the sample used for the QNST-3 is not geographically reflective of the United States.

The number of individuals in several specific age groups of the QNST-3 national sample is troubling. Although a stated intention of the third edition of this test was to extend the age range to geriatric populations, examination of the sample's age groupings indicates the majority of 1,289 individuals in the national sample, 923 individuals were 4 to 17 years old (about 72%) and 366 individuals

(about 28%) were in the 18- to 99-year-old age groups. There is also concern about the size of three of the age groups involved in the national sample. The 17-year-old age group had 28 individuals, the 19-year-old age group had 12 individuals, and the 90- to 99-year-old age group had 10 individuals.

The QNST-3 manual provides evidence of two types of reliability, internal consistency and test-retest. Due to limited variability in the scores, a 0, 1, or 3 is independently assigned to each QNST-3 task. An item difficulty index approach was employed to assess the test's internal consistency. This approach suggests the QNST-3 has good internal consistency. The second presented form of reliability for the QNST-3 is test-retest. A sample of 56 individuals were assessed twice by their initial examiner within a 20-day span. The test-retest correlation coefficients ranged from .49 to .96, with a total raw score coefficient of .87. The test-retest correlation coefficients for 8 of the 15 QNST-3 tasks were below .80, which suggests the temporal stability of the majority of the QNST-3 tasks were below the typically accepted level for evidence of adequate stability over time.

The QNST-3 manual includes information on content, criterion, and construct validity. Content validity is adequately presented in the form of developmental tasks commonly used in neurological and neuropsychological evaluations of balance and motor skills. Evidence concerning the QNST-3's construct and criterion-related validity is provided through comparison with other tests of motor skills, visual spatial processing, adaptive behaviors, and cognitive ability. The correlations between the QNST-3 and the other measures used for comparative purposes yielded coefficients that ranged from .02 to -.34. The test manual states low and possibly negative correlations between the QNST-3 and the other comparative measures were expected. Although negative correlations would be expected as QNST-3 results are recorded errors and the comparative instruments award points for accurate performance, it stands to reason negative correlations between the instruments would be at least moderate if they were assessing similar traits. The low magnitude of the coefficients presented in the test manual suggests the QNST-3 has strong divergent validity as it is measuring traits not being measured by the comparative instruments used in its standardization.

COMMENTARY. The latest version of the QNST-3 was designed to extend the normative age range of earlier versions of this test. There are concerns the test's normative sample is not reflective of the United States population. Additionally, the small number of individuals in several age groups and the small number of participants in the adult age categories gives rise to concern for its use with adult populations.

The evidence presented in the test manual suggests the QNST-3 has adequate reliability. The reported QNST-3 validity evidence suggests it is measuring different traits compared to other instruments.

The QNST-3 record forms are easy to use and score. The interpretation guides provide numerous examples to assist in making judgments about an examinee's performance. The prescribed remedial guidelines may assist clinicians in developing treatment plans for clients displaying severe deficits.

SUMMARY. The QNST-3 is the latest version of a popular neurological screening instrument. The third edition of this test has expanded age groups compared to earlier versions. The QNST-3 national sample does not appear to be reflective of the population of the United States in several ways, which raises questions about its generalizability. It has adequate reported reliability and validity properties. It is a well-established instrument that can be used as a screening instrument to determine if an individual is displaying neurological soft signs associated with deficits in balance and motor skills.

REVIEWER'S REFERENCE

Seidl, U., Thomann, P.A., & Schröder, J. (2009). Neurological soft signs in nursing home residents with Alzheimer's disease. *Journal of Alzheimer's Disease, 18*, 525–532.

[140]

Quick Picture Reading Test.

Purpose: Designed "to quickly characterize an individual's general reading ability" through a picture-matching task.

Publication Date: 2010.

Acronym: QPRT.

Scores: Total score only.

Administration: Group.

Price Data, 2009: $65 per complete kit including 10 Adult AutoScore forms, 10 Child AutoScore forms, and manual (56 pages); $32 per 25 AutoScore forms (specify Adult or Child); $50 per manual.

Time: (10) minutes.

Authors: Amber M. Klein and David S. Herzberg.

Publisher: Western Psychological Services.

a) CHILD FORM.

Population: Ages 8-19.

b) ADULT FORM.

Population: Ages 17-89.

Review of the Quick Picture Reading Test by KATHLEEN QUINN, Professor of Education, Director, Fall and Spring Reading Clinic, Holy Family University, Philadelphia, PA:

DESCRIPTION. The Quick Picture Reading Test (QPRT) is an individually or group-administered measure of reading ability, based on test takers' abilities in vocabulary, phrase-reading, and picture matching. It is designed for use with persons ages 8 to 89. The test authors believe it provides a quick estimate of reading ability in workplace, clinical, academic, and research settings. The test has two forms, identical in items and length. They differ only in the norms for scoring. One form is for use with children ages 8 to 19 and the other is for use with adults, ages 17 to 89. The test authors note that although there is overlap for ages 17 to 19, the administrator should determine which form to use based on the setting. For example, in a school setting, use the child form for an 18-year-old; in a workplace setting, use the adult form. The test is administered identically to both individuals and groups. There are 26 phrases arranged in a vertical column labeled A–Z with lines for written responses next to the letter of each phrase. The instructions, written at about a third grade level, appear in a box on that page as well. If the examinee is unable to read the instructions or does not understand them, the administrator may read them to the examinee. On the facing page, there is an array of 35 clip art pictures, numbered from 1–35. The examinee is to select the picture that best matches the phrase and write its corresponding number on the line next to the phrase/letter. The test authors state that although the examiner times the test for 10 minutes, it is not a timed test. Based on the standardization study, the test authors assert that most examinees can complete the test in that time frame, although, it is not stated what to do if the individual is not finished in 10 minutes. The test is easy to administer with clear instructions. Scoring is also easy to do. The test protocol has a "carbon" backing that transfers the examinees' answers directly to the attached scoring sheet. The scoring sheet has the answer key next to each item. The administrator then just circles all correct answers and tallies them for a total raw score. The raw score is then converted to a Reading Index score, percentile rank, and grade equivalency score using the tables provided on the score sheet, taking only about 2 minutes per examinee. In addition, in the manual the test authors have provided sample score sheets, three case studies, and clear examples of how to interpret each type of score along with a caution to use confidence intervals in this process.

DEVELOPMENT. In developing the QPRT, the authors wanted to design a brief measure of general reading skills for a wide age range that could be used for a variety of appropriate settings and purposes. The test authors state that the "first inspiration for the QPRT was found in a desire to ensure that patients taking a psychological test had sufficient reading skill to understand the questions" (manual, p. 11).

A series of pilot studies was conducted to refine both the phrases and the picture arrays in order to ensure accurate progression of level of item difficulty, especially regarding the grammatical structure of the phrases, and to create a scale that would represent elementary through secondary levels of ability. Rasch methodology (WINSTEPS software) was used to calibrate items at each stage of development enabling the test authors to eliminate redundant items and create new ones at various levels. Developers also used the EDL Core Vocabularies (Taylor, Frackenpohl, & White, 1989) to determine the most difficult word in each phrase as well as revising the phrases for length, structural complexity, literal correspondence to the pictures, item bias, discrimination ability of the phrases, and the possible selection of the distracter pictures in the array. In the first pilot study, children were included in the sample for norming purposes; however, the test authors realized that the QPRT could be used to screen their reading ability as well. This realization altered the focus of their assessment to include more items for children so that the QPRT might be used successfully with them as well. The test authors do a good job of explaining this process as well as providing several examples. However, the manner in which the pictures were selected or revised is mentioned only briefly.

TECHNICAL. The standardization sample for the QPRT included 1,203 adults (ages 17–89) and 1,876 children (ages 7–19) from 16 states largely from schools, churches, sports and social clubs, and various community organizations. The standardization sample approximately reflects U.S. population data. Demographic tables are provided with a clear breakdown of both the adult and child standardization samples regarding gender, race/ethnic background, educational level (adults) or parents' educational level (children), U.S. geographic region, and age. Educational level or parents' educational level was used as an indicator

of socioeconomic status. Individuals with limited English language ability were not included and the QPRT is not recommended for use with English Language Learners as a result. Effect sizes for each variable were analyzed and these determined that gender was not significant for adults and was not clinically meaningful for children; however, race/ethnicity and SES were both clinically meaningful. The interpretation of effect size follows standard recommendations from Coe (2002) and seems appropriate. Therefore, this test must be used with caution when testing African American, Hispanic, and low SES populations.

Reliability is reported for internal consistency using the split-half method resulting in high coefficients for the adult forms (.85 to .92) and for 11- to 19-year-olds (.80 to .89) in the child form. Correlation coefficients for children ages 8 to 10 were somewhat weaker (.71 to .72). Test-retest reliability was examined using two testing sessions and a 10-day (1- to 2-week range) interval. Results produced somewhat higher values for adults (coefficients ranged from .89 to .94) than for children (coefficients ranged from .77 to .87). Standard error of measurement (*SEM*) was higher for children (median of 6.43) than adults (median of 5.27). This finding suggests that the assessment is more suited for use with adults than children, especially children in the 8- to 10-year age range.

Evidence for content validity is reported in the discussion of the development of the phrase items particularly. However, no true discussion of the test authors' philosophical and theoretical underpinnings as to their definition of reading is included. They frequently mention "a broad range of reading abilities" and emphasize vocabulary and syntax in the test items, but they should establish a more direct link between their beliefs about reading and the development of the QRPT to make a stronger case for the use of their test.

As a result, construct validity evidence is again discussed with regard to the change in the level of difficulty of the items (phrases) as the examinee progresses through the scale. The level of difficulty (as shown by raw score means) seems to increase steadily in the child sample, but differences in the difficulty gradients for children and adults prompted some reordering of items. Even so, items J, K, O, L, and M all fall in the same level of difficulty and very few items (A, B, and C) tap into the lower levels of ability measured by the test. The test authors may want to make further adjustments in ordering items and revise the test to include more items at the lower level if they truly want this test to be useful with younger children. At this time, there are not enough items at the lower levels to justify this use.

Concurrent validity evidence derives from findings that the QPRT correlates moderately to strongly with various achievement subtests of the Wechsler Individual Achievement Test–Second Edition, Wide Range Achievement Test 3 and 4, and the Woodcock Johnson III Tests of Achievement. Again, the correlations are stronger for higher age ranges. Additional evidence of test score validity is offered, based on the correlations between QPRT scores and tests of cognitive ability such as the Wechsler Adult Intelligence Scale, Third Edition, the Wechsler Intelligence Scale for Children, Fourth Edition, the Wechsler Abbreviated Scale of Intelligence, the Shipley-2, and the Wonderlic Personnel Test. In all cases, higher coefficients were observed for the adult scales than for the child scales, again indicating that this test may not be appropriate for use with younger children. The QPRT is also highly loaded relative to verbal intelligence based on a study conducted by Firmin, Hwang, Evens, Keyser, and Bennington (2009).

COMMENTARY. The QPRT is a brief and easy test to administer and score for both individuals and groups. Its use as a screening device to determine a general estimate of reading ability for adults is adequate; however, the test authors need to provide more information about their theoretical and philosophical understanding of the reading process in order for the test development process to be more fully supported. A large and mostly representative standardization sample along with good explanations of the QPRT's development and technical characteristics are provided. Use with African Americans, Latinos, English Language Learners, and Low SES is not recommended. There is not enough support nor are there enough items to use this test with children ages 8 to 10. The case studies and samples are very helpful in demonstrating appropriate use and interpretation of test results.

SUMMARY. The QPRT was designed to provide an easy to score and administer, brief assessment of general reading ability for varied purposes with people ages 8 to 89. It includes items that generally increase in difficulty across the order of administration based on vocabulary and grammatical structure for most age groups. The reliability and validity data provide support for its use with

11- to 89-year-olds. Use with younger children (8 to 10) along with the aforementioned subgroups is not recommended. In comparison to other brief reading measures such as the WRAT-III and IV, the QPRT offers more ecologically valid items for screening for general reading ability; however, more information about the theoretical and philosophical basis for the QPRT is needed.

REVIEWER'S REFERENCES
Coe, R. (2002). *It's the effect size, stupid. What effect size is and why it is important.* Paper presented at the Annual Conference of the British Educational Research Association, University of Exeter, England [Retrieved from http://www.leeds.ac.uk/educol/documents/00002182.htm, June 27, 2011].
Firmin, M., Hwang, C., Evens, J., Keyser, S., & Bennington, J. (2009). Correlations among the Quick Picture Reading Test, The Shipley Institute of Living Scale, and the Slosson Intelligence Test-Revised-R-3. *Eastern Educational Journal, 38,* 11-19.
Taylor, S. E., Frackenpohl, H., & White, C. E. (1989). *EDL core vocabularies in reading, mathematics, science, and social studies.* New York: McGraw-Hill.

Review of the Quick Picture Reading Test by TIMOTHY SHANAHAN, *Professor of Urban Education, University of Illinois at Chicago, Chicago, IL:*

DESCRIPTION. The Quick Picture Reading Test (QPRT) is an individually or group-administered measure of general reading ability for use with children and adults, ages 8 to 89. The test provides a single reading score, meant to reflect word reading, vocabulary, and reading comprehension abilities. There are two forms of the test, one for children (ages 8–19) and one for adults (ages 17–89); those in the 17–19 age range are matched to form based on whether or not they have completed high school.

The forms differ only in the test interpretation data that are provided. The instructions, format, and test items are identical. The sealed AutoScore Forms are opened by peeling one edge of the back page. The booklet opens to a two-page display; on the left are instructions and a list of 26 phrases of 2–8 words each, on the right is an array of 35 numbered drawings (5 pictures in each of 7 rows). After responses are recorded on the left-hand page, a perforated strip is removed to reveal a scoring sheet that includes the correct answers and a series of tables for determining standard score, percentile rank, grade-equivalent, and other information. A carbon strip transfers item responses to the test interpretation page.

The test administration instructions are scripted. The examiner is directed to read a brief introduction, which concludes with the examinees being told to open the booklet and read the instructions (which, according to the publisher, are written at a third-grade level); the timing begins when the booklets are opened. However, if an examinee cannot read the instructions or asks for help, the examiner is to read them aloud and provide additional explanation.

To complete the test, examinees read a phrase and then search through 35 pictures to find the one that best matches the phrase meaning. Items become progressively more difficult as the test proceeds; this increasing difficulty is due to later phrases using increasingly less common words, greater grammatical complexity (e.g., passive voice, prepositional and conditional phrases), and the plausibility of the picture distractors increases, too.

The test takes 10 minutes to administer, and it is not a speed test. Thus, examinees are likely to complete the task well within the time limit.

DEVELOPMENT. Originally, the QPRT was intended for adults, but children were the focus of the pilot studies to allow for an accurate scaling of items. Because the QPRT is meant to quickly place individuals along a reading continuum, it is important that the test items be maximally discriminating. For this reason Rasch methodology was used, which required three pilot studies to determine item difficulties: one with 478 children (ages 7–14), another with 351 students (ages 11–15), and a third with 66 upper elementary students. Because the QPRT assesses recognition, the test manual notes, the words had to be more difficult than the intended target reading ranges. To establish fourth-grade discrimination the words had to be representative of seventh-grade curriculum.

TECHNICAL. The QPRT used adult (n = 1,203) and children's (n = 1,876) standardization samples. Standardization took place across 16 states. Both samples were reflective of U.S. demographics in terms of gender, race/ethnicity, and education level. The adult sample (ages 17–89) included varying education levels, from less than high school graduate through 4 years of college or more. The children's sample (ages 7–19) represented wide variations in levels of parents' education.

Reliability was estimated by calculating internal consistency statistics for age-group samples. Split-half coefficients (corrected for length using the Spearman-Brown formula) for the adult groups ranged from .85 to .92. Children's estimates ranged from .71 to .89. These coefficients are acceptable, but were markedly lower for children in the 8- to 10-year age group (those for the older children were nearly as high as the adult statistics). Test-retest reliabilities were calculated over an approximately 10-day interval with a sample of 132 children and 146 adults. The test-retest coefficients ranged from

.77 to .94 for the age-level samples, again higher for the adults than the children. The standard errors of measurement were fairly large (median values were 5.27 for adults, 6.43 for the children). Thus, the 95% confidence interval represents a range of performance from the 25th to the 75th percentile, a very wide interpretive range indicating that the test would have limited utility for fine-grained comparisons or high-stakes decisions.

Validity evidence for the QPRT test scores was shown in many ways. First, the common demographic patterns of performance usually obtained with reading measures (e.g., Kirsch, Jungeblut, Jenkins, & Kolstad, 2002; National Center for Education Statistics, 2010) were evident with the QPRT: No gender differences for adults, though girls slightly outperformed boys; African Americans and Hispanics underperformed Whites by about one-half of a standard deviation; and a significant relationship with socioeconomic status. Test performance on the QPRT showed clear age differences, and the ordering of items generally reflected the scaling identified by Rasch analysis.

Additionally, an extensive array of studies provided concurrent evidence of QPRT scores with various adult and child reading measures. The correlation of the QPRT Reading Index scores and the Word Reading score from the Wechsler Individual Achievement Test, Second Edition (WIAT-II) with 98 adults was .74 (.78 for corresponding grade-equivalent scores). Correlations of the QPRT scores with scores from the Wide Range Achievement Test 3 (WRAT-3) with 180 adults yielded coefficients of .79 for Word Reading and .74 for Spelling, whereas the correlation coefficient of the Wide Range Achievement Test 4 (WRAT-4) Sentence Comprehension subtest scores with 47 adolescents was .54 (corrected for range restriction). The correlation coefficient obtained between the QPRT scores and the Passage Comprehension subtest scores of the Woodcock-Johnson III Tests of Achievement (WJ-III) with a sample of 43 children from special education classes was .56 (.52 for corresponding grade-equivalent scores). In a second analysis with 29 students, the Broad Reading Composite score of the WJ-III and the QPRT produced correlation coefficients of .51.

COMMENTARY. The QPRT is easy to administer, and it results in a reasonably reliable and valid estimate of the word reading skills of children and adults. Unlike other word reading measures, it can be administered to groups and does not require that an examiner monitor oral reading performance. That feature makes it more practical for classroom use and in many adult testing situations (e.g., human resources, medicine). The results of the validity studies suggest that the QPRT would be best used as a screener or in other low-stakes testing situations, such as when a clinician is trying to determine a starting level for a regimen of testing (a situation that would allow easy adjustment if the prediction were incorrect). However, this test correlates most strongly with measures of word reading or pronunciation and does less well in estimating reading comprehension (QPRT performance explained about 25% of the variance in reading comprehension and this in small studies with wide age ranges that should maximize such explanation). The reliabilities are lowest for children and are not high enough to justify individual decisions about children 10 years of age and younger.

Although the overall estimates of word reading performance appear to be sound, the percentile ranks and grade level equivalent scores were puzzling and suggest that care should be used in their interpretation. The QPRT manual provides an example of scoring sheet calculations for a 37-year-old who tested in the "average range," which was equivalent to the 18th percentile, and reflected a grade-equivalent reading score of 11th grade. I can find no studies of adult literacy that would place an 11th-grade reading level at the 18th percentile rank, nor would it be common to suggest that those who perform better than only 18% of a test-taking population are average. One problem, of course, is with the misleading nature of grade equivalent (GE) scores generally. The QPRT indicates that the GEs could be used to estimate whether a prospective employee can read and understand a technical manual written at a particular level of readability. In fact, that is exactly what it cannot provide given the relatively low correlation of the test with reading comprehension measures and the limited evidence offered to support the validity of the GE scores (though they are reliable).

SUMMARY. The QPRT was designed to provide a quick estimate of general reading ability across a wide range of age levels. Validity studies suggest that it performs more like a word reading or word pronunciation test than a general reading test, and that it provides a reliable and valid measure of such performance. That makes the QPRT a useful screener and would allow it to be used to make rela-

tively low impact decisions about examinees' reading abilities. The clever design of the instrument makes it a useful alternative to traditional word reading tests, allowing it to be used as a group measure and one that may be relatively more motivational to older students and adults.

REVIEWER'S REFERENCES

Educational Testing Service, & National Center for Education Statistics. (2010). *Grade 12 reading and mathematics 2009 national and pilot state results.* Washington, DC: National Center for Education Statistics, Institute of Education Sciences, U.S. Dept. of Education.
Kirsch, I. S., Jungeblut, A., Jenkins, L., & Kolstad, A. (2002). *Adult literacy in America: A first look at the findings of the National Adult Literacy Survey.* Washington, DC: U.S. Department of Education.

[141]

Receptive One-Word Picture Vocabulary Test–4: Spanish-Bilingual Edition.

Purpose: Designed to assess "an individual's ability to match a spoken word–in either Spanish or English–to an image of an object, action, or concept shown in a color illustration."

Population: Ages 2–70+.

Publication Dates: 2001–2013.

Acronym: ROWPVT-4: SBE.

Scores: Total score only.

Administration: Individual.

Price Data, 2013: $175 per kit, including manual (2013, 97 pages), test plates, and 25 Spanish-Bilingual record forms; $55 per manual; $40 per 25 record forms; $80 per test plates.

Time: (20-25) minutes.

Comments: Co-normed with the Expressive One-Word Picture Vocabulary Test–4: Spanish-Bilingual Edition (19:70).

Author: Nancy A. Martin.

Publisher: Academic Therapy Publications.

Cross References: For reviews by S. Kathleen Krach and María del R. Medina-Díaz of an earlier edition, see 16:209.

Review of the Receptive One-Word Picture Vocabulary Test-4: Spanish-Bilingual Edition by JOHN ANDERSON, Professor, Department of Educational Psychology, University of Victoria, Victoria, British Columbia, Canada:

DESCRIPTION. The Receptive One-Word Picture Vocabulary Test-4: Spanish-Bilingual Edition (ROWPVT-4: SBE) consists of 180 ordered items, each of which requires the respondent to listen to a word in either Spanish or English and select one of four illustrations that best represents the word spoken. It complements and is co-normed with the Expressive One-Word Picture Vocabulary Test-4: Spanish-Bilingual Edition (EOWPVT-4: SBE; 19:70). The ROWPVT-4: SBE is designed to be individually administered by a bilingual professional with understanding of both the psycho-metric and cognitive developmental aspects of the assessment, such as a speech-language pathologist, school psychologist, or clinical psychologist. The test generally takes about 20 minutes to administer, and it is intended for use with individuals who range in age from 2 to 70 years or more.

The test administrator is to determine the respondent's dominant language–either English or Spanish–and use this dominant language to speak the stimulus word for each item. However, the administrator may switch languages if the respondent does not appear to understand the word when first spoken. The ROWPVT-4: SBE provides some bilingual questions on the record form for the test administrator to ask if the respondent's dominant language is not clearly known before test administration.

The test kit is neatly packaged in a plastic case and consists of the test booklet containing the 180 items in a flip-page, spiral-bound format for test administration, 25 single-use recording and scoring sheets, and a test manual that provides an overview of the test and vocabulary testing, administration instructions, description of test and norms development, reliability and validity information, and age-based norms tables. All materials in the kit also can be purchased separately.

A respondent's score reflects the highest item correctly completed. As noted, the test consists of 180 items ordered by difficulty, so the further the respondent proceeds in the test with correct responses, the higher the level of receptive vocabulary. To derive a score, the number of errors is subtracted from the number corresponding to the highest item answered correctly in the test. However, because respondents of different ages start the test at different points, there is some complexity in determining start and end points. An essential part of test administration is determining where in the test to start (age-based start points are provided) and then determining the final item reached. The start point–termed the *basal* location–is defined as the point in the test where the respondent correctly identifies 8 consecutive items; all items below this point are assumed to be correctly answered. This location would likely be the suggested age-based start point. The highest item, or *ceiling*, is defined as the location in the test where the respondent makes four errors within 6 consecutive items. Examples are provided in the test manual that clarify the score process.

DEVELOPMENT. The development of the test is described in the test manual. It is based upon previous editions of the test, which consisted primarily of nouns along with some gerunds, verbs, and modifiers. The manner in which words were identified for inclusion and the evaluation of the representativeness of the word pool for Spanish and English vocabularies is not described. Analyses were conducted on responses presumably derived from the norming sample. Item analyses were conducted using both classical and 1-parameter item response theory approaches. Item difficulties were used to order the items within the test booklet. Differential item functioning was evaluated for gender, urban/rural residence, and ethnicity for the English language version (Receptive One-Word Picture Vocabulary Test-4; 19:142); no evidence of item bias was detected. It was assumed by the test developers that the Spanish language items, all of which were taken from the same item pool, would show similar results.

The test was normed on a sample of 1,260 Spanish/English bilingual individuals ages 2 to 70 years and older, yielding age-based samples of less than 100 people per group. Participants were recruited from 14 states within the U.S. The total sample demographics were compared to U.S. Census data for the U.S. Hispanic population, and the sample characteristics were similar to those of the population. Sixty-nine individuals were tested on two occasions 2 to 4 weeks apart to allow for evaluating test-retest reliability.

Test results were reported as raw scores, age-based percentile ranks, standard scores ($M = 100$; $SD = 15$), and age-equivalent scores.

TECHNICAL. The internal consistency of the test was estimated using coefficient alpha for each age group. All coefficients were greater than .90 with a median value of .95. The alpha coefficients were used to calculate age-specific standard errors of measurement for test scores. To evaluate temporal stability, the correlation coefficient between the test scores and retest scores for a cross-age subsample of 69 test takers was calculated, with resultant values greater than .90.

Validity was evaluated from a couple of perspectives. What the test manual terms construct validity (but could present as concurrent validity) was evaluated by correlating scores of 23 respondents on the ROWPVT-4: SBE with the 2001 edition ($r = .60$). Scores of 100 respondents were correlated with their scores on the EOWPVT-4: SBE, yielding a coefficient of .67. Criterion-related validity was evaluated by comparing scores across age groups, with an increase in scores as age increased up to 50 years of age. Further, a sample of 11 respondents with attention-deficit/ hyperactivity disorder (ADHD) and a sample of 57 respondents with autism/pervasive developmental disorder (PDD) were compared to same-aged samples without such diagnoses. Significant differences were found indicating the expected lower performance levels of the respondents with ADHD or Autism/PDD.

COMMENTARY. The ROWPVT-4: SBE is a relatively straightforward test of receptive vocabulary with all items focused on the equivalent task of matching a word to an illustration with variation in difficulty based on the nature of the word used. The uniformity of task demands as reflected in item format likely accounts for the high levels of internal consistency reported.

The test seems to be easily administered to a wide range of respondents. The use of age-relevant start points allows for test administration times of about 20 minutes, which is not only convenient and attractive to test users, but also minimizes issues of test fatigue or boredom.

Because the test can be administered in either Spanish or English or both languages, it is essentially testing two vocabularies, yet only one score is generated. It appears that there is an assumption of equivalence of test items using Spanish and English words that have the same meaning. However, this assumption is not evaluated empirically and should be. Also, the extent to which the pool of words that form the basis of this test was evaluated by an expert panel or compared to other recognized tests or vocabulary sets is not reported.

The age-based norms are derived from small samples of respondents (sample sizes of 31 to 95 participants) from 14 states in the U.S. This brings into question the representativeness of the norms and the extent to which derived percentile ranks reflect score distributions within the target population. More work that uses nationally representative samples of respondents should be conducted if intended users are interested in generating national normed scores for the wide range of age groups reported for the measure.

SUMMARY. The ROWPVT-4: SBE is a readily understood test of receptive vocabulary that is easily administered on an individual level. The psychometric evidence presented in the test manual is generally supportive of the use of its scores in the manner suggested by the test publisher.

[142]

Receptive One-Word Picture Vocabulary Test, 4ᵗʰ Edition.

Purpose: Designed to assess an individual's English hearing vocabulary.
Population: Ages 2 to 80 years and older.
Publication Dates: 1985–2011.
Acronym: ROWPVT-4.
Scores: Total score only.
Administration: Individual.
Price Data, 2012: $175 per kit, including manual (2011, 93 pages), 25 record forms, and test plates in vinyl portfolio; $80 per set of test plates; $40 per 25 record forms; $55 per manual.
Foreign Language Edition: Spanish-Bilingual version available.
Time: (20) minutes.
Authors: 1985 edition by Morrison F. Gardner; 2000 edition prepared by Rick Brownell; 4ᵗʰ Edition by Nancy A. Martin and Rick Brownell.
Publisher: Academic Therapy Publications.
Cross References: For reviews by Doreen W. Fairbank and Sheila Pratt of the 2000 Edition, see 15:205; see also T5:2190 (9 references) and T4:2239 (1 reference); for reviews by Janice A. Dole and Janice Santogrossi of an earlier edition, see 10:312; for reviews by Laurie Ford and William D. Schafer of an earlier edition of the upper level, see 11:329.

Review of the Receptive One-Word Picture Vocabulary Test, 4ᵗʰ Edition by RONALD A. MADLE, Licensed Psychologist, Mifflinburg, PA, and Adjunct Associate Professor of School Psychology, The Pennsylvania State University, University Park, PA:

DESCRIPTION. The Receptive One-Word Picture Vocabulary Test, 4ᵗʰ Edition (ROWPVT-4) is a single-word receptive language measure for individuals from 2-0 to 80+ years old. It measures an individual's ability to match a spoken word with a picture of an object, action, or concept. Stated uses include documenting vocabulary development, screening for early language delay, examining word/ concept retrieval in aphasics, indirectly assessing reading skill and some aspects of cognitive skills, and evaluating intervention programs. The untimed measure takes about 15 to 20 minutes to administer, with an additional 5 to 10 minutes needed for scoring. Speech-language pathologists, school psychologists, counselors, learning specialists, and similar professionals can administer the test. Only a professional with training in psychometrics and knowledge of derived score limitations should interpret the test results.

The ROWPVT-4 complete kit includes a full-color stimulus book, a manual, and 25 test forms. The manual provides clear administration instructions. The manual discusses the various scores and how to interpret them.

The test plates are contained in a wire-bound easel that is reversed to present the second half of the items. The full color, numbered item plates are presented horizontally across the page. Test plates are turned from front to back.

The bifold 8.5 by 11-inch record form contains all identifying and summary information on the front page, with instructions and starting points at the top of the second page. The 190 items take the remainder of the test booklet. Spaces are provided for standard scores, confidence levels, percentile ranks, and age-equivalents. All standard scores have a mean of 100 and standard deviation of 15.

Administration begins with four sample items regardless of entry point. Re-administration of the sample items is permitted until the task demands are understood. Responses involve pointing to one of four pictures that corresponds to the word spoken by the examiner. After starting at the person's age entry point, a basal is established by getting eight consecutive correct responses. If an error occurs within the first eight items, the examiner tests backwards until eight consecutive correct answers are obtained and then returns to the highest item not yet administered. Testing is discontinued when there are six errors within eight successive items.

Scoring criteria are objective; no subjective judgments or querying are needed. The ROWPVT-4 yields a single score–the Receptive Standard Score (RSS)–with tables for percentiles, age-equivalents, and 90% or 95% confidence intervals. In contrast to many measures, test-specific descriptors are not included for standard score intervals and the user can use any system with which they are comfortable for descriptive labels. The test was conormed with a companion measure—the Expressive One-Word Picture Vocabulary Test, 4ᵗʰ Edition (EOWPVT-4, Martin & Brownell, 2011; 19:71)—and allows for comparisons between receptive and expressive vocabulary.

DEVELOPMENT. ROWPVT-4 development goals are not specifically delineated in the manual. It appears that the primary goals were to extend the age range both up and down (the clear emphasis on adding older individuals to the norms), to decrease floor and ceiling limitations in the prior edition, and to update norms. The ROWPVT-4 continues to start with toddlers, but the age range has been extended to cover adult and geriatric populations in response to practitioners' requests.

The number of items was increased from 174 in the 2000 edition to 194 in the standardization version. Both easier and more difficult items were written to extend the range as well as to provide improved floors and ceilings. The vast majority of the test items remain unchanged. The words used were predominantly nouns, with some gerunds, verbs, and modifiers. All new words were administered to standardization participants below age 13 for easy items and ages 13 and above for harder ones.

After item analyses using both classical test theory (CTT) and item response theory (IRT), some items were eliminated, and the final version of 190 developmentally sequenced items was prepared. The analyses also showed no evidence of item bias.

TECHNICAL.

Standardization. The ROWPVT-4 standardization sample consisted of 2,394 individuals who were stratified on race/ethnicity, geographic region, and educational level using the 2000 U.S. Census (U.S. Bureau of Census, 2000), as the 2010 Census was not yet available. Hispanics, residents of the Northeast and West regions, and rural populations were somewhat overrepresented. Underrepresentation is evident in the categories of Asian American, Caucasian, and Native American; the North Central region; and urban/suburban populations. Although educational level overall is a good approximation of the Census, there were more with a postgraduate education and fewer with a bachelor's degree than in the Census.

The age distribution was reported at 1-year increments up to age 13. Sample sizes for those ages ranged from 82 to 214. The mean group size was 117.67. After that there were only six age groups reported (15, 17, 20, 50, 70, 80). These appear to represent age spans rather than specific ages because the manual notes that the oldest individual in the standardization sample was 103 years old. Overall, there were an average 28.5 individuals for each age range in developing the norms tables.

Standard scores were derived by plotting the cumulative frequency of each raw score at each age group, then plotting percentile ranks against the range of raw scores. Lines were smoothed to reduce irregularities and new percentile ranks were developed for each raw score. Finally, these were transformed to obtain both z-scores and standard scores (mean = 100; *sd* = 15). Age equivalents were determined from the age group median raw scores.

Norm tables provide scores at 2-month intervals at ages 2 years through 4 years 11 months, 3-month intervals at 5 years through 15 years 11 months, 6-month intervals at ages 16 years through 19 years 11 months, and 5-year intervals for ages 20 and older.

Examination of the norm tables shows the ROWPVT-4 has floors of at least 3 standard deviations (SS = 55) at all levels except age 2. Lower scores, except for the designation SS < 55, are not included in any of the tables. With regard to ceiling, standard scores of 145 or >145 can be obtained until age 50 and then once again at age 65. The ceilings may be to some extent tenuous, however, once age 20 is reached because few if any items can be missed to reach the ceiling. Examinations of the norm tables generally suggest item gradients are acceptable.

Reliability. The median internal consistency coefficient (.97) of the ROWPVT-4 is good, with reliabilities of .94 to .98 for different age groups. The test-retest stability in a group of 78 individuals was .91 over a mean of 19 days. Unfortunately, the manual provides no information about mean changes in scores on retesting.

Validity. Content evidence of validity was established based on item development procedures and appears to be quite good. Information on other types of validity is more limited, especially considering the fairly extensive studies conducted with the previous edition. Initial construct validity evidence presented consisted of the correlation between the ROWPVT-4 and the previous edition (*r* = .93) in a sample of 229 children between the ages of 5 and 15. A second study, using a sample of 23 children, correlated the ROWPVT-4 with the Verbal Comprehension Index on the Wechsler Intelligence Scale for Children, Fourth Edition (WISC-IV; Wechsler, 2003). A moderate correlation of .39 was obtained. Finally, scores on the ROWPVT-4 were correlated with scores on the conormed EOWPVT-4 for the entire normative sample. Moderately strong correlations of .69 for standard scores and .86 for raw scores were obtained.

Several pieces of criterion-related validity information were presented as well. First, there were age-related increases on raw scores until late adulthood followed by a decline in old age for the standardization sample, although this seems to better address construct validity. Further analyses showed

correlations of .69 with the STAR Reading measure (*N* = 33) and of .35 with the WISC-IV Full Scale IQ (*N* = 24). Finally, data for individuals with disabilities where language is typically impaired, such as Speech/Language Impairment (mean = 79.79), Autism (mean = 83.39), Reading Disability (mean = 85.53), and Learning Disability (mean = 83.54), showed appropriately reduced standard scores on the ROWPVT-4. Children with Attention Deficit Disorders (mean = 90.82) showed some reduction but less than the other groups.

COMMENTARY AND SUMMARY. Overall, the ROWPVT-4 appears to be a solid measure of single-word receptive vocabulary that covers most of the life span. It is well designed, easily administered and scored, reliable, and valid. Floors, ceilings, and item gradients are respectable except at the extremes, where floors for 2-year-olds and ceilings for 50- to 65-year-olds suggest results should be interpreted cautiously. Generally, however, the ROWPVT-4 continues to show the psychometric soundness of its predecessor.

If there is a weakness, it is that, compared with the previous edition, limited new validation data were collected. In addition, validation data presented relied mostly on preexisting test results submitted by standardization examiners rather than proactive, planned studies. A particular absence, which certainly can be addressed postpublication, is the lack of correlations with other receptive picture vocabulary tests, such as the Peabody Picture Vocabulary Test, Fourth Edition (Dunn & Dunn, 2007; 18:88).

Finally, although a minor point, it would have been preferable to use more updated information for the standardization sample stratification. Although the final 2010 Census was unavailable, regular updates for population statistics are available online.

REVIEWER'S REFERENCES

Dunn, L. M., & Dunn, D. M. (2007). Peabody Picture Vocabulary Test, Fourth Edition. Minneapolis, MN: Pearson.
Martin, N. A., & Brownell, R. (2011). Expressive One-Word Picture Vocabulary Test, Fourth Edition. Novato, CA: Academic Therapy Publications.
U.S. Bureau of the Census. (2000). *Statistical abstract of the United States.* Washington, DC: U.S. Department of Commerce.
Wechsler, D. (2003). Wechsler Intelligence Scale for Children–Fourth Edition. San Antonio, TX: The Psychological Corporation.

Review of the Receptive One-Word Picture Vocabulary Test, 4ᵗʰ Edition by JONATHAN SANDOVAL, Emeritus Professor of Education, University of California, Davis, Davis, CA:

DESCRIPTION. The Receptive One-Word Picture Vocabulary Test, 4ᵗʰ Edition (ROWPVT-4) consists of 190 vocabulary words ordered by difficulty. The authors designed it to measure the hearing or receptive vocabulary of U.S. English speakers, rather than the ability to define words verbally (expressively). The examiner reads the word to the test taker who must identify a picture illustrating the meaning of the word. Three other incorrect full color illustrations serve as distracters. The examinee may respond verbally or by pointing. The materials include a manual, a record form, and a spiral-bound book of 190 sets of pictures. Administration requires 15 to 20 minutes and scoring requires 5 to 10 minutes. The test begins with four practice trials. Then examiners, guided by suggested age-based starting points, establish a basal level of eight consecutive correct answers and continue testing until they determine a ceiling of six errors within eight consecutive responses. The raw score is the number correct.

Examinees may range from ages 2 years through 80 years and above. ROWPVT-4 raw scores convert to standard scores (with a mean of 100 and standard deviation of 15), percentiles, and age-equivalent scores.

The test authors intend for the test to aid in the identification of language delay or impairment associated with such conditions as autism, delayed cognitive development, reading difficulties, or schizophrenia. When used with a co-normed sister test, the Expressive One-Word Picture Vocabulary Test, 4th Edition (EOWPVT-4; 19:71), test users may find discrepancies in scoring stemming from aphasia or other neurological conditions. The manual contains tables of differences between the tests significant at the .05 level for each of 17 age groupings.

DEVELOPMENT. The ROWPVT-4 is a revision of previous editions and is identical in format and structure. However, the number of items increased from 174 to make the norms applicable to the geriatric population. Of the 190 words/images in this edition, as many as 28 are new. The normative edition contained 194 items. The authors ultimately eliminated 4 items for the final version; the manual does not say whether those deleted were old or new words, although the deletions were based upon item analyses. Presumably, extra items were not needed or did not add appreciably to the reliability or validity of the measure. ROWPVT-4 items seem to be free of bias based on gender, urban versus rural residence, and race. The manual reports no evidence of bias based on analyses of item difficulty, item discrimination,

Rasch modeling, and differential item functioning. No data were provided to substantiate the claim, but it seems credible.

TECHNICAL. The ROWPVT-4 standardization sample consisted of 2,394 individuals from ages 2 years 0 months to 103 years. Speech and language pathologists, school psychologists, educational specialists, and supervised graduate students conducted the norming at 84 sites in 26 states across the U.S. Developers attempted to match U.S. demographic characteristics with respect to gender, ethnicity, geographical region, type of community, level of education, and disability status. In the final normative sample of 2,394, females, Hispanic examinees, those from the West and the Northeast, those from rural areas, and those holding postgraduate degrees were represented slightly more frequently than they were in the general population, but the discrepancies were not dramatic. The examinees at each of 18 age ranges numbered from 82 at age 2 to 279 at ages 20 to 49. Standard score conversions appear at 2-month intervals for ages 2-0 through 4-11, 3-month intervals for ages 5-0 through 15-11, 6-month intervals for ages 16-0 through 19-11, and 5-year age intervals for ages 20 and older up to age 85 and older. Assuming an equal spread across an age span, one would expect norms to be based on approximately 14 examinees at age 2, and as many as 139 for the ages 20–50. The norms themselves were the result of curve smoothing.

The internal consistency reliability coefficient alphas range from .94 in young and middle-aged adults to .98 for most other ages tested, with a median of .97. These high coefficients indicate the test measures its construct very reliably. The test-retest correlation at .97 for raw scores in a sample of 78 is also quite good suggesting that test results are stable over the 2- to 3-week short run (with an average intervening time period of 19 days). The authors have calculated the standard error of measurement for each age level as well as the 90% and 95% confidence level and provided these values in the manual.

Validity evidence comes from information obtained during the standardization process. A correlation of .93 between the previous edition and the current edition for 229 school-aged examinees provides evidence for concurrent validity. How the test correlates with other measures of receptive vocabulary, such as the Peabody Picture Vocabulary Test, Fourth Edition (Dunn & Dunn, 2007) or the Comprehensive Receptive and Expressive Vocabulary Test–Third Edition (Wallace & Hammill, 2012) would be useful additional evidence. Because the test does not require a verbal or written response, it would not be expected to correlate as highly with vocabulary tests requiring a verbal response, but it should have a moderately high correlation with such tests. The ROWPVT-4 raw scores correlated .86 with the EOWPVT-4 but only .39 with a small sample (23) of students on the Wechsler Intelligence Scale for Children–Fourth Edition (WISC-4; Wechsler, 2003) Verbal Comprehension Index, which includes a test of expressive vocabulary. This later finding plus the correlation of .35 with WISC-4 Full Scale for presumably the same sample plus an additional student ($n = 24$) suggests that the ROWPVT-4 is measuring a fairly discrete verbal ability associated with general mental ability. It would be reassuring to have evidence from a larger, representative study looking at the correlation between scores on the test and, for example, the WISC-4 Vocabulary Test (Wechsler, 2003). With respect to construct validity, data in the manual show that the test reflects the hypothesized growth progression of vocabulary, and how various groups with known vocabulary and language difficulties score significantly lower than matched control children on the ROWPVT-4. The groups tested included students with Attention Deficit Disorder, Learning Disability, Reading Disability, Autism, and Specific Language Impairment. There is also a moderately strong correlation (.69) with a test of reading ability.

COMMENTARY. The ROWPVT-4 is a quick and easy-to-administer and score test of a discrete verbal skill, the ability to recognize a picture associated with a vocabulary word. It has been expanded to cover a larger age range and has undergone more refinement in item selection. Its utility is enhanced by a conormed expressive vocabulary test. The norms are reasonably representative of the U.S. population and seem adequate for clinical use. The reliability of the measure, based on the evidence in the manual, is excellent. More validity information would be useful, particularly regarding ways in which scores on the measure compare to similar tests, to nonverbal measures of cognition, and to other expressive vocabulary tests. The usefulness of the test depends greatly on the validity of information derived from the discrepancy between receptive and expressive vocabulary. This topic is not discussed deeply in the manual. Test users would benefit from more validity information about the meaning of a significant discrepancy.

SUMMARY. The fourth edition of the ROWPVT is an improvement over earlier editions and now includes norms for a wider range of ages. The authors developed it using modern test theory, and it is a very good measure of receptive vocabulary or word knowledge out of context. Although users may wish for more evidence of validity, the test will likely be useful to speech and language clinicians, school psychologists, and educators as they study vocabulary development. When used with the conormed EOWPVT-4 it may provide insight into a number of clinical conditions. The test is a reasonable alternative to the popular Peabody Picture Vocabulary Test, Fourth Edition (Dunn & Dunn, 2007; 18:88).

REVIEWER'S REFERENCES
Dunn, L. M., & Dunn, D. M. (2007). Peabody Picture Vocabulary Test, Fourth Edition. Minneapolis, MN: Pearson.
Wallace, G., & Hammill, D. D. (2012). Comprehensive Receptive and Expressive Vocabulary Test–Third Edition. Austin, TX: PRO-ED.
Wechsler, D. (2003). Wechsler Intelligence Scale for Children–Fourth Edition. San Antonio, TX: The Psychological Corporation.

[143]

Repeatable Battery for the Assessment of Neuropsychological Status Update.

Purpose: Designed to measure "attention, language, visuospatial/constructional abilities, and immediate and delayed memory."

Population: Ages 12–89 years.

Publication Dates: 1998–2012.

Acronym: RBANS Update.

Scores, 6: Immediate Memory, Visuospatial/Constructional, Language, Attention, Delayed Memory, Total Scale.

Subtests, 12: List Learning, Story Memory, Figure Copy, Line Orientation, Picture Naming, Semantic Fluency, Digit Span, Coding, List Recall, List Recognition, Story Recall, Figure Recall.

Administration: Individual.

Forms: 4 Parallel Forms: Form A, Form B, Form C, Form D.

Price Data, 2013: $549 per RBANS Update combo kit, including stimulus books A, B, C, and D, scoring templates A, B, C, and D, and manual (2012, 196 pages); $309 per RBANS Update kit (Form A, B, C, or D), including manual, stimulus book, 25 record forms, scoring template; $199 per RBANS Update Form A upgrade kit, including new manual and stimulus book A with new norms (designed for current users; record forms and scoring templates remain the same).

Foreign Language Edition: Forms A and B available in Spanish.

Time: (20-30) minutes.

Author: Christopher Randolph.

Publisher: Pearson.

Cross References: For reviews by Stephen J. Freeman and Timothy J. Makatura of an earlier edition, see 14:315.

Review of the Repeatable Battery for the Assessment of Neuropsychological Status Update by BRIAN F. FRENCH, Professor of Educational Psychology, and CHAD M. GOTCH, Clinical Assistant Professor of Educational Psychology, Washington State University, Pullman, WA:

DESCRIPTION. The Repeatable Battery for the Assessment of Neuropsychological Status Update (RBANS Update) is a brief, individually administered assessment with the purposes of providing (a) early detection of dementia, (b) a brief neuropsychological evaluation, and (c) longitudinal assessment of neuropsychological status. RBANS Update technical documentation notes advantages over other measures including reduced administration time, availability of patient profiles, and theoretical support. The RBANS Update can be used to detect, characterize, and track dementing disorders; to provide medical professionals a quick screener; and to track recovery during rehabilitation or progress of degenerative diseases. The RBANS Update can be used with individuals ages 12 to 89 years, includes two Spanish forms (Forms A and B), and offers normative scores for subtests, which were not previously available. The assessment requires 20 to 30 minutes to administer by examiners familiar with standardized clinical assessments and who have professional training in psychological assessment or speech language pathology.

The RBANS Update consists of five domains—Immediate Memory, Visiospatial/Constructional, Language, Attention, and Delayed Memory—measured across 12 subtests. Standard scores are available for nine age groupings for each domain and at an aggregated total level. Scoring, completed by the examiner, follows thorough and clear instructions for awarding credit, calculating scores for the subtests, and converting raw subtest scores to standard subtest ($M = 10$, $SD = 3$), index ($M = 100$, $SD = 15$), and total scores ($M = 100$, $SD = 15$).

DEVELOPMENT. The RBANS was constructed based on empirically identified correlates of dementia and the idea that distinct profiles of cognitive deficits may exist based on differing etiologies of dementias. The RBANS was developed to bridge the gap between more extensive dementia measures and screeners that are often insensitive to mild impairments. Clear documentation of item development for subscales, including any content updates, was not provided. There are detailed descriptions of the subtests in the test manual, but the user must possess knowledge of other measures to make sense of statements such as, "The content and formats of RBANS subtests are similar in nature to tasks contained in some of the most frequently administered clinical tests, such as WAIS-III (Wechsler, 1997), WMS-III, *Boston Naming Test* (BNT; Kaplan, Goodglass, & Weintraub, 1983), *Judgment of Line Orientation* (Benton, Hamsher, Varney, & Spreen, 1983), and verbal fluency tests" (manual, p. 55).

TECHNICAL. The RBANS was standardized based on individuals ($N = 690$) who had no evidence of recent decline in cognitive/functional abilities, no uncorrected hearing/visual impairment, ability to comprehend English, no current diagnosis/history of alcohol/drug dependence, and no history of several characteristics that would influence test performance (e.g., head injury, psychiatric illness, stroke). The RBANS Update sample is the original adult sample plus 150 adolescents ages 12–19. Adult and adolescent samples are representative of the U.S. population in sex and broad race/ethnic categories based on 1995 and 2010 Census data, respectively. Individuals with less than a high school education are slightly overrepresented. As well, there appears to be some misalignment by geographic region. The technical manual provides two sets of percentages (for adults and adolescents), but the reported percentages do not appear to align with U.S. Census Bureau data.

Internal consistency reliability (split-half) evidence is provided by age groups with coefficients that range from .55 to .91, with an average range across ages on subtests of .78 to .85. Estimates for three subtests and one domain were derived from a clinically based sample, not the standardization sample, and should be viewed cautiously. The Total scale reliability estimates were .90 or above for all age groups. Standard errors of measurement across ages and scores are presented, aiding score interpretation. Test-retest reliability is reported for index scores for the 12–19 age group ($N = 55$; 14 to 31 day interval) and the adult age groups ($N = 40$; 38.7 weeks average interval) with corrected coefficients that range from .63 to .85 and .68 to .84, respectively, with varying levels of practice effects. There is a text to table discrepancy in the adult values; the publisher confirmed the values in the table are correct. Interrater agreement was provided for the Figure Copy subtest with a coefficient of .85. Score differences were discussed in terms of statistically significant differences between domain scores or subtest scores to assist the user in knowing what differences likely are not due to error. No information was provided about practically relevant differences.

Validity evidence is provided in various forms. Most importantly, the user is reminded that the RBANS Update scores provide information to be used in conjunction with the collection of medical and psychosocial histories and direct behavioral observations. The five domain scores are recommended for use in the clinical setting, and the 12 subtest scores are provided with caution to the user not to "overinterpret one or two low scores" (manual, p. 84). Content validity evidence relies on tasks being similar to other measures without detail on how similarity was judged. There is no evidence provided for the factor structure.

Validity evidence derived from associations with other variables is provided across several measures (e.g., Wechsler Adult Intelligence Scale–Revised [WAIS-R; 9:1348], Wechsler Memory Scale–Revised [WMS-R; 11:465], BNT; 10:15). The correlation coefficient between the WAIS-R short form Full IQ score and the RBANS Update Total score was .78 with coefficients for subscales ranging from .57 to .66. Correlation coefficients with the WMS-R were similar (.24 to .70). Generally, there was good support for the RBANS scores. Correlations between RBANS Update subtests and relevant subtests from other tests yielded coefficients that often fell in the .40 to .60 range, while coefficients were lower between subtests not expected to be strongly related. Evidence of small mean differences between English speakers and Spanish speakers was provided as evidence that the English norms were appropriate for Spanish speakers for Form A only. However, a lack of mean differences is not evidence that a form or items function equally well across groups (Thissen, Steinberg, & Gerrard, 1986). Information was provided concerning the equating study used in developing the Spanish version.

COMMENTARY. The RBANS, in updated form, appears to hold promise for the stated purpose by overcoming obstacles of other measures in the area of dementia. The technical manual provides good commentary and appropriate cautions around score use. The testing materials are well prepared, and information on scoring, sample, technical qualities, and test use was mostly clear. The guidelines and sample cases that were provided that consider the typical pattern of performance associated with

various diseases within dementia work and likely will be helpful in acquainting the clinician with this instrument. Concurrent and discriminant evidence of score functioning is provided with an appropriate caveat from the test author that such outcomes should be considered "preliminary rather than conclusive" (manual, p. 58) because of small sample sizes.

The test manual did leave reviewers wanting more information, particularly validity evidence. Some support for the use of the scores is provided, but an attempted validation of use would be incomplete if based on the information currently provided. There is little description available to evaluate content coverage. In general, clearer information about the differences between the RBANS Update and the RBANS would be valuable. Equating of forms was mentioned, but it is unclear whether forms were actually equated (i.e., a score on one form is placed on the same scale as another form). There is no validity evidence provided for adolescents' scores in terms of association with other measures.

The need for additional evidence is most acute in support of the internal structure of the RBANS Update and the derived profiles. One must base use of the profiles and their component domain scores on perceived content associations and reported correlations between scores on subtests and domains and among domain scores. In support of the former, correlation coefficients are only provided for 8 of the 12 subtests. Across the age span these associations range in magnitude from .34 to .55 for intended subtest-domain relationships and from .21 to .44 between subtests and domains to which they do not belong. Correlation coefficients between observed domain scores range from .29 to .64 across the age span. The suite of correlations generally indicates domains are composed of the appropriate subtests and discriminate patterns of item responses. No support is presented, however, for claims that the scores represent distinct underlying aspects of neuropsychological functioning. Furthermore, only three subtest reliability estimates met the criteria typically required for making decisions about individuals (e.g., Nunnally & Bernstein, 1994). Given issues related to measurement error and internal structure, serious caution is warranted against the use of subtest and domain scores as stand-alone diagnostic criteria in deriving profiles.

SUMMARY. The RBANS is designed to detect, characterize, and track disorders related to dementia. Given its grounding in similar measures, its shorter administration time, expanded age range, and Spanish forms, the RBANS Update should be welcomed by users who are engaged in such assessment. Generally, appropriate psychometric information is provided to support the RBANS Update. However, concerns raised in past reviews of the RBANS still exist for the RBANS Update including issues with reliability estimates, differentiation from other similar tests, and a need for stronger evidence of unique profiles. The RBANS Update may be appropriate for use in combination with other criteria but cannot be recommended as a stand-alone product in deriving patient profiles and determining individual patient care. Of course, continual gathering of validity evidence (e.g., response processes, internal structure, consequences of score use) will add support for the RBANS Update over time.

REVIEWERS' REFERENCES

Nunnally, J. C., & Bernstein, I. H. (1994). *Psychometric theory* (3rd ed.). New York, NY: McGraw-Hill.
Thissen, D., Steinberg, L., & Gerrard, M. (1986). Beyond group-mean differences: The concept of item bias. *Psychological Bulletin, 99*, 118-128.

Review of the Repeatable Battery for the Assessment of Neuropsychological Status Update by JOHN F. LINCK, Staff Neuropsychologist, Oklahoma City VAMC, Oklahoma City, OK:

DESCRIPTION. The Repeatable Battery for the Assessment of Neuropsychological Status Update (RBANS Update) is an individually administered standardized pencil-and-paper measure designed to assess immediate and delayed memory, attention, language, and visuospatial/constructional abilities. It is purported to be useful in the assessment of individuals ages 12–89 and can be administered in approximately 20–30 minutes. The RBANS Update measures a number of discrete neurocognitive domains (or indices) and allows for multiple administrations with the availability of alternate forms that are helpful in assessing individuals in rehabilitation settings or individuals who may be experiencing an exacerbation of an existing neurodegenerative disease process.

The RBANS Update comprises 12 subtests that can generate a Total Scale score along with discrete domain-specific index scores consisting of Immediate Memory (two subtests), Visuospatial/Constructional (two subtests), Attention (two subtests), Language (two subtests), and Delayed Memory (four subtests). As it was designed for portability, the examiner requires only the stimulus booklet and record form for administration. The

RBANS Update provides alternate forms (Forms A-D) along with a Spanish version.

Scoring instructions are straightforward and included in the test manual. The record form contains a score conversion page that allows for calculation of the Total Scale score and five additional index scores. The test manual provides administration and scoring criteria for each subtest. Scoring criteria for the figure copy and figure recall portions are included in as appendix of the stimulus booklet. Another appendix contains the normative tables for the RBANS Update. A new addition to the RBANS Update is the ability to calculate scaled scores for 8 of 12 subtests and percentile band norms (i.e., cumulative percentages) for the remaining 4 subtests. Finally, a supplemental discrepancy analysis page is provided for examiners interested in calculating and analyzing the differences between scores on each index.

DEVELOPMENT. As reported in the test manual, the author's review of the literature suggested that some existing dementia measures were less sensitive to mild cognitive changes early in the course of dementia. The RBANS was developed to address these issues and limitations with the purpose of creating a portable, stand-alone screening battery that was sensitive to mild dementia and could be administered in a brief amount of time.

The RBANS Update attempts to provide several improvements to the existing measure. Because of the potential utility with younger populations, the RBANS Update includes a downward extension of age to include individuals 12 years and older. Additionally, equating studies for Forms C and D and Spanish Forms A and B were conducted. Further, the RBANS Update now includes normative tables for 8 of 12 subtests, and percentile band norms (i.e., cumulative percentages) for the remaining 4 subtests (i.e., subtests previously purported to have a restricted range in the normal population). Finally, the test manual was updated to include information about adolescents as well as an RBANS-specific review of the literature since the test was published in 1998.

TECHNICAL.

Standardization. Originally developed and normed for use with individuals ages 20 to 89 years, the RBANS Update now includes expanded norms for individuals ages 12 to 19. The original standardization sample included 540 adults ages 20–89 divided into six age groups containing 90

participants in each group: 20–39, 40–49, 50–59, 60–69, 70–79, and 80–89. For the RBANS Update, an additional sample was included consisting of 150 adolescents ages 12–19 divided into three age groups containing 50 participants in each group: 12–13, 14–15, and 16–19. Both samples were stratified by gender, geographic region, educational level, and ethnicity, and the latter is purported to be similar to U.S. Census Bureau proportions. Exclusionary criteria are listed in the test manual, although little is mentioned regarding how participants were screened for inclusion. Users should be aware that there are only 50–90 individuals in each age group in the normative sample.

Reliability. Split-half reliability coefficients were calculated for each index by age group; the average reliability coefficients range from .75 to .93. For the Line Orientation, Picture Naming, Semantic Fluency, and List Recognition subtests, reliability coefficients were calculated using a group of clinical patients with various neurologic diagnoses; the standardization sample was used for computing reliability estimates for the remaining subtests. No further description is offered by the test author on this issue. The average subtest-level reliability coefficients range from .50 to .85 and are generally lower than index-level reliability estimates. Users should be aware that the reliability estimates are low for some subtest/age group combinations. Test-retest reliability based on 55 adolescents ages 12 to 19 who were administered Form A twice within 14 to 31 days produced coefficients that ranged from .63 to .85. Subtest-level retest correlation coefficients for adolescents ranged from .49 to .79. For adults, corrected test-retest reliability estimates (33–43 week interval) for a group of 40 adults (Mean age = 70.7, SD = 7.9) ranged from .68 to .84. Users should be aware that the retest correlation coefficients among the subtests ranged from .27 to .76. Interrater reliability for Figure Copy was .85 among three trained scorers who blindly scored 20 Figure Copy/Figure Recall subtests.

Alternate form equating studies were conducted with 100 participants from the original sample for Forms A and B. Using the RBANS Update sample, studies compared Form A to Form C and Form A to Form D (n = 135 and 146, respectively). Corrected alternate form correlation coefficients for the index scores between Form A and Form B ranged from .46 to .82. Corrected alternate form correlation coefficients between

Form A and Form C ranged from .24 to .75. Corrected alternate form correlation coefficients between Form A and Form D ranged from .58 to .80. In all instances the differences between the different forms were not anticipated to impact clinical decision making.

The RBANS Update includes Spanish Forms A and B. An equating study using Form A included 89 U.S. Spanish-speaking examinees. Overall, a slightly lower performance for Spanish speakers on Delayed Memory was noted. Although the difference approached statistical significance ($p < .10$) the difference was not believed to impact clinical decision making.

Validity. As documented in the test manual, the RBANS Update demonstrates adequate content validity given the similarities between the subtests and those contained in other existing standardized measures commonly used in clinical practice. Construct validity evidence derived from the resulting correlation coefficients for the indices, which ranged from .29 to .64. The highest values emerged among the memory measures as expected, suggesting that each index measures a distinct factor. However, evidence supporting the interpretability of the five indices has been limited (Strauss, Sherman, & Spreen, 2006) with some studies identifying evidence for a two-factor solution (Duff et al., 2009; Schmitt et al., 2010).

Correlations between the RBANS and other existing standardized measures suggest that the RBANS has adequate construct validity; however, no updated comparisons have been conducted. This is concerning as certain measures such as the Wechsler Scales (i.e., Wechsler Adult Intelligence Scale-Fourth Edition; WAIS-IV; 18:151) have undergone significant changes in both factor structure and item content. However, Strauss et al. (2006) suggest that comparisons between the RBANS and more recently updated versions of these tests reveal strong correlations. Remarkably, no comparisons between the RBANS performances of those ages 12 to 19 and other child assessment measures were included, calling into question the construct validity of the RBANS Update for those in that age range.

COMMENTARY.

Strengths. The RBANS Update is a well-researched measure that includes a broad assessment of several neurocognitive domains in a relatively short period of time. It is sensitive to a number of disorders. The presence of alternate forms allows for repeat administrations that minimize practice effects. Updated tables allow for additional scores to be computed for individual subtests. A Spanish version and the expanded normative data allow for the RBANS Update to be used with additional populations. Finally, the RBANS-specific review of the literature is a useful addition for those interested in using this measure.

Weaknesses. Users should expect to need additional measures (i.e., to evaluate executive functioning, premorbid levels of functioning, mood) when using the RBANS Update. Ceiling effects continue to be present across subtests calling into question the test's utility in more clinically intact populations. (At the same time, the fact that no changes were made in the actual test items allows for continued use of existing research.) Subtest reliabilities are generally lower than the index score reliabilities, and the test author warns against over reliance on the subtest scores during interpretation. Additional research is needed with Forms C and D and the Spanish Forms A and B prior to more consistent use in clinical practice. Likewise, the test would benefit from studies addressing construct validity in the 12- to 19-year age group as well as updated comparison studies of those ages 20 to 89. Finally, minor inconsistencies exist between the text and tables regarding test-retest coefficients for those ages 20-89.

SUMMARY. Overall, the RBANS Update is considered a reliable and well-validated neurocognitive screening measure. It continues to be widely used in both clinical and research settings and remains useful in screening those in acute-care settings, for tracking recovery in rehabilitation settings or for tracking disease progression in degenerative conditions. The measure may also be useful for non-neuropsychologists needing a screening measure. For test users who are aware of the test's strengths and weaknesses, the RBANS Update continues to be a valuable screening tool in the armamentarium of testing professionals who conduct neuropsychological assessments.

REVIEWER'S REFERENCES

Duff, K., Langbehn, D. R., Schoenberg, M. R., Moser, D. J., Baade, L. E., Mold, J. W., ... Adams, R. L. (2009). Normative data on and psychometric properties of verbal and visual indexes of the RBANS in older adults. *The Clinical Neuropsychologist, 23*(1), 39-50.
Schmitt, A. L., Livingston, R. B., Smernoff, E. N., Reese, E. M., Hafer, D. G., & Harris, J. B. (2010). Factor analysis of the Repeatable Battery for the Assessment of Neuropsychological Status (RBANS) in a large sample of patients suspected of dementia. *Applied Neuropsychology, 17*(1), 8-17.
Strauss, E., Sherman, E. M. S., & Spreen, O. (2006). *A compendium of neuropsychological tests: Administration, norms, and commentary* (3rd ed.). New York, NY: Oxford University Press.
Wechsler, D., Coalson, D. L., & Raiford, S. E. (2008). *WAIS-IV technical and interpretive manual.* San Antonio, TX: Pearson.

[144]
Retail Sales Evaluation.

Purpose: Designed to "examine how well the test-taker is suited for a career in the retail field."

Population: Potential retail sales workers.

Publication Date: 2011.

Acronym: RESALE.

Scores, 37: Attitude Towards Teamwork, Communication Skills, Self-Discipline, Time Management, Neatness, Meticulousness, Honesty Attitude, Honesty Ownership, Adaptability/Flexibility, Stress Reaction, Comfort with Routine, Comfort with Authority, Conflict Resolution, Optimism, Helpfulness, Hostility, Patience, Reaction to Criticism, Salesmanship, Drive, Self-Monitoring, Agreeableness, Assertiveness with Clients, Hardiness, Friendliness/Approachability, Extroversion, Social Skills, Comfort with Pressure Sales Tactics, Impression Management, Acquiescence, Work Attitude, Interpersonal Skills, Organizational Skills, Coping Skills, Self-Control Skills, Integrity, Overall Score.

Administration: Individual.

Price Data: Available from publisher.

Time: (30) minutes.

Comments: Self-administered online assessment. The test publisher advises that the test manual is being updated to include more information about methodology and theoretical background used in the development of the test. The test publisher also advises that this information is available to clients, as are benchmarks for relevant industries and racial/ethnic group comparison data. However, this information was not provided to Buros or the reviewer.

Author: PsychTests AIM, Inc.

Publisher: PsychTests AIM, Inc. [Canada].

Review of the Retail Sales Evaluation by GYPSY M. DENZINE, Assistant Vice Provost and Professor of Educational Psychology, Northern Arizona University, Flagstaff, AZ:

DESCRIPTION. The test authors developed the Retail Sales Evaluation (RESALE) to assess whether a test taker's personality traits and abilities match those required to be successful in the area of retail sales.

The RESALE is published by PsychTests AIM, Inc.; however, test authors' names are not provided. According to the test manual, the purpose of the RESALE is to "examine how well the test-taker is suited for a career in the retail field" (p. 1). The manual also states that another application of the RESALE is for "HR testing (screening and training)" (p. 1).

The RESALE contains 131 items, plus additional questions. The questions include both situational and self-assessment types. The RESALE is an online self-administered test that generates a computer-scored report summary.

The score report contains a general score that purports to be an overall indicator of the test taker's suitability for a career in retail. The Overall Score is composed of six subfactors and 28 subscales. This reviewer found the process of reading the instructions and completing the items in the online test to be a straightforward task that took approximately 30 minutes to complete.

Scores are not intended to be interpreted in a normative manner, and the manual does not contain norms for any groups of individuals.

DEVELOPMENT. This reviewer found no information in the manual, or in the literature, related to the theoretical background underlying the RESALE. Moreover, the present reviewer found no information describing the item and/or scale development. The manual contains no references, and the RESALE is seemingly noticeably missing any theoretical connections to personality and/or career development theory, as reflected in the manual.

TECHNICAL. The test manual contains descriptive statistics from an uncontrolled sample of 1,536 participants who took the RESALE online and agreed to particpate in a validation study. The data reported include means, standard deviations, minima, and maxima for the Overall Score, the six subfactors, the 28 subscales, and two validity scales.

The test manual contains a table with reliability analyses in the form of alpha coefficients for the twenty-eight 5-item subscales. The authors do not report how they handled issues of any missing data, nor do they address the extent to which the items met assumptions related to normality, homogeneity of variance, and so forth. Alpha coefficients ranged from .39 (Social Skills) to .85 (Friendliness/Approachability). Six of the 28 subscales had a reported alpha value below .50. The authors do not report alpha coefficients for the two 10-item validity scales: Impression Management and Acquiescence. Nowhere in the test manual do the authors address which items comprise these two subscales nor do they report how the scales were developed. The authors report an alpha coefficient of .96 for the Overall Score, which is said to contain 126 items. However, the test manual indicates the RESALE includes 131 items plus additional questions. There is no mention in the test manual about why the 5 additional items are not included in the Overall Score. No evidence of test-retest reliability is reported in the test manual.

Under the heading of "validity analysis," means and standard deviations together with corresponding analyses of variance (ANOVA) and t-test results are reported to explore differences between groups based on gender, age, position, experience in the retail field, and employer/supervisor ratings of performance.

Age is used as the dependent variable to conduct dozens of ANOVA tests on the subscales for a sample of 1,387 participants. However, age appears to have been artificially collapsed into six categories (under 17 years, 18–24, 25–29, 30–39, 40–49, and 50 and older) without any theoretical or empirical justification for doing so. Although the test authors note on the second page of the manual that t-test and ANOVA analyses are dependent on sample size, the test manual does not include any effect sizes necessary for interpreting practical significance. In yet another set of analyses, 31 t tests were conducted to determine whether subscale scores were significantly different for respondents who answered "yes" to the question of whether they had ever worked in retail sales as compared with those who answered "no."

Beyond the statistical results provided in the test manual for the uncontrolled sample, this reviewer found no published articles about the psychometric properties of the inventory and no empirical studies in which the scale was used.

COMMENTARY AND SUMMARY. In general, the manual contains an inadequate description of the procedures and decisions used to develop the items and the inventory. Persons hoping for an in-depth treatment of personality theory applied to career development will be disappointed in the test manual and the instrument itself. The absence of any factor analytic investigations to explore the underlying structure of the 131 items is concerning, as is the lack of evidence in support of construct and predictive validity. A shortcoming of the materials received by this reviewer was that there was no information about the cost of the test and associated results.

Given the research to date on item and scale development, the RESALE cannot be recommended for use with populations of adults interested in sales positions. The authors have not provided sufficient evidence that the RESALE meets even the bare minimum standards for educational and psychological testing (AERA, APA, & NCME, 1999). This review of the RESALE leads this writer to warn others that the use of the RESALE for employment screening might be unethical and put someone at risk for legal problems.

Although the RESALE is fairly straightforward in its administration, scoring, interpretation, and suggestions for use, the test does not appear to be a psychometrically sound measure of the extent to which an individual is well suited for a career in the retail field.

REVIEWER'S REFERENCE

American Educational Research Association, American Psychological Association, & National Council on Measurement in Education. (1999). *Standards for educational and psychological testing.* Washington, DC: American Educational Research Association.

[145]

Reynolds Child Depression Scale-2nd Edition and Short Form.

Purpose: "Designed to screen for depression in children."
Population: Ages 7-13 years.
Publication Dates: 1981-2010.
Acronyms: RCDS-2; RCDS-2:SF.
Scores: Total score only.
Administration: Individual or group.
Forms, 2: Reynolds Child Depression Scale-2nd Edition; Reynolds Child Depression Scale-2nd Edition: Short Form.
Price Data, 2013: $150 per complete kit including 25 full length test booklets, 25 short test forms, and manual (2010, 133 pages); $60 per 25 full length test booklets; $42 per 25 short forms; $62 per manual.
Time: (10-15) minutes for full length form; (2-3) minutes for short form.
Comments: Both forms should be administered orally to children in Grades 2 through 4; test items have not been revised since the original version, although Short Form has been added, which contains 11 of the 30 items on the full form.
Author: William M. Reynolds.
Publisher: Psychological Assessment Resources, Inc.
Cross References: See T5:2231 (7 references) and T4:2275 (3 references); for reviews by Janet F. Carlson and Cynthia A. Rohrbeck of an earlier edition, see 11:334 (1 reference).

Review of the Reynolds Child Depression Scale–2nd Edition and Short Form by ERIC S. BUHS, Associate Professor of Educational Psychology, University of Nebraska-Lincoln, Lincoln, NE:

DESCRIPTION. The original Reynolds Child Depression Scale was developed beginning in 1981 (publication in 1989) to assess depression in children. The Reynolds Child Depression Scale–2nd Edition and Short Form (RCDS-2; RCDS-2:SF)

self-report instruments published in 2010 are designed for professional assessment of the severity of depressive symptomatology in children ages 7 to 13 (Grades 2–6) and to support clinical decisions regarding children's mental health. The RCDS-2 and RCDS-2:SF (30 items and 11 items, respectively) are intended for use by trained psychologists, researchers, and other mental health professionals.

The instrument is a pencil-and-paper measure and may be administered either in individual or group settings with the full measure estimated to require approximately 10 minutes to complete and with the short form requiring approximately 2 to 3 minutes to complete. Group administration to groups larger than about 20–25 children is not advised. Examinees generally receive instructions and then read the forms and respond to items using a 4-point, Likert-type scale, but the items are intended to be read aloud for children in Grades 2–4 or for those with limited reading ability. Materials include the professional manual and the *About Me* test booklet or Short Form. The booklets are designed to be easily handscored using built-in scoring keys.

The RCDS-2 and RCDS-2:SF both yield total raw scores, a Critical Items subscale, and standard scores (*T*-scores and percentile ranks). The RCDS-2:SF is also designed for group screening using a multiple-gate screening procedure as recommended. Respondents endorsing clinical levels of depression in the group screening (Gate 1) are then selected for small group assessment with the RCDS-2 (Gate 2) and, given further clinical-level endorsement, selected for individual clinical evaluations/interviews and/or referrals (Gate 3). The test authors stress that the measures are to be used to indicate children who demonstrate "clinically relevant levels of depressive symptomatology" (professional manual, p. 4) and do not provide a formal diagnosis. The professional manual provides thorough instructions for detailed score interpretation and presents appropriate cutoff scores for normal, mild, moderate, and severe clinical levels of depressive symptoms. The Critical Items score may be used as "double check" for children scoring below the clinical cutoff but who still may be at risk for depression or require additional evaluation.

DEVELOPMENT. The original RCDS item content was developed for use with children in Grades 3–6 using the symptoms described in the DSM-III (APA, 1980) and standardized with a large sample. Development of the current, revised version was begun in 2008 and standardized using a stratified sample designed to emulate 2007 U.S. Census distributions of ethnicity. No item revisions were made for the RCDS-2/RCDS-2:SF. The items are written at approximately a second-grade reading level. Items are designed to be consistent with the developmental experiences of children in the 8- to 12-year range and to cover both diagnostic and clinical childhood depressive symptoms. Standard scores were added to include scores for the total standardization sample (by grade and gender), the clinical-level cutoff scores were revised, a carbonless booklet with a self-scoring page was developed, and the brief RCDS-2:SF was developed and published.

The test authors provide a relatively thorough description of the conceptual framework used for the RCDS development, and their theoretical overview presents the contention that childhood depression is likely expressed as a cluster of symptoms that include anhedonia, lowered self-esteem, social withdrawal, fatigue, crying spells, sleeping and eating disturbances, and self-destructive impulses. The test authors note that adjustment difficulty in school, family, and peer contexts may also be apparent. The item content reflects these assumptions and the attendant *DSM* criteria. The test authors also provide a clear description of their view of the distinction between describing the severity of depressive symptomatology (the intended use of this measure) and a formal diagnosis of depression. The scores provided by the RCDS-2 and RCDS-2:SF are designed to indicate the severity of depressive symptoms and to provide a cutoff score that identifies those levels consistent with a clinically relevant level of depressive symptoms.

TECHNICAL. The standardization samples for the RCDS-2/RCDS-2:SF included a school sample (n = 1,367) and a total standardization sample (n = 1,100) from representative U.S. states (11 total). Both samples were heterogeneous and ethnically diverse (approximately 40–43% non-Caucasian), and the total standardization sample was designed to approximate 2007 U.S. Census ethnic-group proportions. The school sample included 146 students from Grades 7 and 8. Total raw scores and item-level means, standard deviations, medians, and skewness statistics are provided for the total standardization sample only.

Reliability statistics are provided for the first edition standardization sample, the total standardization sample, and the total school sample, and are broken down by gender, grade, and ethnic group. Estimates of coefficient alpha for the total scores ranged from .83 to .95 for the RCDS-2 and from .73 to .93 for the RCDS-2:SF across all reported groups. Test-retest correlation coefficients for grade-level groups (Grades 3-6) across 2- to 4-week intervals ranged from .81 to .92 for the original RCDS (some test-retest data were drawn from smaller samples and external studies), and the RCDS-2:SF displayed estimates of .72 to .90 across a 3.5–4.5-week interval. No estimates of test-retest reliability were given for the RCDS-2, specifically. The RCDS, RCDS-2, and RCDS-2:SF all appear to display acceptable evidence of reliability and the RCDS and RCDS-2:SF appear to present relatively stable estimates of self-rated depression over periods of a few weeks.

Validity evidence is presented across a thorough range of forms, a subset of which are summarized here. Content validity was demonstrated via item-content congruence with *DSM-IV* (APA, 2000) symptomology and other established clinical sources. Items also displayed acceptable item-total scale correlations and indicated that all items appeared to contribute meaningfully to scale totals (estimates from .32–.64, median = .47, for the RCDS-2; estimates from .44–.64, median = .52, for the RCDS-2:SF). The RCDS-2 and RCDS-2:SF also showed acceptable criterion-related validity evidence and demonstrated relatively high correlation coefficients when compared with other established self-report and interview measures of depression. Estimates ranged from .76 to .83 for the RCDS-2 and from .73 to .81 for the RCDS-2:SF. Convergent validity evidence using measures of related constructs also appeared acceptable, and both measures returned absolute-value estimates with established measures of anxiety, hope, social support, aspects of self-concept, and victimization that ranged from .40 to .60 (correlations with positive constructs/variables were inverse). Clinical validity/efficacy for both of the current scales and for the attendant cutoff scores also appears good, and the levels of sensitivity and specificity reported were strong. Depressed groups (identified through clinical interviews), for example, consistently reported much higher scores than nondepressed groups and the published RCDS-2 cutoff score (65T, or +1.5 SD) correctly identified 91.2% of clinically depressed respondents.

Factor analyses of the RCDS-2 (none were conducted for the RCDS-2:SF) using the total standardization sample indicated a potential 4-factor structure, and the test authors labeled the factors generally as (1) discouragement, self-harm, and low self-worth; (2) anhedonia; (3) sadness, crying, and anxiety; and (4) general somatic complaints. The factor structure for the RCDS and RCDS-2 apparently differed slightly; however, the test authors offered no explanation for this apparent finding. Factor scores were generally moderately intercorrelated both among each other and with the RCDS-2 Total score. Subgroup analyses of the factor structure and confirmatory factor models were apparently not estimated.

COMMENTARY. The RCDS-2 and RCDS-2:SF are well-established and thoroughly examined indices of childhood depressive symptoms. Both scales display acceptable to strong reliability and validity evidence with large, diverse samples and across the subgroups examined. If evidence from the original RCDS is included, there is also a notable level of supporting evidence from external studies as well that suggest the RCDS-2 is likely a reasonable measure of depressive symptomology (the RCDS-2:SF appears to be too new for there to be significant useful information from external studies/findings). There is somewhat less evidence for the equivalent functioning of scale items in gender and ethnic subgroups and it was unfortunate that more thorough and sophisticated analyses of the factor structure and item-level performance were not conducted, especially for the larger ethnic groups, where structural-equation-modeling-based invariance analyses would likely have been appropriate and informative. This is especially relevant for a measure intended for use with an increasingly diverse U.S. school population.

The conceptual support for the development of the RCDS measures also appears strong and is clearly explained and logical. The framework is grounded in theory that is well-established and widely accepted by psychologists. The link between the theoretical framework and the derived factor structure was less thoroughly explained, however; and a well-grounded confirmatory analysis of the factor structure may have clarified potential interpretation issues (i.e., provided better support for the one-dimensional model). This is, however, one relatively minor issue with an otherwise generally high level of reliability and validity for a well-designed pair of measures.

The RCDS-2 and RCDS-2:SF provide easy-to-use indices of depressive symptomatology that require minimal time for administration and scoring. The generally strong support for reliability and validity should provide mental health professionals confidence in using the measures to screen for depressive symptoms and to identify children in need of further testing and clinical interviews—an approach that appears consistent with U.S. Preventive Services Task Force (2009) recommendations.

SUMMARY. Clinicians and researchers examining or using the RCDS-2 series will find that the measure has been thoughtfully developed and that the test authors have provided a high level of documentation and support. Although the psychometric evidence supporting use for non-Caucasian ethnic groups could have been more thorough, the RCDS-2 and RCDS-2:SF are, overall, well-established and thoroughly supported self-report measures that should perform well both in terms of ease of administration and confidence in interpretation. Overall, these appear to be excellent screening indices that are competitive with other well-designed, established screening instruments (e.g., Children's Depression Inventory and Beck Depression Inventory).

REVIEWER'S REFERENCES

American Psychiatric Association. (1980). *Diagnostic and statistical manual of mental disorders* (3rd ed.). Washington, DC: Author.
American Psychiatric Association. (2000). *Diagnostic and statistical manual of mental disorders* (4th ed., text rev.). Washington, DC: Author.
U.S. Preventive Services Task Force. (2009). *Screening for depression in adults: Recommendation statement* (AHRQ Publication No. 10-05143-EF-2). Retrieved from: http://www.uspreventiveservicestaskforce.org/uspstf09/adultdepression/addeprrs.htm

Review of the Reynolds Child Depression Scale–2nd Edition and Short Form by ROBERT WRIGHT, Professor Emeritus, Measurement & Statistics, Widener University, Chester, PA:

DESCRIPTION. The Reynolds Child Depression Scale–2nd Edition (RCDS-2) and its abbreviated form, the RCDS-2 Short Form (RCDS-2:SF), are self-report measures of possible symptoms of depression among children between the ages of 7 and 13 years (2nd through 6th grades). The scale is composed of 30 items that ask children about the intensity or severity of factors related to depression. The intensity levels include four descriptors: *almost never, sometimes, a lot of the time,* and *all the time.*

Each of the first 29 items on this intensity scale begins with the word "I" followed by a short statement of personal feelings or self-observation. Six of the questions have a positive valence, whereas the 23 others have a negative valence. Positive valence items have an inverse numerical valuation to provide a consistent metric. The final item, Number 30, presents the child with a 5-level visual analogy scale designed to measure general feelings (euphoric to dysphoric mood). The RCDS-2 requires 10 minutes to administer and another few minutes to score. The RCDS-2:SF has 10 items, 9 with a negative valence, and 1 question employing a 5-level visual analogy. This abbreviated version of the RCDS-2 requires only 3 minutes to administer.

Both the RCDS-2 and the RCDS-2:SF provide carbonless, handscorable forms integrated into the question booklets that are completed by children being assessed. The items are written on a second grade reading level. The items are printed in colored ink on a light background making them difficult to read for children with low vision. The test manual instructs administrators of the RCDS-2 to read the test directions and items aloud to younger children, as well as those with learning problems and other disabling conditions. Overall, the RCDS-2 manual is a clearly written, user-friendly publication, providing directions, scoring examples, and psychometric information.

Scoring the RCDS-2 is simplified by the carbonless copying of the answers onto a scoring key. This edition of the RCDS provides simplified tables for converting all raw score totals to T scores ($M = 50$, $SD = 10$) and percentile ranks. These scores are presented for the total normative sample and are broken down by grade level and gender.

The RCDS-2 manual suggests that a T score 1.5 standard deviations over the mean of the norm group (T equal to or greater than 65) be used as an indicator of possible significant depressive symptomology. The cutscore for the Short Form is a T score equal to, or greater than 62. Studies of clinical efficacy have shown these cutscores minimize false negative findings.

DEVELOPMENT. The RCDS-2 is built using the framework provided by the American Psychiatric Association for describing depression. That framework is provided in the *Diagnostic and Statistical Manual of Mental Disorders, IV–TR* (APA, 2000). The RCDS-2 also shares measurement objectives with the structured clinical interview approach of Poznanski and colleagues (Children's Depression Rating Scale–Revised, reviewed by Dowd, 2001, and Stovall, 2001), and the 10 criteria of depression among children developed by Weinberg and associates (Weinberg, Harper, Emslie, & Brumback, 1997).

The RCDS-2 author has researched the field of childhood depression since the early 1980s and published the first version of a childhood depression scale in 1989. Like the first edition of the Reynolds Child Depression Scale, the RCDS-2 and the RCDS-2:SF were not developed to provide a formal diagnosis of childhood depression (for reviews of first editition, see Carlson, 1992; and Rohrbeck, 1992). These scales were empirically derived to provide a norm-based screening method for identifying children who are potentially at risk for various forms of clinical depression. The instruments simply provide cutoff scores indicating the severity of depressive symptoms.

TECHNICAL. The normative sample was made up of children from 11 states and was stratified by gender, grade level, and ethnicity. The total sample was well-matched to U.S. Census data from 2007 and consisted of 1,100 children between the ages of 6 and 13 years. The test author focused on stratification by grade level. This is a small problem as there is typically a 24-month span of ages in any classroom. This is a result of such issues as the recent trend for parents to employ a strategy of academic red-shirting to provide an age advantage for their children, and the spike in the number of children who are not grade-promoted as a function of low scores on high-stakes tests (Jimerson, 2001a, 2001b; Katz, 2000; Russell & LaCoste-Caputo, 2006).

The RCDS-2 reports good levels of internal consistency (reliability) with alpha coefficients ranging from .83 to .95. The results of several test-retest reliability (stability) studies reported in the RCDS-2 manual provide evidence that the first edition of the RCDS was a stable measure (Reynolds, 2010). One study using original data from the first edition was reanalyzed to provide evidence that the RCDS-2:SF is a stable measure. This was possible as all the items on the RCDS-2:SF also appeared on the original RCDS. That reanalysis found that the Short Form has a reasonable level of test-retest reliability (r_{tt} = .80) based on a retest interval ranging from 3.5 to 4.5 weeks. No new studies with fresh data were reported for the test-retest reliability of the RCDS-2.

As to be expected, the standard error of measurement (*SEM*) for the RCDS-2:SF is larger than for the RCDS-2. *SEMs* for the Short Form over five grade levels range from 3.32 to 5.10, with a total sample *SEM* of 3.87. *SEMs* range from 2.83 to 3.87, with a total sample *SEM* of 3.16.

The RCDS-2 manual provides a number of validity studies. As was noted above, the RCDS-2 is aligned with the principal framework for the diagnosis of depression from the APA DSM-IV-TR (APA, 2000) and the Weinberg Criteria. The

RCDS-2 manual presents several criterion-related validity studies using the first edition of the RCDS. The manual also includes some recent studies with the second edition and the Short Form.

The RCDS-2 and the Short Form correlate well with other measures of depression including structured clinical interviews and self-report assessments. With the exception of a study of the relationship between psychological distress and the RCDS-2, there were no studies reported concerning convergent validity evidence for the second edition.

The structures of the first edition and the second edition of the RCDS were investigated with factor analysis. The analysis with the two measures identified similar factor models for interpreting data from the RCDS and RCDS-2. This investigation could have been improved by including a measure of factor fit such as the Bentler-Bonett Index or the Normed Fit Index for the concordance of the two factor structures. The four factors identified in the RCDS-2 include: demoralization, anhedonia, cognitive-behavioral manifestations of sadness, and somatic-vegetative symptoms.

COMMENTARY. The Reynolds Child Depression Scale-2nd Edition is an appropriate measure for the construct of childhood depression. The test author assumes the optimistic perspective that childhood depression is a "state" that once identified can be modified through appropriate interventions. The test author notes that, as a self-report measure requiring reflective insight by children, RCDS-2 scores may not always reflect the reality of the child's life. The test manual makes it clear that the RCDS-2 is not an appropriate method for making a clinical diagnosis of depression, but instead provides empirically determined cutscores for assessing the degree of depressive symptomology for individual children.

The instrument may appear to lend itself to classroom administration, but most classroom teachers and many school counselors do not have the training needed to administer and use scores from the RCDS-2. As with all tests involving sensitive information, great care must be used to protect the confidential nature of scores and their interpretations for children who are asked to take the RCDS-2.

Under the Family Educational Rights and Privacy Act, 1974 (FERPA as amended 2011; 20 U.S.C. § 1232g; 34 CFR Part 98), an instrument such as the RCDS-2 may not be used as a general screening instrument in a public school without providing advance notice to parents or guardians together with an opportunity to "opt out" of the evaluation. If the survey is funded by the U.S. Department of Education in any way, then specific written approval by the parent or guardian of each child involved is required. Thus, the RCDS-2 is unlikely to be used for wide screening. The RCDS-2 is likely to be professionally employed by school psychologists working one-on-one with referred children, and by licensed pediatric therapists in private practice. There continues to be an important role for the RCDS-2 in research and policy development for mental health.

SUMMARY. The reliability and validity of the Reynolds Child Depression Scale-2nd Edition is well-established and involves over 30 years of ongoing research. It is well-standardized and appropriate for children between the ages of 7 and 13 (2nd through 6th grades). The normative sample of 1,100 was carefully developed and provides a good model for the standardization of the RCDS-2. It is easy to administer and score, and the cutscores are easy to determine. In this reviewer's opinion, clinical interview skills with children are required to make full use of data derived from the use of the RCDS-2.

REVIEWER'S REFERENCES
American Psychiatric Association. (2000). *Diagnostic and statistical manual of mental disorders, Fourth edition, DSM-IV-TR, Text revision.* Washington, DC: Author.
Carlson, J. F. (1992). [Review of the Reynolds Child Depression Scale]. In J. J. Kramer & J. C. Conoley (Eds.), *The eleventh mental measurements yearbook* (pp. 769-770). Lincoln, NE: Buros Institute of Mental Measurements.
Dowd, E. T. (2001). [Review of the Children's Depression Rating Scale, Revised]. In B. S. Plake & J. C. Impara (Eds.), *The fourteenth mental measurements yearbook* (pp. 251-253). Lincoln, NE: Buros Institute of Mental Measurements.
Jimerson, S. R. (2001a). Meta-analysis of grade retention research: Implications for practice in the 21st century. *School Psychology Review, 30,* 420–437.
Jimerson, S. R. (2001b). A synthesis of grade retention research: Looking backward and moving forward. *The California School Psychologist, 6,* 47–59.
Katz, L. G. (2000). Academic redshirting and young children. *ERIC Digest.* Clearinghouse on Elementary and Early Childhood Education, U.S. Department of Education, [Document No. EDO-00-13]. Retrieved from http://ceep.crc.uiuc.edu/eecearchive/digests/2000/katzred00.pdf
Rohrbeck, C. A. (1992). [Review of the Reynolds Child Depression Scale]. In J. J. Kramer & J. C. Conoley (Eds.), *The eleventh mental measurements yearbook* (pp. 770–771). Lincoln, NE: Buros Institute of Mental Measurements.
Russell, J., & LaCoste-Caputo, J. (2006). More kids repeating kindergarten. *San Antonio News Express.* Retrieved December 6, 2006, from www.mysanantonio.com
Stovall, D. L. (2001). [Review of the Children's Depression Rating Scale, Revised]. In B. S. Plake & J. C. Impara (Eds.), *The fourteenth mental measurements yearbook* (pp. 253–255). Lincoln, NE: Buros Institute of Mental Measurements.
Weinberg, W. A., Harper, C. R., Emslie, G. J., & Brumback, R. A. (1997). Depression and other affective illnesses as a cause of school failure and maladaptation in learning disabled children, adolescents, and young adults. Retrieved from http://www.depressedchild.org/weinberg%20chapter.htm

[146]

SalesMax.

Purpose: A computerized testing system designed "to measure personality traits and sales knowledge that contribute to effectiveness in the sales role."

Population: Potential employees for consultative sales positions (selection) or current employees (development reports available).

Publication Dates: 1998-2010.

Scores, 25: Sales Personality (Energetic, Follows Through, Optimistic, Resilient, Assertive, Social, Expressive, Serious-Minded, Self-Reliant, Accommodating, Positive About People), Sales Knowledge (Prospecting/Pre-qualifying, First Meetings/First Impressions, Probing/Presenting, Overcoming Objections, Influencing/Convincing, Closing), Sales Motivations (Recognition/Attention, Control, Money, Freedom, Developing Expertise, Affiliation, Security/Stability, Achievement).

Administration: Group.

Price Data, 2011: $150 one-time fee for account set-up and user training; reports are $128 to $170 each.

Foreign Language Editions: Portuguese, Hungarian, and Dutch versions available.

Time: [90] minutes for all modules; [20] minutes for 1 or 2 modules.

Comments: Earlier version entitled SalesMax System Internet Version.

Author: Assess Systems.

Publisher: Bigby, Havis & Associates, Inc., d/b/a Assess Systems.

Cross References: For reviews by Gerald R. Schneck and Michael Spangler of an earlier version called SalesMax System Internet Version, see 15:213.

Review of the SalesMax by DAVID J. PITTENGER, Dean, The College of Liberal Arts, Marshall University, Huntington, WV:

DESCRIPTION. SalesMax, a screening instrument of applicants for sales positions, purports to assess the candidate's Sales Personality, Knowledge of best sales practices, and Sales Motivations. Data presented in the technical manual indicate that the Sales Personality score predicts sales performance in a variety of industries and for various products. The test can be completed online and consists of three components. The first component consists of 36 items that assess the applicant's knowledge of best sales practices. Each item presents a stem related to a sales tactic followed by four options that the applicant ranks from best to worst. The second section contains 28 stems followed by six statements from which the respondent rank orders three that are "like me." The final section contains 149 statements that the respondent affirms or denies. The applicant's Sales Personality score places the applicant into one of five ordinal categories of sales potential (Avoid, OK, Good, Better, Best). The report generated for the employer consists of several pages of summary data for each of the three categories and the facets within each. In addition, the report includes descriptive statements about the applicant and recommended probe questions, based upon the less desirable components of the applicant's responses, for subsequent interviews. A second report can be generated for an employee–presumably for those who have been hired–that provides a similar overview of the potential strengths and liabilities of the employee's responses. In addition, the employee receives a bibliography of recommended readings related to improving sales skills. The test also has versions that have been used in Portugal, Hungary, and the Netherlands.

DEVELOPMENT. The development of SalesMax began with a survey of sales managers from three disparate industries who were asked to identify the personality characteristics of a successful sales person. There is little information indicating how the specific items were subsequently developed and tested. For example, the manual indicates that the Sales Personality factor consists of 11 scales, but reading the manual does not reveal whether the scales were developed through statistical analysis or some other means. Indeed, readers grounded in psychometrics may become frustrated with the paucity of information describing the creation of the instrument.

TECHNICAL. The SalesMax manual presents no information about how the test is scored. Specifically, there is no information indicating which items load onto each scale within each component and whether there are specific weightings of the items.

The test authors present little definitive data regarding the reliability of the instrument. Alpha coefficients ranging from .42 to .74 are presented for the 11 scales that make up the Sales Personality score. The test manual also indicates test-retest reliability data will be published in subsequent reports. The latter statement is somewhat confusing as there is a separate report several pages later in the manual that reviews a test-retest reliability study for 164 college students tested twice over a 14-day period.

Data regarding validity are limited to predictive validity, specifically different measures of sales success. Although it does appear that there is a positive relationship between the sales potential categories and sales, one should note that much of the data appears to come from small samples and represents an undisclosed time frame. An exception is a report of sales success for a telephone-based personal insurance sales force. In that example, data for 71 and 67 cases are presented for first and second quarter sales, respectively. The correlation coefficient between sales and the SalesMax success index are .33 for the first quarter and .26 for the second quarter. For the most part, the presentation of psychometric information regarding the test is limited and inconsistently presented. Although the manual presents data for different industries and products, the information is not presented in a consistent manner that would allow for aggregation of the data for a more robust analysis.

COMMENTARY. As with any test, Sales-Max measures something. The questions this reviewer faces are whether the test measures what it purports to measure and whether its performance is superior to other instruments. Unfortunately, the data presented in the manual do not provide definitive answers. Certainly, the scored component of the test is a measure of personality. It is not clear, however, whether the scales identified in the test (i.e., Energetic, Optimistic, Expressive, and so forth) are the product of rigorous empirical testing such as factor analysis or structural equation modeling. Reviewing these facets, one wonders whether they are merely components of the Big Five–extroversion, agreeableness, openness to experience, neuroticism, and conscientiousness–commonly observed in many measures of personality. That is, the Energetic, Social, and Expressive facets may be little more than measures of extroversion whereas the Follow Through facet may be a measure of conscientiousness. This question cannot be resolved because simple tests of convergent and discriminate validity were not reported in the test manual.

Measures of personality may well predict success at sales, but it is not clear that this test is a better predictor than other personality measures readily available. It is also curious that the test includes scales for Sales Knowledge and Sales Motivations, but it does not appear to use the information to determine the final (Sales Personality) score or show how scores on these scales relate to sales performance. [Editor's Note: The publisher advises that Sales Knowledge and Sales Motivations are presented for developmental and/or onboarding purposes, not as performance predictors.]

SUMMARY. The goals of employment screening are to reduce subjective decision-making and to maximize the link between an applicant's aptitudes and the necessary and sufficient attributes for a job. Personality may well be linked to sales effectiveness, but so may intelligence, communication skills, and specialized knowledge. The relationship among these variables and sales is complex and the focus of scholarly research (e.g., Conte & Gintoft, 2005; Furnham & Fudge, 2008; and Verbeke, Belschak, Bakker, & Dietz, 2008). Those promoting SalesMax presume that certain personality characteristics are an essential attribute of a successful sales person and that SalesMax is a unique measure of those attributes. Unfortunately, little in the technical material provides a convincing argument for either claim.

REVIEWER'S REFERENCES
Conte, J. M., & Gintoft, J. N. (2005). Polychronicity, Big Five personality dimensions, and sales performance. *Human Performance, 18*(4), 427–444. doi:10.1207/s15327043hup1804_8
Furnham, A., & Fudge, C. (2008). The Five Factor model of personality and sales performance. *Journal of Individual Differences, 29*(1), 11–16. doi:10.1027/1614-0001.29.1.11
Verbeke, W. J., Belschak, F. D., Bakker, A. B., & Dietz, B. (2008). When intelligence is (dys)functional for achieving sales performance. *Journal of Marketing, 72*(4), 44–57. doi:10.1509/jmkg.72.4.44

Review of the SalesMax by STEVEN W. SCHMIDT, Associate Professor of Adult Education, East Carolina University, Greenville, NC:

DESCRIPTION. SalesMax is a computerized testing system for professional sales job applicants. The authors of SalesMax have more than 30 years of experience in assessing salespeople and sales managers for a variety of organizations. This assessment tool was based on their experience. SalesMax was designed to measure three areas: Sales Personality, Sales Knowledge, and Sales Motivations.

Sales Personality is defined as "relatively stable characteristics which impact sales behaviors. These core characteristics do not change easily over time, even with training" (manual, p. 1). Scales in this construct include Energetic, Follows Through, Optimistic, Resilient, Assertive, Social, Expressive, Serious-Minded, Self-Reliant, Accommodating, and Positive About People.

Sales Knowledge is "the understanding of effective strategies at key stages of the sales cycle" (manual, p. 1). Characteristics of the overall Sales Knowledge construct include Prospecting/Pre-qualifying, First Meetings/First Impressions, Probing/Presenting, Overcoming Objections, Influencing/Convincing, and Closing.

Sales Motivations are defined as "motivations which drive the person" (manual, p. 1). Scales in this construct include Recognition/Attention, Control, Money, Freedom, Developing Expertise, Affiliation, Security/Stability, and Achievement.

Instructions for completing the SalesMax are clear and easy to follow. The first 36 questions relate to sales situations. Scenarios or questions are listed, along with four possible responses for each, and respondents are asked to rank all possible responses from best to worst. In the second section, titled "Most Like Me," respondents are asked to rank their top three choices (the choices most like them) out of the six options provided for each of 28 statements. Statements deal with personal values, opinions, and beliefs. For the final 149 questions, respondents are given a series of statements and asked whether they agree or disagree.

DEVELOPMENT. Drawing on their expertise in assessing professional sales candidates, advice from sales trainers and the published literature on selecting successful sales candidates, the authors developed a preliminary version of the SalesMax. This survey consisted of 45 sales knowledge items, 28 sales motivation items, and 216 work-related personality survey items. The authors also developed a performance evaluation survey asking sales managers to rate their employees on the same list of sales behaviors, sales effectiveness and sales performance dimensions. Sales managers also provided information regarding how familiar they were with the individual's performance. Sales professionals and sales managers in three companies participated in the survey as part of a research/development project. Results from this project served as the foundation for the SalesMax system.

The three participating companies were in the following industries: business products, business services, and home siding sales. In order to qualify for use in the development study, a sales professional had to have completed a pilot SalesMax survey, and that sales professional's manager had to have completed the performance evaluation for that particular sales professional. The survey and evaluation together made up one "packet." In total, 151 packets were completed. A larger pilot study would have been recommended, and as there are many different types of sales positions, a wider variety of participating industries would have been beneficial. The demographic profile of respondents showed that 96 percent of those completing the pilot identified themselves as Caucasian. More diversity of respondents, with regard to ethnicity, would be beneficial, as well.

As a result of the pilot, one original scale in the Sales Personality construct (Restraint) was divided into two scales, Serious-Minded and Expressive. Of the 11 Sales Personality scales, eight were found to predict sales performance in the pilot study. The other three scales, Self-Reliant, Accommodating, and Positive about People, remain in the instrument. The authors note that these constructs

were retained because they can provide potentially useful information for managing the candidate, if that candidate is hired. The Sales Knowledge and Sales Motivation constructs were unchanged as a result of the pilot study.

TECHNICAL. As noted above, a total of 151 packets of data were used to develop this survey instrument. Reliability coefficients (coefficient alpha) for the 11 Sales Personality scales ranged from .42 to .74. Reliability coefficients for the eight Sales Motivation scales were computed using the split-half method and ranged from .67 and .83 (one was below .70). Reliability coefficients for the six subconstructs included in Sales Knowledge were not included in the test manual.

A standard held by this reviewer is that "For research purposes, a rule of thumb is that reliability should be above .70 and preferably higher" (Wallen & Fraenkel, 2001, p. 101). All but one of the reliability coefficients reported for the Sales Personality construct were below the acceptable point. For the Sales Motivation construct, one was below the .70 acceptable point. Adequate reliability is an issue with this instrument. The fact that reliability coefficients for the subconstructs that comprise the overall Sales Knowledge construct were not provided is troubling, as well.

"Validity is the most important idea to consider when preparing or selecting an instrument for use" (Wallen & Fraenkel, 2001, p. 88). In the technical manual, the SalesMax authors discuss their experience in assessing professional sales candidates. They also worked with a variety of experts in the development of this survey. All of the above are forms of content-related evidence of validity (or at least face validity). The test authors note that sales income was selected as the prime criterion for the development and validation of the Sales Personality Index. Because the validation study was conducted across a group of companies, each with different compensation packages, they used a relative measure to examine validity. Additionally, three small validation studies were conducted (each among organizations with similar compensation methods). These studies do show relationships between higher scores on the Sales Personality construct and higher sales income.

Content-related evidence of validity was used to justify the Sales Knowledge construct.

Construct evidence of validity was used to evaluate the Sales Motivation construct. Participants were asked to self-rank the importance of a set of motivations. The ranked motivations corresponded to the set of eight motivations measured by the survey items in the Sales Motivation section of the SalesMax. With one exception (Recognition/Attention), all subconstructs were significantly correlated with self-ratings.

No information about the validity of the overall instrument was presented. This lack is troubling, as validity is extremely important in assessing this type of instrument. Validity of the constructs when examined individually is important, but the instrument as a whole also should be validated. [Editor's Note: The publisher advises that Sales Knowledge and Sales Motivations are presented for developmental and/or onboarding purposes, not as performance predictors.]

COMMENTARY. The SalesMax instrument has promise; however, there are several issues that should be addressed. Most important of these is the lack of information regarding validity of the overall instrument. Also in question is the reliability of the subconstructs of each of the three major constructs that comprise the SalesMax instrument. A larger, more diverse pilot study would be beneficial, followed by thorough presentation of validity and reliability data.

It is unclear as to why the internal consistency reliability coefficients for the Sales Motivation construct were not presented (when reliability coefficients for the other two major constructs were). Also, it would be helpful to learn more about the sales manager piece of the validation study.

There is inconsistency in the way the statements on the SalesMax are worded, which could be confusing to respondents (and which is somewhat awkward to read). Some questions are worded in first-person narrative (e.g., "I believe…"), and others are worded in second-person narrative (e.g., "You are…"). The first 36 questions, for which respondents are asked to rank each potential response from best to worst, may be confusing, as respondents are asked to fill in corresponding circles using each response option only once. Other than the wording issue, SalesMax is fairly easy for respondents to complete.

SUMMARY. The SalesMax was designed to be a testing system for professional sales job applicants. Unfortunately, little evidence of validity of the overall instrument was presented in the test manual. The data on reliability presented indicates that many subconstructs were below what might be considered an acceptable limit. More information must be presented before this survey instrument can be recommended.

REVIEWER'S REFERENCE

Wallen, N. E., & Fraenkel, J. R. (2001). *Educational research: A guide to the process.* Mahwah, NJ: Lawrence Erlbaum Associates.

[147]

Salesperson Personality Profile.

Purpose: Designed to assess "whether a person has the skills, traits, and knowledge to make it in the field of sales."
Population: Under 25 through adult.
Publication Date: 2011.
Acronym: SPPP.
Scores, 45: Comfort with Public Speaking, Comfort with Risk-Taking, Comfort with Decision-Making, Comfort with Rejection/Criticism, Confidence, Adaptability, Assertiveness, Communication Skills, Persuasiveness, Networking Skills, Goal Orientation, Initiative, Energy, Research Skills, Problem-Solving, Competitiveness, Emotional Intelligence, Sales Techniques Knowledge, Neatness, Time Management, Meticulousness, Listening Skills, Integrity, Emotional Control, Helpfulness, Canned Presentation Style vs. Free-Flowing Presentation Style, Resourcefulness, Diplomacy, Memory for Names, Memory for Physical Details, Memory for Personal Details, Impression Management, Self-Efficacy, Sales Aptitude, Conscientiousness, Cooperativeness, Consultative Selling, Relationship Building, Resolving Objectives, Negotiating, Questioning Skills, Positioning, Getting Referrals, Memory Skills, Overall Score.
Administration: Individual.
Price Data: Available from publisher.
Time: (40) minutes.
Comments: Self-administered online assessment. The test publisher advises that the test manual is being updated to include more information about methodology and theoretical background used in the development of the test. The test publisher also advises that this information is available to clients, as are benchmarks for relevant industries and racial/ethnic group comparison data. However, this information was not provided to Buros or the reviewers.
Author: PsychTests AIM, Inc.
Publisher: PsychTests AIM, Inc. [Canada].

Review of the Salesperson Personality Profile by WARREN BOBROW, President, All About Performance, LLC, Los Angeles, CA:

DESCRIPTION. The Salesperson Personality Profile is an online pre-employment test for selecting sales people. It is designed to assess aspects of a person's personality, skills, and knowledge regarding selling products and services. It is meant to help companies evaluate an applicant's fit for a job when making hiring decisions or to determine where an employee may need additional training. The test contains 180 items. Most of the questions appear as personality questions on a 5-point Likert-type scale. Some items test memory for visual and written details, whereas others ask how the test taker would act in a particular situation. The estimated completion time of the test is 40 minutes, which will depend upon how quickly a person answers the questions and the speed of the Internet connection.

The administration instructions were clear and easy to follow. However, the default window in which some of the items were presented was small and required scrolling. Test takers may stretch the window to make it larger. Because the test is scored via computer just after the test administration, the report was generated quickly.

The report opens in a window with six tabs: Summary, Intro, Graphs, Detailed Results, Strengths & Limitations, and Advice. Summary provides information about the test taker's approach to prospects and about his/her presentation style. A description of the test taker's "type" is included as well. The test manual does not provide information as to how test takers are categorized. The Intro tab provides some information about what it takes to be a good salesperson and how the test measures those things. The Graphs section visually shows the test taker's overall results along with five factors with subscales and nine other scales that are not aggregated, including a faking-good scale.

The Detailed Results tab provides a narrative description of the factors and scales with the text varying based on the score. The Strengths & Limitations tab groups statements regarding strengths, potential strengths, and limitations based on the scores. The Advice tab provides general tips on selling techniques.

DEVELOPMENT. The test manual provides no indication of how the test items were developed or why particular items were chosen.

TECHNICAL. The test manual reports using a self-selected group of 1,247 participants. Of these, 593 (48%) reported being female, 503 (40%) reported being male, and 151 (12%) did not indicate gender. The age group breakdown was as follows: 395 (31%) reported being 25 and under, 244 (20%) reported being 25-39 (there is overlap in these two categories, so it is unclear where those aged 25 would have put themselves), 250 (20%) reported being 40 or above, and 358 (29%) did not report their age group.

The manual provides descriptive statistics on a 0 to 100 scale. No information is provided as to how the scores are scaled in this manner. The coefficient alpha data are of an acceptable size. The authors do not provide information on the intercorrelations between the subparts/scales or a rationale for combining any of the subparts into scales.

The evidence of validity in the manual is lacking. What the authors call "validity analysis" is an analysis of group differences by gender, age, and sales experience. In the analyses, it is reported that 336 people fall into the "sales experience" and 336 into the "no sales experience" categories (based on self report). Although several of the scales share the same name as accepted constructs, no data are provided that demonstrate their discriminate or convergent validity. Also, because no intercorrelations of the subparts or scales are provided, it is impossible to determine whether each of them measures a distinct construct. The manual does not provide any predictive validity evidence conducted subsequent to the normative sample. Without documentation of a job analysis, there is no evidence to support the content evidence of validity for the test or its scoring. In sum, the manual does not provide evidence that the test measures what it says it does or that what it does measure is indicative of sales performance.

COMMENTARY. The Salesperson Personality Profile is an easy-to-take online test. However, the purchaser of the test is given no indication as to whether the test is a valid predictor of sales performance or what passing scores should be used. A test user would have no idea what the scores mean or how to use them in selecting salespeople. Nor would test users know in which areas the person taking the test would require development.

The test has potential in that it seemingly covers several areas and combines assessment types (personality, perceived skill, attitudes, and memory). However, a meta-analysis indicates that the number of sales predictors is smaller than what is being proposed here (Verbeke, Dietz, & Verwaal, 2011).

SUMMARY. There are numerous online personality tests available. This particular one is easy to use and provides a great deal of feedback. However, there is no validity evidence to support its claims to be indicative of sales performance, so the Salesperson Personality Profile cannot be recommended for screening sales candidates.

REVIEWER'S REFERENCE
Verbeke, W., Dietz, B., & Verwaal, E. (2011). Drivers of sales performance: A contemporary meta-analysis. Have salespeople become knowledge brokers? *Journal of the Academy of Marketing Science, 39*(3), 407-428.

Review of the Salesperson Personality Profile by PAUL MUCHINSKY, Joseph M. Bryan Distinguished Professor, University of North Carolina at Greensboro, Greensboro, NC:

DESCRIPTION. The purpose of this test is for the selection and training of sales personnel. The test is administered online, consists of 180 questions, and takes 40 minutes to complete. The test consists of questions in two formats. The primary format consists of short self-report statements, which the examinee responds to on a 5-point scale. In the second item format, the examinee is presented with a graphic image (a photograph) or line of print (e.g., information from a business card). The examinee is given 10 seconds to study the image. Following the presentation of the image, several self-report questions are presented, followed by one or two questions regarding details of the previously seen image (e.g., manner of dress of a person depicted, correct spelling of the person's name). As such, the test is structured in a series of three-part sequences: (1) image; (2) self-report questions; and (3) questions about the image. The questions about the image are designed to measure memory. The length of exposure to the image is timed; responding to the questions is untimed. The test yields 45 scale scores, with some being aggregates of others. The major scales include Self-Efficacy, Sales Aptitude, Conscientiousness, Cooperativeness, and Memory Skills. Upon completion of the test, a feedback report is made available to the examinee. This online report includes detailed scale results, graphed data, and statements about the examinee's strengths, potential strengths, and limitations. Finally, there is a section on "advice" regarding how to be a good salesperson.

DEVELOPMENT. The introduction to the test report states, "In some circles, selling is considered an 'art,' in others, an evolved form of deception and trickery ... Top salespeople in big companies make big money ... most successful salespeople share a set of common characteristics and skills, and most of these can actually be learned and honed to perfection." The test report says success in selling is based on the possession of "natural instincts" that the test purports to measure.

No information is provided about how the questions were developed, whether the items measure the attributes ("natural instincts") stated, or why the particular attributes were deemed desirable or necessary to be measured at all. There are no clear operational definitions for any of the scales. There is no information about which items are measures

of which scale, or which subscales were aggregated to form larger scales. The test manual does not contain a theoretical basis for the questions, references to other scientific research supporting the relevance of the measured attributes to sales, or any other information that informs how the test was developed. The developmental basis of the test is simply the apparent manifest need for such a test in selecting and training sales personnel.

TECHNICAL. A manual provides information about validational evidence regarding examinee performance on the test. The manual is 120 pages long and consists solely of statistical data. The manual states 1,247 people took this test: 593 women, 503 men, and 151 of unknown gender. The modal age group was 25 and under. The validation sample is described as "uncontrolled" (manual, p. 2), the participants were "self-selected," and all data were self-report. Descriptive statistics are reported on the minimum, maximum, and mean scores per scale, along with the standard deviation. Internal consistency reliability estimates are reported for each scale. The number of items per scale range from 4 to 70. The bulk of the manual consists of frequency distributions of scale scores and mean differences in scale scores by gender and age. The only self-report variable that approximates a criterion is a single "yes/no" question about whether the participant in the validation study had sales experience. No further information was available as to the meaning of a "yes" response to this question, such as what jobs constituted sales experience, the type of sales (e.g., telemarketing vs. face-to-face), length of employment in sales, degree of success in sales, or whether the respondent was still in sales. Of the 1,247 participants in the validation study, 336 indicated prior sales experience. Among those with no sales experience, individuals were randomly selected to create an equal sample size for statistical comparison. Those participants who reported having sales experience scored significantly higher than those who had no sales experience on 39 of the 45 scales, as determined by t tests (at varying levels of statistical significance).

Aside from scale means, standard deviations, and t test differences by gender and age, no other standardization data are presented. Scoring is proprietary, so there is no information about such possible features as reverse-scored items to reduce acquiescence bias. No item analysis data are provided.

COMMENTARY. This test is built on a series of assumptions. The creator of this test states that success in selling is based on individuals possessing certain attributes, that a critical amount of these attributes is needed to be successful in sales (no cut scores or even percentiles are provided), and that the items comprising the test are adequate measures of the attributes purportedly assessed. The two-group validational design is particularly disappointing. In the introduction the reader is told that not everyone can succeed in sales, and that the field has a high turnover rate. The criterion group that had sales experience could consist of currently successful salespeople, floundering salespeople, and former salespeople. By specifically citing occupational turnover as a critical problem in sales, the creators of the test missed an opportunity to make an important validational assessment. To learn that people who are not in sales have lower scale scores than people who are now or once were in sales is not particularly useful if the former group has no intention of entering sales in the first place. Furthermore, having "had sales experience" is a contaminated criterion. A multicriterion research design would have been far more useful, consisting of the following groups: people with no interest in sales, interest in sales but no experience, prior unsuccessful sales experience, and current successful sales experience. The weak validational evidence merely provides information that two groups differ for unexplained reasons and it is even more troubling given the stated intention of the test. The Canned Presentation Style vs. Free-Flowing Presentation Style scale is extremely confusing. There is no information about how this scale was created, what items define it, whether one style is preferable to the other, or what conditions under which each style might be used. Additionally, it is difficult to imagine what interpretive use can be made of 45 scale scores. The validation sample is described as being uncontrolled, suggesting participants had no motive to slant their responses in a manner they perceived to be desired by the organization. An actual employment setting (the context for which this test was designed) provides an opportunity for response distortion among ambitious job seekers, which could serve to lessen the difference between the two groups. There are no internal validity scales (e.g., fake good) to assess the occurrence of response distortion. The fact that more than 10% of the validation sample are of unknown gender suggests the standards used to create the test were less than rigorous. Finally, this reviewer found the use of several phrases in the test report (e.g., "natural instincts," "deception and trickery," "honed to perfection") to be rather unseemly language for professional test developers.

SUMMARY. The premise for this test is correct; not everyone is suited for sales work. Such can be said about any occupation. Perhaps this test does measure attributes related to success in sales, but there is only the slightest validational evidence to support such a conclusion. Other than face validity, there is little evidence the items assess the attributes they purport to measure and no evidence that high scores on this test are associated with successful performance in sales. The purpose of this test is laudable, but the validational evidence in support of its value is oversold.

[148]

SELECT Associate Screening System.

Purpose: Designed to assist organizations in making employee selection decisions for associate and entry-level positions.

Publication Dates: 1995-2010.

Acronym: SELECT.

Administration: Group.

Price Data, 2011: $150 one-time fee for account set-up and user training. Report costs are $15 to $40 each (depending on quantity of order and complexity of report). Annual licenses for larger volume usage are also available.

Time: (15-40) minutes depending on survey.

Authors: Bigby, Havis & Associates, Inc., d/b/a Assess Systems.

Publisher: Bigby, Havis & Associates, Inc., d/b/a Assess Systems.

a) SELECT FOR ADMINISTRATIVE SUPPORT.

Purpose: "A personality-based survey designed to measure characteristics that have been found to predict job effectiveness in administrative or clerical positions."

Population: Applicants for administrative support positions.

Scores, 2: Provides Overall Performance and Integrity indices with recommended ranges; subscale results for Energy, Multi-Tasking, Attention to Detail, Self-Reliance, Task Focus, Interpersonal Insight, Criticism Tolerance, Acceptance of Diversity, Self-Control, Productive Attitude; optional modules available for willingness to perform job tasks and Counterproductive Behaviors.

b) SELECT FOR ENTRY LEVEL RETAIL MANAGERS.

Purpose: Designed to measure "personality characteristics related to effective job performance in managerial jobs that require individuals to produce sales, lead associates, and build customer loyalty."

Population: Applicants for entry level retail management positions.

Scores, 2: Provides Overall Performance and Integrity indices with recommended ranges; subscale results for Energy, Frustration Tolerance, Persuasiveness, Positive Sales Attitude, Leadership, Good Judgment, Organization and Attention to Detail; optional modules available for Retail Manager Math and Counterproductive Behaviors.

c) SELECT FOR RETAIL SALES ASSOCIATES.

Purpose: Designed to measure "personality characteristics related to effective job performance in sales-oriented jobs that require associates to sell and build customer loyalty."

Population: Applicants for retail sales associate positions.

Scores, 2: Provides Overall Performance and Integrity indices with recommended ranges; subscale results for Energy, Frustration Tolerance, Initiative, Positive Sales Attitude, Leadership, Persuasiveness, Good Judgment; optional modules available for Retail Math, willingness to perform job tasks, and Counterproductive Behaviors.

d) SELECT FOR RETAIL CLERK/CASHIER.

Purpose: Designed to measure "personality characteristics related to effective job performance in retail jobs that require employees to enjoy serving the customer."

Population: Applicants for clerk or cashier positions in a retail store.

Scores, 2: Provides Overall Performance and Integrity indices with recommended ranges; subscale results for Positive Service Attitude, Energy, Accommodation to Others, Frustration Tolerance, Acceptance of Diversity; optional modules available for Retail Math, willingness to perform job tasks, and Counterproductive Behaviors.

e) SELECT FOR PRODUCTION AND DISTRIBUTION.

Purpose: "A personality-based survey designed to measure characteristics important to team-oriented manufacturing and distribution jobs."

Population: Applicants for production, manufacturing, and distribution positions.

Scores, 2: Provides Overall Performance and Integrity indices with recommended ranges; subscale results for Energy, Frustration Tolerance, Acceptance of Diversity, Self-Control, Productive Attitude, Acceptance of Structure; optional modules available for willingness to perform job tasks and Counterproductive Behaviors

f) SELECT FOR LEASING AGENTS.

Purpose: Designed to measure "personality characteristics related to effective job performance in rental property sales positions."

Population: Applicants for leasing agent positions.

Scores, 2: Provides Overall Performance and Integrity indices with recommended ranges; subscale results for Energy, Assertiveness, Positive Sales Attitude, Social Comfort, Accommodation to Others, Frustration Tolerance, Criticism Tolerance, Self-Reliance, Acceptance of Diversity; optional modules available for Leasing Agent Math, willingness to perform job tasks, and Counterproductive Behaviors.

g) SELECT FOR HEALTH CARE.

Purpose: "A work-personality survey designed to measure characteristics important in most health care jobs."

Population: Applicants for jobs in hospitals or care-giving environments that have high patient (or patient family) contact.

Scores, 2: Provides Overall Performance and Integrity indices with recommended ranges; subscale results for Positive Service Attitude, Energy, Accommodation to Others, Frustration Tolerance, Accountability, Rapport, Empathy, Acceptance of Diversity, Multi-Tasking; optional modules available for willingness to perform job tasks and Counterproductive Behaviors.

h) SELECT FOR CUSTOMER SERVICE.

Purpose: Designed to measure personality characteristics that contribute to success in customer service jobs.

Population: Applicants for general customer service representative positions.

Scores, 2: Provides Overall Performance and Integrity indices with recommended ranges; subscale results for Energy, Frustration Tolerance, Accommodation to Others, Acceptance of Diversity, Positive Service Attitude; optional modules available for Retail Math, willingness to perform job tasks, and Counterproductive Behaviors.

i) SELECT FOR PERSONAL SERVICE.

Purpose: Designed to measure personality characteristics that contribute to success in customer service jobs.

Population: Applicants for positions that require providing high quality customer service as well as developing and maintaining a client base.

Scores, 2: Provides Overall Performance and Integrity indices with recommended ranges; subscale results for Energy, Frustration Tolerance, Accommodation to Others, Acceptance of Diversity, Positive Service Attitude, Social Comfort; optional modules available for willingness to perform job tasks and Counterproductive Behaviors.

j) SELECT FOR RECEPTIONISTS.

Purpose: Designed to measure personality characteristics that contribute to success in customer service jobs.

Population: Applicants for receptionist or information clerk positions.

Scores, 2: Provides Overall Performance and Integrity indices with recommended ranges; subscale results for Energy, Frustration Tolerance, Accommodation to Others, Acceptance of Diversity, Positive Service Attitude, Social Comfort; optional modules available for willingness to perform job tasks and Counterproductive Behaviors.

k) SELECT FOR CALL CENTERS—INBOUND SERVICE.

Purpose: Designed to "measure personality characteristics related to effective job performance in call center positions."

Population: Applicants for service-oriented jobs in call centers.

Scores, 2: Provides Overall Performance and Integrity indices with recommended ranges; subscale results for Energy, Frustration Tolerance, Accommodation to Others, Acceptance of Diversity, Positive Service Attitude; optional modules available for willingness to perform job tasks and Counterproductive Behaviors.

l) SELECT FOR CALL CENTERS—INBOUND SALES.

Purpose: Designed to "measure personality characteristics related to effective job performance in call center positions."

Population: Applicants for jobs that require answering calls and using effective selling and persuasion techniques.

Scores, 2: Provides Overall Performance and Integrity indices with recommended ranges; subscale results for Energy, Accountability, Positive Sales Attitude, Preference for Structure, Influence, Social Comfort, Frustration Tolerance; optional modules available for willingness to perform job tasks and Counterproductive Behaviors.

m) SELECT FOR CALL CENTERS—OUTBOUND SALES.

Purpose: Designed to "measure personality characteristics related to effective job performance in call center positions."

Population: Applicants for jobs that require actively soliciting and selling to potential customers.

Scores, 2: Provides Overall Performance and Integrity indices with recommended ranges; subscale results for Energy, Multi-Tasking Ability, Accountability, Positive Sales Attitude, Assertiveness, Social Comfort, Diplomacy, Acceptance of Diversity, Frustration Tolerance, Criticism Tolerance; optional modules available for willingness to perform job tasks and Counterproductive Behaviors.

n) SELECT FOR CALL CENTERS—HELP DESK.

Purpose: Designed to "measure personality characteristics related to effective job performance in call center positions."

Population: Applicants for help desk and technical phone support positions.

Scores, 2: Provides Overall Performance and Integrity indices with recommended ranges; subscale results for Energy, Frustration Tolerance, Accountability, Criticism Tolerance, Assertiveness, Collaboration, Problem Solving, Multi-Tasking, Acceptance of Diversity; optional modules available for willingness to perform job tasks and Counterproductive Behaviors.

o) SELECT FOR CONVENIENCE STORE MANAGERS.

Purpose: "Work-personality survey designed to measure characteristics important in convenience store jobs."

Population: Applicants for convenience store manager positions.

Scores, 2: Provides Overall Performance and Integrity indices with recommended ranges; subscale results for Energy, Frustration Tolerance, Persuasiveness, Positive Sales Attitude, Leadership, Good Judgment, Organization and Attention to Detail; optional modules available for math and Counterproductive Behaviors.

p) SELECT FOR CONVENIENCE STORE ASSOCIATES.

Purpose: "Work-personality survey designed to measure characteristics important in convenience store jobs."

Population: Applicants for convenience store associate positions.

Scores, 3: Provides Overall Performance, Integrity, and Math Ability indices with recommended ranges; subscale results for Positive Service Attitude, Accommodation to Others, Frustration Tolerance, Acceptance of Diversity, Self-Control, Energy; optional modules available for willingness to perform job tasks and Counterproductive Behaviors.

q) SELECT FOR BANKING SALES ASSOCIATES.

Purpose: "Personality-based survey designed to measure characteristics that have been found to predict job effectiveness for positions in retail banking work environments."

Population: Applicants for positions responsible for handling transactions and selling banking services.

Scores, 2: Provides Overall Performance and Integrity indices with recommended ranges; subscale results for Positive Service Attitude, Acceptance of Diversity, Accommodation to Others, Energy, Resilience/Frustration Tolerance, Interpersonal Influence, Social Comfort, Preference for Objective Measures, Dependability, Process Focused, Multi-Tasking, Self-Reliance, Leadership, Responsibility, Flexible Thinking; optional modules available for Retail Banking Associate Math, willingness to perform job tasks, and Counterproductive Behaviors.

r) SELECT FOR IN-STORE SALES ASSOCIATES.

Purpose: "Personality-based survey designed to measure characteristics that have been found to predict job effectiveness for positions in retail banking work environments."

Population: Applicants for sales associate positions within an in-store banking environment.

Scores, 2: Provides Overall Performance and Integrity indices with recommended ranges; subscale results for Positive Service Attitude, Acceptance of Diversity, Accommodation to Others, Energy, Resilience/Frustration Tolerance, Interpersonal Influence, Social Comfort, Preference for Objective Measures, Dependability, Process Focused, Multi-Tasking, Self-Reliance, Leadership, Responsibility, Flexible Thinking; optional modules available for Retail Banking Associate Math, willingness to perform job tasks, and Counterproductive Behaviors.

s) SELECT FOR BRANCH MANAGERS.

Purpose: "Personality-based survey designed to measure characteristics that have been found to predict job effectiveness for positions in retail banking work environments."

Population: Applicants for positions that require managing daily operations of a bank branch and promoting customer service.

Scores, 2: Provides Overall Performance and Integrity indices with recommended ranges; subscale results for Positive Service Attitude, Acceptance of Diversity, Accommodation to Others, Energy, Resilience/Frustration Tolerance, Interpersonal Influence, Social Comfort, Preference for Objective Measures, Dependability, Process Focused, Multi-Tasking, Self-Reliance, Leadership, Responsibility, Flexible Thinking; optional modules available for Retail Banking Manager Math, Job Experience Checklist, and Counterproductive Behaviors.

t) SELECT FOR BANKING SERVICE ASSOCIATES.

Purpose: "Personality-based survey designed to measure characteristics that have been found to predict job effectiveness for positions in retail banking work environments."

Population: Applicants for service-only positions, including bank tellers.

Scores, 2: Provides Overall Performance and Integrity indices with recommended ranges; subscale results for Positive Service Attitude, Acceptance of Diversity, Accommodation to Others, Energy, Resilience/Frustration Tolerance, Interpersonal Influence, Social Comfort, Preference for Objective Measures, Dependability, Process Focused, Multi-Tasking, Self-Reliance, Leadership, Responsibility, Flexible Thinking; optional modules available for Retail Banking Associate Math, willingness to perform job tasks, and Counterproductive Behaviors.

Cross References: For reviews by James T. Austin and Vicki S. Packman of an earlier version called SELECT Associate Screening System-Internet Version, see 14:344.

Review of the SELECT Associate Screening System by S. ALVIN LEUNG, Department of Educational Psychology, The Chinese University of Hong Kong, Shatin, N.T., Hong Kong:

DESCRIPTION. The SELECT Associate Screening System (SELECT) is a series of personality and work-related surveys designed to measure characteristics associated with job effectiveness in entry-level positions. SELECT provides test scores to users in the forms of indices and descriptive data that can be used by organizations in personnel and employee selection. Test takers respond to a series of items to which they indicate they "agree" or "disagree" and to multiple-choice items asking them to report job-related experiences and preferences. Test findings are summarized via Integrity and Performance indices. The Integrity Index is an attitudinal measure tapping into personal integrity and work ethics. A high Integrity Index (Good range) suggests positive work ethics; a low score (Avoid range) indicates that the test taker might not "give it their all" and tends to just "get by" in performing job duties (SELECT for Administrative Support manual, p. 5). The Performance Index measures personality attributes that are associated with positive performance in the position for which a job candidate is being considered. A high or average score suggests that the test taker is likely to perform well on the job (OK and Good ranges), and a low score suggests otherwise (Avoid range). Using the "Avoid" category of the Performance and Integrity indices as a criterion to screen out applicants would eliminate roughly less than 20% of applicants depending on specific SELECT surveys (e.g., for Call Centers inbound service, inbound sales, outbound service, and outbound sales, the elimination range was between 12% and 17%). If the bar is raised to include test takers whose scores fall in the "OK" category on the Performance Index, less than 40% of the applicants would be eliminated without introducing significant adverse impact (e.g., for the call center job positions above, the elimination range was between 23% and 39%).

There are a number of common performance subscales (or dimensions) across SELECT surveys: Productive Attitude, Energy, Frustration and Criticism Tolerance, Acceptance of Diversity, Self-Control, Acceptance of Structure, Empathy, Interpersonal Insight, Multi-Tasking, Integrity, Influence, Sociability, and Good Judgment. It seems that the mix of subscales for different occupation groups is unique, consisting of some of the common subscales as well as other job-specific subscales identified through specific job analyses. The inclusion of subscales for a specific occupation is based on whether the subscales were found to predict performance. For instance, the subscales for health care occupations are Positive Service Attitude, Energy, Accommodation to Others, Frustration Tolerance, Accountability, Rapport, Empathy, Acceptance of Diversity, and Multi-Tasking; the subscales for leasing agents are Energy, Assertiveness, Positive Sales Attitude, Social Comfort, Accommodation to Others, Frustration Tolerance, Criticism Tolerance, Self-Reliance, and Acceptance of Diversity. The Performance Index is derived from the performance subscales, but it is not clear how the exact calculation is done (e.g., simple summation of subscales or weighting of subscales).

A brief description is offered in the various technical manuals to define the performance subscale scores. In the test report, a test taker's performance on each subscale is classified as either "OK" or "Flag." It is possible that a candidate might have an overall Performance Index that falls in the "OK" or "Good" range, while also having one or more subscale scores that are flagged. At the end of the test report, interview questions are suggested to follow up on scores that are flagged and to explore whether the low scores are indeed concerns.

Several optional modules or components are available. The Job Tasks module asks test takers whether they are willing to perform specific job tasks. The Counterproductive Behaviors module consists of items on topics such as drug use, theft, job commitment, work ethics, resistance to direction, and safety. It is stated in the various test manuals that admission-based questions related to counterproductive behavior should not be included in regions where such inquiry is legally prohibited. The SELECT report also contains interview probes and a structured interview guide to help in conducting employment interviews so that consistency and objectivity can be achieved when multiple candidates are assessed and interviewed.

There are two safeguards to check the validity of responses. First, in order to assess whether a test taker is responding to items randomly, a Random Response Index is included. If the test profile is indicated as "invalid," test users are encouraged to look for possible explanations (e.g., reading skill deficits). Second, a positive response pattern warning alerts test users when a test taker may have a tendency to present himself or herself in an overly positive manner. When a positive response pattern is identified, test users are encouraged to verify test findings through other channels (e.g., interviews, reference checks). It is, however, not clear what specific items or questions are used in compiling these two indices.

DEVELOPMENT. The organizational psychologists and consultants of Bigby, Havis & Associates developed SELECT. The development of the various specific job-position surveys followed a standard protocol encompassing the following steps: job analysis; identifying desirable attribute dimensions; assembling preliminary test battery; choosing samples to administer test battery and collect job performance measures; statistical analysis to examine validity, adverse impact, and utility; and finalizing of test battery. For instance, for SELECT for Health Care, the general steps for developing items are reported in a "Study One" (manual, p. 17) yet there is no specific information in the test manual regarding how job analysis transformed into items and scales. The three studies and the "validation updates" reported for SELECT for Health Care offered information on the correlation between the Performance and Integrity indices and performance ratings, but information on the psychometric properties of the performance subscales used are not reported in the test manual (technical manual for SELECT Associate Screening System for Health Care). A review of the test development information recorded in the various specific occupation manuals suggests that test development details and psychometric information are not available.

To monitor for adverse impact, selection data with breakdowns based on White vs. Minority and Men vs. Women are presented in the various technical manuals. The general findings are that the selection ratios were within the "four-fifths rule." In some of the occupational groups, additional selection analyses on specific minority groups are presented (e.g., for "Production and Distribution" occupations, pp. 27–32 of technical manual).

TECHNICAL.

Standardization. There are two concerns related to standardization. First, it is not clear how test scores (subscale scores and indices) were computed and whether test scores were transformed into standardized scores or whether raw scores were used. Second, because test scores are summarized into descriptive categories such as "OK" and "Flag," it is not clear if and what normative populations were used as references to place scores in these respective categories. Overall, there is very little (if any) normative information presented in the various test manuals, including means and test scores used for standardization.

Reliability. The test manuals did not offer information about test reliability. Certain basic reliability information typical in standardized test batteries is missing, including internal consistency reliability of scales and subscales, as well as test-retest reliability information. The lack of such basic reliability information is a major concern.

Validity. SELECT is not a theory-based personality instrument, and the composition and configuration of scales to be used for different occupations are identified through empirical observation. Hence, validity based on concurrent and predictive evidence is the most crucial aspect to examine. For each of the specific SELECT occupation measures, the test manuals reported findings on both concurrent and predictive validity. A majority of the reported studies dealt with concurrent validity where incumbent samples were used and the correlations between the SELECT indices and performance criteria were examined. Across these validation studies, it was stated that the expected strength of correlation between performance measures and the test survey scales should be .20 to .40. The justification for this expected correlation range is missing. A review of the reported correlation coefficients between test scores and performance criteria suggested that the coefficients fell mostly within the expected range. For instance, the range of correlation coefficients between SELECT indices and performance ratings for Retail occupations was .17 to .47 in two studies with entry retail managers, and between .20 and .32 for retail sales associates (Retail technical manual). The range of correlation coefficients for Retail Banking was .25 to .42 (Retail Banking technical manual).

In some of the validation studies (e.g., Health Care occupations), follow-up validation was conducted in which candidates selected via the SELECT system were measured again after they settled into their positions. In the Health Care follow-up study, the correlation coefficients between the indices and performance ratings were .34 and .39, respectively (Heath Care technical manual).

COMMENTARY AND SUMMARY. The SELECT Associate Screening System aspires to be a personality-based measure with application to a wide array of service-, support-, and administrative-related occupations. It provides users with information on the degree of fit between job applicants and target positions. Test users also may make use of optional features including interview guides to assess the suitability of candidates and to followup on concerns.

However, SELECT suffers from at least three major limitations. First, the process of item and scale development could be more rigorous. For instance, procedures such as factor analysis could be performed to examine the validity of the performance subscale structures. Such analyses would add evidence on the construct validity of the instrument. Second, almost all of the validation studies used the Performance and Integrity indices as key variables, and the various performance subscales and validity measures (e.g., Random Response Index) were not included in the analysis or reported in the manuals. Because the performance subscales are key aspects of the SELECT reports, it is important for findings on their concurrent and predictive validity to be examined and summarized. Third, SELECT should provide basic normative data, reliability information, and details about how scoring was carried out (e.g., if raw or standard scores were used). These are fundamental psychometric sources of information expected of instruments aiming for either research or industrial applications.

[149]

Self-Esteem Assessment.

Purpose: "Designed to evaluate an individual's general level of self-esteem."

Population: Under age 17 through adult.

Publication Date: 2011.

Acronym: SEA.

Scores, 9: Feelings of Inadequacy, Sense of Self-Worth, Need for Approval, Unrealistic Self-Expectations, Sense of Social Acceptance, Narcissism, Defensiveness, Self-Deception, Overall Score.

Administration: Individual.

Price Data: Available from publisher.

Time: (30) minutes.

Comments: Self-administered online assessment. The test publisher advises that the test manual is being updated to include more information about methodology and theoretical background used in the development of the test. The test publisher also advises that this information is available to clients, as are benchmarks for relevant industries and racial/ethnic group comparison data. However, this information was not provided to Buros or the reviewers.

Author: PsychTests AIM, Inc.

Publisher: PsychTests AIM, Inc. [Canada].

Review of the Self-Esteem Assessment by ERIC S. BUHS, Associate Professor of Educational Psychology, University of Nebraska–Lincoln, Lincoln, NE:

DESCRIPTION. The Self-Esteem Assessment reviewed here is an online, internet-based instrument composed of 79 items that yield an overall Self-Esteem score and a set of eight scale scores designed to tap Feelings of Inadequacy, Sense of Self-Worth, Need for Approval, Unrealistic Self-Expectations, Sense of Social Acceptance, Narcissism, Defensiveness, and Self-Deception. No hard copy or pencil-and-paper version was available at the time of this review. The accompanying materials presented a one-page outline of the measure's features and also reported scale scores and means comparisons from an uncontrolled, self-selected sample using data drawn from a single online data collection.

The test authors state that the measure, "Evaluates how you view and feel about yourself" (manual, p. 1). This definition of the self-esteem construct is broad and appears more general than many current definitions of self-esteem. Brief, one-sentence definitions or descriptions of all of the scales are given but no explanation is given as to how these fit within established definitions of the construct(s) in the current psychology literature nor is there a description of how the subscale constructs should relate to the higher order construct. The definition of Sense of Self-Worth ("The degree to which one feels valuable and worthy of love and respect"), for example, exhibits considerable conceptual and semantic overlap with the typical definition of self-esteem (e.g., a global judgment one makes about one's self-worth). The introduction to the score report that is automatically generated for test takers cites self-esteem as a central component of Maslow's self-actualization process and suggests that self-esteem is a core characteristic affecting "personal happiness, success, relationships with others, achievement, creativity, dependencies, even our sex lives" (report introduction). The same report materials suggest that the test authors view the eight subscales listed above as potential indicators of fragile self-esteem.

The test publisher states that the measure may be used for personal interest, counseling, and therapy purposes. No manual for professional use is provided and there are thus no detailed instructions presented to guide clinical use. No information about clinical pilot studies or any prior use of the measure in clinical settings was provided. All the descriptive materials provided by the publisher, including the computer-generated score report, appear intended for use directly by the test taker. No information is given regarding the item-level composition of the subscales/scores and it is thus unclear what the item content or details for the targeted constructs of the overall score (composed of a 36-item subset of the 79 items) or the subscales (9–19 item subsets) may be. The intended age range for the measure is not specifically described, but the sample statistics presented in the test materials, drawn from a self-selected online sample of test takers, are identified as having been drawn from groups ranging from "below 17" through "40+."

The 79-item measure is designed to be completed in approximately 30 minutes using an electronic, online format. Respondents use a 5-point Likert-type scale to indicate the degree to which each item applies to them or to indicate their level of agreement with the statement. No information is provided on scoring procedures (subscale composition, calculations, examples, etc.). Scoring is completed by an automatic, online scoring algorithm upon test completion. The scale scores apparently are computed from item responses for specific scales (composed of from 9 to 36 items). The reported scores range from 0 to 100. No guidance for interpretation of scores is given other than the information contained in the end user report. Score reports summarize the overall score and separate subscale scores and generate a single set of general advice that the test authors suggest will improve self-esteem and overall psychological well-being. In the absence of detailed professional guidelines, score reports from the three sample trials allowed the reviewer were examined. Feedback for a low scoring evaluation trial was clearly negative, indicating "no strengths detected" and "no potential strengths detected," and followed by a detailed list of "limitations" to the respondent's self-concept, personality, and behavior. The moderate score trial returned a somewhat more positive feedback set indicating "no strengths detected," a detailed list of potential strengths, and no limitations. The high scoring trial generated a score report that detailed a list of strengths and no potential strengths or limitations. The "advice" intervention profile generated for all three trials/scores was identical.

DEVELOPMENT. No information was presented describing the conceptual framework or specific theoretical perspectives supporting the development and construction of this measure.

Specifically, no conceptual or measurement sources for attitudinal or behavioral items were indicated. No pilot studies or samples were listed or described and no factor analytic procedures or item loadings for scale items are reported.

TECHNICAL. No standardization information was presented. All statistics reported were drawn from a single, uncontrolled, nonrandom, self-selected group of 12,920 participants (7,627 women, 4,152 men, and 1,141 individuals of unknown gender) who completed the measure online via several different weblinks/portals used to recruit the participant group.

The measure has not been normed using accepted professional standards, as there has been no evaluation using data from randomly selected groups, for example. The descriptive statistics and validity information reported are limited to reports of score means for gender, age, socioeconomic, educational, and grade/achievement (i.e., based on possible self-reports of grades from unspecified school settings) groups. No ethnic group scores were reported or evaluated. No score comparisons or correlational statistics with external, alternate, or established measures of similar or related constructs are reported. No interpretations of the mean score differences discovered are offered.

Reliability information was limited to estimates of internal consistency for the overall score and for the subscale scores. The reported alpha coefficients appeared acceptable and ranged from .75 to .96. No reliability estimates were generated for the participant subgroups. Overall and subscale score means and standard deviations were reported. Means were between 37.1 and 63.8 on a scale of 0–100. Standard deviations and distributions appeared to indicate adequate variability but no skewness statistics were reported. No test-retest or other stability information is presented.

COMMENTARY. The Self-Esteem Assessment presented for evaluation here appears to be in the preliminary stages of development. It presents a quick and easy to administer measure and generates immediate feedback directly to the test taker. The test authors do not appear to have examined many of the psychometric or applied properties of the measure that are typically present for instruments designed for professional or clinical use. It is not possible, given the information provided, to assess whether or not the scores generated and presented to test takers accurately reflect aspects of self-esteem or self-concept relative to other commonly used, psychometrically evaluated self-esteem measures. An additional limitation is that the test authors have provided no empirical or psychometric evidence that the scores generated by their instrument are predictive of the outcomes suggested by their score reports. Given that low scale scores generate feedback that suggests that respondents may have significant problems with psychological adjustment and mental health, it is possible that the experience of taking this test may exacerbate mental health problems that tend to be associated with high levels of negative self-concept. The fact that the feedback algorithm apparently generates identical "advice" profiles across a range of possible scores also suggests that the instrument is unlikely to support effective, individualized intervention plans or mental health guidance that would mitigate potential harm for respondents or support use by clinicians.

SUMMARY. The lack of thorough psychometric support for the instrument's validity and reliability is a significant limitation of the measure. There is no professional manual provided (only a brief report of summary statistics), and there do not appear to have been any instances of prior clinical or professional use. Given these features, it appears unlikely that this test would be chosen for use by psychologists, researchers, or other trained mental health professionals.

Review of the Self-Esteem Assessment by AMY SCOTT, Assistant Professor of Educational and School Psychology, Benerd School of Education, University of the Pacific, Stockton, CA:

DESCRIPTION. The Self-Esteem Assessment (SEA) is a self-administered online assessment that evaluates an individual's overall self-esteem as well as self-esteem in eight areas: Feelings of Inadequacy, Sense of Self-Worth, Need for Approval, Unrealistic Self-Expectations, Sense of Social Acceptance, Narcissism, Defensiveness, and Self-Deception. The test authors indicate that it can be used for personal interest or for counseling and therapy purposes. There is one form of the assessment, which has 79 items. No information is provided in the test manual as to how individuals rate each item (i.e., Likert scale, yes/no, multiple choice, etc.). According to the test authors, the SEA takes about 30 minutes to complete. After completing the test the individual receives a computer-generated report that contains an introduction, a general score, interpretations for each of the eight subscales, and advice. No information is provided regarding how the general score or subscale scores are computed. It appears that some items are used to compute scores for multiple subscales, as the number of items reflected in one of the tables sums to more than 79 items. The introduction and advice given appears to be the same for each individual, as the three score reports provided for review all contained the same introduction and advice despite low, average, and high self-esteem scores.

DEVELOPMENT. No information is provided about the development of the SEA. For example, no information is offered regarding the theoretical basis for the assessment, why a general score is computed as well as a score in eight areas, or why or how the eight areas were chosen as subscales.

TECHNICAL. The standardization sample consisted of 12,920 individuals who self-selected to take the assessment through an online website. For some analyses a subset of this sample was used. The majority of the sample consisted of women (59%) and 9% of the sample was of unknown gender. The sample age ranges were from less than 17 (21%), 18–24 (35%), 25–29 (9%), 30–39 (12%), 40+ (11%), and unknown age (12%). No information was provided about race/ethnicity of the sample. Although the section of the test manual titled "Sample Description" does not include other variables, such as socioeconomic status, the validity evidence presented includes analyses by gender, age, education, grades, socioeconomic status, and performance in current field. Therefore, it is assumed that data on these variables were collected as part of the standardization process. All information collected was based on self-report.

Descriptive statistics are provided for each subscale using histogram displays. Each histogram includes the mean and standard deviation for the subscale. No written information or analysis is provided for the descriptive statistics for each subscale. A reliability analysis is provided in the form of a table indicating alpha coefficients for the overall scale (.96) and each subscale (.75–.95). No written information or analysis regarding reliability is provided beyond this table.

Limited validity evidence is provided in the SEA manual. The only analyses conducted were to examine group differences for those in the standardization sample. T-tests indicated that women and men differed significantly on five of the eight subtests. ANOVAs were conducted on the remaining variables of age, education, school grades, socioeconomic status, and performance in current field. Each of these variables was grouped categorically. Significant differences were found on all eight subscales and the overall scale for age, five scales and the overall scale for education, six of the subscales and the overall scale for grades, four scales and the overall scale for SES, seven scales and the overall scale for performance in current field. No additional validity information was provided, including evidence in support of content, criterion-related, concurrent, or construct validity.

COMMENTARY. The SEA is a brief and easy assessment to administer online. Its strengths are that it can be self-administered and a score report is generated immediately through the website. However, the test manual is lacking in detail that is needed to make informed decisions about using this assessment. No information is provided related to the theoretical basis for this assessment. More information needs to be provided about the standardization of the measure and how the measure is scored. In further development of this assessment the test authors may want to consider describing how the measure is scored and what the cutoff points are for low, average, and high self-esteem. They should also describe how these cutoff scores were determined. Additionally, reliability and validity data are extremely limited. The test authors may want to consider examining test-retest reliability in the future. They may also want to examine split-half reliability as another measure of internal consistency. The test authors may want to consider examining convergent or divergent validity by examining how this measure correlates with other measures of self-esteem or measures that do not evaluate self-esteem. Although the test manual indicates that there are group differences based on gender, age, education, grades, socioeconomic status, and performance in current field, the manual would benefit from inclusion of information concerning how to appropriately interpret scores given these group differences.

SUMMARY. The SEA was designed to be a self-administered measure of self-esteem that can be taken online. Little information is provided in the test manual regarding the description of the test, the development of the test, or, most importantly, the reliability and validity of test score use. The SEA cannot be recommended for clinical use at this time.

[150]
Sensory Processing Measure–Preschool.

Purpose: "Enables assessment of sensory processing issues, praxis, and social participation in children of preschool age."

Population: Children ages 2-5 who have not started kindergarten.

Publication Date: 2010.

Acronym: SPM-P.

Scores: 8 for each form: Social Participation, Vision, Hearing, Touch, Body Awareness, Balance and Motion, Planning and Ideas, Total Sensory Systems.

Administration: Individual.

Forms, 2: Home, School.

Price Data, 2013: $141 per complete kit including 25 Home AutoScore forms, 25 School AutoScore forms, and manual (94 pages); $46 per 25 AutoScore forms (Home or School); $72.50 per manual.

Time: (15–20) minutes.

Comments: The Home and School forms are intended for use together, but each form may also be used separately; the SPM-P is "the companion instrument to the Sensory Processing Measure [18:119], which facilitates assessment of sensory processing issues for elementary school-aged children."

Authors: Cheryl Ecker and L. Diane Parham (Home Form); Heather Miller Kuhaneck, Diana A. Henry, and Tara J. Glennon (School Form).

Publisher: Western Psychological Services.

Review of the Sensory Processing Measure–Preschool by SHERRY K. BAIN, Associate Professor, Department of Educational Psychology and Counseling, and ALLISON HUNT, Doctoral Student in School Psychology, The University of Tennessee, Knoxville, TN:

DESCRIPTION. The Sensory Processing Measure–Preschool (SPM-P) is a brief rating scale developed by occupational therapists to identify problems with sensory processing, bodily movement, and social participation among preschool children ages 2 to 5. Its predecessor, the Sensory Processing Measure (SPM; Parham, Ecker, Miller Kuhaneck, Henry, & Glennon, 2007; 18:119) is appropriate for children from 5 to 12 years of age. The test authors suggest using the SPM-P when 5-year-olds have not yet started kindergarten.

A Home form and a School form are provided. Each takes about 15–20 minutes to complete. The School form is completed by a staff member who is familiar with the child; the Home form is typically filled out by a parent or home care provider. Each record form has an attached summary sheet, which should be removed before administering the form and used later for scoring.

Each form contains 75 Likert-type items that include the following subscales: Social Participation (SOC), Vision (VIS), Hearing (HEA), Touch (TOU), Body Awareness (BOD), Balance and Motion (BAL), and Planning and Ideas (PLA). Additionally, there are 4 or 5 items measuring tasting and smelling behaviors that are used in the overall composite score, labeled Total Sensory Systems (TOT). The TOT score includes the Vision, Hearing, Touch, Body Awareness, and Balance and Motion, but not the Social Participation and Planning and Ideas subscales.

The SPM-P manual provides a scored example and instructions for scoring the record forms. Scoring instructions are also included within each record form. We found that scoring was easy, and took only about 10 minutes or less per record form. The summary sheet contains the information needed to convert raw scores into T-scores and allows scores to be graphed for visualization and interpretation. Scores are classified within three ranges: Typical, Some Problems, or Definite Dysfunction. If both forms are completed, the Home form summary sheet includes an Environment Difference (DIF) score to evaluate differences in sensory reports across home and school settings.

DEVELOPMENT. The SPM-P and SPM were developed based upon the Ayres Sensory Integration theory (Ayres, 2005), which emanates from the field of occupational therapy. Scale items for the SPM-P were adapted for preschool ages from the SPM and the Evaluation of Sensory Processing (ESP; Johnson-Ecker & Parham, 2000). Fourteen preschool teachers served as a panel of experts, providing suggestions and comments during item development. Following this review, 119 items were developed for the School research form and 114 for the Home research form.

TECHNICAL. The standardization group consisted of 651 children from regular preschool classrooms and a clinical sample of 242 children, not yet in kindergarten, who were being treated by occupational therapists. One parent and one school staff member completed a form for each child. Structural equation modeling and factor-analytic procedures were used to select the final 75 items for each form.

The manual includes tables of demographic information for the standardization and clinical groups, as well as means, standard deviations, and effect sizes for the differences between nonclinical and clinical groups. The authors note that they attempted to match the 2006–2007 U.S. Census for demographic characteristics in their normative sample; however, Whites are overrepresented among the ethnic groups. Gender groups from the nonclinical sample are evenly distributed, but approximately twice as many males as females make up the clinical sample.

The SPM-P raw scores are converted into T-scores, with a mean of 50 and a standard deviation of 10. There are three interpretive ranges among the T-scores: Typical (T-score range of 40 to 59), Some Problems (T-score range of 60 to 69), and Definite Dysfunction (T-score range of 70 to 80). The authors recommend examining individual item responses to establish sensory integration vulnerabilities.

Reliability. The authors offer reliability information in the forms of tabled data and thorough discussion for internal consistency, test-retest reliability, and the standard error of measurement (SEM) with confidence intervals for subtests and the Total Sensory Systems (TOT). Interrater reliability and interform reliability between Home and School forms are not provided in the manual.

Internal consistency analyses produced adequate to good alpha coefficients ranging from .72 to .94 across all subtests for both Home and School forms. Data from a 2-week-interval trial for test-retest produced correlations at or above .90 for all subtests. SEMs were calculated based upon test-retest correlations, and also on internal consistency correlations. SEMs are generally larger for the internal consistency-based results, reaching above 4 points for some subtests. The authors provide 95% confidence interval ranges for both methods of calculating the SEM but they recommend using SEMs derived from test-retest data, providing a brief rationale for this recommendation.

Validity. The authors' efforts to address content evidence of validity are summarized above in the Development section of this review. In the manual, the authors briefly discuss results of confirmatory factor analyses based on a predecessor instrument, the ESP, before describing the results of exploratory factor analyses using SPM-P standardization data. They provide factor loadings and discuss their initial 10-factor solution. The Touch Scale produced some problematic loadings for the Home form, and the Touch, Taste, Smell, and Vision items had some inconsistent loadings for the School form. The authors offer brief rationales for the disparate loadings for the Home Touch items and the School Vision items.

The authors also examined test items based upon item response theory or the Rasch model, presenting a graphed analysis of the probability curves for items based upon data from the School form collected during standardization. For psychometricians not familiar with the model, the authors offer a fairly explicit explanation of how the results should be interpreted. A graphed analysis of the Home form was not included in the manual; the authors stated the results were similar to the School form.

Convergent validity is examined by the authors based upon comparisons of the SPM-P with the Short Sensory Profile (SSP; Dunn, 1999), and the Infant/Toddler Sensory Profile (I/TSP; Dunn, 2002). If one examines the tabled correlations for the comparisons, some of the subtests of the SPM-P correlate the strongest with subtests from the comparison tests in a manner that does not seem to be completely rational. For instance, based on a somewhat small sample ($N = 105$), the SPM-P Home Form TOU correlates at .59 with the SSP Tactile Sensitivity Scale, but SPM-P VIS correlates highest with Seeks Sensation, Auditory Filtering, and Auditory Sensitivity (.54, .55, and .56, respectively). Apparently, there is no discrete SSP equivalent for the SPM-P VIS subscale, and perhaps there is a viable explanation for these strong correlations but the present test reviewers could not locate it in the text. The correlations for the SPM-P VIS scale and the I/TSP Visual Processing scale were reduced at .33 relative to a previous correlation of .53 between SPM-P VIS and I/TSP Auditory Processing. Based upon the convergent evidence of validity, some questions can be raised concerning the construct validity of SPM-P VIS, and it would be preferable to have more discussion in the manual regarding these findings.

Criterion-related evidence of validity is provided by comparing scores for children from clinical and nonclinical samples. Specific clinical subsamples included children with sensory processing deficits, disorders on the autism spectrum, speech/language impairments, and mental retardation or developmental delays. Tabled effect sizes for the differences between these groups and the nonclinical sample fell in the medium to large effect ranges across all subscales for the School and Home forms. A cutoff score of $T = 60$ for the Home TOT scale demonstrated adequate sensitivity and specificity levels of .64 and .84, respectively. The School TOT scale demonstrated slightly lower sensitivity of .52 and a similar level of specificity as the Home scale, .82.

The test authors present an evaluation of the differences between Home and School form TOT scores for samples from the standardization and clinical groups. Approximately 70% of the standardization sample and 68% of the clinical sample obtained difference scores between -9 and 9, which were considered to be in the No Difference range.

COMMENTARY. The SPM-P appears to be an efficient way to assess sensory processing deficits among preschool-aged youth. The manual offers information regarding what seems to be an adequate standardization sample, and some in-depth information regarding specific forms of reliability and validity. Among the strengths of this measure are its quick and easy administration and scoring procedures. Information regarding interrater reliability and correlations across the Home and School forms are mostly lacking in the manual.

The authors briefly mention how the SPM-P scores might guide sensory-based interventions, providing five case studies as examples. A bibliography of additional intervention-based case studies would be welcome.

SUMMARY. The SPM-P was developed by occupational therapists to provide assessment for problematic behaviors in sensory processing, bodily movement and balance, and social participation among preschool children across home and school settings. This instrument should provide a welcome addition to the testing library of assessment teams that provide early intervention services for toddlers. Administration, scoring, and interpretation are straightforward. Some additional reliability information would be welcome.

REVIEWERS' REFERENCES

Ayres, J. A. (2005). *Sensory integration and the child, 25ᵗʰ anniversary edition.* Los Angeles, CA: Western Psychological Services.

Dunn, W. (1999). *Sensory Profile: User's manual.* San Antonio, TX: Psychological Corporation.

Dunn, W. (2002). *Infant/Toddler Sensory Profile: User's manual.* San Antonio, TX: Psychological Corporation.

Johnson-Ecker, C. L., & Parham, L. D. (2000). The evaluation of sensory processing: A validity study using contrasting groups. *American Journal of Occupational Therapy, 54,* 494-503.

Parham, L. D., Ecker, C., Miller Kuhaneck, H., Henry, D. A., & Glennon, T. J. (2007). *Sensory Processing Measure (SPM): Manual.* Los Angeles, CA: Western Psychological Services.

Review of the Sensory Processing Measure–Preschool by REBECCA GOKIERT, Assistant Professor and Assistant Director, Faculty of Extension, and REBECCA GEORGIS, Ph.D. Candidate, Department of Educational Psychology, University of Alberta, Edmonton, Alberta, Canada:

DESCRIPTION. The Sensory Processing Measure–Preschool (SPM-P) is an individually completed set of rating forms (Home and School) that is designed to measure sensory processing issues, praxis, and social participation of children prior to kindergarten entry (aged 2 to 5). When the forms are used together, the test authors suggest that it is of value to educational, clinical, and research settings as they "support the identification and treatment of sensory processing difficulties" (manual, p. 4) across multiple environments. The two forms consist of 75 items each and they take approximately 15–20 minutes to complete and 5–10 minutes to score. The responses are transferred via carbon paper to a scoring worksheet utilizing AutoScore™ forms. Eight norm-referenced SPM-P standard scores are calculated on the worksheet: Social Participation (SOC), Vision (VIS), Hearing (HEA), Touch (TOU), Body Awareness (BOD), Balance and Motion (BAL), Planning and Ideas (PLA), and Total Sensory Systems (TOT). The child's functioning can be classified in three ways: *Typical, Some Problems,* or *Definite Dysfunction.* The authors provide a rich description and interpretive guide for understanding each of the eight standard scores but recommend that this be done by an occupational therapist with post-professional training in sensory integration. Separate norms are provided for 2- and 3- to 5-year-olds. Adding the items and plotting the corresponding *T*-scores and percentile ranks produce standard scores. To determine a child's sensory functioning across different environments, an Environment Difference (DIF) score is calculated and interpreted as *no difference, probable difference,* or *definite difference.* In addition to the eight standard scores, SPM-P items are sensitive to additional sensory integration difficulties such as overresponsiveness, underresponsiveness, sensory seeking, and perceptual problems. The authors provide very detailed scoring instructions and examples throughout the manual, and case studies to support interpretation.

DEVELOPMENT. The authors developed the SPM-P as a preschool companion to the Sensory Processing Measure (SPM; Parham, Ecker, Miller Kuhaneck, Henry, & Glennon, 2007), used to measure the same constructs in children aged 5 to 12 years. The authors provide a description of the Ayres Sensory Integration theory, upon which the SPM-P is conceptually based (Ayres, 2005), and the SPM School-aged form and the Evaluation of Sensory Processing (ESP; Johnson-Ecker & Parham, 2000) from which the items were derived. Selected items were edited and additional items were created to reflect preschool skills and contexts. Combined, these items made up the Home and School research forms. Fourteen preschool teachers reviewed the School research form and their feedback was used to modify or delete items on both forms. The resulting research forms consisted of 119 School items and 114 Home items. The goals that guided the development of the final scales for the Home and School forms are briefly described, and the various analytic methods used are listed (e.g., exploratory factor analysis). However, the reader is referred to the next chapter of the manual to review the analyses, which are all based on the already reduced forms. The method by which each form was reduced by over 40 items is not described and this reviewer found the Development chapter confusing.

TECHNICAL.

Standardization. The standardization sample consists of 651 typically developing children aged 2 to 5 years from regular education preschools and daycares. Five-year-olds were included if they had not yet started kindergarten. The sample is representative of the larger population with respect to age and gender, and a reasonable approximation of geography, ethnicity, and parental education (SES indicator). As part of the standardization process, the authors describe analyses to determine if demographic variables (gender, age, ethnicity, clinically referred, parental education, and geography) could lead to clinically significant differences. Medium to large effect size calculations indicated the need for separate age-based norms for 2- and 3- to 5-year-olds, with no other variables producing meaningful differences. A sample of 242 clinically referred children are described as contributing to clinical validity and utility studies, which are described in a chapter of the manual entitled, Psychometric Properties.

Reliability. The authors report internal consistency utilizing coefficient alpha for both forms across the eight scales for the entire standardization sample, entire clinical sample, and separately for the 2-year-old age group. The Home form resulted in reliability coefficients greater than or equal to .73 across all samples. The School form produced similar results across all samples with coefficients greater than or equal to .72. Given that there are separate norms provided for the 2- and 3- to 5-year-old samples it is unclear why reliability estimates were not provided for the 3- to 5-year age sample. The

authors examined the stability of the SPM-P over a 2-week time period (test-retest reliability) for a small sample ($n = 49$), which resulted in high correlations greater than or equal to .90. Overall, the Home and School forms demonstrate adequate reliability.

Validity. The authors provide extensive validity evidence under the main categories of content, construct, and criterion. Content evidence of validity is demonstrated by grounding tool development in the Ayres theory, previous validated tools, and item analysis by content experts. To provide evidence for the constructs measured, three different analyses were conducted on the standardization sample (exploratory factor analysis [EFA], interscale correlations, and item-scale correlations). The authors describe each process in a detailed fashion and provide supporting documentation through tables of factor loadings (greater than or equal to .40), interscale correlations (.29–.63 for the Home form and .44–.71 for the School form), and correlations across the eight scales between forms (cross-rater correlations ranged from .18 for BAL to .49 for SOC). Similar factor structure was found for the Home and School forms; however, the final eight standard scales are not reflective of the reported EFA results (i.e., they found 10 factors for both forms). Although the EFA revealed promising results with respect to multiple constructs, a confirmatory factor analysis for each normative age group across the scales would be more convincing evidence. All sources of evidence suggest that the SPM-P is multidimensional, and more meaningful inferences can be generated when the scale is interpreted across the eight scales.

The manual reports on convergent evidence for the SPM-P Home form in comparison to the Short Sensory Profile (Dunn, 1999) and the Infant/Toddler Sensory Profile (Dunn & Daniels, 2002). The Short Sensory Profile correlates highly with the TOT score ($r = .62$) as well as similar content scales. It is not surprising that less similar content scales produced low correlations. Although the TOT SPM-P score correlates with the Infant/Toddler Sensory Profile ($r = .35–.51$), weak correlations were found between similar content scales. A small sample ($n = 20$) was used to compare the SPM-P School form to the Sensory Profile (SPM) School companion; although some similar scales resulted in statistically significant correlations, other similar scales did not. Sample sizes are provided for all comparisons; however, it is not clear what ages were used. Given that the Short Sensory Profile is a measure of 3- to 5-year-olds and the Infant/Toddler Sensory Profile is a measure of 2-year-olds, it would have made more sense to compare the appropriate normative sample. The standardization sample was compared against the clinical sample, and large effect sizes suggest good discriminant validity for children with known deficits. Furthermore, the sensitivity and specificity values were calculated at different cutoff points to determine disorders of sensory processing or sensory integration. As the *T*-score cutoffs approach the clinically significant range (75) the sensitivity is lower on the Home and School forms (.14 and .01, respectively), and specificity is higher on both forms (.99).

COMMENTARY. The SPM-P is a brief, easy-to-administer and score test that is useful for distinguishing sensory processing difficulties in preschool children. Given the variability in development in the early years, this tool is promising for use across multiple environments and to inform intervention and programming. The tool draws its strength from its theoretical grounding in the Ayres theory of sensory integration and its predecessor (SPM). Scoring and interpretation are relatively easy as detailed instructions and interpretive case studies are provided. The reliability evidence is convincing with estimates greater than .70. Although the reliability and validity evidence is extensive, the unit of analysis is not always consistent and not well described in the manual. For example, separate norms for 2- and 3- to 5-year-olds are provided, but many of the analyses are conducted with the entire standardization sample. The test authors could enhance this evidence by conducting additional analyses on the separate normative samples. Given that the tool is relatively new, there is room for research to continue to enhance the reliability and validity evidence provided by the manual. The developers have already published two articles examining the use of the tool to support collaborative processes, which enhances the validity of the inferences that can be drawn from the SPM-P (see Glennon, Kuhaneck, & Herzberg, 2011).

SUMMARY. The SPM-P was designed as a preschool (aged 2 to 5 years) measure of sensory processing and integration across the Home and School/care environments. The tool has utility in discriminating between typically developing and clinically referred children with reasonable sensitivity and specificity. The tool should not be used in isolation for clinical decision making but can contribute meaningful information to a comprehensive assessment process that includes direct performance assessments of a child's sensorimotor function. Because the tool engages both parents and teachers/care providers, it can support collaborative intervention planning across the home and school environments. The manual provides adequate reliability and validity evidence to support the inferences that are generated from the SPM-P eight scale scores and children's progress can be monitored into school using the companion SPM measure. The tool is recommended for use; however, additional construct evidence of validity, specifically for the separate age-based normative groups and in comparison to direct measures of function, would further enhance the utility of the tool.

REVIEWERS' REFERENCES

Ayres, A. J. (2005). *Sensory integration and the child. 25th anniversary edition.* Los Angeles, CA: Western Psychological Services.
Dunn, W. (1999). *Sensory Profile: User's manual.* San Antonio, TX: Psychological Corporation.
Dunn, W., & Daniels, D. (2002). Initial development of the Infant/Toddler Sensory Profile. *Journal of Early Intervention, 25,* 2-41.
Glennon, T. J., Miller Kuhaneck, H., & Herzberg, D. (2011). The sensory processing measure–preschool (SPM-P)–part one: Description of the tool and its use in the preschool environment. *Journal of Occupational Therapy, Schools, and Early Intervention, 4,* 42-52.
Johnson-Ecker, C. L., & Parham, L. D. (2000). The evaluation of sensory processing: A validity study using contrasting groups. *American Journal of Occupational Therapy, 54,* 494-503.
Parham, L. D., Ecker, C., Miller Kuhaneck, H., Henry, D. A., & Glennon, T. J. (2007). *Sensory Processing Measure (SPM): Manual.* Los Angeles, CA: Western Psychological Services.

[151]

Sleep Disorders Inventory for Students.

Purpose: Designed to "determine risk level for sleeping disorders, including bedwetting and sleepwalking."

Publication Date: 2004.

Acronym: SDIS.

Administration: Individual.

Forms: 2 forms.

Price Data, 2012: $324.55 per kit, including 25 child record forms, 25 adolescent record forms, and technical manual (93 pages) with scoring and reporting on CD-ROM; $41.20 per 25 record forms (child or adolescent).

Foreign Language Edition: Record forms available in Spanish.

Time: (8-10) minutes.

Author: Marsha Luginbuehl.

Publisher: Pearson.

a) SLEEP DISORDERS INVENTORY FOR STUDENTS—CHILDREN'S FORM.

Population: Ages 2–10.

Acronym: SDIS-C.

Scores, 5: 4 Sleep Scales (Obstructive Sleep Apnea Syndrome, Periodic Limb Movement Disorder, Delayed Sleep Phase Syndrome, Excessive Daytime Sleepiness); Total Sleep Disturbance Index.

b) SLEEP DISORDERS INVENTORY FOR STUDENTS—ADOLESCENT FORM.

Population: Ages 11–18.

Acronym: SDIS-A.

Scores, 6: 5 Sleep Scales (Obstructive Sleep Apnea Syndrome, Periodic Limb Movement Disorder/Restless Legs Syndrome, Delayed Sleep Phase Syndrome, Excessive Daytime Sleepiness, Narcolepsy); Total Sleep Disturbance Index.

Review of the Sleep Disorders Inventory for Students by MICHAEL SACHS, Professor, Department of Kinesiology, Temple University, Philadelphia, PA:

DESCRIPTION. The Sleep Disorders Inventory for Students–Children's Form (SDIS-C) and Adolescent Form (SDIS-A) were designed to "help determine risk level for sleeping disorders, including bedwetting and sleepwalking" (quote from publisher's website). The two tests were published in 2004. The SDIS-C is designed for children ages 2 through 10 years and the SDIS-A for adolescents ages 11 through 18 years. The SDIS-C has four sleep scales (Obstructive Sleep Apnea Syndrome, Periodic Limb Movement Disorder, Delayed Sleep Phase Syndrome, and Excessive Daytime Sleepiness) and a Total Sleep Disturbance Index. It has 41 items and is projected to be able to be completed in 8–10 minutes. The SDIS-A has five sleep scales (Obstructive Sleep Apnea Syndrome, Periodic Limb Movement Disorder/Restless Legs Syndrome, Delayed Sleep Phase Syndrome, Excessive Daytime Sleepiness, and Narcolepsy) and a Total Sleep Disturbance Index. It has 41 items and is projected to be able to be completed in 8–10 minutes.

Instructions for both tests require parents to complete the forms based on the child's behaviors for the past 6–12 months. Some parents may be able to answer the questions based on observance of their child over many days/weeks/months. Instructions for some questions recommend observing the "child sleep on two different nights for two hours, beginning approximately 1–2 hours after s/he falls asleep, and then again for 60 minutes around 4:00 or 5:00 a.m." (test form). Responses are provided by parents on a 7-point Likert type rating scale ranging from 1 (*Never*) to 7 (*Always*).

DEVELOPMENT. Development of the SDIS encompassed an impressive array of experts, including sleep clinic technicians and directors. An Expert Test Review Panel also provided feedback on development of the Inventory. An excellent technical manual provides extensive development information for the Inventory.

First, an initial set of sleep constructs was identified, with items then developed for the Inventory. An Expert Test Review Panel evaluated all items extensively. After completion of several drafts, a panel of sleep specialists reviewed the measure and judged its content

Pilot testing was conducted with 226 children ages 3–18 years of age. Children came from four different sampling groups. An Exploratory Factor Analysis was conducted with the pilot test responses. Results were used to revise item and test content.

TECHNICAL.

Standardization. The normative sample encompassed 595 children and adolescents. Ethnic diversity is present, although Caucasians provided 74.58% of participants, with 9.93% African Americans and 7.91% Latinos. Gender specification is provided: 60.34% males, 39.66% females. Participants came from five groups/settings in different geographical locations. Participants were primarily 6–10 years old (age at which most initial sleep disorder referrals occur), with many respondents from the 3–5, 11–14, and 15–18 age ranges as well. Additional demographic information is provided in the technical manual, including information on primary language of parents/guardians, family income, educational level of parents, educational classification of participants, mental health/medical diagnoses of the participants, as well as sleep disorder diagnoses of participants.

Reliability. Reliability for the SDIS was demonstrated through internal consistency as well as test-retest reliability. Alpha coefficients for 412 SDIS-C and 182 SDIS-A were high for the total SDIS Sleep Disturbance Index (SDI), .91 for the younger group (SDIS-C) and .92 for the older group (SDIS-A). In considering the relationship between SDIS subscale scores and total SDIS, coefficients were reported to range from .51 to .91 for the SDIS-C, and from .74 to .95 for the SDIS-A. Alpha coefficients for SDIS subscales ranged from .76 to .90 for SDIS-C and .71 to .92 for SDIS-A.

Test-retest reliability was evaluated over a 2- to 5-month time interval. A total of 54 inventories completed by parents were analyzed, with 30 SDIS-C and 24 SDIS-A. Stability coefficient for the group as a whole was .92, with .97 for the younger group (SDIS-C) and .86 for the older group (SDIS-A).

Validity. Evidence of content validity was addressed through the use of the Expert Test Review Panel, described in the Development section of this review. Construct validity encompassed Exploratory Factor Analysis as well as Confirmatory Factor Analysis. The Exploratory Factor Analysis was conducted in a pilot study with 226 children ages 3–18 years. Results of the EFA analysis suggested a 5-factor solution was most consistent with Sleep Theory. A 5-factor solution was used to develop the SDIS-A (Obstructive Sleep Apnea Syndrome, Periodic Limb Movement Disorder/Restless Legs Syndrome, Delayed Sleep Phase Syndrome, Excessive Daytime Sleepiness, Narcolepsy, and a Total Sleep Disturbance Index), and a 4-factor solution (the above factors minus the factor of Narcolepsy) was applied to the SDIS-C.

Criterion-related validation was also addressed, with evidence of both concurrent and predictive validity presented. Concurrent validity evidence was based on comparisions between the SDIS–Obstructive Sleep Apnea Syndrome scale and Polysomnography measures, in particular the Respiratory Distress Index (RDI) and the Snore Index. The correlation coefficient for 106 children on the SDIS-C and the RDI was .33 ($p < .0005$). For 48 adolescents on the SDIS-A and the RDI, the correlation coefficient was .57 ($p < .0001$). For the Snore Index, coefficients were higher–for the SDIS-C and 98 in the children's group $r = .43$ ($p < .0001$), whereas for the SDIS-A and 43 in the adolescent group $r = .64$ ($p < .0001$).

Discriminate Function Analysis with a Jacknife process was used with 411 participants on the SDIS-C to evaluate predictive validity. When considering medically diagnosed sleep disorders of Obstructive Sleep Apnea Syndrome, Periodic Limb Movement Disorder, Delayed Sleep Phase Syndrome, and Narcolepsy, participants had higher mean scores than a "no sleep study" group. Further analysis of 111 children with a medically diagnosed sleep disorder or a sleep concern indicated 85.6% were correctly predicted for referral to sleep specialists for evaluation. Furthermore, the predictive accuracy increased to 93% for those disorders screened by the SDIS.

A similar analysis was conducted on 182 adolescents on the SDIS-A. Of the 182, 50 had a medically diagnosed sleep disorder or a sleep concern. Here again, means were higher than the "no sleep study" group. The correct prediction rate for referral to sleep specialists for evaluation was 96%.

COMMENTARY. The test author makes clear that the SDIS is only a screening instrument and is NOT designed to serve as a diagnostic tool per se. Most children/adolescents have only one sleep disorder, although their scores on this disorder may result in elevated scores on multiple scales,

suggesting other sleep disorders may be present. The 93-page technical manual provides an impressive wealth of information on test development as well as validity and reliability of the Inventory.

An important strength of the SDIS is assessment of sleep characteristics across a broad range of ages (2–18 years) and encompassing five major sleep disorders. The SDIS appears to have higher specificity than other inventories available. The SDIS also appears to be the most comprehensive instrument available in this area and was validated across a wide range of participants with varying demographic characteristics in varying geographical locations. A Spanish version of the SDIS is available.

No apparent weaknesses are present for this Inventory. The web site for the test publisher appears to be somewhat more exuberant in depiction of what the SDIS can offer, but parents with children with these issues may find the cost-effective test to be extremely helpful (and unlikely to hurt in terms of possibly providing valuable information relatively inexpensively). There are other inventories available, such as the Iowa Sleep Disturbances Inventory (Koffel & Watson, 2010), which may be considered for assessment in this area as well.

SUMMARY. The Sleep Disorders Inventory for Students–Children's Form (SDIS-C) and Adolescent Form (SDIS-A) were designed to "help determine risk level for sleeping disorders, including bedwetting and sleepwalking" (quotation from publisher's website: http://www.pearsonassessments. com/HAIWEB/Cultures/en-us/Productdetail. htm?Pid=015-8149-22X&Mode=summary). This Inventory has undergone extensive development and establishment of validity and reliability. The Inventory appears to cover the range of sleep disturbances and disorders in which most parents would be interested. The Inventory has many strengths and is relatively inexpensive as well, potentially providing valuable information to parents and clinicians at low cost.

REVIEWER'S REFERENCE
Koffel, E., & Watson, D. (2010). Development and initial validation of the Iowa Sleep Disturbances Inventory. *Assessment, 17*(4), 423-439.

Review of the Sleep Disorders Inventory for Students by MARC A. SILVA, Neuropsychologist, James A. Haley Veterans' Hospital, Mental Health & Behavioral Sciences Service, Tampa, FL:

DESCRIPTION. The Sleep Disorders Inventory for Students (SDIS) is a parent-rated screening instrument of sleep disorders in children ages 2–18. Per the test author, the SDIS is designed for use by sleep specialists and other health care and educational professionals (e.g., psychologists, guidance counselors) who are concerned about possible sleep-related problems in children.

There are 2 forms: a 41-item child form (SDIS-C) for ages 2–10 years and a 46-item adolescent form (SDIS-A) for ages 11–18 years. Parents/caregivers are instructed to observe the child/adolescent sleeping for 2 hours on two different nights. Most items are rated on a 7-point scale, measuring the frequency with which a particular behavior occurs, from "never" to "multiple times per hour." Scores from 25 items from the SDIS-C and 30 items from the SDIS-A are summed to yield the Total Sleep Disturbance Index (TSDI) and the following subscales: Delayed Sleep Phase Syndrome (DSPS); Excessive Daytime Sleepiness (EDS); Narcolepsy (NARC); Obstructive Sleep Apnea Syndrome (OSAS); Periodic Limb Movement Disorder (PLMD); and Periodic Limb Movement Disorder/Restless Leg Syndrome (PLMD/RLS). The SDIS-C yields 4 subscale scores (DSPS, EDS, PLMD, and OSAS). The SDIS-A yields 5 subscale scores (DSPS, EDS, NARC, PLMD/RLS, and OSAS). Raw scores are converted to T-scores for the TSDI and each subscale, with the following classifications: normal sleep ($T < 60$), caution/some risk ($T = 60$–64), and high risk of sleep disorder ($T > 64$).

Both forms contain additional items not included in TSDI and subscale score computations: 5 items that screen for 5 parasomnias (i.e., teeth grinding, sleep walking, sleep talking, sleep/night terrors, and nocturnal enuresis) and 11 dichotomously related items that provide more information about the possibility of OSAS.

Per the test manual, the SDIS-C is written at a 4th–5th grade reading level, and the SDIS-A is written at a 5th grade reading level. Observation time notwithstanding, the SDIS can be rated in about 15 minutes and computer scored in 3–5 minutes.

The SDIS Start Up Kit includes 25 SDIS-A forms, 25 SDIS-C forms, plus a CD-ROM containing scoring software and the technical manual. It is stated that the CD-ROM software is compatible with Windows 98, 2000, ME, Vista, and XP, or Macintosh with Windows and Virtual PC 5.0+. Hand-scoring instructions and T-score conversion tables are provided in the manual. Spanish forms are also available for purchase from the test publisher.

DEVELOPMENT. According to the test manual, the SDIS developed over a period of 4 years. The test authors state the SDIS was designed to identify common sleep disorders that potentially impair cognitive and behavioral functioning. The sleep disorders included in the SDIS were identified via review of research literature, consultation with 5 sleep medicine specialists, and review of 2 existing sleep disorder screening instruments. An initial pool of 54 items were written based on definitions and common characteristics of each sleep disorder. An expert review panel of 9 (i.e., 6 national sleep experts and 3 test development experts) rated the initial set of items for content and clarity. Items not fitting any sleep disorder construct were deleted. Ambiguous, nonessential, poorly written, and redundant items were rewritten or deleted. The second draft of the SDIS contained 49 items divided into two sections: (a) 38 items rated on a 7-point scale, and (b) 11 dichotomously rated items. The expert review panel rated Section 1 of the second draft for content, resulting in deletion of 2 items and addition of 6 new items for Section 1. The third draft underwent exploratory factor analysis (EFA) and confirmatory factor analysis (CFA) leading to additional item changes, resulting in the current versions of the SDIS-A and SDIS-C.

TECHNICAL. The standardization sample for the SDIS consisted of 595 children and adolescents, recruited from hospitals (30%) and schools and private practices (70%) nationwide. Per the test authors, purposive sampling was used to ensure adequate sample sizes of children with sleep disorders given low base rates in the general population. Five regions of the U.S. were represented. The test manual provides detailed information about sociodemographic characteristics of child's age, grade level, gender, ethnicity, primary language, sleep disorder diagnoses, educational and psychiatric diagnoses, parents' annual income, and parents' educational attainment. Selected study demographics are compared to 2000 U.S. Census data, and in general they are comparable. Normative data are provided separately for children and adolescents. The test manual includes tables with means, standard deviations, standard errors of measurement indices, hand-scoring instructions, and raw score/T-score conversion tables.

Reliability. For the TSDI, coefficient alpha was reported as .92 for the SDIS-A and .91 for the SDIS-C. For the SDIS-A, subscale alphas reportedly ranged from .71 (DSPS) to .92 (NARC). For the SDIS-C, the alpha coefficient for DSPS was reported as .76, whereas the remaining subscales reportedly demonstrated alpha coefficients of .90, .85, and .84 for OSAS, PLMD, and EDS, respectively. Luginbuehl, Bradley-Klug, Ferron, Anderson, and Benbadis (2008) reported different subscale alpha coefficients (e.g., .76 for the DSPS on the SDIS-C) although they are purported to have used the same study sample. Subscales of the SDIS-A correlated with total SDIS yielded coefficients that ranged from .74 (DSPS) to .95 (NARC). Subscales of the SDIS-C correlated with total SDIS yielded coefficients that ranged from .51 (DSPS) to .91 (OSAS and PLMI).

Test-retest reliability estimates were based on results from a subgroup of the study sample (n = 54). Time interval between test and retest ranged from 2–5 months. For the TSDI, Pearson r was .86 for the SDIS-A and .97 for the SDIS-C. Test-retest coefficients were not provided for subscales.

Validity. EFA was conducted during the development phase of the SDIS, using 226 SDIS inventories, combining children and adolescent forms. Limited data are provided in the test manual, but the authors state that a 5-factor solution best described the factor structure. More technical information is provided in Luginbuehl et al. (2008), who reported that a 4-factor solution better described the SDIS-C, and accounted for 70% of the variance. EFA was not conducted separately for adolescents.

CFA of a 4-factor model was conducted for the SDIS-C, on a separate subsample of 201 children, and CFA of a 5-factor model was conducted on the study sample of 182 adolescents (Luginbuehl et al., 2008). Several fit indices are reported, and all were within acceptable ranges for both the SDIS-A and SDIS-C (per study manual). R-squared values at the item level ranged from .33 to .86 (Luginbuehl et al., 2008). Standardized path coefficients are depicted and reported to indicate moderate to strong relationships between items and factors.

Subscale clinical elevations ($T > 65$) were evaluated in terms of whether they predicted sleep specialists' diagnoses based on overnight sleep studies, sleep diaries, or physician judgment. For the SDIS-C, hit rates ranged from 70% (PLMD) to 100% (DSPS). For the SDIS-A, hit rates ranged from 78% (PLMD/RLS) to 100% (DSPS, NARC, and OSAS). Additional classification accuracy information is provided by Luginbuehl et al. (2008). For the SDIS-C, sensitivity ranged from .50 (PLMD/RLS) to 1.00 (DSPS); specificity ranged from .62

(OSAS) to .98 (DSPS and NARC); positive predictive power ranged from .54 (PLMD/RLS) to .75 (OSAS); and negative predictive power ranged from .84 (OSAS) to 1.00 (DSPS). For the SDIS-A, sensitivity ranged from .55 (PLMD/RLS) to 1.00 (DSPS); specificity ranged from .88 (OSAS) to .95 (DSPS); positive predictive power ranged from .70 (NARC) to .78 (DSPS); and negative predictive power ranged from .87 (PLMD/RLS) to 1.00 (DSPS).

In addition, the OSAS subscale score was correlated with the Polysomnography Respiratory Distress Index at a statistically significant level for the SDIS-C (r = .33, p < .001, n = 106) and the SDIS-A (r = .57, p < .001, n = 48). An item assessing snoring from the OSAS subscale was correlated with the Polysomnography Snore Index, and results were statistically significant (r = .43, p < .001, n = 98 for the SDIS-C, and r = .64, p < .001, n = 43 for the SDIS-A).

COMMENTARY. The SDIS has many strengths, such as inclusion of several sleep disorders affecting pediatric populations, wide age range coverage, methodological rigor in its development, psychometric properties, and relatively easy scoring. Detailed study data are presented in the test manual and subsequent publication (Luginbuehl et al., 2008) permitting prospective test users to critically evaluate the SDIS. The instrument's development was consistent with many of the recommendations by Spruyt and Gozal (2011), including consideration of target population, readability, response scale type, and efforts to minimize subjectivity. The test authors wisely conducted and described validation efforts, including comparison to polysomnography data. The OSAS subscale has the most validity support at present, although validity data are presented for use of all subscale scores. There are some weaknesses as well. The SDIS may be burdensome to complete, requiring 2 hours of observation by the rater. Also, there is scant research on the instrument beyond studies of its original development, raising questions regarding replicable study findings. As well, some sleep disorder diagnoses were underrepresented, but this is not unexpected given low base rates of certain sleep disorders.

SUMMARY. The SDIS has promise as a screening instrument for various sleep disorders in children and adolescents. It meets its goals of screening for several common sleep disorders that may impair cognitive and behavioral functioning across a wide age range of children. It may be particularly useful in the identification of Obstructive Sleep Apnea. Its development was methodologically rigorous, and initial validity evidence supporting use of test scores is promising, but more research is recommended to support its clinical use across the disorders it purports to measure.

REVIEWER'S REFERENCES

Luginbuehl, M., Bradley-Klug, K. L., Ferron, J., Anderson, W. M., & Benbadis, S. R. (2008). Pediatric sleep disorders: Validation of the Sleep Disorders Inventory for Students. *School Psychology Review, 37,* 409–431.

Spruyt, K., & Gozal, D. (2011). Development of pediatric sleep questionnaires as diagnostic or epidemiological tools: A brief review of Dos and Don'ts. *Sleep Medicine Reviews, 15,* 7–17.

[152]

Social Emotional Assets and Resilience Scales.

Purpose: Designed as "a cross-informant system for measuring the social-emotional competencies and assets of children and adolescents."

Publication Date: 2011.

Administration: Individual.

Price Data, 2014: $310 per long form/short form introductory kit, including professional manual (118 pages), 25 of each rating booklet (SEARS-C, SEARS-A, SEARS-P, and SEARS-T), 25 of each summary/profile form (SEARS-C, SEARS-A, SEARS-P English & Spanish, and SEARS-T) 25 of each short form (SEARS-C, SEARS-A, SEARS-P, and SEARS-T); $240 per long form introductory kit, including professional manual, 25 of each rating booklets (SEARS-C, SEARS-A, SEARS-P, and SEARS-T), 25 of each summary/profile form (SEARS-C, SEARS-A, SEARS-P English & Spanish, and SEARS-T); $120 per short form introductory kit, including professional manual and 25 of each short form (SEARS-C, SEARS-A, SEARS-P, and SEARS-T short forms); $130 per score reporting CD-ROM; $55 per professional manual; $40 per 25 rating booklets (SEARS-C, SEARS-A, SEARS-P, SEARS-P Spanish, or SEARS-T); $16 per 25 summary/profile forms (SEARS-C, SEARS-A, SEARS-P, or SEARS-T); $22 per 25 short forms (SEARS-C, SEARS-A, SEARS-P, SEARS-P Spanish, or SEARS-T short forms).

Time: (10-12) minutes.

Author: Kenneth W. Merrell.

Publisher: Psychological Assessment Resources, Inc.

a) SEARS-CHILD.

Purpose: Designed "to obtain a global assessment of a child's social-emotional assets and resilience."

Population: Ages 8-12 years.

Acronym: SEARS-C.

Scores: Total score only.

Comments: Child self-report.

b) SEARS-ADOLESCENT.

Purpose: "Designed to measure an adolescent's perception of his or her self-awareness, metacognition, intrapersonal insight, self-management, and self-direction."

Population: Ages 13-18 years.

Acronym: SEARS-A.

Scores, 5: Self-Regulation, Social Competence, Empathy, Responsibility, Total.

Comments: Adolescent self-report.

c) SEARS-TEACHER.

Population: Teachers of students ages 5-18 years.

Acronym: SEARS-T.

Scores, 4: Self-Regulation, Social Competence, Empathy, Responsibility.

Comments: Focused on school context and designed to be completed by classroom teachers or other educators who know the student well.

d) SEARS-PARENT.

Population: Parents or guardians of children ages 5-18 years.

Acronym: SEARS-P.

Scores, 3: Self-Regulation/Responsibility, Social Competence, Empathy.

Foreign Language Edition: Spanish version available.

Comments: Focused on home and community context and designed to be completed by home-based caregivers.

e) SHORT FORMS.

Acronyms: SEARS-C-SF, SEARS-A-SF, SEARS-T-SF, SEARS-P-SF.

Scores: Total score only.

Time: (2) minutes.

Comments: "Developed primarily for use in intervention outcome measurement and progress monitoring."

Review of the Social Emotional Assets and Resilience Scales by ELIZABETH BIGHAM, Program Director, Department of Human Development, California State University San Marcos, San Marcos, CA:

DESCRIPTION. The Social Emotional Assets and Resilience Scales (SEARS) are designed to assess perceptions of a child's social-emotional functioning. There are two self-report and two observer-report forms as follows:

SEARS-Child (SEARS-C): This form is designed to obtain a global assessment of a child's self-concept regarding his or her social-emotional assets and resilience. This assessment is appropriate for use with children in Grades 3 to 6 or between the ages of 8 and 12 years. It has 35 items that contribute to one overall score.

SEARS-Adolescent (SEARS-A): This form is designed to measure an adolescent's perception of his or her self-awareness and ability to communicate, engage socially, empathize, and accept responsibility. This assessment is appropriate for use with youth in Grades 7 to 12 or between the ages of 13 and 18 years. It has 35 items that contribute to four subscale scores: Self-Regulation, Social Competence, Empathy, and Responsibility.

SEARS-Teacher (SEARS-T): This form is designed to assess the perspective of those who know the student well, such as teachers, school counselors, and speech pathologists. The form is designed to be used for assessment of students in grades K to 12 or ages 5 to 18 years. It has 41 items comprising four subscale scores: Self-Regulation, Social Competence, Empathy, and Responsibility.

SEARS-Parent (SEARS-P): This form is designed to assess the perspective of those who know the child in home and community contexts, such as parents, guardians, and caregivers. The form is designed to be used for assessment of children in Grades K to 12 or ages 5 to 18 years. It has 39 items comprising three subscale scores: Self-Regulation/ Responsibility, Social Competence, and Empathy. It is also available in Spanish.

Short forms also are available for all four SEARS forms. The short forms each have 12 items that produce one overall score. The full-length profile forms have convenient T-score and percentile rank charts that can be used to illustrate how the child's scores compare to the normative sample.

The SEARS-C and SEARS-A can be administered individually or in a group. Individuals are asked to indicate on the carbonless form how frequently (*never, sometimes, often,* or *always*) a circumstance occurs. All responses are automatically transferred to the scoring sheet. Scores are calculated by summing the columns into raw scores. The manual provides easy to use charts for looking up the T-scores and percentile ranks. The format and content are similar across all four forms so they can be used together for a multiple-perspective assessment.

The test authors indicate that most professional psychologists, school counselors, licensed professional counselors, and psychometricians would be qualified to use the SEARS. More specifically, users must be knowledgeable about the underlying theories of social and emotional competence, peer acceptance, empathy, problem-solving abilities, and social maturity; understand the nature and limitations of assessment; be trained in assessment and interpretation; and have a working knowledge of the concepts of reliability of validity.

DEVELOPMENT. The SEARS manual includes a detailed description of the steps taken to ensure the integrity of the measure. Initially, 100 items were identified to cover the broad construct of social-emotional assets and resilience. Analysis of these items revealed 12 clusters, and overlapping items were deleted. Additional items were deleted to balance the representation of the clusters. The remaining 54 items were reviewed by experts in the field to address content validity. These reviews resulted in an increase to 64 items and modifications to several items. Items were also reworded to fit into the cross-informant type format. After normative data were collected and factor analyses conducted, the number of items was reduced to 35 to 41 per form, and scales were constructed.

TECHNICAL. Norms for the SEARS were based on four separate similarly sized samples (1,224 for SEARS-C; 1,727 for SEARS-A; 1,400 for SEARS-T; and 1,204 for SEARS-P). The test manual includes detailed demographic information about the normative samples and highlights how closely the samples match the U.S. Census Bureau's demographic figures. Overall, there were slightly more males (51% for SEARS-C, 50% for SEARS-A, 51–53% for SEARS-T, and 52–54% for SEARS-P) and more than half were Caucasian (55% for SEARS-C, 55% for SEARS-A, 53–58% for SEARS-T, and 55% for SEARS-P). The geographic distribution was across multiple regions of the U.S. for all four samples. The test authors statistically evaluated the influence of sex and ethnicity on the normative data and found no notable effect sizes.

The test manual reports estimates of internal consistency and test-retest reliability. The internal consistency estimates for the SEARS are very strong. The test manual reports alpha coefficients for the subscales, total scores, and short forms as ranging from .80 to .98. Test-retest reliability for the SEARS-C and SEARS-A was examined in a study that included four assessments, each 2 weeks apart. The 83 SEARS-C participants were in Grade 6, primarily Caucasian (95%), and male (54%). The 86 SEARS-A participants were in Grade 7 or 8, primarily Caucasian (84%), and male (65%). Resulting stability coefficients ranged from adequate (.63) to strong (.89).

Test-retest reliability for the SEARS-T and SEARS-P was examined in studies that included two assessments, 2 weeks apart. The 30 SEARS-T participants were K–5 teachers with an average of 15 years of teaching experience, whose students were considerably diverse (56% Caucasian, 11% Hispanic/ Latino, 20% African American, 4% Asian/Pacific

Islander, 9% multiracial). The SEARS-P participants were the parents of 76 children and adolescents between the ages of 5 and 18 years. The sample was diverse (46% Caucasian, 20% Hispanic/Latino, 17% African American, 7% Asian/Pacific Islander, 11% multiracial). The SEARS-T and SEARS-P demonstrated strong temporal stability across two administrations (.84 to .94).

The test manual provides a detailed explanation of the strategies used to provide evidence of validity. During the development stage, deliberate steps were taken to ensure the content validity of the SEARS. These steps included a systematic scale refinement method, use of a content validation panel, and a readability analysis/revision phase.

Factor analyses were conducted on each of the SEARS measures. The exploratory factor analyses (EFAs) were estimated using principal axis factoring (PAF) with an oblique rotation (direct Oblimin method). This method was chosen because PAF is useful for identifying latent variables, and the Oblimin oblique rotation assumes that other factors will correlate, both appropriate choices for this analysis. In an analysis of SEARS-C responses from a sample of 1,628 elementary school students, no EFAs resulted in interpretable factor structures. After additional analyses, the test authors decided to reduce the number of items while still representing the broad construct of social-emotional resilience and assets. A similar analysis was conducted on SEARS-A forms completed by a nationwide sample of 2,356 adolescents. Results of the analysis, examination of the scree plot, and clinical relevance guided the test authors to identify four factors that were subsequently identified as Self-Regulation (explained 26.28% of the variance), Social Competence (explained 6.11% of the variance), Empathy (explained 4.53% of the variance), and Responsibility (explained 2.43% of the variance). Confirmatory factor analyses (CFAs) confirmed the stability of the factors.

Factor analysis of the SEARS-T used the initial nationwide sample (n = 1,673). Multiple EFAs, examination of the scree plots, and attempts at clinical interpretation of the factors were conducted and resulted in a four-factor solution. The factor labels were identified as Responsibility (explained 49.88% of the variance), Social Competence (explained 6.91% of the variance), Self-Regulation (explained 3.8% of the variance), and Empathy (explained 2.6% of the variance. CFAs confirmed the stability of the factors. For the factor analysis

of the SEARS-P, the initial nationwide sample (n = 2,022) was randomly divided into two halves. Eight factors were initially extracted from the first half of the data set and examined for clinical relevance. Then a series of EFAs and item reduction procedures resulted in a three-factor solution with the factors labeled Self-Regulation/Responsibility (explained 39% of the variance), Social Competence (explained 5.86% of the variance), and Empathy (explained 3.56% of the variance). A CFA was performed on the second half of the data set to confirm the stability of the factors.

The subscale and total scores from the normative data sets for the three multidimensional SEARS measures (i.e., SEARS-A, SEARS-T, and SEARS-P) were analyzed for intercorrelations using bivariate Pearson product-moment correlations. Moderate to strong associations were revealed for every combination of subscale and/or total scale score within each of the multidimensional SEARS measures. Intercorrelations for SEARS-A ranged from .44 to .94, SEARS-T ranged from .61 to .98, and SEARS-P ranged from .59 to .97.

COMMENTARY. The SEARS measures are designed as a brief cross-informant assessment of perceptions of a child's social-emotional resilience and assets. These strength-based assessment measures identify levels of desirable and important social-emotional competencies. The SEARS would be particularly useful for educational planning teams. Deficits in the assessed areas can be easily used to write positively worded education-plan goals, and subscale scores (available on SEARS-A, SEARS-T, and SEARS-P) can provide additional clarification and rationale for the support strategy. Reliability and validity evidence were based on the initial national sample used to develop the normative data. Normative studies should continue to add to the current data. Future normative studies should include participants with different levels of cognitive functioning and English language competency.

SUMMARY. The SEARS measures are designed to assess perceptions of a child's social-emotional strengths. Child/adolescent self-report, teacher report, and parent report forms can be used alone or together for a cross-informant analysis. Short forms can be used for brief screenings. The SEARS-C results in an overall score, whereas the SEARS-A, SEARS-T, and SEARS-P have multiple subscales (i.e., Self-Regulation/Responsibility, Social Competence, and Empathy). Reliability and validity information provide justification for the use of these measures. A scoring program is available but was not included in this review.

Review of the Social Emotional Assets and Resilience Scales by KATHY J. BOHAN, Associate Professor of Educational Psychology–School Psychology, Northern Arizona University, Flagstaff, AZ:

DESCRIPTION. The Social Emotional Assets and Resilience Scales (SEARS) was developed by Kenneth W. Merrell. The strength-based assessment system measures competencies, skills, and positive attributes of children and adolescents ages 5 to 18 years across raters and settings. The test developer suggests that focusing on a child's assets, strengths, resiliency, and positive characteristics can reduce disorder-oriented stigmas, guide intervention, engage parents and teachers, and empower the child. The system includes four rating scales of 35 to 41 items each designed to be completed by teachers (SEARS-T), parents (SEARS-P), the child (SEARS-C; ages 8 to 12 years), or the adolescent (SEARS-A; ages 13 to 18 years). Additional short form versions (12 items) are available to assist with progress monitoring and outcome assessments. The parent form also is available in Spanish. The scales can be used in a response to intervention model to assist with determining the tier of intervention the child or adolescent may need in the school or home environment.

The scales can be completed in approximately 10–12 minutes. Each item is rated on a 4-point scale. The examiner hand scores the responses, calculating a *T*-score, percentile rank, confidence interval, and tier based on the total raw score.

DEVELOPMENT. Using rational-theoretical procedures, the test author and a team of graduate students generated a pool of 100 potential items. The items were then grouped into 12 clusters based on commonalities, and the item pool was subsequently reduced to 54 items. An expert panel reviewed the selected items to address content validity. Items were revised and organized into cross-informant scales. After the scales were administered to a normative pool, factor analysis reduced the item pool to the final rating scale versions. For the short forms, 12 items with high correlations to the long form Total score and that represented the various constructs of the scales were selected for each corresponding form.

The normative sample consisted of 1,224 children for the SEARS-C and 1,727 adolescents for the SEARS-A. Although attempts were made to collect a representative sample aligned with U.S. Census Bureau demographics, almost half of the sample lived in western states and only 13% of the SEARS-A normative sample lived in the Midwest. For the SEARS-C, African American and Hispanic children were underrepresented, whereas "other" ethnicity children were overrepresented. The SEARS-A normative sample ethnic percentages approximated national Census data, but also included a higher percentage of "other" designations. Similarly, the SEARS-P sample underrepresented African American and Hispanic ethnicities, but included a significantly higher percentage of parents whose children were identified as "other." The test author performed MANOVAs and post hoc analyses to verify that any differences accounted for were not practically significant.

Although the factor structure varies across the four rating scales, all four scales provide aggregate information about the individual's assets, skills, and attributes. All forms produce a Total *T*-score, and additional scale scores are available for most measures. For example, the SEARS-A and the SEARS-T also provide Self-Regulation, Social Competence, Empathy, and Responsibility subscale *T*-scores. The SEARS-P combines Self-Regulation/Responsibility into one subscale, and includes Social Competence and Empathy. The SEARS-C produces only a Total score.

TECHNICAL. Total score internal consistency coefficients for each of the long form measures ranged from .92 to .98. The short form coefficients ranged from .82 to .93. The various scale score coefficients ranged from .80 to .95. The test manual provides evidence of test-retest reliability using two samples of middle school students of approximately 85 students each. The appropriate child or adolescent forms were administered using repeated measures at 2 weeks, 4 weeks, and 6 weeks after the initial administration. The correlation coefficients ranged from .67 to .81 (child form) and .63 to .89 (adolescent form). Parent and teacher form temporal reliability was studied using a 2-week interval and a sample of teachers in Washington state (.84 to .94) and another sample of parents in Florida (.88 to .93). Thus, the measure appears to be reliable with coefficients similar to those obtained with other behavioral measures.

The test manual provides details of convergent validity studies comparing the SEARS with other strength-based measures. Small to moderate

Social Personality and Skills Assessment [153]

positive correlations were found with the various versions of the SEARS. The results suggest that the forms measure assets and skills, but also may offer a unique perspective into understanding the child or adolescent's social, emotional, and behavioral strengths. The test manual also describes two preliminary studies using the SEARS to measure intervention outcomes. Significant pretest to posttest differences were identified with medium to large effect size gains in social-emotional assets and resiliency. Thus, the measures show promise for assisting with progress monitoring efforts in educational settings.

COMMENTARY. Both the long and short form versions of the SEARS are quick and easy to complete, score, and interpret. The test author acknowledges that the strength-based approach has not been well studied in practice. He invites researchers and practitioners to use the measure for setting goals and designing interventions, as well as monitoring progress. Certainly, the focus on a child's assets, skills, and resiliency offers a unique approach for designing interventions and treatments.

SUMMARY. The SEARS offers examiners a unique multisystem perspective on a child or adolescent's positive attributes, competencies, and skills. As a strength-based tool, the approach aligns well with the positive psychology movement (Seligman & Csikszentmihalyi, 2000). The system has potential for contributing to implementation of tiered behavioral and academic intervention models in educational settings.

REVIEWER'S REFERENCE
Seligman, M. E. P., & Csikszentmihalyi, M. (2000). Positive psychology: an introduction. *American Psychologist, 55*, 5–14.

[153]
Social Personality and Skills Assessment.

Purpose: Designed "to measure how well developed" a test-taker's social skills are in areas including "social awareness, communication, and conflict management."
Population: Under 17 through adult.
Publication Date: 2011.
Acronym: SPSA.
Scores, 8: Communication Skills, Body Language, Conflict Resolution Skills, Relationship Skills, Social Insight, Social Behavior, Social Comfort, Overall Score.
Administration: Individual.
Price Data: Available from publisher.
Time: (30) minutes.
Comments: Self-administered online assessment. The test publisher advises that the test manual is being updated to include more information about methodology and theoretical background used in the development of

the test. The test publisher also advises that this information is available to clients, as are benchmarks for relevant industries and racial/ethnic group comparison data. However, this information was not provided to Buros or the reviewer.
Author: PsychTests AIM, Inc.
Publisher: PsychTests AIM, Inc. [Canada].

Review of the Social Personality and Skills Assessment by KENNETH S. SHULTZ, Professor of Psychology, Department of Psychology, California State University, San Bernardino, San Bernardino, CA:

DESCRIPTION. The Social Personality and Skills Assessment (SPSA) provides a measure of social skills primarily in adults. The test authors claim that it has a variety of applications for the workplace including pre-employment testing, personal and professional development, team building, and leadership development, as well as sales and customer service training. The SPSA has seven scales including Communication Skills, Body Language, Conflict Resolution Skills, Relationship Skills, Social Insight, Social Behavior, and Social Comfort. The 75-item measure is administered individually via the Internet and takes approximately 30 minutes to complete. After reading the instructions and clicking "Next," a separate pop-up window appears on the computer screen and the items are presented in small blocks of 3 to 10 questions per screen. At the end of the test the respondent can print a roughly 10-page report that provides a summary, introduction/overview, and graphs showing the respondent's scores on a 0 to 100 scale for the overall test as well as for each of the seven scales. Subsequent pages of the report detail the respondent's scores on each of the seven scales in about one paragraph. The final two pages provide a brief discussion of the respondent's "Strengths and Limitations" and several paragraphs of "Advice."

DEVELOPMENT. The SPSA was developed to assess the broad concepts of social skills and social competence. Specifically, the SPSA assesses seven dimensions including Communication Skills (17 items evaluating the ability to converse with others in a clear and concise manner), Body Language (7 items that assess whether a person's body language hinders or helps during interactions with others), Conflict Resolution Skills (16 items that assess the ability to resolve conflict effectively and appropriately), Relationship Skills (17 items that assess whether a person knows what it takes to maintain positive relationships with others), Social Insight (11 items assessing whether a person picks up on social cues and interacts with others in a sensitive manner), Social Behavior (13 items that assess whether a person conducts himself/herself in social situations in a mature and professional manner), and Social Comfort (6 items that assess a person's level of comfort in social situations). The stated goal of the test is "to bring any weak areas to [the test taker's] attention so that [he or she] will know where to begin to improve [his or her] social skills." A two-page supplement to the technical manual notes, "The test was developed based on research as well as group discussions meant to flesh out the various aspects of social skills, in order to develop an assessment that covers all areas of this construct." Unfortunately, little additional information is provided in terms of the underlying theoretical rationale for the seven dimensions that appear in the final version of the measure.

TECHNICAL. Although the overall sample size reported in the technical manual is impressive at 9,041, the test authors did not use the entire sample in many of the analyses reported. Instead, when making group comparisons they chose the smallest subgroup and then took a random sample from the other subgroups so that the subgroups had approximately equal sample sizes. This was not necessary; they should have been more concerned about the equality of variances across the samples, which could have been easily assessed with a Levene's test for homogeneity of variance. The data were collected online via three web sites. No information is provided in the technical manual that indicates when the data were collected. As a result of the unproctored Internet data collection, it is unclear how conscientious the respondents were when they completed the assessment. Descriptive data are provided on several demographic variables such as gender (54% women, 31% men, and 15% unknown sex) and age (23% age 17 and below, 27% ages 18–24, 10% ages 25–29, 13% ages 30–39, 9% ages 40–49, 6% age 50 and over, and 12% of unknown age).

Descriptive statistics such as minimum scores, maximum scores, means, and standard deviations are provided for each of the seven scale scores, as well as for the Overall Score. Frequency histograms with the normal curve imposed are also presented for all seven scales, as well as for the Overall Score. Each frequency histogram reported has a different y-axis score range (some as narrow as 64–70, whereas another goes from 0–80) despite the fact that all scales have a potential range from 0 to 100. Coef-

ficient alpha reliability estimates are provided for the overall test (.90) and each of the seven scales, which range from .42 for Body Language, .65 for Social Behavior, .71 for Conflict Resolution Skills, .89 for Social Comfort, to .90 for Communication Skills, Relationship Skills, and Social Insight. No other reliability estimates are provided in the technical manual.

What the test authors term "validity analysis" consists of a series of tables depicting t-tests for gender and one-way ANOVA's for age groups, education groups, self-reported grades (top grades, good grades, average grades, and below average grades), current position (entrepreneur, managerial position, nonmanagerial position, and not officially employed), socioeconomic status ($75,000 or more, $50,000 to $75,000, $25,000 to $50,000, and $25,000 or less), satisfaction with current field (unsatisfied, somewhat satisfied, and satisfied), and performance in the field (poor, average, and good). Not surprisingly given the large sample sizes, most results are statistically significant at the $p < .05$ level. Although the technical manual does not provide any estimates of effect size, a quick calculation of eta squared for the statistically significant t-test results for gender differences on the scale scores shows values ranging from .007 (for Social Comfort) to .054 (for Relationship Skills). These results indicate extremely small effect sizes for gender, despite the statistically significant t-test results. Thus, although the authors claim the SPSA can be used for a wide variety of applied purposes in the workplace, such as pre-employment screening, personal and professional development, team building, and leadership development, as well as sales and customer service training, extremely limited validity evidence is provided to support those inferences about test score use.

COMMENTARY. The SPSA is a relatively brief 75-item, self-administered (via the Internet) assessment of social competence and skills that shows some promise. However, little is known about its theoretical framework, as well as the practical steps that were taken to develop it. Although coefficient alpha reliability estimates are generally adequate (except for the Body Language and Social Behavior scales), extremely limited validity evidence is presented to support inferences made from SPSA scores, particularly for employment applications. Additional validity analyses need to be conducted, including those that will provide concurrent and predictive validity evidence with key outcome variables, as well as construct and factorial validity evidence based on confirmatory factor analyses.

SUMMARY. The SPSA was designed to provide an individually computer-administered (via the Internet) evaluation of social skills and competence that would be of particular interest to employers. Although the 75 items do appear to assess social skills and competence, there is little in the way of supporting evidence provided for the seven factors reported. As a result, the SPSA cannot be recommended for the numerous employment purposes suggested by the publisher.

[154]

Social Responsiveness Scale, Second Edition.
Purpose: Designed as a "measure of symptoms associated with autism."
Population: Ages 2-6 to adult.
Publication Dates: 2005-2012.
Acronym: SRS-2.
Scores, 7: Social Communication and Interaction, Restricted Interests and Repetitive Behavior, Social Awareness, Social Cognition, Social Communication, Social Motivation, Total.
Administration: Individual.
Forms, 4: Preschool, School-Age, Adult, Adult Self-Report.
Price Data, 2012: $240 per hand-scored kit, including 25 School-Age AutoScore forms, 25 Preschool AutoScore forms, 25 Adult AutoScore forms, 25 Adult Self-Report AutoScore forms, and manual (2012, 117 pages); $340 per software kit, including all of the above plus unlimited-use scoring CD; $50 per 25 AutoScore forms (Preschool, School-Age, Adult, or Adult Self-Report); $130 per unlimited-use scoring CD; $82 per manual.
Time: (15-20) minutes.
Authors: John N. Constantino and Christian P. Gruber.
Publisher: Western Psychological Services.
Cross References: For reviews by Francine Conway and John J. Venn of an earlier edition, see 17:173.

Review of the Social Responsiveness Scale, Second Edition by KATHRYN E. HOFF, Adjunct Faculty, Department of Psychology, and KARLA J. DOEPKE, Associate Professor of Psychology, Illinois State University, Normal, IL:

DESCRIPTION. The Social Responsiveness Scale, Second Edition (SRS-2) is a 65-item rating scale designed to assess the social, communication, and repetitive/stereotypic behaviors associated with autism spectrum disorders (ASD) in individuals ages 2 1/2 years through adulthood. The SRS-2 is designed for use in naturalistic settings as a time-efficient, cross-informant measure to provide a continuous assessment of behavior, ranging from minor social impairments and difficulties in reciprocal social behavior to severe forms of ASD. Purported uses of the measure include screening a child at risk for ASD, incorporating results within a comprehensive evaluation to support clinical diagnoses, delineating the social characteristics of children with ASDs, differential diagnoses of psychiatric concerns, conducting research, generating behavioral treatment goals and targeting areas for intervention, and monitoring intervention effectiveness over time.

The reported administration time is between 15 and 20 minutes, with an additional 5 to 10 minutes to score and graph results. The test kit contains a professional manual, four types of profile sheets, and optional scoring software. The profile sheets include a preschool form (ages 2 1/2 to 4 1/2 years) and a School-Age form (ages 4–18 years; male and female versions) for collecting ratings from parents and/or teachers. Two adult profile sheets also are included: an Adult Self-Report form (age 19 and up) and an Adult form, which is completed by a rater who is familiar with the individual. Behaviors are rated on a 4-point Likert scale reflecting frequency of occurrence. Scoring is accomplished by obtaining raw scores for each of the five treatment subscales: (a) Social Awareness, (b) Social Cognition, (c) Social Communication, (d) Social Motivation, and (e) Restricted Interests and Repetitive Behavior. All five treatment subscales are summed to determine the SRS-2 Total raw score, and raw scores are then converted to T-scores. The Total score is to be used for assessment purposes, and subscale scores are intended for treatment planning, progress monitoring, or research examining treatment effectiveness. In addition, users can determine two subscales that are compatible with the *Diagnostic and Statistical Manual of Mental Disorders* (5th ed.; *DSM-5*; American Psychiatric Association [APA], 2013): Social Communication and Interaction (based on the sum of the first four treatment subscales) and Restricted Interests and Repetitive Behavior (the final treatment subscale score). However, the clinical or research utility of these *DSM-5* (APA, 2013) subscales is yet to be established.

DEVELOPMENT. The SRS-2 was developed as a tool to assess symptoms associated with ASD. The SRS-2 represents an update of the SRS, which was published in 2005. In the updated version, the test authors retained the original School-Age form, expanded the normative sample and range of assessment to include younger children and adults (the Preschool and Adult forms are new), and updated the test manual to reflect additional research conducted on the measure. All forms contain essentially the same items; however, the test authors reworded 14 items on the Preschool form and 19 items on the Adult form to correspond to developmentally appropriate behavior. Additionally, the items on the Adult Self-Report form were reworded to first person format. Items on the SRS-2 initially were created by the first author based on his extensive clinical experience with children on the autism spectrum and appear to have excellent face validity. Items were examined more explicitly by an expert panel of 25 judges with a range of professional degrees working directly with children with ASDs. The expert panel placed items into clusters corresponding to the treatment subscales. A comparison of the judges' placements with the initial placements was significant, suggesting strong agreement. However, because of the high degree of overlap in treatment subscales, it is noted that these subscales may not represent unique symptoms, but rather may be useful ways to categorize and conceptualize treatment goals.

TECHNICAL.

Standardization. The standardization sample includes 474 parent and teacher ratings of 247 preschoolers; 2,025 parent and teacher ratings of 1,014 school-aged children; and 2,210 ratings of 702 adults. The samples were fairly equally distributed across age, gender, geographic region, and level of parents' education. Diversity closely represented the U.S. Census figures, with the exception of Asians, who were underrepresented in the preschool and adult samples. The test authors do not provide diagnostic information for the standardization sample; thus, information about how well the standardization sample reflects clinical and nonclinical members of the population is lacking. An evaluation of moderator effects revealed gender differences in teacher ratings for the school-age group; therefore, norms for the School-Age form were calculated separately by child gender and informant, whereas norms for the Preschool and Adult forms were calculated from the mean and standard deviation for the respective total sample across gender, age, and type of informant.

Reliability. The test manual includes information about internal consistency, interrater reliability,

and test-retest reliability from three information sources: (a) the standardization sample; (b) a clinical sample examining the School-Age form (data were obtained from the Interactive Autism Network Research Database: children with ASD n = 4,891; unaffected siblings n = 3,030); and (c) evidence from independent research studies examining the School-Age form. In general, reliability coefficients were excellent (alpha coefficients above .90), suggesting strong internal consistency of the SRS-2 across gender, age, and type of informant. Similar to results obtained from other cross-informant rating scales, interrater reliability evidence indicates a moderate degree of convergence between informant reports in the standardization sample (Total sample School-Age r = .61; Preschool r = .77; Adult form informants range r = .66–.95) and from published research (r = .61–.91). The test authors present evidence of test-retest reliability from independent research studies, and moderate to strong correlation coefficients were obtained, ranging from .72 to .95, depending on the study and retest intervals, which ranged from 2 weeks to 5 years. Although the aforementioned results are promising, additional research is necessary to establish test-retest reliability of the Preschool and Adult forms.

Validity. The test authors examined "test validity" by comparing mean scores of children with ASD in the clinical sample with scores of their nonaffected siblings and found a significant contrast in scores (effect size of 2.7). Results from published research collectively demonstrate a similar pattern of findings, as children with ASD score significantly higher on the SRS-2 than non-ASD clinical samples and typically developing children (effect size of 1.0 or higher). A receiver operating characteristics analysis indicated excellent sensitivity (.84–.93) and specificity (.90–.95) of the scale across mild to severe cutoff scores for both genders. To provide evidence of convergent validity, the developers document findings from published research demonstrating a moderate degree of overlap between scores from the SRS-2 and other well-established social/communication rating scales. Comparisons of SRS-2 scores with those from the Autism Diagnostic Observation Schedule and the Autism Diagnostic Interview–Revised were more variable with correlation coefficients ranging from low (r = .26–.40) to moderate (r = .77), providing some limited evidence for convergent validity. Initial comparisons of the SRS-2 with the Child

Behavior Checklist and the Vineland Adaptive Behavior Scales demonstrate preliminary evidence of divergent validity in the predicted patterns of relations (moderate correlations where there is overlap in symptoms associated with ASD, and low correlations between subscales not associated with ASD); however, continued validation studies are necessary.

COMMENTARY. The SRS-2 represents a beneficial tool to assess social, communication, and repetitive/stereotypic behaviors that interfere with everyday social interactions. The test manual is well organized and easy to understand. Administration and scoring are straightforward and user friendly, with all necessary information included on the profile forms. Further, the test manual provides numbered directions for administration and scoring, case examples that assist in interpretation and application of scores, and some interpretative text and sample language that may be helpful for communicating results. Reliability data are encouraging, and results from multiple studies demonstrate that the SRS-2 can adequately discriminate school-age children with and without ASDs. Additional research is necessary supporting the use of the SRS-2 for differential diagnoses. Importantly, no test-retest reliability or validity information was provided for the Preschool and Adult forms, thus users should exercise caution when interpreting results. Because the SRS-2 allows one to assess a range of problem behaviors, from subclinical levels to those with more severe intensity, it may be sensitive to social communication problems in mild cases of ASD. The comprehensive list of behaviors compiled by the test authors appears useful in treatment planning, and the continuous rating scale may be helpful for assessing change over time and responsiveness to intervention for children with ASDs.

SUMMARY. The Social Responsiveness Scale, Second Edition (SRS-2) is a rating scale designed to assist in the assessment and intervention of individuals on the autism spectrum, from preschool age through adulthood. Reliability results are impressive, and although the psychometric integrity of the School-Age form is encouraging, additional research is necessary to firmly establish the utility of the Preschool and Adult forms. Time efficiency and ease of administration make the SRS-2 optimal for use in naturalistic contexts, and the measure is one of the few autism-specific instruments that can be used with multiple informants. In summary, the

SRS-2 appears to be a beneficial tool for assessing severity of social impairment and nature of social communication skills in the ASD population.

REVIEWERS' REFERENCE

American Psychiatric Association. (2013). *Diagnostic and statistical manual of mental disorders* (5th ed.). Arlington, VA: American Psychiatric Publishing.

Review of the Social Responsiveness Scale, Second Edition by GEORGETTE YETTER, Associate Professor, Applied Health and Educational Psychology, Oklahoma State University, Stillwater, OK:

DESCRIPTION. The Social Responsiveness Scale, Second Edition (SRS-2) is a 65-item rating scale assessing symptoms associated with autism in individuals ages 30 months to 89 years. It is intended to be completed by adults familiar with an individual's social functioning in natural settings.

The SRS-2 consists of four forms: Preschool (ages 30–54 months), School-Age (ages 4–18 years), Adult (ages 19–89 years), and Adult Self-Report. All forms produce two cluster scores: Social Communication and Interaction (SCI; 53 items) and Restricted Interests and Repetitive Behavior (RRB; 12 items), as well as a Total score. The SCI items are divided into four treatment subscales: Social Awareness (8 items), Social Cognition (12 items), Social Communication (22 items), and Social Motivation (11 items). These four subscales were formed based on clinical judgment rather than on statistical analysis, and they are included to assist with intervention development and evaluation in treatment settings.

All items are rated on a 4-point Likert scale anchored by *not true* and *almost always true*, where high scores indicate greater dysfunction. Scoring is done by hand and is straightforward. Raw scores are converted into *T*-scores for interpretation. A summary profile sheet is provided for recording and graphing SCI, RRB, and Total *T*-scores and for classifying them as *within normal limits* ($T = 59$ or lower), *mild* ($T = 60$–65), *moderate* ($T = 66$–75), or *severe* ($T = 76$ or higher). Raters can complete the questionnaire in 15–20 minutes. Scoring and graphing can be completed in 5–10 minutes.

DEVELOPMENT. The SRS-2 is an extension of the SRS (Constantino & Gruber, 2005), a well-established screener for autism symptoms for ages 4–18 years. The SRS-2 School-Age form is the same as the original SRS. New Preschool and Adult forms were developed by adapting the wording of items from the School-Age form, generally maintaining item wording to be as similar as possible across the forms.

Diagnostic criteria in the *Diagnostic and Statistical Manual of Mental Disorders* (5th ed.; American Psychiatric Association, 2013) specified two distinct areas of impairment for Autism Spectrum Disorder (ASD): social communication and interaction impairment and restricted, repetitive patterns of behavior. The appropriateness of the two-dimensional framework for the SRS-2 School-Age form (parent report) was examined with approximately 5,000 school-age children diagnosed with ASDs and 3,000 non-ASD siblings. Results suggested a moderate separation of the SCI and RRB domains. Confirmatory factor analyses with preschool, school-age, and adult samples indicated adequate fit to the two-dimensional model, supporting the interpretation of separate SCI and RRB indices for the various SRS-2 forms.

TECHNICAL. Standardization samples representative of the 2009 U.S. Census according to gender, race, U.S. geographic region, and parents' educational level were gathered to provide evidence of the technical soundness of the Preschool (n = 247), School-Age (n = 1014), and Adult (n = 702) forms. For each form, the mean ratings were compared by gender, ethnicity, age, and respondent (e.g., parent, teacher, self). The norm samples included too few Asians and Native Americans to support the analysis of ethnic differences with these populations. Using a 3-point T-score difference in mean scores as the criterion for developing separate norm tables, the test authors concluded that whereas for the School-Age form separate norm tables were warranted by respondent and gender, a single norm table was most appropriate for each of the other forms.

The internal consistency of all SRS-2 forms is excellent across gender, age, and respondent for both nonclinical and clinical samples; coefficient alpha values were consistently in the .92–.95 range. Correlation coefficients reflecting interrater agreement for school-age children with ASD were .91 for mothers with fathers and from .72 to .82 for parents with teachers. Interrater reliability of the Preschool form ranged from .70 to .79 for parents with teachers in 6-month age increments. Interrater reliability for the Adult form was fair to good, with correlation coefficients ranging from .66 (comparing self-rating with all other informants) to .88 (comparing mother's rating with all other informants). Small sample sizes for some age clusters in the adult sample precluded analysis of interrater reliability by respondent and age simultaneously.

Evidence for temporal stability is strong, indicating reliability over time in school-age clinical samples where correlation coefficients ranged from .88 to .95 for periods of 3 months to 5 years. Test-retest reliability coefficients for school-age general population samples also are acceptable. The test manual does not document the temporal stability of the Adult form or the Preschool form.

Support for the validity of the SRS-2 School-Age form was provided through its convergence with other measures of autism-related symptoms. Correlations with the Social Communication Questionnaire (Rutter, Bailey, & Lord, 2001) yielded coefficients between .58 and .68. Correlation coefficients for the SRS-2 and the Children's Communication Checklist (Bishop, 1998) ranged from -.49 to -.75. Concordance with the Childhood Autism Rating Scale (Schopler, Reichler, DeVellis, & Daly, 1980) was r = .61. Relationships with the Autism Diagnostic Interview-Revised (ADI-R; Rutter, Le Couteur, & Lord, 2003) were varied, but generally supported the validity of the SRS-2 School-Age form. Correlation coefficients for the SRS-2 and ADI-R domain scores ranged from .26 to .77. Coefficients for the SRS-2 and Autism Diagnostic Observation Schedule domain scores (ADOS; Lord, Rutter, DiLavore, & Risi, 2001) also were variable, ranging from .15 to .58. The relationship of the SRS-2 School-Age form with the Vineland Adaptive Behavior Scales (Sparrow, Balla, & Cicchetti, 1984) was moderate in magnitude (r = -.36 for the Vineland composite and -.34 to -.43 for the subscales) but in the anticipated direction.

The validity of the SRS-2 School-Age form was further evidenced by substantial differences between mean Total SRS-2 scores for children with ASD and those without ASD; M = 106.6 (SD = 30.0) for a group of approximately 5,000 children with ASD versus M = 24.6 (SD = 24.7) for their unaffected siblings. Studies of the Preschool and Adult forms also reported mean scores substantially higher for individuals with ASD or at risk of developmental problems. An area of concern pertains to evidence of higher mean scores for adults ages 60 and over on the Adult form. The mean Total raw score for older adults (n = 127) in the standardization sample was 61, more than 20 points higher than for the overall adult sample.

A receiver operating characteristics (ROC) analysis of the School-Age form revealed test sensitivity of .93 and specificity of .91 when a cutoff score of 60 was used and a sensitivity of

.84 and specificity of .94 with a cutoff of 75. ROC analyses have yet to be reported for the Preschool and Adult forms.

COMMENTARY. The original SRS is widely used in both clinical and research settings to measure the severity of ASD symptoms. By extending its age range, the SRS-2 has the potential to expand its applicability. Several concerns with the SRS-2 are noted. First, the item development procedures for the new Preschool and Adult forms were less than optimal. The assumption that items that adequately distinguish ASD symptoms among school-age children will also be appropriate for individuals at other ages (with minimal rewording) is questionable, insofar as the diagnostic utility of items depends on the developmental appropriateness of the behaviors they address. The adequacy of items at both ends of the age range (younger children and older adults) is not sufficiently demonstrated. The representation of older adults in the standardization sample is small, and their mean scores were inexplicably elevated.

Secondly, the test manual offers relatively little evidence supporting the validity of the Preschool and Adult forms. Studies with larger clinical samples are needed, and ROC analyses are needed to establish the test's sensitivity and specificity at these ages.

SUMMARY. The SRS-2 is a brief, easy-to-administer Likert rating instrument that may be useful for screening individuals for symptoms of ASDs. The second edition has expanded the age range of the original SRS downward to include preschoolers and upward to include individuals up to age 89. Ample evidence supports its validity and sensitivity for predicting individuals' ASD-related symptomology for school-age children. Further study is needed, however, before the new forms can be used with confidence with adults and preschool children.

REVIEWER'S REFERENCES

American Psychiatric Association. (2013). *Diagnostic and statistical manual of mental disorders* (5th ed.). Arlington, VA: American Psychiatric Publishing.

Bishop, D. V. M. (1998). Development of the Children's Communication Checklist (CCC): A method for assessing qualitative aspects of communicative impairment in children. *Journal of Child Psychology and Psychiatry, 39,* 879–891.

Constantino, J. N., & Gruber, C. P. (2005). The Social Responsiveness Scale. Los Angeles, CA: Western Psychological Services.

Lord, C., Rutter, M., DiLavore, P. C., & Risi, S. (2001). Autism Diagnostic Observation Schedule (ADOS). Los Angeles, CA: Western Psychological Services.

Rutter, M., Bailey, A., & Lord, C. (2001). Social Communication Questionnaire (SCQ). Los Angeles, CA: Western Psychological Services.

Rutter, M., Le Couteur, A., & Lord, C. (2003). Autism Diagnostic Interview-Revised (ADI-R). Los Angeles, CA: Western Psychological Services.

Schopler, E., Reichler, R., DeVellis, R., & Daly, K. (1980). Toward objective classification of childhood autism: Childhood Autism Rating Scale (CARS). *Journal of Autism and Developmental Disorders, 10,* 91–103.

Sparrow, S. S., Balla, D. A., & Cicchetti, D. V., (1984). Vineland Adaptive Behavior Scales. Circle Pines, MN: American Guidance Service.

[155]
Sport Personality Questionnaire.

Purpose: "Designed to provide information about the personality and mental factors that contribute to elite performance in sport. It is intended to be used by sport psychologists and coaches to help athletes understand and develop the mental skills needed to perform successfully in competition."

Population: Athletes ages 16 to 65.

Publication Date: 2011.

Acronym: SPQ20.

Scores, 27: 20 Scale scores (Competitiveness, Aggressiveness, Self-Efficacy, Flow, Achievement, Power, Conscientiousness, Ethics, Adaptability, Self-Awareness, Intuition, Relationships, Empathy, Emotions, Managing Pressure, Fear of Failure, Burnout, Self-Talk, Visualization, Goal Setting); 7 Summary scores (Overall Mental Skills, Leadership Potential, Achievement and Competitiveness, Confidence and Resilience, Interaction and Sportsmanship, Power and Agressiveness, Response Style).

Administration: Group.

Price Data, 2011: $14.95 per test.

Time: [15-20] minutes.

Comments: Assessment, scoring, and feedback conducted online.

Author: MySkillsProfile.com, Ltd.

Publisher: MySkillsProfile.com, Ltd. [United Kingdom].

Review of the Sport Personality Questionnaire by STEPHEN AXFORD, Executive Officer for Special Services, Falcon School District 49, Colorado Springs, CO, and Adjunct Professor, University of Colorado at Colorado Springs, Colorado Springs, CO:

DESCRIPTION. The Sport Personality Questionnaire (SPQ20) "is designed to provide information about the personality and mental factors that contribute to elite performance in sport" (user manual, p. 4). Questionnaire items were developed from a concept model of six key mental skills domains associated with exceptional athletic performance: Dynamism, Motives and Values, Openness, Sociability, Anxieties, and Techniques. Based on a statistically determined four-factor model representing clusters of 20 scales related to these mental skills, the SPQ20 was shown to measure: Power and Aggressiveness, Achievement Drive and Competitiveness, Interaction and Sportsmanship, and Confidence and Resilience. The 20 specific scales are: Competitiveness, Aggressiveness, Self-Efficacy, Flow (performance immersion), Achievement (training motivation), Power (authority and leadership), Conscientiousness, Ethics, Adaptability, Self-Awareness, Intuition, Relationships, Empathy,

Emotions (affective regulation), Managing Pressure, Fear of Failure, Burnout, Self-Talk, Visualization, and Goal Setting. The SPQ20 is designed to be used by sports psychologists and coaches, although it is also directly available to athletes through a website (www.sportsconfidence.biz). When administered by a sports psychologist or coach, the athlete is provided emailed directions for accessing a test administration hyperlink. For the direct access online option, athletes may download a PDF format interpretive report or request test results via email.

DEVELOPMENT. In the user manual, the test developers provide a detailed summary of the development of the SPQ20. This includes a clear description of each scale, and essentially rubrics for low, moderate, and high scorers corresponding to the six individual Key Areas or domains of sport mental skills identified by the authors as part of the concept model. These domains were identified from review of the sport psychology literature. Factor analysis was then used to place items into four identified clusters. Each scale has eight items, with equal numbers that are negatively or positively keyed.

Across the dimensions related to sport mental skills, high scorers, to capsulate: enjoy competition, fantasize about winning, long to be the best, play aggressively and intimidate opponents, display confidence and recover quickly from setbacks, feel they are "playing in the zone," invest total commitment and are willing to sacrifice, are motivated by exercising authority, train vigorously, display sportsmanship, stay abreast of technical development to enhance skills, take risks to succeed, are aware of personal strengths and weaknesses, use intuition to guide performance, use sport to build relationships, support the growth of others, regulate their emotions, manage stress before competitions, are confident in their performance, follow a healthy lifestyle, use positive self-talk, rehearse performance by using visualization, progress monitor performance in setting goals, and answer questions in an honest and self-critical fashion. Of course, moderate scorers endorse items indicating internalization of these mental skills to a lesser extent, and low scorers endorse answers indicating an absence of these skills. For example, low scorers, related to the Anxieties Key Area, report "difficulty staying calm and in control before important events" (user manual, p. 23).

For interpretation and application, the SPQ20 yields sten scores, based on the Standard Ten scoring approach. Five sten score ranges are identified (Green, Amber Green, Amber, Amber Red, Red), corresponding to Red-Amber-Green (RAG) "traffic light" assessment ratings, with Green representing mental skills available for the athlete to capitalize upon in realizing a competitive edge; and Red representing an area of sport mental skills needing marked improvement. A "feedback report" is provided with specific interventions recommended for developing these skills. Also provided is a table indicating the percentage of athletes in the international comparison group corresponding to each of the 10 sten scores. For example, a sten score of 10 indicates the athlete scored higher than 99% of athletes in the comparison group, and a sten score of 6 indicates the athlete scored higher than 60% of athletes in the comparison group. In addition, the feedback report includes a mental skills matrix that provides a "visual summary of an athlete's mental toughness and what they need to do and how far they need to travel to become a Confident Achiever" (user manual, p. 31). The matrix is divided into four quadrants: Confident Achiever, Tense Achiever, Easygoing Contestant, and Tense Contestant. In addition, the feedback report identifies specific areas to target for improvement, development (i.e., "work on"), and for capitalizing upon (i.e., strengths).

TECHNICAL. With regard to standardization, the SPQ20 uses an online format with clear and specific test instructions. Respondents are directed to answer all 168 questions. A 5-point Likert-type rating scale is used for answering test items, with a rating of 1 being "Never/Almost never" and a rating of 5 being "Nearly always/Always." The individual items seem to be well constructed and to have face validity. As noted earlier, test items were developed following review of the related sport psychology literature and development of a concept model based on identification of six key sport mental skills domains. Factor analysis yielded four main factor loadings.

The user manual provides technical information related to reliability and validity with several well-constructed tables summarizing these results. Internal consistency reliability estimates ($n = 8,927$), based on coefficient alphas, range from .63 to .82, with a median value of .72. Standard errors of measurement for sten scores range from .84 to 1.31, with a median value of 1.08. From these data, the test authors suggest that a difference of two stens between scores of two athletes is needed to surmise a reliable difference on a scale. Limited information is provided regarding the standardization sample.

Using the same standardization sample (n = 8.927), scale intercorrelations for the SPQ20 range from -.31 to .77, indicating satisfactory independence. Positive correlations with the greatest magnitude are observed between scales comprising the four statistical factors. In addition, 76% of the SPQ20 primary scale pairs share less than 50% common variance. This result indicates the SPQ20 scales exhibit reasonable independence. Collectively, these results offer evidence of construct validity that supports test score uses suggested in the user manual.

The median Standard Error of Difference for the SPQ20 primary scales is 1.51 stens. Thus, on average, a difference of 3 stens is required to establish a meaningful difference corresponding to comparison scales. The test authors provide an example using a 3-point sten score difference between Visualization and Self-Talk, favoring the latter. Such a difference can be interpreted to mean that the athlete uses Self-Talk more than Visualization to enhance athletic performance.

To conduct the factor analysis, the test authors utilized principal components extraction with varimax rotation (n = 8,927). Indicating a sufficient factor analysis, the Kaiser-Meyer-Olkin Measure of Sampling Adequacy was .94. As noted earlier, four factors were extracted (eigenvalues of 1 and higher, accounting for 67% of the variance). With a median value of .71, communality values ranged from .55 to .81. All 20 of the scales loaded on at least one of the four factors. The Relationships and Empathy scales loaded on more than one factor.

As an additional means of addressing construct validity, the SPQ20 was correlated with items from the International Personality Item Pool (IPIP; n = 725; 66% males/34% females; ages 16–65 years; mean age of 25.7). Correlation coefficients were in the range of .40 to .73 (median value of .60), indicating that the SPQ20 and IPIP items measure similar constructs, supporting the construct validity of the SPQ20.

Addressing predictive validity, the SPQ20 was correlated with assessments of athletic performance. Athletic performance was measured through self-report and coach's assessments using a 4-point Likert-type scale survey. Median correlation coefficients ranged from .22 to .29. Coach assessment scores were slightly lower than self-ratings, with an overall correlation coefficient of .61. Using the combined assessment (self-ratings and coach assessment), 18 scales yielded statistically significant scores at the .01 level.

The impact of response style was also addressed by the test developers. Significant differences related to response style were observed. This information was used to make score adjustments for the computer-generated interpretive report.

The test authors also considered age and gender effects. Correlation coefficients were all below .22 (n = 8,927). Additional details related to these coefficients are provided in the user manual. The overall finding related to age and gender effects was that there was no need to develop separate norms for either demographic.

The user manual includes a section describing the sample used in developing norms. The original international sample consisted of just fewer than 10,000 athletes who completed the online assessment. Participants over age 65 or under age 16 were omitted, and duplicate cases were also deleted. This left a sample of 8,927 athletes to be used in standardizing the SPQ20. The international sample was limited to English-speaking nations: 38% from the United Kingdom, 34% from the United States, 12% from Australia, and 7% from Canada. Nearly twice as many (65%) of the participants were male as compared to females. Several well-developed tables are provided summarizing norms for the SPQ20.

COMMENTARY AND SUMMARY. The SPQ20 promises to be a useful tool for sport psychologists and coaches in advising and working with athletes for the purpose of enhancing athletic performance. It is recommended by this reviewer that even for the direct access option, where no test administrator is involved, the participating athlete should be given the opportunity to consult or debrief with an expert familiar with the SPQ20. Such a policy would help to ensure test results are appropriately interpreted and applied.

With regard to technical adequacy, the test developers have gone a long way in standardizing and validating the SPQ20. Subsequent validation efforts should include correlating the SPQ20 with additional tests measuring similar constructs, besides the IPIP items. In addition, although limited validation research was conducted involving correlating the SPQ20 with actual athletic performance as measured by self and coach surveys, additional credibility would be gained through empirical research examining the use of the SPQ2O in developing interventions and in looking at related outcomes. In other words, does use of the SPQ20 and interventions derived from it actually result in better athletic performance?

Review of the Sport Personality Questionnaire by CLAUDIA R. WRIGHT, Professor Emerita, California State University, Long Beach, CA:

DESCRIPTION. The Sport Personality Questionnaire (SPQ20) is a self-assessment constructed to identify one's mental approach and style when engaged in a chosen sport. It was designed for 16- to 65-year-olds who are elite athletes or athletes seeking to improve their performance in competitive sports. The 168-item, 4-factor SPQ20 comprises 20 scale scores and 7 summary scores: Overall Mental Skills, Leadership Potential, Confidence and Resilience (Factor 1), Achievement Drive and Competitiveness (Factor 2), Interaction and Sportsmanship (Factor 3), Power and Aggressiveness (Factor 4), and Response Style. Computerized feedback from SPQ20 scores can be viewed and downloaded by the individual or by coaches and sport psychologists to assist the athlete in gaining a broader, personal understanding of those psychological dynamics that may affect success in sports and to facilitate training.

Test administration and scoring. The examinee registers on the website www.myskillsprofile.com and pays a modest fee using a credit card. Testing may be initiated by the individual or by a coach or sport psychologist, depending on the purpose of the assessment. The examinee is given access to the 168-item questionnaire and instructed to respond to each statement with respect to how he or she thought or felt during or after sporting situations in which he or she competed. The examinee is encouraged to not overthink the item-statements and to avoid a middle response set. The questionnaire takes approximately 20 minutes to complete. Personal information is collected regarding gender, age, sport, country, ethnic group, and the respondent's self-performance assessment over the last year and his/her estimate of his/her coach's assessment over the same time period. Within minutes of completion, responses to the SPQ20 are analyzed, and a 13-page SPQ20 Mental Skills Report is generated that can be downloaded or can be emailed either to the examinee or to the coach/sport psychologist. The report provides an introduction to the questionnaire and an explanation for interpreting the results including a brief review of the Standard Ten (sten) scoring system with a corresponding color-coded, 5-point competence level ranging from 1 "very low" (red, "improve") to 3 (yellow, "work on") to 5 "very high" (green, "capitalize on"); and a definition for each of the 20 scales organized by

factor. A respondent's personal "Sport Personality Profile Summary" provides a classification and a brief explanation for each of the 7 summary scores.

The summary for Overall Mental Skills incorporates results from two factor scale scores, Confidence and Resilience (Factor 1) and Achievement and Competitiveness (Factor 2), and represents the findings in both a narrative form and as a detailed, color-coded 2x2 matrix with axes ranging from "less preferred" to "preferred." The respondent's relative position is clearly marked in the matrix. Additional pages of feedback are provided regarding obtained "level" related to each of the respondent's 7 scale scores associated with Achievement and Competitiveness and for each of the 8 scale scores associated with Confidence and Resilience. A similar summary profile is generated for Leadership Potential, which includes matrices for Interaction and Sportsmanship and for Power and Aggressiveness. Finally, an SPQ20 "Psychometric Scorecard" lists for each scale the respondent's raw score, sten score, and the meaning of the score; for example, a sten score of 5 is "higher than about 40% of the comparison group" (Sample report, p. 12).

DEVELOPMENT. Little information is provided regarding the selection of the SPQ20 item-statements or the theoretical model or models supporting test development. The test author offers online a list of recommended readings and "practical tips and suggestions for performance improvement" that correspond to areas covered by the SPQ20 items. Whatever decisions were made for compiling items for the questionnaire, a substantial effort was undertaken to study the psychometric properties of the questionnaire and to develop norms.

Data were obtained from a sample of 8,927 respondents and subjected to a principal components factor analysis, using varimax rotation. Four factors were extracted. Factor 1, Confidence and Resilience, accounted for 44.7% of the variance and includes 8 scales: Managing Pressure, Self-Efficacy, Fear of Failure, Flow, Burnout, Emotions, Self-Talk, and Self-Awareness. Factor 2, Achievement and Competitiveness, accounted for 9.2% of the variance and is made up of 7 scales: Achievement, Adaptability, Competitiveness, Conscientiousness, Visualization, Intuition, and Goal Setting; although the Empathy scale loaded on this factor and met the criterion, it was not included. Factor 3, Interaction and Sportsmanship, accounted for 7.9% of the variance and included 3 scales: Ethics, Empathy, and Relationships; Factor 4, Power and Aggressiveness, accounted for 5.3% of the variance and is made up of 3 scales: Relationships, Aggressiveness, and Power; Factors 3 and 4 share the Relationships scale. The findings from the factor analysis have been used to structure the personal profile feedback provided by the online analysis.

TECHNICAL.

Norms. Data were collected over a 7-year period from 10,000 athletes, who completed an online assessment. After eliminating redundant respondents and individuals under 16 and over 65 years of age, the resulting sample was made up of 8,927 respondents representing 10 countries. About 65% were male and 35% were female; with ages 16–20 (53.2%), 21–30 (23.6%), 31–40 (11.4%), and 41–65 (11.9%). Respondents were predominately from the United Kingdom (39%) and the U.S. (34%); with about 22% accounted for by those from Australia (12%), Canada (7%), New Zealand (3%); and the remaining 5% from India, Ireland, Malaysia, Philippines, and South Africa (each about 1% or less). Although data were collected regarding a broad spectrum of sports and ethnic group affiliation, no separate analyses have been reported for these descriptions.

Reliability. Adequate evidence of internal-consistency estimates of reliability (coefficient alpha) was reported for each of 21 scales (in addition to the 20 scales listed in the descriptive information, an additional scale was included called "Impression Management," although it is not clear what items, if any, apply to this scale). Coefficients ranged from .63 to .82 (median value of .72).

Validity. To examine construct validity, a sample of 725 respondents between the ages of 16 and 65 (m = 25.7, sd = 11.4), 66% male, provided responses to the SPQ20 and to "marker variables," the content of which was obtained from the International Personality Item Pool (IPIP, 2001; www.ipip.ori.org), an online site for accessing test items in the public domain with emphasis upon personality and other individual differences measures. No specific information has been provided by the test author that clarifies the basis for the selected markers from IPIP, whether each of the "marker variables" employed represents a single item or a scale score, and how the IPIP "markers" were administered to the sample. Moderate correlation coefficients between each of the SPQ20 scales with a selected IPIP "marker variable" ranged from .40 to .73 (median value of .60). The test author concluded that the SPQ20

scale scores and the IPIP "marker variables" are measuring similar constructs.

To examine concurrent validity, 215 athletes' (64% males; more than 80% white; ages ranged from 16–65, m = 26.3, sd = 11.5) SPQ20 scale scores were correlated with responses to two item-statements as well as an average of the two, to assess the respondent's athletic performance: (1) the respondent's self-assessment and (2) the respondent's estimate of his or her coach's assessment. Each item-statement employed the same 4-point response scale that ranged from "excellent" to "not satisfactory." The following low-moderate correlation coefficients were reported for the self-assessment, rating with each of the following SPQ20 scale scores: Self-Efficacy (r = .39), Flow (r = .41), Managing Pressure (r = .37), and Burnout (r = .33), all p < .01; and, for the coach's assessment rating with SPQ20 scales: Self-Efficacy (r = .31), Flow (r = .34), Achievement (r = .31), Conscientiousness (r = .32), Burnout (r = .36), and Goal Setting (r = .30), all p < .01.

COMMENTARY. Over the past decade or two, there has been a growing body of research focused on how the psychological characteristics of elite athletes affect performance. The SPQ20 appears to offer a promising step toward the development of an instrument with utility for athletes and their coaches. Discussion is lacking linking the various scales of the SPQ20 or the resulting factor structure with theoretical models and research in the field. Additional validity evidence supporting the construct and concurrent validities of SPQ20 scale scores would be helpful.

SUMMARY. The Sport Personality Questionnaire (SPQ20) shows promise as an additional tool for athletes, coaches, and sports psychologists, who seek to describe and improve athletic performance. Adequate evidence supports the reliability of scores and the resulting factor structure of the SPQ20 and offers a starting point for validity studies. Modest construct validity evidence was offered among SPQ20 scale scores and IPIP "marker variables" (IPIP, 2001).

REVIEWER'S REFERENCE

International Personality Item Pool. (2001). *A scientific collaboratory for the development of advanced measures of personality and other individual differences.* http://ipip.ori.org.

[156]

State-Trait Anger Expression Inventory-2: Child and Adolescent.

Purpose: Designed to "assess state and trait anger with anger expression and control."

Population: Ages 9 to 18 years.

Publication Date: 2009.
Acronym: STAXI-2 C/A.
Scores, 9: State Anger, State Anger-Feelings, State Anger-Expression, Trait Anger, Trait Anger-Temperament, Trait Anger-Reaction, Anger Expression-Out, Anger Expression-In, Anger Control.
Administration: Group.
Price Data, 2010: $155 per introductory kit including professional manual (87 pages), 25 rating booklets, and 25 profile forms; $52 per professional manual; $80 per 25 rating booklets; $36 per 25 profile forms.
Time: (10-15) minutes.
Authors: Thomas M. Brunner and Charles D. Spielberger.
Publisher: Psychological Assessment Resources, Inc.

Review of State-Trait Anger Expression Inventory-2: Child and Adolescent by STEPHANIE STEIN, Professor and Chair, Department of Psychology, Central Washington University, Ellensburg, WA:

DESCRIPTION. The State-Trait Anger Expression Inventory-2: Child and Adolescent (STAXI-2 C/A) is a self-report rating scale intended for children ages 9 to 18 years. The purpose of the measure is to "assess both state and trait anger along with anger expression and control" (professional manual, p. 11). The STAXI-2 C/A is adapted from the STAXI-2 (Spielberger, 1999; 15:244).

The test authors recommend the STAXI-2 C/A for the purposes of screening, diagnosis, and/or monitoring of anger in children and adolescents. The 35-item rating scale can be administered in either individual or group settings, with an estimated time frame of 15 minutes or less. All items are phrased in the first person (i.e. "I feel…"). Responses are given on a 3-point scale, either "Not at all/Somewhat/Very much" or "Hardly ever/Sometimes/Often." The questionnaire is a 2-page multiple-sheet carbonless form, which provides the questions on the top answer sheet and scoring on the second sheet.

Raw scores are converted to percentile ranks and T scores for five scales: State Anger (S-Ang, 10 items), Trait Anger (T-Ang, 10 items), Anger Expression-Out (AX-O, 5 items), Anger Expression-In (AX-I, 5 items), and Anger Control (AC, 5 items). In addition, scores are computed for four subscales: State Anger-Feelings (S-Ang/F, 5 items), State Anger-Expression (S-Ang/VP, 5 items), Trait Anger-Temperament (T-Ang/T, 5 items), and Trait Anger-Reaction (T-Ang/R, 5 items). In addition, qualitative descriptors are provided for scores on each scale/subscale (Low, Average, Elevated, or Very High). A two-sided Profile Form can be used to plot the scores as percentile ranks and T scores. The test manual provides clear guidelines for administering the STAXI-2 C/A and procedures for dealing with missing responses, as well as detailed scoring and interpretation guidelines.

DEVELOPMENT. The STAXI-2 C/A represents an adaptation of the STAXI-2, with the purpose of developing a version of the instrument appropriate for use with children and adolescents. Although the STAXI-2 has been used to assess anger in older adolescents, it has been limited in usefulness with children and younger adolescents because of the challenging readability level of some items. In addition to simplifying items, the test authors' goal in developing the STAXI-2 C/A included "revalidating the basic conceptual components that were first identified with the original STAXI" (professional manual, p. 11). Furthermore, the STAXI-2 C/A was developed to address contemporary societal problems related to school violence and youth suicide by specifically examining the internalization of anger by youth.

The constructs underlying the development of the STAXI-2 C/A are largely unchanged from Spielberger's state-trait theory of anger operationalized in the original STAXI (Spielberger, 1988) and later in the STAXI-2. However, the test authors also explicitly identify a number of dissimilarities between the STAXI-2 and the STAXI-2 C/A. Some of the changes were intended to make the STAXI-2 C/A more appropriate for younger individuals, including simplifying instructions and decreasing the number of items from 57 in the STAXI-2 to 35 in the STAXI-2 C/A. Other differences between the instruments include reducing the number of scales from six to five, reducing the number of State Anger subscales from three to two (based on results of factor analyses), and the development and replacement of a few items to better reflect the concept of anger in juveniles. Finally, the test authors eliminated the total score (Anger Expression Index) from the STAXI-2 to recognize the multidimensional nature of anger delineated by the separate scales and subscales of the STAXI-2 C/A.

TECHNICAL.

Standardization. The weighted normative sample for the STAXI-2 C/A consisted of 838 public school students, ages 9–18, with a mean age of 13.77 years. Fifty-one percent of the normative sample was male. Ethnicity of the normative sample was 60% Caucasian, 18% Hispanic, 15%

African American, and 7% Other. No information was provided about geographic location or SES demographics of the normative sample. Given the paucity of data regarding the normative sample, it is difficult to determine how well the sample represents the general population. Scale and subscale *T* scores (means, standard deviations, and standard errors of measurement) are provided for the normative sample by age/gender subgroups for ages 9–11, 12–14, and 15–18.

In addition, scale and subscale *T* score means and standard deviations are provided for a small clinical sample consisting of 52 adolescents, ages 11–18 (mean age of 15.21), with "delinquent behavior or chronic anger problems" (professional manual, p. 25) from outpatient and inpatient treatment facilities. Forty percent of the clinical sample was male, and ethnicity representation was 67% Caucasian, 21% African American, 6% Hispanic, and 6% Other. The clinical sample was drawn from six Northeastern, Midwestern, and Southern states.

Reliability. Internal consistency reliability coefficients of each scale and subscale were provided for the entire unweighted normative sample and were further broken down by age/gender groups. The State Anger (S-Ang) scale demonstrated the highest alpha coefficients, ranging from .83 (age 9–11 females) to .90 (age 12–14 females), with an overall coefficient of .87. Though slightly lower, the Trait Anger (T-Ang) scale demonstrated mostly moderate to high coefficients, ranging from .76 (age 12–14 males) to .83 (age 12–14 females), with an overall coefficient of .80. In contrast, the Anger Expression-Out (AX-0) and Anger Expression-In (AX-I) scales showed the lowest alpha coefficients ranging from .57 (AX-I, age 9–11 males) to .76 (AX-I, age 12–14 males), with overall coefficients of .70 and .71, respectively. Overall, internal consistency coefficients are acceptable for all scales and subscales on the entire normative sample but are unacceptable (<.70) for eight of the age/gender subgroup scale or subscale scores. In the clinical sample as a whole, internal consistency coefficients for all of the scale and subscale scores were in the moderate (.74 on AX-I) to high range (.94 on S-Ang). Surprisingly, no evidence for temporal reliability (test-retest) was provided, even though one of the major constructs (Trait Anger) is largely based on the assumption of stability over time. Instead, the test authors attempt to minimize the need for these data, claiming that numerous prior test-retest studies on the earlier instruments

(STAXI and STAXI-2) "have consistently found that the Trait scales are relatively stable over time" (professional manual, p. 21). Though that may be true for the earlier instruments, the STAXI-2 C/A is normed on a much younger population and one cannot just assume that similar temporal stability in scores will be found in this age group on this particular instrument.

Validity. Several types of validity assertions were provided for the STAXI-2 C/A. The test authors claim that this instrument has content validity, largely because prior research has supported the content validity of the STAXI-2 for use with children and adolescents. However, no research of this sort is provided on the STAXI-2 C/A. Most of the validity data provided in the test manual focus on discriminant and convergent validity, relying on data from the clinical sample of 52 adolescents with disruptive behavior problems. Scores on the scales and subscales of the STAXI-2 C/A were correlated with those on the Youth Self-Report form (YSR; Achenbach & Rescorla, 2001). As expected, the T-Ang scales and subscales and AX-O had significant, moderately strong positive correlations with YSR Syndrome scales of Aggressive Behavior and Externalizing and YSR DSM-oriented scales of Oppositional Defiant and Conduct Problems. Furthermore, these same YSR scales had significant negative correlations with the AX-I and AC scales, suggesting that higher levels of internalized anger and anger control are associated with lower levels of externalizing behavior disorders in youth.

For the small clinical sample of adolescents, these findings provide evidence for convergent and discriminant validity for several of the STAXI-2 C/A scales/subscales in comparison to an established measure of aggressive and disruptive behavior in youth. However, this validity claim cannot automatically be extended to the general population of youth. The test authors did, however, compare the clinical sample of the STAXI-2 C/A with a same size matched control sample from the normative sample and found statistically significant differences between the groups for T-Ang and AX-O scales/subscales and, to a lesser degree, the S-Ang scale and S-Ang/F subscale. This suggests that the STAXI-2 C/A has the potential to discriminate between adolescents identified with behavior disorders and those in the general population.

COMMENTARY. The apparent strengths of the STAXI-2 C/A include a solid conceptual state/trait anger framework based on decades of research. The test manual is clear, well organized, and thorough in describing theoretical foundations, development of the instrument, scoring, and interpretation. The test authors have addressed several criticisms of the earlier STAXI-2 in this current instrument through the inclusion of demographic information on ethnicity and information regarding standard error of measurement. The STAXI-2 C/A takes very little time to complete, and the items are simple enough to be read and understood by fourth graders. In addition, the STAXI-2 C/A has acceptable to good internal consistency reliability on most scales, which is impressive, given the brevity of the measure and the relatively few items within each scale/subscale. Finally, the test authors provide data that offer convergent and discriminant evidence of validity of parts of the STAXI-2 C/A, at least when administered to adolescents with documented behavior problems.

On the other hand, the STAXI-2 C/A also has some weaknesses. The normative sample for the instrument is not well-defined, especially with regard to geographical location and SES. Therefore, it is difficult to determine how well the sample represents the general population. In addition, no data exist to support the test-retest reliability of the instrument. This lack of reliability data is especially problematic in the scales/subscales in which temporal stability is a defining feature (i.e., Trait Anger). Furthermore, the evidence for validity is limited to a small, clinical sample of adolescents and cannot be generalized to the overall population of school-age children. This lack of validity evidence is unfortunate, given the stated purpose of screening for anger problems in children and adolescents. We can already conclude that adolescents with externalizing behavior problems are likely to have anger issues, but it would be much more helpful if we knew that the STAXI-2 C/A scores provide a valid measure of screening for anger in nonidentified youth. Finally, one of the most potentially important stated purposes of the STAXI-2 C/A is to identify internalized anger in children and adolescents that could result in violent behavior towards self and others (i.e., school violence). However, the relevant scale for measuring internalized anger (AX-I) does not discriminate between clinical and normal populations, nor does it correlate positively with any measure of adolescent dysfunction.

SUMMARY. The STAXI-2 C/A provides a brief, simple, and easy-to-administer measure of anger in children and adolescents. Though this instrument has potential as a useful screening, diagnostic, and monitoring tool, the test authors do not provide sufficient evidence to support the validity of using scores from the STAXI-2 C/A for these purposes, especially in the general population of school-age youth. Additional validation studies are needed to support the clinical use of this instrument. In addition, studies on the temporal reliability of the STAXI-2 C/A are warranted. In the meantime, clinicians who chose to use the STAXI-2 C/A to assess anger problems in youth should be very cautious in interpreting the results.

REVIEWER'S REFERENCES

Achenbach, T. M., & Rescorla, L. A. (2001). *Manual for the ASEBA school-age forms and profiles.* Burlington, VT: University of Vermont, Research Center for Children, Youth, and Families.
Spielberger, C. D. (1988). *State-Trait Anger Expression Inventory (STAXI) professional manual.* Lutz, FL: Psychological Assessment Resources.
Spielberger, C. D. (1999). *State-Trait Anger Expression Inventory-2 (STAXI-2) professional manual.* Lutz, FL: Psychological Assessment Resources.

Review of the State-Trait Anger Expression Inventory–2: Child and Adolescent by JEREMY R. SULLIVAN, Associate Professor of Educational Psychology, University of Texas at San Antonio, San Antonio, TX:

DESCRIPTION. The State-Trait Anger Expression Inventory–2: Child and Adolescent (STAXI-2 C/A) is a 35-item, self-report scale designed to assess anger among children and adolescents ages 9 to 18 years. Anger is defined in the test manual as "an emotional state or condition that consists of feelings that vary in intensity from mild irritation or annoyance to intense fury and rage, accompanied by activation and arousal of the autonomic nervous system. As an experiential state or process, anger occurs in response to real or imagined frustration, threat, or perceived injustice" (professional manual, p. 5). Based on Spielberger's state-trait theory, the "state" dimension describes anger that is transitory, variable in intensity, and experienced in response to some specific event or stressor, whereas the "trait" dimension captures anger that is more stable across time and situation and is characterological in nature. Children who are higher in trait anger are more prone to experience state anger more frequently and intensely, as they are more likely to perceive more situations or events as anger-inducing.

The scale also is multidimensional in that it separates the process of anger into the dimensions of experience, expression, and control. The experience component includes the State Anger scale (10 items total), which is divided into State Anger-Feelings (5 items assessing the intensity of current angry feelings) and State Anger-Expression (5 items assessing current feelings regarding verbal or physical expressions of anger), and the Trait Anger scale (10 items total), which is divided into Trait Anger-Temperament (5 items assessing the experience of anger in the absence of a specific stressor or provocation) and Trait Anger-Reaction (5 items assessing the experience of anger in reaction to frustration or negative evaluation). The expression component includes the Anger Expression-Out (5 items assessing the expression of anger through verbal or physical aggression) and Anger Expression-In (5 items assessing the suppression of angry feelings) scales. Finally, the control component includes only the Anger Control scale, which is based on 5 items assessing attempts to control the inward or outward expression of anger. This multidimensionality means that the STAXI-2 C/A goes beyond the feelings or experience of anger to also assess how anger is expressed and controlled.

The test authors suggest that clinical uses of the STAXI-2 C/A include differentiating temporary anger states from more stable characteristics, describing the intensity of anger as it relates to a range of clinical diagnoses that are characterized by angry feelings, measuring anger within the context of risk assessment and predicting aggressive behaviors, identifying specific triggers of anger, distinguishing between externalizing and internalizing styles for coping with anger, using the subscales to place children into appropriate treatment groups based on their score profiles, and providing a pre-post measure for assessing treatment effectiveness. Appropriate populations include children and adolescents in outpatient settings, youth involved in the juvenile justice system, and the general population. The test is appropriate for school and clinical settings.

Test materials include the professional manual, rating booklet, and profile form. Administration may be conducted in either individual or group situations, and items may be read aloud if necessary. The examinee completes the rating booklet by circling 1, 2, or 3 for each item. Items are presented in three parts: Part 1 includes items related to intensity of current feelings of anger (i.e., the State dimension), Part 2 includes items related to frequency and situational characteristics of angry feelings (i.e., the Trait dimension), and Part 3 includes items related to frequency of various modes of expression and control of anger (e.g., losing temper versus trying to calm down). Thus, the ratings of 1, 2, and 3 are defined differently

for each part (with 1 meaning either "Not at all" or "Hardly ever," 2 meaning either "Somewhat" or "Sometimes," and 3 meaning either "Very much" or "Often"), and examinees must pay attention to the specific directions and definitions for each section. Scoring involves the examiner opening the rating booklet to reveal a scoring sheet (onto which the examinee's responses have been transferred), adding the item responses within each scale to generate raw scores, and converting raw scores to T-scores and percentile ranks. These score conversions can be completed using the total normative sample, or subsamples based on gender and age (i.e., 9–11 years, 12–14 years, and 15–18 years); the test authors suggest that the age-by-gender norms are most appropriate. The profile form is then used to plot T-scores and percentile ranks for a visual representation of the examinee's scores.

The chapter on interpretation includes a consideration of how the STAXI-2 C/A can be used with other methods to provide a comprehensive assessment; this discussion provides a useful picture of how the test "fits in" with the larger assessment process. The interpretation chapter also provides definitions and possible interpretive hypotheses for each scale, in addition to patterns or relationships among the scales that may be especially informative. A step-by-step guide for profile analysis is included, which seems to provide sufficient information to permit profile interpretation. Finally, several distinct and complex case studies are provided to illustrate the interpretation process.

DEVELOPMENT. The development process was largely informed by the State-Trait Anger Expression Inventory (STAXI; Spielberger, 1988) and the State-Trait Anger Expression Inventory–2 (STAXI-2; Spielberger, 1999), both of which were developed based on the state-trait theory of emotions and have a history of being used to assess anger among clinical groups of children and adolescents. The test authors summarize some of the correlational and clinical group studies that support the structure and content of the STAXI and STAXI-2, thereby supporting the use of these instruments to guide the development of the STAXI-2 C/A. The development of the STAXI-2 C/A was deemed necessary due to the reading level of some of the STAXI-2 items; thus, the STAXI-2 may be seen as the adult version and the STAXI-2 C/A is more appropriate for children and adolescents. Most of the items were adapted from the STAXI-2 in order to maintain the content and structure of that scale, but some new items were added to increase relevance for children and adolescents. Final items were selected based on readability analyses; the test authors' judgment regarding content validity; and psychometric indices such as item-total correlations, internal consistency, and results of exploratory factor analysis. Unfortunately, specific results of these initial analyses, and the specific criteria used for some of these decisions, are not described in the test manual.

TECHNICAL.

Standardization. The norms are based on data gathered from 836 children and adolescents ranging from 9 to 18 years of age. Approximately half of the participants were female, 60% were Caucasian, 15% were African American, 18% were Hispanic, and 7% were Other. Participants were selected from public school settings, and data were gathered in small group formats. The sample is described as coming from "multiple sites around the country" (professional manual, p. 17), but the test manual does not indicate how many (or which) states were represented. Similarly, SES was not reported as a demographic variable. Regression analyses indicated that age and gender accounted for very little variance in STAXI-2 C/A raw scores, but age- and gender-based norms are still provided in order to permit more specific norm-referenced interpretation.

Reliability. Score reliability was assessed with internal consistency and standard error of measurement (*SEM*). Notably, no analyses of test-retest reliability were conducted. Internal consistency was based on alpha coefficients and scale and subscale intercorrelations. All alpha coefficients were .70 or above based on the total normative sample, but 8 coefficients fell below .70 when considering the separate age-by-gender groups (including a coefficient of .57 for the Anger Expression-In scale with males ages 9-11). No information is provided regarding similarity of alpha coefficients across ethnic groups. Scale and subscale intercorrelations were generally in the expected direction and of the expected magnitude. Many of the *SEM*s are rather large (i.e., above 5 points), suggesting that confidence intervals constructed around obtained *T*-scores may be very wide for some scales.

Validity. Evidence for validity is divided into content, construct, and criterion-related validity. With regard to content evidence, the test authors suggest that evidence related to the validity of the STAXI, STAXI-2, and state-trait taxonomy supports the appropriateness of the content and

structure of the STAXI-2 C/A. Other scales used to assess anger among youth also were consulted during the item generation phase. Readability analyses of items contribute to content validity by providing evidence that the items are developmentally appropriate for children and adolescents. This is especially important because most of the items were adapted from previous adult versions of the test.

Construct validity evidence consisted of a discriminant and convergent analysis using a clinical sample of 52 children and adolescents with disruptive behaviors or anger problems. The sample completed the STAXI-2 C/A in addition to the widely used Youth Self-Report (Achenbach & Rescorla, 2001), and correlations between these scales were examined to determine whether scores correlated in theoretically expected ways. In general, results support construct validity. For example, STAXI-2 C/A scores were most strongly correlated with scales such as Aggressive Behavior, Externalizing, and Oppositional Defiant Problems, and showed relatively little correlation with scales related to more affective or internalizing symptoms.

Finally, criterion-related evidence derived from a comparison of scores from the clinical sample described above with scores obtained by a matched control group drawn from the larger normative sample. Statistically significant differences in mean *T*-scores were observed for most of the scales, with the clinical sample reporting more anger than the control sample. The largest group differences were observed for the scales assessing trait anger and the outward expression of anger (e.g., verbal or physical aggression). Group differences were not observed for the State Anger-Expression, Anger Expression-In, or Anger Control scales.

COMMENTARY. The STAXI-2 C/A shows promise as a multidimensional measure of anger among children and adolescents. The test seems to have some intuitive utility for differentiating temporary, situational feelings of anger from more chronic, stable characteristics, and for assessing methods of anger expression and control. All of this information is likely to be useful in planning interventions. For example, if the scale identifies an adolescent as having a tendency to internalize anger rather than express it outwardly, this distinction may take the clinician in certain treatment directions. Similarly, knowing whether angry feelings may be best characterized as a "state" versus a "trait" may inform treatment efforts that focus on specific stressors or on coping with precipitating events. Potential users need to keep in mind that although the STAXI-2 C/A is not a diagnostic measure (and does not claim to be), it may be helpful in assessing characteristics of anger from a norm-referenced perspective among individuals with various diagnoses.

Despite its promise, the STAXI-2 C/A is limited by several weaknesses. Perhaps the most salient limitation is that a number of areas in the test manual seem incomplete and preliminary. For example, potential users need more detail about the development process, such as specific results of the factor analyses with the initial pool of items, so they have a better understanding of why the test authors made certain decisions regarding item selection and subscale development. Similarly, the test manual does not provide important information about the standardization sample and norming procedures (e.g., SES, geographic distribution of participants). The current lack of information makes it difficult to evaluate the appropriateness of the procedures used and decisions made. Also notably absent are analyses of test-retest reliability. The test authors cite results of stability analyses using the STAXI and STAXI-2, but these analyses do not inform potential users about the stability of scores on the STAXI-2 C/A. Additional research also will be necessary to provide further evidence for construct and criterion-related validity. The studies presented in the test manual are limited by small sample sizes, and relationships with scores on other anger scales need to be examined to provide further convergent evidence of test score validity. Finally, as a more minor issue, the STAXI-2 C/A does not include formal scales that assess validity of responses. Examiners are instructed to look for incongruent item responses, but including more formal validity scales would provide a more sophisticated way of looking at response patterns.

SUMMARY. The STAXI-2 C/A provides a unique perspective on the assessment of anger among youth by examining the state and trait dimensions separately, in addition to considering different modes of expressing and controlling anger. Unfortunately, the test manual seems incomplete in terms of providing justification for decisions made during the test development process; this is especially true for the exploratory factor analyses, which are only briefly described without the presentation of specific data such as factor loadings. This lack of detail is particularly conspicuous when contrasted with the abundance of information provided on interpretation. Further, more research on psycho-metric properties will be necessary before the test can be recommended for clinical decision making. For example, the test manual suggests the scale could be used to inform risk assessment by contributing to the prediction of aggressive behaviors, but more evidence is needed to demonstrate that the test should be used for these types of decisions.

REVIEWER'S REFERENCES

Achenbach, T. M., & Rescorla, L. A. (2001). *Manual for ASEBA school-age forms & profiles.* Burlington, VT: University of Vermont, Research Center for Children, Youth, & Families.
Spielberger, C. D. (1988). *State-Trait Anger Expression Inventory (STAXI) professional manual.* Lutz, FL: Psychological Assessment Resources.
Spielberger, C. D. (1999). *State-Trait Anger Expression Inventory–2 (STAXI-2) professional manual.* Lutz, FL: Psychological Assessment Resources.

[157]

Store Manager Aptitude Personality & Attitude Profile.

Purpose: Designed "to assess whether a test-taker's preferences and personality traits match those required to work as a store manager."

Population: Potential store managers.

Publication Date: 2011.

Acronym: SMAPAP.

Scores, 15: Adherence to Rules, Approachability, Communication, Conscientiousness, Cultural Sensitivity, Goal-Orientation, Go-Getting, Innovation, Leading, Logical Thinking, Organizing, Salesmanship, Self-Efficacy, Staffing, Overall Score.

Administration: Individual.

Price Data: Available from publisher.

Time: (25) minutes.

Comments: Self-administered online assessment. The test publisher advises that the test manual is being updated to include more information about methodology and theoretical background used in the development of the test. The test publisher also advises that this information is available to clients, as are benchmarks for relevant industries and racial/ethnic group comparison data. However, this information was not provided to Buros or the reviewers.

Author: PsychTests AIM, Inc.

Publisher: PsychTests AIM, Inc. [Canada].

Review of the Store Manager Aptitude Personality & Attitude Profile by PHILLIP L. ACKERMAN, Professor of Psychology, Georgia Institute of Technology, Atlanta, GA:

DESCRIPTION. The Store Manager Aptitude Personality & Attitude Profile (SMAPAP) is a 127-question self-report measure designed for self-assessment, and the intended application is "pre-employment testing" (manual, p. 1) for personnel who aspire to store manager positions. The measure provides scores on 14 different scales, including personality traits (e.g., Conscientiousness), aptitude (Logical Thinking), and attitudes (Self-Efficacy and Cultural Sensitivity), along with an aggregated Overall Score. A report of the individual's responses is provided graphically (in terms of absolute score), along with provision of a narrative paragraph on each scale and an interpretation of the individual's score. A final narrative is provided with a summarized list of the individual's strengths, potential strengths, and limitations. The items on the SMAPAP include standard personality assessment questions, questions about attitudes regarding how one interacts with customers and co-workers, attitudes toward management, attitudes toward diversity among staff, and a small number of problem-solving items. Raw scores for each scale are generated along with an Overall Score, the derivation of which is not described.

DEVELOPMENT. No information is provided in the manual about the development of the instrument.

TECHNICAL.

Standardization. The manual notes that the SMAPAP was not standardized in a conventional fashion. The data reported in the manual are based on an "uncontrolled" sample who "self-selected to take the assessment and opted in to participate in the validation study" (manual, p. 2). Responses were collected from 1,250 participants, of whom 11% were of unknown gender and 9% were of unknown age. In addition, 230 of the respondents were under the age of 21. Descriptive statistics (minimum, maximum, mean, and standard deviation) for the 14 individual scales and the Overall Score are provided. The descriptive statistics indicate that for most of the scales, score distributions are skewed, with substantial ceiling effects (e.g., for the Overall Score, the mean is 77.19, the *SD* is 10.26, and the maximum score is 95, less than 2 *SD* above the mean). Gender differences, age differences, and educational attainment differences are also described in the manual. Women scored significantly higher than men on 11 scales, including the Overall Score. Significant differences also were found on a variety of the scales when the scores were examined by age and by educational attainment.

Reliability. The full extent of reliability analyses reported in the manual is a set of coefficient alpha statistics for the individual scales and the Overall Score. The alpha coefficients range from .12 (Logical Thinking) to .88 (Conscientiousness), with a coefficient of .95 for the Overall Score (computed at the item level, rather than by scale). The reliability

of .12 for Logical Thinking is a substantial concern, indicating almost no significant correlations across the items. In contrast, most extant tests of aptitudes have much higher internal consistency reliabilities. No indications of test-retest reliability were reported.

Validity. The only data that could conceivably be considered as validity information were mean comparisons between respondents identified as in a "managerial position" and those in a "non-managerial position"–presumably a concurrent validity approach to validation. The differences reported between these groups, although several were significantly different from zero, were extremely small (e.g., the difference between the groups on the Overall Score was 2.16 points, corresponding to a Cohen's $d = .23$, barely above the threshold for what Cohen [1988] considered a small effect). That result, along with the fact that gender differences in the Overall Score were of a similar magnitude (2.02 points, $d = .21$), suggests that the instrument is problematic from a validity perspective. Also, given that several scales showed no significant differences between manager and nonmanager groups, and given the small effect size differences on the remaining scales, there is a clear lack of demonstrated validity for the instrument. No intercorrelations among the scales were provided, nor were there any construct or other criterion-related validity data (e.g., correlations with job performance) provided in the manual. It is not clear what theoretical or pragmatic justification there is for aggregating scales of diverse content (e.g., personality, attitudes, and aptitude) to arrive at an Overall Score.

COMMENTARY. Given the lack of traditional standardization data, reliability information beyond internal consistency statistics, and demonstrable validity information, it is not clear what valid use can be made of this instrument. The small differences between managerial and nonmanagerial groups and the differences between gender groups of similar magnitude, give reasons for concern about the adequacy of the instrument. The narrative report is extensive and descriptive, but there is no indication of the validity of the statements made to the respondent or to the manager engaged in pre-employment screening of respondents.

The manual is mostly made up of frequency distributions for the norming sample on each scale and autoscaled bar graphs with two or three bars separately indicating means for gender, educational, managerial, and manager-aspiration groups. No indications of standard errors of the differences between groups are provided, and little material is included to aid interpretation of the data, except for comments about sample sizes and statistical significance of *t*-tests. No effect size data are presented for the differences between groups.

SUMMARY. The SMAPAP appears to be a rationally derived self-report measure that is intended to provide feedback to respondents with store manager aspirations, and pre-screening information to managers about the suitability of employees for managerial positions. The lack of job analysis data, suitable standardization data, construct validity data (e.g., correlations with extant measures), validity data in terms of correlations with criteria, or any other information to aid interpretation suggests that this measure is not suitable for providing informative feedback to the respondent and is not suitable for pre-employment testing without extensive local efforts regarding job analysis, standardization, validation, bias analysis, and utility analysis.

REVIEWER'S REFERENCE

Cohen, J. (1988). *Statistical power analysis for the behavioral sciences.* Hillsdale, NJ: Erlbaum.

Review of the Store Manager Aptitude Personality & Attitude Profile by MICHAEL J. SCHEEL, Associate Professor, Department of Psychology, University of Nebraska-Lincoln, Lincoln, NE:

DESCRIPTION.

Purpose. The Store Manager Aptitude Personality & Attitude Profile (SMAPAP) is a 127-item self-report instrument designed to screen applicants for employment as store managers. It requires approximately 25 minutes to complete. The stated purpose is "to assess whether a test-taker's preferences and personality traits match those required to work as a store manager" (manual, p. 1).

Scales and scoring. The SMAPAP includes 14 scales and an overall scale score. The scales are Adherence to Rules, Approachability, Communication, Conscientiousness, Cultural Sensitivity, Goal-Orientation, Go-Getting, Innovation, Leading, Logical Thinking, Organizing, Salesmanship, Self-Efficacy, and Staffing. An accompanying test report provides scores for each subscale, a total score, a store manager occupational description, a list of strengths and limitations based on subtest scores, and generic advice in the form of tips to improve store management skills.

Descriptions were not available through the manual of item format or methods by which scores are totaled and scaled. The total score for each scale is converted from raw scores to a scale of 100 with means and standard deviations for each scale based on the standardization sample.

DEVELOPMENT.

Underlying assumptions and theories. The SMAPAP does not appear to use a theory of effective store management aptitudes and personality traits that would serve to ground the test scientifically. Instead, test construction is seemingly guided by common sense assumptions about appropriate personality, attitudes, and aptitudes of good store managers. The test report includes a short description, organized by subscales, of effective store manager qualities. For instance, Approachability is defined as possessing the demeanor to display friendliness and being inviting as opposed to displaying an intimidating posture or being standoffish. Go-Getting means being motivated, focused on the goals of the organization, and having an eye on the finish line. Organizing means juggling organizational tasks and keeping track of details. Staffing means understanding the theory of recruiting and training employees.

Item development. A Likert-type scale (Items 1 through 92; 1 = *completely agree*, 2 = *mostly agree*, 3 = *somewhat agree/disagree*, 4 = *mostly disagree*, and 5 = *completely disagree*) is used to self-report work-related tendencies, personality traits, personal beliefs, and values. Items 93 through 103 ask the respondent to rate the impact (1 = *no impact* to 5 = *major impact*) of characteristics and conditions on the hiring of applicants to a culturally diverse staff. Items 104 and 105 are exercises in reasoning about two hypothetical work scenarios. Items 106 through 111 are true/false items designed to test logical reasoning ability. Items 112 through 117 are hypothetical scenarios about work situations in which the respondent is given choices about how he or she might act. Items 118 through 127 are self-estimates of ability (e.g., memory for faces; memory for names) and personal beliefs/values.

TECHNICAL.

Standardization. The standardization sample consists of 1,250 respondents (50% male; 39% female; 11% unknown). A wide age range is noted with 19% of respondents listed as below 21 years and 24% as older than 41. The sample is described as "uncontrolled." The mean overall score of the standardization sample is 77.19 (*SD* = 10.26) with a minimum score of 39 and maximum of 95 on a 100-point scale. Frequency distributions show a positive skew for all subscales and for the overall scale.

Reliability. Nine of 14 subscales of the SMAPAP achieved a coefficient alpha (internal consistency reliability) of .70, and 4 of the other 5 subscales had alpha coefficients above .60. The overall scale achieved an alpha of .95. The internal consistency of the Logical Thinking scale was an exception to an otherwise positive trend with a problematic alpha of .12. Low internal consistency of the scale may be due to the nature of the items seemingly requiring right or wrong responses to test the reasoning ability of the respondent. Reliability estimates of the SMAPAP measure over time (i.e., test-retest reliability) were not included in the manual.

Validity. Evidence for the validity of the SMAPAP consists solely of the criterion-related type using comparison tests of selected variables. Inexplicably, women scored significantly higher than men ($p < .05$) on 11 of 15 scales including the overall scale. There was no explanation for why women should score higher on store manager traits, aptitudes, and attitudes. A significant trend was found on a number of scales indicating older respondents scored higher than younger respondents. Exceptions include Logical Thinking, Goal Orientation, and Salesmanship. Respondents under 21 scored markedly lower than the other age groups on all scales. The standardization sample was divided into three education groups (i.e., high school or lower; junior college/college/trade school; and associate degree or higher). The junior college/college/trade school group and the associate degree or higher group significantly outscored ($p < .05$) the high school or lower group on all scales except Logical Thinking. In addition, the junior college/college/trade school group scored higher than the associate degree or higher group on all scales except the Logical Thinking scale. This result seems counter to an expectation of higher education being associated with higher scores for an area such as store management. A comparison of respondents in managerial positions ($n = 240$) with those in nonmanagerial positions ($n = 237$) indicated significantly higher scores ($p < .05$) for managerial position respondents on seven scales including the overall scale. A comparison was also made between those who rated aspirations to store manager as "Yes, a great deal" ($n = 300$) and those rating aspirations as "Yes, somewhat" with the more strongly aspiring group significantly outscoring ($p < .001$) the more moderate aspiring group on all scales except for Logical Thinking.

COMMENTARY. The SMAPAP ambitiously attempts to measure 14 different dimensions described as qualities of an effective store manager. The test takes on multiple purposes by measuring, all in a single instrument, aptitudes, attitudes, and personality characteristics of store managers. The SMAPAP demonstrates ability to differentiate between groups defined by gender, age, education, aspiring to store manager, and managerial versus nonmanagerial positions. The result of women scoring significantly higher than men is not explained, and no rationale for this finding is advanced. A second counterintuitive result came from comparisons of education levels achieved, with the junior college/college/trade school group scoring higher than the more highly educated group achieving a college degree. Again, reasons are not posed for why this result might be observed. Thus, the comparisons by gender and by education constitute evidence that the instrument may be measuring something other than the purported constructs.

On the more positive side, criterion-related evidence of validity was represented through findings that individuals in management positions and individuals with higher aspirations to become store managers scored higher than nonmanagers and those with lower aspirations. The overall internal consistency reliability of the test is high (alpha = .95) with all scales in the acceptable range except Logical Thinking.

The consistency over time of the instrument was not assessed. This omission represents a shortcoming because test-retest reliability seems relevant for the constructs being measured. The Logical Thinking scale is problematic because of low internal consistency reliability and failure to differentiate between the groups tested in the standardization sample.

The viability of the constructs being measured is difficult to determine. Little evidence was available supporting the distinctiveness of individual scales. Evidence of discriminant validity could be determined through correlational analyses of the scales and factor analysis to realize the factor structure of the instrument. The items of the SMAPAP also do not appear to be written on the basis of a theoretical structure for an effective store manager. Information is missing about how subjects of the standardization were recruited (a self-selection based on website recruitment), leaving open the possibility of sampling bias. The test also seems vulnerable to response bias. The test is transparent in that a respondent could answer in socially desirable ways in an effort to be hired. Finally, even though the face validity of the measure is strong, future research is needed to determine whether the SMAPAP can accurately predict or select effective store managers.

SUMMARY. The SMAPAP is a multidimensional instrument designed for selection of effective store managers. The item and scale structure seems in line with common sense understandings of the ingredients of successful store managers, but construct evidence of validity is not available to provide support for the construct. The instrument is easily taken and available online for a fee. Results are provided as a profile of scores with interpretation that communicates the strengths and limitations of the respondent along 14 dimensions and an Overall Score. More research is needed to determine more clearly the validity of the measure. Finally, the Logical Thinking scale is problematic, and refinement of the scale or replacement with a more reliable and valid measure seems important.

[158]

Stress Assessment Questionnaire.

Purpose: Designed to "provide an integrated multifactor stress assessment measure for counseling and self-development."
Population: Ages 16-65.
Publication Date: 2010.
Acronym: SAQ.
Scores, 16: Work, Relationship, Parenting, Emotional Symptoms, Behavioral Symptoms, Physical Symptoms, Social Support, Self-Regulation, Problem Solving, Distraction, Health, Procrastination, Perfectionism, Self-Esteem, Depression, Anxiety.
Administration: Group.
Price Data, 2011: $14.95 per assessment.
Time: (10-15) minutes.
Comments: Assessment, scoring, and feedback conducted online.
Author: MySkillsProfile.com.
Publisher: MySkillsProfile.com Limited [England].

Review of the Stress Assessment Questionnaire by JAMES A. ATHANASOU, Adjunct Professor, Faculty of Arts & Social Sciences, University of Technology, Sydney, Australia:

DESCRIPTION. There is no prize for guessing that the Stress Assessment Questionnaire (SAQ) provides a standardized report on the sources and symptoms of stress, the strategies used to cope with stress, the personality strategies linked with stress, and the mental health or stability consequences of stress. The SAQ is designed for guidance and

support; the output provided to the respondent states clearly: "This report is designed to develop your understanding of stress and help you decide whether you should seek professional help." It is one of 16 global online assessments provided by the distributor direct to the public, to organizations, or to psychologists for their clients.

The target population is largely adult (16-65 years), English-speaking, and probably employed. Because it is administered as an online commercial questionnaire, there is also a requirement for reasonable literacy, minimal computer skills, and the capacity to pay for the detailed report.

The SAQ is intended to provide a comprehensive assessment of the stress background and experiences of the individual. It is intended to assist individuals in better understanding the context of their stressful reactions and to indicate whether they should seek professional help.

Respondents rate their reactions to 128 items on a 5-point scale (*hardly ever, seldom, sometimes, often, nearly always*). The items are in the format "I have …" or "When I have …." There is no formal scoring procedure for the administrator or the recipient as the results of this online questionnaire are tabulated automatically.

The results on 16 dimensions are grouped under the four main headings of sources, symptoms, strategies, and stability. The results are reported on 10-point scales categorized as lower (1-3), average (4-7), and higher (8-10). These are actually sten scores, but this technical detail is not advertised to the recipient nor is it necessary information for most laypersons. Although the user's manual provided to the reviewer refers to breaking "the sten range into five categories" (manual, p. 25), the results were presented in three categories.

DEVELOPMENT. The development of the SAQ used a unique bootstrapping procedure in the original (and not statistical) sense of advancing by its own efforts. A draft version of the SAQ was advertised as "a free stress assessment" and piloted on the Internet. There are no details on the initial sample size or the number of revisions, but the development appears to have been iterative.

The underlying theory behind the SAQ is that there are four major domains of stress that encompass 16 traits or facets. The model is represented as two-dimensional and orthogonal, but this may be for the purposes of illustration rather than a theoretical statement. In any event, the four domains listed in the manual (p. 4) did not appear to be consistent with the four labels provided in the results. Moreover, five domains (sources, symptoms, strategies, personality, and stability) are listed in Table 1 of the manual (p. 6); possibly some are amalgamated. Finally, 17 dimensions are indicated in the results, one more than the 16 listed throughout the manual. These inconsistencies warrant some minor clarification.

The construct of stress has biological and behavioral concomitants. Since its recognition by Hans Selye around 1926, stress has been a difficult construct to define with universal agreement. In the SAQ, stress is defined in terms of the psychosocial perception its causes (e.g., dissatisfaction with work) and its outcomes (e.g., emotional symptoms) bring about, but it is noted that these are tempered by the coping strategies used by an individual.

A prototype inventory was produced based on writing items for the 16 scales on an a priori basis. The subsequent descriptions of the scales are comprehensive. They provide characterizations of low and high scorers, typical items for low and high scorers, the key behaviors associated with low, moderate, and high scorers, and a verbal description of the scales with which each dimension has positive or negative correlations. Users will find that the items cover many everyday contexts.

Detailed results of the pilot testing were not provided. The criteria for the selection of items were focused on the reliability of the scales and the factor structure. The initial factor structure was two stress dimensions, which at face value contradicts the four major domains.

TECHNICAL. The normative sample is indicated as 5,000 male and 5,000 female international respondents with a mean age of 34 (SD = 12) who completed the SAQ between 2003 and 2011. This group was selected randomly from a larger sample of more than 25,000 respondents. The final cohort comprised more than 70 occupations, with an over representation of education, health services, and government. The respondents were mainly from the United States, United Kingdom, Australia, and Canada. It is likely that the sample will match the intended population given the process of online development and use of the SAQ.

The findings of reliability may require further evidence. Only alpha coefficients were calculated (n = 10,000), and these ranged from .60 to .94 with a median of .80. The low coefficients are of concern for any important practical decisions. Coefficient alpha is only an evaluation of internal consistency

or homogeneity and is not as useful an indicator of stability as test-retest reliability. The median standard error of measurement for the sten scores was cited as .89 or "about one sten either side of the observed score" (p. 27). Results are shown graphically in terms of confidence intervals in the report provided to test takers.

Some validity evidence is offered in support of the accuracy of the findings. This discussion mainly addresses issues of construct validity and concurrent validity. There is no evidence of the accuracy of predictions resulting from use of test scores as prescribed. The results of a principal components analysis with oblique rotation on a sample of 4,554 complete responses provided a two-factor solution accounting for 60.24% of the total variance. The first factor was described as symptoms of stress and mental health; the second factor was interpreted as coping style. In addition, evidence was offered in the form of correlations between seven SAQ scales and marker variables from the *Diagnostic and Statistical Manual of Mental Disorders* and items in the International Personality Item Pool. The median correlation coefficient between eight SAQ scales and the weighted sum of the incidents from the well known Holmes-Rahe Stress Scale was .25.

COMMENTARY. The overall strength of this assessment is that it provides a consumer-friendly, self-perception evaluation of the sources, symptoms, strategies, and stability associated with stress. It is useful in those contexts where online administration is feasible and acceptable. The readability level is Grade 3–4, according to the Flesch-Kincaid Grade Level Formula. The SAQ is easy to use, and the self-scoring is timesaving for group administration. The substantive feedback that is computer-generated will be quite impressive to laypersons in its detail, although some professional users likely will think that it is reminiscent of boilerplate descriptions.

The SAQ will find greatest application as a precursor to a formal psychological assessment. The scope of the content makes it useful in a range of everyday contexts, especially those related to employment settings. Professional users have ready access to an online user's manual.

The weaknesses of the SAQ relate to technical aspects. The definitions of the domains and their component traits may warrant attention. The internal consistency reliabilities of some scales are far too low for any high stakes assessment. Data on test-retest reliability were not cited, which is considered a major omission. The evidence for validity would be bolstered by a confirmatory factor analysis and further evidence deriving from correlations with other scales. The present scoring is based on a simple Likert methodology rather than more up-to-date item response theory.

SUMMARY. With its broad content coverage, the SAQ has advantages over those stress inventories that are focused only on employment such as the Job Stress Survey (15:132) or the Occupational Stress Inventory-Revised Edition (14:260). It does not make ambitious claims beyond being a self-perception inventory, and as such should find wide application as an initial stress assessment. The claims for reliability and validity require further evidence, especially in light of the measure's reported use by more than 25,000 respondents. As such it is recommended for corporate use but not for individual assessment in clinical settings.

REVIEWER'S REFERENCE

Holmes, T. H., & Rahe, R. H. (1967). The social readjustment rating scale. *Journal of Psychosomatic Research, 11,* 213-218.

Review of the Stress Assessment Questionnaire by JEAN POWELL KIRNAN, Professor of Psychology, The College of New Jersey, Ewing, NJ:

[The reviewer would like to thank Christine L. Bastedo for her contributions to this review. Her hard work and perspectives contributed greatly to the critique.]

DESCRIPTION. The Stress Assessment Questionnaire (SAQ) was designed to provide an integrated multifactor assessment of the respondent's stress by measuring four broad domains: sources and symptoms, coping strategies, personality factors, and mental health. According to the test authors, the SAQ differs from traditional stress assessments that measure only one or two of these domains. The instrument is available online only and suggested for adults, ages 16–64, for both individual self-development and as a tool for professional counselors.

The SAQ's 128 statements are answered on a 5-point Likert scale *hardly ever, seldom, sometimes, often,* and *nearly always.* The instrument's wording, format, and instructions are clear and easy to follow, and it requires fewer than 20 minutes to complete. Items are worded using both positive and negative statements, a good technique for reducing "yea" and "nay" response sets, but by the end of the test, there is a feeling of repetition. Finally, respondents indicate which of 40 traditional life stress events (from the Holmes-Rahe Scale) they have experienced in the past 2 years.

The test manual is fairly comprehensive and presents scale descriptions defining the meaning of low, moderate, and high scores, key behaviors associated with scores, and relationships with other scales. There are 8 items per scale, and scores are reported using the standard ten or "sten" process. In this reviewer's opinion, the reporting lacks consistency, as the test manual presents the sten scores in five levels, but the score report groups them into three levels.

The score report provides an interpretive statement for each of the 16 subscales (Work, Relationship, Parenting, Emotional Symptoms, Behavioral Symptoms, Physical Symptoms, Social Support, Self-Regulation, Problem Solving, Distraction, Health, Procrastination, Perfectionism, Self-Esteem, Depression, and Anxiety), and discusses the respondent's answers relative to average. This report is followed by a summary table of modified "sten" scores with confidence intervals, displaying the respondent's scores graphically for each of the subscales. The graph is somewhat difficult to interpret as the dimensions measured by the scales differ as to whether high, moderate, or low scores are desirable. The final page of the report contains a Stress Symptom Checklist the purpose of which is unclear. This personalized score report is produced immediately online, or it can be emailed, a benefit of the SAQ's online access. Although the test manual consistently refers to 16 subscales, the score report provides information on an additional scale, Stressful Incidents.

DEVELOPMENT. The SAQ was constructed in several phases beginning with the generation of items to represent the 16 scales that cover the four-dimensional model of stress. A prototype questionnaire was developed and made available on the Internet. Based on responses to this free assessment, changes were made, deleting or revising ineffective items. Little detail is provided about the type of item analysis conducted. A factor analysis revealed two factors (generalized measure of one's stress experience including symptoms and mental health; and coping style), but the test authors cite four factors in their concept model (sources and symptoms, personality, coping, and mental health) and the score report shows five factors with sources and symptoms reported separately.

A literature search revealed information on a 2002 edition of an instrument published by Test Agency Limited, also called the Stress Assessment Questionnaire. The similarities between the two instruments are striking, leaving one to assume that the current SAQ was derived from this earlier version. The test manual for the earlier version cites 17 subscales. The additional scale, Stressful Incidents, is the same scale that appears in the current SAQ report, adding to the need for clarification about the SAQ's subscales.

TECHNICAL. The normative sample for the SAQ was obtained over the Internet. Although the test authors cite efforts to eliminate duplicate cases and haphazard response protocols, additional information on the administration is needed. There has been much discussion in both the testing and research communities regarding the use of Internet samples. Administration of a survey or research protocol via the Internet has its own issues, but the development of a normative sample from the Internet expands these concerns. The two dominant issues are the representativeness of the normative group and the quality of survey responses (Paolacci, Chandler, & Ipeirotis, 2010). The test authors should provide information on ethnicity, education, and socioeconomic status, as these variables have been correlated with Internet use and could compromise the representativeness of the sample. Information on participant compensation, recruitment, and the public nature of the Internet site would shed light on concerns regarding the motivational level and honesty of respondents. The normative sample consists of equal numbers of men and women (5,000 each) and was randomly drawn from a larger sample of more than 25,000 respondents who completed the SAQ between 2003 and 2011. Age and occupation distributions suggest a diverse sample for these variables.

Acceptable measures of reliability are reported for the 16 scales using coefficient alpha; values ranged from a low of .60 (Health, Perfectionism) to a high of .94 (Social Support). These internal measures of reliability could be supplemented by a test-retest reliability to demonstrate stability. Several aspects of stress will change over time and it would be informative to know how often the SAQ should be retaken. The test manual provides additional information such as standard errors of measurement and scale intercorrelations that supports the reliability and differentiation of the scales.

Validity evidence supporting the use of SAQ scores is demonstrated through several different methodologies. A factor analysis revealed two factors, noted above, which seems at odds with the theory of four stress domains. Although it is not unusual for a factor analysis to identify different numbers or types of factor, authors should address such discrepancies. Additionally, this analysis was conducted on a subset of the normative sample; the 4,554 respondents who answered all of the items (eliminating individuals without a husband/wife/partner or children).

Two "marker variables" from the DSM-IV-TR (*Diagnostic and Statistical Manual of Mental Disorders*) and two items from the IPIP (International Personality Item Pool) were included in the Emotional Symptoms and Anxiety scales, respectively. Seven relevant SAQ subscales demonstrated expected relationships with these variables. Although this information is offered as evidence of validity, the quality of this evidence is difficult to evaluate without knowing exactly what these items are. Also, there remains a question as to whether the items contributed to the scale score for Emotional Symptoms and Anxiety—a situation that would artificially inflate the correlation between scale score and item.

The SAQ subscales correlate appropriately with the Holmes-Rahe Scale that measures exposure to critical life events associated with stress. The SAQ also has been analyzed for its relationship with variables such as age and gender.

COMMENTARY. According to the test authors, the SAQ is different from other measures of stress in that it attempts to integrate four domains of sources and symptoms, coping strategies, personality factors, and mental health. However, these four domains are not supported by statistical analysis. Strengths include a comprehensive test manual, ease of administration, and score reporting, as well as thoughtful development of the instrument and strong reliability evidence. Weaknesses include the source of the normative sample, clarification of validity studies, and potential issues associated with any self-diagnostic test taken without professional guidance. If the purpose of the SAQ is to identify individuals in need of professional counseling, a useful exercise would be a comparison of SAQ scores to independently derived counselor evaluations of client stress.

The test manual indicates that the SAQ's main function is "to help develop the client's understanding of stress and whether they should seek professional help" (p. 5). The manual adds, "The SAQ report is intended to help clarify things for the client but it cannot in any way replace a formal assessment by a qualified mental health professional." This cautionary note is important as there are concerns regarding the use of the Internet in the measurement of psychological disorders. Naglieri et al. (2004) raised issues such as assessment by unqualified persons and lack of adequate interpretation of test results. Inaccurate scores may lead some respondents to avoid seeking help when they need it or wrongly identify others for counseling. A professional would know circumstances under which someone took the test and could, thus, gauge the validity and reliability of the results.

The SAQ does not consider stress levels relating to the absence of a partner or children. Two items inquire whether the respondent has a husband/wife or partner and children; a "no" response disables future items on these topics. The instrument also makes the assumption that the only relationship that can cause stress is one with a partner, ignoring other relationships. Curiously, the "disable" feature that applies to items regarding spousal/partner and parental relationships is not applied to worklife, apparently assuming all respondents are employed.

SUMMARY. The SAQ is a well-developed instrument that measures distinct aspects of stress including sources and symptoms, coping strategies, personality factors, and mental health. Although it may prove useful as a self-diagnostic tool, this reviewer is hesitant to promote the measurement of psychological disorders without the guidance of a trained professional. A counselor might find the SAQ useful as a screening tool to identify factors associated with stress and to provide a basis for a more in-depth conversation with a client. In any event, the utility of the SAQ should be affirmed by the professional counseling community.

REVIEWER'S REFERENCES

Cameron, A. (2002). *Stress Assessment Questionnaire (SAQ): Professional manual*. Retrieved from: The Test Agency Limited website: http://www.stressdiagnosis.com/SAQ20%20Manual%20Version%201.0.pdf
Naglieri, J. A., Drasgow, F., Schmit, M., Handler, L., Prifitera, A., Margolis, A., & Velasquez, R. (2004). Psychological testing on the Internet: New problems, old issues. *American Psychologist, 59,* 150–162.
Paolacci, G., Chandler, J., & Ipeirotis, P. G. (2010). Running experiments on Amazon Mechanical Turk. *Judgment and Decision Making, 5,* 411–419.

[159]

Structured Interview of Reported Symptoms, 2nd Edition.

Purpose: Designed to "evaluate feigning of psychiatric symptoms" and "the manner in which it is likely to occur."
Population: Ages 18 and over.
Publication Dates: 1986-2010.
Acronym: SIRS-2.
Scores, 14: Primary Scales (Rare Symptoms, Symptom Combinations, Improbable or Absurd Symptoms, Blatant Symptoms, Subtle Symptoms, Selectivity of Symptoms, Severity of Symptoms, Reported vs. Observed Symptoms), Classification Scale (Rare Symptoms-Total), Supplementary Scales (Direct Appraisal of Honesty, Defensive Symptoms, Improbable Failure, Overly Specified Symptoms, Inconsistency of Symptoms); plus 2 indexes (Modified Total Index, Supplementary Scale Index).
Administration: Individual.
Price Data, 2010: $285 per complete kit including 25 interview booklets, 2 security templates, and manual (2010, 130 pages); $220 per 25 interview booklets; $10 per set of 2 security templates; $80 per manual.
Foreign Language Edition: Interview booklet available in Spanish.
Time: (30-45) minutes.
Authors: Richard Rogers (interview booklet and manual), Kenneth W. Sewell (manual), and Nathan D. Gillard (manual).
Publisher: Psychological Assessment Resources.
Cross References: For reviews by David N. Dixon and Ronald J. Ganellen of an earlier edition, see 12:375.

Review of the Structured Interview of Reported Symptoms, 2nd Edition by JEFFREY A. JENKINS, Professor of Justice Studies, Roger Williams University, Bristol, RI:

DESCRIPTION. The second edition of the Structured Interview of Reported Symptoms (SIRS-2) seeks to improve upon its predecessor for the measurement of malingering or feigned response styles. The primary changes in the second edition involve expansion of the professional manual, which is an integral component of SIRS-2 for the evaluation of malingering, as well as changes in classification categories, scales, and indexes. In particular, the SIRS-2 professional manual incorporates research published since the introduction of the SIRS involving feigned mental disorders, as well as further explanation and updating of scoring, interpretation, and classification. New descriptive data on the use of the instrument with reference groups also allows for norm-referenced interpretation.

Like the SIRS, SIRS-2 seeks to help examiners determine whether a respondent is likely to be malingering or feigning a mental illness or cognitive deficit. As is typical of such instruments, the SIRS-2 seeks to accomplish this goal by examining whether a respondent reports the existence of very rare psychological symptoms or whether a respondent reports the existence of symptoms at a much higher rate than do nonfeigning patients.

The SIRS-2 consists of an interview booklet and the professional manual. The items in the interview booklet are divided between "detailed inquiries" (32 items) and "general inquiries" (108 items). The "detailed inquiries" are those that relate to plausible symptoms and comprise four scales: Selectivity of Symptoms, Severity of Symptoms, Blatant Symptoms, and Subtle Symptoms. The "general inquiries" relate to symptoms that occur infrequently in clinical populations and comprise four primary scales (Rare Symptoms, Symptom Combinations, Improbable or Absurd Symptoms, Reported vs. Observed Symptoms) and four supplementary scales (Direct Appraisal of Honesty, Defensive Symptoms, Improbable Failure, Overly Specified Symptoms). In addition, the "detailed inquiries" are repeated, and responses are recorded as separate items that are listed in the booklet as "repeated inquiries." The purpose of "repeated inquiries" is to establish disparities in responses; inconsistencies are noted and form the Inconsistency of Symptoms scale.

SIRS-2 items are simple questions that are read aloud to examinees; most items require yes/no responses. Space on the interview booklet is also provided for nonresponses and response to a follow-up question relating to severity.

The professional manual for the SIRS-2 contains an overview of response styles and the measurement of feigning, as well as specific instructions on the use of the interview booklet and administration and scoring of the SIRS-2. A separate chapter on interpretation of responses and classification presents a Decision Model with step-by-step instructions on its use. Integration of results with other methods and measures (such as the MMPI-2, PAI, and M-FAST) is discussed, and interpretive case studies are presented. A Spanish version of the interview booklet is also available.

DEVELOPMENT. The professional manual notes that SIRS was originally developed as a measure of classification of psychological feigning that was conceptually based. That is, SIRS stemmed from a growing literature on empirical methods and case studies of malingering and related response styles to identify strategies for detection. Fifteen strategies were identified and were organized as scales for which a pool of items was created. Each item was drafted to employ a single detection strategy, and the content of items was devised to reflect a range of psychopathology.

SIRS-2 incorporates four major changes to the instrument. These include a Rare Symptoms-Total scale that is designed to differentiate between feigned symptoms and genuine but atypical ones in order to reduce the number of false positives and increase the number of true negatives. A

Modified Total Index, composed of the sum of Rare Symptoms, Symptom Combinations, Improbable or Absurd Symptoms, and Blatant Symptoms, was created to produce an index that best places examinees in one of four classifications: Feigning, Indeterminate-Evaluate, Indeterminate-General, and Genuine Responding. A Supplementary Scale Index (the sum of Direct Appraisal of Honesty, Defensive Symptoms, Improbable Failure, and Overly Specified Symptoms) was added for the purpose of identifying feigners who use disengagement to produce "too-good-to-be-true" response profiles. The Improbable Failure scale was added as a sum of individual items (word opposites and word rhymes) scored on a scale of 1 to 5 to provide a supplementary scale to distinguish genuine responders from feigners.

TECHNICAL. The technical characteristics of the original SIRS and SIRS-2, particularly evidence of validity, are discussed throughout the professional manual, but an extensive discussion of updated reliability and validity pertaining to the SIRS-2 is presented in Chapter 6. The reliability for the SIRS-2 is reported in terms of internal consistency, interrater reliability, and test-retest reliability.

Internal consistency estimates (coefficent alphas) were derived from the original validation study for SIRS and numerous subsequent studies reported in the test manual. For the primary scales, weighted averages ranged from .74 to .91, and from .62 to .89 for the supplementary scales. Generally speaking, such estimates are acceptable for a psychological measure. However, as the test authors point out, the SIRS scales are indirect measures of response style that examine patterns of responses. As such, it is unclear whether internal consistency estimates reflect the reliability of measurement of the underlying construct: malingering.

The test manual also examines interrater reliability, perhaps a more important way of assessing reliability for a measure of malingering because it is based on comparisons of evaluators using the SIRS to distinguish feigned from genuine responses. Based on the original SIRS validation sample and several subsequent studies, interrater reliability estimates ranged from .89 to 1.00 for both the primary and supplementary scales. These are certainly high and reflect consistent measurement using SIRS.

Test-retest reliability estimates were also reported. Using data from two studies with a 5–13-day retest interval resulted in primary scale coefficients of .24 to .91. The test authors note that low test-retest reliabilities for three scales were due to circumscribed ranges.

The professional manual provides an extensive discussion of evidence of validity for the SIRS-2. Several studies provided evidence to support construct validity through the examination of the factor structure underlying the SIRS. These studies demonstrated the utility of SIRS for classifying examinees in terms of two underlying dimensions: spurious presentations and plausible presentations. In addition, the discriminant and convergent validity of the SIRS was examined by comparisons with the MMPI-2, the PAI, the SIMS, and the M-FAST. In sum, the results of these studies showed correlations in the expected direction to support the SIRS' ability to differentiate genuine from feigning responders.

COMMENTARY. The SIRS-2 offers a welcome update to an already useful instrument. Although the learning curve for administration and interpretation is somewhat steep, the professional manual is a valuable source of guidance for users of the SIRS-2. Indeed, with its extensive discussion of the conceptual framework and summary of relevant research, the test manual is a useful resource for those who wish to learn more about the theory and practice of identifying malingering of psychological symptoms. With mastery of the interview booklet, an examiner can readily obtain a classification for suspected feigners. The research-based development of the instrument and the ongoing examination of its strong technical characteristics recommend the SIRS-2 to users with a need for response style measurement.

SUMMARY. The SIRS-2 is a measure of malingering or feigning response styles relating to psychological symptoms. The development of the SIRS-2 reflects extensive study of the response styles, and demonstrates a sound and professional approach to psychological measurement. For evaluations of patient-reported psychological symptoms, the SIRS-2 may be used confidently to help evaluate malingering or feigned response styles.

Review of the Structured Interview of Reported Symptoms, 2nd Edition by GEOFFREY L. THORPE, Professor of Psychology, University of Maine, Orono, ME:

DESCRIPTION. The Structured Interview of Reported Symptoms, 2nd Edition (SIRS-2) is used to assess patterns of feigning in interviewees with apparent mental disorders. It consists of an interview booklet and a professional manual, both of which represent significant revisions of the original SIRS materials (Rogers, 1986, 1992; Rogers, Bagby, & Dickens, 1992). The interviewer presents 172 items from the interview booklet, including 32 repeated items and others that compare an interviewee's reported and observed behavior within the test setting, both variations intended as consistency checks. Scores on eight primary scales are drawn from an examinee's responses to 69 of the 140 unique items: Rare Symptoms, Symptom Combinations (unlikely pairings of symptoms), Improbable or Absurd Symptoms, Blatant Symptoms (presenting many significant symptoms, each as a major concern), Subtle Symptoms (presenting many common symptoms, each as a major concern), Selectivity of Symptoms (endorsing an unusually large number of symptoms), Severity of Symptoms (describing many symptoms as unmanageable), and Reported vs. Observed Symptoms (consistently reporting more symptoms than are, in fact, observed by the examiner).

Examples of the five supplementary scales are Overly Specified Symptoms (with items similar to: "Do you see strange visions only on Tuesdays?"), Direct Appraisal of Honesty (with items similar to: "Are you trying to fake having a serious mental illness?"), and Improbable Failure, consisting of cognitive tasks: four questions, each with five components, asking either for antonyms or for words rhyming with those presented.

About 20% of the items are either divided questions or rule-out questions. In a divided question, the examiner asks a threshold question and presents the other component only if the interviewee responds affirmatively. The rationale is to avoid presenting the most bizarre material to all examinees. For example, a question similar to those on the Improbable or Absurd Symptoms scale would be presented as follows: "Do you have any unusual beliefs about flowers?" If the response is "No," the examiner moves to the next question; if the response is "Yes," the examiner asks: "Do you believe they have their own government?" A question similar to the SIRS-2 rule-out items would be: "Do the faces of your friends change suddenly and look distorted and grotesque?" An affirmative reply would prompt a rule-out question such as: "Is this only when you are delirious because of a high fever?" Most items are coded by the interviewer on a 0, 1, or 2 scale to reflect increasing levels of endorsement, with "X" used to denote "No Answer." Colored indicators in the interview booklet facilitate the calculation of scale scores.

To classify feigning, the test authors set the cutoff scores high enough to minimize false positives. Feigning is likely when one or more of the primary scale scores is in the "definite feigning" range, or when three or more primary scale scores fall in the "probable feigning" range. These general rules are supplemented by a Decision Model that takes advantage of additional indexes, specific combinations of either primary or supplementary scale scores.

The interview booklet provides straightforward and convenient instructions for recording raw scores, summing these to form scale scores, transferring the primary scale scores to a profile on the front, and checking boxes as appropriate in a Decision Model flow chart. The profile immediately indicates the categorization of primary scale scores as genuine, indeterminate, probable feigning, and definite feigning.

DEVELOPMENT. Examination of case studies, research on deception, and studies of simulators identified 22 dissimulation strategies, 15 of which were applicable to feigned mental disorders and suitable for development as scales for the original SIRS. An initial pool of 330 items was generated and reduced to 152 items prior to pilot testing. The structured interview format was shown to have advantages over a self-report protocol. Informal pilot testing with 35 forensic inpatients was followed by rationally based refinements and the development of specific scales. Eight experts allocated items to strategies, with an overall concordance rate of 88%. Item-scale correlations below .20 in the data from seven samples from community, clinical, and correctional settings led to the elimination of 12 items; the final version of the scale comprises 140 unique items. Acceptable values for internal consistency and interrater reliability were observed on all scales. The construct validity of the SIRS was established by a series of studies with known-groups and simulation designs.

The SIRS-2 authors note the success of the original SIRS as a preeminent measure of feigning and comment on the enormous growth of the pertinent professional literature since 1992. Because of significant modifications in the scales and the resulting classifications, the SIRS-2 is a "substantive revision" (professional manual, p. 1) of the SIRS. The manual presents an update of the literature on malingering and an expanded conceptual framework for approaching the clinical assessment of feigning. It supplements the original

validation data with information from 2,298 SIRS respondents in college, community, correctional, and forensic settings.

The SIRS-2 preserves the structure and standardization of the SIRS but adds a Rare Symptoms Total (RS-Total), a Modified Total Index (MT Index), a Supplementary Scale Index (SS Index), and the revived supplementary scale Improbable Failure. Part of the rationale for these additions was the need to distinguish severe but genuine psychopathology (as in some cases of posttraumatic stress disorder with dissociative features) from feigned presentations. For example, on the 15 items selected for the RS-Total scale, false positives had markedly lower scores than true positives. The MT Index is a composite of four primary scales that (among other things) minimize false positives. The SS Index assesses a response style of disengagement in which examinees consistently disavow common problems or difficulties.

TECHNICAL. The standard data set for the SIRS-2 comprises test protocols from the following settings: clinical-general ($n = 236$), clinical-forensic ($n = 1,232$), correctional ($n = 613$), and community/college ($n = 217$). A subset of 167 respondents from all settings except clinical-forensic were administered the test with instructions to simulate feigning. The test authors note that the sociodemographic information from the four standard composite groups broadly reflects the age, gender, racial, and ethnic distributions observed in similar studies with such samples. Specifically, in the clinical-forensic group "the large majority of the study was men of European American ethnicity" (professional manual, p. 60). A majority of this group (77%) were male and European American (76%).

Means and standard deviations of scale, classification, and index scores are tabulated for each of the four standard composite groups responding with standard instructions, the 167 with instructions to simulate feigning, and a sample of 36 identified feigners, so test users can calculate standard scores from the appropriate groups if they wish. Normally the scale scores are classified and interpreted directly from the work areas, Profile, and Decision Model in the interview booklet.

The weighted average alpha values for the internal consistency of six of the eight primary scales ranged from .74 to .91 across eight studies from 1992 to 2008. (The Selectivity of Symptoms and Severity of Symptoms scales draw from items across several scales, so the unidimensionality assumptions required for alpha were not satisfied.) Eight studies produced extremely high interrater reliability coefficients, with the weighted averages ranging from .95 to 1.00. Standard errors of measurement for individual scores were very low and within the limits of 95% confidence intervals. In a 2009 study, overall values for test-retest reliability (5 to 7 days) were high (SIRS-2 total score, $r = .82$), but there was marked variability within the subscales. The test authors point out that the circumstances of individuals who feign mental disorders are likely to change abruptly within brief periods of time.

The convergent validity of the SIRS-2 primary scales with the Minnesota Multiphasic Personality Inventory-2 validity scales is satisfactory, with most correlation coefficients exceeding .50. The average correlation between SIRS-2 primary scale scores and the total score on the Structured Inventory of Malingered Symptomatology is .73. Studies of the SIRS comparing simulators to clinical respondents have produced large or very large values for effect size, with a mean value for Cohen's d of 1.74 in the original standardization sample. The same mean value was obtained when the scores of small samples of probable malingerers were compared with those of clinical respondents.

The RS-Total scale improved the identification of true positives when a cutoff score was established with the development sample and tested with the cross-validation sample. Three score ranges of the MT Index were found to be effective in classifying respondents as feigners or in one of two levels of the "indeterminate" category, and a fourth (lowest) range of scores was highly effective in identifying genuine respondents when used in conjunction with the SS Index.

COMMENTARY. The original SIRS has been cited as "the gold standard of measures of feigning" (Green & Rosenfeld, 2011, p. 95). However, those authors report on a meta-analysis of 26 SIRS studies that have collectively shown higher sensitivity but lower specificity rates than those described by Rogers et al. (1992). Studies of respondents simulating feigning have produced more compelling results than those focused on suspected malingerers.

In developing the SIRS-2 from its predecessor, the test authors were able to draw from 16 years of research on feigning in general and on the SIRS in particular. The first chapter of the test manual presents a detailed and valuable review of the pertinent concepts, clarifying and distinguishing malingering,

factitious disorders, feigning, dissimulation, overreporting, secondary gain, symptom magnification, and disengagement. The large SIRS-2 development sample has expanded the SIRS standardization data base significantly. However, only 36 known malingerers were included (Rubenzer, 2010). The manual documents the strong psychometric basis of the test and its scales in 32 pages and 23 tables within two chapters.

The SIRS-2 interview booklet presents the same items as the SIRS, but makes use of many items that previously were not always scored or that did not contribute to scale scores. The addition of new composite scales and a refined Decision Model is intended to improve classification accuracy, especially in reducing false positives. Test users will applaud the test authors' efforts to validate the SIRS-2 with complex clinical presentations. An examinee may report a history of physical and sexual abuse in early childhood, with clinical records documenting serious head injuries. Distinguishing a genuine from a feigned pattern of dissociative, posttraumatic, and neurological symptoms in such a case is a challenging task for the clinician.

Replicating the SIRS-2 decision rules with new samples of respondents would be a difficult and complex endeavor. For example, three (or more) of the eight primary scale scores falling in the probable feigning range is one component of the classification of feigning. But drawing any three from a list of eight scales creates 56 distinct patterns, surely too many to evaluate individually.

This may be a trivial point, but the absence of an index in the manual sometimes makes it frustratingly difficult to retrieve specific information.

SUMMARY. The SIRS-2 represents a significant revision of the SIRS, itself commonly referred to as the "gold standard" in the evaluation of feigning in mental health and forensic settings. A richly detailed professional manual presents a valuable review of pertinent concepts and thoroughly documents the development of new composite scales and decision rules from 16 years of research and from a new development sample of more than 2,000 respondents from various settings. The interview booklet conveniently provides all the information necessary to administer and score the test and to interpret its results.

REVIEWER'S REFERENCES

Green, D., & Rosenfeld, B. (2011). Evaluating the gold standard: A review and meta-analysis of the Structured Interview of Reported Symptoms. *Psychological Assessment, 23,* 95-107.

Rogers, R. (1986, 1992). *SIRS: Structured Interview of Reported Symptoms: Interview booklet.* Lutz, FL: Psychological Assessment Resources, Inc.

Rogers, R., Bagby, R. M., & Dickens, S. E. (1992). *SIRS: Structured Interview of Reported Symptoms: Professional manual.* Odessa, FL: Psychological Assessment Resources, Inc.

Rubenzer, S. (2010). Review of the Structured Inventory of Reported Symptoms–2 (SIRS-2). *Open Access Journal of Forensic Psychology, 2,* 273-286.

[160]
Supplementary Spelling Assessments.

Purpose: Designed to "augment the assessments of spelling teachers make on the basis of how, and how well, children spell in their writing."

Population: Years 4-8.

Publication Dates: 2007–2010.

Acronym: SSpA.

Administration: Group.

Price Data, 2013: A$50 per starter set including teacher manual (2010, 47 pages), administration and scoring guide (2010, 35 pages), plus one of each test booklet and diagnostic assessment; $10.95 per 10 test booklets (specify Year 4, 5, 6, 7, or 8; $27.50 per 10 Diagnostic Assessments (specify 1 or 2); $25.95 per teacher manual; $19.95 per administration and scoring guide.

Author: Cedric Croft.

Publisher: New Zealand Council for Educational Research [New Zealand].

a) PART 1: ACHIEVEMENT AND PROGRESS.

Time: (35) minutes.

Population: Years 4-8.

1) *Test 1.*

Scores, 4: Dictated Words, Beginning Sounds, Recognising Errors in Words, Recognising Errors in Sentences.

2) *Test 2.*

Scores, 5: Dictated Words, Dictated Paragraph, Recognising Errors in Words, Recognising Errors in Sentences, Recognising Correct Words.

3) *Test 3.*

Scores, 5: Dictated Words, Dictated Paragraph, Recognising Errors in Words, Recognising Errors in Sentences, Recognising Correct Words.

4) *Test 4.*

Scores, 4: Dictated Words, Correcting Errors in Paragraph, Recognising and Classifying Errors in Sentences, Correcting Errors in Words.

5) *Test 5.*

Scores, 4: Dictated Words, Correcting Errors in Paragraph, Recognising and Classifying Errors in Sentences, Correcting Errors in Words.

b) PART 2: DIAGNOSTIC ASSESSMENTS.

Time: Untimed.

Population: Years 5-6.

Scores, 6: Beginning Sounds/Initial Consonants, Beginning Sounds/Prefixes, Ending Sounds/Suffixes, Short and Long Vowel Sounds, Silent Letters, Shortened Words/Contractions.

Review of the Supplementary Spelling Assessments by KATHLEEN D. ALLEN, Associate Professor of Education and Professional Psychology, and MAUREEN SIERA, Associate Professor of Education and Professional Psychology, Saint Martin's University, Lacey, WA:

[Editor's Note: This review was prepared prior to receipt of materials for the 2010 update for this test and so reflects information in the 2007 edition.]

DESCRIPTION. The Supplemental Spelling Assessments (SSpA) are designed to augment teacher writing-based assessments of student spelling by providing standardized tests for additional information about achievement and developmental progress. These tests are for New Zealand school Years 4, 5, and 6 (ages 8–10).

There are two parts to the SSpA. Part 1: Achievement and Progress is composed of three separate tests. Test 1 is for Year 4 and has four subtests. Test 2 is for Year 5 and has five subtests. Test 3 is for Year 6 and has five subtests. The six subtests from all the tests are: (a) Dictated Words–the teacher dictates the word to be spelled; (b) Beginning Sounds (Test 1)–students provide initial letters based on a partly spelled word with an illustration prompt; (c) Dictated Paragraph (Tests 2 and 3)–"cloze style" response, the teacher reads the passage and students write the correct contraction; (d) Recognizing Errors in Words–students identify the misspelled word in each row; (e) Recognizing Errors in Sentences–students identify the word in a sentence that is either spelled or used incorrectly; and (f) Recognizing Correct Words (Tests 2 and 3)–students identify correctly spelled words.

Part 2: Diagnostic Assessments has six subtests for struggling spellers, Year 5 (age 9) and older. Diagnostic 1 includes Beginning Sounds/Initial Consonants, Beginning Sounds/Prefixes, and Ending Sounds/Suffixes. Diagnostic 2 includes Vowel Sounds, Silent Letters, and Contractions.

The Administration and Scoring Guide provides explicit directions. Tests are untimed and are administered to groups or individuals. A portion of the test is teacher-directed and students work independently on the remaining sections. Scoring is "0" incorrect or "1" correct. Raw scores are recorded on the students' answer sheets. The last subtest in each test provides formative information and is not included in the total test score. The raw score is converted into both a scale score and stanine using tables in the teacher manual.

The components of the SSpA are the teacher manual, the Administration and Scoring Guide, Part 1: Achievement and Progress with three tests (one test for each year), and Part 2: Diagnostic Assessments with two tests (Diagnostic 1 and Diagnostic 2). Test booklets are included for students to write their answers.

DEVELOPMENT.

Theoretical framework. The Supplementary Spelling Assessments were designed to provide a focused and detailed evaluation of spelling proficiency and developmental spelling levels. The test author notes that during the writing process, poor spellers often only use words that are easily spelled, which limits their writing vocabulary. Therefore, to assess spelling using writing samples alone may not produce an accurate picture of a student's ability. By using a preselected list of words, the teacher can determine the pattern of errors and developmental spelling level in relation to peers. This formative assessment helps the teacher plan instruction. Additional tests diagnose specific issues for students who are below expected developmental spelling levels.

Task development. For the Part 1 assessment, as part of the test development process 180 words were selected by the test author for each test from a list of words used most frequently by primary school writers. This list was from a national survey of New Zealand primary school writing (Croft, 1998). These words were selected to measure developmental spelling level and spelling achievement in comparison to peers. The test author conducted pilot studies and trial tests to develop the format and structure of Part 1. During this trial phase, teacher comments and student performance on the tests were analyzed. Afterward, the word list was refined, one section was replaced, and a decision was made to exclude one subtest in each year's test from the total score.

TECHNICAL.

Standardization. The norm sample for standardization consisted of 3,096 students in New Zealand Years 4–7. A stratified random sample was utilized with the criteria of school size, school type, and community type. Each school was asked to identify the class "which best reflected the full range of achievement in literacy at that year level in school" (teacher manual, p. 41). Some schools provided data for all of the classes, and a repeated subsampling technique was used to guard against overrepresentation of any particular subgroup. Although there is a comparison of scores according to gender, there is no evidence of language, ethnic, or culture group comparisons.

To provide comparable results at different times during the school year, stanines from the standardization data were calculated, and a regression analysis was done of mean scale scores through Years 4–7. There was a very good fit (R^2 = .99) to growth across Year levels, and satisfactory fit (R^2 = .81) for standard deviation estimates at each year level.

Reliability. Evidence of internal consistency reliability is provided in the teacher manual. Scores from the three Part 1 tests administered during the standardization trial were used to determine the reliability coefficient. The reliability coefficient for each Part 1 test is calculated at .96, which indicates very good internal consistency. However, calculations appear to be based on a single score for the entire Part 1 test, which includes Dictated Words, Beginning Sounds, and error analysis. Therefore, the reliability associated with each component is not provided. No reliability evidence is offered for the final subtest of Part 1 as this score is not included in the total score. The test author states that this subtest measures a different part of spelling ability than the other subtests, so it is not an acceptable part of the scale score. However, it still provides valuable information for teachers. There is also no reliability evidence provided for Part 2, which is meant to be an individualized diagnosis, and not part of the SSpA scale.

Validity. Content validity evidence is exhibited by evaluating the words selected for the assessment. At least 90% of the words selected are from studies of most frequently used words by New Zealand primary students (Croft, 1998). It is stated that because the test is designed to supplement assessment within the context of writing, the inclusion of words that students will often use while writing indicates content validity. This premise seems reasonable, but other validity evidence should also be gathered. For example, concurrent validity could be shown by independent evaluations of a student's developmental spelling level at the time of the assessment. Differential validity for diverse groups also is not reported. Although not described in the validity section of the manual, evidence of construct validity is provided in the SSpA scale descriptors. Spelling knowledge and skills at scale score levels are described in the language of the developmental spelling continuum (teacher manual, p. 11) with explicit examples of words mastered and typical errors.

COMMENTARY. One of the major strengths of the SSpA is that it attempts to measure a range of student spelling skills that goes beyond the words students use in their writing. The SSpA assesses frequently used words and places the results on a template with detailed scale descriptors to provide a broad report of student spelling achievement and developmental progress. Results are expressed with a single score. However, in order for a teacher to identify specific skills needed for effective instruction, a more thorough analysis of the results would have to be completed.

The construct for the SSpA includes using the results to place students on a research-based spelling developmental stage continuum. According to the cited stage theory developed by Gentry (1981), almost all of the students would be in the "transitional" stage of spelling development. This stage is not delineated enough for explicit spelling pattern feedback. To provide this feedback, the research on spelling developmental stages could be expanded to include more descriptive definitions of the spelling stages (Henderson & Beers, 1980; Henderson & Templeton, 1986). In addition, adding research on spelling demands (Gentry & Gillet, 1993) could inform instructional strategies. These could be correlated with the SSpA subtests to create a profile of students' strengths and needs in historical, semantic, phonological, and visual demands.

To make the results of the SSpA more generalizable, the degree to which the norm sample reflects the diversity of the students tested should be verified. Separate analyses of students across ethnic and cultural groups would add to the value of the assessment. There is no mention of ELL students, and this would be an important subgroup to analyze. Also, there are only three decile groups of schools (high, medium, and low) represented in the standardization trial. A more specific and inclusive analysis of the decile groups would add to the usefulness of the norms and the SSpA.

According to the manual, the words in the test are from a list of most frequently used words by New Zealand primary students, but the test author does not provide a convincing case for the selection of these particular words. Inclusion of a detailed item analysis and corroborating research confirming the use of high frequency words would add to the construct validity of this assessment.

SUMMARY. The Supplementary Spelling Assessments are easy to administer and score in the classroom setting. To increase the effectiveness of the SSpA, the norm sample needs to clearly describe ethnic, cultural, and language groups, and the instrument should be validated for these populations. [Editor's Note: The publisher advises that separate analyses for such groups are not part of achievement testing in New Zealand.] Research on the construct could also be updated and expanded. Additional efforts could be made that would make the SSpA generalizable to other populations. Consequential validity would be enhanced by making the assessment more useable for teaching spelling strategies. Bear, Invernizzi, Templeton, and Johnston (2007) have produced a program that combines assessment of developmental spelling level, spelling feature analysis, and spelling instruction. Adding the feature analysis, clear guidelines on how the results can inform effective instruction, and a list of suggested teacher resources would be welcome additions to the SSpA.

REVIEWERS' REFERENCES

Bear, D. R., Invernizzi, M., Templeton, S., & Johnston, F. (2007). *Words their way: Word study for phonics, vocabulary, and spelling instruction* (4th ed.). Boston, MA: Pearson.
Croft, C. (1998). *Spell-Write: An aid to writing and spelling–revised.* Wellington, NZ: New Zealand Council for Educational Research.
Gentry, J. R. (1981). Learning to spell developmentally. *The Reading Teacher, 34,* 378-381.
Gentry, J. R., & Gillet, J. W. (1993). *Teaching kids to spell.* Portsmouth, NH: Heinemann.
Henderson, E. H., & Beers, J. W. (1980). *Developmental and cognitive aspects of learning to spell: A reflection of word knowledge.* Delaware: International Reading Association.
Henderson, E. H., & Templeton, S. (1986). A developmental perspective of formal spelling instruction through alphabet, pattern and meaning. *The Elementary School Journal, 86,* 305-316.

Review of the Supplementary Spelling Assessments by JEFFREY K. SMITH, Professor of Education, University of Otago College of Education, Dunedin, New Zealand:

[Editor's Note: This reviewer had access to the 2010 edition of this assessment and supporting documents.]

DESCRIPTION. The Supplementary Spelling Assessments (SSpA) are a set of measures designed to augment the information about student spelling ability that teachers would gather from examination of the students' writing–hence, the use of the word "supplementary" in the title of the measure. The tests are published by the New Zealand Council for Educational Research, and are intended for use in Years 4–8 of the New Zealand educational system, which is equivalent to Grades 3–7 in the United States.

There are two components to the SSpA: Part 1 is an overall measure of ability in spelling and Part 2 is a diagnostic assessment. Part 1 requires students to spell dictated words, provide beginning letters of words, identify misspelled words in sentences, identify spelling errors, and so on. There are five separate tests for Part 1, which equate roughly to Years 4–8, but teachers have some flexibility in deciding which test to administer to which students, depending upon ability.

Part 2, which is intended for Years 5 through 8, assesses the students' ability to spell word beginnings and endings, identify silent letters, recognize and write words with short and long vowel sounds, and so on. It is intended to help teachers with instruction in spelling. There are two tests for Part 2, each of which has three sections. Teachers can administer individual sections of Part 2 to students, depending on their instruction program and students' needs.

The tests in both parts are administered by classroom teachers in a group or individual setting. There are no strict time limits for the test, but the teacher manual suggests that Part 1 tests will take roughly 35 minutes to administer. Scoring is completed by teachers and then raw scores are related to scale scores using the Rasch model of test analysis, and then to norms via standardization samples. There is a teacher manual and an administration and scoring guide for the assessment.

DEVELOPMENT. SSpA is based on research into word use and spelling and published as a classroom resource for students: Spell-Write: An Aid to Writing and Spelling–Revised (Croft, 1998), and a Teacher Manual (Croft, 2002) was also developed by the author of the SSpA. The development of the subscales and virtually all of the words chosen for spelling come from this research, which is not described in detail in the teacher manual. This is unfortunate for those who might want to examine the issues in the assessment outside New Zealand, but who are not necessarily interested in the classroom resource. The words, and their placement, were based on a national survey of spelling ability in New Zealand, and the technical evidence provided indicates that the levels of difficulty were appropriate for use in New Zealand.

TECHNICAL. With the exception of the fact that the development of the measures is not discussed in the actual test materials, and the lack of much in the way of validity evidence, the technical materials for the SSpA are very good.

Standardization. Standardization of the SSpA was conducted in two separate studies, one in 2006 for Tests 1–3, and a second in 2009 for Tests 4–5.

The 2006 study involved more than 3,000 students from a stratified random sample of schools. The 2009 study included more than 1,000 students, again from a stratified random sample of schools. Although these students are from New Zealand, the resulting norms should provide a good rule of thumb for other English-speaking countries. The nature of the standardization studies is explained in detail, and they appear to have been rigorously conducted.

Reliability. The SSpA uses the Rasch model as the basic tool for psychometric analysis of results. Extensive material on these results is available, and accompanying tables and graphs detailing performance levels are presented. Users of the SSpA can link the performance of students to individual items on the SSpA using the information provided. Teachers score students' performance and then look up the scale scores and norming information through tables in the teacher manual. Although teachers may not be initially familiar with such materials, the documentation presented is clear and useful. Classical reliability coefficients are presented as well, and they are quite high, as would be expected for a measure assessing a clear latent construct with a large number of items. Reliabilities for the five tests in Part 1 range from .96 to .97. The Part 2 diagnostic measures, designed for use as adjuncts to classroom spelling programs, do not have accompanying information about reliability.

Validity. There is very little available on validity studies associated with the SSpA. An argument that supports content validity stems from the fact that 90% of the words were selected from existing lists of words that are commonly misspelled. The paucity of validity evidence is not unusual for school-based testing programs, even ones from large testing companies. Basically, the argument here appears to be that because the tests form a strong scale across the years given (which they certainly do), educators should examine the tests themselves and look to see how they compare to their instructional goals and practices.

COMMENTARY. Although spelling is not a high priority area in many educational programs, it is often a component of a writing program, and various approaches to writing instruction exist. The SSpA is clearly tied to the Spell-Write program by the same author, which is used in a number of schools in New Zealand. The SSpA appears to be a well-conceptualized and professionally executed set of measures, with strong standardization materials and an excellent application of the strengths of the Rasch approach to measurement. If it had additional validity evidence to accompany the standardization and Rasch information, it would be easy to give the SSpA a ringing endorsement. Unfortunately, it falls slightly short of that mark. However, it should be noted that lack of validity evidence does not mean lack of validity. Educators looking for a strong measure of spelling ability for students between the ages of 8 and 12 should definitely consider the SSpA. It should be noted that a few of the words in the SSpA have a clear New Zealand flavor to them.

SUMMARY. The SSpA presents a set of measures for spelling assessment of students from roughly ages 8 to 12. It has an exemplary set of standardization materials and applications for interpretation using Rasch-based test analysis. It is easy to administer and score and can be used by classroom teachers. It does not present strong validity evidence, but gives every appearance of being a solid set of measures of overall spelling ability and a provider of useful diagnostic information.

REVIEWER'S REFERENCES

Croft, C. (1998). *Spell-Write: An aid to writing and spelling–revised.* Wellington, New Zealand: New Zealand Council for Educational Research.
Croft, C. (2003). Teachers manual: Spell-Write—Revised. Wellington, NZ: New Zealand Council for Educational Research.

[161]
Surgical Weight Loss Psychological Screening.

Purpose: Designed to identify "suitable candidate[s] for Bariatric Surgery."
Population: Potential candidates for bariatric surgery.
Publication Date: 2011.
Acronym: SWLPS.
Scores, 34: Overall Results, Compliance [Sense of Control Over Health, Adherence History, Self-Discipline, Procrastination], Self-Motivation [Reward Dependence, Proactive Attitude, Self-Efficacy], Emotional Strength [Resilience, Anger Control, Tolerance for Frustration, Emotional Eating], Coping Skills [Problem Solving, Information Seeking, Negotiation, Support Seeking, Positive Cognitive Restructuring, Emotional Regulation, Distraction, Rumination, Avoidance, Helplessness, Opposition, Social Withdrawal], Current Mental Health Issues, Suicide Concern, Mental Disorder History, Drug History, Substance Use History, Impression Management.
Administration: Individual.
Price Data: Available from publisher.
Time: (45) minutes.
Comments: Self-administered online assessment. The test publisher advises that the test manual is being updated to include more information about methodology and theoretical background used in the development of the test. The test publisher also advises that this information is available to clients, as are benchmarks for relevant industries and racial/ethnic group comparison data. However, this information was not provided to Buros or the reviewers.
Author: PsychTests AIM, Inc.
Publisher: PsychTests AIM, Inc. [Canada].

Review of the Surgical Weight Loss Psychological Screening by STEPHEN J. FREEMAN, Professor, Department of Psychology, Counseling & Special Education, Texas A&M University-Commerce, Commerce, TX:

DESCRIPTION AND DEVELOPMENT. The Surgical Weight Loss Psychological Screening (SWLPS) is an individually administered online screening measure of various psychological and behavioral factors that can influence the outcome of bariatric surgery. The purpose of the SWLPS is to identify "suitable candidate[s] for bariatric surgery" (manual, p. 1). Demographic information regarding target population is not included in the test manual; however, sample age ranges are reported as below 16 to 40+. The instrument contains 177 questions and uses a Likert-type response format that takes approximately 45 minutes to complete. Online instructions are clear and easy to follow. The computer-generated report produces 34 scores on 10 scales, 23 subscales, and an overall score: Compliance (Sense of Control Over Health, Adherence History, Self-Discipline, Procrastination); Self-Motivation (Reward Dependence, Proactive Attitude, Self-Efficacy); Emotional Strength (Resilience, Anger Control, Tolerance for Frustration, Emotional Eating); Coping Skills (Problem Solving, Information Seeking, Negotiation, Support Seeking, Positive Cognitive Restructuring, Emotional Regulation, Distraction, Rumination, Avoidance, Helplessness, Opposition, Social Withdrawal); Current Mental Health Issues (Depression Diagnosis, Anxiety Diagnosis, Binge Eating Diagnosis); Suicide Concern (Suicide Ideation, Suicidal Planning, Suicidal Attempt); Mental Disorder History (Depression, Anxiety, Bipolar, OCD, Other Mental Health Disorder); Drug History (Marijuana, Magic Mushrooms, LSD, Ecstasy, Hashish, Cocaine, Speed or Ice, Heroin, PCP, Other Substance); Substance Use History (Tobacco, Alcohol, Painkillers). The last section listed in the manual under "report" is Advice; however, the computer-generated report also includes an Impression Management scale, which indexes validity of the overall screening, and Strengths & Limitations. The Details section includes a brief interpretation of the scale and subscale scores. The test manual contains no information on scoring, how scores are determined, or how they are interpreted. The test manual also contains no information about test development. Reliability was reported using coefficient alpha, and validity evidence was presented by reporting the statistical significance of group comparisons. The Psychometric Report section also contains approximately 120 pages of graphs displaying the group comparisons.

TECHNICAL. The sample used to compute means, standard deviations, and frequencies for the SWLPS consisted of 2,017 participants, 1,228 (60.9%) female, 530 (26.3%) male, 259 (12.8%) unknown. The sample is described as "uncontrolled," in that participants chose to complete the measure and opted to contribute their data to the validation study. No other information regarding ethnicity or other factors was provided.

Normative data are provided separately by age group. Age distribution was reported as below 16 to 40+. The sample was subdivided into 7 age bands: below 16 (n = 269); 17–20 (n = 366); 21–24 (n = 184); 25–29 (n = 264); 30–39 (n = 286); 40+ (n = 335); Unknown (n = 313).

Reliability. The alpha coefficients for most scales were good (.71–.95) with an alpha coefficient for overall score of .98. No stability (test-retest) or other reliability measures were reported.

Validity. Validity was reported as statistically significant mean differences (*t*-tests and ANOVA) between scale and subscale scores and comparison variables: gender (n = 530 in each of two groups), body weight (n = 70 in each of two groups), age (n = 1,504 total across six groups), watching diet (n = 289 in each of three groups), frequency of exercise (n = 1,619 total across four groups), and socioeconomic status (n = 1,110 total). The test authors acknowledge sample size does affect findings of significance and significance does not connote practical impact. Additionally, large differences in sample sizes were acknowledged, and the test authors state that "a smaller, random sample was selected from the large groups whenever possible, in order to level out the numbers and conduct the analyses effectively" (manual, p. 3). No further elucidation was included.

COMMENTARY. The SWLPS is one of the first instruments designed for use as a screening measure offering a broad assessment across psychological and behavioral indicators associated with morbid obesity. It is an online self-report screening instrument intended to fill the need for clinically useful information related to the suitability of individuals for bariatric surgery. The broad basis for the measure appears consistent with published reviews examining psychological and behavioral assessment practices in bariatric surgery (Greenberg, Perna, Kaplan, & Sullivan, 2005; Pull, 2010); however, development of the SWLPS was not addressed. This oversight is a serious and possible fatal flaw owing to the fact that validity evidence is a requirement for any test and that the 1999 *Standards* define validity as "the degree to which evidence and theory (development) support the interpretation of test scores" (AERA, APA, & NCME, 1999; p. 9). Minimally, information regarding test content and item and scale development should be included in the test manual. The standardization sample raises some major concerns such as the disparity between genders (61% female & 26% male) and the 250 (13%) participants whose gender is listed as unknown. The normative data expressed by age group raises similar concerns, specifically the 313 (15%) participants for whom age was unknown. The population for which a test is appropriate should be clearly delimited, and this is a problem for the SWLPS.

Overall, the instrument evidences good reliability; however, evidence of the test's stability is not included and should be addressed. Little solid evidence to support validity is offered. As noted by the test authors, statistical significance often does not relate to practical differences, leaving the validity analysis of questionable value. Lacking information on instrument development rules out evidence based on test content as well as internal structure. Evidence based on comparison of the SWLPS scales with other measurement devices with well-established validity (e.g., Eating Inventory, State-Trait Anger Expression Inventory-2, Millon Behavioral Medicine Diagnostic) would yield greater support for the instrument's validity.

SUMMARY. The SWLPS is an online, individually administered screening instrument with very good face validity. However, significant criticisms can be made regarding the demographic information on the normative sample as well as the sample size. The 1999 *Standards* (AERA, APA, & NCME, 1999) define the concept of unitary validity as "the degree to which evidence and theory support the interpretation of test scores" (p. 9). The lack of information on test development rules out the availability of theoretical support, and reliance on group comparisons and statistical significance fails to provide adequate support. This lack of validity evidence makes supporting the use of the SWLPS difficult; however, given the significant rise in the rate of obesity in the United States it could be argued that there exists a strong need for instrumentation assessing the suitability of individuals for bariatric surgery. Further research and refinement of the SWLPS is strongly recommended.

REVIEWER'S REFERENCES

American Educational Research Association, American Psychological Association, & National Council on Measurement in Education. (1999). *Standards for educational and psychological testing.* Washington, DC: American Educational Research Association.

Greenberg, I., Perna, F., Kaplan, M., & Sullivan M. A. (2005). Behavioral and psychological factors in the assessment and treatment of obesity surgery patients. *Obesity Research, 13* (2), 244–249.

Pull, C. B. (2010). Current psychological assessment practices in obesity surgery programs: What to assess and why. *Current Opinions in Psychiatry, 23,* 30–36.

Review of the Surgical Weight Loss Psychological Screening by MICHAEL G. KAVAN, Professor of Family Medicine and Professor of Psychiatry, Associate Dean for Student Affairs, Creighton University School of Medicine, Omaha, NE:

DESCRIPTION. The Surgical Weight Loss Psychological Screening (SWLPS) is a 177-item web-based, self-report instrument designed to assess "whether a person would be a suitable candidate for Bariatric Surgery" (professional manual, p. 1). More specifically, the SWLPS is intended to "assess personality factors, coping mechanisms, and mental as well as physical health issues to ensure appropriate pre- and post-operative care for Bariatric Surgery" (online Assessment Solutions manual, p. 57, http://corporate.psychtests.com/pdf/catalog_arch_b.pdf). The SWLPS includes an overall score, nine scales along with 47 subscales (Compliance [Sense of Control over Health, Adherence History, Self-Discipline, Procrastination], Self-Motivation [Reward Dependence, Proactive Attitude, Self-Efficacy], Emotional Strength [Resilience, Anger Control, Tolerance for Frustration, Emotional Eating], Coping Skills [Problem Solving, Information Seeking, Negotiation, Support Seeking, Positive Cognitive Restructuring, Emotional Regulation, Distraction, Rumination, Avoidance, Helplessness, Opposition, Social Withdrawal], Current Mental Health Issues [Depression Diagnosis, Anxiety Diagnosis, Binge Eating Disorder], Suicide Concern [Suicide Ideation, Suicidal Planning, Suicidal Attempt], Mental Disorder History [Depression, Anxiety, Bipolar, OCD, Other Mental Health Disorder], Drug History [Marijuana, Magic Mushrooms, LSD, Ecstasy, Hashish, Cocaine, Speed or Ice, Heroin,

PCP, Other Substance], Substance Use History [Tobacco, Alcohol, Painkillers]), and an Impression Management scale. In all, 34 scores are generated, as not all subscales produce scores.

The SWLPS is accessed online at the test developer's website. The website provides no information as to who may purchase the exam for administration. Once purchased, the examinee logs in and begins to answer 177 mostly Likert-type questions. The SWLPS takes approximately 45 minutes to complete, and examinees must complete the entire assessment in one sitting. Once completed, a report is then saved and made available to the examinee. The website notes that the manager who assigned the SWLPS to the examinee has immediate access to all results excluding answers to individual questions. The report includes a summary of overall results, an introduction statement covering general psychological issues related to bariatric surgery, graphs of all scales and subscale results including overall results and an impression management score, detailed narrative results for all scales and subscales, strengths and limitations, and advice. The advice section seems to be general advice that is not specifically based on the results of the individual examinee. Scores appear to range from 0 to 100. No alternative language versions of the SWLPS are available from the publisher.

DEVELOPMENT. The PsychTests AIM, Inc. website (http://corporate.psychtests.com/tests/science_validity) reports that tests are developed by a team of experienced developers led by Ilona Jerabek, PhD. It is also reported that professional tests offered are "rigorously developed and based on a thorough statistical analysis" and that each test is "well researched and designed according to the APA (American Psychological Association) standards for educational and psychological testing." No specific information is provided on the website or within the test manual on the development of the SWLPS.

TECHNICAL. Normative data consisting of means, standard deviations, and frequency distributions for the overall score, nine scales, and 29 of the subscales are provided within the test manual (*n* range from 1,289 to 2,017). Limited information is available on the normative sample. The test manual notes that the sample was uncontrolled and that participants "self-selected" to complete the instrument on one of two websites. Of the 2,017 persons taking the SWLPS, 60.9% were women, 26.3% were men, and 12.8% were unknown. The age ranges of those taking the instrument were fairly evenly divided among several age groups between "below 16" and "40+" years of age. A considerable number of participants ($n =$ 269) were younger than 16 years old, and there was no age information on 313 participants. Internal consistencies (coefficient alpha) are provided for the overall score, 7 of the 9 scales (Mental Disorder History and Drug History are not included), and 29 of the subscales. Coefficient alpha for the Overall score is .98. Internal consistencies for the scales range from .47 (Substance Use History) to .95 (Coping Skills), whereas those for the subscales range from .60 (Distraction) to .90 (Depression Diagnosis). No test-retest data are provided within the test manual.

The test manual includes what it describes as a "validity analysis" (t-tests for dichotomous variables and ANOVAs for continuous variables) in which significant differences were noted between certain comparison groups on the various subscales. Comparison variables included gender, obese versus healthy weight, age, watching diet, frequency of exercise, and socioeconomic status. These are followed by means and standard deviations for each of these comparisons. No other validity data are provided within the test manual or on the publisher's website. The author (I. Jerabek, personal communication, June 5, 2012) suggests that additional analyses are currently being conducted using variables such as history of bariatric surgery, but these data are not yet available.

COMMENTARY. The SWLPS was developed to assess the suitability of a person for bariatric surgery. Promotional materials also suggest that it is meant to "ensure appropriate pre and post-operative care" for this surgery as well. Approximately two-thirds of the adult population in the United States is overweight (Body Mass Index: BMI $\geq$ 25). Of these, 35.7% are considered obese (BMI $\geq$ 30) and 6.3 % are considered extremely obese (BMI $\geq$ 40; Flegal, Carroll, Kit, & Ogden, 2012). Although bariatric surgery is typically reserved for those patients with BMIs greater than 35 and possessing significant comorbidity, patients with BMIs as low as 32 may be appropriate for bariatric surgery when specific selection criteria are met (e.g., patients with the most severe category of diabetes; Yermilov, McGory, Shekelle, Ko, & Maggard, 2009). Therefore, the availability of a reliable and valid measure to determine the best candidates for successful bariatric surgery along

with strategies to enhance their recovery from surgery would be useful.

Although the SWLPS attempts to fill these needs, it fails on many accounts. First, no normative data are presented within the test manual on patients being considered for bariatric surgery. Second, although the SWLPS does appear to be a reliable measure, limited validity data are provided by the test authors and include "validity analysis" conducted between a select number of comparison variables. No data are provided within the test manual or on the website regarding exploratory or confirmatory factor analyses, convergent or discriminant evidence, or test-criterion evidence (i.e., concurrent and predictive evidence). Third, no evidence is presented within the test manual on whether using the SWLPS enhances a user's ability to predict the "suitability" of a patient for bariatric surgery or whether using the SWLPS enhances patient preparation or recovery from surgery. Therefore, further research is necessary to support the use of the SWLPS in the clinical setting.

SUMMARY. The SWLPS is a 177-item, web-based, self-report instrument designed to assess a person's suitability for bariatric surgery. Specifically, it is intended to assess personality factors, coping mechanisms, mental health status, and physical health issues in order to ensure appropriate pre- and postoperative care for bariatric surgery. Although internal consistency reliability data are good, the SWLPS manual provides no normative data on patients being considered for bariatric surgery. Nor are validity data available demonstrating the use of the SWLPS in patients being considered for or recovering from bariatric surgery. Therefore, the SWLPS cannot be recommended for use at this time until further validation studies are conducted with this population. Instead, instruments such as the Minnesota Multiphasic Personality Inventory-2 (MMPI-2) should be considered more appropriate and only when used as part of a full clinical assessment that includes a larger battery of tests and consideration of medical selection criteria and risk factors (cf. Tsushima, Bridenstine, & Balfour, 2004).

REVIEWER'S REFERENCES

Flegal, K. M., Carroll, M. D., Kit, B. K., & Ogden, C. L. (2012). Prevalence of obesity and trends in the distribution of body mass index among US adults, 1999–2010. *Journal of the American Medical Association, 307*, 491–497.

Tsushima, W. T., Bridenstine, M. P., & Balfour, J. F. (2004). MMPI-2 scores in the outcome prediction of gastric bypass surgery. *Obesity Surgery, 14*, 528–532.

Yermilov, I., McGory, M. L., Shekelle, P. W., Ko, C. Y., & Maggard, M. A. (2009). Appropriateness criteria for bariatric surgery: Beyond the NIH guidelines. *Obesity, 17*, 1521–1527.

[162]
Symbol Imagery Test.

Purpose: "Designed to measure a student's symbol imagery for letters in both random and orthographically regular combinations."
Population: Ages 6-0 to 17-11.
Publication Date: 2010.
Acronym: SI Test.
Scores: Total score only.
Administration: Individual.
Price Data, 2011: $149.95 per complete kit, including letters and words cards, 25 examiner's record booklets, and examiner's manual (128 pages); $99.95 per examiner's manual.
Time: (10-20) minutes.
Author: Nanci Bell.
Publisher: Gander Publishing.

Review of the Symbol Imagery Test by C. DALE CARPENTER, Interim Dean and Professor of Special Education, College of Education and Allied Professions, Western Carolina University, Cullowhee, NC:

DESCRIPTION. The Symbol Imagery Test (SI Test) is a standardized, individually administered, norm-referenced test intended to measure a child's "symbol imagery for letters" (manual, p. 27). The SI Test is normed on children ages 6-0 through 17-11 and yields standard scores, age equivalents, and percentile ranks. Five sections with 50 total items comprise the test, which can be administered in 10 to 20 minutes.

Section A includes 10 items in which examinees are presented with cards showing two to seven random letters, then asked to orally recall the letters. Section B uses the same format for 12 nonwords. Section C is the only section in which students hear, rather than see, nonwords and are asked to spell them aloud. Section D presents 8 one-syllable nonwords on cards and asks questions about the letters in the words such as, "What is the fourth letter you saw?" Section E continues the format of Section D, but uses 3 multisyllable nonwords for the 8 items like those in Section D. A total raw score is used to calculate derived scores for the SI Test. Section standard scores are not available.

DEVELOPMENT. The examiner's manual devotes fully a quarter of the approximately 100 pages of narrative to explain the rationale, theory, and research leading to the development of the Symbol Imagery Test. Potential users should carefully review this section because the SI Test is a new test rather than a revision or modification or slightly different version of another instrument. The test author utilizes an extensive history of clinical work at the Lindamood-Bell Learning Centers with oral and written literacy combined with empirical studies to establish the need for the current instrument. The link between a student's ability to create visual mental representations of alphabetical symbols in response to oral- and written-language stimuli and success in reading and spelling is documented in the research presented.

The test manual contains the rationale for each section of the test and the item format; however, the particular choice of items such as why some nonword letter combinations were used and not others is not provided. The test manual presents data on item properties as a group rather than individually with information about the range of item difficulty, discrimination indexes, and data showing that items were not differentially biased for major subgroups based on gender and race. The manual does not describe a field-testing process used in the development of the SI Test.

TECHNICAL.
Standardization. The SI Test was normed on 1,058 students between 2000 and 2008, representing national demographic characteristics in 12 states of the United States of America. There were 90 or more students at each of the age levels with the exception of a low of 76 students aged 13 years. The test manual does not indicate how students were selected to be included in the norm sample.

Reliability. Internal consistency (coefficient alpha) and temporal stability estimates are reported in the test manual. Internal reliability coefficients for the entire norm sample (.94) and for gender and ethnic subgroups are all above .90, and the coefficients for those identified as gifted and talented and those with learning disabilities were .89 and .88, respectively. Two-week test-retest reliability coefficients were all above .80 for 125 children tested.

Validity. As a new test, the SI Test has a burden to establish evidence of content validity, which the test authors address in sections describing the theory behind the test and the rationale for each of the sections that make up the test. The research narrative appears to support the structure used. Both conventional and differential item analyses are provided as further evidence of content validity. Differential item function analyses were used to determine whether the SI Test items differentially discriminated among important subgroups (gender, race, and ethnicity), and the data indicated that they did not.

Concurrent criterion-related evidence of validity accrues from a study of the correlation of SI Test scores with scores on seven other measures taken from the Gray Oral Reading Tests–Fourth Edition, Slosson Oral Reading Test–Revised, Wide Range Achievement Test–Third Edition, and Woodcock Reading Mastery Tests–Revised: Normative Update. Correlations are very good, above .68 for all but one. In fact, the SI Test scores for 717 students in the study correlated well with orthographic and literacy measures relying on visual imagery and for those with strong phonetic components.

Construct validity evidence is demonstrated through correlation of the SI Test with phonological measures: Lindamood Auditory Conceptualization Test–Third Edition and the Comprehensive Test of Phonological Processing. Correlation coefficients ranged from .49 to .72. Construct validity is also supported by the evidence that higher scores are associated with higher chronological age, demonstrating that the construct assessed is developmental.

COMMENTARY. As a new instrument measuring a skill not assessed by another known instrument, validity is critical for the Symbol Imagery Test, and the test author includes substantial information in the test manual to describe the theory and rationale for the SI Test. In addition, the author presents information showing that the constructs measured are diagnostically useful for reading and spelling. Assessment results have been used to develop instructional interventions that have been empirically successful and are documented in a chapter titled "Results of Explicit Instruction in Symbol Imagery." Similar research published in peer-reviewed journals will help to establish the validity of the instrument. The process of identifying and writing items and field-testing the instrument are not explained in the test manual, which represents a significant omission.

The format of the SI Test is appropriate and convenient, and the psychometric properties are generally satisfactory. Two improvements should be considered in possible future revisions. Section C requires the examiner to pronounce nonwords and the examinee to orally spell the word he or she heard. A recording of the nonwords that can be presented to examinees would assure consistency so that examinees hear a standard pronunciation. A less desirable alternative would be online access to a digital recording of the nonword stimuli for examiners so they can train themselves in the standard pronunciation.

A second improvement would be to include interrater reliability estimates. Whenever the responses are oral and do not result in a permanent product, interrater reliability coefficients would inform consumers about the consistency of scoring procedures and results.

SUMMARY. The Symbol Imagery Test provides consumers with an easily administered norm-referenced instrument that measures imagery for letters seen and heard. These skills are assessed by subtests of other instruments, but the SI Test presents the ability to get one score representing the skill of symbol imagery critical to reading and spelling. Psychometric properties are generally satisfactory. The format and resulting scores are convenient and potentially useful for instructional diagnosis and research.

Review of the Symbol Imagery Test by THOMAS McKNIGHT, Psychologist, Private Practice, Spokane, WA:

DESCRIPTION. According to the test author, symbol imagery is "the ability to create mental imagery for the sounds and letters within words" (manual, p. 5) and "a silent partner in reading and spelling" (manual, p. ix). She notes the ability is "not easily accessed by everyone" (manual, p. ix) because of individual differences in symbol imagery ability. The Symbol Imagery Test is purported to measure processing ability in "both the phonology and the orthography of words" (manual, p. 1), reportedly an "essential factor related to competency in literacy" (manual, p. ix). From reading the test manual, it appears the Symbol Imagery Test is another product of the Lindamood-Bell Learning Centers. The test author indicates the test manual "represents a marriage between instructional practice, theory, and research" (p. ix), but, on review, this is not entirely clear.

DEVELOPMENT. The test contains 50 items divided into five functions (seeing and recalling unconnected letters, seeing and recalling letters in nonwords, hearing and spelling nonwords, seeing and manipulating one-syllable nonwords, and seeing and manipulating multisyllable nonwords). It is unclear how the items were chosen. The age range for which the test is recommended is broad (6 years 0 months through 17 years 11 months); thus, the limited number of items is a serious concern. The normative study occurred between 2000 and 2008 and included 1,058 people in 12 states. Stratification of the sample included age, race, geographic region, and gender, but several of the race/age cells were limited to one case.

TECHNICAL ASPECTS. Test results are reported in standard scores, age equivalents, and percentile ranks. T scores, z scores, and stanines can be determined as well, using a table in the appendix. Internal consistency is adequate (coefficient alpha ranged from .85 to .89 for each age group), but the *SEM* is rather large for the limited number of items in the test. Test-retest reliability is excellent, based on a sample size of 125 from a single school system in California. Coefficients ranged from .90 to .95 over approximately a 2-week interval during the 2001–2002 school year. There is no report of interrater reliability, possibly unneeded with the apparent simplicity of scoring but technically necessary if the instrument is to be taken seriously. Concurrent validity evidence is adequate but would be more impressive if more than one subtest (Word Attack) from the Woodcock had been included with the other measures (Gray Oral Reading Tests–Fourth Edition: Reading Rate, Reading Accuracy, Reading Fluency, Reading Comprehension; Slosson Oral Reading Test–Revised; Wide Range Achievement Test–Third Edition: Spelling). There was a report of research comparing the instrument with various measures, including some measures of "auditory conceptualization and phonological processing" (manual, p. 79), using 717 people. Correlation coefficients for the Symbol Imagery Test and the Comprehensive Test of Phonological Processing were modest (.54–.64) and somewhat higher with the Lindamood Auditory Conceptualization Test. The test manual includes additional validity information. In a regression study the test author found that the Symbol Imagery Test accounted for 47%–58% of the variance in spelling and various reading skills and that the addition of scores on the Lindamood Auditory Conceptualization Test–Third Edition and the Comprehensive Test of Phonological Processing essentially added nothing to the equation.

COMMENTARY AND SUMMARY. Those who purchase this instrument may also be interested in supporting teaching material, specifically the "Seeing Stars" program, available from the same publisher. Experimental/control outcome data suggest the amount of instruction, with this material, has some impact on degree of improvement in reading-related areas but this finding is somewhat inconsistent across different outcome measures. Instructions are clear, and ease of administration is obvious for those with experience in individual testing.

In time, the Symbol Imagery Test might add significantly to the diagnosis of reading and related problems, but there is limited supporting data in the manual. Predictive validity studies using this instrument at the beginning of first grade and scores on reading, spelling, and language measures in third grade are needed. If additional independent research supports its diagnostic utility, wide-spread use in preschools and language instruction programs can be expected. Overall, the test would benefit from additional research, using large sample sizes and complete tests rather than selected subtests.

[163]

Systematic Analysis of Language Transcripts 2010 Bilingual SE Version.

Purpose: Designed to assess the expressive language proficiency of native Spanish-speaking bilingual (Spanish/English) children by providing a series of analyses comparing their English and Spanish language samples to samples from age- or grade-matched bilingual peers.

Population: Preschool-Grade 3 native Spanish-speaking bilingual children.

Publication Dates: 2009–2010.

Acronym: SALT 2010 Bilingual SE version.

Scores, 2: Subordination Index, Narrative Scoring Scheme.

Administration: Individual.

Price Data, 2010: $99 per SALT Bilingual SE Version including software and printed SALT manual (2009, 115 pages).

Foreign Language and Other Special Editions: English, Research, and Instructional editions available.

Time: Unlimited.

Comments: Computer software for Windows® 2000, XP, Vista, 7.

Author: Jon F. Miller and Aquiles Iglesias.

Publisher: SALT Software, LLC.

Review of the Systematic Analysis of Language Transcripts 2010 Bilingual SE Version by JEANETTE W. FARMER, Professor of Special Education, Marshall University Graduate College, South Charleston, WV:

DESCRIPTION. Students who are bilingual, with Spanish being their native language, and English as their second language, are the targeted group for this assessment. The Systematic Analysis of Language Transcripts 2010 Bilingual SE Version (SALT) examines oral language proficiency in both languages. The assessment is completed on an individual basis with students in kindergarten through Grade 3. A model narrative following pages of the picture book *Frog, Where are You?* by

Mercer Mayer is provided either directly by the examiner, or via an audio recording. After hearing the narrative, the examinee must retell the story, first in Spanish, and then in English. It is estimated that the administration for each retell will take 20 minutes. A 3–5-minute audio file is produced and transcribed. The transcription time is approximately 1 hour per file.

The picture book is provided with the assessment kit, along with the test manual and software that provides training in transcription rules. The SALT software also prints out a standard set of analyses, generated in 5 minutes. Examiners may refer to the lengthy list of codes in the test manual, or can save time by using SALT transcription services at a cost of about $25 per transcript. Web sites are available as well as consulting services with licensed speech-language pathologists who can help clinicians, instructors and researchers.

DEVELOPMENT. Databases consisted of narratives of more than 2,000 students from public schools in urban Texas, border Texas, and urban California. Although not included in the test manual, the test author indicates that "age, grade and gender data is [*sic*] available for all children, and mother's education is available for many" (manual, p. 2). It is reported that students were in regular education, and represented the diverse socioeconomic levels of the regions in the samples. Ages of participants in the norm group ranged from 5–0 to 9–9 years. Analyses of the norm databases were completed by the collaborative work of several speech-language pathologists.

TECHNICAL. Critical components of the test manual are the story script in Spanish and English (Appendix A), and a summary of SALT transcription conventions (Appendix B). With regard to the former, a script is presented for each page of the picture book–one version in Spanish and the other version in English. For the latter, 14 categories of codes are organized. The transcriber is to become fluent in the given codes in order to quantify the expressive language efforts of the students.

COMMENTARY. Although case studies are provided for transcribers to practice scoring passages, it appears that considerable training is required for one to develop expertise with this assessment. The use of a picture book is an appealing and creative way of eliciting responses from children in a relaxed setting.

SUMMARY. The SALT was designed to assess the possible oral language disorders among a select group of students–bilingual Spanish/English, with Spanish being the native language. Because normative data regarding Spanish or English proficiency have not been used before with this population, earlier assessments have misdiagnosed the students who may need specialized instruction in Language Arts in either or both languages. The administration is intended for a narrow grade range of students (K-3). Administration is relatively easy, with students first hearing a narrative while following a pictures-only book. The student repeats the story first in his or her native Spanish, and then in the English language. The second retelling may occur several weeks after the first.

Audio recordings are made, and then detailed notes are made by transcribers who translate the students' narrative. Errors are coded by an extensive system. Data are analyzed. Support for administrators is given via case studies in the test manual, coding keys, and administration guidelines, including tips for establishing rapport with the students. Additionally, a website is available and a training compact disk is part of the original package. Analysis of the language samples yields detailed information that could be interpreted by trained speech-language therapists. With the growing population of bilingual students, the need for quality assessments is imperative. It is noteworthy that other norm-referenced instruments for this special population are nonexistent at this time.

Review of the Systematic Analysis of Language Transcripts 2010 Bilingual SE Version by TIFFANY L. HUTCHINS, Assistant Professor, and MICHAEL S. CANNIZZARO, Associate Professor, Department of Communication Sciences and Disorders, University of Vermont, Burlington, VT:

DESCRIPTION. The Systematic Analysis of Language Transcripts 2010 Bilingual SE (SALT-SE) is offered as an assessment tool to aid in the identification of language disorders among native Spanish-speaking bilingual (Spanish-English) children from kindergarten through third grade. It also might be used to identify areas of relative strength and weakness in bilingual children's productive language. The SALT-SE is unique for these purposes because it provides a normative database of Spanish-English bilinguals as means for estimating a child's proficiency in each language using a narrative retelling procedure. Materials included in the SALT-SE include the Windows-based software program with installation guide, an audio CD with

Spanish and English narrative elicitation scripts, the examiner's manual, and a wordless picture book (described below). Supplemental and support materials (e.g., descriptions of the different language sample analysis comparison databases, case study examples, and extensive training materials with both text and video support) also can be accessed from the SALT-SE website at http://www.SALTSoftware.com.

The SALT-SE makes use of the wordless picture book *Frog, Where are You?* (Mayer, 1969) to elicit narratives using a procedure that is best described as semistructured. Two options for elicitation are available. The first option is recommended only for examiners who are fluent in the language in which the story is told. This option involves telling the story "loosely following the story script" (manual, p. 6) provided in the appendix. Users are directed to "tell (not read) the story to the child" (manual, p. 7) and although memorization is not required, the examiner should become "familiar enough [with the story] to tell a similar story" (manual, p. 7). The test authors note that this method is preferred because it mirrors the method used to collect the samples for the Bilingual Story Retell reference database. The second option, which is recommended when the examiner is not "sufficiently fluent" (manual, p. 7) in the language in which the story is told, is to play an audio recording of the story to a child (available on the accompanying DVD or online).

Regardless of the elicitation procedure used, participants are to listen to the narrative as they view the picture book, which is controlled by the examiner. They are then asked to retell the story in the language of the model. Short, nonleading, and openended prompts (e.g., "Just do your best" and "Tell me what you can") can be provided if the child does not respond or responds in a way suggesting that more guidance or encouragement is needed (e.g., says "I don't know," lists items from the story without using a narrative form). Elicitation is conducted first in Spanish and then in English because it is expected that eliciting a retelling in the native tongue (Spanish) provides maximum support for producing a narrative in a second language. Stories are audio recorded for subsequent transcription and analysis. Elicitation of each narrative takes approximately 20 minutes.

Because language sample size is expected to vary with age and proficiency in each language, no particular number of utterances is recommended. According to the test manual, "at least one complete and intelligible verbal utterance" (p. 6) in which

80% of words are in the target language (i.e., no more than 20% of words are code switched) is needed for the language sample to be considered valid. Although the test manual states that a valid language sample is a representative one, no guidance regarding the minimal number of utterances needed to establish confidence in representativeness is offered, and representativeness cannot be achieved using the earlier criterion of a single intelligible utterance. Data for the number of utterances characteristic of the normative sample are not offered in the test manual; however, correspondence with the developers (personal communication with Aquiles Iglesias, September 2011) revealed that for data collapsed across language and grade level, the number of utterances ranged from 1–116 (means ranged from 28.0 to 42.0). The sample should be transcribed by someone who is fluent in the language being transcribed and "proficient" (manual, p. 10) in the other language to identify instances of code switching. Transcription for each sample takes approximately one hour and involves careful adherence to the SALT-SE transcript conventions (e.g., notation for utterance segmentation, punctuation, identification of morphemes, mazes, unintelligible utterances, transcriber comments). Additional hand-coded analyses can be performed to identify the presence of story grammars using the Narrative Scoring Scheme (NSS) and to calculate the subordination index (a measure of syntactic complexity). The examiner's manual provides detailed instructions for transcription conventions and a number of clear webbased resources are also provided on the SALT-SE website (e.g., video tutorials, coding and transcript entry, numerous examples).

Once the transcripts have been coded according to the SALT-SE conventions, they can be submitted to the database for comparison to age or grade-level matched peers. Several different reports can be generated depending on the needs of the examiner. For example, the Standard Measures report provides information regarding the number of coded occurrences of 25 language features within seven broader categories of language sample analysis. Categories include transcript length, syntax/morphology, semantics, intelligibility, mazes and abandoned utterances, verbal facility and rate, and omissions and error codes for which several descriptive statistics (e.g., mean, range, standard deviation) are available. Scores that fall below one standard deviation of the comparison population are highlighted for easy identification. Another example of a report is a Transcript Summary that itemizes particular utterance types (e.g., statements, exclamations, questions) and reports the frequency and percent of occurrence of each. Still another report known as the Word and Morpheme Summary calculates mean length of utterance (MLU), Number of Different Words (NDW), Total Number of Words (TNW), and Type Token Ratio (TTR), which are measures that have gained some currency in language sample analysis (LSA) for the purpose of identifying language disorders. Other reports that are available include, but are not limited to, the Maze Summary, Word Code Tables, and reports for Subordination Index and the Narrative Scoring Scheme. SALT-SE reports are intended to be interpreted in light of the child's unique personal history, which includes consideration of the time and degree of exposure to each language. Users are encouraged to construe language disorders in relation to seven general typologies for which SALT offers variables of clinical relevance.

DEVELOPMENT. The SALT-SE is a software tool based on the earlier (Systematic Analysis of Language Transcript [SALT; Miller, 2008]) and original (Miller & Chapman, 1982) versions that were intended as tools for analyzing language transcripts in English. The SALT-SE was developed to respond to a number of unique challenges posed in the diagnosis of language impairment in bilingual children. Chief among these is a paucity of measures with normative data for English-language-learning children that allow for a comparison of the child's proficiency in each language. Historically, bilingual children "have often been either over diagnosed, failing to consider English as the second language, or under diagnosed, assuming that more time was needed to master English" (manual, p. 1). Like its predecessors, the SALT-SE is offered as a method to manage LSA. The authors of the SALT-SE argue that "LSA is the assessment procedure of choice because … it uses real communication contexts; the same context can be used to elicit a sample of Spanish and English, [and] it allows for tracking performance over time in each language" (manual, p. 1).

TECHNICAL.

Standardization. The SALT-SE manual describes a database that consists of English and Spanish story-retell narratives from over 2,070 native Spanish-speaking bilingual children who ranged in age from 5 years to 9 years, 9 months and represent Grades K-3. More detailed information

about the breakdown of number of children by grade and age is not available in the test manual; however, correspondence with the test authors indicated that the number of children representing each grade and age level were as follows: $n = 617$ for Grade K ages 5-0 to 6-8, $n = 298$ for Grade 1 ages 6-3 to 7-9, $n = 900$ for Grade 2 ages 7-0 to 8-9, and $n = 255$ for Grade 3 ages 8-3 to 9-9.

As described in the test manual, children were drawn from "public school ELL classrooms in urban Texas (Houston and Austin), border Texas (Brownsville), and urban California (Los Angeles)" (manual, p. 2). The test authors argue that "the children reflect the diverse socio-economic status of these areas" (manual, p. 2) but, unfortunately, no data for income and parental education are available in the test manual. According to the manual, inclusion criteria required that children be identified as typically developing as determined by normal progress in school and the absence of special education services.

Reliability. No evidence for the reliability of the SALT-SE is offered in the test manual. However, a study examining the transcription accuracy and reliability of the narrative retellings has been reported elsewhere. Using a sample of 40 narratives drawn from the larger SALT-SE normative sample, Heilmann et al. (2008) documented high degrees of agreement between two transcriptionists who independently identified utterance segments, words and morphemes, words and morphemes within mazes, and maze placement in both English and Spanish (all levels of point-to-point agreement were 90% or above). Heilmann et al. (2008) also examined test-retest reliability using 241 pairs of narrative retellings (115 in English and 126 in Spanish) from children who were representative of the larger sample with regard to gender and grade level. The test-retest interval was approximately 2 months ($M = 62$ days, range = 11–84). All Pearson correlation coefficients for MLU, NDW, NTW, and words per minute at Time 1 and Time 2 were significantly correlated in both English and Spanish, although the overall magnitude of the coefficients was moderate (ranging from .37–.79), which may reflect growth in language skills over the 2-month test-retest lag (Heilmann et al., 2008). Although these data are encouraging, it must be noted that in the Heilmann et al. (2008) study, transcriptionists completed an approximate 10-hour training procedure and narrative samples were elicited from a script. Thus, the procedures employed in this study were "designed for accuracy and efficiency" (manual, p. 186) and differ from the examiner training and semistructured elicitation procedures described in the SALT-SE manual.

Validity. No evidence in support of the validity of the SALT-SE is offered in the test manual. However, examination of the indices yielded by SALT-SE offer evidence of the tool's content validity. With regard to measures commonly derived from LSA, the SALT-SE is comprehensive. A wide range of indices can be assessed (e.g., story grammars, MLU, NDW, questions, statements, pauses, mazes), which can often be reported using a variety of descriptive statistics. In addition, a study by Miller et al. (2006) provides some evidence for the tool's convergent validity. They utilized a subset of more than 1,500 of the Spanish-English-speaking children from the larger normative sample. Among the results was the finding that measures of LSA in Spanish predicted reading scores in Spanish and that measures of LSA in English predicted reading scores in English. Given the connection between language disorder and literacy outcomes, these data are relevant in light of the tool's stated goal, which is to serve as "an assessment tool for identifying language disorder among bilingual children" (manual, p. 1). Of course, further evidence in support of this tool's validity is warranted and an examination of the measure's sensitivity and specificity is desirable. In particular, a contrasting-groups method of construct validation seems crucial. This analysis would compare bilingual Spanish-English-speaking typically developing children to bilingual Spanish-English-speaking children diagnosed with language disorder on the most relevant LSA measures.

COMMENTARY. The SALT-SE is a unique tool for the management of LSA in Spanish and English. It is one of the only tools available with normative data for a large group of bilingual children, although the characteristics of the normative sample are underspecified. The SALT-SE also appears to have good content validity and is capable of analyzing a broad range of language performance features in both languages. In addition, the coding conventions are clearly described in the test manual, and those developed to credit morphological advances among speakers of a highly inflected language are well-reasoned.

Weaknesses of the SALT-SE include the fact that the sampling, transcription, coding, analysis, and interpretation of language data require a significant time investment. The time investment

is particularly heavy among first-time or novice users who will require a great deal of training to conduct the procedures with confidence. Time can be expected to drop substantially for experienced users who may spend approximately 2–3 hours to complete elicitation, transcription, and analysis. In a related vein, it is not clear what procedures are needed to ensure reliability. Heilmann et al. (2008) showed that a 10-hour training procedure yielded reliable transcription and data entry but what level is expected for users who simply purchase the test manual? Similarly, evidence in support of the reliability and validity of the measure using the procedures described in the test manual and those most comparable to the procedures used for the normative sample will be important in efforts to further develop the SALT-SE. It is also a concern that clinicians using this tool could potentially make diagnostic decisions based on a language sample consisting of a single utterance. As such, discussion and guidance for considering the representativeness of a language sample seems important for understanding a child's proficiency in each language and for informing diagnostic decisions.

SUMMARY. The SALT-SE holds promise as an assessment tool for the identification of language disorders among young bilingual Spanish-English-speaking children and it may prove useful for documenting a variety of language production deficits not captured through traditional standardized testing. Nonetheless, more convincing evidence in support of the tool's validity is needed before the SALT-SE can be recommended as a diagnostic tool. Particularly important will be evidence of reliability and validity using procedures that adhere to those presented in the test manual and those used to generate norms. As noted previously, a contrasting-groups method of construct validation (comparing typically developing bilingual children and bilingual children with language disorders) is needed. This analysis also may be useful for establishing empirically supported minimal language sample sizes and the development of specific criteria (e.g., cutoff scores) that might be used to guide diagnostic decisions. At present, use of the SALT-SE to document strengths and weaknesses in children's productive forms for the purposes of treatment planning seems better justified.

REVIEWERS' REFERENCES

Heilmann, J., Miller, J. F., Iglesias, A., Fabiano-Smith, L., Nockerts, A., & Digney Andriacchi, K. (2008). Narrative transcription accuracy and reliability in two languages. *Topics in Language Disorders, 28,* 178-188.
Mayer, M. (1969). *Frog, where are you?* New York, NY: Dial Books for Young Readers.

Miller, J. (2008). Systematic Analysis of Language Transcripts (SALT), English Version 2008 [Computer Software], SALT Software, LLC.

Miller, J., & Chapman, R. (1982). Systematic Analysis of Language Transcripts-Harris computer version [Computer program]. Madison, WI: University of Wisconsin-Madison, Waisman Center, Language Analysis Laboratory.

Miller, J. F., Heilmann, J., Nockerts, A., Iglesias, A., Fabiano, L., & Francis, D. J. (2006). Oral language and reading in bilingual children. *Learning Disabilities Research & Practice, 21*, 30-43.

[164]
Systematic Analysis of Language Transcripts 2010 English Version.

Purpose: Aids the transcription process and provides a series of analyses comparing an individual language sample to samples from age or grade-matched peers whose primary language is English.

Population: Preschool through high school.

Publication Dates: 2009-2010.

Acronym: SALT 2010 English version.

Scores: 3 handscoring: Subordination Index, Narrative Scoring Scheme, Expository Scoring Scheme; 5 computer analyses: Syntax, Morphology, Lexicon, Fluency and Rate, Discourse.

Administration: Group.

Price Data, 2010: $99 per SALT English Version including software and printed SALT manual.

Foreign Language and Other Special Editions: Bilingual (Spanish/English), Research, and Instructional editions available.

Time: Unlimited.

Comments: Computer software for Windows® 2000, XP, Vista, 7.

Author: Jon F. Miller.

Publisher: SALT Software, LLC.

Review of the Systematic Analysis of Language Transcripts 2010 English Version by ABIGAIL BAXTER, Professor of Special Education, University of South Alabama, Mobile, AL:

DESCRIPTION. The Systematic Analysis of Language Transcripts (SALT) is a Windows®-based software program that helps clinicians and researchers analyze children's language samples. Language samples are important components of a complete assessment of children's abilities to communicate (Price, Hendricks, & Cook, 2010; p. 206). In addition to providing an analysis of a specific child's language skills, the SALT is capable of providing normative comparison data. Although there is no need for the use of standardized conditions to elicit the language sample, if the user desires to compare the results to one of the normative groups, standardized elicitation protocols are provided in the software manual. Comparisons can be made based on age, grade, gender, language sample context (conversation, child-selected narrative, story retell, expository, and others), and transcript length. The

SALT can be used to assist in the diagnosis of expressive language disorders as well as to monitor the effectiveness of interventions or therapy. The test manual and available online training both include an overview of SALT, elicitation procedures, transcription coding conventions, description of available analysis reports, interpretation of SALT results, directions for hand-calculating analyses that are not available in SALT, example transcripts, and a case study. Guidelines for interpreting the SALT reports in terms of language disorders are included.

Using the SALT is relatively straightforward. After a language sample has been conducted, an orthographic transcription using special codes that are recognized by the SALT software is created. The coding system is easily learned (Miller, 2007). SALT includes extensive training, both through the software manual and through online resources, to help transcribers develop the abilities to produce accurate transcriptions. SALT also allows for users to develop their own additional codes that can be analyzed. The transcript is then analyzed. There is a great deal of flexibility in the types of analyses that can be completed. Transcripts can be analyzed individually, compared to normative samples or reference databases, using user-defined variables, and/or compared to another transcript for the same child. SALT uses different menus to allow users to specify the type(s) of analysis they would like to generate. SALT also equates transcripts that differ in number of words, number of utterances, or length of time of the sample to create valid comparisons across transcripts. Clinical, instructional, and research versions are available.

DEVELOPMENT. Language samples have long been used to understand children's expressive language abilities. However, the variability in the collection of language sample data, scoring procedures, reference groups, and interpretation have limited its use. In addition, hand calculations led to inaccuracies and results were difficult to interpret (Heilmann, Miller, & Nockerts, 2010; Long, 2001). These limitations and difficulties led to the development of computer analysis programs (Heilmann, Miller, & Nockerts, 2010). One of these was SALT. SALT was originally used by graduate students and researchers but as more people had access to computers, it also became available to clinicians working with students with communication problems (Miller, 2007). The goal was to "develop a standardized method of transcription that incorporated the entire sample: the language of the child and the communication partner..." based upon "...an accurate orthographic record of the recorded sample with minimal coding so the result was a readable transcript accessible to anyone" (Miller, 2007, p. 318).

There is not a great deal of information about the development of SALT in the test manual. The results of research studies investigating methods for collecting language samples, scoring such samples, the development of norm groups, and the use of language sample analysis data were used to develop SALT. The transcription rubrics were developed in such a manner that users may add their own codes. The analyses routines were developed so that there were a set of standard analyses available. Additional standard analyses were added with time, as was the ability for users to conduct exploratory analyses (Miller, 2007). The development of the normative data (the reference databases) began with studies of expressive language in conversation and narrative contexts using samples of children from Wisconsin between the ages of 3 and 13 years (Heilmann, Miller, & Nockerts, 2010). Additional work developed databases for story retell using children from Wisconsin and California. Three other databases were also developed (one with Spanish-speaking English language learners, one that was collected to norm the Test of Narrative Language, and one each from Canada and New Zealand). Most recent changes have impacted how the user controls the menus and the interface. In sum, SALT consists of the software and a manual as well as a great deal of online support focused on training and support.

TECHNICAL. SALT has seven different reference databases that include language sample analyses, elicited in different contexts for different samples of children. It is these databases that can be chosen for the normative comparisons available in SALT. These reference databases are described in the manual and appendices as well as online. The numbers of children in the databases vary from a low of 87 to a high of 612. Children's ages range from 2 years 8 months to 15 years 9 months in the different samples. The databases include performance samples from children from different areas in the U.S., but they were primarily from Wisconsin and California. There is a database from Canada and one from New Zealand. Many of these databases are described in an article by Heilmann, Miller, and Nockerts (2010). The manual and online sources report that information about grades, ages, and gender of children in the reference databases is

available but it is not included in these materials. Although the descriptions of the databases include information on the SES backgrounds of students, different metrics were used in different reference databases, making it difficult to compare across databases. In addition, there are discrepancies in the descriptions of the ages of the children in the New Zealand sample.

There is evidence in the literature (e.g., Long, 2001) that language sample analyses conducted by computers are more reliable than hand-calculated analyses. SALT's reliability is tied to the reliability of the transcripts created by users. Studies have indicated that individuals can learn to create language sample transcripts that are reliable in terms of interrater, test-retest, and internal consistency reliability estimates (e.g., Gavin & Giles, 1996; Heilmann, Miller, Iglesias, Fabiano-Smith, Nockerts, & Andriacchi, 2008; Heilmann, Nockerts, & Miller, 2010; Miller, 2007; Ukrainetz & Blomquist, 2002). The reliability of the SALT assessment, however, depends upon the reliability of the transcription of the language sample. The SALT transcription conventions appear to be easy to learn and use. The SALT system clearly describes their transcription coding system in the manual, in online training materials, and with examples that SALT users can access. SALT includes samples that can be used to obtain interrater reliability estimates for transcripts. Case studies are also included to ensure reliability for the user. There is also an FAQ section on the website as well as a way to submit questions about SALT and its use.

The analysis of language samples is viewed as a very ecologically valid assessment of children's language abilities (Heilmann, Miller, & Nockerts, 2010; Ukrainetz & Blomquist, 2002). The elicitation protocols available with SALT reflect the varied purposes of language use in young children. The validity of SALT relies on the validity of the different characteristics of language it assesses. The basic variables coded in SALT are important components of language but their validity rests upon the transcriptionists' abilities to detect and mark them in the transcript.

COMMENTARY. SALT appears to be a very useful assessment tool for analyzing children's language samples in a time-efficient and accurate manner that also produces normative comparisons, if desired. There is a plethora of training information and support to users available in the software manual as well as online. This material should be very helpful to SALT users. After completing training, the first step in using SALT is collecting the language sample. The manual and online sources provide great detail about how to elicit the sample in order to make comparisons to their reference databases. The sample is then transcribed using well-defined coding conventions. The transcript is then analyzed using prepared and/or individually designed analyses. The report format is complete and easy to understand. The information provided by SALT is useful for both researchers and clinicians. In addition to research, the information available from SALT can be used to plan treatment or educational interventions as well as to monitor their effectiveness.

SUMMARY. SALT is a computerized analysis tool for language samples. It is very flexible in terms of what is recorded, transcribed, and analyzed. It provides ipsative and norm-referenced information about children's language that is easily used in the development of educational and/or therapeutic goals. It also is able to provide documentation of the progress toward and/or accomplishment of these goals.

REVIEWER'S REFERENCES

Gavin, W. J., & Giles, L. (1996). Sample size effects on temporal reliability of language sample measures of preschool children. *Journal of Speech & Hearing Research, 3*, 1258-1262.

Heilmann, J. J., Miller, J. F., Iglesias, A., Fabiano-Smith, L., Nockerts, A., & Andriacchi, K. D. (2008). Narrative transcription accuracy and reliability in two languages. *Topics in Language Disorders, 28*, 178-188. doi:10.1097/01.TLD.0000318937.39301.76

Heilmann, J. J., Miller, J. F., & Nockerts, A. (2010). Using language sample databases. *Language, Speech and Hearing Services in Schools, 41*, 84-95. doi:10.1044/0161-1461 (2009/08-0075)

Heilmann, J., Nockerts, A., & Miller, J. F. (2010). Language sampling: Does the length of the transcript matter? *Language, Speech and Hearing Services in Schools, 41*, 393-404. doi:10.1044/0161-1461(2009/09-0023)

Long, S. H. (2001). About time: A comparison of computerized and manual procedures for grammatical and phonological analysis. *Clinical Linguistics & Phonetics, 15*, 399-425. doi: 10.1080/02699200010027778

Miller, J. (2007). Documenting progress in language production: The evolution of a computerized language analysis system. In R. Paul (Ed.), *Language disorders from a developmental perspective: Essays in honor of Robin S. Chapman* (pp. 315-329). Mahwah, NJ: Erlbaum.

Price, L. H., Hendricks, S., & Cook, C. (2010). Incorporating computer-aided language sample analysis into clinical practice. *Language, Speech and Hearing Services in Schools, 41*, 206-222. doi:10.1044/0161-1461(2009/08-0054)

Ukrainetz, T. A., & Blomquist, C. (2002). The criterion validity of four vocabulary tests compared to a language sample. *Child Language Teaching and Therapy, 18*, 59-78. doi:10.1191/0265659002ct227oa

Review of the Systematic Analysis of Language Transcripts 2010 English Version by KATHY L. SHAPLEY, Assistant Professor of Speech Pathology, University of Arkansas Little Rock/University of Arkansas for Medical Sciences, Little Rock, AR:

DESCRIPTION. The Systematic Analysis of Language Transcripts (SALT) is a software program used to aid the analysis of language samples. The software provides analysis at the morpheme, word, utterance, and discourse level. In addition, there are seven databases that can be used for age-matched peer comparisons. The software is compatible with Windows platform (2000, XP, Vista & 7) and requires 64MB of RAM and 40MB of space on the hard drive.

The software manual provides detailed descriptions of how to elicit, transcribe, and analyze a language sample. Information is included on how to interpret the results of the language analysis. A clinical typology is included that summarizes seven types of language disorders and associated characteristics; however, as stated in the manual, these typologies have not been validated through research.

The SALT software has 8 coding conventions with which the user must be familiar in order to use the software effectively. These conventions include: transcription format (e.g., identify the speakers, demographic information, time), end of utterance punctuation (e.g., period, question mark), comments within an utterance (i.e., to mark nonverbal utterances-head nod), unintelligible segments; bound morphemes (e.g., plurals, possessives, past tense), mazes (e.g., false starts, pauses), omissions (e.g., partial words or omitted words), overlapping speech (e.g., when both speakers are talking), root identification (e.g., root words of irregular verb forms-went for "goed"), and codes (to make the utterance for error types).

The software manual provides detailed description of each of the coding conventions and provides two case studies. Training is included in the manual and consists of 10 modules: Lesson 1–How to use the training materials on the website; Lesson 2–How to enter a language transcript (entering demographic and speaker information, utilizing help, typing in a short transcript, checking for errors); Lesson 3–How to analyze a transcript (word and morpheme summary, etc.); Lesson 4–Comparing a transcript to a reference database (the age match is plus or minus 6 months) and provides information on how to interpret the results. The same language sample can be compared to multiple databases once the transcript has been entered and coded into SALT; Lesson 5–Linking transcripts for comparison, demonstrates how to link two language samples from the same speaker (Time 1 and Time 2) to show changes/growth; Lesson 6–Coding a transcript and analysis of the codes; these codes do not alter the transcript but provide additional qualitative information to the user (e.g., verb type used past, present, future); Lesson 7–Exploring the transcript provides additional practice for analyzing code types; Lesson 8–Subordination index, which provides instruction on how to measure syntactic complexity of the transcription; Lesson 9–Analyze the NSS scores, provides an analysis of the narrative scoring scheme; Lesson 10–Setup menu provides instruction on changing the default folder to allow the user to customize the program for individual clients. Web training for the software is also provided and allows the user to practice transcription skills using SALT conventions and coding skills.

The amount of time it takes to transcribe and code a language sample using the SALT software will vary depending on how familiar the user is with the system.

DEVELOPMENT. The technical manual does not provide information on how the software was developed.

TECHNICAL. There are seven databases that can be used for comparisons. Each database provides a description of the protocol used to collect the sample. The technical manual does not provide any evidence of reliability or validity regarding the databases, or the analyses.

The conversation database provides 612 language samples collected from typically developing children ages 2:8–13:3 from Wisconsin and ages 4:4–9:11 from California. The description of the sample states that samples were collected from urban and rural areas and SES status was determined by mother's highest level of education; age, gender, and grade data are available for the sample. However, no detailed information regarding how the sample was stratified is provided in the manual. The narrative student selects story (NSS) database consists of narrative samples from 330 typically developing 5-year-old through 13-year-old students from urban and rural Wisconsin schools. Again, no detailed information regarding how the sample was stratified is provided. The narrative story retell reference database contains samples from 346 typically developing children in Grades P–4; ages 4:4–10:0 collected in Wisconsin and California. Age, gender, and grade data are reported to be available for each individual in the sample; however, no detailed information is reported in the technical manual.

The expository reference database includes 87 samples collected from typically developing students, ages 12:7–15:9, who were enrolled in public schools located in Wisconsin. The sample is not nationally representative but reportedly reflects the population from which it is drawn: 80.5% White,

9.2% African American, 8% Hispanic, and 2.3% Asian. Demographic characteristics from the U.S. Census for Wisconsin are not provided in order to determine if the characteristics of the sample do reflect the actual population. There were 43 females and 44 males in the sample, and 18% of the sample qualified for the free and reduced-price lunch program.

The Gillam narrative task reference database consists of narrative samples from 500 children ages 5:0–11:11. The database contains samples from 50 children at ages 5, 9, 10, and 11 as well as 100 children at ages 6, 7, and 8. There are an equal number of boys and girls at each age. Reportedly the sample came from four regions of the U.S. although the percentage from each region is not listed. The race/ethnicity of the sample is 71% White, 11% African American, 10% Hispanic, and 8% other. No census data are provided to make comparisons regarding national representation race/ethnicity.

The New Zealand reference database includes conversational and narrative samples from 256 typically developing children ages 4:6–7:6. Reportedly, there was an even gender representation in the sample, and race/ethnicity is 62% New Zealand European, 22% Maori, 5% Pacific Island, 3% Asian, and 8% other.

COMMENTARY. The SALT software is a unique tool to aid in the analysis of language samples. Although it takes some time to learn the transcription conventions once mastered the software provides valuable and detailed information that would otherwise be difficult and time-consuming to obtain. The SALT software is most likely to be used by researchers at this time.

Clinicians should exercise caution when using the databases for comparisons as the population in the database may not be representative of the individual being assessed. If more robust databases were available that provided detailed demographic characteristics reflecting current ethnic, minority, and socioeconomic status distributions in the United States, comparisons could be made without concern regarding representation of the sample.

SUMMARY. The SALT is a well-supported software program that aids in the detailed analysis of language samples. The developers provide multiple formats for training (detailed manual and training on the website). This is not a tool that is currently used to diagnose a language disorder. Rather, it is a tool that is used to provide more detailed, qualitative information for clinicians.

[165]

Tasks of Executive Control.

Purpose: Designed to "assess attention, working memory, and inhibitory control."

Population: Ages 5 to 18.

Publication Dates: 2006-2010.

Acronym: TEC.

Administration: Individual.

Forms, 5: Forms 1, 2, and 3 are statistically equivalent; Forms 4 and 5 are to be used in research.

Price Data, 2012: $675 per introductory test kit CD-ROM including unlimited use TEC software program with onscreen help, professional manual (2010, 188 pages), 1 set of keytops, and quick start guide; $80 per professional manual.

Time: (20-30) minutes.

Comments: The TEC is a computer-administered test and requires the following technical supports: CD-ROM drive for installation; keyboard (USB/wireless not recommended); 60Hz noninterlaced (16.76 ms) refresh rate; 12.5-inch diagonal CRT or LCD (14.5-inch diagonal widescreen); AGP or PCI Express video card with 32MB on-board RAM, 128MHz RAMDAC; 16-bit, 1024x768 (XGA) display.

Authors: Peter K. Isquith, Robert M. Roth, and Gerard A. Gioia.

Publisher: Psychological Assessment Resources, Inc.

a) AGES 5 TO 7 YEARS.

Scores, 23: 3 Factor Scores: Response Control, Selective Attention, Response Speed; 10 Summary Scores: Accuracy, Target Correct, Standard Correct, Target Omissions, Standard Omissions, Incorrect, Commissions, Target RT, Standard RT, Standard RTSD, Standard ICV; 10 Task Scores: Target Correct, Standard Correct, Target Omissions, Standard Omissions, Incorrect, Commissions, Target RT, Standard RT, Standard RTSD, Standard ICV.

b) AGES 8 TO 18 YEARS.

Scores, 24: 4 Factor Scores: Sustained Accuracy, Selective Attention, Response Speed, Response Variability; 10 Summary Scores: Accuracy, Target Correct, Standard Correct, Target Omissions, Standard Omissions, Incorrect, Commissions, Target RT, Standard RT, Standard RTSD, Standard ICV; 10 Task Scores: Target Correct, Standard Correct, Target Omissions, Standard Omissions, Incorrect, Commissions, Target RT, Standard RT, Standard RTSD, Standard ICV.

Review of the Tasks of Executive Control by RAMA K. MISHRA, Neuropsychologist, Department of Psychiatry, Medicine Hat Regional Hospital, Medicine Hat, Alberta, Canada:

DESCRIPTION. The Tasks of Executive Control (TEC) is a computer-administered test of working memory and inhibitory control, two main aspects of executive function. It also measures attentional processes such as vigilance and sustained attention over time. This test is designed for children/adolescents between the ages of 5 and 18 years.

There are four sequential tasks for 5- to 7-year-olds and six tasks for older children. There are three equivalent forms with norms and two additional forms developed for research purposes. The software program calculates performance accuracy, response time, and time variability for each task condition and across the entire battery with normative data for Factor and Summary scores.

For this test, participants are presented with colored pictures briefly on a computer screen and are required to press the right side shift key to put the standard objects in a blue box or press the left side shift key to put the target objects in a red box. The instructions for the six conditions vary and require the test taker to withhold responses for various intervals when the image appears inside a box. Red and blue stickers are provided to place on the shift keys of the keyboard for convenience.

This instrument is expected to be used along with other neuropsychological tests for identifying deficits for developmental disorders, attention disorders, learning disabilities, autism spectrum disorders, traumatic brain injuries, and other psychiatric and behavioral disorders.

DEVELOPMENT. The test authors report that they wanted to develop a novel approach to assessment of working memory and inhibitory control, as these executive functions are impaired in a broad range of the pediatric clinical population. They reviewed numerous clinical studies, particularly from the field of cognitive neuroscience. They found that n-Back is used to assess working memory and a go/no-go task is used for inhibitory control frequently in neuroimaging studies. The test authors' goal was to develop a computer-administered test incorporating these two aspects of executive functioning. They also decided to develop five alternate forms for repeated administration. Selection of task stimuli was completed by examining word frequency, naming agreement, familiarity, and semantic categories. Selection of task parameters such as exposure time, time interval between objects, size of objects, working memory load, and inhibitory control demand were determined by reference to existing literature and by maximizing the expected specificity and sensitivity indices.

TECHNICAL. The Tasks of Executive Control was administered to 1,107 children and adolescents between the ages of 5 and 18 years from six states (Colorado, Florida, Maryland, Virginia, New Hampshire, Vermont) and the District of Columbia through schools and youth or community organizations. Potential participants with a history of developmental disability, neurological disorders, head injury or loss of consciousness, and severe psychiatric disorders were excluded from the normative sample. Participants with incomplete protocols or missing race/ethnicity information were also excluded from the sample. Out of the total sample of 1,107 participants, 835 participants completed Form 1, 138 participants completed Form 2, and 134 participants completed Form 3. The TEC standardization sample was reported to be very similar to the 2007 U.S. population distribution with respect to age, gender, and race/ethnicity. Several clinical samples including individuals with learning disabilities, attention deficit/hyperactivity disorder, fragile-X syndrome, or traumatic brain injury were also used in validity studies. The five forms contain identical task parameters with respect to timing of stimulus presentation, time between stimuli, and stimulus position. The only differences between the forms are the stimulus objects employed in the forms. The objects were matched with respect to word frequency, naming agreement, and familiarity among the five forms. During standardization, the first three forms were randomly assigned to groups of participants. The between-form effects at the .01 level were reported to account for less than 1% of the variance in TEC score. (The test authors do not explain why more than 75% of participants were given Form 1, whereas only about 12% of participants were given Form 2 or Form 3.)

Extensive reliability and validity information (65 pages) is presented in the test manual. Internal consistency coefficients for factor scores were reported to be in the .80s and .90s. The only exception was the Response Control factor for 5- to 7-year-olds, which was .75. The test authors explain that this result could be due to the fact that very young children are more variable in their accuracy. The reported test-retest reliability coefficients were generally in the .60s and .80s for Form 1, based on 100 participants who were tested across an interval of between 5 and 34 days (most were retested after 7 days). The test authors point out that test-retest reliability is adequate for Standard stimuli measures such as Correct, RT, RTSD, and ICV. However, the values were somewhat lower for Target stimuli

measures due to restricted range with only 20 possible Target responses in each task. Alternate form test-retest reliabilities were reported to be in the .70s to .80s (Forms 1 and 2) and in the .70s to .90s (Forms 1 and 3). When analyzed by task (e.g., 0B, 1B, and 2B), some of the Standard stimuli accuracy measures (e.g., omissions, incorrect) were found to have lower reliability coefficients.

Validity evidence is reported based on content, developmental changes, response processes, relationships to other variables, internal structure, and performance in clinical samples. In terms of the content of the Tasks of Executive Control, the test authors cite several studies to demonstrate that the n-Back paradigm used in the TEC manipulates working memory load and that the go/no-go paradigm manipulates inhibitory control most efficiently. With regard to evidence based on developmental changes, the test authors report that there are strong linear associations between age and TEC variables such as accuracy, response speed, and response speed variability. The correlation coefficients of age with Target Correct and Standard Correct were reported to range from .49 to .58, with RT between -.21 and -.55, and with RTSD between -.26 and -.56 (all $p < .05$).

In terms of response process, it has been found that as working memory load increased or respondents were required to exercise inhibitory control, their performance measures showed a significant degree of decline. For example, there was strong multivariate within subjects main effects and interactions effects for three levels of working memory load (e.g., 0-back, 1-back, 2-back) and two levels of inhibitory demand (e.g., no inhibit and inhibit) for Target Correct, RTSD, and Target RT (all $p < .001$). Moreover, the interaction between working memory load and inhibitory control accounted for 50% of the variance in how participants responded to Target stimuli and 36% of the variance in how participants responded to Standard stimuli.

Extensive convergent and discriminant validity data have been presented, as the test authors report significant correlations between the TEC and other measures that are similar in traits and low correlations with measures that are dissimilar in traits. For example, select TEC measures were found to have modest to moderate correlations (.25 to .48) with primary scales of the Behavior Rating Inventory of Executive Function (BRIEF) Parent Form, Conners' Parent Rating Scales

(CPRS), Child Behavior Checklist (CBCL), Post-Concussion Symptom Inventory (PCSI), Everyday Situations Survey (ESS), and Family Assessment Device (FAD).

TEC measures (Factor and Summary scores) were also found to have significant relationships (.21 to .59) with several neuropsychological measures such as the Digit Span subtest of the Wechsler Intelligence Scale for Children (WISC-IV), Symbol Digit Modalities Test (SDMT), Woodcock-Johnson III Tests of Achievement (WJ III) Reading Fluency and Math Fluency, California Verbal Learning Test–Children's Version (CVLT-C), and Auditory Consonant Trigrams (ACT). The test authors claim that negligible relationships of TEC measures with recognition scores of CVLT-C, and the short delay/distractor condition of ACT, provide evidence of discriminant validity.

With regard to internal structure of TEC, it was reported that a three-factor solution (Response Control, Selective Attention, and Response Speed) had the best fit for the younger group of 5- to 7-year-olds and a four-factor solution (Sustained Accuracy, Selective Attention, Response Speed, and Response Variability) had the best fit for the older group of 8- to 18-year-olds. The test authors have explained that this difference in factor structure is consistent with the idea that executive functioning is less differentiated in younger children.

Finally, the Tasks of Executive Control was found to capture different types of deficits in executive functioning among different samples of clinical populations. For example, the test authors reported that children and adolescents with mild traumatic brain injury showed the slowest RTs and high response time variability. However, they were among the most accurate and error-free compared to other groups. Individuals with ADHD-Inattentive subtype were found to be less accurate, slower, and more variable than typically developing children. Individuals with ADHD-Combined subtype were faster in responding but were found to be inaccurate and variable. Children with fragile X syndrome or learning disabilities were found to be similar to ADHD-Inattentive subtype. The test authors have claimed that these findings are consistent with expected conceptual differences among the clinical groups.

COMMENTARY. The Tasks of Executive Control is an easy and short test to administer. It generates extensive data automatically. The program computes 3 Factor scores for younger children and 4 Factor scores for older children and 10 summary scores. The three report options (Score Report, Protocol Summary Report, and Client Report) provide T-scores, percentiles, and interpretive descriptors (elevated, typical), as well as line and bar graphs for the Factor scores and Summary scores. It would be a very useful tool for neuropsychological evaluation of executive functioning.

The test authors provide extensive reliability and validity data. However, it was somewhat surprising that they did not use well-known neuropsychological tests such as the Delis-Kaplan Executive Function System (Delis, Kaplan, & Kramer, 2001), the Category Test (Choca, Laatsch, Garside, Gupta, & Fenstermacher, 2008), or the Wisconsin Card Sorting Test (Heaton, Chelune, Talley, Kay, & Curtiss, 1993) to demonstrate concurrent validity.

The writer of this review administered this test to a small number of typically developing children and found that most of them found it very difficult. None of them reported that it was fun and they did not want to take it again even after a month's time. Therefore, the popularity of this test, particularly for retesting, may be somewhat limited compared to other automated tests such as the Wisconsin Card Sorting Test or the Category Test.

Continuing research is necessary to develop well-defined markers of TEC measures (Factor scores and Summary scores) for different clinical populations so that it can be part of a comprehensive test battery for diagnosis and monitoring treatment effectiveness.

SUMMARY. In spite of some limitations, the Tasks of Executive Control will be very popular for neuropsychological evaluation for three reasons: (a) It is fully automated and may feel like playing a game, (b) it takes only about 20 minutes to complete, and (c) it measures aspects of executive functioning that are not assessed by most popular tests currently available. This test should be part of most psychoeducational and neuropsychological test batteries. The test authors have done an excellent job in developing this brief but powerful test, which is expected to generate much clinical and research interest.

REVIEWER'S REFERENCES

Choca, J., Laatsch, L., Garside, D., Gupta, R., & Fenstermacher, J. (2008). Category Test. North Tonawanda, NY: Multi-Health Systems, Inc.

Delis, D. C., Kaplan, E., & Kramer, J. H. (2001). Delis-Kaplan Executive Function System. San Antonio, TX: Pearson.

Heaton, R. K., Chelune, G. J., Talley, J. L., Kay, G. G., & Curtiss, G. (1993). Wisconsin Card Sorting Test. Lutz, FL: Psychological Assessment Resources, Inc.

Isquith, P. K., Roth, R. M., & Gioia, G. A. (2010). Tasks of Executive Control. Lutz, FL: Psychological Assessment Resources, Inc.

Review of the Tasks of Executive Control by GABRIELLE STUTMAN, Private Practice, Westchester and Manhattan, NY:

DESCRIPTION. The Tasks of Executive Control (TEC) is a standardized computer-administered and scored measure of working memory and inhibitory control suitable for use with children from 5 to 18 years of age. These functions are two of the most fundamental aspects of executive control processes. The instrument is useful as an aid in diagnosing, structuring intervention, monitoring progress, and measuring the development of executive functions for diagnostic and research purposes. It consists of a go/no-go task to measure inhibitory control combined with an n-Back task to measure working memory. The n-Back task is composed of separate 0-Back, 1-Back, and 2-Back conditions, and is presented as a game-like sorting task. (Some objects go in the red [Target] box and some in the blue [Standard] box.) The test materials include a manual, the TEC software, colored keyboard stickers, a software guide, and an on-screen help/guidance system. The clinician must provide a computer that meets hardware and system specifications.

Three (normed) equivalent forms and two (unnormed) additional research forms are included, along with reliable change statistics to interpret repeated measures. The first task is a basic choice reaction time task that allows vigilance and sustained attention to be assessed and provides a baseline. Each n-Back condition is first presented without the need for inhibitory response, and later with an infrequent no-go stimulus. In this way the TEC differentially provides information regarding an individual's working memory and inhibitory control. Because 5- to 7-year-old children have difficulty performing the 2-Back task, this task was eliminated for this age group. Administration time varies from 20 to 25 minutes depending on age.

The TEC calculates multiple performance accuracy, response time, and response time variability measures within each Task and across performance as a whole (Factor and Summary Scores). Scores take age, gender, and age by gender interactions into account. Raw values, T scores, percentiles, and 90% confidence interval values for Factor, Summary, and Task scores are automatically generated by the TEC software, which also provides Client, Protocol Summary, and Score Reports. Raw scores chart accuracy and response time for each quartile of a task and for the task as a whole. All available

Factor Score, Summary Score, Task Score variables, as well as scores of change within and across tests/administrations are listed in a table along with their meanings; significant deviations from the norm are bolded and have an asterisk (*). If inadequate effort is suspected, a warning will appear at the beginning of the report. Automatically generated change scores enable the examiner to review change in performance (relative to expected change) within each administration across working memory load for each "inhibit" condition. Normed retesting can be done with statistically equivalent Forms 2 and 3 that are identical except for different stimulus content. Forms 4 and 5 are not normed, and are for research purposes only. The process of score interpretation and the meaning of variance are facilitated by interpretive case illustrations in the test manual.

DEVELOPMENT. The TEC was developed to create a computer-generated and psychometrically sound measure of executive functions. Inhibitory control (including sustained and selective attention) and working memory are the executive functions of primary concern. These developmentally evolving functions are generally believed to be basic to executive functioning, and neurological disorders appear to result in somewhat different patterns of executive dysfunction over the life span; early performance on inhibitory tasks is highly correlated with working memory performance in 5- to 6-year-old children, but not in 8- to 9-year-olds. Further, working memory continues to develop well into late adolescence. The alternation of tasks allows the user to gauge how an individual responds to increased working memory load with and without the need for inhibitory control. Picture stimuli with low visual complexity and high frequency words that are familiar to young children were chosen from a large set; the 13 stimuli for each of the five TEC forms showed no significant differences on any characteristic. The overall probability of a Target stimulus occurring is the same across all six tasks, as the stimuli are in a fixed, pseudo-randomized order. Pilot testing with computers (no background programs running; no wireless and/or USB keyboards) showed only minimal variations in stimulus duration.

TECHNICAL. Standardization data were collected between December 2005 and October 2008, based on the Current Population Survey (U.S. Census Bureau, 2007), and 1,188 participants between the ages of 5 and 18 years were chosen who had no history of diagnosis or treatment for developmental disability, neurological disorder, severe psychiatric disorder, and history of brain injury or loss of consciousness. Form equivalence was evaluated using a random groups design. Forms 1, 2, or 3 showed no appreciable differences between forms. Younger children were less accurate, slower, and had more variable response times accounting for as much as 32% of the variance. Gender differences were more pronounced at younger ages; girls were more accurate, slower, and had slightly more variable response speed (5% of the variance). Race/ethnicity accounted for no more than 5% of the variance. Separate age-by-gender norms were generated. Distributions were appropriate for all variables except Standard Omissions and Target Omissions, which had a strong positive skew. Cutoff scores were placed at the 95th percentile for these variables, and the rest were transformed into non-normalized T-score distributions with a mean of 50 and standard deviation of 10. Percentiles were assigned and confidence intervals were calculated.

Reliability measures included split-half, which tended to be somewhat better for the older than for the younger group (generally .80–.90 vs. .75–.97), and test-retest (5–34 days with an average interval of about 11 days; generally stable). Alternate form test-retest revealed adequate Summary Score stability. For Form 1, Incorrect Responses and Commissions are relatively stable over time across tasks (.92 to .94 and .86 to .90, respectively), with RT the most stable (.92 to .99). Reliability coefficients were generally adequate for Standard stimuli, but dropped for target score measures. The SRB change scores were variable beyond the 80% confidence limit.

Evidence for validity of the TEC included excellent content evidence. At all ages respondents became less accurate, slower, and more variable in response speed with increased working memory load (74% of the variance for Target stimuli; 55% for Standard stimuli) and inhibitory demand (27% of variance for Target, 44% for Standard stimuli). The interaction between working memory and inhibition accounted for 50% of the Target and 36% of the Standard variance. Accuracy, speed, and consistency increase with increasing age. In addition, relationships between TEC performance measures and parent and self-report measures and appropriate neuropsychological assessment measures showed multiple lines of convergence.

A factor analysis gave a three-factor solution for 5- to 7-year-olds of Response Control, Selective Attention, and Response Speed (61.3% of the variance). A four-factor solution for the 8- to 18-year-olds consisted of Sustained Accuracy, Selective Attention, Response Speed, and Response Variability (60.9% of the variance). Each of these factors is only moderately correlated with one other. In addition, TEC scores correlate in the expected direction with measures of similar functions across modalities, but not with measures of distinct functions, thus providing good evidence of convergent and discriminant validity.

COMMENTARY. The TEC is a time-effective tool for measuring the acquisition and development of working memory, response inhibition, and selective/sustained attention. It appears appropriate for its intended population, practitioners, and uses. The research performed adds credence to the developmental hypothesis of working memory and inhibitory control. It is also well correlated with assessments of similar functions, but, because it is able to parcel out the variables of attention, working memory, and inhibitory control, it gives a more nuanced set of data than is currently available in other similar measures. The necessary computer characteristics are probably difficult for the lay person to assess, but the instrument can probably be used on any relatively new Mac or PC computer with an attached keyboard, CD drive, and 32MB RAM. The test manual is fully informative with regard to set-up, administration, scoring, and norms. Interpretive guidelines and case studies assist the clinician's understanding. Theoretical foundations and data are sufficiently reviewed, and reliability and validity data are generally acceptable to good. Also helpful are alternative forms that enable one to retest individuals in order to measure developmental progress and/or intervention effectiveness.

SUMMARY. The TEC has an advantage over other similar measures in that it parcels out increased working memory load, inhibitory control, and sustained attention in a progressive manner. Consequently, users may prefer it to the Conners' CPT and the IVA, which are relatively simpler tasks. Test users who are nervous about computer-generated tests can rest assured that technical support is available and the set-up is fairly simple.

REVIEWER'S REFERENCE

U.S. Census Bureau. (2007). *Current population survey, March 2007* [Data File]. Washington, DC: U.S. Department of Commerce.

[166]
Team Skills (Form AR-C).

Purpose: Designed to evaluate a candidate's ability to work as a member or leader of a team.

Population: Applicants and incumbents for jobs requiring knowledge of team principles.

Publication Dates: 1998-2009.

Scores: Total score only covering 7 areas: Conflict Resolution, Group Dynamics, Team Decision Making, Productivity and Motivation, Communication Skills, Leader & Member Skills, Interpersonal Skills.

Administration: Group.

Price Data, 2011: $14 per consumable self-scoring test booklet or online test administration (minimum order of 20); $24.95 per manual (2009, 15 pages).

Foreign Language Edition: Available in Spanish.

Time: (30-50) minutes.

Comments: Self-scoring instrument; available for online test administration.

Author: Roland T. Ramsay.

Publisher: Ramsay Corporation.

Cross References: For a review by Gerald Tindal of an earlier edition, see 17:181.

Review of the Team Skills (Form AR-C) by NEETA KANTAMNENI, Assistant Professor, and NICHOLE SHADA, Doctoral Student, University of Nebraska-Lincoln, Lincoln, NE:

DESCRIPTION. The Ramsay Corporation Job Skills Team Skills (Form AR-C) was developed to measure the knowledge and skills necessary to work successfully in teams. The test is intended "for use for pre-employment selection or for assessing incumbents in jobs where the knowledge of team principles is a required part of training or job activity" (manual, p. 1). The test includes 35 multiple-choice items measuring seven areas of knowledge of team principles including Conflict Resolution, Group Dynamics, Team Decision Making, Productivity and Motivation, Communication Skills, Leader and Member Skills, and Interpersonal Skills. The test can be administered online or via paper and pencil. The Team Skills assessment is available in English, Spanish, and French and can be administered in a group setting. Test administration should not take more than an hour, and there is no time limit.

Test items are formatted as questions or scenarios with four possible answers. Respondents are asked to select the best answer. Each test item has only one correct response. Items receiving multiple responses are scored as incorrect. The paper-and-pencil version of Team Skills (Form AR-C) includes a self-scoring grid at the end of the test booklet.

Scoring instructions are clear: correct responses are counted in each of the seven areas and added together to determine the individual's total score. Detailed and concrete instructions for administration and test scoring are provided in the manual.

DEVELOPMENT. Team Skills (Form AR-C) is a revised version of Team Skills (Form A). Team Skills Form A was developed in 1997; it was renamed Team Skills (Form A-C) when a self-scoring format was developed in 1998. Initially, test items for seven knowledge areas of team skills were developed by two industrial/organizational psychologists. The seven knowledge areas were selected based on a review of undisclosed periodicals and texts. Of the 35 test items, 8 items have been revised by two industrial/organizational psychologists for the current version of the test (Form AR-C), which was released in 2009. Item revisions were based on item-analysis data from more than 1,000 participants.

TECHNICAL. Standardization, reliability, and validity information provided in the test manual reflects information from the previous version of the test (Team Skills [Form A-C], 1998). Eight test items have been revised in the current version (Team Skills [Form AR-C], 2009); however, information on the standardization, reliability, and validity of the revised items and the current version of the test were not reported.

Standardization. Normative data were gathered from a group of male and female applicants for production employment (N = 2,173) in 1997. The manual provides only cumulative percentages and percentile ranks for raw scores. Little demographic information is provided regarding the standardization sample. Although the manual specifies that the sample included both men and women, no information regarding the number or percentage of men and women in the sample is reported. Furthermore, no information is provided about the race/ethnicities or ages included in the sample.

Reliability. The manual reports reliability information regarding the previous version (Team Skills [Form A-C], 1998); no data or tests for reliability are provided in the manual for the current form of the test. Data from 2,173 test takers were used to examine reliability and item analysis. The Kuder–Richardson Formula 20 reliability coefficient was reported to be .70, the odd-even, split-half reliability was reported to be .71, and the standard error of measurement was reported to be 2.5. Item analyses tested each item for difficulty and point-biserial coefficients. Point-biserial indices examined the correlation between a correct/incorrect response and the score on a specific subtest. Results found difficulty to range from .20 to .92 and uncorrected point-biserial coefficients to range from .40 to .66. The table providing these scores noted that eight items were changed since these analyses were conducted.

Validity. The manual reported a summary table of content validation studies for various forms of the Team Skills assessment. Although no discussion of these studies is included in the manual, it appears that these studies examined how the assessment was related to job duties in various industries. Between 6 and 10 raters were used to evaluate relatedness, and intraclass correlation rater agreement ranged from .85 to .93; no statistical evidence was provided in these studies to discuss the significance of these findings. The manual reported that no criterion-related or construct validity studies have been conducted.

COMMENTARY. The Team Skills (Form AR-C) is an easy-to-administer assessment tool with very clear administration and scoring instructions. Unfortunately, these are the only clear strengths that this instrument possesses. The manual for Team Skills (Form AR-C) does not provide a thorough overview of the constructs being assessed nor does it provide a strong rationale for the utility of this assessment. Very little information is provided regarding test development and construction. Further, no rationale is provided as to why the test measures the seven chosen areas of team skills; these areas also are not clearly defined, leaving the reader uncertain as to what constructs are being measured. The information presented in the manual regarding the standardization sample is inadequate; no demographic information is reported, and information is missing regarding how participants were recruited, leaving open the possibility of sampling bias. Although the manual provides information on percentile ranks for raw scores in the normative sample, these percentile ranks are not broken down by gender or race/ethnicity. More alarmingly, appropriate cut-off scores or "passing" scores are not provided, thus making it very difficult to interpret test results.

The reliability and validity data presented in the manual are inadequate. The internal consistency of items within subtests should be provided so the reader can assess the reliability of each subtest. More importantly, the reliability estimates provided in the manual are estimates from an earlier version of the test; eight items have been revised

in this version. These estimates are not applicable to the current test. The manual's discussion of validity is also insufficient. No specific information is provided about the content validation studies presented in the manual; thus, readers are not informed about how these studies were conducted or whether any statistically significant results were found. The studies presented do not provide scientific evidence of validity for the Team Skills (Form AR-C), calling into question whether this assessment is actually measuring team skills. Further, the test appears to be developed for and normed on workers in production jobs; it is questionable whether the reliability and validity data apply to other industries.

SUMMARY. The Ramsay Corporation Job Skills Team Skills (Form AR-C) was developed to evaluate an individual's ability to work as a member or leader of a team. It includes 35 multiple-choice items measuring seven areas of team principles including Conflict Resolution, Group Dynamics, Team Decision Making, Productivity and Motivation, Communication Skills, Leader and Member Skills, and Interpersonal Skills. Although this test provides clear instructions for administration and scoring, the manual does not provide an essential overview of constructs of interest, theoretical frameworks underlying the measure, or information regarding test development, reliability, and validity. Serious concerns regarding test development and construction, reliability, and validity were noted within the manual, and most of the information provided was based on earlier versions of the test. More research is needed to (a) test the standardization, reliability, and validity of the current version and (b) examine the test's use with test takers from various ethnic/racial groups, ages, and industries within the U.S.

Review of Team Skills Forms A (1997), A-C (1998), and AR-C (2009) by TRACY KANTROWITZ, Director of Research & Development, SHL, Atlanta, GA:

DESCRIPTION. The Team Skills Forms A, A-C, and AR-C are measures of knowledge of team principles for use in pre-employment selection and employee testing contexts. Based on job analytic research, the test was developed primarily for use with supervisor roles although the technical manual shows content evidence of validity for a variety of other jobs (customer engineers, production technicians, trainers, operators, utility workers). The test uses 35 situational judgment items to assess principles of team knowledge. Form A was the original format, Form A-C is a self-scoring format, and Form AR-C includes eight revised items. The test is available in paper-and-pencil and web-based formats with clear instructions to administrators regarding conditions under which to administer the test. The test is untimed, but the test authors indicate no more than one hour should be needed. Instructions for scoring the paper-and-pencil format are easy to follow.

DEVELOPMENT. The authors sought to develop a test of principles of team knowledge, and they reviewed books and periodicals to identify seven domains of team knowledge. Two industrial/organizational psychologists generated test items to map to the seven domains. Very little detail is provided, however, about the development of Team Skills. The construct or operational definition of team knowledge is not provided, even though a sizable literature exists on the topic in the area of industrial/organizational psychology (see, for example, Ilgen, Hollenbeck, Johnson, & Jundt, 2005; Salas, Goodwin, & Burke, 2008). In addition, no information is provided about the theoretical or empirical support for the seven domains, citations of articles describing the nomological network of team knowledge, rationale for the use of the situational judgment item format, how scoring was determined, how items were piloted and the final set of items selected, and the nature of the revisions to a selected number of items for Form AR-C.

TECHNICAL. The standardization sample for Team Skills (Form A-C) consisted of 2,173 applicants to production positions. Normative data are presented for the overall sample in the form of percentile ranks. No details are provided about the composition of the normative sample in terms of gender, race/ethnicity, and age makeup, so the norm group may or may not be representative of the larger population. In addition, no information is provided about norms for the subsequent forms of Team Skills, particularly Form AR-C, which includes revisions to a substantial number of the original items.

Item analysis statistics are provided for Form A-C for a large sample of 2,173 job applicants. Item difficulty and item total correlations are shown in the technical manual and indicate that most items substantially relate to the overall test scores and that a range of difficulty exists in the items. Item statistics are shown for the eight items that were

subsequently revised for Form AR-C. Additional information should be provided for how the new items performed.

Reliability evidence is presented for Form A-C in the form of measures of internal consistency. Reliability estimates were calculated using a sample of 2,173 (presumably the same group of applicants used to generate the normative data noted above). The test exhibits slightly lower than traditionally accepted levels of internal consistency reliability ($KR20$ = .70; odd/even, split-half item reliability = .71). According to published texts (e.g., Gatewood & Feild, 2000), tests used for pre-employment selection should reach a reliability threshold of .80.

Validity evidence is presented in the form of multiple content validation studies conducted between 1997 and 2006. Studies were conducted to determine the extent to which behaviors required on the test were also performed on the job. Results are presented in terms of interrater agreement and average job relatedness statistics. Few details are provided to interpret the meaningfulness of the job relatedness statistics. No information is given about who served as raters in the studies (incumbents, supervisors, or otherwise). If a value of 3 (on a 0-5 scale) constitutes "job related" then all studies indicated evidence of job relatedness, but the rating scale is unknown. In terms of the interrater agreement statistics, results are presented as intraclass correlation coefficients, and all values meet traditional levels of acceptability. The authors indicate reliance on content-related evidence of validity to support the use of the test for the intended purposes on the basis of job relatedness findings. No criterion-related or construct evidence of validation is provided, but such studies should be conducted to fully support the use of the test. Demonstrating criterion-related validation is particularly important to organizations wishing to understand the relationship between test scores and job performance criteria, such as team performance, so they understand the usefulness of the test for their applications. Furthermore, no information is provided about subgroup differences resulting from use of this test that may provide the potential for adverse impact to legally protected classes.

COMMENTARY. The Team Skills test is brief and easy to administer. It measures a knowledge domain reflective of changes in the world of work given the increased prevalence of team-based work (see Salas et al., 2008). The normative data are based on a large group of job applicants, but these data need to be updated to reflect the most current form of the test. Similarly, the reliability estimates are based on a large group of applicants, but item performance should be reviewed to identify methods of improving reliability. The test has been found to be job relevant for a variety of jobs. Most critically, however, validity evidence is extremely limited, and the theoretical basis supporting the assessment is unknown. In future development, the authors should consider conducting additional research on the instrument so the psychometric properties of the test reflect the latest version and provide more information to consumers about its usefulness.

SUMMARY. The Team Skills test was designed to measure principles of team knowledge for use in selection and development of employees. The test shows evidence of job relatedness through content validation. Unfortunately, very little evidence is provided to support the inferences made about the Team Skills test. More information is needed for critical evaluation.

REVIEWER'S REFERENCES

Gatewood, R., & Feild, H. S. (2000). *Human resource selection*. Mason, OH: South-Western College Publishers.
Ilgen, D. R., Hollenbeck, J. R., Johnson, M., & Jundt, D. (2005). Teams in organizations: From Input-Process-Output models to IMOI models. *Annual Review of Psychology, 56*, 517–543.
Salas, E., Goodwin, G. F., & Burke, C. S. (Eds.). (2008). *Team effectiveness in complex organizations*. New York, NY: Routledge.

[167]

Team vs. Individual Orientation Test.

Purpose: Designed to evaluate "work style."
Population: Under age 18 through adult.
Publication Date: 2011.
Acronym: TIOT.
Scores, 21: Overall Results, Self-Confidence, Interpersonal Discomfort, Feeling Inferior, Fear of Accountability, Peer Confidence, Unwillingness to Depend on Others, Issues with Consulting Others, Need to Compromise, Fear of Criticism, Having to Adjust for the Group, Loss of Control, Unfairness, Concern About Being Held Back, Not Getting Due Credit, Unfair Workload, Communication Issues, Meeting the Need to Communicate, Issues with Listening to Team Members, Fear of Speaking up in Front of Group, Worry About Unclear Roles.
Administration: Individual.
Price Data: Available from publisher.
Time: (20) minutes.
Comments: Self-administered online assessment. The test publisher advises that the test manual is being updated to include more information about methodology and theoretical background used in the development of the test. The test publisher also advises that this information is available to clients, as are benchmarks for relevant industries and racial/ethnic group comparison

data. However, this information was not provided to Buros or the reviewers.
Author: PsychTests AIM, Inc.
Publisher: PsychTests AIM, Inc. [Canada].

Review of the Team vs. Individual Orientation Test by THEODORE L. HAYES, Personnel Research Psychologist, U.S. Office of Personnel Management, Washington, DC:

DESCRIPTION. The Team vs. Individual Orientation Test (TIOT) is a web-administered 86-item, self-report purported measure of "[T]he work setting in which a person is most motivated (individual work or in a team setting), along with potential concerns" (manual, p. 1). The target respondent audience includes working-age adults. The test and its supporting materials are written in English, although because the test publisher is based in Quebec one might have anticipated a companion French-language version. The 86 items are measured through varying Likert-type scales resulting in an "overall Team Orientation score" as well as six scale scores (Self-Confidence, Peer Confidence, Need to Compromise, Unfairness, Communication Issues, and Worry About Unclear Roles), and 14 subscale scores. The publisher's test catalog refers to a "second revision" of the TIOT, a designation not made in the test manual, but the second revision seems to be based on the same standardization sample and scales as reported in the test manual. The catalog states that the TIOT "complies" with American Psychological Association standards as well as U.S. Equal Employment Opportunity Commission standards for disability and gender; no mention is made of Canadian fair employment standards. Test-taker feedback includes an autogenerated report for each score, summary comments about one's overall team orientation, and notes about strengths and developmental areas. Other general test feedback materials and advice include potential interview questions for managers.

DEVELOPMENT. TIOT data were gathered from 18,868 respondents who came across the TIOT on any of three general interest websites (e.g., www.queendom.com). No timeframe for data collection is mentioned. No information is provided regarding the proportion of respondents who took the assessment more than once across the three websites. Within the development sample, 47% were female, 27% were male, and 26% did not disclose gender; 19% of respondents were under 18 years of age, 14% were at least 40 years old, 22% did not indicate age, and the age range for the remainder (45%) was between 18 and 39. The test manual does not state how many items comprised the initial version of the TIOT. Reliability information presented in the manual claims there are 74 TIOT questions counted for the overall score, though the five subscales combined (the sixth is never mentioned in the reliability analyses) apparently have 85 questions. Some new question may have been added as well, according to the manual.

TECHNICAL.

Standardization. Contrary to what the catalog states and/or alludes to–the TIOT's test catalog and test manual are frequently inconsistent with each other–no analyses of data by disability category or of data administered under accommodated conditions are presented. No "benchmarks for 35 industries" as claimed were made available nor is there an attempt at any sort of normative table. Mean difference analyses by age include the five categories (e.g., "18–24") out of the original respondent sample, but, apparently in an attempt to have comparable-sized categories, not all respondent data within each category were analyzed; no rationale is given for this omission or for the basis by which some cases were dropped. No analyses compare those 40 years of age and older to those under 40. There are no analyses of scores according to respondent race/national origin. There are analyses of variance and *t*-test analyses with the full respondent sample by gender at the total score, scale, and subscale levels.

Reliability. The test publisher has chosen an internal consistency reliability model. The coefficient alphas for five main scales (sixth scale not reported) range from .82 to .90, and the coefficient alpha for the total score is .95. Given that the test publisher claims the TIOT could be used for team building and training as well as pre-employment assessment, one should expect to see stability coefficients as well as coefficient alpha. The very high coefficient alpha for the overall score indicates that the TIOT is homogeneous generally, which likely lessens the diagnostic utility of scale and subscale scores.

Validity. The content-oriented approach to validity of the TIOT is debatable. There is no indication of how these items were developed. The items are lengthy and phrased to reflect extremes of concerns and anxieties about working with others in teams. The items are also less subtle than other more psychologically sophisticated items (compare to, for example, the "Big 5" items at www.ipip.ori. org). Consequently, when responding to the TIOT items, one might "strongly disagree" not with the sentiment assessed but with the extremity of the wording of an item. That is, I might be unsure about the roles of team members but I would strongly disagree that I was "very concerned" about these roles, as the item might be stated.

The conceptual or construct-level evidence of validity of the TIOT is a matter of taste. Being a "good team player" may be a corporate or social virtue, but its diffuse nature is not easily operationalized. Will I, as a high scorer on the TIOT, be successful in a team situation? Would I, as a low scorer, never be able to work in any team? Will those with low scores be successful as individual contributors? Would teams with higher overall TIOT scores be more successful than teams with lower overall scores? Will those with high TIOT scores challenge poor or malfeasant leadership, which after all would mean disrupting the team? Can training lead me to change my team orientation, and if so to what extent? These are important issues for an assessment such as the TIOT where there are either potential adverse consequences for low scores in pre-employment testing or the TIOT is used as part of personal development.

The criterion-oriented evidence of validity of the TIOT ranges from none to suspect. The publisher apparently had initial respondents indicate whether they were "popular at work" (3-point scale) and whether they had ever "declined to work with a team" (dichotomous). These are offered as "criteria" (referred to as comparison variables in the manual) without further elaboration or consideration of their adequacy and contamination. Furthermore, as with analyses of age, the number of cases is dramatically reduced for these criterion-focused analyses to create equal numbers of respondents per outcome category. No rationale is provided for this approach or for the reduction strategy to create these equal-sized groups. Separately, the TIOT scoring algorithm is unusual. High scores on the scales and subscales seem to be "bad" but the overall TIOT score is scaled so that higher scores, presumably based on scale and subscale scores, are "good." Technically, this is not necessarily problematic, but when viewed on a feedback report it is not obvious and can be confusing.

COMMENTARY. The test manual for the TIOT is probably less than adequate. There is no rationale provided for why the TIOT items, scales, subscales, or reliability models were chosen. Analyses are only tangential and are provided without logic or rationale, though with an eye toward proving analyses were conducted. There is no explanation or data to show what the measure should be related to from either a nomological network or business perspective. Instead, the manual presents several dozen pages of *t*-tests and score distributions with no apparent logic other than to present *t*-tests and score distributions.

Although the TIOT items are nominally focused on teamwork, its constructs are indistinguishable from "Big 5" measures of emotional stability and extraversion. Some users may not find that to be problematic. However, those users would also need more support regarding cutscores and interpretation guidelines than is available in the TIOT manual or website.

The publisher has positioned the TIOT as being useful for "pre-employment testing" (manual, p. 1). The publisher should be more forthcoming that there is no such thing as a "pre-validated" test in general nor is there any cumulative validation evidence specifically for the TIOT. However, if an organization's occupational analysis and competency model support the type of constructs assessed in the TIOT, practitioners may wish to examine the TIOT's psychometric adequacy and demographic fairness in their organizations. But these practitioners at the same time cannot rely on what is in the manual.

Finally, the TIOT and the feedback it provides would be impressive for a previous generation of web-based tests. Given how much technical expertise the catalog and website claim the publisher has, and what else is available on the market, the TIOT should be expected to have next generation web-based test technology such as adaptive testing or even avatars.

SUMMARY. Not everyone can work successfully in teams. Team success requires coordinated effort, complementary skills, and emotional resilience. None of that is necessarily measured in the TIOT.

Review of the Team vs. Individual Orientation Test by JEAN POWELL KIRNAN, Professor of Psychology, The College of New Jersey, Ewing, NJ:

[The reviewer would like to thank Steven Siminerio for his contributions to this review. His diligence and insights were greatly appreciated.]

DESCRIPTION. The Team vs. Individual Orientation Test, TIOT, is a self-administered, online pre-employment measure designed to gauge

test takers' team and individual work styles. The test, which is not timed, can be completed in approximately 20 minutes. The visual layout of the assessment is standard of most online surveys. Test takers answer the majority of 86 items (68) using a 5-point Likert scale, with additional questions presented in multiple-choice format. One problem test takers may face is the labeling of the Likert scale. The first 3 of the 5 points on the scale are *completely true, strongly true*, and *somewhat true/ false*. Respondents may read the first two options as meaning nearly the same thing, as both "completely" and "strongly" are absolute and strong adjectives. Additionally, the third option could be interpreted three different ways: *somewhat true, somewhat false*, and *neutral* (as it is the middle of five options). This may lead to some test takers defaulting to Option 3. A standard *strongly agree, agree, neutral*, etc. may work better.

The TIOT measures individuals on six different scales: Self-Confidence, Peer Confidence, Need to Compromise, Unfairness, Communication Issues, and Worry about Unclear Roles. Within each of the six scales, except Worry about Unclear Roles, there are further subscales provided. Score reports are divided into six sections: summary, introduction, graphs, detailed interpretive statements for each of the 21 scores, strengths and limitations, and advice. The graphs section presents scores for the overall score, the six main scales, and each of the subscales on a number line scaled 0–100. However, no information is provided about how the test taker's score on each of the subscales contributes to the main scales or to the overall score, a point needing clarification because adding subscales does not yield main scale scores and adding the six main scales does not produce the total score.

In addition, the report provides test takers with information and suggestions about how to use the feedback to better themselves as employees in the workplace. This material conflicts with the stated purpose of the TIOT as a pre-employment measure, which calls for a score report with directives for the employer and not one with self-help guides.

DEVELOPMENT. No information is provided about the development of the TIOT and thus the measure and scales lack context for evaluation. The six major scales and various subscales suggest a concept or theory about how people work in teams as they touch on obstacles, concerns, and strategies associated with teamwork. However, an explanation is needed. Are there specific theories, observations, research, or professional experiences that guided the authors in writing items and determining subscales? There is no evidence to support what the TIOT or its subscales, in fact, measure. A review of the items by subject matter experts, a basis in theory, or statistical evidence (such as a factor analysis) is needed.

TECHNICAL. The norms are really descriptive statistics based on an uncontrolled sample of 18,868 subjects: 47% female, 27% male, and 26% of unknown gender. Similarly, 22% of the subjects did not report age. Knowing the gender and age distribution of a normative sample is vital for prospective test users. The manual also states that 19% of the normative sample was below the age of 18. As the TIOT was designed to be an employment tool, the inclusion of these individuals is questionable for the target population. In addition, no information was reported on the ethnicities, geographic locations, years of employment, or occupations of the subjects in the sample, which would be important information to include based on the purpose of the assessment. This is especially true in a web-based sample where there are concerns that select ethnic and socioeconomic groups are underrepresented.

There appears to be inconsistent administration of the assessment in the norming process. The test was offered on three different test-taking websites, and subjects selected the TIOT from various tests and quizzes available. However, no information was provided on whether or not the test appeared aesthetically the same for all subjects or was advertised similarly on the three websites. The type of websites the assessment was offered on was also inconsistent: test publisher, *Psychology Today* magazine, and Queendom, which advertises itself as an "interactive venue for self-exploration with a healthy dose of fun," ("About Queendom," n.d.). Although it is stated on the website that Queendom is a subsidiary company of the test publisher, it appears as though the purpose of the Queendom website is more fun and lighthearted than for purposes of norming a potential employment tool.

The use of the Internet for any data collection has concerns, but the use for developing a normative sample presents unique challenges. The most important concerns are the quality of the survey responses and the representativeness of the sample (Paolacci, Chandler, & Ipeirotis, 2010). One has to question the motivation and honesty of individuals who frequent free testing websites. Yet, there is no indication of validity checks or elimination of duplicate responses. The authors themselves describe the sample as "uncontrolled; the subjects self-selected to take the assessment and opted in to participate in the validation study" (manual, p. 2).

Excellent internal reliability estimates are provided using coefficient alpha. The coefficients were reported as .95 for Overall Score, .88 for Self-Confidence, .85 for Peer Confidence, .90 for Need to Compromise, .82 for Unfairness, and .85 for Communication Issues. No reliability data are reported for Worry about Unclear Roles or the 14 subscales. It is recommended that the authors address this oversight and also demonstrate the stability of the TIOT through a test-retest reliability methodology.

The authors' attempt at providing construct evidence of validity falls far short of the requirements, despite the fact that exhaustive statistical analyses and graphs are provided. TIOT scores are compared for select variables of gender, age, "declined opportunity to work on a team," and "popularity at work." It is unclear how the last two variables were measured. For example, is declined opportunity "ever declined," "often declined," "declined in the last year"? The Y-axes on the graphs vary in range across the 21 scores. Thus, what visually appears to be a large difference is often less than a point, but looks the same as a statistically significant difference of several points. The authors highlight which of the 21 scores differ on the variables tested without any reference to whether the existence of differences or direction of differences is, in fact, hypothesized or expected with the construct. These problems trace back to the fact that no theory of work orientation has been proposed. Presenting differences and lack of differences in a vacuum does not prove validity.

If this instrument was indeed intended for use in an employment setting, a much more rigorous demonstration of validity and fairness would be required. Yet, even as a self-exploration tool, the TIOT has inadequate validity.

COMMENTARY. The TIOT is a quick, easy-to-administer, face-valid instrument. All of the questions on the test would be the types of questions one would expect on an assessment about teamwork. That being said, the TIOT has many shortcomings. The lack of any information about the theory supporting the test severely impacts the validity as well as an understanding of the instrument's development. The normative sample is inadequately described and questionably obtained.

Although the manual lists the application of the TIOT as "pre-employment testing," there is no information provided as to how these scores might be used in a selection or placement context. Indeed, many team measures are used by employers for employee personal development or facilitation of work teams with existing employees. However, this shift from employee development to employee selection brings with it the burden of EEO laws and professional guidelines related to validity, protected groups, alternatives search, adverse impact–none of which are addressed by the authors. Items are also transparent, a common situation in counseling or self-development tools where we assume honesty and motivation for self-improvement on the part of the respondent. If the TIOT were used as a part of the selection or placement process, the transparency would likely lead to faking and threaten the reliability and validity of the instrument. The TIOT may work better as a self-help quiz as opposed to a pre-employment measure based on the layout of the score report and the websites through which the test was normed.

SUMMARY. There is little to endorse in the TIOT as currently presented. The reviewer is left to ponder whether there was adequate development, whether the development was based on theory, or whether the instrument was haphazardly developed as appears from the lack of information provided. This reviewer is still unclear as to the TIOT's purpose: pre-employment testing or self-exploration. If intended as part of a selection process, much more rigorous statistical analyses are required. If intended as self-exploration and not selection, then one has to question whether the TIOT is an improvement over existing, well-established measures of general style such as the Myers-Briggs Type Indicator (MBTI; 14:251).

REVIEWER'S REFERENCES

About Queendom. (n.d.) Retrieved August 10, 2012, from http://www.queendom.com/about/about/about.htm
Paolacci, G., Chandler, J., & Ipeirotis, P. G. (2010). Running experiments on Amazon Mechanical Turk. *Judgment and Decision Making, 5,* 411-419.

[168]

Test of Auditory Processing Skills 3: Spanish-Bilingual Edition.

Purpose: Designed to assess "auditory skills commonly utilized in academic and everyday activities."
Population: Spanish-bilingual children ages 5-0 to 18-11.
Publication Dates: 1985-2009.
Acronym: TAPS-3:SBE.
Scores, 13: Word Discrimination, Phonological Segmentation, Phonological Blending, Number memory Forward, Number Memory Reversed, Word Memory, Sentence Memory, Auditory Comprehension, Auditory Reasoning, Phonologic Index, Memory Index, Cohesion Index, Overall Score.
Subtests, 9: Word Discrimination, Phonological Segmentation, Phonological Blending, Number memory Forward, Number Memory Reversed, Word Memory, Sentence Memory, Auditory Comprehension, Auditory Reasoning.
Administration: Individual.
Price Data, 2010: $140 per complete kit including manual (2009, 104 pages), 25 test booklets, and Auditory Figure-ground CD; $50 per manual.
Foreign Language Edition: English edition available.
Time: 60 (10) minutes.
Comments: Spanish edition, based on but not a translation of the English-language Test of Auditory Processing Skills–Third Edition (18:137).
Author: Nancy A. Martin.
Publisher: Academic Therapy Publications.
Cross References: For reviews by Timothy R. Konold and Rebecca Blanchard and by Dolores Kluppel Vetter of the Test of Auditory Processing Skills–Third Edition, see 18:137; for reviews by Annabel J. Cohen and by Anne R. Kessler and Jaclyn B. Spitzer of the Test of Auditory-Perceptual Skills, Revised, see 13:324 (2 references).

Review of the Test of Auditory Processing Skills 3: Spanish Bilingual Edition by VICTORIA A. COMERCHERO, Assistant Professor of School Psychology, Touro College, New York, NY:

DESCRIPTION. The Test of Auditory Processing Skills 3: Spanish-Bilingual Edition (TAPS-3:SBE) is an individually administered test measuring auditory skills in Spanish-speaking bilingual children (5-0 to 18-11). The test author reports that the skills measured by the TAPS-3:SBE correlate significantly with those that students use in "academic and everyday activities" (manual, p. 9). The structure of the test is similar to that of the TAPS–3 (Martin & Brownell, 2005) in that both consist of nine core subtests organized in order of task difficulty as well as one optional subtest on a CD-ROM. The instructions are presented verbally and students respond orally; however, a benefit of this test is that students do not need to read or write in order to be tested. The TAPS-3:SBE subtests were created to assess auditory processing skills as they relate to both "cognitive and communicative aspects of language" (manual, p. 11). Specifically the subtests provide information in four major domains: auditory attention, basic phonological skills, auditory memory, and auditory cohesion. The latter three areas comprise the scoring indices reflecting different skill sets. The test author notes that before administration begins, it should be confirmed that the examinee (child) is able to accurately hear the sounds presented and can attend to what was heard, thus ruling out problems with peripheral hearing and/or attention deficits.

The administration instructions are presented clearly and systematically. The protocol is well-organized and has clear directions and practice items and the front page of the protocol has two noteworthy sections: "Administration Reminders" and "How this Booklet is Organized." Estimated time of completion is about 1 hour for the nine core subtests (approximately 7 minutes per subtest) but no time limit is imposed. Four key indices are computed. The Phonologic Index provides a relatively quick assessment of some basic phonological abilities. This index represents a sum of the first three subtests (Word Discrimination, Phonological Segmentation and Phonological Blending). The Memory Index entails the next four subtests (Number Memory Forward, Number Memory Reversed, Word Memory, and Sentence Memory) measuring basic memory processes and sequencing skills. For the Cohesion Index, the last two subtests (Auditory Comprehension and Auditory Reasoning), comprising the most complex tasks, assess higher order linguistic constructs. When scoring the items some changes made from the TAPS-3 include allowing for partial credit for some test responses, three new index scores (Phonological Skills, Memory, and Cohesion), and finally, the Overall Score is based on the sum of all subtest scaled scores, which are conversions from raw scores. The Index and Overall scores are based on sums of scaled scores and are reported as Standard Scores. To avoid scoring errors, a calculator is needed because no computer scoring software for this test exists to date.

DEVELOPMENT. The test author cites Hambleton and Patsula's (1999) research regarding translating retests vs. constructing new tests in a second language and notes that this research guided the development and revision of test items. A translation service was used along with feedback from bilingual professionals in the field. Based on the aforementioned review, the Compound Words portion of the Phonological Segmentation subtest was eliminated. New passages and queries also were added to the Sentence Memory, Auditory Comprehension, and Auditory Reasoning subtests.

As described by the test author, the Word Memory subtests were chosen to match as closely as possible the difficulty levels of words in the English version. Word frequencies, based on a "published frequency dictionary" (manual, p. 47), were used to assist with word arrangement and order of word presentation. After the norming study, all bilingual examiner comments were incorporated into a prepublication version that was then reviewed by an additional panel of bilingual professionals proficient in testing and with the English TAPS-3.

After extensive statistical analyses were performed, items that performed poorly were eliminated and the final sequence of the items for the published edition of the test was produced. The test author discussed multi-stage qualitative and quantitative procedures that were utilized to limit the test's bias. The Pearson's point biserial analysis and Rasch analysis of TAPS-3:SBE items showed no evidence of bias. Finally, the test author utilized differential item functioning analysis, which was deemed appropriate because the TAPS-3:SBE was normed on one ethnicity group (Hispanic) using the contrast method, described extensively in the test manual (p. 49). Results yielded no bias in any of the contrasts used to evaluate the TAPS-3:SBE.

A final item analysis was performed after all normative data were received in order to determine which items would be retained (and in what presentation order) for the final, published version of the TAPS-3:SBE. Selection of items involved careful consideration of item analyses and differential item functioning statistics along with the comments made by the examiners and reviewers. According to the test author, "The items chosen were those that were shown to be highly discriminating, culturally balanced, and sensitive to a wide range of ability" (manual, p. 50).

TECHNICAL. The standardization sample for the TAPS-3:SBE consisted of 851 Spanish bilingual children between the ages of 5 years 0 months and 18 years 11 months residing in the United States and Puerto Rico. The majority of the sample was from the west coast region of the U.S. (n = 671). The test author did not provide information regarding the race/ethnicity of the sample, and although she attempted to obtain a diverse sample there may be some mismatch with respect to the ethnicity of the Hispanic population living in the United States and the normed sample because (a) no data regarding the subcategory of Hispanic culture are provided, and (b) the majority of the sample is from the west coast (79.2%), yet according to the data obtained from the U.S. Census (2006), which the test author stated "closely approximates the demographics of the U.S. Hispanic population" (manual, p. 53), only 42% of Hispanics live in the West. Additionally, there are some other approximations that do not completely match the U.S. Hispanic population parameters for demographic characteristics. In examining Table 6.1 "Demographic Characteristics of the Normative Sample" (manual, p. 54), there are some other instances in which the percentage of the normed sample representing a certain characteristic deviates from the comparative parameters (e.g., gender, type of residence). Additionally, the normative percentage of Hispanic population residing in Puerto Rico was not provided by the test author.

Normative data are provided separately by age group in increments of 1 and 2 years and for each of the 9 subtests as well as for the total raw scores. Scaled and standard scores were obtained using a statistically sound method (Angoff, 1971) in which the derived scaled scores were based on a distribution having a normal mean ($M = 10$; $SD = 3$). Standard scores yielded were also based on the normal curve ($M = 100$; $SD = 15$). The test author also provides percentile ranks that corresponded to the standard scores and age equivalents in separate appendices. Overall, although the standardization sample may have some slight mismatches in terms of representing the Hispanic demographic population, strengths in using a large sample size as well as careful selection of examiners and checking of protocols bolsters the overall quality of the standardization sample.

Strong reliability evidence was documented. Using the normative sample ($n = 851$), internal consistency using coefficient alpha yielded moderate to high reliability with the majority of subtests above .80 and ranging from .78–.97 across all ages. Additionally, temporal stability was documented using a sample of 63 examinees who were retested by the same examiner over an average interval of 14 days. The test-retest correlations ranged from .60 to .95 for each subtest, and .53 to .90 for indices. Additionally, the small standard error of measurement for each subtest and index further bolsters the reliability of this test. Overall, the procedures used to obtain reliability are thoroughly described in the TAPS-3:SBE manual.

Validity evidence for the TAPS-3:SBE is reported extensively by the test author in three main areas. First, content evidence is reflected as the items and tasks were carefully developed to reflect measurement of auditory processing skills related to those required in academic settings. In establishing content validity, item analysis resulted in selection of nonbiased items that ranged in difficulty levels commensurate with a wide range of abilities. Second, concurrent evidence is reported. The test author used the English version of the TAPS-3 because there are no other tests in Spanish that assess the same blend of auditory skills. A sample of 36 students who were determined to be at a similar language proficiency in both languages were tested with both the English and Spanish-Bilingual version. Correlations ranged from .70 to .94 reflecting similarity between the abilities measured by the two tests.

Finally, the test author organized the construct evidence into three sections. First, in terms of developmental progression, the median raw scores showed positive correlations between age and TAPS-3:SBE raw scores. Next, studies representing academic skills were conducted, specifically with the WJ-III (Woodcock-Johnson III) by comparing Broad Reading and Writing scores. Moderate correlations between the Broad Reading and TAPS-3:SBE scores for the Word Discrimination subtest ($r = .46$) and Phonological Segmentation ($r = .52$) were obtained with lower coefficients for other subtests deemed less related to reading/writing skills. WJ-III Writing scores also demonstrated moderate correlations with TAPS-3:SBE Word Discrimination scores ($r = .47$) and lower with the remaining tasks. However, the small sample sizes ($n = 16$) call for caution on the part of the test user in interpreting these studies. The test author presented the validity evidence in well-organized tables in the manual.

Exceptional group differences were also found by administration of the TAPS-3:SBE, further adding to the construct validity of the test. Specifically, scores for students with CAPD (Central Auditory Processing Disorder) were significantly lower on eight of the TAPS:3-SBE subtests and all four of the indices compared to scores obtained by students in the normative sample. Students with Attention Deficit Disorder diagnoses also showed significantly lower scores for six of the subtests and three of the indices when compared to the normative sample. Again, small sample sizes ($n = 48$ and $n = 37$, respectively) limit the value of this evidence.

The test author also noted that students in the special education group performed similarly to the ADD groups, scoring significantly lower on seven subtests and three indices when compared to the matched sample. Again the limited sample size ($N = 36$) compared to the larger matched sample ($N = 851$) is an area of weakness. The test author widely encourages "users of the TAPS-3:SBE … to submit studies pertaining to the validity of the test" (manual, p. 68), thus acknowledging that the small number of published studies to date makes the findings somewhat tenuous in terms of interpretation. Additional evidence supporting validity of the construct was obtained through use of a two-fold factor analytic process. Based on the results of factor analysis, the three TAPS-3:SBE constructs were found to be the same as those in the English version: Basic Phonological Skills, Auditory Memory, and Auditory Cohesion.

COMMENTARY. The TAPS-3:SBE is a strong adaptation of the original TAPS-3. The test author provides extensive psychometric data with a large normative sample for bilingual students. Presenting concurrent evidence of validity using individualized achievement tests (e.g., WJ-III Reading and Writing) bolsters the rationale for using this test to determine the practical utility in terms of how the results directly relate to everyday academic skills, which was one of the TAPS-3:SBE's stated purposes. Administration and scoring instructions are clearly written and easy to follow. Reminders on the protocol help the examiner to stay attuned to some of the common errors made, especially by newer testers (e.g., do not repeat after x number of trials).

SUMMARY. The TAPS-3:SBE is an adaptation of the TAPS-3 intended to be used to assess everyday auditory skills related to practical and academic functioning amongst Spanish-English bilingual speakers. The test meets its goal of assessing the major domains (basic phonological abilities, basic memory processes, and higher order auditory comprehension and reasoning skills) that underlie the larger construct of auditory processing. In adapting the test to meet the needs of the exponential rise of Spanish-speaking students, the TAPS-3:SBE will be well-received by speech pathologists, psychologists, and other professionals who need to assess the functional auditory processing skills that are pivotal to academic success as well as everyday daily functioning.

REVIEWER'S REFERENCES
Angoff, W. (1971). Scales, norms and equivalent scores. In R. L. Thorndike (Ed.), *Educational measurement, 2nd ed.* Washington, DC: National Council on Education.
Hambleton, R. K., & Patsula, L. (1999). Increasing the validity of adapted tests: Myths to be avoided and guidelines for improving test adaptation practices. *Journal of Applied Testing Technology, 1,* 1–30.
Martin, N. A., & Brownell, R. (2005). Test of Auditory Processing Skills, 3rd Edition. Novato, CA: Academic Therapy Publications.

Review of the Test of Auditory Processing Skills 3: Spanish-Bilingual Edition by S. KATHLEEN KRACH, Associate Professor, Troy University, Montgomery, AL:

DESCRIPTION. The purpose of the Test of Auditory Processing Skills 3: Spanish-Bilingual Edition (TAPS-3:SBE) is to determine "how well a child uses and understands what is heard" (manual, p. 14). The test was designed based on two separate models of auditory processing. Richard's (2001) model focuses on central auditory processing and language processing, whereas the Bellis/Ferre model (Bellis, 2002) expands on the typologies of auditory disorders. The test author was clear that the TAPS-3:SBE was not designed as a language proficiency test, nor was it designed as a standalone measure to diagnose a Central Auditory Processing Disorder (C)APD. Instead, it was designed to provide one piece of information in comprehensive language and/or psychological evaluations. Different from the TAPS-3, the TAPS-3:SBE was specifically designed for Hispanic children ages 5 years, 0 months through 18 years, 11 months who are from the United States.

The TAPS-3:SBE consists of nine required subtests, one optional subtest, and four indices. The Phonological Index is composed of the Word Discrimination, Phonological Segmentation, and Phonological Blending subtests. The Memory Index is composed of the Number Memory Forward, Number Memory Reversed, Word Memory, and Sentence Memory subtests. The Cohesion Index is composed of the Auditory Comprehension and Auditory Reasoning subtests. An Overall Index score is available consisting of all of the subtests except the optional Figure-Ground subtest. The Figure-Ground subtest stands alone and is not included in any of the indices.

The entire test takes approximately 45 to 60 minutes to complete. The TAPS-3:SBE is administered in Spanish; however, if the test taker cannot understand Spanish instructions, the examiner can repeat them in English. Although instructions can be provided in English, questions are to be administered in Spanish. If the child answers the question in English, full credit will be provided for the answer. Given the bilingual nature of this test, the examiner must speak fluently in English and Spanish. All of the test items are presented in an auditory manner. This is done either by the administrator reading items from the blank test form (core subtests) or by presenting information from an audio CD-ROM (optional Figure-Ground subtest). In order to interpret the core subtests it is necessary to convert the raw scores to scaled scores (mean = 10, standard deviation = 3), percentile ranks, or age equivalents. Index raw scores are converted to a standard score (mean = 100, standard deviation = 15) and percentile ranks. The optional Figure-Ground subtest is interpreted by counting the number of errors; if there are more than two errors, the test administrator is requested to check for attention problems in the test taker.

DEVELOPMENT AND TECHNICAL INFORMATION.

Development. According to Konold and Blanchard (2010), the English TAPS-3 is an updated version of Gardner's Test of Auditory Perceptual Skills, Revised (TAPS-R) from 1996. Significant changes were made to Gardner's original version in the updated third edition. According to Martin (2009), the Spanish-Bilingual version is a direct adaptation of the TAPS-3. For more information on the TAPS-3 in English, see *The Mental Measurements Yearbook* reviews (18:137).

Standardization. The sample consisted of 851 Spanish-English bilingual children living in the United States and Puerto Rico. Participants were chosen to match the demographic characteristics within the U.S. Hispanic population across the parameters of region, race/ethnicity, parent education, gender, and residence as was described by the information provided by the U.S. Census Bureau in 2006 and the U.S. Department of Education in 2000.

Reliability. Internal consistency data were obtained through the use of coefficient alpha. All of the index coefficients indicated high internal consistency across all categories (.80–.99). The subtests provide solid evidence for internal consistency in all areas for all age categories with the exception of the memory subtests. For some ages, the memory subtests have coefficients as low as .55. These coefficients indicate that although modestly reliable, the memory subtest score should be interpreted more broadly than the other scores provided.

Test-retest reliability data were provided with an average of 14 days separating test administra-

tions. Reliability coefficients indicate strong temporal stability for all of the composites, except the Cohesion Index (.53), which demonstrates modest stability. Temporal stability evidence was better than internal consistency evidence for the memory subtests (lowest one is Sentence Memory at .62).

Validity. The author of the test presented multiple types of evidence to support validity of test score use. Content evidence was provided first for the TAPS-3. A panel of judges evaluated the Spanish translation version across each of the content areas of concern. Item changes were made based on recommendations by the panel. Items were then analyzed using Rasch and differential item functioning analyses. These analyses determined item difficulty and affected item selection. Concurrent evidence of validity was demonstrated for the TAPS-3:SBE by administering the TAPS-3 and the TAPS-3:SBE to children who were determined to be equally proficient in each language. All but one correlation coefficient was .80 or above. The exception was the Word Discrimination subtest, which had a correlation coefficient of .70. Predictive validity data indicated that the TAPS-3:SBE scores provide statistically significant differences in scores for individuals with and without a diagnosed disability. Construct validity evidence was shown through factor analysis data. Three main factors were expected from the test scores (basic phonological skills, auditory memory, and auditory cohesion), as these were the factors found in the TAPS-3. Principal Components Analysis supports these three factors.

COMMENTARY. The TAPS-3, English-only version was previously reviewed in *The Mental Measurements Yearbook.* Konold and Blanchard (2010) described the TAPS-3 as having weak evidence of validity. However, Vetter (2010) felt that although the psychometric properties were not superb, the need for the instrument outweighed the faults. In a separate study, Edwards (2006) found that the TAPS-3 may not actually measure strictly auditory processing. Instead, it was stated that the test may measure verbal cognitive ability as well. Therefore, it appears that the English version upon which the TAPS-3:SBE was built may have some underlying weaknesses that extend to the adapted version of the test as well.

These weaknesses seem to carry over at a minor level to the TAPS-3:SBE. The TAPS-3:SBE also demonstrated some psychometric weaknesses in terms of validity and reliability data presented in the test manual. However, none of these appear to be as significant of a problem as previously noted in the English version. Also, the test author did a fantastic job of accurately representing the desired population (Hispanics living within the United States) within the normative group. Therefore, this reviewer agrees with Vetter's (2010) evaluation of the TAPS-3 that this instrument may not be perfect, but it is sufficient for the current assessment needs of the field given the lack of few better options.

SUMMARY. The TAPS-3:SBE was built to be a psychometrically sound companion to the English-only TAPS-3 assessment tool. The test developers built the Spanish-bilingual version using updated item selection and item analysis as well as appropriate norms for the target population of Hispanics from the United States. The test author describes the purpose of the TAPS-3:SBE as measuring what a child hears and understands. In addition, she is very clear that the TAPS-3:SBE is only one tool that can be used as part of a comprehensive battery of tests for the bilingual child. To this end, it appears that the TAPS-3:SBE does a solid job of meeting these goals. However, further research examining the psychometric properties of this instrument should be conducted.

REVIEWER'S REFERENCES

Bellis, T. (2002). *When the brain can't hear: Unraveling the mystery of auditory processing disorder.* New York: Pocket Books.
Edwards, K. M. (2006). *The Test of Auditory Processing Skills–Third Edition (TAPS-3): Validity analyses and reconceptualization based on the Cattell-Horn-Carroll model of cognitive abilities* (Unpublished doctoral dissertation). Auburn University, Auburn, AL.
Martin, N. A. (2009). *Test of Auditory Processing Skills, Third Edition: Spanish-Bilingual Edition (TAPS-3:SBE) manual.* Novato, CA: Academic Therapy Publications.
Konold, T. R., & Blanchard, R. (2010). [Review of the Test of Auditory Processing Skills-Third Edition.] In R. A. Spies, J. F. Carlson, & K. F. Geisinger (Eds.), *The eighteenth mental measurements yearbook* (pp. 619-622). Lincoln, NE: Buros Institute of Mental Measurements.
Richard, G. (2011). *The source for processing disorders.* East Moline, IL: LinguiSystems.
Vetter, D. K. (2010). [Review of the Test of Auditory Processing Skills-Third Edition.] In R. A. Spies, J. F. Carlson, & K. F. Geisinger (Eds.), *The eighteenth mental measurements yearbook* (pp. 622-624). Lincoln, NE: Buros Institute of Mental Measurements.

[169]

The Test of Infant Motor Performance.

Purpose: Designed to test "postural and selective motor control needed for functional performance in daily life during infancy."

Population: Ages birth to 17 weeks (term-born infants); 34 weeks postmenstrual age through 4 months post-term (premature infants).

Publication Dates: 2001-2012.

Acronym: TIMP; TIMPSI.

Score: Total score only.

Administration: Individual.

Forms, 2: Test of Infant Motor Performance, Version 5.1; TIMP Screening Items, Version 1.0.

Price Data, 2013: $36 per manual (2012, 65 pages); $65 per 25 TIMP test forms; $10 per 100 Percentile Rank score sheets; $85 per self-instructional Compact Disc V. 4; $15 per age calculator; $60 per 50 TIMPSI test forms.

Foreign Language Editions: French and Portuguese editions available for the TIMP.

Time: (21-45) minutes.

Comments: Additional materials required for administration but not included: rattle, squeaky object, shiny red ball, age calculation wheel; after getting a total raw score, it is possible to obtain standard scores based on age norms as well as percentile rank scores; electronic version of the TIMP available (the TIMP Online).

Authors: Suzann K. Campbell, Gay L. Girolami, Thubi H. A. Kolobe, Elizabeth T. Osten, and Maureen C. Lenke.

Publisher: Infant Motor Performance Scales, LLC.

Review of the Test of Infant Motor Performance by KORESSA KUTSICK MALCOLM, School Psychologist, The Virginia School for the Deaf and the Blind, Staunton, VA:

[Editor's Note: This review is based on Version 2.0 of the test user's manual. Version 3.0, which was released in 2012, was not available at the time the review was written.]

DESCRIPTION. The Test of Infant Motor Performance (TIMP) is an individually administered assessment system designed to measure motor functioning in newborns. The purpose of the TIMP is to determine the postural control and motor movements of infants, particularly for those who experienced premature birth or other birth trauma. The test was developed to be used by health professionals such as occupational and physical therapists who work with infants in special care settings. The TIMP may be administered to infants born prematurely at 34 weeks postmenstrual age to age 17 weeks post full-term delivery.

The TIMP is divided into two separate parts. There are 13 observed test items as well as 29 elicited items that comprise the test. Administration begins with a 2- to 3-minute observation session where examiners note an infant's spontaneous movements, watching for specific actions. A checklist is provided to record whether given movements occur. Observations for these movements can continue throughout the assessment of the elicited items and examiners may give credit for any movements that occur after the initial observation session. For the elicited items, examiners position infants in various situations, noting their motor responses. The responses in the elicited section of the TIMP are rated given specific scoring criteria on a 4- to 7-point scale provided for each item. Examiners complete a comprehensive test record that includes photos of targeted movements that illustrate criteria for each rating. Raw scores are obtained by adding the awarded points for each item. An infant's relative performance on the TIMP is determined through comparison of the raw score to a table of age standards followed by completion of a series of mathematical formulae to obtain the score difference from the mean. A cutoff score of -.5 *SD* from the mean is suggested for identification of infants at risk for motor delay although it is recommended by the test authors that local cutoff points be determined.

Because administration of the TIMP involves the physical handling of newborns, some of whom may be medically fragile due to prematurity or birth complications, the test authors caution that examiners need to be well trained and experienced in working with this population. Examiners must be knowledgeable about typical developmental patterns of motor functioning in newborns. In addition, examiners should be well versed in signs of infant stress and fatigue. To participate in an evaluation using the TIMP, infants need to be tested when they are in states of alertness and relative calm. A screening version of the TIMP is available for use with those infants whose medical conditions might cause them to fatigue quickly during testing or if they are so fragile that they should not be handled too much.

Extensive training videos that highlight scoring criteria for each item and proper techniques for holding and moving infants during TIMP assessments are available from the test developers. The test authors note that 10 or more hours should be devoted to training before examiners attempt to administer the TIMP. Examiners need to gather a few items, such as a rattle with a soft sound and a small red ball, to complete a test kit. These items may be purchased from sources that are recommended by the test authors. In addition, a firm but comfortable surface, such as a crib mattress, needs to be available on which to place the infant during the assessment session.

DEVELOPMENT. The current edition of the TIMP is the fifth version of the test. This version reflects the refinement of items and scoring procedures that have occurred over the course of almost three decades of TIMP research and use. The original version of the TIMP, which was called the Supplemental Motor Test, was developed in 1983 for use in a study on neurodevelopmental theory. Subsequent revisions of this scale were generated

to expand item content for a wider age range of infants and to refine tasks of the evaluation. The test manual presents a detailed discussion of the rationales involved in item and scoring revisions over the years. Items were designed to reflect naturally occurring movements when infants interact with caregivers in their daily lives. The test authors maintain that 92% of the items have been observed to mimic motor functioning found when caregivers bathe, change, and dress infants. If infants do not exhibit these specific behaviors during the testing sessions, it was felt that the TIMP would be a good indicator of developmental delay and support the need for early interventions.

TECHNICAL. The TIMP was normed on a sample of 990 infants selected from 13 hospitals in 11 cities throughout the United States. The infants in this sample were reported to represent the racial and ethnicity distribution of low birth weight infants born in the United States based on the 1996 data from the National Center for Health Statistics. Fifty-two percent were male. Other details of this sample, such as information on SES levels, hospital sites, and cities, were not provided.

A few studies are summarized in the test manual to support the reliability of the TIMP. These include test-retest and interrater reliability. In one study of test-retest reliability conducted with 106 infants, pairs of test administrations over a 3-day interval yielded correlation coefficients of .89. The test authors note it is difficult to demonstrate test-retest reliability over longer periods of time as rapid changes in infant development can account for more of the variance in scores than would be attributed to characteristics of the test itself. Interrater reliability for the TIMP can be high given the type and level of training available to examiners. The test authors note studies with intraclass correlation coefficients above .95 given a variety of examiner training experiences.

Evidence for the validity of test score use is presented from a review of studies with previous versions of the test as well as from the current version. Studies noting evidence supporting content, construct, discriminant, concurrent, and predictive validity of the TIMP are presented in the test manual. The TIMP has been found to be sensitive to the effects of interventions.

COMMENTARY. The TIMP should prove to be a valuable tool for early detection of motor delays in infants who experience birth complications. The test is based on theoretical constructs of early development as well as practical observations of infant/caregiver interactions. It would take some time to become proficient in the administration of the TIMP; however, the test authors provide well-developed training materials and technical support for examiners to become skilled in their observations and ratings of the test tasks. Scoring procedures for the TIMP are rather complex. Expansion of the age comparison tables to ease the process of determining an infant's relative standing in relation to the mean would be a good goal for any future revisions of the test. The examiner record form is very detailed. A positive feature of this is that examiners can use the form to indicate to parents what their child could do and development that could occur in the next stages, in a very concrete form. This level of detail, however, results in a visually complex profile. The small type and fold-out pages make it difficult for examiners to find items for scoring. Perhaps a different organization of the record form could be considered in a future edition. In addition, more descriptive information about the normative group would be helpful. Reliability and validity studies of the TIMP conducted to date are promising. Additional research in these areas, especially in terms of the concurrent and predictive validity of the test, would strengthen the psychometric properties of the TIMP.

SUMMARY. The TIMP was designed to be a measure of postural control and motor movements in infants at risk for delays in their physical development. The test has emerging psychometric support. Specific examiner qualifications and extensive training are needed for those wishing to administer the TIMP to newborns. Supportive training materials are available from the test authors to assist prospective examiners in acquiring the necessary testing skills. The TIMP would be a useful assessment device to provide very early indicators of motor delays in infants at risk for developmental difficulties. It would provide reliable and valid scores to demonstrate support for the need for early intervention services.

Review of the Test of Infant Motor Performance by CATHERINE RUTH SOLOMON SCHERZER, Associate Professor, Department de Psychologie, Université de Montreal, Montreal, Quebec, Canada:

[Editor's Note: This review is based on Version 2.0 of the test user's manual. Version 3.0, which was released in 2012, was not available at the time the review was written.]

DESCRIPTION. The Test of Infant Motor Performance (TIMP) is a test of posture and movement in infants. It was "designed for use by health professionals such as physical therapists and occupational therapists" (test user's manual, p. 1) who are knowledgeable about infants and have experience examining and intervening with preterm and full-term high-risk infants. Settings suggested for the use of the test are "newborn and special care nurseries, diagnostic follow-up clinics for infants at risk for delayed motor development, and community-based early-intervention and rehabilitation programs" (test user's manual, p. 1). The test user's manual has a section on the extra care that should be taken when evaluating fragile infants and indicates infants for whom the test is not suitable. The purpose of the test is to provide an assessment of functional motor performance in infants from 34 weeks postmenstrual age (PMA) through 4 months postterm in premature infants or up to 17 weeks chronological age for term-born infants. According to the test authors, it can be used to "1) identify infants under the age of 4–5 months…with delayed motor development or atypical motor performance, 2) measure change in typically developing infants with precision over two-week periods of time, 3) develop intervention goals for infants with delayed motor development, 4) measure change resulting from interventions, and 5) educate parents about infant motor development" (test user's manual, p. 2) and provide them with anticipatory guidance regarding the next developments they should expect from their children.

The test authors report research that shows that test scores are sensitive and "change with maturation, discriminate among infants with differing degrees of risk for poor motor outcome and predict with a high degree of accuracy motor performance at 12 months of age, at preschool age, and at early school age from TIMP testing at 3 months" (test user's manual, p. 1). The test authors state that the conceptual basis of the test is that "the human infant is a self-organizing being and that multiple systems interact to create the actions of the…muscles, joints, neural components, and cognitive/emotional aspects of movement…Self-organization occurs in a task context which also contributes to shaping the movements used to accomplish a purposeful action" (test user's manual, p. 3). The test authors cite research showing "that the sensorimotor areas of the brain reorganize in response to … specific practice … The tasks presented to the infant in the TIMP are posed as problems for the infant to solve. Responses reveal how the infant uses organization of posture and movement and how functional synergies change with development or intervention" (test user's manual, p. 3).

The TIMP was designed for use in clinical practice. The test user's manual provides general directions for the test and the necessary conditions for testing infants. There are three scoring forms available for use with the TIMP. The first form is used when an infant is to be evaluated using all the test items. This form presents technical descriptions of 42 items, 13 observed items and 29 elicited items, and photographs illustrating how the infant should be placed or held for each item. The items provide an assessment of developing head and neck control as well as selective control of arms and legs. The items were chosen and shown to reflect the movement demands experienced by infants in naturalistic interactions with caregivers such as bathing, dressing, and play. Some items are original, others are based on previous tests of motor development. Observed items, those that are spontaneously emitted by the infant, are scored 0 (not observed) or 1 (observed). Elicited items present infants with tasks to which they are expected to respond with appropriate postural alignment or movement. These items are scored with rating scales with from 4 to 7 levels according to the quality of the responses. The average testing time is 33 minutes.

A table of age standards for performance on the TIMP gives typical and below average performance ranges in terms of raw score performance at the different ages for which the test can be used. The table permits the determination of how well an infant performs relative to the normative sample. The second form is used for a 22-minute screening test for infants too fragile for testing with the full TIMP (the TIMP screening items; TIMPSI). The test authors provide information about how to translate the results of scores on the TIMPSI screening test items to results on the TIMP had the infant been given the entire test. The TIMPSI uses the best 11 items, based on Rasch psychometric analysis, drawn from the whole TIMP test to screen infants. Based on raw score on the screening items, a second set of either 10 easier or 8 harder items is given to round out an assessment of performance on a variety of tasks involving postural control. As part of the national normative study, 990 infants were tested using the TIMPSI within 3 days of being tested using the full TIMP test. The correla-

tion coefficient between the TIMP score and total score on the TIMPSI was .88.

The simple correlation between adjusted age (AA) at testing and TIMPSI score was .72. The third scoring form permits situating the infant according to his or her percentile rank. The administration instructions for the TIMP observed and elicited items on the scoring sheets are clear, but the scoring sheet for the elicited items does not lend itself easily to scoring. The photographs and total raw score entries are on pages that differ from and are on the backs of pages presenting the descriptions of the items and the scores to be attributed. The general directions on the scoring sheet require that the infant be in certain states for the test to be carried out, but these states are not described in the test manual, only references are given. There is no space provided to note the total scores on the front sheet. The TIMPSI score sheet requires using the descriptors on the TIMP score sheet when evaluating infants with the TIMPSI. The test manual elaborates little on how to use the score sheet and provides little supplementary information on testing procedures.

DEVELOPMENT. The TIMP has gone through four revisions to date. The original version was designed for use in the study of the effectiveness of neurodevelopmental therapy in improving the motor performance of premature infants at term-equivalent age at high risk for poor motor outcome. Later versions expanded the content to cover a wider range of infants, added items to improve the assessment of quality of movement and of selective control of arms and legs, and deleted some unreliable items (Version 2). The first large-scale research on the test (Version 3) was conducted with 59 items: 28 observed and 31 elicited items. The 59 ordinally scaled items were transformed into an interval-level scale using Rasch psychometric analysis, which revealed that certain items were redundant or did not distinguish infants on the basis of age or ability. Such items were deleted from the TIMP, leaving the 42-item Version 4. Age-related standards were first established based on the performance on Version 4 of 98 white (non-Hispanic), black (African and African American), and Latino (Mexican and Puerto Rican) infants from the Chicago metropolitan area who were tested repeatedly on a weekly basis up to 4 months AA plus 60 infants tested only once. Age-related standards were established for the TIMP Version 5 and the TIMPSI in 2002–2004 based on a cross-sectional sample of 990 low birthweight infants from 13 hospitals in 11 cities across the United States. Infants were selected to reflect the distribution of race/ethnicity in the low birthweight population of newborns according to 1996 data from the National Center for Health Statistics (Centers for Disease Control and Prevention, 1998). The test authors recommend using the test for infants represented in the normative sample although Latino infants achieved variable results in different studies. No sex differences were found.

TECHNICAL.

Content validity evidence. Following development of an early draft of Version 2 of the TIMP, the elicited items were submitted to review by 25 experts in pediatric physical therapy, occupational therapy, or psychology. Twenty-one experts replied and supported the content validity of the TIMP by indicating that they believed the items to be sensitive to developmental change over time (84% of the items) and to be useful for detecting developmental deviance in young infants (96% of the items).

Item analysis. The test authors report that 92% of the TIMP Elicited Item administration instructions were similar in the demands placed on infants to those that occurred naturally in caregiver-infant interactions. These demands include those involved in diapering, dressing, encouraging the infant to use eyes and head to track moving objects or to look at still objects, and those evoking orientation to sounds such as the caregiver's voice or a rattle.

Data from 174 tests on 137 infants were submitted to Rasch psychometric analysis. The analysis showed no floor or ceiling effects in a sample of infants ranging in age from 32 weeks PMA through 3.5 months post term, and that infants could be divided into at least six different levels of overall ability by the items on the TIMP. Further analysis was conducted in 2002–2004 on 1,719 tests on children across the age range of the test, which showed that children could be separated into at least four to five distinctly different levels of ability.

Construct validity evidence. TIMP motor scores are highly correlated with age. In the normative study, the correlation between age and the TIMP raw score was shown to be .81. The test authors also report the test to be sensitive to the results of intervention.

Discriminative validity evidence. TIMP scores differentiate infants with high biologic risk for poor motor outcome from those infants with lower risk.

Concurrent validity evidence. Concurrent validity evidence was based on a comparison of TIMP with the Alberta Infant Motor Scale (AIMS). A correlation coefficient of .64 was reported.

Predictive validity evidence. The test manual presents tables that illustrate the predictive validity of 3-month TIMP scores (standard scores) with AIMS percentile ranks at 12 months and variations of diagnostic efficiency of the 3-month TIMP for predicting performance on the AIMS below the 5th percentile at 12 months ($N = 82$) and on the Peabody Total Motor Quotient at 4–5 years ($N = 61$). Tables in the test user's manual illustrate that using a -.5 standard deviation (SD) as the cutoff, infants who tested poorly on the TIMP at 3 months are likely to have motor development below the 5th percentile on the AIMS at 12 months. Infants who tested poorly on the TIMP at 3 months have a 75% chance of being below the cut-off of -2 SD on the Peabody at 4–5 years. Infants who perform well on the TIMP at 3 months have a 98% chance of performing above the 5th percentile in motor development on the AIMS at 12 months and a 91% chance of performing above -2 SD on the Peabody at 4–5 years.

COMMENTARY. The TIMP appears to be well grounded in current research concerning the development of the infant motor system. The photographs on the scoring forms provide an excellent guide about how to handle the infants for testing. The descriptions of the scoring criteria for the elicited items are clear for experienced practitioners. On the other hand, the user's manual should be revised. It was published in 2005, making some references out of date for research in progress or submitted. Of more importance, the manual should clearly explain the concept of infant states and how they relate to testing procedures. The manual should also expand the section on test administration and scoring by providing more detailed explanations of the scoring criteria and the infant signals to which the test administrator must be sensitive.

SUMMARY. The TIMP appears to be a good test of posture and movement for evaluating the motor development and motor potential of preterm and full-term high risk infants. The user's manual requires some revision in order to make it more informative and user friendly.

REVIEWER'S REFERENCE

Centers for Disease Control and Prevention: Health, United States, 1998 with socioeconomic status and health chartbook. Hyattsville, MD: National Center for Health Statistics, U.S. DHHS Pub (PHS) 98–1232, 1998.

[170]

Test of Information Processing Skills.

Purpose: Designed to assess "how well a person learns and retains new information and the effects of interference on those processes."
Population: Ages 5-0 and over.
Publication Dates: 1981-2009.
Acronym: TIPS.
Scores, 6: Visual Modality, Auditory Modality, Delayed Recall, Word Fluency, Modality, Process.
Administration: Individual.
Parts, 4: Part 1: Visual Modality, Part 2: Auditory Modality, Part 3: Delayed Recall, Part 4: Word Fluency.
Price Data, 2010: $140 per test kit including manual (2009, 224 pages), plates, and 25 protocols; $50 per manual.
Time: 30(15) minutes.
Comments: Based on the Learning Efficiency Test.
Author: Raymond E. Webster.
Publisher: Academic Therapy Publications.
Cross References: For information on the Learning Efficiency Test, see T5:1462 (3 references); for reviews by Alice J. Corkill and Gregory Schraw of the 1992 Revision of the Learning Efficiency Test, see 12:215; see also T4:1423 (1 reference); for a review by Robert G. Harrington of an earlier form of the Learning Efficiency Test, see 9:601.

Review of the Test of Information Processing Skills by MARY (RINA) M. CHITTOORAN, Associate Professor, Department of Education, Saint Louis University, St. Louis, MO:

DESCRIPTION. The Test of Information Processing Skills (TIPS) is a norm-referenced, standardized, individually administered measure of the ability to retain and retrieve visual and auditory information, both with and without interference. The TIPS may be used by psychologists, occupational therapists, speech-language pathologists, and other clinicians with individuals between 5 and 90 years of age. The TIPS is composed of four parts: Visual Modality, Auditory Modality, Delayed Recall, and Word Fluency. Using the TIPS, an individual's learning and memory can be characterized along the following seven parameters: Ordered and Unordered Recall (measures of sequential memory), Short-Term Memory (a measure of visual and auditory short-term memory), Working Memory 1 (a measure of the impact of a verbal interference task and a 15- to 20-second delay on retrieval of strings of letters), Working Memory 2 (a measure of the impact of a verbal interference task and a 30- to 35-second delay on retrieval of short sentences), Delayed Recall (a measure of a 3-minute delay on

retrieval of information presented in the Working Memory 2 recall task), Word Fluency (a measure of spontaneously generated oral and written semantic processing efficiency), and Analysis of Acoustic Intrusion and Proactive Interference (measures of the ability to discriminate among similar sets of information presented in the same modality).

A complete TIPS kit consists of the manual, stimulus card booklet, and 25 protocols. Included in the manual are an Administration and Scoring Tutorial, norms tables, information about participants, test sites for norm and validation samples, and characteristics of validity samples, as well as several case studies. Training needs for administration and scoring are relatively simple, whereas interpretation requires some background in psychometrics. The TIPS can be completed in approximately 20–45 minutes and can be scored in under 15 minutes. Subtest raw scores are converted to scaled scores; Visual and Auditory Modality scores are based on sums of scaled scores, Visual, Auditory, Delayed, and Fluency Process scores are based on sums of standard scores, and Modality and Process scores are reported as standard scores (Mean = 100; *SD* = 15). Percentile ranks and age equivalents are also provided in the manual.

DEVELOPMENT. The TIPS has its foundation in the Learning Efficiency Test, developed by the same author and first published in 1981. Based on new research in the field as well as changes in clinical practice, the TIPS has two new subtests, Delayed Recall and Word Fluency, new scoring analyses, including error analyses, and several subtest name and content changes.

TECHNICAL. The TIPS was standardized between February and December of 2007 with data from 3,314 individuals (1,874 females and 1,440 males) between 5 and 97 years of age. The sample was stratified in accordance with the most recent U.S. Census divisions of gender, ethnicity, educational level, geographic region (Northeast, North Central, South, and West), and residence (urban and suburban/rural).

With regard to reliability, interitem correlations and factor analysis were used to examine internal consistency of the TIPS, with Visual items correlating strongly (.81 to .99) with each other, but not with Auditory items (.42 to .56) or Word Fluency (.31 to .36). Test-retest reliability, with a sample of 387 and a test-retest interval ranging from 14 to 21 days, resulted in reliability coefficients of .67 to .91 for ages 5–10, .73 to .94 for ages 11 through 19, and .78 to .93 for age 20 and older. The standard error of measurement ranged from a low of .74 on Auditory Unordered Working Memory 1 to a high of 1.72 on Auditory Ordered Working Memory 2, with 10 *SEM*s at or under 1.00. Standard error of estimation ranged from a low of 3.25 on Auditory Unordered to a high of 6.31 on Auditory Ordered.

Content validation evidence was presented by linking TIPS subtests to the information processing abilities required for academic tasks and everyday activities, by ensuring that the TIPS was assessing discrete instead of overlapping skills, and by ruling out problems related to lack of proficiency in English or hearing loss. Concurrent validity was examined by comparing scores on the TIPS to scores on related tests of academic achievement, cognitive functioning, memory, and speech fluency. The manual reports moderate correlations with the Wide Range Achievement Test 3 (WRAT-3), low to moderate correlations with cognitive measures such as the Wechsler Intelligence Scale for Children–Fourth Edition (WISC-IV) and the Wechsler Adult Intelligence Scale–Third Edition (WAIS-III), low to high correlations (although perhaps higher) with the Wechsler Memory Scale-III and with Trails A and B of the Halstead Reitan Neuropsychological Battery, and low to moderate correlations with tests of speech and fluency. Construct-related validation was begun by comparing TIPS scores to measures of cognitive functioning and academic achievement. In addition, TIPS raw and subtest scores increased, as expected, with changes in developmental functioning. Individuals with certain disabilities (Auditory Processing Disorder, ADD, learning disabilities, and mild and moderate Alzheimer's) were found to have significantly lower scores on subtests that assessed relevant skills such as attention and memory. Finally, principal components factor analysis showed that all TIPS subtests loaded heavily on one factor and that 93.06% of the total variance was explained by four factors. Maximum likelihood analysis showed that 89.96% of the total variance was explained by four factors, with the highest loadings (.82 to .89) on the Visual factor. Why the argument is made that one principal component accounts for the majority of the variance and is the best solution seems somewhat incongruous with the presentation of the four-factor solution.

COMMENTARY. The TIPS is one of the few norm-referenced, standardized measures available that is designed to assess information process-

ing skills. This focus is important, given the move away from global measures of cognitive functioning and an increasing emphasis on the way individuals process, learn, and memorize information. It also addresses these skills in the very young as well as the very old. The subtests seem to be based on the current literature in the area of processing skills and memory. The standardization sample is large, diverse, and representative of the national population. Studies using the TIPS reveal good reliability that is confirmed by a low standard error of measurement. The test is quickly administered, thereby alleviating the chance of fatigue or boredom in examinees. The stimulus booklet has an easel back that aids in ease of administration and the protocol is of good quality and is, for the most part, nicely laid out. The manual is comprehensive and provides detailed information about administration and scoring. Subtests include several practice and teaching items and stopping rules are clearly outlined. The inclusion of sample scoring sheets and the score calculation page on the back of the eight-page protocol simplify the scoring process. Examiners do not have to administer all parts of the TIPS if it is not feasible with certain examinees; that is, separate area-specific scores are available. The inclusion of case studies sheds additional light on how the TIPS might be effectively used.

Despite its positive aspects, the TIPS has some problematic features. First, the manual includes very little information on test development, although it refers readers to the Learning Efficiency Test on which the TIPS is based. It would be helpful for readers to have this information more easily available instead of having to go elsewhere to find it. The stimulus card booklet is of some concern, as well. For one thing, the booklet is very small (about 4 in. x 6 in.), and the thinness of the paper does not lend itself to turning the pages in an efficient manner. The first card that is presented to examinees to determine if they know their alphabet is busy, with letters crowded into a small space. One wonders about the impact on examinees who are older, have attention problems, or experience processing difficulties. Further, it would be difficult to distinguish between examinees with processing difficulties and those with attention problems. Subsequent revisions of the TIPS might include repeating the content of a card on the page that faces the examiner; this change would facilitate administration. As it stands, it is difficult for the examiner to determine what the examinee is seeing on the other side of the booklet. As for the protocol, it too, is somewhat busy and there is little room provided for the examiner to record responses or other comments. This could contribute to errors in the recording or reading of scores. [Editor's Note: The publisher has provided·Buros with a revised, larger stimulus booklet designed to alleviate some of these concerns.]

Although the author has offered some convincing evidence as to the technical merits of the test, it must be noted that validity is not as impressive; this is interesting, given that reliability is rather high. What these findings may mean is that the test is consistent in what it measures, but that it may not be measuring what it purports to measure. It would be a good idea–as the author acknowledges–to continue gathering validity data to strengthen the evidence supporting this measure.

Verbal directions to examinees are simply worded, but they are lengthy and there is a lot of information for examinees, especially young ones, to process. In addition, item complexity seems manageable for examinees who are in middle school or higher; however, task demands may be beyond the capabilities of most kindergartners and elementary school students.

SUMMARY. The TIPS is unique in that it assesses visual and auditory information processing skills in both children and adults. It has several positive features as well as some undesirable ones. Given the previously noted comments, it is recommended that results be interpreted with caution, that it be used with adolescents and adults rather than with very young children, and that it be administered as part of a comprehensive psychoeducational battery, rather than as a stand-alone measure.

Review of the Test of Information Processing Skills by AMANDA NOLEN, Associate Professor, Educational Foundations/Teacher Education, College of Education, University of Arkansas at Little Rock, Little Rock, AR:

DESCRIPTION. The Test of Information Processing Skills (TIPS) is an individually administered test. Its author reports that it measures information processing skills related to acquiring, organizing, retrieving, using, and managing visual and auditory information in children from age 5 through adulthood. TIPS consists of four parts: Visual Modality, Auditory Modality, Delayed Recall, and Word Fluency. Measurement across these four parts indicates whether an individual's memory pro-

cessing deficits are generalized or discrete compared with same-aged peers. Subtest results are reported as scaled scores with a mean of 10 and a standard deviation (*SD*) of 3 points. Overall functionality across the four areas is reported as standard scores with a mean of 100 and *SD* of 15 points. Error analyses of acoustic intrusion (AI) and proactive interference (PI) are conducted to evaluate how well the person can distinguish among similar sets of information presented in the same modality.

The TIPS is intended to be used as both an assessment and a diagnostic tool for psychologists, occupational therapists, rehabilitation specialists, speech/language pathologists, school psychologists, and others who assess cognitive functioning. Administering the test requires no specialized training; however, scoring and interpretation of the scores requires some formal training in psychometrics. The instrument takes approximately 20 to 45 minutes to administer, although the examiner is cautioned to allow for multiple sessions when administering it to young children.

The only requirements for the examinee described by the author are that the individual must be at least 5 years of age and must be able to identify all of the letters of the alphabet correctly. This second qualification is verified by the examiner prior to administering any portion of the TIPS. Presumably, other implied requirements are full or only minimally impaired hearing and visual abilities. There are no instructions or provisions if an examinee is impaired in either of these areas.

Visual and Auditory Modality subtests consist of strings of letters that vary in length. For the Visual Modality subtest each letter string is revealed to the examinee on a stimulus card, then it is removed during the recall activities. For the Auditory Modality subtest, the string of letters is read to the examinee by the examiner. The recall activities include the ability to recall the letters in the order they were presented, recalling the letters in any order, recalling the letters (ordered or unordered) after a series of increasingly complex interfering acts such as counting to 10 or repeating a sentence. The raw scores across these two subtests can be compared to determine if there are any discrepancies in how the person acquires, stores, and retrieves new linguistic information based on the modality of presentation.

The Delayed Recall subtest requires the examinee to recall the animal and fruit names embedded in the sentences the examinee repeated during the

Modality subtests. These activities occur exactly 3 minutes after completing the Modality subtests.

The Word Fluency subtests are to be administered only to examinees 9 years of age and older. The examinee is to recall as many words as possible within 60 seconds that begin with a certain letter provided by the examiner. This activity is first completed orally and then repeated using a different prompt letter and requiring the examinee to write the words.

Each subtest can generate a number of different scores, each with different scoring schemes. In the opinion of this reviewer, this complexity in scoring is a flaw in this instrument as it requires training and understanding of scaled scores. However, the technical manual includes a scoring tutorial for those examiners unfamiliar with the instrument. Examiners are advised to read the entire manual carefully prior to administering and scoring the TIPS.

TECHNICAL. Internal consistency was measured using split-half correlations rather than the more traditional coefficient alpha due to the repetition of prompts throughout the instrument and the "unusual scoring features" (manual, p. 66). Scores on the visually presented strings correlated strongly with each other (r = .81 to r = .99), but not with the Word Fluency tasks (r = .31 to r = .36). Likewise, the auditory strings correlated moderately to strongly with each other (r = .42 to r = .56). Test-retest reliability was measured by retesting 387 individuals by the same respective examiner after 14–21 days. The reliability coefficients across the subtests ranged from .67 to .94 across the different age groups. The coefficients were stronger across the composite scores ranging from .82 to .95 across the age groups. These values demonstrate a respectable homogeneity and stability within the instrument.

Content validation was described by the author as being established by screening the examinees for peripheral hearing loss and for accurate knowledge of the English alphabet. In the opinion of this reviewer, this appears to be insufficient evidence. Providing external review from experts in the field of the representativeness of the items would have been more appropriate here.

An abundance of evidence establishing criterion-related validity is provided for the TIPS. Data describing the relationship between performances on the TIPS subtest and composite scores with scores from other widely used tests are summarized in easy-to-read tables. These tests include achievement tests (i.e., WRAT-3 and WIAT-2), cognitive tests (i.e., WISC-4 and WAIS-3), memory tests (i.e., WMS-3), and tests of fluency and speech. The authors provide a detailed discussion on each comparison noting where the comparisons are high and proposing possible explanations where the comparisons are weak.

A maximum likelihood factor analysis (with a Varimax Rotation) of the subtest scores across the normative sample revealed a solution supporting the four-factor model. The Visual, Auditory, Word Fluency, and Delayed Recall subtests all load on separate factors, although the factor loadings for the Delayed Recall were much weaker compared to the other three factors.

A strength of the TIPS, based on its psychometric properties is that the instrument was developed, normed, and tested for reliability all with different samples. This test development process suggests that the authors were meticulous and deliberate to bring the instrument to publication. The inclusion of the abundance of concurrent validation data responds to questions about the utility of the instrument further strengthening properties of the TIPS.

COMMENTARY. The TIPS was developed to provide a norm-based diagnostic assessment instrument for assessing a number of executive functions related to learning, acquisition, recall, and retention of information presented orally or visually. The flexibility of the instrument allows its use across the lifespan, from the age of 5 years and older, and makes this a potentially valuable tool for researchers, practitioners, and diagnosticians alike. The stability of the instrument should allow for a seamless longitudinal tracking of cognitive development as well as screening for decay in functionality due to trauma, disease, or maturation. The instrument is easy to administer; however, it is complex to score and requires specialized knowledge to do so.

SUMMARY. The TIPS was developed to assess information processing skills related to acquiring, organizing, retrieving, using, and managing visual and auditory information in children from age 5 through adulthood. The instrument has sufficient evidence of homogeneity of subtest items and temporal stability that make it a possibly useful screening instrument for generalized or discrete impairments in the acquisition, storage, and retrieval of visual or auditory information.

Test of Nonverbal Intelligence, Fourth Edition.

Purpose: "Developed to assess aptitude, intelligence, abstract reasoning, and problem solving in a completely language-free format."
Population: Ages 6-0 to 89-11.
Publication Dates: 1982–2010.
Acronym: TONI-4.
Scores: Total score only.
Administration: Individual.
Forms, 2: Form A, Form B.
Price Data, 2010: $361 per kit including examiner's manual (2010, 107 pages), picture book, Critical Reviews and Research Findings (1982-2009), 50 Form A answer booklets and record forms, and 50 Form B answer booklets and record forms.
Foreign Language Editions: Spanish, French, German, Chinese, Vietnamese, Korean, Tagalog instructions available.
Time: (15-20) minutes.
Author: Linda Brown, Rita J. Sherbenou, and Susan K. Johnsen.
Publisher: PRO-ED.
Cross References: For reviews by Jeffrey A. Atlas and Gerald E. DeMauro of the Third Edition, see 14:393; see also T5:2704 (47 references) and T4:2775 (10 references); for reviews by Kevin K. Murphy and T. Steuart Watson of the Second Edition, see 11:439 (9 references); for reviews by Philip M. Clark and Samuel T. Mayo of the original edition, see 9:1266.

Review of the Test of Nonverbal Intelligence, Fourth Edition by TAWNY N. EVANS-McCLEON, Assistant Professor of School Psychology, Mississippi State University, Mississippi State, MS:

DESCRIPTION. The Test of Nonverbal Intelligence, Fourth Edition (TONI-4) is a measure of general intelligence relying heavily on a nonverbal format and limited motor responses. The TONI-4 is designed to assess abstract/figural problem-solving skills of children and adults (ages 6 to 89 years) who have language, hearing, and motor difficulties. The TONI-4 has two equivalent versions, Form A and Form B, each of which consists of 60 items listed in order from easy to difficult with six additional training items. Using verbal or nonverbal instructions, the examinee is required to respond to a series of novel abstract figures using pointing "motor-minimized" (manual, p. 2) gestures. Although the authors consider the TONI-4 to be a nonverbal measure, verbal instructions are provided in English, Spanish, French, German, Chinese, Vietnamese, Korean, and Tagalog.

Overall, the administration guidelines for the TONI-4 are clear and easy to understand. There is no time limit for examinees to respond during administration; however, it is estimated that the average administration process for each form takes approximately 15 minutes. The authors suggest that the TONI-4 can be administered using two formats: oral directions or nonverbal directions. The explanations for each format are presented in an easy to follow step-by-step fashion. The administration process for the training items along with suggestions for starting points for different age groups, individuals suspected of intellectual difficulties, and examinees experiencing difficulty passing training items are provided. However, the passing rate for the training items is not clearly stated in the examiner's manual.

Completing the answer and record form during the administration process may cause several challenges for the test administrator. One concern is related to lack of inclusion of the recording of the training items responses on the answer and record form, which may pose difficulty for the administrator tracking the passing rate for each trial. Secondly, although the response choice numbers that correspond with the answer and record form are shown in the manual (p. 8), the lack of numbers in the picture book may increase the chances for administrator errors when recording the correct responses. Several subtests on the Wechsler Adult Intelligence Scale–Fourth Edition provide an excellent example of numbered responses in the stimulus book (Wechsler, 2008). Including numbers for the responses in the picture book minimizes the motor requirements for individuals with such impairments. Finally, there are errors noted on the answer and record form for both Forms A and B. The number of responses included in the picture book on Item 49 on Record Form A and Item 41 on Record Form B are inconsistent with the number of answer choices on the answer and record form. The same error is reflected in the manual (p. 9). [Editor's Note: The publisher advises that these errors have been corrected in the second printing.]

The scoring guidelines for the TONI-4 are very simple and clear with detailed instructions for establishing the basal and ceiling rules; several case examples with visual graphics were provided. The raw score is converted into one Index score (mean = 100; standard deviation = 15).

DEVELOPMENT. The TONI-4 has undergone several revisions since 1982. In developing the original version of the TONI (Brown, Sherbenou, & Johnsen, 1982), the authors' goals were to address the need for a measure of intelligence without language and complex motor requirements. Due to the problem-solving nature and novice effect of the items, this measure is viewed as an adequate representation of Spearman's theory of general intelligence and Horn and Cattell's theory of fluid intelligence. The content of the original TONI was developed to fit Jensen's (1980) seven properties of culture-free tests in which content-validation procedures led to the inclusion of 50 items per form. To address the need for lower flooring, larger ceiling effect, and greater discriminating power, original items have been added and removed over several revisions. Based on critical reviews and expert opinions, several changes were made to the TONI-4, including new norms and adding 15 items to improve the floor and ceiling effects. Also, items on each form of the TONI-4 are evenly distributed based on difficulty and across five areas of problem solving: Matching, Analogy, Progression, Classification, and Intersection.

TECHNICAL. The standardization for the TONI-4 was conducted with 2,272 individuals ages 6 to 89 years. The demographic characteristics of the normative sample corresponded with the U.S. Census across several variables (i.e., geographic region, gender, race, Hispanic status, educational attainment, family income, and exceptionality status). Representativeness of the normative sample was supported by the stratification of each demographic variable for each age group (e.g., 6-18 years and 19-89 years) and clear tables are provided. The TONI-4's normative data are reported across a total of 19 age intervals. Of the total normative sample, 77% of the examinees were assessed using the oral instructions (English version only) and 23% were assessed using the nonverbal instructions. No additional information was provided regarding the demographic characteristics of those in the normative sample who were nonverbally administered the TONI-4.

Reliability for the TONI-4 was evaluated using several methods, such as internal consistency, alternative forms, test-retest, and interscorer. Using the Fisher z-transformation technique, the internal consistency for the TONI-4 was examined across all age intervals and the coefficient alphas fell at the highly acceptable level for both forms (Average r = .96.). On the TONI-4, the authors expanded the evaluation of internal consistency for 13 subgroups

(e.g., gender, race, ethnicity, and exceptionality) and the coefficient alphas ranged from .92 to .97 (Form A) and .94 to .98 (Form B). Using the entire normative sample, an evaluation of alternate forms reliability for immediate administration revealed an average corrected coefficient of .81 (ranging from .67 to .89). During the delayed administration (1 to 2 weeks) for both forms, using 63 individuals ranging from ages 9 to 72 years, the average corrected coefficient was .84 for all ages. The test-retest reliability was examined using the same population and data collected during the delayed administration for alternative forms, and the correlation coefficient was .86 for Form A and .89 for Form B. Although the test-retest reliability falls within an acceptable range, the sample did not include all age groups or a representation of the U.S. Census. Interscorer reliability for randomly selected pairs of Form A and Form B (reviewed by two publishing staff members) revealed a correlation coefficient of .99.

Validity was determined by content-description, criterion-prediction, and construct-identification. First, evidence for content validity was supported by examining the variation of the TONI-4's administration formats (e.g., verbal and nonverbal instructions) utilizing a sample of 188 English-speaking individuals (ages 6 through 8; ages 12 through 14; and ages 18 and over) without hearing impairments, and statistically significant differences were found for the age group 6 through 8 years only. More studies with homogenous groups are needed to examine further differences between individuals receiving verbal and nonverbal instructions. Similar to the previous version, the median percentage of difficulty (median = .58; .57; ranging from .28–.83; .27–.83) and median discrimination coefficients (median = .58; .55; ranging from .45–.66; .48–.69) fell within the acceptable range for both forms. Secondly, for an evaluation of criterion-related (predictive) validity, correlations between the TONI-4 with the Comprehensive Test of Nonverbal Intelligence-Second Edition (CTONI-2; r_c = .79) and the TONI-3 (r_c = .74) were in the high range and comparison of the standard scores, means, and standard deviations indicated that the TONI-4 is predicted to produce similar scores to the CTONI-2 and the TONI-3. Finally, evidence supporting the TONI-4 for construct validity is presented across several areas. The authors provided support for the correlation with age and calculated raw scores on the TONI-4 have the tendency to increase over the years until age 60 years, and significant differences are found in the performance of intellectually gifted and cognitively disabled individuals. Also, evidence of construct validity for the relationship between the TONI-4 and several measures of school achievement was found through positive correlations. Data to support factor analysis and item validity were presented in a table format. In comparison with the validity studies on previous versions (Johnsen, Brown, & Sherbenou, 2010), the authors have expanded the technical evidence and support for the TONI-4.

COMMENTARY. The TONI-4 is designed on the foundation of the previous editions (TONI, TONI-2, and TONI-3) and shows similar strengths; it is brief and easy to administer and score. The normative data for the TONI-4 were updated, representative of the U.S. population and stratified across several demographic variables. Traditionally, the TONI has been considered a "language-free measure of cognitive ability" (Brown et al., 1982; p. 2); however, the newer version utilizes oral instructions in the standardized procedures. The inclusion of verbal instructions in a variety of languages in the administration process may expand the usefulness for other populations, but may lead to other questions: (a) Is the TONI-4 a true nonverbal measure of intelligence, and (b) do the results of the TONI-4 produce unbiased scores for language-impaired and non-English-speaking individuals? These questions are not clearly supported by the information provided by the authors in the normative data, reliability, and validity studies. The following evidence for reliability and validity strongly support caution for the use of the TONI-4 with children under the age of 9 years: (a) the exclusion of individuals younger than 9 years in the alternative-form, delayed-administration, and test-retest reliability studies, and (b) evidence that supports statistically significant differences in mean standard scores for ages 6 through 8 years during the verbal instructions (106.4) and the nonverbal instructions (103.5).

SUMMARY. Similar to earlier versions, the TONI-4 is brief, simple, and highly beneficial for assessing abstract reasoning and problem-solving skills for individuals with language and hearing difficulties and motor impairments. The addition of verbal instructions in several languages may increase the interest of using the TONI-4 for screening intellectual functioning for gifted and nondisabled individuals with educational, cultural, or experiential disadvantages. Unfortunately, the lack of inclusion

of normative data for nonverbal administrations and the limited validity evidence for the inclusion of individuals with exceptionalities (e.g., language impairments) raises a concern for potential bias for using the TONI-4 with individuals who have language barriers and difficulties, especially children under the age of 9 years.

REVIEWER'S REFERENCES
Brown, L., Sherbenou, R. J., & Johnsen, S. K. (1982). Test of Nonverbal Intelligence. Austin, TX: PRO-ED.
Jensen, A. R. (1980). Bias in mental testing. New York, NY: Free Press.
Johnsen, S. K., Brown, L., & Sherbenou, R. J. (2010). Test of Nonverbal Intelligence: Critical reviews and research findings, 1982–2009. Austin, TX: PRO-ED.
Wechsler, D. (2008). Wechsler Adult Intelligence Scale–Fourth Edition. San Antonio, TX: NCS Pearson.

Review of the Test of Nonverbal Intelligence, Fourth Edition by CLEBORNE D. MADDUX, Foundation Professor of Counseling and Educational Psychology, University of Nevada, Reno, Reno, NV:

DESCRIPTION. This measure is the fourth version of the Test of Nonverbal Intelligence (TONI-4), a test intended to measure general intelligence in a nonverbal, motor-reduced format "that would make it possible to assess intelligence without the effects of a person's linguistic or motor skills confounding the results and yielding a potentially inaccurate assessment of cognitive ability" (examiner's manual, p. v). The examiner's manual goes on to assert that the test is appropriate for use with those with aphasia or other expressive language disorders; those who are deaf or hearing impaired; those who do not speak proficient English or who are unable to read or write Standard English; and individuals with speech, language, or motor impairments as a result of neurological conditions such as cerebral palsy, stroke, or head trauma.

The test items require abstract reasoning and figural problem solving. The TONI-4 is intended to be free of language, complex motor requirements, and significant cultural influence. Consequently, the authors maintain that it is ideal for use with individuals who have language, hearing, or motor disabilities or who are not familiar with mainstream U.S. culture. They further maintain that the test is useful for screening and for verifying the validity of referrals for special services, treatment, or therapy. The test should not be used with examinees with serious visual impairments.

The TONI-4 consists of two alternate, 60-item forms. It is untimed and is to be administered individually in approximately 15 minutes. The test is normed for examinees whose ages are between 6 years, 0 months and 89 years, 11 months. Nonverbal directions were used for all previous editions. Oral directions were added in this edition, and are the recommended directions for examinees who are proficient in English or the other languages for which verbal instructions are provided (English, Spanish, French, German, simplified Chinese, Vietnamese, Korean, and Tagalog). Over 85% of the items are the same across all four editions of the test.

The test comes attractively and compactly packaged, and the materials are sturdy, well-organized, and easy to use. The directions for administering, scoring, and interpreting the TONI-4 are clear, straightforward, and well-written. In fact, the materials are so complete and so well-designed that they provide a model for ideal test packaging. A unique and welcome inclusion in the test materials is a 65-page, bound monograph (including a comprehensive reference list) that presents and discusses research literature and test reviews that address the previous three editions of the TONI (Johnsen, Brown, & Sherbenou, 2010). Also welcome is advice found in this manual to present the test results in confidence intervals, rather than as point estimates known as an Index Score. The record form lists the mean standard error of measurement (3) next to the blank for the index score. Unfortunately, the record form has a blank only for the point estimate or Index Score.

The test consists of six training items and 60 test items making use of abstract/figural content. Items are easy to administer and are reminiscent of those used in the Raven's Progressive Matrices (T8:2233). Using the oral directions, the examiner presents the appropriate stimulus item from the picture book, runs a finger over the response items at the bottom of the page saying "Which one of these," then points back to the stimulus item and says "goes in this box?" Examinees can answer by pointing to the correct answer or making some other meaningful response.

Testing begins with Item 1 for children ages 6 to 9 years and those suspected of having a significant intellectual impairment or who had difficulty with the training items. All other examinees begin with Item 20. The basal level is the highest level in which an examinee makes five consecutive correct responses. Testing continues until all items are administered or until there are three errors in five consecutive items. The ceiling is the highest numbered error.

The test yields three normative scores. These include (a) index scores, which are standard scores with a mean of 100 and a standard deviation of 15

(called quotients in previous editions); (b) percentile ranks; and (c) age equivalents (included because some regulatory agencies require them). The manual includes a full and satisfactory description of how these scores were developed.

DEVELOPMENT. The TONI-4 is based on a conceptualization of general intelligence operationally defined as problem-solving ability applied to abstract figural content. By making use of abstract/figural items, the goal was to eliminate both language and motor ability as a component of test administration. Item development of the first edition of the test was also guided by Jensen's (1980) seven properties of culture-free tests. The authors suggest:

> Eliminating language and reducing motor activity significantly mitigated the cultural loading of the test. Jensen's other criteria were met by creating something other than a traditional paper-and-pencil test; by incorporating nonverbal instructions; by building novel, abstract items requiring reasoning and problem-solving abilities; and by eliminating any timed components. (examiner's manual, p. 48)

In general, and in the opinion of the reviewer, the manual for the TONI-4 is exemplary. It is well-written and complete and does an excellent job of presenting the psychometric qualities of the test, which are themselves quite good. However, one omission is the absence of detail about how the figural items were generated for the original TONI. Readers wanting more detail are referred to the 1990 manual. The TONI-4 manual does, however, do a good job of describing the conventional item-analytic techniques used and the differential item functioning (DIF) analyses that were used to detect and eliminate items that might be seen as biased. DIF was used to detect group differences by gender, by African American versus non-African American, and by Hispanic versus non-Hispanic subjects.

The manual suggests that the tasks involved in the items can be broadly categorized as *matching* (both simple and complex), *analogy, progression, classification,* and *intersection,* and asserts that these tasks were sorted according to difficulty level before assignment to Form A and Form B so that each form contains similar items at similar difficulty levels. A table shows the number of items in each of these categories found in each Form.

TECHNICAL.

Standardization. The TONI-4 was renormed using a sample of 2,272 people from 31 states tested between 2005 and 2008. The sample was stratified by geographic region, gender, race and ethnicity, income, and educational level. A table shows the sample is representative of the U.S. as a whole with regard to the above and with regard to exceptionality status (no disability, specific learning disability, speech-language disorder, intellectual disability, and other disability). About 3/4 of the normative data were collected using the new English oral instructions; the remainder were collected using the nonverbal instructions. The manual provides index scores (mean of 100, standard deviation of 15) for 21 age groups. For ages 6-0 to 6-11, these are divided by 6-month intervals and from 7-0 to 89-11 by 12-month intervals. The manual also includes tables to convert index scores to percentile ranks and to convert raw scores to age equivalents for school-age examinees.

Reliability. Alpha coefficients were calculated for each form of the test for 19 age intervals. All exceed .90. The average alpha is .96, providing some evidence that the test measures a single unidimensional construct—that of general intelligence. The standard error of measurement ranges from 2 to 4 with a median of 3. Alphas were also calculated for 13 subgroups reflecting gender, racial, ethnic, and exceptionality characteristics. These range from .92 to .98. Alternate-forms reliability, both immediate and delayed, was studied. Coefficients from immediate administration range from .67 to .89 with a mean coefficient across age categories of .81. Delayed administration produced similar coefficients with average coefficients for school-age, adult, and combined groups of .84, .81, and .84, respectively. Test-retest coefficients are also provided and are similar in magnitude.

Validity. In terms of content validity, the authors discuss the development of the test and how it reflects Jensen's (1980) properties of culture-free tests: (a) by eliminating language and reducing motor activity, (b) by creating a test that does not rely on paper and pencil responses, (c) by including nonverbal instructions, (d) by using novel, abstract items that require problem-solving ability, and (e) by eliminating timing. Details of item analyses and differential item functioning analyses are also presented as evidence of content validity.

As criterion-related validation efforts, the authors correlated TONI-4 scores with the Comprehensive Test of Nonverbal Intelligence–Second Edition (CTONI-2; Hammill, Pearson, & Wiederholt, 2009) and the third edition of the TONI. In a study of school-age individuals, correlations between

three scales of the CTONI-2 (Pictorial, Geometric, and Full Scale) and TONI-4 were all between .70 and .79. Correlations between TONI-4 and TONI-3 were also very high. Means of the TONI-4 and the criterion measure means were compared with *t*-tests. Means of TONI-4 versus CTONI-2 were not significantly different. The *t*-test comparing TONI-4 with TONI-3 was significant, but with a small effect size (.23). Binary classification analyses comparing the TONI-4 with the CTONI-2 and TONI-3 were conducted and offered as evidence of acceptable predictive validity. Sensitivities were .71 and .83, specificities were .82 and .92, positive predictive values were .71 and .74, and negative predictive values were .82 and .95, respectively.

Construct validity was addressed by a discussion of the five basic constructs thought to underlie the TONI-4 and evidence for the existence of these constructs. First, the relationship of examinee age to TONI-4 scores is shown to be similar to that of other intelligence tests. Second, mean scores for gender and ethnic subgroups and for disability subgroups with no intellectual impairments are all average. They are above average for gifted and talented subgroups and are below average for subgroups with intellectual disabilities. Third, the correlations between TONI-4 scores and school achievement as measured by a number of popular achievement tests range from .55 to .78. Fourth, factor-analytic results show the TONI-4 items load heavily on a single factor. Fifth, TONI-4 items are highly correlated with the total test scores, as expected when items measure the same trait.

COMMENTARY. The TONI-4 is a quick and easy test to administer. Its psychometric qualities are sound and are well-presented in the test manual. The test materials are excellent and the inclusion of a 65-page bound summary and discussion of previous reviews and research conducted between 1982 and 2009 on earlier versions of the test will be highly appreciated by potential users. A minor suggestion for the future would be a section in the manual listing and discussing all differences between the current and past editions and a brief explanation for each difference.

SUMMARY. There is little to criticize about the TONI-4, and it is evident that valid criticisms of earlier editions have been used to change and improve the test. If forced to be critical, one might point out that the test is based on a conceptualization of intelligence that is somewhat dated, and that is no longer the only way to think about intellectual functioning. On the other hand, it is an unavoidable fact that special services, especially in schools, continue to rely heavily on assessments based on such conceptualizations. Therefore, when a quick assessment of general intellectual functioning is needed for individuals who have language or motor impairments or who are not familiar with U.S. culture, the TONI-4 would be a good choice.

REVIEWER'S REFERENCES

Hammill, D. D., Pearson, N. A., & Wiederholt, J. L. (2009). Comprehensive Test of Nonverbal Intelligence (2nd ed.). Austin, TX: PRO-ED.
Jensen, A. R. (1980). *Bias in mental testing.* New York, NY: Free Press.
Johnsen, S. K., Brown, L., & Sherbenou, R. J. (2010). *Test of Nonverbal Intelligence: Critical reviews and research findings, 1982-2009.* Austin, TX: PRO-ED.

[172]

Test of Visual-Motor Skills–3rd Edition.

Purpose: Designed to assess visual-motor skills.
Population: Ages 3 to 90.
Publication Dates: 1986–2010.
Acronym: TVMS–3.
Scores, 2: Accuracy, Errors.
Administration: Group.
Price Data, 2013: $135 per kit, including manual (2010, 96 pages), 15 test booklets, and 15 record forms; $70 per manual; $48 per 15 test booklets; $17 per 15 record forms.
Time: (20–30) minutes.
Comments: Third edition combines lower and upper levels and extends age range.
Authors: Nancy A. Martin (TVMS-3); earlier editions by Morrison F. Gardner.
Publisher: Academic Therapy Publications.
Cross References: For reviews by Deborah Erickson and Janet E. Spector of an earlier edition, see 13:337 (2 references); see also T4:2791 (1 reference).

Review of the Test of Visual-Motor Skills—3rd Edition by AYRES G. D'COSTA, Emeritus Associate Professor of Educational Research, Evaluation, and Measurement, Department of Educational Policy and Leadership, College of Education and Human Ecology, The Ohio State University, Columbus, OH:

DESCRIPTION. The Test of Visual-Motor Skills—3rd Edition (TVMS-3) is a paper-and-pencil test that assesses visual and motor skills specific to eye-hand coordination needed to copy special designs. These designs are presumed to be common in academic and everyday activities. However, as stated in the technical manual, "The emphasis is not to evaluate visual memory...per se, but to note if there are any systematic distortions or gross inaccuracies seen in the copied design that could be attributed to difficulties in visual perception, motor planning, and/or motor execution" (p. 8). A set of 39 designs arranged in difficulty level

and developmental order is presented one design at a time. The copying is done while each design remains in sight and does not require memory. Only one design is presented on each page of the test booklet. TVMS-3 focuses on two types of examiner-judged scores: Accuracy of the copied design and the type(s) of Errors committed by the examinee out of nine possible categories of errors. The test is intended for use in educational and clinical assessment for ages 3 to 90 years and even older. The test is untimed; testing is stopped after four consecutive scores of 0 (incorrect responses).

TVMS-3 comes as a kit consisting of the manual, 15 test booklets, and 15 record forms. The manual comprises chapters intended to provide a detailed overview of the purpose and rationale of the test, specifics on examiner qualifications and training for administration and scoring, instructions on how to administer and score the test in a standardized manner, and psychometric details about the development of the test and its proper use and interpretation. In addition to a list of references, the appendices include a list of the participant test sites used for the standardization sample, norms tables, and a tutorial on scoring the test. Although the test is untimed, the typical administration time is 20 to 30 minutes with an additional 15 minutes required for scoring. The test can be administered individually or in a group setting.

The test manual's scoring tutorial emphasizes that the scoring procedures for the TVMS-3 are significantly different from the earlier editions of this test. Careful scoring is imperative to ensure proper interpretation. Each of the designs is scored independently in terms of accuracy (from 0 to 2), and in terms of the types of errors committed (from nine different types). Accuracy is scored as 2 if the copied design is almost perfect, 1 if some distortion is present, and 0 if the design is unrecognizable or not attempted. Error types include wrong closure of the lines drawn, incorrect angle, line quality/characteristics, or some critical modification of the design's shape/size including reversals or overlaps. Multiple errors may be recorded. Both Accuracy and Error scores are provided norm-referenced interpretations.

DEVELOPMENT. TVMS-3 development is based on the experience and concerns gathered from several years of clinical use of the previous editions of this test. Specifically, two major kinds of concerns were addressed by TVMS-3. The first concern relates to the time-consuming and cumbersome nature of the scoring procedures required in previous editions. The manual states that scoring past editions required the use of a ruler and protractor. The TVMS-3 manual highlights its new "scoring scheme," which does not "require complex measurements" (p. 28). Examinees were trained in this new scoring method, and it was found to be empirically no different from the older scoring protocols. No details or empirical data have been presented in the test manual to justify this assertion, which should be of interest to all clinical users of the older editions. The second concern addressed by the TVMS-3 was the problem of multiple scales geared to different age levels, which resulted in some awkward overlaps in results that could at best be said to be difficult to explain. The items in TVMS-3 now include all the items in the two earlier editions, specifically TVMS-R (the lower level test) and TVMS-UL (the upper level test). Items are presented in their original order with three exceptions. Two TVMS-R items were placed higher, and one TVMS-UL item was placed lower; however, no empirical justification for this decision is presented in the manual.

The selection of the 39 designs, perhaps because they came entirely from previous editions of the test, is not justified in this manual. Likewise, their hierarchical order, although claimed to be developmentally age-based and also related to everyday and academic challenges, is not discussed in the manual. Although the manual states that the order is justified by item analysis discussed in a later section of the manual, this reviewer did not find a relevant table of item-based means or item-response-theory-based difficulty values to substantiate this statement. Factor analyses shown in the manual indicate that combining the two earlier editions into TVMS-3 seems to have created a test with two factors, providing some good content evidence of validity. However, these insights also detract from, rather than justify, a single test for all ages from 3 to 90+. The manual dismisses the need for subtests stating that "the TVMS-3 items vary primarily in complexity, with no additional tasks required" (p. 46).

The special scoring strategy used in the TVMS-3 by which testing for an examinee is stopped after four consecutive scores of 0 would appear to make an earlier segment of the 39-item test more relevant for certain and presumably younger examinees than others. The TVMS-3 manual does not discuss this change, nor does it present data to clarify what types of examinees were administered only certain segments of the test, or what lengths these segments might have been. Such information would seem to be useful for clinicians. It also raises issues related to research analyses using incomplete or missing data. [Editor's Note: The test publisher advises that all participants in the normative study were administered all 39 items.]

TECHNICAL. The standardization sample of 2,610 individuals ages 3 to 100 was drawn from some 75 test sites in 70 cities from 28 states. The test was administered by 80 examiners, most of whom were occupational therapists. Demographic characteristics of the sample are presented and compared with U.S. population data from the 2000 Census. The demographics table in Appendix D of the manual is valuable to clinicians and should have merited more discussion in the body of the manual.

The interpretation of test results is based on normalized techniques to provide standardized scores such as age equivalents, percentile ranks, T-scores, and stanines. The score related to Accuracy is used in developing these standard scores. Neither the Error type nor its frequency are used in its computation. Because the maximum score per design (item) is 2, the highest possible score on the TVMS-3 should be 78. As expected, the manual demonstrates that the maximum score rises and peaks for test takers in their 20s and 30s, and thereafter falls in older individuals. This information is useful, but it would also have been useful to see a frequency distribution of raw scores, especially as the derived scores presented for clinical use are based on the assumption of normal distribution.

There are no norms data presented other than by age. Although the normative sample was presumably stratified by gender and other important socioeconomic criteria, no norms are presented for these groups, leading clinicians to believe that age is the only criterion that needs to be considered in interpreting visual-motor skills and their development. Given the single peak seen in the statistics presented in the manual, one should ask if this finding is entirely explained by a single variable, and if so, what its nature might be. Interestingly, the introduction in the manual stipulates that "TVMS-3 does not separate the visual-perceptual from the motor or planning components but rather it shows how well those separate systems are integrated during the execution of one particular type of skill: copying" (p. 8). This statement has profound significance in interpreting the results of this test and for recognizing its focus on Copying, given the multi-factor theories that are found in the literature related to visual perception (Hammill, Pearson, & Voress, 1993; Leonard, Foxcroft, & Kroukamp, 1988). The pertinent research question then is whether the TVMS-3 is simply a measure of copying skill, as opposed to visual perception, and if so, what are the implications for its use in clinical settings where perception is a critical factor. Furthermore, does the copying of designs have the same relevance for mature adults as for young children? An answer to this question might explain why mature test takers do less well on the TVMS-3 as they age.

Reliability was estimated using coefficient alpha and a split-half index using the Spearman-Brown prophecy coefficient, presumably computing these internal consistency measures at each age level. A table in the manual shows reasonably high reliability coefficients; however, these values are not reported for individual age levels, but rather for various sized groups, ranging from 1 year to 10 years per group. It is not clear whether these coefficients were initially computed for each age level or for aggregated age groups as shown.

Another measure of reliability presented is test-retest (average interval was 20 days). The values reported start with age 6, and then continue in 4- and then 3-year intervals up to age 19. No values are reported beyond the age of 19, except for an overall coefficient of .71. Because there were 120 test takers in the test-retest analysis, this study may have been limited to participants in this age range. If so, a statement in the test manual that the test-retest correlation was ".71 across all ages" (p. 37) is somewhat misleading. Also, it is noted that most of the values are asterisked indicating significance at the 5% level, but two of the values (.69 for age 6 and .91 for ages 17–19) are left without any asterisks, leaving this reviewer to wonder why.

Interrater reliability is also an important measure of reliability for this test. Scoring is done by examiners manually using some modicum of subjectivity, and their scoring is dependent upon the quality of training that they may have received. The scoring tutorial shown as Appendix C in the manual appears to be rigorous, and this reviewer was impressed by the examples presented. The manual also presents a concordance coefficient (not defined) of .72 (n = 64), using two different scorers trained by the test publisher.

Validity was reported in terms of content, criterion, and construct validity. The manual states

that information about a careful analysis of tasks utilized is presented in the development section of the manual. Unfortunately, this reviewer found no such section or discussion. The manual also says that "the TVMS-3 task is simple and discrete enough so as to minimize any confounding variables, and that factor analysis confirmed the task similarity for all items" (p. 43). As mentioned earlier in this review, this statement appears to be incorrect, given the two-factor solution presented in a table in the manual. Furthermore, the test manual says that "Inspection of item difficulties and factor analyses ensured that the presentation order of the designs progressed from easiest to more difficult and complex" (p. 43). Nowhere are the item difficulties presented, and the factor analyses do not appear to corroborate this statement.

Criterion-related evidence of validity is asserted based on a single study (n = 26). Clearly more and better validation studies are suggested. The literature in this field has numerous validity studies related to clinical applications for similar tests. Comparisons presented in the manual show nondisabled test takers scored significantly higher than test takers with learning disabilities and attention-deficit/hyperactivity disorder. These studies are worthwhile, and the demographic characteristics reported in the manual are good, but in this reviewer's opinion this comparison should have elicited more discussion, and the test authors should have presented related research references.

COMMENTARY. TVMS-3 promises to be a welcome addition to the complex process of standardizing the assessment of visual-motor skills. Its approach to developing a statistically based scoring system is commendable. This reviewer lauds the effort expended in defining, measuring, and reporting error types. It would have been especially worthwhile if this effort were documented with research references. As a general comment on the statistical analyses and the psychometric quality of the TVMS-3, this reviewer found several deficiencies and inaccurate statements in the manual.

The presentation of an appropriate rationale for a clinical test such as the TVMS-3 is critically important. Users must understand its theoretical basis, and this component is missing from the manual. The section in the manual on background and rationale does not address the choice of the tested variable, design copying. The other two sections on visual-motor problems in children and in adults address the need for such a test, but they do not address the rationale for the psychometric construct utilized in TVMS-3. There is no rationale presented, nor empirical justification, for combining the two precursor tests, TVMS-R and TVMS-UL, into a single TVMS-3 to include all ages from 3 to 90. The updated literature review in the manual is limited to half a page and the only reference cited there is the *Diagnostic and Statistical Manual of Mental Disorders, Fourth Edition* (1994). A good discussion of theoretical and clinical issues related specifically to the measurement of visual-motor skills would be an important addition to the manual. Such a discussion cannot be presumed to have been presented in the earlier editions of this test. It must be included in the current manual. Most importantly, the TVMS-3 has a serious construct validity challenge because its factor analyses would appear to demonstrate it is two-dimensional, not unidimensional, and therefore scoring should not be represented by a single score. In this sense, the older editions, TVMS-R and TVMS-UL, seem to retain their justification and utility.

SUMMARY. The TVMS-3 was intended to serve as an accurate, reliable, and valid measure of visual-motor skills for ages 3 to 90. Its goal was to untangle the complexities of scoring and reporting experienced by users of its previous editions. It is targeted for use by clinicians in various educational and psychological settings. This reviewer does not recommend the use of the TVMS-3 in its current state. Much work remains to be done to justify its psychometric quality and its validity for use in clinical settings. The current manual needs significant updates and corrections.

REVIEWER'S REFERENCES

Bonifacci, P. (2004). Children with low motor ability have lower visual-motor integration ability but unaffected perceptual skills. *Human Movement Science, 23,* 157–168.

Tsai, C., & Wu, S. (2008). Relationship of visual perceptual deficit and motor impairment in children with developmental coordination disorder. *Perceptual and Motor Skills, 107,* 457–472.

Hammill, D. D., Pearson, N. A., & Voress, J. K. (1993). Developmental Test of Visual Perception, Second Edition. Toronto, Canada: Mind Resources, Inc.

Leonard, P., Foxcroft, C., & and Kroukamp, T. (1988). Are visual-perceptual and visual-motor skills separate abilities? *Perceptual and Motor Skills, 67,* 423–426.

Review of the Test of Visual-Motor Skills—3rd Edition by KENNETH M. HANIG, Staff Psychologist, Logansport Joint Special Services, South Bend, IN:

DESCRIPTION. The Test of Visual-Motor Skills—3rd edition (TVMS–3) is an assessment of visual-motor skills that can be administered to small groups or individuals. It assesses eye-hand coordination, specifically copying skills that are used in everyday and academic activities. The test is untimed and requires examinees to copy 39 target designs that remain in sight (i.e., it does not assess memory). Each attempt is scored based on Accuracy and the type of Errors made. To assist in scoring, numerous examples of each error type are shown in the test manual. Norms are based on a nationally derived sample of 2,610 participants ages 3–90 years and older. The test is designed to be used by occupational therapists, rehabilitation specialists, educators, school psychologists, clinical psychologists, neuropsychologists, and other clinicians. The Accuracy score is reported as an overall standard score; percentile ranks and age equivalents also are provided. Error analyses are interpreted using cutoff scores that were derived from the frequency of error occurrence in the normative sample. The TVMS–3 can be administered in 20 to 30 minutes; an additional 15 minutes are required for scoring. Administration and scoring directions are fairly straightforward, and scoring examples are easily followed. This revision replaces the TVMS (1986), the TVMS-UL (1992), the TVMS-R (1995), and the TVMS-R-ASM (1997).

DEVELOPMENT. The TVMS–3 is described as emphasizing the roles that visual-motor skills play in activities such as handwriting, reading, reaching, and grasping, many job-related tasks, and everyday activities of children and adults. The development of this measure drew on the normative functional skill approach to understanding behavior. This approach, influenced by the works of Gesell, Piaget, and McGraw that "described the acquisition and development of both sensorimotor and cognitive functions related to age norms" (manual, p. 10), is often used when assessing movement, according to the test authors. Visual-motor disorders are evident in learning difficulties, and according to the test manual, 5% to 15% of school-age children are estimated to experience such difficulties. The test manual provides an impressive description of the background for visual-motor deficiencies in various populations along with academic problems associated with them. The review in the manual is comprehensive, short, and to the point. Background information about adult disorders associated with visual-motor deficits is covered as well, although this subject is given a shorter treatment.

Two considerations were addressed in developing the current version of the test: time-consuming and difficulty scoring and the presence of age-based test levels. Previous editions required the use of a protractor and ruler to get precise measurements, but these tools no longer are needed with the new scoring method used in the

TVMS–3. Addressing the age-based test levels, the test manual says, "Anytime two or more age-based 'levels' of a test exist, there is a risk that a child at the upper age limit of one test will 'top out' because the items are relatively easy, but will 'bottom out' when given the upper level of a test which contains much more difficult items" (p. 28). Therefore, the TVMS–3 combines the two sets of designs (lower and upper levels) from the earlier editions. An test manual's updated literature review provides references to current trends in therapeutic approaches.

TECHNICAL. The standardization sample consisted of 2,610 individuals ages 3 to 90 years and older. Tests were administered at 75 sites in 70 cities in 28 states across the U.S. According to the test manual, most of the data were collected from group administrations, with the exception of the youngest children. Of the total participants, 57% were female, and 68.6% were Caucasian. Hispanics made up 15.5% of the sample, African Americans 9.5%, Asian Americans 4.2%, and Native Americans 0.8%. Most participants (62.3%) were urban-centered, and 37.7% were from rural areas. Disabled participants made up 3.65% of the 3- to 18-year-old age group and .4% of those 19 and older. The sample was compared to population data from the 2000 U.S. Census, and when necessary, statistical weighting procedures were applied to make the sample as representative as possible of the appropriate U.S. population. Standard scores were developed, along with percentile ranks, and age equivalents. Because there are no subtests, scale scores were not developed. Raw score to standard score conversion tables are provided in the appendix, as well as Error score interpretation tables. There were no specific tables in the test manual to be used for interpreting scores from disabled populations.

Reliability. Test-retest reliability data noted corrected correlation coefficients for various age groups that ranged from .50 to .91 across two test administrations averaging 20 days apart. The corrected coefficient across all ages was .71. The standard error of measurement (*SEM*) is reported with a high value of 9.28 for age 3 and a low value of 3.39 for the 30–39-year age group. The overall *SEM* was 3.79. Interrater reliability was examined to determine whether the TVMS-3 could be scored consistently by different raters. The mean raw scores of 64 testing from the normative sample that were scored by two different raters showed a correlation of .78. Lin's concordance coefficient between these scores was .72.

Validity. Three types of validity evidence were provided for the TVMS-3, those being based upon content evidence, criterion-referenced evidence, and construct evidence. In terms of content evidence of validity, the test author noted that the TVMS-3 tasks and format are unchanged from prior editions of the measure. Further, the test manual says item difficulty and factor analyses of the items show items are presented from easy to difficult to complex. Regarding criterion-referenced evidence of validity, scores (*n* = 26) from the TVMS-3 were compared to scores from the VMI-4 and demonstrated a correlation coefficient of .63. Regarding construct evidence of validity, the test author noted developmental changes in visual-motor skills that occur with age. Correlation coefficients between TVMS-3 raw scores and age were .80 for ages 3-6, .51 for ages 7–39, and -.40 for ages 40 and above. Group differences also were examined as TVMS-3 standard scores from clinical and matched samples were compared. Children with a learning disability (LD; *n* = 66) scored significantly lower (*p* < .01) than a matched sample (*n* = 67) from the normative group. Likewise, children with attention-deficit/hyperactivity disorder (ADHD; *n* = 15) scored significantly lower (*p* < .05) than the matched sample (*n* = 15). Finally, children with both LD and ADHD (*n* = 15) scored significantly lower than the matched sample (*p* < .05). Factor analyses resulted in a two-factor solution, which the test authors attributed to items that are simpler to copy and those that are more complex.

COMMENTARY. Overall, the test seems to serve its intended purpose, and if one is interested in using the test in a school or clinical setting, this reviewer would endorse it. However, this reviewer was somewhat surprised that a flyer was attached to the scoring report forms indicating errors on certain pages of the test manual regarding interpretations of some scores. Corrections to the headings of the manual's Error analysis and interpretation tables were also noted on the flier. Hopefully, these errors will be corrected in a future printing of the manual. This reviewer especially liked the scoring guidelines in the manual that indicate exactly how to score certain errors. The information provided is far better than some other measures. However, this reviewer would like to see validity studies conducted using more than one similar measure. Although the norm samples appear to represent the U.S. population well, this reviewer would have preferred larger numbers (an overrepresentation) of

Hispanics and African Americans in that sample. Because the majority of students referred to school psychologists are members of these two groups, using results from the TVMS–3 in determining special education placement may be a cause for concern. Likewise, the number of participants in the clinical groups, especially the ADHD group and the comorbid group needs to be increased with additional research using revisions of the test for clinicians to be comfortable with referring students to special education using this instrument. Finally, examiners should keep in mind that the majority of the participants in the normative sample did not take the test individually, but rather did so in small group settings.

SUMMARY. In sum, the TVMS-3 is designed to measure how well a person age 3 to 90 years and up can coordinate visually guided fine motor movements to copy designs that are in sight and to document errors that are made. Because visual-motor skills play a significant role in everyday tasks, a measure such as this aids in determining a test taker's level of ability. Standard scores, percentile ranks, and age-equivalent scores can be derived. The standardization sample included 2,610 people, but this reviewer would prefer larger numbers of participants from African American, Hispanic, and disabled groups. Reliability and validity data are respectable, and the factor analysis lends credence to the veracity of the measure.

[173]
TPRI.

Purpose: Designed to "measure students' progress in the acquisition of important skills related to early reading."
Population: K-3.
Publication Date: 2010.
Acronym: TPRI.
Scores, 5: Phonemic Awareness, Graphophonemic Knowledge, Word Reading, Listening Comprehension, Reading Accuracy/ Fluency/ and Comprehension.
Administration: Group.
Levels, 2: Progress Monitoring for Beginning Readers, Progress Monitoring for Emergent Readers.
Price Data, 2010: $69.95 per Progress Monitoring for Emergent Readers kit including PMER Teacher's Guide and Task Card Booklet; $69.95 per Progress Monitoring for Beginning Readers kit including PMBR Teacher's Guide and Story Comprehension Booklet; $29.95 per 15 PMER Student Record Sheets; $29.95 per 15 PMER Student Record Sheets.
Time: Administration time not reported.

Comments: The assessment has an administration schedule that can assess progress at the beginning of the year, middle of the year, and end of the year.
Author: Texas Education Agency.
Publisher: Paul H. Brookes Publishing Co., Inc.

Review of the TPRI by JAMES DEAN BROWN, Professor of Second Language Studies, University of Hawai'i at Mānoa, Honolulu, HI:

DESCRIPTION. The TPRI [Texas Primary Reading Inventory] is an individually administered test of reading development for kindergarten to third grade (K–3) children. The teacher's guide recommends the TPRI be administered at the beginning, middle, and end of each school year. Two separate score interpretations are available: screening and inventory. The Screening Section assesses key concepts: for children in K, they include Letter Sound, and Blending Onset-Rimes and Phonemes; in Grade 1, they include Letter Sound, Word Reading, and Blending Phonemes; in Grades 2 and 3, only Word Reading is used for this purpose. The Screening Section provides scores of Developed (D–meaning that the student is performing the task successfully) or Still Developing (SD–for students who have not yet fully developed a particular skill or concept). The teacher's guide encourages further assessment of students who receive SD scores so that instructional goals can be matched to student needs. The Inventory Section provides the recommended follow-up assessment with separate scores for eight key concepts: Book and Print Awareness (BPA for Grade K only), Listening Comprehension (LC for K), Phonemic Awareness (PA for Grades K–1), Graphophonemic Knowledge (GK for K–3), Word Reading (WR for K–3), Reading Accuracy (RA for 1–3), Reading Fluency (RF for 1–3), and Reading Comprehension (RC for 1–3). The progression through the subsections varies by grade as follows: Kindergarten-Screening Section to BPA to PA to GK to LC to WR; Grade 1-Screening Section to PA to GK to WR to RA/RF/RC; Grade 2-Screening Section to GK to WR to RA/RF/RC; Grade 3-Screening Section to GK to WR to RA/RF/RC. The teacher's guide (pp. 93–120) also helps teachers shift from assessment to appropriate instruction.

DEVELOPMENT. The teacher's guide briefly covers the history of the TPRI by explaining how the stories were developed, piloted, and researched with about 3,000 Texas students. A more complete history of the TPRI is provided in the 2010–2014 technical report. All in all, the history of the TPRI is covered well, but the actual development of the TPRI is described less fully. For example, it is not clear how grade equivalents were determined, how items/tasks were developed, and how individual items/tasks were analyzed and selected for the current TPRI.

TECHNICAL. The most recent 2010-2014 technical report was supplied with the test kit (also available at: http://www.tpri.org/resources/documents/20102014TechnicalReport.pdf). One problem with all three of the TPRI technical reports described in this section is that they only cover Grades K–2, whereas the assessment materials are for K–3. Moreover, the 2010–2014 technical report provides no descriptive statistics (i.e., no means, standard deviations, ranges) and no standardization data.

Reliability estimates, in the form of coefficients, are supplied in abundance for all possible combinations of subtests and totals for Grades K, 1, and 2, separately for genders and ethnicities. The alpha estimates ranged from .47 to .95 for various subtests and samples, except for the Book and Print Awareness subtest, which produced reliability estimates as low as .32. Because this subtest is used only for warm-up, its low reliabilities do not pose a particular problem. The test authors interpret alpha estimates rather generously: "Poor (0–.39), Adequate (.40–.59), Good (.60–.79) and Excellent (.80–1.0)" (2010-2014 technical report, p. 5). By those standards, the reliability estimates for the TPRI subtests generally range from Good to Excellent. The reader may want to apply other standards.

In addition, differential item functioning (DIF) was studied. However, no explanation is supplied for what sort of DIF analysis was used or how it was performed. As the test authors put it, "Item response theory (IRT) models were employed for detecting differential item bias" (p. 8). Because there are many ways to do IRT DIF, the test authors should have explained the process used in much more detail. DIF results are reported for male/female, White/Black, and White/Hispanic biases for Grades K, 1, and 2, separately. Overall, about 5% of items show bias one way or the other.

In terms of validity, the 2010–2014 technical report (p. 3) seems to sidestep validity issues when the test authors write that, "Given the research underlying the development of the TPRI and the analysis of validity completed in the first study (see 1997–1998 technical report [http://www.tpri.org/resources/documents/19971998TechnicalManual.pdf]), validity was not viewed as a major issue."

That earlier 1997–1998 technical report did describe a concurrent validity study that concluded that, "The pattern of correlations among inventory tasks and the independent measures were statistically significant and in the expected direction, providing support for the validity of the TPRI. Tasks that showed reduced validity were generally those with less than adequate reliability" (p. 10). The "pattern of correlations" ranged from weak to moderate coefficients among the subtests on the TPRI and between each of those subtests and a number of other reading and comprehension tests. This report also describes the development and piloting ($n = 30$) of a questionnaire designed to study teachers' perceptions of the strengths and weaknesses of the TPRI, the administration procedures, and TPRI training. A larger scale study ($n = 287$) was reported in the 1998–1999 technical report (available at http://www.tpri.org/resources/documents/19981999TechnicalReport.pdf). The responses to the questionnaires were generally neutral to positive.

The validity evidence and arguments presented in previous technical reports probably should not be accepted in lieu of new evidence that should have been supplied in the 2010–2014 technical report that accompanies the TPRI testing kit. The test authors do present decision-validity information in the 2010–2014 technical report labeled as "predictive validity of TPRI screens" (pp. 10–13). By "predictive validity," the test authors mean comparing dichotomous at-risk vs. not-at-risk decisions based on the TPRI Screening section to decisions made with end-of-year Woodcock-Johnson Broad Reading Cluster scores (with a 20th percentile cut point). The TPRI correctly identified whether children were at-risk or not 61%–79% of the time for Grades K–2. Sensitivity was between 89%–94%; specificity was between 56%–77%; false negatives between 6%–11%; and false positives between 23%–44%. This report was quite upbeat about these results: "While the TPRI screens would have correctly identified over 70% of those students, it is more instructive to consider that the TPRI screens would have failed to identify only 43 out of 3,767 (~1%) through the use of short assessments that take less than 3 to 5 minutes per student" (p. 15).

COMMENTARY. Positive features of the TPRI include: (a) Perhaps the most important positive feature of the TPRI is that it is closely linked to a reading curriculum. The teacher's guide and other materials in the TPRI kit directly supply considerable information that teachers can use to provide effective instruction based on the diagnostic results of the test. (b) The TPRI provides abundant online resources including downloadable versions of some of the disposable TPRI materials, videos, FAQs, and so on for teachers, trainers, and researchers (http://www.tpri.org/resources/ACSS.html). (c) The technical reports are readily available (http://www.tpri.org/resources/researchers-resources.html). (d) The teacher's guide carefully explains how teachers should go about selecting the appropriate grade level test and interpreting the results for their particular group of students. (e) The teacher's guide carefully explains the importance of accommodating special needs and special education students, as well as the need for being sensitive to dialectal and cultural differences. (f) The Screening Section allows for quick assessment of individual students by identifying those most likely to not require the additional assessment details provided by the more time-consuming Inventory Section.

However, the TPRI also has negative characteristics: (a) Foremost among these is the inexplicable fact that the technical reports only provide information on K–2, whereas the TPRI reviewed here covers K–3. No explanation is provided for why Grade 3 was left out of the 2010–2014 technical report. (b) No explanation is provided for how the grade levels of the passages and test items were determined in the TPRI, or how items/tasks were selected. (c) The 2010-2014 technical report provides: No descriptive statistics, no standardization data, no discussion of what the many moderate reliability estimates mean with regard to the consistency of TPRI scores and decisions based on those scores, no confidence intervals to help with cut point screening decisions, and no explanation of how IRT was used to study DIF. (d) The 2010–2014 technical report largely sidesteps validity issues, seemingly in the belief that they had already been covered in previous technical reports about a previous version of the TPRI. Instead, the validity study focuses on the validity of the cut points in the Screening Section of the test.

SUMMARY. The TPRI may prove to be a useful test for teachers who need to screen quickly for at-risk readers in Grades K–3 and diagnose their reading difficulties. It may be particularly useful because it is closely linked to teaching strategies for addressing those difficulties. The TPRI provides abundant online resources including all three of the technical reports that have been written over the years, and the teacher's guide is helpful as far as

it goes. In addition to the fact that the technical reports cover only K–2, the 2010–2014 technical report conspicuously lacks important technical details. Nonetheless, for users who value the decision making and pedagogical features of the test over technical details, the TPRI may prove useful.

Review of the TPRI by CARLEN HENINGTON, Associate Professor of School Psychology, and CARMEN D. REISENER, Assistant Professor of School Psychology, Mississippi State University, Mississippi State, MS:

DESCRIPTION. The TPRI [Texas Primary Reading Inventory] is a teacher–administered assessment of reading for children in kindergarten through third grade (K–3). The TPRI identifies children at-risk for reading difficulties and may be used to help develop learning objectives and instructional plans. The TPRI can also be used during intervention for progress monitoring at either 2- or 6-week intervals. The TPRI consists of (a) a screen that allows rapid assessment of individual children with a designated status of "developed" (low risk) and "still developing" (at-risk), (b) an inventory that is a detailed assessment of reading and reading-related skills, and (c) an intervention guide. The TPRI is a criterion–referenced instrument with phonic and grammar elements that increase in difficulty across and within grades.

The TPRI screens are a brief assessment used to quickly (i.e., typically in 3 to 5 minutes) identify students most at-risk for falling behind or failure to reach grade-level performance. The screens identify students for whom additional assessment data are needed to determine whether intervention is necessary. There are eight forms of the TPRI screens, which include: beginning (BOY) and end (EOY) of the year for kindergarten (K), first (1), second (2), and third (3) grades. Areas assessed with the screens include Book and Print Awareness (optional), Listening Comprehension, Letter Sound, Letter-to-Sound Linking, Blending Onset-Rimes and Phonemes, Rhyming, Blending Phonemes, Deleting Initial Sounds, Deleting Final Sounds, Letter Name Identification, Blending Words Parts (beginning, middle, end), Spelling, and Word and Story Reading.

The inventory facilitates assessment for specific instructional needs in the areas of Phonemic Awareness (K–1), Graphophonemic Knowledge (K–3), Word Reading (K–G), Listening Comprehension (K), and Reading Accuracy, Fluency, and

Comprehension (1–3). There is a Book and Print Awareness task (K). The same inventory form is used across the year in each grade.

The intervention activities guide provides teachers with multiple direct-instruction activities across all assessed reading areas. In addition to details for some 276 interventions across the seven broad areas of reading-related skills, the intervention guide provides tips for setting up work stations for small group instruction, managing the classroom during multiple reading group activities, and providing differentiated instruction to students. The materials for intervention include a number of aids to determine ability group for intervention, a time management example to assist in planning for interventions across multiple groups, and individual student summary tools to document students' progress within intervention and across the school year.

The TPRI kit includes a number of booklets and stimulus materials: the teacher's guide for administration (for both the screen and inventory), intervention activities guide, teacher's guides for Progress Monitoring of Emergent Readers (K–1) and Beginning Readers (1–3), two administration booklets (a task card for screening, and a story booklet for story comprehension), four cards used in screening for letter and word knowledge, student progress monitoring and summary booklets for each grade, and a class summary sheet.

Instructions for administration for each task in the TPRI are clear, sequential, and easy to follow. Administration begins at the child's grade level and with tasks appropriate to the time of year. For example, at the beginning of the year in Grade 1, the teachers begin the screening with the Letter Sound Task, but at the end of the year the teacher begins with Word Reading. If the child is unsuccessful with the beginning task, the teacher follows the branching rules (typically still progressing forward in the sequence). All items are scored as 0 (incorrect) or 1 (correct). The item scores are totaled for a section (typically 5 to 10 items) and "branching rules" guide the teacher to specific inventory tasks to best determine the student's instructional needs. Based upon these identified needs the teacher may use any intervention materials available to them including the TPRI intervention activities guide to develop an instructional plan used with small groups with similar instructional needs.

DEVELOPMENT. The TPRI is the current version of a reading assessment tool developed by the Texas Education Agency in collaboration with a number of other agencies within Texas to provide a research-based assessment tool of early reading skills. Originally developed in 1997, the TPRI has been refined each year to address identified areas of weakness in reliability, validity, and test bias (i.e., gender, ethnicity). The test authors provide a technical report with details of development and technical aspects of the TPRI (Children's Learning Institute and Texas Institute for Measurement, Evaluation, and Statistics, n.d.). This report indicates that the 2008–2009 development study included data on 3,234 children from 169 classrooms (K–2) in 16 schools located in the Houston, Texas area.

TECHNICAL. As a measure of reliability, alpha coefficients for the screen and inventory tasks were calculated by grade, by gender, and by each ethnicity within each grade across all tasks. Coefficients ranged from .58 to .98 across all tasks; only Book and Print Awareness (an optional task) demonstrated alphas at unacceptable levels (e.g., in the low .30s). Of the screening tasks, all showed acceptable alphas (i.e., above .70), and 22 of 29 inventory tasks were acceptable.

To determine item bias, differential item functioning (DIF) was computed for each item comparing gender, White to Black, and White to Hispanic. The overall DIF for all items was below 5% except for 9 items at first grade (White to Hispanic) in which the results were split as to which ethnicity was favored (4 favored White and 5 favored Hispanic students).

Using a linear discriminant function analysis of all possible combinations of predicting outcomes at the end of the year, the test authors examined the (a) squared canonical correlation testing strength of relationship between predictor (fall) and outcome (spring) variables and (b) the identification matrices resulting from predicting outcomes case-by-case for the screens (K–3). From this process, a set of predictor variables were determined (i.e., those with high squared canonical correlation and low numbers of false positive/negative errors) and "cut scores" were set with the goal of using the least number of predictors to establish the lowest possible false positive error rate with negative error rates below 10%. Using a comparison to the Woodcock-Johnson Broad Reading cluster score (below 20th percentile), the five screens at all grades for 3,767 students correctly identified more than 70% of at-risk students. Most errors involved incorrectly identifying students as at-risk (false positives);

only 43 students were incorrectly identified as not at-risk (false negatives).

COMMENTARY. Educational professionals who seek early identification and targeted Tier II (small group) or Tier III (individualized) intervention for students at-risk for falling behind and/or failing reading are likely to find the TPRI very useful. The TPRI screens when combined with the corresponding grade level inventory provide educators with a very comprehensive and brief tool for determining students at risk for reading failure. This is not particularly unique to tools already available to educators. However, the specificity in the identification of skills targeted for intervention is remarkable, given the very brief administration time required. The teacher's ability to link specific identified skills with a large array of interventions via the intervention activities guide is possibly the most valuable aspect of the TPRI. Once a teacher has learned the aspects of the TPRI, it is likely he or she will more thoroughly understand the skills of all the students in the classroom. The additional aids provided (e.g., suggestions for setting up ability groups and managing the schedules for intervention, at-a-glance summary for tracking the entire class) are another attractive aspect of the TPRI.

The materials, spiral bound and mostly of durable card stock, are nicely packaged such that a teacher at each grade level will have only those materials pertinent to his or her classroom. The stories are interesting and the tasks are appropriate for the identified grade level. The individual student summary sheets are concise and user friendly for tracking students across skills within the year as they master each reading skill. Teachers can use the TPRI for all students in the classroom, including those who are not at-risk but still need specifically designed instruction during small group activities because skill assessments across all aspects of reading are addressed by grade. The test authors make no case for the validity of the interventions provided in the intervention activity guide.

SUMMARY. The TPRI is a brief criterion-based assessment tool that is used for early identification of reading skill deficits and student- and skill-specific program development. Materials allow for tracking students' skills throughout the year, including progress monitoring at either 2- or 6-week increments. The TPRI has undergone regular refinement to address weaknesses such that the current version appears to be relatively free of gender and ethnic bias while providing high levels of accuracy for identification of reading deficits.

REVIEWERS' REFERENCE

Children's Learning Institute & Texas Institute for Measurement, Evaluation, and Statistics. (n.d.). *Technical report: TPRI (2010-2014 edition).* Retrieved January 1, 2011, from http://tpri.org/resources/respurces/researchers-resources.html.

[174]

Trauma Symptom Inventory-2.

Purpose: Designed to evaluate "acute and chronic symptomatology … associated with trauma at any point in the respondent's lifespan."

Population: Ages 18 years and older.

Publication Dates: 1995-2011.

Acronym: TSI-2.

Administration: Group.

Forms: 2 forms.

Price Data, 2014: $212 per TSI-2 or TSI-2-A introductory kit including 10 reusable item booklets, 25 hand-scorable answer sheets, 25 profile forms, and manual (2011, 111 pages); $50 per 10 reusable item booklets; $64 per 25 hand-scorable answer sheets; $50 per 25 profile forms; $64 per manual; $365 per downloadable scoring program or CD-ROM.

Time: (20-30) minutes.

Comments: Revisions include new scales, subscales, and norms. Alternate form TSI-2-A contains no sexual symptom items.

Author: John Briere.

Publisher: Psychological Assessment Resources, Inc.

a) TSI-2.

Scores, 30: Validity Scales (Response Level, Atypical Response); Factors (Self-Disturbance, Posttraumatic Stress, Externalization, Somatization); Clinical Scales/Subscales [Anxious Arousal (Anxiety, Hyperarousal), Depression, Anger, Intrusive Experiences, Defensive Avoidance, Dissociation, Somatic Preoccupations (Pain, General), Sexual Disturbance (Sexual Concerns, Dysfunctional Sexual Behavior), Suicidality (Ideation, Behavior), Insecure Attachment (Relational Avoidance, Rejection Sensitivity), Impaired Self-Reference (Reduced Self Awareness, Other-Directedness), Tension Reduction Behavior].

b) TSI-2-A.

Scores, 27: Validity Scales (Response Level, Atypical Response); Factors (Self-Disturbance, Posttraumatic Stress, Externalization, Somatization); Clinical Scales/Subscales [Anxious Arousal (Anxiety, Hyperarousal), Depression, Anger, Intrusive Experiences, Defensive Avoidance, Dissociation, Somatic Preoccupations (Pain, General), Suicidality (Ideation, Behavior), Insecure Attachment (Relational Avoidance, Rejection Sensitivity), Impaired Self-Reference (Reduced Self Awareness, Other-Directedness), Tension Reduction Behavior].

Cross References: For reviews by Ephrem Fernandez and Jack E. Gebart-Eaglemont of an earlier edition, see 14:402; see also T5:2782 (3 references).

Review of the Trauma Symptom Inventory-2 by JODY L. KULSTAD, Clinical Coordinator/Adjunct Clinical Professor, Seton Hall University, South Orange, NJ:

DESCRIPTION. The Trauma Symptom Inventory-2 (TSI-2) purports to assess the multiple impacts of trauma through both acute and chronic symptoms of traumatic stress and to assess traumatic response without having it tied to a specific stressor or point in time. The TSI-2 is a revision of the earlier TSI. Both the TSI and the TSI-2 include an "A" form, which does not include the sexual items. The TSI-2 has 136 questions (TSI-2A has 126) and is appropriate for individuals ages 18–90 who can read at least at a fifth-grade level. Respondents are asked to rate frequency of occurrence in the previous 6 months, with 0 being *no occurrences* and 3 being *it has happened often* in the past 6 months. The average respondent can complete the TSI-2 in 20–30 minutes. The TSI-2 profile form displays scale, subscale, factor, and validity scores, converted from raw scores to *T*-scores and percentile ranks, with visible guides for score interpretation at the normal, problematic, and clinically elevated ranges. There is also a Reliable Change Score summary form that allows evaluation of change between scores from two time points.

DEVELOPMENT. Per the test manual, major revisions were made to the TSI content to update items, expand coverage, and address the complexity of trauma symptoms in response to growing knowledge and new developments in the field. The test author was also mindful of maintaining downward compatibility between the TSI-2 and the TSI. In the revision, many items were rewritten, new items were written, one scale was dropped in its entirety, and two scales were combined into one. New scales also were added. More specifically, the 100-item TSI with its three validity scales and 10 clinical scales was revised to the TSI-2 with 136 items, two validity scales, 12 clinical scales, 12 subscales, and four factors.

With the revision, the three validity or control scales became two: the Inconsistent Response validity scale was dropped, major revisions were made to the Atypical Response scale to better address posttraumatic stress disorder (PTSD) symptom misrepresentation and overreported trauma symptoms, and the Response Level scale was retained. Three new scales were added (Somatic Preoccupations, Suicidality, and Insecure Attachment), two sexual symptom scales were collapsed into one scale (Sexual Disturbance), and the remaining scales (Anxious-Arousal, Depression, Anger, Intrusive Experiences, Defensive Avoidance, Dissociation, Impaired Self-Reference, Tension-Reduction Behavior) were revised. The TSI-2 also includes 12 subscales: Anxiety and Hyperarousal (Anxious Arousal scale); Pain and General (Somatic Preoccupations scale); Sexual Concerns and Dysfunctional Sexual Behavior (Sexual Disturbance scale); Ideation and Behavior (Suicidality scale); Relational Avoidance and Rejection Sensitivity (Insecure Attachment scale); and Reduced Self Awareness and Other-Directedness (Impaired Self-Reference scale). The scales also were statistically organized into four factors: Self-Disturbance, Posttraumatic Stress, Externalization, and Somatization.

The 233-item pool for the TSI-2 consisted of some of the original TSI's 100 items, either rewritten or as originally worded, as well as a number of entirely new items. Eighty-three items were dropped due to redundancy, poor phrasing, or because they did not match the intent of the content domains, leaving 150 items. The remaining items were administered to the standardization sample of 678 respondents, obtained via the Internet by a national survey sampling company employed by the test publisher. The sample generally reflected the 2007 U.S. Census Bureau statistics across age, gender, race, educational attainment, and geographic region. Each item was then evaluated for its contribution to scale-specific internal consistency and its content value. Fourteen items were dropped leaving 136 items.

TECHNICAL. The remaining 136 items were subjected to further psychometric studies, alone and combined with other samples procured by the test author and publisher. Findings regarding reliability and validity follow, but before addressing these findings, some notes regarding standardization are warranted. As noted, the standardization sample comprised 678 individuals, demographically similar to the 2007 Census. Based on analysis of results from the standardization sample, two key issues were identified. First, significant main effects of gender and age led to the development of separate norms that are broken out by gender and age (ages 18–54 and 55–90). Second, though not unexpected, many of the scores were not normally distributed, resulting in the need to transform the scores to obtain norms. Per the test manual, the raw scores for each interpretable area (validity scales, factors, scales, and subscales) were converted to non-normalized linear T scores. Unfortunately, because this conversion did not allow for a T-score conversion to percentile ranks, percentile ranks were calculated based on raw scores, many of which were negatively skewed, creating a less valuable tool for interpretation. Psychometrics were evaluated using the standardization sample and five other samples including clinical samples, college students, and incarcerated women.

Reliability. Using data from the standardization sample only, the TSI-2 evidenced overall good internal consistency with clinical scale and subscale alpha coefficients between .74 and .94, with most trending toward the upper end of this range. Alpha coefficients for the validity scales were adequate (.72–.81), and for factors the alpha coefficients were in the good to excellent range (.77–.93, only Somatization was in the adequate range). Average item-total correlations for all scales, subscales, and factors were moderate or better, further suggesting good internal consistency. A small subsample of the standardization sample retook the TSI-2 at an interval of 1 to 13 days, with a mean of 5 days. Test-retest correlation coefficients were significant (at the .01 level) and good (.66–.96) for all but the Suicidality-Behavior subscale ($r = .15$). Per the test manual, the latter finding was not unexpected because of the low level of suicidality in the nonclinical population.

Validity. Validity evidence was shown through studies and analyses addressing convergent, concurrent, factorial, and criterion validity.

TSI and TSI-2 scores were correlated to provide evidence related to convergent validity. Scales, subscales, and factors all demonstrated significant correlations with their counterparts with a few exceptions. The TSI Self-Disturbance factor was more highly correlated with the TSI-2 Externalization factor, and the TSI Dysphoria factor was more highly correlated with the TSI-2 Self-Disturbance factor. The test author suggests that the revision of the scale altered contributions to the factors. Additional evidence supporting convergent validity was shown through high intercorrelations among the scale, subscale, and factor scores.

Comparisons of the TSI-2 scales and factors with other relevant clinical instruments, including the Multiscale Dissociation Inventory (MDI; 16:156), PTSD Checklist-Civilian Version (PCL-C), Borderline Orientation scale of the Personality Assessment Inventory (PAI; 18:93), Impact Events Scale–Revised (IES-R), Experiences in Close

Relationships–Revised (ECR-R), and the Health Symptom Checklist (HSC) were used to provide concurrent validity evidence. Scores across TSI-2 scales and factors correlated as expected with the scales on the other measures with the exception of the PCL-C Avoidance scale, which correlated marginally higher with the Intrusive Experiences scale (.69) than with the Defensive Avoidance scale (.66). The test author notes that this finding shows discriminant validity; however, the difference is so small as to be weak evidence.

Confirmatory factor analysis (CFA) in the standardization sample provided support for factorial validity. The initial four factor model was a good fit (chi square ratio = 3.56, CFI = .94), leaving no significant unexplained variance and path coefficients to scales were significant at $p < .001$ (Godbout, Hodges, Briere, & Runtz, 2010, as cited in Briere, 2011b). Replication of the CFA in the university and online samples supported this structure across groups.

Comparisons of TSI-2 scale scores among four separate populations (i.e., combat veterans, survivors of sexual assault, survivors of domestic violence, and clients diagnosed with borderline personality disorder) provided criterion validity evidence of the TSI-2 scores. All participants with trauma histories endorsed more TSI-2 items than did those without trauma histories. The only variable that did not discriminate was the Dysfunctional Sexual Behavior subscale of the Sexual Disturbance scale. This is not wholly unexpected, because not all trauma events have a sexual component. Also, in comparison to matched, nonclinical control groups, scale, subscale, and factor score differences produced the expected pattern based on group membership. Lastly, comparison of the T-score classification ranges (normal, problematic, and clinically elevated) were made, though not through statistical analysis. Per the test author, clear differences regarding classification were seen between the groups and their nonclinical counterparts.

The last aspect of validity covered in the test manual is predictive validity. Using the PTSD Checklist (PCL), participants were identified as having PTSD (PCL scores of 50 or higher) or not (PCL scores under 50). Scores on the TSI-2 posttraumatic stress scales (Anxious Arousal-Hyperarousal, Intensive Experiences, and Defensive Avoidance) were submitted to discriminant function analysis and significantly predicted PTSD status at the $p < .001$ level with a sensitivity of 1.00 and a specificity of .88. Further, receiver-operator curve analysis of the Posttraumatic Stress factor and PTSD status yielded an area under the curve of .98, suggesting the TSI-2 is an excellent predictor of classification. In fact, TSI-2 Posttraumatic Stress factor scores of 50 or above had a sensitivity of 1.00 and specificity of .86 for those identified with PTSD on the PCL.

COMMENTARY. The TSI-2 manual provides evidence of a solid standardization process reflective of the general population as well as sound psychometrics. Although reliability evidence was restricted to the standardization sample and it would be good to obtain further evidence with outside samples, validity was evaluated and evidenced through a variety of comparisons among clinical and nonclinical samples and across similar or related measures. Perhaps the only criticism of the TSI-2 is that the measure does not specifically ask respondents to consider their responses in relation to a particular trauma or traumas. An earlier review of the TSI (Fernandez, 2001) noted this is a possible weakness as it relates to diagnostic criteria for PTSD. This is of further concern with the new diagnostic criteria in the *Diagnostic and Statistical Manual of Mental Disorders* (5th ed.; American Psychiatric Association, 2013) being more restrictive of type of traumatic event. For clinicians or researchers not intending to diagnose based on the responses, this is not a concern, but the test manual should address this issue, and caution should be used in extrapolating a diagnosis of PTSD based on scores on the TSI-2, even with the predictive validity being so strong.

SUMMARY. The TSI-2 is designed to assess multiple impacts of trauma through both acute and chronic symptoms of traumatic stress in individuals ages 18 to 90 years. Responses are based on frequency of various behavioral, inter- and intrapersonal experiences from the past 6 months related to trauma symptomatology. Psychometric evidence, although generally supportive, did not include reliability evidence derived from samples beyond the normative sample. The test manual reports numerous studies that were used to provide evidence of validity of test score use. Overall, the measure provides a wealth of information for the clinician to use in assisting a client who presents with trauma-related symptoms.

REVIEWER'S REFERENCES

American Psychiatric Association. (2013). *Diagnostic and statistical manual of mental disorders* (5th ed.). Arlington, VA: American Psychiatric Publishing.
Briere, J. (2011). *Trauma Symptom Inventory–2 professional manual.* Lutz, FL: Psychological Assessment Resources.

Fernandez, E. (2001). Test review of the Trauma Symptom Inventory. In B. S. Plake & J. C. Impara (Eds.), *The fourteenth mental measurements yearbook.* Lincoln, NE: Buros Institute of Mental Measurements. Retrieved from the Buros Institute's Test Reviews Online website: http://www.buros.org/

[175]
Wechsler Abbreviated Scale of Intelligence— Second Edition.

Purpose: Designed as "a short and reliable measure of intelligence in clinical, psychoeducational, and research settings."

Population: Ages 6-90.

Publication Dates: 1999-2011.

Acronym: WASI-II.

Administration: Individual.

Price Data, 2013: $320 per complete kit, including stimulus book, 25 record forms, set of nine blocks, and manual (2011, 257 pages) in canvas bag; $77 per 25 record forms, $166 per stimulus book, $180 per manual.

Author: David Wechsler.

Publisher: Pearson.

a) TWO SUBTEST FORM.

Scores, 3: Vocabulary, Matrix Reasoning, Full Scale IQ-2.

Time: (15) minutes.

b) FOUR SUBTEST FORM.

Scores, 7: Verbal Comprehension Index (Vocabulary, Similarities), Perceptual Reasoning Index (Block Design, Matrix Reasoning), Full Scale IQ-4.

Time: (30) minutes.

Cross References: For reviews by Timothy Z. Keith and by Cederick O. Lindskog and Janet V. Smith of the original edition, see 14:414.

Review of the Wechsler Abbreviated Scale of Intelligence–Second Edition by KATHLEEN M. JOHNSON, Psychologist, Lincoln Public Schools, Lincoln, NE:

DESCRIPTION. The Wechsler Abbreviated Scale of Intelligence–Second Edition (WASI-II) is an individually administered and abbreviated measure of intelligence, designed for use with individuals from 6 through 90 years of age. Similar to the original WASI, the purpose of this revised instrument is to provide a standard set of subtests yielding a fast and reliable screening measure of intelligence for use in clinical, educational, and research settings. The author stated the following specific revision goals: enhancing the links to the WISC-IV and the WAIS-IV (in terms of administration, scoring, and normative data), increasing user-friendliness, and improving psychometric properties (manual, p. 3).

The WASI-II test kit includes the manual, the stimulus book, a set of nine standard two-color blocks, and 25 record forms in a carrying bag. The test is composed of four standard Wechsler subtests: Block Design, Vocabulary, Matrix Reasoning, and Similarities. The subtests were selected for the original edition because they correlated strongly with general intelligence (i.e., *g* factor) and also tap a range of cognitive abilities (e.g., verbal and performance, fluid and crystallized). The Vocabulary and Similarities subtests combine to yield the Verbal Comprehension Index; similarly, Block Design and Matrix Reasoning combine to yield the Perceptual Reasoning Index. The names of the Index scores on the WASI-II have been updated to be consistent with other Wechsler scales. The Full Scale score is derived from the scores of all four subtests (FSIQ-4). The Full Scale IQ scores range from 40 to 160. An even more abbreviated measure can be obtained using only the Vocabulary and Matrix Reasoning subtests, which yields the FSIQ-2. Administration time is estimated at 30 minutes for the entire test with all four subtests, and 15 minutes when only two subtests are used.

In the manual, the author provides a thorough description of administration details. The specific directions are printed in contrasting, bold print and are easy to read and follow. Within each subtest the test items are sequenced by difficulty. Age-related starting points are provided to minimize the time needed for a thorough yet efficient assessment. The basal and ceiling rules, reversal rules, and age-based starting and stopping points are printed in the record form for easy reference. Sample items, demonstrations, and corrective feedback (on certain teaching items) are provided to help ensure that examinees understand the tasks. Standard queries and prompts are specifically outlined in the manual, along with presentation procedures (described and illustrated) for all of the subtests. General as well as specific scoring guidelines are provided in the manual; common responses are also provided to aid in the scoring of the verbal items. *T*-scores for each subtest are derived from the raw scores. The sums of the respective subtest *T*-scores are converted to the index and overall scores (VCI, PRI, and FSIQ-4, or FSIQ-2). Corresponding percentile ranks and confidence bands are also provided in the normative tables.

DEVELOPMENT. Several steps were taken in the development process to address the WASI-II revision goals. Experts and examiners were surveyed and pilot studies were conducted using research versions of the revised scale. More than half of the items from the WASI were retained

and combined with new items. Final adjustments in the start and discontinue points were based on empirical review of the data collected. Examiners who had extensive experience with intelligence testing were selected and training was provided to ensure quality test administration. A national tryout (stratified sample, *N* = 564) was conducted with a revised scale containing the new, retained, and modified items for all four subtests. Scale revisions included improved floor and ceiling levels, updated artwork, and simplified directions. Various administrative and scoring procedures were modified to make the WASI-II more consistent with the Wechsler Intelligence Scale for Children–Fourth Edition (WISC-IV) and Wechsler Adult Intelligence Scale–Fourth Edition (WAIS-IV). The tryout data were thoroughly analyzed with regard to item scoring, item statistics, differential item functioning, subtest score reliability, and clinical utility based upon classical test theory and item response theory methods. The overall results indicated that the tryout version had adequate quality for use in the standardization process.

TECHNICAL. The WASI-II was standardized using a U.S. representative sample of 2,300 examinees. The participating individuals were English-speaking, 6 to 90 years of age. Census data were used to stratify the sample based on the following demographic variables: age, sex, race/ethnicity, self or parent education level, and geographic region. The child portion of the sample consisted of 1,100 examinees. The adult portion of the sample consisted of 1,200 examinees. Data in the manual detail the standardization sample, which corresponded fairly closely to 2008 U.S. Census population data. To better differentiate levels of ability represented by the subtest total raw scores, *T*-scores (mean of 50, standard deviation of 10) were derived from the standardization data. The sums of age-corrected *T*-scores were used to generate the composite scores. Scaled score equivalents were also generated to allow examiners to compare WASI-II *T*-scores to WISC-IV and WAIS-IV subtest scaled scores (mean of 10, *SD* of 3). The author proposes that the parallel subtest design (with the WISC-IV and WAIS-IV), which was developed and validated through linking studies, make it possible to substitute the WASI-II subtest (scaled) scores into a WISC-IV or WAIS-IV comprehensive scale and administer only the remaining subtests.

Reliability and validity evidence is summarized in the WASI-II manual. Internal consistency coefficients for the subtest and the composite scores are reported and reflect moderate to high levels of internal consistency. The values were generally lower for the youngest ages and for the subtests (e.g., .83 for age 6 on Block Design), as compared to the coefficient values for the composite scores (.90 and above for all ages). Test-retest reliability data indicated adequate score stability (over the 12–88 days intervening period), but with some practice effect noted. The average test-retest coefficients were .90 to .96 for the composite scores in the adult sample and .87 to .95 for the composite scores in the child sample. Interscorer reliability data were high, indicating clear, well-articulated scoring procedures and guidelines. To facilitate accurate test interpretation, tables are provided in the manual so examiners can identify statistically significant differences between subtest scores and identify the base rate frequencies of known score differences.

Validity evidence provided in the manual includes data relevant to test content (described in earlier sections), internal structure data, and data reflecting the relationship of the WASI-II to other variables and measures. With regard to internal structure evidence for the WASI-II, the intercorrelation patterns found among the subtest scores and the sums of subtest scores (corresponding to the index and full scale scores) provided evidence of convergent and discriminant validity: a common *g* ability factor measured by the contributions of four different aspects of intellectual ability. Factor-analytic studies (exploratory and confirmatory) provided support that a two-factor model (verbal and perceptual factors) fit the data best for the overall sample and all age bands. Analyses were also conducted to determine the relationship of the WASI-II scores and the scores of other intelligence measures such as the WASI, WISC-IV, WAIS-IV, and the Kaufman Brief Intelligence Test–Second Edition (KBIT-2; 17:102). The WASI-II overall composite (FSIQ-4) appears to measure the same construct as the previous edition, based on a high correlation (.91) between the scores on the two tests for a subgroup (*N* = 142) of the standardization sample. Similarly, strong positive correlations were also found between the overall WASI-II composite (FSIQ-4) and the FSIQ on the WISC-IV (.91) and the WAIS-IV (.92) for examinees in the linking studies. The author presented data on the relationship of the WASI-II with the Wechsler Fundamentals: Academic Skills. Moderate posi-

tive correlations were found between the Reading Composite and the WASI-II Index and the Full Scale scores for children and adults. Tables in the manual list the predicted academic scores based upon the WASI-II obtained scores. Several small group studies took place during the standardization process to examine the scores obtained on the WASI-II by individuals with various disabilities, as compared to scores obtained by demographically matched controls. The results were as expected; for example, the mean FSIQ-4 for individuals with moderate intellectual disability was 51.4, whereas the matched control mean was 100.2, showing adequate clinical utility for this group.

COMMENTARY. The Wechsler Abbreviated Scale of Intelligence–Second Edition is a normative update and revision of the WASI and continues to be a useful instrument for quickly estimating intelligence when such a screening is needed and justified. It can be used with individuals from 6 to 90 years of age. In keeping with other Wechsler tests, the WASI-II materials, documentation, test development, standardization, and technical elements are of high quality. Having a bookstand built into the manual, similar to the WISC-IV, would be helpful albeit more expensive. The elements that this test has in common with the WISC-IV and WAIS-IV (e.g., subtest format, directions, and test structure) make it easy to learn and interpret for experienced examiners. The WASI-II FSIQ-4 appears to have the most predictive strength when screening or estimating intelligence, whereas the FSIQ-2, Index scores (Verbal and Perceptual), and Subtest scores (Block Design, Vocabulary, Matrix Reasoning, and Similarities) have less predictive value, as expected.

Although this abbreviated IQ test has the advantage of being quick to administer, it may not provide enough information and more testing may be needed. The test author proposes that the parallel subtest design of the WASI-II with the WISC-IV and WAIS-IV allows an examiner to substitute the already administered WASI-II subtest scores for the corresponding subtest scores on the comprehensive scales (WISC-IV or WAIS-IV) when a more comprehensive assessment of intelligence is needed. Linking studies and equating methods were used to provide data for this parallel subtest design concept. Efforts were made in the test development and standardization stages to increase the likelihood that the WASI-II scores correlate well with those of the WISC-IV and WAIS-IV. Score differences required for statistical significance between VCI and PRI, as well as base rates for the score differences are provided in the manual to facilitate test interpretation. Examiners should only consider using the WASI-II when they truly just need an estimate of intellectual abilities, such as to verify previous IQ results or when the referral question at hand does not center around an examinee's intelligence level. The time factor (getting an IQ quickly) should not be used as the deciding factor. When a comprehensive assessment of intelligence is needed, a full test battery should be utilized from the start, rather than beginning with the WASI-II and then supplementing it with parts of another test battery. The test author notes that combining the two tests to obtain comprehensive IQ scores is a deviation from standardized procedures and examiners are cautioned in using this procedure. As compared to using Wechsler short forms of the comprehensive batteries, the advantages of using the WASI-II include the independent norms and the controlled content (using the subtests with the highest loading on the g factor). As also noted by the test author, the WASI-II is not a comprehensive measure of intelligence and the results should not be viewed as such.

SUMMARY. The Wechsler Abbreviated Scale of Intelligence–Second Edition (WASI-II) is an individually administered, abbreviated measure of intelligence designed for use with individuals from 6 through 90 years of age. Administration time is approximately 30 minutes for all four subtests, and 15 minutes for the even more abbreviated form consisting of only two subtests. The test battery yields T-scores for the subtests and composite standard scores (Verbal Comprehension Index, Perceptual Reasoning Index, and Full Scale IQ). The WASI-II normative update also includes revisions and improvements in terms of administrative, scoring, and other technical qualities. It is well standardized, reliable, and valid for its purported use as an intellectual screening tool.

Review of the Wechsler Abbreviated Scale of Intelligence—Second Edition by JONATHAN SAN-DOVAL, Emeritus Professor of Education, University of California, Davis, Davis, CA:

DESCRIPTION. The test developers created the Wechsler Abbreviated Scale of Intelligence—Second Edition (WASI-II) to be an individually administered, brief but accurate measure of intelligence or general cognitive ability (g). Examiners may use the test for screening to determine the likelihood that an individual's intellectual functioning is within the normal range or if more comprehensive testing is needed. The test is appropriate for screening in schools, correctional facilities, clinics, and other settings. The WASI-II is a parallel short form of both the Wechsler Intelligence Scale for Children–Fourth Edition (WISC-IV) and the Wechsler Adult Intelligence Scale–Fourth Edition (WAIS-IV). It is a revision of a 1999 test and consists of the same four subtests with similar item types: a 13-item Block Design subtest, a 31-item expressive Vocabulary subtest, a 30-item Matrix Reasoning subtest, and a 24-item Similarities subtest. The subtests are similar in format to their corresponding WISC-IV and WAIS-IV subtests, although the items are different. The test materials include a comprehensive and well-organized manual, a spiral-bound stimulus book, record forms, and a set of red and white patterned cubes. Examinees may be as young as 6 and as old as 90.

The WASI-II yields T scores (mean of 50 and standard deviation of 10) for each subtest, and standard IQ scores with a mean of 100 and a standard deviation of 15 for Verbal Comprehension Index (based on Vocabulary and Similarities), Perceptual Reasoning Index (based on Block Design and Matrix Reasoning), and Full Scale IQ based on the total score of all the subtests administered. Users have the choice of a two-subtest form (Vocabulary and Matrix Reasoning; FSIQ-2) or a four-subtest form (FSIQ-4). The manual states the two-subtest form requires approximately 15 minutes, and the four-subtest form requires 30 minutes.

The manual includes tables of the 90% and 95% confidence intervals for the Verbal Comprehension Index scores (VCI), the Perceptual Reasoning Index scores (PRI), and the FSIQ scores; the age equivalents of subtest raw scores for ages 6 to 29; the expected ranges of the Full Scale IQ on the WISC-IV and WAIS-IV based on the WASI-II FSIQ-4; the significance of differences between VCI and PRI scores; and the base rate of VCI-PRI differences by percentages of the normative sample at different ability levels. Of interest to examiners screening for learning disabilities is a set of tables in Appendix D providing information about discrepancies between WAIS-II scoring and performance on the Wechsler Fundamentals: Academic Skills subtests of Word Reading, Reading Comprehension, Spelling, Numerical Operations, and Reading Composite.

DEVELOPMENT. The revision focused on improving and bringing the measure up to date. The developers' goals were to simplify the administration and to improve the psychometric properties. To this end, the developers created 30 new items across the four subtests (e.g., 45% of the items in Similarities are new). They created new items at the extremes of difficulty for subtests to extend the ceiling and floor of the test. They modified and simplified the administration rules to make them more consistent with other current Wechsler tests, and simplified the verbatim instructions to examinees. They also reduced or simplified the discontinue rules and the rules for establishing a floor. The publisher collected new representative norms for the WASI-II and collected new reliability and validity information.

A further important goal was to link the test with other Wechsler scales. The developers equated subtest norms with those on the WISC-IV and WAIS-IV so that results from the WASI-II could be legitimately compared with these tests, and the parallel subtest scores from the WASI could be substituted in the administration of the other tests when a subtest is "spoiled." In addition, should an examiner wish to administer a full WISC-IV or a WAIS-IV after administering the WASI-II, the WASI-II subtests may be used to estimate IQ scores, so there is no need to administer the parallel subtests. A final goal was to link the WASI-II to a measure of academic achievement.

The development process included surveying professional users and scholars, pilot testing versions of the test, and conducting a national tryout version of the WASI-II with a stratified sample of 564 individuals. The national tryout permitted the evaluation of the several changes in the new version, differential item functioning studies, and item response theory studies of bias. After completing the tryout study, the test was administered to a larger standardization sample. Based on data from this final sample, the developers eliminated unneeded items, determined start points and discontinue rules to minimize the length of test administration, and determined time bonuses for quick performance. The publisher also undertook several quality assurance procedures to recruit competent examiners and to produce accurate scoring and data entry.

TECHNICAL. The WASI-II standardization sample consisted of 2,300 individuals aged 6 to 90. Ages were grouped into 23 spans, each with 100 examinees. Consistent with cognitive developmental theory, the age spans were by year up to age 16, then in 3-year, 5-year, and from age 45, in 5- to 10-year intervals. Based on U.S. Census data from 2008, the developers stratified the sample on gender, race/ethnicity, educational level, and geographical region. Data in the manual indicate that the norms are reasonably representative of the English-speaking U.S. population. Raw scores were converted to *t*-scores using the method of inferential norming, along with curve smoothing.

The internal consistency reliability of the WASI-II was determined using the split-half method. The average corrected coefficients on the subtests ranged from .87 for children on Matrix Reasoning to .92 for adults on Vocabulary. Coefficients were higher, in the mid .90s for the composites, with the FSIQ-4 average corrected split-half correlation having the highest value at .97. The reliabilities are consistent across the age span, but slightly more stable among middle-aged adults. These high coefficients suggest that the test measures its construct very reliably. The results of correlations between two administrations of the test over a short period of time (possibly averaging 2 weeks, the manual is not clear [Editor's Note: The test publisher advises that the test-retest interval ranged from 12 to 88 days with a mean of 21.2 days]) indicate the subtests and composites are measuring a stable construct. The manual reports the least stable subtest as Block Design among young children (.80), and the most stable as Vocabulary among older adults (.95). The remainder of the subtest values are in between and high. The highest values among the composites are .94 (children) and .96 (adult) for the FSIQ-4, suggesting these scores can be trusted to yield consistent information over intervals of weeks. All of these coefficients were corrected for sample variability.

The manual presents several lines of evidence for judging the validity of the WASI-II. The test content is typical of other measures of intellectual functioning and the item types have historically proven useful in measuring intelligence in U.S. populations. The intercorrelation of the subtests and composite scores shows the same pattern for children and adults as on the WISC-IV and WAIS-IV. The fact that all the subtests are moderately correlated supports the construct of *g*, but with the tests making up the VCI and PRI correlating higher with each other, justifying a dichotomy, related to two-factor theories of intelligence. Factor-analytic studies reported in the manual, including both an exploratory study and a confirmatory study, support the structure of the test and the use of the composite scores. The WASI-II correlates highly with its predecessor, the WASI, the WISC-IV, and the WAIS-IV. In all of these comparisons, the lowest correlation of around .70 was for Matrix Reasoning, and the highest, around .92 for FSIQ-4. The WASI-II also correlates as expected with a similar test, the Kaufman Brief Intelligence Test–Second Edition (KBIT-2; 17:102). The parallel composite scores correlate in the .80s, and the FSIQ-4 correlates .91 with KBIT-2 IQ. The developers also examined the correlation between the WAIS-II scales and the Wechsler Fundamentals: Academic Skills achievement measures. The obtained relationships were similar to those found with other Wechsler tests and the Wechsler Individual Achievement Test. Subtests making up the WASI-II VCI correlated relatively highly with Word Reading, Reading Comprehension, and Spelling. Subtests making up the PRI have a moderate correlation with achievement, but the FSIQ-4 correlates .79 with the Reading composite. The FSIQ-4 correlation with Numerical Operations was .62 for children and adolescents, and was .68 for adults. These results speak to the construct validity of the test as predictive of academic achievement.

Studies of the performance on the test by individuals with established diagnoses also appear in the manual. Individuals with mild and moderate intellectual disability score lower than two and three standard deviations below the mean, respectively, score significantly lower than matched controls, and have less variability in their scores. This is the case for both subtests and composites. Individuals identified as intellectually gifted scored significantly higher than matched controls. The mean for the 36 individuals in this group was VCI = 129.6, PRI = 122.6, and FSIQ-4 = 128.4. As expected, these scores are close to two standard deviations above the mean. Brief studies of the performance on the WASI-II by individuals with Attention-Deficit/Hyperactivity Disorder, Learning Disorders, and Traumatic Brain Injury compared to match controls also show validity evidence. Score patterns on the WASI-II comport with theory by showing predicted patterns of lower scoring in the latter two groups.

COMMENTARY. From the reliability and validity data, it is clear that administering the four-subtests form is preferable to administering the two-subtests form. Nevertheless, both forms will serve as the test developers intended, as a brief screening measure of intellectual functioning. The

WASI-II has excellent psychometric properties and a comprehensive manual. A major advantage of the test is the link to the WISC-IV and WAIS-IV, where scores on these two tests can be predicted, and the WASI-II subtests can be substituted if the examiner decides after screening that a more comprehensive test is needed. Most of the validity evidence focuses on the relationship of the WASI-II to other Wechsler scales. More evidence will be needed looking at other measures developed using other theoretical models of intelligence. The special group studies should be treated as pilot studies, and there is a need for more careful looks at the adequacy of the WASI-II as a screening measure. Although it is possible to estimate achievement-ability discrepancies, the use of the WASI-II in the initial special education placement decision-making process is not a good idea, because WISC-IV and WAIS-IV yield useful information on additional intellectual factors (i.e., Working Memory and Processing Speed).

SUMMARY. Readers familiar with the Wechsler family of measures of intellectual functioning will recognize the WASI-II as the latest addition in a distinguished line. The revision process yielded several improvements over its predecessor with greater precision at the extremes of age and ability. The test has excellent reliability, and validity evidence suggests it compares favorably with the longer Wechsler scales. Examiners familiar with the WISC-IV and WAIS-IV will be able to administer and interpret it with relative ease. It is not a replacement for these tests, but particularly in the four-subtest form, it is a superior brief measure of intelligence suitable for screening and use in research.

[176]

Wechsler Preschool and Primary Scale of Intelligence—Fourth Edition.

Purpose: Designed "for measuring the intelligence of children."
Publication Dates: 1949-2012.
Acronym: WPPSI-IV.
Administration: Individual.
Price Data, 2012: $1,120 per complete box kit, including administration and scoring manual (2012, 342 pages), technical and interpretive manual (2012, 272 pages), 3 stimulus books, 25 of each record form (ages 2-6 through 3-11 and ages 4-0 through 7-7), 25 of each response booklet (1, 2, and 3), scoring keys, block set, puzzle set, zoo location set, and 2 ink daubers; $1,170 per complete box kit with 25 web-based score reports;

$205 per administration and scoring manual; $205 per technical and interpretive manual; $79 per 25 record forms (ages 2-6 through 3-11); $99 per 25 record forms (ages 4-0 through 7-7); $47 per 25 response booklets (3, Animal Coding); $79 per 25 response booklets (1 and 2, Bug Search and Cancellation); $125 per stimulus book (1, 2, or 3); $3 per ink dauber; $129 per 25 record forms with web-based score report usages (ages 2-6 through 3-11); $149 per 25 record forms with web-based score report usages (ages 4-0 through 7-7).

Author: David Wechsler.

Publisher: Pearson.

a) 2-6 THROUGH 3-11 AGE BAND.

Population: Ages 2-6 through 3-11.

Scores, 9 to 14: Primary Index Scales: Verbal Comprehension Index (Receptive Vocabulary, Information, Total), Visual Spatial Index (Block Design, Object Assembly, Total), Working Memory Index (Picture Memory, Zoo Locations, Total); Ancillary Index Scales: Vocabulary Acquisition Index (Receptive Vocabulary, Picture Naming, Total), Nonverbal Index (Block Design, Object Assembly, Picture Memory, Zoo Locations, Total), General Ability Index (Receptive Vocabulary, Information, Picture Naming [supplemental], Block Design, Object Assembly, Total); Full Scale IQ consists of Verbal Comprehension Index (with supplemental Picture Naming), Visual Spatial Index, and Working Memory Index (with supplemental Zoo Locations).

Time: [30-45] minutes

b) 4-0 THROUGH 7-7 AGE BAND.

Population: Ages 4-0 through 7-7.

Scores, 12 to 25: Primary Index Scales: Verbal Comprehension Index (Information, Similarities, Total), Visual Spatial Index (Block Design, Object Assembly, Total), Fluid Reasoning Index (Matrix Reasoning, Picture Concepts, Total), Working Memory Index (Picture Memory, Zoo Locations, Total), Processing Speed Index (Bug Search, Cancellation, Total); Ancillary Index Scales: Vocabulary Acquisition Index (Receptive Vocabulary, Picture Naming, Total), Nonverbal Index (Block Design, Object Assembly [supplemental], Matrix Reasoning, Picture Concepts, Picture Memory, Zoo Locations [supplemental] Bug Search, Cancellation [supplemental], Animal Coding [supplemental], Total), General Ability Index (Information, Similarities, Vocabulary [supplemental], Comprehension [supplemental], Block Design, Object Assembly [supplemental], Matrix Reasoning, Picture Concepts [supplemental], Total), Cognitive Proficiency Index (Picture Memory, Zoo Locations, Bug Search, Cancellation, Animal Coding [supplemental], Total); Full Scale IQ consists of Verbal Comprehension Index (with supplemental Vocabulary, Comprehension), Visual Spatial Index (with supplemental Object Assembly), Fluid Reasoning Index (with supple-

mental Picture Concepts), Working Memory Index (with supplemental Zoo Locations), and Processing Speed Index (with supplemental Cancellation and Animal Coding).

Time: [45-60] minutes.

Cross References: For reviews by Ronald A. Madle and by Merilee McCurdy and Lynae A. Johnsen, of the previous edition, see 16:267; see also T5:2864 (146 references) and T4:2941 (38 references); for reviews by Bruce A. Bracken and Jeffery P. Braden of an earlier edition, see 11:466 (118 references); for a review by B. J. Freeman, see 9:1356 (33 references); see also T3:2608 (280 references), 8:234 (84 references), and T2:538 (30 references); for reviews by Dorothy H. Eichorn and A. B. Silverstein, and excerpted reviews by C. H. Ammons and by O. A. Oldridge and E. E. Allison, see 7:434 (56 references).

Review of the Wechsler Preschool and Primary Scale of Intelligence–Fourth Edition by GARY L. CANIVEZ, Professor of Psychology, Department of Psychology, Eastern Illinois University, Charleston, IL:

DESCRIPTION. The Wechsler Preschool and Primary Scale of Intelligence-Fourth Edition (WPPSI-IV) is the latest edition of the individually administered early childhood intelligence test with origins dating back to the Wechsler Preschool and Primary Scale of Intelligence (Wechsler, 1967). The WPPSI-IV continues the traditional design and structure with numerous subtests each providing an estimate of general intelligence consistent with Wechsler's "global capacity" definition of intelligence (Wechsler, 1939, p. 229), but it also incorporates new and innovative methods purporting to measure dimensions consistent with more contemporary explications of intelligence structure. The WPPSI-IV is a major revision and re-standardization with many new and interesting tasks and changes that clinicians likely will appreciate. The WPPSI-IV is divided into two distinct age bands (2 years, 6 months to 3 years, 11 months and 4 years, 0 months to 7 years, 7 months) corresponding to different subtest batteries due to significant cognitive ability and developmental changes during the age range covered.

DEVELOPMENT. Major revision goals noted in the *WPPSI-IV Technical and Interpretive Manual* included updating theoretical foundations, increasing developmental appropriateness, increasing user-friendliness, improving psychometric properties, and enhancing clinical utility. To accomplish these goals major changes included deleting subtests, adding new subtests, and modifying subtest content, administration, and scoring. Four

WPPSI-III (T8:2911; Wechsler, 2002) subtests (Word Reasoning, Picture Completion, Symbol Search, and Coding) were deleted to reduce redundancy, to decrease emphasis on speed, and to make room for tasks that would better measure working memory and processing speed. Five new subtests were added, including Picture Memory, Zoo Locations, Bug Search, Cancellation, and Animal Coding. Application of contemporary theory was noted in the *WPPSI-IV Technical and Interpretive Manual* and the resulting structure articulated is a higher-order model with links to Carroll (1993, 2003, 2012), Cattell and Horn (1978), Horn (1991), and Horn and Blankson (2012) in what has come to be known as Cattell-Horn-Carroll (CHC; McGrew, 1997, 2005) theory. Measurement of intelligence from this model is illustrated by narrow ability subtests combining to measure various broad abilities that in turn combine to measure general intelligence (Spearman, 1904, 1927).

WPPSI-IV stimuli are visually engaging, and several game-like activities that appear relatively easy to administer and score should be helpful in gaining and maintaining child cooperation and participation. To minimize fine motor control effects on processing speed tasks, an ink dauber was incorporated for children to quickly mark objects on response booklets. With this change, children are not required to manipulate a pencil. Core subtests associated with the Full Scale IQ score are administered first, followed by supplemental subtests and then optional subtests.

TECHNICAL.

Standardization. The *WPPSI-IV Technical and Interpretive Manual* presents extensive and detailed information on the standardization procedures and the normative sample, which included 1,700 children divided into nine age groups. The standardization sample was obtained through stratified proportional sampling across key demographic variables of age, sex, race/ethnicity, parent education level (a proxy for socioeconomic status), and geographic region. Inspection of *WPPSI-IV Technical and Interpretive Manual* tables indicated a close match to the 2010 U.S. Census data. A list of exclusionary criteria also is presented and included, among other factors, language and communication limitations, visual or hearing impairments, upper extremity disability, and physical or medical conditions or medications that might impact test performance.

Subtest scaled scores ($M = 10$, $SD = 3$, range = 1 to 19) for each of 19 age groups were derived

from an "inferential norming" (manual, p. 45) procedure. This procedure used raw score means, standard deviations, and skewness estimates that were examined from 1st through 4th order polynomial regressions. The best fitting model was selected with comparison to theoretical distributions and growth curve patterns that produced percentiles for each raw score. Minor irregularities were reportedly corrected through smoothing, but the method (statistical vs. hand/visual) was not specified. Composite scores for children ages 2:6 to 3:11 include the Full Scale IQ (FSIQ); primary index scores of Verbal Comprehension (VCI), Visual Spatial (VSI), and Working Memory (WMI); and Ancillary Index scores of Vocabulary Acquisition (VAI), Nonverbal (NVI), and General Ability (GAI). Composite scores for children ages 4:0 to 7:7 include the Full Scale IQ (FSIQ); primary index scores of Verbal Comprehension (VCI), Visual Spatial (VSI), Fluid Reasoning (FRI), Working Memory (WMI), and Processing Speed (PSI); and ancillary index scores of Vocabulary Acquisition (VAI), Nonverbal (NVI), General Ability (GAI), and Cognitive Proficiency (CPI). Composite scores ($M = 100$, $SD = 15$) were derived from sums of scaled scores from appropriately included subtests, and standard score distributions were visually smoothed to eliminate irregularities and ensure they were approximately normal. Some composite scores range from 45–155; others range from 40–160. Overall, a wide range (7.3–8.0 SDs) is represented.

Interpretation methods are delineated including reporting and describing the FSIQ and index scores and then evaluating index score strengths and weaknesses, index score pairwise comparisons, ipsative subtest strengths and weaknesses, and pairwise subtest comparisons, long a part of clinical tradition. Ability-achievement discrepancy analysis is discussed in assessment of specific learning disability, as is the pattern of strengths and weaknesses (PSW). No statistical analyses of reliability, validity, or diagnostic utility of these strengths or weaknesses, pairwise comparisons, or PSWs were provided to judge the value of such comparisons. Notwithstanding the numerous methods for clinical interpretation promoted in the *Technical and Interpretive Manual* and by others in textbooks and clinical guidebooks, there was a selective reporting of literature. Relevant empirical literature on the overwhelming shortcomings and failures of these ipsative and pairwise comparison methods to inform clinical practice (see Canivez, 2013a; Macmann &

Barnett, 1997; Watkins, 2003; Watkins, Glutting, & Youngstrom, 2005) was notably absent and should be duly considered. Specific psychometric evidence for the WPPSI-IV interpretations demands strong empirical evidence for application to individuals but is absent.

Reliability. Three methods of estimating reliability of WPPSI-IV scores are reported in the *Technical and Interpretive Manual*: internal consistency, test-retest stability, and interscorer agreement. Internal consistency estimates were produced by Spearman-Brown corrected split-half coefficients for all subtests except Bug Search, Cancellation, and Animal Coding, as these are speeded tests where test-retest stability served as the reliability estimate. A table in the *Technical and Interpretive Manual* presents subtest, process, and composite score reliability coefficients for each of the nine age groups as well as average reliability coefficients across the age groups. Internal consistency coefficients across the nine age groups were .95–.96 for the FSIQ and ranged from .85 to .96 for index scores and from .71 to .95 for the subtest scores. Standard errors of measurement based on the reliability coefficients are also included in the *Technical and Interpretive Manual* but should be considered best-case estimates because they do not consider other major sources of error such as long-term temporal stability, administration errors, or scoring errors (Hanna, Bradley, & Holen, 1981) that influence test scores in clinical assessments. Short-term test-retest stability of WPPSI-IV scores was examined with a sample of 172 children in three age bands with retest intervals of 7–48 days (*M* = 23 days). Stability coefficients (uncorrected) for all ages were .88 for the FSIQ, .78–.88 for index scores, and .69–.81 for the subtests. Corrected coefficients were slightly higher. Mean differences across the retest interval were mostly small but reflected some practice effects as typically observed. All standardization sample record forms were double scored by two independent scorers and, as noted in the *Technical and Interpretive Manual*, the overall interscorer agreement was very high (.98–.99) due to most subtests containing simple and objective scoring. A random sample of 60 cases was used to examine interscorer agreement for Information, Similarities, Vocabulary, Comprehension, and Picture Naming subtests where judgment is involved. Resultant intraclass correlations ranged from .96 to .99, reflecting very strong agreement in application of scoring criteria.

Estimated true score confidence intervals (90% and 95%) based on the standard errors of measurement are provided in the *Administration and Scoring Manual*, but the *Technical and Interpretive Manual* noted that there may be a preference for using the obtained score confidence interval. In fact, when the assessment question is concerned with estimating the true score of the individual at the time of the evaluation (rather than the long-term estimate), the obtained score confidence interval is appropriate (Glutting, McDermott, & Stanley, 1987; Sattler, 2008). Although a table of obtained score confidence intervals was not included in the manual, the formula for its calculation and an example were provided. For most WPPSI-IV scores, both confidence intervals will be quite close due to the generally high reliability indices.

Validity. Consistent with *Standards for Educational and Psychological Testing* (American Educational Research Association [AERA], American Psychological Association [APA], & National Council on Measurement in Education [NCME], 1999), evidence for validity was structured around areas of test content, response processes, internal structure, relations with other variables, and consequences of testing. As anticipated, subtest intercorrelations were all positive for both age bands and reflected Spearman's (1904) positive manifold and measurement of general intelligence (*g*). Factor index score intercorrelations were also moderately high for both age bands as observed in other Wechsler scales and intelligence tests in general (Canivez, 2013a). Results from exploratory factor analyses (EFA) were not reported in the *WPPSI-IV Technical and Interpretive Manual* despite the fact that four former subtests were deleted and five new ones were added. Confirmatory factor analysis (CFA) preference was argued and evidence for the internal structure relied exclusively on CFA. CFA was examined separately for the two age bands due to different subtest compositions. One issue present in CFA modeling was the fact that with only two subtests representing Visual Spatial (VS) and Working Memory (WM) dimensions in the 2:6 to 3:11 age group and only two subtests representing VS, Fluid Reasoning (FR), and WM dimensions in the 4:0–7:7 age group, models appear only just identified. Including one additional subtest to each of these latent dimensions would provide for overidentification recommended in CFA. Based on the theoretical models reported for the 2:6 to 3:11 age band, results from CFA with all subtests supported the higher-order model with a general intelligence dimension and three broad first-order dimensions (Verbal Comprehension [VC], VS, and WM). Based on the theoretical models reported for the 4:0 to 7:7 age band, results from CFA with all subtests supported the higher-order model with a general intelligence dimension and four (traditional Wechsler model like the WISC-IV [Wechsler, 2003] or WAIS-IV [Wechsler, 2008a]) or five (CHC inspired) broad first-order dimensions. Large differences between these two higher-order models were not apparent. To examine the latent structure of the WPPSI-IV further, CFA was used with only the primary index subtests for the two age bands. The respective higher-order g with first-order VC, VS, and WM dimensions (2:6–3:11) or first-order VC, VS, FR, WM, and Processing Speed (PS) dimensions (4:0–7:7) both produced well fitting models according to contemporary standards for goodness-of-fit statistics (Hu & Bentler, 1998, 1999).

Numerous small sample comparative studies of the WPPSI-IV in relation to other intelligence or neuropsychological tests were reported in the *Technical and Interpretive Manual*, and preliminary evidence for convergent and divergent validity was present. Correlations between subtest and composite scores from the WPPSI-IV and the Wechsler Individual Achievement Test-Third Edition (WIAT-III; 18:153; Pearson, 2009) were presented for generally small samples of children ages 4:0–7:6. Zero-order correlations between the WPPSI-IV FSIQ and WIAT-III subtest and composite scores were similar to those obtained with older children and adolescents who were administered the WISC-IV. Incremental validity (Hunsley, 2003; Hunsley & Meyer, 2003) of factor index scores was not reported. Small sample special groups and matched controls were compared to test for distinct group differences. Special groups included individuals identified with giftedness, mild and moderate intellectual disability, developmental delay-cognitive, developmental risk factors, attention-deficit/hyperactivity disorder, autistic disorder, and Asperger's disorder as well as some others. Mean differences were typically what one would expect with groups of individuals with giftedness scoring appreciably higher and children with disabilities or risk factors scoring lower than the matched control group. However, distinct group differences are a necessary but not sufficient condition for diagnostic utility and individual clinical application, and analyses examining

diagnostic efficiency statistics (Kessell & Zimmerman, 1993) and/or receiver operator characteristic curves (Swets, 1996; Treat & Vicken, 2012) will need to be examined.

COMMENTARY. In the Forward of the WPPSI-IV *Administration and Scoring Manual*, Alan Kaufman and Nadeen Kaufman quoted the WPPSI-IV research director as saying, "We wanted to give the clinician more insight with broader construct coverage, but not at the expense of him, her, or the child" (p. x). In their opinion, this goal was achieved. Although there are many notable changes and improvements including new engaging subtests that are geared to early childhood, ease of administration and scoring, the outstanding large and representative standardization sample, strong estimates of score reliability, and some preliminary evidence for validity, there are a number of important and disconcerting omissions in the *WPPSI-IV Technical and Interpretive Manual* that should have been included and must be addressed in the future. Some omissions are the same as those pointed out in a review of the WAIS-IV (Canivez, 2010).

With the deletion of four WPPSI-III subtests and the addition of five new subtests, this reviewer considered it disappointing to see, as with the WAIS-IV (Wechsler, 2008b), that EFA results were not reported. Although CFA is informative and tests theory, EFA and CFA answer different questions, and Gorsuch (1983) noted the complementary nature of the two approaches and general confidence in the latent structure when both were in agreement. It would have been useful to have seen evidence for factor extraction based on Cattell's scree test (Cattell, 1966), Horn's parallel analysis (Horn, 1965), and minimum average partials (Velicer, 1976), which help to guard against overextraction observed by Frazier and Youngstrom (2007). Further, presentation of oblique rotation factor pattern and structure coefficients for subtests would illustrate the degree to which subtests were uniquely associated with their theoretically postulated dimension. Presentation of variance accounted for by extracted factors would also assist clinicians in judging the merits of the factors. Absence of EFA results indicates that WPPSI-IV data were not allowed to speak for themselves. Failure to present Schmid and Leiman (1957) apportioned subtest variance to the general intelligence dimension and to the three, four, or five first-order dimensions (as insisted by Carroll, 1995) does not allow WPPSI-IV users the opportunity to judge for themselves whether sufficient variance is captured by index score factors for interpretation beyond the FSIQ.

Schmid and Leiman decomposed variance estimates were also absent from the CFA presentation. Such analysis results would have illustrated what subtest variance is associated with the higher-order g factor and what remains in the first-order factors. This decomposition is necessary to understand the higher-order dimensionality better. Also disappointing was the exclusive presentation of only higher-order measurement models that conceive general intelligence as a superordinate construct (Gignac, 2008) that has influences on subtests fully mediated through the first-order factors. Rival alternate bifactor (Holzinger & Swineford, 1937)/nested factor (Gustafsson & Balke, 1993; Keith, 2005)/direct hierarchical (Gignac, 2005, 2006, 2008) models should have been tested and often are equally or better fitting. Gignac and others (i.e., Brunner, Nagy, & Wilhelm, 2012; Reise, 2012; Watkins, 2010) have made compelling arguments regarding superiority of the direct hierarchical (bifactor/nested factors) model in that the general factor having direct subtest influences is easy to interpret, both general and specific influences on subtests can be simultaneously examined, and psychometric properties necessary for determining scoring and interpretation of subscales can be evaluated. The direct hierarchical model can also be considered a more parsimonious model (Gignac, 2006). Also missing is estimation of latent factors reliability from CFA by calculating coefficient omega and omega hierarchical (Brunner et al., 2012; McDonald, 1999; Reise, 2012; Zinbarg, Revelle, Yovel, & Li, 2005; Zinbarg, Yovel, Revelle, & McDonald, 2006), which is also critical in judging whether latent constructs are sufficiently precise for interpretation beyond the g estimate (FSIQ).

Absent also were hierarchical multiple regression analyses examining the relationships between WPPSI-IV index scores and WIAT-III scores after the effects of the FSIQ were accounted for to test the incremental validity of factor index scores as illustrated by Glutting, Watkins, Konold, and McDermott (2006) with the WISC-IV or Canivez (2013b) with the WAIS-IV. Understanding the relative contribution of FSIQ and index scores in predicting achievement is necessary in determining interpretive weight of FSIQ and lower-order index scores.

SUMMARY. Although the WPPSI-IV is an outstanding revision overall with many positive attributes and much of the *WPPSI-IV Technical and Interpretive Manual* can be considered a model for presentation of important information, like the *WAIS-IV Technical and Interpretive Manual* (Wechsler, 2008b), it falls short of fully disclosing critical statistical analyses and results necessary for clinicians to judge the adequacy of provided scores and interpretation methods. Such information is readily available. This reviewer believes that there can be no justifiable rationale for not including key pieces of information such as proportion of variance apportioned to the FSIQ, factor indexes, and subtests from EFA with Schmid and Leiman (1957) transformation, proportions of variance explained in subtests by the latent g dimension and latent first-order factors from CFA, or factor index score incremental prediction of WIAT-III achievement scores beyond the FSIQ. These results are critical in guiding clinicians in their selection and utilization of the WPPSI-IV. As such clinicians must wait for such information to emerge from the extant literature. In the meantime, if following the methods of interpretation articulated in the *Technical and Interpretive Manual,* they risk overinterpretation and misinterpretation of WPPSI-IV scores in clinical application. Empirical evidence for the WPPSI-IV clinical interpretation schemes (ipsative strengths and weaknesses, pairwise comparisons, PSW) was also lacking. Perpetuation of these subtest and profile analyses continues clinical test interpretation tradition that appears more a shared professional myth of subtest and profile utility and belief without empirical evidence. Subtest and profile interpretation methods are not consistent with *Standards for Educational and Psychological Testing* (AERA, APA, NCME, 1999) and should not be used in clinical decision-making until psychometric support for them is provided. In the words of Weiner (1989), the ethical psychologist will "(a) know what their tests can do and (b) act accordingly" (p. 829).

REVIEWER'S REFERENCES

American Educational Research Association, American Psychological Association, & National Council on Measurement in Education. (1999). *Standards for educational and psychological testing.* Washington, DC: American Educational Research Association.

Brunner, M., Nagy, G., & Wilhelm, O. (2012). A tutorial on hierarchically structured constructs. *Journal of Personality, 80,* 796–846.

Canivez, G. L. (2010). [Review of the Wechsler Adult Intelligence Test–Fourth Edition.] In R. A. Spies, J. F. Carlson, and K. F. Geisinger (Eds.), *The eighteenth mental measurements yearbook* (pp. 684–688). Lincoln, NE: Buros Institute of Mental Measurements.

Canivez, G. L. (2013a). Psychometric versus actuarial interpretation of intelligence and related aptitude batteries. In D. H. Saklofske, C. R. Reynolds, & V. L. Schwean (Eds.), *The Oxford handbook of child psychological assessments* (pp. 84–112). New York, NY: Oxford University Press.

Canivez, G. L. (2013b). Incremental validity of WAIS-IV factor index scores: Relationships with WIAT-II and WIAT-III subtest and composite scores. *Psychological Assessment, 25,* 484–495. doi:10.1037/a0032092

Carroll, J. B. (1993). *Human cognitive abilities: A survey of factor-analytic studies.* Cambridge, UK: Cambridge University Press.

Carroll, J. B. (1995). On methodology in the study of cognitive abilities. *Multivariate Behavioral Research, 30,* 429–452.

Carroll, J. B. (2003). The higher-stratum structure of cognitive abilities: Current evidence supports g and about ten broad factors. In H. Nyborg (Ed.), *The scientific study of general intelligence: Tribute to Arthur R. Jensen* (pp. 5–21). New York, NY: Pergamon Press.

Carroll, J. B. (2012). The three-stratum theory of cognitive abilities. In D. P. Flanagan & P. L. Harrison (Eds.), *Contemporary intellectual assessment: Theories, tests, and issues* (3rd ed., pp. 883–890). New York, NY: Guilford Press.

Cattell, R. B. (1966). The scree test for the number of factors. *Multivariate Behavioral Research, 1,* 245–276.

Cattell, R. B., & Horn, J. L. (1978). A check on the theory of fluid and crystallized intelligence with description of new subtest designs. *Journal of Educational Measurement, 15,* 139–164.

Frazier, T. W., & Youngstrom, E. A. (2007). Historical increase in the number of factors measured by commercial tests of cognitive ability: Are we overfactoring? *Intelligence, 35,* 169–182.

Gignac, G. E. (2005). Revisiting the factor structure of the WAIS-R: Insights through nested factor modeling. *Assessment, 12,* 320–329.

Gignac, G. E. (2006). The WAIS-III as a nested factors model: A useful alternative to the more conventional oblique and higher-order models. *Journal of Individual Differences, 27,* 73-86.

Gignac, G. E. (2008). Higher-order models versus direct hierarchical models: g as superordinate or breadth factor? *Psychology Science Quarterly, 50,* 21-43.

Glutting, J. J., McDermott, P. A., & Stanley, J. C. (1987). Resolving differences among methods of establishing confidence limits for test scores. *Educational and Psychological Measurement, 47,* 607–614.

Glutting, J. J., Watkins, M. W., Konold, T. R., & McDermott, P. A. (2006). Distinctions without a difference: The utility of observed versus latent factors from the WISC-IV in estimating reading and math achievement on the WIAI-II. *Journal of Special Education, 40,* 103–114.

Gorsuch, R. L. (1983). *Factor analysis* (2nd ed.). Hillsdale, NJ: Erlbaum.

Gustafsson, J.-E., & Balke, G. (1993). General and specific abilities as predictors of school achievement. *Multivariate Behavioral Research, 28,* 407-434. doi:10.1207/s15327906mbr2804_2

Hanna, G. S., Bradley, F. O., & Holen, M. C. (1981). Estimating major sources of measurement error in individual intelligence scales: Taking our heads out of the sand. *Journal of School Psychology, 19,* 370–376.

Holzinger, K. J., & Swineford, F. (1937). The bi-factor method. *Psychometrika, 2,* 41–54.

Horn, J. L. (1965). A rationale and test for the number of factors in factor analysis. *Psychometrika, 30,* 179–185.

Horn, J. L. (1991). Measurement of intellectual capabilities: A review of theory. In K. S. McGrew, J. K. Werder, & R. W. Woodcock (Eds.), Woodcock-Johnson technical manual (Rev. ed., pp. 197–232). Itasca, IL: Riverside.

Horn, J. L., & Blankson, A. N. (2012). Foundations for better understanding of cognitive abilities. In D. P. Flanagan & P. L. Harrison (Eds.), *Contemporary intellectual assessment: Theories, tests, and issues* (3rd ed., pp. 73–98). New York, NY: Guilford Press.

Hu, L.-T., & Bentler, P. M. (1998). Fit indices in covariance structure modeling: Sensitivity to under parameterized model misspecification. *Psychological Methods, 3,* 424–453.

Hu, L.-T., & Bentler, P. M. (1999). Cutoff criteria for fit indexes in covariance structure analysis: Conventional criteria versus new alternatives. *Structural Equation Modeling: A Multidisciplinary Journal, 5,* 1–55.

Hunsley, J. (2003). Introduction to the special section on incremental validity and utility in clinical assessment. *Psychological Assessment, 15,* 443–445.

Hunsley, J., & Meyer, G. J. (2003). The incremental validity of psychological testing and assessment: Conceptual, methodological, and statistical issues. *Psychological Assessment, 15,* 446–455.

Keith, T. Z. (2005). Using confirmatory factor analysis to aid in understanding the constructs measured by intelligence tests. In D. P. Flanagan & P. L. Harrison (Eds.), *Contemporary intellectual assessment: Theories, tests, and issues* (2nd ed., pp. 581–614). New York, NY: Guilford.

Kessel, J. B., & Zimmerman, M. (1993). Reporting errors in studies of the diagnostic performance of self–administered questionnaires: Extent of the problem, recommendations for standardized presentation of results, and implications for the peer review process. *Psychological Assessment, 5,* 395–399. doi:10.1037/1040-3590.5.4.395

Macmann, G. M., & Barnett, D. W. (1997). Myth of the master detective: Reliability of interpretations for Kaufman's "Intelligent Testing" approach to the WISC-III. *School Psychology Quarterly, 12,* 197-234.

McDonald, R. P. (1999). *Test theory: A unified treatment.* Mahwah, NJ: Erlbaum.

McGrew, K. S. (1997). Analysis of the major intelligence batteries according to a proposed comprehensive Gf-Gc framework. In D. P. Flanagan, J. L. Genshaft, & P. L. Harrison (Eds.), *Contemporary intellectual assessment: Theories, tests, and issues* (pp. 151–179). New York, NY: Guilford.

McGrew, K. S. (2005). The Cattell-Horn-Carroll theory of cognitive abilities: Past, present, and future. In D. P. Flanagan & P. L. Harrison (Eds.), *Contemporary intellectual assessment: Theories, tests, and issues* (2nd ed., pp. 136–181). New York, NY: Guilford.

Pearson. (2009). Wechsler Individual Achievement Test-Third Edition. San Antonio, TX: Author.

Reise, S. P. (2012). The rediscovery of bifactor measurement models. *Multivariate Behavioral Research, 47,* 667–696.

Sattler, J. M. (2008). *Assessment of children: Cognitive foundations* (5th ed.). San Diego, CA: Author

Schmid, J., & Leiman, J. M. (1957). The development of hierarchical factor solutions. *Psychometrika, 22,* 53–61.

Spearman, C. (1904). "General intelligence": Objectively determined and measured. *American Journal of Psychology, 15,* 201–293.

Spearman, C. (1927). *The abilities of man.* New York, NY: Cambridge.

Swets, J. A. (1996). *Signal detection theory and ROC analysis in psychological diagnostics: Collected papers.* Mahwah, NJ: Erlbaum.

Treat, T. A., & Viken, R. J. (2012). Measuring test performance with signal detection theory techniques. In H. Cooper, P. M. Camic, D. L. Long, A. T. Panter, D. Rindskopf, & K. J. Sher (Eds.), *Handbook of research methods in psychology: Volume 1 Foundations, planning, measures, and psychometrics* (pp. 723–744). Washington, DC: American Psychological Association.

Velicer, W. F. (1976). Determining the number of components form the matrix of partial correlations. *Psychometrika, 41,* 321–327.

Watkins, M. W. (2003). IQ subtest analysis: Clinical acumen or clinical illusion? *The Scientific Review of Mental Health Practice, 2,* 118–141.

Watkins, M. W. (2010). Structure of the Wechsler Intelligence Scale for Children–Fourth Edition among a national sample of referred students. *Psychological Assessment, 22,* 782–787.

Watkins, M. W., Glutting, J. J., & Youngstrom, E. A. (2005). Issues in subtest profile analysis. In D. P. Flanagan and P. L. Harrison (Eds.), *Contemporary intellectual assessment: Theories, tests, and issues* (2nd ed., pp. 251–268). New York, NY: Guilford.

Wechsler, D. (1939). *The measurement of adult intelligence.* Baltimore, MD: Williams & Wilkins.

Wechsler, D. (1967). Wechsler Preschool and Primary Scale of Intelligence. New York, NY: The Psychological Corporation.

Wechsler, D. (2002). Wechsler Preschool and Primary Scale of Intelligence-Third Edition. San Antonio, TX: The Psychological Corporation.

Wechsler, D. (2003). Wechsler Intelligence Scale for Children-Fourth Edition. San Antonio, TX: The Psychological Corporation.

Wechsler, D. (2008a). Wechsler Adult Intelligence Scale—Fourth Edition. San Antonio, TX: NCS Pearson, Inc.

Wechsler, D. (2008b). *Wechsler Adult Intelligence Scale—Fourth Edition technical and interpretive manual.* San Antonio, TX: NCS Pearson, Inc.

Weiner, I. B. (1989). On competence and ethicality in psychodiagnostic assessment. *Journal of Personality Assessment, 53,* 827–831.

Zinbarg, R. E., Revelle, W., Yovel, I., & Li, W. (2005). Cronbach's alpha, Revelle's beta, and McDonald's omega h: Their relations with each other and two alternative conceptualizations of reliability. *Psychometrika, 70,* 123–133.

Zinbarg, R. E., Yovel, I., Revelle, W., & McDonald, R. P. (2006). Estimating generalizability to a latent variable common to all of a scale's indicators: A comparison of estimators for omega. *Applied Psychological Measurement, 30,* 121–144.

Review of the Wechsler Preschool and Primary Scale of Intelligence–Fourth Edition by TRACY THORNDIKE, Associate Professor of Special Education and Education Leadership, Western Washington University, Bellingham, WA:

DESCRIPTION. The Wechsler Preschool and Primary Scale of Intelligence–Fourth Edition (WPPSI-IV) is an individually administered intelligence test designed for use with children ages 2 years, 6 months (2:6) to 7 years, 7 months (7:7). The WPPSI-IV is a substantially revised version of the Wechsler Preschool and Primary Scale of Intelligence–Third Edition (WPPSI-III; T8:2911). As with the WPPSI-III, the WPPSI-IV is divided into two age bands (2:6 to 3:11 and 4:0 to 7:7) with the second age band extended upward to overlap more fully with the Wechsler Intelligence Scale for Children–Fourth Edition (WISC-IV; 16:262). The scale includes 15 subtests with different batteries of subtests used for each age band.

Scores can be interpreted at three levels: full scale, index scale, and individual subtest. Scores on multiple core subtests are combined to yield up to five primary, factor-based composite index scores reflective of different aspects of intellectual functioning and a second-order factor-based composite score representing general cognitive ability (i.e., *g* or Full Scale IQ [FSIQ]). Available supplemental and optional subtests allow for a broader sampling of specific intellectual skills and make possible the computation of up to four additional theoretically based ancillary index scores. The breadth and depth of information provided by the primary and ancillary index scores, in the hands of a skilled user, could increase the clinical utility of the WPPSI-IV as a component of a comprehensive neuropsychological assessment of cognitive and/or adaptive functioning in young children.

DEVELOPMENT. The Wechsler intelligence scales—the Wechsler Adult Intelligence Scale (WAIS), Wechsler Intelligence Scale for Children (WISC), and the Wechsler Preschool and Primary Scale of Intelligence (WPPSI)—are among the instruments most widely used to measure intellectual functioning in English-speaking populations and have been revised frequently over the past seven decades. The WPPSI-IV is the newest revision of the scale designed to measure intelligence in young children.

Goals of this revision were to: (a) update the scale to reflect more accurately current structural models of intelligence, theories of working memory, and findings from neurodevelopmental and neuro-cognitive research; (b) increase the developmental appropriateness and user-friendliness of the materials and administration and scoring procedures; (c) improve the psychometric properties of the scale; and (d) enhance the clinical utility of the scale for use in various types of psychological evaluation. The scope of these goals necessitated substantial modifications to the scale including removal of four subtests, addition of five new subtests, and revision of item content and administration and/or scoring procedures on all subtests retained from the WPPSI-III.

The major alterations to subtests for the WPPSI-IV involved those measuring working memory (two new subtests) and processing speed (three new subtests). Both working memory subtests now employ proactive interference rather than sequencing as the means of increasing cognitive processing demands. The new processing speed subtests were designed to be more developmentally appropriate than the subtests they replaced. Specifically the tasks are more play-like, realistic stimuli are favored over abstract stimuli, and level of fine motor skill needed to generate a response quickly has been decreased through use of an ink dauber instead of a pencil.

Multiple rounds of revision, piloting, and refinement, all clearly described in the test manual, were conducted to arrive at the WPPSI-IV. Major revisions to items, administration procedures, and scoring were first tested in pilot studies before moving to a national tryout phase of development.

TECHNICAL. Normative information for the WPPSI-IV is based on a stratified sample of 1,700 children ages 2:6 to 7:7 years. The sample is representative of the U.S. population of English-speaking children in this age range in terms of race/ethnicity, parent education level, and geographic region and includes an equal number of males and females. The sample was divided into nine age groups with 200 children each for the 2:6–2:11 through 6:0-6:11 groups and 100 children for the 7:0–7:7 group.

Scores on individual subtests are scaled to a metric with a mean of 10 and a standard deviation of 3. Composite scores are scaled with a mean of 100 and a standard deviation of 15. Age equivalent scores are provided for 1-month intervals across the full 2:6 to 7:7 age range. Percentile ranks, standard errors of measurement, and confidence intervals also are available to aid interpretation of scores.

The reliability of scores on the individual subscales and composites was examined separately. Internal consistency for all scores except those measuring processing speed was estimated using the split-half method later adjusted with the Spearman-Brown formula to estimate reliability of the full-length scales. Reliability coefficients ranged from .85 to .93 for the subscales and from .86 to .94 for the composite scores. Reliability estimates for the processing speed subtests were based on test-retest data and ranged from .75 to .83. The values were somewhat lower than the other subtests, but still in an acceptable range given that they were based on test-retest data.

A subset of the standardization sample (N = 172) took the WPPSI-IV on two occasions to estimate score stability over time. Test-retest reliability of subtest and composite scores was calculated for three age ranges (2:6–3:11, 4:0–5:5, and 5:6–7:7) over an interval of an average of 23 days. Reliability coefficients were in the .70s and .80s for the subtests, .80s for the primary index scores, and over .90 for the FSIQ score indicating acceptable to excellent levels of stability over time for all age ranges. Evidence of interscorer agreement is also presented for the five subtests that require judgment in scoring. A sample of 60 cases was randomly selected from the norming sample and scored independently by nine scorers with no prior experience with the WPPSI-IV scoring rules. Inter-rater reliability coefficients ranged from .96 to .99, indicating that these subtests can be reliably scored.

Extensive validation evidence is provided to support proposed interpretations and uses of scores from the WPPSI-IV. Expert and advisory panel reviews were employed at each stage of development to help ensure that test content adequately sampled all relevant domains of intellectual functioning and that items and administration procedures were developmentally appropriate. Evidence describing the internal structure of the instrument is available for each of the two age bands. Confirmatory factor analysis was used to generate and test a variety of structural models. A model with three first-order factors (Verbal Comprehension, Visual Spatial, and Working Memory) and one second-order factor (g) best fit the data for the 2:6 to 3:11 age band. For the 4:0 to 7:7 age band, a model with five first-order factors (Verbal Comprehension, Visual Spatial, Fluid Reasoning, Working Memory, and Processing Speed) and one second-order factor (g) best reproduced the observed correlations among subtest scores. Both the WISC-IV and WAIS-IV have a four-factor structure, but the test manual notes that evidence collected since the publication of these scales is more compatible with the five-factor model observed on the WPPSI-IV for the older age band.

Strong evidence of convergent concurrent validity was demonstrated by the strength of relationship between scores on the WPPSI-IV and scores on multiple other measures of cognitive ability (e.g., WPPSI–III, Bayley Scales of Infant and Toddler Development–Third Edition [Bayley–III; 17:17], and Differential Ability Scales–Second Edition [DAS–II; 18:45]). Additional validation evidence in the form of correlations with scores on tests of achievement, executive functioning, and emotional and behavioral functioning commonly used clinical application in conjunction with the WPPSI-IV is also presented for 13 "special groups" of children. Although based on relatively small, nonrandom samples, the "special group" evidence generally supports the clinical utility of the WPPSI-IV as part of a comprehensive diagnostic evaluation of cognitive functioning in young children.

COMMENTARY. The WPPSI-IV is a psychometrically strong instrument that yields scores that estimate both overall cognitive ability and more specific intellectual skills. New norms are based on a large, representative sample of the U.S. population of English-speaking children ages 2 years 6 months to 7 years 7 months. Extensive evidence is provided to support both the reliability of scores and the validity of a wide range of score-based inferences. The test manual includes detailed information about administration, scoring, and score interpretation presented so clearly that even inexperienced test users should find it easy to understand. Of particular note is the chapter in the manual on interpretative considerations with step-by-step instructions for interpreting and reporting scores and important cautions that, if heeded, would decrease dramatically the likelihood of score misinterpretation and misuse. The major goals of this revision–updating the scale to reflect current structural models of intelligence, increasing developmental appropriateness and user-friendliness, improving psychometric properties, and expanding the evidence base supporting clinical application–have largely been achieved.

SUMMARY. The WPPSI-IV is a substantially revised version of the Wechsler Preschool and Primary Scale of Intelligence, an individually administered test battery used to measure cognitive ability in young children. The structure of the test has been updated to reflect accurately current theoretical conceptualizations of intellectual functioning. Changes to items, subtests, and administration and scoring procedures have resulted in a more developmentally appropriate instrument that is psychometrically stronger than its predecessors. Evidence supporting the use of the WPPSI-IV with a wide variety of groups enhances the clinical utility of the scale for diagnostic and intervention planning purposes.

[177]

WeldTest (Form AC).

Purpose: Designed for selecting and evaluating journey-level, industrial welders.
Population: Welding job applicants.
Publication Dates: 1984-2007.
Scores: 7 areas: Print Reading, Welding/Cutting Torch and Arc Air Cutting, Welder Maintenance and Operation, Tools/Machines/Material and Equipment, Mobile Equipment and Rigging, Production Welding Practices, Total.
Administration: Group.
Price Data, 2011: $22 per consumable self-scoring test booklet or online test administration; $24.95 per manual (2005, 16 pages).
Time: (60-70) minutes.
Comments: Self-scoring instrument; available for online test administration.

Author: Roland T. Ramsay.
Publisher: Ramsay Corporation.
Cross References: For reviews by John Peter Hudson, Jr. and David C. Roberts of an earlier edition, see 13:360.

Review of the WeldTest (Form AC) by JAMES WITTE, Professor of Adult Education, Auburn University, Auburn, AL:

DESCRIPTION. The WeldTest (Form AC) is a 60-item version of the Ramsay Corporation Job Skills Welding Test (Form A; 13:360) first developed in the 1980s by the Ramsay Corporation as part of a series of skills tests for production employees in a Midwestern equipment manufacturing plant. The RCJS WeldTest (Form AC) is provided in a self-scoring format developed in 1998.

The test instructions are clear, inclusive, and easy to follow. The test may be administered individually or to a group. The authors recommend that group administration not exceed 20 persons at a single setting. With a larger number of participants, one assistant test administrator is recommended for each additional 20 persons. A testing can be performed using the administration instructions, two (recommended) sharpened Number 2 pencils per examinee and the test booklets. No additional testing support equipment or materials (e.g., calculator or electronic equipment) are required. There is no time limit for the examination; however, the authors state that examinees should not need more than one hour to complete the measure.

DEVELOPMENT. The development of the WeldTest (Form AC) followed the development of the RCJS Welding Test (Form A). Portions of content areas were kept the same from Form A to Form AC. The test's content was derived through the use of an expert panel. Four job experts were given a list of knowledge and skill areas appropriate for the intended participants. Job experts were defined as incumbent production workers or supervisors of production workers. The job experts edited the list and independently ranked the importance of the knowledge and skill areas. These values were averaged across raters. Each rater also independently estimated the percentage of items that should be developed for each knowledge and skill area. The responses were then averaged and multiplied by the number of items contemplated for the test. This number then became the number of planned items for the test.

Job experts, working in groups of two, then selected relevant items from the corporate item bank. From a list of pertinent items, the job experts selected items for each category that they believed reflected appropriate content and difficulty. The job experts were asked to include a safety item for each test section where applicable. They then marked the correct answer and submitted their selections for verification.

After 38 individuals were tested with the RCJS Welding Test (Form A), two industrial psychologists selected the best 60 items based on item point-biserial discrimination indices and item difficulty information. The resultant 60 items constitute the RCJS WeldTest (Form AC).

TECHNICAL. Internal consistency reliability was calculated using the Kuder-Richardson 20 formula. The reliability coefficient and standard error of measurement table provided in the test manual reports on data collected from two groups, both identified as production employees in a Midwestern equipment plant. It appears, however, that the first group (N = 38) represents applicants, and the second group (N = 34) represents production line workers. The *KR20* scores (.92 and .89, respectively) indicate acceptable estimates of internal consistency reliability for the instrument (Huck, 2000).

Evidence of validity was determined by using a panel of experts. Item difficulty analyses and point-biserial discrimination indices indicate satisfactory instrument performance. The difficulty analyses and discrimination indices were calculated based on scores from 38 applicants. Normative data were developed by examining scores from 38 welding applicants and 34 production employees. Data were analyzed, reported and deemed appropriate.

COMMENTARY. The WeldTest (Form AC) is a self-scoring instrument also available for online test administration. The accompanying Manual for Administration & Scoring is a well written, easy to use publication. The WeldTest (Form AC) demonstrates a great deal of promise. The questions are clear and concise, and the figures used are also clear and replicate what a worker may find on the job. The evidence supporting reliability and validity is encouraging and should be further examined. Once further evidence of validity and reliability are established, the instrument should meet expectations in all regards. The small sample (with no reported effect size) brings into question the reliability data. Although the internal consistency reliability of the instrument is acceptable based on the data, as reported, another examination using a larger sample size would be appropriate.

SUMMARY. The WeldTest (Form A) was designed as part of a series of skills tests for production employees in a Midwestern equipment plant. Form AC was developed as a shortened version in a self-scoring format. Despite the need for further reliability and validity assessment, the initial findings (using a small sample size) are sufficiently encouraging to recommend using the instrument for its intended purpose. The well-written Manual for Administration & Scoring helps to establish consistency in administration and scoring of the test. In spite of the low sample size used for initial instrument assessment, the instrument appears to do what it claims to do and is, therefore, recommended for use in the welding trades.

REVIEWER'S REFERENCE

Huck, S. W. (2000). *Reading statistics and research.* (3rd ed.). New York, NY: Longman.

[178]

Winslow Profiles.

Purpose: Designed to measure personality characteristics to aid in applicant selection, employee development, personal coaching and individual self-improvement.

Publication Dates: 1968-2012.

Administration: Individual or group.

Time: (30-45) minutes.

Authors: John Stahl, Andria Brown, Richard Sudweeks, Joseph Olsen, and Scott Thayn (technical manuals).

Publisher: Winslow Research Institute.

a) WINSLOW DYNAMICS PROFILE.

Purpose: Measures 24 personality characteristics to aid in applicant selection, employee development, personal coaching, and self-improvement "to assist individuals in achieving career success and personal contentment."

Population: Applicants for positions, current employees, coaching program participants.

Scores: Assessment Validity (Objectivity, Accuracy), Interpersonal Traits (Sociability, Recognition, Conscientiousness, Exhibition, Trust, Nurturance); Organizational Traits (Alertness, Structure, Order, Flexibility, Creativity, Responsibility); Dedication Traits (Ambition, Endurance, Assertiveness, Boldness, Coachability, Leadership); Self-Control Traits (Self-Confidence, Composure, Tough-Mindedness, Autonomy, Contentment, Control).

Administration: Individual or group.

Price Data, 2014: Fees range from $195-$145 per report depending on quantity purchased. Fee includes the Assessment Profile, free re-takes (when the participant's answers to the Profile are invalid), Participant's Report, Manager's Report, Executive Report, Position Compatibility Summary Report, Group Profiles, and Sub-group Profiles.

Time: (45) minutes or less.

Comments: Previously listed as Personal Dynamics Profile; internet-based administration and delivery or reports on confidential website provided free of charge to clients.

Authors: Denis Waitley, Lem Burnham, Charles C. Kaufman, J. Michael Priddy, Joan L. Francis, Thomas A. Tutko, Bruce C. Ogilvie, and Leland P. Lyon.

b) WINSLOW DISCOVERY PROFILE.

Purpose: Measures 16 personality characteristics to assist in hiring the best available applicants for many hourly positions in organizations and for personnel development.

Population: Applicants for hourly positions, current employees, coaching program participants.

Scores: Assessment Validity (Objectivity, Accuracy), Interpersonal Traits (Sociability, Recognition, Conscientiousness, Exhibition, Trust, Nurturance); Organizational Traits (Alertness, Structure, Order, Flexibility, Creativity, Responsibility); Dedication Traits (Ambition, Endurance, Assertiveness, Boldness, Coachability, Leadership); Self-Control Traits (Self-Confidence, Composure, Tough-Mindedness, Autonomy, Contentment, Control).

Administration: Individual or group.

Price Data, 2014: $75 to $95 per report depending on quantity purchased. Fee includes the Assessment Profile, free re-takes (when the participant's answers to the Profile are invalid), Participant's Report, Manager's Report, Executive Report, Position Compatibility Summary Report, Group Profiles, and Sub-group Profiles.

Time: (30) minutes.

Comments: Internet-based administration and results are immediately available online.

Authors: Denis Waitley, Lem Burnham, Charles C. Kaufman, J. Michael Priddy, Linda G. Griggs, Joan L. Francis, Thomas A. Tutko, Leland P. Lyon, and Bruce C. Ogilvie.

c) WINSLOW SUCCESS PROFILE.

Purpose: A personality assessment instrument designed to measure 11 personality characteristics of individuals; can be utilized by organizations in hiring the best available applicants for minimum hourly positions and developing current employees in those positions to their potential.

Population: Current personnel and potential employees.

Scores: Assessment Validity (Objectivity, Accuracy), Competitiveness Traits (Drive, Assertiveness, Determination, Leadership), Self-Control Traits (Self-Confidence, Emotional Control, Mental Toughness), Dedication Traits (Coachability, Conscientiousness, Responsibility, Trust), Composite Traits (Competitiveness, Self-Control, Dedication).

Price Data, 2014: Fee per participant ranges from $25-49 depending on quantity of Profile Passwords purchased; fee includes assessment profile, free retakes (when participant's answers are invalid) Participant's Report, Manager's Report, Executive Report, PCS Summary Forms, Group Profiles, and Subgroup Profiles.

Foreign Language Editions: Available in English, Spanish, and French.

Time: (30) minutes or less.

Comments: Previously listed as Personal Success Profile; short version of comprehensive Winslow Dynamics Profile; derivation of Athletic Success Profile (aka The Athletic Motivation Inventory, AMI), which measures the mental attitudes of individuals participating in competitive sport; internet-based administration and delivery of reports.

Authors: Denis Waitley, Lem Burnham, Charles C. Kaufman, J. Michael Priddy, Linda G. Griggs, Joan L. Francis, Thomas A. Tutko, Leland P. Lyon, and Bruce C. Ogilvie.

d) PERSONAL SUCCESS SURVEY.

Scores, 3: Ambition, Self-Confidence, Mental Toughness.

Price Data: Available from publisher.

Time: (10) minutes.

Comments: This is a paper-and-pencil, self-scoring assessment, measuring 3 of the 11 personality traits in the Winslow Success Profile; derivation of the Athletic Success Profile. Note: The Publisher advises that the Personal Success Survey is no longer available.

Review of the Winslow Profiles by FRED-ERICK T. L. LEONG, Professor of Psychology and Psychiatry, Michigan State University, East Lansing, MI, and DZENANA HUSREMOVIC, Assistant Professor of Psychology, University of Sarajevo, Bosnia and Hercegovina:

DESCRIPTION. The Winslow Profiles is a comprehensive personality assessment instrument designed to improve the validity and accuracy of organizational decisions in different areas of human resource management such as selection, need analysis, development, promotions, evaluations, team building planning, and termination decisions. It is also intended to be used by individuals as a self-awareness tool for better understanding of one's own personality traits and modes of behavior with the aim to utilize personal growth, career advancement, stress or conflict management, or for archiving personal contentment.

Winslow Profiles is designed to measure normal dimensions of personality and is not intended to be used in clinical diagnostic purposes. The measure is to be used for males and females, age 18 and older, in any type of organization and career in American culture. Winslow Profiles is a package that includes two main portions: questionnaire kit and report. [Editor's note: The publisher advises that the assessment and reports are now Internet-based and that results are immediately available upon completion.]

The questionnaire package includes questionnaire, completion instructions for participants, personal data form, and The Winslow Profiles answer sheet (both forms to be completed by participant). The questionnaire can be completed as paper-and-pencil form or using an Internet system with proper authorization. After conclusion of the administration of paper-and-pencil questionnaire, the assessment forms may be mailed, air expressed, faxed, or emailed to Winslow Research Institute.

The output report comes in two forms: a report for manager and a report for participant. The report for manager gives a detailed interpretation of a participant's profile; description for all traits as well as the participant's profile fit to position description for which the applicant applied or at which he or she works; and an executive report and Group and Subgroup profiles (if requested by client for specific groups of employees or applicants).

There are three main instruments in the Winslow Profiles:

1. Winslow Dynamic Profile. This is the most comprehensive instrument with 260 questions for measuring 24 personality traits grouped in four composite trait-groups. The approximate time for testing (as reported by authors) is less than an hour (technical manual, p. 9).

2. Winslow Success Profile. This is a shorter version of the Winslow Dynamics Profile. It measures 11 traits designed for the same purposes as the Winslow Dynamic Profiles. It has the same profiles. The required time for completing the questionnaire is 30 minutes or less. However, there is no description of how the authors decided which traits to include in the shorter version.

3. The Personal Success Survey. This is a short self-coring survey with 30 questions measuring three traits. It is intended for personal use. Its goal is to introduce participants to personality assessment and provide some feedback on three characteristics important for personal success.

This review is about the Winslow Dynamics Profile because data for the two other Profiles were not provided in the materials for review.

DEVELOPMENT. The Winslow Profiles is based on the assumption that each of the above mentioned 24 personality traits can be conceptually distinguished from other attributes measured by other scales. The instrument was developed following the studies on personality and athletics by Bruce Ogilvie and Thomas Tutko. Two criteria for selecting personality traits for the Dynamic Profile were: (a) the trait received empirical support as being related to success in careers and contentment in personal lives and (b) the trait was valued by consulted managers and employers. Twenty-four traits are included in the Winslow Profiles: Interpersonal Traits: Sociability, Recognition, Conscientiousness, Exhibition, Trust, and Nurturance; Organizational Traits: Alertness, Structure, Order, Flexibility, Creativity, and Responsibility; Dedication Traits: Ambition, Endurance, Assertiveness, Boldness, Coachability, and Leadership; and Self-Control Traits: Self-Confidence, Composure, Tough-Mindedness, Autonomy, Contentment, and Control.

In addition to measures of 24 traits, two additional measures, Accuracy and Objectivity, are included in order to check if a participant's responses on the main scales were valid and accurate. The Accuracy scale consists of 10 items that ask about knowledge regarding obvious facts. The Objectivity scale consists of items that indicate socially desirable response tendency (impression management). Problems identified on these two scales will stop the process of further interpretation of the main results, and participants must retake the Profile to obtain a report.

The items for the scales were constructed in the way that the test authors first made a hypothesis about the nature of the constructs, then decided on behavioral and attitudinal expectations, and finally generated the item pool with an effort to retain original meaning and sense of the characteristics defined by more general personality tests (like the 16PF). The selection of items for the final form was based on criteria of item difficulty, homogeneity, career specificity, hypothesized behavior, and retention of the original meaning of the trait. For each of 24 traits, 10 items were selected based on three statistical properties: item discrimination, convergent validity, and divergent validity (with other scales).

TECHNICAL. The norms were compiled from a sample of 815 participants in several Personal Coaching Programs, who were between the ages of 21 and 82 in mostly white collar positions. These participants declared themselves as "middle class" and were chosen based on their performance on the Accuracy and Objectivity scales. The results of the norming procedure are reported in the technical manual.

Reliability estimates were reported twice in two technical manuals. In the first technical manual—written by Computer Adaptive Technologies—in which the sample of 815 participant's results were used, the authors reported alpha coefficients for all 24 scales as well as Rasch model analyses. The alpha coefficients reported for separate scales ranged from .34 (Alertness) to .87 (Exhibition) with a median of .75. Rasch reliability ranged from .40 (Alertness) to .86 (Exhibition) with the median value of .76.

In the second technical manual—written by Certified Management Consultants—the authors calculated psychometric properties using a sample of 1,000 records in the data base for which there are no data on demographic composition. Alpha coefficients were between .59 (Ambition) to .87 (Exhibition), and Rykov's Rho, as another measure of reliability, was between .69 (Ambition) and .90 (Exhibition). Test-retest reliability is not reported in any of the documentation.

Evidence of construct validity was addressed in Technical Manual II. The factor loadings for scales are reasonably high, except for the items mentioned in the report itself as invalid. The evidence of convergent validity of the test was examined in the first technical manual by comparing the Winslow Profiles with 16PF and PRF (Personality Research Form) and reported in tables, but the authors have not given the synthetic conclusion about convergent validity. By analyzing the tables, these reviewers conclude that the scales from the Winslow Profiles reasonably correlate with the corresponding scales from PRF and these correlations are moderate to high (from .46 to .77).

In tables presenting correlations between the Winslow Profiles and 16PF the authors of the manual presented the data separately for two draft forms (Form A and Form B) with 16PF traits. By analyzing these data, these reviewers conclude that scales from the Winslow Profiles correlate in expected fashion with the scales from 16PF. It can be said that there is enough supporting evidence for convergent and divergent validity of the instrument. The profile authors did not conduct any data analyses to support criterion related evidence of validity using external criteria for which the test is intended.

COMMENTARY. The authors of the Winslow Profiles have followed standard test development procedure to construct a measure that is reliable and in concordance with other typical personality measures like 16PF and PRF. The authors also wrote clear recommendations for test improvement by correcting some of the items, which affected factor structure and reliability of the scales adversely. The report produced after the completion of testing is very user-friendly, easy to interpret, and very informative in terms of describing individual and group characteristics. The participant report is a valuable source of information for every employee who would like to develop the career and the skills.

However, there are some concerns regarding the norming sample in Technical Manual I and Technical Manual II. In the first manual, the sample is predominantly white collar middle class, which means that the test might not be representative of some culturally diverse groups. In the second technical manual there are no data about how the sample was stratified and what characteristics of the participants were included in the sample.

The other important concern is that this test is intended to predict worker performance, but the authors provide no data on actual correlation between test and the main outcomes for which the test is intended. It seems that, by correlating the results of the Winslow Profile and the 16PF and PRF, the authors just assume that their test will be as valid as other already proven measures.

The Winslow Profiles is actually a package of tests including the main test with 24 scales and two shorter versions. The authors did not provide any argument that would explain how they chose the scales for shorter versions and no data on usefulness of these shorter versions, so it is going to be difficult for the test buyer to decide what are the gains and losses if he or she chooses one over another.

SUMMARY. Winslow Profiles was developed as a personality measure for work and organizational settings. The intent of the measure aims to increase accuracy and objectivity of different personnel decisions. The test authors claim that 24 traits measured by the Winslow Profiles are strongly related to organizational behavior. But there is little or no evidence of such because the test was neither validated against performance measures nor did it provide any evaluative evidence of increasing the accuracy of personnel decisions.

Review of the Winslow Profiles by STEVEN V. ROUSE, Professor of Psychology, Pepperdine University, Malibu, CA:

DESCRIPTION. The Winslow Profiles include a family of interrelated measures. The most comprehensive of these measures is the Winslow Dynamics Profile (WDP), which was created to assess a variety of personality traits that had been previously linked to success in occupational and athletic settings. These 24 traits are organized into four rationally derived Trait Groups: Interpersonal Traits (i.e., Sociability, Recognition, Conscientiousness, Exhibition, Trust, and Nurturance), Organizational Traits (i.e., Alertness, Structure, Order, Flexibility, Creativity, and Responsibility), Dedication Traits (i.e., Ambition, Endurance, Assertiveness, Boldness, Coachability, and Leadership), and Self-Control Traits (i.e., Self-Confidence, Composure, Tough-Mindedness, Autonomy, Contentment, and Control). Each trait is described in paragraph-long passages in the manual, along with paragraph-long explanations of the prior research that led to this trait's inclusion in the WDP. The Winslow Discovery Profile is a shorter version of the Winslow Dynamics Profile, providing a full measurement of 16 of the traits above (omitting Exhibition, Nurturance, Creativity, Alertness, Boldness, Leadership, Autonomy, and Self-Control). Finally, the Winslow Success Profile provides a full measurement for 3 of the 24 traits (i.e., Ambition, Self-Confidence, and Toughness) that were chosen specifically because of their linkage with success in athletics. Because the traits measured in the Discovery and Success profiles use the same items used in the WDP, the remainder of the review focuses on the full set of traits as measured by the WDP.

The WDP can be completed on a paper-and-pencil form (which can be faxed to the scoring center or locally scanned and scored if the user has appropriate optical scanning hardware and software). There is also a very user-friendly online administration, scoring, and report system available at www.winslowresearch.com. [Editor's Note: The publisher advises that the assessments are now exclusively Internet-based.] Scores are obtained based on responses to 250 items for which the respondent answers on a 4-point scale, ranging from "*Agree*" to "*Disagree*." Although some of the individuals who completed the demonstration administrations provided for review complained that the item-by-item presentation was tedious for 250 items, all acknowledged that it was easy to access and complete, and the interpretive report was easily accessed and read.

The interpretive results are provided in three different formats. First, the Participant's Report provides both profile charts and paragraph-long interpretive comments for each of the 24 traits, along with page-long discussions of how the person's most "influential traits" (i.e., those for which the person obtained very high or very low scores) might affect his or her behavior in both career and social settings. Second, the Manager's Report also provides both profile charts and interpretive comments (albeit more succinct than those interpretive comments given on the Participant's Report) for each of the scales. Third, the Executive Report provides only the profile chart.

The test user can opt to include a Position Compatibility Summary (PCS) for each respondent. This additional chart designates the respondent's score as being in a "Desirable," "Favorable," "Neutral," "Caution," or "Concern" range for several different types of occupational positions, such as Sales Representative, Administrative Assistant, and Supervisor. Unlike other aspects of the WDP, which as described in the following sections, generally have sufficient documentation in the manual, no information is provided to explain how these optimal score levels were determined. In the absence of support from the manual, in the opinion of this reviewer the use of this option for applied purposes of personnel screening or selection is not recommended.

DEVELOPMENT. The project that eventually resulted in the Winslow Profiles started as an effort to identify and measure personality traits related to athletic motivation and success. From there, it was developed to be used more broadly as a measure of traits related to occupational success. On the basis of a literature search, the 24 traits listed above were identified and rationally clustered into Trait Groups. For each of the 24 traits, 15 items were initially created; of these, items were eliminated if they correlated more highly with another scale than with the parent scale or if response percentages were dramatically uneven across the four response options. Of the remaining candidate items, the 10 with the highest item discrimination statistics were selected for inclusion on the final scale to maximize the internal consistency reliability. Ten additional items were included to identify test-takers who were inattentive or careless in their responses or who were intentionally presenting themselves in a favorable or unfavorable way.

Additional statistical information would be valuable to examine the extent to which the scale development procedure resulted in a measure that aligns with the goals set for the measure. Because the individual scales were created by (in part) eliminating candidate items that correlated higher with a different scale more than it did with its intended scale, it is likely that the scale intercorrelations are low. Nevertheless, because the set of 24 constructs was chosen rationally based on a literature review, an intercorrelation matrix for the 24 scales would be a valuable addition to the manual to ensure that these scales are measuring distinct constructs. Moreover, because the 24 scales were rationally organized into four Trait Groups, a scale-level confirmatory factor analysis would be valuable to ensure that this rational grouping of traits is a meaningful one.

TECHNICAL.

Standardization. Scant information is provided about the normative sample. The manual indicates that the sample consisted of 1,016 individuals, of which 815 individuals were included in the final sample, with a roughly even representation of men and women. The ages ranged from 21 to 82, with the majority of the participants between ages 25 and 50, and the careers of the participants were described as varying widely, though most held administrative, technical, sales, and management positions. Most reported midlevel incomes, and the manual states that the "(e)thnic representation in the sample approximately equals ethnic representation in 'white collar' positions in U.S. populations" (p. 19). From this initial normative sample, a subset of 815 participants was selected on the basis of acceptable scores on the items that measure invalid response styles. Although this test boasts a large and potentially diverse normative sample, the characteristics of this sample are only given as generalized descriptions; precise descriptive statistics would bolster confidence in making generalizations beyond the normative sample.

Reliability. Two forms of reliability data are provided. First, internal consistency alpha coefficients were calculated for each of the 24 traits. These ranged from .34 (obtained for the Alertness scale) to .87 (obtained for the Exhibition scale), with a mean of .64. Although the manual concludes that these values indicate "good internal consistency for the scales," these are relatively low for tests of this type. On the other hand, the coefficients obtained for the four Trait Group scores ranged .79 (obtained for Organization Traits) to .91 (obtained for Self-Control Traits), with a mean of .86, reaching appropriate levels for applied assessment purposes.

Second, reliability indices were calculated based on an Item Response Theory analysis that used the Rasch model; these reliability statistics estimate the proportion of total test score variance that can be attributed to a test-taker's True Score (as opposed to Error Variance). These coefficients ranged from .40 (for Alertness) to .86 (for Exhibition), with a mean of 65. Again, the Trait Group reliability estimates were higher, ranging from .79 (for Organization Traits) to .90 (for Self-Control Traits), with a mean of .86.

Validity. Criterion-related evidence of validity is provided in the form of theory-relevant correlations between the PDP scales and scales from the Personality Research Form (Jackson, 1967) and the 16 Personality Factor Questionnaire (Cattell & Stice, 1962). Although each of the four Trait Group scales had substantial correlations with counterpart scales on these external measures, as did 17 of the 24 Trait scales, 7 of the traits (i.e., Conscientiousness, Trust, Alertness, Creativity, Responsibility, Ambition, and Coachability) did not have any substantial theory-consistent correlates. The manual simply states that these two external measures did not have any scales measuring these constructs. As a result, one cannot be fully confident that these scales measure the intended constructs.

SUMMARY AND COMMENTARY. The WDP was designed to measure 24 traits (clustered into four Trait Groups) that had been linked to occupational success in past research and theoretical writings; shorter versions (measuring fewer traits) are also available. Its strengths include a very well-developed online system for purchasing, administering, and reporting test results. Although it boasts a large normative sample, additional statistical information would help in evaluating the robustness of this sample. The manual also lacks important information, including the method of identifying cutoff levels for designating compatibility between the test-taker's scores and those recommended for various careers. Although some of the 24 Trait Scales produced relatively low reliability estimates (averaging around .65), the 4 Trait Group scales yielded higher reliability estimates (averaging around .85). These Trait Group scores also correlated well with theory-consistent external measures; however, no external evidence of validity was presented for 7 of the 24 Traits. Although the

WDP shows promise, confidence in the use of this test would be strengthened if additional supporting information were included in the manual.

REVIEWER'S REFERENCES

Cattell, R. B., & Stice, G. G. (1962). *Handbook for the Sixteen Personality Factor Questionnaire.* Champaign, IL: Institute for Personality and Ability Testing.
Jackson, D. N. (1967). *Personality Research Form: Manual.* Goshen, NY: Research Psychologists Press.

[179]

Woodcock Reading Mastery Tests, Third Edition.

Purpose: Designed "to measure reading readiness and reading achievement."

Population: Pre-kindergarten through Grade 12; ages 4-6 through 79-11.

Publication Dates: 1973-2011.

Acronym: WRMT-III.

Scores: 9 individual test scores: Letter Identification, Phonological Awareness, Rapid Automatic Naming, Word Identification, Word Attack, Listening Comprehension, Word Comprehension, Passage Comprehension, Oral Reading Fluency; 4 cluster scores: Readiness, Basic Skills, Reading Comprehension, Total Reading.

Administration: Individual.

Forms, 2: A, B.

Price Data, 2013: $632 per Form A and B combined kit including administration manual (2011, 685 pages), 1 set Rapid Automatic Naming Cards, record forms (25 Form A and 25 Form B), Oral Reading Fluency forms (25 Form A and 25 Form B), Form A stimulus book with audio CD, and Form B Stimulus Book with audio CD in carrying case; $394 per Form A or Form B kit; $60 per 25 record forms (A or B); $30 per 25 Oral Reading Fluency forms (A or B); $150 per administration manual.

Time: (15-45) minutes for complete battery.

Comments: Tests may be administered individually or in combination.

Author: Richard W. Woodcock.

Publisher: Pearson.

a) LETTER IDENTIFICATION.

Population: Pre-kindergarten through Grade 1.

Time: (1) minute.

b) PHONOLOGICAL AWARENESS.

Population: Pre-kindergarten through Grade 2.

Time: (9) minutes.

c) RAPID AUTOMATIC NAMING.

Population: Pre-kindergarten through Grade 2.

Time: (4) minutes.

d) WORD IDENTIFICATION.

Population: Grade 1 through age 79:11.

Time: (2) minutes.

e) WORD ATTACK.

Population: Grade 1 through age 79:11.

Time: (2) minutes.

f) LISTENING COMPREHENSION.

Population: Grade 1 through age 79:11.

Time: (12) minutes.

g) WORD COMPREHENSION.
Population: Grade 1 through age 79:11.
Time: (10) minutes.
h) PASSAGE COMPREHENSION.
Population: Grade 1 through age 79:11.
Time: (7) minutes.
i) ORAL READING FLUENCY.
Population: Grade 1 through age 79:11.
Time: (4) minutes.
Cross References: For reviews by Linda Crocker and Mildred Murray-Ward of the 1998 Normative Update, see 14:423; see also T5:2905 (123 references) and T4:2976 (34 references); for reviews by Robert B. Cooter, Jr. and Richard M. Jaeger of an earlier edition, see 10:391 (38 references); see also T3:2641 (17 references); for reviews by Carol Anne Dwyer and J. Jaap Tuinman, and excerpted reviews by Alex Bannatyne, Richard L. Allington, Cherry Houck (with Larry A. Harris), and by Barton B. Proger of the 1973 edition, see 8:779 (7 references).

Review of the Woodcock Reading Mastery Tests, Third Edition by BETHANY BRUNSMAN, Assessment/Evaluation Specialist, Lincoln Public Schools, Lincoln, NE:

DESCRIPTION. The Woodcock Reading Mastery Tests, Third Edition (WRMT-III) consists of nine measures of reading achievement. They are individually administered, typically as a battery, and include Letter Identification (letter names and sounds), Phonological Awareness (first- and last-sound matching, rhymes, blending, and deletion), Rapid Automatic Naming, Word Identification (sight words), Word Attack (nonsense words), Word Comprehension (vocabulary), Passage Comprehension (sentence comprehension), Listening Comprehension, and Oral Reading Fluency. The tests vary in length from 17 items to 86 items, but examinees often answer many fewer items per test because of basal and discontinue rules. Administration time is 45 minutes or less. There are two parallel forms, A and B. Items are ordered by difficulty, and grade level starting points are clearly marked in the materials.

The WRMT-III is a revision of the Woodcock Reading Mastery Tests-Revised [1998 Normative Update]. The revisions include new items, new pictures, two new subtests (Phonological Awareness and Rapid Automatic Naming), and new norms. The test manual references substantial research to support each of the WRMT subscales.

According to the test author, the WRMT-III may be used to plan instructional interventions for individuals with reading problems, for educational placement, to screen for Kindergarten readiness, to assess growth in reading skills over short or long time spans, to evaluate reading program effectiveness, or as a reading measure in research studies. The test author recommends that examiners have a background in education or psychology (e.g., school psychologists, special education teachers, reading specialists) and have completed at least Bachelor's-level training in the administration and interpretation of tests. This recommendation seems reasonable given the amount of judgment required in scoring the tests and the age range of examinees (ages 4 years, 6 months through 79 years, 11 months).

All of the items are selected response or short answer, with the exception of Oral Reading Fluency, which requires examinees to read one to two passages aloud. For most of the tests, the examiner reads the item aloud and the respondent references letters, words, and/or pictures on an easel before responding. The Listening Comprehension test also includes some items recorded on a CD. The pictures, which are full-color drawings, were updated for this edition of the WMRT and include people from diverse backgrounds.

Raw scores, standard scores, percentile ranks, and age and grade equivalents are available. Five norming windows per year are provided for examinees in Grades K-1, and three per year are provided for older examinees. Growth Scale Values can be used for growth comparisons. The Relative Performance Index is based on the probability of success for the examinee on items that the average student at the same grade level performs with 90% accuracy. Score clusters (Readiness, Basic Skills, Reading Comprehension, and Total Reading) can also be calculated if the appropriate subtests are given. The basal and discontinue rules are adequately explained in the test manual and should be relatively easy to implement because they are mostly consistent across tests. Scoring for many of the tests includes an analysis of examinee errors. Space is available on the paper/pencil answer document or on a separate worksheet to track the types of errors examinees make to allow the examiner to determine patterns. The error analysis may be of limited usefulness, however, if examinees make few errors because of the discontinue rules.

The test manual contains detailed directions for hand scoring. In addition, an online scoring and reporting system is available. Examiners can enter examinee responses into the online system and receive individual score reports, including error analysis and comparisons of Growth Scale

Value scores over time. Because hand scoring is somewhat complicated and involves a number of different calculations, worksheets, and several tables, the online scoring system might be preferable. The reports generated from the online system contain narrative explanations and comparisons among scores that would be helpful to examiners in interpreting scores.

The test manual also includes specific guidance for interpreting scores and developing an instructional program based on examinee results. Recommendations are based on a solid research base, and a number of case studies are presented to facilitate use of results. The recommendations include specific instructional strategies to improve deficit skills. The test author suggests using scores along with other measures to develop programs for examinees.

DEVELOPMENT. The development process was comprehensive and included pilot studies, a tryout, and expert reviews, allowing for revisions throughout the process. Results of the pilot studies and tryout conducted before the norming study were used to verify appropriateness of item and presentation formats; check artwork, directions, and the level of reading passages; calibrate items; and run statistical bias analyses. Items were revised or removed based on item statistics and feedback from examiners. The administration rules (e.g., discontinue rules) were also simplified based on data collected. A panel of 13 experts with backgrounds in curriculum and reading achievement assessments and experience working with students with disabilities and English language learners reviewed the items for content match and to detect bias.

TECHNICAL. The normative data were collected in 2009–2010 from 5,000 individuals ages 4 years, 6 months to 79 years, 11 months, with half of the examinees taking each form of the test. The norm group adequately represented the U.S. population in terms of geography, ethnicity, gender, socioeconomic status, mother's/examinee's educational level, and disability. The issue of testing accommodations is not addressed in the test manual. It is not clear whether accommodations were allowed for participants in the norm group or how they might affect scores for examinees. Recommendations about score interpretation if particular accommodations are used (e.g., large print, repetition of items) would help examiners to more effectively use test scores. A sample of 451 examinees who were reasonably representative of

the U.S. population and who took both forms of the tests allowed for statistical equating so that scores, including Growth Scale Values, across forms would be comparable.

Data are provided based on the norming study and other studies to support the reliability of scores. Split-half indices ranged from .64 to .97 (slightly higher for cluster scores), with most values in the .85 to .95 range. Alternate form indices based on the 451 examinees who took both test forms ranged from .62 to .94. Test-retest indices for a group of 155 examinees in prekindergarten through Grade 12 with a 2-week minimum interval ranged from .52 to .97. Interrater reliability coefficients for scores on the Oral Reading Fluency test calculated with 9–11 raters and 220 passages were .99 for both forms.

The test author collected several kinds of construct-related evidence to support the validity of score interpretations for measuring reading achievement. Analyses of scores in the norm group showed an increasing pattern over age and grade level. As expected, older examinees received higher scores on all of the tests compared to younger examinees. Correlations among test scores and cluster scores were moderate and positive in each of the age ranges studied in the norm group. Six studies in which examinees took the WRMT-III and another similar measure of reading achievement or aptitude generally found moderate to strong positive correlations among the measures. Finally, three clinical samples yielded expected results for score differences among groups. Gifted students received higher average scores than those in the norm group and students identified with mild intellectual disabilities or learning disabilities in reading scored lower on average on the tests than did the norm group.

COMMENTARY. The validity studies and related evidence, in conjunction with other research cited in the test manual, provide support for uses of the WRMT-III in identifying individuals with reading difficulties, placing them in appropriate instructional levels, and developing interventions for them. There is less support for the use of test scores to measure growth over short or long time spans. Although average scores increase with age/grade group, it is not clear whether two forms are sufficient for frequent testing. With so few items and quite a bit of overlap between items administered at contiguous grade levels, practice effects may interfere with progress monitoring over time. Combining the WRMT-III with other measures, including classroom assessments, to reduce the repeated use of the WRMT-III over time might be more prudent.

It is not clear why interrater reliability was calculated only for the Oral Reading Fluency test. Many of the tests require some amount of judgment for scoring. Evidence that scores can be generated in a consistent manner based on the directions in the manual would be helpful for all of the tests.

Another question relates to whether the WRMT-III is well aligned with state and national standards that increasingly require more critical thinking skills in reading. The WRMT-III is designed to measure the building blocks of reading. Although there is some inference involved in the format used for listening and passage comprehension, the amount of critical thinking required is minimal. Additionally, the "passage" length of one or two sentences is limited in applicability to tasks that require individuals to read and make inferences about much longer narrative and expository text. The WRMT-III seems better suited to identify deficits than to measure reading proficiency as defined in state and national standards. The claim on page 43 of the test manual that the test "provides a comprehensive, standardized basis for evaluating an individual's reading proficiency..." seems overstated. Some empirical evidence that scores on the WRMT-III relate to more complicated reading tasks would lend credence to the test author's claim.

SUMMARY. The WRMT-III is a well-constructed set of tests that can be used to identify individuals with reading difficulties and to develop instructional interventions. If supplemented by other educational assessments, it also can provide information about individuals' progress over time. In addition to administration and scoring guidelines for the tests, the test manual offers research-supported suggestions and case studies that will be helpful in interpreting scores and supporting instruction to develop reading skills.

Review of the Woodcock Reading Mastery Tests, Third Edition by TAWNYA MEADOWS, Pediatric Psychologist, Geisinger Health System, Danville, PA:

DESCRIPTION. The Woodcock Reading Mastery Tests, Third Edition (WRMT-III) evaluates reading readiness and reading achievement to assist schools in developing effective and personalized reading intervention programs. The WRMT-III has been re-normed several times since its initial development in 1973. In addition to

norm updates, changes to this most recent version were intended to assess reading acquisition skills in younger examinees via the addition of Phonological Awareness and Rapid Automatic Naming tests. Listening Comprehension and Oral Reading Fluency were added to increase the comprehensiveness of the test. Finally, an expansion of error analysis was designed to include Phonological Awareness, Listening Comprehension, Passage Comprehension, and Oral Reading Fluency.

The combined test kit includes two parallel forms designed to increase the test's utility as a source of instructional planning. The test kit includes a 685-page manual, a set of Rapid Automatic Naming Cards, 25 record forms, 25 Oral Reading Fluency forms, Form A stimulus book with audio CD, and Form B stimulus book with audio CD in a sturdy canvas carrying case. Stimulus materials provide large easy-to-see illustrations that keep examinees interested without excessive distracting details.

Bachelor's level examiners are qualified to administer this comprehensive battery of tests to prekindergarteners (age 4 years, 6 months) and students through Grade 12 and beyond (i.e., through age 79 years, 11 months). Administration takes 15 to 45 minutes. Most test items are administered with the stimulus book and are presented in order of difficulty with recommended start items specified by grade level. Scoring may be completed either by hand or through the WRMT-III online scoring and reporting system. Norm-referenced scores are provided; standard scores have a mean of 100 and a standard deviation of 15.

Results from testing are scored on four hierarchical levels: qualitative, level of development, quality of performance, and position in a group. Scores on individual tests are combined to form cluster scores to allow for more global interpretation. The four cluster scores are Readiness, Basic Skills, Reading Comprehension, and Total Reading. It is unclear whether these clusters were identified through statistical analysis or by the opinion of the test author.

DEVELOPMENT. The development of the WRMT-III was designed to update norms, extend error analysis, and extend the age range downward. As noted by the test author, influences included the National Reading Panel's *Teaching Children to Read* report (National Institute of Child Health and Human Development, 2000) and the *Standards for the Assessment of Reading and Writing* (International Reading Association & National Council of Teachers of English, 2009). These influences led to coverage across five primary reading areas: phonics, phonemic awareness, reading fluency, text comprehension, and vocabulary. The test was formatted to provide data upon which to base an individual's reading program.

The battery consists of nine tests that can be administered individually or combined into four cluster scores. Letter Identification measures the ability to recognize lowercase and upper case letters. Phonological Awareness consists of five sections: first-sound matching, last-sound matching, rhyme production, blending, and deletion. Rapid Automatic Naming is a timed test that measures the speed and accuracy of naming familiar letters, numbers, colors, and objects. Word Identification consists of increasingly difficult words for the examinee to read. Similarly, Word Attack consists of increasingly difficult nonsense words for the examinee to read. Six examiner-read passages and 21 passages presented on an audio CD comprise the Listening Comprehension test, which assesses literal and inferential comprehension. Word Comprehension is a measure of reading vocabulary evaluated via analogies, antonyms, and synonyms. Passage Comprehension uses a modified cloze procedure to assess an individual's ability to study a sentence or short passage and identify a missing word. Finally, Oral Reading Fluency involves an examinee reading appropriate-level passages and assesses fluency according to three categories (expression, phrasing, and smoothness) to evaluate one's skills to integrate reading abilities such as decoding, expression, and phrasing.

TECHNICAL. The WRMT-III examiner's manual provides clearly presented, appropriate information about the normative sample and the psychometric properties of the test.

Over the course of a year, 5,000 examinees between the ages of 4 years, 6 months and 79 years, 11 months were administered one of the parallel forms of the WRMT-III. Data from these examinees contributed to the normative sample and/or reliability or validity studies. This sample size appears to be sufficient and allows for ample examinees at each age and grade level. Approximately 50% of examinees completed both forms of the test. Collection of standardization data occurred in more than 1,000 sites across 45 states. All examinees identified English as their most commonly spoken language; therefore, the WRMT-III should not

be used with individuals who are not identified as speaking English most frequently. Participants were selected from a pool of potential examinees using stratified random sampling procedures and were provided financial compensation for participating. The test publisher attempted to ensure the quality of data collection through reviewing each examiner's first two test administrations, checking accuracy in administration and scoring, and randomly calling examinees to ensure they participated in the testing session. However, no information was provided regarding the frequency of poor quality incidents and recommended remedies.

The WRMT-III manual provides normative data based on both grade level and age. The norm sample reflects the U.S. population, based on data from the 2008 U.S. Census, for demographic characteristics including race/ethnicity, parent's education or examinee's education, age, and geographic region. Gender in the normative sample is fairly balanced across all age levels and grade levels. The highest level of education of the mother or female caregiver was used as a measure of socioeconomic status. The test publisher made reasonable efforts to ensure that each race/ethnicity and SES group be representative of the U.S. population by grade and age. However, ethnicity is not presented as a function of gender. Although individuals with a diagnosis of attention-deficit/hyperactivity disorder are somewhat underrepresented in the norm sample, the test author claims that all other educational diagnoses or educational classifications are representative of the U.S. special education population. Examination of the test manual suggests there were fewer individuals with special education status than exist in the general population of high school students.

Standardization data demonstrated that Kindergarten examinees on Word Identification and Word Attack had inadequate floors; thus, no norms were derived for these tests at this grade level. In addition, norms for Letter Identification for second graders were not calculated due to an inadequate ceiling. This reviewer also questions whether there is an inadequate (i.e., low) ceiling on tasks such as Letter Identification for Kindergarteners because a perfect raw score in winter/spring yields a standard score of only 106 (less than 1 standard deviation above the mean). For first graders during winter, a perfect raw score results in a standard score of 103 while one item wrong results in a standard score of 77. There are instances also found in the scoring tables that demonstrate a high floor whereby an examinee can miss all items on a subtest yet receive a standard score in the upper 70s to lower 80s. These issues tend to occur at the lower ages and grades and typically involve one or two subtests consistently (e.g., Word Comprehension and Word Attack).

The WRMT-III uses several acceptable methods to establish reliability. First, the split-half reliability method established adequate internal consistency estimates for all tests except Rapid Automatic Naming due to the inappropriateness of using the split-half technique for timed tasks. Reliability for Rapid Automatic Naming was established using the alternate form correlation. Reliability estimates are considered very good whether considering age-based values or grade-based values. Total Reading yielded an average reliability estimate of .97 over all grades with cluster score estimates averaging .93 to .95. There do not appear to be any attempts to provide reliability data for specific demographic groups.

As noted by the test author, comparison data between Form A and Form B appear to be adequate due to similar mean and standard deviation values by subtest, as well as gradual increases in scores from lower ages and grade levels to higher ones. However, there are noticeable differences between the two forms. For instance, the mean raw score for Form A Word Comprehension for 26- to 30-year-olds was 28.0, whereas the mean score on Form B was significantly higher at 59.8. [Editor's Note: The publisher has informed the Buros Center that the reported mean of 28.0 is a misprint in the manual that will be corrected in subsequent printings. The publisher reported that the correct Form A mean is 58.0.]

Alternate form reliability evidence based on data from examinees in prekindergarten through Grade 12 supported the equivalence of Forms A and B. The test author concludes that there is a strong possibility that an examinee will obtain the same score on either form of the test as demonstrated by strong to very strong corrected correlation coefficients for cluster scores (.84 to .90) and test scores (.62 to .93), as well as small effect size values of standard differences. For the younger elementary grade levels, a small to moderate effect (.43) was found for Listening Comprehension. Listening Comprehension, Word Attack, and Passage Comprehension generally demonstrated the lowest corrected correlation coefficients.

Test-retest reliability was also computed. A total of 155 examinees from prekindergarten to high school were each administered one form of the test at least 14 days apart. Although the test author provided the average number of days, the test manual was unclear as to the range of days between test administrations. The test author disclosed that the younger sample was underrepresented in terms of African Americans, children of mothers with less than a high school education, and children from the Western region of the United States. In addition, children with mothers with 1–3 years of college education and children from the South were underrepresented in Grades 3 through 8. For Grades 9 through 12, females, Hispanic children, children whose mothers had an education level below high school, and children from the South were underrepresented. Despite some slight under-representations, the test author made a respectable effort to conduct test-retest reliability with a sample representative of the U.S. population. The test author made a reasonable conclusion that the test battery is stable over short periods of time with relatively small practice effects. Demonstration of stability over a long period of time is not to be expected for tests of academic performance as educational achievement is a dynamic construct.

Interrater reliability was computed for Oral Reading Fluency due to the subjective nature of its scoring. Intraclass correlation coefficients were .99 for both forms, indicating a very high level of interrater reliability.

Similar to the test author's extensive efforts to establish reliability using a variety of acceptable formats, the test author demonstrated sufficient validity of the test battery as a reading measure. The test author reports development of the test based upon information presented from recent influential publications that define the current field of reading. Construct validity evidence was presented by the test author through three different formats. The WRMT-III demonstrated developmental gains as predicted based upon reading theory with rapid acceleration of scores on the test from students in the lower grades and a deceleration of growth in upper grades.

Comparison studies of the WRMT-III and six different achievement tests provided convergent validity evidence. It is important to note that the test author found WRMT-III scores to be one third to one fifth of a standard deviation lower than corresponding scores on the Kaufman Test of Educational Achievement–Second Edition (KTEA-II; 16:124) and the Woodcock Reading Mastery Tests–Revised [1998 Normative Update] (WRMT-R/NU; T8:2956). The author indicates this finding may be due in part to the Flynn Effect.

Previous reviews of this instrument have expressed concern regarding the test author's claim that the test data can be used to develop instructional plans as there has been no study conducted that validates this claim. Again, there does not appear to be any empirical support for this claim.

SUMMARY. The Woodcock Reading Mastery Tests, Third Edition attempts to provide a major revision updating its norms and providing better support for validity and reliability. It appears as though the test author made several improvements that would satisfy some criticism from previous reviews (see Crocker, 2001 and Murray-Ward, 2001) such as including a larger normative sample and greater representation of the U.S. population. Many test items were updated or replaced, but little information is available to describe methods used to select or keep items other than those deemed by experts to be outdated or biased. Two significant limitations to the instrument are: (a) there is no empirical support for use of this test to determine individualized educational plans, and (b) oftentimes standard scores reach their maximum or minimum score less than 1 standard deviation from the mean thus making it difficult for school systems that may determine instructional intervention eligibility based upon performance 2 standard deviations below the mean or in comparison to cognitive ability scores.

REVIEWER'S REFERENCES

Crocker, L. (2001). Test review of the Woodcock Reading Mastery Tests–Revised [1998 Normative Update]. In B. S. Plake & J. C. Impara (Eds.), *The fourteenth mental measurements yearbook*. Retrieved from the Buros Institute's Test Reviews Online website: http://www.buros.org/

International Reading Association & National Council of Teachers of English. (2009). *Standards for the assessment of reading and writing*. Newark, DE: Author.

Murray-Ward, M. (2001). Test review of the Woodcock Reading Mastery Tests–Revised [1998 Normative Update]. In B. S. Plake & J. C. Impara (Eds.), *The fourteenth mental measurements yearbook*. Retrieved from the Buros Institute's Test Reviews Online website: http://www.buros.org/

National Institute of Child Health and Human Development. (2000). *Report of the National Reading Panel. Teaching children to read: An evidence-based assessment of scientific-research literature on reading and its implications for reading and instruction.* NIH Publication No 00-4769, 3–1 to 3–43. Washington, DC: U.S. Government Printing Office.

[180]

Work Accident Likelihood Assessment.

Purpose: Designed to assess "how risky the test-taker's decisions are, whether she/he takes unnecessary chances, and how likely she/he is to have an accident."

Population: Under age 17 through adult.

Publication Date: 2011.

Acronym: WALA.

Scores, 7: Overall Results, Sensation-Seeking, Harm-Avoidance, Conscientiousness, Attitudes Towards Safety, Attentiveness, Responsibility.

Administration: Individual.

Price Data: Available from publisher.

Time: (30) minutes.

Comments: Self-administered online assessment. The test publisher advises that the test manual is being updated to include more information about methodology and theoretical background used in the development of the test. The test publisher also advises that this information is available to clients, as are benchmarks for relevant industries and racial/ethnic group comparison data. However, this information was not provided to Buros or the reviewers.

Author: PsychTests AIM, Inc.

Publisher: PsychTests AIM, Inc. [Canada].

Review of the Work Accident Likelihood Assessment by BERT A. GOLDMAN, Professor Emeritus, University of North Carolina Greensboro, Greensboro, NC:

DESCRIPTION. The Work Accident Likelihood Assessment (WALA) is a 62-item situational and self-assessment designed for the purpose of determining how risky the test-taker's decisions are, whether the respondent takes unnecessary chances, and how likely the respondent is to have an accident.

Psychtests, Inc. in Montreal (Quebec, Canada) copyrighted the WALA in 2011. The WALA is self-administered in approximately 30 minutes online by using Queendom.com, Psychtests.com, or PsychologyToday.com.

No portion of the test is timed. Within a few minutes following completion of the WALA, the on-line program provides results on the six subscales comprising the instrument. The subscales include Sensation-Seeking, Harm Avoidance, Conscientiousness, Attitudes Towards Safety, Attentiveness, and Responsibility. The results are expressed as level of desire for novel and exciting experiences; level of desire to steer clear of negative experiences; degree to which one is willing to be rule-abiding, careful, responsible, and less likely to take unwise and dangerous risks; a person's reactions to rules and regulations in the workplace; how well and for how long a person reports being able to concentrate on taxing mental tasks; and whether a test-taker views the consequences of her or his actions as her or his own responsibility or has a tendency to blame outside forces.

Actually, there is a total of 11 scales, which includes the 6 subscales that the manual claims comprise the test. There is no description of the additional 5 scales, but alpha coefficients are given for all 11 scales. There is no explanation regarding the number of subscores being 6 scales or 11.

DEVELOPMENT. There is no description of the WALA's development including, for example, such elements as the stages in its development, the length of time involved in its development, and the person or persons responsible for its development. There is no indication of whether there are alternate forms of the test.

TECHNICAL. Data were collected from 4,945 self-selected test-takers who went online to take the self-administered WALA. This population consisted of 41% women and 24% men, with 35% of unknown gender. There were 32% whose ages ranged from 18 to 39. There were 22% who were below age 17, but the youngest age included is not provided. Also, 13% were 40 years and older, but the oldest age included is not given. In addition, 33% were of unknown age. Further, the geographic location or locations of the participants is unknown.

The 4,945 participants self-administered, online each of the 11 subtests. Graphs depicting the statistical results are presented for each subtest. Given that the test is self-administered online as well as scored and interpreted by the online computer program, there are no directions in the manual for administering, scoring, and interpreting the results.

Coefficient alpha was used to determine the instrument's internal consistency. Alpha coefficients were calculated for each of the 11 scales. This reviewer holds the following standards for alpha reliability coefficients: Excellent alpha coefficients are those in the .90s; those in the .80s are good; fair coefficients are those in the .70s; and those in the .60s and below are considered poor. Five of the scales had good coefficients ranging from .82 to .86. Three scales had fair coefficients ranging from .73 to .76, and the remaining three scales had poor coefficients ranging from .62 to .65. The overall score based upon all 63 items produced an excellent alpha coefficient of .91. No other methods for determining reliability are reported such as test-retest or alternate forms.

Sources for determining the validity of this test consist of the significant differences, found between those who were fired for unsafe behavior and those who were not fired for unsafe behavior, on the sensation seeking, challenger, past accidents, safety risk, rule-breaking risk, negligence risk scales, and on the overall score. Those fired had significantly

higher scores on these scales. By similar token, additional sources for determining the validity of the scores produced by this instrument consist of the significant differences, found between those who were not fired and those who were fired for unsafe behavior, on the Harm-Avoidance, Conscientiousness, Attitudes Towards Safety, Attentiveness, and Responsibility scales. Those not fired had significantly higher scores on these scales. Additional data presented reveal differences in certain scale scores within age levels, genders, education levels, and employment position levels.

COMMENTARY AND SUMMARY. All validity data are subject to the same weakness as the reliability data in that there is no complete description of the population who took the tests such as age, gender, education, employment, and geographic location. In summary, the Work Accident Likelihood Assessment (WALA) test provides useful information for pre-employment testing, especially for physically dangerous work. However, the test manual contains myriad omissions. There is no description of the test's development such as who developed it and over what time period it was developed. There is a rather incomplete description of the subjects to whom the test was administered. There is neither a description of how the test is scored nor is there a description of how to interpret the results.

The reliability data are based only upon alpha coefficients, which ranged from good to poor, but with an overall alpha coefficient that was excellent. Validity data are acceptable. However, both reliability and validity data are based upon the scores of participants whose clear identity is not given. Anyone using this test should use the results cautiously until such time when the manual has been revised to contain all missing information.

Review of the Work Accident Likelihood Assessment by RONALD S. LANDIS, Nambury S. Raju Chair of Psychology, Illinois Institute of Technology, Chicago, IL:

DESCRIPTION. The Work Accident Likelihood Assessment (WALA) published by PsychTests is designed for use in organizational settings in which one is interested in measuring the riskiness of a test taker's decisions, whether the test taker takes unnecessary chances, and how likely the test taker is to have an accident. This test is likely to be of interest to those seeking a pre-employment (i.e., selection) test, particularly for physically dangerous jobs, or for counseling purposes. The WALA is composed of 62 items, of varying formats, and is administered online through the test publisher's website. The estimated time limit for administering the test is 30 minutes but the test is untimed. An overall test score is provided as well as scores on six subscales and an assessment of the extent to which the test taker engaged in Impression Management. The first subscale is Sensation-Seeking and indicates the test taker's level of desire for novel and exciting experiences. Harm Avoidance provides an assessment of an individual's desire to steer clear of negative experiences, and Conscientiousness indicates a test taker's willingness to follow rules and to be careful and responsible. A fourth subscale, Attitudes Towards Safety, assesses a person's reactions to workplace rules and regulations. Fifth, the Attentiveness subscale indicates how well and for how long a person reports being able to concentrate on difficult mental tasks. The final subscale, Responsibility, assesses whether the test taker views consequences of actions as primarily her or his own, or tends to blame outside sources.

The online interface for this test is professional, easy to read, and the instructions are easy to follow. The 62 items are presented through a series of screens. Items are grouped by similar response options, which leads to relatively few items on any given page. A progress bar assists the test taker in identifying how many more screens/items are remaining. Overall, the test formatting and instructions should prove relatively straightforward for most test takers. Following completion of the test, a report provides an interpretation of the test taker's responses. This interpretation is provided as an overall assessment, scores and interpretations for each of the six primary subdimensions, and the Impression Management items. Each score is presented numerically and also visually on a scale from 0–100. Individual sections then provide a qualitative summary of each score.

As stated by the publisher, use of this test is most likely in pre-employment (hiring) contexts in which the purpose is to screen out those individuals with a predisposition toward risky behaviors. Though the publishers provide results of a validation study regarding observed differences in response patterns between groups of individuals, organizations seeking to use this test for pre-employment testing may want to consider carefully whether there is adequate evidence for the job-relatedness of this measure in the particular context (i.e., the degree of content

validity) and/or may also want to collect additional evidence for the construct validity of the measure.

DEVELOPMENT. The validation report provides definitions of the six content areas assessed by the WALA, but does not describe how the test was developed or how items were written/selected. The manual does not provide any supporting references or logic regarding why the particular content areas were chosen or what defines the construct space. No qualitative (e.g., theory-based) or quantitative (e.g., item-analysis, factor analysis) evidence is provided in support of the overall score or the six dimensions.

TECHNICAL. Normative data collected as part of a "validation" study in support of the WALA are presented and are based on responses provided by 4,945 test takers. The manual reports that the sample was uncontrolled and it is not well-defined.

The test developers report reliability (coefficient alpha) for the overall score (.91) and each of the six dimensions (Sensation Seeking = .82; Harm Avoidance = .64; Conscientiousness = .86; Attitudes Towards Safety = .74; Attentiveness = .86; and Responsibility = .62). Without item-level information or factor-analytic evidence, it is difficult to determine whether the rather modest values for Harm Avoidance and Responsibility are due to a few poor items or possible multidimensionality. Reliability evidence for additional scales is also provided in the manual. This information should be clarified as there is ambiguity with respect to how these scales are connected to scores on the WALA. It appears that some of these measures were used to "validate" the WALA scores, but greater explanation would be helpful.

The validity evidence presented includes a comparison of mean scores across several groups including: gender, age, education, position, job performance, and whether an individual had ever been fired for unsafe work behavior. Of particular note to those considering this test for use in a pre-employment context, significant mean differences were observed across (a) gender for the overall score as well as several subscales and (b) age categories for the overall score and all of the subscales. Of note, no data or analyses were presented for racial/ethnic subgroups.

Evidence is provided that mean differences were observed for the overall score as well as all subscales with respect to self-reported job performance (coded as poor, satisfactory, and good). In terms of whether individuals had ever been fired for unsafe behavior (collected through self-report), significant differences in responses were observed for the overall score and for all of the subscales.

COMMENTARY. The WALA has clear instructions, the online interface is professional and easy to navigate, and the score reporting and interpretation is easy to understand. Psychometric evidence is limited and should be strengthened through additional studies. At a minimum, evidence should be provided regarding the conceptual underpinnings of the focal construct(s) measured by this test and should include quantitative evidence regarding the factor structure of the items. Evidence is provided regarding the extent to which this test produces mean differences across gender and subgroups, as well as differences between individuals fired for unsafe behaviors and those who have not been fired. Additional criterion-related validity evidence would be valuable. In particular, evidence regarding whether the test produces differences between other protected subgroups (e.g., ethnic and race) as well as correlating scores with criterion variables measured using something other than self-report means of assessment.

SUMMARY. The WALA purports to measure an individual's propensity to engage in risky behaviors and/or make risky decisions. Scores on this measure could be used by organizations for purposes of prehire testing and/or an assessment of attitude or behavior change that might occur in the context of safety training. Despite the ease of administration, scoring, and report generation, several aspects of the test may limit its utility. More information should be provided in support of the underlying conceptual foundation and logic for the reported dimensions. Additional quantitative results (e.g., factor analysis) would also be helpful in establishing support for the validity of the WALA. Finally, efforts would be well-directed toward collecting criterion data through methods beyond self-report.

[181]

Work Engagement Profile.

Purpose: Designed to measure "intrinsic rewards and... work engagement."
Population: Employees.
Publication Dates: 1993-2009.
Acronym: WEP.
Scores, 4: Sense of Meaningfulness, Sense of Choice, Sense of Competence, Sense of Progress.
Administration: Individual.
Price Data, 2011: $14.95 per Work Engagement Profile including 1 self-scorable assessment and 1 interpretive information booklet; $141.50 per 10 copies of Work Engagement Profile including self-scorable assessments and interpretive information booklets.
Time: (12) minutes.
Comments: Earlier versions were entitled Empowerment Inventory and Profile of Intrinsic Motivation.
Authors: Kenneth W. Thomas and Walter G. Tymon, Jr.
Publisher: CPP, Inc.
Cross References: For reviews by Leslie Eastman Lukin and Patricia Schoenrade of the Empowerment Inventory, see 13:119.

Review of the Work Engagement Profile by GARY J. DEAN, Professor and Chairperson, Department of Adult and Community Education, Indiana University of Pennsylvania, Indiana, PA:

DESCRIPTION. The Work Engagement Profile (WEP) is a self-report, self-scoring, 24-item instrument with scaled responses on a 7-point scale from *strongly disagree* to *strongly agree*. The instrument consists of a 20-page booklet that includes directions for completing the instrument, the instrument, a scoring grid, an explanation of the underlying theory, an interpretive scale with norms, and a guide to using the findings from the profile for self-development.

DEVELOPMENT. The WEP's development dates back to 1988 and the work of the primary author, Kenneth W. Thomas. The instrument has seen considerable development over its lifespan including several iterations of the title and purpose. The WEP was introduced as the Empowerment Inventory in 1993. The name was changed to the Profile of Intrinsic Motivation in 2005 and then to the Work Engagement Profile in 2009. The name changes reflect changes in the literature and the market for the instrument.

Theoretical foundation. Changes in the economy, including a shift from an industrial base to an informational economy, have changed the nature of work and the rewards that workers receive from it. The test authors state that today's jobs are better understood not only in terms of their purpose, but also as activities that workers perform. In today's workforce, workers are increasingly expected to exercise self-management in their work. The test authors draw a connection between self-management and engagement in work by suggesting that workers who self-manage are more engaged in their work. Workers who self-manage and are engaged in their work rely more heavily on intrinsic as opposed to extrinsic rewards for motivation. The WEP measures intrinsic rewards related to well-being (intrinsic rewards related to job satisfaction and the sense of well-being that stems from it), job performance (higher levels of intrinsic rewards lead to higher levels of job performance), and commitment (intrinsic rewards result in more commitment to the profession and the organization).

Development. Four intrinsic rewards are measured by the WEP: Competence, Choice, Meaningfulness, and Progress. These rewards were measured in a 1994 study in which factor analysis supported that the four rewards were separate entities. This study was conducted with 384 employees in both supervisory (49% of the sample) and nonsupervisory positions (51% of the sample) enrolled in MBA courses. The sample had a median age category of 26–30 and was 64% male and 36% female. The test authors provide a detailed description of the supervisory portion of the sample but no details on the nonsupervisory portion. The instrument consisted of six items per scale and the correlation coefficients ranged from .84 to .88 for Competence, .72 to .91 for Choice, .64 to .85 for Meaningfulness, and .72 to .79 for Progress. No information was provided regarding the process of item development.

Two other factorial studies were cited. One, with a French translation of the WEP, involved 122 French Quebec government workers and the second employed an English version of the WEP administered to 4,811 workers in India. Although no specifics were reported in the *Technical Brief for the Work Engagement Profile*, the test authors state that results of these studies confirm the four intrinsic rewards identified in the original 1994 study.

TECHNICAL.

Validity. Validity was established primarily through concurrent validity studies that sought to establish relationships between the WEP and other measures of motivation, the WEP's relationship to outcome variables, and the WEP's relationship to antecedent variables. Studies to establish validity were conducted with earlier versions of the WEP as well as the current version.

Concurrent evidence of WEP test score validity derived from studies in which the WEP was compared with three motivational instruments. The test authors report that the WEP scales correlated positively with the appropriate scales and negatively with the inappropriate scales for each of the instruments cited. No specific information was provided regarding the studies including the

nature of the instruments to which the WEP was compared, the samples involved, or the actual correlation coefficients.

To provide evidence of test score validity of the WEP in relationship to outcomes variables, the WEP was correlated with job satisfaction, professional development, career success, commitment to the organization, stress, retention, and work effectiveness. Three studies, conducted in 1991, 1994, and 2008, were cited to establish the relationship between the WEP and job satisfaction. Correlation of the WEP to professional development was established in a 1991 study. Career success was studied in the 2008 study of 4,811 Indian workers whose self-ratings of their own career success were correlated with an aggregate WEP measure. Two studies from 2008 were cited to establish validity with commitment to the organization. The study of French government workers showed a high correlation with affective commitment (proud to be a part of the organization). Low correlations resulted from comparison with normative commitment (feeling it would be morally bad to leave the organization) and continuance (feeling they would have too much to lose to leave the organization). Data from the study of the 4,811 Indian workers indicated that the WEP correlated positively with an organizational satisfaction/commitment factor. The 1994 and 1991 studies indicated that all four intrinsic motivations measured by the WEP were negatively correlated with measures of stress symptoms in the workplace. The relationship of the WEP with retention was established in 1991 and 1994 through studies correlating the scales of the WEP with intent to leave the organization. Negative correlations were noted as expected. The relationship between the WEP and work effectiveness is based on 1988 and 1994 studies in which supervisors' ratings of employees were correlated with WEP scales.

The WEP's relationship to antecedent variables was shown in studies to establish a shared sense of meaningfulness, autonomy afforded by supervisors, team conflict versus cooperation, managerial effectiveness, constructive task-related organization culture, and interpretive styles. The studies cited in this section attempted to establish the relationship of the WEP with the concepts that underlie the instrument's theoretical foundation.

Reliability. Reliability studies were reported for the initial, intermediate, and final versions of the WEP. The same studies that were used to establish validity were cited to establish reliability. All reliability studies were conducted using coefficient alpha. Four of the studies used the final version of the WEP. Coefficient alphas for the four scales in these studies were quite good: Meaningfulness correlations ranged from .85 to .92; Choice correlations ranged from .85 to .95; Competence correlations ranged from .88 to .95; and Progress correlations ranged from .83 to .93.

Norms. Norms were established based on the 1994 study of 384 MBA students. As noted earlier, some details were provided on the supervisory portion of this sample (49%) but no information was provided on the nonsupervisory portion of the sample (51%).

COMMENTARY. The WEP has a long history of development and has undergone three major iterations. The initial theoretical formulation appears to have been developed with care and with an ear to the nature of work in the post-industrial economy of the United States. The validity and reliability studies cited are extensive and cover a considerable period of time, from 1988 to 2008. Some of the studies used substantial sample sizes lending credibility to the findings. In general, the validity studies substantiate the usefulness of the WEP to measure the four scales of internal motivation. The reliability correlations are also substantial and lend credibility to the instrument.

There are some areas of concern, however. The information provided in the *Technical Brief for the Work Engagement Profile* is incomplete, especially regarding the validity studies. Following are some areas in which additional information could have been provided.

A key to understanding the validity of the WEP is its development over time. There have been three major iterations of the instrument, each with different language used to describe the WEP's purpose, and ultimately, interpretations of it. Validity studies were cited that cover the entire life span of the instrument. The test authors cite the relevance of the earlier studies to support the validity of the current version of the WEP by stating that the changes in items over time have been minimal and that the original intention of the items was maintained. This means that the changes to the WEP are image only and do not represent changes in the basic motivations or how they are measured.

A second area of concern is that no information was provided on how the item pool for the WEP was originally developed. One assumes that

the original investigators developed the items, but no explanation is provided to substantiate this assumption. In addition, there is no information on how, or which, items have been changed over time. This is particularly problematic with regard to applying earlier validity studies to the current version of the WEP.

Third, there is a lack of detail in the reporting of the validity studies in general. Sample sizes are reported, but detailed descriptions of the samples are lacking. More descriptive information on the demographic characteristics of the samples and the way in which the studies were conducted would be helpful. For example, in several studies an aggregate WEP score is referenced, but there is no indication of how this score was computed. The lack of detail regarding the studies cited makes it problematic to compare intended users of the WEP to the norm sample.

SUMMARY. The WEP is a short, easy-to-use assessment of four intrinsic motivators for engagement in work. The instrument is well-designed and easy to use. The 20-page booklet includes the instrument, scoring grid, norms table, and interpretation guide. The WEP has a long history of development spanning more than 20 years. There have been three major iterations of the instrument in that time: the Empowerment Inventory, the Profile of Intrinsic Motivation, and the Work Engagement Profile. Validity and reliability data are presented spanning this entire period of time. Although the validity and reliability data are voluminous, there are questions regarding the completeness of the information in the studies cited and regarding the relevance of earlier studies to the intended uses of the current version of the WEP.

Review of the Work Engagement Profile by JU-LIA Y. PORTER, Professor of Counselor Education, Mississippi State University-Meridian, Meridian, MS:

DESCRIPTION. The Work Engagement Profile (WEP) measures an individual's perceptions about the psychological factors of work engagement using a 24-item pencil-and-paper self-report questionnaire that can be self-scored. Items are based on The Self-Management Process adapted from Thomas, Jansen, and Tymon (1997) to measure the intrinsic work rewards of: (a) Meaningfulness (whether you perceive your job to have worth), (b) Choice (self-determination for how work will be accomplished), (c) Competence (ability to perform work tasks competently), and (d) Progress (moving toward completion of work goals). For each of the four scales measured, scores can range from 6 (very low) to 42 (very high). Items on the WEP measure perceptions about psychological aspects of work using a Likert 7-point scale with responses ranging from 1 *Strongly Disagree* to 7 *Strongly Agree*. Scores are reported as percentiles that indicate how well a job is working for the individual and for the organization. A percentile chart based on responses of the original norm sample (N = 384) is included in the WEP booklet as a reference point to help participants understand the meaning of their questionnaire results. Low WEP scores indicate a drain on work satisfaction and accomplishment, whereas high scores indicate energy and satisfaction for work. Designed for adults 18 and over, WEP estimated administration time is 12 minutes.

DEVELOPMENT. The WEP is based on over 30 years of research that began in the 1980s examining the concept of psychological empowerment through intrinsic rewards. The four intrinsic rewards were identified through factor analysis in a study conducted by Thomas and Tymon in 1994 using a sample of 384 (N = 384) employees from managerial/supervisory and nonsupervisory positions. Although the initial study indicated that the four intrinsic rewards were separate, meaningful constructs, the researchers continued conducting research studies to refine the items included in the WEP until the current version with 24 items measured by 6 items per scale was released in 1993 under the title "Empowerment Inventory." Additional research that focused on development and refinement of the conceptual model for the Empowerment Inventory found that intrinsic motivation more accurately described the concepts being measured. Thomas and Tymon changed the name of the inventory to the "Profile of Intrinsic Motivation (PIM)" in 2005. Although the items on the questionnaire remained the same, new interpretive materials for scores focused on self-management and intrinsic rewards instead of empowerment. In 2009, the Work Engagement Profile (WEP) was published and included interpretive information about the concepts of self-management and intrinsic rewards. The interpretive information also included "building blocks," which are ways respondents may raise levels of intrinsic rewards in areas for which a respondent scores low.

TECHNICAL. The original norm sample of 384 (N = 384) part-time MBA students had a median age category of 26–30, included 64% male

and 36% female, and included employees in 51% nonsupervisory positions and 49% supervisory or managerial positions (Thomas, 2009). Another normative study (N = 122) was conducted by Forest in 2008 in Canada using a French version of the WEP administered to French-speaking government employees. In Forest's 2008 study, the four factors identified in the original study explained 76% of the variance in the 24 items. Another study in 2008 by Stumpf using a sample from India (N = 4,811) found that the four factors explained 61% of the variance in the 24 items. The final version of the WEP has reliability coefficients of .83 or higher for each of the four scales measured. Administration of the WEP in the U.S. resulted in coefficients that were .90 or higher for the four scales compared to the overall average of .83. In the WEP technical brief, Thomas (2009) reports that the validity scores have remained constant over time for the scales being measured. In studies conducted by Forest, the WEP correlated significantly with the intrinsic scale of Deci's model of intrinsic motivation (Gagne & Deci, 2005), with "harmonious passion at work" described by Vallerand and Houlfort in 2003, and with positive work experience as defined in the PANAS measure. These correlations provide construct evidence for test score validity (Thomas, 2009).

COMMENTARY. The WEP instrument includes well-organized, easy-to-follow administration and score interpretation instructions that include practical suggestions for effective use of score results. The administration booklet clearly defines and explains the importance of intrinsic motivation in the satisfaction and retention of effective employees, which is important for the employee and the employer. The online technical brief for the WEP is also well-prepared and easy to understand.

Although the reliability coefficients indicate a high correlation of reliability for the original norm sample and two subsequent norm samples, the samples used to date may not be representative of groups who do not share the same characteristics as the part-time MBA students, French-speaking government employees, or Indian employees included in previous norm samples. Additional studies with a more diverse sample representative of the U.S. and global employees would lend greater strength to the reliability findings. Likewise, the validity evidence presented offers support for the use of test scores in the manner prescribed in the WEP materials. However, validity studies that examine the predictive validity of the four scales of intrinsic motivation as they relate to employee retention and success would help professionals better determine the appropriate usefulness of the WEP.

SUMMARY. The Work Engagement Profile (WEP) assesses the intrinsic psychological motivation of workers on four scales to evaluate the individual's tendency to be successful in a work setting based on his or her perceptions of whether the job contains activities and purposes that provide opportunities and a sense of accomplishment for the worker. The 24-item questionnaire is presented as part of a booklet that includes self-scoring instructions and score interpretation materials. An additional 15-page customized interpretive report may be purchased to better help individuals understand their scores and the practical use of score results. The WEP may provide useful information for human resource personnel and career counselors who are helping individuals develop career plans as well as for employers interested in assessing and developing the intrinsic motivation of employees as a way to help increase employee satisfaction and retention.

REVIEWER'S REFERENCES

Forest, J. (2008). *Technical brief on the French version of the PIM for Dr. Kenneth W. Thomas.* Unpublished manuscript.

Gagne, M., & Deci, E. L. (2005). Self-determination theory and work motivation. *Journal of Organizational Behavior, 26,* 331-362.

Thomas, K. W. (2009). Technical brief for the Work Engagement Profile. Printed January 25, 2011, from: www.cpp.com/pdfs/WEP-Tech_Brief.pdf

Thomas, K. W., Jansen, E., & Tymon, W. G., Jr. (1997). Navigating in the realm of theory: An empowering view of construct development. *Research in Organizational Change and Development, 10,* 1-30.

Thomas, K. W., & Tymon, W. G., Jr. (1994). Does empowerment always work: Understanding the role of intrinsic motivation and personal interpretation. *Journal of Management Systems, 6*(2) 1-13.

Vallerand, R. J., & Houlfort, N. (2003). Passion at work: Toward a new conceptualization. In W. Gilliland, D. D. Steiner, & D. P. Skarlicki (Eds.), *Emerging perspectives on values in organizations* (pp. 175-204). Greenwich, CT: Information Age Publishing.

[182]

Work Integrity Test.

Purpose: Designed to assess "potential for dishonest behavior in the work environment."
Population: Under age 17 through adult.
Publication Date: 2011.
Acronym: WINT.
Scores, 5: Overall Results, Lenient Attitude Towards Dishonest Behavior, Perceived Frequency of Dishonest Behavior, Rationalizing of Dishonest Behavior, Self-Reported Dishonesty.
Administration: Individual.
Price Data: Available from publisher.
Time: (30) minutes.
Comments: Self-administered online assessment. The test publisher advises that the test manual is being updated to include more information about methodology and theoretical background used in the development of the test. The test publisher also advises that this infor-

mation is available to clients, as are benchmarks for relevant industries and racial/ethnic group comparison data. However, this information was not provided to Buros or the reviewers.
Author: PsychTests AIM, Inc.
Publisher: PsychTests AIM, Inc. [Canada]

Review of the Work Integrity Test by BRITTON D. MILES, Adjunct Professor, Industrial Psychology, Director of ADHD Consulting, Alabama State University, Montgomery, AL:

DESCRIPTION. The Work Integrity Test (WINT) is a multiple-choice, situational judgment test proposed for pre-employment screening "intended to provide supplemental information on a person's potential for dishonest behavior in the work environment" (manual, p. 1). The WINT manual describes the test in only 168 words. The "norming" sample is described on a second page. The rest of the manual consists of bar graphs and tables.

DEVELOPMENT. The WINT manual does not discuss the integrity construct or how the authors of this instrument attempt to measure it. The WINT manual provides no description of item creation, theory testing, or pilot testing.

The concepts in each WINT scale, including its validity scale, exactly match the concepts described by the Sackett and Harris review of integrity tests. Sackett and Harris (1984) categorized the schemes of 10 overt integrity tests as delving into the applicant's thoughts on the following: the frequency of theft in society; how stringently theft should be punished; cover-up of the thefts of others; rationalizations about theft; and assessments of one's own honesty.

The wording of the Work Integrity Test items closely follows the wording in the sample integrity test items provided by Sackett and Harris (1984, p. 223). Many of the overt tests Sackett and Harris reviewed directly asked the applicant to admit thefts. The WINT also asks for overt theft admissions using similar wording.

Sackett and Harris (1984) also reported that some of these integrity tests included a "lie" scale and, similarly, the Work Integrity Test also contains a "lie scale."

TECHNICAL.

Test standardization. The WINT manual does not discuss the standardization of its scales. The manual does provide a brief description of the norm sample. It also discusses significant differences for test items between contrasted groups based on "admission of theft," "being fired for theft," and other touchstone admissions by those who took the test on their website. However, the manual does not show correlations between test items and these touchstone admissions, or the intercorrelations between test items. As the manual does not provide the WINT's standard error of measurement (*SEM*), the reviewer attempted to compute it. It is shared in the Reliability section and discussed in the Commentary section in this review.

Norms. The norms for the WINT are not appropriate for pre-employment screening. Its standardization sample is self-selected (instead of randomly sampled). In addition, the norm-group for the WINT appears different from that of the general workforce. The WINT's norm sample described in the manual is much younger than that of the average job applicant. Almost half (46%) of the sample is age 24 or younger. Almost one quarter (23%) of the norm sample is "under age 17" and likely are individuals who are not employed. The inclusion of subjects who are not likely to apply for jobs decreases the evidence of validity of the instrument. These scores should have been eliminated before test norms were developed, unless the instrument was intended to assess academic dishonesty.

To be useful, pre-employment test norms should be derived from a randomly selected sample of the general applicant population, or from a stratified-random sample of persons that highly resembles the general job-applicant population. Given its significant limitations, relying on the WINT's norms may lead to inaccurate conclusions.

Reliability. The author of this review calculated the mean, standard deviation, and the standard errors of measurement for the WINT overall score and its four subscales. In the reviewer's opinion, the standard errors of measurement are too large for the instrument to adequately differentiate candidates at the pre-employment stage, even though the coefficient alpha was found to be .92 for the Overall Score and .75 to .88 for the four subscales.

Criterion validity. The WINT manual provides no evidence of criterion validity. Neither WINT manual nor this reviewer's search of the literature produced any WINT criterion validity studies. A search of the term "Work Integrity Test" produced no published study of the WINT in the EBSCO Psychology and Behavioral Sciences Collection.

COMMENTARY. This reviewer's two greatest concerns about the WINT are its scoring accuracy in correctly classifying job applicants based on its own criteria, and the problems with the WINT norms that have already been described.

The WINT manual indicates that persons who were "Fired for Dishonesty" averaged 59.2 on the Overall Score (of Integrity), 10.45 points lower than the Overall Score mean of 69.6. The range of scores on the instrument is sufficiently small and the standard error of measurement sufficiently large that this reviewer does not believe that the instrument can adequately differentiate those likely to be honest from those who are not so likely, even if one presumes it is valid. In short, if used as a pre-employment screen, the WINT's poor discrimination could label many honest applicants as dishonest and vice versa.

It appears to this reviewer that the WINT scales inaccurately assess both honest and dishonest applicants over much of the test scales' ranges. The following WINT scales have accuracy problems in the following ranges: the Overall Score scale between 49 and 69, the Lenient Towards Dishonesty scale between 20 and 57, the Perceived Frequency of Dishonesty scale between 26 and 59, the Rationalizing Dishonesty scale between 6 and 60, and the Self-Reported Dishonesty scale between 11 and 54.

SUMMARY. This reviewer found no criterion-related validity studies for the Work Integrity Test (WINT). Its high measurement error means that it misclassifies on much of its range. The WINT's norms are not useful, and its manual provides no guidelines on the validity of its interpretations. The WINT fails to meet minimum standards for published psychological tests described in the SIOP (2003) *Principles* and the Evers, Sijtsma, Lucassen, and Meijer (2010) review process for psychological tests.

REVIEWER'S REFERENCES

Evers, A., Sijtsma, K., Lucassen, W., & Meijer, R. R. (2010, October-December). The Dutch review process for evaluating the quality of psychological tests: History, procedure, and results. *International Journal of Testing, 10,* 295-317.

Sackett, P. R., & Harris, M. M. (1984). Honesty testing for personnel selection: A review and critique. *Personnel Psychology, 37,* 221-245.

Society for Industrial and Organizational Psychology (SIOP). (2003). *Principles for the validation and use of personnel selection procedures* (4th ed.). Bowling Green, OH: Author.

Review of the Work Integrity Test by DAVID J. PITTENGER, Dean, The College of Liberal Arts, Marshall University, Huntington, WV:

DESCRIPTION. The developers of the Work Integrity Test (WINT) claim that the instrument predicts an individual's propensity for workplace dishonesty. More specifically, the test presents five subscales that assess "lenient attitude towards dishonest behavior," "perceived frequency of dishonest behavior," "rationalizing of dishonest behavior," "self-reported dishonesty," and a "validity scale" (manual, p. 1). It is difficult to determine the total number of items in the instrument as the test description indicates 59, the overall score data indicate 48, and the total of the subscales equal 56. According to the manual, the Lenient Attitude Towards Dishonest Behavior scale contains 11 items that assess the individual's tolerance of others' dishonest behavior; the Perceived Frequency of Dishonest Behavior scale, which includes 16 items, assesses the individual's perception of the frequency of others' dishonesty; the Rationalizing of Dishonest Behavior scale consists of 9 items measuring the extent to which the individual excuses others' dishonesty; and the Self-Reported Dishonesty scales uses 20 items to assess the individual's self-assessment of how he or she might react when tempted to engage in malfeasance. There is no additional information regarding the validity scale and the manual does not provide samples of the items used in the instrument. Also absent from the manual are any normative data and guidance for how best to interpret the results.

DEVELOPMENT. Readers of the manual will find no information regarding the development of the WINT. The manual indicates only that the instrument was completed by 1,672 who volunteered through means that are not disclosed.

TECHNICAL. The manual presents no information on how the test is scored, the rationale for linking specific items to specific traits, the scale used for responses, and other information that would allow one to understand the empirical foundations of the instrument. The manual does include information regarding coefficient alphas, which range from .75 for the rationalization scale to .92 for the overall scale.

The vast majority of the manual is a procession of frequency distributions for the subscales as well as other dimensions that are not described such as "covering up for others." The validity assessment consists of an odd assortment of simple statistical tests. For example, the first set of tests compares the difference between men and women on the four subscales and the overall scale. The differences (men generally score higher) are presented without commentary. Particularly disconcerting are the notable differences among the degrees of freedom reported for each of the eight t-tests. If the dataset were complete, the

degrees of freedom for each test should have been 1,445. Nevertheless, the reported degrees of freedom are extremely variable with no explanation for the discrepancy.

Equally vague and perplexing are the sections examining differences among age groups and differences among those who had or had not been fired for dishonesty. The latter analysis deserves particular attention as it is the only comparison that might demonstrate construct validity for the instrument. According to the report, 73 people who had been fired due to malfeasance were compared to 73 people who, presumably, had not been fired. The manual provides no information regarding how these people were identified and selected for the study or a verification of their work history. As with the previous comparisons, the degrees of freedom for the various t-tests are inconsistent and only occasionally at the correct value of 144.

COMMENTARY. The Employee Polygraph Protection Act of 1988 prevents most private employers from using devices to measure the physiological reactions of people as they answer various screening questions (see http://www.dol.gov/compliance/laws/comp-eppa.htm). These lie detector tests are of dubious validity and are, therefore, prejudicial when used to screen job applicants or to conduct internal investigations. There is no credible evidence presented in the manual for the WINT suggesting it measures any propensity for dishonest behaviors. As such, using this instrument to form any conclusion or inference about a potential or current employee is not supported by empirical evidence.

SUMMARY. If employees were angels there would be no need for internal audits, surveillance, policy training, and tests of employee dishonesty. Unfortunately, we all have a measure of evil as well as good, but not the fair scale and blind justice to measure the respective weight of each. Karren and Zacharias (2007) outlined the many methodological, ethical, and potentially legal liabilities associated with paper-and-pencil integrity tests and found that even when the data are well-analyzed, the value of integrity tests is highly suspect. As we know nothing of what the WINT measures, users wishing to find an honest employee will need to await the arrival of a reputable Diogenes.

REVIEWER'S REFERENCE

Karren, R. J., & Zacharias, L. (2007). Integrity tests: Critical issues. *Human Resource Management Review, 17*, 221-234.

[183]

Youth Level of Service/Case Management Inventory 2.0.

Purpose: Designed for use in "assessing risk, need, and responsivity factors in youth and in the formulation of a case plan."

Population: Juvenile offenders, ages 12-18.

Publication Dates: 2002-2011.

Acronym: YLS/CMI 2.0.

Scores: 9 Risk Ratings: Prior and Current Offenses/Dispositions, Family Circumstances/Parenting, Education/Employment, Peer Relations, Substance Abuse, Leisure/Recreation, Personality/Behavior, Attitudes/Orientation, Total.

Administration: Individual.

Parts, 7: Assessment of Risks and Needs, Summary of Risks and Needs, Assessment of Other Needs and Special Considerations, Final Risk/Need Level and Professional Override, Program/Placement Decision, Case Management Plan, Case Management Review.

Price Data, 2011: $195 per complete kit including 25 interview guides, 25 Quikscore forms, 25 case management forms, and user's manual (2011, 92 pages); $79 per 25 interview guides; $47 per 25 Quikscore forms; $28 per 25 case management forms; $63 per user's manual.

Time: [30-40] minutes.

Comments: Reflects the theory and structure of the Level of Service Inventory–Revised (17:107).

Authors: Robert D. Hoge and D. A. Andrews.

Publisher: Multi-Health Systems, Inc.

Cross References: For reviews by Pam Lindsey and Stephen E. Trotter of an earlier edition, see 16:282.

Review of the Youth Level of Service/Case Management Inventory 2.0 by MARK A. ALBANESE, Professor Emeritus of Population Health Sciences, University of Wisconsin School of Medicine and Public Health, Madison, WI:

DESCRIPTION. The Youth Level of Service/Case Management Inventory 2.0 (YLS/CMI 2.0) is used by probation officers or other professionals to evaluate youth offenders and plan for their management through all phases of the judicial decision-making process. Sources of information used to complete the YLS/CMI 2.0 include interviews with the youth and his/her parents or teachers; school, institutional, or criminal records; aptitude, achievement, or personality tests; and behavioral ratings by credible individual(s). It consists of seven parts: I. Assessment of Risks and Needs; II. Summary of Risks and Needs; III. Assessment of Other Needs and Special Considerations; IV. Final Risk/Need Level and Professional Override; V. Program/Placement Decision; VI. Case

Management Plan; and VII. Case Management Review. There are three separate sets of materials that comprise the YLS/CMI 2.0: Interview Guide (58 open questions), Parts I through VI, and Part VII. Although the instrument is very well organized and user-friendly, it is complex to describe with each part having items tailored to the particular nature of the task. The key operational sections are Parts I and II, which together produce the total score used with the normative data. It is critical that the YLS/CMI 2.0 is completed by a professional who must exercise judgment in evaluating whether there are strengths that might mitigate an otherwise poor prognosis. There is also a professional override added with the latest version that enables professionals to override the number total score if, in their opinion, it is warranted.

DEVELOPMENT. The YLS/CMI 2.0 is a third generation instrument based upon the General Personality and Social Psychological Model of Criminal Conduct, a model that is based upon two assumptions: (a) a young person's criminal activity is caused by a complex network of six interacting variables of the individual's characteristics and circumstance and (b) interventions can reduce the chances of future antisocial activity if they are targeted to the criminologic needs of the young person and they are delivered effectively. The assessment and treatment implications of the model are expressed through four principles of case classification: Risk, Need, Responsivity, and Professional Override. The first generation instrument was composed of 112 risk/need checklist items divided into 10 subsections. The second generation instrument was reduced to 42 checklist items based upon considerable research. It also added a professional override option. The current version expanded some sections and upgraded the normative data, but most significantly, left Parts I and II intact as well as the professional override. With Parts I and II intact, the total score is the same as in the previous generation. Because the research and norms are based upon the total score, this is a critical feature that did not require demonstrating the equivalence of the new form to the old form.

Scoring. The total score from the YLS/CMI 2.0 is generated in Part II, the Summary of Risks and Needs, but in large part it is created from Part I. Part I covers two pages and consists of 42 checklist items grouped into eight areas: Prior and Current Offenses/Dispositions, Family Circumstances/Parenting, Education/Employment, Peer Relations,

Substance Abuse, Leisure/Recreation, Personality/ Behavior, and Attitudes/Orientation. The number of checklist items varies between 3 and 7 within areas. All items reflect negative attributes. For each of the eight sections, there is an overall box that allows the person completing the instrument to register whether the area comprises a particular strength for the youth that may help him or her to demonstrate restraint in the face of temptation. Each area also has a box on the right with space for comments and sources of the information used in making checklist responses.

Part II consolidates the information from Part I into a one-page overview and a classification into one of four risk/need levels: low, moderate, high, or very high. The classification is based upon the sum of the number of items checked in Part I and is conditional upon gender and whether the youth is in a community or custodial setting.

TECHNICAL.

Standardization. Normative data (means and *SD*s) for Part I, the assessment of risks and needs, from a sample of more than 10,300 youth in community settings and more than 2,200 youth in custodial settings are provided in the test manual. Separate norms are provided for males and females. More detailed normative data (percentile ranks) are provided in three appendices (D, E, and F).

Reliability. Internal consistency coefficients for the total score have been found to range from .73 to .91 with a median value of .89 across eight studies. Coefficients associated with interrater reliability analyses of the total score range from .72 to .98 with a median value of .82 across five studies.

Validity. The inventory's convergent and predictive validity have been assessed by various independent researchers and meta-analyses, providing what might be considered almost surprisingly strong support. Convergent validity was assessed by correlating YLS/CMI 2.0 with 27 other risk assessment scales and subscales, producing 51 correlation coefficients ranging from -.01 to .91 with a median value of .47. Coefficients below .30 occurred exclusively on subscores in only four cases. Of the 51 correlation coefficients, 45 were statistically significant beyond the .05 level and 39 beyond the .001 level. Ten of the coefficients were .71 or above. Predictive validity evidence was derived from correlations between the YLS/CMI 2.0 and indices of reoffending. Some 14 studies yielded 27 coefficents ranging from -.42 to .46, with a median value of .30. Of these values, 8 were .40 or greater;

23 correlations were statistically significant at the .05 level and 5 beyond the .001 level. Examples of the highest correlation coefficients were with charges and convictions (.46, $p < .001$), months to new offense ($r = -.42$, $p < .01$) and violent recidivism ($r = .40$, $p < .01$). Two studies used linear discriminant analysis with the eight YLS/CMI subscores to predict reoffending and found a 75.38% correct classification value. In addition, the YLS/CMI demonstrated an accuracy rate of 56% in prediction of serious reoffense. The validity analyses also examined differences in mean scores for youth under differing levels of supervision. The results were all statistically significant beyond .001 and produced effect sizes (Cohen's *d*) ranging from .43 to 1.47 in the normative sample. Separate, but comparable, norms for males and females indicate that the YLS/CMI 2.0 is gender neutral and does not show significant cultural bias. Whites versus non-whites had Cohen's *d* values that were at most .18, a value that is less than what Cohen classified as a small effect size. A study by the instrument authors found relatively strong support for the Risk-Need-Responsivity principle of case classification that involved matching services to the identified needs of the offender. The correlation between the matching of services to youth needs and rates of recidivism was -.48, $p < .001$ (the better the matching, the lower the rate of recidivism). The availability of data from several meta-analyses to support the validity of the YLS/CMI 2.0 was particularly impressive. The instrument has clearly become a major tool for assessing offending youths.

COMMENTARY. The Youth Level of Service/Case Management Inventory 2.0 (YLS/ CMI 2.0) is used by probation officers or other professionals to evaluate youth offenders and plan for their management through all phases of the judicial decision-making process. Poor decisions from such evaluations can ruin the lives of youth who, perhaps, could turn to a better path with proper management. Alternately, poor decisions may unleash dangerous individuals on society if they are not identified as posing such a risk. Such high risk decisions demand an instrument that meets the highest psychometric standards. Generally, the YLS/CMI 2.0 rises to the challenge.

The YLS/CMI 2.0 is based upon principles and theory that have been tested and found to have merit. It is the third generation instrument that has benefited from 29 years of use and research, decreasing from 112 risk elements to 42 from this refinement. Since the first generation instrument called the Level of Supervision Inventory (LSI) was published (Andrews, 1982), there have been numerous studies conducted in at least three countries (U.S., Australia [Thompson & Pope, 2005], and the U.K. [Marshall, Egan, English, & Jones, 2006]) that have studied the validity of the underlying principles and concepts of the YLS/CMI 2.0 and found support for the use of the instrument. A 2010 comprehensive literature review identified over 100 articles and conference presentations describing YLS/CMI research. A study for the U.S. Department of Justice involving 960 youth reported that YLS/CMI scores significantly predicted general rearrests and felonies, reincarcerations, treatment program completion, and institutional and technical violations (Flores, Travis, & Latessa, 2004). From a technical perspective the YLS/CMI 2.0 has a strong theoretical and empirical basis for its structure and use. Its broad adoption further reinforces its utility.

From a user-friendliness perspective, the YLS/CMI 2.0 also has substantial merit. The technical report contains a substantial amount of highly technical information, but it is extremely well-written and is a relatively easy document to read for anyone with a basic knowledge of measurement practice. The test manual includes several examples of cases and how the YLS/CMI 2.0 would be completed for these individuals. Even though the instrument contains eight parts, they are organized in a sequence that facilitates the decision and process being developed from risk assessment to case recommendations and management.

Ironically, the main weakness of the instrument may stem from its strengths. The data in support of its validity and utility are fairly compelling. One could easily take information from the YLS/CMI 2.0 at face value without looking too deeply into the manner in which it is completed. However, its results are only as good as the effort put into its completion. The instrument depends upon a best information approach where the individual completing it attempts to get the best information possible for its completion from the myriad of sources that can be used. However, even with a good faith effort (let alone a hurried and cursory effort) the information may not be the best and it may not even be very good. It will depend upon how much effort was put into its completion and the availability of best sources. The YLS/CMI 2.0 has room for noting the sources of information used in making a rating, so one should be careful to

review that section before offering conclusions. The best information provided may not be good enough to support the high risk assessment being made.

SUMMARY. The Youth Level of Service/Case Management Inventory 2.0 (YLS/CMI 2.0) is a theory-based and heavily researched, yet user-friendly instrument for probation officers or other professionals to evaluate youth offenders and plan for their management through all phases of the judicial decision-making process. It provides a large, geographically representative norm sample for offenders 12 to 18 years of age, and for four separate subgroups based on gender and institutional status. The psychometric properties of the YLS/CMI 2.0 are surprisingly strong for such a complex instrument that relies heavily upon professional judgment. Generally, the YLS/CMI 2.0 has been shown to be effective in diagnosing and managing the needs of youth offenders so as to reduce the likelihood of repeat offenses. The YLS/CMI 2.0 is based upon a best evidence model that includes room for noting the source of information that ratings are based upon. Anyone interpreting the results of the YLS/CMI 2.0 should consider the sources used for the ratings to be confident that the best source used is good enough to support the decisions being made.

REVIEWER'S REFERENCES

Andrews, D. A. (1982). *The Level of Supervision Inventory (LSI): The first follow-up.* Toronto, Ontario, Canada: Multi-Health Systems.
Flores, A. W., Travis, L. F., III, & Latessa, E. J. (2004). *Case classification for juvenile corrections: An assessment of the Youth Level of Service/Case Management Inventory (YLS/CMI), final report.* Retrieved from http://www.ncjrs.gov/pdffiles1/nij/grants/204005.pdf
Marshall, J., Egan, V., English, M., & Jones, R. M. (2006). The relative validity of psychopathy versus risk/needs-based assessments in the prediction of adolescent offending behavior. *Legal and Criminological Psychology, 11,* 197-210.
Millon, T. (1983). *Modern psychopathology.* Prospect Heights, IL: Waveland Press.
Thompson, A. P., & Pope, Z. (2005). Assessing juvenile offenders: Preliminary data for the Australian adaptation of the Youth Level of Service/Case Management Inventory (Hoge & Andrews, 1995). *Australian Psychologist, 40,* 201-214.

Review of the Youth Level of Service/Case Management Inventory 2.0 by GENE N. BERG, Adjunct Instructor Psychology, Chapman University, Riverside, CA:

DESCRIPTION. The Youth Level of Service/Case Management Inventory 2.0 (YLS/CMI 2.0) is a checklist composed of multiple categories and domain areas used to evaluate juvenile offenders from the ages of 12 to 18. The YLS/CMI 2.0 includes a test manual, an interview guide, profile forms, and case management sheets.

The YLS/CMI 2.0 is designed to assess risk, needs, and responsivity factors in youth and can assist in the formulation of case plans for youthful offenders. The test publisher suggests that the YLS/CMI 2.0 is relatively easy to use and allows the practitioner to assess and review a wide range of information about a juvenile offender. The interview guide contains a series of questions relating to criminal and disposition history, family circumstances/parenting, education/employment, peer relations, substance abuse, leisure/recreation, personality/behavior, and attitudes, values, and beliefs that can be asked of the youthful offender. Responses are recorded on the interview guide. Collaborative information from family, records, legal documentation, and other sources can be added to information obtained from the youth.

In turn, a profile form is filled out relating to Part I: Assessment of Risks and Needs, Part II: Summary of Risks and Needs, Part III: Assessment of Other Needs and Special Considerations, Part IV: Final Risk/Need Level and Professional Override, and Part V: Program/Placement Decision. The profile form assists with the analysis of information, and, once completed, the Total Risk/Need Levels can be tabulated for custodial males, custodial females, community males, and community females. The risk/need level can be reviewed in relationship to the normative data included in an appendix of the test manual. The appendices also include information about the norm group for the YLS/CMI 2.0 and for Part II of the norm group for the YLS/CMI. The case management sheets can be filled out relating to risk/need in various areas and interventions.

DEVELOPMENT. The YLS/CMI 2.0 is based on the General Personality and Social Psychological Model of Criminal Conduct (Andrews & Bonta, 2006; Andrews, Bonta, & Hoge, 1990). The test incorporates the underlying assumption that a young person's criminal activity results from "a complex network of interacting variables" relating to the "individual's characteristics and circumstances" (manual, p. 1), including the individual's developmental history; family situation; personality, behavioral, and cognitive attributes; educational and employment experiences; peer group associations; and beliefs and attitudes. The second underlying assumption of the model is that interventions with high risk youth can effectively reduce the likelihood of future antisocial activity. Much of the research by Andrews and Bonta (2006) is fairly consistent with most theoretical thinking relating to delinquency factors.

The YLS/CMI 2.0 inventory was developed from the original Level of Supervision Inventory (LSI; Andrews, 1982), which was "developed to assist in decisions about parole release and parole supervision for adult offenders by assessing the level of risk for reoffending" (manual, p. 2). Several revisions were made of the LSI. "An earlier version of the LSI was adapted for use with children and adolescents" and was renamed "the Youth Level of Service Inventory (YLSI, Andrews, Robinson, & Hoge, 1984)" (manual, p. 2). This instrument was composed of 112 risk/need items divided into 10 subsections (manual, p. 2). Another version of this test–the Youth Level of Service/Case Management Inventory (YLS/CMI)–incorporated 42 of the 112 risk/need items from the YLSI; "selected items were those that previous research had indicated as most strongly associated with youthful criminal activity" (manual, p. 3). The YLS/CMI was revised into the YLS/CMI 2.0.

TECHNICAL. The YLS/CMI 2.0 was standardized on a larger norm group than was the YLS/CMI. The original norms for the YLS/CMI were developed in 1996 using a sample consisting mostly of community offenders and provided guidelines (i.e., risk cutoffs) for the classification of young offenders. Data were added to those norms, expanding the age range from 12- to 17-year-olds to 12- to 18-year-olds and creating separate norms for four groups based on gender and institutional status (i.e., custodial vs. community). The final normative sample for the YLS/CMI 2.0 was updated with 12,798 young offenders from various correctional agencies in seven states between 2001 and 2008 with 72.1% of the participants being male, the majority of whom were White although there was some representation of Blacks, Latinos, and Asians. The test manual provides a number of descriptive statistics for YLS/CMI 2.0 scores relating to male custodial and male community offenders and female custodial and female community offenders and respective cutoff scores.

The inventory includes new recommended cutoffs for various risks/need levels and provides cutoffs and ratings relating to Very High, High, Moderate, and Low Risk/Need ratings that are specific to juveniles within custody settings or juveniles within the community. With respect to reliability, a number of statistics and research studies are cited relating to the reliability of the YLS/CMI 2.0. The majority of findings indicate that the test has high internal consistency and a high degree of interrater agreement. With respect to validity evidence, ANCOVA (one-way analysis of covariance) was conducted in reference to institution status (i.e., custodial vs. community) using age and race as covariates. MANCOVA (multivariate analyses of covariance) were also conducted with subcomponents of the test. Statistics summarized in the test manual indicate that the test clearly differentiates between custodial and community offenders in relationship to risk/need variables. With respect to evidence of predictive validity, the manual reports multiple studies that collectively indicate the total risk/need score on the YLS/CMI 2.0 is highly correlated with rates of recidivism and reoffending.

COMMENTARY. The YLS/CMI 2.0 is easy to administer, yet does require some time to conduct interviews and collect information from numerous sources. Once an interview is completed and collaborative information is gathered, profile sheets and ratings need to be completed. This requires doing a thorough comprehensive analysis of multiple factors relating to delinquency. The interview guide provides direction with respect to content questions and recording responses and obtaining collaborative information. Profile sheets assist in focusing on risk/need factors across various areas along with the Total Risk/Need Score.

The YLS/CMI 2.0 meets its goal for the comprehensive assessment of a juvenile's level of criminality in relationship to multiple criminal factors and risk. The YLS/CMI 2.0 follows in the tradition of inventory checklists that have been used over the past several years to assess risk factors and potential risk for reoffending and potential for violence. Although this is not a new approach, the YLS/CMI 2.0 is a very comprehensive measure with considerable research with a large subject population. Additionally, the YLS/CMI 2.0 is an excellent assessment resource for a correctional, court, or legal setting that requires a comprehensive risk assessment for potential dispositions, ongoing care, and supervision of offenders.

SUMMARY. The YLS/CMI 2.0 is a standardized comprehensive inventory checklist with norms based on a large expanded representative sample of male and female juvenile offenders ages 12 to 18 from institutional and community settings. The YLS/CMI 2.0 assists the examiner in providing a comprehensive review and analysis of need/risk factors relating to recidivism and reoffending. The instrument assists the examiner by providing multiple risk/need ratings and a Total Score of risk/need level. Scores can be compared to the normative sample of male and female juvenile offenders. In turn, a plan of intervention and case management can be formulated. The inventory demonstrates a high degree of reliability. As well, evidence supporting use of its scores in the prescribed manner is provided and is at least moderately compelling.

REVIEWER'S REFERENCES

Andrews, D. A. (1982). *The Level of Supervision Inventory (LSI): The first follow-up.* Toronto, Ontario, Canada: Multi-Health Systems.
Andrews, D. A., & Bonta, J. (2006). *The psychology of criminal conduct* (4th ed.). Markham, Ontario, Canada: LexisNexis.
Andrews, D. A., Bonta, J., & Hoge, R. D. (1990). Classification for effective rehabilitation: Rediscovering psychology. *Criminal Justice and Behavior, 17,* 19-52.

APPENDIX

TESTS LACKING SUFFICIENT TECHNICAL DOCUMENTATION FOR REVIEW

Effective with The Fourteenth Mental Measurements Yearbook *(2001), an additional criterion was added for tests reviewed in* The Mental Measurements Yearbook. *Only those tests for which at least minimal technical or test development information is provided are now reviewed. This list includes the names of new and revised tests received since publication of* The Eighteenth Mental Measurements Yearbook *that are lacking this documentation. The publishers have been advised that these tests do not meet our review criteria.*

[184]
American Mathematics Contest 10.
Publisher: Mathematical Association of America; American Mathematics Competitions.

[185]
Assessing Reading: Multiple Measures–Second Edition.
Publisher: Consortium on Reading Excellence, Inc. (CORE).

[186]
BRIGANCE® Early Childhood Complete System.
Publisher: Curriculum Associates, LLC.

[187]
BRIGANCE® Head Start and Early Head Start Complete System.
Publisher: Curriculum Associates, Inc.

[188]
BRIGANCE® Transition Skills Inventory.
Publisher: Curriculum Associates, Inc.

[189]
Career Matchmaker.
Publisher: Career Cruising.

[190]
Careers for Me.
Publisher: Career Kids.

[191]
Classroom Reading Inventory, Twelfth Edition.
Publisher: McGraw-Hill Higher Education.

[192]
Diagnostic Mathematics Assessment.
Publisher: Scholastic Testing Service, Inc.

[193]
Diagnostic Reading Assessment.
Publisher: Scholastic Testing Service, Inc.

[194]
Practical Test of Articulation and Phonology.
Publisher: Cambridge Speech and Language Pathology, Inc.

[195]
RIASEC Inventory.
Publisher: JIST/EMS Publishing.

[196]
The SCERTS Model: A Comprehensive Educational Approach for Children with Autism Spectrum Disorders.
Publisher: Paul H. Brookes Publishing Co., Inc.

[197]

STEM Careers Inventory.
Publisher: JIST/EMC Publishing.

[198]

3-Minute Reading Assessments.
Publisher: Scholastic Inc.

TESTS TO BE REVIEWED FOR THE TWENTIETH MENTAL MEASUREMENTS YEARBOOK

By the time each new Mental Measurements Yearbook *reaches publication, the staff at the Buros Center have already collected many new and revised tests destined to be reviewed in the next* Mental Measurements Yearbook. *Following is a list of tests that meet the review criteria and that will be reviewed, along with additional tests published and received in the next year, in* The Twentieth Mental Measurements Yearbook.

BRIGANCE® Inventory of Early Development III
BRIGANCE® Screens III

Clinical Evaluation of Language Fundamentals—5
Clinical Evaluation of Language Fundamentals—Fifth Edition Screening Test
Cognitive Assessment of Young Children
Comprehensive Receptive and Expressive Vocabulary Test—Third Edition
Comprehensive Test of Nonverbal Intelligence—Second Edition
Comprehensive Test of Phonological Processing—Second Edition

Delis Rating of Executive Function
Developmental Assessment of Young Children—Second Edition
Developmental Test of Auditory Perception
Developmental Test of Visual Perception—Third Edition

Early Reading Assessment
Emergenetics Profile
Emotional and Behavioral Screener

FIRO Business [Fundamental Interpersonal Relations Orientation]
Functional Vision and Learning Media Assessment

Gilliam Autism Rating Scale–Third Edition
Goal-Oriented Assessment of Lifeskills
Gray Oral Reading Tests, Fifth Edition

i-Ready K-12 Diagnostic and K-8 Instruction

Leiter-3

MacArthur Competence Assessment Tool—Criminal Adjudication
Mini-Mental State Examination, Second Edition
Minnesota Multiphasic Personality Inventory—2 Restructured Form
Myers-Briggs Type Indicator Step III

Parenting Interactions with Children: Checklist of Observations Linked to Outcomes
Parents' Evaluation of Developmental Status, Second Edition
Parents' Evaluation of Developmental Status: Developmental Milestones
PTSD and Suicide Screener

The Roll Evaluation of Activities of Life
Ross Information Processing Assessment—Geriatric: Second Edition

Scales for Assessing Emotional Disturbance–Second Edition
Scales for Rating the Behavioral Characteristics of Superior Student—Third Edition
Scales of Cognitive and Communicative Ability for Neurorehabilitation
Self-Directed Search, 5th Edition
Standardized Assessment of Miranda Abilities

Test of Early Communication and Emerging Language
Test of Early Written Language—Third Edition
Test of Mathematical Abilities—Third Edition
Test of Orthographic Competence
Test of Reading Comprehension—Fourth Edition
Test of Silent Contextual Reading Fluency—Second Edition
Test of Silent Reading Efficiency and Comprehension
Test of Silent Word Reading Fluency—Second Edition
Test of Word Reading Efficiency—Second Edition
Test of Written Language—Fourth Edition
Test of Written Spelling—Fifth Edition
Transition Planning Inventory—Second Edition

Universal Multidimensional Abilities Scales

Verbal Behavior Milestones Assessment and Placement Program
Vocabulary Assessment Scales—Expressive
Vocabulary Assessment Scales—Receptive

Work Personality Inventory

NEW TESTS REQUESTED BUT NOT RECEIVED

The staff of the Buros Center endeavor to acquire copies of every new or revised commercially available test. Descriptions of all tests are included in Tests in Print, *and reviews for all tests that meet our review criteria are included in* The Mental Measurements Yearbook. *A comprehensive search of multiple sources of test information is ongoing, and test materials are regularly requested from publishers. Many publishers routinely provide review copies of all new test publications. However, some publishers refuse to provide materials and others advertise tests long before the tests are actually published. Following is a list of test titles that have been requested but not yet provided.*

The Abel Assessment for Sexual Interest-2
The Abel-Blasingame Assessment for Individuals with
    Intellectual Disabilities
Abilities Forecaster
Ability Test
Accuracy Level Test
AccuRater
AccuVision
ACER General Ability Tests (AGAT)
Achiever
ACT Assessment
The ACT Survey Services [Revised]
Acumen Leadership WorkStyles
Acumen Team Skills
Acumen Team WorkStyles
Adaptiv Resilience Factor Inventory
Adaptive Behavior Evaluation Scale, Revised Second
    Edition
Adaptive Matrices Test
Adaptive Spatial Ability Test
Adaptive Tachistoscopic Traffic Perception Test
Adaptive Test for Assessment of Numerical Flexibility
Admitted Student Questionnaire and Admitted Student
    Questionnaire Plus
The Adolescent Multiphasic Personality Inventory
Adolescent Self-Report and Projective Inventory
Adolescent Substance Abuse Subtle Screening Inven-
    tory–2
Adult Health Nursing
Adult Life Skills
Adult Measure of Essential Skills
Adult Reading Test
Adult Youth Engagement Survey
Advanced Management Tests
Advanced Placement Examination in Computer Sci-
    ence A
Advanced Placement Examination in Statistics
Advanced Placement Examination in United States
    Government and Politics
The Advanced Problem Solving Tests
Affective Go/No-go
Aggressive Driving Behavior

Agression Assessment Method
AIMSweb Testing Materials
Alcoholic Selection Procedure
Algebra Readiness Assessment
Allied Health Aptitude Test
Analytical Aptitude Skills Evaluation
Analytical Reasoning Skills Battery
Apperceptive Personality Test
Applicant Potential Test
Applied Technology Series
Aptitude Assessment
Aptitude Test Battery for Pupils in Standards 6 and 7
Aptitude Tests Portfolio
The Arabic Speaking Test
The Area Coordinator Achievement Test
Arizona Basic Assessment and Curriculum Utilization
    System for Young Handicapped Children
Armed Services Vocational Aptitude Battery [Revised]
Arno Profile System
ASPENS: Assessing Student Proficiency in Early
    Number Sense
Assertiveness Profile
Assessing Levels of Comprehension
Assessing Semantic Skills Through Everyday Themes
Assessment and Intervention Materials–Basic Language
    and Social Skills (AIM)
Assessment in Speech-Language Pathology
The Assessment of Basic Language and Learning
    Skills–Revised
Assessment of Collaborative Tendencies [Revised]
Assessment of Competencies and Traits
Assessment of Developmental Delays and Intervention
    Strategies in Early Childhood, Volume I and II
Assessment of Dual Diagnosis
Assessment of Functional Living Skills
Assessment of Grandparenting Style
Assessment of Organizational Readiness for Mentoring
Assessment of Sound Awareness and Production
Assessment of Stuttering Behaviors
Asset Individual
Asset Organisational
Assurance of Learning Assessment

Attention Battery for Children
Attention Index Survey
Attention Switching Task
Attitude Survey
Attitude Towards Work
Auditory Discrimination and Lip Reading Skills Inventory
Auditory Selective Attention Test
Autism Diagnostic Interview: Revised
Autism Screening Instrument for Educational Planning–Third Edition
The Autism Spectrum Disorders-Adult Version
The Autism Spectrum Disorders-Child Version
Autistic Disorder Evaluation Scale
Automated Working Memory Assessment, 2nd Edition
AVIATOR 3

The b Test
The Baby and Infant Screen for Children with aUtIsm Traits
Baccalaureate Achievement
Basic Achievement Skills Inventory Comprehensive Version
Basic English Literacy Skills Test
Basic Intelligence Functions
Basic Nursing Care I and II
The BASICS Behavioral Adjustment Scale
Bayley–III Motor Scale
Beck Depression Inventory–Fast Screen
Beginning College Survey of Student Engagement
Beginning Literacy Reading Assessment
Behavior Assessment Battery for School-Age Children Who Stutter
Behavior Dimensions Scale, Second Edition
Behavior Disorders Identification Scale–Second Edition: Renormed
Behavior Forecaster
Behavior Style Analysis
Behavioral Characteristics Progression (BCP) Assessment Record
Behavioral Intervention Plan
Behaviors & Attitudes Drinking & Driving
Bennett Hand-Tool Dexterity Test
Big Five Profile
Bilingual Classroom Communication Profile
Bilingual Communication Assessment Resource
Bilingual Health and Developmental History Questionnaire
Bilingual Language Proficiency Questionnaire, English/Spanish Version
Bilingual Verbal Ability Tests Normative Update
Bilingual Vocabulary Assessment Measure
Birkman 360
Birkman Abilities Inventory
The Birkman Method [Revised]
Birmingham Object Recognition Battery
Blind Spots Assessments

Bloom Sentence Completion Attitude Survey
Bloomer Learning Test–Neurologically Enhanced
BOP ESL Placement Test
Bracken School Readiness Assessment–Third Edition
Braille Reading Assessment
Brief Cognitive Status Exam
British Picture Vocabulary Scale: Third Edition
British Spelling Test Series: Second Edition
Business Personality Indicator

C.I.T.E. Academic Learning Styles
CAHSEE Readiness Tests
Calculating with Symbols
Call Center Survey
Callier-Azusa Scale: H Edition
The Camden Memory Tests
Campbell-Hallam Team Leader Profile
"Can-Do" Attitude Test
Candidate and Officer Personnel Survey
CANTAB Alzheimer's
Cardiff Pediatric Acuity Test
Cardiff Pediatric Contrast Test
Care of the Adult Client
Care of the Client During Childbearing and Care of the Child
Care of the Client with a Mental Disorder
Career Assessment Battery
Career Automotive Retailing Scale
Career Competency Scale for College Students
Career Competency Scale–Sales and Marketing
Career Exploration Inventory, Fourth Edition
Career Finder
Career Guidance Inventory II
Career Interest Profiler
Career Interests, Preferences, and Strengths Inventory (CIPSI)
Career Mapper
Career Personality Questionnaire
Career Portfolio Builder
Career Preference Scale
Career Quest Analysis
Career Test
Career Values Scale
Caregiver-Administered Communication Inventory
CASI Second Edition
The Category-Specific Names Test
Central Test Personality Inventory
Chally Assessment
Change Agent Questionnaire
Change Management Effectiveness Profile
Change Readiness Assessment
Change Style Indicator
Character Development Scale
Checklist for Autism Spectrum Disorder (CASD)
Chemical Abuse Scale
Child and Adolescent Diagnostic Scales
Child and Adolescent Functional Assessment Scale

Child Health Nursing

Child Health Questionnaire

Child Observation Record (COR) for Infants and Toddlers

Child-focused Toddler and Infant Experiences: Revised Form

Children's Assessment of Participation and Enjoyment/ Preferences for Activities of Children

Children's Depression Scale, Third Edition

Children's Interaction Matrix

Children's Progress Academic Assessment

Children's Progress Academic Assessment

Children's Self-Report and Projective Inventory

Choice Reaction Time

Citizenship

Classification of Violence Risk

CLEP Education Assessment Series

Clerical Series Test Modules

Clerical Series Test: Oral Instructions Forms Completion

Clerical Test Battery

Clinical Assessment of Interpersonal Relationships

Cloze Reading Tests 1-3, Second Edition

Coaching Competencies Questionnaire

Coaching Effectiveness Profile

Cognitive (Intelligence) Test: Nonverbal

The Cognitive Assessment of Minnesota

Cognitive Performance Test (CPT)

Cognitive Stability Index

Cognitive, Linguistic and Social-Communicative Scales

Cognitrone

College Board Institutional SAT II: Biology E/M Subject Test

College Board Institutional SAT II: Chemistry Subject Test

College Board Institutional SAT II: Chinese with Listening Subject Test

College Board Institutional SAT II: English Language Proficiency Test

College Board Institutional SAT II: French Subject Test

College Board Institutional SAT II: German with Listening Subject Test

College Board Institutional SAT II: Italian Subject Test

College Board Institutional SAT II: Japanese with Listening Subject Test

College Board Institutional SAT II: Latin Subject Test

College Board Institutional SAT II: Literature Subject Test

College Board Institutional SAT II: Mathematics Level IC Subject Tests, and SAT II: Mathematics Level II C Subject Tests

College Board Institutional SAT II: Modern Hebrew Subject Test

College Board Institutional SAT II: Physics Subject Test

College Board Institutional SAT II: Spanish Subject Test

College Board Institutional SAT II: Spanish with Listening Subject Test

College Board Institutional SAT II: World History Subject Test

College Board Institutional SAT II: Writing Subject Test

College Board Institutional SAT Subject Test in French with Listening

College Board Institutional SAT Subject Test in U.S. History

College Board Institutional SAT: Spanish Subject Test

College Board SAT I Reasoning Test

College Board SAT II: American History and Social Studies Subject Test

College Board SAT II: Biology E/M Subject Test

College Board SAT II: Biology Subject Test

College Board SAT II: Chemistry Subject Test

College Board SAT II: English Language Proficiency Test

College Board SAT II: French Subject Test

College Board SAT II: French with Listening Subject Test

College Board SAT II: German Subject Test

College Board SAT II: German with Listening Subject Test

College Board SAT II: Korean with Listening Subject Test

College Board SAT II: Latin Subject Test

College Board SAT II: Literature Subject Test

College Board SAT II: Mathematics Level IC and SAT II: Mathematics Level IIC

College Board SAT II: Modern Hebrew Subject Test

College Board SAT II: Physics Subject Test

College Board SAT II: Spanish Subject Test

College Board SAT II: Spanish with Listening Subject Test

College Board SAT II: Subject Test in Chinese with Listening

College Board SAT II: Subject Test in Italian

College Board SAT II: Subject Test in Japanese with Listening

College Board SAT II: World History Subject Test

College Board SAT II: Writing Subject Test

College Board SAT Program

College Entrance Test

College Majors Scorecard

College Portfolio Builder

College Success

Collegiate Assessment of Academic Proficiency [Revised]

Colorado Malingering Tests

Colorado Neuropsychology Tests

The Communication Behaviors Inventory II

Communication Checklist–Adult

Communication Checklist–Self-Report

Communication Competency Assessment Instrument

Communication Effectiveness Profile

Communication Effectiveness Scale

Communication Independence Profile for Adults

Communication Style Inventory

Community Health Nursing

Compass

COMPASS Managerial Practices Profile

Competence Assessment to Stand Trial for Defendants

with Mental Retardation
Competency-Based Position Analysis
Comprehensive Nursing Achievement Test for Practical
   Nursing Students
Comprehensive Nursing Achievement–PN
Comprehensive Nursing Achievement–RN
Comprehensive Personality Analysis
Comprehensive Test of Adaptive Behavior–Revised
The Computer Category Test
Computer Optimized Multimedia Intelligence Test
Computer Programmer Ability Battery
Computer-Assisted SCID-Clinician Version for Win-
   dows (CAS-CV)
The Concise Learning Styles Assessment
Concussion Resolution Index
Conflict Style Instrument
Contextual Probes of Articulation Competence-Spanish
Continuous Attention
Continuous Visual Recognition Task
Controller Staff Selector
Copeland Symptom Checklist for Attention Deficit
   Disorders, Adult Version
Copeland Symptom Checklist for Attention Deficit
   Disorders, Child and Adolescent Version
COPS Interest Inventory (1995 Revision)
COPSystem Picture Inventory of Careers
Core Abilities Assessment
Core Knowledge Curriculum-Referenced Tests
Corporate Communication Assessment
Corsi-Block-Tapping-Test
Counterproductive Behavior Index
Creating a Great Place to Learn
Creativity Questionnaire
Creativity/Innovation Effectiveness Profile
Credit and Blame Type Assessment
Criterion-Referenced Articulation Profile
Critical Thinking in Clinical Nursing Practice–PN
Critical Thinking in Clinical Nursing Practice–RN
Critical Thinking Test
Cultural Diversity and Awareness Profile
Culture and Climate Survey for Organizations
Culture for Diversity Inventory
Customer Care Ability Test
Customer Satisfaction Practices Tool
Customer Service Commitment Profile
Customer Service Listening Skills Exercise
Customer Service Simulator
Customer Service Skills Assessment
Customer Service Survey
Customer ServiceStyles

Data Entry and Data Checking Tests
Data Entry Test
Dealing With Conflict Instrument
DecideX
Delayed Matching to Sample
Dementia Questionnaire for People with Learning

Disabilities
Denison Leadership Development Survey
Denison Organizational Culture Survey
Detailed Assessment of Speed of Handwriting
Determination Test
Determination Test for Children
Developmental Assets Profile
Developmental Eye Movement Test
Developmental Reading Assessment
Diagnostic Assessment for the Severely Handicapped II
Diagnostic Evaluation of Articulation and Phonology,
   U.K. Edition
Diagnostic Evaluation of Articulation and Phonology,
   U.S. Edition
The Diagnostic Inventory of Personality and Symptoms
Diagnostic Prescriptive Assessment
Diagnostic Readiness Test–PN
Diagnostic Readiness Test–RN
The Diana Screen
Differential Aptitude Tests for Guidance
Differential Aptitude Tests for Schools
Differential Aptitude Tests for Selection
Differential Assessment of Autism & Other Develop-
   mental Disorders
Differential Attention Test
Differential Screening Test for Processing
Differential Stress Inventory
Discovering Diversity Profile
Disruptive Behavior Rating Scale
Diversity & Cultural Awareness Profile
Diversity Survey
DOMA–Diagnostic Online Mathematics Assessment
The Dot Counting Test
Double Labyrinth Test
Draw A Person Questionnaire
Drug/Alcohol Attitude Survey
Dynamic Assessment and Intervention: Improving
   Children's Narrative Abilities
Dynamic Loewenstein Occupational Therapy Cognitive
   Assessment (DLOTCA Battery)
Dynamic Loewenstein Occupational Therapy Cognitive
   Assessment for Geriatric Use (DLOTCA)
Dynamic Occupational Therapy Cognitive Assessment
   for Children
Dynamic Screening for Phonological Awareness
Dyslexia Portfolio
Dyslexia Screener
Dyslexia Screening Test-Junior
Dyslexia Screening Test-Secondary

E.Q. Test
Early Learning Success Essential Skills Inventories
Early Literacy Diagnostic Test
Early Motor Control Scales
Early Repetition Battery
Easy Assessments
easyCBM

ECHOS Early Childhood Observation System
Ecologically Oriented Neurorehabilitation of Memory (EON-MEM)
Edinburgh Reading Tests [2002 Update]
Edinburgh Reasoning Series
Educational Assessment of School Youth for Occupational Therapists
Educational Development Series–Revised Edition
Educational Interest Inventory II
Efron Visual Acuity Test
eMeasures of Vocabulary Growth
Emerging Literacy & Language Assessment
Emo Questionnaire [Revised]
Emotion Recognition Task
Emotional Competence Inventory–University Edition
Emotional Intelligence Profile
Emotional Intelligence Style Profile
Emotional Quotient Scale for Children
Emotional Quotient Scale for Employee
Emotional Smarts!
Employability Competency System (ECS) Reading and Math
Employability Skills Inventory
Employee Adjustment Survey
Employee Empowerment Survey
Employee Evaluation of Management Survey
Employee Opinion Survey
Empowerment Development Gauge and Evaluation
Empowerment Management Inventory
Entrepreneur Test
Entry Level Police Officer Examination
Essential Skills Screener
The Ethical Type Indicator
Evaluating Acquired Skills in Communication–Third Edition
eWrite Computer-Based Writing Test
Exam Preparation Inventory
Examining for Aphasia–Fourth Edition
Express Assessments
Expression, Reception, and Recall of Narrative Instrument
The Expressive Language Test, Second Edition
Extended DISC
Eysenck Personality Scales

Facial Recognition
Faculty Survey of Student Engagement
Family Child Care Environment Rating Scale
Family Crisis Oriented Personal Evaluation Scales
Family Evaluation Form
Family History Analysis
Farnsworth Lantern Color Vision Test
Fieldwork Performance Evaluation for the Occupational Therapy Student/Fieldwork Performance Evaluation for the Occupational Therapy Assistant Student
15FQ+
Fifteen Factor Questionnaire

Filipino Family Relationship Scale
Filipino Professional/Technical Employee Needs Inventory
Financial Literacy Inventory
Fire Engineer
Fire Inspector and Senior Fire Inspector
Fire Service Administrator (Battalion Chief)
Fire Service Administrator (Captain) 574
Fire Service Administrator (Chief) 578
Fire Service Administrator (Deputy Chief)
Fire Service Supervisor (Sergeant, Lieutenant)
Firefighter Examinations 275.1 and 275.2
Firefighter Test: B-3
Firefighter Test: B-4
Flicker/Fusion Frequency
Focus Energy Balance Indicator
Following Instructions Test
Form 130 Employability Competency System Appraisal for Reading and Math
Form 230 Workforce (WLS) Appraisal for Reading and Math
Form 30 Life Skills Appraisal for Math
Form 80 Appraisal for Reading and Listening
Form CR (Creativity)
Form L (Learning How You Learn)
Form RR (Reading Readiness)
Foundations of Nursing
4-Dimensional Personality Inventory
Four-Lenses Assessment
Four Sigma Qualifying Test
French Reading Comprehension Tests
The French Speaking Test
Full Engagement Self Profile
Functional Analysis of Behavior
Functional Assessment for Multiple CausaliTy
Functional Assessment of Communication Skills for Adults (ASHA-FACS)
Functional Communication Profile–Revised
Functional Evaluation of Assistive Technology
Functional Hearing Inventory
Functional Independence Skills Handbook
Functional Language Assessment and Intervention Sourcebook
Functional Writing Assessment
Further Education Reasoning Test

Gardner Social (Maturity) Developmental Scale
Gates-MacGinitie Reading Test, Second Canadian Edition
General Clerical Test–Revised
General Education Performance Index
General Interest Structure Test
General Reasoning Test
The German Speaking Test
Gestalt Perception Test
Gifted Evaluation Scale–Third Edition
Global Assessment Inventory

Global Mindset Inventory
Global Perspective Inventory
Goal/Objective Setting Profile
Golden Personality Type Profiler
Graded Naming Test
The Graduate and Management Problem Solving Series
Graduate Appraisal Questionnaire
Graduate Reasoning Test
Group Literacy Assessment
Group Mathematics Test, Third Edition
Group Perceptions Inventory
Group-Level Team Assessment

Halstead Russell Neuropsychological Evaluation System, Revised
Hare P-SCAN Research Version
Hare P-Scan Research Version 2
Hare Self-Report Psychopathy Scale III
HCR-20: Assessing Risk for Violence, Second Edition
Health and Illness: Adult Care
Healthcare Employee Productivity Report
Help for Preschoolers Assessment Strands: Ages 3-6
HELP Strands (Hawaii Early Learning Profile): Ages Birth-3
The HELP Test-Elementary
High Performing Organizations Assessment
The Highlands Ability Battery
The Highly Effective Meeting Profile
Hill Interaction Matrix [Revised]
Hilson Adolescent Profile–Version D
Hilson Adolescent Profile–Version S
Hilson Background Investigation Inventory, Revised
Hilson Career Satisfaction Index
Hilson Career Stress Inventory
Hilson Caregiver's Questionnaire
Hilson Cognitive Abilities Test
Hilson Job Analysis Questionnaire
Hilson Law Enforcement History Questionnaire
Hilson Life Adjustment Profile
Hilson Life Stress Questionnaire
Hilson Management Inventory
Hilson Management Survey
Hilson Parent/Guardian Inventory
Hilson Personal History Questionnaire
Hilson Relationship Inventory for Public Safety Personnel
Hilson Safety/Security Risk Inventory
Hilson Spouse/Mate Inventory
The Hindi Proficiency Test
Hiskey-Nebraska Test of Learning Aptitude [Renormed]
Hodder Group Reading Tests 1-3
Hogan Business Reasoning Inventory
Honesty Survey
Honesty Test
Human Job Analysis
Hyperkinetic Syndrome Assessment Method

I-7 Impulsiveness Questionnaire

ICT Self-Rating Scale
IDEL (Indicadores Dinamicos del Exito en la Lectura) (7a Edicion)
In-Law Relationship Scale
Individualized Mathematics Program
Inductive Reasoning
Influencing Skills Index
The Influencing Skills Inventory
Influencing Skills Profile
Influencing Strategies and Styles Profile
The Influencing Style Clock
Information and Communications Technology Literacy Assessment
Initial Assessment: An Assessment for Reading, Writing and Maths [New Version]
Insight Pre-School
Insight Primary
Insight Secondary
Insights Discovery
Insights Navigator
Integrated Visual and Auditory Continuous Performance Test–Advanced Edition
Integrity Survey
Intelligence Structure Battery
Intercultural Communication Inventory
Intercultural Development Inventory (aka IDI v3)
Interest Check List
Interest Inventory
Interest-A-Lyzer Family of Instruments
Interference Test
Internal Customer Service Survey
InterSurvS
Interventions For All: Phonological Awareness
Interview Style Inventory
Inventory for Assessing a Biblically Based Worldview of Cultural Competence Among Healthcare Professionals
Inventory for Assessing the Process of Cultural Competence Among Healthcare Professionals–Revised
Inventory for Assessing the Process of Cultural Competence Among Healthcare Professionals–Student Version
Inventory for Personality Assessment in Situations
Inventory of Classroom Style and Skills (INCLASS)
Inventory of Driving Related Personality Traits
Inventory of Gambling Situations
Inventory of Leadership Styles
Inventory of Program Stages of Development
Inventory of Religious Activities and Interests
IInwald Personality Inventory–Clinical
nwald Personality Inventory–Short Version
Inwald Survey 2
Inwald Survey 2-Adolescent Version
Inwald Survey 3
Inwald Survey 4
Inwald Survey 5
Inwald Survey 6

Inwald Survey 8
Iowa Assessments, Form E
IS Manager/Consultant Skills Evaluation

The Janus Competency Identification & Assessment
    System
The Japanese Speaking Test
Job Observation and Behavior Scale: Opportunity for
    Self-Determination
Job-O Enhanced
Job Requirements Questionnaire
Job Skills Training Needs Assessment
Job Values Inventory
Jonico Questionnaire
Jordan Dyslexia Assessment/Reading Program
Judgment of Line Orientation
Jung Type Indicator
Junior Scholastic Aptitude Test Battery (Standard 5)
Juvenile Interview for Functioning
Juvenile Treatment Outcome

K-3 Screening for Learning and Thinking Abilities
    (SOI Screening)
The Kaufman Speech Praxis Test for Children
Kaufman Test of Educational Achievement, Second
    Edition Brief Form
Kendrick Assessment Scales of Cognitive Ageing
Kilmann Insight Test
Kilmann-Covin Organizational Influence Survey
Kilmanns Personality Style Instrument
Kilmanns Team-Gap Survey
Kilmanns Time-Gap Survey
Kindergarten Readiness Checklists for Parents
Kohlman Evaluation of Living Skills–Third Edition
Kuder Career Search
Kuder Skills Assessment

Langdon Adult Intelligence Test
Language Assessment for Grades 3 & 4
Language Processing Test–Revised
Language-Free Programmer/Analyst Aptitude Test
LanguageLinks: Syntax Assessment and Intervention:
    Levels 1-6
[Law Enforcement] Personal History Questionnaire
Law School Survey of Student Engagement
Leader Action Profile
Leader Behavior Analysis II for Team Leaders
Leadership Competency Inventory [Revised]
Leadership Development Profile
Leadership Development Report
Leadership Development Series
Leadership Effectiveness Analysis [Revised]
Leadership Effectiveness Profile
Leadership Impact
Leadership Qualities Scale
Leadership Skills Test
Learning & Study Strategies Inventory (LASSI) for

Learning Online
Learning Climate Questionnaire
Learning Disability Diagnostic Inventory
Learning Disability Evaluation Scale, Renormed Second
    Edition
Leatherman Leadership Questionnaire II
Legendary Service Leader Assessment
Life Skills Math
Lifespace Access Profile
Lifestyle Questionnaire
Light Industrial Skills Test
LinguiSystems Articulation Test
Linking Skills Index
Linking Skills Profile
The Listening Comprehension Test 2
Listening & Literacy Index
Listening Effectiveness Profile
Literacy Probe 7–9
The Logical Rorschach
Logramos, Second Edition
Lore Leadership Assessment II
Lowenstein Occupational Therapy Cognitive Assessment
    Battery [Second Edition]

Magellan 6
Making a Terrific Career Happen (MATCH)
Management Behavior Assessment Test
Management Development Questionnaire
Management Effectiveness Profile
Management Practices Inventory II
Management Training Needs Analysis
Management/Impact
The Managerial and Professional Profiles
Managing Performance
Mann Assessment of Swallowing Ability (MASA)
Marketing Aptitude Test
Marriage Assessment Inventory
Marshalla Oral Sensorimotor Test
Maternity and Child Health Nursing
Maternity Infant Nursing
Math Grade-Placement Tests
Mathematical Achievement Test
Mathematics in Practice
Matson Evaluation of Drug Side-effects
Matson Evaluation of Social Skills for Individuals with
    sEvere Retardation
Matson Evaluation of Social Skills in Youngsters-II
Matson Evaluation of Social Skills With Youngsters
Matson Evaluation of Social Skills with Youngsters, Hard
    of Hearing Version
McGhee-Mangrum Inventory of School Adjustment
The McQuaig System
Me and My World
Measured Success
Measures in Health Psychology Portfolio
Measures of Children's Mental Health & Psychological
    Wellbeing

Measures of Guidance Impact
Measures of Student Development (MSD)
Measuring Success In Maths
Measuring Success in Science
Mechanical Ability Test
Mechanical-Technical Perceptive Ability
Medical College Admission Test
Meeting Effectiveness Questionnaire
Member Satisfaction Survey
Mental Health Concepts
Mental Rotation
Mentoring Dynamics Survey Online
Metric Assessment of Personality
Michigan Screening Profile of Parenting
Michigan State Suggestibility Profiles
Mill Hill Vocabulary Scales
MindStreams
Mini-Hilson Life Adjustment Profile
Minnesota Cognitive Acuity Screen
Minnesota Developmental Programming System Behavioral Scales
Montgomery Assessment of Vocabulary Acquisition
Moray House Tests
Motivation Questionnaire
Motor Performance Series
Motor Screening Task
Movement ABC
Movement Assessment Battery for Children–Second Edition
MR/DD Profile
The MSFI College of Law Admission Test
Multi-Digit Memory Test
Multi-Dimensional Pain Scale
Multi-Level Management Surveys
Multi-Motive Grid
Multi-Tasking Ability Test
Multidimensional Personality Questionnaire
Multidimensional Verbal Intelligence Test
Multimedia Occupational GOE Assessment Series
Multiphasic Environmental Assessment Procedure [1998 Revision]
Myself as a Learner Scale Digital

N-Test Alpha
Naglieri Nonverbal Ability Test–Second Edition
The National Corrections Officer Selection Test
The National Firefighter Selection Test & National Firefighter Selection Test–Emergency Medical Services
The National First- and Second-Line Supervisor Tests
The National Police Officer Test [Revised]
NCTE Cooperative Test of Critical Reading and Appreciation
Negotiating Style Instrument
Negotiation Style Instrument
Neitz Test of Color Vision
Nelson Assessment: Mathematics

NEO Personality Inventory, Spanish Edition
Network Technician Staff Selector
Networking & Relationship Building Profile
Neuropsychological Aging Inventory
The New Jersey Test of Children's Reasoning
The New Jersey Test of Reasoning [Adult Version]
New Workers Inventory
NOCTI Experienced Worker Assessments
NOCTI Job Ready Assessments
Non-Verbal Learning Test
The Nonspeech Test
Normative Adaptive Behavior Checklist–Revised
Norris-Ryan Argument Analysis Test
Numeracy Progress Tests
Numerical Computation Test
Nursing Care During Childbearing and Nursing Care of the Child
Nursing Care in Mental Health and Mental Illness
Nursing Care of Adults, Parts I, II, and III
Nursing Care of Children
Nursing the Childbearing Family

O*Net Ability Profiler
O*NET Career Interests Inventory, Second Edition
Objective Achievement Motivation Test
Occupational Interest Profile
Occupational Personality Profile
Occupational Preference Inventory
Occupational Therapy Driver Off-Road Assessment Battery
Occupational: Administrative Personnel
Occupational: Customer Service
Odor Memory Test
Ohio Vocational Competency Assessment
Online Sales Effectiveness Profile
Ontario Numeracy Assessment Package
Ontario Writing Assessment
The Opportunities-Obstacles Profile
Oral Communication Battery
The Oral Language Acquisition Inventory, Second Edition
Organisational Transitions
Organizational Climate Survey
Organizational Courage Assessment
Organizational Focus Questionnaire
Organizational Survey System
The Overexcitability Questionnaire-II
Overseas Assignment Inventory

P.A.S.S. III Survey
Pacesetter
Paediatric Activity Card Sort
Paediatric Index of Emotional Distress
Pair Behavioral Style Instrument
Parent as a Teacher Inventory [2012 Revision]
Parent Report Card
Parental Involvement in Education Scale

Punctuation and Grammar (PAT-SPG)
Proof Reading Test
ProWrite
Psychiatric Mental Health Nursing
Psycho-Moral and Self-Regulation Scale
Psycholinguistic Assessments of Language Processing in Aphasia
Psychology in Education Portfolio
Pulse Surveys

QO2 Profile [Opportunities/Obstacles Quotient]
QPASS: The Quick Psycho-Affective Symptoms Scan
Qualitative Reading Inventory
Quality Customer Service Assessment
Quality Customer Service Test
Quality Effectiveness Profile
Quality Healthcare Employee Inventory
Quality of Communication Life Scale (ASHA-QCL)
Quality of Life Questionnaire
Quality of Student Life Questionnaire
Questionnaire Concerning Reaction to Pain
Questionnaire for the Determination of Suicide Risk
Questionnaire on Functional Drinking
Questions About Behavior Function
Questions About Behavior Function–Mental Illness
Quick Assessments for Neurogenic Communication Disorders

Radio Operator and Senior Radio Operator
Randot Stereotests
Rate Level Test
Rauding Efficiency Level Test
Reaction Test
Reaction Time Analysis
Reading Efficiency Level Battery
Reading Grade-Placement Tests
Reading Now
Reading Observation Scale
Reading Power Essentials
Reading Progress Scale
Ready School Assessment
Real Estate Instructor Examination
Reasoning 5-7 Test Series
Recruitment Personality Test
Reid Report [29th Edition]
Reinstatement Review Inventory-II
Reiss Profile of Fundamental Motives
Reiss Scales
Reiss Screen
Reiss Screen for Maladaptive Behavior
The Relationship Report Card
Relationship Selling Skills Inventory
Reliability Test
Restaurant Manager Assessment Report
Retail Skills Test
Right-Left Orientation
Risk Choice

Rivermead Behavioural Memory Test, Third Edition
Riverside Early Assessments of Learning
Riverside Interim Assessments
The Roberts Personality and Motivation Questionnaire
The Roberts Workstyles Profiler
Rookwood Driving Battery
Rorschach's Inkblot Test, Third Edition
Rossetti Infant-Toddler Language Scale
RTI: Assessments & Remediation for K-2

Safety Effectiveness Profile
Sage Vocational Assessment System
Sahlgren's Saturation Test
Sales Effectiveness Profile
Sales Indicator
Sales Profile
Sales Skills Profile
Salford Sentence Reading Test (Revised)
Saville Consulting Wave
Scale for the Evaluation and Identification of Seizures, Epilepsy, and Anticonvulsant Side-effects-B
Scales for Service and Client Orientation
Scales for the Registration of Subjective Strain and Dissatisfaction
Scholastic Proficiency Test–Higher Primary Level
Scholastic Reading Inventory
School Child Stress Scale
School Diversity Inventory
School Readiness Tests for Blind Children
SCID II Patient Questionnaire for Windows and Computer-Assisted SCID II Expert System for Windows
Science Research Temperament Scale
Science, Social Studies, and Mathematics Academic Reading Test (SSSMART)
Scoreboard
Screening for Central Auditory Processing Difficulties (SCAPD)
The Screening Tool of fEeding Problems
Secondary Level Assessment
Secondary Reading Assessment Inventory
Secord Contextual Articulation Tests
Self Starter Profile
Self-Assessment and Program Review for Positive Behavior Interventions and Supports
Self-Directed Learning Readiness Scale [Revised]
Self-Directed Team Assessment
Self-Image Profile for Adults
Self-Perceptions Inventory [2006 Revision]
Seligman Attributional Style Questionnaire
Sensomotor Coordination
SEPO (Serial Position) Test for the Detection of Guilty/ Special Knowledge
Serial Digit Learning
Servant Leadership Inventory Forms A&B
Service Ability Inventory for the Healthcare Industry
Service Skills Indicator

Severe Impairment Battery–Short Form
The Sexual Abuse Interview for the Developmentally Disabled
SF-12: Physical and Mental Health Summary Scales
SF-36: Physical and Mental Health Summary Scales
Shore Handwriting Screening for Early Handwriting Development
The Shorr Couples Imagery Test
The Shorr Parent/Child Imagery Test
SigmaRadius 360° Feedback
Signal-Detection
Simulated Oral Proficiency Interview (SOPI-7 languages)
Simultaneious Capacity/Multi-Tasking
Single Word Reading Test 6-16
Situational Leadership II Leadership Skills Assessment
Situational Leadership® [Revised]
Six Factor Automated Vocational Assessment System
16+ PersonalStyle Profile
Skil Scale Inventory
SkillCheck Professional Plus
Skills Profiler
Slosson Auditory Perceptual Skill Screener
Slosson Intelligence Test–Primary
Slosson Intelligence Test–Revised (SIT-R3)
Slosson Oral Reading Test–Revised 3
Slosson Phonics and Structural Analysis Test
Slosson Visual Perceptual Skill Screener
Slosson Visual-Motor Performance Test
Slosson Written Expression Test
Slosson–Diagnostic Math Screener
Smell Threshold Test
Social Communication Questionnaire
Social Competency Rating Form
Social Emotional Evaluation
Social Influence Questionnaire
Social Language Development Test, Adolescent
Social Performance Survey Schedule
Social Use of Language Programme: Revised Edition
Somatic Inkblot Series
Sourcebook for Speech and Language Assessment
Spanish Articulation Measures–Revised Edition
Spanish Language Assessment Procedures, Third Edition
The Spanish Speaking Test
The Spanish Structured Photographic Expressive Language Test 3
The Spanish Structured Photographic Expressive Language Test–Preschool
Spanish Substance Abuse Subtle Screening Inventory
Spanish Test for Assessing Morphologic Production
Spatial Orientation
Spatial, Temporal, and Physical Analysis of Motor Control
Special Abilities Scales
Speech and Language Checklists PLUS
SSIS Performance Screening Guide
Staff Burnout Scale for Police and Security Personnel
Stages of Concern Questionnaire

Stanford Spanish Language Proficiency Test
Step One Survey
Stephen's Oral Language Screening Test
Strategic Leadership Type Indicator [including 360-Degree Feedback Profile]
Strength Deployment Inventory: Easy-Read Edition
Strength Deployment Inventory: Standard Edition
Stress Management Questionnaire [Revised]
Student Aspiration Inventory
Student Educational Assessment Screening
Stuttering Severity Instrument–Fourth Edition
Super's Work Values Inventory–Revised
Supervisory Aptitude Test
Supervisory Proficiency Tests
Supervisory Skills Inventory
Supervisory Skills Test
The Supplementary Shorr Imagery Test
SureHire
Surgical Weight Loss Psychological Screening
Survey of Beliefs
Survey of Implementation
Survey of Student Resources & Assets
Sutherland Phonological Awareness Test, Revised (SPAT-R)
Symptom Checklist-90 Analogue Derogatis Psychiatric Rating Scale (SCL-90 Analogue DPRS)
System for Testing and Evaluation of Potential
System of Interactive Guidance Information, Plus
Systematic Assessment of Voice

TABE Complete Language Assessment System–English (TABE CLAS-E)
Tajma Personality Profile
Tangent Screen
TapDance
Teacher and Student Technology Surveys
Teacher Performance Assessment [2006 Revision]
Team Assessment System
Team Charter Checkup
Team Climate Inventory
Team Culture Analysis
Team Dimensions Profile
Team Effectiveness Inventory
Team Empowerment Practices Test
Team Leader Competencies
Team Leader Skills Assessment
Team Management Index
Team Management Profile
Team Member Behavior Analysis
Team Performance Assessment
Team Performance Index
Team Performance Profile
Team Performance Questionnaire
Team Skills Indicator
Team Success Profile
Team-Building Effectiveness Profile
Team-Review Survey

Teamable

Teambuilding Effectiveness

Teamwork Skills Inventory

Technology and Internet Assessment

Telemarketing Ability Test

Temperament Comparator [Revised]

Temporal Orientation

TerraNova Online

Test Alert (Test Preparation)

Test for Reception of Grammar–Version 2

Test of Academic Achievement Skills-Revised

Test of Adult Literacy Skills

Test of Auditory Reasoning and Processing Skills

Test of Grocery Shopping Skills

Test of Inductive Reasoning Principles

Test of Language Development–Intermediate–Fourth Edition

Test of Language Development–Primary–Fourth Edition

Test of Leadership Ability

Test of Memory and Learning: Senior Edition

Test of Oral Reading and Comprehension Skills

Test of Oral Reading Comprehension-4

Test of Pictures/Forms/Letters/Numbers Spatial Orientation and Sequencing Skills

Test of Pragmatic Language–Second Edition

Test of Problem Solving 2–Adolescent

Test of Reading Comprehension Plus (TORCH Plus)

Test of Relational Concepts [Norms for Deaf Children]

Test of Semantic Skills–Intermediate

Test of Semantic Skills–Primary

Test of Silent Reading Skills

Test of Variables of Attention (TOVA-8)

Test of Verbal Conceptualization and Fluency

Test of Visual-Motor Skills–Upper Level

Tests of General Educational Development [The GED Tests]

Tests of Reading Comprehension, Second Edition

The Texas Oral Proficiency Test

Theological School Inventory

360 By Design

360 Degree Assessment and Development

360° Feedback Assessment

Thurston Cradock Test of Shame

Time Management Effectiveness Profile

Time Management Inventory

Time Mastery Profile

Time-Movement Anticipation

Titmus Stereo Fly Test

Total Quality Management Survey

TotalView

TotalView Assessment System

Training Needs Assessment for Modern Leadership Skills

Training Needs Assessment Test

Training Proficiency Scale

Truck Driver Inventory

Trustworthiness Attitude Survey

25 Quick and Formative Assessments for a Differential

Classroom

The Two Cultures Test

Two-hand Coordination

Types of Work Index

Types of Work Profile

Undergraduate Assessment Program: Business Test

Urban District Assessment Consortium's Alternative Accountability Assessments

Valpar Computerized Ability Test

Value Assessment Scale

Value Development Index Form A and Form B

Value Development Index Form C

Values and Motives Questionnaire

Vanderbilt Assessment of Leadership in Education

Verbal Dyspraxia Profile

VESPAR: A Verbal and Spatial Reasoning Test

Victim Index

Vienna Risk-Taking Test Traffic

Vienna Risk-Taking Test–Revised Version

Vigilance

Visual Analogue Scales

Visual Form Discrimination

Visual Memory Test

Visual Pursuit Test

Visualization

The Vocabulary Gradient Test

Vocational Interest, Experience and Skill Assessment (VIESA), 2nd Canadian Edition

Voice Impact Profile

Wechsler Intelligence Scale for Children–IV Spanish

What About You?

The Whitener Group Industrial Assessments

Window on Work Values Profile

Wisconsin Card Sorting Test: Computer Version 4, Research Edition

Wisconsin Personality Disorders Inventory-IV

Wonderlic Interactive Skills Evaluations, Keyboard and Office Skills

Wonderlic Interactive Skills Evaluations, Software Skills

Woodcock-Johnson III Normative Update

Word Analysis Diagnostic Tests

Word Processing Aptitude Battery

The WORD Test 2-Adolescent

Words List

Work Expectations Profile

Work Habits, Attitudes and Productivity Scale [Employee and Student Editions]

Work Performance Series

Work Personality Profile & Computer Report

Work Preference Questionnaire [1990 Revision]

Work-Readiness Cognitive Screen

Work Skills Series Manual Dexterity

Work Smarts: Using Multiple Intelligences To Make Better Career Choices

Work Team Simulator
Workforce Learning Systems–Reading and Math
Workforce Skills Certification System (WSCS)
Working Memory Rating Scale
Workplace Aptitude Test
Workplace Ergonomics Profile
Workplace Essentials Profile
Workplace Personality Inventory II
Workplace Personality Profile
Workplace Skills Survey–Form E

Workplace Speaking
WPS Electronic Tapping Test
Writing and Reading Assessment Profile (W.R.A.P.)
Written Language Observation Scale

Xyting In Sight

York Assessment of Reading for Comprehension (YARC Secondary)

DISTINGUISHED REVIEWERS

Based on the recommendation of our National Advisory Council, the Buros Center for Testing is now making special recognition of the long-term contributions made by individual reviewers to the success of the Mental Measurements Yearbook series. To receive the "Distinguished Reviewer" designation, an individual must have contributed to six or more editions of this series beginning with The Ninth Mental Measurements Yearbook. *The first list below includes those who have now achieved Distinguished Reviewer status by their contribution to six or more editions as of the current* Nineteenth Mental Measurements Yearbook. *The second list includes those reviewers who qualified with their contribution to an earlier volume of the* Mental Measurements Yearbook *series (those who also reviewed in* The Nineteenth Mental Measurements Yearbook *are indicated with an asterisk). By virtue of their long-term service, all these individuals exemplify an outstanding dedication in their professional lives to the principles of improving the science and practice of testing.*

Frank M. Bernt
James Dean Brown
Ric Brown
Collie Wyatt Conoley
Andrew A. Cox
Rosemary Flanagan
Stephen J. Freeman
Robert K. Gable
John S. Geisler
Kate Hattrup
Carlen Henington
Thomas P. Hogan

Ashraf Kagee
Joseph C. Kush
Aimée Langlois
Theresa Graham Laughlin
Ronald A. Madle
Mildred Murray-Ward
Gretchen Owens
David J. Pittenger
Cynthia A. Rohrbeck
John J. Vacca
James P. Van Haneghan
Martin J. Wiese

DISTINGUISHED REVIEWERS FROM PREVIOUS MENTAL MEASUREMENTS YEARBOOKS

(* Also reviewed for *Nineteenth Mental Measurements Yearbook*)

* Phillip L. Ackerman
* Caroline M. Adkins
* Mark Albanese
* John O. Anderson
* Jeffrey A. Atlas
* James T. Austin
* Stephen N. Axford
* Patricia A. Bachelor
* Laura L. B. Barnes
Phillip G. Benson
Ronald A. Berk

Brian F. Bolton
Gregory J. Boyle
* Susan M. Brookhart
Albert M. Bugaj
* Michael B. Bunch
Linda K. Bunker
Carolyn M. Callahan
Karen T. Carey
Janet F. Carlson
JoEllen V. Carlson
* C. Dale Carpenter

* Mary "Rina" Mathai Chittooran
  Joseph C. Ciechalski
  Gregory J. Cizek
* Mary M. Clare
  Alice J. Corkill
* Merith Cosden
  Kevin D. Crehan
* Rik Carl D'Amato
* Ayres G. D'Costa
* Gary J. Dean
  Gerald E. DeMauro
* Beth Doll
* George Engelhard, Jr.
  Deborah B. Erickson
  Doreen Ward Fairbank
  Robert Fitzpatrick
  John W. Fleenor
* Michael J. Furlong
  Ronald J. Ganellen
* Bert A. Goldman
  J. Jeffrey Grill
  Thomas W. Guyette
  Richard E. Harding
  Patti L. Harrison
  Michael R. Harwell
* Theodore L. Hayes
* Sandra D. Haynes
  Allen K. Hess
  Robert W. Hiltonsmith
* Anita M. Hubley
* Jeffrey A. Jenkins
  Samuel Juni
  Randy W. Kamphaus
* Michael G. Kavan
  Timothy Z. Keith
  Mary Lou Kelley
* Jean Powell Kirnan
  Howard M. Knoff
* Matthew E. Lambert
  Suzanne Lane
  Joseph G. Law, Jr.
* Frederick T. L. Leong
* S. Alvin Leung
  Cederick O. Lindskog
  Steven H. Long
* Cleborne D. Maddux
* Koressa Kutsick Malcolm
  Rebecca J. McCauley
  William B. Michael

* M. David Miller
  Patricia L. Mirenda
* Judith A. Monsaas
  Kevin L. Moreland
* Paul M. Muchinsky
  Anthony J. Nitko
  Janet A. Norris
  Salvador Hector Ochoa
  Judy Oehler-Stinnett
  D. Joe Olmi
  Steven Ira Pfeiffer
  James W. Pinkney
* G. Michael Poteat
  Nambury S. Raju
  Paul Retzlaff
  Cecil R. Reynolds
  Bruce G. Rogers
  Michael J. Roszkowski
* Darrell L. Sabers
  Vincent J. Samar
* Jonathan Sandoval
* Eleanor E. Sanford-Moore
  William I. Sauser, Jr.
  Diane J. Sawyer
* William D. Schafer
* Gregory Schraw
  Gene Schwarting
* Steven R. Shaw
* Eugene P. Sheehan
* Jeffrey K. Smith
  Jayne E. Stake
* Stephanie Stein
  Terry A. Stinnett
  Richard B. Stuart
* Gabrielle Stutman
* Hoi K. Suen
  Mark E. Swerdlik
* Gerald Tindal
  Roger L. Towne
  Michael S. Trevisan
  Wilfred G. Van Gorp
* Chockalingam Viswesvaran
* Sandra B. Ward
  T. Steuart Watson
  William K. Wilkinson
* Claudia R. Wright
  James E. Ysseldyke
* Sheldon Zedeck

CONTRIBUTING
TEST REVIEWERS

PHILLIP L. ACKERMAN, Professor of Psychology, Georgia Institute of Technology, Atlanta, GA

SANDRA T. ACOSTA, Assistant Professor of Bilingual Education, Educational Psychology, Texas A&M University, College Station, TX

CAROLINE M. ADKINS, Professor Emeritus, School of Education, Hunter College, City University of New York, New York, NY

MARK A. ALBANESE, Professor Emeritus of Population Health Sciences, University of Wisconsin School of Medicine and Public Health, Madison, WI

KATHLEEN D. ALLEN, Associate Professor of Education and Professional Psychology, Saint Martin's University, Lacey, WA

JOHN ANDERSON, Professor, Department of Educational Psychology, University of Victoria, Victoria, British Columbia, Canada

MARTIN W. ANDERSON, Deputy Commissioner, Connecticut Department of Administrative Services, Hartford, CT

CHRISTOPHER ANTHONY, Doctoral Candidate, School Psychology Program, Pennsylvania State University, University Park, PA

JAMES A. ATHANASOU, Adjunct Professor, Faculty of Arts & Social Sciences, University of Technology, Sydney, Australia

JEFFREY A. ATLAS, Director, Mental Health Services, SCO Family of Services, Queens, NY

JAMES T. AUSTIN, Senior Research Specialist and Director of Assessment Services, Center on Education and Training for Employment, The Ohio State University, Columbus, OH

STEPHEN AXFORD, Executive Officer for Special Services, Falcon School District 49, Colorado Springs, CO, and Adjunct Professor, University of Colorado at Colorado Springs, Colorado Springs, CO

PATRICIA A. BACHELOR, Professor Emeritus, California State University, Long Beach, Long Beach, CA

SHERRY K. BAIN, Associate Professor, Department of Educational Psychology and Counseling, The University of Tennessee, Knoxville, TN

LUCY BARNARD-BRAK, Associate Professor, Education EPL, Texas Tech University, Lubbock, TX

LAURA L. B. BARNES, Associate Professor of Research and Evaluation, School of Educational Studies, Oklahoma State University, Tulsa, OK

ABIGAIL BAXTER, Associate Professor of Special Education, University of South Alabama, Mobile, AL

NICHOLAS F. BENSON, Assistant Professor of School Psychology, The University of South Dakota, Vermillion, SD

GENE N. BERG, Adjunct Instructor Psychology, Chapman University, Riverside, CA

NANCY BERGLAS, Research Scientist, UC Public Health Institute, Berkeley, CA

IRA H. BERNSTEIN, Professor of Clinical Sciences, The University of Texas Southwestern Medical Center at Dallas, Dallas, TX

FRANK M. BERNT, Professor, Education Department, Saint Joseph's University, Philadelphia, PA

ELIZABETH BIGHAM, Program Director, Department of Human Development, California State University San Marcos, San Marcos, CA

BRUCE BISKIN, Senior Associate, Delaware Valley Career Solutions, Newtown, PA, and Adjunct Assistant Professor of Graduate Education, Leadership, and Counseling, Rider University, Lawrenceville, NJ

MICHELLE P. BLACK, doctoral student in school psychology, Department of Educational Psychology and Counseling, The University of Tennessee, Knoxville, TN

WARREN BOBROW, President, All About Performance, LLC, Los Angeles, CA

KATHY J. BOHAN, Associate Professor of Educational Psychology-School Psychology, Northern Arizona University, Flagstaff, AZ

SARAH M. BONNER, Associate Professor, Department of Educational Foundations and Counseling Programs, Hunter College, City University of New York, New York, NY

SUSAN M. BROOKHART, Consultant, Brookhart Enterprises LLC, Helena, MT

JAMES DEAN BROWN, Professor of Second Language Studies, University of Hawai'i at Manoa, Honolulu, HI

NINA W. BROWN, Professor and Eminent Scholar of Counseling, Old Dominion University, Norfolk, VA

RIC BROWN, Adjunct Faculty, Statistics and Higher Education, Department of Educational Psychology, Northern Arizona University, Flagstaff, AZ

BETHANY BRUNSMAN, Assessment/Evaluation Specialist, Lincoln Public Schools, Lincoln, NE

ERIC S. BUHS, Associate Professor of Educational Psychology, University of Nebraska-Lincoln, Lincoln, NE

EMILY BULLOCK-YOWELL, Associate Professor of Psychology, University of Southern Mississippi, Hattiesburg, MS

MICHAEL BUNCH, Senior Vice President, Measurement Incorporated, Durham, NC

GARY L. CANIVEZ, Professor of Psychology, Department of Psychology, Eastern Illinois University, Charleston, IL

MICHAEL S. CANNIZZARO, Associate Professor, Department of Communication Sciences and Disorders, University of Vermont, Burlington, VT

C. DALE CARPENTER, Interim Dean and Professor of Special Education, College of Education and Allied Professions, Western Carolina University, Cullowhee, NC

JERRELL C. CASSADY, Professor of Psychology, Department of Educational Psychology, and Director, Academic Anxiety Resource Center, Ball State University, Muncie, IN

FELICIA CASTRO-VILLARREAL, Assistant Professor of Educational Psychology, University of Texas at San Antonio, San Antonio, TX

TONY CELLUCCI, Professor and Director of the ECU Psychological Assessment and Specialty Services (PASS) Clinic, East Carolina University, Greenville, NC

MARY (RINA) M. CHITTOORAN, Associate Professor, Department of Education, Saint Louis University, St. Louis, MO

DAVID F. CIAMPI, Post Doctoral Intern, Valley Mental Health Associates, Inc., Springfield, MA

MARY M. CLARE, Professor of Counseling Psychology, Lewis & Clark College, Portland OR

JEAN N. CLARK, Associate Professor of Educational Psychology, University of South Alabama, Mobile, AL

LORA CLAYWELL, Associate Professor, Rueckert-Hartman College for Health Professions (RHCHP), Regis University, Denver, CO

MARTA J. COLEMAN, Teacher and Researcher, Gunnison High School, Gunnison, CO

VICTORIA A. COMERCHERO, Assistant Professor of School Psychology, Touro College, New York, NY

COLLIE W. CONOLEY, Professor of Counseling, Clinical and School Psychology, University of California, Santa Barbara, Santa Barbara, CA

NORMAN A. CONSTANTINE, Research Program Director, Public Health Institute, Oakland, CA, and Clinical Professor of Community Health and Human Development, University of California, Berkeley, Berkeley, CA

MERITH COSDEN, Professor, Department of Counseling, Clinical, & School Psychology, University of California, Santa Barbara, Santa Barbara, CA

ANDREW A. COX, Professor, Counseling and Psychology, Troy University, Phenix City, AL

NANCY L. CRUMPTON, Adjunct Professor, Walden University, School of Counseling and Social Service, Mental Health Counseling Program; Troy University, College of Education, Counseling Department, Montgomery, AL

RIK CARL D'AMATO, Editor-in-Chief of the International Journal of School and Educational Psychology, Professor of School Psychology, Chicago School of Professional Psychology, Chicago, IL

AYRES G. D'COSTA, Emeritus Associate Professor of Educational Research, Evaluation, and Measurement, Department of Educational Policy and Leadership, College of Education and Human Ecology, The Ohio State University, Columbus, OH

M. MEGHAN DAVIDSON, Assistant Professor of Counseling Psychology, University of Nebraska-Lincoln, Lincoln, NE

ANDREW S. DAVIS, Associate Professor, Department of Educational Psychology, Ball State University, Muncie, IN

HEATHER DAVIS, Doctoral Student, Special Education Program, Texas A&M University, College Station, TX

R. EVAN DAVIS, Adjunct Instructor of Management, Spears School of Business, Oklahoma State University, Stillwater, OK

GARY J. DEAN, Professor and Chairperson, Department of Adult and Community Education, Indiana University of Pennsylvania, Indiana, PA

SHARON HALL deFUR, Professor of Special Education, Curriculum and Instruction, The College of William and Mary, Williamsburg, VA

GYPSY M. DENZINE, Assistant Vice Provost and Professor of Educational Psychology, Northern Arizona University, Flagstaff, AZ

STEPHAN DILCHERT, Assistant Professor, Department of Management, Baruch College, City University of New York, New York, NY

JAMES C. DiPERNA, Associate Professor, School Psychology Program, Pennsylvania State University, University Park, PA

JOE W. DIXON, Licensed Psychologist, Private Practice, Tuscaloosa, AL

KARLA J. DOEPKE, Associate Professor of Psychology, Illinois State University, Normal, IL

BETH DOLL, Associate Dean, College of Education and Human Sciences, University of Nebraska-Lincoln, Lincoln, NE

STEFAN C. DOMBROWSKI, Professor and Director, School Psychology Program, Rider University, Lawrenceville, NJ

ANTHONY T. DUGBARTEY, Adjunct Associate Professor, Department of Psychology, University of Victoria, Victoria, British Columbia

GEORGE ENGELHARD, JR., Professor of Educational Measurement and Policy, Emory University, Atlanta, GA

JENNIFER L. ENGELLAND, Doctoral Student, Illinois State University, Normal, IL

CONNIE T. ENGLAND, Professor, Graduate Counseling & Guidance, Lincoln Memorial University, Knoxville, TN

TAWNY N. EVANS-McCLEON, Assistant Professor of School Psychology, Mississippi State University, Mississippi State, MS

JEANETTE W. FARMER, Professor of Special Education, Marshall University Graduate College, South Charleston, WV

RAY FENTON, President, FentonResearch, Tucson, AZ

W. HOLMES FINCH, Assistant Professor, Department of Educational Psychology, Ball State University, Muncie, IN

ROSEMARY FLANAGAN, Associate Professor, Touro College, Graduate School of Psychology, New York, NY

STEPHEN J. FREEMAN, Professor, Department of Psychology, Counseling, & Special Education, Texas A&M University-Commerce, Commerce, TX

BRIAN F. FRENCH, Professor of Educational Psychology, Washington State University, Pullman, WA

BRENT A. FUNK, Postdoctoral Fellow, Henry Ford Health System, Detroit, MI

MICHAEL J. FURLONG, Professor Counseling/Clinical/School Psychology Department, University of California-Santa Barbara, Santa Barbara, CA

ROBERT K. GABLE, Director, Center for Research and Evaluation, Johnson & Wales University, Alan Shawn Feinstein Graduate School, Providence, RI

MARY L. GARNER, Professor of Mathematics, Kennesaw State University, Kennesaw, GA

JOHN S. GEISLER, Professor Emeritus, Western Michigan University, Kalamazoo, MI

REBECCA GEORGIS, PhD Candidate, Department of Educational Psychology, University of Alberta, Edmonton, Alberta, Canada

REBECCA GOKIERT, Assistant Professor and Assistant Director, Faculty of Extension, University of Alberta, Edmonton, Alberta, Canada

BERT A. GOLDMAN, Professor Emeritus, University of North Carolina Greensboro, Greensboro, NC

JORGE E. GONZALEZ, Associate Professor, School Psychology Program, Texas A&M University, College Station, TX

VICTORIA M. GONZALEZ, Doctoral Student, Counseling/Clinical/School Psychology Department, University of California-Santa Barbara, Santa Barbara, CA

MARTA GONZALEZ-LLORET, Professor in Spanish, University of Hawai'i at Manoa, Honolulu, HI

MONICA GORDON PERSHEY, Associate Professor, Speech and Hearing Program, School of Health Sciences, Cleveland State University, Cleveland, OH

CHAD M. GOTCH, Clinical Assistant Professor of Educational Psychology, Washington State University, Pullman, WA

ZANDRA S. GRATZ, Professor of Psychology, Kean University, Union, NJ

AMANDA GRAY, Ph.D. Candidate in School Psychology, Texas Woman's University, Denton, TX

MALINDA HENDRICKS GREEN, Professor of Educational Sciences, Foundations and Research, University of Central Oklahoma, Edmond, OK

KENNETH M. HANIG, Staff Psychologist, Logansport Joint Special Services, South Bend, IN

SANDRA M. HARRIS, Assessment Coordinator, College of Social and Behavioral Sciences, Walden University, Minneapolis, MN

KATE HATTRUP, Professor, Department of Psychology, San Diego State University, San Diego, CA

JOHN K. HAWLEY, Engineering Psychologist, U.S. Army Research Laboratory, Ft. Bliss Field Element, Ft. Bliss, TX

LESLIE R. HAWLEY, Postdoctoral Trainee, Nebraska Center for Research on Children, Youth, Families and Schools, University of Nebraska-Lincoln, Lincoln, NE

THEODORE L. HAYES, Personnel Research Psychologist, U.S. Office of Personnel Management, Washington, DC

SANDRA D. HAYNES, Dean, School of Professional Studies, Metropolitan State University of Denver, Denver, CO

CYNTHIA E. HAZEL, Associate Professor of Child, Family, and School Psychology, University of Denver, Denver, CO

CARLEN HENINGTON, Associate Professor of School Psychology, Mississippi State University, Mississippi State, MS

KATHRYN E. HOFF, Adjunct Faculty, Department of Psychology, Illinois State University, Normal, IL

THOMAS P. HOGAN, Professor of Psychology, University of Scranton, Scranton, PA

JILL HOLTZ, Doctoral Student, Department of Educational Psychology, University of Nebraska-Lincoln, Lincoln, NE

JANET HOUSER, Academic Dean of the Rueckert-Hartman College for Health Professions (RHCHP), Regis University, Denver, CO

ANITA M. HUBLEY, Professor of Measurement, Evaluation, and Research Methodology, University of British Columbia, Vancouver, British Columbia, Canada

ALLEN I. HUFFCUTT, Caterpillar Professor of Psychology, Bradley University, Peoria, IL

ALLISON HUNT, doctoral student in school psychology, Department of Educational Psychology and Counseling, The University of Tennessee, Knoxville, TN

DZENANA HUSREMOVIC, Assistant Professor of Psychology, University of Sarajevo, Bosnia and Hercegovina

TIFFANY L. HUTCHINS, Assistant Professor, University of Vermont, Burlington, VT

JASON C. IMMEKUS, Assistant Professor, California State University, Fresno, Fresno, CA

JEFFREY A. JENKINS, Professor of Justice Studies, Roger Williams University, Bristol, RI

CHRISTOPHER JOHNSON, Professor of Music Education and Music Therapy & Director, Music Research Institute, The University of Kansas, Lawrence, KS

KATHLEEN M. JOHNSON, Psychologist, Lincoln Public Schools, Lincoln, NE

STEPHEN B. JOHNSON, Senior Psychometrician, Castle Worldwide, Inc., Greensboro, NC

ASHRAF KAGEE, Professor, Department of Psychology, Stellenbosch University, Stellenbosch, South Africa

NEETA KANTAMNENI, Assistant Professor, University of Nebraska-Lincoln, Lincoln, NE

TRACY KANTROWITZ, Director of Research & Development, SHL, Atlanta, GA

MICHAEL G. KAVAN, Professor of Family Medicine and Professor of Psychiatry, Associate Dean for Student Affairs, Creighton University School of Medicine, Omaha, NE

KARL N. KELLEY, Professor of Psychology, North Central College, Naperville, IL

MEGHAN KILEY, Admissions Associate, The Wheeler School, Providence, RI

JEAN POWELL KIRNAN, Professor of Psychology, The College of New Jersey, Ewing, NJ

ANNETTE S. KLUCK, Assistant Professor, Auburn University, Auburn, AL

TIMOTHY R. KONOLD, Professor of Research, Statistics, and Evaluation, University of Virginia, Charlottesville, VA

S. KATHLEEN KRACH, Associate Professor, Troy University, Montgomery, AL

JODY L. KULSTAD, Clinical Coordinator/Adjunct Clinical Professor, Seton Hall University, South Orange, NJ

ANTONY JOHN KUNNAN, Professor, California State University, Los Angeles, CA

JOSEPH C. KUSH, Associate Professor and Director of the Doctoral Program in Instructional Technology and Educational Leadership, Duquesne University, Pittsburgh, PA

SUSAN N. KUSHNER BENSON, Associate Professor of Educational Research, Assessment, and Evaluation, University of Akron, Akron, OH

MARIA I. KUZNETSOVA, Assistant Lecturer of Psychology, University of Wyoming, Casper, WY

BRENDA LAGUNAS, Doctoral Student in School Psychology, Texas A&M University, College Station, TX

MATTHEW E. LAMBERT, Texas Tech University Health Sciences Center, Department of Neuropsychiatry, Lubbock, TX

RONALD S. LANDIS, Nambury S. Raju Chair of Psychology, Illinois Institute of Technology, Chicago, IL

AIMÉE LANGLOIS, Professor Emerita, Department of Child Development, Humboldt State University, Arcata, CA

THERESA GRAHAM LAUGHLIN, Adjunct Faculty, Nebraska Methodist College of Nursing, Omaha, NE

TARA LAYMON, Doctoral Student, Counseling Psychology Program, Department of Educational Psychology, University of Nebraska-Lincoln, Lincoln, NE

FREDERICK T. L. LEONG, Professor of Psychology and Psychiatry, Michigan State University, East Lansing, MI

S. ALVIN LEUNG, Department of Educational Psychology, The Chinese University of Hong Kong

JOHN F. LINCK, Staff Neuropsychologist, Oklahoma City VAMC, Oklahoma City, OK

GREGORY A. LOBB, Clinical Director and Licensed Psychologist, Family Psychological Associates, Kittanning, PA

GIULIANA LOSAPIO, Assistant Professor of School Psychology, Touro College, New York, NY

KELLY BREY LOVE, Faculty Psychologist, Lincoln Family Medicine Program/Lincoln Behavioral Health Program, Lincoln, NE

JUSTIN LOW, Assistant Professor of Educational and School Psychology, University of the Pacific, Stockton, CA

LESLEY LUTES, Clinical Health Psychology Faculty, East Carolina University, Greenville, NC

CLEBORNE D. MADDUX, Foundation Professor of Counseling and Educational Psychology, University of Nevada, Reno, Reno, NV

RONALD A. MADLE, Licensed Psychologist, Mifflinburg, PA, and Adjunct Associate Professor of School Psychology, The Pennsylvania State University, University Park, PA

JENNIFER N. MAHDAVI, Associate Professor of Special Education, Sonoma State University, Rohnert Park, CA

KORESSA KUTSICK MALCOLM, School Psychologist, The Virginia School for the Deaf and Blind, Staunton, VA

DENISE E. MARICLE, Professor of School Psychology, Director of Clinical Training, Doctoral Program in School Psychology, Texas Woman's University, Denton, TX

NORMA MARTINEZ, Graduate Research Assistant, Teacher Education Department, University of Texas at El Paso, El Paso, TX

MICHAEL S. MATTHEWS, Associate Professor of Gifted Education, Department of Special Education and Child Development, University of North Carolina at Charlotte, Charlotte, NC

HELEN MAYO, Research and Liaison Librarian, The University of Texas Southwestern Medical Center at Dallas, Dallas, TX

MERILEE McCURDY, Associate Professor, Department of Educational Psychology, University of Nebraska-Lincoln, Lincoln, NE

SUSAN McDONALD, Doctoral Student, Child, Family, and School Psychology, University of Denver, Denver, CO

THOMAS McKNIGHT, Psychologist, Private Practice, Spokane, WA

MARY J. McLELLAN, Department of Educational Psychology, Northern Arizona University, Flagstaff, AZ

TAWNYA MEADOWS, Pediatric Psychologist, Geisinger Health System, Danville, PA

MARÍA DEL R. MEDINA-DÍAZ, Professor, Program of Educational Research and Evaluation, Department of Graduate Studies, Faculty of Education, University of Puerto Rico-Río Piedras, San Juan, PR

BRADLEY MERKER, Neuropsychology Division Head, Henry Ford Health System, Detroit, MI

OREN MEYERS, Psychologist, Case Western University, Department of Psychiatry, and SOLUTIONS (private practice), Beechwood, OH

BRITTON D. MILES, Adjunct Professor, Industrial Psychology, Director of ADHD Consulting, Alabama State University, Montgomery, AL

M. DAVID MILLER, Professor, Research and Evaluation Methods, University of Florida, Gainesville, FL

RAMA K. MISHRA, Neuropsychologist, Department of Psychiatry, Medicine Hat Regional Hospital, Medicine Hat, Alberta, Canada

CAROLYN MITCHELL-PERSON, Associate Professor in the Speech-Language Pathology Department at Southern University and A&M College, Baton Rouge, LA

JUDITH A. MONSAAS, Executive Director, Assessment and Evaluation, Office of Access and Success, Board of Regents of the University System of Georgia, Atlanta, GA

LAUREN D. MOORE, Doctoral Student, Counselor Education, Seattle Pacific University, Seattle, WA

BENJAMIN MORSA, Graduate Student, The George Washington University, Washington, DC

PAUL MUCHINSKY, Joseph M. Bryan Distinguished Professor, University of North Carolina at Greensboro, Greensboro, NC

THOMAS D. MULDERINK, Doctoral Student, Illinois State University, Normal, IL

MILDRED MURRAY-WARD, Professor of Education, Retired, California State University, Stanislaus, Turlock, CA

AMANDA NOLEN, Associate Professor, Educational Foundations/Teacher Education, College of Education, University of Arkansas at Little Rock, Little Rock, AR

ARTURO OLIVÁREZ, JR., Professor, Teacher Education Department, University of Texas at El Paso, El Paso, TX

AMY M. OLSON, Doctoral Student, University of Arizona, Tucson, AZ

FREDERICK L. OSWALD, Professor of Psychology, Rice University, Houston, TX

GRETCHEN OWENS, Professor of Child Study, St. Joseph's College, Patchogue, NY

THANOS PATELIS, Vice President of Research and Analysis, Research and Development Department, The College Board, and Research Scholar, Graduate School of Education, Fordham University, New York, NY

AMINAH PERKINS, Ph.D. candidate, Educational Studies, Emory University, Atlanta, GA

DAVID J. PITTENGER, Dean, The College of Liberal Arts, Marshall University, Huntington, WV

SAMEANO F. PORCHEA, Test Development Manager, American Nurses Association/American Nurses Credentialing Center, Silver Spring, MD

JULIA Y. PORTER, Professor of Counselor Education, Mississippi State University-Meridian, Meridian, MS

G. MICHAEL POTEAT, Associate Professor, Department of Psychology, East Carolina University, Greenville, NC

SHAWN POWELL, Dean, Social and Behavioral Sciences, Casper College, Casper, WY

KATHLEEN QUINN, Professor of Education, Director, Fall and Spring Reading Clinic, Holy Family University, Philadelphia, PA

GLEN E. RAY, Professor of Psychology, Auburn University Montgomery, Montgomery, AL

JANET S. REED, Board Certified Clinical neuropsychology, Division of Neuropsychology, Henry Ford Behavioral Health Services, Detroit, MI

LAURA W. REID, Graduate Student, The George Washington University, Washington, DC

NORA P. REILLY, Professor of Psychology, Radford University, Radford, VA

RICHARD REILLY, Professor Emeritus, Stevens Institute of Technology, Hoboken, NJ

CARMEN D. REISENER, Assistant Professor of School Psychology, Mississippi State University, Mississippi State, MS

DAVID M. RICHMAN, Chair of the Burkhart Center, Texas Tech University, Lubbock, TX

CYNTHIA A. ROHRBECK, Associate Professor of Psychology, The George Washington University, Washington, DC

STEVEN V. ROUSE, Professor of Psychology, Pepperdine University, Malibu, CA

RICHARD RUTH, Associate Professor of Clinical Psychology, The George Washington University, Washington, DC

DARRELL L. SABERS, Professor Emeritus of Educational Psychology, University of Arizona, Tucson, AZ

MICHAEL SACHS, Professor, Department of Kinesiology, Temple University, Philadelphia, PA

LIA E. SANDILOS, Postdoctoral Scholar, Temple University, Philadelphia, PA

JONATHAN SANDOVAL, Emeritus Professor of Education, University of California, Davis, Davis, CA

ELEANOR E. SANFORD-MOORE, Senior Vicepresident of Research and Development, MetaMetrics, Inc., Durham, NC

WILLIAM SCHAFER, Affiliated Professor (Emeritus), University of Maryland College Park, College Park, MD

MICHAEL J. SCHEEL, Associate Professor, Department of Psychology, University of Nebraska-Lincoln, Lincoln, NE

CHARLES A. SCHERBAUM, Associate Professor of Psychology, Baruch College, City University of New York, New York, NY

STEVEN W. SCHMIDT, Associate Professor of Adult Education, East Carolina University, Greenville, NC

PATRICIA SCHOENRADE, Professor of Psychology, William Jewell College, Liberty, MO

GREGORY SCHRAW, Professor, Department of Educational Psychology, University of Nevada-Las Vegas, Las Vegas, NV

STEPHEN T. SCHROTH, Assistant Professor of Educational Studies, Knox College, Galesburg, IL

AMY SCOTT, Assistant Professor of Educational and School Psychology, Benerd School of Education, University of the Pacific, Stockton, CA

NICHOLE SHADA, Doctoral Student, University of Nebraska-Lincoln, Lincoln, NE

TIMOTHY SHANAHAN, Professor of Urban Education, University of Illinois at Chicago, Chicago, IL

KATHY L. SHAPLEY, Assistant Professor of Speech Pathology, University of Arkansas Little Rock/University of Arkansas for Medical Sciences, Little Rock, AR

STEVEN R. SHAW, Associate Professor of Educational and Counselling Psychology, McGill University, Montreal, Quebec, Canada

EUGENE P. SHEEHAN, Dean, College of Education and Behavioral Sciences, University of Northern Colorado, Greeley, CO

KATHAN SHUKLA, Doctoral Student in Research, Statistics, and Evaluation, University of Virginia, Charlottesville, VA

KENNETH S. SHULTZ, Professor of Psychology, Department of Psychology, California State University, San Bernardino, San Bernardino, CA

MAUREEN SIERA, Associate Professor of Education and Professional Psychology, Saint Martin's University, Lacey, WA

JONATHON SIKORSKI, Doctoral Student, Department of Educational Psychology, University of Nebraska-Lincoln, Lincoln, NE

MARC A. SILVA, Neuropsychologist, James A. Haley Veterans' Hospital, Mental Health & Behavioral Sciences Service, Tampa, FL

CHRISTOPHER A. SINK, Professor and Chair, School Counseling and Psychology, Seattle Pacific University, Seattle, WA

JEFFREY K. SMITH, Professor of Education, University of Otago College of Education, Dunedin, New Zealand

LISA F. SMITH, Professor of Education and Dean, University of Otago College of Education, Dunedin, New Zealand

CATHERINE RUTH SOLOMON SCHERZER, Associate Professor, Department de Psychologie, Université de Montreal, Montreal, Quebec, Canada

RAYNE A. SPERLING, Associate Professor of Educational Psychology, The Pennsylvania State University, State College, PA

STEPHEN STARK, Associate Professor, I/O Psychology & Quantitative Methods, University of South Florida, Tampa, FL

F. STASKON, Adjunct Faculty, Saint Xavier University, Chicago, IL

STEPHANIE STEIN, Professor and Chair, Department of Psychology, Central Washington University, Ellensburg, WA

KAY B. STEVENS, Associate Professor, Texas Christian University, Fort Worth, TX

JENNIFER M. STRANG, Traumatic Brain Injury Program Manager, Northern Regional Medical Command, Fort Belvoir, VA

GABRIELLE STUTMAN, Private Practice, Westchester and Manhattan, NY

HOI K. SUEN, Distinguished Professor of Educational Psychology, Pennsylvania State University, University Park, PA

JEREMY R. SULLIVAN, Associate Professor of Educational Psychology, University of Texas at San Antonio, San Antonio, TX

CAROLYN H. SUPPA, Licensed Psychologist, Coordinator of Human Services Education, Office of Career and Technical Instruction, West Virginia Department of Education, Charleston, WV

WILLIAM TANGUAY, Professor, School Psychology Program, Rider University, Lawrenceville, NJ

TRACY THORNDIKE, Associate Professor of Special Education and Education Leadership, Western Washington University, Bellingham, WA

GEOFFREY L. THORPE, Professor of Psychology, University of Maine, Orono, ME

GERALD TINDAL, Castle-McIntosh-Knight Professor of Education, College of Education, University of Oregon, Eugene, OR

NANCY T. TIPPINS, Senior Vice President and Managing Principal, CEB, Greenville, SC

RENÉE M. TOBIN, Professor of Psychology, Illinois State University, Normal, IL

KATHLEEN TORSNEY, Associate Professor, Department of Psychology, William Paterson University, Wayne, NJ

JOHN J. VACCA, Associate Professor of Education, Saint Joseph's University, Philadelphia, PA

JAMES P. VAN HANEGHAN, Professor and Director of Assessment and Evaluation, College of Education, University of South Alabama, Mobile, AL

ELISA VASQUEZ, Doctoral Student, University of California, Santa Barbara, Santa Barbara, CA

CHOCKALINGAM VISWESVARAN, Professor of Psychology, Florida International University, Miami, FL

ROMEO VITELLI, Psychologist, private practice, Hamilton, Ontario, Canada

CHRISTINE CALDERON VRIESEMA, Doctoral Student, University of Arizona, Tucson, AZ

ELVIS WAGNER, Assistant Professor, Temple University, Philadelphia, PA

YUAN YUAN WANG, completing her PhD in Psychology in the Faculty of Social Sciences and Humanities, University of Macau, Macau SAR, China

SANDRA WARD, Professor of Education, The College of William & Mary, Williamsburg, VA

CHRISTA E. WASHINGTON, Associate Professor of Psychology, Saint Augustine's University, Raleigh, NC

KEITH F. WIDAMAN, Professor of Psychology, University of California, Davis, CA

MARTIN J. WIESE, School Psychologist, Lincoln Public Schools, Lincoln, NE

LYNN WIMETT, Professor, Rueckert-Hartman College for Health Professions (RHCHP), Regis University, Denver, CO

JAMES WITTE, Professor of Adult Education, Auburn University, Auburn, AL

CLAUDIA R. WRIGHT, Professor Emerita, California State University, Long Beach, CA

ROBERT WRIGHT, Professor Emeritus, Measurement & Statistics, Widener University, Chester, PA

TONY C. WU, Faculty, College of Social and Behavioral Sciences, Walden University, Minneapolis, MN

TRACEY WYATT, Academic Dean and Associate Professor of Psychology at York College, York, NE

GEORGETTE YETTER, Associate Professor, Applied Health and Educational Psychology, Oklahoma State University, Stillwater, OK

SUZANNE YOUNG, Professor of Educational Research, University of Wyoming, Laramie, WY

PETER ZACHAR, Professor of Psychology, Auburn University Montgomery, Montgomery, AL

SHELDON ZEDECK, Professor of the Graduate School, University of California at Berkeley, Berkeley, CA

YUANZHONG ZHANG, Faculty, Miami-Dade College, Miami, FL

INDEX OF TITLES

This title index lists all the tests included in The Nineteenth Mental Measurements Yearbook. *Citations are to test entry numbers, not to pages (e.g., 54 refers to test 54 and not page 54). Test numbers along with test titles are indicated in the running heads at the top of each page, whereas page numbers, used only in the Table of Contents but not in the indexes, appear at the bottom of each page. Superseded titles are listed with cross references to current titles, and alternative titles are also cross referenced.*

Some tests in this volume were previously listed in Tests in Print VIII *(2011). An (N) appearing immediately after a test number indicates that the test is a new, recently published test, and/or that it has not appeared before in any Buros Center publication other than* Tests in Print VIII. *An (R) indicates that the test has been revised or supplemented since last included in a Buros publication.*

Adult Self-Report Inventory-4, 1 (N)
Advanced Multi-Dimensional Personality Matrix Abridged–Big 5 Personality Test, 2 (N)
American Mathematics Contest 10, 184 (R)
Anger Regulation and Expression Scale, 3 (N)
ASSESS Expert Assessment System Internet Version 1.3, see Assess Expert System, 4
Assess Expert System, 4 (R)
Assessing Reading: Multiple Measures–Second Edition, 185 (N)
Assessment of Multiple Intelligences, 5 (N)
Assessment of Spirituality and Religious Sentiments, 6 (N)
Auditory Skills Assessment, 7 (N)
Autism Spectrum Rating Scales, 8 (N)

Barkley Adult ADHD Rating Scale-IV, 9 (N)
Barkley Deficits in Executive Functioning Scale–Children and Adolescents, 11 (N)
Barkley Deficits in Executive Functioning Scale, 10 (N)
Barkley Functional Impairment Scale–Children and Adolescents, 13 (N)
Barkley Functional Impairment Scale, 12 (N)
BarOn Emotional Quotient Inventory, see Emotional Quotient Inventory 2.0, 62
The Beery-Buktenica Developmental Test of Visual-Motor Integration, Sixth Edition (Beery VMI), 14 (R)

Behavior Intervention Monitoring Assessment System, 15 (N)
Behavioral Assessment of Pain-2 Questionnaire, 16 (R)
Behavioral Summary, 17 (N)
Bell Relationship Inventory for Adolescents, 18 (R)
BEST Literacy, 19 (N)
Brain Injury Rehabilitation Trust Memory and Information Processing Battery, 20 (N)
BRIGANCE® Comprehensive Inventory of Basic Skills II, 21 (R)
BRIGANCE® Diagnostic Comprehensive Inventory of Basic Skills, Revised, see BRIGANCE® Comprehensive Inventory of Basic Skills II, 21
BRIGANCE Diagnostic Employability Skills Inventory, see BRIGANCE® Transition Skills Inventory, 188
BRIGANCE® Diagnostic Inventory of Early Development-II, see BRIGANCE® Inventory of Early Development II, 22
BRIGANCE® Diagnostic Life Skills Inventory, see BRIGANCE® Transition Skills Inventory, 188
BRIGANCE® Early Childhood Complete System, 186 (R)
BRIGANCE Early Preschool Screen-II, see BRIGANCE® Early Childhood Complete System, 186
BRIGANCE Early Preschool Screen-II, see BRIGANCE® Head Start and Early Head Start Complete System, 187

INDEX OF ACRONYMS

This Index of Acronyms refers the reader to the appropriate test in The Nineteenth Mental Measurements Yearbook. *In some cases tests are better known by their acronyms than by their full titles, and this index can be of substantial help to the person who knows the former but not the latter. Acronyms are listed only if the author or publisher has made substantial use of the acronym in referring to the test, or if the test is widely known by the acronym. A few acronyms are registered trademarks (e.g., SAT); where this is known to us, only the test with the registered trademark is referenced. There is some danger in the overuse of acronyms. However, this index, like all other indexes in this work, is provided to make the task of identifying a test as easy as possible. All numbers refer to test numbers, not page numbers.*

CLASSIFIED SUBJECT INDEX

The Classified Subject Index classifies all tests included in The Mental Measurements Yearbook *into 18 major categories: Achievement, Behavior Assessment, Developmental, Education, English and Language, Fine Arts, Foreign Languages, Intelligence and General Aptitude, Mathematics, Miscellaneous, Neuropsychological, Personality, Reading, Science, Sensory-Motor, Social Studies, Speech and Hearing, and Vocations. This Classified Subject Index for the tests reviewed in* The Nineteenth Mental Measurements Yearbook *includes tests in 16 of the 18 available categories. (The categories of Science and Social Studies had no representative tests in this volume.) Each category appears in alphabetical order and tests are ordered alphabetically within each category. Each test entry includes test title, population for which the test is intended, and the test entry number in* The Nineteenth Mental Measurements Yearbook. *All numbers refer to test numbers, not to page numbers. Brief suggestions for the use of this index are presented in the introduction and definitions of the categories are provided at the beginning of this index.*

Achievement

Tests that measure acquired knowledge across school subject content areas. Included here are test batteries that measure multiple content areas and individual subject areas not having separate classification categories. (Note: Some batteries include both achievement and aptitude subtests. Such batteries may be classified under the categories of either Achievement or Intelligence and Aptitude depending upon the principal content area.)

See also Fine Arts, Intelligence and General Aptitude, Mathematics, Reading, Science, and Social Studies.

Behavior Assessment

Tests that measure general or specific behavior within educational, vocational, community, or home settings. Included here are checklists, rating scales, and surveys that measure observer's interpretations of behavior in relation to adaptive or social skills, functional skills, and appropriateness or dysfunction within settings/situations.

Developmental

Tests that are designed to assess skills or emerging skills (such as number concepts, conservation, memory, fine motor, gross motor, communication, letter recognition, social competence) of young children (0-7 years) or tests which are designed to assess such skills in severely or profoundly disabled school-aged individuals. Included here are early screeners, developmental surveys/profiles, kindergarten or school readiness tests, early learning profiles, infant development scales, tests of play behavior, social acceptance/social skills, and preschool psychoeducational batteries. Content specific screeners, such as those assessing readiness, are classified by content area (e.g., Reading).

See also Neuropsychological and Sensory-Motor.

Education

General education-related tests, including measures of instructional/school environment, effective schools/teaching, study skills and strategies, learning styles and strategies, school attitudes, educational programs curriculae, interest inventories, and educational leadership.

Specific content area tests (i.e., science, mathematics, social studies, etc.) are listed by their content area.

English and Language

Tests that measure skills in using or understanding the English language in spoken or written form. Included here are tests of language proficiency, applied literacy, language comprehension/development/proficiency, English skills/proficiency, communication skills, listening comprehension, linguistics, and receptive/expressive vocabulary. (Tests designed to measure the mechanics of speaking or communicating are classified under the category Speech and Hearing.)

Fine Arts

Tests that measure knowledge, skills, abilities, attitudes, and interests within the various areas of fine and performing arts. Included here are tests of aptitude, achievement, creativity/talent/giftedness specific to the Fine Arts area, and tests of aesthetic judgment.

Foreign Languages

Tests that measure competencies and readiness in reading, comprehending, and speaking a language other than English.

Intelligence and General Aptitude

Tests that measure general acquired knowledge, aptitudes, or cognitive ability and those that assess specific aspects of these general categories. Included here are tests of critical thinking skills, nonverbal/verbal reasoning, cognitive abilities/processing, learning potential/aptitude/efficiency, logical reasoning, abstract thinking, creative thinking/creativity; entrance exams and academic admissions tests.

Mathematics

Tests that measure competencies and attitudes in any of the various areas of mathematics (e.g., algebra, geometry, calculus) and those related to general mathematics achievement/proficiency. (Note: Included here are tests that assess personality or affective variables related to mathematics.)

Miscellaneous

Tests that cannot be sorted into any of the current MMY categories as listed and defined above. Included here are tests of handwriting, ethics and morality, religion, driving and safety, health and physical education, environment (e.g., classroom environment, family environment), custody decisions, substance abuse, and addictions. (See also Personality.)

Neuropsychological

Tests that measure neurological functioning or brain-behavior relationships either generally or in relation to specific areas of functioning. Included here are neuropsychological test batteries, questionnaires, and screening tests. Also included are tests that measure memory impairment, various disorders or decline associated with dementia, brain/head injury, visual attention, digit recognition, finger tapping, laterality, aphasia, and behavior (associated with organic brain dysfunction or brain injury).

See also Developmental, Intelligence and General Aptitude, Sensory-Motor, and Speech and Hearing.

Personality

Tests that measure individuals' ways of thinking, behaving, and functioning within family and society. Included here are projective and apperception tests, needs inventories, anxiety/depression scales; tests assessing substance use/abuse (or propensity for abuse), risk taking behavior, general mental health, emotional intelligence, self-image/-concept/-esteem, empathy, suicidal ideation, schizophrenia, depression/hopelessness, abuse, coping skills/stress, eating disorders, grief, decision-making, racial attitudes; general motivation, attributions, perceptions; adjustment, parenting styles, and marital issues/satisfaction.

For content-specific tests, see subject area categories (e.g., math efficacy instruments are located in Mathematics). Some areas, such as substance abuse, are cross-referenced with the Personality category.

Reading

Tests that measure competencies and attitudes within the broadly defined area of reading. Included here are reading inventories, tests of reading achievement and aptitude, reading readiness/early reading ability, reading comprehension, reading decoding, and oral reading. (Note: Included here are tests that assess personality or affective variables related to reading.)

Science

Tests that measure competencies and attitudes within any of the various areas of science (e.g., biology, chemistry, physics), and those related to general science achievement/proficiency. (Note: Included here are tests that assess personality or affective variables related to science.)

Sensory-Motor

Tests that are general or specific measures of any or all of the five senses and those that assess fine or gross motor skills. Included here are tests of manual dexterity, perceptual skills, visual-motor skills, perceptual-motor skills, movement and posture, laterality preference, sensory integration, motor development, color blindness/discrimination, visual perception/organization, and visual acuity.

See also Neuropsychological and Speech and Hearing.

Social Studies

Tests that measure competencies and attitudes within the broadly defined area of social studies. Included here are tests related to economics, sociology, history, geography, and political science, and those related to general social studies achievement/proficiency. (Note: Also included here are tests that assess personality or affective variables related to social studies.)

Speech and Hearing

Tests that measure the mechanics of speaking or hearing the spoken word. Included here are tests of articulation, voice fluency, stuttering, speech sound perception/discrimination, auditory discrimination/comprehension, audiometry, deafness, and hearing loss/impairment.

See also Developmental, English and Language, Neuropsychological, and Sensory-Motor.

Vocations

Tests that measure employee skills, behaviors, attitudes, values, and perceptions relative to jobs, employment, and the work place or organizational environment. Included here are tests of management skill/style/competence, leader behavior, careers (development, exploration, attitudes); job- or work-related selection/admission/entrance tests; tests of work adjustment, team or group processes/communication/effectiveness, employability, vocational/occupational interests, employee aptitudes/competencies, and organizational climate.

See also Intelligence and General Aptitude, and Personality and also specific content area categories (e.g., Mathematics, Reading).

ACHIEVEMENT

BRIGANCE® Comprehensive Inventory of Basic Skills II; Ages 5-12; 21

i-Ready Diagnostic and Instruction; Students in Grades K-8 (Diagnostic) and K-6 (Instruction); 86

BEHAVIOR ASSESSMENT

Autism Spectrum Rating Scales; Ages 2 to 18; 8
Barkley Adult ADHD Rating Scale-IV; Ages 18 to 89; 9
Barkley Deficits in Executive Functioning Scale; Ages 18 to 81; 10
Barkley Deficits in Executive Functioning Scale–Children and Adolescents; Ages 6 to 17; 11
Barkley Functional Impairment Scale; Ages 18 to 89; 12
Barkley Functional Impairment Scale–Children and Adolescents; Parents of children ages 6 to 17; 13
Behavior Intervention Monitoring Assessment System; Ages 5 to 18; 15

Behavioral Summary; Students in Grades K-12; 17
Comprehensive Executive Function Inventory; Ages 5 to 18; 41
Developmental Teaching Objectives and Rating Form—Revised, 5th Edition; Ages Birth to 16 years; 52
Garos Sexual Behavior Inventory; Ages 18 and over; 74
PDD Behavior Inventory–Screening Version; Ages 1-6 to 12-5; 128
Social Responsiveness Scale, Second Edition; Ages 2-6 to adult; 154

DEVELOPMENTAL

Auditory Skills Assessment; Ages 3-6 to 6-11; 7
BRIGANCE® Inventory of Early Development II; Developmental ages birth to age 7; 22
The Capute Scales; 1 month to 36 months; 26
Developmental Indicators for the Assessment of Learning–Fourth Edition; Ages 2-6 to 5-11; 51
Gesell Developmental Observation–Revised; Ages 2-6 through 9 years; 75
Gesell Early Screener; Ages 3 to 6; 76
Harris Infant Neuromotor Test; 2.5 months to 12.5 months; 83

MacArthur-Bates Communicative Development Inventories, Second Edition; 8 months to 37 months; 93
NICU Network Neurobehavioral Scale; Infants between 30 to 48 weeks corrected or conceptional age; 118
The Test of Infant Motor Performance; Ages birth to 17 weeks (term-born infants); 34 weeks postmenstrual age through 4 months post-term (premature infants); 169

EDUCATION

ENGLISH AND LANGUAGE

FINE ARTS

FOREIGN LANGUAGES

INTELLIGENCE AND GENERAL APTITUDE

MATHEMATICS

MISCELLANEOUS

NEUROPSYCHOLOGICAL

PERSONALITY

READING

SENSORY MOTOR

SPEECH AND HEARING

VOCATIONS

PUBLISHERS DIRECTORY
AND INDEX

This directory and index gives the names and test entry numbers of all publishers represented in The Nineteenth Mental Measurements Yearbook. *Current addresses are listed for all publishers for which this is known. This directory and index also provides telephone and FAX numbers and e-mail and Web addresses for those publishers who responded to our request for this information. Please note that all test numbers refer to test entry numbers, not page numbers. Publishers are an important source of information about catalogs, specimen sets, price changes, test revisions, and many other matters.*

Academic Therapy Publications
20 Commercial Boulevard
Novato, CA 94949-6191
Telephone: 800-422-7249
FAX: 415-883-3720
E-mail: sales@academictherapy.com
Web: www.academictherapy.com
Tests: 48, 70, 71, 90, 139, 141, 142, 168, 170, 172

Behavioral-Developmental Initiatives
14636 North 55th Street
Scottsdale, AZ 85254
Telephone: 800-405-2313
FAX: 602-494-2688
E-mail: bdi@temperament.com
Web: www.b-di.com
Tests: 117

Bigby, Havis & Associates, Inc., d/b/a Assess Systems
12750 Merit Drive, Suite 300
Dallas, TX 75251
Telephone: 972-233-6055
FAX: 972-233-3154
E-mail: kcapelle@assess-systems.com
Web: www.assess-systems.com
Tests: 4, 146, 148

Brain Injury Rehabilitation Trust
Kerwin Court, Five Oaks Road
Slinfold, Nr Horsham, West Sussex RH13 0TP
England
Telephone: 01403 799163
FAX: 01403 791738
E-mail: michael.oddy@thedtgroup.org
Web: www.birt.co.uk
Tests: 20

Cambridge Speech and Language Pathology, Inc.
3450 Palmer Drive, Suite 4-288
Cameron Park, CA 95682
Telephone: 530-306-7773
FAX: 530-677-3195
Web: www.cambridgeslp.com
Tests: 194

Cambridge Michigan Language Assessments
CaMLA, 535 West William Street, Suite 310
Ann Arbor, MI 48103-4978
Telephone: 734-615-9629
FAX: 734-763-0369
E-mail: info@cambridgemichigan.org
Web: www.cambridgemichigan.org
Tests: 68, 69, 106

Career Cruising
1867 Yonge Street, Suite 1002
Toronto, Ontario M4S 1Y5
Canada
Tests: 189

Career Kids
PO Box 7032
Auburn, CA 95604-7032
Telephone: 800-537-0909
FAX: 916-624-7267
E-mail: info@careerkids.com
Web: www.careerkids.com
Tests: 190

CASAS
5151 Murphy Canyon Road, Suite 220
San Diego, CA 92123-4339
Telephone: 858-292-2900
FAX: 858-292-2910
E-mail: bwalsh@casas.org
Web: www.casas.org
Tests: 29, 30

Center for Applied Linguistics
4646 40th Street, NW
Washington, DC 20016-1859
Telephone: 202-362-0700
FAX: 202-363-7204
E-mail: info@cal.org
Web: www.cal.org
Tests: 19, 42

Checkmate Plus, Ltd.
P.O. Box 696
Stony Brook, NY 11790-0696
Telephone: 800-779-4292
FAX: 631-360-3432
E-mail: info@checkmateplus.com
Web: www.checkmateplus.com
Tests: 1

Consortium on Reading Excellence, Inc. (CORE)
2560 Ninth Street, Suite 220
Berkeley, CA 94710
Tests: 185

CPP, Inc.
1055 Joaquin Road, 2nd Floor
Mountain View, CA 94043
Telephone: 800-624-1765
FAX: 650-969-8608
E-mail: custserve@cpp.com
Web: www.cpp.com
Tests: 181

Curriculum Associates, LLC
153 Rangeway Road, P.O. Box 2001
North Billerica, MA 01862-0901
Telephone: 800-225-0248
FAX: 800-366-1158
E-mail: info@cainc.com
Web: www.curriculumassociates.com
Tests: 21, 22, 86, 186, 187, 188

Developmental Therapy Institute, Inc.
P.O. Box 5153
Athens, GA 30604-5153
Tests: 52

Educational Records Bureau
470 Park Ave. South, Front 2,
New York, NY 10016-6819
Telephone: 212-672-9800
FAX: 212-370-4096
E-mail: info@erbtest.org
Web: www.erbtest.org
Tests: 87

Gander Publishing
P.O. Box 780 or 450 Front St.
Avila Beach, CA 93424
Telephone: 805-541-5523
FAX: 805-782-0488
Tests: 162

Gesell Institute of Child Development
310 Prospect Street, 2nd Floor
New Haven, CT 06511
Telephone: 203-777-3481
FAX: 203-776-5001
E-mail: mguddemi@gesellinstitute.org
Web: www.gesellinstitute.org
Tests: 75, 76

GIA Publications, Inc.
7404 South Mason Avenue
Chicago, IL 60638
Telephone: 708-496-3800
FAX: 708-496-3828
E-mail: custserv@giamusic.com
Web: www.giamusic.com
Tests: 107

Green's Publishing Inc.
Suite 201, 17010-103 Ave.
Edmonton, Alberta T5S 1K7
Canada
Telephone: 780-484-5550
FAX: 780-484-5631
E-mail: drpgreen@telus.net
Web: www.wordmemorytest.com
Tests: 77, 78, 79, 80

Guilford Publications, Inc.
72 Spring Street
New York, NY 10012
Telephone: 212-431-9800
FAX: 212-966-6708
E-mail: estefeni.estremera@guilford.com
Web: www.guilford.com
Tests: 9, 10, 11, 12, 13

Hogan Assessment Systems, Inc.
2622 East 21st Street
Tulsa, OK 74114
Telephone: 800-756-0632
Web: www.hoganassessments.com
Tests: 84

Infant Motor Performance Scales, LLC
1301 W. Madison St., #526
Chicago, IL 60607
Telephone: 312-733-9604
FAX: 312-733-0565
E-mail: skc@thetimp.com
Web: www.thetimp.com
Tests: 83, 169

JIST/EMC Publishing
875 Montreal Way
Saint Paul, MN 55102-4245
Telephone: 800-648-5478
FAX: 800-547-8329
E-mail: educate@emcp.com
Web: jist.emcp.com
Tests: 39, 67, 121, 195, 197

Mathematical Association of America; American Mathematics Competitions
Steven R. Dunbar, Director, University of Nebraska–Lincoln, 1740 Vine Street
Lincoln, NE 68588-0658
Telephone: 800-527-3690; 402-472-2257
FAX: 402-472-6087
E-mail: amcinfo@unl.edu
Web: www.unl.edu/amc
Tests: 184

MATRICS Assessment, Inc.
914 Westwood Blvd. #512
Los Angeles, CA 90024
FAX: 310-312-1535
E-mail: matricsassessment@gmail.com
Web: www.matrics.org
Tests: 98

McGraw-Hill Higher Education
2 Penn Plaza, 20th Floor
New York, NY 10121
Tests: 191

Multi-Health Systems, Inc.
P.O. Box 950
North Tonawanda, NY 14120-0950
Telephone: 800-456-3003
FAX: 888-540-4484
E-mail: customerservice@mhs.com
Web: www.mhs.com
Tests: 3, 8, 15, 33, 41, 62, 113, 136, 183

MySkillsProfile.com Limited
23 Dunkeld Road
Ecclesall, Sheffield S11 9HN
England
FAX: 44-114-238-5559
Web: MySkillsProfile.com
Tests: 96, 155, 158

New Zealand Council for Educational Research
Education House West, 178-182 Willis Street, Box 3237
Wellington, 6011
New Zealand
Telephone: 00 64 4 384 7939
FAX: 00 64 4 384 7933
E-mail: karyn.dunn@nzcer.org.nz
Web: www.nzcer.org.nz
Tests: 137, 138, 160

Pain Assessment Resources
4790 Caughlin Parkway Ste 173
Reno, NV 89519-0907
Telephone: 800-782-1501 or 775-828-2955
FAX: 775-828-4275
Web: www.painassessmentresources.com
Tests: 16

Paul H. Brookes Publishing Co., Inc.
P.O. Box 10624
Baltimore, MD 21285-0624
Telephone: 800-638-3775
FAX: 410-337-8539
E-mail: custserv@brookespublishing.com
Web: www.brookespublishing.com
Tests: 26, 36, 54, 55, 93, 118, 120, 129, 134, 173, 196

Pearson
19500 Bulverde Road
San Antonio, TX 78259
Telephone: 800-627-7271 or 952-681-3232
FAX: 800-632-9011 or 952-681-3299
E-mail: pearsonassessments@pearson.com
Web: www.pearsonassessments.com
Tests: 7, 14, 23, 38, 51, 130, 131, 132, 133, 143, 151, 175, 176, 179

Dr. Ralph L. Piedmont
Loyola University Maryland, Pastoral Counseling Department, 8890 McGaw Road,
Columbia, MD 21045
Telephone: 410-617-7625
FAX: 410-617-7644
E-mail: rpiedmont@loyola.edu
Tests: 6

PRO-ED
8700 Shoal Creek Blvd.
Austin, TX 78757-6897
Telephone: 800-897-3202
FAX: 800-397-7633
E-mail: info@proedinc
Web: www.proedinc.com
Tests: 171

Psychological Assessment Resources, Inc.
16204 N. Florida Avenue
Lutz, FL 33549-8119
Telephone: 800-331-8378
FAX: 800-727-9329
E-mail: custsupp@parinc.com
Web: www.parinc.com
Tests: 24, 25, 50, 56, 60, 72, 88, 105, 108, 116, 125, 127, 128, 145, 152, 156, 159, 165, 174

PsychTests AIM, Inc.
9001 Boulevard de l'Acadie, Suite 802
Montreal, Quebec H4N 3H5
Canada
Telephone: 514-745-3189
FAX: 514-745-6242
E-mail: ilona@psychtests.com
Web: corporate.psychtests.com/
Tests: 2, 5, 27, 28, 37, 40, 44, 45, 47, 61, 63, 65, 66, 73, 81, 89, 91, 92, 97, 110, 111, 114, 115, 119, 144, 147, 149, 153, 157, 161, 167, 180, 182

Ramsay Corporation
Boyce Station Offices, 1050 Boyce Road,
Pittsburgh, PA 15241-3907
Telephone: 412-257-0732
FAX: 412-257-9929
E-mail: sales@ramsaycorp.com
Web: www.ramsaycorp.com
Tests: 31, 57, 58, 59, 94, 95, 99, 100, 101, 102, 103, 104, 109, 112, 135, 166, 177

Research Press
2612 N Mattis Ave.
Champaign, IL 61822
Telephone: 800-519-2707
FAX: 217-352-1221
E-mail: rp@researchpress.com
Web: www.researchpress.com
Tests: 85

SALT Software, LLC
23441 Gingers Drive
Muscoda, WI 53573-5591
Telephone: 888-440-7258
FAX: 608-739-3676
E-mail: info@saltsoftware.com
Web: www.saltsoftware.com
Tests: 163, 164

Scholastic Inc.
557 Broadway
New York, NY 10012
Tests: 198

Scholastic Testing Service, Inc.
480 Meyer Road
Bensenville, IL 60106-1617
Telephone: 1-800-642-6787
FAX: 630-766-8054
E-mail: sts@mail.ststesting.com
Web: www.ststesting.com
Tests: 192, 193

Schoolhouse Educational Services, LLC
1052 Forest Oak Drive, Suite 200
Onalaska, WI 54650
Telephone: 608-787-5636
E-mail: cpps@psychprocesses.com
Web: www.schoolhouseeducationalservices.com
Tests: 35

Schuhfried
Hyrtlstrasse 45
2340 Moedling,
Austria
Telephone: +43 2236 42315
FAX: +43 2236 46597
E-mail: info@schuhfried.at
Web: www.schuhfried.at
Tests: 82

SHL
The Pavilion, 1 Atwell Place,
Thames Ditton, Surrey KT7 0NE
United Kingdom
Telephone: +44 (0) 20 8335 8000
FAX: +44 (0) 20 8335 7000
E-mail: info@shl.com
Web: www.shl.com
Tests: 122

SIGMA Assessment Systems, Inc.
P.O. Box 610757
Port Huron, MI 48061-0757
Telephone: 800-265-1285
FAX: 800-361-9411
E-mail: SIGMA@SigmaAssessmentSystems.com
Web: www.SigmaAssessmentSystems.com
Tests: 53

Professor Paris Strom
Dept. of Educational Foundations, Leadership & Technology, 4036 Haley Center,
Auburn University, AL 36849-5221
Telephone: 334-844-3077
E-mail: stromps@auburn.edu
Web: www.teamworkskillsinventory.org
Tests: 126

Western Psychological Services
625 Alaska Ave.
Torrance, CA 90503-5124
Telephone: 424-201-8800
FAX: 424-201-6950
E-mail: customerservice@wpspublish.com
Web: www.wpspublish.com
Tests: 17, 18, 32, 34, 43, 46, 49, 64, 74, 123, 124, 140, 150, 154

Winslow Research Institute
1933 Windward Point
Discovery Bay, CA 94505
Telephone: 925-516-8686
FAX: 925-516-7015
E-mail: winslow@winslowresearch.com
Web: www.winslowresearch.com
Tests: 178

INDEX OF NAMES

This index indicates whether a citation refers to authorship of a test, a test review, or a reviewer's reference for a specific test. Numbers refer to test entries, not to pages. The abbreviations and numbers following the names may be interpreted as follows: "test, 73" indicates authorship of test 73; "rev, 86" indicates authorship of a review of test 86; "ref, 45" indicates a reference in one of the "Reviewer's References" sections for test 45. Reviewer names mentioned in cross references are also indexed.

Abbott, R. D.: ref, 90
Abbott-Shim, M.: ref, 55
Abidin, R. R.: test, 127
Accardo, P. J.: test, 26; ref, 26
Achenbach, T. M.: ref, 13, 51, 156
Ackerman, P. L.: ref, 116; rev, 59, 157
Acosta, S. T.: rev, 42, 106
Adams, B. N.: ref, 43
Adams, R. L.: ref, 139, 143; rev, 139
Adkins, C. M.: rev, 27
Adriaanse, M. A.: ref, 61
Agras, W. S.: ref, 61
Aguilar-Gaxiola, S.: ref, 34
Albanese, M. A.: rev, 78, 183
Allen, K. D.: rev, 7, 160
Allen, L.: ref, 80
Allen, M. D.: ref, 80
Allington, R. L.: rev, 179
Allison, E. E.: rev, 176
Allison, J. A.: rev, 127
Allport, G. W.: ref, 6, 116
Alpert, B.: ref, 4
Als, H.: ref, 118
Aluwahlia, S.: ref, 13
Amatruda, C. S.: ref, 26
Ambrosini, P.: ref, 13
American Council on the Teaching of Foreign Languages: ref, 42
American Educational Research Association: ref, 2, 5, 16, 20, 31, 33, 37, 38, 44, 47, 48, 63, 69, 73, 80, 85, 89, 90, 98, 99, 100, 108, 111, 117, 119, 130, 133, 144, 161, 176
American Management Association: ref, 82
American Psychiatric Association: ref, 1, 8, 9, 13, 33, 34, 84, 85, 128, 145, 154, 174

American Psychological Association: ref, 2, 5, 16, 20, 31, 33, 37, 38, 44, 47, 48, 63, 69, 73, 80, 85, 89, 90, 98, 99, 100, 108, 111, 117, 119, 130, 133, 144, 161, 176
American Speech-Language-Hearing Association: ref, 7
Amiel-Tison, C.: ref, 118
Ammons, C. H.: rev, 130, 176
Anastasi, A.: ref, 12, 24, 48
Anastasopoulos, L.: test, 55; ref, 55
Anderson, D. O.: rev, 99
Anderson, J.: rev, 141
Anderson, J. R.: ref, 57
Anderson, M. W.: rev, 10, 56
Anderson, W. M.: ref, 151
Andrew, D. M.: ref, 37
Andrews, D. A.: test, 183; ref, 121, 183
Andriacchi, K. D.: ref, 164
Angoff, W.: ref, 168
Anthony, C.: rev, 110
Arena, J.: test, 48
Arnow, B.: ref, 61
Ashton, R. S.: ref, 108
Asparouhov, T.: ref, 116
Assess Systems: test, 148
Astner, K.: ref, 80
Athanasou, J. A.: ref, 117; rev, 103, 117, 158
Atkinson, J. W.: ref, 27
Atlas, J. A.: ref, 33, 60; rev, 33, 60, 171
Austin, J. T.: rev, 37, 100, 148
Axford, S.: rev, 84, 155
Axford, S. N.: ref, 117; rev, 117
Ayres, J. A.: ref, 150

Baade, L. E.: ref, 98, 143
Babyak, M. A.: ref, 6
Bachelor, P. A.: rev, 96, 101

SCORE INDEX

This Score Index lists all the scores, in alphabetical order, for all the tests included in The Nineteenth Mental Measurements Yearbook. *Because test scores can be regarded as operational definitions of the variable measured, sometimes the scores provide better leads to what a test actually measures than the test title or other available information. The Score Index is very detailed, and the reader should keep in mind that a given variable (or concept) of interest may be defined in several different ways. Thus the reader should look up these several possible alternative definitions before drawing final conclusions about whether tests measuring a particular variable of interest can be located in this volume. If the kind of score sought is located in a particular test or tests, the reader should then read the test descriptive information carefully to determine whether the test(s) in which the score is found is (are) consistent with reader purpose. Used wisely, the Score Index can be another useful resource in locating the right score in the right test. As usual, all numbers in the index are test numbers, not page numbers.*

A Words: 20
A1-A5 Total: 20
A6: 20
Abrasiveness: 63
AC/DC Theory & Schematics: 59
Academic Functioning: 15
Academic Habits: 17
Academic Performance: 17
Academic/Cognitive: Literacy Subdomain: 22
Academic/Cognitive: Mathematical/General Concepts Subdomain: 22
Acceptability: 127
Acceptable Designs: 24
Acceptance of Diversity: 148
Acceptance of Structure: 148
Accident Proneness: 63
Accommodating: 146
Accommodation to Others: 148
Accountability: 148
Accuracy: 90, 165, 172, 178
Achievement: 27, 46, 146, 155
Achievement and Competitiveness: 155
Achievement Striving: 116
Achieving: 122
Acids/Bases & Salts: 31
Acquiescence: 28, 37, 89, 144

Action Agents: 75
Action Response: 105
Actions: 22, 116
Actions and Gestures: 93
Activity: 116
Activity Interference-Domestic/Household Activities: 16
Activity Interference-Heavy Activities: 16
Activity Interference-Personal Care Activities: 16
Activity Interference-Personal Hygiene Activities: 16
Activity Interference-Social Activities: 16
Activity Level: 32, 117
Adaptability: 63, 65, 89, 117, 127, 147, 155
Adaptability/Flexibility: 144
Adaptability/Trainability: 37
Adaptable: 122
Adaptable Social Skills: 110
Adaptation to Change: 32
Adaptation to Change/Restricted Interests: 32
Adapting and Coping with Pressure: 96
ADHD-EF Index: 10, 11
Adherence History: 161
Adherence to Rules: 157
Adolescent in Middle: 125
Adult Socialization: 8
Advanced High: 42
Advanced Low: 42